# PRENTICE HALL
# WORLD HISTORY
## CONNECTIONS TO TODAY

**Elisabeth Gaynor Ellis and Anthony Esler**
With Senior Consultant Burton F. Beers

PRENTICE HALL
Simon & Schuster Education Group
A VIACOM COMPANY

## The World History Team

Core Team: Lynda Cloud, Kathryn Dix, Anne Falzone, Monduane Harris, Carol Leslie, Emily Rose, Frank Tangredi, Elizabeth Torjussen

Advertising and Promotion: Carol Leslie, Rip Odell

Art and Design: Laura Jane Bird, Paul Gagnon, Monduane Harris, AnnMarie Roselli, Gerry Schrenck, Kira Thaler

Computer Test Bank Technology: Greg Myers, Cleasta Wilburn

Editorial: Tom Barber, Jim Doris, Anne Falzone, Nancy Gilbert, Mary Ann Gundersen, Barbara Harrigan, Rick Hickox, Naomi Kisch, Marion Osterberg, Kirsten Richert, Luess Sampson-Lizotte, Amit Shah, Frank Tangredi

Manufacturing: Rhett Conklin, Matt McCabe

Marketing: Laura Asermily, Lynda Cloud

Media Resources: Martha Conway, Libby Forsyth, Vickie Menanteaux, Emily Rose

Pre-Press Production: Carol Barbara, Kathryn Dix, Annette Simmons

Production: Christina Burghard, Joan McCulley, Marilyn Stearns, Elizabeth Torjussen, Cynthia Weedel

Text Permissions: Doris Robinson

ISBN 0-13-803271-8

12 13 14 15    04 03 02 01 00

PRENTICE HALL
Simon & Schuster Education Group
A VIACOM COMPANY

Upper Saddle River, New Jersey
Needham, Massachusetts

**ACKNOWLEDGMENTS**

Grateful acknowledgment is made to the following for permission to reprint copyrighted material:

Excerpt from "Requiem," translated by Robin Kemball, Copyright © 1974 by Robin Kemball, from *Selected Poems* by Anna Akhmatova, edited and translated by Walter Arndt. Reprinted by permission of **Ardis.** Excerpt from "No Time" by Nguyen Sa, from *A Thousand Years of Vietnamese Poetry*, translated by Nguyen Ngoc Bich with Burton Raffel and W. S. Merwin, edited by Nguyen Ngoc Bich. Copyright © 1962, 1967, 1968, 1969, 1970, 1971, 1974 by The Asia Society, Inc. Reprinted by permission of Nguyen Ngoc **Bich.** From "A

Doll's House," from *The Complete Major Prose Plays of Henrik Ibsen* by Henrik Ibsen, translated by Rolf Fjelde. Translation copyright © 1965, 1970, 1978 by Rolf Fjelde. Used by permission of **Dutton Signet, a division of Penguin Books USA Inc.** From *Book of Songs*, translated by Arthur Waley. Copyright © 1937 by Arthur Waley. Used by permission of **Grove/Atlantic, Inc.** From "The Heirs of Stalin," from *The Collected Poems, 1952–1990*, Yevgeny Yevtushenko, edited by Albert C. Todd with the author and James Ragan. Copyright © 1991 by Henry Holt and Co. Reprinted by permission of **Henry Holt and Co.** From *Casualties* (**Longmans,** 1970). Lines from "Year after year I have Watched," by Li Ch'ing Chao, translated

by Kenneth Rexroth from *Love and the Turning Year: One Hundred More Poems from the Chinese* by Kenneth Rexroth. Copyright © 1970 by Kenneth Rexroth. Reprinted by permission of **New Directions Publishing Company.** Excerpts from "The Prologue" to *The Canterbury Tales* by Geoffrey Chaucer, translated by Nevill Coghill (Penguin Classics, 1951, Fourth revised edition, 1977), copyright © Nevill Coghill, 1951, 1958, 1960, 1975, 1977. Reprinted by permission of **Penguin Books Ltd.** From *The Misadventures of Alonso Ramirez*, translated by Edwin H. **Pleasants** (Mexico, 1962). From *Sundiata: An Epic of Old Mali* by D. T. Niane, translated by G. D. Pickett. © **Présence Africaine** 1960 (original French version:

*Soundjata, ou l'Epopée Mandingue).* © Longman Group Ltd. (English Version) 1965. Reprinted by permission of **Présence Africaine.** Four lines of "In Memory of W. B. Yeats," from *W. H. Auden: Collected Poems* by W. H. Auden. Copyright © 1940 and renewed 1968 by W. H. Auden. Reprinted by permission of **Random House, Inc. and Faber and Faber Limited.** From "We Crown Thee King" by Rabindranath Tagore from *The Hungry Stones and Other Stories*, published by The Macmillan Company, 1916. Reprinted by permission of **Simon & Schuster, Inc. and Macmillan Publishers Ltd.** Four lines

(Acknowledgments continue on page 1034.)

# PRENTICE HALL
# WORLD HISTORY
## CONNECTIONS TO TODAY

## AUTHORS

### Elisabeth Gaynor Ellis

Elisabeth Gaynor Ellis is a historian and writer. She is a co-author of *World Cultures: A Global Mosaic*. Ms. Ellis, a former social studies teacher and school administrator, has taught world cultures, Russian studies, and European history. She holds a B.A. from Smith College and an M.A. and M.S. from Columbia University.

### Anthony Esler

Anthony Esler is Professor of History at the College of William and Mary. He received his Ph.D. from Duke University and received Fulbright Fellowships to study at the University of London and travel to Ivory Coast and Tanzania. Besides publishing numerous works of fiction, Dr. Esler has written histories, including *The Human Venture: A World History* and *The Western World: A History*.

### Senior Consultant
### Burton F. Beers

Burton F. Beers is Professor of History at North Carolina State University. He has taught European history, Asian history, and American history. Dr. Beers has published numerous articles in historical journals and several books, including *The Far East: A History of Western Impacts and Eastern Responses*, with Paul H. Clyde, and *World History: Patterns of Civilization*.

# Program Reviewers

# Contents

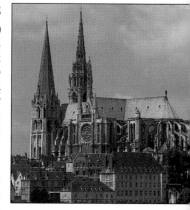

## THE BIG PICTURE

### THE BIG PICTURE

# UNIT 5  Enlightenment and Revolution

## THE BIG PICTURE

## UNIT 7 World Wars and Revolutions

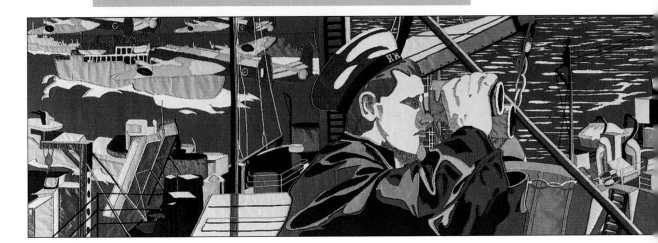

# Special Features

## PARALLELS THROUGH TIME

**Going Shopping**

Some complain that the marketplace is loud, busy, crowded. But for merchants selling their wares, shoppers looking for bargains, and people who just want to be with people, this is the place to be.

**Linking Past and Present** What advantages does an enclosed mall have over an open-air marketplace? Why are some open-air markets still popular?

**PAST** *Muslim bazaars, or marketplaces, sold local goods as well as imports made available by a vast trading network. In major cities, such as Baghdad and Istanbul, the bazaar consisted of miles of streets enclosed by a roof. In this illustration, we see, from left to right, a jeweler, a druggist, a butcher, and a baker.*

**PRESENT** *The giant, multilevel, indoor mall is a modern version of the bazaar. Within its great expanse, you may shop, dine, see a movie, or perhaps even ice skate.*

## Up Close

▶ *In-depth stories bring history alive.*

## Art History

▶ *Works of art reveal the talents and creativity
of artists and artisans around the world.*

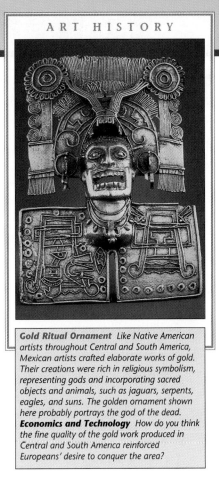

**Gold Ritual Ornament** *Like Native American artists throughout Central and South America, Mexican artists crafted elaborate works of gold. Their creations were rich in religious symbolism, representing gods and incorporating sacred objects and animals, such as jaguars, serpents, eagles, and suns. The golden ornament shown here probably portrays the god of the dead.* **Economics and Technology** *How do you think the fine quality of the gold work produced in Central and South America reinforced Europeans' desire to conquer the area?*

## World Literature

▶ *Literature selections offer insights into diverse
world cultures throughout history.*

# Skills for Success

# Charts, Graphs, and Time Lines

# Maps

## Economic Activity in Argentina

Meatpacking and food processing · Textiles · Metals · Chemicals · Car assembly · Wheat · Corn

## GEOGRAPHY AND HISTORY

Since the 1980s, Argentina has regained its position as the most stable economy in Latin America. Its economic success stems from a wide variety of resources and industries.

1. **Location** On the map, locate (a) Buenos Aires, (b) Falkland Islands, (c) Chile.
2. **Region** Using longitude and latitude, describe the major agricultural region of Argentina.
3. **Critical Thinking** **Making Inferences** Based on this map, name two cities that you might expect to attract a great many workers from rural areas.

# About This Book

***World History: Connections to Today*** is organized into 8 units, made up of 37 chapters, as well as an introduction. The Table of Contents lists the titles of the units and chapters. It also lists You Decide and other special features, skill lessons, maps, charts, and graphs. In addition, the Table of Contents offers a guide to the Reference Section at the back of the book.

## IN EACH UNIT

**Unit Opener** Each unit opens with a two-page introduction that includes a list of the chapters in the unit, as well as a map and series of illustrations. The map shows the world during a certain era in history. The illustrations link locations in the world at that time to important themes.

**World Literature** Each unit features an extended excerpt from a well-known piece of literature, written during the period covered in the unit.

**The Big Picture** Each unit ends with a six-page wrap-up. The features include:

- **The Unit-in-Brief,** which presents a short summary of each chapter in the unit.
- **A Global View,** which includes a thematic essay and a regional time line. The essay addresses an essential question raised by the unit content. The regional time line shows key events in the years covered in the unit.
- **You Decide,** which uses primary sources and pictures to explore viewpoints about an enduring global issue.

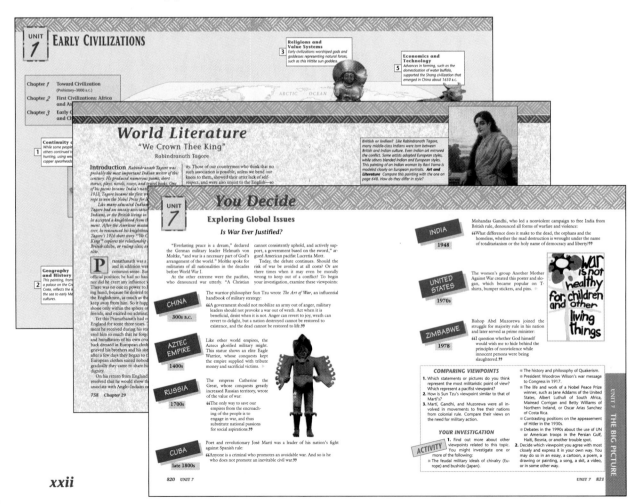

## IN EACH CHAPTER

**Chapter Opener**  Each chapter begins with a Chapter Outline that lists the numbered sections of the chapter. It also sets the time and place covered in the chapter with the use of a locator map and a time line. A large illustration sets the tone of the period, while the Humanities Link lists important works of art and literature included in the chapter. The Chapter Opener also provides Focus On questions, based on important themes, which will help direct your reading of the chapter.

**To Help You Learn**  Several features help you read and comprehend the chapter:
- *Find Out* questions at the beginning of each section guide your reading.
- *Important terms and vocabulary words* are printed in blue type and are defined the first time they are used. They also appear in the Glossary, which begins on page 996.
- *Section Review* questions at the end of each section test your understanding of what you have read and sharpen your critical thinking skills.
- *Issues for Today* contain questions to link content in the chapter to enduring issues facing us today.
- *Global Connections* show how events and ideas are connected over time and place.

**Maps, Graphs, and Charts**  These graphics bring to life major events and developments in history. Captions provide important background and also include questions to sharpen your map, graph, and chart, as well as critical thinking, skills.

**Skills for Success**  A step-by-step skill lesson at the end of each chapter helps you to understand and practice important skills.

**Chapter Review**  The Chapter Review helps you to review the main ideas and themes of the chapter and to strengthen your critical thinking skills. The Chapter Review also provides an opportunity to apply your skills and understandings to real-life situations through the For Your Portfolio activity.

**Special Features**  There are several kinds of special features throughout the book:
- *Parallels Through Time* presents groups of pictures to compare daily life in different world regions at different times in history.
- *Art History* presents works of art that exemplify the talents and creativity of artists around the world throughout history.
- *Up Close* provides a vivid, in-depth look at an interesting person or event in world history.
- *Cause-and-Effect Charts* show graphically the many long-term and short-term causes and effects of key events and developments in history. Each Cause-and-Effect Chart connects the event or development to the world today.
- *Quick Study Charts* provide a quick graphic overview of a historical development or phenomenon. Each Quick Study Chart also shows how the development or phenomenon connects to today.

## REFERENCE SECTION

At the back of the book, you will find a section of reference materials for use in the course. It includes an Atlas, a Glossary, charts that make connections between *World History: Connections to Today* and literature and science, and an Index.

# The Big Picture

## FOCUS ON THEMES

Events that happened hundreds of years ago, or thousands of miles away, can have a powerful impact on our lives. Ancient Greeks pioneered democratic ideas that influenced the framers of our Constitution. American rock 'n' roll grew out of the music brought to North America by Africans in the time of slavery. Today, decisions made by a Brazilian planter, a Saudi Arabian oil minister, or a Japanese manufacturer can have a direct impact on our daily lives.

This textbook can help you understand how today's complex world came to be. To make the past easier to comprehend, this text emphasizes nine themes. They can help you to focus on key features of each society you read about. The nine themes are

- Continuity and Change
- Geography and History
- Political and Social Systems
- Religions and Value Systems
- Economics and Technology
- Diversity
- Impact of the Individual
- Global Interaction
- Art and Literature

In the following pages, you will learn what these themes are and how they can help you to understand world history.

 Turn to the following pages in your textbook and identify how one or more of the themes listed above is highlighted on that page: pages 74–75, page 282, page 429, page 542, page 897.

# CONTINUITY AND CHANGE

Human history is a story of change. Some changes are quick. For example, in 1532, Spanish conquerors toppled the vast Incan empire of Peru, transforming South America forever. Other changes take place over centuries, such as the spread of democratic ideas or the shifting role of women in many societies. While change is always happening, enduring traditions and concerns link people across time and place. In India, current politics are affected by a social system more than 3,000 years old. And the question of how to get a good education was as important to a youth in ancient Egypt, Rome, or China as it is to you.

**ACTIVITY** Interview a parent or any other older acquaintance. Ask them to identify three ways in which your community or the world has changed in the last 25 years.

Migration has been taking place since the beginning of history. One of the most common migrations has been the movement from farming villages (left) to crowded industrial cities (right).

In the 1940s, the government of South Africa imposed apartheid, a system of strict racial separation. In the 1990s, apartheid was abolished, and Nelson Mandela, far right, became president of South Africa.

# GEOGRAPHY AND HISTORY

Geography influences the work people do, the clothes they wear, the food they eat, and how they travel. Since the time of the pharaohs, for example, Egyptians have used the Nile River to transport people and goods. But people also try to master their surroundings. They have built dams to control flooding and cut highways through rugged mountains. More recently, pollution and other environmental issues have caused heated debate. The uneven distribution of vital natural resources, such as oil or gold, is another way geography has helped to shape history.

**ACTIVITY**

With a partner, create a Geographic Profile for your local area. You might list location, climate, type of land, nearest waterways, plant and animal life, resources, and outstanding geographic features.

▷ Geography plays a key role in military strategy. Using knowledge of geographic conditions, the French general Napoleon Bonaparte seized control of the high ground to win the Battle of Austerlitz.

▷ The cutting down of tropical rain forests, like this one in Costa Rica, has become an urgent economic and environmental issue of our time.

▷ The Sahara is the world's largest desert. Since early times, it has served as a highway for trade and migration among widely separated African civilizations.

## Battle of Austerlitz, 1805

| | |
| --- | --- |
| → French forces | ⇒ Russian-Austrian forces |
| ⇒ Fake French retreat | ⇒ Russian-Austrian retreat |
| ○ Hills | ☐ Swamps |

1. French fake retreat to lure Russian-Austrian forces off Pratzen Heights.
2. Russian-Austrian forces chase French.
3. French take Pratzen Heights.
4. Russian-Austrian forces attack, but are repulsed.
5. More French troops join in to defeat Russian-Austrian forces.

## GEOGRAPHY AND HISTORY

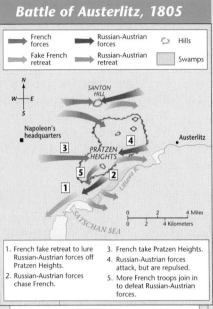

In December 1805, Napoleon's forces fought a combined Russian-Austrian army at the Battle of Austerlitz. Thanks to Napoleon's superior leadership, his outnumbered troops won an outstanding victory.

1. **Location** On the map, locate (a) Austerlitz, (b) Pratzen Heights, (c) Satschan Sea, (d) Napoleon's headquarters.
2. **Movement** How were Napoleon's troops able to defeat the Russian-Austrian forces south of Pratzen Heights?
3. **Critical Thinking Making Generalizations** Why is control of the high ground important in a battle?

# POLITICAL AND SOCIAL SYSTEMS

Kings and queens, presidents and dictators, elected congresses and tribal councils—each society has a way to govern itself. A government tries to keep order within a society and protect it from outside threats. Societies have other important institutions, including the most basic one of all, the family. Social classes—which rank people based on wealth, ancestry, occupation, or education—are also important. Nobles, priests, merchants, workers, and slaves were common social classes in early societies. In addition, most societies have made sharp distinctions between the roles of women and men.

**ACTIVITY** Draw a political cartoon describing a current political issue in your country, state, or community.

▷ *Modern democracy has its roots in the Greek city-state of Athens, left, where every adult male citizen was expected to take part in government. In 1994, Haitians celebrated a return to democratic government after years of military rule.*

▽ *Describe the type of political system you think this cartoon represents.*

PALOMO
Mexico City
MEXICO

Cartoonists & Writers Syndicate

▽ *A feudal social system is based on rigid classes and mutual obligations. This chart shows the feudal system developed in Japan in the 1100s.*

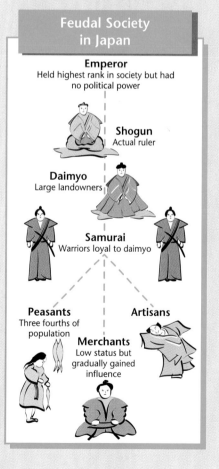

**Feudal Society in Japan**

**Emperor**
Held highest rank in society but had no political power

**Shogun**
Actual ruler

**Daimyo**
Large landowners

**Samurai**
Warriors loyal to daimyo

**Peasants**
Three fourths of population

**Artisans**

**Merchants**
Low status but gradually gained influence

# RELIGIONS AND VALUE SYSTEMS

How was the world created? How can we tell right from wrong? What happens to us after death? Since early times, people have turned to religion for answers to such questions. Religious ideas—such as the belief in a single true God, shared by Jews, Christians, and Muslims—have exerted a powerful influence on human life. Other kinds of value systems have also shaped societies. The ancient Chinese thinker Confucius preached duty, respect for parents, and loyalty to the state. In the 1800s, a strict code of "middle-class values"—including hard work, thrift, and good manners—came to dominate western society. Through their religions and value systems, people define their vision of a good society.

**ACTIVITY** Make a list of 10 values that you think are shared by most people in your community. Compare your list with those of others in the class.

*Jesus, pictured at left, the founder of Christianity, was born in Palestine about 4 B.C. Today, Christianity is the most widely practiced religion in the world, with over a billion followers.*

*Sacred books help pass religious beliefs and values from one generation to the next. Above, a Jewish boy studies the Torah. Below, Muslim children learn to read the Quran.*

*Two major world religions emerged in India: Hinduism, below left, and Buddhism, below right. Buddhism gradually became the dominant religion in much of East Asia and Southeast Asia.*

# ECONOMICS AND TECHNOLOGY

Early humans lived by hunting animals and gathering plants. When people learned how to grow crops, they settled in farming villages. Thousands of years later, the steam engines of the Industrial Revolution created millions of factory jobs. These examples all show the impact of technology. Technology is often related to economic questions. Who controls vital resources? How are goods exchanged? Are people fairly rewarded for the work they do? Economic motives have forged trading networks, caused wars, and contributed to the rise or decline of nations.

**ACTIVITY**

Skim through a recent news magazine. Locate two advertisements or articles that deal with advances in technology and two articles that deal with economic issues. Identify the topics addressed by each article in a one-sentence summary.

Inventions that changed the course of history include, in clockwise order, wheeled vehicles, block printing, the magnetic compass, the steam engine, and the automatic machine gun.

What do you think is the meaning of this cartoon?

One major economic trend of the past 50 years has been a sharp rise in the number of women who work outside the home.

**Women Working Outside the Home**

Percentage Working

Canada   France   Italy   Sweden   United Kingdom   United States

■ 1963   ■ 1993

Source: U.S. Bureau of Labor Statistics

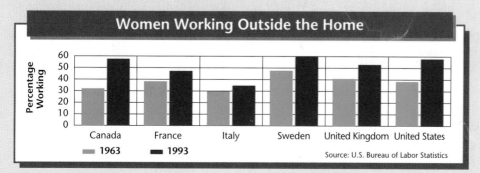

# DIVERSITY

How many languages can you think of? English, Spanish, and Japanese are easy. But what about Urdu, Quechua, Gaelic, or Wolof? Today, as in the past, the diversity of human culture is shown by the hundreds of languages people speak. Diversity is also reflected in religions, social systems, art, customs, and forms of government. Within each nation, there may also be a mix of cultures. India, for example, has 16 official languages and hundreds of other regional languages. While diversity has enriched human experience, cultural or ethnic differences can also lead to conflict.

**ACTIVITY** Make a list of six examples that show diversity in your community. The list might include languages, religions, buildings, clothing styles, foods, or cultural events.

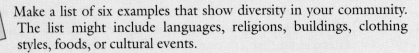

| Comparing Languages | | | | | | |
|---|---|---|---|---|---|---|
| **English** | month | mother | new | night | nose | three |
| **German** | Monat | Mutter | neu | Nacht | Nase | drei |
| **Persian** | māh | mādar | nau | shab | bini | se |
| **Sanskrit** | mās | matar | nava | nakt | nās | trayas |
| **Spanish** | mes | madre | nuevo | noche | nariz | tres |
| **Swedish** | månad | moder | ny | natt | näsa | tre |

*Many diverse languages—stretching from Western Europe to India—came from a common root. Word similarities show the relationship of these "Indo-European" languages.*

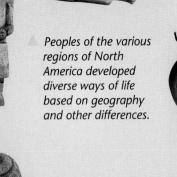

*Peoples of the various regions of North America developed diverse ways of life based on geography and other differences.*

*Russia is the world's largest country, spanning both Europe and Asia. This drawing from the early 1800s shows the diverse peoples of Russia.*

# IMPACT OF THE INDIVIDUAL

Some people have such an impact on events that we remember them long after they die. Vietnam still honors the Trung sisters who fought against Chinese invaders nearly 2,000 years ago. In the 1400s, the voyages of Christopher Columbus and Vasco da Gama launched new patterns of world trade and conquest. The 1900s saw such important political leaders as Mohandas Gandhi, Adolf Hitler, Franklin Roosevelt, Mao Zedong, Juan and Eva Perón, Gamel Abdel Nasser, and Margaret Thatcher. For good or for ill, these individuals have shaped our world.

**ACTIVITY** Skim the Index of this book (pages 1010–1033) and find three people whose names you recognize. Try to identify the reason that each of these people is famous. Then check your responses against the book.

Nearly 4,000 years ago, the Babylonian king Hammurabi became the first person in history to collect all the laws of one civilization into a single legal code.

In the 1300s, Mansa Musa built the West African kingdom of Mali into one of the most prosperous empires in the world.

As prime minister of India, Indira Gandhi led the world's largest democracy from 1966 to 1977 and again from 1980 until her assassination in 1984.

In the 1400s, Joan of Arc, a teenage peasant woman, led French troops to battle in an effort to liberate France from its English conquerors.

In the late 1800s, Polish-born chemist Marie Curie was one of the first scientists to conduct experiments in radioactivity.

Benjamin Franklin was an inventor, writer, diplomat, and political thinker whose ideas helped shape the young United States of America.

Jomo Kenyatta led the Kikuyu people in their struggle against British rule and, in 1963, became the first president of an independent Kenya.

Simón Bolívar led the battle to liberate Venezuela, Ecuador, Bolivia, and other South American nations from Spanish rule in the early 1800s.

# GLOBAL INTERACTION

Coffee was first grown in the 1300s in the Middle East. Two hundred years later, Portuguese settlers carried coffee beans to Brazil. Today, Brazil is the world's leading exporter of coffee. This is one example of global interaction. Nations may interact in many ways—through trade, through migration, or through war and conquest. When people traveled by oxcart or sailing ship, interaction was slow. Today, communication and transportation networks can instantly link all parts of the globe. Organizations such as the United Nations and the World Bank show the growing interdependence of the world.

**ACTIVITY** Look through a current newspaper and find three articles concerning interaction between the United States and other countries. Locate these countries on the maps on pages 984–985.

▲ How can a war in one part of the world affect people living in other parts of the world?

© Punch/ROTHCO

▲ Starting in the 1400s, European powers gained outposts along the African coast. This ivory carving from Benin depicts Portuguese soldiers and was probably sold to them.

▼ For 1,500 years, the city of Constantinople (present-day Istanbul, Turkey) was a center of world trade, attracting merchants from as far away as China and Britain.

# ART AND LITERATURE

From early times, people have created art and literature to reflect their lives and values. Stone by stone, Europeans of the Middle Ages raised soaring cathedrals dedicated to the glory of God. In West Africa, griots, or professional poets, recited ancient stories, preserving both histories and traditional folk tales. In the 1920s, the murals of the Mexican painter Diego Rivera depicted the history of Mexico and the lives of its people. Throughout this book, you will see what poems, stories, songs, paintings, sculpture, and architecture show us about other times and other places.

Skim through the pages of this book and find one example of painting, sculpture, or architecture that appeals to you. Freewrite a brief description of how you respond to it.

▶ During the Renaissance, Italian artists such as Michelangelo developed new ways to represent humans in a realistic way. This statue of Moses is almost eight feet tall.

▲ Japanese paintings such as this one give us a detailed look at life during a time when Japan was isolated from the rest of the world.

▼ The ancient Chinese poem at left describes the emotions of parents whose children have gone off to war. Almost 2,500 years later, the German artist Käthe Kollwitz explored the same theme in her print The Parents, at right.

❝My mother is saying,
  'Alas, my young one
  is on service;
Day and night he gets
  no sleep.
Grant that he is being
  careful of himself,
So that he may come
  back, and not be cast
  away.'❞

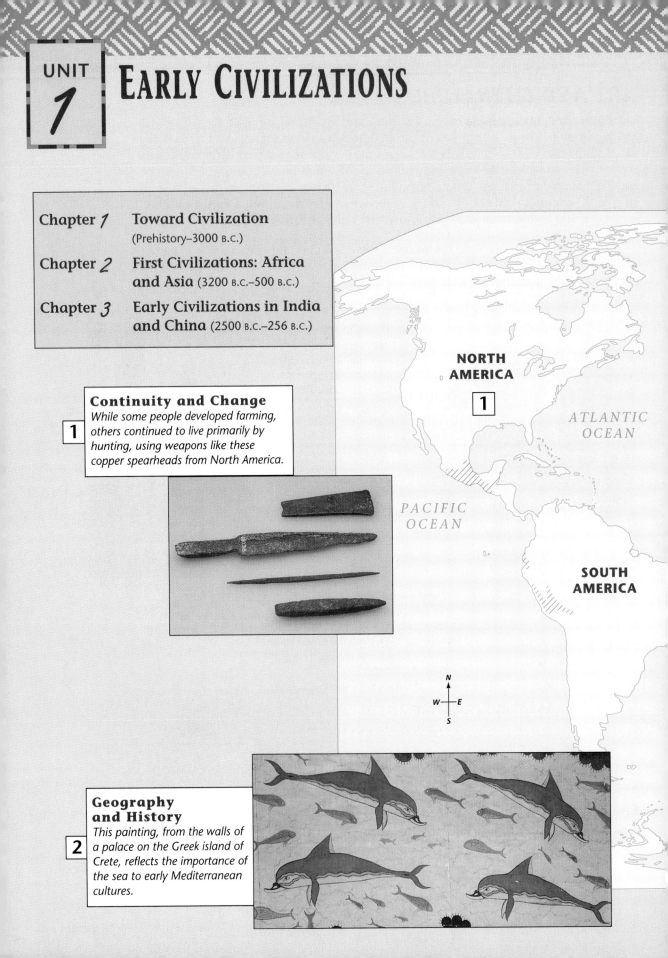

**Continuity and Change**
*While some people developed farming, others continued to live primarily by hunting, using weapons like these copper spearheads from North America.*

**1**

NORTH AMERICA

**1**

ATLANTIC OCEAN

PACIFIC OCEAN

SOUTH AMERICA

N
W — E
S

**Geography and History**
*This painting, from the walls of a palace on the Greek island of Crete, reflects the importance of the sea to early Mediterranean cultures.*

**2**

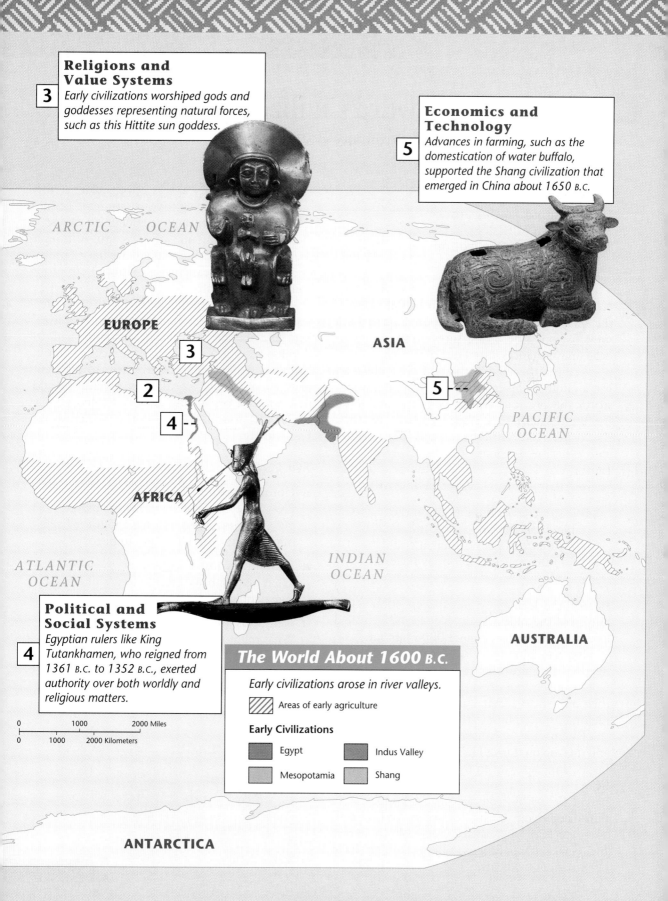

### Religions and Value Systems

**3** *Early civilizations worshiped gods and goddesses representing natural forces, such as this Hittite sun goddess.*

### Economics and Technology

**5** *Advances in farming, such as the domestication of water buffalo, supported the Shang civilization that emerged in China about 1650 B.C.*

ARCTIC   OCEAN

EUROPE

**3**

**2**

**4** --

ASIA

**5** ---

PACIFIC OCEAN

AFRICA

ATLANTIC OCEAN

INDIAN OCEAN

AUSTRALIA

### Political and Social Systems

**4** *Egyptian rulers like King Tutankhamen, who reigned from 1361 B.C. to 1352 B.C., exerted authority over both worldly and religious matters.*

0        1000        2000 Miles
0    1000    2000 Kilometers

## The World About 1600 B.C.

*Early civilizations arose in river valleys.*

▨ Areas of early agriculture

**Early Civilizations**

■ Egypt          ■ Indus Valley

■ Mesopotamia    ■ Shang

ANTARCTICA

# Toward Civilization

## (Prehistory–3000 B.C.)

## CHAPTER OUTLINE

1  **Understanding Our Past**
2  **The Dawn of History**
3  **Beginnings of Civilization**

On an autumn day in 1991, a German couple was tramping through a high pass in the Alps when they came upon a gruesome sight. At one side of the snowy trail, a human head and shoulders jutted out of the ice.

At first, the couple thought that the man was an unlucky hiker who had frozen in a snowstorm the previous winter. Soon, police freed the body from its icy grave. A helicopter took the corpse, along with the remains of his clothes and other possessions, to the University of Innsbruck. There, Professor Konrad Spindler realized that the man had not died recently:

> **66**We stood around the body on the table. I saw the stone tools and the copper ax and said: 'I think it could be 4,000 years old.' Nobody believed me.**99**

In fact, the Iceman, as newspapers soon called him, was the oldest body ever found. He had frozen to death more than 5,000 years ago.

Experts think that the Iceman was sleeping near his campfire when a sudden storm struck. Cold winds freeze-dried the body. Winter snows then buried the Iceman until 1991, when heavy melting exposed him to the gaze of the world.

Fascinated, scientists studied the Iceman and his belongings. His deerskin coat, warm boots, and cape woven from long grass showed he was used to a cold climate. Other evidence gave clues to his skills. He had a copper ax, a flint dagger, a bow, and 14 arrows. In his backpack, he may have carried hot coals to start a fire. Flakes of tree fungus in his pack might have been ancient medicines.

Few discoveries are as spectacular as this one. Yet in the past 200 years, students of history have found enough evidence to create a picture of life thousands of years ago. Although the picture remains incomplete, we have a pretty clear idea of how early people slowly built more complex ways of life.

The Iceman, huddled by his fire to keep warm, may seem far removed from our lives. Yet, like us, he and his descendants had to develop ways to meet their basic needs — food, clothing, shelter, and good health. In different places around the world, new inventions and new ways of organizing activity helped people build the foundations for the societies we know today.

**FOCUS ON** these questions as you read:

■ **Continuity and Change**
How have archaeologists, historians, and geographers helped us learn about the lives of people at different stages in history?

■ **Economics and Technology**
What breakthrough technologies did Stone Age peoples develop?

■ **Religions and Value Systems**
What religious beliefs and practices were developed by early peoples?

■ **Political and Social Systems**
What are the basic features of civilization?

## TIME AND PLACE

*"Cave of the Hands"* People of the Paleolithic age, or Old Stone Age, relied on gathering and hunting for their existence. In this South American cave painting, ancient hands seem to reach out for a herd of guanaco. The guanaco, an animal closely related to the llama, provided early Native Americans with meat and wool for clothing. **Political and Social Systems** Why do you think Paleolithic hunters needed to unite in small bands?

## HUMANITIES LINK

*Art History* Lascaux cave paintings (page 10).
*Literature* In this chapter, you will encounter passages from the following works of literature: Agatha Christie, *Come, Tell Me How You Live* (page 4); *Hymn to Varuna* (page 14).

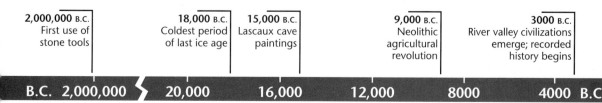

**2,000,000** B.C.
First use of stone tools

**18,000** B.C.
Coldest period of last ice age

**15,000** B.C.
Lascaux cave paintings

**9,000** B.C.
Neolithic agricultural revolution

**3000** B.C.
River valley civilizations emerge; recorded history begins

B.C. **2,000,000** **20,000** **16,000** **12,000** **8000** **4000** B.C.

# 1 Understanding Our Past

## Guide for Reading

- What methods do scientists use to find out about early peoples?

- How do historians reconstruct the past?

- How are geography and history linked?

- **Vocabulary** *prehistory, archaeology, artifact, technology, historian, geography, latitude, longitude*

They knew they were standing on a mountain of hidden treasure. Eagerly, they set up their equipment and began drilling. A 1,300-pound bucket plunged into the mountain, bringing up heaps of "wonderful things." Despite the foul smell that rose from the mound, the scientists sorted eagerly through each pile.

These treasure hunters were members of the University of Arizona Garbage Project. On this day, they were exploring the Fresh Kills landfill on Staten Island, New York—the world's largest garbage dump. Layer by layer, the drill bored into the recent past. At 35 feet, the bucket was bringing up newspapers, grass clippings, and hot dogs from 1984. At 60 feet, the drill had reached debris from the 1940s. From each layer, the team carefully collected and labeled samples.

Members of the Garbage Project learn about our society by studying the things we have thrown away. In a similar way, other scientists find and study the objects left behind by early peoples, from their garbage to their artwork. Through such research, we are slowly learning how people lived at the dawn of human history.

## How Do We Know?

The search for our ancient past has led us all over the globe and far back in time. The Iceman, whom you read about on page 2, lived in prehistoric times. Prehistory refers to the long period of time before people invented systems of writing. Prehistoric people had no cities, countries, organized central governments, or complex inventions.

About 5,000 years ago, some people in different parts of the world began to keep written records. That event marked the beginning of recorded history. Although these early records are often scanty, they do give us a narrative of events, as well as a number of names and dates.

**Kinds of evidence.** In the past 200 years, a new science, archaeology, has emerged to help us understand our past. Archaeology (ahr kee AHL uh jee) is the study of the ways of life of early peoples through the examination of their physical remains. Archaeologists have learned about the human past by studying artifacts, or objects made by people. Artifacts include tools, weapons, pottery, clothing, and jewelry. By analyzing such artifacts, archaeologists draw conclusions about the beliefs, values, and activities of our ancestors.

Mystery writer Agatha Christie, who was married to an archaeologist, wrote that artifacts and other evidence were just a way for people of the past to tell us how they lived:

66'In this big silo we kept our grain.'
'With these bone needles we sewed our clothes.' 'These were our houses, this our bathroom, here our system of sanitation!' . . . 'Here, in this little jar, is my make-up.' 'All these cook-pots are of a very common type. You'll find them by the hundred. We get them from the potter at the corner. Woolworth's, did you say? Is that what you call him in your time?'99

**Archaeologists at work.** Analyzing ancient artifacts is difficult, but archaeologists have devised many useful techniques. In the 1800s and early 1900s, archaeologists picked a likely site, or place, to look for human remains. Then they began digging. The farther down they dug, the older the artifacts they found. Sometimes, the long-buried objects crumbled as soon as they were exposed to light and air. Today, scientists have discovered ways of preserving such fragile artifacts.

By studying thousands of items, archaeologists have traced how early people developed new technologies. Technology refers to the skills and tools people use to meet their basic needs. The first stone tools, for example, were

crudely made with jagged edges and rough surfaces. Stone tools from later times are smooth and polished, showing improved skills.

Archaeologists today also make detailed maps locating every artifact they find. By analyzing this evidence, they can tell what went on at different locations within a site. Flint chips, for example, might suggest the workplace of a tool-maker. Piles of shells or gnawed bones may show where prehistoric people threw their garbage.

**Technology and the past.** Archaeologists use modern technology to study and interpret their findings. Computers can be used to store and sort data or to develop accurate site maps. Aerial photography can reveal patterns of how people used the land. Techniques for measuring radioactivity help chemists and physicists determine the age of objects.

Geologists, or experts on earth science, help archaeologists date artifacts by determining the age of nearby rocks. Botanists and zoologists, experts on plants and animals, examine seeds and animal bones to learn about the diet of early people. Experts on climate determine what conditions early people faced on the plains of Africa or in ice-covered parts of Europe. Biologists analyze human bones, as well as bloodstains found on old stone tools and weapons.

## Historians Reconstruct the Past

While archaeologists have uncovered useful information about the past, most of what goes into a textbook like this one comes from the work of historians. Historians study how people lived in the past. Like archaeologists, historians study artifacts, from clothing and coins to artwork and tombstones. However, they rely even more on written evidence, such as letters or

Today, most historians and nations officially use the Christian Era calendar, based on the life of Jesus Christ. Years are dated either B.C. (before Christ) or A.D. (*anno domini*, "year of the Lord"). But the Christian calendar is not the only one used in the world. For example, the Chinese, Jews, and Muslims have their own dating systems. The year 2000 on the Christian calendar will overlap the Muslim year 1371, the Chinese year 4637, and the Jewish year 5761.

" '. . . . A record for posterity?' Man, are you cracked? Who's going to want to read about *this* war a hundred years from now?"

© Punch/ROTHCO

tax records. Historians of the recent past also use such evidence as photographs or films.

**Historical detection.** Robin Winks, a noted historian, has described the thrill of historical discovery:

> ❝The historian must collect, interpret, and then explain his evidence by methods which are not greatly different from those techniques employed by the detective.❞

Like a detective, the historian must evaluate the evidence to determine if it is reliable. Do records of a meeting between two officials tell us exactly what was said? Who was taking notes? Does a videotape of an event show everything that happened? Was a letter writer really giving an eyewitness report or just passing on rumors? Could the letter even be a forgery? The historian tries to find the answers.

Historians then must interpret the evidence, explaining what it means. Often, the historian's goal is to determine the causes of a certain development or event, such as a war. By explaining why things happened in the past, the historian can help us understand what is going on today and what may happen tomorrow.

Generally, historians try to give a straightforward account of events. Sometimes, though, their personal experiences, cultural backgrounds, or political opinions may affect their interpretations. At times, historians disagree about what the evidence proves. Such differences can lead to lively debates.

**The "great" and the "small."** The first historians began writing thousands of years ago. These early historians wrote mostly about the deeds of well-known people such as monarchs, politicians, and generals.

Today, historians still write about famous people whose actions have had wide influence. Yet other historians are studying the lives of ordinary people. How did farmers or workers earn a living? What holidays did they celebrate? What was family life like? The answers to such questions have increased our understanding of the past.

## Geography and History

Geography is one key to understanding history because it is the stage on which all history takes place. In its broadest sense, geography is the study of people, their environments, and the resources available to them. Five themes sum up the impact of geography on the human story: location, place, human-environment interaction, movement, and region.

**Location.** Location tells where a place is on the surface of the Earth. You can locate any place on a map using latitude and longitude. Latitude measures distance north or south of the Equator. Longitude measures distance east and west of the Prime Meridian, an imaginary line that runs north to south through Greenwich, England. For example, you can locate the city of Seoul, South Korea, at 37° N latitude and

127° E longitude. These numbers give its exact location.

Relative location, where one place is located in relation to another, is sometimes more important than exact location. Ancient Athens, for example, was located on the eastern Mediterranean Sea, near much older civilizations in Egypt and the Middle East. This relative location influenced the Athenians' way of life because they acquired valuable skills and ideas from their neighbors.

**Place.** Geographers describe places in terms of their physical features and human characteristics. Physical features of a place include landforms, bodies of water, climate, soil quality, resources, and plant and animal life. Human characteristics include where most people live, their economic activities, religious beliefs, and languages.

**Human-environment interaction.** Since prehistoric times, people have interacted with their environment. That is, they have shaped and been shaped by the places in which they lived. Early farmers, for example, used water from rivers to irrigate their crops. Much later, European settlers in the Americas cut down trees to clear land for farms. As technology has advanced, we have changed the environment in

*Geography Makes a Difference*  Where people live affects how they live. Differences in landforms, bodies of water, climate, and natural resources help shape a variety of human cultures. Note some of the differences between life in Siberia (right) and life in Vietnam (above).
*Diversity*  Identify two cultural differences shown by these photos. How might geography help create this cultural diversity?

more complex ways. Today, roads slice through deserts, and canals link distant bodies of water. The impact of these changes has led people to look at the environment in new ways.

**Movement.** The movement of people, goods, and ideas is another key link between geography and history. In early times, people followed herds of deer or buffalo on which they depended for food. In more recent times, people have migrated, or moved, from farms and villages to cities in search of jobs. Others have fled from one place to another to escape war or religious persecution.

In ancient times, as today, traders have carried goods from one part of the Earth to another. Ideas also move, carried by people like missionaries or settlers. Today, communications satellites and television cables carry ideas faster and farther than ever before.

**Region.** Geographers divide the world into many types of regions. Some regions are based on physical features. The Gulf States, for example, are those countries bordering the Persian Gulf. They are part of a larger region of southwestern Asia, which we today call the Middle East. Regions may also be defined by political, economic, or cultural features. Culturally, the Gulf States are part of two larger regions, the Arabic-speaking world and the Muslim world.

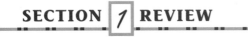

## SECTION 1 REVIEW

1. **Define** (a) prehistory, (b) archaeology, (c) artifact, (d) technology, (e) historian, (f) geography, (g) latitude, (h) longitude.
2. How do archaeologists learn about the lives of prehistoric people?
3. What kinds of evidence do historians use to study the past?
4. Give two examples of how people interact with their environment.
5. *Critical Thinking* **Linking Past and Present** Historians and archaeologists have worked to piece together the human story from prehistory up to today. Why do you think it is important to understand our past?
6. *ACTIVITY* Make a list of artifacts that you might find in the weekly trash from your community. Then, describe what archaeologists of the future might learn from these artifacts.

# 2  The Dawn of History

## Guide for Reading

■ What advances did people make during the Old Stone Age?

■ What can we learn about the religious beliefs of early people?

■ Why was the agricultural revolution a turning point in history?

■ **Vocabulary** *nomad, glacier*

A small band of hunters and food gatherers were camped on the shore of Lake Turkana in East Africa. One member of the group picked up a stone and chipped it with another stone to make a sharp, jagged edge. The toolmaker may have used this simple tool to cut meat from a dead animal or to sharpen a stick for digging up edible roots.

The toolmaker left the chipped stone near the lake. Some three million years later, archaeologist Richard Leakey picked it up. Leakey later described how he felt holding the tool:

&&It is a heart-quickening thought that we share the same . . . heritage with the hand that shaped the tool that we can now hold in our own hands, and with the mind that decided to make the tool that our minds can now contemplate.&&

Very slowly, early people learned to make better tools and weapons from stone, bone, and wood. They also developed new skills. Technological advances like these helped more people to survive.

## Hunters and Food Gatherers

Historians call the earliest period of human history the Old Stone Age, or Paleolithic age. This long period dates from the time of the first stone toolmakers to about 10,000 B.C.

**African beginnings.** In the last few decades, archaeologists have found startling evidence of early human life in East Africa. In 1959, Mary and Louis Leakey found pieces of bone embedded in ancient rock at Olduvai (OHL duh way) Gorge in Tanzania. After careful testing, they determined that the bone belonged to early humans. In 1974, Donald Johanson found the oldest complete human skeleton in Ethiopia. He named his find "Lucy" after a Beatles song.

Because of such evidence, scientists think that the earliest people lived in East Africa. Later, their descendants migrated north and east into Europe and Asia. In time, people reached the Americas, Australia, and the islands of the Pacific.

**Nomads on the move.** Paleolithic people lived in small hunting and food-gathering bands numbering about 20 or 30 people. Everyone contributed to feeding the group. In general, men hunted or fished. Women, with their small children, gathered berries, fruit, nuts, wild grain, roots, or even shellfish. This food kept the band alive when game was scarce. Paleolithic people were nomads, moving from place to place as they followed game animals and ripening fruit.

People depended wholly on their environment for survival. At the same time, they found ways to adapt to their surroundings. Men and women made simple tools and weapons such as digging sticks, spears, and axes out of the materials at hand—stone, bone, or wood. At some point, Stone Age people developed spoken language, which let them cooperate during the hunt and perhaps discuss plans for the future.

**Environmental changes.** Prehistoric people faced severe challenges from the environment. During several ice ages, the Earth cooled. Thick glaciers, or sheets of ice, spread across parts of Asia, Europe, and North America. To endure the cold, Paleolithic people invented clothing. Wrapped in animal skins, they took refuge in caves or under rocky overhangs during the long winters. They also learned to build fires for warmth and cooking. In this harsh life, only the hardy survived.

**Early religion and art.** About 30,000 years ago, people began to leave evidence of their belief in a spiritual world. To them, the world was full of spirits like those of the animals they hunted. Ancient artists may have expressed those beliefs in the pictures that they painted on cave walls.

In France, Spain, and northern Africa, cave paintings vividly portray animals such as deer, horses, and buffalo. Some cave paintings show stick-figure people, too. The paintings lie deep in the caves, far from a band's living quarters. Cave paintings may have been part of religious rituals in which hunters sought help from the spirit world for an upcoming hunt. (See the picture on page 10.)

Archaeologists have also found small stone statues that probably had religious meaning. Statues of pregnant women, for example, may have been symbols meant to ensure survival of the band. They suggest that early people worshiped earth-mother goddesses, givers of food and life.

**Belief in an afterlife.** Toward the end of the Old Stone Age, some people began burying their dead with great care. This practice suggests a belief in life after death. They probably believed the afterlife would be similar to life in this world, so they provided the dead with tools, weapons, and other needed goods. Burial customs like these survived in many places into modern times.

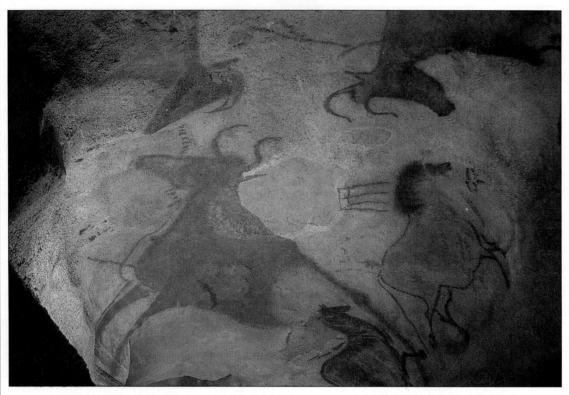

**Lascaux Cave Paintings** *This dramatic view of an ancient hunt exists deep within a cave in Lascaux, France. Religious beliefs probably inspired the Stone Age artists who created the scene by using paints made from crushed minerals and plants. The artists lighted their way by burning animal fats in stone dishes, and climbed wooden scaffolds to reach high walls and ceilings.* **Art and Literature** *What religious purpose do you think this cave painting might have served?*

## The First Farmers

About 11,000 years ago, nomadic bands made a breakthrough that had far-reaching effects. They learned to farm. By producing their own food crops, they could remain in one place. Farmers thus settled into permanent villages and developed a whole new range of skills and tools. This change from nomadic to settled farming life ushered in the New Stone Age, or Neolithic age.

**Planting seeds.** No one knows when and how people began to plant seeds for food. Some scholars think that farming started in the Middle East and then spread. Others argue that farming developed independently in different regions. No matter which way it occurred, the change had such dramatic effects that historians call it the Neolithic agricultural revolution.

Food-gathering women may have made the crucial discovery. They may have noticed that if seeds were scattered on the ground, new plants would grow the next year. They may also have seen that removing some plants enabled nearby ones to grow stronger. Perhaps if game animals were scarce, a band might camp at a place where plants grew and might begin cultivating them season after season.

**Domesticating animals.** The Neolithic revolution included a second feature. People learned to domesticate, or tame, some of the animals they had once hunted. Rather than wait

**ISSUES** *For* **TODAY** Farming technology transformed the lives of Neolithic people. How does technology change the way that people meet their basic need for food?

for migrating animals to return each year, hunters rounded them up. Then they herded the animals to good grasslands or penned them in rough enclosures. The animals provided people with a source of protein.

The Neolithic agricultural revolution enabled people to become food producers for the first time. It led to a growth in population, which in turn led to more interaction among human communities. No greater change in the way people lived took place until the Industrial Revolution, which began in the late 1700s.

## Skara Brae, A Neolithic Village

On a windy blue bay in the Orkney Islands, north of Scotland, lies a cluster of half-buried stone houses. Their roofs are long gone. Sheep browse on a green hillside to one side of the houses. On the other side, the chilly waters of the bay wash against the gravel shore.

About 5,000 years ago, a Neolithic village stood on this site. Buried among the ruins of Skara Brae (SKA ruh BRAY), archaeologists have found artifacts that give us clues to the lives of these early farmers.

Skara Brae is tiny. The entire village covers an area about equal to three classrooms. Each house is similar to its neighbor, showing that people were relatively equal in social status. Its single room contains a central, square fireplace, two or three stone shelves against the wall, and a sleeping area set off by stone slabs.

**At work and play.** If you had visited Skara Brae in the New Stone Age, you would have seen some people planting barley or wheat in the fields near their homes. Children might be tending pigs, cows, or sheep like the ones that graze there today. Other villagers might have been fishing along the shore. In a village such as Skara Brae, cooperation was essential. Families lived close together and depended on one another for survival.

At nightfall, each family probably gathered around its own hearth. They cooked meat or fish in clay pots and baked bread in a small stone oven. Smoke quickly filled the tiny hut, but its walls protected the family from the blustering winds outside.

Gathered around the fireplace, the family might talk over the day's events or make plans for the next day. Perhaps an adult told stories passed down from generation to generation. Children and adults might also have played games. Among the artifacts archaeologists found at Skara Brae were two bone cubes with markings like those on modern dice.

**In the village workshop.** At one end of the village, chips of flint and chert, a local stone,

**A Neolithic Home** This photograph shows the remains of a one-room house at the Neolithic village of Skara Brae. To the rear of the house are stone shelves for storing possessions, and to the left is a sleeping area. The house was buried within a mound of dirt for protection from the harsh climate.
**Geography and History** What role did geography play in the use of stone rather than wood for buildings in Skara Brae?

indicate the location of a workshop. There, villagers made tools, including smooth, polished ax heads and chipped arrowheads.

Like Neolithic people elsewhere, the villagers of Skara Brae made clay pots. They had not, however, mastered another basic technology, weaving cloth. In other parts of the world, Neolithic people had learned to weave cloth from animal hair or vegetable fibers. The people of Skara Brae, on the other hand, sewed together animal skins to make clothing, as their Paleolithic ancestors had.

Archaeologists have found many bone beads at Skara Brae. Some were strung into necklaces, while others may have decorated fur or leather clothing. Some stone objects remain mysterious. They are smooth, polished, and marked with patterns of lines, bumps, and hollows. Possibly village religious leaders used these stones in their ceremonies.

**Respect for the dead.** Villagers buried their dead in earthen tombs surrounded by stone walls. Like other Neolithic people, they showed respect for the dead and may have called on the spirits of their buried ancestors to help them in this world. ■

## Changing Ways of Life

How did the lives of Neolithic farmers differ from those of Paleolithic hunters and gatherers? They probably divided up the work much as their ancestors had done, by gender and age. Still, important differences began to emerge. In settled farming communities, the status of women declined as men came to dominate family, economic, and political life.

**Village leaders.** Heads of families, probably older men, formed a council of elders. They were responsible for important decisions, such as when to plant or harvest. In time, a village headman, or chief, may have emerged.

During times of economic scarcity, warfare increased and some men gained great prestige as warriors. These elite warriors asserted power over both women and other men. The changes did not mean that women lost all their influence or rights. Rather, they show that village life was reshaping the roles of both women and men.

**More possessions.** Settled people accumulated more personal property than their nomadic ancestors. The beads, pottery bowls, and other prized objects displayed on the stone shelves at Skara Brae may have made some families feel wealthier than their neighbors. Great differences among social classes did not yet exist, however.

**New technologies.** To farm successfully, people had to develop new technologies. Like farmers today, they had to find ways to protect their crops and measure out enough seed for the next year's harvest. They also needed to measure time accurately so that they would know when to plant and harvest. Gradually, they created the first calendars. In some places, farmers learned to use animals such as oxen or water buffalo to plow the fields.

Inventions did not take place everywhere at the same time. Technologies might travel slowly from one area to another, taking thousands of years to spread across continents. Other technologies may have been invented separately in different parts of the world.

By about 5,000 years ago, the advances made by early farming communities led people to a new stage of development—the emergence of civilizations.

## SECTION 2 REVIEW

1. **Identify** (a) Paleolithic age, (b) Neolithic age, (c) Skara Brae.
2. **Define** (a) nomad, (b) glacier.
3. How did Paleolithic people learn to adapt to their environment?
4. What do burial customs suggest about the beliefs of early peoples?
5. (a) What were the key features of the agricultural revolution? (b) How did it change people's lives?
6. *Critical Thinking* **Recognizing Causes and Effects** (a) Why might economic scarcity lead to increased warfare? (b) Why do you think this change may have affected the status of women in Stone Age societies?
7. *ACTIVITY* With a classmate, prepare and act out a conversation between someone who lived in Paleolithic or Neolithic times and someone living today. Discuss what you each do every day, what you eat, how you dress, or how you spend your leisure time.

# Beginnings of Civilization

## Guide for Reading

- What are the basic features of civilizations?

- How did the first cities emerge?

- What developments can cause cultures to change?

- **Vocabulary** *bureaucracy, polytheistic, artisan, pictogram, scribe, city-state, empire, steppe, cultural diffusion*

Perhaps the best-known monuments of the ancient world are the great pyramids of Egypt. More than 100,000 workers labored for years under the hot North African sun to build these giant tombs. Without modern machinery, they fit into place more than two million stones *weighing an average of 2 ½ tons each!*

Clearly, pyramid building required a society more highly organized and technologically advanced than Neolithic farming villages. In fact, the pyramids were created by one of the world's first civilizations. In Egypt, as in other parts of the world, people were taking a giant step from prehistory into history.

*Dawn of Civilization  The development of cities marked the beginning of civilization. In the Americas, cities such as this Mayan one at Uxmal served as political and religious centers. The temple-pyramid towering above the surrounding landscape offers lasting evidence of Mayan devotion to their gods.*
***Religions and Value Systems*** *Why do you think nature gods were so important to people of early civilizations?*

## Features of Civilization

What do we mean by civilization? What did the early civilizations that rose in different parts of the globe have in common? Historians distinguish eight basic features found in most early civilizations. These eight features are (1) cities, (2) well-organized central governments, (3) complex religions, (4) job specialization, (5) social classes, (6) arts and architecture, (7) public works, and (8) writing.

**Rise of cities.** The central feature of civilization was the rise of cities. The first cities emerged after farmers began cultivating fertile lands along river valleys and producing surplus, or extra, food. These surpluses in turn helped populations to expand. As populations grew, some villages swelled into cities.

**River valley civilizations.** Cities rose independently in the valleys of the Tigris and Euphrates rivers in the Middle East, the Nile River in Egypt, the Indus River in India, and the Yellow River, or Huang He, in China. (See the map on page 1.) Conditions in these river valleys favored farming. Flood waters spread silt across the valleys, renewing the soil and keeping it fertile. The animals that flocked to the rivers to drink were another source of food. In addition, rivers provided a regular water supply and a means of transporting people and goods.

Rivers also posed challenges. Farmers had to control flooding and channel waters to the fields. To meet these challenges, cooperation was needed. Early farmers worked together to build dikes, dig canals, and carve out irrigation ditches. Such large-scale projects required leadership and a well-organized government.

**Civilizations in the Americas.** Unlike the civilizations in Asia, Africa, and Europe, civilizations in the Americas often did not rise in river valleys. Two major civilizations, the Aztecs and Incas, eventually emerged in the highlands of Mexico and Peru.

In the Americas, the first cities may have begun as religious centers. There, powerful priests inspired people from nearby villages to build temples to their gods. Villagers would gather at the temples for regular worship. In time, many may have remained permanently, creating cities like those elsewhere.

## Organized Governments

As cities grew, they needed to maintain a steady food supply. To produce large amounts of food and oversee irrigation projects, new forms of government arose. City governments were far more powerful than the councils of elders and local chiefs of farming villages.

At first, priests probably had the greatest power. In time, warrior kings emerged as the chief political leaders. They took over the powers of the old councils of elders and set themselves up as hereditary rulers who passed power from father to son.

Almost always, rulers claimed that their right to rule came from the gods. They thus gained religious power as well. Darius the Great, ruler of the vast Persian empire, proclaimed that his power came directly from Ahura Mazda, the supreme Persian god:

> 66Ahura Mazda bestowed the kingdom upon me. Ahura Mazda bore me aid until I got possession of this kingdom. By the favor of Ahura Mazda I hold this kingdom.99

Government became more complex as rulers issued laws, collected taxes, and organized systems of defense. To enforce order, rulers relied on royal officials. Over time, government bureaucracies evolved. A bureaucracy is a system of managing government through departments run by appointed officials. Separate departments oversaw tax collection, irrigation projects, or the military.

## Complex Religions

Like their Stone Age ancestors, most ancient people were polytheistic. That is, they be-

lieved in many gods. People appealed to sun gods, river goddesses, and other spirits that they believed controlled natural forces. Other gods were thought to control human activities such as birth, trade, or war.

In ancient religions, priests and worshipers sought to gain the favor of the gods through complex rituals such as ceremonies, dances, prayers, and hymns. In one hymn of ancient India, a sick man humbly appeals to the god Varuna for help:

> 66Let me not go to the House of Clay,
>    O Varuna!
> Forgive, O gracious Lord,
>    forgive! . . .
> Whatever sin we mortals have
>    committed against . . . the gods,
> If, foolish, we have thwarted your
>    commands,
> O god, do not destroy us in your
>    anger!99

To ensure divine help, people built temples and sacrificed animals, crops, or sometimes other humans to the gods. Sacrifices and other ceremonies required the full-time attention of priests, who had special training and knowledge.

## Job Specialization and Social Classes

The lives of city dwellers differed from those of their Stone Age ancestors. Urban people developed so many new crafts that a single individual could no longer master all the skills needed to make tools, weapons, or other goods.

**Skilled artisans.** For the first time, individuals began to specialize in certain jobs. Some became artisans, or skilled craftworkers, who made pottery or finely carved or woven goods. Among the crafts that developed in cities, metalworking was particularly important. People learned to make tools and weapons, first out of copper, then later out of bronze, a more durable mixture of copper and tin.

Cities had other specialists, too. Bricklayers built city walls. Soldiers defended them. Merchants sold goods in the marketplace. Singers, dancers, and storytellers entertained on public occasions. Such specialization made people dependent on others for their various needs.

# PARALLELS THROUGH TIME

## Jewelry

Since the rise of civilization, skilled artisans have engaged in many different crafts. One such craft is the creation of jewelry for the personal adornment of both men and women. With the passage of time, styles may change, but the human desire for beauty endures.

**Linking Past and Present**  What precious materials have artisans of both the past and present used in their jewelry? Why do people consider these materials so valuable?

**PAST**  *The jade and gold necklace with a pair of female dancers was crafted during the Zhou dynasty in China more than 2,000 years ago. Some 1,000 years earlier, skillful Egyptian artisans made necklaces of multicolored glass, such as the one shown below.*

**PRESENT**  *Today's artisans continue to create necklaces of gold, silver, and other materials. They often imitate the designs and styles of ancient civilizations.*

**Social ranking.** In cities, social organization became more complex. People were ranked according to their jobs. Such ranking led to the growth of social classes. Priests and nobles usually occupied the top level of an ancient society. Next came a small class of wealthy merchants, followed by humbler artisans. Below them stood the vast majority of people, peasant farmers who lived in the surrounding villages and produced food for the city.

Slaves occupied the lowest social level. Slaves sometimes came from poor families who sold themselves into slavery to pay their debts. Others were prisoners captured in war. Since male captives were often killed, women and children made up the largest number of these slaves.

## Arts, Architecture, and Public Works

The arts and architecture of ancient civilizations expressed the beliefs and values of the people who created them. Temples and palaces dominated the city scenery. Such buildings reassured people of the strength and power of their government and religion.

Skilled workers built and decorated these massive buildings. In museums today, you can see statues of gods and goddesses, temple wall paintings, as well as furniture and jewelry found in ancient tombs from around the world. They give ample evidence of the artistic genius of the first civilizations.

Closely linked to temples and palaces were vast public works that strong rulers ordered to be built. Such projects included irrigation systems, roads, bridges, and defensive walls. Although they were costly in human labor and even lives, such projects were meant to benefit the city, protecting it from attack and ensuring its food supply.

## Writing

A critical new skill developed by the earliest civilizations was the art of writing. It may have begun in temples, where priests needed to record amounts of grain collected, accurate information about the seasons, and precise rituals and prayers.

Archaeologists have found masses of ancient writings, ranging from treaties and tax rolls to business and marriage contracts. Early writing was made up of pictograms, or simple drawings to show the words represented. In time, symbols were added. They might stand for sounds of words or for ideas that could not be expressed easily in pictures.

As writing grew more complex, only specially trained people called scribes learned to read and write. Scribes were educated in temple schools and kept records for priests, rulers, and merchants. In only a few societies were women permitted to attend temple schools. As a result, women were generally excluded from becoming scribes, an occupation that could lead to political power.

## Spread of Civilization

As ancient rulers gained more power, they conquered territories beyond their cities. This expansion led to the rise of the city-state, a political unit that included a city and its surrounding lands and villages. Rulers, nobles, and priests often controlled the land outside the city and forced peasants to grow crops on it. A large portion of each harvest went to support the government and temples.

**The first empires.** Rival leaders often battled for power. Sometimes, ambitious rulers conquered many cities and villages, creating the first empires. An empire is a group of states or territories controlled by one ruler. For the conquered people, defeat was painful and often cruel. At the same time, empire building also brought benefits. It helped end war between neighboring communities and created common bonds among people.

**Interactions with nomadic peoples.** The first cities were scattered islands in a sea of older, simpler ways of life. Most peoples lived as their Stone Age ancestors had. They hunted, gathered food,

▲ Replica of ancient Egyptian reed boat

or lived in simple farming villages. On some less-fertile lands or on sparse, dry grasslands, called steppes, nomadic herders tended cattle, sheep, goats, or other animals. Because the lands were poor in water and grass, these nomads had to keep moving to find new pasture.

Nomadic cultures were not "civilized," in the sense that they did not exhibit the characteristics of city life. However, many nomadic peoples developed sophisticated traditions in oral poetry, music, weaving, animal raising, and other areas of the arts and sciences.

Throughout history, relations between nomads and city dwellers have been complex. At times, the two groups cooperated in political, economic, or military matters. At other times, they have been in conflict, with cities subduing nomadic peoples or nomads overrunning cities. You will read about such encounters in later chapters.

## Civilizations and Change

All societies and civilizations change. In fact, history itself might be defined as the story of these changes. Ancient civilizations changed in many ways over the centuries. Among the chief causes of change were shifts in the physical environment and interactions among people.

**Environmental changes.** Like their Stone Age ancestors, people of early civilizations depended heavily on the physical environment. They needed rain and fertile soil to produce crops. Resources such as stone, timber, or metals were also essential. Changes in the environment could have an immediate impact on people's lives.

At times, sudden, drastic events devastated a community. A tremendous volcano may have wiped out Minoan civilization on the island of Crete in the Mediterranean Sea. (See Chapter 5.) Overfarming could destroy soil fertility, or rivers might become too salty. Cities would then suffer famine, and survivors would be forced to move away.

If people used up nearby timber or ran out of other building resources, they would have to adapt to this scarcity. They might, for example, trade with areas where such resources were available. Or they might use alternate building materials such as reeds.

**Interactions among people.** An even more important source of change was cultural diffusion, the spread of ideas, customs, and technologies from one people to another. Cultural diffusion occurred through migration, trade, and warfare.

As famine, drought, or other disasters led people to migrate, they came into contact with others whose lives differed from their own. As a result of such interactions, people often shared and adapted customs. Trade, too, introduced people to new goods or better methods of producing them. In ancient times, skills such as working bronze and writing, as well as religious beliefs, passed from one people to another.

Warfare also brought change. Often, victorious armies forced their way of life upon the people they defeated. On other occasions, the victors adopted the ways of conquered people. Sometimes, nomadic rulers would become absorbed in city life. At other times, they would rule from camps outside the city limits, keeping their own customs.

**Looking ahead.** In the next two chapters, you will read about the earliest civilizations that developed in the river valleys of Africa and Asia. They differed in significant ways, each developing its own traditions. At the same time, the civilizations of Egypt, Mesopotamia, India, and China all fit our definition of a civilization.

## SECTION 3 REVIEW

1. **Define** (a) bureaucracy, (b) polytheistic, (c) artisan, (d) pictogram, (e) scribe, (f) city-state, (g) empire, (h) steppe, (i) cultural diffusion.
2. How did conditions in some river valleys favor the rise of civilization?
3. How were government and religion linked in early civilizations?
4. What are three causes of cultural change?
5. *Critical Thinking* **Recognizing Causes and Effects** How did job specialization lead to the emergence of social classes?
6. *ACTIVITY* Draw a three-column chart. In the first column, list the eight basic features of a civilization. In the second column, describe each feature. In the third column, give an example of each feature from modern society.

# Skills for Success

## Recognizing Causes and Effects

Causes are the reasons why an event or development happened. Effects are what followed as a result of the event. Key words can help you recognize causes and effects. The words *since, because,* and *due to* often indicate causes. The words *therefore* and *as a result* often indicate effects.

Causes and effects may be either immediate or long-term. Immediate causes generally happened just before an event and had a direct role in bringing it about. Immediate effects generally happened just after an event and as a direct result of that event. Long-term causes and effects develop over a longer period of time.

Cause-and-effect charts, like the one here, give brief summaries of events or developments. While they cannot provide all information about causes and effects, they can organize such information into usable form. Use the chart and the information in Chapter 1 to answer the following questions.

**1** **Identify the immediate and long-term causes and effects.** (a) What is the subject of the chart? (b) What were two long-term causes? (c) What were two immediate causes? (d) What effects are still felt today?

**2** **Analyze the causes and effects.** (a) How were geographic causes linked to the emergence of river valley civilizations? (b) What role did technology play in the rise of civilization? (c) How did civilizations lead to a more complex system of social classes?

**3** **Draw conclusions based on the cause-and-effect relationship.** (a) What do you think was the most important effect of the rise of civilizations? (b) Why do you think cities can now exist far from fertile river valleys?

*Beyond the Classroom* Look through a newspaper or magazine and locate an article that discusses an event of interest to you. Look for the key words mentioned above. Then, prepare a cause-and-effect chart. What information would you need to make your chart more complete?

## CAUSE AND EFFECT

**Long-Term Causes**

Silt deposits create fertile soil in river valleys
Neolithic agricultural revolution
Hunters and gatherers settle into farming communities

**Immediate Causes**

New technologies improve farming
Food surpluses support rising populations
First cities built in fertile valleys
Farmers cooperate to control flooding and channel water

### RISE OF RIVER VALLEY CIVILIZATIONS

**Immediate Effects**

Complex forms of government develop
Arts become more elaborate
Job specialization leads to social classes
Invention of writing

**Long-Term Effects**

Government bureaucracies emerge
Early civilizations conquer neighboring lands
Civilizations clash with nomadic peoples

**Connections Today**

Archaeologists mine rich stores of information in Egypt, Middle East, India, China
Large cities such as Cairo and Baghdad still flourish in river valley regions

## Building Vocabulary

Review the vocabulary words in this chapter. Then, use *ten* of these words to create a crossword puzzle. Exchange puzzles with a classmate. Complete the puzzles and then check each other's answers.

## Reviewing Chapter Themes

1. **Continuity and Change** (a) What are two tasks facing historians? (b) How do historians draw on the work of archaeologists and geographers? (c) How has the work of historians and archaeologists changed in recent years?
2. **Economics and Technology** (a) Why is the Neolithic agricultural revolution considered to be a turning point in history? (b) Compare the way Neolithic and Paleolithic people interacted with their environment.
3. **Religions and Value Systems** (a) What does archaeological evidence suggest about the religious beliefs of Stone Age people? (b) How did religious practices become more complex in early civilizations?
4. **Political and Social Systems** (a) What are the eight basic features of civilization? (b) Why was the growth of cities linked to the rise of strong, well-organized central governments? (c) Why did bureaucracies develop in early governments?

## Thinking Critically

1. **Identifying Main Ideas** Review the story of the discovery of the Iceman on page 2. Then, write a sentence stating the main idea of the story.
2. **Recognizing Points of View** Thomas Carlyle, a Scottish writer of the 1800s, defined history as "the biography of great men." Ibn Khaldun, a Muslim historian of the 1300s, wrote that history was "information about human social organizations." (a) What is the main difference between Khaldun's definition of history and Carlyle's? (b) How might their viewpoints have affected the way each man wrote about history? (c) Which of these two points of view do you most agree with? Explain. (★ See *Skills for Success,* page 280.)
3. **Applying Information** (a) Describe the area where you live in terms of each of the five themes of geography. (b) Explain two ways that geography affects your own way of life.
4. **Recognizing Causes and Effects** Make a list of five major social or technological developments of the Old Stone Age and the New Stone Age. Then, for each development, identify one short-term and one long-term effect. (★ See *Skills for Success,* page 18.)
5. **Linking Past and Present** (a) Describe three ways that cultural diffusion occurs. (b) Give three examples of cultural diffusion in today's world. (c) Why do you think cultural changes occur more quickly today than ever before?

## For Your Portfolio

A television news magazine is preparing a show about major archaeological discoveries. You and a classmate will work together to prepare a segment for the show. One of you will conduct the interview; the other will play the archaeologist.

1. Select an archaeologist, such as Louis or Mary Leakey (Olduvai Gorge), Charles Leonard Woolley (Ur), Kathleen Kenyon (Jericho), Howard Carter (the tomb of Tutankhamen), Heinrich Schliemann (the ruins of Troy), or Edward Herbert Thompson (Chichén Itzá). Look at recent books or articles on archaeology for other possible choices.
2. Use the library to research the life and work of the archaeologist you have chosen.
3. Write a series of questions that an interviewer might ask the archaeologist. Topics might include: (a) how the archaeologist became interested in uncovering the past, (b) where he or she worked, (c) important findings he or she made, (d) how he or she felt about these findings, (e) the lasting value of his or her work. Organize your questions and prepare answers. (★ See *Skills for Success,* page 444.)
4. Prepare visual aids for the interview. These may include maps and diagrams of the site, as well as photographs and drawings of artifacts.
5. Present the interview to the class. Afterward, discuss what you have learned about the work of archaeologists.

# First Civilizations: Africa and Asia

### (3200 B.C.–500 B.C.)

## CHAPTER OUTLINE

1  **Ancient Kingdoms of the Nile**
2  **Egyptian Civilization**
3  **City-States of Ancient Sumer**
4  **Invaders, Traders, and Empire Builders**
5  **The World of the Hebrews**

The dying man listened intently as the scribe read the words written on the scroll. The scroll contained the Book of the Dead, which Egyptians believed would prepare them for the perilous journey after death. Without knowing the right magical spells, the dead soul could not defeat fearsome monsters, cross a lake of fire, or outwit the sinister ferryman who piloted the dead through the underworld. One mistake and the journey was over.

Yet a still greater ordeal lay ahead. With dread, the deceased entered the hall of Osiris, god and judge of the dead. Osiris and his tribunal weighed the conscience of each soul. Eternal happiness awaited all who passed the test. To fail meant torture and extinction.

Fearfully, the deceased offered his defense:

66I have made no man to suffer hunger. I have made no one to weep. I have done no murder. . . . I have not encroached upon the fields of another. I have not added to the weights of the scales to cheat the seller. I have not misread the pointer of the scales to cheat the buyer.

I have not turned back water when it should flow. I have not cut a cutting in a canal of running water. . . . I am pure. I am pure. I am pure.99

Like people in every society throughout history, the ancient Egyptians grappled with questions of life and death. Through the spells in the Book of the Dead, they tried to overcome earthly mortality and gain a blissful afterlife.

Egyptian civilization emerged more than 5,000 years ago. At about the same time, another center of civilization emerged in the Middle East, in Sumer. Both rose in river valleys and had the basic features of civilization that you read about in Chapter 1. While they differed from each other in significant ways, both made distinct contributions to our world today.

**FOCUS ON** these questions as you read:

■ **Geography and History**
What role did rivers play in shaping the first civilizations of Egypt and Mesopotamia?

■ **Global Interaction**
How did trade, warfare, and migration spread ideas and inventions among early civilizations?

■ **Impact of the Individual**
How did powerful rulers influence political, military, and religious developments in Egypt and the Fertile Cresent?

■ **Diversity**
What contributions to civilization were made by small groups such as the Phoenicians and the Hebrews?

## TIME AND PLACE

***Egyptian Tomb Painting*** *Paintings found in the tombs of Egypt's rulers provide evidence of Egyptian religious beliefs. Here, the goddess Hathor, protector of lovers, sits next to the hawk-headed sun god Re-Harakhti. In his right hand, Re-Harakhti holds an ankh, symbol of eternal life.* ***Religions and Value Systems*** *What other symbols appear to have been important in ancient Egyptian religion? What are some important symbols in present-day religions?*

## HUMANITIES LINK

***Art History*** Queen Nefertiti (page 30).
***Literature*** In this chapter, you will encounter passages from the following works of literature: Book of the Dead (page 20); *Instructions of the Vizier Ptah-hotep* (page 23); *The Tale of Sinuhe* (page 30); *The Epic of Gilgamesh* (pages 31, 34); Book of Exodus (page 45).

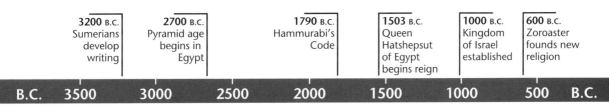

**3200 B.C.** Sumerians develop writing

**2700 B.C.** Pyramid age begins in Egypt

**1790 B.C.** Hammurabi's Code

**1503 B.C.** Queen Hatshepsut of Egypt begins reign

**1000 B.C.** Kingdom of Israel established

**600 B.C.** Zoroaster founds new religion

B.C.  3500     3000     2500     2000     1500     1000     500   B.C.

# 1 Ancient Kingdoms of the Nile

## Guide for Reading

■ How did geography influence Egyptian life?

■ What were the main periods of early Egyptian history?

■ How did trade and warfare affect the Egyptians?

■ Vocabulary *silt, cataract, delta, dynasty, pharaoh, vizier*

Every year, the great Nile River in northeastern Africa flooded its banks. As the waters rose, the people of ancient Egypt offered thanks: "Hail to thee, O Nile, that issues from the earth and comes to give life to Egypt." They praised the Nile for nourishing their land and cattle and for filling their storehouses with food.

The fertile lands of the river valley attracted Stone Age farmers. In prehistoric times, migrating people reached Egypt from the Mediterranean area, from hills and deserts along the Nile, and from other parts of Africa. As these early farmers produced more food, populations grew. In the Nile Valley, a powerful civilization emerged that depended on the control of river waters.

## Geography: The Nile Valley

Egypt, said the ancient Greek historian Herodotus, "is wholly the gift of the Nile." Without the Nile, Egypt would be swallowed up by the barren deserts that surround it. While the desert protected Egypt from invasion, it also limited where people could settle.

In ancient times, as today, farming villages dotted the narrow band of land watered by the Nile. Beyond the rich, irrigated "Black Land," generally no more than 10 miles (16 km) wide, lay the "Red Land," a sun-baked desert that stretches across North Africa.

Farmers took advantage of the fertile soil of the Nile Valley to grow wheat and flax, a plant whose fibers were used for clothing. By the time of Herodotus, Egypt had been producing large amounts of food for thousands of years. It had become known as a "breadbasket," exporting food to other parts of the Mediterranean world.

**Yearly floods.** The Nile rises in the highlands of Ethiopia and the lakes of central Africa. Every spring, rains in this interior region send water racing down streams that feed the Nile River. In ancient times, Egyptians eagerly awaited the annual flood. It soaked the land with life-giving water and deposited a layer of rich silt, or soil. An Egyptian hymn expressed the happiness of the people during this season:

> ❝If the Nile smiles, the Earth is joyous,
> Every stomach is full of rejoicing,
> Every spine is happy
> Every jawbone crushes its food.❞

People had to cooperate to control the Nile floods. They built dikes, reservoirs, and irrigation ditches to channel the rising river and store water for the dry season.

**Uniting the land.** Ancient Egypt had two distinct regions, Upper Egypt in the south and Lower Egypt in the north. Upper Egypt stretched from the first cataract, or waterfall, of the Nile northward to within 100 miles (160 km) of the Mediterranean. Lower Egypt covered the delta region where the Nile empties into the Mediterranean. A delta is a triangular area of marshland formed by deposits of silt at the mouth of some rivers.

About 3100 B.C., Menes, the king of Upper Egypt, united the two regions. He and his successors used the Nile as a highway linking north and south. They could send officials or armies to towns along the river. The Nile thus helped make Egypt the world's first unified state.

The river also served as a trade route. Egyptian merchants traveled up and down the Nile in sailboats and barges, exchanging the products of Africa, the Middle East, and the Mediterranean world.

## The Pyramid Age

The history of ancient Egypt is divided into three main periods: the Old Kingdom (about 2700 B.C.–2200 B.C.), the Middle Kingdom (about 2050 B.C.–1800 B.C.), and the New

Kingdom (about 1550 B.C.–1100 B.C.). During these periods, power passed from one dynasty, or ruling family, to another, but the land generally remained united.

**Old Kingdom.** During the Old Kingdom, pharaohs (FAIR ohz), as Egyptian rulers were called, organized a strong, centralized state. Pharaohs claimed divine support for their rule. Egyptians believed the pharaoh was a god. The pharaoh thus had absolute power, owning and ruling all the land.

Pharaohs of the Old Kingdom took pride in preserving justice and order. A pharaoh depended on a **vizier,** or chief minister, to supervise the business of government. Under the vizier, various bureaus looked after matters such as tax collection, farming, and the all-important irrigation system. Thousands of scribes carried out the vizier's instructions.

A wise vizier, Ptah-hotep (tah HOH tehp), took an interest in training young officials. Based on his vast experience of government, he wrote a book, *Instructions of the Vizier Ptah-hotep.* In it, he advised ambitious young people to avoid the errors he had seen all too often among officials:

> **❝**Let not your heart be puffed up because of your knowledge; be not confident because you are wise. Take counsel with the ignorant as well as the wise.**❞**

**Majestic tombs.** The Old Kingdom is sometimes called the Pyramid Age because during this period the Egyptians built the majestic pyramids that still stand at Giza, near present-day Cairo. The pyramids were tombs for eternity. Because Egyptians believed in an afterlife, they preserved the bodies of their dead rulers and provided them with everything they would need in their new lives.

To complete the pyramids, workers hauled and lifted millions of limestone blocks that weighed an average of 2 ½ tons each. The pyramid builders had no iron tools or wheeled vehicles. Workers quarried each stone by hand, pulled them on sleds to the site, and hoisted them up earthen ramps to be placed on the slowly rising structure. Building a pyramid took so many years that often a pharaoh would begin building his tomb as soon as he inherited the throne.

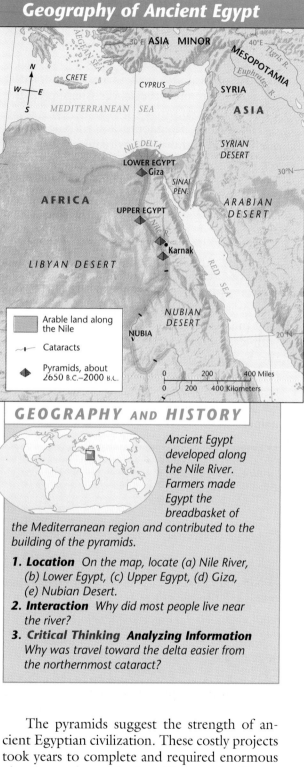

## Geography of Ancient Egypt

Arable land along the Nile

Cataracts

Pyramids, about 2650 B.C.–2000 B.C.

### GEOGRAPHY AND HISTORY

Ancient Egypt developed along the Nile River. Farmers made Egypt the breadbasket of the Mediterranean region and contributed to the building of the pyramids.

1. **Location** On the map, locate (a) Nile River, (b) Lower Egypt, (c) Upper Egypt, (d) Giza, (e) Nubian Desert.
2. **Interaction** Why did most people live near the river?
3. **Critical Thinking** *Analyzing Information* Why was travel toward the delta easier from the northernmost cataract?

The pyramids suggest the strength of ancient Egyptian civilization. These costly projects took years to complete and required enormous planning and organization. Thousands of farmers, who had to be fed each day, worked on the pyramids when not planting or harvesting crops.

## The Middle Kingdom

Power struggles, crop failures, and the cost of building the pyramids contributed to the collapse of the Old Kingdom. After more than a century of disunity, new pharaohs eventually emerged to reunite the land, ushering in the Middle Kingdom.

The Middle Kingdom was a turbulent period. The Nile did not rise as regularly as it had. Corruption and rebellions were common. Still, strong rulers did organize a large drainage project, creating vast new stretches of arable, or farmable, land. Egyptian armies occupied part of Nubia, the gold-rich land to the south. Traders also had greater contacts with the peoples of the Middle East and the Mediterranean island of Crete.

Catastrophe struck about 1700 B.C. when foreign invaders, the Hyksos (HIHK sohs), occupied the delta region. They awed the Egyptians with their horse-drawn war chariots. In time, the Egyptians would master this new military technology. The Hyksos, in turn, were so impressed by Egyptian civilization that they soon adopted Egyptian customs, beliefs, and even names.

The Hyksos dominated Egypt for more than 100 years. Finally, new Egyptian leaders arose, drove out the foreigners, and set up the New Kingdom.

## The Egyptian Empire

During the New Kingdom, powerful and ambitious pharaohs created a large empire. At its height, the Egyptian empire reached the Euphrates River. This age of conquest brought Egypt in greater contact with the Middle East as well as other parts of Africa.

**Queen Hatshepsut.** Among the outstanding rulers of the New Kingdom was Hatshepsut (hat SHEHP soot), daughter of one pharaoh and widow of another. Like some earlier Egyptian queens, Hatshepsut began by ruling in the name of a male heir too young to take the throne. However, she then took the bold step of declaring herself pharaoh and won the support of key officials. Because Egyptians saw kingship as a male privilege, she donned a false beard as a sign of authority.

*Great Sphinx at Giza* The Great Sphinx silently guards the pyramid tombs of Egyptian pharaohs. Originally painted in vivid colors, this figure of a crouching lion bears the face of King Khafre. **Political and Social Systems** What does the portrayal of the king as a lion suggest about the nature of kingship in ancient Egypt?

On the walls of her beautiful funeral temple, Hatshepsut left a record of her reign from 1503 B.C. to 1482 B.C. Carvings and writings proclaim her power and right to rule:

66Lo, the god knows me well,
    Amon, Lord of Thrones-of-the-
    Two Lands.
He made me rule Black Land and Red
    Land as a reward.
No one rebels against me in all lands.99

Other carvings describe how she encouraged trade with eastern Mediterranean lands. Her greatest triumph was an expedition sent to Punt, down the Red Sea coast of Africa. We do not know exactly where Punt was, but ships returned loaded with ebony, ivory, spices, leopard skins, and live monkeys for private zoos. They also brought back incense, medicines, and myrrh trees, much valued for their perfume. Hatshepsut had the fragrant trees planted near her temple.

**Ramses II.** A later pharaoh, Ramses II, won fame for his military victories. Between 1290 B.C. and 1224 B.C., he pushed Egyptian rule northward through Palestine and as far as Syria. On temples and other monuments, he boasted of his conquests, though his greatest victory may not have actually taken place. In a battle against the Hittites of Asia Minor, only the desperate bravery of Ramses himself prevented a crushing defeat. Back home, however, Ramses had inscriptions carved on a monument that made the near defeat sound like a stunning victory.

After years of fighting, the Egyptians and Hittites finally signed a peace treaty, the first such document to have survived in history. The treaty declared

66Egypt, with the land of Hatti [the Hittites], shall be at peace and in brotherhood forever. Hostilities shall not occur between them forever.99

**Decline.** After Ramses II, Egyptian power slowly declined. Invaders, such as the Assyrians and Persians, conquered the Nile region. (See the map on page 39.) Later, Greek and Roman armies marched into the rich Nile Valley. Each new conqueror was eager to add the Egyptian breadbasket to a growing empire.

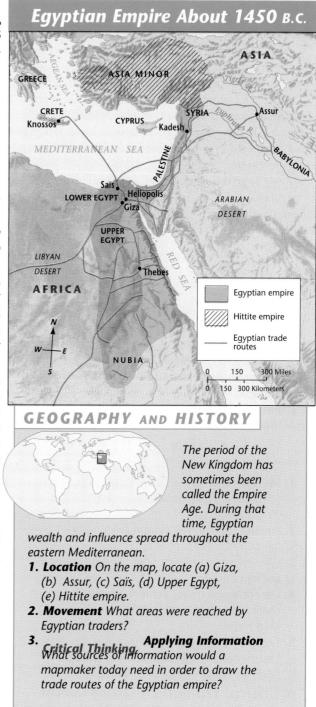

## Egyptian Empire About 1450 B.C.

Egyptian empire

Hittite empire

Egyptian trade routes

## GEOGRAPHY AND HISTORY

The period of the New Kingdom has sometimes been called the Empire Age. During that time, Egyptian wealth and influence spread throughout the eastern Mediterranean.

1. **Location** On the map, locate (a) Giza, (b) Assur, (c) Saïs, (d) Upper Egypt, (e) Hittite empire.
2. **Movement** What areas were reached by Egyptian traders?
3. **Critical Thinking. Applying Information** What sources of information would a mapmaker today need in order to draw the trade routes of the Egyptian empire?

## Egypt and Nubia

To the south, the Nile kingdom of Nubia (also known as Kush) developed in the shadow of Egypt. You will read more about Nubian civilization in Chapter 12. Here, we will look at the relationship between the two kingdoms.

For centuries, Egyptians traded or fought with their southern neighbor. From Nubia, they acquired ivory, cattle, and slaves. Egyptian armies conquered Nubia during the New Kingdom. The pharaoh Ramses II used gold from Nubia to pay foreign charioteers in his army. Nubians served in Egyptian armies and left their mark on Egyptian culture. Much Egyptian art of this period shows Nubian soldiers, musicians, or prisoners.

As Egypt declined, Nubia regained its independence. In about 750 B.C., Nubian kings marched north, adding Egypt to their own lands. For 100 years, Nubian kings ruled an empire that stretched from what is today Sudan to the Mediterranean.

The Nubians saw themselves not as foreign conquerors but as restorers of Egyptian glory. They ruled Egypt like the pharaohs of earlier centuries, respecting ancient Egyptian traditions. About 650 B.C., Assyrians, armed with iron weapons, descended on Egypt. They pushed the Nubians back into their original homeland, where Nubian monarchs ruled for 1,000 years more.

## SECTION 1 REVIEW

1. **Identify** (a) Menes, (b) Ptah-hotep, (c) Giza, (d) Hatshepsut, (e) Punt, (f) Ramses II.
2. **Define** (a) silt, (b) cataract, (c) delta, (d) dynasty, (e) pharaoh, (f) vizier.
3. Give two examples of how the Nile shaped ancient Egypt.
4. Describe one major achievement of Egyptian civilization during each of the three ancient kingdoms.
5. Explain how Egypt was affected by its contacts with each of the following groups: (a) Hyksos, (b) Hittites, (c) Nubians.
6. *Critical Thinking* **Drawing Conclusions** How are colossal monuments such as the pyramids a source of information about ancient Egypt?
7. *ACTIVITY* Write an instruction of your own that the vizier Ptah-hotep might have written to advise a political leader of today. The topic might be how to work effectively with other people or how to govern fairly.

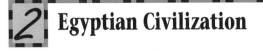

# 2 Egyptian Civilization

## Guide for Reading

■ How did religious beliefs shape the lives of Egyptians?

■ How was Egyptian society organized?

■ What advances did Egyptians make in learning and the arts?

■ **Vocabulary** *mummification, hieroglyphics, demotic, papyrus*

From an early age, Egyptian children heard stories about their gods and goddesses. A popular tale concerned the god Osiris (oh SĪ rihs), who had ruled Egypt until he was killed by his jealous brother, Set. The wicked Set then cut Osiris into pieces, which he tossed all over Egypt.

Osiris was saved by his faithful wife, the goddess Isis (Ī sihs). She reassembled her husband's body and brought him back to life. Since Osiris could no longer rule over the living, he became god of the dead and judge of the souls seeking admission to the afterlife.

The symbol of the goddess Isis was the ankh, a cross with a loop above the bar. To Egyptians, an ankh placed on a dead person assured the soul of eternal life. "The blood of Isis," they prayed, "the charms of Isis, the power of Isis are a protection unto me." The Egyptians' belief in eternal life had a profound effect on their civilization.

## *Egyptian Religion*

Egyptians inherited from their earliest ancestors a variety of religious beliefs and practices. Inscriptions on monuments and wall paintings in tombs reveal how Egyptians appealed to the divine forces that they believed ruled this world and the afterlife.

**Chief gods and goddesses.** In the sun-drenched land of Egypt, the chief god was the sun god Amon-Re (AH muhn RAY). The pharaoh, whom Egyptians viewed as a god as well as a monarch, was closely linked to Amon-Re.

Only the pharaoh could conduct certain ceremonies for the sun god.

Most Egyptians identified more easily with Osiris and Isis, whose story touched human emotions such as love, jealousy, and fear of death. According to the myth of Osiris and Isis, their son, Horus, later took revenge on the wicked god Set, killing his uncle.

To Egyptians, Osiris was especially important. Not only did he rule over the underworld, but he was also god of the Nile. In that role, he controlled the annual flood that made the land fertile. Isis had special appeal for women, who believed that she had first taught women to grind corn, spin flax, weave cloth, and care for children. Like Osiris, Isis promised the faithful they would have life after death.

**A fateful test.** Belief in the afterlife affected all Egyptians, from the highest noble to the lowest peasant. To win eternal life, each soul had to pass a test. Osiris weighed a soul's heart against the feather of truth. Those he judged to be sinners were fed to the crocodile-shaped Eater of the Dead. Worthy souls entered the Happy Field of Food. Egyptians believed that the afterlife would be much like life on Earth, so they buried the dead with everything they would need for eternity.

To give a soul use of its body in the afterlife, Egyptians perfected skills in mummification (muhm mih fih KAY shuhn), the preservation of the dead. Skilled embalmers removed vital organs, then dried and wrapped the body in strips of linen. This costly process took months to complete. At first, mummification was a privilege reserved for rulers and nobles. Eventually, ordinary Egyptians also won the right to mummify their dead.

**Evidence of the tombs.** Many pharaohs were buried in the desolate Valley of the Kings. Their tombs, filled with fantastic riches, were a temptation to robbers in ancient times. As a result, most royal tombs were stripped of their treasures long ago. Then, in 1922, the British archaeologist Howard Carter unearthed the tomb of the pharaoh Tutankhamen (too tahng KAH muhn), which had remained almost untouched for more than 3,000 years. The tomb and its treasures have provided a wealth of evidence about Egyptian civilization.

The body of the 18-year-old "King Tut" had been placed in a solid-gold coffin, nested within richly decorated outer coffins. Today, the dazzling array of objects found in the tomb fills several rooms in the Egyptian Museum in Cairo. They include chariots, weapons, furniture, jewelry, toys, games, and food. Tutankhamen was a minor king. Imagine the treasures that must have filled the tombs of great pharaohs like Ramses II.

**A religious rebel.** About 1380 B.C., a young pharaoh challenged the powerful priests of Amon-Re. He devoted his life to the worship of Aton, a minor god whose symbol was the sun's disk. The pharaoh took the name Akhenaton (ah kuh NAH tuhn), meaning "he who serves Aton." With the support of his wife, Queen Nefertiti, Akhenaton tried to sweep away all other gods in favor of Aton.

Scholars disagree about whether or not Akhenaton was trying to introduce a new religion based on worship of a single god. Akhenaton's radical ideas had little success, however. Priests of Amon-Re resisted the revolutionary changes. Nobles also deserted the pharaoh because he paid little attention to defending the empire. After Akhenaton's death, the priests of the old gods reasserted their power.

*Mummified Cat* Archaeologists have discovered an ancient Egyptian cemetery filled with mummified cats, like this one. Some Egyptians prayed to the cat goddess Bastet for protection against diseases and demons. The religious significance of cats greatly intensified Egyptians' devotion to their pets. **Continuity and Change** Can you think of any interesting beliefs that some people have about cats today?

## Board Games

A benefit that accompanied the rise of civilization was an increase in leisure time. People invented games of skill and chance to occupy their free time. Many board games today are similar to their ancient ancestors.

**Linking Past and Present**  What games today resemble the ancient Egyptian game of "twenty squares"? Explain the similarities.

**PAST**  *The Egyptian game of "twenty squares" had a set of specially shaped game pieces that were stored in a built-in drawer. Players threw sticks to determine how they might move their pieces. We do not know the exact rules of the game, but players probably needed both luck and skill to win. The game board shown here was found in the tomb of Tutankhamen.*

**PRESENT**  *Today, board games continue to entertain and challenge us. Here, two opponents ponder their upcoming moves in a contest of Chinese chess. In this game, skill is more important than luck.*

## Egyptian Society

Like other early civilizations, Egypt had its own class system. As both a god and an earthly leader, the pharaoh stood at the top of Egyptian society. Directly under the pharaoh were the high priests and priestesses, who served the gods and goddesses. Next came the nobles, who fought the pharaoh's wars. A tiny class of merchants, scribes, and artisans developed slowly. They provided for the needs of the rich and powerful.

**The life of the farmer.** Most Egyptians were peasant farmers. Many were slaves. Men and women spent their days working the soil and repairing the dikes. In the off-season, peasants were expected to serve the pharaoh, laboring on palaces, temples, and tombs. Besides working in the fields, women also spent much time raising children, collecting water, and preparing food—similar to the tasks of peasant women today.

An ancient record describes the life of a typical Egyptian peasant:

> 66When the water is full he irrigates [the fields] and repairs his equipment. He spends the day cutting tools for cultivating barley, and the night twisting ropes. Even his midday hour is spent in farm work.99

**Social changes.** During the New Kingdom, society grew more fluid as trade and warfare increased. Trade offered new opportunities to the growing merchant class. Foreign conquests brought riches to Egypt, which in turn meant more business for artisans. These skilled craftsworkers made fine jewelry, furniture, and fabrics for the palaces and tombs of pharaohs and nobles.

**Women.** Egyptian women generally enjoyed a higher status and greater independence than women elsewhere in the ancient world. Ramses II declared, "The foot of an Egyptian woman may walk where it pleases her and no one may deny her." Under Egyptian law, women could inherit property, enter business deals, buy and sell goods, go to court, and obtain a divorce.

Although there were often clear distinctions between the occupations of women and men, women's work was not confined to the home. They manufactured perfume and textiles, managed farming estates, and served as doctors. Women could also enter the priesthood, especially in the service of goddesses. Despite this equality of rights, few, if any, women learned to read and write. Even if they were literate, they were excluded from becoming scribes or holding other government jobs.

## Lasting Records

Like other early civilizations, the ancient Egyptians developed a form of picture writing.

Hieroglyphics (hī er oh GLIHF ihks) were used to keep important records. Early on, priests and scribes carved hieroglyphics on stone. Inscriptions on temples and other monuments preserved records of Egyptian culture for thousands of years.

**Scribes.** Besides learning to read and write, scribes also acquired skills in mathematics, medicine, and engineering. Temple scribes kept records of ceremonies, taxes, and gifts. Other scribes served nobles or the pharaoh. With skill and luck, a scribe from a poor family might become rich and powerful.

Over time, scribes developed demotic, a simpler form of writing for everyday use. They also learned to make a paperlike writing material from papyrus (puh PĪ ruhs), a plant that grows along the banks of the Nile. (Paper would not be invented until about A.D. 100, in China.) Writing with reed pens and ink on the smooth surface of papyrus strips was much easier than chiseling words onto stone. When writing official histories, however, scribes continued to carve hieroglyphics.

**The Rosetta Stone.** After the New Kingdom declined, Egyptians forgot the meanings of ancient hieroglyphics. Not until the early 1800s did a French scholar, Jean Champollion (ZHAHN shahm poh LYOHN), unravel the mysterious writings on Egypt's great monuments.

Champollion managed to decipher, or decode, the Rosetta Stone. This flat, black stone has the same message carved in three different forms of script—hieroglyphics, demotic, and Greek. By comparing the three versions, Champollion patiently worked out the meanings of many hieroglyphic symbols. As a result of that breakthrough, scholars could begin to read the thousands of surviving records from ancient Egypt.

## The Wisdom of the Egyptians

The records reveal that the ancient Egyptians accumulated a vast store of knowledge in fields such as medicine, astronomy, and mathematics. They were a practical people. When they had a problem, they used trial and error to find a solution.

**Medicine.** Like most doctors until recent times, Egyptian physicians believed in various

**Queen Nefertiti** *This painted limestone sculpture of Nefertiti, wife of the pharaoh Akhenaton, reflects a change in Egyptian art. For centuries, Egyptian artists had been preoccupied with scenes of death and the afterlife. During the New Kingdom, artists turned toward portraits and representations of living people. This likeness of the queen also shows the artist's concept of an ideal of beauty.* **Art and Literature** *How did the artist use exaggeration to emphasize the beauty of Nefertiti?*

changes, this ancient Egyptian calendar became the basis for our modern calendar.

**Mathematics.** Nile floods forced Egyptians to redraw the boundaries of fields each year. To do this, they developed practical geometry to survey the land. Egyptian engineers also used geometry to calculate the exact size and location of each block of stone to be placed in a pyramid or temple. Huge building projects such as pyramids and irrigation systems required considerable skills in design and engineering.

## Literature and the Arts

Literature and art tell us much about Egyptian values and attitudes. The oldest literature includes hymns and prayers to the gods, proverbs, and love poems. Other writings tell of royal victories in battle or, like *Instructions of the Vizier Ptah-hotep*, give practical advice.

**The Tale of Sinuhe.** Folk tales were popular, especially *The Tale of Sinuhe*. It relates the wanderings of Sinuhe (sihn oo HAY), an Egyptian official forced to flee into what is today Syria. He fights his way to fame among the desert people, whom the Egyptians consider uncivilized. As he gets older, Sinuhe longs to return home. The story ends happily when the pharaoh welcomes him back to court. As Sinuhe sheds the life of the desert nomad for that of an Egyptian noble, he says:

> ❝Years were made to pass away from my body. I was shaved, my hair was combed. . . . And I was dressed in the finest linen and anointed with the best oil. I slept on a bed, and gave up the sand to those who live [in the desert].❞

The story helps us see how Egyptians viewed both themselves and the people of the surrounding desert.

**Painting and sculpture.** The arts of ancient Egypt included statues, wall paintings in tombs, and carvings on temples. Some show everyday scenes of trade, farming, family life, or religious ceremonies. Others boast of victories in battles.

Painting styles remained almost unchanged for thousands of years. The pharaoh and gods were always much larger than any other human figures. Artists usually drew people with their

kinds of magic. Yet, through their knowledge of mummification, they learned a lot about the human body. They also became skilled at observing symptoms, diagnosing illnesses, and finding cures. Doctors performed complex surgical operations, which they described on papyrus scrolls. Many medicines that Egyptian doctors prescribed are still used, including anise, castor beans, and saffron.

**Astronomy.** Egyptian priest-astronomers studied the heavens, mapping constellations and charting the movements of the planets. With this knowledge, they developed a calendar that had 12 months of 30 days each and 5 days added at the end of each year. With a few

heads and limbs in profile but their eyes and shoulders facing the viewer.

Statues often depicted people in stiff, standard poses. Some human figures have animal heads that represent special qualities. The Sphinx, which crouches near the pyramids at Giza, portrays an early pharaoh as a powerful lion. (See the photograph on page 24.)

Besides the pyramids, Egyptians erected other great buildings. The magnificent temple of Ramses II at Karnak contains a vast hall with towering 80-foot columns. Much later, the Romans would adopt building techniques like those used at Karnak.

### Looking Ahead

Long after its power declined, Egypt remained a center of learning and culture in the African and Mediterranean worlds. It also retained economic importance as a source of grain and other riches. In later ages, new Egyptian cities like Alexandria and Cairo would attract scholars, traders, and other visitors. Yet, from ancient times to today, foreigners have gazed in awe at the monuments of a culture that flourished for 3,000 years.

## SECTION 2 REVIEW

1. **Identify** (a) Osiris, (b) Isis, (c) Amon-Re, (d) Tutankhamen, (e) Akhenaton, (f) Jean Champollion, (g) Rosetta Stone, (h) *The Tale of Sinuhe.*
2. **Define** (a) mummification, (b) hieroglyphics, (c) demotic, (d) papyrus.
3. (a) Which gods and goddesses were especially important to the ancient Egyptians? (b) What role did they play in Egyptian life?
4. (a) What social classes existed in Egypt? (b) What rights did women have?
5. Describe three achievements of ancient Egyptians in the arts or learning.
6. *Critical Thinking* **Synthesizing Information** How were religion, government, and the arts linked in ancient Egypt?
7. *ACTIVITY* Write a headline and brief news account about the decoding of the Rosetta Stone. Include quotations from historians or archaeologists explaining why this discovery is so valuable.

# 3 City-States of Ancient Sumer

## Guide for Reading

■ How did geographic features encourage the rise of civilization in the Fertile Crescent?

■ How were Sumerian government and society organized?

■ What were the main achievements of Sumerian civilization?

■ **Vocabulary** *ziggurat, hierarchy, cuneiform*

To the northeast of the Nile lay the cities of Sumer, in the ancient Middle East. There, people passed down stories about a hero named Gilgamesh. In time, these stories were collected into a long narrative poem, *The Epic of Gilgamesh,* which is one of the oldest works of literature in the world.

The epic tells of his fantastic adventures and daring exploits. At one point, the goddess Inanna falls in love with the young hero and proposes marriage:

> 66Come to me, Gilgamesh, and be my bridegroom. . . . I will harness for you a chariot of lapis lazuli [a semiprecious stone] and of gold, with wheels of gold and of copper; and you shall have mighty demons of the storm for draft mules.99

When Gilgamesh rejects Inanna's offer, her love turns to rage and Gilgamesh suffers miseries and heartaches.

*The Epic of Gilgamesh* is filled with supernatural figures and events. Yet it offers a glimpse into Sumerian civilization. We learn that the people believed in powerful goddesses who exhibited very human emotions. The Sumerians valued gold, copper, and gems, rode in wheeled chariots, and used mules to carry goods. Archaeologists have confirmed much of what the epic tells us about Sumer, the oldest civilization of the Middle East.

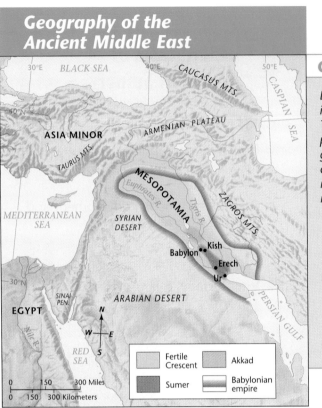

## Geography of the Ancient Middle East

### GEOGRAPHY AND HISTORY

*Like the Nile River in Egypt, the Tigris and Euphrates rivers gave rise to early civilizations. The rivers made the land fertile and provided avenues for trade.*

1. **Location**  On the map, locate (a) Tigris River, (b) Euphrates River, (c) Fertile Crescent, (d) Sumer, (e) Akkad, (f) Mesopotamia, (g) Egypt.
2. **Place**  What physical features may have helped limit the expansion of Akkad?
3. **Critical Thinking**  **Comparing**  Look at the map on page 25. Compare the location, physical features, and size of the Egyptian and Babylonian empires.

## Geography: The Fertile Crescent

If you look at the map above, you will notice an arc of land that curves from the Persian Gulf to the eastern Mediterranean coast. The dark, rich soils and golden wheat fields earned it the name the Fertile Crescent.

Nomadic herders, ambitious invaders, and traders easily overcame the few natural barriers across the Fertile Crescent. As a result, the region became a crossroads where people and ideas met and mingled. Each new group that arrived made its own contributions to the turbulent history of the region.

**The land between the rivers.** The first known civilization in the Fertile Crescent was uncovered in the 1800s in Mesopotamia. The Tigris and Euphrates rivers define Mesopotamia, which means "between the rivers" in Greek. The two rivers flow from the highlands of modern-day Turkey through Iraq into the Persian Gulf.

In Sumer, as in Egypt, the fertile land of a river valley attracted Stone Age farmers from neighboring regions. In time, their descendants produced the surplus food needed to support growing populations. More than 5,000 years ago, busy cities emerged in the southern part of Mesopotamia.

**Floods and irrigation.** Just as control of the Nile was vital to Egypt, control of the Tigris and Euphrates was key to developments in Mesopotamia. The rivers frequently rose in terrifying floods that washed away topsoil and destroyed mud-brick villages. To survive and protect their farmland, villages along the riverbanks had to work together. Even during the dry season, the rivers had to be controlled to channel water to the fields.

Temple priests or royal officials provided the leadership to ensure cooperation. They organized villagers to build dikes to hold back flood waters and irrigation ditches to carry water to their fields.

Gradually, Sumerian civilization emerged as the first of many to flourish in the Fertile Crescent. Its achievements would influence all later Mesopotamian civilizations.

## Sumerian Civilization

The Sumerians made remarkable strides. They had few natural resources, but they made the most of what they had. They lacked building materials, such as timber or stone, so they built with earth and water. They made bricks of clay, shaped in wooden molds and dried in the sun. These bricks were the building blocks for great cities like Ur and Erech.

**The first cities.** Sumerian cities were often rectangular in shape, surrounded by high, wide walls. Inside the city gates were broad avenues used for religious processions or victory parades. The largest buildings were ziggurats (ZIHG uh rats), pyramid-temples that soared toward the heavens. Their sloping sides had terraces, or wide steps, that were sometimes planted with trees and shrubs. On top of each ziggurat stood a shrine to the chief god or goddess of the city.

Rulers lived in magnificent palaces with spacious courtyards. Most people, though, lived in tiny houses packed in a tangled web of narrow alleys and lanes. Artisans who practiced the same trade, such as weavers or carpenters, lived and worked in the same street. These shop-lined streets formed a bazaar, the ancestor of today's shopping mall.

**Economic life.** Trade brought riches to the cities. Traders sailed along the rivers or risked the dangers of desert travel to carry goods to distant regions. (Although the wheel had been invented by some earlier unknown people, the Sumerians made the first wheeled vehicles.) Archaeologists have found goods from as far away as Egypt and India in the rubble of Sumerian cities.

**Government.** Sumer included many independent city-states. Rival cities often battled for control of land and water. For protection, people turned to courageous and resourceful war leaders. Over time, these war leaders evolved into hereditary rulers.

In each city-state, the ruler was responsible for maintaining the city walls and the irrigation

*Stairway to the Gods* Sumerian ziggurats were artificial mountains reaching skyward toward the heavens. At the summit of each was a shrine where priests honored their city's chief god or goddess. The sketch reconstructs a ziggurat to the goddess Inanna in the city of Ur. **Continuity and Change** Are there religious structures of today that also seem to reach to the heavens? Explain.

systems. He led its armies in war and enforced the laws. As government grew more complex, he employed scribes to carry out functions such as collecting taxes and keeping records. The ruler also had religious duties. He was seen as the chief servant of the gods and led ceremonies designed to please them.

**Social classes.** Each Sumerian city-state had a distinct social hierarchy (HĪ uh rahr kee), or system of ranks. The highest class included the ruling family, leading officials, and high priests. A small middle class was made up of merchants, artisans, and lesser priests and scribes.

At the base of society were the majority of people, peasant farmers. Some had their own land, but most worked land belonging to the king or temples. Sumerians also owned slaves. Most slaves had been captured in war. Some, though, had sold themselves into slavery to pay their debts.

**Women.** In the earliest Sumerian myths, a mother-goddess was the central figure of creation. She may have reflected the honored role of mothers in early farming communities. An ancient proverb advised, "Pay heed to the word of your mother as though it were the word of a god."

As large city-states emerged with warrior-leaders at their head, male gods who resembled early kings replaced the older mother-goddess. Still, in the early city-states, wives of rulers enjoyed special powers and duties. Some supervised palace workshops and ruled for the king when he was absent. One woman, Ku-Baba, became a ruler herself, rising from the lowly position of tavern owner to establish a ruling family in Kish.

Over time, as men gained more power and wealth, the status of women changed. Because they devoted their time to household duties and raising children, women became more dependent on men for their welfare. Despite these changes, women continued to have legal rights. Well-to-do women, for example, engaged in trade, borrowed and loaned money, and owned property.

## Sumerian Religion

Like most ancient peoples, the Sumerians were polytheistic, worshiping many gods. These gods were thought to control every aspect of

life, especially the forces of nature. Sumerians believed that gods and goddesses behaved like ordinary people. They ate, drank, married, and raised families. Although the gods favored truth and justice, they were also responsible for violence and suffering.

To Sumerians, their highest duty was to keep these divine beings happy and thereby ensure the safety of their city-state. Each city-state had its own special god or goddess to whom people prayed and offered sacrifices of animals, grain, and wine.

People celebrated many holy days with ceremonies and processions. The most important ceremony occurred at the new year when the king sought and won the favor of Inanna, the life-giving goddess of love. The king participated in a symbolic marriage with the goddess. This ritual, Sumerians believed, would make the new year fruitful and prosperous.

Like the Egyptians, the Sumerians believed in an afterlife. At death, they believed, a person descended into a grim underworld from which there was no release. In *The Epic of Gilgamesh*, which you read about on page 31, a character describes the underworld as

> **❝**the house where one goes in and
>         never comes out again,
>     the road that, if one takes it, one never
>         comes back, . . .
>     the place where they live on dust,
>         their food is mud;
>     . . . and they see no light, living
>         in blackness:
>     on the door and door-bolt, deeply
>         settled dust.**❞**

The gloomy Sumerian view of an afterlife contrasts with the Egyptian vision of the Happy Field of Food. Possibly differences in geography help account for this contrast. The floods of the Tigris and Euphrates were less regular and more destructive than the Nile floods. As a result, Sumerians may have developed a more pessimistic view of the world.

**ISSUES** *For* **TODAY**

In Sumer, as in Egypt, rulers fulfilled important religious duties. How do religious values and institutions influence government?

## School for Scribes

The scribe bent over the clay tablet. His hand held a stylus, or reed pen, and moved swiftly across the wet clay, leaving small wedge-shaped marks. When he had finished, he read over the text and then called an assistant to place the tablet to dry.

**The first writing.** By 3200 B.C., the Sumerians had invented the earliest known form of writing. This type of writing was later called cuneiform (kyoo NEE uh form) from the Latin word *cuneus* for "wedge."

Cuneiform grew out of a system of pictographs that priests used to record goods brought to temple storehouses. Later, priests developed symbols to represent more complicated thoughts. (See the chart below.) As their writing evolved, the Sumerians were able to use it to record not only grain harvests but also myths, prayers, laws, treaties, and business contracts.

**School days.** Sumerian scribes had to go through years of strict schooling to acquire their skills. One scribe wrote an essay describing his school days in the *edubba*, or "tablet house."

"When I arose early in the morning," he recalled, "I faced my mother and said to her: 'Give me my lunch, I want to go to school!'" He then hurried to school, knowing that if he were late he could be beaten with a cane:

> **❝** The fellow in charge of punctuality said: 'Why are you late?' Afraid and with pounding heart, I entered before my teacher and made a respectful bow. **❞**

With that hurdle cleared, the boy worked hard copying his tablets. The "school-father" (teacher) and "big brother" (assistant teacher) monitored his work with a sharp eye. If he wrote untidily or talked without permission, he could be "caned." Once he even begged his father to pay the teacher more so that he would be treated more kindly.

## Cuneiform Writing

| Meaning | Outline character about 3000 B.C. | Sumerian about 2000 B.C. | Assyrian about 700 B.C. | Baby-lonian about 500 B.C. | |
|---|---|---|---|---|---|
| Sun | | | | | |
| God or heaven | | | | | |
| Mountain | | | | | |
| Ox | | | | | |
| Fish | | | | | |

***Interpreting a Chart*** *Sumerian writing developed gradually, from simple outline pictures to the wedged symbols of cuneiform. Later Mesopotamian peoples, like the scribes shown here, adapted Sumerian cuneiform to their own needs.* ■ *Based on this chart, describe how cuneiform changed between 2000 B.C. and 500 B.C.*

Each day had its routine, the student later recalled:

> **"**I recited my tablet, ate my lunch, prepared my [new] tablet, wrote it, finished it . . . and in the afternoon my exercise tablets were brought to me. When school was dismissed, I went home, entered the house, and found my father sitting there. I explained my exercise-tablets to my father, recited my tablet to him, and he was delighted.**"**

**Advances in learning.** Young scribes-in-training learned by copying and reciting. Most students were boys, but a few girls from wealthy families learned to read and write. Some students left school after learning simple arithmetic so that they could keep accounts. Gifted students went on to gain a wide range of knowledge about religion, medicine, mathematics, geography, astronomy, and literature.

Over the centuries, inventive Sumerians made advances in mathematics. To measure and solve problems of calculation, they developed basic algebra and geometry. They based their number system on six, dividing the hour into 60 minutes and the circle into 360 degrees, as we still do today.

Priests studied the skies, recording the movement of heavenly bodies. This knowledge enabled them to make accurate calendars, which are so essential to a farming society. In Sumerian society, as in most early civilizations, educated scribes enjoyed respect and could sometimes reach high positions. Such benefits made the long, difficult years of schooling worthwhile. ▨

### Looking Ahead

Armies of conquering peoples swept across Mesopotamia and overwhelmed the Sumerian city-states. Often the newcomers settled in the region and adopted ideas from the Sumerians. The myths and gods of these people became mingled with those of Sumer. In the process, names changed. The Sumerian goddess Inanna, for example, became Ishtar.

The newcomers adapted cuneiform to their own languages and helped spread Sumerian learning across the Middle East. Building on Sumerian knowledge of the constellations and planets, later Mesopotamian astronomers developed ways to predict eclipses of the sun and moon.

Later peoples also elaborated on Sumerian literature, including *The Epic of Gilgamesh*. In other episodes, Gilgamesh travels the world in search of eternal life. On his journey, he meets the sole survivor of a great flood that destroyed the world. (Archaeologists have found evidence suggesting that a catastrophic flood devastated Mesopotamia somewhere about 4,900 years ago.) By the end of the story, Gilgamesh has learned the greatest truth of all—that even heroes must die.

By means of the various peoples who conquered the Middle East, Sumerian knowledge passed on to the Greeks and Romans. They, in turn, had a powerful impact on the development of the western world.

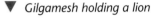
▼ *Gilgamesh holding a lion*

## SECTION 3 REVIEW

1. **Identify** (a) *The Epic of Gilgamesh,* (b) Inanna, (c) Ku-Baba.
2. **Define** (a) ziggurat, (b) hierarchy, (c) cuneiform.
3. How did geography influence the city-states of Sumer?
4. (a) What were the duties of Sumerian rulers? (b) How were religion and government linked?
5. Describe three accomplishments of Sumerian civilization and explain how each influenced later peoples.
6. *Critical Thinking* **Comparing** Compare school life in ancient Sumer to life in your school. How are they similar? How are they different?
7. *ACTIVITY* Review the chart on page 35. Then, create pictographic and cuneiform symbols for three objects or concepts that are important in your own life.

# 4 Invaders, Traders, and Empire Builders

## Guide for Reading

- How did strong rulers shape the civilizations of the Fertile Crescent?
- What advances in government and technology did early civilizations make?
- How did warfare and trade influence the ancient Middle East?

- **Vocabulary** *civil law, satrap, barter economy, colony*

If you had visited the palace of the ancient Assyrian king Assurbanipal (ah soor BAH nuh pahl), you would have found the walls decorated with magnificent carvings. One scene shows Assurbanipal and his queen enjoying a picnic in their lush palace garden. Nearby, musicians entertain the royal couple.

The scene is relaxed and elegant. Look carefully, though, and you will see something startling. Hanging from a tree branch, just behind a harp player, is the head of a defeated king.

In the ancient Middle East, as elsewhere, bloody warfare and advanced culture went hand in hand. In this section, we will look at the accomplishments of Middle Eastern civilizations across 3,000 years of war and peace.

## Ruling a Large Empire

Invasion and conquest were prominent features in the history of the ancient Middle East. Again and again, nomadic peoples or ambitious warriors descended on the rich cities of the Fertile Crescent. While many invaders simply looted and burned, some stayed to rule. Powerful leaders created large, well-organized empires, bringing peace and prosperity to the region.

**The first empire builder.** About 2300 B.C., Sargon, the ruler of neighboring Akkad, invaded and conquered the city-states of Sumer. He built the first empire known to history. His astonishing achievement did not last long, however. Soon after his death, other invaders swept

into the wide valley between the rivers, tumbling his empire into ruin.

In time, the Sumerian city-states revived, and their power struggles resumed. Eventually, however, new conquerors followed in the footsteps of Sargon and imposed unity over the Fertile Crescent.

**Hammurabi.** About 1790 B.C., Hammurabi (hah moo RAH bee), king of Babylon, brought much of Mesopotamia under his control. He took steps to unite the Babylonian empire by publishing a remarkable set of laws, known as the Code of Hammurabi.

Hammurabi was not the author of the code. Most of the laws had been around since Sumerian times. Hammurabi, however, wanted people to know the legal principles his government would follow. So he had artisans carve the 300 laws on a stone pillar for all to see. On it, he proclaimed his goals:

> 66To cause justice to prevail in the land,
> To destroy the wicked and evil,
> That the strong may not oppress the weak.99

**Code of Hammurabi** *"If a man breaks into a house, he shall be killed in front of that break-in and buried there."* This law and the rest of Hammurabi's code were cut into a seven-foot-tall pillar nearly 4,000 years ago. At the top of the pillar, this carving shows King Hammurabi dealing justice to one of his subjects. **Political and Social Systems** *Why do you think Hammurabi displayed his laws in such a public way?*

**Crime and punishment.** Hammurabi's Code was the first major collection of laws in history. It listed both criminal laws, dealing with murder and theft, and civil laws, dealing with private rights and matters, such as business contracts, property inheritance, taxes, marriage, and divorce.

By today's standards, the laws often seem cruel, following the principle of "an eye for an eye and a life for a life." For example, if a house collapsed because of poor construction and the homeowner was killed, the builder of the house could be put to death. Still, such a legal code was more orderly than older traditions, which permitted unrestricted personal vengeance. (▮ See *You Decide,* "How Should Society Deal With Lawbreakers?" pages 72–73.)

**Laws for women.** Hammurabi's Code did try to protect the powerless, including women and slaves. One law spelled out the rights of a married woman:

66If a woman so hated her husband that
she has declared, 'You may not have
me,' her record shall be investigated at
her city council, and if she . . . was not at
fault . . . that woman, without incurring
any blame at all, may take her dowry and
go off to her father's house.99

If the woman was not found blameless, she could be thrown into the river. Still, under Hammurabi's Code, divorce laws were fairer to women than those found in many countries until recent times. Other laws allowed a woman to own property and pass it on to her children.

In general, the code strictly regulated the behavior of women. It expected a woman to remain in her husband's home and be dependent on him. A husband, however, had a legal duty to support his wife. The code also gave a father nearly unlimited authority over his children. The Babylonians believed that an orderly household headed by a strong father was necessary for a stable empire.

**Other accomplishments.** Although most famous for his law code, Hammurabi took other steps to unite his empire. He improved irrigation and organized a well-trained army. He had temples repaired and promoted the chief Babylonian god, Marduk, over older Sumerian gods.

## Warfare and the Spread of Ideas

Later empires shaped the Middle East in different ways. Often, conquerors uprooted the peoples they defeated. By forcing people to move elsewhere, these invaders helped spread ideas. Other conquerors, like the Hittites, brought new skills to the region.

**The secret of ironworking.** The Hittites pushed out of Asia Minor into Mesopotamia about 1400 B.C. While they were less advanced than the peoples of Mesopotamia, they had learned to extract iron from ore. The Hittites heated iron ore and pounded out impurities before plunging it into cold water. The tools and weapons they made with iron were harder and had sharper edges than those made out of bronze or copper. Because iron was plentiful, the Hittites were able to arm more people at less expense.

The Hittites tried to keep this valuable technology secret. But as their empire collapsed about 1200 B.C., Hittite ironsmiths migrated to serve customers elsewhere. The new knowledge thus spread across Asia, Africa, and Europe, ushering in the Iron Age.

**Savage warriors.** The Assyrians, who lived on the upper Tigris, learned to forge iron weapons. By 1100 B.C., they were expanding their power across the Fertile Crescent. For 500 years they terrorized the region, earning a lasting reputation as one of the most warlike people in history.

Perhaps to frighten their enemies, Assyrian rulers boasted of their brutal treatment of the peoples they conquered:

66I built a pillar over against his city gate
and I flayed all the chief men . . . and
I covered the pillar with their skins;
some I walled up within the pillar,
some I impaled upon the pillar on
stakes . . . and I cut off the limbs of
the officers. . . .99

**Assyrian society.** Despite their brutality, Assyrian rulers encouraged a well-ordered society. They were the first rulers to develop extensive laws regulating life within the royal household. Riches from trade and war loot paid for the splendid palaces in well-planned cities. The women of the palace, though, were confined

# Assyrian and Persian Empires

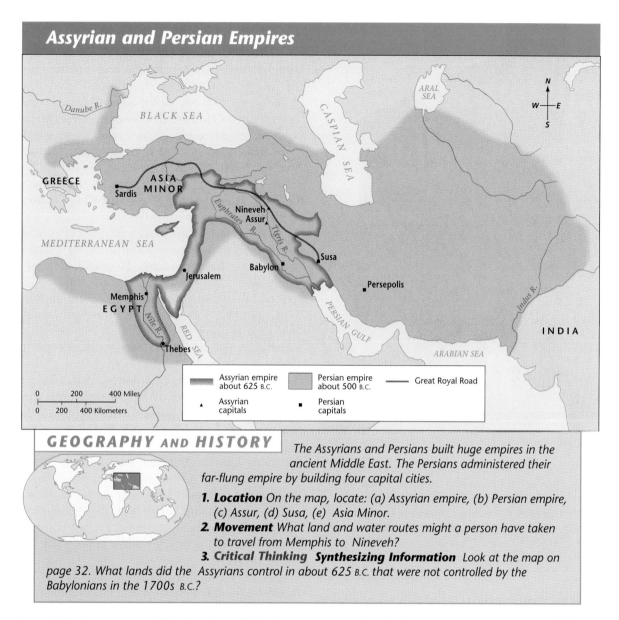

**GEOGRAPHY AND HISTORY**

The Assyrians and Persians built huge empires in the ancient Middle East. The Persians administered their far-flung empire by building four capital cities.

**1. Location** On the map, locate: (a) Assyrian empire, (b) Persian empire, (c) Assur, (d) Susa, (e) Asia Minor.

**2. Movement** What land and water routes might a person have taken to travel from Memphis to Nineveh?

**3. Critical Thinking Synthesizing Information** Look at the map on page 32. What lands did the Assyrians control in about 625 B.C. that were not controlled by the Babylonians in the 1700s B.C.?

in secluded quarters and had to be veiled when they appeared in public.

At Nineveh (NIHN uh vuh), King Assurbanipal founded one of the first libraries. He ordered his scribes to collect cuneiform tablets from all over the Fertile Crescent. Those tablets have given modern scholars a wealth of information about the ancient Middle East.

**Babylon revived.** In 612 B.C., shortly after Assurbanipal's death, neighboring people joined forces to crush the once-dreaded Assyrian armies. An aggressive and ruthless king, Nebuchadnezzar (neh buh kuhd NEHZ uhr), revived the power of Babylon. His new Babylonian empire stretched from the Persian Gulf to the Mediterranean Sea.

Nebuchadnezzar rebuilt the canals, temples, walls, and palaces of Babylon. Near his chief palace were the famous Hanging Gardens, known as one of the wonders of the ancient world. The gardens were probably made by planting trees and flowering plants on the steps of a huge ziggurat. According to legend, Nebuchadnezzar had the gardens built to please his wife, who was homesick for the hills where she had grown up.

**Astronomy.** Under Nebuchadnezzar, the Babylonians pushed the frontiers of learning into new areas. Priest-astrologers were especially eager to understand the stars and planets, which they believed had a great influence on all events on Earth. Their observations of the

**Royal Guardian** *This huge, bull-like figure guarded the palace of an Assyrian king. Such mythical creatures stood in front of all Assyrian palaces as protection against evil spirits. Sculptors carved the bull with five legs so that, seen from the front, it appeared to be standing, while seen from the side, it appeared to be walking.* **Art and Literature** *Based on what you have read, how does this sculpture reflect the values of Assyrian society?*

heavens contributed to the growing knowledge of astronomy.

## The Persian Empire

The thick walls built by Nebuchadnezzar failed to hold back new conquerors. In 539 B.C., Babylon fell to the Persian armies of Cyrus the Great. Cyrus and his successors went on to conquer the largest empire yet seen. The Persians eventually controlled a wide sweep of territory from Asia Minor to India, including what is today Turkey, Iran, Egypt, Afghanistan, and Pakistan. (See the map on page 39.)

In general, the Persians were tolerant of the people they conquered. They respected the customs and religious traditions of the diverse groups in their empire.

**Uniting many peoples.** The real unification of the Persian empire was accomplished under the Persian emperor Darius, who ruled from 522 B.C. to 486 B.C. A skilled organizer, Darius set up a government that became a model for later rulers. He divided the Persian empire into provinces, each headed by a governor called a satrap. Each satrapy, or province, had to pay taxes based on its resources and wealth. Special officials, "the Eyes and Ears of the King," visited each province to check on the satraps.

Like Hammurabi, Darius adapted laws from the people he conquered and drew up a single code of laws for the empire. To encourage unity, he had hundreds of miles of roads built or repaired. Roads made it easier to communicate with different parts of the empire. Darius himself kept moving from one royal capital to another. In each, he celebrated important festivals and was seen by the people.

**Economic life.** To improve trade, Darius set up a common set of weights and measures. He also encouraged the use of coins, which the Lydians of Asia Minor had first introduced. Most people continued to be part of the barter economy, exchanging one set of goods or services for another. Coins, however, brought merchants and traders into an early form of a money economy, replacing barter with the exchange of money. By setting up a single Persian coinage, Darius created economic links among his far-flung subjects.

**A new religion.** Religious beliefs put forward by the the Persian thinker Zoroaster (zoh roh AS tuhr) also helped to unite the empire. Zoroaster lived about 600 B.C. He rejected the old Persian gods. Instead, he taught that a single wise god, Ahura Mazda (ah HOO ruh MAHZ duh), ruled the world. Ahura Mazda, however, was in constant battle against Ahriman (AH rih muhn), the prince of lies and evil. Each individual, said Zoroaster, had to choose which side to support.

Zoroaster's teachings were collected in a sacred book, the *Zend-Avesta*. It taught that in the end Ahura Mazda would triumph over the forces of evil. On that day, all individuals would be judged for their actions. Those who had done good would enter paradise. Evildoers would be condemned to eternal suffering. Two later religions that emerged in the Middle East,

# Contributions of the Fertile Crescent

| Contribution | People | Description | Connections Today |
|---|---|---|---|
| **Wheeled vehicles** | Sumerians | Sumerians first used wheeled vehicles to transport goods in trade. | A vital development in human history, wheeled vehicles are used by billions today. |
| **Cuneiform** | Sumerians | The Sumerian cuneiform was made up of wedge-shaped symbols. Its "alphabet" included about 300 symbols representing syllables. | Writing has developed from cuneiform to hand-writing and mechanical printing to computer-generated images and text. |
| **Alphabet** | Phoenicians | This alphabet contained 22 symbols standing for consonant sounds, written in vertical columns from right to left. | Later peoples adapted the Phoenician alphabet to produce our 26-letter alphabet. |
| **Ironworking** | Hittites | Hittites learned to extract iron from ore and fashion tools and weapons that were harder than bronze or copper ones. They helped spread knowledge of iron. | Today, iron is used to make steel products—such as cars, building materials, and utensils—and a few iron products—such as decorative railings. |
| **Advanced knowledge of astronomy** | Babylonians | Using advanced geometry, astronomers could predict eclipses of the sun and moon and the positions of planets in relation to the sun. | Today, astronomers still use geometry in the study of the moon, stars, and planets. They get much of their data from powerful telescopes and satellites. |
| **Coins** | Lydians, Persians | Early coins were made of electrum, an alloy, or natural mix, of gold and silver. The image on a coin showed its value. | Coins replaced barter, leading to the money economy of today. Now we also use paper money, plastic credit cards, and electronic transfers. |

***Interpreting a Chart*** *Ancient civilizations of the Fertile Crescent made breakthroughs in writing, science, and technology. Trade and warfare spread these ideas to neighboring lands.* ■ *Which contribution on the chart do you think was most important? Explain.*

Christianity and Islam, stressed similar ideas about heaven, hell, and a final judgment day.

## Brave Sea Traders

While powerful rulers subdued large empires, many small states made their own contributions to civilization. The Phoenicians (fuh NEE shuhns), for example, gained fame as sailors and traders. They occupied a string of cities along the eastern Mediterranean coast, in what is today Lebanon and Syria.

**Manufacturing and trade.** The coastal land, though narrow, was fertile and supported farming. Still, the resourceful Phoenicians became best known for manufacturing and trade. They made glass from coastal sand. From a tiny sea snail, they produced a widely admired purple dye, called "Tyrian purple" after the city of Tyre. Phoenicians also used papyrus from Egypt to make scrolls, or rolls of paper, for books. The words *Bible* and *bibliography* come from the Phoenician city of Byblos.

Phoenicians traded with people all around the Mediterranean Sea. To promote trade, they set up colonies from North Africa to Sicily and Spain. A colony is a territory settled and ruled by people from a distant land. (★ See *Skills for Success*, page 46.)

**Daring voyages.** A few Phoenician traders braved the stormy Atlantic and sailed as far as England. There, they exchanged goods from the Mediterranean for tin. About 600 B.C., one Phoenician expedition may have sailed down the Red Sea and then followed the African coast around the southern tip. That historic voyage was forgotten for centuries. (In the late 1400s, Europeans claimed to be the first to round the southern tip of Africa.)

**The alphabet.** Historians have called the Phoenicians "carriers of civilization" because they spread Middle Eastern civilization around the Mediterranean. Yet the Phoenicians made their own contribution to our world, giving us our alphabet.

Phoenician traders needed a quick, flexible form of writing to record business deals. The wedges of cuneiform were too clumsy, so they adapted the idea of using symbols to represent spoken sounds. Their system of 22 symbols for consonant sounds became the first real alphabet.

Later, the Greeks adapted the Phoenician alphabet and added symbols for the vowel sounds. From this Greek alphabet came the letters in which this book is written. (See the chart on page 109.)

## Looking Ahead

The Middle East continued to be a vital crossroads, where warriors and traders met, clashed, and mingled. Under Persian rule, scholars drew on 3,000 years of Mesopotamian learning and added their own advances to this rich heritage. In time, the achievements of this culture filtered eastward into India and westward into Europe. The chart on page 41 summarizes the impact of some Middle Eastern contributions.

Other conquerors would overwhelm the Persian empire, although different leaders revived Persian power at various times down to the present. The Middle East remained a region where diverse peoples came into close contact. Though these people lived thousands of years ago, some of their beliefs and ideas survived to shape our modern world.

## SECTION 4 REVIEW

1. **Identify** (a) Sargon, (b) Hammurabi, (c) Assurbanipal, (d) Nebuchadnezzar, (e) Cyrus the Great, (f) Darius, (g) Zoroaster.
2. **Define** (a) civil law, (b) satrap, (c) barter economy, (d) colony.
3. Describe how each of the following leaders unified his empire: (a) Hammurabi, (b) Darius.
4. How did the Hittites introduce a new age of technology?
5. Why are the Phoenicians called "carriers of civilization"?
6. *Critical Thinking* **Making Inferences** Why do you think Darius supported the spread of Zoroastrianism throughout the Persian empire?
7. *ACTIVITY* Using information in this section and Section 3, create a time line of the ancient Middle East. Include the rise and fall of empires, important individuals, and turning points in technology or religion.

# The World of the Hebrews

## Guide for Reading

■ What were the main events in the history of the Hebrews?

■ How were Hebrew religious beliefs unique in the ancient world?

■ What moral values did the Hebrew prophets preach?

■ Vocabulary *monotheistic, covenant, prophet, ethics, diaspora*

The Book of Genesis records a vow made by God to the Hebrew leader Abraham:

66I will give you many descendants, and some of them will be kings. You will have so many descendants that they will become nations. . . . I will keep my promise to you and your descendants in future generations as an everlasting covenant. I will be your God and the God of your descendants.99

This promise of a unique relationship with God helped shape the history of the Hebrew people to the present.

## *At the Crossroads*

The Hebrews were among the many peoples who occupied the Fertile Crescent. Living at the crossroads of civilization, they came into contact with many people and ideas. Over time, the Hebrews developed their own ideas, which reflected a blend of many traditions.

The early Hebrews came to believe that God was taking a hand in their history. As a result, they recorded events and laws in the Torah,* their most sacred text. Like many Mesopotamian peoples, the Hebrews told of a great flood that devastated the land. They believed that God had sent the flood to punish the wicked.

*The Torah contains five books: Genesis, Exodus, Leviticus, Numbers, and Deuteronomy. Christians later adopted these as the first five books of the Old Testament.

**A nomadic people.** According to the Torah, the Hebrews had lived near Ur in Mesopotamia. About 2000 B.C., they migrated, herding their flocks of sheep and goats into a region known as Canaan (later called Palestine).

The Book of Genesis tells that around 1800 B.C. a famine in Canaan forced many Hebrews to migrate to Egypt. There, they were eventually enslaved. In time, Moses, the adopted son of the pharaoh's daughter, led the Hebrews in their escape, or exodus, from Egypt. For 40 years, the Hebrews wandered in the Sinai Peninsula. After Moses died, they entered Canaan and defeated the people there, claiming for themselves the land they believed God had promised them.

**The kingdom of Israel.** By 1000 B.C., the Hebrews had set up the kingdom of Israel. Among the most skillful rulers of Israel were David and Solomon. According to Hebrew tradition, David was a humble shepherd who defeated a huge Philistine warrior, Goliath. Later, David became a strong and shrewd king who united the feuding Hebrew tribes into a single nation.

David's son Solomon turned Jerusalem into an impressive capital. He built a

**David and Goliath**
*The story of David's victory over Goliath has had an enduring appeal. In this thirteenth-century French illustration, the Hebrew shepherd boy David prepares to battle the giant Philistine champion. The story provides hope and inspiration for those facing difficult challenges.*
**Continuity and Change** *What is inaccurate about this portrayal of figures from the Bible?*

**The Torah** *Over time, Jewish people migrated to diverse lands. Nevertheless, Jewish communities around the world remained united by their common traditions and faith in God. Here, the sacred Torah scroll is elevated for all to see.*
**Global Interaction** *As shown by the illustration, what other element of Jewish culture has helped unite Jews of many lands?*

During their captivity, the Hebrews became known as the Jews.

Years later, when the Persian ruler Cyrus conquered Babylon, he released the Jews from captivity. Many Jews returned to Palestine, where they rebuilt King Solomon's temple in Jerusalem. Yet, like other small groups in the region, they continued to live under a series of foreign rulers, including the Persians, Greeks, and Romans.

## *A Covenant With God*

What you have just read is an outline of early Jewish history. To the Hebrews, history and religion were interconnected. Each event reflected God's plan for the Hebrew people. In time, Hebrew beliefs evolved into the religion we know today as Judaism. Judaism differed in fundamental ways from the beliefs of nearby peoples.

**Belief in one true God.** Judaism was monotheistic, teaching a belief in one God. At the time, most other people worshiped many gods and goddesses. A few religious leaders, like Zoroaster in Persia and the Egyptian ruler Akhenaton, believed in a single powerful deity. However, their ideas did not have the worldwide impact that Hebrew beliefs did.

The ancient Hebrews prayed to God to save them from their enemies. Many other ancient people had also turned to particular gods or goddesses as their special protectors. But they thought of such gods as tied to certain places or people. The Hebrews believed in an all-knowing, all-powerful, male God who was present everywhere.

**A chosen people.** As you read, Jews believed that God had made a covenant, or binding agreement, with Abraham. As a result, Jews considered themselves to be God's "chosen people." Moses later renewed this covenant. He told the Hebrews that God would lead them to Canaan, the "promised land," in exchange for their faithful obedience.

**The Ten Commandments.** At the heart of Judaism are the Ten Commandments, laws that Jews believed God gave them through Moses. The laws set out both religious duties toward God and rules for moral conduct toward other people:

splendid temple dedicated to God, as well as an enormous palace for himself. King Solomon won praise for his wisdom and understanding. He also tried to increase Israel's influence by negotiating with powerful empires in Egypt and Mesopotamia.

**Division and conquest.** The kingdom of Israel paid a heavy price for Solomon's ambitions. His building projects required such heavy taxes and so much forced labor that revolts erupted soon after his death about 930 B.C. The kingdom then split into Israel in the north and Judah in the south.

Weakened by this division, the Hebrews could not fight off invading armies. In 722 B.C., Israel fell to the Assyrians. In 586 B.C., Babylonian armies captured Judah. King Nebuchadnezzar destroyed the great temple in Jerusalem and forced many Hebrews into exile in Babylon.

**❝**I the Lord am your God who brought
you out of the land of Egypt, the
house of bondage: You shall have
no other gods beside Me. . . .
Honor your father and your mother,
as the Lord your God has
commanded. . . .
You shall not murder.
You shall not steal.**❞**

**Other laws.** The Torah set out many other
laws. Some dealt with everyday matters such as
cleanliness and food preparation. Others were
criminal laws. Like Hammurabi's Code, many
Hebrew laws required an eye for an eye. At the
same time, preachers called on leaders to enforce laws with justice and mercy.

Some laws were meant to protect women.
The Ten Commandments, for example, made
respect for mothers a basic law. Still, as in many
other religions, most laws treated women as
subordinate to men. The male head of a family
owned his wife, or wives, and his children. A father could sell his daughters into marriage, and
only a husband had the right to seek a divorce.

Early in Hebrew history, a few women
leaders, such as the judge Deborah, won honor
and respect. Later on, however, women were
not allowed to participate in many religious
ceremonies.

**Justice and morality.** Often in Jewish
history, prophets, or spiritual leaders, emerged
to interpret God's will. The prophets warned
that failure to obey God's law would lead their
people to disaster.

Prophets preached a strong code of ethics,
or moral standards of behavior. They urged
both personal morality and social justice, calling

on the rich and powerful to protect the poor
and weak. All people, they said, were equal before God. Unlike many ancient societies where
the ruler was seen as a god, Jews saw their leaders as fully human and bound to obey God's law.

## Looking Ahead

Almost 2,000 years ago, many Jews were
forced to leave their homeland in Palestine. (See
Chapter 6.) This diaspora (di AS puhr uh), or
scattering of people, sent Jews to different parts
of the world. Wherever they settled, Jews maintained their identity as a people by living in
close-knit communities and obeying their religious laws and traditions. These traditions set
Jews apart from other people. Yet they also
helped them survive centuries of persecution.

Judaism is numbered among the world's
major religions for its unique contribution to religious thought as well as its influence on two
later religions, Christianity and Islam. Both
those faiths, which also emerged in the Middle
East, were monotheistic. Jews, Christians, and
Muslims all honor Abraham, Moses, and the
prophets, and they all teach the ethical world
view developed by the Hebrews.

## SECTION 5 REVIEW

1. **Identify** (a) Torah, (b) Moses, (c) David,
   (d) Solomon, (e) Ten Commandments,
   (f) Deborah.
2. **Define** (a) monotheistic, (b) covenant,
   (c) prophet, (d) ethics, (e) diaspora.
3. Why did Israel become a divided kingdom?
4. Describe three basic teachings of Judaism.
5. What was the status of women under Hebrew
   law?
6. *Critical Thinking* **Linking Past and
   Present** Compare the ethical beliefs of the
   Hebrews to those commonly accepted in our
   society today. How are they similar? How are
   they different?
7. *ACTIVITY* With a partner, act out a conversation between a Hebrew parent and child
   in Egypt or Babylon. The parent should try to
   explain why, even though they are in exile,
   the Hebrews believe they are "the chosen
   people."

**GLOBAL CONNECTIONS**

As a result of the diaspora, by A.D. 300 Jewish
communities existed as far east as India and as
far west as Spain. The first Jewish settlers in the
Americas arrived in Brazil in the early 1500s.
Meanwhile, a separate group converted to Judaism in Ethiopia. These African Jews, now
known as the Falasha, strictly observed Jewish
laws and traditions for centuries. In the 1980s,
most of the surviving Falasha left their famine-
stricken homeland to settle in Israel.

# Skills for Success

## Interpreting a Thematic Map

Thematic maps are special-purpose maps that illustrate specific characteristics of a place aside from physical features and political boundaries. Examples of thematic maps include population maps, resource maps, trade maps, and/or battle maps. Thematic maps can help you draw conclusions about civilizations and events.

The most important parts of a thematic map are the title and the map key. The title identifies the topic of the map, while the key contains details that will help in reading the map. Use the following questions as a guide to interpreting the map below.

**1** **Identify the subject of the map.** (a) What land area is pictured on the map? (b) What is the topic of the map?

**2** **Use the key to read the map.** (a) What do the arrows on the map show? (b) Describe the extent of Phoenician trade in 700 B.C. (c) What color is used to illustrate Phoenician colonies?

(d) Where did the Phoenicians have colonies in about 700 B.C.? (e) What towns or trading centers did the Phoenicians control in Africa?

**3** **Analyze the information on the map and draw conclusions.** (a) How did geography influence the type of economy that the Phoenicians developed? (b) What information on the map supports the claim that the Phoenicians were skilled sailors? (c) Why were the Phoenicians in a good position to become "carriers of civilization"? (d) What geographic factors would make it difficult for the Phoenicians to maintain control of their colonies?

***Beyond the Classroom*** Thematic maps appear regularly in newspapers and magazines as an aid to understanding the information in news articles. Look through a recent copy of a news magazine or newspaper and locate a thematic map. Report to the class on what the topic of the map was, what information the map illustrated, and what conclusions can be drawn from the map.

## Phoenician Trade and Colonies

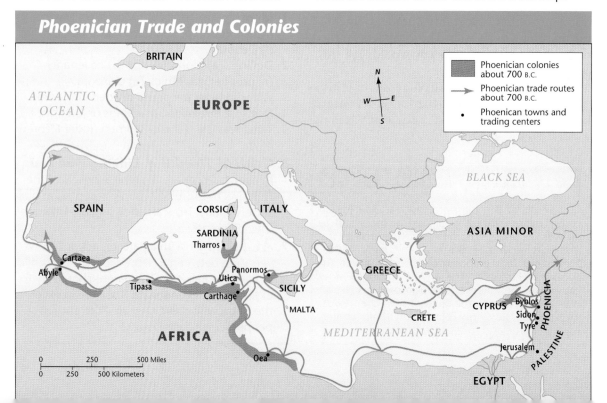

Key:
- Phoenician colonies about 700 B.C.
- Phoenician trade routes about 700 B.C.
- Phoenican towns and trading centers

# CHAPTER 2 REVIEW

## Building Vocabulary

Review the vocabulary words in this chapter. Then, use *ten* of these vocabulary words and their definitions to create a matching quiz. Exchange quizzes with another student. Check each other's answers when you are finished.

## Reviewing Chapter Themes

1. **Geography and History** Describe the influence of rivers on the development of (a) Egypt and (b) Mesopotamia.
2. **Global Interaction** Give two examples of how trade and warfare spread ideas and technology through the ancient Middle East.
3. **Impact of the Individual** Choose three rulers of Mesopotamia or Egypt. (a) Describe one achievement of each ruler. (b) Make a generalization about the power of rulers in many early civilizations.
4. **Diverslty** (a) What impact did the Phoenicians have on the Middle East? (b) What contributions did the Hebrews make to later religious thinking?

## Thinking Critically

1. **Linking Past and Present** (a) How was the building of the pyramids in ancient Egypt similar to public building projects today? (b) How was it different?
2. **Comparing** Compare the view of the afterlife in the Sumerian and Egyptian religions. (a) What differences do you see between the two views? (b) Why do you think they might have been so different?
3. **Analyzing Primary Sources** One of Hammurabi's laws states, "If outlaws collect in the house of a wine-seller, and she does not arrest these outlaws and bring them to the palace, that wine-seller shall be put to death." (a) What was the purpose of this law? (b) Would you consider this a harsh law? Why or why not? (c) What similar laws do we have in our society today?
4. **Analyzing Information** (a) What rights did women have in Egyptian, Sumerian, and Hebrew societies? (b) How were these rights restricted? (c) What do these facts suggest about the status of women in ancient civilizations?

5. **Drawing Conclusions** According to the Book of Esther, an adviser to the king of Persia warned, "There is a certain people scattered and dispersed among the other peoples in all the provinces of your realm, whose laws are different from those of any other people and who do not obey the king's laws." (a) How does this passage help explain why the Jews were often persecuted? (b) How do you think their sense of uniqueness helped the Jews survive?

## For Your Portfolio

A local museum is preparing a data bank. As part of this project, you have been asked to contribute a high-interest chart illustrating the features of an early civilization of Africa or Asia. (Your teacher will advise you whether to work alone or with a partner.)

1. Choose one of the following civilizations that you have read about in this chapter: Egyptian (Old, Middle, or New Kingdom), Sumerian, Babylonian, Assyrian, Hittite, Persian, Phoenician, Hebrew.
2. Review the eight basic features of a civilization described on pages 13–16. Using the information in this chapter, list ways in which these features apply to the civilization you have chosen. For example, if you chose Sumer, you might list *cuneiform* under the feature Writing and *worship of local gods and goddesses* under the feature Complex Religions.
3. Use library resources to fill in more details about the civilization you have chosen.
4. Look for pictures, charts, or diagrams that you can use to illustrate your chart. For example, if you chose Egypt, a picture of a pharaoh might illustrate Central Government and a diagram of the levels of Egyptian society might illustrate Social Classes. Copy these pictures for use in your chart.
5. Classify the information you have gathered under each of the features of a civilization. Decide which information and illustrations you want to include on your chart.
6. Create your chart. (You might first wish to make a small sketch in pencil or on computer.) Make sure that you identify the civilization and that the chart is clear and easy to read.

# Early Civilizations in India and China

## (2500 B.C.–256 B.C.)

## CHAPTER OUTLINE

1 **Cities of the Indus Valley**
2 **Kingdoms of the Ganges**
3 **Early Civilization in China**

On New Year's Day more than 3,000 years ago, the king, known to his people as the Son of Heaven, mounted the high earth platform and entered the brightly decorated wooden temple. Helped by priests whose prayers echoed his, he made offerings of food and wine to the powerful forces of Heaven and Earth. As cold winds rustled his brilliant green robes, he descended to a nearby field, took up a plow, and cut a furrow into the earth. The people watching these ceremonies felt reassured.

New Year's Day in the Chinese calendar was the beginning of spring. The king's prayers to Shang Di, the Supreme Being, were essential for bringing good harvests.

To the ancient Chinese, the king stood between Heaven and Earth. His sacrifices alone could keep the powerful forces of nature in harmony. An ancient Chinese history explains the link between the king, the powers above, and the people below:

66Heaven and Earth are the parents of all creatures, and of all creatures, people are the most highly endowed. . . . Heaven had to help the inferior people by providing rulers and teachers that they might be able to aid Shang Di and secure the peace of the kingdom. . . . Furthermore, the One Man [king] having offered special sacrifice to Heaven and performed the due services to Earth, leads the people to execute the will of Shang Di.99

Like leaders in other ancient civilizations, early Chinese rulers served as both priests and kings. Traditions like those surrounding the Son of Heaven continued until A.D. 1911. Every New Year's Day, a Chinese ruler plowed a furrow near the Temple of Heaven to ensure favorable harvests.

As civilizations took shape in the Nile Valley and Fertile Crescent, very different civilizations emerged in India and China. Like ancient Egypt and Sumer, Indian and Chinese civilizations rose in fertile river valleys and influenced nearby lands. These two remarkable civilizations grew up in widely separate areas, one in South Asia and the other in East Asia. In each, people evolved distinct ways of life and thought whose influence can still be seen today.

**FOCUS ON** these questions as you read:

■ **Geography and History**
How did geographic forces help shape early civilizations in India and China?

■ **Art and Literature**
How do the great epics of ancient India express basic social and religious values?

■ **Continuity and Change**
How did early Chinese traditions form the basis for a long-lasting civilization?

## TIME AND PLACE

***Dragon's Head*** *Chinese artisans of the Zhou dynasty crafted this dragon head of bronze overlaid with gold. According to Chinese myth, dragons flew across the heavens, gathering clouds and showering the Earth with life-giving rain. Like other early peoples, the Chinese recognized the importance of nature to their lives and thought that it was controlled by powerful outside forces.* **Art and Literature** *How did the artist convey the image of the dragon as a powerful beast?*

## HUMANITIES LINK

***Art History*** Shang bronze sculpture (page 60).
***Literature*** In this chapter, you will encounter passages from the following works of literature: the *Vedas* (pages 54–55); the *Mahabharata* (page 56); *Book of Songs* (pages 63, 64–65).

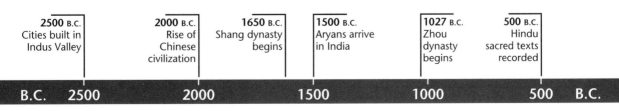

| 2500 B.C. Cities built in Indus Valley | 2000 B.C. Rise of Chinese civilization | 1650 B.C. Shang dynasty begins | 1500 B.C. Aryans arrive in India | 1027 B.C. Zhou dynasty begins | 500 B.C. Hindu sacred texts recorded |
|---|---|---|---|---|---|

| B.C. | 2500 | 2000 | 1500 | 1000 | 500 | B.C. |
|---|---|---|---|---|---|---|

# Cities of the Indus Valley

## Guide for Reading

- How has geography influenced India?
- How have archaeologists learned about early cities of the Indus Valley?
- Why do so many questions about Indus Valley civilization remain unanswered?
- **Vocabulary** *subcontinent, monsoon*

In 1922, archaeologists made a startling discovery in northwestern India. While digging in the Indus River valley, they unearthed bricks, small statues, and other artifacts unlike any they had seen before. They soon realized that they had uncovered a "lost civilization"—forgotten for some 3,500 years. Though later discoveries have added to our knowledge of the cities of the Indus Valley, many mysteries remain.

## Geography: The Indian Subcontinent

The Indus Valley is located in the region known as South Asia or the subcontinent of India. A subcontinent is a large landmass that juts out from a continent. The Indian subcontinent is a huge, wedge-shaped peninsula extending into the Indian Ocean. Today, it includes 3 of the world's 10 most populous countries—India, Pakistan, and Bangladesh—as well as the island nation of Sri Lanka (SREE LAHNG kah) and the mountain nations of Nepal and Bhutan.

Towering, snow-covered mountain ranges arc across the northern border of the subcontinent, including the Hindu Kush and the Himalayas. These mountains limited contacts between India and other lands and helped its people develop a distinct culture. Yet the mountains were not a complete barrier. Steep passes through the Hindu Kush served as gateways to migrating and invading peoples for thousands of years.

**Three regions.** The Indian subcontinent is divided into three major zones. They are the well-watered northern plain, the dry triangular Deccan plateau, and the coastal plains on either side of the Deccan. (See the map on page 51.)

The northern plain lies just south of the mountains. This fertile region is watered by mighty rivers: the Indus, which gives India its name, the Ganges (GAN jeez), and the Brahmaputra (brahm uh POO truh). These rivers and their tributaries carry melting snow from the mountains to the plains, making agriculture possible. To the people of the Indian subcontinent, rivers are sacred, especially the Ganges. An Indian name for river is *lok-mata,* or "mother of the people."

The most recognizable feature on any map of India is the Deccan, the triangular plateau that juts into the Indian Ocean. The Deccan lacks the melting snows that feed the rivers of the north and provide water for irrigation. As a result, much of the region is arid, unproductive, and sparsely populated.

The coastal plains, India's third region, are separated from the Deccan by low-lying mountain ranges, the Eastern and Western Ghats. Rivers and heavy seasonal rains provide water for farmers in the coastal plains. From very early times, coastal people used the seas for fishing and as highways for trade.

**The monsoons.** Today, as in the past, a defining feature of Indian life is the monsoon, a seasonal wind. In October, the winter monsoon blows from the northeast, bringing a flow of hot, dry air that withers crops. In late May or early June, the wet summer monsoon blows from the southwest. These winds pick up moisture over the Indian Ocean and then drench the land with daily downpours.

The monsoon has shaped Indian life. Each year, people welcome the rains that are desperately needed to water the crops. If the rains are late, famine and starvation may occur. More than 1,000 years ago, a poet hailed the arrival of monsoon rains after a long dry spell:

66The summer sun, who robbed the
     pleasant nights,
And plundered all the water of the
     rivers,
And burned the earth, and scorched
     the forest-trees
Is now hiding; and the rain-clouds,
Spread thick across the sky to track him
     down,
Hunt for the criminal with lightning
     flashes.99

Yet if the rains are too heavy, rushing rivers unleash deadly floods.

**Cultural diversity.** India's great size and diverse landscapes made it hard to unite. Many groups of people, with differing languages and traditions, settled in different parts of India. At times, ambitious rulers conquered much of the subcontinent, creating great empires. Yet the diversity of customs and traditions remained.

## Indus Valley Civilization

The first Indian civilization is cloaked in mystery. It emerged in the Indus River valley, in present-day Pakistan, about 2500 B.C. This civilization flourished for about 1,000 years, then vanished without a trace. Only in this century have its once prosperous cities emerged beneath the archaeologists' picks and shovels.

Archaeologists have not fully uncovered many Indus Valley sites. Nor have they deciphered the fragments of its writing found on stone seals. We have no names of kings or queens, no tax records, no literature, no accounts of famous victories. Still, we do know that the Indus Valley civilization covered the largest area of any civilization until the rise of Persia more than 1,000 years later. We know, too, that its great cities were as impressive as those of Sumer.

**Well-planned cities.** The two main cities, Harappa and Mohenjo-Daro (moh HEHN joh DAH roh), may have been twin capitals. Both were large, some three miles in circumference. Each was dominated by a massive hilltop structure, probably a fortress or temple. Both cities had huge warehouses to store grain brought in from outlying villages. Clearly, farmers produced enough surplus food to support tens of thousands of city dwellers.

The most striking feature of Harappa and Mohenjo-Daro is that they were so carefully planned. Each city was laid out in a grid pattern,

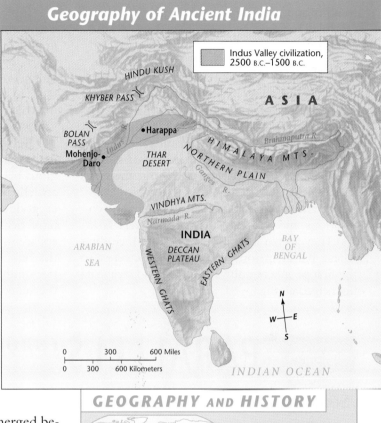

### Geography of Ancient India

Indus Valley civilization, 2500 B.C.–1500 B.C.

HINDU KUSH
KHYBER PASS
BOLAN PASS
Mohenjo-Daro
•Harappa
THAR DESERT
HIMALAYA MTS.
Brahmaputra R.
Ganges R.
NORTHERN PLAIN
ASIA
VINDHYA MTS.
Narmada R.
ARABIAN SEA
INDIA
DECCAN PLATEAU
WESTERN GHATS
EASTERN GHATS
BAY OF BENGAL
INDIAN OCEAN

0    300    600 Miles
0  300  600 Kilometers

### GEOGRAPHY AND HISTORY

As in Egypt and Mesopotamia, the Indus Valley civilization grew up in a fertile river valley. Indus people built great cities and carried on farming and trade.

1. **Location** On the map, locate (a) Himalaya Mountains, (b) Deccan Plateau, (c) Indus River, (d) Ganges River, (e) Mohenjo-Daro, (f) Harappa.
2. **Place** How has India's geography helped protect the people living in the Deccan Plateau?
3. **Critical Thinking** **Making Inferences** Why do you think the Indus River valley was a more inviting location for the development of a civilization than was the Narmada River valley?

with rectangular blocks larger than modern city blocks. All houses were built of uniform oven-fired clay bricks. Over the centuries, houses were built and rebuilt to the same pattern. Houses had surprisingly modern plumbing systems, with baths, drains, and water chutes that led into sewers beneath the streets. Merchants in the marketplaces used a uniform system of weights and measures—additional evidence of careful planning.

From such evidence, archaeologists have concluded that the Indus Valley cities had a well-organized government. Powerful leaders, perhaps priest-kings, made sure the cities had a steady supply of grain from the villages. The rigid pattern of building and the uniform brick sizes suggest government planners at work. These experts must also have developed skills in mathematics and surveying to lay out the cities so precisely.

**Farming and trade.** As in other early civilizations, most Indus Valley people were farmers. They grew a wide variety of crops, including wheat, barley, melons, and dates. They were also the first people to cultivate cotton and weave its fibers into cloth.

Some people were merchants and traders. Their ships carried cargoes of cotton cloth, grain, copper, pearls, and ivory combs to distant lands. By hugging the Arabian Sea coast and sailing up the Persian Gulf, Indian vessels reached the cities of Sumer. Contact with Sumer may have stimulated Indus Valley people to develop their own system of writing.

**Religious beliefs.** From clues such as statues, archaeologists have speculated about religious beliefs of Indus Valley people. Like other ancient people, they were polytheistic. A mother goddess, the source of creation, seems to have been widely honored. Indus people also apparently worshiped sacred animals, including the bull. Some scholars think these early practices influenced later Indian beliefs, especially the veneration, or special regard, for cattle.

# PARALLELS THROUGH TIME

## Seals and Logos

Many artisans and businesses mark their products with a trademark, brand, logo, or other identifying label. In this way, they and their customers can easily distinguish their products from those of competitors.

**Linking Past and Present**  List three animals that are used as company trademarks or logos today.

 **PAST**  Archaeologists have recovered more than 2,000 seals from the Indus cities of Harappa and Mohenjo-Daro. They think each merchant family used its own unique seal to stamp labels on its trade goods. The stone seals often bore images of animals, along with symbols whose meaning remains a mystery.

### PRESENT

The Sower logo identifies books published by Simon and Schuster. (You can see it on the copyright page of this textbook.) The Seal of Cotton appears on products made of 100 percent United States cotton. Both of these symbols are registered trademarks that cannot be used by other businesses.

## Decline and Disappearance

By 1750 B.C., the quality of life in Indus Valley cities was declining. The once orderly cities no longer kept up the old standards. Crude pottery replaced the finer works of earlier days.

We do not know for sure what happened, but scholars have offered several explanations. Ecological disasters may have contributed to the decline. Possibly too many trees were cut down to fuel the ovens of brickmakers. Tons of river mud found in the streets of Mohenjo-Daro suggest that a volcanic eruption blocked the Indus, flooding the city. Other evidence points to a devastating earthquake.

Scholars think that the deathblow fell about 1500 B.C., when nomadic people arrived in ever larger numbers from the north. The newcomers were the Aryans, whose ancestors had slowly migrated with their herds of cattle, sheep, and goats from what is today southern Russia. The Aryans may have completed the destruction begun by nature. With their horse-drawn chariots and superior weapons, the Aryans overran the cities and towns of the Indus region. The cities were soon abandoned.

As the ruined cities disappeared beneath the silt of the Indus, all memory of them faded. Only vague references to the conquest of city dwellers survived in Aryan oral traditions.

## SECTION 1 REVIEW

1. **Define** (a) subcontinent, (b) monsoon.
2. Describe two ways in which geography has influenced the people of South Asia.
3. What evidence shows that Indus Valley civilization had a well-organized government?
4. Why do we know so little about Indus Valley civilization?
5. *Critical Thinking* **Linking Past and Present** (a) How could natural disasters have contributed to the decline of Indus Valley civilization? (b) What ecological problems does the world face today?
6. *ACTIVITY* Imagine that you are an archaeologist digging in the Indus region. Write a "wish list" of three items you would like to uncover to learn more about Indus Valley civilization.

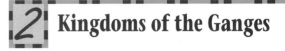

# 2 Kingdoms of the Ganges

## Guide for Reading

- How did the Aryans build a new civilization in India?
- How did Aryan life change between 1500 B.C. and 500 B.C.?
- What do India's ancient epics reveal about Aryan life?
- **Vocabulary** *caste, brahman, mystic, rajah*

The Aryans were warlike people. Their hymns praised their warriors as brave heroes and successful looters:

66Hail to the lord of thieves . . . hail to the destructive ones armed with spears, hail to the lord of plunderers.

Hail to the archers, to those who stretch the bowstring, and to those who take aim.99

Over the centuries, the Aryans who destroyed and looted the cities of the Indus Valley became the builders of a new Indian civilization. It rose in the northeast along the Ganges River, rather than in the northwest along the Indus.

## The Vedic Age

The Aryans were among many groups of Indo-European people who migrated across Europe and Asia seeking water and pasture for their horses and cattle. (See the map on page 54.) The early Aryans built no cities and left no statues or stone seals. Most of what we know about them comes from the Vedas, a collection of prayers, hymns, and other religious teachings. Aryan priests memorized and recited the Vedas for a thousand years before they were written down. As a result, the period from 1500 B.C. to 500 B.C. is often called the Vedic age.*

---

*Our knowledge about the Aryans is very limited. Historians have re-created a picture of Aryan life from studying their language, but many conclusions are still open to debate.

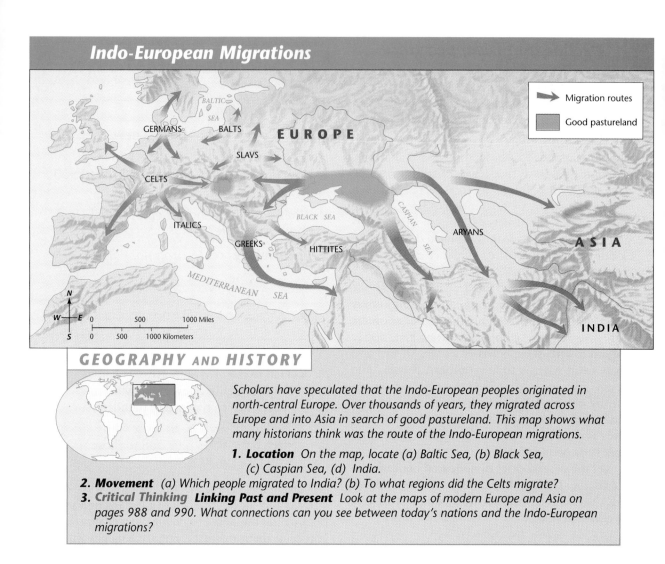

## Indo-European Migrations

Migration routes

Good pastureland

GERMANS    BALTS    **EUROPE**

SLAVS

CELTS

ITALICS    BLACK SEA

GREEKS    HITTITES    ARYANS    **ASIA**

MEDITERRANEAN    SEA

0    500    1000 Miles
0    500    1000 Kilometers

**INDIA**

## GEOGRAPHY AND HISTORY

*Scholars have speculated that the Indo-European peoples originated in north-central Europe. Over thousands of years, they migrated across Europe and into Asia in search of good pastureland. This map shows what many historians think was the route of the Indo-European migrations.*

**1. Location**  *On the map, locate (a) Baltic Sea, (b) Black Sea, (c) Caspian Sea, (d) India.*

**2. Movement**  *(a) Which people migrated to India? (b) To what regions did the Celts migrate?*

**3. Critical Thinking  Linking Past and Present**  *Look at the maps of modern Europe and Asia on pages 988 and 990. What connections can you see between today's nations and the Indo-European migrations?*

In the Vedas, the Aryans appear as warriors who fought in chariots with bows and arrows. They loved eating, drinking, music, chariot races, and dice games. These nomadic herders valued cattle, which provided them with food and clothing. Later, when they became settled farmers, families continued to measure their wealth in cows and bulls.

**Aryan society.** From the Vedas, we learn that the Aryans divided people by occupation. The three basic groups were the Brahmins, or priests; the Kshatriyas (kuh SHAT ree yuhz), or warriors; and the Vaisyas (VĪS yuhz), or herders, farmers, artisans, and merchants. At first, warriors enjoyed the highest prestige, but priests eventually gained the most respect. Their power grew because Brahmins claimed that they alone could conduct the ceremonies needed to win the favor of the gods.

The Vedas also show that the Aryans felt vastly superior to the Dravidians, the people they conquered. Many scholars think that the Dravidians may have been descended from the original inhabitants of the Indus Valley. Although the Dravidians had built an advanced civilization, the nomadic Aryans had no use for city dwellers. The Aryans therefore separated non-Aryans into a fourth group, the Sudras (SOO druhz). This group included farmworkers, servants, and other laborers who occupied the lowest level of society.

A Vedic hymn explains how Aryans believed their society came to be divided into four distinct classes:

66When the gods divided the Man,
        into how many parts did they
            divide him?

What was his mouth, what were his
    arms, what were his thighs and his
    feet called?
The Brahmin was his mouth, of his
    arms was made the warrior,
    his thighs became the Vaisya, of his
    feet the Sudra was born. **99**

During the Vedic age, class divisions came to reflect social and economic roles more than racial differences between Aryans and non-Aryans. As these changes occurred, they gave rise to a more complex system of castes,* or social groups into which people are born and from which they cannot change. You will read about the caste system in Chapter 4.

**Aryan religious beliefs.** The Vedas show that the Aryans were polytheistic. They worshiped gods and goddesses that embodied natural forces such as sky and sun, storm and fire. The Aryans also honored animals, such as monkey gods and snake gods. Fierce Indra, the god of war, was the chief Aryan deity. Indra's weapon was the thunderbolt, which he used not only to destroy demons but to announce the arrival of rain, so vital to Indian life. Other major gods included Varuna, the god of order and creation, and Agni, the god of fire. Agni also served as the messenger who communicated human wishes to the gods.

Brahmins offered sacrifices of food and drink to the gods. Through the correct rituals and prayers, the Aryans believed, they could call on the gods for health, wealth, and victory in war.

As the lives of the Aryans changed, so, too, did their beliefs. Some religious thinkers were moving toward the notion of a single spiritual power beyond the many gods of the Vedas, called brahman, that resided in all things. There was also a move toward mysticism. Mystics are people who devote their lives to seeking spiritual truth. Through meditation and yoga, or spiritual and bodily discipline, Indian mystics sought direct communion with divine forces. The religions that emerged in India after the Vedic age reflected the impact of mysticism as well as the notion of brahman.

_____

*Indians use the word *jati* to describe their social system. The Portuguese, who reached India in the late 1400s, used the word *caste,* which other Europeans adopted.

## Expansion and Change

Over many centuries, waves of Aryans went through the mountain passes into northwestern India. Aryan tribes were led by chiefs called rajahs. A rajah was often the most skilled war leader, elected to his position by an assembly of warriors. He ruled with the advice of a council of elders made up of heads of families.

**From nomads to farmers.** Despite their racial pride, Aryans mingled with the people they conquered. Gradually, they gave up their nomadic ways and settled into villages to grow crops and breed cattle. From the local people, they learned farming and other skills and developed new crafts of their own.

In time, Aryans spread eastward to colonize the heavily forested Ganges basin. By about 800 B.C., they had learned to make tools out of iron. Equipped with iron axes and weapons, restless pioneers carved farms and villages out of the rain forests of the northeast.

**Cities in the jungle.** Tribal leaders fought to control trade and territory across the northern plain. Some rajahs became powerful hereditary rulers, extending their influence over many villages. Walled cities filled with multistory houses rose above the jungle.

By 500 B.C., a new Indian civilization had emerged. Although it consisted of many rival kingdoms, the people shared a common culture rooted in both Aryan and Dravidian traditions. By this time, too, the Indian people had developed a written language, Sanskrit. (See the chart on page 56.) Priests now began writing down their sacred texts.

## Heroic Deeds and Moral Lessons

 On the eve of battle, the young warrior Arjuna gazes out across a silent battlefield, his heart filled with doubt. These enemies are not invaders from a far-off land. They are friends and relatives, people he has known and loved all his life. Now he must face them in battle and perhaps kill them. Where will he ever find the strength?

For thousands of years, people in India have shared Arjuna's agony. Families today, watching the story on television, are as anxious to know what Arjuna will do as the ancient Aryans were when priests told the story.

**India's greatest epic.** Arjuna is one of the heroes of the *Mahabharata* (muh HAH bah rah tuh), the greatest Indian epic. Almost 100,000 verses long, the *Mahabharata* was told and re-told for centuries before it was written down. Through it, we hear echoes of the battles that rival Aryan tribes fought to gain control of the Ganges region.

Like other epics, such as *The Epic of Gil-gamesh* (see page 31), the *Mahabharata* mixes history, mythology, and religion. Characters in-clude mortals, gods, goddesses, animals, and demons. The plot swirls around five royal broth-ers, the Pandavas, who have lost their kingdom to their cousins but struggle to regain it.

**Preparing for battle.** Arjuna, one of the Pandavas, at last faces his cousins and rivals in a great battle. Just before the battle, Arjuna con-fides to Krishna, his charioteer, that he does not want to fight even though he knows that his cause is just:

66O Krishna, when I see my kinsmen thus arrayed for battle, my mind is all awhirl. These I would not kill even though they might seek to kill me.99

Krishna, who is actually a god in human form, then instructs Arjuna about life and death. The soul, Krishna says, cannot be killed:

66It is never born and never dies, nor, once it exists, does it cease to be. Unborn, eternal, abiding, and an-cient, it is not slain when the body is slain. . . . Weapons do not destroy it, fire does not burn it, waters do not wet it, wind does not dry it.99

While Arjuna hesitates, Krishna presses his point home. The warrior, he says, has a duty to fulfill. No matter what, he must fulfill that duty: "For there is more joy in doing one's duty badly than in doing another man's duty well." Most important, Krishna advises Arjuna to detach himself from personal desire and ambition and to concentrate on duty. This episode of the *Ma-habharata*, known as the *Bhagavad-Gita* (BUHG uh vuhd GEE tuh), reflects important Indian re-ligious beliefs.

Strengthened in resolve, Arjuna goes into battle. The fighting lasts for 18 days and results in the complete victory of the Pandavas. As the *Mahabharata* ends, the brothers have restored peace to India.

**Rama and Sita.** A much shorter, but equally memorable, epic is the *Ramayana* (rah MAH yuh nuh). It recounts the fantastic deeds of the daring hero Rama and his beautiful bride Sita.

Not long after their wedding, Sita is kid-napped by the demon-king Ravana. The rest of the story tells of Rama's efforts to rescue Sita

## Comparing Languages

| English | month | mother | new | night | nose | three |
|---------|-------|--------|-----|-------|------|-------|
| **German** | Monat | Mutter | neu | Nacht | Nase | drei |
| **Persian** | māh | mādar | nau | shab | bini | se |
| **Sanskrit** | mās | matar | nava | nakt | nās | trayas |
| **Spanish** | mes | madre | nuevo | noche | nariz | tres |
| **Swedish** | månad | moder | ny | natt | näsa | tre |

*Interpreting a Chart* Similarities in words are one clue that Sanskrit shared a common root with Persian and most modern European languages. These languages are today called the Indo-European family. ■ How might the map on page 54 help explain the word similarities shown on this chart?

**Epic Romance** *The marriage of the courageous Rama to the beautiful Sita is joyously celebrated in this eighteenth-century illustration from the Ramayana. Excitement and suspense soon follow as the evil, 10-headed Ravana kidnaps Sita, and the noble Rama sets out to rescue his love.* **Diversity** *How does this picture reflect India's ethnic diversity?*

with the aid of the monkey general Hanuman. Ravana tries to ward off the attack by killing a duplicate of Sita before Rama's eyes. But Rama presses on, winning the battle and rescuing his bride.

Like Aryan religion, these epics evolved over thousands of years. Priest-poets added new morals to the tales to teach different lessons about morality. For example, they turned Rama into a model of virtue. In some versions, he appears as an ideal king. Likewise, Sita came to be honored as an ideal woman who remained loyal and obedient to her husband through many hardships. "May you be like Sita" is a common blessing still given to young women in India. ■

## Looking Ahead

The Aryans were the first of many people to filter into India through passes in the Hindu Kush. Even though scholars recognize that our knowledge of the Aryan migrations is very limited, most accept that Aryan traditions and beliefs formed a framework for later Indian civilization.

Aryan religious beliefs would evolve into major world religions. Just as the Middle East gave rise to three world religions—Judaism, Christianity, and Islam—South Asia was the birthplace of two influential faiths, Hinduism and Buddhism. You will read about these religions in Chapter 4.

## SECTION 2 REVIEW

1. **Identify** (a) Vedas, (b) Brahmins, (c) Kshatriyas, (d) Vaisyas, (e) Sudras, (f) Indra, (g) Sanksrit, (h) *Mahabharata*, (i) *Bhagavad-Gita*, (j) *Ramayana.*
2. **Define** (a) caste, (b) brahman, (c) mystic, (d) rajah.
3. What do the Vedas tell us about classes in Aryan society?
4. How did Aryan life change in the centuries after the Aryans invaded India?
5. *Critical Thinking* **Analyzing Information** Why might epic poems like the *Mahabharata* and *Ramayana* be good vehicles for teaching moral lessons?
6. *ACTIVITY* According to the *Ramayana*, Rama and Sita possess the qualities of the "ideal" man and woman. Make a list of at least four qualities that you think today's ideal man or woman should have. Do any of the qualities of Rama or Sita appear on your list?

**GLOBAL CONNECTIONS**

The *Ramayana* bears some resemblance to the *Iliad*, the ancient Greek epic. Both are long heroic tales in verse that were recited for centuries before being written down. Both epics revolve around efforts to recapture kidnapped brides, though Helen of Troy in the *Iliad* bears little resemblance to the admirable Sita. Some scholars think that both the *Ramayana* and the *Iliad* may have derived from a common Indo-European legend.

# 3 Early Civilization in China

## Guide for Reading

- How did geography help shape early Chinese civilization?
- What ideas about government did the Chinese develop?
- What were some achievements of early Chinese civilization?
- **Vocabulary** *loess, clan, ideograph, oracle bone, calligraphy, dynastic cycle, feudalism*

In very ancient times, relates a Chinese legend, flood waters rose to the top of the highest hills. Yu, a hard-working official, labored for 13 years to drain the waters:

> **❝**I opened passages for the streams throughout the nine provinces, and conducted them to the sea. I deepened channels and canals, and conducted them to the streams.**❞**

While taming the rivers, Yu did not once go home to see his wife and children. As a reward for his selfless efforts, he later became ruler of China.

The legend of Yu offers insights into early China. The ancient Chinese valued the ability to control flood waters and to develop irrigation systems for farming. The legend also shows how highly the Chinese prized devotion to duty. Both these values played a key role in the development of Chinese civilization.

## Geography: The Middle Kingdom

The ancient Chinese called their land Zhongguo (JONG goo AW), the Middle Kingdom. China was the most isolated of the civilizations you have studied so far. Long distances and physical barriers separated it from Egypt, the Middle East, and India. This isolation contributed to the Chinese belief that China was the center of the Earth and the sole source of civilization.

**Geographic barriers.** To the west and southwest of China, high mountains—the Tien Shan and the Himalayas—and brutal deserts blocked the easy movement of people. To the southeast, thick jungles divided China from Southeast Asia. To the north lay the forbidding Gobi Desert. To the east, the vast Pacific Ocean rolled endlessly. (See the map on page 59.)

Despite formidable barriers, the Chinese did have contact with the outside world. They traded with neighboring people and, in time, Chinese goods reached the Middle East and beyond. More often, though, the outsiders whom the Chinese encountered were nomadic invaders. To the Chinese, these nomads were barbarians who did not speak Chinese and lacked the skills and achievements of a settled society. Even the invaders accepted the superiority of Chinese culture. Nomads conquered China from time to time, but they were usually absorbed into the advanced Chinese civilization.

**Main regions.** As the Chinese expanded over an enormous area, their empire came to include many regions with a variety of climates and landforms. The Chinese heartland lay along the east coast and the valleys of the Huang He (HWAHNG HAY), or Yellow River, and the Yangzi (yahng DZEE). In ancient times, as today, these fertile farming regions supported the largest populations. Then, as now, the rivers provided water for irrigation and served as transportation routes.

Beyond the heartland are the outlying regions of Xinjiang (sheen jee AHNG), Mongolia, and Manchuria. The first two regions have harsh climates and rugged terrain. Until recent times, they were mostly occupied by nomads and subsistence farmers. All three outlying regions played a key role in China's history. Nomads repeatedly attacked and plundered Chinese cities. At times, powerful Chinese rulers conquered or made alliances with the people of these regions. China also extended its influence over the Himalayan region of Tibet, which the Chinese called Xizang (shee DZAHNG).

**"River of Sorrows."** Chinese history began in the Huang He Valley, where Neolithic people learned to farm. As in other places, the need to control the river through large water projects probably led to the rise of a strong central government.

# Geography of Ancient China

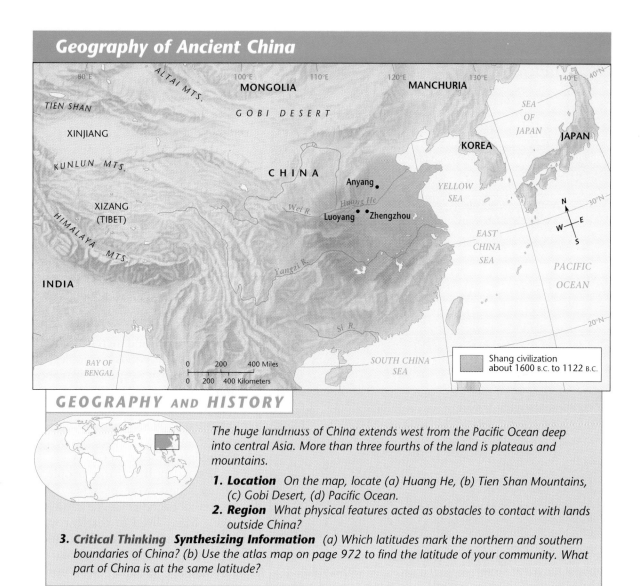

## GEOGRAPHY AND HISTORY

The huge landmass of China extends west from the Pacific Ocean deep into central Asia. More than three fourths of the land is plateaus and mountains.

1. **Location** On the map, locate (a) Huang He, (b) Tien Shan Mountains, (c) Gobi Desert, (d) Pacific Ocean.
2. **Region** What physical features acted as obstacles to contact with lands outside China?
3. **Critical Thinking** **Synthesizing Information** (a) Which latitudes mark the northern and southern boundaries of China? (b) Use the atlas map on page 972 to find the latitude of your community. What part of China is at the same latitude?

The Huang He got its name from the loess, or fine windblown yellow soil, that it carries eastward from Siberia and Mongolia. Long ago, the Huang He earned a bitter nickname, "River of Sorrows." As loess settles to the river bottom, it raises the water level. Chinese peasants labored constantly to build and repair dikes that kept the river from overflowing. However, when heavy rains swelled the river, it ran high above the surrounding plain.

If the dikes broke, flood waters burst over the land. Such disasters destroyed crops and brought mass starvation. Fear of floods is reflected in Chinese writing. The character, or written symbol, for misfortune, 川, represents a river with a blockage that causes flooding.

## China Under the Shang

About 1650 B.C., a Chinese people called the Shang gained control of a corner of northern China, along the Huang He. The Shang dynasty dominated this region until 1027 B.C. During the Shang period, Chinese civilization took shape. Despite many changes, ideas and achievements of this early civilization have survived to the present.

**Government.** Archaeologists have uncovered large palaces and rich tombs of Shang rulers. Shang kings led other noble warriors in battle. From their walled capital city at Anyang, they emerged to drive off nomads from the northern steppes and deserts.

**Shang Bronze Sculpture** *This bronze bucket shows the exceptional skill of Shang artists. It is decorated with carved symbolic figures, including serpents, cats, and a small deer. The main figure seems to be some sort of demon in the form of a tiger or bear. Art historians disagree, though, about whether the demon is swallowing the man or protecting him.* **Art and Literature** *What does this bronze suggest about the view of humans in ancient China?*

ancestor. Thus, Shang China probably more closely resembled the small kingdoms of Aryan India or the city-states of Sumer than the centralized government ruled by the Egyptian pharaohs.

**Social classes.** Shang society mirrored that in other early civilizations. Alongside the royal family was a class of noble warriors who owned the land. Shang warriors used leather armor, bronze weapons, and horse-drawn chariots. The chariots may have come from outside China through contacts with people of western Asia. Noble families lived in large timber or stone houses.

Early Chinese cities supported a class of artisans and merchants. Artisans produced goods for nobles, including bronze weapons, silk robes, and jade jewelry. Merchants organized trade, exchanging food and crafts made by local artisans for salt, cowrie shells, and other goods not found in northeastern China.

**Peasant life.** Most people in Shang China were peasants. They clustered together in farming villages. Many lived in thatch-roofed pit houses whose earthen floors were dug several feet below the surrounding ground. Such homes preserved the heat in winter and remained cool in summer.

Peasants led grueling lives. All family members worked in the fields, using stone tools to prepare the ground for planting or to harvest grain. When they were not in the fields, peasants had to repair the dikes. If war broke out between noble families, men had to fight alongside their lords. (📖 See *World Literature,* "Book of Songs," pages 64–65.)

In one Shang tomb, archaeologists discovered the burial place of Fu Hao (FOO HOW), wife of the Shang king Wu Ding. Artifacts show that she owned land and helped to lead a large army against invaders. This evidence suggests that noblewomen had considerable status during the Shang period.

Shang kings probably controlled only a small area. Princes and nobles loyal to the Shang dynasty governed most of the land. They were most likely the heads of important clans, or groups of families who claimed a common (often mythical)

### Religious Beliefs

By Shang times, the Chinese had developed complex religious beliefs. They prayed to many gods and nature spirits. Chief among them were Shang Di (SHAHNG DEE) and a mother goddess who brought plants and animals to Earth. As you read on page 48, the king was seen as the link between the people and Shang Di.

**Veneration of ancestors.** Gods as great as Shang Di, the Chinese believed, would not respond to the pleas of mere mortals. Only the spirits of the greatest mortals, such as the ancestors of the king, could get the ear of the Lord of Heaven. Thus, the prayers of rulers and nobles to their ancestors were thought to be essential to the community as a whole, ensuring good harvests or victory in war.

The ruler's power grew out of this veneration of ancestors. At first, only the royal family and other nobles had important enough ancestors to influence the gods. Gradually, other classes shared in these rituals. The Chinese called on the spirits of their ancestors to bring good fortune to the family. To honor their ancestors' spirits, they offered them sacrifices of food and other necessities. When westerners reached China, they mistakenly called this practice "ancestor worship."

**Yin and yang.** The Chinese believed the universe reflected a delicate balance between two forces, yin and yang. Yin was linked to Earth, darkness, and female forces, while yang stood for Heaven, light, and male forces. To the Chinese, these forces were not in opposition. Rather, the well-being of the universe depended on harmony between yin and yang. People could play a role in maintaining this harmony. For example, the king had to make the proper sacrifices to Heaven while at the same time taking practical steps to rule well.

## System of Writing

The ancient Chinese developed a system of writing. It used both pictographs and ideographs, signs that expressed thoughts or ideas.

**Consulting the ancestors.** The oldest examples of Chinese writing are on oracle bones, used by priests to predict the future. On animal bones or turtle shells, Shang priests wrote questions addressed to the gods or the spirit of an ancestor. These questions generally required a yes or no answer. Priests then heated the bone or shell until it cracked. By interpreting the pattern of cracks, they could provide answers or advice from the ancestors.

**A difficult study.** Written Chinese took shape almost 4,000 years ago. Over time, it evolved to include tens of thousands of characters. Each character represented a word or idea and was made up of a number of different strokes. In recent years, the Chinese have simplified their characters, but Chinese remains one of the most difficult languages to learn. Students must still memorize up to 10,000 characters to read a newspaper. By contrast, languages based on an alphabet, such as English or Arabic, contain only two dozen or so symbols representing basic sounds.

Not surprisingly, in earlier times, only the well-to-do could afford the years of study needed to master the skills of reading and writing. Working with brush and ink, Chinese scholars turned calligraphy, or fine handwriting, into an elegant art form.

**A force for unity.** Despite its complexity, the written language fostered unity. Isolated by geographic barriers, people in different parts of China often could not understand one another's spoken language, but they all used the same system of writing.

## The Zhou Dynasty

In 1027 B.C., the battle-hardened Zhou (JOH) people marched out of their kingdom on the western frontier to overthrow the Shang. They set up the Zhou dynasty, which lasted until 256 B.C.

**The Mandate of Heaven.** To justify their rebellion against the Shang, the Zhou promoted the idea of the Mandate of Heaven, or the divine right to rule. The cruelty of the last Shang king, they declared, had so outraged the gods that they had sent ruin on him. The gods then passed the Mandate of Heaven to the Zhou, who "treated the multitudes of the people well."

▲ Tortoise shell used as an oracle

## The Dynastic Cycle in China

### The New Dynasty

Restores peace
Appoints loyal officials
Redistributes land to peasants
Builds canals, irrigation systems,
    and roads
Repairs defensive walls

**New dynasty claims the Mandate of Heaven.**

**After several generations, the new dynasty becomes an aging dynasty.**

### Problems

Floods, famine, earthquakes
Invasions
Armed bandits in the provinces
Peasant revolts

**Aging dynasty loses the Mandate of Heaven.**

### The Aging Dynasty

Neglects government duties
Ignores corrupt officials
Loses control of the provinces
Imposes heavy taxes to pay for
    luxuries
Allows defensive walls to decay

**Interpreting a Chart** *The Chinese believed that their emperor had received the Mandate of Heaven to rule his people. However, they also believed that the emperor was obligated to govern wisely and preserve order.* ■ *According to this flow chart, how did a new dynasty try to repair the problems left by an aging dynasty?*

might seize power and set up a new dynasty. His success and strong government showed the people that the new dynasty had won the Mandate of Heaven. The dynastic cycle would then begin again. (See the chart at left.)

**A feudal state.** The Zhou rewarded their supporters by granting them control over different regions. Thus, under the Zhou, China developed into a feudal state. Feudalism (FYOO duhl ihz uhm) was a system of government in which local lords governed their own lands but owed military service and other forms of support to the ruler. (In later centuries, feudal societies also developed in Europe and Japan.)

In theory, Zhou kings ruled China, and for about 250 years, they actually did enjoy great power and prestige. After about 771 B.C., though, feudal lords exercised the real power and profited from the lands worked by peasants within their domains.

**Economic growth.** During the Zhou period, China's economy grew. Knowledge of ironworking reached China about 500 B.C. As iron axes and ox-drawn iron plows replaced stone, wood, and bronze tools, farmers produced more food. Peasants also began to grow new crops, such as soybeans. Some feudal lords organized large-scale irrigation works, making farming even more productive.

Commerce expanded, too. The Chinese began to use money for the first time. Chinese copper coins had holes in the center so they could be strung on cords. This early form of a cash, or money, economy made trade easier. Merchants also benefited from new roads and canals built by feudal lords.

**The dynastic cycle.** The Chinese later expanded the idea of the Mandate of Heaven to explain the dynastic cycle, or the rise and fall of dynasties. As long as a dynasty provided good government, it enjoyed the Mandate of Heaven. If the rulers became weak or corrupt, the Chinese believed that Heaven would withdraw its support.

Floods, famine, or other catastrophes were signs that a dynasty had lost the favor of Heaven. In the resulting chaos, an ambitious leader

**ISSUES** *For* **TODAY**

According to the dynastic cycle, a dynasty would fall if it failed to fulfill its duties. What services should government provide for its citizens?

Economic expansion led to an increase in population. People from the Huang He heartland overflowed into central China and began to farm the immense Yangzi basin. Feudal nobles expanded their territories and encouraged peasants to settle in the conquered territories. By late Zhou times, China was increasing in size, population, and prosperity.

## Chinese Achievements

The Chinese made progress in many areas during the Shang and Zhou periods. For example, astronomers studied the movement of planets and recorded eclipses of the sun. Their findings helped them develop an accurate calendar with 365¼ days. The Chinese also made remarkable achievements in the art and technology of bronzemaking. (See Art History, page 60.)

**Silkmaking.** By 1000 B.C., the Chinese had discovered how to make silk thread from the cocoons of silkworms. Soon, the Chinese were cultivating both silkworms and the mulberry trees on which they fed. Women did the laborious work of tending the silkworms and processing the cocoons into thread. They then wove silk threads into a smooth cloth that was colored with brilliant dyes. Only royalty and nobles could afford luxurious silk robes.

Silk became China's most valuable export. The trade route that eventually linked China and the Middle East became known as the Silk Road. (See pages 96–97.) To protect this profitable trade, the Chinese kept the process of silkmaking a secret.

**The first books.** Under the Zhou, the Chinese made the first books. They bound thin strips of wood or bamboo together and then carefully drew characters on the flat surface with a brush and ink.

The earliest Chinese books included histories and religious works. *I Ching,* a handbook for diviners, is still used by people who want to foretell the future.

Among the greatest Zhou works is the lovely *Book of Songs.* Many of its poems describe such events in the lives of farming people as planting and harvesting. Others praise kings or describe court ceremonies. The book also includes tender or sad love songs. In one lyric, a young woman complains that her family is forcing her into a marriage she does not want:

> 66 My heart is not a mirror, To reflect
> what others will.
> Brothers too I have; I cannot be
> snatched away.
> But lo, when I told them of my plight
> I found that they were angry
> with me. 99

## Looking Ahead

By 256 B.C., China was a large, wealthy, and highly developed center of civilization. Chinese culture was already dominant in East Asia. Yet the Zhou dynasty was too weak to control feudal lords who ignored the Son of Heaven and battled each other in savage wars. Out of these wars rose a ruthless leader who was determined to impose political unity on China. His triumphs would leave a lasting imprint on Chinese civilization.

## SECTION 3 REVIEW

1. **Identify** (a) Zhongguo, (b) Shang, (c) yin and yang, (d) Zhou, (e) Mandate of Heaven, (f) *Book of Songs.*
2. **Define** (a) loess, (b) clan, (c) ideograph, (d) oracle bone, (e) calligraphy, (f) dynastic cycle, (g) feudalism.
3. How did the Huang He earn the nickname "River of Sorrows"?
4. What role did veneration of ancestors play in ancient Chinese life?
5. How did China's economy expand during the Zhou period?
6. *Critical Thinking* **Predicting Consequences** Give three examples of how your life and schooling might be different if you had had to learn a language written in characters like Chinese rather than a language using an alphabet.
7. *ACTIVITY* Using the simple, direct style of the poems above and on pages 64–65, write a short poem to add to the *Book of Songs.* Your poem might be about floods, rulers, war, or the deeds of an ancestor.

# World Literature
## Book of Songs

**Introduction**  *The poems in the* Book of Songs *were compiled sometime around 500* B.C., *though many poems are much older. From Zhou times to the present, Chinese have taken pleasure in reciting these ancient songs. In earlier times, scholars had to memorize all 305 poems to show their mastery of Chinese literature.*

*Most of these poems were originally folk songs. They offer glimpses into the lives of women and men from all social classes. Men sing of wooing and winning their wives. Women tell of joyful love and heartbreaking losses. Farmers celebrate harvests, while princes reflect on the responsibilities of ruling. The five poems below all deal with the subject of war. Song 100 is the lament of a wife whose husband is away at war; song 117 is a rousing song for the start of a military campaign; while songs 122, 124, and 127 are complaints by common soldiers who have been forced to leave home on a long expedition.*

### 100
My lord is on service;
He did not know for how long.
Oh, when will he come?
The fowls are roosting in their holes,
Another day is ending,
The sheep and cows are coming down.
My lord is on service;
How can I not be sad?

My lord is on service;
Not a matter of days, nor months.
Oh, when will he be here again?
The fowls are roosting on their perches,
Another day is ending,
The sheep and cows have all come down,
My lord is on service;
Were I but sure that he gets drink and food!

### 117
Firmly set are the rabbit nets,
Hammered with a *ting, ting.*
Stout-hearted are the warriors,
Shield and rampart of our elder and lord.

Firmly set are the rabbit nets,
Spread where the paths meet.
Stout-hearted are the warriors,
Good comrades for our elder and lord.

Firmly set are the rabbit nets,
Spread deep in the woods.
Stout-hearted are the warriors,
Belly and heart of our elder and lord.

### 122
How few of us are left, how few!
Why do we not go back?
Were it not for our prince and his concerns,
What should we be doing here in the dew?

How few of us are left, how few!
Why do we not go back?
Were it not for our prince's own concerns,
What should we be doing here in the mud?

### 124
I climb that wooded hill
And look towards where my father is.
My father is saying, "Alas, my son is on
   service;
Day and night he knows no rest.
Grant that he is being careful of himself,
So that he may come back and not be left
   behind!"

I climb that bare hill
And look towards where my mother is.
My mother is saying, "Alas, my young one is
   on service;
Day and night he gets no sleep.
Grant that he is being careful of himself,
So that he may come back, and not be cast
   away."

I climb that ridge
And look towards where my elder brother is.
My brother is saying, "Alas, my young
   brother is on service;
Day and night he toils.
Grant that he is being careful of himself,
So that he may come back and not die."

*Jade Figures* Like the poems in the Book of Songs, *these carved jade figures give us a glimpse into the lives of early Chinese people. Actually, human figures like these were rare except in the outlying regions of southern and western China. Most sculptures of the Shang and early Zhou periods represented birds and animals of religious significance.* **Economics and Technology** *Why do you think museums and private collectors consider such jade sculptures very valuable today?*

**127**

Minister of War,
We are the king's claws and fangs.
Why should you roll us on from misery to
    misery,
Giving us no place to stop in or take rest?

Minister of War,
We are the king's claws and teeth.
Why should you roll us on from misery to
    misery,
Giving us no place to come to and stay?

Minister of War,
Truly you are not wise.
Why should you roll us on from misery to
    misery?
We have mothers who lack food.

Source: Book of Songs, translated from the Chinese
by Arthur Waley (New York: Grove Press, 1960).

## Thinking About Literature

1. **Vocabulary** Use the dictionary to find the meanings of the following words: stout-hearted, rampart.
2. (a) What does song 117 say about the relationship between soldiers and their feudal lords? (b) How do the soldiers in songs 122 and 127 feel about serving their lords?
3. Give three examples of how these poems show the effects of war on the family.
4. *Critical Thinking* **Linking Past and Present** Do you think the thoughts and feelings expressed in these ancient Chinese poems have meaning for people in our society today? Explain.

# Skills for Success

Critical Thinking | **Writing and Researching** | Maps, Charts, and Graphs | Speaking and Listening

## Using the Writing Process

Writing that is clear, logical, and interesting goes through a three-stage process: prewriting, writing, and revising. During the **prewriting** stage, the writer decides what to write about, gathers information, and begins to organize it. During the **writing** stage, the writer makes choices about the purpose of the writing, the audience, and the form the writing will take. The writer then prepares a first draft. During the **revising** stage, the writer reviews the draft for sense, style, and errors in spelling, punctuation, and grammar. The writer may also make changes based on new ideas or the response of readers.

The chart below is one of several prewriting tools that can help you organize your information. It is especially helpful when your writing involves comparisons of topics or ideas.

**1** **Develop ideas for writing and organize your information in preparation for writing.** Look at the chart below. (a) What idea has the writer come up with for an essay topic? (b) What kinds of details has the writer listed in the chart? (c) How has the writer organized the details so that they make sense?

**2** **Identify who your audience is and what your purpose is and write a first draft.** (a) Who are the likely readers of this writer's work? (b) How will that affect the writing? (c) Would the writer be more likely to use an eyewitness approach, an analytical approach, or a biographical approach? Why? (d) What would be a good topic sentence for the first paragraph of this essay?

**3** **Review your writing to see if it makes sense.** Ask one of your classmates to listen to and respond to your topic sentence. (a) What changes, if any, were suggested? (b) Rewrite your sentence based on these suggestions.

***Beyond the Classroom*** Job applications often contain questions that require you to write a paragraph or essay. Employers may ask these questions not only to learn your answers, but to evaluate your writing skills. Imagine that a job application asks you to describe your strengths as an employee. Use the above steps to write an answer.

| Features of Aryan civilization | Features of both civilizations | Features of Shang civilization |
|---|---|---|
| • believed in reincarnation | • rigid class system | • power was handed down through family dynasties |
| • religion moved toward monotheism | • developed written language | • polytheistic |
| • status of women deteriorated over time | • lived in extended families | • venerated ancestors |
| • warfare dominated life | • households headed by oldest male | • long period of peace allowed arts and sciences to flourish |
| • rajahs were elected | | • women farmed and practiced some crafts |

# CHAPTER 3 REVIEW

## Building Vocabulary

Select *five* vocabulary words from the chapter. Write each word on a separate slip of paper. Then, write the definition for each word on other slips of paper. Scramble the slips and exchange them with another student. Match the words with their definitions, and then check each other's results.

## Reviewing Chapter Themes

1. **Geography and History** Describe how each of the following geographic features influenced the development of civilization in India and China: (a) rivers, (b) physical barriers, (c) regions.
2. **Art and Literature** Describe what each of the following reveals about Aryan life and ideas: (a) religious texts such as the Vedas, (b) epics such as the *Mahabharata* and the *Ramayana.*
3. **Continuity and Change** Describe the role played by *three* of the following in the development of a unique Chinese civilization: (a) veneration of ancestors, (b) written language, (c) the dynastic cycle, (d) advances in technology.

## Thinking Critically

1. **Linking Past and Present** Based on the evidence uncovered by archaeologists, how were the cities of the Indus Valley similar to and different from cities today?
2. **Applying Information** In the Vedas, "breaker of cities" is one of the titles of honor given to the god Indra. How might this title have linked Indra to actual events in the history of the Aryans?
3. **Recognizing Points of View** Review the summary of the *Bhagavad-Gita* on page 56. (a) Restate Krishna's advice to Arjuna in your own words. (b) How does this advice help Arjuna resolve his doubts? (c) What does this excerpt from the *Bhagavad-Gita* suggest about the Aryans' view of the self? (★ See *Skills for Success*, page 280.)
4. **Analyzing Information** The Chinese symbol for yin and yang is ☯. (a) How does this symbol convey the meaning of yin and yang? (b) What role did the concept of yin and yang play in Chinese thought?

5. **Making Generalizations** Based on what you have read about the ancient societies of Egypt, Sumer, China, and the Indus Valley, make three generalizations about the role of religion and priests in early river valley civilizations.
6. **Analyzing Literature** Reread song 100 on page 64. (a) What is the setting and situation of this poem? (b) What are the main concerns of the woman who is speaking? (c) How has she spent her days while her husband has been away? (d) What does this poem suggest about the relationship between husbands and wives in rural China at that time? (e) How is the mood of this poem similar to that of other selections from the *Book of Songs?* (★ See *Skills for Success*, page 234.)

### For Your Portfolio

A local Asian cultural center is sponsoring a contest called Geography, History, and Life. You have been asked to contribute an entry dealing with the impact of geography on either India or China.

1. Select a specific geographic feature of either India or China. You might select a river, such as the Indus or Huang He; a region, such as the Deccan plateau or Mongolia; a mountain range, such as the Hindu Kush or the Himalayas; a mountain pass, such as the Khyber; a desert, such as the Gobi; or a feature of climate, such as the monsoon.
2. Do research at your local or school library to find out more about the impact of that feature on history or daily life in India or China. Then, select a specific topic, such as *The Huang He Floods* or *Farming the Deccan Plateau.*
3. Use the information you have found to create a contest entry. It may be in the form of a brief written report, an illustrated map, a song or poem, a letter or diary entry, a story, or a visual display such as a collage.
4. Divide into groups of five students. Present your entry to the other students as if they were the panel of judges. Then, briefly explain to the panel why you picked your topic, how you researched it, and what you found most interesting. Conclude by adding your entry to a classroom display.

# UNIT 1

# *Unit-in-Brief*

# Early Civilizations

## Chapter 1 Toward Civilization
### (Prehistory–3000 B.C.)

Archaeologists, historians, and other scholars are learning about our ancient human past through careful research. When the evidence that they find is gathered, pieced together, and interpreted, a fascinating story of the emergence of civilization unfolds.

- Archaeologists analyze artifacts to trace how early people developed new technologies and ways of life.
- Historians also study how people lived in the past, but they rely more heavily on written evidence to interpret past events.
- Geographers use the themes of location, place, human-environment interaction, movement, and region to explain the impact of geography on the human story.
- People made tools, learned to build fires, and developed spoken languages during the Paleolithic period, or Old Stone Age, the earliest period of human history.
- About 11,000 years ago, during the Neolithic period, or New Stone Age, people learned to farm, a dramatic breakthrough that transformed the way people lived.

- By about 5,000 years ago, the advances made by early farming communities led to the rise of civilizations.
- Historians define eight basic features common to most early civilizations: (1) cities, (2) well-organized central governments, (3) complex religions, (4) job specialization, (5) social classes, (6) arts and architecture, (7) public works, and (8) writing.
- Cities, the central feature of civilization, first rose in river valleys in the Middle East, Africa, and Asia, where conditions favored farming and a surplus of food could be grown.

## Chapter 2 First Civilizations: Africa and Asia
### (3200 B.C.–500 B.C.)

The first civilizations to develop emerged in river valleys in Egypt and the Middle East more than 5,000 years ago. In these places, people developed a complex way of life and beliefs that continue to affect our world today.

- A rich civilization emerged in the valley of the Nile River in Egypt that depended on control of the river waters.

- During the Old Kingdom, Egyptian pharaohs organized a strong, centralized state and built majestic pyramids.
- During the Middle Kingdom and the New Kingdom, trade and warfare brought Egypt into contact with other civilizations and helped spread ideas.
- Egyptians worshiped many gods and goddesses and believed in an afterlife.
- Egyptian society was organized into classes with the pharaoh, who was considered both a god and king, at the top of the hierarchy and farmers and slaves at the bottom.
- Independent Sumerian city-states developed in Mesopotamia, an area of rich, fertile land between the Tigris and Euphrates rivers.
- The Sumerians invented the earliest form of writing, known as cuneiform, and made great strides in mathematics and astronomy.
- Mesopotamia's location at a geographical crossroads made it vulnerable to a succession of invaders—including the Babylonians, the Assyrians, and the Persians—who built great empires.
- Warfare and trade in Mesopotamia helped to spread ideas and technology—including codified laws, ironworking, and the Phoenician alphabet—around the Mediterranean.
- The Hebrews developed Judaism, a monotheistic religion based on the worship of one God, whose laws are set out in the Torah and the Ten Commandments.

## Chapter 3  Early Civilizations in India and China
### (2500 B.C.–256 B.C.)

As civilizations took shape in the Nile Valley and Fertile Crescent, people in India and China carved out their own civilizations. These two remarkable civilizations evolved distinct ways of life and thought that would exert a powerful influence on other civilizations.

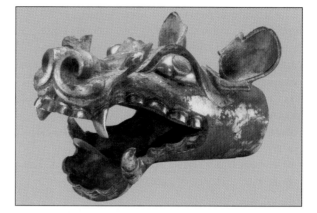

- India's first civilization, which emerged in the Indus River valley, flourished for about 1,000 years and then vanished.
- Excavations show that the Indus Valley covered the largest area of any ancient civilization and that its two main cities, Mohenjo-Daro and Harappa, were carefully planned.
- The nomadic Aryans, who overran the Indus Valley, eventually created a new Indian civilization along the Ganges River.
- The Vedas and the great Aryan epic poems, the *Mahabharata* and the *Ramayana,* reveal much about the lives and religious beliefs of the early Aryans.
- Long distances and physical barriers separated China from the other ancient civilizations and contributed to the Chinese belief that it was the sole source of civilization.
- Early on, the Chinese developed the idea of the dynastic cycle, which explained the rise and fall of the many dynasties that came to rule China.
- Chinese religious practices centered around the veneration of ancestors and the concept of balance of two opposing forces, yin and yang.
- During the Shang and Zhou periods, the Chinese made achievements in astronomy and bronzework, discovered how to make silk and books, and developed a complex system of writing.

# A Global View

## How Did the First Civilizations Evolve?

The first humans were wanderers. Clad in animal skins, equipped with rude spears and digging sticks, they followed game animals and ripening fruit, roots, and wild grain from season to season. Over thousands of generations, they learned to chip stone tools, to make fire, and to decorate cave walls with pictures of animals.

### Farming Villages

Then, about 10,000 years ago, some human beings abandoned the wandering life of hunter-gatherers. Settling into tiny villages of stone or mud huts, they raised crops and herded or penned up animals. Thanks to these dependable food sources, agricultural villages grew in number. Some of them began to specialize in arts and crafts, trade, and war.

The next step, from scattered farming villages to city-based civilizations, came a little more than 5,000 years ago. Here and there around the world, cities and city-states emerged. Kings, priests, and traders rose to wealth and power. And the invention of writing symbolized the emergence of a new way of life. We call it civilization.

### Ancient Societies

Early civilizations took shape in North Africa, the Middle East, India, and China. Though they emerged in isolation across a widely scattered area, these first civilized societies had much in common.

Politically, the first civilizations turned increasingly to hereditary monarchs for leadership. These rulers depended on priests, officials, aristocrats, or merchants for support.

Priests provided divine sanction for royal rule, asserting that the kings of Sumerian city-states were "stewards of the gods" or that Egypt's pharaohs were gods themselves. Royal officials carried out the ruler's decrees, collected taxes, and supervised large-scale public works, including city walls and irrigation projects. Landowning aristocrats dominated agriculture and often served as military officers in royal armies.

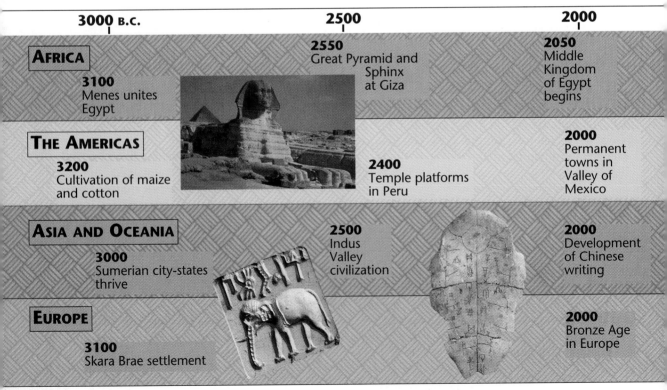

| 3000 B.C. | 2500 | 2000 |
|---|---|---|
| **AFRICA** | **2550** Great Pyramid and Sphinx at Giza | **2050** Middle Kingdom of Egypt begins |
| **3100** Menes unites Egypt | | |
| **THE AMERICAS** | | **2000** Permanent towns in Valley of Mexico |
| **3200** Cultivation of maize and cotton | **2400** Temple platforms in Peru | |
| **ASIA AND OCEANIA** | **2500** Indus Valley civilization | **2000** Development of Chinese writing |
| **3000** Sumerian city-states thrive | | |
| **EUROPE** | | **2000** Bronze Age in Europe |
| **3100** Skara Brae settlement | | |

The merchants of Mesopotamia, India, and elsewhere grew wealthy from trade, paid taxes, and strengthened the state economically.

Cities like Mohenjo-Daro or Babylon became the centers of political power and economic development. Most people, however, continued to live in small villages and cultivate the soil. These peasant majorities provided a foundation for the more elaborate lifestyles of their social superiors.

## Ancient Cultures

These early civilizations built on the cultural achievements of the simpler societies from which they grew. Architects constructed elaborate royal palaces, temples like the ziggurats of Mesopotamia, and royal tombs like the pyramids of Egypt. Sculptors carved beautiful statues of gods, goddesses, and rulers. Painters depicted scenes of everyday life or military victories. The development of writing preserved some of the world's oldest literature, from the Egyptian *Tale of Sinuhe* and the Sumerian *Epic of Gilgamesh* to India's *Mahabharata* and ancient China's *Book of Songs*.

Major advances in science and technology may also be traced to ancient times. From metalworking and textiles to mathematics and astronomy, early civilizations added greatly to humanity's store of skills. Religions also grew more complex, producing early scriptures like the Vedas of India. While most ancient societies were polytheistic, the Hebrew people of Mesopotamia introduced monotheism, the worship of one single, all-powerful God.

## Looking Ahead

A thousand years before the time of Jesus, civilization was still a rare phenomenon. Most people on all continents still lived in food-gathering bands, in farming villages, or as nomadic herders. But the future belonged to the islands of civilization that were emerging here and there around the world.

**ACTIVITY** Choose two events and two pictures from the time line below. For each, write a sentence explaining how it relates to the themes expressed in the Global View essay.

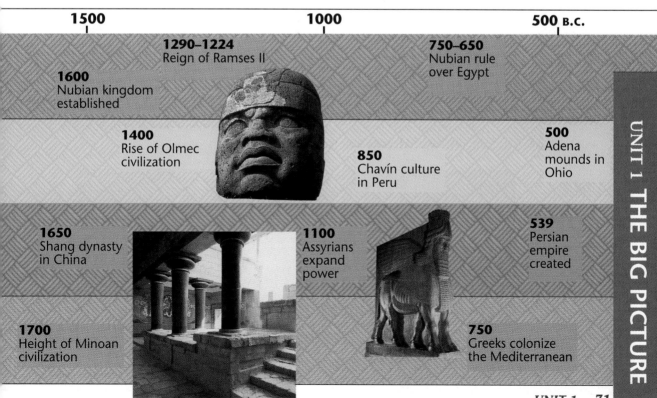

**1500**        **1000**        **500** B.C.

**1290–1224**
Reign of Ramses II

**1600**
Nubian kingdom established

**750–650**
Nubian rule over Egypt

**1400**
Rise of Olmec civilization

**850**
Chavín culture in Peru

**500**
Adena mounds in Ohio

**1650**
Shang dynasty in China

**1100**
Assyrians expand power

**539**
Persian empire created

**1700**
Height of Minoan civilization

**750**
Greeks colonize the Mediterranean

# You Decide

## Exploring Global Issues

### How Should Society Deal With Lawbreakers?

"Let the punishment fit the crime." To many people, this seems like the only fair and just way to deal with lawbreakers. The idea appears again and again in the Code of Hammurabi, history's first formal system of law. (See pages 37–38.) To others, though, punishments like Hammurabi's seem primitive and brutal.

The question of how to deal fairly and effectively with lawbreakers is as old as society itself. To begin your own investigation, examine these viewpoints.

**CANAAN**

**700s B.C.**

The ancient Hebrews looked to the Torah as God's authority on the law. The book of Leviticus states:

❝When a man causes a disfigurement in his neighbor, as he has done it shall be done to him, fracture for fracture, eye for eye, tooth for tooth; as he has disfigured a man, he shall be disfigured.❞

**CHINA**

**200s B.C.**

Hanfeizi, an influential scholar, believed that people were basically corrupt and that the only way to ensure an orderly society was to enforce strict laws:

❝People become naturally spoiled by love, but are submissive to authority. . . . That being so, rewards should be rich and certain that the people will be attracted to them; punishments should be severe and definite so that the people will fear them; and laws should be uniform and steadfast so that the people will be familiar with them.❞

**FRANCE**

**1600s**

Artist Jacques Callot depicted the mass hanging of a group of thieves. The caption warns that "it is the fate of vice-ridden men to experience the justice of Heaven sooner or later." ▼

**ITALY**

**1764**

Cesare Beccaria was one of the first reformers to argue against torture, capital punishment, and harsh treatment of criminals:

66 The purpose [of punishment] can only be to prevent the criminal from inflicting new injuries on its citizens and to deter others from similar acts. . . . Such punishments and such methods of inflicting them ought to be chosen, therefore, which will make the strongest and most lasting impression on the minds of men, and inflict the least torment on the body of the criminal. 99

**GREAT BRITAIN**

**1959**

After decades of heated debate, Great Britain abolished its death penalty in 1969. The picketers shown here were demonstrating outside a prison where a hanging was scheduled to take place. ▶

**SINGAPORE**

**1994**

In 1994, an American teenager living in Singapore was sentenced to a painful flogging for acts of vandalism. A Singaporean official defended his country's harsh penalties:

66 Unlike some other societies which tolerate acts of vandalism, Singapore has its own standards of social order as reflected in our laws. We are able to keep Singapore relatively crime free. We do not have a situation where acts of vandalism are commonplace, as in cities like New York, where even police cars are not spared the acts of vandals. 99

---

## COMPARING VIEWPOINTS

**1.** Which viewpoints here seem closest to Hammurabi's code?

**2.** On what point would Cesare Beccaria agree with Hanfeizi? With the official in Singapore?

**3.** How do the two pictures convey opposing messages?

## YOUR INVESTIGATION

**ACTIVITY**

**1.** Find out more about one of the viewpoints above or another viewpoint related to this topic. You might investigate:

■ Criminal provisions of the Sharia, the Islamic system of law.

■ Other law codes, such as the Code of Justinian or the Napoleonic Code.

■ The work of a prison reformer, such as Elizabeth Fry of England or Dorothea Dix of the United States.

■ The declaration of Pope John Paul II against capital punishment issued in April 1995.

■ Recent articles and editorials about capital punishment or prison conditions.

**2.** Decide which viewpoint you agree with most closely and express it in your own way. You may do so in an essay, a cartoon, a poem, a drawing or painting, a song, a skit, a video, or some other way.

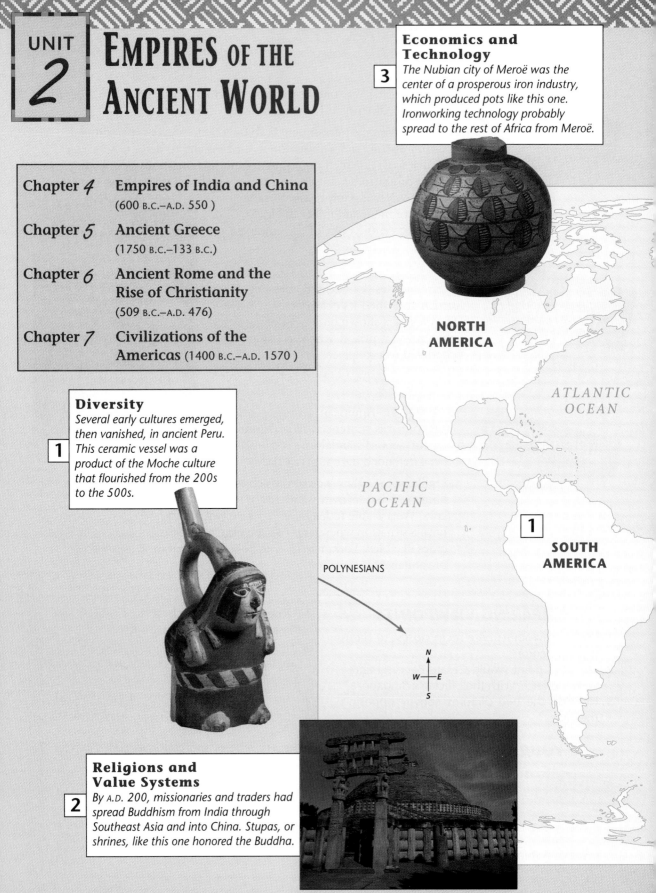

# EMPIRES OF THE ANCIENT WORLD

## Economics and Technology

**3** *The Nubian city of Meroë was the center of a prosperous iron industry, which produced pots like this one. Ironworking technology probably spread to the rest of Africa from Meroë.*

**NORTH AMERICA**

*ATLANTIC OCEAN*

## Diversity

*Several early cultures emerged, then vanished, in ancient Peru.* **1** *This ceramic vessel was a product of the Moche culture that flourished from the 200s to the 500s.*

*PACIFIC OCEAN*

**1**

**SOUTH AMERICA**

POLYNESIANS

N
W   E
S

## Religions and Value Systems

**2** *By A.D. 200, missionaries and traders had spread Buddhism from India through Southeast Asia and into China. Stupas, or shrines, like this one honored the Buddha.*

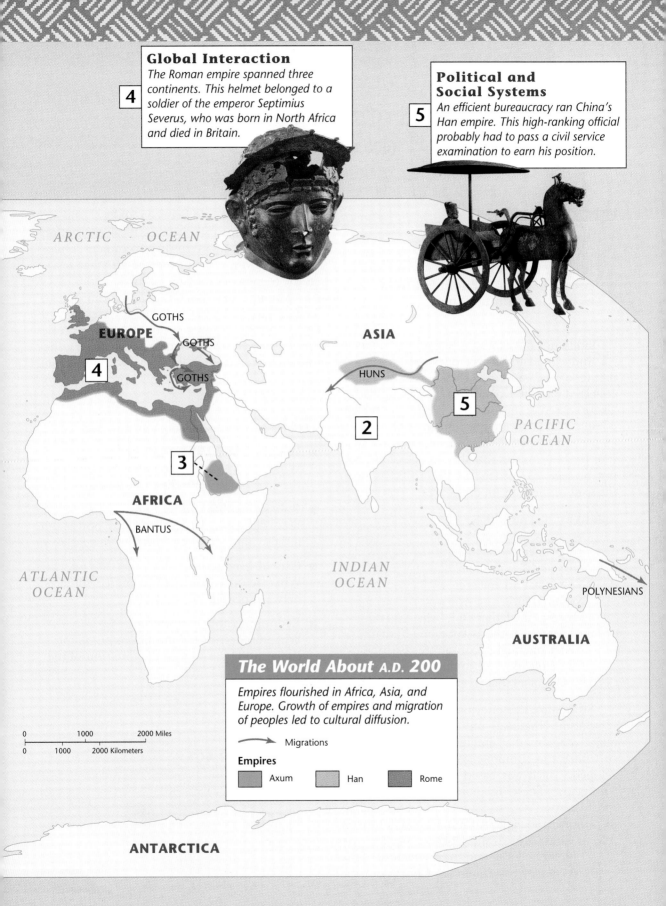

**Global Interaction**

4

The Roman empire spanned three continents. This helmet belonged to a soldier of the emperor Septimius Severus, who was born in North Africa and died in Britain.

**Political and Social Systems**

5

An efficient bureaucracy ran China's Han empire. This high-ranking official probably had to pass a civil service examination to earn his position.

ARCTIC     OCEAN

GOTHS

EUROPE

GOTHS

4

GOTHS

ASIA

HUNS

5

2

PACIFIC OCEAN

3

AFRICA

BANTUS

INDIAN OCEAN

ATLANTIC OCEAN

POLYNESIANS

AUSTRALIA

**The World About A.D. 200**

*Empires flourished in Africa, Asia, and Europe. Growth of empires and migration of peoples led to cultural diffusion.*

→ Migrations

**Empires**

Axum     Han     Rome

| 0 | 1000 | 2000 Miles |
| 0 | 1000 | 2000 Kilometers |

ANTARCTICA

# Empires of India and China

## (600 B.C. – A.D. 550)

**CHAPTER OUTLINE**

1 Hinduism and Buddhism
2 Powerful Empires of India
3 Pillars of Indian Life
4 Three Schools of Thought in China
5 Strong Rulers Unite China

Thousands of years ago, religious teachers in India tried to answer questions about the nature of the universe. Their ideas were later collected into the Upanishads (oo PAN ih shadz). These sacred texts use vivid images to explain complex ideas about the human soul and the connectedness of all life. In one story, a man tries to show his son that the essence of life cannot be seen. He orders the boy to break open the fruit of the banyan, or fig, tree:

66'What do you see?'
  'Very tiny seeds, sir.'
  'Break one.'
  'I have broken it, sir.'
  'Now, what do you see?'
  'Nothing, sir.'
  'My son,' the father said, 'what you do
  not perceive is the essence, and in that
  essence the mighty banyan tree exists.
  Believe me, my son, in that essence is
  the soul of all that is.'99

Stories like this one convey the teachings of Hinduism. Hinduism and Buddhism were two major religions that emerged in ancient India. In China, too, a unique system of thought developed, which was based on the teachings of Confucius. These religions and philosophies spread across Asia, where their influence still affects modern societies from India and Southeast Asia to China, Korea, and Japan.

Complex belief systems were a feature of the civilizations that rose in India, China, and the Mediterranean world between 500 B.C. and A.D. 500. Historians call them classical civilizations because they set patterns in government, philosophy, religion, science, and the arts that served as the framework for later cultures.

Though they differed greatly from one another, classical civilizations had features in common. Strong leaders brought vast territories under their control. To unify their empires, they organized efficient bureaucracies, built strong armies, and improved systems of transportation and communication.

**FOCUS ON** these questions as you read:

- **Religions and Value Systems**
  What religious and moral ideas helped shape the civilizations of India and China?

- **Political and Social Systems**
  How did strong leaders centralize power and impose unity on diverse peoples?

- **Global Interaction**
  What factors encouraged or limited contacts between peoples across Asia?

- **Economics and Technology**
  What discoveries and inventions put Gupta India and Han China in the forefront of the world's technology?

**TIME AND PLACE**

***The Buddha Preaching the Law*** *From India, the Buddha's disciples spread his teachings to China, Korea, Japan, and other Asian lands. This painting from the* A.D. *700s was found in a cave temple in China. The Buddha sits under a beautiful canopy as he preaches to his devoted disciples.* **Art and Literature** *How does this painting suggest that the Buddha is a holy and important figure?*

## HUMANITIES LINK

*Art History* Kailasa Temple (page 86).
*Literature* In this chapter, you will encounter passages from the following works of literature: the Upanishads (page 76); the *Tripitaka* (page 81); Avvaiyar, "The weapons of my king are blunt" (page 85); Kalidasa, *Shakuntala* (pages 86–87); Confucius, *The Analects* (page 90); "My people have married me" (page 95).

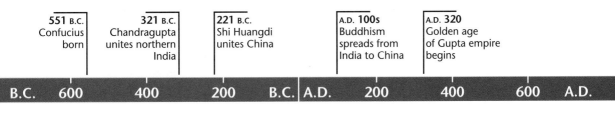

| 551 B.C. Confucius born | 321 B.C. Chandragupta unites northern India | 221 B.C. Shi Huangdi unites China | A.D. **100s** Buddhism spreads from India to China | A.D. **320** Golden age of Gupta empire begins |

| B.C. | 600 | 400 | 200 | B.C. | A.D. | 200 | 400 | 600 | A.D. |

# 1 Hinduism and Buddhism

## Guide for Reading

- Why is Hinduism such a complex religion?

- What are the central teachings of Hinduism and Buddhism?

- How did Buddhism become a major world religion?

- **Vocabulary** *atman, reincarnation, karma, dharma, ahimsa, nirvana*

As Hinduism evolved over 3,500 years, it absorbed diverse beliefs and forms of worship. If you visited a Hindu temple in India today, you would see people place offerings before the statues of many gods and goddesses. Yet a priest might begin a service with this prayer:

> 66 O Lord, forgive the sins that are due to my human limitations. You are everywhere, but I worship you here. You are without form, but I worship you in these forms. You need no praise, yet I offer you these prayers. 99

Like Hinduism, Buddhism includes a wide variety of beliefs. The ethical and spiritual message of these religions profoundly shaped the civilization of India.

## Hinduism: Unity and Diversity

Unlike most major religions, Hinduism has no single founder and no single sacred text. Instead, it grew out of the overlapping beliefs of the diverse groups who settled India. The process probably began when the Aryans added the gods of the Indus Valley people to their own. Later people brought other gods, beliefs,

and practices. As a result, Hinduism became one of the world's most complex religions, with countless gods and goddesses and many forms of worship existing side by side. Despite this diversity, all Hindus share certain basic beliefs.

**Many gods—or one?** "God is one, but wise people know it by many names." This ancient proverb reflects a central feature of Hinduism. By the late Vedic age, Hindu thinkers came to believe that everything in the universe was part of the unchanging, all-powerful spiritual force called brahman. (See page 55.) To Hindus, brahman is too complex an idea for most people to understand, so they worship gods that give a concrete form to brahman.

The most important Hindu gods are Brahma, the Creator; Vishnu, the Preserver; and Shiva, the Destroyer. Each represents aspects of brahman. Each of these gods can take many forms, human or animal, and each also has his own family. Some Hindus, for example, worship Shakti, the powerful wife of Shiva. She is both kind and cruel, a creator and destroyer.

**The goal of life.** To Hindus, every person has an essential self, or **atman** (AHT muhn). But atman is really just another name for brahman. The ultimate goal of existence, Hindus believe,

**Shiva: Lord of the Dance** *This bronze sculpture portrays the god Shiva dancing to destroy and re-create the universe. With his feet, he crushes a demon into submission. The circle of fire represents the Hindu belief in an endless cycle of creation, death, and rebirth.* **Diversity** *Why do you think various cultures use the circle to symbolize continuity?*

is achieving *moksha* (MAHK shuh), or union with brahman. In order to do that, individuals must free themselves from selfish desires that separate them from brahman. Most people cannot achieve moksha in one lifetime, but Hindus believe in reincarnation, or the rebirth of the soul in another bodily form. Reincarnation allows people to continue working toward moksha through several lifetimes.

**Karma and dharma.** In each existence, Hindus believe, a person can come closer to achieving moksha by obeying the law of karma. Karma refers to all the actions of a person's life that affect his or her fate in the next life. To Hindus, all existence is ranked. Humans are closest to brahman. Then come animals, plants, and objects like rocks or water. People who live virtuously earn good karma and are reborn at a higher level of existence. Those who do evil acquire bad karma and are reborn into suffering. In Indian art, this endless cycle of death and rebirth is symbolized by the image of the wheel.

To escape the wheel of fate, Hinduism stresses the importance of dharma (DAHR muh), the religious and moral duties of an individual. These duties vary according to class, occupation, gender, or age. By obeying one's dharma, a person acquires merit for the next life. As you will read, the concepts of karma and dharma helped ensure the social order by supporting the caste system.

**Sacred texts.** Over several thousand years, Hindu teachings were recorded in sacred texts such as the Vedas and Upanishads. The *Bhagavad-Gita* (see page 56) spells out many ethical ideas central to Hinduism. In that poem, you will recall, the god Krishna instructs Prince Arjuna on the importance of duty and the unimportance of the self.

Another key moral principle of Hinduism is ahimsa (uh HIM sah), or nonviolence. To Hindus, all people and things are aspects of brahman and should therefore be respected. Many holy people have tried to follow the path of nonviolence. The teacher Mahavira (muh hah VEE ruh) developed an extreme form of ahimsa. About 500 B.C., he founded Jainism (JIN ihz um), a new religion that grew out of Hindu traditions. Jain teachings emphasized meditation and self-denial. To avoid accidentally killing a living thing, even an insect, Jains carried brooms to sweep the ground in front of their feet.

**Opposition to the Brahmins.** Mahavira lived in a time of frequent warfare. During this troubled period, Brahmin priests acquired great power by insisting that they alone could perform the sacred rites to bring victory in battle or ensure adequate rainfall. Reformers like Mahavira rejected Brahmin domination and offered other paths to truth. In the foothills of the Himalayas, another reformer, Siddhartha Gautama (sihd DAHR tuh  go TUH muh), founded a new religion, Buddhism. His teachings eventually spread across Asia to become one of the world's most influential religions.

## *Gautama Buddha: The Enlightened One*

The facts of Gautama's life are buried in legend. We know that he was born about 566 B.C. into a high-ranking family of the Kshatriya caste. According to tradition, his mother dreamed that a radiant white elephant descended to her from heaven. Because of this dream and other signs, a prophet predicted that the young boy would someday become a wandering holy man. To stop that from happening, Gautama's father kept him in the palace, surrounded by comfort and luxury. Prince Gautama enjoyed a happy life. He married a beautiful woman and had a son who filled his hours with joy.

**The search.** Then one day, as Gautama rode beyond the palace gardens, he saw for the first time a sick person, an old person, and a dead body. This new awareness of human suffering deeply disturbed him. Late that night, he whispered farewell to his sleeping wife and child and left the palace, never to return. He set out to discover "the realm of life where there is neither suffering nor death."

Gautama wandered for years, vainly seeking answers from Hindu scholars and holy men. He tried fasting, but succeeded only in making himself ill. Eventually, he sat down to meditate under a giant tree, determined to stay there until

**ISSUES** *For* **TODAY**

The teachings of both Hinduism and Buddhism emphasize the need to overcome individual desires and ambitions. What value do different cultures place on the individual?

he understood the mystery of life. For 48 days, evil spirits tempted him to give up his meditations. Then, he suddenly believed that he understood the cause and cure for suffering and sorrow. When he rose, he was Gautama no longer, but the Buddha, the "Enlightened One."

**Four Noble Truths.** The Buddha spent the rest of his life teaching others what he had learned. In his first sermon after reaching enlightenment, he explained the Four Noble Truths that stand at the heart of Buddhism:

1. All life is full of suffering, pain, and sorrow.
2. The cause of suffering is the desire for things that are really illusions, such as riches, power, and long life.
3. The only cure for suffering is to overcome desire.
4. The way to overcome desire is to follow the Eightfold Path.

The Buddha described the Eightfold Path as "right views, right aspirations, right speech, right conduct, right livelihood, right effort, right mindfulness, and right contemplation." The first two steps involved understanding the Four Noble Truths and committing oneself to the Eightfold Path. Next, a person had to live a moral life, avoiding evil words and actions. Through meditation, a person might at last achieve enlightenment. For the Buddhist, the final goal is nirvana, union with the universe and release from the cycle of rebirth.

The Buddha saw the Eightfold Path as a middle way between a life devoted to pleasure and one based on harsh self-denial. He emphasized moral and ethical rules such as honesty, charity, and kindness to all living creatures.

**Shared traditions.** Buddhism, like Hinduism, grew out of Vedic religious traditions. Both Hindus and Buddhists accepted the law of karma, dharma, and moksha and believed in a cycle of rebirth. Nonviolence was also central to Buddhism.

Yet Buddhism differed from Hinduism in several important ways. The Buddha rejected the priests, formal rituals, and the existence of the many gods of Hinduism. Instead, he urged each individual to seek enlightenment through meditation. Buddhists also rejected the caste system, offering the hope of nirvana to all regardless of birth.

## Spread of Buddhism

The Buddha attracted many disciples, or followers, who accompanied him as he preached across northern India. Many men and women who accepted the Buddha's teachings set up monasteries and convents for meditation and study. Some Buddhist monasteries grew into major centers of learning.

**Reclining Buddha** Traditionally, images of the Buddha lying down represent his achievement of nirvana. Here, a Buddha of carved granite lies amidst the natural beauty of a botanical garden in Sri Lanka. **Religions and Value Systems** Why do you think a garden was chosen as the site for this sculpture?

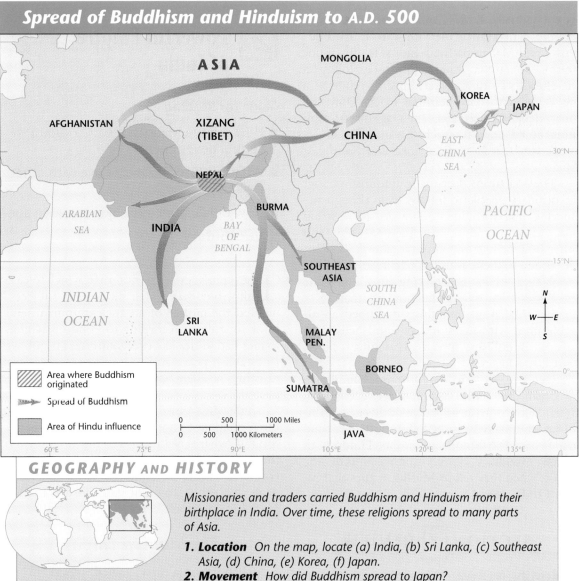

## Spread of Buddhism and Hinduism to A.D. 500

**ASIA**

MONGOLIA

AFGHANISTAN

XIZANG (TIBET)

KOREA

JAPAN

CHINA

NEPAL

*EAST CHINA SEA*

30°N

BURMA

*ARABIAN SEA*

INDIA

*BAY OF BENGAL*

*PACIFIC OCEAN*

*INDIAN OCEAN*

SRI LANKA

SOUTHEAST ASIA

*SOUTH CHINA SEA*

15°N

MALAY PEN.

N
W — E
S

BORNEO

0°

SUMATRA

JAVA

Area where Buddhism originated

Spread of Buddhism

Area of Hindu influence

0     500     1000 Miles
0   500   1000 Kilometers

60°E          75°E          90°E          105°E          120°E          135°E

## GEOGRAPHY *AND* HISTORY

*Missionaries and traders carried Buddhism and Hinduism from their birthplace in India. Over time, these religions spread to many parts of Asia.*

**1. Location**  On the map, locate (a) India, (b) Sri Lanka, (c) Southeast Asia, (d) China, (e) Korea, (f) Japan.
**2. Movement**  How did Buddhism spread to Japan?
**3. Critical Thinking  Drawing Conclusions**  Review the information about the spread of Buddhism on pages 81–82. Which arrows on the map probably represent the spread of Theravada Buddhism?

The Buddha's death, like his birth, is clouded in legend. At age 80, he is said to have eaten spoiled food in the home of a poor family. As he lay dying, he told his disciples, "Decay is inherent in all things. Work out your own salvation with diligence."

**Sacred texts.** After the Buddha's death, some of his followers collected his teachings into a sacred text called the *Tripitaka*, or "Three Baskets of Wisdom." One of the "baskets" includes sayings like this one, which echoes the Hindu emphasis on duty:

66Let no one forget his own duty for the sake of another's, however great. Let a man, after he has discerned his own duty, be always attentive to his duty.99

Other sayings give the Buddha's version of the golden rule: "Overcome anger by not growing angry. Overcome evil with good. Overcome the liar by truth."

**Two schools.** Missionaries and traders spread Buddhism across India to many parts of

Asia. Gradually, Buddhism split into two major schools, Theravada (ther uh VAH duh) Buddhism and Mahayana (mah huh YAH nuh) Buddhism. Theravada Buddhism closely followed the Buddha's original teachings. It required a life devoted to hard spiritual work. Only the most dedicated seekers, such as monks and nuns, could hope to reach nirvana. The Theravada sect spread to Sri Lanka and Southeast Asia.

The Mahayana sect made Buddhism easier for ordinary people to follow. Even though the Buddha had forbidden followers to worship him, Mahayana Buddhists pictured him and other holy beings as compassionate gods. People turned to these gods for help in solving daily problems as well as in achieving salvation. While the Buddha had said little about the nature of nirvana, Mahayana Buddhists described an afterlife filled with many heavens and hells. Mahayana Buddhism spread to China, Tibet, Korea, and Japan.

**Decline in India.** Although Buddhism took firm root across Asia, it slowly declined in India. With its great tolerance of diversity, Hinduism eventually absorbed Buddhist ideas and made room for Buddha as another Hindu god. A few Buddhist centers survived until the 1100s, when they fell to Muslim armies that invaded India. (See Chapter 11.)

## SECTION 1 REVIEW

1. **Identify** (a) Shiva, (b) Jainism, (c) Siddhartha Gautama, (d) Four Noble Truths, (e) Theravada, (f) Mahayana.
2. **Define** (a) atman, (b) reincarnation, (c) karma, (d) dharma, (e) ahimsa, (f) nirvana.
3. What are three basic teachings of Hinduism?
4. According to the Buddha, what actions would allow people to escape worldly suffering?
5. How did Buddhism spread beyond India?
6. *Critical Thinking* **Drawing Conclusions** How do you think Mahayana teachings increased the appeal of Buddhism?
7. *ACTIVITY* Make a chart or diagram comparing Hinduism and Buddhism. Place a star next to any beliefs or practices that the two religions have in common.

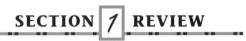

# 2 Powerful Empires of India

## Guide for Reading

- How did the Mauryas create a strong central government?

- What contacts did India have with other civilizations?

- How did Gupta India enjoy a golden age?

- **Vocabulary** *stupa*

“The king's good is not that which pleases him, but that which pleases his subjects," insisted the author of an ancient Indian handbook for rulers. According to Hindu teachings, a ruler had duties like everyone else. His job was to establish peace and order by enforcing laws, resisting invaders, and encouraging economic growth.

Achieving those goals was difficult. More often than not, northern India was a battleground, where rival rajahs fought for control of the rich Ganges Valley. Then, in 321 B.C., a young adventurer, Chandragupta Maurya (chun druh GUP tuh MOW uhr yuh), forged the first great Indian empire.

## The Maurya Empire

Chandragupta first gained power in the Ganges Valley. Building a large army, he then conquered northern India. His son and grandson later pushed south, adding much of the Deccan to their empire. From 321 B.C. to 185 B.C., the Maurya dynasty ruled over a vast, united empire.

**Record of the Greek ambassador.** We know about Chandragupta largely from reports written by Megasthenes (meh GAS thuh neez), a Greek ambassador to the Maurya court. He described the great Maurya capital at Pataliputra (pah tah lih POO trah), probably the largest and most prosperous city in the world at that time. It boasted schools and a library as well as splendid palaces, temples, and parks. An awed Megasthenes reported that a huge wall surrounding the city "was crowned with 570 towers and had 64 gates."

Chandragupta maintained order through a well-organized bureaucracy. Royal officials supervised the building of roads and harbors to benefit trade. Other officials collected taxes and managed state-owned factories and shipyards. People sought justice in royal courts and from the emperor himself. A brutal but efficient secret police reported on corruption, crime, and dissent within the empire.

Chandragupta's rule was effective but harsh. Fearful of his many enemies, he had specially trained women warriors guard his palace, while servants tasted his food to protect him from poisoning. Secret passages in the palace let him slip about unseen.

**The "philosopher king."** The most honored Maurya emperor was Chandragupta's grandson, Asoka (uh SOH kuh). A few years after becoming emperor in 268 B.C., Asoka fought a long, bloody war to conquer the Deccan region of Kalinga. Then, horrified at the slaughter—over 100,000 dead—Asoka turned his back on further conquests. He converted to Buddhism, rejected violence, and resolved to rule by moral example.

Asoka had stone pillars set up across India, announcing laws and promising righteous government. On one, he proclaimed:

> 66All people are my children, and just as I desire for my children that they should obtain welfare and happiness, both in this world and the next, so do I desire the same for all people.99

Asoka took steps to help his "children" by building roads, rest houses for travelers, and hospitals. "I have had banyan trees planted on the roads to give shade to people and animals," he noted. "I have planted mango groves, and I have had [wells] dug and shelters erected along the roads."

True to the Buddhist principle of respect for all life, Asoka became a vegetarian and limited Hindu animal sacrifices. He sent missionaries, women as well as men, across India and to Sri Lanka. He thus paved the way for the later spread of Buddhism throughout Asia. Although Asoka promoted Buddhism, he preached tolerance for other religions.

Asoka's rule brought peace and prosperity, and helped unite the diverse people within his

*Pillars of Asoka* Along roads and near towns all over India, Asoka's massive stone pillars reached skyward for all to see. Atop the columns sat sculptures of lions, elephants, or other symbols. Buddhist virtues and ideals of justice were inscribed into each pillar. **Political and Social Systems** What methods do modern governments use to communicate with citizens?

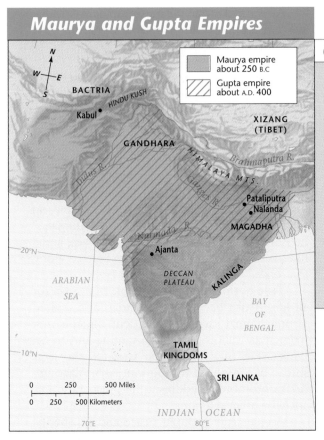

## Maurya and Gupta Empires

Maurya empire about 250 B.C

Gupta empire about A.D. 400

### GEOGRAPHY AND HISTORY

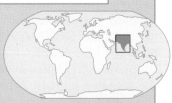

India's diverse people were seldom united. Yet the Mauryas and, later, the Guptas were able to unite much of the subcontinent. Both empires arose in the north and spread southward.

1. **Location** On the map, locate (a) Hindu Kush, (b) Kalinga, (c) Gandhara, (d) Ganges River, (e) Deccan plateau.
2. **Region** What lands included in the Maurya empire were not part of the Gupta empire?
3. **Critical Thinking** *Analyzing Information* What physical features prevented further expansion by the Maurya rulers?

empire. After his death, however, Maurya power declined. By 185 B.C., rival princes again battled for power across the northern plain.

## Division and Unity

During its long history, India has seldom been united. In ancient times, as today, the subcontinent was home to many peoples and cultures. Although the Aryan north shared a common civilization, fierce local rivalries kept it divided. In the Deccan south, other cultures thrived. Distance and geographic differences further separated the north and south.

Adding to the turmoil, foreign invaders frequently pushed through mountain passes into northern India. Some came to plunder rich Indian cities but stayed to rule. The divided northern kingdoms could not often resist such conquerors.

Despite invasions and war, India developed into a center of world trade. By 100 B.C., Indian textiles, gems, incense, and spices were widely in demand. Merchants sent Indian goods overland into Central Asia and China. Others took cargoes by sea to the Middle East, Egypt, East Africa, and Southeast Asia.

Shortly before Chandragupta gained power, Alexander the Great had expanded his empire from Europe across Persia, then into northwestern India. (See Chapter 5.) Alexander controlled the Indus Valley for only a few years, but his conquests opened up a trade corridor between India and the Mediterranean world. After Alexander's death, descendants of his soldiers set up kingdoms in northwestern India, where Greek styles influenced Buddhist art.

Later, during Maurya times and after, Rome conquered much of the Middle East. There, Romans acquired a taste for Indian goods, stimulating trade between the two regions. Indian merchants sent fine textiles and other luxuries westward to eager Roman buyers.

## Kingdoms of the Deccan

Most goods produced and shipped to Rome came from Indian cities in the Deccan. Like the northern plain, the Deccan was divided into many kingdoms. Each had its own capital with magnificent temples and bustling workshops. Unlike the peoples of the Aryan north, the peoples of the Deccan were Dravidians with very different languages and traditions. Women, for example, enjoyed a high status and economic power. The Tamil kingdoms, which occupied much of the southernmost part of India, were sometimes ruled by queens.

Over the centuries, Hindu and Buddhist traditions and Sanskrit writings drifted south and blended with local cultures. Deccan rulers generally tolerated all religions as well as the many foreigners who settled in their busy ports.

The Tamil kingdoms have left a rich literature. Tamil poets described fierce wars and festive occasions along with the routines of peasant and city life. One noted Tamil poet, Avvaiyar (ahv vī yahr), praised the virtues of her king:

66My king, when rich, freely gives food away,
    when poor he eats with his men.
He is the head of the family of the poor,
    yet great is he. . . .99

## *Golden Age of the Guptas*

Although many kingdoms flourished in the Deccan, the most powerful Indian states rose in the north. About 500 years after the Mauryas, the Gupta dynasty again united much of India. (See the map on page 84.) Under the Guptas, who ruled from A.D. 320 to about 550, India enjoyed a golden age. Gupta emperors presided over a dazzling court in the old Maurya capital at Pataliputra. More important, they organized a strong central government that ensured peace and prosperity.

**Peace and prosperity.** Gupta rule was probably looser than that of the Mauryas. Much power was left in the hands of individual villages and of city governments elected by merchants and artisans.

Faxian (FAH shee EHN), a Chinese Buddhist monk who visited India in the 400s, left behind a detailed record of life under the Guptas. He reported on the mild nature of Gupta rule:

66The people are very well off, without poll tax or official restrictions. Only those who till the royal lands return a portion of the profit of the land as tax. If they desire to go, they go. If they like to stop, they stop. The kings

govern without corporal punishment. Criminals are fined, according to circumstances, lightly or heavily.99

The Chinese visitor noted that the wealthy set up hospitals for the poor and that, in accordance with Buddhist teachings, most of the people were vegetarians.

Trade and farming flourished across the Gupta empire. Farmers harvested crops of wheat, rice, and sugar cane. In cities, artisans produced cotton cloth, pottery, and metalware for local markets and for export to East Africa, the Middle East, and Southeast Asia. The prosperity of Gupta India contributed to a flowering in the arts and learning.

**Advances in learning.** In India, as elsewhere during this period, students were educated in religious schools. In Hindu and Buddhist centers, learning was not limited to religion and philosophy. The large Buddhist monastery-university at Nalanda, which attracted students from other parts of Asia, taught mathematics, medicine, physics, languages, literature, and other subjects.

Indian advances in mathematics had a wide impact on the world. Gupta mathematicians devised the simple system of writing numbers that is used today. These numerals are now called "Arabic" numerals because it was Arabs who carried them from India to the Middle East and Europe. Indian mathematicians originated the concept of zero. They also developed the decimal system based on the number 10, which we still use today.

By Gupta times, Indian physicians had pioneered the use of herbs and other remedies to treat illness. Surgeons were skilled in setting bones and in simple plastic surgery to repair facial injuries. Doctors also began vaccinating people against smallpox about 1,000 years before this practice was used in Europe.

**Architecture.** Rajahs sponsored the building of magnificent stone temples. Sometimes, cities grew up around the temples to house the thousands of artisans and laborers working there. Hindu temples were designed to reflect cosmic patterns. The ideal shape was a square inscribed in a circle to symbolize eternity.

Buddhists built splendid stupas, large dome-shaped shrines that housed the sacred

**Kailasa Temple** *Indians considered caves holy and often built temples inside them. Inspired by this tradition, Indian stonemasons cut directly into rock cliffs to create Kailasa Temple and its dark cavernous rooms. Artists decorated the temple with numerous sculptures of Hindu gods, legendary heroes, and mythical creatures.* **Art and Literature** *Where in the temple do you see areas that appear like caves?*

remains of the Buddha or other holy people. The stupas were ringed with enclosed walkways where Buddhist monks slowly walked, chanting their prayers.

**Magnificent carvings.** While stupas were quite plain, their gateways featured elaborate carvings that told stories of the life of the Buddha. He was portrayed with a gentle smile symbolizing the inner peace of someone who has reached nirvana. Hindu temples, too, were covered with carvings of gods and goddesses, elephants, monkeys, and ordinary people. A familiar figure is the four-armed god Shiva, who dances the world out of existence and then re-creates it again. (See the picture on page 78.)

**Paintings at Ajanta.** On the walls of the cave temples at Ajanta in western India, Buddhist artists painted rich murals recalling Buddhist stories and legends. The wall paintings also reveal scenes of life in Gupta India, from beg-

gars with bowls to sailors at sea to princes courting princesses in lovely flowered gardens. (See the picture on page 88.)

**Literature.** During Gupta times, many fine writers added to the rich heritage of Indian literature. They collected and recorded fables and folk tales in the Sanskrit language. In time, Indian fables were carried west to Persia, Egypt, and Greece.

The greatest Gupta poet and playwright was Kalidasa. His most famous play, *Shakuntala*, tells the moving story of a king who marries the lovely orphan Shakuntala. Under an evil spell, the king forgets his beloved bride. After many plot twists, he finally recovers his memory and is reunited with her. At the end of the play, the king's wise adviser blesses the royal couple:

66For countless ages may the god of
   gods,

Lord of the atmosphere, by plentiful
    showers
Secure abundant harvest to your
    subjects;
And you by frequent offerings
    preserve
The Thunderer's friendship! Thus,
    by interchange
Of kindly actions, may you both
    confer
Unnumbered benefits on Earth and
    Heaven!**"**

## *Looking Ahead*

The Gupta empire reached its height just as the Roman empire in the west collapsed. (See Chapter 6.) Before long, Gupta India also declined under the pressure of civil war, weak rulers, and foreign invaders. From central Asia came the White Huns, a nomadic people who overran the weakened Gupta empire, destroying its cities and trade.

Once again, India split into many kingdoms. It would see no great empire like those of the Mauryas or Guptas for almost 1,000 years. Then, as you will read in Chapter 11, another wave of invaders pushed into India and created a powerful new empire.

## SECTION 2 REVIEW

1. **Identify** (a) Chandragupta Maurya, (b) Asoka, (c) Avvaiyar, (d) Kalidasa.
2. **Define** stupa.
3. (a) What steps did Chandragupta take to unite his empire? (b) How did Asoka's rule differ from that of his grandfather?
4. Give three examples of interactions between India and other civilizations.
5. *Critical Thinking* **Defending a Position** "All faiths deserve to be honored for one reason or another," proclaimed Asoka. How do you think Asoka's policy of toleration helped him unite his empire?
6. *ACTIVITY* Imagine that you are either Chandragupta, Asoka, or one of the Gupta emperors. Write a list of three to five "Rules for Governing an Empire."

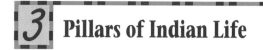

# 3 Pillars of Indian Life

## Guide for Reading

- How was caste linked to Hindu beliefs?
- How were Indian villages organized?
- What values influenced family life?
- **Vocabulary** *joint family, patriarchal*

Most Indians knew nothing of the dazzling courts of the Mauryas or Guptas. The vast majority were peasants who lived in the countless villages that dotted the Indian landscape. In Gupta times, as today, the village ensured stability and order. Two other pillars of Indian life were the caste system and the family.

## *A Complex Caste System*

In Chapter 3, you read how the Aryans had divided society into four occupational classes. Non-Aryans were considered outcastes and held the lowest jobs. By Gupta times, many additional castes and subcastes had evolved. As invaders were absorbed into Indian society, they formed new castes. Other castes grew out of new trades, occupations, and religions. By modern times, major castes numbered in the hundreds, with thousands of minor or local subcastes.

**Complex rules.** Caste was closely linked to Hindu beliefs, although other religious groups also accepted it. To Hindus, people in different castes were different species of beings. A high-caste Brahmin, for example, was purer and therefore closer to moksha than someone from a lower caste. To ensure spiritual purity, a web of complex rules developed within the caste system.

Caste rules governed every aspect of life—where people lived, what they ate, how they dressed, and how they earned a living. Rules forbade marrying outside one's caste or eating with members of another caste. High-caste people had the strictest rules to protect them from the spiritually polluted, or impure, lower castes.

For the lowest-ranked outcastes, or "Untouchables," life was harsh and restricted. To them fell the jobs that were considered "impure," such as digging graves, cleaning streets, or turning animal hides into leather. Other castes feared that even the shadow of an Untouchable could spread pollution. Untouchables not only had to live apart, but they also had to sound a wooden clapper to warn of their approach.

**Effects.** Despite its inequalities, caste ensured a stable social order. People believed that the law of karma determined their caste. While they could not change their status in this life, they could reach a higher state in a future life. The road to improvement lay in faithfully fulfilling the duties of their present caste.

The caste system gave people a sense of identity. Each caste had its own occupation and its own leaders. Caste members cooperated to help one another. Further, each caste had its own special role in Indian society as a whole. Although strictly separated, different castes depended on one another for their basic needs. A lower-caste carpenter, for example, built the home of a higher-caste scholar.

*A Diverse People* In the Ajanta caves in western India, artists painted murals to illustrate Buddhist beliefs and aspects of Indian life. This mural includes people of the many castes and ethnic groups of Indian society. **Religions and Value Systems** How does this mural reflect the Buddha's rejection of the caste system?

The caste system also adapted to changing conditions, absorbing foreigners and new occupations into their own castes. This flexibility allowed people with diverse customs and practices to live side by side in relative harmony.

## Village Life

Throughout India's history, the village was at the heart of life. A typical village included a cluster of homes made of earth or stone. Beyond these dwellings stretched the fields, where farmers grew wheat, rice, cotton, sugar cane, or other crops according to region. In most of India, farming depended on the rains brought by the summer monsoons. Too much or too little rain meant famine. Villagers cooperated to build or maintain vital irrigation systems, as well as roads and temples.

Each village ran its own affairs based on caste rules and tradition. It faced little outside interference as long as it paid its share of taxes. A village headman and council made decisions and dealt with outside authorities when necessary. Members of the council included the most respected people of the village. In early times, women served on the village council, but as Hindu law began to place greater restrictions on women, they were later excluded.

## Family Life

Within the village, the basic unit was the joint family, in which parents, children, grandchildren, uncles, and their offspring shared a common dwelling. The joint family was usually achieved only by the wealthy. In poor families, people often died young, so several generations seldom survived long enough to live together. Still, even when relatives did not share the same house, close ties linked brothers, uncles, cousins, and nephews.

The Indian family was patriarchal; that is, the father or oldest male headed the household. Because he was thought to have wisdom and experience, the head of the family enjoyed great authority. Still, his power was limited by sacred laws and tradition. Usually, he made decisions after consulting his wife and other family members. Property belonged to the whole family.

**Children and parents.** The joint family fostered a sense of security and unity. From an early age, children learned their family duties, which included obeying caste rules. Family interests came before individual wishes.

Children worked with older relatives in the fields or at a family trade. While still young, a daughter learned that as a wife she would be expected to serve and obey her husband and his family. A son learned the rituals to honor the family's ancestors. Such rites linked the living and the dead, deepening family bonds across the generations.

For parents, an important duty was arranging good marriages for their children, based on caste and family interests. Marriage customs varied. In northern India, a bride's family commonly provided a dowry, or payment to the bridegroom, and financed the costly wedding festivities. After marriage, the daughter left her home and became part of her husband's family.

**Women.** Attitudes and customs affecting women changed over time and varied across India. In early Aryan society, women seem to have enjoyed a higher status than in later times. Women even composed a few Vedic hymns. By early Gupta times, upper-caste Hindu women could still move freely in society and some were well educated.

Women were thought to have *shakti*, a creative energy, that men lacked. Poets acknowledged a woman's power:

> **66**The wife is half the man, the best
>     of friends,
>   the root of . . . all that will help him
>     in the other world.
>   With a wife a man does mighty deeds,
>   with a wife a man finds courage.**99**

Still, shakti might also be a destructive force. A husband's duty was to channel his wife's energy in the proper direction. For a woman, rebirth into a higher existence was gained through devotion to her husband.

**Growing restrictions.** By late Gupta times, upper-class women were increasingly restricted to the home. When they went outside the home, they were supposed to cover themselves

**Hindu Women** *Hindu society valued the creative power of women. In a religious ritual called* dohada, *a woman nurtured a tree with gifts of wine to help increase its fruitfulness. In this sculpture, the two women on the balcony observe a woman who may be performing* dohada. **Religions and Value Systems** *Why do you think one of the women is holding her finger to her lips?*

from head to foot. Lower-class women, however, labored in the fields or worked at spinning and weaving.

As customs changed, a high-caste widow was forbidden to remarry. In parts of India, she was sometimes expected to become a *sati,* or "virtuous woman," by joining her dead husband on his funeral fire. Some widows accepted this painful death as a noble duty that wiped out their own and their husbands' sins. Eyewitness accounts, however, show that other women bitterly resisted the custom.

## SECTION 3 REVIEW

1. **Define** (a) joint family, (b) patriarchal.
2. (a) Describe the development of the caste system after Aryan times. (b) How did the caste system provide a sense of order?
3. Describe the government of an Indian village.
4. How did the lives of Indian women change over time?
5. *Critical Thinking* **Analyzing Information** How did the Hindu doctrines of karma and dharma support the caste system?
6. *ACTIVITY* With a partner, act out a conversation between a father and son or a mother and daughter in an Indian village on the child's wedding day. The parent should share information about family and social traditions.

# 4 Three Schools of Thought in China

## Guide for Reading

■ What were the teachings of Confucius?

■ How did Confucian ideas help shape Chinese life?

■ How did Legalist and Daoist views differ?

■ **Vocabulary** *filial piety, alchemy*

> **❝**Lead the people by laws and regulate them by punishments, and the people will simply try to keep out of jail, but will have no sense of shame. Lead the people by virtue . . . and they will have a sense of shame and moreover will become good.**❞**

The great philosopher Confucius* offered this advice to China's rulers about 500 B.C. Government, he felt, was more than enforcing laws. Rulers must also set a good example.

Confucius lived in late Zhou times, when war raged across China. Economic and social changes were also disrupting old ways of life. Seeing the chaos, thinkers put forward ideas about how to end conflict and restore social order. Their ideas would shape Chinese civilization for the next 2,500 years.

## The Wisdom of Confucius

China's most influential philosopher, Confucius, was born in 551 B.C. to a noble but poor family. A brilliant scholar, Confucius hoped to become an adviser to a local ruler. For years, he wandered from court to court talking to rulers about how to govern. Perhaps because he was too outspoken in his views, he never got a permanent position at court. Instead, he turned to teaching. As his reputation for wisdom grew, he attracted many loyal students.

**The Analects.** Like two other influential thinkers who lived about the same time, Gautama Buddha in India and Socrates in Greece, Confucius never wrote down his ideas. After his death, students collected his sayings in *The Analects.*

Unlike the Buddha, Confucius took little interest in religious matters such as salvation. Instead, he was concerned with worldly goals, especially how to ensure social order and good government. Confucius studied ancient texts to learn the rules of conduct that had guided the ancestors.

**Five relationships.** Confucius taught that harmony resulted when people accepted their place in society. He stressed five key relationships: father to son, elder brother to younger brother, husband to wife, ruler to subject, friend to friend. Confucius believed that, except for friendship, none of these relationships was equal. Older people were superior to younger ones; men were superior to women. Confucius did bolster the status of women by teaching that mothers of sons should be respected.

According to Confucius, everyone had duties and responsibilities, depending on his or her position. Superiors should care for their inferiors and set a good example, while inferiors owed loyalty and obedience to their superiors. A woman's duty was to ensure the stability of the family and promote harmony in the home. Correct behavior, Confucius believed, would bring order and stability.

Confucius put *filial piety,* or respect for parents, above all other duties, even loyalty to the state. "While a father or mother is alive, a son should not travel far," he said. Other Confucian values included honesty, hard work, and concern for others, which would promote harmony. "Do not do to others," he declared, "what you do not wish yourself."

**Government.** Confucius believed that people were naturally good. The best ruler was a virtuous man who led by example:

> **❝**If a ruler is upright, all will go well without orders. But if he himself is not upright, even though he gives orders, they will not be obeyed.**❞**

Confucius put great faith in education for men. "By nature, men are pretty much alike," he said. "It is learning and practice that set them apart." He urged rulers to take the advice of

---

*The name Confucius is the western version of the name Kong Fuzi, or Master Kong.

**Confucius and His Students** This drawing from the 1700s suggests the Chinese people's lasting respect for Confucius. Confucius sought to replace the conflict of his time with harmony and order. He believed that education should train people in proper values and rules of conduct. **Continuity and Change** Do you think that teachers today should instruct students in values and rules of conduct? Why or why not?

wise, educated men. Education would become the road to advancement in Chinese society.

**Spread of Confucianism.** In the centuries after Confucius died, his ideas influenced every area of Chinese life. Confucianism never became a religion, as Buddhism did. But Chinese rulers would base their government on Confucian ideas, choosing Confucian scholars as officials. The Confucian emphasis on filial piety bolstered traditional customs such as reverence for ancestors.

As Chinese civilization spread, hundreds of millions of people in Korea, Japan, and Vietnam accepted Confucian beliefs. Close to a third of the world's population came under the influence of these ideas.

## The Harsh Ideas of Legalism

A very different school of thought grew out of the teachings of another Chinese philosopher, Hanfeizi (HAHN fay DZEE), who died in 233 B.C. According to Hanfeizi, "the nature of man is evil. His goodness is acquired." Greed, he declared, was the motive for most actions and the cause of most conflicts. Hanfeizi scoffed at the Confucian idea that people would follow the example of a good ruler. The only way to achieve order, he insisted, was to pass strict laws and enforce them with harsh punishments. Because of their emphasis on law, Hanfeizi's teachings were known as Legalism.

To Legalists, strength, not goodness, was a ruler's greatest virtue. "The ruler alone possesses power," declared Hanfeizi, "wielding it like lightning or like thunder."

Many feudal rulers chose Legalism as the most effective way to keep order. It was the official policy of the Qin (CHEENG) emperor who united China in 221 B.C. His laws were so cruel that later generations despised Legalism. Yet Legalist ideas survived in laws that forced people to work on government projects and punished those who shirked their duties.

## Daoism: The Unspoken Way

A third Chinese philosophy, Daoism (DOW ihz uhm), differed from both Confucianism and Legalism. Daoists had no interest in bringing order to human affairs. Instead, they sought to live in harmony with nature.

The founder of Daosim was a mysterious figure known as Laozi (LOW DZEE), or "Old Master." He is said to have "lived without leaving any traces" at the time of Confucius. Although we know little about him, he is credited with writing *The Way of Virtue,* a book that had enormous influence on Chinese life.

**Seeking "the Way."** Laozi looked beyond everyday worries to focus on the *Dao,* or "the way" of the universe as a whole. How does one find the Dao? "Those who know the Dao do not speak of it," replied Laozi. "Those who speak of it do not know it." Daoists often gave such seemingly puzzling answers to show the conflict between human desires and the simple ways of nature.

Daoists rejected the world of conflict and strife. Instead, they emphasized the virtue of yielding. Water, they pointed out, does not resist, but yields to outside pressure. Yet it is an unstoppable force. In the same way, Daoists might give way in a conflict, only to return again, like water, to their natural course. Many Daoists turned away from the "unnatural" ways of society. Some became hermits, mystics, artists, or poets.

**Government.** Daoists viewed government as unnatural and, therefore, the cause of many problems. "If the people are difficult to govern," Laozi declared, "it is because those in authority are too fond of action." To Daoists, the best government was one that governed the least.

**A popular religion.** Although scholars kept to Laozi's teachings, Daoism evolved into a popular religion with gods, goddesses, and magical practices. Chinese peasants turned to Daoist

*Yin and Yang* "One must learn to be without desires beyond the immediate and simple needs of nature," wrote Laozi, founder of Daoism. Here, a group of wise Daoists ponder the circular symbol for yin and yang. (See page 61.) **Religions and Value Systems** How does the ancient Chinese concept of yin and yang accord with Daoist beliefs?

priests for charms to protect them from unseen forces. Instead of accepting nature as it was, Daoist priests searched for a substance to bring immortality and experimented with alchemy (AL kuh mee), trying to transform ordinary metals into gold.

To achieve this goal, alchemists mixed chemistry and magic. Sometimes, their experiments led to advances in science. Efforts to find the key to eternal life may have contributed to discoveries in medicine. Daoists are thought to have invented gunpowder, which they first used in firecrackers to frighten ghosts.

**A blend of ideas.** Confucian and Daoist ideas influenced everyone from nobles and scholars to the poorest peasants. Although the two philosophies differed, people took beliefs and practices from each. Confucianism showed them how to behave. Daoism influenced their view of the natural world.

## Buddhism in China

By A.D. 100, missionaries and merchants had spread Mahayana Buddhism from India into China. At first, the Chinese had trouble with the new faith. For example, Chinese tradition valued family loyalty, while Buddhism honored monks and nuns who gave up family life for solitary meditation. In addition, the Chinese language had no word for an unfamiliar, mystical concept like nirvana.

Despite obstacles such as these, Buddhism became more popular, especially in times of crisis. Its great appeal was the promise of escape from suffering. Mahayana Buddhism offered the hope of eternal happiness and presented Buddha as a compassionate, merciful god. Through prayer, good works, and devotion, anyone could hope to gain salvation. Neither Daoism nor Confucianism emphasized this idea of personal salvation.

In China, Buddhism absorbed Confucian and Daoist traditions. Some Chinese even believed that Laozi had gone to India, where he taught the Buddha. Chinese Buddhist monks stressed filial piety and honored Confucius as a person who had achieved enlightenment.

By A.D. 400, Buddhism had spread throughout China. From time to time, Chinese rulers persecuted Buddhists, but the new religion was

▲ *Figures of dancing peasants*

generally tolerated. Large Buddhist monasteries became important centers of learning, literature, and the arts.

SECTION 4 REVIEW

1. **Identify** (a) *The Analects,* (b) Legalism, (c) Daoism.
2. **Define** (a) filial piety, (b) alchemy.
3. Explain how each of these thinkers believed an orderly society could be achieved: (a) Confucius, (b) Hanfeizi, (c) Laozi.
4. What ethical code of conduct did Confucius promote?
5. (a) Why did Buddhism appeal to many people in China? (b) How did Buddhism adapt to Chinese traditions?
6. *Critical Thinking* **Analyzing Information** "Rewards should be rich and certain so that the people will be attracted by them. Punishments should be severe and definite so that the people will fear them." Which of the philosophers discussed in this section expressed these ideas? Explain.
7. *ACTIVITY* Write a dialogue between Confucius, Hanfeizi, and Laozi on the proper role of government.

# 5 Strong Rulers Unite China

## Guide for Reading

- How did Shi Huangdi unite China?
- How did Han rulers shape Chinese government?
- What advances did Han China make?
- **Vocabulary** *monopoly*

From his base in western China, the powerful ruler of Qin rose to unify all of China. An ancient Chinese poet and historian described how Zheng (JUHNG) crushed all his rivals:

66 Cracking his long whip, he drove the universe before him, swallowing up the eastern and the western Zhou and overthrowing the feudal lords. He ascended to the highest position . . . and his might shook the four seas. 99

In 221 B.C., Zheng proclaimed himself Shi Huangdi (SHEE hoo ahng DEE), or "First Emperor." Though his methods were brutal, he ushered in China's classical age.

## Triumph of the First Emperor

Shi Huangdi was determined to end the divisions that had splintered Zhou China. He spent 20 years conquering most of the warring states. Then, he centralized power with the help of Legalist advisers. Using rewards for merit and punishments for failure, he built a strong, authoritarian government.

**Sweeping changes.** The emperor abolished the old feudal states and divided China into 36 military districts, each ruled by appointed officials. Inspectors, who were actually more like spies, checked on local officials and tax collectors. Shi Huangdi forced noble families to live in his capital at Xianyang, where he could keep an eye on them, and divided their lands among peasants. Still, peasants had to pay high taxes to support Shi Huangdi's armies and building projects.

To promote unity, the First Emperor standardized weights and measures and replaced the diverse coins of the Zhou states with Qin coins. He also had scholars create uniformity in Chinese writing. Workers repaired and extended roads and canals to strengthen the transportation system. A new law even required cart axles to be the same width so that wheels could run in the same ruts on all Chinese roads.

**Crackdown on dissent.** Shi Huangdi moved harshly against critics. He jailed, tortured, and killed many who opposed his rule. Hardest hit were the feudal nobles and Confucian scholars who despised his laws. To end dissent, Shi Huangdi approved a ruthless campaign of book burning, ordering the destruction of all works of literature and philosophy. Only books on medicine and agriculture were spared.

**The Great Wall.** Shi Huangdi's most remarkable and costly achievement was the Great Wall. In the past, individual feudal states had built walls to defend their lands against raiders. Shi Huangdi ordered the walls to be joined together. Hundreds of thousands of laborers worked for years through bitter cold and burning heat. They pounded earth and stone into a mountainous wall almost 25 feet high topped with a wide brick road. Many workers died in the harsh conditions.

Over the centuries, the wall was extended and rebuilt many times. Eventually, it snaked for thousands of miles across China.

While the wall did not keep invaders out of China, it did show the emperor's ability to mobilize vast resources. In the long run, the Great Wall became an important symbol to the Chinese, dividing their civilized world from the nomadic bands north of the wall.

**Collapse.** Shi Huangdi thought his empire would last forever. But when he died in 210 B.C., anger over heavy taxes, forced labor, and cruel policies exploded into revolts. As Qin power collapsed, Liu Bang (LEE OO BAHNG), an illiterate peasant leader, defeated rival armies and founded the new Han dynasty. Like earlier Chinese rulers, Liu Bang claimed the Mandate of Heaven. (See page 61.)

## The Han Dynasty

As emperor, Liu Bang took the title Gao Zu (GOW DZOO) and set about restoring order and justice to his empire. Although he continued earlier efforts to unify China, he lowered taxes and eased the Qin emperor's harsh Legalist policies. In a key move, he appointed Confucian scholars as advisers. His policies created strong foundations for the Han dynasty, which lasted from 206 B.C. to A.D. 220.

**Strengthening the government.** The most famous Han emperor, Wudi, took China to new heights. During his long reign from 141 B.C. to 87 B.C., he strengthened the government and economy. Like Gao Zu, he chose officials from Confucian "men of wisdom and virtue." To train scholars, he set up an imperial university at Xian.

Wudi furthered economic growth by improving canals and roads. He had granaries set up across the empire so the government could buy grain when it was abundant and sell it at stable prices when it was scarce. He reorganized finances and imposed a government monopoly

**Army in a Tomb** More than 8,000 terra cotta foot soldiers, cavalry, and chariots stand guard inside the tomb of Emperor Shi Huangdi. This life-sized army was expected to protect the First Emperor even after death. The tomb was uncovered accidentally in 1974 by a farmer who was digging a well. **Impact of the Individual** How does this tomb reflect the power of Shi Huangdi?

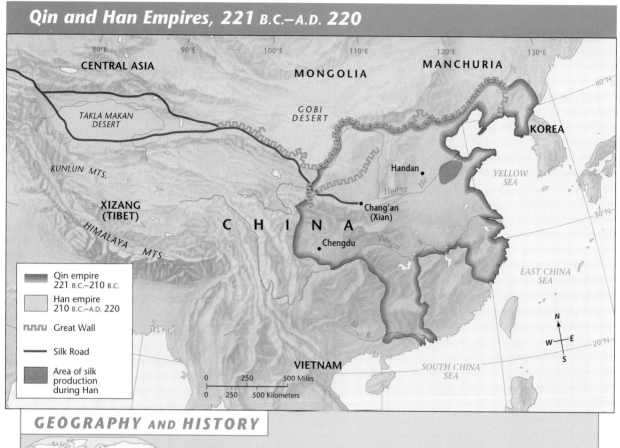

## Qin and Han Empires, 221 B.C.–A.D. 220

**CENTRAL ASIA**

**MONGOLIA**

**MANCHURIA**

TAKLA MAKAN DESERT

GOBI DESERT

KOREA

KUNLUN MTS.

Handan

Huang He

YELLOW SEA

XIZANG (TIBET)

HIMALAYA MTS.

**C H I N A**

Chang'an (Xian)

Chengdu

Yangzi R.

EAST CHINA SEA

Qin empire
221 B.C.–210 B.C.

Han empire
210 B.C.–A.D. 220

Great Wall

Silk Road

Area of silk production during Han

Si R.

**VIETNAM**

SOUTH CHINA SEA

N  W  E  S

0    250    500 Miles
0    250    500 Kilometers

### GEOGRAPHY AND HISTORY

Under the Qin and Han dynasties, China expanded to roughly its present-day borders. Still, Chinese territory would be lost and regained many times over the centuries.

1. **Location**  On the map, locate (a) the Silk Road, (b) the Great Wall, (c) Chang'an, (d) Korea, (e) Qin empire, (f) Huang He.
2. **Region**  In which regions of the Han empire was silk production carried on?
3. **Critical Thinking  Linking Past and Present**  Study the map of Asia on page 988. Compare the extent of the Han empire with the extent of China today.

on iron and salt. A **monopoly** is the complete control of a product or business by one person or group. The sale of iron and salt gave the government a source of income other than taxes on peasants.

**Expansion.** Wudi earned the title "the Warrior Emperor" because of his endless campaigns to secure and expand China's borders. He fought many battles to drive nomadic peoples beyond the Great Wall. Chinese armies added outposts in Manchuria, Korea, northern Vietnam, Tibet, and Central Asia. Soldiers, traders, and settlers slowly spread Chinese influence across these areas. (See map above.)

To cement alliances with nomads on the western frontier, Wudi and later emperors arranged marriages between nomad chiefs and noble Chinese women. The loneliness of these brides became a popular theme in Chinese poems like this one:

66My people have married me
In a far corner of Earth;
Sent me away to a strange land . . .
A tent is my house,
Of felt are my walls;
Raw flesh my food
With mare's milk to drink.
Always thinking of my own country,
My heart sad within.
Would I were a yellow stork
And could fly to my old home!99

# PARALLELS THROUGH TIME

## Success Stories

What is the road to success? There are as many answers to that question as there are successful people. Enterprising people have always found new and interesting ways to achieve economic prosperity. Their success is often based on ingenuity, hard work, and perseverance.

**Linking Past and Present**  Do you think one needs to "dress for success"? How do today's attitudes about proper business attire differ from those of the past?

**PAST**  *Sima Qian, a historian of the Han dynasty, studied prosperous business people. He marveled at their many roads to success, which included plowing fields, slaughtering swine, shipping bamboo, making silk, tanning hides, sharpening knives, and drying sheep stomachs.*

*"Wealth finds its way to the man of ability like the spokes of a wheel converging upon the hub."*
—Sima Qian

**PRESENT**  *Wally Amos of the United States achieved success in the 1970s and 1980s by way of chips—chocolate chips! His cookie business started out as just a way to make a living, but quickly became a multimillion-dollar operation. After selling his first cookie company, Amos started a new one based in Hawaii.*

*"I tried really hard to make it. That determination is all it takes."*
—Wally Amos

---

### Silk Road to the West

The emperor Wudi listened intently to the tales told by the traveler Zhang Qian (JAHNG chee EHN). Zhang had spent a dozen years among the barbarians of Central Asia. Far to the west, he told the emperor, was a land with an amazing breed of "heavenly horses," stronger than any known in China.

To Wudi, the horses were an irresistible lure. He sent a huge army 2,500 miles (4,025 km) into Central Asia to get some of the marvelous beasts. His forces pushed into the Takla Makan desert, bringing oases under their control. The emperor sent gifts of silk to help secure allies among the nomadic rulers of those distant lands.

Wudi's efforts paid off handsomely—he got his horses. He had also opened up a trade route, later called the Silk Road, that would link China and the west for centuries.

**Wondrous goods.** Strange and tempting things came to the emperor along the great Silk Road. A Chinese historian reported on one gift from a Persian ambassador:

    **&#6622;**To the Chinese court he presented an ostrich egg and some conjurers from

Li-Chien [a Chinese name for the Roman Empire]. The Son of Heaven took great pleasure in these."

During the Han period, new foods such as grapes, figs, cucumbers, and walnuts flowed to China from western Asia. At the same time, the Chinese sent tons of silk westward to fill a growing demand for the prized fabric.

**A long, hard journey.** Setting out from China along the Silk Road, fearful travelers might begin the journey with a prayer. Beyond the borders of the Middle Kingdom lurked not only bandits and harsh terrain, but evil spirits and strange gods as well. Still, the possible rewards made the risk worth taking. So the travelers would tighten the straps on their pack animals—horses, mules, camels, or yaks laden with bundles of silk or packets of jewels and spices. In a band of 50 or more, protected by a bodyguard of archers, the caravan set forth.

Week after week, month after month, the journey continued. The traders would roast in the deserts of the Takla Makan and freeze in the snowy passes of the Pamirs. Along the way, the caravan passed lonely soldiers huddled in clay-walled forts, ever on the lookout for bands of hostile nomads.

Eventually, the Silk Road stretched for 4,000 miles (6,400 km), linking China to the Fertile Crescent. Still, few traders covered the entire distance. Instead, goods were relayed in stages from one set of traders to another. At the western end, trade was controlled by various people, including the Persians.

**Back to China.** At the end of the journey, weary merchants could complete their business and begin the journey home. Lucky traders might return to China bearing furs from Central

◀ *Woman in silk robe*

Asia, muslin from India, or glass from Rome. Unlucky traders might not return at all. Some died of fever under a felt tent on the steppes, or froze in snowy mountain passes, or were killed by bandits. These brave merchants had paid a grave price to keep up the flow of goods on the great Silk Road. ■

## *Han Society*

Han rulers left their stamp on all areas of Chinese life. Han China made such tremendous advances in so many fields that the Chinese later called themselves "the people of Han."

**Scholar-officials.** Han emperors made Confucianism the official belief system of the state. They relied on well-educated scholars to run the bureaucracy. A scholar-official was expected to match the Confucian ideal of a gentleman. He would be courteous and dignified and possess a thorough knowledge of history, music, poetry, and Confucian teachings.

**Civil service examinations.** Han emperors adopted the idea that officials should win positions by merit rather than through family background. To find the most qualified officials, they set up a system of exams. In time, these civil service exams were given at the local, provincial, and national levels. To pass, candidates studied the Confucian classics, a collection of histories, poems, and handbooks on customs that Confucius was said to have compiled.

**GLOBAL CONNECTIONS**

China and Rome shared goods indirectly by way of the Silk Road. Yet the two empires never made formal contact. They came close in A.D. 97, when a Han general led an army to the edge of the Caspian Sea, the nearest any Chinese army ever came to Europe. He sent an ambassador to learn more about Rome. But when Persian sea captains warned that the journey back would be long and dangerous, the ambassador turned back.

In theory, any man could take the exams. In practice, only those who could afford years of study, such as the sons of wealthy landowners or officials, could hope to succeed. Occasionally, a village or wealthy family might pay for the education of a brilliant peasant boy. If he passed the exams and obtained a government job, he, his family, and his clan all enjoyed immense prestige and moved up in society.

The civil service system had enormous impact on China for almost 2,000 years. It put men trained in Confucian thought at every level of government and created an enduring system of values. Dynasties rose and fell, but Confucian influence survived.

**Women.** Confucian teachings about filial piety and the superiority of men kept women from taking the civil service exam. As a result, government positions were closed to women. Still, a few women did receive an education, mostly nuns or members of the imperial court.

The proper behavior of both women and men was carefully spelled out. Around A.D. 100, Ban Zhao (BAHN JOW) wrote *Lessons for Women,* an influential handbook of behavior. While she did argue in favor of equal education for boys and girls, Ban Zhao stressed obedience and submission. "Let a woman modestly yield to others," she advised. "Let her respect others."

## Han Achievements

The Han period was one of the golden ages of Chinese civilization. Han scientists wrote texts on chemistry, zoology, botany, and other subjects. Han astronomers carefully observed and measured movements of the stars and planets, which enabled them to improve earlier calendars and invent better timekeeping devices.

The scientist Wang Chong disagreed with the widely held belief that comets and eclipses showed Heaven's anger. "On the average, there is one moon eclipse about every 180 days," he wrote, "and a solar eclipse about every 41 or 42 months. Eclipses . . . are not caused by political action." Wang Chong argued that no scientific theories should be accepted unless they were supported by proof.

**Advances in technology.** In its time, Han China was the most technologically advanced civilization in the world. Cai Lun, an official of the Han court, invented a method for making durable paper out of wood pulp. His basic method is still used to manufacture paper today. The Chinese also pioneered advanced methods of shipbuilding and invented the rudder to steer. Other practical inventions included bronze and iron stirrups, fishing reels, wheelbarrows, suspension bridges, and chain pumps. Some of these ideas moved west slowly, reaching Europe hundreds of years later.

**Medicine.** Chinese physicians diagnosed diseases, experimented with herbal remedies and other drugs, and developed anesthetics. Some doctors explored the uses of acupuncture. In this medical treatment, the doctor inserts needles under the skin to relieve pain or treat various illnesses.

**The arts.** The walled cities of Han China boasted splendid temples and palaces amid elegant parks. Although these wooden buildings have not survived, Han poets and historians have described their grandeur. Artisans produced delicate jade and ivory carvings and fine ceramic figures. Bronzeworkers and silkmakers improved on earlier techniques and set high standards for future generations.

## Collapse of the Han Empire

As the Han dynasty aged, signs of decay appeared. Court intrigues undermined emperors who could no longer control powerful warlords in the provinces. Weak rulers let canals

*A Dutiful Wife* This figure of a servant was buried with a Chinese princess. The lamp she is holding symbolizes eternal fidelity. Under Confucianism, wives were expected to give eternal devotion to their husbands. **Political and Social Systems** According to Confucian ideas, how did women contribute to the stability of society?

# CAUSE AND EFFECT

### Long-Term Causes

Confucian ideas dominate education
China's isolation permits development without much outside interference
Common system of writing evolves

### Immediate Causes

Zheng conquers eastern and western Zhou and overthrows feudal lords
Zheng proclaims himself Shi Huangdi ("first Emperor")

## UNIFICATION OF CHINA

### Immediate Effects

Shi Huangdi standardizes weights and measures and money
Roads and canals unify distant provinces
Government cracks down on dissenters

### Long-Term Effects

Han dynasty is founded by Liu Bang
China makes advances in government, trade, and transportation
Confucian-educated officials gain monopoly of government offices
Common culture helps China survive upheavals

### Connections Today

Mainland China remains a large, politically united country
Chinese still share a common written language

*Interpreting Charts Under Shi Huangdi, most of China united under a single ruler. Although China's borders continued to shift under later rulers, the First Emperor's goal of a unified state endured.*
■ *How did political unification encourage advances in government, trade, and technology?*

and roads fall into disrepair. Burdened by heavy taxes, peasants revolted. In A.D. 220, ambitious warlords overthrew the last Han emperor. After 400 years of unity, China broke up into several kingdoms. Adding to the disorder, invaders poured over the Great Wall and set up their own states. In time, many of these newcomers were absorbed into Chinese civilization.

During this turbulent period, Buddhism took root in China. It appealed to nomads and Chinese alike. A common faith created links among these diverse groups.

## Looking Ahead

Shi Huangdi and Gao Zu forged a vast and varied land into a united China. The two rulers established the pattern of government that would survive until 1912.

Han rulers created an empire roughly the size of the continental United States. China would undergo great changes. It would break up and be painfully reassembled over and over. But, on the whole, Chinese civilization flourished in a united land. After periods of disunity, a new dynasty would turn to Confucian scholars to revive the days of Han greatness.

## SECTION 5 REVIEW

1. **Identify** (a) Shi Huangdi, (b) Great Wall, (c) Gao Zu, (d) Wudi, (e) Silk Road (f) Ban Zhao (g) Wang Chong.
2. **Define** monopoly.
3. What were three steps Shi Huangdi took to unify China?
4. How did Han emperors increase the influence of Confucianism in China?
5. Why is the Han period considered a golden age of Chinese civilization?
6. *Critical Thinking* **Synthesizing Information** How did the ideas of Wang Chong challenge the ancient Chinese concept of the Mandate of Heaven? (See page 61.)
7. *ACTIVITY* Imagine that you are a Chinese trader traveling along the Silk Road during the Han dynasty. Write a poem or a letter home describing how you feel about your journey.

# Skills for Success

Critical Thinking | Writing and Researching | Maps, Charts, and Graphs | Speaking and Listening

## Classifying Sources of Information

To learn about the past, historians rely on two types of information: primary sources and secondary sources. **Primary sources** include official documents, as well as firsthand accounts of events by people who witnessed or participated in them. Autobiographies, letters, and diaries are examples of primary sources. Primary sources may also include visual evidence, such as a news photo or a painting by an eyewitness.

**Secondary sources** are written after events have occurred by people who did not witness or participate in them. They are usually based on primary sources. While secondary sources do not provide direct evidence, they may offer a broader view than primary sources. Examples of secondary sources include encyclopedias, biographies, articles or books by historians, and history textbooks. A picture based on historical accounts, such as a reconstruction of what an ancient city might have looked like, is also a secondary source.

Below are a list of sources about India and two passages written by Sima Qian, an official historian of Han China. Use them to answer the following questions.

**1** **Identify primary sources.** (a) Which sources on the list are primary sources of information about India? (b) Why is Reading B a primary source? Explain.

**2** **Identify secondary sources.** (a) Which sources on the list are secondary sources? (b) Why is Reading A a secondary source? Explain.

**3** **Decide how each kind of source might be used.** (a) If you were writing a paper about Gupta India, how would Faxian's report be useful? (b) What kind of information about Maurya India might you get from the encyclopedia that you could not get from the laws of Asoka? (c) How does Sima Qian use other sources of information to tell the story of Bo Yi and Shu Qi?

***Beyond the Classroom*** Television news programs use both primary and secondary sources to present current events. Watch a segment of a news show and list the various sources of information presented. Identify who is providing primary information and who is providing secondary information.

---

*Sources of information about India*

This textbook
One of Asoka's pillars
An encyclopedia entry about Asoka
A report on the Maurya court by the Greek ambassador Megasthenes (see page 82)
*The Wonder That Was India*, a book written by the scholar A. L. Basham in 1963
A report on Gupta India by the Chinese monk Faxian (see page 85)

*Reading A*

❝Confucius said, 'Bo Yi and Shu Qi never bore old ills in mind and had not the faintest feelings of hatred.' . . . The tales of these men state that Bo Yi and Shu Qi were two sons of the ruler of Kuchu. Their father wished to set up Shu Qi as his heir, but when he died, Shu Qi yielded in favor of Bo Yi.❞

*Reading B*

❝Li Ling and I were both stationed in the palace, but we never had a chance to become friends. Our duties kept us apart; we never shared so much as a cup of wine, let alone enjoyed a closer friendship. But I observed that he conducted himself as no ordinary gentleman. He was filial toward his parents, honest with his colleagues.❞

# CHAPTER 4 REVIEW

## Building Vocabulary

Write sentences using *five* of the vocabulary words from this chapter, leaving blanks where the vocabulary words would go. Exchange your sentences with another student and fill in the blanks on each other's lists.

## Reviewing Chapter Themes

1. **Religions and Value Systems**   Describe three ways that each of the following belief systems influenced the civilization of India or China: (a) Hinduism, (b) Buddhism, (c) Confucianism.
2. **Political and Social Systems**   Choose one Indian and one Chinese ruler and describe how their policies helped to unify and strengthen their empires.
3. **Global Interaction**   (a) How did India develop into a major center of trade? (b) How did the Silk Road become a major trade route across Asia? (c) What obstacles did travelers face on the Silk Road?
4. **Economics and Technology**   Describe three scientific or technological advances made in Han China.

## Thinking Critically

1. **Synthesizing Information**   A modern Indian writer noted, "We believe that the worst of all evils is the ego, the 'I am.' The more we can squash it, the better." (a) Do you think the information given in this chapter about Indian religious beliefs supports this statement? Explain. (b) How did each of the three pillars of Indian life—caste, village, and family—place the community or group above the individual? (★ See *Skills for Success*, page 896.)
2. **Applying Information**   Using the chart on page 41 as a model, create a Quick Study Chart summarizing some of the main achievements of the Gupta golden age.
3. **Analyzing Information**   An ancient Indian law states, "Though he has not virtue . . . or has not good qualities, a husband nevertheless must be constantly worshiped as a god by a faithful wife." (a) What does this law suggest about the status of women in ancient Indian society?

(b) How might this law relate to the Hindu idea of dharma? (c) Do you think most women accepted such a law? Why or why not?
4. **Comparing**   Both Indian and Chinese rulers faced difficult challenges in uniting their lands. How were these challenges similar? How were they different?
5. **Defending a Position**   Confucius argued that people were basically good and could be led by virtuous example. Hanfeizi believed that people were basically evil and had to be controlled by strict laws. Express your viewpoint on this issue. Give examples from history, current events, or your own experience to support your view.
6. **Understanding Causes and Effects**   (a) What actions of Shi Huangdi were an attempt to erase China's Confucian traditions? (b) Why did he pursue this policy? (c) What were the long-term effects of this policy? (★ See *Skills for Success*, page 18.)
7. **Linking Past and Present**   (a) How did education become a key to advancement in Chinese society? (b) Is education a key to advancement in modern American society? Explain. (c) Compare the Chinese system of civil service examinations to that used in the United States today.

## For Your Portfolio

You have been asked to write an article for a book titled *Continuity and Change: The Heritage of India and China.*

1. Choose one of the following topics: (a) Hindu traditions in modern India, (b) Buddhist traditions in modern Tibet or Southeast Asia, (c) the caste system today, (d) the current status of women in India or China, (e) the influence of Indian ideas about nonviolence, (f) Confucian ideas in modern China, (g) Chinese medical techniques today. (Your teacher may suggest other topics.)
2. Research your topic at the public library. Use the *Readers' Guide to Periodical Literature* or a computerized newspaper and magazine index to find recent articles.
3. Write a two- to three-page article describing what you have learned. You should show both how classical traditions have survived and how they have been adapted.

# Ancient Greece

## (1750 B.C. – 133 B.C.)

## CHAPTER OUTLINE

1 **Early People of the Aegean**
2 **The Rise of Greek City-States**
3 **Victory and Defeat in the Greek World**
4 **The Glory That Was Greece**
5 **Alexander and the Hellenistic Age**

In the hot, dusty summer afternoon, all eyes watched the athletic young men sprint across the meadow. A great cheer burst from the crowd as the lead runner shot ahead in a final dash to glory. The winner proudly accepted his prize, a wreath made of olive leaves.

That summer day in 776 B.C., a cook named Corroebus won the 200-yard dash. His victory brought honor and prestige to him and to his hometown of Elis. His name has survived the centuries as the first recorded victor in the Greek Olympic Games. Centuries later, the poet Pindar captured the joy of victory:

66 He who wins, of a sudden,
    some noble prize
In the rich years of youth
Is raised high with hope . . .
He has in his heart what is better
    than wealth. . . .
When god-given splendor visits him
A bright radiance plays over him, and
    how sweet is life.99

Every four years, in the sacred valley of Olympia, the ancient Greeks held athletic contests to honor Zeus (zoos), their chief god. The competitive spirit mirrored the rivalries that kept dozens of small Greek city-states in a state of near-constant war. Yet the Olympic Games also helped unify the Greek world. As the time for the games drew near, the Greeks called a truce so that athletes and spectators could reach Olympia safely.

Unlike the other civilizations we have studied so far, Greek civilization did not rise in a fertile river valley. Instead, it emerged in a rugged, remote corner of southeastern Europe. Like the Gupta empire in India and the Han empire in China, Greece gave rise to a classical civilization that set a standard for later civilizations. Faith in the individual strongly influenced Greek thought. The Greeks tried out many forms of government. Among others, they created a system based on the right of each individual citizen to speak out about issues.

**FOCUS ON** these questions as you read:

■ **Geography and History**
   How did geography influence the Greek way of life and interaction between the Greeks and other people?

■ **Impact of the Individual**
   What role did individual political leaders, philosophers, and writers play in shaping Greek civilization?

■ **Political and Social Systems**
   What Greek ideas about government influenced later societies?

■ **Global Interaction**
   How did Greek civilization affect peoples across many regions?

## TIME AND PLACE

*A Classical Style* Artists of ancient Greece developed a style that stressed the search for balance and perfection. This "classical" style had a lasting influence on later European cultures. The two sculptured heads shown here represent Greek ideals of perfect male and female beauty.
**Art and Literature** What qualities do these two sculptures have in common?

## HUMANITIES LINK

*Art History* Greek vase painting (page 111).
*Literature* In this chapter, you will encounter passages from the following works of literature: Pindar, *Victory Ode* (page 102); Homer, *the Iliad* (page 107); Herodotus, *History of the Persian Wars* (page 114); Plato, *Euthyphro* and *Apology* (pages 117, 118); Sophocles, *Antigone* (page 120).

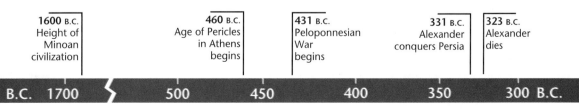

| **1600** B.C. Height of Minoan civilization | **460** B.C. Age of Pericles in Athens begins | **431** B.C. Peloponnesian War begins | **331** B.C. Alexander conquers Persia | **323** B.C. Alexander dies |

B.C.   1700          500          450          400          350          300  B.C.

# Early People of the Aegean

## Guide for Reading

- What civilizations influenced the Minoans?

- How did Mycenaean civilization affect the later Greeks?

- What do the epics of Homer tell us about the Greeks?

- **Vocabulary** *strait*

Europa, the beautiful daughter of the king of Phoenicia, was gathering flowers with her friends when she saw a bull quietly grazing with her father's herds. The bull was actually Zeus, king of the gods, who had fallen in love with her. When Europa reached to place flowers on his horns, he suddenly bounded into the air and carried the weeping princess far across the Mediterranean Sea to the island of Crete. Eventually, Europa married the king of Crete and gave her name to a new continent—Europe.

This Greek legend carries seeds of truth. Crete was the cradle of an early civilization that later influenced Greeks on the European mainland. The people of Crete, however, had absorbed many ideas from the older civilizations of Egypt and Mesopotamia. Europa's journey from Phoenicia to Crete thus suggests the diffusion of ideas from east to west.

## Minoan Civilization

Washed by the warm waters of the Aegean (uh JEE uhn) Sea, Crete was home to a brilliant early civilization. We do not know what the people who built this civilization called themselves. However, the British archaeologist who unearthed its ruins called them Minoans after Minos, a legendary king of Crete. The success of the Minoans was based on trade, not conquest. Minoan traders set up outposts throughout the Aegean world, including the Greek mainland. (See the map on page 108.)

Location affected these early people. From their island home in the eastern Mediterranean, they crossed the seas to the Nile Valley and the Middle East. Through contact with Egypt and Mesopotamia, they acquired ideas and technology that they adapted to their own culture. Minoan civilization reached its height between about 1750 B.C. and 1500 B.C.

**The palace at Knossos.** The rulers of this trading empire lived in a vast palace at Knossos (NAHS uhs). It housed rooms for the royal family, religious shrines, banquet halls, and working areas for artisans. Colorful wall paintings show dolphins leaping through Aegean waters or young Minoan nobles strolling through gardens. In another painting, we see men and women practicing for an unusual athletic contest—jumping through the horns of a charging bull.

The paintings suggest that women appeared freely in public and may have enjoyed more rights than women in most ancient civilizations. Perhaps their status was linked to the important role of a mother goddess in Minoan religious beliefs.

**A civilization disappears.** By about 1400 B.C., Minoan civilization had vanished. Archaeologists are not sure of the cause. A sudden volcanic eruption on a nearby island may have rained flaming death on Knossos. Or an earthquake may have destroyed the palace, followed by a tidal wave that drowned the inhabitants of the island.

However, invaders certainly played a role in the destruction of Minoan civilization. These intruders were the Mycenaeans (mī suh NEE uhnz), the first Greek-speaking people of whom we have a record.

## Rulers of Mycenae

The Mycenaeans were an Indo-European people, like the Aryans who swept into India. (See the map on page 54.) The Mycenaeans conquered the Greek mainland before overrunning Crete.

**Successful sea traders.** Mycenaean civilization dominated the Aegean world from about 1400 B.C. to 1200 B.C. Like the Minoans, the Mycenaeans were sea traders. They reached out beyond the Aegean to Sicily, Italy, Egypt,

and Mesopotamia. The newcomers learned many skills from the Minoans, including the art of writing. They, too, absorbed Egyptian and Mesopotamian influences, which they passed on to later Greeks.

The Mycenaeans lived in separate city-states on the mainland. In each, a warrior-king built a thick-walled fortress from which he ruled the surrounding villages. Wealthy rulers amassed hoards of treasure, including fine gold ornaments that archaeologists have unearthed from their tombs.

**The Trojan War.** The Mycenaeans are best remembered for their part in the Trojan War, which took place around 1250 B.C. The conflict may have had its origins in economic rivalry between the Mycenaeans and Troy, a rich trading city in present-day Turkey. Troy controlled the vital straits, or narrow water passages, that connect the Mediterranean and Black seas.

Greek legend attributes the war to a more romantic cause. After the Trojan prince Paris kidnapped Helen, the beautiful wife of a Greek king, the Mycenaeans sailed to Troy to rescue her. For 10 years, Greeks and Trojans fought outside the city's well-defended walls. Finally, the Greeks tricked the Trojans into hauling a giant wooden horse inside the city. Hidden inside the "Trojan Horse" were a few Greek warriors. At night, the soldiers slipped out to open the city gates to the Greeks, who quickly overwhelmed Troy and burned the city to the ground.

For centuries, most people regarded the Trojan War purely as a legend. Then, in the 1870s, a wealthy German businessman, Heinrich Schliemann (HĪN rihk SHLEE mahn), set out to prove that the legend was rooted in fact. As he excavated the site of ancient Troy, Schliemann discovered that the city had been rebuilt many times. At the layer dating to about 1250 B.C., he found evidence of fire and war. Though most of the details still remain lost in legend, modern scholars agree that the Trojan War was an actual event.

## The Age of Homer

Not long after the fall of Troy, Mycenaean civilization crumbled under the attack of sea raiders. About the same time, another wave of Greek-speaking people, the Dorians, invaded from the north. As Mycenaean power faded, people abandoned the cities, and trade declined. People forgot many skills, including the art of writing. From 1100 B.C. to 800 B.C., Greek civilization seemed to step backward.

**An oral record.** We get hints about life during this period from two great epic poems, the *Iliad* and the *Odyssey*. These epics may have been the work of many people, but they are credited to the poet Homer, who probably lived about 750 B.C.

According to tradition, Homer was a blind poet who wandered from village to village, playing his harp and singing of heroic deeds. Like the great Indian epics (see pages 56–57), Homer's tales were passed orally for generations before they were finally written down.

## The Hero

In various cultures, epics tell of heroes who overcome obstacles to achieve important goals. The hero succeeds through a special combination of personal characteristics. Legends about the hero endure and inspire others.

**Linking Past and Present** Name some legendary heroes of the past and present. What special human qualities do they typically possess?

**PAST** Odysseus, hero of the Odyssey, was known for his cleverness in the face of danger. Here, he outwits the siren, a legendary bird-woman whose bewitching song lured passing sailors to their doom. Odysseus filled his crew's ears with beeswax. He then had himself tied to the ship's mast so that he himself could listen to the siren's song without endangering his ship.

**PRESENT** Indiana Jones is a popular American film hero. By using his wits, he narrowly escapes all obstacles and emerges victorious.

**Epics for all time.** The *Iliad* is our chief source of information about the Trojan War, although the story involves gods, goddesses, and even a talking horse. At the start of the poem, Achilles (uh KIHL eez), the mightiest Greek warrior, is sulking in his tent because of a dispute with his commander. Although the war soon turns against the Greeks, Achilles stubbornly refuses to listen to pleas that he rejoin the fighting. Only after his best friend is killed does Achilles again charge into battle to strike down many Trojans.

The *Odyssey* tells of the struggles of the Greek hero Odysseus (oh DIHS ee uhs) to return home to his faithful wife, Penelope, after the fall of Troy. On his long voyage, Odysseus encounters a sea monster, a race of one-eyed giants, and a beautiful sorceress who turns men into swine.

The *Iliad* and *Odyssey* reveal much about the values of the ancient Greeks. The heroes display honor, courage, and eloquence, as when Achilles rallies his troops:

> **66**Every man make up his mind to fight
> And move on his enemy! Strong as I am,
> It's hard for me to face so many men
> And fight with all at once. . . .
> And yet I will!**99**

For almost 3,000 years, the epics of Homer have inspired European writers and artists.

## Looking Ahead

For centuries after the Dorian invasions, the Greeks lived in small, isolated villages. They had no writing and few contacts with the outside world. From this unpromising start, they would develop a civilization that influenced many parts of the world. As they emerged from obscurity, they benefited from the legacy of earlier civilizations. Over time, the stories they heard about Crete and Mycenae underwent changes and became part of the Greek heritage.

## SECTION 1 REVIEW

1. **Identify** (a) Trojan War, (b) Heinrich Schliemann, (c) Homer.
2. **Define** strait.
3. Describe one similarity and one difference between Minoan and Mycenaean civilizations.
4. How did trade contribute to a blending of cultures in the Aegean world?
5. *Critical Thinking* **Drawing Conclusions** Do you think the epics of Homer are a reliable source of information about the ancient Greeks? Why or why not?
6. *ACTIVITY* Imagine that you are Heinrich Schliemann. Design a newspaper advertisement to attract helpers for your expedition to discover the ruins of Troy.

# 2 The Rise of Greek City-States

## Guide for Reading

■ How did geography influence the Greek city-states?

■ What kinds of government did the Greeks develop?

■ How did Sparta and Athens differ?

■ **Vocabulary** *polis, acropolis, monarchy, aristocracy, oligarchy, phalanx, democracy, tyrant, legislature*

**66**Whatever the Greeks have acquired from foreigners," boasted the Greek thinker Plato, "they have, in the end, turned into something finer." The ancient Greeks absorbed many ideas and beliefs from older civilizations in Mesopotamia and Egypt. At the same time, they evolved their own ways that differed greatly from those of the river valley empires. In particular the Greeks developed unique ideas about how best to govern a society.

## Geography: The Greek Homeland

As you have read, geography helped to shape the river valley civilizations early. There, strong rulers organized irrigation works that helped farmers produce the food surpluses needed to support large cities. A very different set of geographic conditions influenced the rise of Greek civilization.

**Mountains and valleys.** Greece is part of the Balkan peninsula, which extends southward into the eastern Mediterranean Sea. Mountains divide the peninsula into isolated valleys. Beyond the rugged coast, hundreds of rocky islands spread toward the horizon. (See the map on page 108.)

The Greeks who farmed the valleys or settled on the scattered islands did not create a large empire as the Egyptians or Mesopotamians had. Instead, they built many small city-states, cut off from one another by land or water. Each included a city and its surrounding

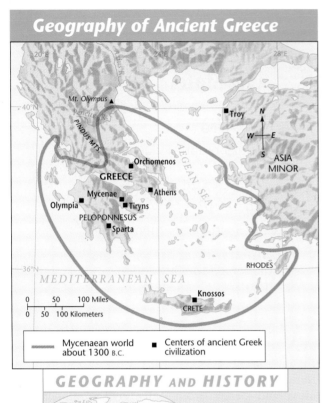

## Geography of Ancient Greece

**GEOGRAPHY AND HISTORY**

Islands in the Aegean Sea were home to the earliest Greek civilizations. Later, proudly independent Greek city-states, such as Athens and Sparta, arose on the Balkan peninsula.

1. **Location** On the map, locate (a) Aegean Sea, (b) Greece, (c) Knossos, (d) Troy, (e) Athens, (f) Sparta, (g) Pindus Mountains.
2. **Region** How did the geography of Greece present obstacles to the development of a large Greek empire?
3. **Critical Thinking** **Comparing** How did the geography of ancient Greece differ from that of other ancient civilizations?

With its hundreds of bays, the Greek coastline provided safe harbors for ships. Like the Phoenicians, the Greeks became skilled sailors. Carrying cargoes of olive oil, wine, and marble, Greek traders sailed to Egypt, the Middle East, and Asia Minor. They returned not only with grains and metals, but also with ideas, which they adapted to their own needs. For example, the Greeks expanded the Phoenician alphabet. The resulting Greek alphabet became the basis for all western alphabets. (See the chart on page 109.)

By 750 B.C., rapid population growth was forcing many Greeks to leave their own overcrowded valleys. With fertile land limited, the Greeks expanded overseas. Gradually, a scattering of Greek colonies took root all around the Mediterranean from Spain to Egypt. Wherever they traveled, Greek settlers and traders carried their ideas and culture.

### The Polis

As their world expanded after 750 B.C., the Greeks evolved a unique version of the city-state, which they called the polis. Typically, the city itself was built on two levels. On a hilltop stood the acropolis (uh KRAHP uh lihs), or high city, with its great marble temples dedicated to different gods and goddesses. On flatter ground below lay the walled main city with its marketplace, theater, public buildings, and homes.

The population of each city-state was fairly small, which helped citizens share a sense of responsibility for its triumphs and defeats. In the warm climate of Greece, free men spent much time outdoors in the marketplace, debating issues that affected their lives. The whole community joined in festivals honoring the city's special god or goddess.

**Early governments.** Between 750 B.C. and 500 B.C., Greeks evolved different forms of government. At first, the ruler of the polis, like those in the river valley empires, was a king. A government in which a king or queen exercises central power is a monarchy. Slowly, though, power shifted to a class of noble landowners. They were also the military defenders of the city-states, because only they could afford bronze weapons and chariots. At first these nobles defended the king. In time, they won power for

countryside. Greeks felt strong loyalty to their tiny city-states and fiercely defended their independence. Endless rivalry led to frequent wars between the city-states—and, in time, to the conquest of Greece by outsiders.

**The seas.** "We live around the sea like frogs around a pond," noted Plato. The Mediterranean and Aegean seas were as central to the Greek world as the Nile to Egypt. While mountains divided Greeks from one another, the seas provided a vital link to the world outside.

themselves. The result was an aristocracy, or rule by a landholding elite.

As trade expanded, a new middle class of wealthy merchants, farmers, and artisans emerged in some cities. They challenged the landowning nobles for power and came to dominate some city-states. The result was a form of government called an oligarchy. In an oligarchy, power is in the hands of a small, powerful elite, usually from the business class.

**Changes in warfare.** Changes in military technology contributed to the increased power of the middle class. In about 650 B.C., iron weapons and tools replaced bronze ones. Because iron was cheaper, ordinary citizens could afford iron helmets, shields, and swords. Meanwhile, a new method of fighting emerged. The phalanx was a massive formation of heavily armed foot soldiers. It required long hours of drill. Shared training created a strong sense of unity among citizen-soldiers.

By putting the defense of the city-state in the hands of ordinary citizens, the phalanx reduced class differences. The new type of warfare, however, led the two most influential city-states to develop very different ways of life. While Sparta stressed military virtues and stern discipline, Athens glorified the individual and extended political rights to more citizens.

## Sparta: A Nation of Soldiers

The Spartans were Dorians who conquered Laconia. This region lies in the Peloponnesus (pehl uh puh NEE suhs), the southern part of Greece. The invaders turned the conquered people into state-owned slaves, called helots, and made them work the land. Because the helots greatly outnumbered their rulers, the Spartans set up a brutal system of strict control.

The Spartan government included two kings and a council of elders who advised the monarchs. An assembly made up of all citizens approved major decisions. Citizens were male, native-born Spartans over the age of 30. The assembly also elected five ephors, officials who held the real power and ran day-to-day affairs.

**The rigors of citizenship.** From childhood, a Spartan prepared to be part of a military state. Officials examined every newborn, and sickly children were abandoned to die. Spartans wanted future soldiers or mothers of soldiers to be healthy.

At the age of seven, boys began training for a lifetime in the military. They moved into barracks, where they endured a brutal existence. Toughened by a coarse diet, hard exercise, and rigid discipline, Spartan youths became excellent soldiers. To develop cunning and supplement their diet, boys were encouraged to steal food. If caught, though, they were beaten.

At the age of 20, a man could marry, but he continued to live in the barracks for another 10 years and to eat there for another 40 years. At the age of 30, after further specialized training, he took his place in the assembly.

**Women.** Girls, too, had a rigorous upbringing. As part of a warrior society, they were

### Early Alphabets

| Phoenician | Greek | Roman |
|:---:|:---:|:---:|
| ⟨K⟩ | A | A |
| ⟨4⟩ | B | B |
| ⟨△⟩ | △ | D |
| ⟨Ψ⟩ | K | K |
| ⟨l⟩ | ∧ | L |
| ⟨9⟩ | N | N |
| ⟨φ⟩ | G | Q |
| ⟨9⟩ | P | R |

**Interpreting a Chart** *Our alphabet came to us from the Phoenicians by way of the Greeks. The word* alphabet *itself comes from the first two Greek letters, alpha and beta.* ■ *Which of the letters shown here changed the least over time?*

expected to produce healthy sons for the army. They therefore were trained to exercise and strengthen their bodies—something no other Greek women did.

Like other Greek women, Spartan women had to obey their fathers or husbands. Under Spartan law, though, they had the right to inherit property. Because men were occupied with war, some women took on responsibilities such as running the family's estates.

**Sparta and its neighbors.** The Spartans isolated themselves from other Greeks. They looked down on trade and wealth, forbade their own citizens to travel, and had little use for new ideas or the arts. While other Greeks admired the Spartans' military skills, no other city-state imitated their rigorous way of life. "Spartans are willing to die for their city," some suggested, "because they have no reason to live."

In the long run, Sparta suffered from its rigid ways and inability to change. In time, its warrior class shrank, and its power declined.

## Athens: A Limited Democracy

Athens was located in Attica, just north of the Peloponnesus. As in many Greek city-states, Athenian government evolved from a monarchy into an aristocracy. Around 700 B.C., noble landowners held power and chose the chief officials. Nobles judged major cases in court and dominated the assembly.

**King Leonidas** *This bronze monument honors Leonidas, a great warrior-king of ancient Sparta. It stands today as a reminder of the city's militaristic past. A primary duty of a Spartan king was to lead citizen-soldiers in war.* **Continuity and Change** *Name some government leaders of the past or present who are usually shown in military dress.*

**Demands for change.** Athenian wealth and power grew under the aristocracy. Yet discontent spread among ordinary people. Merchants and soldiers resented the power of the nobles. They argued that their service to Athens entitled them to more rights. Foreign artisans, who produced many goods that Athens traded abroad, were resentful that Athenian law barred foreigners from becoming citizens.

Demand for change also came from farmers. During hard times, many farmers were forced to sell their land to nobles. A growing number even had to sell themselves and their families into slavery to pay their debts.

As discontent spread, Athens moved slowly toward democracy, or government by the people. As you will see, the term had a different meaning for the ancient Greeks than it does for us today.

**Solon's reforms.** Solon, a wise and trusted leader, was appointed archon (AHR kahn), or chief official, in 594 B.C. Athenians gave Solon a free hand to make needed reforms. He outlawed debt slavery and freed those who had already been sold into slavery for debt. He opened high offices to more citizens, granted citizenship to some foreigners, and gave the Athenian assembly more say in important decisions.

Solon introduced economic reforms as well. He encouraged the export of wine and olive oil. This policy helped merchants and farmers by increasing demand for their products.

Although Solon's reforms ensured greater fairness and justice to some groups, citizenship remained limited, and only the wealthy landowners could serve in many positions. Widespread and continued unrest led to the rise of tyrants, or people who gained power by force. Tyrants often won support of the merchant class and the poor by imposing reforms to help these groups. (Although Greek tyrants

**Greek Vase Painting** *Most of the ancient Greek painting that survives today is found on vases like this one. It was done in the "red-figure" style of the 400s B.C. The vase itself is made of red clay. The artist then covered the vase with black glaze, letting the red show through to create a detailed scene. Unlike earlier paintings that often depicted gods or warfare, these works focused more on domestic scenes. Here, a group of women prepare a bride for her wedding feast.* **Art and Literature** *How does this vase painting differ from the painting of Odysseus on page 106?*

often governed well, the word *tyrant* has come to mean a vicious and brutal ruler.)

**Later reforms.** The Athenian tyrant Pisistratus (pi SIHS truh tuhs) seized power in 546 B.C. He helped farmers by giving them loans and land taken from nobles. New building projects gave jobs to the poor. By giving poor citizens a greater voice, he further weakened the aristocracy.

In 507 B.C., another reformer, Cleisthenes (KLĪS thuh neez), broadened the role of ordinary citizens in government. He set up the Council of 500, whose members were chosen by lot from among all citizens. The council prepared laws for the assembly and supervised the day-to-day work of government. Cleisthenes made the assembly a genuine legislature, or lawmaking body, that debated laws before de-

ciding to approve or reject them. All male citizens over 30 were members of the assembly.

**Limited rights.** By modern standards, Athenian democracy was quite limited. Only male citizens could participate in government, and citizenship was severely restricted. Also, tens of thousands of Athenians were slaves without political rights or personal freedom. In fact, it was the labor of slaves that gave citizens the time to participate in government. Still, Athens gave more people a say in decision making than the other ancient civilizations we have studied.

**Women.** In Athens, as in other Greek city-states, women had no share in public life. "The loom is women's work, and not debate," observed a Greek man. The respected thinker Aristotle saw women as imperfect beings who lacked the ability to reason as well as men. He wrote:

> **"The man is by nature fitter for command than the female, just as an older person is superior to a younger, more immature person."**

Although some men disagreed, most Greeks accepted the view that women must be guided by men. In well-to-do Athenian homes, women lived a secluded existence, shut off and "protected" from the outside world.

Within their homes, women managed the entire household. They spun and wove, cared for their children, and prepared food. Their slaves or children were sent to buy food and to fetch water from the public well. Poorer women worked outside the home, tending sheep or working as spinners, weavers, or assistant potters.

**Education for democracy.** Unlike girls, who received little or no formal education, boys attended school if their families could afford it. Besides learning to read and write, they studied music and memorized poetry. They studied to become skilled public speakers because, as citizens in a democracy, they would have to voice their views. Young men received military training and, to keep their bodies healthy, participated in athletic contests. Unlike Sparta, which put military training above all else, Athens encouraged young men to explore many areas of knowledge.

## Forces for Unity

Strong local ties, an independent spirit, and economic rivalry led to fighting among the Greek city-states. Despite these divisions, Greeks shared a common culture. They spoke the same language, honored the same ancient heroes, participated in common festivals such as the Olympic Games, and prayed to the same gods.

**Religious beliefs.** Like most other ancient people, the Greeks were polytheistic. They believed that the gods lived on Mount Olympus in northern Greece. The most powerful Olympian was Zeus, who presided over the affairs of gods and humans. His wife, Hera, was goddess of

▲ *Athena, goddess of wisdom*

marriage, and his brother Poseidon (poh SĪ duhn) was god of the sea. Zeus' children included Aphrodite (af ruh DĪ tee), goddess of love, and Ares, god of war. His daughter Athena, goddess of wisdom, gave her name to Athens.

Greeks honored their gods with temples and festivals. To discover the will of the gods, Greeks consulted the oracles, priests or priestesses through whom the gods were thought to speak. Although religion was important, some Greek thinkers came to believe that the universe was regulated, not by the will of gods, but by natural laws.

**View of non-Greeks.** As trade expanded and Greek colonies multiplied, the Greeks came in contact with people who spoke different languages and had different customs. Greeks felt superior to non-Greeks and called them *barbaroi*, people who did not speak Greek. The English word *barbarian* comes from this Greek root. These "barbarians" included such people as the Phoenicians and Egyptians, from whom the Greeks borrowed important ideas and inventions. Still, this sense of uniqueness would help the Greeks face a threat from the mightiest power in the Mediterranean world—the Persian empire.

## SECTION 2 REVIEW

1. **Identify** (a) Solon, (b) Cleisthenes, (c) Zeus.
2. **Define** (a) polis, (b) acropolis, (c) monarchy, (d) aristocracy, (e) oligarchy, (f) phalanx, (g) democracy, (h) tyrant, (i) legislature.
3. Describe how geography affected Greece.
4. (a) How did noble landowners gain power in Greek city-states? (b) How did the development of the phalanx affect Greek society and government?
5. What cultural ties united the Greek world?
6. *Critical Thinking* **Comparing** Compare Athens and Sparta in terms of (a) government, (b) education, (c) the role of women, and (d) values.
7. *ACTIVITY* Create a dialogue between an Athenian and a Spartan in which they discuss the responsibilities of a citizen.

# 3 Victory and Defeat in the Greek World

## Guide for Reading

■ What were the results of the Persian and Peloponnesian wars?

■ Why did Athens enjoy a golden age under Pericles?

■ What led to the outbreak of the Peloponnesian wars?

■ **Vocabulary** *direct democracy*

In 492 B.C., King Darius of Persia sent messengers to the Greek city-states, demanding gifts of "earth and water" as a symbol of surrender. Many city-states obeyed. But Athens and Sparta were not so quick to submit. Saying that the Persians could collect their own earth and water, the Athenians threw Darius' messengers into a well, while the Spartans tossed them into a pit.

The Greek historian Herodotus (hih RAHD uh tuhs) told this story of Greek defiance and pride. Despite their cultural ties, the Greek city-states were often bitterly divided. Yet, when the Persians threatened, the Greeks briefly put aside their differences to defend their freedom.

## The Persian Wars

By 500 B.C., Athens had emerged as the wealthiest Greek city-state. But Athens and the entire Greek world soon faced a fearsome threat from outside. The Persians, you will recall, conquered an empire stretching from Asia Minor to the border of India. (See page 39.) Their subjects included Greek city-states of Ionia in Asia Minor. When these Ionian Greeks rebelled against Persian rule in 499 B.C., Athens sent ships to help them. As Herodotus wrote some years later, "These ships were the beginning of mischief both to the Greeks and to the barbarians."

**Victory at Marathon.** The Persians soon crushed the rebel cities. Later, the emperor Darius sent a huge force across the Aegean to punish Athens for its interference. The mighty

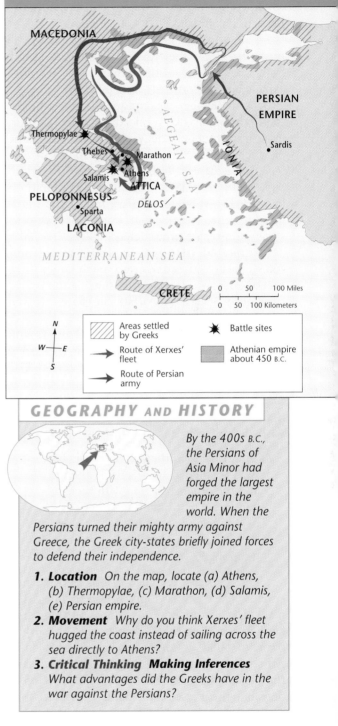

### Persian Wars, 490 B.C.–479 B.C.

### GEOGRAPHY AND HISTORY

By the 400s B.C., the Persians of Asia Minor had forged the largest empire in the world. When the Persians turned their mighty army against Greece, the Greek city-states briefly joined forces to defend their independence.

1. **Location** On the map, locate (a) Athens, (b) Thermopylae, (c) Marathon, (d) Salamis, (e) Persian empire.
2. **Movement** Why do you think Xerxes' fleet hugged the coast instead of sailing across the sea directly to Athens?
3. **Critical Thinking Making Inferences** What advantages did the Greeks have in the war against the Persians?

Persian army landed at Marathon, north of Athens, in 490 B.C.

The Persians outnumbered Athenian forces two to one. Yet the invaders were amazed to see "a mere handful of men coming on at a run

*Chapter 5* **113**

without either horsemen or archers." Overwhelmed by the fury of the Athenian assault, the Persians hastily retreated to their ships.

The victorious Greeks sent Pheidippides (fī DIHP ih deez), their fastest runner, to carry home news of the stunning victory. Though exhausted, he sprinted 26.2 miles (32 km) to Athens. "Rejoice, we conquer," he gasped—then dropped down dead. In his honor, marathon runners today still cover the same distance that Pheidippides ran 2,500 years ago.

The Athenian leader, Themistocles (thuh MIHS tuh kleez), knew the victory at Marathon had bought only a temporary lull in the fighting. He urged Athenians to build a fleet of warships and prepare other defenses.

**Renewed attacks.** In 480 B.C., Darius' son Xerxes (ZERK seez) sent a much larger force to conquer Greece. By this time, Athens had convinced Sparta and other city-states to join the fight.

Once again, the Persians landed an army in northern Greece. A small Spartan force guarded the narrow mountain pass at Thermopylae (thuhr MAHP uh lee). Led by King Leonidas, (see page 111), they held out heroically against the enormous Persian force. Herodotus described the heroic stand of the Spartans:

66They defended themselves to the last, such as still had swords using them, and the others resisting with their hands and teeth; till the barbarians . . . overwhelmed and buried the remnant that was left beneath showers of missile weapons.99

The Persians marched south and burned Athens. The city was empty, however. The Athenians had withdrawn to safety, putting their faith in the fleet that Themistocles had urged them to build. In the nearby strait of Salamis, Athenian warships trapped, rammed, and sank the Persian fleet. The following year, the Greeks defeated the Persians on land. In a brief moment of unity, the Greek city-states had saved themselves from the Persian threat.

**Results.** Victory in the Persian Wars increased the Greek sense of their own uniqueness. The gods, they felt, had protected their superior form of government—the city-state—against invaders from Asia.

Athens emerged from the war as the most powerful city-state in Greece. To meet continued threats from Persia, it organized the Delian League, an alliance with other Greek city-states. Athens dominated the league, slowly using its position to create an Athenian empire. It moved the league treasury from the island of Delos to Athens and forced its allies to remain in the league against their will. Athenians even used money contributed by other city-states to rebuild their own city. Yet, while Athens was enforcing its will abroad, Athenian leaders were championing political freedom at home.

## Athens in the Age of Pericles

The years after the Persian Wars were a golden age for Athens. Under the able statesman Pericles (PEHR uh kleez), the economy thrived and the government became more democratic. Because of his wise and skillful leadership, the period from 460 B.C. to 429 B.C. is often called the Age of Pericles.

**Political life.** Pericles believed that all male citizens, regardless of wealth or social class, should take part in government. Athens therefore began to pay salaries to men who held public office. This reform enabled poor men to serve in government.

By the time of Pericles, the assembly met several times a month and needed at least 6,000 members present before deciding important issues. Athenians had a direct democracy in which a large number of male citizens took part in the day-to-day affairs of government. By contrast, in most democratic countries today, citizens participate in government indirectly through elected representatives. (☑ See *You Decide*, "How Should a Society's Leaders Be Chosen?" pages 180–181.)

**The Funeral Oration.** Thucydides (thoo SIHD uh deez), a historian who lived in the Age of Pericles, recorded a speech given by Pericles at the funeral of Athenians slain in battle. In this famous Funeral Oration, Pericles praised the Athenian form of government:

66Our constitution is called a democracy because power is in the hands not of a minority but of the whole people. When it is a question of settling private

**Symbols of Democracy** *This stone relief depicts Democracy crowning the people of Athens with a wreath. The image reminded Athenians of their duty to participate in government. Athenians used tokens like the one shown here to cast their votes on important issues.* **Continuity and Change** *Do people in modern democracies need reminders about the value of voting? Explain.*

disputes, everyone is equal before the laws. When it is a question of putting one person before another in positions of public responsibility, what counts is not membership of a particular class, but the ability the man possesses. **"**

Pericles pointed out that Athenian citizens bore a special responsibility. "We alone," he stated, "regard a man who takes no interest in public affairs, not as a harmless but as a useless character."

**Economic and cultural life.** Athens prospered during the Age of Pericles. With the riches of the Athenian empire, Pericles hired the best architects and sculptors to rebuild the Acropolis, which the Persians had destroyed. Magnificent new temples rose to remind citizens that the gods had favored the Athenians. Building projects further increased prosperity by creating jobs for artisans and workers.

With the help of an educated foreign-born woman named Aspasia, Pericles turned Athens into the cultural center of Greece. Pericles and Aspasia surrounded themselves with thinkers, writers, and artists. Through building programs and public festivals, they supported the arts. In the next section, you will read about Greek contributions to the arts, literature, and philosophy.

## Greek Against Greek

The power of Athens contained the seeds of disaster. Many Greeks resented Athenian domination. Before long, the Greek world split into rival camps. To counter the Delian League, Sparta and other enemies of Athens formed the Peloponnesian League. Sparta encouraged oligarchy in the cities of the Peloponnesian League, while Athens supported democracy among its allies.

In 431 B.C., warfare broke out in earnest between Athens and Sparta. The 27-year Peloponnesian War engulfed all of Greece.

**Peloponnesian War.** Despite its riches and powerful navy, Athens faced a serious geographic disadvantage. Sparta was located inland, so it could not be attacked from the sea. Yet Sparta had only to march north to attack Athens by land.

When Sparta invaded Athens, Pericles allowed people from the surrounding countryside

**ISSUES** *For* **TODAY** | Pericles boasted that it was the duty of every Athenian citizen to participate in government. How have the responsibilities of a citizen changed over time?

to move inside the city walls. The overcrowded conditions soon led to disaster. A terrible plague broke out, killing at least a third of the population, including Pericles himself. His successors were much less able leaders. Their power struggles quickly undermined the city's democratic government.

As the war dragged on, each side committed savage acts against the other. Sparta even allied itself with Persia, the longtime enemy of the Greeks. Finally, in 404 B.C., with the help of the Persian navy, the Spartans captured Athens. The victors stripped Athenians of their fleet and empire.

**The aftermath of war.** The Peloponnesian War ended Athenian greatness. Although the Athenian economy revived, its spirit and vitality declined. In Athens, as elsewhere in the Greek world, democratic government suffered. Corruption and selfish interests replaced older ideals such as service to the city-state.

Fighting continued to disrupt the Greek world. Sparta itself soon suffered defeat at the hands of Thebes, another Greek city-state. As Greeks fought among themselves, a new power rose in Macedonia (MAS uh dohn ee yuh), a kingdom to the north. By 359 B.C., its ambitious ruler stood poised to conquer the quarrelsome city-states.

## SECTION 3 REVIEW

1. **Identify** (a) Marathon, (b) Themistocles, (c) Delian League, (d) Aspasia.
2. **Define** direct democracy.
3. Describe two effects of the Persian Wars.
4. What are three ways in which Pericles contributed to Athenian greatness?
5. How did the growth of Athenian power contribute to the outbreak of the Peloponnesian War?
6. *Critical Thinking* **Linking Past and Present** Compare Athenian democracy under Pericles to American democracy today. (a) How are they similar? (b) How are they different?
7. *ACTIVITY* Draw a political cartoon commenting on the causes or effects of the Peloponnesian War, from the viewpoint of either Athens or Sparta.

# 4 The Glory That Was Greece

## Guide for Reading

- What political and ethical ideas did Greek philosophers develop?
- What were the goals of Greek architects and artists?
- How did Greek theater evolve?
- **Vocabulary** *rhetoric, tragedy, comedy*

Despite wars and political turmoil, Greeks had great confidence in the power of the human mind. "We cultivate the mind," declared Pericles. "We are lovers of the beautiful, yet simple in our tastes." Driven by curiosity and guided by a belief in reason, Greek thinkers, artists, and writers explored the nature of the universe and the place of people in it.

## Lovers of Wisdom

As you have read earlier, some Greek thinkers denied that events were caused by the whims of gods. Instead, they used observation and reason to find causes for what happened. The Greeks called these thinkers philosophers, meaning "lovers of wisdom."

Philosophers explored many subjects, from mathematics and physics to music and logic, or rational thinking. Through reason and observation, they believed they could discover laws that governed the universe. Much modern science traces its roots to the Greek search for principles explaining how the universe works.

Other philosophers were more interested in ethics, or moral behavior. Their debates centered on questions such as what was the best kind of government and what standards should govern people's behavior.

In Athens, one group of thinkers, the Sophists, questioned accepted ideas about truth and justice. To them, success was more important than moral truths. They urged students to develop skills in rhetoric, the art of skillful speaking. Ambitious men could use clever words to advance their careers within the city-state. The turmoil of the Peloponnesian War led many young Athenians to follow the Sophists. Older citizens, however, condemned the Sophists for undermining traditional values. An outspoken critic of the Sophists was Socrates, an Athenian stonemason and philosopher, who lived from 469 B.C. to 399 B.C.

## Death of a Philosopher

 "The unexamined life is not worth living," declared Socrates. True to his word, he encouraged those around him to examine their deepest beliefs and ideas. Eventually, this commitment to truth cost Socrates his life.

**A wandering teacher.** Most of what we know about Socrates comes from his student Plato. Socrates himself wrote no books. Instead, he lounged around the marketplace, questioning fellow citizens about their beliefs and ideas. In one dialogue reported by Plato, Socrates challenges his friend Euthyphro (yoo THIHF roh) to define what actions are pious, or holy. "What is pleasing to the gods is pious," Euthy-

phro immediately responds. But Socrates refuses to accept this simple answer. Through patient questioning, he gets Euthyphro to contradict himself:

66'Have we not said, Euthyphro, that there are quarrels and disagreements and hatreds among the gods?'
  'We have. . . .'
  'Then you say that some of the gods think one thing just, the other another; and that what some of them hold to be honorable or good, others hold to be dishonorable or evil; . . . and the same thing will be displeasing and pleasing to them?'
  'Apparently.'
  'Then, according to your account, the same thing will be pious and impious.'99

**Death of Socrates** Socrates urged his students to question and critically examine all around them. For "corrupting the youth" in this way, an Athenian jury sentenced him to death. This French painting of the 1600s shows the condemned Socrates drinking deadly hemlock. **Impact of the Individual** Why do you think later artists like this one portrayed Socrates as a heroic figure?

This questioning process is known today as the Socratic method. To Socrates, it was a way to help others seek truth and self-knowledge. To many of his students, it was an amusing game. To other Athenians, however, it was an annoyance and a threat to accepted traditions.

**Trial and execution.** When he was about 70 years old, Socrates was put on trial. His enemies accused him of corrupting the city's youth and failing to respect the gods.

Standing before a jury of 501 citizens, Socrates offered a calm defense:

> 66All day long and in all places I am always fastening upon you, stirring you and persuading you and reproaching you. You will not easily find another like me, and therefore I would advise you to spare me.99

To the jurors, Socrates' cool reason seemed like arrogance. They condemned him to death.

His friends urged Socrates to flee. By examining the issue, however, he showed how escape would be morally wrong. "In leaving the prison against the will of the Athenians," he asked, "do I not desert the principles which were acknowledged by us to be just?"

Loyal to the laws of Athens, Socrates accepted the death penalty. He drank a cup of hemlock, a deadly poison. Then, as the poison surged through his body, he chatted with friends and students. According to Plato, his last words were, "Crito, I owe a rooster to Asclepius. Will you remember to pay the debt?" So died the man Plato called the "wisest, justest, and best of all I have ever known."

## Ideas About Government

The death of Socrates so shocked and disturbed Plato that he left Athens for 10 years. When he returned, he set up the Academy, a school that survived for almost 900 years. There, he taught and wrote about his own ideas.

**Plato.** Like Socrates, Plato emphasized the importance of reason. Through rational thought, he argued, people could discover unchanging ethical values, recognize perfect beauty, and learn how to organize an ideal society.

In *The Republic*, Plato described his vision of an ideal state. He rejected Athenian democracy because it had condemned Socrates. Instead, Plato felt the state should regulate every aspect of its citizens' lives in order to provide for their best interests. He divided society into three classes: workers to produce the necessities of life, soldiers to defend the state, and philosophers to rule. This elite class of leaders would be specially trained to ensure order and justice. The wisest of them, a philosopher-king, would have the ultimate authority.

Plato thought that women could rank among the ruling elite of his republic. He claimed that, in general, men surpassed women in mental and physical tasks, but he thought that some women were superior to some men. Talented women, he said, should be educated and put to use by the state. The ruling elite, both men and women, would take military training together and raise their children in communal centers for the good of the republic.

**Aristotle.** Plato's most famous student, Aristotle, developed his own ideas about the best kind of government. He analyzed all kinds of government—from monarchy to aristocracy to democracy—and found good and bad examples of each. Like Plato, he was suspicious of democracy, which he thought could lead to mob rule. In the end, he favored rule by a single strong and virtuous leader.

Like Plato, Aristotle also addressed the question of how people ought to live. In his view, good conduct meant pursuing the "golden mean," a moderate course between extremes. He promoted reason as the guiding force for learning.

Aristotle set up a school, the Lyceum, for the study of all branches of knowledge. He left writings on politics, ethics, logic, biology, literature, physics, and many other subjects. When the first universities evolved in Europe some 1,500 years later, their courses were largely based on the works of Aristotle.

## The Search for Beauty and Order

Plato argued that every object on Earth had an ideal form. The work of Greek artists and architects reflected the same concern with form and order.

**The Parthenon** *Each year, armies of tourists invade Athens to gaze at the temples on the Acropolis. These buildings have been battered by 2,500 years of weather, war, and pollution. Yet they stand as proud monuments to the Greek quest for order and beauty. The most revered temple on the Acropolis is the Parthenon, shown here.* **Continuity and Change** *Based on this picture, what modern buildings were influenced by the style of the Parthenon?*

**Architecture.** The most famous Greek temple, the Parthenon, was dedicated to the goddess Athena. Its builders sought to convey a sense of perfect balance to reflect the harmony and order of the universe. The basic plan was a simple rectangle, with tall columns supporting a gently sloping roof. The delicate curves and placement of the columns added dignity and grace.

Greek architecture has been widely admired for centuries. Throughout the United States today, you can see buildings that have adopted various kinds of Greek columns.

**Sculpture.** In ancient times, a towering figure of Athena, covered in gold and ivory, stood inside the Parthenon. Though this statue has not survived, many other works from this period show Greek sculpture at its best.

Early Greek sculptors carved figures in rigid poses, perhaps imitating Egyptian styles. By 450 B.C., Greek sculptors had developed a new style that emphasized natural poses, such as athletes in motion. While their work was realistic, or lifelike, it was also idealistic. That is, sculptors carved gods, goddesses, athletes, and famous men in a way that showed individuals in their most perfect, graceful form.

**Painting.** The only Greek paintings to survive are on vases and other pottery. They offer intriguing views of Greek life. Women carry water from wells, oarsmen row trading ships, warriors race into battle, and athletes compete in javelin contests. Each scene is designed to fit the shape of the pottery perfectly. (See the picture on page 111.)

## Poetry and Drama

In literature, as in art, the ancient Greeks set the standard for what later Europeans called the classic style. Ever since, writers and artists in the western world have studied the elegance, harmony, and balance of Greek works.

Greek literature began with the epics of Homer, whose stirring tales inspired later writers. Other poets wrote about the joys and sorrows of their own times. Sappho sang of love and of the beauty of her island home. Pindar's poems celebrated the victors in athletic contests. (See page 102.) Perhaps the most important Greek contribution to literature, though, was in the field of drama.

**The beginnings of Greek drama.** The first Greek plays evolved out of religious festivals, especially those held in Athens to honor Dionysus (di uh NĪ suhs), god of fertility and wine. Plays were performed outdoors in large theaters gouged out of the sides of hills. There was little or no scenery. Actors wore elaborate costumes and stylized masks. A chorus responded to the action by singing or chanting commentary between scenes.

Greek dramas were often based on popular myths and legends. Through these familiar stories, playwrights discussed moral and social issues or explored the relationship between people and the gods.

**Tragedy.** The greatest Athenian playwrights were Aeschylus (EHS kuh luhs), Sophocles (SAHF uh kleez), and Euripides (yu RIHP uh deez). All three wrote tragedies, plays that told stories of human suffering that usually ended in disaster. The purpose of tragedy, the Greeks felt, was to excite emotions of pity and fear.

Aeschylus drew on tales of the Trojan Wars in *The Oresteia* (ohr eh STEE uh). This series of three plays unfolded hideous crimes of murder and revenge within a powerful family. The plays showed how pride could bring misfortune and how the gods could bring down even the greatest heroes.

In *Antigone* (an TIHG uh nee), Sophocles explored what happens when an individual's moral duty conflicts with the laws of the state. As the play opens, Antigone's brother has been killed leading a rebellion against the city of Thebes. King Creon forbids anyone to bury the traitor's body. When Antigone buries her brother anyway, she is arrested. She tells Creon that duty to the gods is greater than human law:

❝ For me, it was not Zeus who made that order. Nor did I think your orders were so strong that you, a mortal man, could overrule the gods' unwritten and unfailing laws. ❞

For her defiance, Antigone is put to death. Creon, too, is punished when his actions lead to the deaths of his wife and son.

Both Sophocles and Euripides survived the horrors of the Peloponnesian War. That experience probably led Euripides to question accepted ideas. His plays said little about the gods. Instead, they suggested that people were the cause of human misfortune. In *The Trojan Women*, he stripped war of its glamour by showing the suffering of women who were victims of the war.

**Comedy.** Other Greek playwrights composed comedies, humorous plays that mocked people or customs. Through ridicule, they criticized society, much as political cartoons do today. Almost all surviving Greek comedies were written by Aristophanes (ar ihs TAHF uh neez). In *Lysistrata*, Aristophanes tells what happens when the women of Athens together force their husbands to end a war against Sparta.

### The Writing of History

The Greeks applied observation, reason, and logic to the study of history. Herodotus is often called the "Father of History" in the west-

**Comic Masks** *In this marble relief, the playwright Menander looks at the masks used in one of his comedies. The masks, with their exaggerated facial features, enabled those sitting far from the stage to recognize the characters. A small mouthpiece inside the mask helped project the actor's voice.* **Art and Literature** *What emotions do you see in each of these masks?*

ern world because he went beyond listing rulers or retelling ancient legends. Before writing *The Persian Wars,* Herodotus visited many lands, collecting information from people who remembered the events he chronicled.

Herodotus cast a critical eye on his sources, noting bias and conflicting accounts. Yet his writings reflected his own view that the war was a clear moral victory of Greek love of freedom over Persian tyranny. He also invented conversations and speeches for historical figures.

Thucydides, a few years younger than Herodotus, wrote about the Peloponnesian War, a much less happy subject for the Greeks. He had lived through the war and vividly described its savagery and its corrupting influence on all those involved. Although he was an Athenian, he tried to be fair to both sides.

Both writers set standards for future historians. Herodotus stressed the importance of research. Thucydides showed the need to avoid bias in recording the past.

## SECTION 4 REVIEW

1. **Identify** (a) Socrates, (b) Aristotle, (c) Parthenon, (d) Aeschylus, (e) Sophocles, (f) Euripides, (g) Herodotus, (h) Thucydides.
2. **Define** (a) rhetoric, (b) tragedy, (c) comedy.
3. What standards of beauty did Greek artists follow?
4. (a) How were Greek plays performed? (b) What themes did Greek playwrights explore?
5. (a) Why did Plato reject democracy as a form of government? (b) Describe the ideal government set forth in Plato's *Republic.*
6. *Critical Thinking* **Analyzing Information** Review Socrates' statement about an "unexamined life" on page 117. (a) Restate this idea in your own words. (b) How did his actions reflect this belief? (c) Why was Socrates seen as a danger to the state?
7. *ACTIVITY* Thucydides wrote about an event he had lived through because he believed it would still have an impact years later. Choose an event during your own lifetime that you think historians will write about 100 years from now. Write a paragraph explaining the importance of this event.

## 5 Alexander and the Hellenistic Age

### Guide for Reading

- What were the results of Alexander's conquests?
- Why was Alexandria a center of the Hellenistic world?
- How did individuals contribute to Hellenistic civilization?

Again and again, Demosthenes (dih MAHS thuh neez), the finest public speaker in Athens, tried to warn fellow citizens of the danger they faced. Philip II, the ambitious king of Macedonia, was gradually bringing Greece under his control:

66He is always taking in more, everywhere casting his net round us, while we sit idle and do nothing. When, Athenians, will you take the necessary action? What are you waiting for?99

When the Athenians finally took action against Philip, it was too late. Athens and the other Greek city-states lost their independence. Yet the disaster ushered in a new age that saw Greek influence spread from the Mediterranean to the edge of India.

### *Macedonian Ambitions*

To the Greeks, the rugged, mountainous kingdom of Macedonia was a backward, half-civilized land. The rulers of this frontier land, in fact, were of Greek origin and maintained ties to their Greek neighbors. As a youth, Philip lived in Thebes and came to admire Greek culture. Later, he hired Aristotle to tutor his young son Alexander.

When Philip gained the Macedonian throne in 359 B.C., he dreamed of conquering the prosperous, warring city-states to the south. He built a superb army and hired foreign captains to train his troops. Through threats, bribery, and diplomacy, he formed alliances with many Greek city-states. Others he overpowered. In 338 B.C., when Athens and Thebes finally joined forces against Philip, they suffered a crushing defeat at the battle of Chaeronea (kehr uh NEE uh). Philip then brought all of Greece under his control.

Philip had still grander dreams. He proposed to lead a force of Macedonians and Greeks to conquer the Persian empire. Before he could achieve his plan, however, he was murdered at his daughter's wedding feast. Philip's clever and determined wife, Olympias, then outmaneuvered his other wives and children to put her own son Alexander on the throne.

## A Mighty Conqueror

Although Alexander was only 20 years old, he was already an experienced soldier. As a boy, he had heard tales of Achilles, hero of the *Iliad*. Alexander saw himself as a second Achilles. In the next 12 years, this confident and reckless young man earned the title Alexander the Great.

From Aristotle, Alexander acquired a love of learning and an interest in the arts. But he was first and foremost a warrior. When Thebes rebelled, his punishment was swift and brutal. He ordered

▲ *Alexander and his mother*

the city to be burned and its inhabitants to be killed or sold into slavery. He told his soldiers, though, to spare the house where the poet Pindar had once lived.

**Conquest of Persia.** Like his father, Alexander planned to invade Persia. With Greece subdued, he began organizing the forces needed to achieve that goal. By 334 B.C., he had enough ships to cross the Dardanelles, the strait that separates Europe from Asia Minor.

Persia was no longer the great power it had been. The emperor Darius III was weak, and the satraps who governed the provinces were often rebellious. Still, the Persian empire stretched more than 2,000 miles from Egypt to India.

Alexander won his first victory against the Persians at the Granicus River. He then moved from victory to victory, marching through Asia Minor into Palestine and south to Egypt. In 331

B.C., he took Babylon, then seized the Persian capitals. Before Alexander could capture Darius, however, one of the emperor's satraps murdered him and left his body on the road for Alexander to find. Alexander had the dead emperor buried properly.

**On to India.** With much of the Persian empire under his control, the restless young conqueror headed further east. He crossed the Hindu Kush into northern India. There, in 326 B.C., his troops for the first time faced soldiers mounted on elephants.

Alexander never lost a battle, but his soldiers were growing tired of the long campaign. At a branch of the Indus River, they refused to go further. Reluctantly, Alexander agreed to turn back. A long, grueling march brought them to Babylon, where Alexander began planning a new campaign.

**Sudden death.** Before he could set out again, he fell victim to a sudden fever. As Alexander lay dying, his commanders asked to whom he left his immense empire. "To the strongest," he is said to have whispered.

In fact, no one leader appeared who was strong enough to succeed Alexander. Instead, after years of disorder, three generals divided up the empire. Macedonia and Greece went to one general, Egypt to another, and most of Persia to a third. For 300 years, their descendants competed for power over the lands Alexander had conquered.

## The Legacy of Alexander

Although Alexander's empire soon crumbled, he had unleashed changes that would ripple across the Mediterranean world and the Middle East for centuries. His most lasting achievement was the spread of Greek culture.

**A blending of cultures.** Alexander's conquests linked a vast area. Across his far-flung empire, Alexander founded many new cities, most of them named after him. The generals who succeeded him founded still more. Soldiers, traders, and artisans surged out of Greece

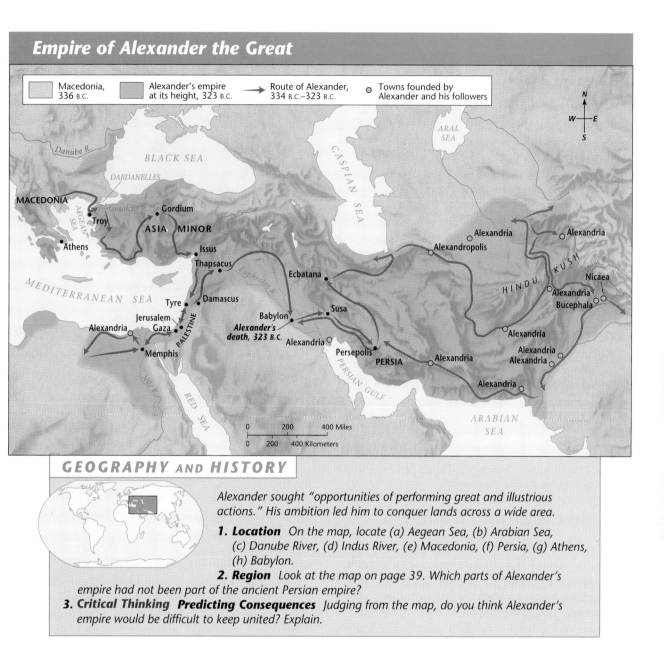

# Empire of Alexander the Great

**Legend:**
- Macedonia, 336 B.C.
- Alexander's empire at its height, 323 B.C.
- Route of Alexander, 334 B.C.–323 B.C.
- Towns founded by Alexander and his followers

## GEOGRAPHY AND HISTORY

*Alexander sought "opportunities of performing great and illustrious actions." His ambition led him to conquer lands across a wide area.*

**1. Location** On the map, locate (a) Aegean Sea, (b) Arabian Sea, (c) Danube River, (d) Indus River, (e) Macedonia, (f) Persia, (g) Athens, (h) Babylon.

**2. Region** Look at the map on page 39. Which parts of Alexander's empire had not been part of the ancient Persian empire?

**3. Critical Thinking Predicting Consequences** Judging from the map, do you think Alexander's empire would be difficult to keep united? Explain.

to settle these new cities. From Egypt to the Fertile Crescent to the borders of India, they built Greek temples, filled them with Greek statues, and held athletic contests as they had in Greece. Local people assimilated, or absorbed, Greek ideas. In turn, Greek settlers adopted local customs.

Gradually, a blending of eastern and western cultures occurred. Alexander had encouraged this blending when he married a Persian woman and urged his soldiers to follow his example. He had also adopted many Persian customs, including Persian dress.

After his death, a vital new culture emerged, which is known as Hellenistic civilization. A blend of Greek, Persian, Egyptian, and Indian influences, Hellenistic civilization would flourish for centuries.

**Alexandria.** At the very heart of the Hellenistic world stood the city of Alexandria, Egypt. Located on the sea lanes between Europe and Asia, its markets boasted a wide range of goods, from Greek marble to Arabian spices to East African ivory.

A Greek architect had drawn up plans for the city, which would become home to almost a million people. Greeks, Egyptians, Persians, Hebrews, and many others crowded its busy streets. Among the city's marvelous sights was the Pharos, an enormous lighthouse that soared 440 feet into the air. Visitors counted the lighthouse among the Seven Wonders of the World.

Alexander had supported and encouraged learning throughout his empire, and his successors also supported the work of scholars. The rulers of Alexandria built the great Museum as a center of learning. (Its name meant "house of the Muses." The Muses were nine Greek goddesses who presided over the arts and sciences.) The Museum boasted laboratories, lecture halls, and a zoo. Its well-stocked library had thousands of scrolls representing the accumulated knowledge of the ancient world. Unfortunately, the library was later destroyed in a fire.

**Opportunities for women.** Paintings, statues, and legal codes reveal that women were no longer restricted to their houses in the Hellenistic period. More women learned to read and write. Some became poets and philosophers. Throughout the Hellenistic world, royal women held considerable power, working alongside husbands or sons who were the actual rulers. In Egypt, the able and clever Cleopatra came to rule in her own right.

## Hellenistic Civilization

The cities of the Hellenistic world employed armies of architects and artists. Temples, palaces, and other public buildings were much larger and grander than the buildings of classical Greece. The elaborate new style reflected the desire of Hellenistic rulers to glorify themselves as godlike, absolute monarchs.

**New schools of thought.** The political turmoil of the Hellenistic age contributed to

**GLOBAL CONNECTIONS**

The list of the Seven Wonders of the World was compiled in the 100s B.C. by a writer who traveled across the Hellenistic world. In addition to the Pharos, the list included the Hanging Gardens of Babylon (see page 39) and the Colossus, a 100-foot bronze statue on the Aegean island of Rhodes. Of all these ancient wonders, only the pyramids of Egypt can still be seen today.

**A New Look** This bronze head, originally part of a full-length statue, reflects a new realistic approach developed by Hellenistic sculptors. They carved every bone and muscle exactly as it looked in real life. For subjects, they preferred ordinary people to gods and heroes. **Art and Literature** Compare this sculpture to the ones on page 103. What changes in artistic style can you see?

the rise of new schools of philosophy. The most influential, Stoicism, was founded by Zeno. He urged people to avoid desires and disappointments and accept calmly whatever life brought. The Stoics believed that all people, including women and slaves, though unequal in society, were morally equal because all had the power of reason. Stoics preached high moral standards that included protecting the rights of fellow humans. Stoicism later influenced many Roman and Christian thinkers.

**Mathematics and the sciences.** The Hellenistic age saw important advances in the sciences and mathematics. Hellenistic thinkers built on earlier Greek, Babylonian, and Egyptian knowledge. Pythagoras (pih THAG uhr uhs) derived a formula $(a^2 + b^2 = c^2)$ that is still used to calculate the relationship between the sides of a right triangle. In Alexandria, Euclid wrote *The Elements*, which became the basis for modern geometry.

Using mathematics and careful observation, the astronomer Aristarchus (ar ihs TAHR kuhs) argued that the Earth rotated on its axis and or-

# CAUSE AND EFFECT

### Causes

Rise of civilizations in Persia, Egypt, and Greece

Macedonian conquest of Greece

Growth of Alexander's empire from Greece to northern India

Growing contacts among kingdoms of eastern Mediterranean and Middle East

## RISE OF HELLENISTIC CIVILIZATION

### Effects

Learning and arts encouraged by Alexander and his successors

Alexandria, Egypt, becomes center of trade and learning

Spread of Greek, Middle Eastern, and Persian religions

Spread of Christianity

### Connections Today

Continued practice of Christianity and Judaism in the region

Alexandria, Egypt, still a center of learning

Greek architecture still visible in ruins across Middle East

*Interpreting a Chart* *Alexander the Great's empire split apart soon after his death. Yet, by creating a common civilization over a vast area, he had an impact that endured for centuries.* ■ *How did the conquests of Alexander encourage contacts among Mediterranean civilizations?*

bited around the sun. This idea was not accepted until almost 2,000 years later. Another astronomer showed that the Earth was round and accurately calculated its circumference.

The most famous Hellenistic scientist, Archimedes (ahr kuh MEE deez), applied principles of physics to make practical inventions. He mastered the use of the lever and pulley. He boasted, "Give me a lever long enough and a place to stand on, and I will move the world." An awed audience watched as he used his invention to draw a ship onto shore.

**Medicine.** About 400 B.C., the Greek physician Hippocrates (hih PAHK ruh teez) studied the cause of illnesses and looked for cures. His Hippocratic oath set ethical standards for doctors. Physicians swore to "help the sick according to my ability and judgment but never with a view to injury and wrong" and to protect the privacy of patients. Doctors today take a similar oath.

## Looking Ahead

During the Hellenistic period, a powerful new state, Rome, came to dominate the Mediterranean world. By then, the Greeks had already made their greatest contributions.

Greek ideas about law, freedom, justice, and government have influenced political thinking to the present day. In the arts and sciences, Greek works became a standard of excellence for later people of Europe. These achievements were especially remarkable because they were produced by a scattering of tiny city-states whose bitter rivalries cost them their freedom. In the chapters ahead, you will see how the Greek legacy influenced the civilizations of Rome and of Western Europe.

## SECTION 5 REVIEW

1. **Identify** (a) Philip, (b) Stoics, (c) Pythagoras, (d) Euclid, (e) Archimedes, (f) Hippocrates.
2. How did Alexander's conquests lead to the rise of a new civilization?
3. Describe three changes in the arts and philosophy during the Hellenistic age.
4. *Critical Thinking* **Ranking** What do you think were the three most important contributions made by Hellenistic scientists and mathematicians? Explain your choices.
5. *ACTIVITY* Imagine that you are a soldier in Alexander's army. Write two postcards to your family. In the first, tell how you feel about the Persian campaign. In the second, tell how you feel about marching into India.

# Skills for Success

## Working in a Group

Both in and out of school, you may often be asked to complete projects that require the work of more than one person. One advantage of working in a group is the opportunity to draw on the talents, ideas, and skills of many people. At the same time, working in a group can present difficulties. Decisions can be harder to reach when many people take part. Some group members may try to dominate the discussion, while others may feel shy about contributing their ideas.

Imagine that you are a member of a group that is planning a textbook chapter about ancient Greece. The following techniques can help your group work more productively:

**1 Identify the group's goals.** Groups work best when they have clearly defined goals. At the first group meeting, choose a group leader and a group recorder. The leader should start the group off by asking group members to discuss the scope of the assignment. The recorder will then take notes on the group's discussion. (a) Define the main goal of your group by completing the following sentence: "Our assignment is to _____." (b) What decisions must be made before you can complete this assignment? (c) List the separate tasks that need to be done in order to complete this assignment.

**2 Use brainstorming to generate ideas.** Groups can make decisions in a number of ways. One effective technique is called **brainstorming.** At the start of a brainstorming session, the group sets a time limit. During that time, members freely suggest any ideas that come to mind, no matter how wild they seem. A recorder writes all the ideas down for everyone to see. Nobody is allowed to reject or criticize any idea until the time is up. Then the group discusses the ideas, gradually eliminating or refining ideas until they develop a plan everyone can accept. (a) What do you think are the advantages of brainstorming? (b) Why is it important that no one reject or criticize any ideas while the group is brainstorming?

**3 Assign tasks and set deadlines.** The list below gives different ways that your group might perform specific tasks. (a) What are the advantages and disadvantages of Plan 3? Of Plan 4? (b) Which plan seems to you to be the least useful? Explain. (c) Which plan seems the most useful? Explain. (d) Why is it important to set clear deadlines for tasks to be completed?

**4 Communicate progress.** When group members are working at different tasks, they should meet regularly to discuss their progress. Why is it important for the group to communicate regularly?

*Beyond the Classroom* Most people belong to several groups, whether in school, on a job, at church, or in the community. Make a list of groups to which you have belonged. Then, briefly summarize a project you have worked on with one of these groups. Describe how your group decided on this project, how it divided up the work, how long the project took, and how successful it was.

---

*Ways to Divide Up Work Within a Group*

**Plan 1.** Have the group leader do everything.

**Plan 2.** Have every person in the group work on every task.

**Plan 3.** Let each person choose what he or she wants to do.

**Plan 4.** Have the group leader assign each person a job.

**Plan 5.** Discuss who should do jobs based on each individual's strengths and talents.

**Plan 6.** Assign jobs by picking names at random.

**Plan 7.** Ask someone outside the group to assign tasks.

# CHAPTER 5 REVIEW

## Building Vocabulary

Write a sentence comparing each of the following pairs of words or describing the relationship between them: (a) *polis* and *acropolis,* (b) *aristocracy* and *oligarchy,* (c) *legislature* and *democracy,* (d) *comedy* and *tragedy.*

## Reviewing Chapter Themes

1. **Geography and History** (a) How did geography lead to isolation in the Greek world? (b) How did geography encourage interaction with the world outside Greece?
2. **Impact of the Individual** Choose three of the following individuals and describe the contribution of each to Greek civilization: (a) Homer, (b) Solon, (c) Cleisthenes, (d) Sophocles, (e) Plato, (f) Aristotle.
3. **Political and Social Systems** (a) Describe three stages of government in the Greek city-states. (b) According to Pericles, what were the outstanding features of the Athenian system of government? (c) In what ways was democracy limited?
4. **Global Interaction** (a) How did trade contribute to the development and spread of Greek culture? (b) How did the conquests of Alexander lead to widespread cultural diffusion? Give two examples.

## Thinking Critically

1. **Analyzing Information** (a) How did Greek culture stress the importance of the individual? Give two examples. (b) How do you think the importance given to the individual might have been related to the development of Greek democracy?
2. **Comparing** Review what you learned about ancient China in Chapters 3 and 4. How was the Greek attitude toward foreigners similar to that of the Chinese?
3. **Recognizing Causes and Effects** (a) Identify two immediate and two long-range causes of the Peloponnesian War. (b) Why might it be said that all Greeks were losers in the Peloponnesian War? (★ See *Skills for Success,* page 18.)
4. **Synthesizing Information** (a) In what ways was the form of government outlined in Plato's *Republic* similar to the government of Sparta? (b) How was it different? (★ See *Skills for Success,* page 896.)
5. **Recognizing Points of View** Imagine that you are preparing to interview Alexander the Great just before his death. List six questions that you would ask him about himself, his goals, and his achievements. Then, write his answers to three of these questions. (★ See *Skills for Success,* page 280.)
6. **Linking Past and Present** Reread the description of the Hippocratic oath on page 125. (a) How did Hippocrates address the question of medical ethics? (b) What moral and ethical issues do doctors face today?

## For Your Portfolio

Imagine that it is the year 425 B.C. You and some of your classmates have been assigned to produce a magazine to be called either *Athenian Life* or *Spartan Life.*

1. Decide which city-state you want to write about. Brainstorm a list of questions about life in that city-state around 425 B.C. Questions might include: How did men and women dress? What were their houses like? Who were the most influential leaders? What was happening on the war front?
2. Divide the questions among members of your group. Use your school or local library to research the answers to your questions.
3. Discuss the results of your research and make a list of possible topics. Use this list to make a table of contents for your magazine. (You might use the table of contents of a news magazine, such as *Time* or *Newsweek,* as a model.) Then, prepare brief articles on *two* of the topics. One article should focus on news, such as war or politics. The other article should focus on daily life or the arts.
4. Plan a cover for your magazine. You may either have a member of your group draw a cover or use photocopies of pictures you have found during your research.
5. In a presentation or bulletin board display, share your cover, table of contents, and articles. Afterward, sum up what you have learned about the Greek city-states.

# Ancient Rome and the Rise of Christianity

### (509 B.C. – A.D. 476)

## CHAPTER OUTLINE

1 **The Roman World Takes Shape**
2 **From Republic to Empire**
3 **The Roman Achievement**
4 **The Rise of Christianity**
5 **The Long Decline**

The poet Virgil wrote the epic poem the *Aeneid* to remind his fellow Romans of their great heritage. As he set out to celebrate the glories of Rome, though, he faced a dilemma. Educated Romans—the people who would read his poem—viewed Greek culture as superior to all others, including their own. After all, what Roman could match Homer's poetry or Plato's philosophy? How could Romans improve on Greek art, rhetoric, or knowledge of astronomy?

It would be best, the poet decided, to acknowledge Greek greatness at the start:

> **66**Others will . . .
>    Bring more lifelike portraits out
>       of marble;
>    Argue more eloquently, use the
>       pointer
>    To trace the paths of heaven
>       accurately
>    And accurately foretell the rising
>       stars. **99**

Having paid his debt to Greece, Virgil reminded Romans of their own special mission in the world:

> **66**Roman, remember by your strength
>       to rule
>    Earth's peoples—for your arts are to
>       be these:
>    To pacify, to impose the rule of law,
>    To spare the conquered, strike down
>       the proud. **99**

Peace, rule of law, mercy for the conquered—those were the achievements of Rome, Virgil concluded. Practical and solid, those achievements were very important indeed for the millions of people who lived under Roman rule.

From a small village, Rome grew into a superstate that stamped its decrees with the proud words "Rome, the City and the World." Rome expanded across the Mediterranean world to build a huge, ethnically diverse empire ruled by law. Rome's 1,000-year history had many lasting effects, but probably none was more important than the spread of important aspects of the civilizations of Greece, Egypt, and the Fertile Crescent westward into Europe.

**FOCUS ON** these questions as you read:

- **Political and Social Systems**
  How did Rome conquer and rule a diverse empire?

- **Global Interaction**
  How was Rome a bridge between the civilizations of east and west?

- **Religions and Value Systems**
  How did Christianity become a central institution of western civilization?

- **Continuity and Change**
  Why did Roman power fade?

## TIME AND PLACE

ARASCANTVS

*Trading Across a Vast Empire* At the height of its power, Rome ruled a vast empire stretching over much of Europe, plus parts of northern Africa and the Middle East. A flourishing trade helped spread Roman culture throughout these diverse lands. Here, a merchant ship in the Roman port of Ostia is loaded with grain. **Global Interaction** How does trade help spread culture?

## HUMANITIES LINK

*Art History* Mosaic of Nile delta scene (page 134).

*Literature* In this chapter, you will encounter passages from the following works of literature: Virgil, the *Aeneid* (page 128); Martial, "By the time the barber Eurus" (page 143); The Gospel According to Matthew (page 145); Paul's Letter to the Romans (page 146); Ovid, *The Metamorphoses* (pages 152–153).

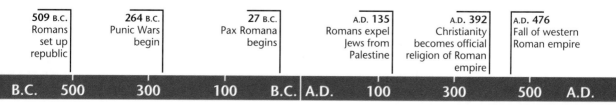

| 509 B.C. Romans set up republic | 264 B.C. Punic Wars begin | 27 B.C. Pax Romana begins | A.D. 135 Romans expel Jews from Palestine | A.D. 392 Christianity becomes official religion of Roman empire | A.D. 476 Fall of western Roman empire |

| B.C. | 500 | 300 | 100 | B.C. | A.D. | 100 | 300 | 500 | A.D. |

# 1 The Roman World Takes Shape

## Guide for Reading

- How did Italy's geography help the Romans unite the peninsula?

- How did the Roman government become more democratic?

- Why was Rome able to conquer a vast empire?

- **Vocabulary** *republic, patrician, consul, dictator, plebeian, tribune, veto, legion*

Romans loved stories about great heroes of the past. One of their favorite heroes was Horatius, who was said to have single-handedly saved Rome from an invading Etruscan army.

As the enemy approached, Horatius rushed to the far end of the bridge that led into the city. Standing alone, he held off the attackers while his fellow Romans tore down the bridge behind him. As the last timber fell, Horatius flung himself into the river below. Dodging the spears raining down all around him, he swam safely to the other side.

The story of Horatius is more legend than it is history. Still, it helps us to understand the virtues that the Romans admired. Courage, loyalty, and devotion to duty were the pillars on which Romans would build an empire.

## The Italian Landscape

Rome began as a small city-state in Italy but ended up ruling the entire Mediterranean world. The story of the Romans and how they built a world empire starts with the land they lived in.

Italy is a peninsula that looks like a boot, jutting into the Mediterranean Sea and kicking the island of Sicily toward North Africa. The peninsula is centrally located in the Mediterranean, and the city of Rome is in the center of Italy. That location helped the Romans as they expanded, first in Italy, and then into lands around the Mediterranean.

Because of its geography, Italy was much easier to unify than Greece. Unlike Greece, Italy is not broken up into small, isolated valleys. In addition, the Apennine Mountains, which run like a backbone down the length of the Italian peninsula, are less rugged than the mountains of Greece. Finally, Italy has the advantage of broad, fertile plains, both in the north under the shadow of the Alps, and in the west, where the Romans settled. These plains supported a growing population.

## Roman Beginnings

The Romans, like the Greeks, were an Indo-European people. (See page 53.) Their ancestors, the Latins, had migrated into Italy by about 800 B.C. The Latins settled along the Tiber River in small villages scattered over seven low-lying hills where they herded and farmed. Those villages would in time grow into Rome, the city on seven hills.

The Romans shared the Italian peninsula with other peoples, whose ideas they adapted. Among them were Greek colonists whose city-states dotted southern Italy and the island of Sicily. But closer neighbors, the Etruscans, who lived north of Rome, were the greatest influence.

The Etruscans, who had come from Asia Minor, ruled much of central Italy, including Rome itself. From them, the Romans learned the alphabet that the Etruscans had earlier acquired from the Greeks. They also learned to use the arch in building and adopted Etruscan engineering techniques to drain the marshy lands along the Tiber. Etruscan gods and goddesses merged with Roman deities.

## The Early Republic

The Romans drove out their hated Etruscan king in 509 B.C. This date is traditionally considered to mark the founding of the Roman state. By this time, Rome had already grown from a cluster of villages into a small city.

Determined never again to be ruled by a monarch, the Romans set up a new government in which officials were chosen by the people. They called it a republic, or "thing of the people." A republic, Romans thought, would keep any individual from gaining too much power.

Later Romans looked back with enormous pride on the achievements of the early republic. Between 509 B.C. and 133 B.C., Rome adapted its republican form of government to meet changing needs. It also developed the military power to conquer not just Italy but the entire Mediterranean world.

**The government takes shape.** In the early republic, the most powerful governing body was the senate. Its 300 members were all patricians, members of the landholding upper class. Senators, who served for life, issued decrees and interpreted the laws.

Each year, the senators elected two consuls. Their job was to supervise the business of government and command the armies. Like senators, consuls came from the patrician class. Consuls, however, could serve only one term. They were also expected to consult with the senate. By limiting their time in office and making them responsible to the people through the senate, Rome had a system of checks on the power of government.

In the event of war, the senate might choose a dictator, or ruler who has complete control over a government. Each Roman dictator was granted emergency powers to rule for six months. At the end of that time, he had to give up power. Romans admired Cincinnatus as a model dictator. As he plowed his fields, a messenger arrived to tell him he had been chosen dictator. Cincinnatus left his plow, organized an army, led the Romans to victory over the attacking enemy, attended victory celebrations, and returned to his fields—all within 16 days.

As Rome grew, it elected other officials to oversee finances, justice, city government, and religious matters. A government censor kept an accurate list of citizens, or census.

**Plebeians demand equality.** At first, all government officials were patricians. Plebeians (plih BEE uhnz), the farmers, merchants, artisans, and traders who made up the bulk of the population, had little influence. The efforts of the plebeians to pry open the doors to power shaped politics in the early republic.

The plebeians' first breakthrough came in 450 B.C., when the government had the laws of Rome inscribed on 12 tablets and set up in the Forum, or marketplace. Plebeians had protested that citizens could not know what the laws

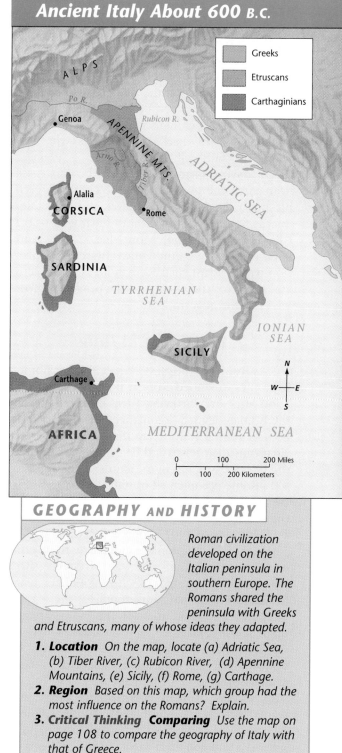

## Ancient Italy About 600 B.C.

Greeks
Etruscans
Carthaginians

### GEOGRAPHY AND HISTORY

Roman civilization developed on the Italian peninsula in southern Europe. The Romans shared the peninsula with Greeks and Etruscans, many of whose ideas they adapted.

1. **Location** On the map, locate (a) Adriatic Sea, (b) Tiber River, (c) Rubicon River, (d) Apennine Mountains, (e) Sicily, (f) Rome, (g) Carthage.
2. **Region** Based on this map, which group had the most influence on the Romans? Explain.
3. **Critical Thinking** **Comparing** Use the map on page 108 to compare the geography of Italy with that of Greece.

were, because they were not written down. The Laws of the Twelve Tables made it possible for the first time for plebeians to appeal a judgment handed down by a patrician judge.

In time, the plebeians gained the right to elect their own officials, called tribunes, to protect their interests. The tribunes could veto, or block, those laws that they felt were harmful to plebeians. Little by little, plebeians forced the senate to choose plebeians as consuls, appoint plebeians to other high offices, and finally to open the senate itself to plebeians who had served the state well.

**A lasting legacy.** Although the senate still dominated the government, the common people had gained access to power and won safeguards for their rights without having to resort to war or revolution. More than 2,000 years later, the framers of the United States Constitution would adapt such Roman ideas as the senate, the veto, and checks on the power of those who run the government.

## Expansion in Italy

As Rome's political system evolved at home, its armies expanded Roman power across Italy. Soon after overthrowing their Etruscan rulers, the Romans gained dominance over their neighbors in central Italy. They then conquered the Etruscans themselves and began moving against the Greek city-states in the south. By about 270 B.C., Rome occupied all of Italy, from the Rubicon River in the north to the tip of the boot in the south.

**Masters of war.** Rome's success was due partly to skillful diplomacy and partly to its efficient, well-disciplined army. As in Greece, Roman armies consisted of citizen-soldiers who fought without pay and supplied their own weapons. The basic unit was the legion, made up of about 5,000 men.

Well trained in military skills and brought up to value loyalty and courage, Roman soldiers chalked up a series of brilliant victories. To ensure success, Roman commanders mixed rewards with harsh punishment. Young soldiers who showed courage in action won praise and gifts. If a unit fled from battle, however, 1 out of every 10 men from the disgraced unit was put to death.

**Conquered lands.** Rome generally treated its defeated enemies with justice. Conquered peoples had to acknowledge Roman leadership, pay taxes, and supply soldiers for the Roman army. In return, Rome let them keep their own customs, money, and local government.

To a few privileged groups among the conquered people, Rome gave the highly prized right of full citizenship. Others became partial citizens, who were allowed to marry Romans and carry on trade in the growing city on the Tiber. Such generous treatment created support for Rome, and even in troubled times most of the conquered lands remained loyal.

To protect its conquests, Rome posted soldiers throughout the land. It also built a network of all-weather military roads to link distant provinces to Rome. As trade and travel increased, local peoples incorporated Latin into their languages and adopted many Roman customs and beliefs. Slowly, Italy began to unite under Roman rule.

## Rivalry With Carthage

Rome's conquest of the Italian peninsula brought it into contact with a new rival, Carthage. Carthage was a city-state on the northern coast of Africa, in present-day Tunisia. Settled by Phoenician traders, it ruled over a trading empire that stretched across North Africa and the western Mediterranean. As Rome spread into the Mediterranean, conflict between these two powers became inevitable.

Between 264 B.C. and 146 B.C., Rome fought three wars against Carthage. They are called the Punic Wars, from *punicus,* the Latin word for Phoenician. In the First Punic War, Rome defeated Carthage, forcing it to surrender Sicily, Corsica, and Sardinia. Peace was short-lived, however. Carthage was seething with rage at its loss, and 23 years later, led by a general named Hannibal, it sought revenge.

## War With Hannibal

According to legend, when Hannibal was nine, his father, the general Hamilcar Barca, had him take a sacred oath. Leading the young boy to the altar of the gods, Hamilcar made him swear himself "an enemy of the Roman people." From that moment, Hannibal dedicated his life to the destruction of Rome.

**A daring expedition.** Several years after his father's death, Hannibal was selected as leader of the Carthaginian army. He commanded a mixed force of troops from Europe and North Africa. Although they had no language or customs in common, reported a historian, "the skill of the commander was such that these great differences did not disturb their obedience to his will."

In 218 B.C., Hannibal embarked on one of the most daring military expeditions in history. Setting out from Spain, he led his troops, including dozens of war elephants, in a march across the Pyrenees, through France, and over the mighty peaks of the Alps into Italy. The Roman historian Livy (LIHV ee) described the descent down the Alps' steep slopes:

> 66The whole way was narrow and slippery, so that the soldiers could not prevent their feet from sliding, nor, if they made the least false step could they, on falling, stop themselves in the placc; and thus mcn and beasts tumbled confusedly over one another. . . . Whenever they attempted to rise, either by aid of the hands or knees, these slipping, they fell again; add to this, that there were neither stumps nor roots within reach, on which they could lean for support; so that they wallowed in the melted snow on one entire surface of slippery ice.99

The trek across the Alps lasted 15 days and cost Hannibal nearly half his army and almost all his elephants. Still, the Carthaginian general had achieved his goal. The Romans had expected an invasion from the south, through Sicily. The bold attack through the Alps caught them completely off guard.

**Battle for Italy.** For 15 years, Hannibal and his army moved across Italy, winning battle after battle in the Second Punic War. The Carthaginians, however, were never able to capture Rome itself. In the end, the Romans outflanked Hannibal by sending an army to attack Carthage. Hannibal returned to defend his homeland, and at the battle of Zama, the Romans defeated him at last.

Under the peace terms ending the war, Carthage gave up all its lands except those in Africa. It also had to pay a huge tribute, or tax, to Rome. For the Romans, however, the most important result of the Second Punic War was that they were now masters of the western Mediterranean.

**Death of Hannibal.** At first, the Romans allowed Hannibal to remain free after the war, and under his leadership, Carthage made a rapid recovery. However, the Romans still feared the Carthaginian general and accused him of plotting with their enemies. Learning of these charges, Hannibal fled to the east. When the Romans tracked him down, he took poison rather than surrender to his hated enemy.

**Carthage destroyed.** Hannibal was dead and Carthage kept to the terms of the peace. Rome, however, still saw Carthage as a rival. Besides, Romans would never forgive the terrible destruction that Hannibal's army had brought to Italy. For years, Cato, a wealthy senator, ended every speech he made with the words "Carthage must be destroyed."

In the end, Rome attacked and completely destroyed the 700-year-old city. Survivors were killed or sold into slavery. The Romans poured salt over the earth so that nothing would grow there again. Carthage and the region surrounding it became the new Roman province of Africa. ◼

*War Elephants* *War elephants, like the one painted on this Roman dish, trampled and crashed through enemy lines. From a tower on the elephant's back, soldiers rained arrows and spears on fleeing enemies. Hannibal hoped his war elephants would terrify Roman armies.* **Global Interaction** *Why might elephants have been more surprising and terrifying to Roman soldiers than to African and Asian soldiers?*

**Mosaic of Nile Delta Scene** Like the Greeks before them, Roman artists decorated walls, floors, and ceilings with multicolored mosaics. Each mosaic consisted of thousands of tiny stone and glass pieces. This detail from a mosaic of the first century B.C. re-creates a scene in Roman Egypt. **Diversity** How does the mosaic show the diversity that existed within the Roman empire?

## Ruler of the Mediterranean World

"The Carthaginians fought for their own preservation and the sovereignty of Africa," observed a Greek witness to the fall of Carthage; "the Romans, for supremacy and world domination." While Rome fought Carthage in the west, it was also expanding into the eastern Mediterranean. There, Romans confronted the Hellenistic rulers who had divided up the empire of Alexander the Great.

Sometimes to defend Roman interests, sometimes simply for plunder, Rome launched a series of wars in the area. One by one, it brought Macedonia, Greece, and parts of Asia Minor under its rule. Other regions, like Egypt, allied with Rome. By 133 B.C., Roman power extended from Spain to Egypt. Truly, the Romans were justified in calling the Mediterranean *Mare Nostrum*—"Our Sea."

## SECTION 1 REVIEW

1. **Identify** (a) senate, (b) Laws of the Twelve Tables, (c) Punic Wars, (d) Hannibal.
2. **Define** (a) republic, (b) patrician, (c) consul, (d) dictator, (e) plebeian, (f) tribune, (g) veto, (h) legion.
3. Describe two ways that the geography of Italy influenced the rise of Rome.
4. (a) Why were plebeians discontented during the early republic? (b) What reforms did they win?
5. *Critical Thinking* **Linking Past and Present** Roman heroes were admired for their courage, loyalty, and devotion to duty. What qualities do American heroes display?
6. *ACTIVITY* Write a series of newspaper headlines announcing the major events in the rise of Rome.

# 2 From Republic to Empire

## Guide for Reading

- How did winning an empire affect Rome?
- Why did the Roman republic decline?
- What were the strengths and weaknesses of the Roman empire?

The historian Appian, who lived in Alexandria about A.D. 150, wrote about the declining years of the Roman republic. Conquering an empire, he noted, had created strains and conflicts in Roman society:

> 66The powerful ones became enormously rich and the race of slaves multiplied throughout the country, while the Italian people dwindled in numbers and strength, being oppressed by poverty, taxes, and military service.99

In the end, the triumphant Romans tore their state apart. Ambitious generals battled for power, and their struggles crushed the republic. Out of the rubble rose the Roman empire and a new chapter in Rome's long history.

## Effects of Expansion

Romans gloried in their successes as they set out to rule the newly acquired provinces. Victory put them in control of busy trade routes, and incredible riches flooded into Rome from the conquered lands. Generals, officials, and traders amassed fortunes from loot, taxes, and commerce. This newly found wealth, however, had disturbing consequences.

**Social and economic consequences.** A new class of wealthy Romans emerged. They built lavish mansions and filled them with luxuries imported from the east. Wealthy families bought up huge estates, called latifundia, which were worked by slaves captured in war.

The widespread use of slave labor hurt small farmers, who were unable to produce food as cheaply as the latifundia could. The farmers' problems were compounded when huge quantities of grain pouring in from the conquered lands drove down grain prices. Many farmers fell into debt and had to sell their land.

In despair, landless farmers flocked to Rome and other cities looking for jobs. There, they joined a restless class of unemployed people. As the gap between rich and poor widened, ambitious men aroused angry mobs to riot.

The new wealth also increased corruption. Greed and self-interest replaced virtues such as simplicity, hard work, and devotion to duty so prized in the early republic.

**Attempts at reform.** Two young patricians, brothers named Tiberius and Gaius Gracchus (GAY uhs GRAK uhs), were among the first to attempt reform. Tiberius, who was elected a tribune in 133 B.C., called on the state to distribute land to poor farmers. He described their plight in moving words:

> 66Even the wild beasts that roam over Italy have a cave to sleep in, but the men who fight and die for Rome enjoy only the air and light, nothing else. They and their wives and children wander about homeless.99

Gaius, elected tribune 10 years later, sought a wider range of reforms, including the use of public funds to buy grain to feed the poor. He also called for extension of full citizenship to some of Rome's allies.

The reforms of the Gracchus brothers angered the senate, which saw them as a threat to its power. The brothers, along with thousands of their followers, were killed in waves of street violence set off by senators and their hired thugs.

**A century of civil war.** The slayings of the Gracchus brothers showed that the republic was unable to resolve its problems peacefully. During the next 100 years, Rome was plunged into a series of civil wars. At issue was who should hold power—the senate, which wanted to govern as it had in the past, or popular political leaders, who wanted to weaken the senate and enact reforms.

The turmoil sparked slave uprisings and revolts among Rome's allies. At the same time, the endless warfare transformed the old legions

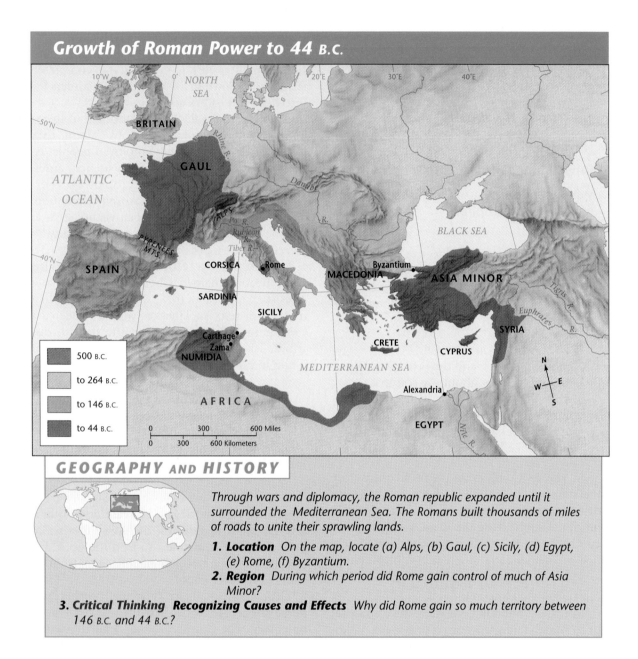

## Growth of Roman Power to 44 B.C.

**Legend:**
- 500 B.C.
- to 264 B.C.
- to 146 B.C.
- to 44 B.C.

0 300 600 Miles
0 300 600 Kilometers

### GEOGRAPHY AND HISTORY

*Through wars and diplomacy, the Roman republic expanded until it surrounded the Mediterranean Sea. The Romans built thousands of miles of roads to unite their sprawling lands.*

**1. Location** On the map, locate (a) Alps, (b) Gaul, (c) Sicily, (d) Egypt, (e) Rome, (f) Byzantium.

**2. Region** During which period did Rome gain control of much of Asia Minor?

**3. Critical Thinking Recognizing Causes and Effects** Why did Rome gain so much territory between 146 B.C. and 44 B.C.?

of citizen-soldiers into highly organized professional armies whose first loyalty was to their commanders. Spurred by their successes abroad, rival generals marched their armies into Rome to advance their ambitions.

### Caesar's Bid for Power

Out of this chaos emerged Julius Caesar, an able commander who combined soaring ambition with a determination to make drastic reforms. For a time, Caesar dominated Roman politics with Pompey, one of Rome's most bril-

liant generals. Then, in 59 B.C., Caesar set out with his army to make new conquests. After nine years of almost constant fighting, he succeeded in bringing all of Gaul—the area that is now France—under Roman control.

**Crossing the Rubicon.** Back home, Pompey grew jealous of Caesar's successes and fearful of his rising fame. He had the senate order Caesar to disband his army and return to Rome.

Caesar decided to defy the order. Acting swiftly and secretly, he led his army across the Rubicon River into northern Italy and then headed toward Rome. With this act, which was considered treason, he committed himself to a life-and-death struggle from which there was no turning back.

Once again, civil war erupted across the empire. Caesar crushed Pompey and his supporters. He then swept around the Mediterranean, suppressing rebellious provinces and strengthening Roman power. "*Veni, vidi, vici*"—"I came, I saw, I conquered"—he announced briefly after one victory. Later, returning to Rome, he forced the senate to make him dictator. Although he kept the senate and other features of the republic, he was in fact the absolute ruler of Rome.

**Caesar's reforms.** Between 48 B.C. and 44 B.C., Caesar pushed through a number of reforms intended to deal with Rome's many problems. He launched a program of public works to employ the jobless and gave public land to the poor. He also reorganized the government of the provinces and granted Roman citizenship to more people. To enact these reforms, however, he packed the senate with his own followers.

Caesar's most lasting reform was the introduction of a new calendar based on Egyptian knowledge. The Julian calendar, as it was later called, was used in western Europe for nearly 1,600 years, and with minor changes is still our calendar today.

**The Ides of March.** Caesar's enemies worried that he planned to make himself king of Rome. In order to save the republic, they plotted against him.

According to legend, early in the year 44 B.C., a fortune-teller warned Caesar to "beware the Ides of March," as the Romans called March 15. The day arrived and nothing happened. "The Ides of March have come," Caesar called out mockingly to the fortune-teller. "They have come," the man replied, "but not yet gone." Moments later, as he arrived in the senate, Caesar's enemies stabbed him to death.

The death of Julius Caesar plunged Rome into a new round of civil wars. Mark Antony, Caesar's chief general, and Octavian, Caesar's grandnephew, joined forces to hunt down the murderers. The two men soon quarreled, however, and a

▲ *Julius Caesar*

bitter struggle for power ensued. In 31 B.C., Octavian finally defeated Antony and his powerful ally Queen Cleopatra of Egypt.

**End of the republic.** The senate proclaimed the triumphant Octavian *Augustus,* or Exalted One, and declared him *princeps,* or first citizen. Although he was careful not to call himself king, a title that Romans had hated since Etruscan times, Augustus exercised absolute power and named his successor, just as a king would do.

Under Augustus, who ruled from 31 B.C. to A.D. 14, the 500-year-old republic came to an end. Romans did not know it at the time, but a new age had dawned—the age of the Roman empire.

## Imperial Rome

Through firm but moderate policies, Augustus helped Rome recover from the long period of civil war. At the same time, he laid the foundation for a stable government.

**A stable government.** While he left the senate in place, Augustus created an efficient, well-trained civil service charged with enforcing the laws. High-level jobs were open to men of talent, regardless of their class. In addition, he cemented the allegiance of cities and provinces to Rome by allowing them a large measure of self-government.

Augustus undertook economic reforms, too. To make the tax system more fair, he ordered a census, or population count, to be taken in the empire. He set up a postal service and issued new coins to make trade easier. He put the jobless to work building roads and temples and sent others to farm the land.

The government that Augustus organized functioned well for 200 years. Still, a serious problem kept arising: Who would rule after an emperor died? Romans did not accept the idea of power passing automatically from father to son. Consequently, the death of an emperor often led to intrigue and violence.

**Bad emperors and good emperors.** Not all of Augustus' successors were great rulers. Indeed, some were weak and incompetent.

Two early emperors, Caligula and Nero, were downright evil and perhaps insane. Caligula, for example, appointed his favorite horse as consul. Nero viciously persecuted Christians and was even blamed for setting a great fire that destroyed much of Rome.

Between A.D. 96 and A.D. 180, the empire benefited from the rule of a series of "good emperors." The emperor Hadrian, for example, codified Roman law, making it the same for all provinces. He also had soldiers build a wall across Britain to hold back attackers from the non-Roman north. You can still walk along Hadrian's Wall on the border between England and Scotland.

The emperor Marcus Aurelius, who read philosophy while on military campaigns, was close to Plato's ideal of a philosopher-king. His *Meditations* show his Stoic philosophy and commitment to duty: "Hour by hour resolve firmly . . .to do what comes to hand with correct and natural dignity."

## The Roman Peace

The 200-year span that began with Augustus and ended with Marcus Aurelius is known as the period of the Pax Romana, or "Roman Peace." During that time, Roman rule brought peace, order, unity, and prosperity to lands stretching from the Euphrates River in the east to Britain in the west, an area equal in size to the continental United States.

The Pax Romana created "a world every day better known, better cultivated, and more civilized than before," glowed one Roman writer. He went on to detail the many benefits of Roman civilization:

> ❝Everywhere roads are traced, every district is known, every country opened to commerce. Smiling fields have invaded the forests . . . the rocks are planted, the marshes drained. There are now as many cities as there were once solitary cottages. Reefs and shoals have lost their terrors. Wherever there is a trace of life, there are houses, well-ordered governments and civilized life.❞

With legions to maintain the roads and fleets to chase pirates from the seas, trade flowed freely to and from distant lands in Africa, India, and China. Egyptian farmers in the Nile Valley supplied Romans with grain. From other parts of Africa came ivory and gold, as well as lions and other wild animals that were used in public entertainments. From India came spices, cotton, and precious stones. Traveling the great Silk Road, caravans brought exotic goods from China. Iranian merchants, successors to the Persians, were a key link in this long-distance trade between the Mediterranean and Asia.

People, too, flowed across the Roman empire, spreading ideas and knowledge, especially the advances of the Hellenistic east. As you will read, ideas from Greece and Palestine would have tremendous impact on Rome and the western world.

## Family and Religion

The family was the basic unit of Roman society. Under Roman law, the male head of the household, usually the father, had absolute power in the family. He enforced strict discipline and demanded total respect for his authority. His wife was subject to his authority and was not allowed to administer her own affairs.

**Changing role of women.** The ideal Roman woman was loving, dutiful, dignified, and strong. During the late republic and early empire, however, women gained greater freedom.

Patrician women, especially, played a larger role in society than did Greek women. They went to the public baths, dined out, and attended the theater or other public entertainments with their husbands. Some imperial women, such as Livia and Agrippina the Younger, had highly visible public roles and exercised significant political influence.

GLOBAL CONNECTIONS

India was one of Rome's major trading partners. Wealthy Romans dyed their finest purple robes with indigo from India. Indian traders also provided elephants, lions, and tigers to perform in Rome's wild animal shows. For their part, wealthy Indians prized Roman gold, wine, and manufactured goods.

# PARALLELS THROUGH TIME

## Hairstyles

The art of hairstyling goes back at least 3,500 years, to the ancient Assyrians. They viewed elaborately shaped hair as a sign of wealth and social position, for both men and women. Since then, every society and every generation have evolved their own unique styles.

**Linking Past and Present**  Does Ovid's comment below about fashions in ancient Rome apply to American society today? Explain.

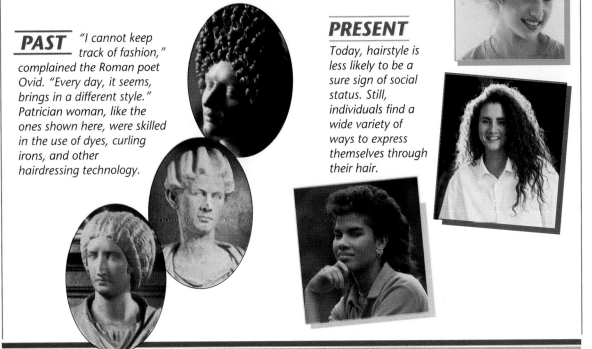

**PAST**  *"I cannot keep track of fashion,"* complained the Roman poet Ovid. *"Every day, it seems, brings in a different style."* Patrician woman, like the ones shown here, were skilled in the use of dyes, curling irons, and other hairdressing technology.

**PRESENT**  *Today, hairstyle is less likely to be a sure sign of social status. Still, individuals find a wide variety of ways to express themselves through their hair.*

---

Women from all classes ran a variety of businesses, from small shops to major shipyards. Those who made their fortunes earned respect by supporting the arts or paying for public festivals. Most women, though, worked at home, raising their families, spinning, and weaving. This memorial pays tribute to an unknown woman named Claudia:

&#10077;This is the unlovely tomb of a lovely woman. Her parents named her Claudia. She loved her husband with her whole heart. She bore two sons, one of whom she leaves on Earth; the other she has placed beneath the ground. She was charming in conversation, yet her conduct was appropriate. She kept house; she made wool.&#10078;

**Education.** Girls and boys alike learned to read and write. Even lower-class Romans were taught to write, as can be seen from the jokes, messages, and other graffiti that archaeologists found scrawled on walls around the city.

By the late republic, many wealthy Romans were hiring private tutors, often Greek slaves, to teach their children. Under their guidance, children memorized major events and developments in Roman history. Rhetoric was an important subject for boys who wanted political careers.

**Religion.** Roman gods and goddesses resembled those of the Etruscans and Greeks. Like the Greek god Zeus, the Roman god Jupiter ruled over the sky and the other gods. Juno, his wife, like the Greek goddess Hera, protected marriage. Romans also prayed to

*Chapter 6*  **139**

**Chariot Race** Speed thrilled the fans who crowded into the Circus Maximus for chariot races. Crashes and bloody collisions added even more excitement. The poet Martial once complained that the names of winning horses and charioteers were legendary among the masses, while his own name remained virtually unknown. **Religions and Value Systems** What does Martial's comment suggest about Roman values at the time?

Neptune, god of the sea, whose powers were the same as those of the Greek god Poseidon. On the battlefield, they turned to Mars, the god of war.

The Roman calendar was full of feasts and other celebrations to honor the gods and to ensure divine favor for the city. As loyal citizens, Romans joined in these festivals, which inspired a sense of community.

"Mystery" religions not associated with the official state gods were also popular, especially with women. For example, the cult of Isis, which originated in Egypt, promised life after death and offered women equal status with men. Becoming a priest in such a cult was a way in which a woman could achieve high office.

## Bread and Circuses

Rich and poor alike loved spectacular entertainments. At the Circus Maximus, Rome's largest racecourse, chariots thundered around an oval course, making dangerously tight turns at either end. Fans bet feverishly on their favorite teams—the Reds, Greens, Blues, or Whites—and successful charioteers were hailed as heroes.

Gladiator contests were even more popular. Many gladiators were slaves who had been trained to fight. Led into the arena, they battled one another, either singly or in groups. Crowds cheered a skilled gladiator, and a good fighter might even win his freedom. But if a gladiator made a poor showing, the crowd turned thumbs down, a signal that he should be killed.

To the emperors who paid for them with the taxes they collected from the empire, these amusements were a way to control the city's restless mobs. In much the same spirit, the government provided free grain to feed the poor. Critics warned against this policy of "bread and circuses," but no one listened.

During the Pax Romana, the general prosperity hid underlying social and economic problems. Later Roman emperors, however, would face problems that could not be brushed away with "bread and circuses."

## SECTION 2 REVIEW

1. **Identify** (a) Tiberius and Gaius Gracchus, (b) Julius Caesar, (c) Augustus, (d) Hadrian, (e) Pax Romana, (f) Circus Maximus.
2. Describe three ways in which empire building affected the Roman republic.
3. What problems did the republic face after the deaths of the Gracchus brothers?
4. (a) What reforms did Julius Caesar undertake? (b) Why did some Romans oppose him?
5. *Critical Thinking* **Analyzing Information** How do you think the founders of the Roman republic would have viewed the Roman empire? Explain.
6. *ACTIVITY* Imagine that you are one of the plotters against Julius Caesar. Create a political cartoon that shows why you oppose him.

# 3 The Roman Achievement

## Guide for Reading

- How did Roman art and literature blend different traditions?

- What were Rome's greatest practical achievements?

- What principles of law did Romans develop?

- **Vocabulary** *aqueduct*

Marcus Tullius Cicero was a philosopher, politician, essayist, orator, and passionate defender of the law. As the republic declined, Cicero attacked ambitious leaders such as Julius Caesar. When Caesar won power, he forgave Cicero for his attack, noting that his critic's contributions were greater than his own:

> 66 How much greater and more glorious to have enlarged the limits of the Roman mind than the boundaries of Roman rule. 99

Caesar was modest about the impact of his own deeds. Through war and conquest, he and other Roman generals spread the Latin language and carried Roman civilization to distant lands. Yet the civilization that developed was not simply Roman. Rather, it blended Greek, Hellenistic, and Roman achievements.

## Greco-Roman Civilization

In its early days, Rome absorbed ideas from Greek colonists in southern Italy, and it continued to borrow heavily from Greek culture after it conquered Greece. To the Romans emerging from their villages, Greek art, literature, philosophy, and scientific genius represented the height of cultural achievement. Their admiration never wavered, leading the Roman poet Horace to note, "Greece has conquered her rude conqueror."

Over time, Romans adapted and transformed Greek and Hellenistic achievements, just as the Greeks had once absorbed and blended ideas and beliefs from Egypt and the Fertile Crescent. The blending of Greek, Hellenistic, and Roman traditions produced what is known as Greco-Roman civilization. Trade and travel during the Pax Romana helped spread this vital new civilization.

**Art.** In the field of art, the Romans owed a great debt to the Greeks. They imported shiploads of Greek statues to decorate their homes, gardens, and public buildings. Roman sculptors adapted the realism of Hellenistic works, portraying their subjects with every wart and vein in place. They also broke new ground, however, with portraits in stone or on coins that revealed an individual's character. A statue of a soldier, a writer, or an emperor might capture an expression of smugness, discontent, or haughty pride.

Some Roman sculpture was more idealistic, like the classic Greek statues of gods and athletes. Sculptors, for example, transformed Augustus, who was neither handsome nor imposing, into a symbol of power and leadership.

▲ *Sculpture of a Roman senator*

**Architecture.** From England to Spain to North Africa to the Middle East, you can see Roman buildings that combine both Greek and Roman elements and ideas. Roman builders used Greek columns, but where the Greeks aimed for simple elegance, the Romans emphasized grandeur. Immense palaces, temples, stadiums, and victory arches stood as mighty monuments to Roman power and dignity.

The Romans improved on devices such as the arch and the dome, which could roof large spaces. The most famous domed structure is the Pantheon, a temple to all the Roman gods, which still stands in Rome. The Romans also introduced new kinds of buildings, such as the Baths of Caracalla, an enormous structure whose vaulted roofs were supported by arches.

**Engineering.** The Romans excelled in the practical arts of building, perfecting their engineering skills as they built roads, bridges, and harbors throughout the empire. Roman roads

**Roman Engineering**
Roman engineers built this bridge, road, and aqueduct across the Gardon River in France. The road stretches across the lowest tier of arches. The aqueduct, a concrete channel that carried fresh water to the town of Nimes, sits atop the entire structure. **Economics and Technology** What natural force caused aqueduct water to flow from highlands down to Roman towns?

were so solidly built that many of them remained in use long after Rome fell.

Roman engineers built many immense aqueducts, or bridgelike stone structures that brought water from the hills into Roman cities. In Segovia, Spain, a Roman aqueduct still carries water along a stone channel supported by tiers of arches.

The availability of fresh water was important to the Romans. Wealthy homes had water piped in, and almost every city boasted both female and male public baths. Here, people gathered not only to wash themselves but to hear the latest news and exchange gossip.

**Science.** The Romans generally left scientific research to the Greeks, who were by that time citizens of the empire. Alexandria, Egypt, remained a center of learning, where Hellenistic scientists exchanged ideas freely. It was in Alexandria that astronomer-mathematician Ptolemy (TAHL uh mee) proposed his theory that the Earth was the center of the universe, an idea that was accepted in the western world for nearly 1,500 years.

The Greek doctor Galen advanced the frontiers of medical science by insisting on experiments to prove a conclusion. He confessed that "the disease from which I have suffered all my life is to trust . . . no statements until, so far as

possible, I have tested them for myself." Galen compiled a medical encyclopedia summarizing what was known at the time. It remained the standard text for more than 1,000 years.

While the Romans rarely did original scientific investigations, they did put science to practical use. They applied geography to make maps, and medical knowledge to help doctors improve public health. Like Galen, they collected knowledge into encyclopedias. Pliny the Elder, a Roman scientist, compiled volumes on geography, zoology, botany, and other topics, all based on other people's works. In A.D. 79, Pliny's eagerness for knowledge led to his death. He ventured too close to Mount Vesuvius, a volcano that was erupting near Pompeii in southern Italy, and was suffocated by volcanic gases. (★ See *Skills for Success*, page 154.)

## Literature, Philosophy, and History

In literature, too, educated Romans admired the Greeks. Many spoke Greek and imitated Greek styles in prose and poetry. Still, the greatest Roman writers used Latin to create their own literature.

**Poetry.** In his epic poem the *Aeneid*, Virgil tried to show that Rome's past was as heroic as that of Greece. (See page 128.) He linked his epic to Homer's work by telling how Aeneas escaped from Troy to found Rome. Virgil wrote the *Aeneid* soon after Augustus came to power. He hoped it would arouse patriotism and help unite Rome after years of civil wars. Another poet, Ovid, also linked Rome to Greece by retelling tales of Greek and Roman gods. (📖 See *World Literature,* "The Metamorphoses," pages 152–153.)

Roman writers like Horace or Juvenal used verse to satirize, or make fun of, Roman society. In the following verse, the poet Martial laughs at chatty barbers:

> **66** By the time the barber Eurus
> Had circled Lupo's face,
> A second beard had sprouted,
> In the first one's place. **99**

**Historians.** Roman historians pursued their own theme—the rise and fall of Roman power. Like the poet Virgil, the historian Livy sought to rouse patriotic feeling and restore traditional Roman virtues by recalling images of Rome's heroic past. In his history of Rome, Livy recounted tales of great heroes such as Horatius and Cincinnatus.

Another historian, Tacitus, wrote bitterly about Augustus and his successors, who, he felt, had destroyed Roman liberty. He admired the simple culture of the Germans who lived on Rome's northern frontier and would later invade the empire.

**Philosophers.** Romans borrowed much of their philosophy from the Greeks. The Hellenistic philosophy of Stoicism impressed Roman thinkers like the emperor Marcus Aurelius. Stoics stressed the importance of duty and acceptance of one's fate. They also showed concern for the well-being of all people, an idea that would be reflected in Christian teachings. (See page 145.)

## Roman Law

"Let justice be done," proclaimed a Roman saying, "though the heavens fall!" Probably the greatest legacy of Rome was its commitment to the rule of law and to justice—ideas that have shaped western civilization to today.

**Two systems.** During the republic, Rome developed a system of law, known as the civil law, that applied to its citizens. As Rome expanded, however, it ruled many foreigners who were not covered under the civil law. Gradually, a second system of law, known as the law of nations, emerged. It applied to all people under Roman rule, citizens and noncitizens. Later, when Rome extended citizenship across the empire, the two systems merged.

During the Roman empire, the rule of law fostered unity and stability. Many centuries later, the principles of Roman law would become the basis for legal systems in Europe and Latin America.

**Common principles.** As Roman law developed, certain basic principles evolved. Many of these principles are familiar to Americans today. Among them are these ideas:

1. People of the same status are equal before the law.
2. An accused person is presumed innocent until proven guilty.
3. The accused should be allowed to face his or her accuser and defend against the charge.
4. Guilt must be established "clearer than daylight" through evidence.
5. Decisions should be based on fairness, allowing judges to interpret the law.

## SECTION 3 REVIEW

1. **Identify** (a) Greco-Roman civilization, (b) Pantheon, (c) Pliny, (d) Virgil, (e) Livy, (f) civil law, (g) law of nations.
2. **Define** aqueduct.
3. How did Roman conquests lead to the birth of a new civilization?
4. Give an example to show how Roman art blended different traditions.
5. What practical skills did Romans develop?
6. *Critical Thinking* **Linking Past and Present** Give two examples of how the principles of law developed by Rome affect life in the United States today.
7. *ACTIVITY* Create a design for a Roman coin celebrating an important achievement of Greco-Roman civilization.

# 4 The Rise of Christianity

## Guide for Reading

- What attitude did Rome take toward the different religions in its empire?
- What was the basic message of Jesus?
- Why did Christianity spread despite persecution?
- **Vocabulary** *messiah, sect, martyr, bishop, pope, heresy*

Early in the Pax Romana, a new religion, Christianity, sprang up in a distant corner of the Roman empire. At first, Christianity was just one of many religions practiced in the empire. But despite many obstacles, the new faith grew rapidly, and by A.D. 392, it had been declared the official religion of the Roman empire.

As it gained strength, Christianity reshaped Roman beliefs. And when the Roman empire fell, the Christian Church took over its role, becoming the central institution of western civilization for nearly 1,000 years.

## Jews and the Roman Empire

Generally, Rome tolerated the varied religious traditions of its culturally diverse empire. As long as citizens showed their loyalty by honoring the gods of Rome and acknowledging the divine spirit of the emperor, they were allowed to worship as they pleased. Since most people at the time were polytheistic, they were content to worship the Roman gods along with their own.

**Deep divisions arise.** Among the peoples in the empire were the Jews. By 63 B.C., the Romans had conquered Palestine, where most Jews of the time lived, and made it into the province of Judea. As with other citizens of the empire, the Romans tolerated the Jews' religion. They even excused the Jews from worshiping Roman gods. They knew that to do so would violate the Jewish faith, which was based on belief in one God.

Among the Jews themselves, however, religious ferment was creating deep divisions. During the Hellenistic age, many Jews absorbed Greek customs and ideas. Concerned about the weakening of their religion, Jewish reformers rejected these influences and called for strict obedience to Jewish laws and traditions.

The turmoil had a political side, too. While Jewish priests struggled to preserve their religion, other Jews, called Zealots, had a different mission. They called on Jews to revolt against Rome and reestablish an independent Israel. Some Jews believed that a messiah, or savior sent by God, would soon appear to lead the Jewish people to freedom.

**Revolt and expulsion.** In A.D. 66, discontent flared into rebellion. Roman forces crushed the rebels, captured Jerusalem, and destroyed the Jewish temple. When revolts broke out again in the next century, Roman armies leveled Jerusalem. In A.D. 135, they drove the Jews out of their homeland and forbade them to return. As you recall, this scattering of the Jews is known as the diaspora.

Although they were defeated in their efforts to regain political independence, Jews survived in scattered communities around the Mediterranean. Over the centuries, Jewish rabbis, or scholars, extended and preserved the religious law, known as the Talmud. In the late 1800s, some Jews took steps to rebuild an independent Jewish state in Palestine, as you will read in Chapter 24.

## The Life of Jesus

As turmoil engulfed the Jews in Palestine, a new religion, Christianity, rose among them. Its founder was a Jew named Jesus.

What little we know about the life of Jesus comes from the Gospels, accounts written by four of his followers. Jesus was born around 4 B.C. in Bethlehem, near Jerusalem, to a family descended from King David. According to the Gospels, an angel had told Jesus' mother, Mary, that she would give birth to the messiah. "He will be great," said the angel, "and will be called the Son of the Most High God."

Growing up, Jesus worshiped the Jewish God and followed Jewish law. As a young man, he worked as a carpenter. Then, at the age of 30, he began preaching to the villagers near the Sea of Galilee. Large crowds gathered to hear his message, especially when word spread that he had performed miracles of healing. After three years, Jesus and his disciples, or loyal followers, traveled to Jerusalem to spread his teachings.

**The message.** The teachings of Jesus were firmly rooted in the Jewish religion. He believed in one God and accepted the Ten Commandments that God had given to the Jews. Jesus preached strict obedience to the law of Moses and defended the teachings of the Jewish prophets.

At the same time, Jesus preached new beliefs. According to his followers, he called himself the Son of God and declared that he was the messiah whose appearance Jews had long predicted. His mission, he proclaimed, was to bring spiritual salvation and eternal life to anyone who would believe in him. In the Sermon on the Mount, Jesus summed up his ethical message, which echoed Jewish ideas of mercy and sympathy for the poor and helpless:

> ❝Blessed are the meek, for they shall inherit the Earth. . . .
> Blessed are the merciful, for they will be shown mercy. . . .
> Blessed are the peacemakers, for they will be called the children of God.❞

Jesus rejected the principle of "an eye for an eye." Instead, he preached forgiveness. "Love your enemies," he told his followers. "If anyone hits you on one cheek, let him hit the other one, too."

**Death on the cross.** Some Jews welcomed Jesus to Jerusalem. Others, however, regarded him as a dangerous troublemaker. Jewish priests, in particular, felt that he was challenging their leadership. To the Roman authorities, Jesus was a revolutionary who might lead the Jews in a rebellion against Roman rule.

Jesus was betrayed by one of his disciples. Arrested by the Romans, he was tried, condemned, and executed Roman-style—nailed to a cross and left to die of shock, loss of blood, and exposure.

Jesus' disciples were thrown into confusion. But then rumors spread through Jerusalem that Jesus was not dead at all. His disciples, the Gospels say, saw and talked with Jesus, who had risen from the dead. He commanded them

**Jesus Healing a Woman** *Jesus promised everlasting life to all who accepted his teachings. Belief in the saving power of Jesus helped early Christians overcome oppression and persecution. This Roman mural depicts Jesus miraculously healing an afflicted woman.* **Religions and Value Systems** *Which social classes do you think were most attracted to Christianity? Why?*

to spread his teachings. Then he ascended into heaven.

The disciples who spread Jesus' message are known as the Apostles, from the Greek word meaning "a person sent forth." Some preached among the Jews of Judea. Others traveled to the communities of the Jewish diaspora, including Rome. Slowly, a few Jews accepted the teaching that Jesus was the messiah, or the Christ, from the Greek for "the anointed one." These people became the first Christians.

## Spread of Christianity

At first, Christianity remained a sect, or small group, within Judaism. Then Paul, a Jew from Asia Minor, began the wider spread of the new faith.

**Work of Paul.** Paul had never seen Jesus. In fact, he had been among those who persecuted Jesus' followers. Then one day, Paul had a vision in which Jesus spoke to him. Immediately converting to the new faith, Paul made an important decision. He would spread Jesus' teachings beyond Jewish communities to gentiles, or non-Jews.

Paul's missionary work set Christianity on the road to becoming a world religion. A tireless traveler, Paul set up churches from Mesopotamia to Rome. In long letters to the Christian communities, he explained and expanded Christian teachings. For example, he emphasized the idea that Jesus had sacrificed his life out of love for humankind.

> 66 We have complete victory through him who loved us! . . . There is nothing in all creation that will ever be able to separate us from the love of God which is ours through Christ Jesus our Lord. 99

Paul promised that those who believed Jesus was the son of God and followed his teachings would achieve salvation, or eternal life.

**Persecution.** Rome's tolerant attitude toward religion did not extend to Christianity. Roman officials suspected Christians of disloyalty to Rome because they refused to make sacrifices to the emperor or to honor the Roman gods. When Christians met in secret to avoid persecution, rumors spread that they were engaged in evil practices.

In times of trouble, persecution increased. Roman rulers like Nero used Christians as scapegoats, blaming them for social or economic ills. Over the centuries, thousands of Christians became martyrs, people who suffer or die for their beliefs. Among them was Paul, who was killed during the reign of Nero.

**Survival.** Despite the attacks, Christianity continued to spread. The reasons were many. Jesus had welcomed all people, especially the humble, poor, and oppressed. They found comfort in his message of love and of a better life beyond the grave.

As they did their work, Christian missionaries like Paul added ideas from Plato, the Stoics, and other Greek thinkers to Jesus' message. Educated Romans, in particular, were attracted to a religion that incorporated the discipline and moderation of Greek philosophy.

Even persecution brought new converts. Observing the willingness of Christians to die for their religion, people were impressed by the strength of their belief. "The blood of the martyr is the seed of the [Christian] Church," noted one Roman.

**Role of women.** Women often led the way to Christianity. Many welcomed its promise that in the Church "there is neither Jew nor Greek . . . neither slave nor free . . . neither male nor female." In early Christian communities, women served as teachers and administrators. Even when they were later barred from any official role in the Church, they still worked to win converts and supported Christian communities across the Roman world.

**The Catacombs** Christians buried their dead in underground vaults and passageways called catacombs. During times of persecution, some worshiped secretly in these hidden tombs. **Religions and Value Systems** How did persecution help strengthen Christianity?

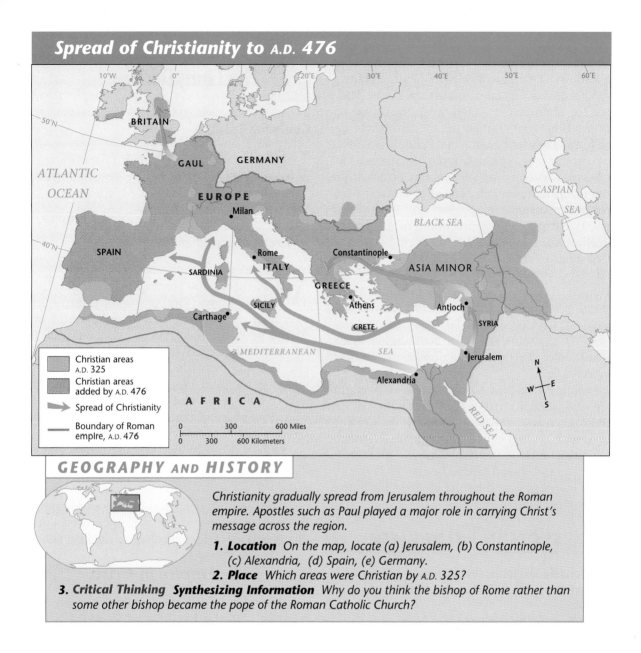

## Spread of Christianity to A.D. 476

Christian areas
A.D. 325

Christian areas
added by A.D. 476

Spread of Christianity

Boundary of Roman
empire, A.D. 476

Christianity gradually spread from Jerusalem throughout the Roman empire. Apostles such as Paul played a major role in carrying Christ's message across the region.

**1. Location** On the map, locate (a) Jerusalem, (b) Constantinople, (c) Alexandria, (d) Spain, (e) Germany.

**2. Place** Which areas were Christian by A.D. 325?

**3. Critical Thinking** **Synthesizing Information** Why do you think the bishop of Rome rather than some other bishop became the pope of the Roman Catholic Church?

## The Early Christian Church

Early Christian communities began to organize a formal Church. Each community had its own priest. Priests came under the authority of a bishop, a Church official who was responsible for all Christians in an area called a diocese (DĪ uh sihs).

Later, bishops of important cities gained even greater authority, presiding as archbishops over the other bishops in their area. Bishops traced their spiritual authority to Peter, the chief disciple of Jesus, and through Peter to Jesus himself. The Christian Church thus developed into a hierarchy, or organization in which officials are arranged according to rank. Only men were allowed to become members of the Christian clergy.

**Divisions and unity.** Rivalry among the bishops of Jerusalem, Antioch, Rome, and Constantinople led to divisions in the Church. In the Latin-speaking west, Christians eventually accepted the bishop of Rome as pope, or head of the Roman Catholic Church. In the Greek-speaking east, Christians acknowledged other leaders, as you will read. (See Chapter 10.)

As the Church grew and evolved, it imposed order and discipline on the scattered

Christian communities. To end disputes over questions of faith, councils of Church leaders met to decide official Christian teachings. They put together the New Testament, the 27 books of the Bible that contain the life and teachings of Jesus. They battled heresies, or beliefs said to be contrary to official Church teachings. The Church also sent out missionaries both within the Roman empire and beyond to convert people to Christianity.

**Triumph.** The persecution of Christians finally ended in A.D. 313, when the emperor Constantine issued the Edict of Milan. It granted freedom of worship to all citizens of the Roman empire. In making his decision, Constantine was influenced by his mother, who was a devout Christian. Some 80 years later, the emperor Theodosius (thee uh DOH shuhs) made Christianity the official religion of the Roman empire.

As the Christian Church grew in strength and influence, Roman power was fading. When the Roman empire finally collapsed, the Church inherited many of its functions. Along with Christian teachings, the Church preserved, adapted, and spread Greco-Roman civilization. That tradition would be the seedbed for a new western civilization.

## SECTION 4 REVIEW

1. **Identify** (a) Jesus, (b) Gospels, (c) Apostle, (d) Paul, (e) New Testament, (f) Edict of Milan.
2. **Define** (a) messiah, (b) sect, (c) martyr, (d) bishop, (e) pope, (f) heresy.
3. (a) How did the Romans treat the Jews of Palestine? (b) Why did divisions arise among the Jews?
4. (a) Describe three basic teachings of Christianity. (b) How were Christian teachings rooted in Jewish traditions?
5. Why did Christianity attract so many diverse converts?
6. *Critical Thinking* **Synthesizing Information** How do you think the unity of the Roman empire, with its extensive system of roads, helped Christianity to spread?
7. *ACTIVITY* Create a diagram showing the hierarchy of the Roman Catholic Church.

## 5 The Long Decline

### Guide for Reading

■ Why did the Pax Romana end?

■ How did Diocletian and Constantine try to restore order?

■ What led to the fall of the Roman empire?

■ **Vocabulary** *mercenary*

More than 1,500 years ago, the western half of the Roman empire stumbled into ruin. Ever since, people have tried to understand why. At the time, the spectacle of decay and defeat left Romans stunned. "For 30 years," lamented one Roman, "war has been waged in the very midst of the Roman empire." Beggars in the street, he noted, had once been "men and women of noble birth." He wondered:

> **66**Who would believe . . . that Rome, built upon the conquest of the whole world, would itself fall to the ground?**99**

The end of greatness was a catastrophe for Romans, but it did not happen overnight. Decay had set in centuries before the final fall.

### *The Empire in Crisis*

After the death of the emperor Marcus Aurelius in 180, the Pax Romana ended. For the next 100 years, political turmoil rocked the Roman empire. One after another, ambitious generals seized power, ruled for a few months or years, and then were overthrown by rival commanders. In one 50-year period, at least 26 emperors reigned. Only one died of natural causes.

At the same time, the empire was shaken by disturbing social and economic trends. High taxes to support the army and the bureaucracy placed heavy burdens on business people and small farmers. Many poor farmers left their land and sought protection from wealthy landowners. Living on large estates, they worked for the landowner and farmed a small plot for themselves. Although technically free, they were not allowed to leave the land.

## Efforts at Reform

The political and economic problems underlying the chaos had existed since the late republic. No ruler had been able to solve them, but reforming emperors did try to reverse the decline.

**Diocletian.** In 284, the emperor Diocletian (DĪ uh KLEE shuhn) set out to restore order. To make the empire easier to govern, he divided it into two parts. He kept control of the wealthier eastern part himself but appointed a co-emperor to rule the western provinces. The co-emperor was responsible to Diocletian, who retained absolute power.

Diocletian tried to increase the prestige of the emperor by surrounding himself with elaborate ceremonies. He wore purple robes embroidered with gold and a crown encrusted with jewels. Anyone who approached the throne had to kneel and kiss the hem of the emperor's robe.

Diocletian also took steps to end the empire's economic decay. To slow the rapid rise of prices, he fixed prices for goods and services. Other laws forced farmers to remain on the land. In cities, sons were required to follow their fathers' occupation. These rules were meant to ensure steady production of food and other goods.

**Constantine.** In 312, the talented general Constantine gained the throne. As emperor, Constantine continued Diocletian's reforms. More important, he took two steps that changed the course of European history.

First, as you have read, Constantine granted toleration to Christians. By doing so, he encouraged the rapid growth of Christianity within the empire and guaranteed its future success.

Second, he built a new capital, Constantinople, on the Bosporus, the strait that connects the Black and Mediterranean seas. By making his capital there, Constantine made the eastern portion of the empire the center of power. The western Roman empire was in decline, but the eastern Roman empire, which had more people and greater resources, would prosper for centuries to come.

**Mixed results.** The reforms of Diocletian and Constantine had mixed results. They revived the economy. And by increasing the power of government, they helped hold the empire together for another century. Still, the reforms failed to stop the long-term decline. In the end, internal problems combined with attacks from outside to bring the empire down.

## Foreign Invasions

For centuries, Rome had faced attacks from the Germanic peoples who lived along its northern borders. When Rome was powerful, it held back the invaders. As the empire declined, however, it was forced to give up its territories. Under pressure from attacks, it surrendered first Britain, then France and Spain. It was only a matter of time before foreign invaders marched into Italy and took over Rome itself.

**A global chain reaction.** As early as A.D. 200, wars in East Asia set off a chain of events that would eventually overwhelm Rome, thousands of miles to the west. Those wars sent the Huns, a nomadic people, migrating across Central Asia. By 350, the Huns reached eastern Europe. These skilled riders fought fierce battles to dislodge the Germanic peoples in their path. People like the Visigoths sought safety by crossing into Roman territory. Men armed with spears moved in bands along with women and

**Art of the Visigoths** *The Germanic peoples who invaded Rome left behind no stone monuments or wall paintings. Instead, they showed their artistic skills in small, portable items, such as the clasps that fastened their clothing. Visigoth artisans crafted these eagle clasps out of gold, bronze, and gemstones.* **Art and Literature** *How are these clasps similar to Greek and Roman mosaics?*

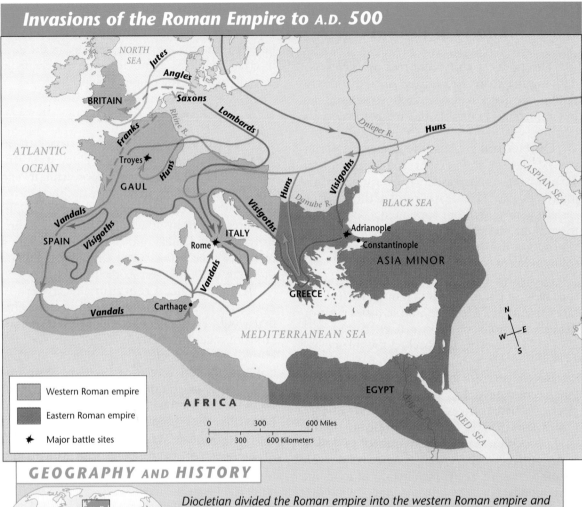

## Invasions of the Roman Empire to A.D. 500

**Map labels:** NORTH SEA · Jutes · Angles · Saxons · Lombards · BRITAIN · Franks · Rhine R. · Troyes · Huns · GAUL · ATLANTIC OCEAN · Dnieper R. · Huns · CASPIAN SEA · Vandals · SPAIN · Visigoths · Visigoths · Danube R. · Huns · Visigoths · BLACK SEA · ITALY · Rome · Adrianople · Constantinople · ASIA MINOR · Vandals · GREECE · Carthage · MEDITERRANEAN SEA · EGYPT · Vandals · AFRICA · RED SEA · Nile R.

**Legend:**
- Western Roman empire
- Eastern Roman empire
- ★ Major battle sites

0   300   600 Miles
0   300   600 Kilometers

### GEOGRAPHY AND HISTORY

*Diocletian divided the Roman empire into the western Roman empire and eastern Roman empire. Under Diocletian and Constantine, the eastern empire prospered, but invasions and internal problems led to the gradual decline of the west.*

**1. Location** *On the map, locate (a) western Roman empire, (b) eastern Roman empire, (c) Rhine River, (d) Danube River, (e) Constantinople.*

**2. Movement** *(a) Which Germanic tribes entered Italy? (b) Where did the Visigoths originate? (c) Describe the route of the Vandals. (d) To which land did the Angles and Saxons migrate?*

**3. Critical Thinking** **Drawing Conclusions** *Foreign invasions hurt the western Roman empire more than they did the eastern Roman empire. How does the map help you draw that conclusion?*

children, carts and herds, hoping to settle on Roman land.

**Retreat.** In 378, when a Roman army tried to turn back the Visigoths at Adrianople, it suffered a stunning defeat. Roman power was fading. New waves of invaders were soon hammering at Rome's borders, especially in the west. In 410, the Visigoth general Alaric overran Italy and plundered Rome. Gradually, other Germanic peoples occupied large parts of the western Roman empire.

**The "scourge of God."** For Rome, the worst was yet to come. Starting in 434, the Hun leader Attila embarked on a savage campaign of conquest across much of Europe. Christians called Attila the "scourge of God" because they believed his attacks were a punishment for the sins of humankind.

Attila died in 453. Although his empire collapsed soon after, the Hun invasion sent still more Germanic peoples fleeing into the Roman empire.

Finally, in 476, Odoacer (oh doh AY suhr), a Germanic leader, ousted the emperor in Rome. Later, historians referred to that event as the "fall" of Rome. By then, however, Rome had already lost many of its territories and Roman power in the west had ended.

## The End of Greatness

Why did Rome "fall"? Modern historians identify a number of interrelated causes.

**Military causes.** Perhaps the most obvious cause of Rome's fall was the Germanic invasions. Still, these attacks were successful in part because Roman legions of the late empire lacked the discipline and training of past Roman armies. To meet its need for soldiers, Rome hired mercenaries, or foreign soldiers serving for pay, to defend its borders. Many were German warriors who according to some historians, felt little loyalty to Rome.

**Political and economic causes.** Political problems also contributed to Rome's decline. First, as the government became more oppressive and authoritarian, it lost the support of the people. Growing numbers of corrupt officials undermined loyalty, too. Perhaps most important, dividing the empire at a time when it was under attack may have weakened it beyond repair.

Economically, the empire suffered as heavier and heavier taxes were required to support the vast government bureaucracy and huge military establishment. The wealth of the empire itself dwindled as farmers abandoned their land and the middle classes sank into poverty. At the same time, reliance on slave labor discouraged Romans from exploring new technology. Finally, the population itself declined as war and epidemic diseases swept the empire.

**Social causes.** For centuries, worried Romans pointed to the decline in values such as patriotism, discipline, and devotion to duty on which the empire was built. The upper class, which had once provided leaders, devoted itself to luxury and self-interest. And besides being costly, providing "bread and circuses" may have undermined the self-reliance of the masses.

**Did Rome fall?** Although we talk of the "fall" of Rome, the Roman empire did not disappear from the map in 476. An emperor still ruled the eastern Roman empire, which later became known as the Byzantine empire and lasted for another 1,000 years. (See Chapter 10.)

The dramatic phrase "the fall of Rome" is, in fact, shorthand for a long, slow process of change from one way of life to another. Roman civilization survived the events of 476. In Italy, people continued to live much as they had before, though under new rulers. Many still spoke Latin and obeyed Roman laws.

Over the next few centuries, however, German customs, ideas, and languages replaced Roman culture. Old Roman cities crumbled, and Roman roads disappeared under mud and weeds. Still, the Christian Church preserved elements of Roman civilization. In Chapters 8 and 9, you will read how Roman and Christian traditions gave rise to a new medieval civilization in western Europe.

## SECTION 5 REVIEW

1. **Identify** (a) Diocletian, (b) Constantine, (c) Huns, (d) Visigoths, (e) Alaric, (f) Attila, (g) Odoacer.
2. **Define** mercenary.
3. Describe conditions in the Roman empire after the Pax Romana ended.
4. (a) List two political and two economic reforms of Diocletian. (b) What effect did Constantine's policies have on the Roman empire?
5. Why did the Roman government lose the support of the people?
6. *Critical Thinking* **Linking Past and Present** Imagine that the United States government in Washington no longer existed. What would be the effects on (a) your life, (b) your state, (c) the United States?
7. *ACTIVITY* Create an illustrated booklet for a fifth-grade class explaining why the Roman empire fell. You may use charts as well as pictures to illustrate your booklet.

**ISSUES** *For* **TODAY** Historians have identified numerous causes for the fall of Rome. What factors can contribute to the decline of a great power?

# World Literature
## The Metamorphoses
### Ovid

**Introduction** *Publius Ovidius Naso, known as Ovid, was born near Rome in 43 B.C. He was educated by the best tutors and trained in the law. Much to his father's annoyance, however, he chose to devote his talents to poetry. For much of his career, he enjoyed the sponsorship of the emperor Augustus. Later, though, Ovid lost favor with the emperor and spent the last years of his life in exile.*

*The Metamorphoses is one of Ovid's greatest works. In it, he weaves together both Greek and Roman myths about gods and humans. The stories are all connected by a shared theme of metamorphoses, or changes. For example, in one story, a young woman named Arachne boasts that her skills as a weaver are greater than those of the goddess Pallas. After Arachne defeats Pallas in a weaving contest, the angry goddess changes Arachne into a spider. (Arachnid, the scientific term for spiders, comes from the name Arachne.)*

*The following excerpt from* The Metamorphoses *tells the story of Midas, a legendary king known for his foolishness. Midas is a crony of the fun-loving god Bacchus (the Roman name for the Greek god Dionysus). Here, Bacchus agrees to grant the king a wish.*

### The Story of King Midas

Then Bacchus, glad to see the old man home,
And like a good adopted son, thanked Midas,
Gave him the choice of making a wish come true:
What would he have? Midas was always sure
To make the worst of every good occasion—
Of turning glory into desperate ill—
So Midas said, "Make everything I touch turn gold."

Bacchus gave him the golden touch, yet thought
"What foolishness; it almost makes me sad."
Meanwhile
The Hero Midas danced on his way, and touched all things
That flashed before his eyes. Could he believe this?
Yes! He plucked a green shoot from a tree—
It was all gold, pure gold, had the right weight and color;
Then a handful of wet clay—he had but to touch it
And it was gold. His trembling fingers plucked
A head of wheat—it might have been the promise
Of golden harvest—and next he took an apple from a tree,
And in his hand it shone as though it were a gift
Transported to him from the Hesperides.[1]
He touched a standing beam that held the roof;
Look sharply now! It was a pillar of gold.
And as he dipped his hand in running water,
A stream of gold rushed out. . . .
Midas' imagination, his hopes, his dreams grew big with gold:
He called his slaves to bring a feast before him,
From wine to meat to bread to fruits to wine.
And as he broke bread, that rich gift of Ceres,[2]

---

[1] In Greek mythology, the Hesperides were a garden where golden apples were grown.
[2] Ceres was an ancient Italian goddess of agriculture. The Romans later merged Ceres with Demeter, the Greek goddess of fertile land.

**A Doomed Love** *This painting depicts a scene from one of the saddest tales of* The Metamorphoses, *the tale of Polyphemus and Galatea. Polyphemus is a Cyclops, or one-eyed giant, who loves the sea nymph Galatea. She, however, loves the handsome Acis. Enraged with jealousy, Polyphemus kills Acis, who is then changed into a river.* **Art and Literature** *How does this painting convey a sense of tragedy and sadness?*

It did not break but was of gold itself,
Beautifully hard, not stale, and as his teeth
Ate into meat, the meat was gold, too
And he could not close his jaws. As he
     poured
Water into wine (Bacchus' own wine) red,
     sunset color,
And raised them to his lips, both turned to
     gold.
Dazed, damned by gold, a golden terror
     took him,
Midas began to hate his wealth, tried to
     escape
The very riches that he prayed for. However
     large
The feast laid out before him, he went
     hungry,
And though his throat burned dry, no drink
     could wet it.
By his own choice gold had become his
     torture.
He lifted glittering hands and arms to
     heaven:
"O Bacchus, Father of your unlucky son!
I have done wrong, wrong from the start,
     wrong, wrong forever,
But take away your gift that shines in gold.
It's damned—it curses me." Because he
     seemed to learn
His way was error, the gods took pity on him.
Bacchus reversed him to what he was before;
He said, "Through your own foolishness you
     wear
A golden coffin, your very body is a tomb of
     gold;
Go to the river . . .

To wash your guilt away." The king obeyed;
And gold fell from him to the waters that ran
     gold.
Even now the golden touch has stained the
     river,
And the soil it waters is as hard as gold.
Midas, no longer lured by dreams of riches,
Took to the woods, became a nature lover.

Source: Ovid, *The Metamorphoses, A Complete New Version by Horace Gregory* (New York: The Viking Press, Inc., 1958).

## Thinking About Literature

1. (a) What request did King Midas make of the god Bacchus? (b) Why did Midas come to regret his wish?
2. (a) How does *The Metamorphoses* show a blending of Greek and Roman culture? Give two examples. (b) Why were the Romans proud of their cultural ties to Greece?
3. *Critical Thinking* **Making Inferences** (a) What human qualities does the god Bacchus display in "The Story of King Midas"? (b) What does the story suggest about the Roman view of the relationship between gods and people?

# Skills for Success

**Critical Thinking**    **Writing and Researching**    **Maps, Charts, and Graphs**    **Speaking and Listening**

## Analyzing a Primary Source

Historians use primary sources to find out about the past. As you have learned, primary sources include official documents, as well as firsthand accounts of events by people who witnessed or participated in them. (★ See *Skills for Success*, page 100.)

The excerpt below is from a letter written by the Roman author Pliny the Younger. Pliny witnessed the eruption of Mount Vesuvius in A.D. 79. Read the excerpt and follow the steps below to analyze it as a primary source.

**1** **Identify the document.** (a) Who wrote the document? (b) When was it written? (c) What event does it describe?

**2** **Interpret the contents of the document.** (a) Based on the document, what happened during the eruption? (b) What did Pliny do when the eruption began? Why? (c) Was Pliny frightened? Explain. (d) Based on the docu-ment, what generalization can you make about the effects of the eruption of Mount Vesuvius?

**3** **Combine primary and secondary sources to draw conclusions about a historical event.** According to the *World Almanac,* heated mud and ash from the eruption of Mount Vesuvius left debris over 60 feet deep in the cities of Pompeii, Herculaneum, and Stabiae. About 10 percent of the population of these towns was killed. (a) Is the *World Almanac* a primary or secondary source? (b) How does the kind of information in the almanac differ from that provided by Pliny? (c) Does the information from the almanac change the conclusions that you drew from Pliny's letter? Explain.

***Beyond the Classroom*** News articles often contain both firsthand and secondhand information. Locate a news article in a newspaper or news magazine. Circle the primary source information in pencil and the secondary source information in pen. Discuss how each source of information helps you to understand the event.

---

### From a Letter to Tacitus by Pliny the Younger

66The buildings round us were already tottering, and the open space we were in was too small for us not to be in real and imminent danger if the house collapsed. This finally decided us to leave the town.... Once beyond the buildings we stopped, and there we had some extraordinary experiences which thoroughly alarmed us....

Ashes were already falling, not as yet very thickly. I looked round: a dense black cloud was coming up behind us, spreading over the Earth like a flood. 'Let us leave the road while we can still see,' I said....

We had scarcely sat down to rest when darkness fell, not the dark of a moonless or cloudy night, but as if the lamp had been put out in a closed room. You could hear the shrieks of women, the wailing of infants, and the shouting of men. . . . A gleam of light returned, but we took this to be a warning of the approaching flames rather than daylight. However, the flames remained some distance off; then darkness came on once more and ashes began to fall again, this time in heavy showers. We rose from time to time and shook them off, otherwise we should have been buried and crushed beneath their weight. I could boast that not a groan or cry of fear escaped me in these perils, but I admit that I derived some poor consolation in my mortal lot from the belief that the whole world was dying with me and I with it.

At last the darkness thinned and dispersed like smoke or cloud; then there was genuine daylight, and the sun actually shone out, but yellowish as it is during an eclipse. We were terrified to see everything changed, buried deep in ashes like snowdrifts.99

## Building Vocabulary

Review the vocabulary words in this chapter. Then, use *ten* of these words to create a crossword puzzle. Exchange puzzles with a classmate. Complete the puzzles and then check each other's answers.

## Reviewing Chapter Themes

1. **Political and Social Systems** Explain how each of the following helped Rome conquer and rule a vast empire: (a) an efficient army, (b) skillful diplomacy, (c) the leadership of strong emperors.
2. **Global Interaction** Give three examples showing how Rome adapted and transformed Greek and Hellenistic achievements.
3. **Religions and Value Systems** (a) What were the basic ethical teachings of Christianity? (b) How did Christians view Jesus? (c) How did Christianity help preserve the Greco-Roman heritage?
4. **Continuity and Change** The causes for the fall of Rome can be divided into four categories: military, political, economic, and social. Identify one cause in each category and explain how it contributed to the collapse of the empire.

## Thinking Critically

1. **Comparing** (a) How did geographic conditions in Italy differ from those in Greece? (b) How did those differences make it easier to unite Italy than it was to unite Greece? (c) How did both Greece and Rome benefit from their location on the Mediterranean Sea?
2. **Defending a Position** Imagine that you were a Roman senator living at the time of Cato. Would you have supported his call to destroy Carthage? Why or why not?
3. **Analyzing Information** Did the Roman republic have a democratic government? Why or why not?
4. **Ranking** (a) Describe four achievements of Augustus. (b) Which of these achievements do you think was the most important? Give reasons for your ranking.
5. **Synthesizing Information** The Roman poet Horace said of Roman civilization, "Greece has conquered its rude conqueror." (a) What did he

mean by this? (b) Give three examples that support his statement. (★ See *Skills for Success*, page 896.)
6. **Linking Past and Present** "History," said Cicero, "illuminates reality, vitalizes memory, provides guidance in daily life, and brings us tidings of antiquity." (a) How did the work of Roman historians like Livy and Tacitus illustrate Cicero's idea? (b) Do you think Cicero's views on the value of history are still valid today? Why or why not?
7. **Making Inferences** (a) How did the Pax Romana help the spread of Christianity? (b) How do you think the decline of Rome's political power helped increase the appeal of Christianity?
8. **Solving Problems** (a) Describe two policies that Rome might have followed to restore its strength in the later years of the empire. (b) Do you think it would have been possible for the Romans to follow such policies? Why or why not?

### For Your Portfolio

Imagine that you are a a member of the Living Latin League, a group dedicated to preserving the Roman heritage. You have been asked to make a presentation on the following topic: "The Spirit of Rome Is Alive in the United States."

1. Select one of the following subject areas as the topic for your presentation: government, law, religion, art, or architecture.
2. Use a dictionary and other reference sources to make a list of Latin-based words or terms that are still in use in your subject area. Collect as many words or terms as possible.
3. Decide on a form for your presentation. For example, you might make a poster, deliver a speech, compile a specialized dictionary, or write and illustrate a magazine article.
4. Develop your presentation, using your word list to show Roman influence today.
5. After you complete the presentation, answer the following questions: (a) What ideas that are part of our everyday life originated in ancient Rome? (b) What parallels exist between life during ancient Roman times and life in the United States today?

# Civilizations of the Americas

## (1400 B.C.–A.D. 1570)

## CHAPTER OUTLINE

1 Civilizations of Middle America
2 The World of the Incas
3 Peoples of North America

In a cave outside Mexico City, an archaeologist made an intriguing discovery. He found the remains of plants that had sprouted more than 5,000 years before. Though the plants were less than an inch long, the archaeologist recognized them for what they were—tiny ears of corn. At other levels, the archaeologist discovered slightly larger ears of corn, then still larger ones. Apparently, early farmers in Mexico gradually cultivated a small grass pod into the full-sized corn plant we know today. In the process, corn became the lifeline of civilization in the Americas.

Many Native American religious beliefs reflect the importance of corn, or maize. The Mayan people of Mexico worshiped a handsome maize god, whose profile and flattened forehead resembled an ear of corn. According to Mayan sacred writings, the gods created the first man and woman from corn. "Of yellow corn and white corn they made their flesh; of cornmeal dough they made the arms and legs of people." A Navajo creation story relates that corn was the first plant to appear on Earth:

66First Man called the people together.
He brought forth the white corn
which had been formed with him.
First Woman brought the yellow
corn. They laid the perfect ears side
by side. . . . [The Turkey] danced
back and forth four times, then
shook his feather coat and there
dropped from his clothing four ker-
nels of corn, one gray, one blue, one
black, and one red.99

By 1500 B.C., the technology of growing corn had spread throughout the Americas. With potatoes and manioc in South America, corn supported the large populations that built the first American civilizations. In time, the crops developed in the Americas would feed much of the world.

Three complex civilizations—the Mayas, Aztecs, and Incas—flourished in Central and South America. Although each had many of the basic features of civilization you read about in Chapter 1, they differed from one another in important ways. Across North America, smaller and less-complex cultures developed their own diverse ways of life.

FOCUS ON these questions as you read:

■ **Diversity**
How did people in different parts of the Americas create distinct civilizations?

■ **Continuity and Change**
How did the Mayas, Aztecs, and Incas build on the achievements of earlier peoples?

■ **Political and Social Systems**
What methods did Aztec and Incan rulers use to organize their large empires?

■ **Religions and Value Systems**
How did religion play a central role in early American societies?

## TIME AND PLACE

**Sacred Bird of Ancient Mexico** *In this colorful mural, a flowery vine pours forth from the mouth of a sacred bird. Murals like this one covered the buildings of Teotihuacán, a city that dominated central Mexico more than 1,000 years ago. In both Central and South America, complex civilizations produced detailed, highly symbolic works of religious art.* **Art and Literature** *How does this mural celebrate nature and fertility? Explain.*

## HUMANITIES LINK

*Art History* Peruvian textile (page 165).

*Literature* In this chapter, you will encounter passages from the following works of literature: Navajo story of creation (page 156); Nezahualcoyotl, "All the Earth is a grave and nothing escapes it" (page 164); Garcilasco de la Vega, *The Royal Commentary of the Incas* (page 168); *Travel Song* (pages 171 and 173); the Iroquois constitution (page 173).

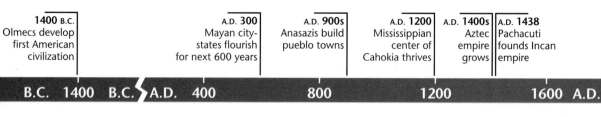

| **1400 B.C.** Olmecs develop first American civilization | **A.D. 300** Mayan city-states flourish for next 600 years | **A.D. 900s** Anasazis build pueblo towns | **A.D. 1200** Mississippian center of Cahokia thrives | **A.D. 1400s** Aztec empire grows | **A.D. 1438** Pachacuti founds Incan empire |

B.C. 1400   B.C. / A.D. 400          800          1200          1600 A.D.

# 1 Civilizations of Middle America

## Guide for Reading

- How did the first people reach the Americas?
- What were the main achievements of Mayan civilization?
- How did the Aztecs build a powerful empire?
- **Vocabulary** *tribute*

The Aztecs of Middle America evolved a complex system of religious beliefs. Their religions, like those of many other people, included a belief that the world would someday come to a fiery end.

According to the Aztec Legend of the Five Suns, the universe had been created and destroyed four times in the past. People living under the First Sun had been destroyed by jaguars. People living under the Second Sun were swept away by wind. People living under the Third Sun perished in the fire and ash of volcanoes, while those living under the Fourth Sun had been swallowed by water. The Fifth Sun represented the time of the Aztec empire:

> **66**This is our Sun, the one in which we now live. And here is its sign, how the Sun fell into the fire, into the divine hearth. . . . And as the elders continue to say, under the Sun there will be earthquakes and hunger, and then our end shall come.**99**

The Legend of the Five Suns reflects the important role of the sun in Aztec religion. It also suggests a feeling of helplessness in the face of the harsh forces of nature. Despite this sense of impending doom, the Aztecs were able to create a remarkable civilization. In order to do so, they built on the achievements of earlier peoples. To understand more about these early American civilizations, we must go far back in time to the arrival of the first people in the Americas.

## Geography: The Americas

Perhaps as early as 30,000 years ago,* small family groups of Paleolithic hunters and food gatherers reached North America from Asia. This great migration took place during the last ice age. At that time, so much water froze into thick ice sheets that the sea level dropped, exposing a land bridge between Siberia and Alaska. Hunters followed herds of bison and mammoths across this land bridge. Other migrating people may have paddled small boats and fished along the coasts.

**Global warming.** About 10,000 B.C., the Earth's climate grew warmer. As the ice melted, water levels rose, covering the land bridge under the Bering Strait. The global warming, along with the hunting skills of the first Americans, may have killed off large game animals like the mammoth. People adapted by hunting smaller animals, fishing, and gathering fruit, roots, and shellfish. These nomadic hunter-gatherers slowly migrated eastward and southward across the Americas.

**Regions.** What lands did the first Americans explore and settle? The Americas are made up of the continents of North America and South America. Within these two geographic regions is a cultural region that historians call Middle America. Middle America, which includes Mexico and Central America, was home to several early civilizations.

Great mountain chains form a spiny backbone down the western Americas. In North America, the Rocky Mountains split into the East and West Sierra Madre of Mexico. The towering Andes run down the length of South America. The continents are drained by two of the world's three longest rivers, the Amazon of South America and the Mississippi of North America.

The first Americans adapted to a variety of climates and resources. Far to the north and south, people learned to survive in icy, treeless lands. Closer to the Equator, people settled in the hot, wet climate and thick vegetation of the Amazon rain forests. Elsewhere, hunters adapted to conditions in deserts like the Atacama of Chile,

---

*Scholars disagree about exactly when the first people reached the Americas. They have proposed dates ranging from 70,000 to 10,000 years ago.

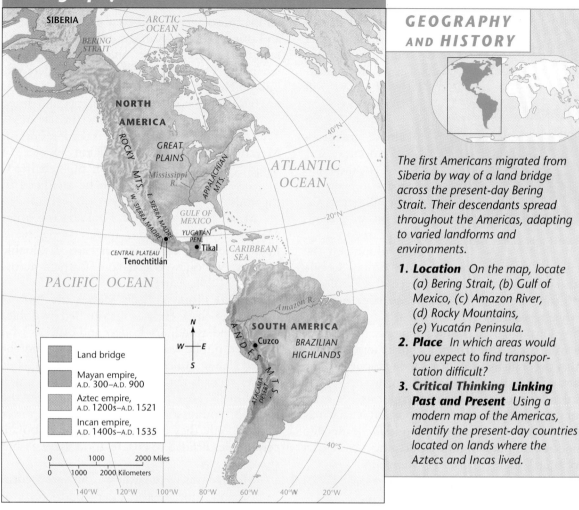

The first Americans migrated from Siberia by way of a land bridge across the present-day Bering Strait. Their descendants spread throughout the Americas, adapting to varied landforms and environments.

1. **Location** On the map, locate (a) Bering Strait, (b) Gulf of Mexico, (c) Amazon River, (d) Rocky Mountains, (e) Yucatán Peninsula.
2. **Place** In which areas would you expect to find transportation difficult?
3. **Critical Thinking** **Linking Past and Present** Using a modern map of the Americas, identify the present-day countries located on lands where the Aztecs and Incas lived.

---

in woodlands like those in eastern North America, and on the fertile plains of both continents.

**The agricultural revolution.** In the Americas, as elsewhere, the greatest adaptation occurred when some people learned to cultivate plants and domesticate animals. Archaeologists think that farming was partly a response to the disappearance of the large mammals. With fewer animals to hunt, people came to depend more on other food sources. In Mexico, or perhaps farther south, Neolithic people began cultivating a range of crops from corn and beans to sweet potatoes, peppers, tomatoes, and squash. These changes took place slowly between about 8500 B.C. and 2000 B.C.

Early American farmers learned to domesticate animals. In South America, domesticated animals include the llama and other creatures valued for their wool. However, the Americas had no large animals such as oxen or horses that

were capable of bearing heavy loads or pulling wagons. This lack of draft animals would limit development in some areas.

In the Americas, as in Africa and Eurasia, the agricultural revolution helped to cause other changes. Farming people settled into villages. Populations expanded. Some villages grew into large religious centers and then into the great cities of the first American civilizations.

## Legacy of the Olmecs

The first American civilization, the Olmecs, emerged in the tropical forests along the Mexican Gulf Coast and lasted from about 1400 B.C. to 500 B.C. Archaeologists know very little about the Olmecs, but rich tombs and temples suggest a powerful class of priests and aristocrats. The Olmecs did not build true cities, but rather they built ceremonial centers made up

▲ *Giant Olmec head*

of pyramid-shaped temples and other buildings. People came from nearby farming villages to work on the temples or attend religious ceremonies.

The most dramatic remains of the Olmec civilization are the giant carved stone heads found in the ruins of a religious center at La Venta. No one knows how the Olmecs moved these colossal 40-ton stones from distant quarries without wheeled vehicles or draft animals.

Through trade, Olmec influence spread over a wide area. The grinning jaguars and serpents that decorate many Olmec carvings appear in the arts of later peoples. The Olmecs also invented a calendar and used carved inscriptions as a form of writing. But their most important legacy may have been the tradition of priestly leadership and religious devotion that became a basic part of later Middle American civilizations.

## The World of the Mayas

Among the peoples influenced by the Olmecs were the Mayas. Between A.D. 300 and 900, Mayan city-states flourished from the Yucatán in southern Mexico through much of Central America.

Scientists have recently determined how Mayan farming methods allowed them to thrive in the tropical environment. Mayan farmers cleared the dense rain forests and then built raised fields that caught and held rainwater. They also built channels that could be opened to drain off excess water. This complex system produced enough maize and other crops to support rapidly growing cities.

**Temples and palaces.** Towering pyramid temples dominated the largest Mayan city of Tikal (tee KAHL), in present-day Guatemala. Priests climbed steep temple stairs to perform sacrifices on high platforms, while ordinary people watched from the plazas far below. Some temples also served as burial places for nobles and priests. The Mayan pyramids remained the tallest structures in the Americas until 1903, when the Flatiron Building, a skyscraper, was built in New York City.

Tikal also boasted large palaces and huge stone pillars covered with elaborate carvings. The carvings, which usually record events in Mayan history, preserve striking images of haughty aristocrats, warriors in plumed headdresses, and captives about to be sacrificed to the gods.

Much of the wealth of Tikal and the other Mayan cities came from trade. Along roads made of packed earth, traders carried valuable cargoes of honey, cocoa, and feathers across most of Middle America.

**Social classes.** Each Mayan city had its own ruling chief. He was surrounded by nobles who served as military leaders and officials who managed public works, collected taxes, and enforced laws. Rulers were usually men, but Mayan records and carvings show that women occasionally governed on their own or in the name of young sons. Priests held great power because only they could conduct the elaborate ceremonies needed to ensure good harvests and success in war.

Most Mayas were farmers. They grew corn, beans, and squash—the basic food crops of Middle America—as well as fruit trees, cotton, and brilliant tropical flowers. Men usually cultivated the crops, while women turned them into food. To support the cities, farmers paid taxes in food and helped build the temples.

**Advances in learning.** Along with their magnificent buildings and carvings, the Mayas made impressive advances in learning. They de-

**GLOBAL CONNECTIONS**

Maize originated in the Americas and only later arrived in Asia, Europe, and Africa. But how much later? Temples in southern India show stone figures offering maize to the gods. These figures were carved in the A.D. 1000s—more than 400 years before the Spanish arrived in Central America. Some historians take these carvings as evidence that there was earlier contact between the Mayas and people of Asia. But how the maize got to India is still a mystery.

## Play Ball!

Kick it. Throw it. Hit it. Roll it. Sink it. Catch it. Dodge it. Through the centuries, sports-minded people all over the world have developed an amazing array of games using a most simple invention—the ball.

**Linking Past and Present** Which of today's ball games share similarities with the Mayan ball game? Describe the similarities.

**PAST** Along with temples and pyramids, ball courts were a key feature of Mayan cities. Spectators watched intently as two teams tried to drive a solid rubber ball through a stone ring that hung from a wall. Opposing players moved the ball across the court by using their bodies, but not their hands or feet. In spite of protective helmets and padding, collisions with other players and the impact of the hard ball resulted in many injuries.

**PRESENT** Ball games today are played on fields, courts, tables, and even in alleys by players using rackets, bats, hammers, cues, clubs, and more. Wherever and however these ball games are played, they thrill both players and spectators alike.

veloped a hieroglyphic writing system, which has only recently been deciphered. Mayan scribes kept their sacred knowledge in books made of bark. Though Spanish conquerors later burned most of these books, a handful were taken to Europe and survive in European museums.

Mayan priests needed to measure time accurately in order to hold ceremonies at the correct moment. As a result, many priests became expert mathematicians and astronomers. They developed an accurate 365-day solar calendar, as well as a 260-day calendar based on the orbit of the planet Venus. Mayan priests also invented a numbering system and understood the concept of zero long before Europeans acquired this idea from India through the Arabs.

**Decline.** About A.D. 900, the Mayas abandoned their cities, leaving their great stone palaces and temples to be swallowed up by the jungle. Not until modern times were these "lost cities" rediscovered.

No one knows for sure why Mayan civilization declined. Possibly, frequent warfare forced the Mayas to abandon their traditional agricultural methods. Or overpopulation may have led to overfarming, which in turn exhausted the soil. Heavy taxes to finance wars and temple building may have sparked peasant revolts. Still, remnants of Mayan culture have survived. Today, millions of people in Guatemala and southern Mexico speak Mayan languages and are descended from the builders of this early American civilization.

## The Valley of Mexico

Long before Mayan cities rose to the south, the city of Teotihuacán (tay oh tee wah KAHN) had emerged in the Valley of Mexico. The Valley of Mexico is a huge oval basin ringed by snow-capped volcanoes, located in the high plateau of central Mexico. Teotihuacán dominated a large area from A.D. 100 to 750.

**Teotihuacán.** The city of Teotihuacán was well planned, with wide roads, massive temples, and large apartment buildings. Along the main avenue, the Pyramid of the Sun and the Pyramid of the Moon rose majestically toward the sky. Citizens of Teotihuacán worshiped a powerful nature goddess and rain god, whose images often appear on public buildings and on everyday objects. Teotihuacán eventually fell to invaders, but its culture influenced later peoples, especially the Aztecs.

**Arrival of the Aztecs.** In the late 1200s, bands of nomadic people, the ancestors of the Aztecs, migrated into the Valley of Mexico from the north. According to Aztec legend, the gods had told them to search for an eagle perched atop a cactus holding a snake in its beak. They finally saw the sign on a swampy island in Lake Texcoco. Once settled, the Aztecs shifted from hunting to farming. Slowly, they built the city of Tenochtitlán (tay nawch tee TLAHN), on the site of present-day Mexico City.

As their population grew, the Aztecs found ingenious ways to create more farmland. They built *chinampas,* artificial islands made of earth piled on reed mats that were anchored to the shallow lake bed. On these "floating gardens," they raised corn, squash, and beans. They gradually filled in parts of the lake and created canals for transportation. Wide stone causeways linked Tenochtitlán to the mainland.

**Conquering an empire.** In the 1400s, the Aztecs greatly expanded their territory. Through a combination of fierce conquests and shrewd alliances, they spread their rule over most of Mexico, from the Gulf of Mexico to the Pacific Ocean. By 1500, the Aztec empire numbered about 30 million people.

War brought immense wealth as well as power. Tribute, or payment from conquered peoples, helped the Aztecs turn their capital into a magnificent city.

## The World of the Aztecs

When the Spanish reached Tenochtitlán in 1519, they were awestruck at its magnificence. Hernan Cortés described the city as it looked then:

66The city has many squares where markets are held and trading is carried on. There is one square . . . where there are daily more than 60,000 souls, buying and selling, and where are found all the kinds of mer-

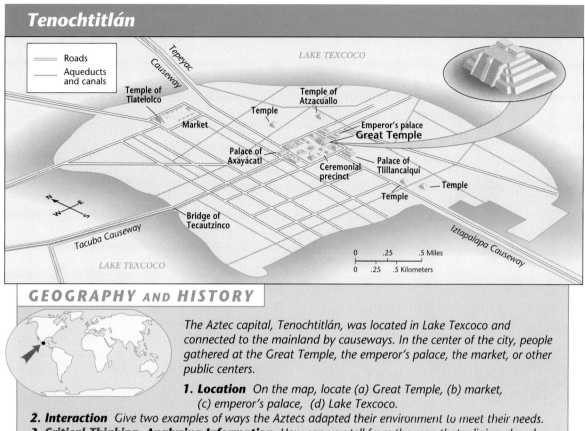

# Tenochtitlán

**Legend:**
- Roads
- Aqueducts and canals

LAKE TEXCOCO

Tepeyac Causeway

Temple of Tlatelolco

Market

Temple

Temple of Atzacuallo

Emperor's palace
**Great Temple**

Palace of Axayácatl

Ceremonial precinct

Palace of Tlillancalqui

Temple

Temple

Bridge of Tecautzinco

Tacuba Causeway

LAKE TEXCOCO

Iztapalapa Causeway

0   .25   .5 Miles
0   .25   .5 Kilometers

## GEOGRAPHY AND HISTORY

The Aztec capital, Tenochtitlán, was located in Lake Texcoco and connected to the mainland by causeways. In the center of the city, people gathered at the Great Temple, the emperor's palace, the market, or other public centers.

1. **Location** On the map, locate (a) Great Temple, (b) market, (c) emperor's palace, (d) Lake Texcoco.
2. **Interaction** Give two examples of ways the Aztecs adapted their environment to meet their needs.
3. **Critical Thinking** **Analyzing Information** How can you tell from the map that religion played an important role in Aztec life?

chandise produced in these countries, including food products, jewels of gold and silver, lead, brass, copper, zinc, bones, shells, and feathers.**"**

From its temples and palaces to its zoos and floating gardens, Tenochtitlán was a city of wonders. It was also the center of a well-ordered empire.

**Government and society.** Unlike the Mayan city-states, each of which had its own king, the Aztecs had a single ruler. The emperor was chosen by a council of nobles and priests to lead in war. Below him, nobles served as officials, judges, and governors of conquered provinces. They enjoyed special privileges such as wearing luxurious feathered cloaks and gold jewelry. Next came the warriors, who could rise to noble status by killing or capturing enemy soldiers. The majority of people were commoners who farmed the land.

At the bottom of society were the slaves, mostly criminals or prisoners of war. Despite their low status, slaves' rights were clearly spelled out by law. For example, slaves could own land and buy their freedom.

Protected by Aztec power, a class of long-distance traders ferried goods across the empire and beyond. From the highlands, they took goods such as weapons, tools, and rope to barter for tropical products such as jaguar skins and cocoa beans. They also served as spies, finding out new areas for trade and conquest.

**Religious beliefs.** The priests were a class apart. They performed the rituals needed to please the many Aztec gods and prevent droughts, floods, or other disasters. The chief Aztec god was Huitzilopochtli (wee tsee loh POHKT lee), the sun god. His giant pyramid-temple towered above central Tenochtitlán.

Huitzilopochtli, the Aztecs believed, battled the forces of darkness each night and was reborn each morning. As the Legend of the Five Suns (see page 158) shows, there was no guarantee that the sun would always win. To give the sun strength to rise each day, the Aztecs offered human sacrifices. Priests offered the hearts of tens of thousands of victims to Huitzilopochtli and other Aztec gods. Most of the victims were prisoners of war, but sometimes a noble family gave up one of its own members to appease the gods.

Other cultures such as the Olmecs and the Mayas had practiced human sacrifice, but not on the massive scale of the Aztecs. The Aztecs carried on almost continuous warfare, using the captured enemy soldiers for a regular source of sacrificial victims. Among the conquered peoples, discontent festered and rebellion often flared up. When the armies from Spain later arrived, they found ready allies among peoples who were ruled by the Aztec empire.

▲ *Aztec shield decorated with a coyote*

**Education and learning.** Priests were the keepers of Aztec knowledge. They recorded laws and historical events. Some ran schools for the sons of nobles. Others used their knowledge of astronomy and mathematics to foretell the future. The Aztecs, like the Mayas, had an accurate calendar.

Like many other ancient peoples, the Aztecs believed that illness was a punishment from the gods. Still, Aztec priests used herbs and other medicines to treat fevers and wounds. Aztec physicians could set broken bones and treat dental cavities. They also prescribed steam baths as cures for various ills, a therapy still in use today.

### Looking Ahead

The Aztec poet-king Nezahualcoyotl (neh tsah wahl cuh YOH tuhl), or "Hungry Coyote," knew his world would not last forever. His poetry of the 1400s reveals a pessimistic viewpoint:

66All the Earth is a grave and nothing escapes it;

Nothing is so perfect that it does not descend to its tomb. . . .
Filled are the depths of the Earth with dust
Once flesh and bone, once living bodies of men
Who sat upon thrones, decided cases, presided in council,
Commanded armies, conquered provinces, possessed treasure, destroyed temples,
Exulted in their pride, majesty, fortune, praise and power.
Vanished are these glories.99

In the next century, the doom that Nezahualcoyotl envisioned engulfed the whole Aztec empire. At the height of Aztec power, word reached Tenochtitlán that pale-skinned, bearded men had landed on the east coast. In Chapter 16, you will read about the results of the encounter between the Aztecs and the newcomers from far-off Spain.

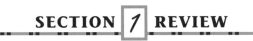

## SECTION 1 REVIEW

1. **Identify** (a) Olmecs, (b) Teotihuacán, (c) Tenochtitlán, (d) Huitzilopochtli, (e) Nezahualcoyotl.
2. **Define** tribute.
3. (a) Describe the migration and settlement of people through the Americas. (b) Describe how early Americans turned from hunting to agriculture.
4. How were religion and learning linked in Mayan society?
5. (a) How did the Aztecs build and control a huge empire in Mexico? (b) Descibe the social structure of the Aztec empire.
6. *Critical Thinking* **Analyzing Information** How can evidence such as artwork and public buildings help archaeologists trace the influence of a civilization like the Olmecs on later peoples?
7. *ACTIVITY* Write five words that an Aztec noble or priest might use to describe the Aztec empire. Then, write five words that someone in a conquered region might use to describe the Aztec empire.

# 2 The World of the Incas

## Guide for Reading

- What regions did the Incas rule?
- How did the Incas organize their empire?
- What role did religion play in Incan civilization?
- **Vocabulary** *quipu*

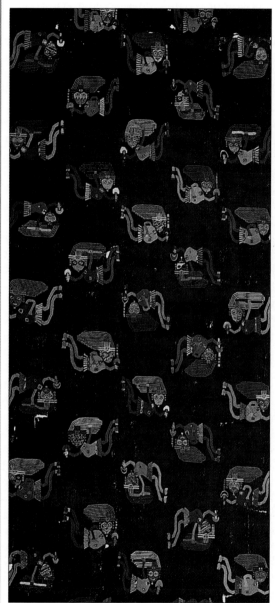

The Sapa Inca lifted a golden cup to the rising sun, a gesture to honor his divine ancestor. He then entered the temple, where sunlight glinted off the golden statues along the walls. A priest placed a bundle of fibers on the altar. With a copper mirror, he directed the magical power of the sun's rays to explode the fibers into flame.

Other rituals followed. Priests sacrificed a llama and prayed for success in the coming year. When the ceremonies ended, horns blared the news to the crowds outside the temple. A shout rose: "*Hailli!*—Victory!" Reed pipes and flutes echoed the joy as people prepared for a day of feasting and dancing.

This ceremony honoring the sun god took place each year in Cuzco, capital of the Incan empire of Peru. By the early 1500s, the Incas, like the Aztecs, ruled a mighty empire.

## Early Peoples of Peru

The Incan empire covered a wide variety of climates and terrains in western South America. The narrow coastal plain is a dry, lifeless desert crossed by occasional river valleys. Further inland, the snow-capped Andes Mountains rise steeply, leveling off into high plateaus that bake by day and freeze at night. East of the Andes lie dense jungles that stretch from Peru into Brazil.

Thousands of years ago, people settled in fishing villages along the desert coast of Peru. Gradually they expanded inland, farming the river valleys up into the highland plateaus. Using careful irrigation, they grew corn, cotton, squash, and beans. On mountain slopes, they cultivated potatoes, eventually producing 700 varieties. In high plateaus, they domesticated

**Peruvian Textile** *Artisans among the Paracas, an early people of Peru, produced this cloak around the 500s B.C. Their work involved many skills. Spinners produced cotton and wool thread, which weavers then turned into cloth. Skillful dyers added color from the more than 150 different shades at their disposal. Finally, embroiderers and painters decorated the fabric with complex and imaginative designs.* **Art and Literature** *Can you find two identical faces in this design? What does this suggest about the work of the artisans who produced it?*

the llama and alpaca. Like the Mayas, they built large ceremonial centers and developed skills in pottery and weaving.

**Chavín.** Through painstaking work at many sites, archaeologists have pieced together a chronology of various cultures that left their mark on the region. The earliest of these was the Chavín (chah VEEN) culture, named for ruins at Chavín de Huantar in the Andes. There, about 850 B.C., people built a huge temple complex. Stone carvings and pottery show that the Chavín people worshiped a ferocious-looking god, part jaguar and part human with grinning catlike features. The arts and religion of the Chavín culture influenced later peoples of Peru.

**Mochica.** Between about A.D. 100 and 700, the Mochica people forged an empire along the arid north coast of Peru. Their leaders had roads built and organized networks of relay runners to carry messages, ideas that the Incas would later adopt.

Remains of Mochica cities and temples dot the land. To build one temple, workers had to produce 130 million sun-dried adobe bricks. The people perfected skills in goldwork and woodcarving. They produced remarkable pots decorated with realistic scenes of daily life. On these painted vases, helmeted warriors go into battle, musicians play pipes and drums, and women weave textiles on small portable looms.

**Clues, but no answers.** Many other cultures left tantalizing clues to their lives and beliefs. In southern Peru, the Nazca people etched giant figures of birds, whales, and other creatures into the sand and gravel hills. These figures may have been family symbols or part of an ancient calendar.

For more than 2,000 years, diverse civilizations rose and fell in Peru. Then, in the mid-1400s, the Incas emerged from high in the Andes. Incan armies rapidly conquered an empire that stretched 2,500 miles (4,025 km) down the Andes and along the Pacific coast. Like the Romans, who also ruled a diverse empire, the Incas drew heavily on the ideas and skills of conquered peoples.

## Ruling an Empire

Pachacuti, a skilled warrior and leader, was the founder of the Incan empire. In 1438, he proclaimed himself Sapa Inca, or emperor, and embarked on a policy of conquest. Once he had subdued neighboring peoples, he enlisted them in his armies for future campaigns. In this way, he and his son extended Incan rule from Ecuador in the north to Chile in the south. (See the map on page 159.)

**Government.** The Sapa Inca exercised absolute power over the empire. Claiming he was divine, the son of the sun itself, he was also the chief religious leader. Like the pharaohs of ancient Egypt, the Incan god-king owned all the land, herds, mines, and people. Gold, the "sweat of the sun," was his symbol. He lived in splendor, eating from golden plates and dressing in richly embroidered clothes. His queen, the Coya, carried out important religious duties and sometimes governed when the Sapa Inca was absent.

From their mountain capital at Cuzco, the Incas ran an efficient government with a chain of command reaching into every village. Nobles ruled the provinces along with local chieftains whom the Incas had conquered. Below them, officials carried out the day-to-day business of collecting taxes and enforcing laws. Specially trained officials kept records on a quipu, a collection of knotted, colored strings. Modern scholars think that quipus noted dates and events as well as statistics on population and crops.

**Roads and runners.** To unite their empire, the Incas imposed their own language, Quechua (KEHCH wuh), and religion on the people. They also created one of the great road systems in history. It wound more than 12,000 miles (19,300 km) through mountains and deserts. Hundreds of bridges spanned rivers and deep gorges. Steps were cut into steep slopes and tunnels dug through hillsides. Even more impressive than the roads that united the Roman empire, the Incan road system was unmatched until modern times.

The roads allowed armies and news to move rapidly throughout the empire. At regular stations, runners waited to carry messages. Relays of runners could carry news of a revolt swiftly from a distant province to the capital. The Incas kept soldiers at outposts throughout the empire. Within days of an uprising, they would be on the move to crush the rebels. Ordinary people, though, were restricted from using the roads at all.

**Cuzco.** All roads led through Cuzco. In the heart of the city stood the great Temple of the Sun, its interior walls lined with gold. Like Incan palaces and forts, the temple was made of enormous stone blocks, each polished and carved to fit exactly in place. The engineering was so precise that, although no mortar was used to hold the stones together, Incan buildings have survived severe earthquakes.

## Lives of the Incas

The Incas strictly regulated the lives of millions of people within their empire. People lived in close-knit communities, called ayllus (ī looz). Leaders of each ayllu carried out government orders, assigning jobs to each family and organizing the community to work the land. Government officials arranged marriages to ensure that men and women were settled at a certain age.

**Farming.** Farmers expanded the step terraces built by earlier peoples. On steep hillsides, they carved out strips of land to be held in place by stone walls. Terraces kept rains from washing away the soil and made farming possible in places where flat land was scarce.

Farmers had to spend part of each year working land for the emperor and the temples as well as for their own communities. The government took possession of each harvest, dividing it among the people and storing part in case of famine.

**Religion.** Like other early peoples, the Incas were polytheistic, worshiping many gods linked to the forces of nature. People offered food, clothing, and drink to the guardian spirits of the home and the village. Religion was tied to the routines of life. Each month had its own festival, from the great ripening and the dance of the young maize to the festival of the water. Festivals were celebrated with ceremonies, sports, and games.

*"Lost City" of the Andes* Some 7,000 feet (2,100 m) above sea level lie the ruins of the Incan city of Machu Picchu. The city's grass roofs are gone, but its sturdy walls have withstood centuries of earthquakes. Incan workers expertly cut and fitted the stones together without the aid of mortar. Abandoned for some 300 years, the ruins of Machu Picchu were not rediscovered until 1911. **Economics and Technology** Where else in the world today must architects design buildings to withstand destructive earthquakes?

A powerful class of priests served the gods, celebrating their special festivals and tending to their needs. Chief among the gods was Inti, the sun god. His special attendants, the "Chosen Women," played a key and honored role in Incan religious rituals.

## Chosen Women of the Sun

The royal official carefully examined the girls parading before him. They were young, only eight years old, but he knew what qualities to look for. Nearby, the girls' parents watched with a mixture of pride and anxiety. Who would the Apopanaca, or He-Who-Chooses, choose?

With great ceremony, he made his selections. This girl belonged to the highest-ranking family in the ayllu. That one had great beauty. Another showed great promise as a weaver. Inti would surely approve of such attendants.

The rejected girls returned to their homes. The girls selected by the Apopanaca went with him to the provincial capital—perhaps never to see their homes or parents again. These girls were now Aclla, the Chosen Women.

**Years of training.** Each provincial capital had its own Acllahuachi, or house of the chosen, not far from the main temple. There, the young Aclla remained in strict seclusion during their period of training. The scholar Garcilasco de la Vega, the son of an Incan mother and Spanish father, later described the house at Cuzco, which admitted only girls of royal blood:

> ❝There was a narrow passage wide enough for two persons that ran the whole length of the building. The passage had many cells on either side which were used as offices where women worked. At each door were trusted doorkeepers, and in the last apartment at the end of the passage where no one entered were the women of the Sun. . . . There were a score of porters to fetch and carry things needed in the house as far as the second door. The porters could not pass this second door under pain of death, even if they were called from within, and no one was allowed to call them in under the same penalty.❞

Within the walls of the Acllahuachi, the young Aclla learned the skills and duties they needed to serve the sun god. They studied the mysteries of the Incan religion, learning the natures and rituals of the many gods and goddesses. They learned to prepare ritual foods and to brew chica, a corn beverage used by priests in their sun ceremonies.

Perhaps most important, the Aclla learned to make the elaborate wool garments and feather headdresses worn by the Sapa Inca and his wife, the Coya. The emperor never wore the same clothing twice, nor could his clothing be passed on to lesser persons. Each garment was worn once, then burned. To meet the constant demand for royal clothing, the Aclla developed legendary skills in the art of weaving. "The luster, splendor, and sheen of the fabrics of featherwork were of such beauty," noted one visitor, "that it is impossible to make them understood, unless by showing them."

**A lifetime of service.** When a Chosen reached the age of about 16, her long period of training came to an end. Then, her future would be decided. In the provincial capitals, some women might be given in marriage to nobles or other allies and friends of the Incas. At Cuzco, a few Aclla might be selected to serve the emperor or the Coya.

Most of the Chosen Women, however, remained in the house of

**The Chosen Women** *The base of this long-necked vase shows several Aclla in their traditional dress. Each Chosen Woman wears a long gown with a cape draping the shoulders. The rich jewelry and embroidery at the waist and hemline indicate the noble rank of these women who served the Sun.* **Religions and Value Systems** *Why do you think the potter did not show the faces of individual Aclla on this vase?*

seclusion. There, they spent their lives using their skills in the service of the Sun. Some Aclla became *mamacuna*, or "noble mothers," within the Acllahuachi. Their sacred duty was to train new generations of Chosen Women.

In old age, a Chosen Woman might gain permission to return to the home she had left so many years before. There, she lived out her days in comfort, venerated by all for her lifetime of service. ■

## *Looking Ahead*

At its height, the Incan civilization, like those of Middle America, was a center of learning. Although the Incas were less advanced in astronomy than the Mayas, they did have a calendar. They also excelled in medicine. They used herbs as antiseptics and performed surgery on the skull to relieve swelling caused by wounds.

Then, in 1525, the emperor Huayna Capac (wī nah  KAH pahk) died suddenly of an unknown plague that swept across the land. As he had not named a successor, civil war broke out between two of his sons. The fighting weakened the empire at a crucial moment. Like the Aztecs to the north, the Incas soon faced an even greater threat from Spanish invaders.

## SECTION 2 REVIEW

1. **Identify** (a) Chavín, (b) Mochica, (c) Pacha-cuti, (d) Inti, (e) Chosen Women.
2. **Define** quipu.
3. How did geography influence the way the Incas ruled their empire?
4. Describe two steps the Incas took to unite their empire.
5. How did religion affect Incan government and daily life?
6. *Critical Thinking* **Recognizing Points of View** To an ordinary person, what might be the advantages and disadvantages of the absolute rule of the Sapa Inca?
7. *ACTIVITY* Draw a time line of ancient Middle America and Peru. Your time line should show when major civilizations flourished, what advances they made, and which civilizations influenced later peoples.

## 3 Peoples of North America

### Guide for Reading

■ How did Middle American civilizations influence cultures in North America?

■ What has archaeological evidence revealed about the Mound Builders?

■ How did cultural traditions differ across North America?

■ **Vocabulary** *kiva, potlatch*

Hundreds of cultural groups emerged in the present-day United States and Canada. For centuries, they lived by hunting, fishing, and gathering wild plants. As farming spread north from Middle America, many people became farmers, raising corn and other food crops. Some people farmed so successfully that they built large permanent settlements. Here, we will look at the earliest of these farming cultures, in the desert southwest and in the Mississippi Valley.

### *The Desert Southwest*

More than 1,000 years ago, fields of corn, beans, and squash bloomed in the desert southwest. The farmers who planted these fields were called the Hohokams, or "Vanished Ones," by their later descendants, the Pimas and Papagos. To farm the desert, they built a complex irrigation system.

The Hohokams lived near the Gila River in present-day Arizona. They may have acquired skills such as irrigation from the civilizations of Middle America. They built temple mounds and ball courts, as the Mayas did. The Hohokams survived until about A.D. 1500, when

**ISSUES** *For* **TODAY** In both North and South America, geographic differences led to the development of different ways of life. How does geography influence cultural diversity?

INUITS
KUTCHINS
INUITS
ARCTIC
INUITS
SUBARCTIC
TLINGITS
INUITS
HUDSON BAY
NORTHWEST COAST
BELLA COOLAS
BEAVERS
CREES
CREES
KWAKIUTLS
BLACKFEET
CHIPPEWAS ALGONQUINS
PLATEAU
MANDANS
HURONS
NEZ PERCÉS
CROWS LAKOTAS
IROQUOIS
COOS
SHOSHONES
CHEYENNES
EASTERN WOODLANDS
PACIFIC OCEAN
POMOS
GREAT BASIN
GREAT PLAINS
MIAMIS LENI-LENAPES
SHAWNEES
ATLANTIC OCEAN
CALIFORNIA
HOPIS
NAVAJOS
ARAPAHOS
OSAGES
CHEROKEES
IROQUOIS
HOHOKAMS PUEBLOS APACHES
COMANCHES
SOUTHEAST
APACHES
NATCHEZ
SOUTHWEST
GULF OF MEXICO
N
W E
S
MIDDLE AMERICA
CARIBBEAN SEA

0   500   1000 Miles
0   500   1000 Kilometers

120°W   110°W   100°W   90°W   70°W

60°N
50°N
40°N
30°N
20°N
10°N

## GEOGRAPHY AND HISTORY

As Native Americans spread out to populate North America, they developed varied cultures. The map shows culture areas in which tribes shared similar ways of life.

1. **Location** On the map, locate (a) Northwest Coast culture area, (b) Eastern Woodlands culture area, (c) Great Plains culture area.
2. **Place** (a) Name two tribes in the southwest culture area. (b) With which culture area are the Cherokees associated?
3. **Critical Thinking  Making Inferences** Make a list of geographic features, such as natural barriers, climate, or vegetation, that might have led to the development of different ways of life.

drought seems to have forced them to leave their settlements.

**Anasazi.** The best-known society of the southwest was that of the Anasazi. They lived in what is today the Four Corners region of Arizona, New Mexico, Colorado, and Utah. Between about A.D. 900 and 1300, the Anasazi built large villages, later called *pueblos* by the Spanish.

Remains of Pueblo Bonita still stand in New Mexico. The village consisted of a huge complex with 800 rooms that housed about 6,000 people. Builders used stone and adobe bricks to erect a crescent-shaped compound rising five stories high. Terraces at each level served as streets.

At the center of the great complex was a plaza. There, the Anasazis dug their kiva, a large underground chamber used for religious ceremonies. Men met in the kiva for religious cere-

monies to ensure rain and good harvests. Paintings on the walls show their concern with weather, including storms that might damage crops.

**Anasazi cliff dwellings.** In the late 1100s, the Anasazi began building housing complexes in the shadow of canyon walls, where the cliffs offered protection from raiders. The largest of these cliff dwellings at Mesa Verde, in present-day Colorado, had over 200 rooms. People had to climb up or down ladders to reach their fields on the flatlands above or the canyon floor below. Women farmed, made pottery and cotton cloth, and replastered the walls of their dwellings. Men and older boys cleared the fields and hunted.

In the late 1200s, a long drought forced the Anasazi to abandon their cliff dwellings. Without rain, they could no longer live in large settlements. Attacks by Navajos and Apaches may have contributed further to their decline. Anasazi traditions survived, however, among the Hopi and other Pueblo Indians of the present-day southwestern United States.

## The Mound Builders

Far to the east of the Anasazi, in the Mississippi and Ohio valleys, other farming cultures emerged as early as 700 B.C. The Adena and Hopewell people left behind giant earthen mounds. Some mounds were cone-shaped, while others were made in the shape of animals. The Great Serpent Mound in Ohio wriggles and twists for almost a quarter of a mile. This enormous monument is evidence of the Adena people's resources and strong leadership.

Objects found in Hopewell mounds show that traders extended their influence over a wide area. They brought back shells and shark teeth from the Gulf of Mexico and copper from the Great Lakes region. Skilled artisans hammered and shaped the copper into fine ornaments.

▲ Snake found in Hopewell mound

**Cahokia.** By A.D. 800, these early cultures had disappeared, but a new people, the Mississippians, had acquired a greater variety of corn and other crops. With a growing food surplus, their civilization prospered. As their culture spread, the Mississippians built clusters of earthen mounds and ever larger towns and ceremonial centers.

Their greatest center, Cahokia in present-day Illinois, housed as many as 40,000 people by about 1200. Cahokia boasted at least 60 mounds. On top of some mounds stood the homes of rulers and nobles. The largest mound probably had a temple on its summit, where priests and rulers offered prayers and sacrifices to the sun. Archaeologists think that this temple mound shows the influence of Middle American civilizations.

**Heirs of the Mound Builders.** The Mississippians left no written records, and their cities had disappeared by the time Europeans reached the area. Still, their traditions survived among the Natchez people, whose ruler, the Great Sun, had absolute power. He and his family lived on the top of pyramid mounds.

## Diverse Regional Cultures

Many other groups of Native Americans emerged in North America prior to 1500. Modern scholars have identified 10 culture areas based on the environments in which people lived: the Arctic, Subartic, Northwest Coast, California, Great Basin, Plateau, Southwest, Great Plains, Southeast, and Eastern Woodlands. In each area, people adapted to geographic conditions that influenced their ways of life.

The chart on page 172 summarizes the characteristics and achievements of peoples who lived in each culture area. Here, we will look in greater detail at ways of life in three regions—the Arctic, the Northwest Coast, and the Eastern Woodlands.

**A frozen world.** In the far north, the Inuits* adapted to a harsh climate, using the resources of the frozen land to survive. Small bands lived by hunting and fishing. Seals and other sea mammals provided them with food, skins for clothing, bones for needles and tools, and oil for cooking. They paddled kayaks in open waters or used dog sleds to transport goods across the ice. An Inuit song describes the life of migrating hunters:

❝Leaving the white bear behind in his
    realm of sea-ice
  we set off for our winter hunting
    grounds . . .

---

* The Inuits were late immigrants from Siberia. Other Native Americans called them Eskimos, "eaters of raw flesh," but they called themselves the Inuits, the "people."

# Native American Culture Groups of North America

| Culture Group/ Selected Tribes | Patterns of Life | Connections Today |
|---|---|---|
| **Arctic/Subarctic** Beavers, Crees, Inuits, Kutchins | Lived as nomadic hunters and food gatherers in cold climate; honored ocean, weather, and animal spirits | In the 1990s, the Canadian government agreed to restore 140,000 square miles of Inuit lands. The Inuits called the new territory Nunavit, or "our land." |
| **Northwest Coast** Bella Coolas, Coos, Kwakiutls, Tlingits | Lived in villages; benefited from rich natural resources in forests, rivers, and ocean; held potlatches, or ceremonial dinners, where host families gave gifts to guests to show wealth and gain status | Artists, such as Jesse Cooday, a Tlingit, are merging many traditional Native American themes with modern styles. Their works are featured in museums and galleries, where they inspire new generations. |
| **California/Great Basin/Plateau** Nez Percés, Pomos, Shoshones | Lived as hunters and gatherers in small family groups; ate mainly fish, berries, acorns | Like many Native Americans, Lillian Valenzuela Robles of southern California is working to stop development of a plot of land that is part of her people's ancestral homeland. |
| **Southwest** Apaches, Hopis, Navajos, Pueblos | Lived in villages in homes made of adobe; built irrigation systems to grow corn and other crops; honored earth, sky, and water spirits | Like many other tribes, Mescalero Apaches in New Mexico have improved the quality of life on their reservation through successful businesses, including a sawmill and a ski lodge. |
| **Great Plains** Arapahos, Blackfeet, Cheyennes, Comanches, Crows, Lakotas, Mandans, Osages | Lived in tepees; animals hunted by men; crops grown by women; relied on buffalo to meet basic needs of food, shelter, and clothing | The Crows in South Dakota have set up a two-year college that teaches such subjects as math, science, and Crow history. It is one of 28 tribally controlled colleges in the United States. |
| **Eastern Woodlands** Algonquins, Chippewas, Hurons, Iroquois, Leni-Lenapes, Miamis, Pequots, Shawnees | Lived in farming villages, but also hunted for food; long houses shared by several families; women held much social and political power | The Pequots in Connecticut, like other tribes around the country, have built a gambling casino. The profits support education and provide health services. |
| **Southeast** Cherokees, Natchez | Grew corn, squash, beans, and other crops; held yearly Green Corn Ceremony to mark end of year and celebrate harvest | Throughout the country, including the Southeast, Native Americans gather at intertribal pow-wows, to celebrate with singing, dancing, food, games, and sports. |

◄ *Interpreting a Chart* *About 500 years ago, a wide range of diverse societies occupied the present-day United States and Canada. Today, Native American cultures no longer dominate North America, but individuals and groups are working to preserve their heritage. The column at the far right gives just one example of recent developments affecting Native Americans in each culture region.* ■ *Choose one artifact shown on the chart and explain how it reflects the pattern of life of the people that produced it.*

We followed the course of the river
  over the flatlands beyond
Where the sleds sank in the deep snow
  up to the cross slats.
It was sweaty work, I tell you,
Helping the dogs. **99**

In some areas, Inuits constructed igloos, or dome-shaped homes made from snow and ice. In others, they built sod dwellings that were partly underground.

**A land of plenty.** The people of the Northwest Coast lived in a far richer environment than the Inuits. Rivers teemed with salmon, while the Pacific Ocean offered other fish and sea mammals. Hunters tracked deer, wolves, and bears in the forests. In this land of plenty, people built large permanent villages with homes made of wood. They traded their surplus goods, gaining wealth that was shared in ceremonies like the potlatch. At this ceremony, which continues in Canada today, a person of rank and wealth distributes lavish gifts to large numbers of guests. By accepting the gifts, the guests acknowledge the host's high status.

**The Iroquois League.** The Eastern Woodlands, stretching from the Atlantic Coast to the Great Lakes, was home to a number of groups, including the Iroquois. They cleared land and built villages in the forests. While women farmed, men hunted and frequently warred against rival nations.

According to Iroquois tradition, the prophet Dekanawidah (deh kan ah WEE dah) urged rival Iroquois nations to stop their constant wars. In the late 1500s, he and his ally Hiawatha formed the unique political system known as the Iroquois League. This was an alliance of five nations who spoke the same language and shared similar traditions. The league's constitu-

tion reflects Dekanawidah's passionate desire to have peace among the nations:

> **66** I, Dekanawidah, and the confederate lords now uproot the tallest tree and into the cavity thereby made we cast all weapons of war. Into the depths of the earth we cast all weapons of strife. We bury them from sight forever and plant again the tree. Thus shall all Great Peace be established and hostilities shall no longer be known between the Five Nations but only peace to a united people. **99**

The Iroquois League did not always succeed in keeping the peace. Still, it was the best-organized political group north of Mexico. Member nations governed their own villages but met jointly in a council when they needed to resolve larger problems. Only men sat on the council, but every clan had a "clan mother" who could name or depose chiefs and members of the council.

The Iroquois League emerged just at the time when Europeans arrived in the Americas. Encounters with Europeans would take a fearful toll on the peoples of North America and topple the Aztec and Incan empires.

## SECTION 3 REVIEW

1. **Identify** (a) Hohokams, (b) Anasazis, (c) Mound Builders, (d) Inuits, (e) Iroquois League.
2. **Define** (a) kiva, (b) potlatch.
3. What evidence suggests that the people of the desert southwest were influenced by Middle American civilizations?
4. How do we know about the lives of the Mound Builders?
5. Give examples of how environmental conditions affected three early cultures of North America.
6. *Critical Thinking* **Linking Past and Present** How do environmental factors affect the way you and others live in your community today?
7. *ACTIVITY* With a partner, create a poster that expresses the ideas behind the formation of the Iroquois League.

# Skills for Success

## Answering Essay Questions

Essay questions, like those found on many tests, require written answers of several sentences or paragraphs. Before you can answer an essay question, you first must understand clearly what the question is asking you to do.

Essay questions contain either *question words* or *instruction words* that are the keys to writing good answers. Some of the most common question and instruction words are listed below, with the type of answer that each one requires.

| | |
|---|---|
| Why: | Give reasons. |
| How: | Tell in what way or by what means something was done. |
| What: | Give specific examples that explain or illustrate. |
| Discuss: | Tell the significance of a person or an event. |
| Describe: | Write a detailed account of what happened. |
| Explain: | Tell how or why an action or event affects something else. |
| Identify: | Give a person's or event's place in time and its relation to other persons or events. |
| Compare: | Give similarities and differences. |

After identifying the type of answer required, look at the question for further clues that limit the topic. Words or phrases might limit you to certain individuals, events, dates, or geographic areas. Look at the list of essay topics given below, then answer the following questions:

**1** **Identify the instruction or question words.** (a) What is the instruction word in sample question C? What is it asking you to do? (b) Which sample questions contain question words? (c) What is the instruction word in question E asking you to do?

**2** **Look for other clues in the question that will help you focus the topic of the answer.** (a) Which words in question A limit the people your answer should focus on? (b) What is the topic of question D?

**3** **Write a thesis statement.** A **thesis statement** is a sentence or two that presents the main point of the essay. It provides focus and a starting point as you answer the essay question. (a) Write a thesis statement for question C. (b) Write a thesis statement for question G.

**4** **Organize supporting detail.** Supporting details are specific facts that support your general thesis statement. (a) List three facts that support your thesis statement for question C. (b) List three facts that support your thesis statement for question G.

***Beyond the Classroom*** Applications for colleges and vocational training schools often include essay questions. Call one of these schools and ask them to send you an application form. Circle the essay questions on the application, underline the instruction words or question word, and highlight the topic words.

---

### Sample Essay Questions

A. Compare the ways the early peoples of North America adjusted to their varied physical environments.

B. What were the religious beliefs of the Aztecs?

C. Describe the status of women among North American Indians.

D. How do historians and scholars account for the decline of the Mayas?

E. Explain what the Incas did to maintain control of their vast empire.

F. Identify the Olmecs and the cultural achievements they passed on to later peoples.

G. Why was farming critical to the development of early civilizations?

## Building Vocabulary

Write a sentence explaining the significance of each of the following words with respect to the civilizations of the Americas: (a) tribute, (b) quipu, (c) kiva, (d) potlatch.

## Reviewing Chapter Themes

1. **Continuity and Change** Describe one way each of the following peoples influenced later societies: (a) the Olmecs, (b) the Mayas, (c) the Mochica people, (d) the Mound Builders.
2. **Political and Social Systems** Describe the political and social system of *either* the Aztec empire or the Incan empire in terms of (a) the role of the ruler, (b) social classes, (c) treatment of conquered people, (d) public works.
3. **Religions and Value Systems** (a) Why did priests have great power in the civilizations of Middle and South America? (b) What role did the sun play in the religious beliefs and rituals of the Aztecs and Incas?
4. **Diversity** (a) What different cultural groups emerged in North America? (b) How did the lives of the Inuits develop differently from those of Native Americans on the Northwest Coast? What contributed to these differences?

## Thinking Critically

1. **Analyzing Information** (a) What advances in agriculture did the Mayas, Aztecs, and Incas make? (b) Why were these farming methods critical to the development of each civilization?
2. **Linking Past and Present** Millions of people visit the Mayan ruins in Mexico each year. Why do you think people are so fascinated by the Mayan civilization and its disappearance?
3. **Solving Problems** (a) How did the geography of the Valley of Mexico pose a challenge to the Aztecs as they built their civilization? (b) What methods did they develop to overcome this challenge? (c) What does their solution suggest about the level of government and learning among the Aztecs?
4. **Comparing** Review Chapter 6. Then, compare the methods used by the Incas and the Romans to unite and control their diverse empires.

5. **Drawing Conclusions** Reread the Up Close on pages 168–169. (a) Why was it a great honor to be chosen as an Aclla? (b) Do you think the Chosen Women had much personal freedom? Explain. (c) Based on your reading, make a generalization about the role of women in Incan society.
6. **Synthesizing Information** Look at the maps on pages 159 and 170 and the chart on page 172. (a) What is the exact location of the land bridge linking Asia and North America? (b) Which North American culture group was located in the region nearest the land bridge? (c) What were the characteristics of this group? (★ See *Skills for Success*, page 896.)

### *For Your Portfolio*

Imagine that you and a group of two or three classmates are time travelers from the next century. You have visited one of the early civilizations of the Americas—the Mayas, the Aztecs, the Incas, or the Anasazis. Now, you have returned home to give a slide show about your trip.

1. With your group, choose a civilization. Then, decide on the date of your visit. Make sure that you choose a time when that civilization was at its height.
2. Do further research on your chosen civilization. Focus on information that can be shown visually, such as what cities looked like and what activities took place there; how temples, palaces, homes, or other structures were designed; how people of various classes and occupations dressed; geographic features.
3. Prepare 8–10 pictures to be used as "slides." You may photocopy pictures of actual buildings, artifacts, or paintings. You may also draw pictures or diagrams based on descriptions by eyewitnesses or historians. Write a short narrative for each picture.
4. Write a brief opening statement for your "slide show," explaining why you chose to visit that civilization. Then, write a brief closing statement summarizing what you learned from your visit.
5. Present your "slide show" to the class. Afterward, invite other members of the class to make comments or ask questions.

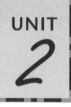

# Unit-in-Brief

## Empires of the Ancient World

**Chapter 4** Empires of India and China
(600 B.C.–A.D. 550)

Between 600 B.C. and A.D. 550, strong, unified empires with complex belief systems emerged in India and China. These civilizations set patterns in government, religion, and philosophy that influenced later cultures.

- Hindu beliefs, including the concepts of reincarnation, kharma, and dharma, profoundly influenced Indian civilization.
- The Buddha, an Indian religious reformer, sought spiritual enlightenment. His teachings gave rise to a new religion, Buddhism, that eventually spread through Southeast and East Asia.
- Under the Maurya and Gupta dynasties, India developed into a center of trade and had contacts with civilizations in Africa, the Middle East, and Central and Southeast Asia.
- The caste system, the village, and the family influenced many aspects of Indian life.
- The teachings of Confucius, based on ideals of duty and social good, influenced Chinese government and society.
- Legalism and Daoism were two other important philosophies that arose in China.
- Shi Huangdi united all of China and built a strong authoritarian government, which laid the groundwork for China's classical age.

- Under Han rulers, the Chinese made huge advances in trade, government, technology, and the arts.

**Chapter 5** Ancient Greece
(1750 B.C.–133 B.C.)

Despite bitter rivalry, Greek city-states gave rise to a civilization that set a standard of excellence for later civilizations. Greek ideas about the universe, the individual, and government still live on in the world today.

- Through trading contacts, Minoan and Mycenaean culture acquired many ideas from older civilizations of Egypt and Mesopotamia.
- Separated by mountains, the Greek city-states often warred with each other but united to defeat the Persians.
- After the Persian Wars, democracy flourished and culture thrived in Athens under the leadership of Pericles.
- Guided by a belief in reason, Greek artists, writers, and philosophers used their genius to seek order in the universe.
- The conquests of Alexander the Great spread Greek civilization throughout the Mediterranean world and across the Middle East to the outskirts of India.

- Greek culture blended with Persian, Egyptian, and Indian cultures to create the Hellenistic civilization, in which art, science, mathematics, and philosophy flourished.

## Chapter 6    Ancient Rome and the Rise of Christianity
### (509 B.C.–A.D. 476)

Rome expanded across the Mediterranean to build a huge, diverse empire. In the process, it spread the civilizations of Greece, Egypt, and the Fertile Crescent westward into Europe.

- After the Romans threw out their Etruscan king, they set up a republic. Eventually, commoners were allowed to be elected to the Roman Senate.
- Conquest and diplomacy helped the Romans to extend their rule from Spain to Egypt. However, expansion created social and economic problems that led to the decline of the republic and the rule of an emperor.
- During the Pax Romana, Roman emperors brought peace, order, unity, and prosperity to the lands under their control.
- Rome acted as a bridge between the east and the west by borrowing and transforming Greek and Hellenistic achievements to produce Greco-Roman civilization.
- Christianity, which emerged in Roman-held lands in the Middle East, spread quickly throughout the Roman empire. The new faith reshaped Roman beliefs.
- Foreign invasions, the division of the empire, a corrupt government, poverty and unemploy-

ment, and declining moral values finally contributed to the downfall of the Roman empire.

## Chapter 7    Civilizations of the Americas
### (1400 B.C.–A.D. 1570)

Three advanced civilizations—those of the Mayas, Aztecs, and Incas—developed in Central and South America. In North America, diverse culture groups emerged.

- The first settlers in the Americas were nomadic hunters who migrated across a land bridge between Siberia and Alaska and gradually populated two vast continents.
- Mayan civilization flourished from southern Mexico through Central America between A.D. 300 and 900. Its system of city-states supported a complex religious structure.
- In the 1400s, the Aztecs conquered most of Mexico and built a highly developed civilization led by a single ruler.
- By the 1500s, the Incas established a centralized government in Peru, ruled by a god-king and a powerful class of priests.
- Ten culture groups developed in the Arctic, Subarctic, Northwest Coast, California, Great Basin, Plateau, Southwest, Great Plains, Southeast, and Eastern Woodlands. Their diverse ways of life were strongly influenced by geography.

# A Global View

## What Characteristics Were Shared by Ancient Empires Around the World?

Empires combining many cities and small countries emerged in various parts of the world in ancient times. Some of the largest of these empires took shape in India, China, Europe, and, later, the Americas.

These larger political structures had many things in common. Most empires were built by military conquest and ruled by hereditary emperors through appointed governors or lesser kings. Empires everywhere developed powerful centralized bureaucracies like those of China or imposed universal legal codes like Roman law. Emperors protected far-flung trade routes and built large cities, canals, highways, and other public works. They also sponsored the spread of major religions, such as Buddhism in India and Christianity throughout the Roman empire.

### Eastern Empires

In India, the Maurya dynasty united the states along the Ganges about 300 B.C. The Hindu faith continued to flourish, but after 500 B.C., followers of a reformer known as the Buddha converted many Indians to Buddhism.

Shi Huangdi unified the states of eastern China around 200 B.C. After that, for most of China's history, the Han and later dynasties ruled a vast united nation. Philosophers like Confucius, as well as Buddhist missionaries, laid the groundwork for many basic Chinese beliefs.

### Classical Civilizations of Europe

The earliest European civilizations emerged among the peoples of two neighboring Mediterranean peninsulas. These people were the Greeks and the Romans. The Greeks built a brilliant civilization centered in independent city-states, while the Romans later constructed a huge empire that spanned three continents.

Two earlier societies—those of the sea-trading Minoans and the warlike Mycenaeans—gave

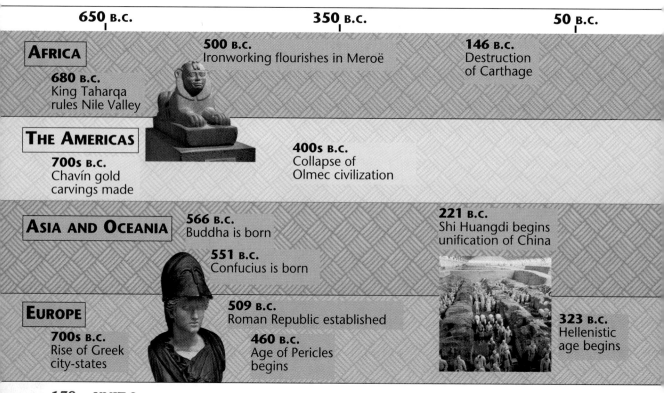

**650 B.C.** | **350 B.C.** | **50 B.C.**

**AFRICA**

**680 B.C.**
King Taharqa rules Nile Valley

**500 B.C.**
Ironworking flourishes in Meroë

**146 B.C.**
Destruction of Carthage

**THE AMERICAS**

**700s B.C.**
Chavín gold carvings made

**400s B.C.**
Collapse of Olmec civilization

**ASIA AND OCEANIA**

**566 B.C.**
Buddha is born

**551 B.C.**
Confucius is born

**221 B.C.**
Shi Huangdi begins unification of China

**EUROPE**

**700s B.C.**
Rise of Greek city-states

**509 B.C.**
Roman Republic established

**460 B.C.**
Age of Pericles begins

**323 B.C.**
Hellenistic age begins

way to the Greek city-states before 500 B.C. Led by Athens and Sparta, the bustling little Greek cities traded with many peoples. Athens also developed an early form of democratic government. Though they often fought with one another, the Greeks created a common body of art, science, and philosophy that laid the foundations of western civilization.

The Romans learned much from the Greeks. Their expanding empire swept around the Mediterranean and then spread northward across western Europe. Dominated first by its aristocratic Senate, Rome came to be ruled by powerful emperors after the reign of Augustus Caesar.

During the reign of Augustus, Jesus was born in the region of Judea. Christianity spread widely in Roman times. The new religion survived the fall of Rome to become the core of European culture in later centuries.

## American Civilizations

Across the Atlantic Ocean, civilizations also emerged in the Americas. Hunters and food-gatherers gradually settled into agricultural villages. In places, religious ceremonial centers emerged, then city-states and empires.

In Mexico, the Mayan city-states built magnificent temples and mastered complex mathematics. Peru saw a number of regional empires flourish. In the A.D. 1300s and 1400s, the Aztecs established a powerful empire in Mexico, while the Incas built an even larger one in the high Andes of Peru.

## Looking Ahead

Some of these mighty empires of Europe, Asia, and the Americas would serve as models for others to come in later centuries. From the Great Wall of China to the Incan royal road through the Andes, these empires left behind impressive monuments. The civilizations of China and India, Greece and Rome, forged cultural legacies that still influence the world.

**ACTIVITY** Choose two events and two pictures from the time line below. For each, write a sentence explaining how it relates to the themes expressed in the Global View essay.

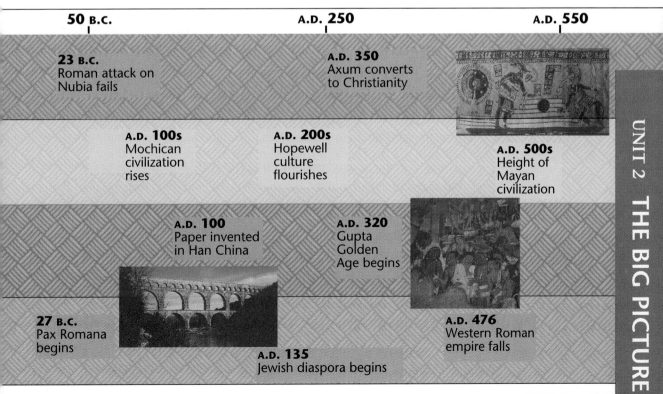

50 B.C.    A.D. 250    A.D. 550

**23 B.C.**
Roman attack on Nubia fails

**A.D. 350**
Axum converts to Christianity

**A.D. 100s**
Mochican civilization rises

**A.D. 200s**
Hopewell culture flourishes

**A.D. 500s**
Height of Mayan civilization

**A.D. 100**
Paper invented in Han China

**A.D. 320**
Gupta Golden Age begins

**27 B.C.**
Pax Romana begins

**A.D. 476**
Western Roman empire falls

**A.D. 135**
Jewish diaspora begins

# You Decide

## Exploring Global Issues

### How Should a Society's Leaders Be Chosen?

Pericles boasted that under Athenian democracy power was "in the hands not of a minority but of the whole people." More than 2,000 years later, Abraham Lincoln expressed this idea as "government of the people, by the people, and for the people." Yet not everyone has agreed that democracy is the best form of government. More often, leaders have inherited their positions, seized power by force, or been chosen by a small group. To begin your own investigation of leadership, examine these viewpoints.

**INDIA**

around 200 B.C.

In the *Mahabharata*, a wise man explains that kings became necessary when people grew too greedy to rule themselves:

> 66To institute order, the gods approached Vishnu, the lord of creatures, and said: 'Indicate to us that one person among mortals who alone is worthy of the highest rank.' Then the blessed lord god Vishnu reflected, and brought forth a glorious son, called Virajas, who became the first king.99

**RUSSIA**

1600s

The theory of divine right was based on the idea that a monarch's authority came directly from God. Many European rulers, like this Russian czar, combined worldly power with religious authority. ▶

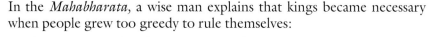

**UNITED STATES**

1787

Alexander Hamilton, a Caribbean-born statesman who helped shape the Constitution, distrusted ordinary citizens:

> 66All communities divide themselves into the few and the many. The first are the rich and well-born, the other the mass of the people. . . . The people are turbulent and changing; they seldom judge or determine right. Give therefore to the first class a distinct, permanent share in the government.99

**GREAT BRITAIN**

1861

The British philosopher John Stuart Mill was a champion of representative government:

> 66The ideally best form of government is that in which the sovereignty, or supreme controlling power in the last resort, is vested in the entire . . . community; every citizen not only having a voice in the exercise of that ultimate sovereignty, but being, at least occasionally, called on to take actual part in the government.99

**TANZANIA**

**1961**

Julius Nyerere, first president of Tanzania, described the practice of government by consensus, or mutual agreement:

> **"**The traditional African society, whether it had a chief or not—and many, like my own, did not—was a society of equals and it conducted its business through discussion. . . . 'They talk till they agree.' That gives you the very essence of traditional African democracy.**"**

**CHILE**

**1986**

Santiago Sinclair, an aide to Chilean military dictator Augusto Pinochet, defended the right of strong leaders to take power into their own hands:

> **"**Command is voice, conscience, justice, and it is made noble by the commitment and personal example of the one who wields it. Command guides spirits and unites wills, carrying them to success in endeavors that often require supreme heroism.**"**

**SOUTH AFRICA**

**1990s**

After years of struggle, the goal of "one person, one vote" was finally achieved by South Africa's black majority. Here, church members learn how to fill out a ballot. ▶

---

## COMPARING VIEWPOINTS

1. Which viewpoints represented here seem closest to the idea of democracy expressed by Pericles? Explain.
2. How is the idea of leadership expressed in the *Mahabharata* similar to divine right?
3. How does a leader emerge according to Hamilton? According to Nyerere? According to Sinclair?

## YOUR INVESTIGATION

**ACTIVITY**

1. Find out more about one of the viewpoints above or another viewpoint related to this topic. You might investigate:
   - The views of government expressed by the Chinese philosopher Confucius.
   - The idea of the "philosopher-king" in Plato's *Republic*.
   - The writings of French bishop Jacques Bossuet on divine right.
   - The Constitution of the United States or another modern constitution.
   - The rise of a charismatic leader such as Napoleon Bonaparte of France, Mustafa Kemal Atatürk of Turkey, or Juan Perón of Argentina.
   - The idea of government expressed by communist thinkers such as Lenin of Russia or Mao Zedong of China.
2. Decide which viewpoint you agree with most closely and express it in your own way. You may do so in an essay, a cartoon, a poem, a drawing or painting, a song, a skit, a video, or some other way.

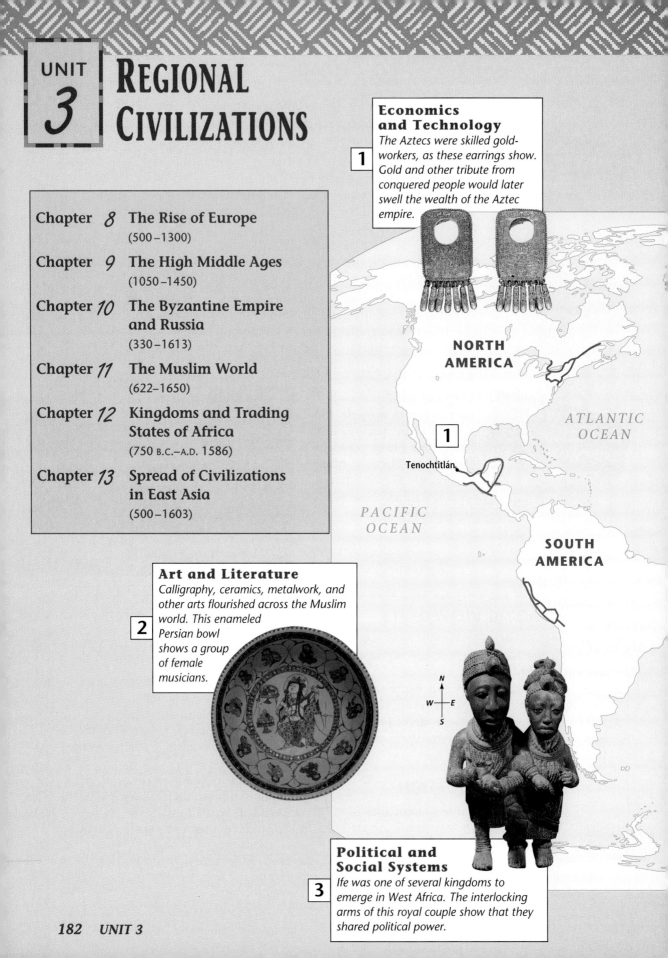

# UNIT 3
# REGIONAL CIVILIZATIONS

**Economics
and Technology**

**1** *The Aztecs were skilled gold-
workers, as these earrings show.
Gold and other tribute from
conquered people would later
swell the wealth of the Aztec
empire.*

NORTH
AMERICA

ATLANTIC
OCEAN

**1**

Tenochtitlán

PACIFIC
OCEAN

SOUTH
AMERICA

**Art and Literature**

*Calligraphy, ceramics, metalwork, and
other arts flourished across the Muslim
world. This enameled*
**2** *Persian bowl
shows a group
of female
musicians.*

**Political and
Social Systems**

**3** *Ife was one of several kingdoms to
emerge in West Africa. The interlocking
arms of this royal couple show that they
shared political power.*

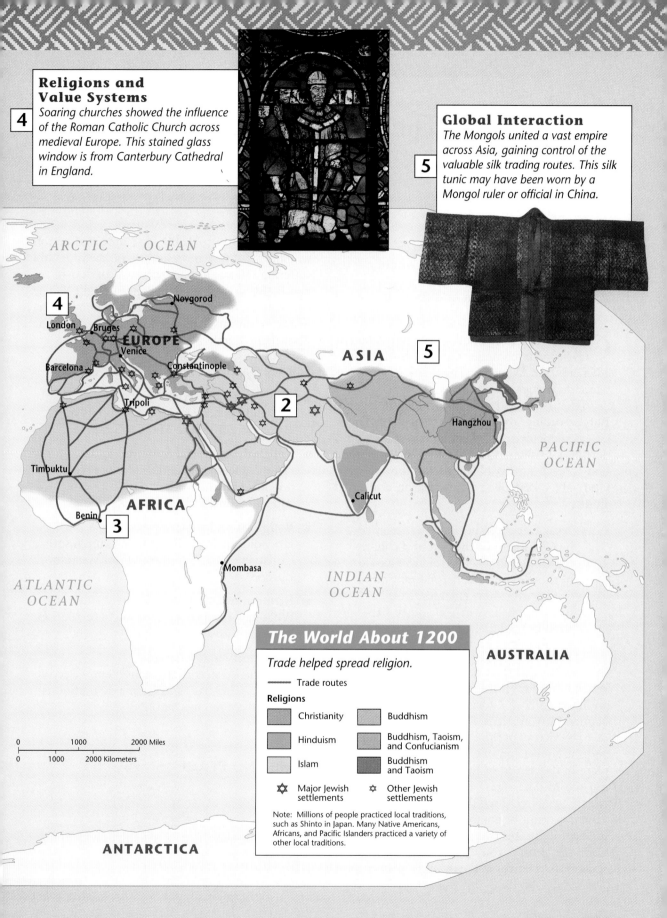

**Religions and Value Systems**

[4] Soaring churches showed the influence of the Roman Catholic Church across medieval Europe. This stained glass window is from Canterbury Cathedral in England.

**Global Interaction**

[5] The Mongols united a vast empire across Asia, gaining control of the valuable silk trading routes. This silk tunic may have been worn by a Mongol ruler or official in China.

ARCTIC OCEAN

[4]
Novgorod
London • Bruges
EUROPE
Venice
Barcelona
Constantinople
Tripoli
[2]

ASIA

[5]

Hangzhou

PACIFIC OCEAN

Timbuktu

AFRICA

Benin
[3]

Calicut

ATLANTIC OCEAN

Mombasa

INDIAN OCEAN

AUSTRALIA

**The World About 1200**

*Trade helped spread religion.*

———— Trade routes

**Religions**

Christianity    Buddhism

Hinduism    Buddhism, Taoism, and Confucianism

Islam    Buddhism and Taoism

✡ Major Jewish settlements    ☆ Other Jewish settlements

Note: Millions of people practiced local traditions, such as Shinto in Japan. Many Native Americans, Africans, and Pacific Islanders practiced a variety of other local traditions.

0   1000   2000 Miles
0   1000   2000 Kilometers

ANTARCTICA

# The Rise of Europe

## (500–1300)

## CHAPTER OUTLINE

1  **The Early Middle Ages**
2  **Feudalism and the Manor Economy**
3  **The Medieval Church**
4  **Economic Expansion and Change**

Clovis, king of the Franks, watched in horror as his men fell under the swords of the hated enemy, the Alamanni. The Frankish army was being destroyed.

What happened next is shrouded in legend. But according to Gregory, bishop of Tours, Clovis suddenly recalled the words of his wife, a devout Christian. Queen Clotilde had urged him to give up his old gods for the one true God. He raised his eyes to heaven and cried aloud:

> 66 Jesus Christ: You who are proclaimed by Clotilde to be the Son of the living God, You who are said to give aid to those in distress, if You grant me victory over these enemies . . . then will I also believe in You and be baptized in Your name. 99

Hardly had he spoken when the Alamanni soldiers "turned their backs and began to flee." When Clotilde learned of the miracle, she arranged to have Clovis and his chief warriors baptized as Christians.

The victory of the Franks over the Alamanni and the conversion of Clovis that followed took place in the period of European history that we call the Middle Ages. The details of the story, which were recorded by Gregory, bishop of Tours, may not be completely accurate. Still, the incident illustrates two major themes of the period: the central role of Christianity and the struggle for control of the dying Roman empire.

The Middle Ages, or medieval period, lasted from about 500 to 1500. The medieval period was a time of war and plunder, of hardship and suffering. It was also, however, a period of renewal. By slow stages, Europeans built a new civilization. It blended Greco-Roman and Germanic traditions within the framework of the Christian Church.

**FOCUS ON** these questions as you read:

■ **Geography and History**
   Why did Western Europe develop its own resources during the Middle Ages?

■ **Political and Social Systems**
   How did feudalism and the manor economy provide a measure of political, economic, and social order?

■ **Religions and Value Systems**
   How did the Roman Catholic Church spread Christian civilization throughout Western Europe?

■ **Economics and Technology**
   What new technologies sparked a revolution in agriculture and commerce?

■ **Continuity and Change**
   How did Western Europeans blend Greco-Roman, Christian, and Germanic traditions to build a new civilization?

## TIME AND PLACE

*Age of Faith*  During the Middle Ages, religion was a central part of everyday living. But the Roman Catholic Church was more than a spiritual guide. It was a powerful organization that helped to unify Western Europe and shaped every aspect of medieval life. This brilliant enamel, portraying Jesus, Mary, and John the Baptist, adorned a medieval church. **Continuity and Change**  Why do you think the fall of Rome helped to strengthen the Catholic Church?

## HUMANITIES LINK

*Art History*  Illuminated manuscript (page 197).
*Literature*  In this chapter, you will encounter passages from the following work of literature: Geoffrey Chaucer, *The Canterbury Tales* (page 196).

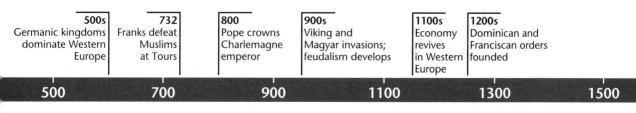

| 500s | 732 | 800 | 900s | 1100s | 1200s |
|---|---|---|---|---|---|
| Germanic kingdoms dominate Western Europe | Franks defeat Muslims at Tours | Pope crowns Charlemagne emperor | Viking and Magyar invasions; feudalism develops | Economy revives in Western Europe | Dominican and Franciscan orders founded |

| 500 | 700 | 900 | 1100 | 1300 | 1500 |

# 1 The Early Middle Ages

## Guide for Reading

- Why was Europe a frontier land in the early Middle Ages?

- How did invasions affect the peoples of Western Europe?

- How did Charlemagne blend Roman, German, and Christian traditions?

Pope Gregory the Great sat at his desk in Rome, thinking about the perils facing Italy. The Lombards were attacking from the north, and once again Rome might fall to plundering invaders. In despair, Gregory wrote:

66Where is the senate? Where are the people? The bones are all dissolved, the flesh is consumed, all the pomp and dignities of this world is gone. The whole mass is boiled away.99

Gregory was writing in about A.D. 600, as waves of invaders swept across Europe. Roman civilization was slowly disappearing. Wars raged constantly. Trade slowed to a trickle, towns emptied, and learning virtually ceased. During the early Middle Ages, from about 500 to 1000, Europe was an isolated, backward region largely cut off from the advanced civilizations that flourished in the Middle East, South Asia, China, and elsewhere.

## A Land of Great Potential

Rome had linked its far-flung European territories with miles of fine roads and had spread classical ideas, the Latin language, and Christianity to the tribal peoples of Western Europe. But Rome was a Mediterranean power. The Germanic peoples who ended Roman rule in the West shifted the focus to the north. There, the peoples of Europe began to create a new civilization.

**Location.** Europe is a relatively small area, although its impact on the modern world has been enormous. It lies on the western end of Eurasia, the giant landmass that stretches from present-day Portugal all the way to China. (See the map on page 187.)

**Resources.** At the dawn of the Middle Ages, Europe had great untapped potential. Dense forests covered much of the north, and the region's rich black earth was better suited for raising crops than the dry soils around the Mediterranean. Beneath the surface of the soil, from Poland to Britain, lay untapped veins of rich minerals.

The seas that surround much of Europe were important to its growth. Coastal people not only fished for food but also used the seas as highways for trade and exploration. Europe's large rivers were ideal for trade, and its many mountain streams seemed made for turning water wheels.

## Germanic Kingdoms

The Germanic tribes who migrated across Europe were farmers and herders. Their culture differed greatly from that of the Romans. They

**The Franks** During the early Middle Ages, many Germanic tribes set up small kingdoms in Italy, Gaul, Spain, Britain, and North Africa. They were constantly at war with one another. Gradually, however, the kingdom of the Franks emerged as strongest and established control over much of the western Roman empire. Shown here is a Frankish warrior. **Geography and History** How did Germanic peoples help to shift the geographic focus of European civilization?

# Geography and Resources of Europe

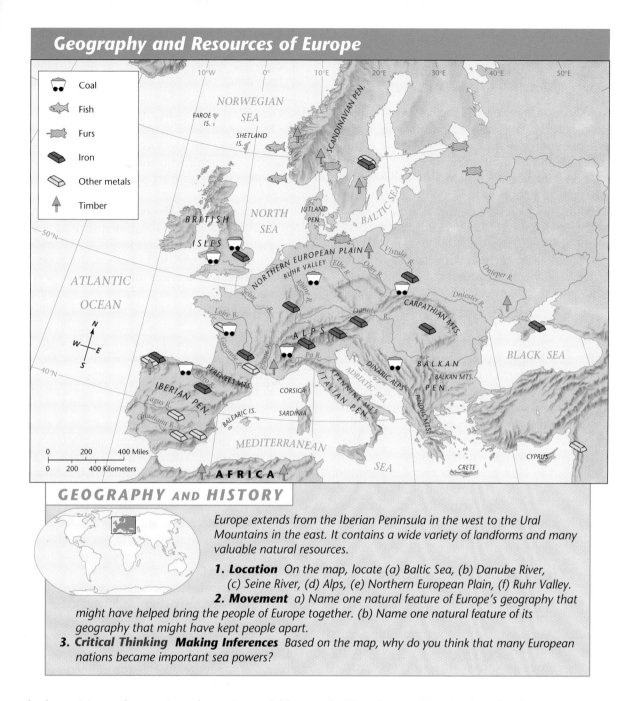

## GEOGRAPHY AND HISTORY

Europe extends from the Iberian Peninsula in the west to the Ural Mountains in the east. It contains a wide variety of landforms and many valuable natural resources.

**1. Location** On the map, locate (a) Baltic Sea, (b) Danube River, (c) Seine River, (d) Alps, (e) Northern European Plain, (f) Ruhr Valley.

**2. Movement** a) Name one natural feature of Europe's geography that might have helped bring the people of Europe together. (b) Name one natural feature of its geography that might have kept people apart.

**3. Critical Thinking Making Inferences** Based on the map, why do you think that many European nations became important sea powers?

---

had no cities and no written laws. Instead, they lived in small communities governed by unwritten customs. They were ruled by elected kings, whose chief role was to lead them in war. Warrior nobles swore oaths of loyalty and fought for the king in exchange for weapons and booty.

Between 400 and 700, the Germanic tribes carved up Western Europe into small kingdoms. The strongest and most successful kingdom was that of the Franks.

In 481, Clovis, a ruler of great energy and ability, became king of the Franks. Under his brilliant but ruthless leadership, the Franks were able to conquer the former Roman province of Gaul. Clovis ruled his new lands according to Frankish custom. At the same time, however, he managed to preserve much of the Roman legacy in Gaul.

Clovis's reign reached an important turning point when he converted to Christianity, the religion of many of his new subjects. (See page 184.) In doing so, he not only earned the support of the Gauls but also gained a powerful ally, the Roman Catholic Church.

## Islam: A New Mediterranean Power

Shortly after the Franks and other Germanic peoples had carved up Western Europe, a powerful new force, Islam, swept out of the Middle East into the Mediterranean world. As you will read in Chapter 11, Islam is a religion that emerged in Arabia in 632. Within 200 years, Muslims, as believers in the Islamic faith are called, had built a great empire and created a major new civilization.

Christians watched with fear as Muslim armies won victories around the Mediterranean. (See the map on page 190.) They overran Christian kingdoms in North Africa and Spain, then headed into France. At the battle of Tours in 732, Frankish warriors led by Charles Martel defeated a Muslim army. Christians saw the victory as a sign that God was on their side. Muslims advanced no farther into Western Europe, although they continued to rule most of Spain.

To European Christians, the Muslim presence was a source of anxiety and anger. Even when Islam was no longer a threat, Christians continued to have a hostile view of the Muslim world. Still, medieval Europeans did learn from the Arabs, whose knowledge in many areas, especially science and mathematics, was superior to their own.

## The Age of Charlemagne

For a time around 800, Western Europe had a moment of unity when the grandson of Charles Martel built an empire reaching across France, Germany, and part of Italy. The founder of this empire is known to history as Charlemagne (SHAHR luh mayn), or Charles the Great.

Standing more than six feet tall, Charlemagne towered over most people of his time.

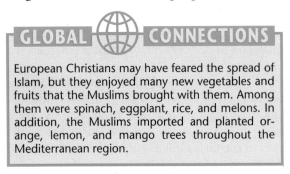

**GLOBAL CONNECTIONS**

European Christians may have feared the spread of Islam, but they enjoyed many new vegetables and fruits that the Muslims brought with them. Among them were spinach, eggplant, rice, and melons. In addition, the Muslims imported and planted orange, lemon, and mango trees throughout the Mediterranean region.

Astride a war horse, he was an awesome sight. He spent much of his 46-year reign fighting the Muslims in Spain, the Saxons in the north, the Avars and Slavs in the east, and the Lombards in Italy. In many ways, Charlemagne was an old-fashioned war chief. He loved battle and was a successful conqueror who reunited much of the old Roman empire in Europe. (See the map on page 189.)

**Emperor of the Romans.** Late in 800, Pope Leo III called on the Frankish king for help against rebellious nobles in Rome. Charlemagne marched south and crushed the rebellious Romans. At services on Christmas Day 800, the pope showed his gratitude by placing a crown on Charlemagne's head and proclaiming him "emperor."

The ceremony would have enormous significance. A Christian pope had crowned a Germanic king successor to the Roman emperors. In doing so, he revived the ideal of a united Christian community.

To the emperor of the eastern Roman empire in Constantinople, however, the pope's action was absurd. The eastern emperor saw himself, and not some backward Frankish king, as the sole Roman ruler. In the long run, Leo's crowning of Charlemagne helped to widen the split between the eastern and western Christian worlds. It also laid the ground for desperate power struggles between the Roman Catholic popes and future Germanic emperors.

**Government.** Charlemagne tried to exercise control over his many lands and create a united Christian Europe. He worked closely with the Church, helping to spread Christianity to the conquered peoples on the fringes of his empire. During his reign, missionaries won converts among the Saxons and the Slavs.

Like other Germanic kings, Charlemagne appointed powerful nobles to rule local regions. He gave them land so that they could offer support and supply soldiers for his armies. To keep control of these provincial rulers, he sent out officials called *missi domenici* (MIH see dohm in NEE kee) to check on roads, listen to grievances, and see that justice was done. He instructed:

66Let the *missi* make a diligent investigation whenever any man claims that an injustice has been done to him by anyone . . . and they shall administer the law fully and justly in the case of the holy churches of God and of the poor, of wards and of widows, and of the whole people.**"**

## A Revival of Learning

Charlemagne hoped to make his capital at Aachen (AH kuhn) a "second Rome." To achieve this goal, he made determined efforts to revive Latin learning throughout his empire.

**Keeping accurate records.** Charlemagne himself could read but not write. He is said to have kept a slate by his bed so that he could practice making letters if he had time before going to sleep at night. Although he made little progress with his own writing skills, he saw the need for officials who could keep complete and accurate records and write clear reports. Education had declined so much that even the supposedly educated clergy were often sadly ignorant, as Charlemagne discovered:

> **"**We have had letters sent to us from Church dignitaries that show a painful weakness in composition. On reading these letters and considering their lack of skill, we began to fear that the writers' knowledge and understanding of the Holy Scriptures might also prove to be much less than it ought to be.**"**

**Promoting education and learning.** To ensure a supply of educated officials, Charlemagne set up a palace school at Aachen. He then asked a respected scholar, Alcuin (AL kwihn) of York, to run the school. Alcuin set up a curriculum of study based on Latin learning, which became the educational model for medieval Europe. It included the study of grammar, rhetoric, logic, arithmetic, geometry, music, and astronomy.

Alcuin also hired scholars to copy ancient manuscripts, including the Bible and Latin works of history and science. These manuscripts served as the textbooks of Europe for the next 700 years.

## Charlemagne's Legacy

After Charlemagne died in 814, his empire soon fell apart. His heirs battled for power for

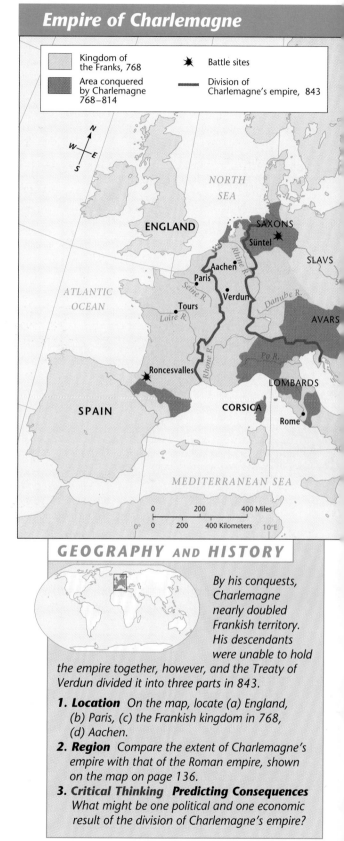

**Empire of Charlemagne**

Kingdom of the Franks, 768

Area conquered by Charlemagne 768–814

Battle sites

Division of Charlemagne's empire, 843

NORTH SEA

ENGLAND

SAXONS
Süntel

SLAVS

ATLANTIC OCEAN

Rhine R.

Aachen
Paris
Seine R.
Verdun
Tours
Loire R.
Danube R.

AVARS

Rhone R.
Po R.

Roncesvalles

LOMBARDS

CORSICA

SPAIN

Rome

MEDITERRANEAN SEA

0        200        400 Miles
0    200    400 Kilometers    10°E
0°

### GEOGRAPHY AND HISTORY

*By his conquests, Charlemagne nearly doubled Frankish territory. His descendants were unable to hold the empire together, however, and the Treaty of Verdun divided it into three parts in 843.*

1. **Location** On the map, locate (a) England, (b) Paris, (c) the Frankish kingdom in 768, (d) Aachen.
2. **Region** Compare the extent of Charlemagne's empire with that of the Roman empire, shown on the map on page 136.
3. **Critical Thinking** **Predicting Consequences** What might be one political and one economic result of the division of Charlemagne's empire?

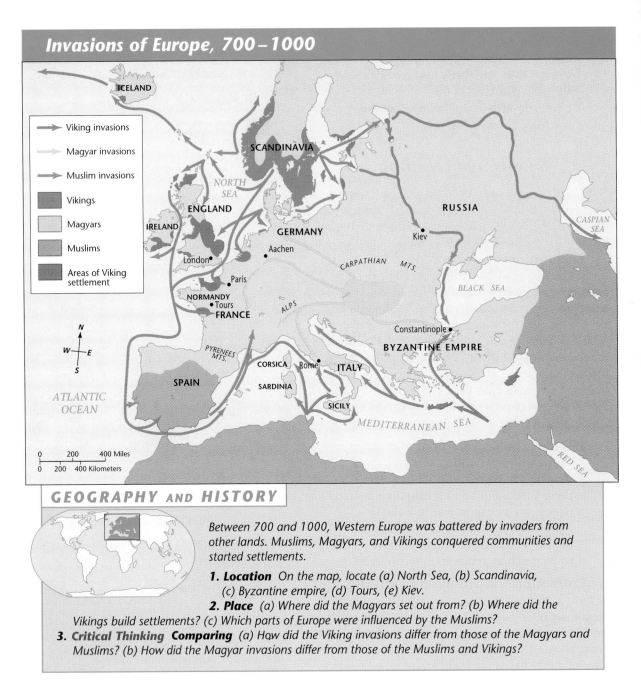

## Invasions of Europe, 700–1000

Viking invasions
Magyar invasions
Muslim invasions
Vikings
Magyars
Muslims
Areas of Viking settlement

ICELAND

SCANDINAVIA

NORTH SEA

ENGLAND

IRELAND

GERMANY

RUSSIA

CASPIAN SEA

Aachen

London

Kiev

CARPATHIAN MTS.

Paris

BLACK SEA

NORMANDY

Tours

FRANCE

ALPS

Constantinople

BYZANTINE EMPIRE

PYRENEES MTS.

CORSICA

Rome

ITALY

SPAIN

SARDINIA

SICILY

ATLANTIC OCEAN

MEDITERRANEAN SEA

RED SEA

0    200    400 Miles
0    200    400 Kilometers

### GEOGRAPHY AND HISTORY

*Between 700 and 1000, Western Europe was battered by invaders from other lands. Muslims, Magyars, and Vikings conquered communities and started settlements.*

**1. Location** On the map, locate (a) North Sea, (b) Scandinavia, (c) Byzantine empire, (d) Tours, (e) Kiev.
**2. Place** (a) Where did the Magyars set out from? (b) Where did the Vikings build settlements? (c) Which parts of Europe were influenced by the Muslims?
**3. Critical Thinking Comparing** (a) How did the Viking invasions differ from those of the Magyars and Muslims? (b) How did the Magyar invasions differ from those of the Muslims and Vikings?

nearly 30 years. Finally, in 843, Charlemagne's grandsons drew up the Treaty of Verdun, which split the empire into three regions. (See the map on page 189.)

Although Charlemagne's empire crumbled, the great Frankish ruler left a lasting legacy. He extended Christian civilization into northern Europe and furthered the blending of German, Roman, and Christian traditions. He also set up a strong, efficient government, and later medieval rulers looked to his example when they tried to centralize their own kingdoms.

## New Attacks

Even after the defeat at Tours in 732, Muslim forces kept up their pressure on Europe. In the late 800s, they conquered Sicily, which became a thriving center of Islamic culture. It was not until the mid-900s, when power struggles in the Middle East diverted attention from Europe, that Muslim attacks finally subsided.

About 896, a new wave of nomadic people, the Magyars, overran Eastern Europe. They moved on to plunder Germany, parts of France, and Italy. Finally after about 50 years, they were turned back and settled in what is today Hungary.

The most destructive raiders, however, were the Vikings. They snapped the last threads of unity in Charlemagne's empire. These expert sailors and ferocious fighters burst out of Scandinavia, a northern region that now includes Norway, Sweden, and Denmark. They looted and burned communities along the coasts and rivers of Europe, from Ireland to Russia.

▲ *Figurehead of a Viking ship*

The Vikings were not just fierce warriors. They were traders and explorers as well. In their far-ranging voyages, they sailed around the Mediterranean Sea and crossed the Atlantic Ocean. Leif Erikson set up a short-lived Viking colony on the continent of North America in about the year 1000. Other Vikings opened trade routes that linked northern Europe to Mediterranean lands. Vikings also settled in England, northern France (Normandy), Ireland, and parts of Russia.

## SECTION 1 REVIEW

1. **Identify** (a) Clovis, (b) Islam, (c) Charlemagne, (d) Alcuin, (e) Treaty of Verdun, (f) Vikings.
2. What resources did Europe have at the dawn of the Middle Ages?
3. (a) What group led the first wave of invasions of Europe? (b) What groups were part of the second wave of invasions? (c) What was the effect of the invasions?
4. What steps did Charlemagne take to improve government and unify his empire?
5. *Critical Thinking* **Recognizing Points of View** The term *Middle Ages* was coined by Europeans to describe the period from 500 to 1500. Do you think that other civilizations, such as that of China or Islam, use the same term for that period? Why or why not?
6. *ACTIVITY* Write a telegram of 25 words or less reporting on the battle of Tours and describing its significance.

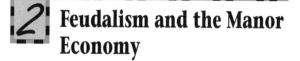

# 2 Feudalism and the Manor Economy

## Guide for Reading

- How did feudalism shape medieval society?
- What status did noblewomen have in medieval Europe?
- What was the basis of the manor economy?
- **Vocabulary** *vassal, fief, knight, chivalry, troubadour, manor, serf*

It was 1127, and Count William had just inherited the rich lands of Flanders, in Western Europe. In April, the nobles of Flanders gathered to pledge loyalty to their new lord. One by one, they knelt before him. "Will you serve me loyally?" asked William. "I will," the noble replied. He then took a solemn oath:

> **❝**I promise on my faith that I will in future be faithful to Count William and will observe my [loyalty] to him completely against all persons in good faith and without deceit.**❞**

The count then touched the noble with a small rod. With that gesture, he granted the noble a parcel of land, including any towns, castles, or people on it.

Although the words might vary, ceremonies like this one took place all across Europe during the Middle Ages. In public, before witnesses, great nobles and lesser lords exchanged vows of loyalty and service. Those vows were part of a new political and social system that governed medieval life.

## A New System of Rule

In the face of invasions by Vikings, Muslims, and Magyars, kings and emperors were too weak to maintain law and order. People needed to defend their homes and lands. In response to that basic need for protection, a new system, called feudalism, evolved.

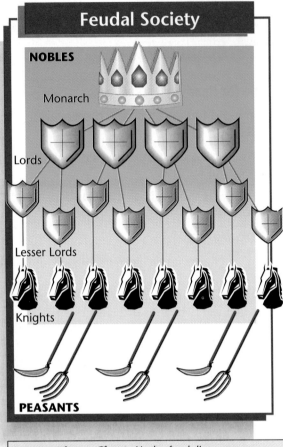

## Feudal Society

**NOBLES**

Monarch

Lords

Lesser Lords

Knights

**PEASANTS**

**Interpreting a Chart** *Under feudalism, everyone had a well-defined place in society. At the head of society was the monarch. Peasants, who made up the bulk of the population, were at the bottom.*
■ *What other groups were part of feudal society?*

As you have read in Chapter 3, feudalism was a loosely organized system of rule in which powerful local lords divided their large land-holdings among the lesser lords. In exchange for land, these lesser lords, or vassals, pledged service and loyalty to the greater lord.

The relationship between lords and vassals was established by custom and tradition. A lord granted his vassal a fief (FEEF), or estate. Estates ranged from a few acres to hundreds of square miles and included peasants to work the land, as well as any towns or buildings on the land. Besides granting the estate, the lord also promised to protect his vassal.

In return, the vassal pledged loyalty to his lord. He also agreed to provide the lord with 40 days of military service each year, certain money payments, and advice.

## Lords, Vassals, and Knights

Everyone had a place in feudal society, as the chart at left shows. Below the monarch were the most powerful lords—dukes and counts—who held the largest fiefs. Each of these lords had vassals, and these vassals in turn had their own vassals. In many cases, the same man was both vassal and lord—vassal to a more powerful lord above him and lord to a less powerful vassal below him.

Because vassals often held fiefs from more than one lord, feudal relationships grew very complex. A vassal who had pledged loyalty to several lords could have serious problems if his overlords quarreled with each other. What was he to do if both demanded his aid? To solve this problem, a vassal usually had a liege lord to whom he owed his first loyalty.

## The World of Warriors

Feudal lords battled constantly for power, and for feudal nobles warfare was a way of life. Many nobles trained from boyhood for a future occupation as a knight, or mounted warrior.

**Training for knighthood.** At the age of seven, a boy slated to become a knight was sent away to the castle of his father's lord. There, he learned to ride and fight. He also learned to keep his armor and weapons in good condition. Training was difficult and discipline was strict. Any laziness was punished with an angry blow or even a severe beating.

When his training was finished, often when he was about age 21, the boy was ready to be made a knight. Kneeling before an older knight, he bowed his head. The knight struck the young man with his hand or the flat side of his sword and declared something like the following: "In the name of God, Saint Michael, and Saint George, I dub thee knight. Be valiant." After this "dubbing," the young knight took his place beside other warriors.

**ISSUES For TODAY** In feudal society, everyone knew his or her place. What are the benefits and drawbacks of a clearly defined social order?

As the fierce fighting of the early Middle Ages lessened in the 1100s, tournaments, or mock battles, came into fashion. A powerful lord would invite knights from the surrounding area to a tournament to enter these contests of fighting skill. At first, tournaments were as dangerous as real battles, and captured knights were held for ransom. In time, they acquired more ceremony and ritual.

**Castles.** During the early Middle Ages, powerful lords fortified their homes to withstand attack. Their strongholds included a keep, or wooden tower, ringed by a fence. The keep was separated from the surrounding area by a moat, or water-filled ditch.

The strongholds gradually became larger and grander. By the 1100s, royal rulers and nobles owned sprawling stone castles with high walls, towers, and drawbridges over wide moats. Wars often centered on seizing castles that commanded strategic river crossings, harbors, or mountain passes. Castle dwellers stored up food and water so that they could withstand a long siege. If attackers failed to starve the defenders into surrender, they might tunnel under the castle walls.

**Role of noblewomen.** Noblewomen as well as noblemen played active roles in this warrior society. The "lady" became "lord of the manor" while her husband or father was off fighting. She supervised vassals, managed the household, and performed necessary agricultural and medical tasks. Sometimes she might even have to go to war to defend her estate.

Some medieval noblewomen, like Eleanor of Aquitaine, took a hand in politics. Eleanor inherited vast lands in southwestern France. Through two marriages, she became, first, queen of France and, later, queen of England. For more than 70 years, Eleanor was a leading force in European affairs.

Women's rights to inheritance were severely restricted under the feudal system. Land was usually inherited by the eldest son in a family. Women did, however, receive land as part of their dowry, and fierce negotiations swirled around an unmarried or widowed heiress. If her husband died before her, a woman regained rights to her land.

Like their brothers, the daughters of nobles were sent to friends or relatives for training. Before her parents arranged her marriage, a young woman was expected to know how to spin, weave, and supervise servants. A few learned to read and write. As a wife, she was expected to bear many children and be dutiful and loyal to her husband.

**Chivalry.** In the later Middle Ages, knights adopted a code of conduct called chivalry. Chivalry required knights to be brave, loyal, and true to their word. In warfare, they had to fight fairly and be generous to their enemies. Knights, for example, agreed not to attack another knight before he had a chance to put on his armor and prepare for battle. Chivalry also dictated that warriors treat a captured knight well or even release him if he promised to pay his ransom. Chivalry had limits, though. It applied to nobles only, not to commoners.

Chivalry raised women to a new status. The code of chivalry called for women to be protected and cherished. Troubadours, or wandering poets, adopted this view. Their love songs

**Knight in Armor** *To do battle, a knight needed armor and helmet, shield, lance, and sword. He also needed several horses, with armor and saddles. Finally, to care for the horses and equipment, he needed the services of a squire, or knight in training.* **Economics and Technology** *What economic reason helps to explain why nobles and not peasants became knights?*

praised the perfection, beauty, and wit of women throughout the ages. Much later, ideas of chivalry would shape our modern ideas of romantic love.

## The Manor

The heart of the medieval economy was the manor, or lord's estate. Most manors included one or more villages and the surrounding lands. Peasants, who made up the majority of medieval society, lived and worked on the manor.

**Peasants and lords.** Most of the peasants on a manor were serfs, who were bound to the land. Serfs were not slaves who could be bought and sold. Still, they were not free. They could not leave the manor without the lord's permission. And if the manor was granted to a new lord, the serfs went along with it.

Peasants and their lords were tied together by mutual rights and responsibilities. Peasants had to work several days a week farming the lord's domain, or lands. They also had to repair the lord's roads, bridges, and fences. Peasants paid the lord a fee when they married, when they inherited their father's acres, or when they used the local mill to grind grain. Other payments fell due at Christmas and Easter. Because money had largely disappeared from medieval Europe, they paid with products such as grain, fruit, honey, eggs, or chickens.

In return for a lifetime of labor, peasants had the right to farm several acres for themselves. They were also entitled to their lord's protection from Viking raids or feudal warfare. Although they could not leave the manor without permission, they also could not be forced off it. In theory, at least, they were guaranteed food, housing, and land.

**A narrow world.** The medieval manor was a small, self-sufficient world. Peasants produced almost everything they needed, from food and clothing to simple furniture and tools. Most peasants never ventured more than a few miles from their village. They had no schooling and no knowledge of the larger world.

A typical manor included a few dozen one-room huts clustered close together in a village. (★ See *Skills for Success*, page 206.) Nearby stood a water mill to grind grain, a tiny church, and the manor house. The fields surrounding the village were divided into narrow strips. Each family had strips of land in different fields so that good and bad land was shared fairly. Half the land was left fallow, or unplanted, each year, to allow the soil to regain its fertility.

## Daily Life

For most peasants, life was harsh. Men, women, and children worked long hours, from sunup to sundown. During planting season, a man might guide an ox-drawn plow while his wife goaded the ox into motion with a pointed stick. Children helped plant seeds, weeded, and took care of pigs or sheep.

The peasant family ate a simple diet of black bread with vegetables such as peas, cabbage, turnips, or onions. They seldom had meat unless they poached wild game at the risk of harsh punishment. If they lived near a river, a meal might include fish. At night, the family and any cows, chickens, pigs, or sheep slept together in their one-room hut.

**Feudal Justice** *Feudal justice was very different from Roman ideas of law. In this illustration of a trial by ordeal, a woman walks over red-hot coals. If she is burned, she is judged guilty. If she emerges unharmed, it is held as proof that God has found her innocent.* **Continuity and Change** *What method is used to try people accused of crimes today?*

**Seasons.** Like farmers everywhere, European peasants worked according to the season. In spring and autumn, they plowed and harvested. In summer, they hayed. At other times, they weeded, repaired fences, and performed chores. Hunger was common, especially in late winter when the harvest was exhausted and new crops had not yet ripened. Disease took a heavy toll, and few peasants lived beyond the age of 35.

**Celebrations.** Despite life's grimness, peasants found occasions to celebrate, such as marriages and births. Welcome breaks came on holidays such as Christmas and Easter, when they had a week off from work.

Dozens of other festivals in the Christian calendar brought days off, too. For these times, people might butcher an animal so that they could feast on meat. There would also be dancing and rough sports, from wrestling to ball games.

**Beliefs.** On the sabbath, peasants might attend chapel. After services, they gossiped or danced, even though the priest might condemn their racy songs or rowdy behavior.

In medieval Europe, people believed in elves, fairies, and other nature spirits. They had faith in love potions and magic charms. Witches, they thought, could cast spells with a mere look.

Priests tried to "Christianize" these old beliefs and practices. They built churches where temples to ancient gods had once stood. Where villagers had once sacrificed to the gods of the sun and rain to ensure good crops, priests might bless the fields in the name of Christ.

## SECTION 2 REVIEW

1. **Define** (a) vassal, (b) fief, (c) knight, (d) chivalry, (e) troubadour, (f) manor, (g) serf.
2. Describe three features of feudal society.
3. How did chivalry affect the status of women?
4. (a) What responsibilities did the peasant have toward the lord? (b) What responsibilities did the lord have toward the peasant?
5. *Critical Thinking* **Recognizing Causes and Effects** How did the breakdown of central authority in Europe lead to the development of feudalism?
6. *ACTIVITY* Imagine that you are a peasant on a medieval manor. Write a diary entry for a typical day of your life.

# 3 The Medieval Church

## Guide for Reading

■ How did the Church dominate life in the Middle Ages?

■ How did monks and nuns influence European life?

■ Why did reform movements spring up within the Church?

■ **Vocabulary** *secular, sacrament, canon law, excommunication, interdict, tithe, anti-Semitism*

The Lady Hirsendis waved goodbye to her husband as he set off for Jerusalem. Then she turned to her own responsibilities, looking after the family's lands in her husband's absence. First, however, she must ride to the monastery of Marmoutier, to pray to St. Martin. She would also pay her respects to the abbot, or head of the monastery.

Religion was woven into the fabric of the medieval world. Indeed, the Middle Ages has often been called Europe's "age of faith." The commanding force behind that faith was the Christian Church.

## A Spiritual and Worldly Empire

After the fall of Rome, the Christian Church split into eastern and western churches. The western church, headed by the pope, became known as the Roman Catholic Church. The Roman Catholic Church grew stronger and wealthier during the Middle Ages. In time, it not only controlled the spiritual life of Christians, but was also the most powerful secular, or worldly, force in Western Europe.

**The Church hierarchy.** The pope was the spiritual leader of the Roman Catholic Church. He also ruled vast lands in central Italy, known as the Papal States. As the spiritual heir and representative of Christ on Earth, the pope claimed to have authority over all secular rulers.

An army of churchmen supervised the Church's many activities. High Church officials were usually nobles. Some archbishops and

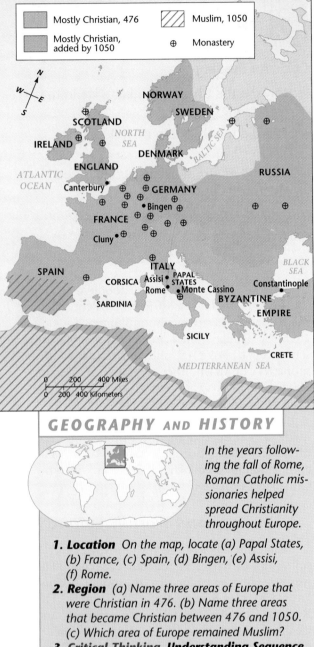

## Spread of Christianity in Europe

Mostly Christian, 476
Mostly Christian, added by 1050
Muslim, 1050
⊕ Monastery

NORWAY
SWEDEN
SCOTLAND
NORTH SEA
IRELAND
DENMARK
ENGLAND
RUSSIA
ATLANTIC OCEAN
Canterbury
GERMANY
Bingen
FRANCE
Cluny
BALTIC SEA
SPAIN
ITALY
CORSICA
Assisi
PAPAL STATES
Rome
Monte Cassino
SARDINIA
BLACK SEA
Constantinople
BYZANTINE EMPIRE
SICILY
CRETE
MEDITERRANEAN SEA

0  200  400 Miles
0  200  400 Kilometers

### GEOGRAPHY AND HISTORY

In the years following the fall of Rome, Roman Catholic missionaries helped spread Christianity throughout Europe.

1. **Location** On the map, locate (a) Papal States, (b) France, (c) Spain, (d) Bingen, (e) Assisi, (f) Rome.
2. **Region** (a) Name three areas of Europe that were Christian in 476. (b) Name three areas that became Christian between 476 and 1050. (c) Which area of Europe remained Muslim?
3. **Critical Thinking** *Understanding Sequence* What device is used on this map to demonstrate a sequence of events? Explain.

bishops had their own territories, like other feudal lords. Since they were often the only educated people, feudal rulers appointed them to administer their own governments.

**Authority of the Church.** Medieval Christians believed that all people were sinners, doomed to eternal suffering. The only way to avoid the tortures of hell was to participate in the sacraments, which are the sacred rituals of the Church. Through faith in Christ and participation in the sacraments, Christians could achieve salvation—eternal life in heaven. Because it decided who could participate in the sacraments, and thus who could gain salvation, the Church had absolute power in the religious life of Christians during the Middle Ages.

The Church had its own body of laws, known as canon law, and its own courts. Canon law applied to religious teachings, the behavior of the clergy, and even marriages and morals.

Anyone who refused to obey Church laws faced a range of penalties. The most severe was excommunication. People who were excommunicated could not receive the sacraments. To people who believed in the tortures of hell, such a punishment was truly terrifying. People who were excommunicated also could not be buried in sacred ground. All other Christians were required to shun them.

A powerful noble who violated Church laws could face an interdict, which excluded an entire town, region, or kingdom from participating in most sacraments and from receiving Christian burial. Even the strongest ruler was likely to give in to that pressure.

### The Church and Daily Life

Most Christians had no contact with the pope or the higher clergy. They saw only their local priest, who supervised their religious life and provided comfort during times of trouble. The English poet Geoffrey Chaucer fondly described a poor town priest:

66Wide was his parish, with
houses far asunder,
But he would not be kept by
rain or thunder,
If any had suffered a sickness
or a blow,
From visiting the farthest,
high or low,
Plodding his way on foot, his
staff in hand,
He was a model his flock could
understand.99

**The village church.** For peasants, religion was linked to the routines of daily life. In the village church, priests baptized their children and performed their marriages. In addition, the church was a social center, where they exchanged news and gossip. In the later Middle Ages, some priests ran schools in the church.

Villagers took pride in the church building, which they decorated with care. Some churches housed relics, the bones or blood of martyrs or other holy figures. Visitors would make pilgrimages, or journeys, to pray before the relics.

**The tithe.** To support itself, the Church required all Christians to pay a tithe, or tax equal to a tenth of their incomes. The idea of a tithe had existed in ancient religions before Christianity. The Church used the tithe to help the poor.

**Women and the Church.** The Church taught that men and women were equal before God. On Earth, however, women were inferior to men. The Church presented women in two extreme roles. On the one hand, women were seen as "daughters of Eve," weak and easily led into sin, and thus needing the guidance of a man. On the other hand, there was the ideal woman, modest and pure in spirit, personified by Mary, "mother of God." Faced with these two extremes, the ordinary woman had little to follow in the way of a realistic role model.

The Church tried to protect women. It set a minimum age for marriage. Church courts fined men who seriously injured their wives. Yet the Church upheld a double standard, punishing women for offenses much more harshly than men.

## Monks and Nuns

Both women and men might withdraw from worldly life to become nuns or monks. Behind the thick walls of monasteries and convents, they devoted their lives to spiritual goals.

**The Benedictine Rule.** About 530, a monk named Benedict founded the monastery of Monte Cassino in Italy. He drew up a set of rules to regulate life there. In time, the Benedictine Rule, as it became known, spread to monasteries and convents across Europe.

Under the Benedictine Rule, monks and nuns took an oath of poverty. They also took vows of chastity, or purity, and of obedience to the abbot. Their chief duties were prayer and

worship of God. However, Benedict also believed in the spiritual value of manual labor, and he required monks to work in the fields or at other physical tasks.

**A life of service.** In a world without hospitals, public schools, or social programs, convents and monasteries provided basic social services. Monks and nuns tended the sick. They gave alms, or charity, to the poor and set up schools for children. Travelers, especially Christian pilgrims traveling to holy shrines, could find food and a night's lodging at many monasteries and convents.

**Centers of learning.** Monasteries and convents performed a vital cultural function by preserving the writings of the ancient world.

ART HISTORY

**Illuminated Manuscript** *Monks, nuns, and other skilled artisans copied books by hand and illuminated, or illustrated, each page. They decorated the letters and framed the text with intricate designs, biblical scenes, or portrayals of daily life.* **Art and Literature** *Describe the decorations on the illuminated manuscript shown here.*

Most often, monks and nuns simply copied the ancient books as a form of labor. Once copied out, the work itself—Virgil's *Aeneid,* for example—might rest unread on a monastery shelf for centuries. Still, it would be there when scholars once again took an interest in such things.

Some monks and nuns were better educated and took a more serious interest in culture. The Italian abbot Cassiodorus, for example, wrote valuable summaries of Greek and Latin works. He also taught the Latin and Greek classics to the monks who served under him.

Other monks, like the Venerable Bede in England, produced scholarly works of their own. Bede was the first to use the designations B.C. and A.D.—meaning before and after the birth of Christ—to date historical events. Bede, a historian, was concerned with the truth. But like all writers of the time, he mixed stories of magical miracles with historical fact.

**Missionaries.** Not all monks and nuns remained isolated from the outside world. During the early Middle Ages, men and women risked their lives to spread Christian teachings across Europe.

St. Patrick was a monk who crossed to Ireland and set up the Irish Church. Pope Gregory the Great sent another monk, St. Augustine, as a missionary to the Angles and Saxons in England. He became the first archbishop of Canterbury. Later, the Church honored some of its missionaries by declaring them saints.

## Hildegard of Bingen: Adviser to Popes and Kings

The very first vision, Hildegard recalled, occurred when she was a child of three. "I kept it hidden until God in His grace willed to have it made public," she later wrote. This vision, soon followed by others, marked the beginning of an extraordinary life. Hildegard would become a composer, writer, abbess, and adviser to the great men and women of her day. Even the pope recognized her special gift as a prophet.

**Commanded by God.** Perhaps in response to her visions, Hildegard's parents placed her in a convent at an early age. There, she would get an education, and if she did not

marry, she might take religious vows. By the age of 14, Hildegard had made her decision: She would become a nun.

During 24 years of convent life, Hildegard followed the daily routine—reading, singing God's praises, and keeping busy copying books, weaving cloth, and doing other manual work. Then, when she was 38 years old, she was named abbess, or head of the convent.

Not long after assuming the duties of abbess, Hildegard had a new vision:

> 66A great flash of light from heaven pierced my brain. . . . In that instant my mind was imbued with the meaning of the sacred books, the Psalter, the Gospel, and the other books of the Old and New Testament.99

A voice accompanying the vision commanded Hildegard to "set down all things according to the secrets of their mysteries."

**The Work of Nuns** *Nuns like Hildegard of Bingen made important contributions to society. Besides advising kings and popes, Hildegard composed more than 80 pieces of religious music, compiled a medical book entitled* Causes and Cures, *and wrote several works criticizing corruption in the Church. Here, a group of nuns waits to receive a blessing.* **Continuity and Change** *Do members of religious orders play a social role today? Explain.*

Certain that the command came from God, Hildegard began writing the first of several books. It dealt with subjects ranging from science, medicine, and philosophy to Christian teachings and morals. Hildegard's writing, expressed in mystical terms, clearly revealed her own extensive knowledge and brilliant mind.

**A sage and prophet.** In 1147, Hildegard founded a new convent, near Bingen, in Germany. Even before moving to Bingen, Hildegard had gained a reputation as a sage and a prophet. Now, reports of her visions and writings spread across Europe. Popes, emperors, kings, and queens sought her advice.

Hildegard did not hesitate to speak her mind and encouraged or scolded churchmen and rulers alike. "Take care that the Highest King does not strike you down because of the blindness that prevents you from governing justly," she warned the German emperor Frederick I. To Eleanor of Aquitaine, who for some 70 years played a central role in European politics, she wrote: "Make peace with God and with men, and God will help you in your tribulations."

**Growing restrictions on women.** Hildegard was not the only nun to raise her voice in the early Middle Ages. Many women with inquiring minds and proud spirits entered convents. But as the Church grew more powerful, it began to restrict nuns' activities. It withdrew rights they had once had to preach the Gospel or hear confession. It frowned on too much learning for women, preferring them to accept the Church's authority. The tradition of women mystical writers continued for a while, but by the early 1400s, the increasingly heavy restrictions on women's activities made it hard for other women to earn a position of power as Hildegard had done. ■

## Reform Movements

The very success of the medieval Church brought serious problems. As its wealth and power grew, discipline weakened. The clergy tended to be worldly, and many lived in luxury. Monks and nuns ignored their vows. Married priests devoted more time to the interests of their families than to their Church duties. The growing corruption and moral decay led to demands for reform.

**The monastery at Cluny.** In the early 900s, the pious Abbot Berno at Cluny, a monastery in eastern France, set out to end abuses. First, he revived the Benedictine Rule. He also announced that he would not permit nobles to interfere in the running of the monastery. Finally, he filled the monastery with men who were devoted solely to religious pursuits. Other monasteries copied the Cluniac program, spreading Abbot Berno's reforms across Western Europe.

In 1073, a new pope, Gregory VII, extended the Cluniac reforms throughout the entire Church. He prohibited simony (SIHM uh nee), the selling of positions in the Church, and outlawed marriage for priests. Gregory then called on Christians to renew their faith. To end outside influence, he insisted that the Church, and not kings and nobles, choose Church officials. That policy would lead to a battle of wills with the German emperor, as you will read.

**Preaching orders.** A different approach to reform was taken by friars, monks who traveled widely, preaching to the poor, especially in Europe's growing towns. The first order of friars, the Franciscans, was founded by a wealthy young Italian known as Francis of Assisi. When he was about 20 years old, Francis underwent a religious conversion. Leaving his father's prosperous home, he devoted himself to preaching the Christian message and teaching by his own examples of good works.

The Spanish reformer St. Dominic also founded a preaching order of friars to work in the larger world. He, too, called for friars to live in poverty as the early Christians had. Dominic was particularly upset by the spread of heresies, religious beliefs or doctrines that differed from accepted Church teachings. The Dominicans dedicated themselves to educating people about Church doctrines and disputing the ideas of the heretics.

Some women responded to the call of reform by creating groups that were independent of the regular Church orders. One such group was the Beguines (BEHG eenz). Most convents accepted only well-born women who gave their dowry to the Church. The Beguines were made up of women who did not have sufficient financial means to enter a convent. Supporting themselves through their weaving and embroidering,

**Seder Plate** *Throughout Europe, Jewish communities observed their unique traditions and customs. This Seder plate belonged to a family living in Muslim Spain. At the Passover holiday each year, the plate was filled with the traditional foods of the Seder, or Passover meal.* **Diversity** *Why does one often need courage to be different from others?*

working Jewish communities, although they taxed them heavily. Early German kings gave educated Jews positions in their courts. Charlemagne, for example, appointed Isaac, a Jew, to serve as interpreter for envoys sent to the Muslim ruler Harun al Rashid in Baghdad.

Often, however, medieval Christians persecuted Jews. As the Church's power increased, it barred Jews from owning land or practicing most occupations, including trade and handicrafts. The Church also charged that Jews were responsible for the death of Jesus, thus laying the foundations for anti-Semitism, or prejudice against Jews.

In bad times, anti-Semitism increased. Christians blamed Jews for all kinds of ills, including diseases and famines. Because many Jews were moneylenders, people blamed them for their own economic hardships. As persecution worsened in Western Europe, large numbers of Jews migrated into Eastern Europe. There, they built communities that survived until modern times. (See the map on page 250.)

the Beguines ministered to the poor and set up hospitals and shelters.

## Jews in Western Europe

Medieval Europe was home to numerous Jewish communities. After the Romans expelled them from Palestine, the Jews had scattered all around the Mediterranean. In their new homes, they preserved the oral and written laws that were central to their faith.

These Mediterranean, or Sephardic, Jews flourished particularly in Spain. The Arab Muslims who gained control of Spain in the 700s were tolerant of both Christians and Jews. Jewish culture flowered in Muslim Spain, which became a major center of Hebrew scholarship. Jews also served as officials in Muslim royal courts.

Jews spread into northern Europe as well. There, they became known as Ashkenazim, or "German" Jews. Many Christian rulers in northern Europe protected or tolerated hard-

## SECTION 3 REVIEW

1. **Identify** (a) Roman Catholic Church, (b) Benedictine Rule, (c) Cluny, (d) Francis of Assisi, (e) Dominicans, (f) Beguines.
2. **Define** (a) secular, (b) sacrament, (c) canon law, (d) excommunication, (e) interdict, (f) tithe, (g) anti-Semitism.
3. Describe three ways in which the Church shaped medieval life.
4. (a) What views did the Church hold about women? (b) How did the Church views of women change over time?
5. How did monks and nuns help build Christian civilization in Europe?
6. *Critical Thinking* **Analyzing Information** Why do you think important leaders accepted the scolding and advice of Hildegard, an "inferior" woman?
7. *ACTIVITY* When copying out old texts, monks and nuns often decorated the first letter of a paragraph and the margins of a page with brilliant designs. (See the picture on page 197.) Imagine that you are a medieval monk. Copy and decorate the Chaucer poem on page 196.

# 4 Economic Expansion and Change

## Guide for Reading

- How did new technologies lead to an agricultural revolution?

- What economic and social changes occurred in the High Middle Ages?

- What was life like in a medieval town?

- **Vocabulary** *charter, capital, usury, guild, apprentice*

The castle of Count William of Flanders was a bustling place. Hundreds of people lived and worked there, from lords and ladies to household knights and servants. Such a large establishment had many needs. As people sought to supply them, the castle became the center of a new town. A medieval chronicler describes the process:

> **66**There began to throng before the gate near the castle bridge, traders and merchants selling costly goods. Then came inn-keepers to feed and house those doing business with the [lord] . . . and these built houses and set up their inns . . . and the houses so increased that there grew up a town.**99**

The appearance of new towns was a symbol of the economic revival that began in Europe about 1000. This period of revival, which spanned from 1000 to 1300, is called the High Middle Ages. These centuries saw remarkable changes that would greatly strengthen Western Europe.

## An Agricultural Revolution

By 1000, Europe's economic recovery was well underway. It had begun in the countryside, where peasants adapted new farming technologies that made their fields more productive. The result was an agricultural revolution that transformed Europe.

**New technologies.** By about 800, peasants were using new iron plows that carved deep into the heavy soil of northern Europe. These were a big improvement over the old wooden plows, which had been designed for the light soils of the Mediterranean region. Also, a new kind of harness allowed peasants to use horses rather than oxen to pull the plows. Because faster-moving horses could plow more land in a day than oxen, peasants could now enlarge their fields and plant more crops.

Looking up, a peasant might have seen another new device, a windmill, turning slowly against the sky. Where there were no fast-moving streams to turn a water mill, the power of the wind had been harnessed to grind the peasants' grain into flour.

**Expanding production.** Other changes brought still more land into use and further increased food production. Feudal lords who wanted to boost their incomes pushed peasants to clear forests, drain swamps, and reclaim wasteland for farming and grazing.

Peasants also adopted the three-field system. They planted one field in grain, a second with legumes, such as peas and beans, and left the third fallow. The legumes restored soil fertility while adding variety to the peasant diet. Unlike the old two-field system, the new method left only a third—rather than half—of the land unplanted.

All these improvements let farmers produce more food. With more food available, the population grew. Between about 1000 and 1300, the population of Europe doubled.

## Trade Revives

Europe's growing population needed goods that were not available on the manor. Peasants needed iron for farm tools. Wealthy nobles wanted fine wool, furs, and spices from Asia. As foreign invasions and feudal warfare declined, traders reappeared, criss-crossing Europe to meet the growing demand for goods.

**New trade routes.** Enterprising traders formed merchant companies that traveled in armed caravans for safety. They set up regular trade routes. Along these routes, merchants exchanged local goods for those from remote markets in Asia and the Middle East.

In Constantinople, merchants bought Chinese silks, Byzantine gold jewelry, and Asian spices. They shipped these goods to Venice on the Adriatic Sea. In Venice, traders loaded their wares onto pack mules and headed north over the Alps and up the Rhine River to Flanders. In Flanders, other traders bought the goods to send on to England and the lands along the Baltic Sea. Northern Europeans paid for the goods with products like honey, furs, fine cloth, tin, and lead.

**Trade fairs.** At first, traders and customers met at local trade fairs. These fairs took place near navigable rivers or where trade routes met.

People from the surrounding villages, towns, and castles flocked to the fairs. Peasants traded farm goods and animals. As they ate and drank, they enjoyed the antics of jugglers, acrobats, or even a dancing bear. They had no money to buy the fine woolens, swords, sugar, and silks offered by the merchants, however. The customers for these luxuries were the feudal rulers, nobles, and wealthy churchmen.

**New towns.** The fairs closed in the autumn when the weather made roads impassable. Merchants might wait out the winter months near a castle or in a town with a bishop's palace. These settlements attracted artisans who made goods that the merchants could sell.

Slowly, these small centers of trade and handicraft developed into the first real medieval cities. Some boasted populations of 10,000, and a few topped 100,000. Europe had not seen towns of this size since Roman times.

The most prosperous cities grew up in northern Italy and Flanders. Both areas were centers of the wool trade and had prosperous textile industries. Each anchored one end of the profitable north-south trade routes across Europe.

To protect their interests, the merchants who set up a new town would ask the local lord, or if possible the king himself, for a charter, or written document that set out the rights and privileges of the town. In return for the charter, merchants paid the lord or the king a large sum of money or a yearly fee or both.

Although charters varied from place to place, they almost always granted townspeople the right to choose their own leaders and control their own affairs. Most charters also had a clause, popular with runaway serfs, that declared that anyone who lived in the town for a year and a day was free. "Town air makes free," was a common medieval saying.

## A Commercial Revolution

As trade revived, money reappeared. This, in turn, led to more changes. Merchants, for example, needed money to buy goods, so they borrowed from moneylenders. In time, their need for capital, or money for investment, spurred the growth of banking houses.

**New business practices.** To meet the needs of the changing economy, Europeans developed new ways of doing business. For example, many merchants joined together in an organization known as a partnership. Under this setup, a group of merchants pooled their funds to finance a large-scale venture that would have been too costly for any individual trader.

Merchants also developed a system of insurance to help reduce business risks. For a small fee, an underwriter would insure the merchant's shipment. If the goods arrived safely, the merchant lost only the small insurance payment. If the shipment was lost or destroyed, the underwriter paid the merchant most of its value.

Europeans adapted other business practices from Middle Eastern merchants. Among the most important was the bill of exchange. A merchant deposited money with a banker in his home city. The banker issued a bill of exchange, which the merchant exchanged for cash in a distant city. A merchant could thus travel without carrying gold coins, which were easily stolen.

**Social changes.** These new ways of doing business were part of a commercial revolution that transformed the medieval economy. Slowly, they also reshaped medieval society.

The use of money, for example, undermined serfdom. Feudal lords needed money to buy fine clothes, weapons, furniture, and other goods. As a result, many peasants began selling farm products to townspeople and fulfilling their obligations to their lords by paying their rent with money rather than with labor. By 1300, most peasants in Western Europe were either tenant farmers, who paid rent for their land, or hired farm laborers.

## Trade in Medieval Europe

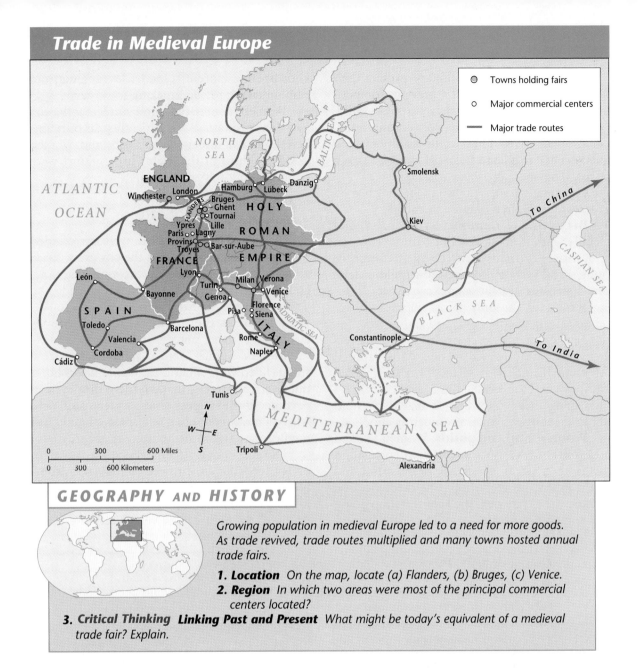

**Legend:**
- ⊙ Towns holding fairs
- ○ Major commercial centers
- ── Major trade routes

## GEOGRAPHY AND HISTORY

Growing population in medieval Europe led to a need for more goods. As trade revived, trade routes multiplied and many towns hosted annual trade fairs.

1. **Location** On the map, locate (a) Flanders, (b) Bruges, (c) Venice.
2. **Region** In which two areas were most of the principal commercial centers located?
3. **Critical Thinking** **Linking Past and Present** What might be today's equivalent of a medieval trade fair? Explain.

---

In towns, the old social order of nobles, clergy, and peasants gradually changed. By 1000, a new class appeared that included merchants, traders, and artisans. They formed a middle class, standing between nobles and peasants. There were a number of independent women. In towns, they had the right to carry on trade and buy and sell their own property.

Nobles and the clergy despised the new middle class. To nobles, towns were a disruptive influence beyond their control. To the clergy, the profits that merchants and bankers made from **usury** (YOO zhuh ree), or lending money at interest, were immoral.

## Role of Guilds

Merchant **guilds,** or associations, dominated life in medieval towns. They passed laws, levied taxes, and decided whether to spend funds to pave the streets with cobblestones, build protective walls for the city, or raise a new town hall.

In time, artisans came to resent the powerful merchants. They organized craft guilds. Each guild represented workers in one occupation, such as weavers, bakers, brewers, sword makers, and goldsmiths. In some towns, the struggles between craft guilds and the wealthier merchant guilds led to riots and revolts.

Guild members cooperated to protect their own economic interests. To prevent competition, they limited membership in the guild. Only guild members could work in any trade. Guilds made rules to ensure the quality of their goods. They regulated hours of labor and even prices. They also provided social services. Besides opening schools and hospitals, they helped widows and children of guild members.

**Becoming a member.** To become a guild member meant many years of hard work as an apprentice, or trainee. At the age of seven or eight, a child was apprenticed to a guild master. The apprentice usually spent seven years learning the trade. The only pay the apprentice received during that time was bed and board.

Few apprentices ever became guild masters unless they were related to one. Most labored for guild members as salaried workers, called journeymen. Journeymen often accused masters of keeping their wages low so that they could not save enough to open a competing shop.

**Women and the guilds.** Women worked in dozens of crafts. A woman often engaged in the same trade as her father or husband and might inherit his workshop if he died. Because she knew the craft well, she kept the shop going and sometimes became a guild master herself.

Girls became apprentices in trades ranging from ribbonmaking to papermaking to surgery.

Women dominated some trades and even had their own guilds. In Paris, they far outnumbered men in the profitable silk and woolen guilds. A third of the guilds in Frankfurt were composed entirely of women.

## City Life

Medieval towns and cities were surrounded by high, protective walls. As the city grew, space within the walls filled to overflowing, and newcomers had to settle in the fields outside the walls. To keep up with this constant growth, every few years the city might rebuild its walls farther and farther out.

Medieval cities were a jumble of narrow streets lined with tall houses. Upper floors hung out over the streets, making them dim even in daytime. In the largest cities, a great cathedral, where a bishop presided, or a splendid guild hall might tower above the humbler residences.

During the day, streets echoed with the cries of hawkers selling their wares and porters grumbling under heavy loads. A wealthy merchant might pass, followed by a procession of servants. At night, the unlit streets were deserted.

**Artisans at Work** *The workers on the left are making a cabinet, while those on the right are producing tapestries. In towns all over medieval Europe, middle-class artisans specialized in a wide variety of crafts.* **Continuity and Change** *How do factories of today differ from medieval workshops?*

## Street Performers

In medieval times, as today, not all entertainers performed on a stage in a theater before a large audience. For some, the stage is a street or a square, a field or a park. Their audience consists of passersby. And their pay is the applause and donations of the crowd.

**Linking Past and Present** Based on the pictures below, has street entertainment changed since the Middle Ages? Explain.

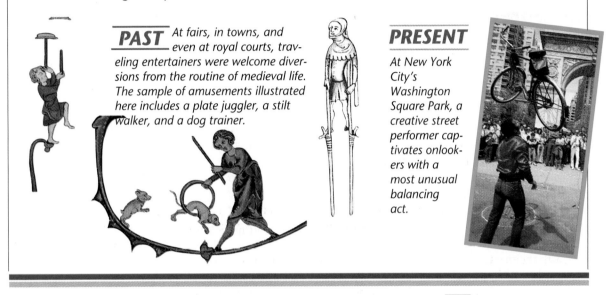

**PAST** At fairs, in towns, and even at royal courts, traveling entertainers were welcome diversions from the routine of medieval life. The sample of amusements illustrated here includes a plate juggler, a stilt walker, and a dog trainer.

**PRESENT** At New York City's Washington Square Park, a creative street performer captivates onlookers with a most unusual balancing act.

---

Even a rich town had no garbage collection or sewer system. Residents simply flung their wastes into the street. Larger cities might pass laws requiring butchers, for example, to dump their garbage on the edge of town. But towns remained filthy, smelly, noisy, and crowded.

### Looking Ahead

By 1300, Western Europe was a different place from what it had been in the early Middle Ages. Although most people had no way of knowing it, slow but momentous changes were sending shock waves through medieval life. Trade, for example, put ideas as well as money into circulation. New riches revised the social structure. In politics, too, new forces were at work.

In the global sphere, the economic revival of the High Middle Ages was bringing Europeans into contact with civilizations much more advanced than their own. From these lands came products, ideas, and technologies that would spark an even greater transformation in how Europeans thought and lived.

## SECTION 4 REVIEW

1. **Identify** High Middle Ages.
2. **Define** (a) charter, (b) capital, (c) usury, (d) guild, (e) apprentice.
3. What were two effects of the agricultural revolution that took place during the Middle Ages?
4. (a) What new ways of doing business evolved in the Middle Ages? (b) Why were they necessary?
5. How did the growth of towns affect the rigid class system of feudal times?
6. *Critical Thinking* **Synthesizing Information** Give three pieces of evidence that prove the High Middle Ages were a time of economic growth.
7. *ACTIVITY* Imagine that a growing medieval city has hired you to attract people to move there. Create an ad that describes opportunities the city provides for merchants, artisans, and peasants.

# Skills for Success

## Interpreting Diagrams

Historians use diagrams to organize and present complex information in a way that can be understood quickly. Study the diagram of a manor below. Then, answer the questions to interpret the diagram.

**1** **Identify the parts of the diagram.**
(a) What is the subject of the diagram?
(b) What kinds of buildings does the diagram show? (c) How many fields does this manor include? (d) What types of livestock were raised?

**2** **Analyze the information in the diagram.**
(a) Use the diagram to compare a serf's house with the manor house. (b) Locate the kitchen garden. What do you think it was used for?

Explain. (c) What was the purpose of the blacksmith's shop? The lord's oven? The mill? Why was it important for the lord to provide the serfs with these facilities? (d) Based on the diagram, how do you know that religion played an important role in manor life?

**3** **Draw conclusions based on the information in the diagram.** (a) What evidence in the diagram supports the statement that each manor was a small, self-sufficient world? (b) How would this affect life in Europe?

***Beyond the Classroom*** Draw a diagram of your neighborhood. Include and label important buildings and geographic features. What conclusions can you draw about life in your neighborhood based on your diagram?

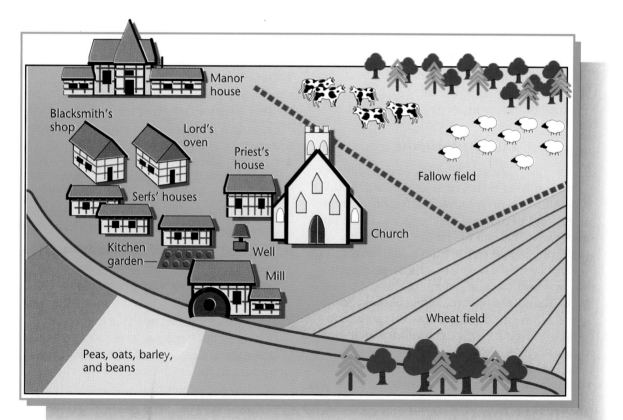

## Building Vocabulary

Review the vocabulary words in this chapter. Then, use *ten* of these vocabulary words and their definitions to create a matching quiz. Exchange quizzes with another student. Check each other's answers when you are finished.

## Reviewing Chapter Themes

1. **Geography and History** (a) Describe the foreign invasions of Western Europe in the early Middle Ages. (b) How did these invasions isolate Western Europeans from the classical heritage of Greece and Rome?
2. **Political and Social Systems** (a) How did feudalism shape the political life of medieval Europe? (b) What were the main features of the manor economy?
3. **Religions and Value Systems** Identify three ways the Church influenced life in medieval Europe.
4. **Economics and Technology** How did each of the following help spur the economic revival of Europe: (a) new farming technologies, (b) growth of trade?
5. **Continuity and Change** Identify one way that each of the following traditions influenced the civilization that emerged in Western Europe during the Middle Ages: (a) Greco-Roman tradition, (b) Germanic tradition.

## Thinking Critically

1. **Analyzing Information** List the accomplishments of Charlemagne. Which do you think had the most lasting importance? Why?
2. **Linking Past and Present** Compare life on a medieval manor with life on an American farm today. Which do you think would be more self-sufficient? Why?
3. **Predicting Consequences** (a) How did feudalism encourage the growth of the Roman Catholic Church? (b) How do you think the weakening of the feudal system might affect the Church? Explain. (★ See *Skills for Success*, page 974.)
4. **Recognizing Causes and Effects** As you have read on page 200, anti-Semitism increased in bad times. Why do you think this was so? (★ See *Skills for Success*, page 18.)
5. **Understanding Sequence** Arrange the following items in the order in which they occurred: new technologies, growth of towns, agricultural revolution, population growth, revival of trade. Then, explain why they occurred in that order.
6. **Comparing** Compare economic life in the early Middle Ages and the High Middle Ages.
7. **Making Decisions** Imagine that you are a European peasant during the Middle Ages. Would you choose to move to a town? Give reasons to support your decision. (★ See *Skills for Success*, page 814.)
8. **Identifying Main Ideas** Choose one section from Chapter 8. Write a sentence describing the main idea of each subsection. Then, write a sentence describing the main idea of the section.

### For Your Portfolio

Work with classmates to develop a radio or TV interview show called "Youth of Medieval Times."

1. Have each member of the group choose a role that represents a social class in medieval society. Some suggested roles: a teenaged peasant, a knight in training, an apprentice in a craft, a young nun or monk, a young nobleman or noblewoman.
2. Provide time for role players to do library or other research about the everyday life of their characters. Players should be able to provide information about where the character lives and what he or she does for a living, as well as about the privileges and limitations associated with belonging to a particular social class.
3. Based on their research, role players should prepare information sheets about their characters. Give these information sheets to a classmate selected to serve as interviewer.
4. Present your show, with the interviewer posing questions based on the information sheets and the role players answering them. You might audiotape or videotape the show for playback to the rest of the class.

# The High Middle Ages

## (1050–1450)

## CHAPTER OUTLINE

Darkness had just fallen when four armed knights burst into Canterbury Cathedral in southern England. "Where is Thomas Becket, traitor to the king and the realm?" they shouted. Becket, the archbishop of Canterbury, stepped forward. "I am here, no traitor, but a priest. Why do you seek me?"

The knights served King Henry II. They had come to make Becket lift the excommunication of several of Henry's supporters. When the archbishop refused their demand, the knights struck him. An eyewitness reported the bloody scene that unfolded:

> 66At the third blow, [Thomas] fell on his knees and elbows, offering himself a living victim, and saying in a low voice, 'For the name of Jesus, I am ready to embrace death.' 99

News of the murder quickly reached the king. Henry was appalled. He realized that his own words had doomed the man who had once been among his closest friends.

Eight years earlier, in 1162, Henry had appointed Becket as archbishop. Once in office, Becket surprised Henry by resisting his attempts to extend royal power over the clergy. A bitter quarrel flared between the two men. Each man used his power to block the other.

At last, Henry's fury exploded. "What a pack of fools and cowards I have nourished," he cried, "that not one of them will avenge me of this turbulent priest." Four hotheaded knights took Henry at his word. Within days, Becket lay

dead. And Henry, forced to live with the consequences of his careless words, had to abandon his efforts to extend royal power at the expense of the Church.

By the High Middle Ages, Western Europe had secured its borders against invaders and planted seeds of economic growth. As conditions improved, feudal monarchs like Henry II increased their power over both the nobles and the Church. They thus took the first steps on the long road toward building the modern nation-state.

FOCUS ON these themes as you read:

- **Political and Social Systems**
  How did feudal monarchs build the foundations for strong national governments?

- **Global Interaction**
  How did Western Europeans come in contact with more advanced civilizations?

- **Art and Literature**
  How did the revival of trade and the growth of towns influence medieval culture?

- **Religions and Value Systems**
  How did Christian scholars try to fit the learning of ancient Greece and the Arab world into their own system of beliefs?

- **Continuity and Change**
  How did the disasters of the late Middle Ages help set the stage for the modern age?

## TIME AND PLACE

**A New Stability for Europe** The High Middle Ages saw the return of orderly society to Europe. As monarchs centralized their power and feudal warfare declined, towns became centers not only of new economic activity but also of a revival of culture. Here, a representative of that revival, the writer Christine de Pizan, presents one of her works to the queen of France. **Art and Literature** How would the return of order encourage cultural pursuits?

## HUMANITIES LINK

*Art History* Chartres Cathedral, France (page 227).
*Literature* In this chapter, you will encounter passages from the following works of literature: "Good King Louis, you held the land under yoke" (page 214); Christine de Pizan, *The City of Ladies* (page 226); *Poem of the Cid* (page 226); Christine de Pizan, *Joan of Arc* (page 232); Geoffrey Chaucer, *The Canterbury Tales* (page 234).

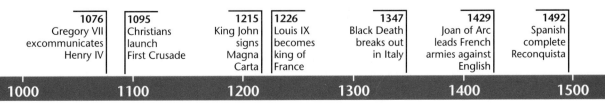

| **1076** Gregory VII excommunicates Henry IV | **1095** Christians launch First Crusade | **1215** King John signs Magna Carta | **1226** Louis IX becomes king of France | **1347** Black Death breaks out in Italy | **1429** Joan of Arc leads French armies against English | **1492** Spanish complete Reconquista |

| 1000 | 1100 | 1200 | 1300 | 1400 | 1500 |

# 1 Growth of Royal Power in England and France

## Guide for Reading

■ How did monarchs in England and France increase royal power?

■ What ideas about government and law emerged in England?

■ Why did royal rulers consult with representative assemblies?

■ **Vocabulary** *common law, jury*

> 66We, who are as good as you, swear to you, who are no better than we, to accept you as our king and sovereign lord; provided you observe our liberties and laws; but if not, not.99

In those blunt words, the nobles of Aragon, a region in what is today Spain, pledged loyalty to their king. Like feudal nobles everywhere, they believed themselves to be the equal of the monarch and were determined to protect their privileges.

In the early Middle Ages, hundreds of feudal nobles ruled over territories of varying size. Most acknowledged a king or other overlord, but royal rulers had little power. During the High Middle Ages, as economic conditions improved, feudal monarchs started to increase their power. Bit by bit over many centuries, they built the framework for what would become the European nations of today.

## Monarchs, Nobles, and the Church

In medieval Europe, kings stood at the head of society. Yet feudal monarchs had limited power. They ruled their own domains but relied on vassals for military support. Nobles and the Church had as much—or more—power than the king. Both nobles and the Church had their own courts, collected their own taxes, and fielded their own armies. They jealously guarded their rights and privileges against any effort by rulers to increase royal authority.

Crafty, ambitious, and determined rulers used various means to centralize power. They expanded the royal domain and set up a system of royal justice that undermined feudal or Church courts. They organized a government bureaucracy, developed a system of taxes, and built a standing army. Monarchs strengthened ties with the middle class. Townspeople, in turn, supported royal rulers, who could impose the peace and unity that were needed for trade and commerce.

The struggles among monarchs, nobles, and the Church lasted for centuries. Here, you will see how a few rulers in England and France moved to strengthen royal power.

## Strong Monarchs in England

During the early Middle Ages, Angles, Saxons, and Vikings invaded and settled in England. Although feudalism developed, English rulers generally kept their kingdoms united.

**Norman conquest.** In 1066, the Anglo-Saxon king Edward died without an heir. His death triggered a power struggle that changed the course of English history. A council of nobles chose Edward's brother-in-law Harold to rule. But Duke William of Normandy, a tough, ruthless descendant of the Vikings, also claimed the English throne. The answer to the rival claims lay on the battlefield.

Duke William raised an army and won the backing of the pope. He then sailed across the English Channel. At the Battle of Hastings, William and his Norman knights triumphed over Harold. On Christmas Day 1066, William the Conqueror, as he was now called, assumed the crown of England.

**William takes control.** Once in power, William exerted firm control over his new lands. Like other feudal monarchs, he granted fiefs to the Church and his Norman lords, or barons, but he kept a large amount of land for himself. He monitored who built castles and where. He required every vassal to swear first allegiance to him rather than to any other feudal lord. Even though William listened to the advice of his chief nobles, he always had the last word.

To learn about his kingdom, William had a complete census taken in 1086. The result was the *Domesday Book* (pronounced doomsday), which listed every castle, field, and pigpen in England. As the title suggests, the survey was as thorough and inevitable as doomsday, believed to be God's final day of judgment that no one could escape. Information in the *Domesday Book* helped William and his successors build an efficient system of tax collecting.

Although William's French-speaking nobles dominated England, the country's Anglo-Saxon population survived. Over the next 300 years, a gradual blending occurred of Norman French and Anglo-Saxon customs, languages, and traditions.

**Increasing royal authority.** William's successors strengthened two key areas of government: finances and law. They created the royal exchequer, or treasury, to collect taxes. Into the exchequer flowed fees, fines, and other dues.

In 1154, an energetic, well-educated king, Henry II, inherited the throne. He broadened the system of royal justice. As a ruler, he could not simply write new laws but had to follow accepted customs. Henry, however, found ways to expand old ideas into law. He then sent out traveling justices to enforce royal laws. The decisions of the royal courts became the basis for English common law, or law that was common—the same—for all people. In time, people chose royal courts over those of nobles or the Church. Since royal courts charged fees, the exchequer benefited from the growth of royal justice.

**Early juries.** Under Henry II, England also developed an early jury system. When traveling justices visited an area, local officials collected a jury, or group of men sworn to speak the truth. (*Juré* in French

means "sworn on oath.") These early juries determined which cases should be brought to trial and were the ancestors of today's grand jury. Later, another jury evolved that was composed of 12 neighbors of an accused. It was the ancestor of today's trial jury.

**A tragic clash.** Henry's efforts to extend royal power led to a bitter dispute with the Church. Henry claimed the right to try clergy in royal courts. Thomas Becket, the archbishop of Canterbury and once a close friend of Henry's, fiercely opposed the king's move.

The conflict simmered for years. Then, as we have seen, in 1170, four of Henry's knights, believing they were doing Henry's bidding, murdered the archbishop in his own cathedral. Henry denied any part in the attack. Still, to make peace with the Church, he eased off his attempts to regulate the clergy. Becket, meantime, was honored as a martyr and declared a saint. Pilgrims flocked to his tomb at Canterbury, where miracles were said to happen.

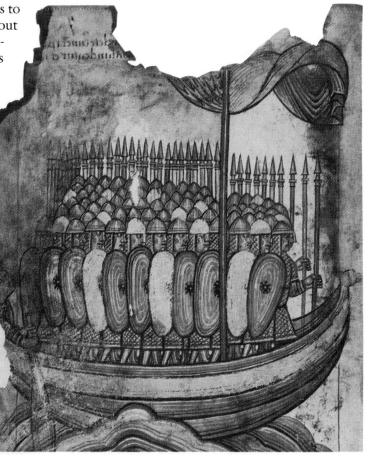

*Invasion* In 1066, hundreds of Norman ships crossed the English Channel to land some 7,000 men, 3,000 horses, and cartloads of supplies on the English coast. The landing was unopposed because the Anglo-Saxon army was busy repelling a Viking invasion in the north. **Impact of the Individual** Why did Normans invade England?

## Evolving Traditions of Government

Later English rulers repeatedly clashed with nobles and the Church. Most battles developed as a result of efforts by the monarch to raise taxes or to impose royal authority over traditional feudal rights. Out of those struggles evolved traditions of government that would influence the modern world.

**John's troubles.** Henry's son John was a clever, greedy, cruel, and untrustworthy ruler. During his reign, he faced three powerful enemies: King Philip II of France, Pope Innocent III, and his own English nobles. He lost his struggles with each.

Ever since William the Conqueror, Norman rulers of England had held vast lands in France. (See the map on page 213.) In 1205, John suffered his first setback when he lost a war with Philip II and had to give up English-held lands in Anjou and Normandy. Next, John battled with Innocent III over selecting a new archbishop of Canterbury. When John attacked the Church, the pope responded by excommunicating him. He also placed England under the interdict—as you recall, a papal order that forbade Church services in an entire kingdom. Even the strongest ruler was likely to give in to that pressure. To save himself and his crown, John had to accept England as a fief of the papacy and pay a yearly fee to Rome.

**The Magna Carta.** Finally, John angered his own nobles with heavy-handed taxes and other abuses of power. In 1215, a group of rebellious barons cornered John and forced him to sign the Magna Carta, or great charter. In this document, the king affirmed a long list of feudal rights. Besides protecting their own privileges, the barons included a few clauses recognizing the rights of townspeople and the Church.

The Magna Carta contained two basic ideas that in the long run would shape government traditions in England. First, it asserted that the nobles had certain rights. Over time, the rights that had been granted to nobles were extended to all English citizens. Second, the Magna Carta made clear that the monarch must obey the law. Among the most significant clauses were those that protected the legal rights of the people:

> 66No freeman shall be arrested or imprisoned or dispossessed or outlawed or . . . in any way harmed . . . except by the lawful judgment of his peers or by the law of the land. . . . To none will we sell, to none deny or delay, right or justice.99

The king also agreed not to raise new taxes without first consulting his Great Council of lords and clergy. Many centuries later, American colonists would claim that those words meant that any taxation without representation was unjust. In 1215, though, neither the king nor his lords could have imagined such an idea.

**Development of Parliament.** During the 1200s, English rulers often called on the Great Council for advice. Eventually, this body evolved into Parliament. Its name comes from the French word *parler,* meaning "to talk." As

**Edward I and Parliament** *In this scene, King Edward I presides over Parliament. On either side of him are his vassals, the rulers of Scotland and Wales. Clergymen sit on the left and lords sit on the right.* **Political and Social Systems** *What other social class was represented in the Model Parliament?*

Parliament acquired a larger role in government, it helped unify England.

In 1295, Edward I summoned Parliament to approve money for his wars in France. "What touches all," he declared, "should be approved by all." He had representatives of the "common people" join the lords and clergy. The "commons" included two knights from each county and representatives of the towns.

Much later, this assembly became known as the Model Parliament because it set up the framework for England's legislature. In time, Parliament developed into a two-house body: the House of Lords with nobles and high clergy and the House of Commons with knights and middle-class citizens.

**Looking ahead.** Like King Edward I, later English monarchs summoned Parliament for their own purposes. Over the centuries, though, Parliament gained the crucial "power of the purse." That is, it won the right to approve any new taxes. With that power, Parliament could insist that the monarch meet its demands before voting for taxes. In this way, it could check, or limit, the power of the monarch.

## Royal Successes in France

Monarchs in France did not rule over a unified kingdom, like William the Conqueror did in England. Instead, the successors to Charlemagne had little power over a patchwork of territories ruled by great feudal nobles.

**The Capetians.** In 987, these feudal nobles elected Hugh Capet, the count of Paris, to fill the vacant throne. They probably chose him because he was too weak to pose a threat to them. Hugh's own lands, the Ile de France around Paris, were smaller than those of many of his vassals.

Hugh and his heirs slowly increased royal power. First, they made the throne hereditary, passing it from father to son. Fortunately, the Capetians enjoyed an unbroken succession for 300 years. Next, they added to their lands by playing rival nobles against each other. They also won the support of the Church.

Perhaps most important, the Capetians built an effective bureaucracy. Government officials collected taxes and imposed royal law over the king's domain. By establishing order, they

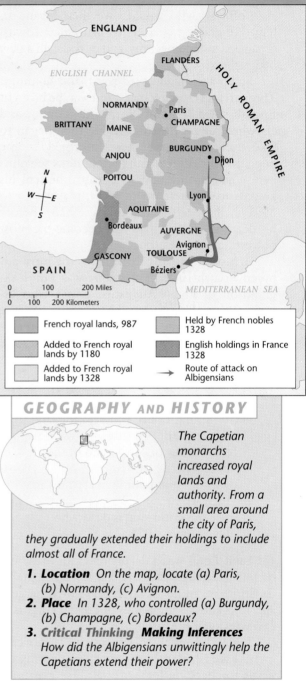

**Royal Lands in France 987–1328**

Key:
- French royal lands, 987
- Added to French royal lands by 1180
- Added to French royal lands by 1328
- Held by French nobles 1328
- English holdings in France 1328
- → Route of attack on Albigensians

### GEOGRAPHY AND HISTORY

The Capetian monarchs increased royal lands and authority. From a small area around the city of Paris, they gradually extended their holdings to include almost all of France.

1. **Location** On the map, locate (a) Paris, (b) Normandy, (c) Avignon.
2. **Place** In 1328, who controlled (a) Burgundy, (b) Champagne, (c) Bordeaux?
3. **Critical Thinking** **Making Inferences** How did the Albigensians unwittingly help the Capetians extend their power?

added to their prestige and gained the backing of the new middle class of townspeople.

**Philip Augustus.** An outstanding French king of this period was Philip II, often called Philip Augustus. A bald, red-faced man who ate and drank too much, Philip was a shrewd and able ruler. He strengthened royal government in many ways. Instead of appointing nobles to fill government positions, he used paid middle-class officials who would owe their loyalty to him. He granted charters to many new towns, organized a standing army, and introduced a new national tax.

Philip also quadrupled royal land holdings. Through trickery, diplomacy, and war, he brought English-ruled lands in Normandy, Anjou, and elsewhere under his control. He then began to take over southern France. Informed by the pope that the Albigensian (al buh JEHN see uhn) heresy had sprung up in the south, he sent his knights to suppress it and add this vast area to his domain. (See the map on page 213.) Before his death in 1223, Philip had become the most powerful ruler in Europe.

**A model monarch.** Perhaps the most admired French ruler of this time was Louis IX, grandson of Philip Augustus. Louis, who ascended to the throne in 1226, embodied the ideal of the perfect medieval monarch—generous, noble, and devoted to justice and the rules of chivalry. Within 30 years of his death, he was declared a saint. France's poets mourned his passing:

> **66**Good King Louis, you held the land
> under yoke
> To the profit of barons and of the
> little folk . . .
> To whom may poor men cry now in
> their woe
> Since the good king is dead who
> loved them so?**99**

Saint Louis was a deeply religious man, and he pursued religious goals that were acceptable to Christians in his day. He persecuted heretics and Jews and led thousands of French knights in two wars against Muslims.

Louis did much to improve royal government. Like Charlemagne, he sent out roving officials to check on local officials. He expanded the royal courts, outlawed private wars, and ended serfdom in his lands. To ensure justice, he even heard cases himself under a tree in the royal park of Vincennes. His enormous personal prestige helped create a strong national feeling among his subjects. By the time of his death in 1270, France was an efficient centralized monarchy.

**Clash with the pope.** Louis's grandson, Philip IV, ruthlessly extended royal power. Always pressed for cash, he tried to collect new taxes from the French clergy. These efforts led to a head-on clash with Pope Boniface VIII.

"God has set popes over kings and kingdoms," declared the pope and forbid Philip to tax the clergy without papal consent. Philip countered by threatening to arrest any clergy who did not pay up. As their quarrel escalated, Philip sent troops to seize Boniface. The pope escaped, but he was badly beaten and died soon afterward. Shortly after, a Frenchman was elected pope. He moved the papal court to the town of Avignon (AH veen yohn) on the border of southern France, ensuring that future French rulers would control religion within their own kingdoms.

**The Estates General.** During this struggle with the pope, Philip rallied French support by setting up the Estates General in 1302. This body had representatives from all three estates, or classes: clergy, nobles, and townspeople. Although later French kings consulted the Estates General, it did not develop the same role that the English Parliament did. It never gained the power of the purse or otherwise served as a balance to royal power.

## SECTION 1 REVIEW

1. **Identify** (a) William the Conqueror, (b) *Domesday Book,* (c) Henry II, (d) Thomas Becket, (e) Magna Carta, (f) Model Parliament, (g) Saint Louis, (h) Philip IV, (i) Estates General.
2. **Define** (a) common law, (b) jury.
3. What steps did William the Conqueror take to exert royal power in England?
4. What principles were established by the Magna Carta?
5. How did the Capetians increase royal power in France?
6. *Critical Thinking* **Linking Past and Present** How is the jury system important to us today?
7. *ACTIVITY* Write a newspaper editorial supporting or opposing the actions of *one* of the following kings: Henry II, John I, Louis IX, or Philip IV.

# 2 The Holy Roman Empire and the Church

## Guide for Reading

■ Why did Holy Roman emperors fail to build a unified state in Germany?

■ What issues led to clashes between emperors and popes?

■ What powers did the Church have at its peak?

■ **Vocabulary** *crusade*

The Church, you will recall, spread its influence across Europe during the early Middle Ages. By the High Middle Ages, both popes and monarchs were extending their authority. In the early 1200s, Pope Innocent III claimed broad new powers:

> 66The priesthood is the sun and the monarchy the moon. Kings rule over their respective kingdoms, but [the pope] rules over the whole Earth.99

With secular rulers advancing their own claims to power, explosive conflicts erupted. The longest and most destructive struggle pitted popes against the Holy Roman emperors who ruled vast lands from Germany to Italy.

## The Holy Roman Empire

In the early Middle Ages, the emperor Charlemagne had brought much of what is today the nation of Germany under his rule. (See Chapter 8.) After Charlemagne's death, Germany dissolved into a patchwork of separate states ruled by a number of powerful counts and dukes. In time, the dukes of one of those states, Saxony, began to extend their power over neighboring German lands. In 936, Duke Otto I of Saxony took the title king of Germany.

Like Charlemagne, Otto I worked closely with the Church. He appointed bishops and abbots to top government jobs. Also like Charlemagne, he took an army south into Italy to help the pope put down a rebellion by Roman nobles. In 962, a grateful pope crowned Otto emperor. Later, Otto's successors took the title Holy Roman emperor—"holy" because they were crowned by the pope, "Roman" because they saw themselves as heirs to the emperors of ancient Rome.

**Emperors and nobles.** The Holy Roman Empire had the potential to be the strongest monarchy in Europe. German emperors claimed authority over much of central and eastern Europe as well as parts of France and Italy. In fact, the real rulers of these lands were the emperor's vassals—hundreds of dukes, counts, archbishops, bishops, and knights. For German emperors, the challenge was to control these nobles. In the end, as you will see, it was a challenge they never met.

**Conflict with the Church.** The close ties between Otto and the Church held the seeds of conflict. Holy Roman emperors saw themselves as protectors of Italy and the pope. They repeatedly crossed the Alps to intervene in Italian affairs. They were tempted, too, by the desire to control the rich cities of northern Italy.

A key conflict between emperors and popes rose over who would control appointments to high Church offices. Like secular rulers in England and France, the Holy Roman emperor often decided who would become bishops and abbots. As the Cluny reforms strengthened the Church, popes attempted to end such outside interference.

**Imperial Crown** *Holy Roman emperors first wore this jewel-encrusted gold crown around the late 900s. Some, however, claimed that Charlemagne had worn it almost two centuries earlier.* **Political and Social Systems** *Why do you think Holy Roman emperors wanted people to believe that the crown had been worn by Charlemagne?*

## Two Determined Rulers

Under the reforming pope Gregory VII, the conflict between emperors and the Church burst into flames. Gregory was one of the greatest medieval popes. He was also among the most controversial. Indeed, few Europeans of his time had a neutral view of him. Many admired and revered him. Among his enemies, however, he probably aroused more hatred and contempt than any other pope of his time.

Gregory was determined to make the Church independent of secular rulers. To do so, he banned the practice of lay investiture. Under this practice, the emperor or another lay person (a person who is not a member of the clergy) "invested," or presented, bishops with the ring and staff that symbolized their office. Only the pope, said Gregory, had the right to appoint and install bishops in office.

**Pope versus emperor.** Pope Gregory's ban brought an angry response from the Holy Roman emperor Henry IV. He argued that bishops held their lands as royal fiefs. Since he was their overlord, Henry felt entitled to give them the symbols of office. The feud heated up as the two men exchanged insulting notes. Mean-while, rebellious German princes saw a chance to undermine Henry by supporting the pope.

In 1076, Gregory excommunicated Henry, freeing his subjects from their allegiance to the emperor. The pope then headed north to crown a new emperor. Faced with revolts at home, Henry was forced to make peace with the pope.

**Barefoot in the snow.** In January 1077, Henry crossed the icy Alps. He found the pope staying at a castle in Canossa and presented himself as a repentant sinner. Gregory later described the scene:

> 66There, having put aside all the trappings of royalty, with bare feet and clad only in a wretched woolen garment, he [Henry] continued for three days to stand before the castle gate . . . beseeching us with tears to grant him absolution and forgiveness.99

Gregory knew that Henry was only trying to save his throne. But according to the tradition and law of the Church, the pope, as a priest, had to forgive a confessed sinner. Gregory thus lifted the order of excommunication. Henry quickly returned to Germany and subdued his rebellious nobles. In later years, he took revenge on Gregory when he led an army to Rome and forced the pope into exile.

**Concordat of Worms.** The struggle over investiture dragged on for almost 50 years. Finally, in 1122, both sides accepted a treaty known as the Concordat of Worms (VOHRMS). In it, they agreed that the Church had the sole power to elect and invest bishops with spiritual authority. The emperor, however, had the right to invest them with fiefs. Although this compromise ended the investiture struggle, new battles were soon raging between popes and emperors.

R exrogat Abbat con. Mathildim Supplicat Atq;

*A Repentant Emperor* In the heat of the investiture conflict, Emperor Henry IV urged Gregory VII to step down as pope, calling for him to be "damned throughout the ages." Gregory's simple, but powerful, response was, "I forbid anyone to serve him as king." Here, Henry is shown at Canossa, humbly begging the pope's forgiveness. Countess Matilda of Tuscany, who helped reconcile the pope and the monarch, is at right. *Religions and Value Systems* Do you think that the conflict between popes and emperors could have been avoided? Explain.

## New Struggles Between Popes and Emperors

During the 1100s and 1200s, ambitious German emperors sought to master Italy. The emperor Frederick I, called Barbarossa, or "red beard," dreamed of building an empire that stretched from the Baltic to the Adriatic. For years, he fought to bring the wealthy cities of northern Italy under his control. With equal energy, they resisted. By joining forces with the pope in the Lombard League, they managed to defeat Barbarossa's armies.

Barbarossa did succeed, however, in arranging a marriage between his son Henry and Constance, heiress to Sicily and southern Italy. That move entangled German emperors even more deeply in Italian affairs.

**Frederick II.** Sicily, a rich island kingdom in the Mediterranean, had a sophisticated court, where Muslim and Christian influences existed side by side. The child of Henry and Constance, Frederick II, was raised in this rich court. Frederick was bright and well educated, fluent in Arabic, Greek, French, and several other languages. He valued the scientific learning of the Muslim world and saw himself as a man of reason. He was also an arrogant, able, and cynical leader, willing to use any means to achieve his ends.

As Holy Roman emperor, Frederick spent little time in Germany. Instead, he pursued his ambitions in Italy. There, he clashed repeatedly and unsuccessfully with several popes. Like his grandfather, Frederick also tried but failed to subdue the cities of northern Italy.

**Consequences.** While Frederick was embroiled in Italy, he gave in to many demands of his German nobles. As a result, they grew increasingly independent. Although the Holy Roman Empire survived, it remained fragmented into many feudal states. The emperors thus lost control of Germany at a time when French and English rulers were building the foundations for stable, unified governments. The German people paid a high price for their emperors' ambitions: They would not achieve unity for another 600 years.

Southern Italy and Sicily, too, faced centuries of upheaval. There, popes turned to the French to overthrow Frederick's heirs. A local uprising against French rule in Sicily led to 200 years of

**A Powerful Pope** Innocent III led the Church to the height of power and prestige. He kept strict control over the bishops and other clergy. He asserted his authority over secular rulers. At the time of his death, Innocent was the unquestioned leader of all Christendom. **Impact of the Individual** What methods did Innocent use to exert control?

chaos as French and Spanish rivals battled for power. The region that had once been a thriving center of European culture was left in ruins.

## The Church Under Innocent III

In the 1200s, the Roman Catholic Church reached its peak of power. Reforming popes like Gregory VII claimed the right to depose kings and emperors. Gregory's successors greatly expanded papal power.

**The height of papal power.** Innocent III, who took office in 1198, embodied the triumph of the Church. As head of the Church, he claimed supremacy over all other rulers. The pope, he said, stands "between God and man, lower than God but higher than men, who judges all and is judged by no one."

Innocent clashed with all the powerful rulers of his day. More often than not, the pope came out ahead. As you have read, when King John of England dared to appoint an archbishop of Canterbury without the pope's approval, Innocent excommunicated the king and placed his kingdom under interdict. Innocent ordered the same punishment for France when Philip II tried unlawfully to annul his marriage. The Holy Roman emperor Frederick II also felt the wrath of the powerful pope.

In 1209, Innocent, aided by Philip II, launched a brutal crusade, or holy war, against the Albigensians in southern France. The Albigensians wanted to purify the Church and return to the simple ways of early Christianity. Tens of thousands of people were slaughtered in the Albigensian Crusade.

**Looking ahead.** For almost a century after Innocent's death, popes pressed their claim to supremacy. During this period, though, the French and English monarchies were growing stronger. In 1296, Philip IV of France successfully challenged Pope Boniface VIII on the issue of taxing the clergy. (See page 214.) After Philip engineered the election of a French pope, the papacy entered a period of decline.

## SECTION 2 REVIEW

1. **Identify** (a) Holy Roman Empire, (b) Gregory VII, (c) Henry IV, (d) Concordat of Worms, (e) Frederick II, (f) Innocent III, (g) Albigensian Crusade.
2. **Define** crusade.
3. (a) Why was the power of German emperors limited? (b) How did the ambitions of German emperors affect the Holy Roman Empire?
4. (a) Describe two issues that led to clashes between popes and Holy Roman emperors. (b) How was each resolved?
5. *Critical Thinking* **Comparing** (a) How did the political development of the Holy Roman Empire differ from that of England and France in the 1100s and 1200s? (b) What were the causes of these differences?
6. *ACTIVITY* On an outline map of Europe, label the places that you have read about in this section. Illustrate your map to show what happened in each location.

# 3 Europeans Look Outward

## Guide for Reading

- What advanced centers of civilizations flourished around the world in 1050?
- What were the causes of the Crusades?
- How did the Crusades affect Western Europe?
- How did Ferdinand and Isabella increase royal power in Spain?

Nearly 23 weeks after setting out from his home in France, Count Stephen of Blois reached the city of Antioch in Syria. There, on March 29, 1098, he dictated a letter to his wife, Adele. "You may be very sure, dearest, that the messenger whom I send you has left me outside Antioch safe and unharmed," he began. He went on to tell of the battles he had fought and the riches he had won. Many more battles lay ahead before he and his fellow knights achieved their goal—the conquest of Jerusalem.

Stephen of Blois was among thousands of Europeans who joined the Crusades, a series of holy wars launched in 1096 by Christian Europe against Muslim lands in the Middle East. For the first time since the fall of Rome, Western Europeans were strong enough to break out of their narrow isolation and take the offensive against other lands. As they streamed eastward over the next 200 years, Western Europeans learned that the world was much larger than they had ever dreamed. Their encounters outside Europe would serve to stimulate the pace of change.

## *The World in 1050*

In 1050, when Western Europe was barely emerging from isolation, several civilizations in the Middle East and Asia had long been major powers. You will read about these civilizations in other chapters. What follows here is an overview of the world at the time that medieval Europe was first beginning to test its strength.

## Good Manners

Books of etiquette, or proper social behavior, date back as far as ancient Egypt and the *Instructions of the Vizier Ptah-hotep.* (See page 23.) Since then, every society has evolved its own system of customs and manners that people are expected to observe. However, ideas about good manners vary from culture to culture and from class to class.

**Linking Past and Present** How does etiquette at your school cafeteria differ from etiquette at a restaurant? Do you think rules of etiquette are still necessary? Explain.

**PAST** *During the late Middle Ages, as monarchs gained greater prestige, royal courts set the standards for good behavior. The first European etiquette books advised nobles how to behave properly at a court banquet:*

> *"A number of people gnaw a bone and then put it back in the dish. This is a serious offense."*
> *"Do not spit over the table in the manner of hunters."*
> *"Refrain from falling upon the dish like a swine while eating, snorting disgustingly, and smacking the lips."*

**PRESENT** *Today, guides to etiquette range from newspaper columns like "Miss Manners" to handbooks for international business travelers. Following are instructions for the proper way to call a waiter in various cultures:*

> *"Africa: Knock on the table."*
> *"Middle East: Clap your hands."*
> *"Japan: Extend your arm slightly upward, palm down, and flutter your fingers."*

---

**Islam: An international civilization.** During Europe's Middle Ages, Islam had given rise to a brilliant new civilization. Islamic civilization reached from Spain across North Africa and the Middle East and on to the borders of India.

Muslim traders and scholars spread goods and ideas even farther afield. Trading caravans regularly crossed the Sahara to West Africa. Arab ships touched at ports on the east African coast and sailed on to India, Southeast Asia, China, and Korea. Through contacts with diverse cultures, Muslims acquired and passed on a whole range of ideas and technologies.

**India and China: Ancient centers of civilization.** Beyond the Muslim world lay India and China. Although it was politically divided, India was a land of thriving cities. Hindu and Buddhist traditions flourished, and wealthy princes financed the building of stunning temples and palaces. Indian mathematicians invented a numbering system, which Arabs adapted. Eventually, Western Europeans adopted these Hindu-Arabic numbers.

China had a strong, central government at a time when Europe was politically fragmented. Under the Tang and Song dynasties, China's culture flourished. Its civilization had an influence on neighboring peoples in Korea, Japan, and Southeast Asia. The Chinese made amazing advances in technology, inventing paper, printing, and gunpowder. In dozens of large cities, traders benefited from the use of coins and paper money, unknown to medieval Europeans.

**African and American civilizations.** In West Africa, the Soninke people were building the great trading empire of Ghana. Its merchants traded goods, especially gold, that would travel across the Sahara to North Africa, the Middle East, and even Europe.

Across the Atlantic, in Central America and southern Mexico, the Mayas had cleared the rain forests and built large cities dominated by towering temples. In Peru, too, Native Americans were carving out empires and creating great works of art, including elegant pottery, textiles, and gold jewelry. The civilizations of the Americas, however, remained outside the contacts that were taking place among Africans, Europeans, and Asians between 1050 and 1250.

**Byzantine civilization.** Closer to Western Europe, Byzantine civilization was a rival to Islam in the eastern Mediterranean. Although pounded by invaders, the Byzantine empire was generally prosperous and united at a time when Western Europe was weak and backward. Its scholars still studied the writings of the ancient Greeks and Romans. In the markets of Constantinople, the Byzantine capital, Byzantine and Muslim merchants mingled with traders from Venice and other Italian cities. Even Vikings made their way to this bustling city.

In the 1050s, the Seljuk Turks invaded the Byzantine empire. The Turks had migrated from Central Asia into the Middle East, where they converted to Islam. By 1071, the Seljuks had overrun most Byzantine lands in Asia Minor (present-day Turkey). The Seljuks also extended their power over Palestine and attacked Christian pilgrims to the Holy Land.*

---

*Christians called Jerusalem and other places in Palestine where Jesus had lived and taught the Holy Land. Jerusalem was also a holy place for Jews and Muslims.

## The Crusades

As the Seljuk threat grew, the Byzantine emperor Alexius I sent an urgent plea to Pope Urban II in Rome. In 1095, he asked for Christian knights to help him fight the Turks. Although Roman popes and Byzantine emperors were longtime rivals, Urban agreed.

At the Council of Clermont in 1095, Urban incited French and German bishops and nobles to action. "From Jerusalem and the city of Constantinople comes a grievous report," he began. "An accursed race . . . has violently invaded the lands of those Christians and has depopulated them by pillage and fire." Urban then called for a crusade to free the Holy Land:

> ❝Seize that land from [the Seljuks], and subject it to yourselves. . . . Undertake this journey eagerly for the [forgiveness] of your sins and with the assurance of everlasting glory in the kingdom of heaven.❞

**Taking up the cross.** *Deus lo volt!* "God wills it!" roared the assembly in response to the pope's words. Soon, thousands of knights were on their way to the Holy Land. Because they sewed large crosses—*cruces* in Latin—on their tunics, they came to be called crusaders. As the crusading spirit swept through Western Europe, armies of ordinary men and women inspired by fiery preachers left for the Holy Land, too. Few returned.

Why did so many people take up the cross? Religious reasons played a large role. Yet many knights also hoped to win wealth and land. Some crusaders sought to escape troubles at home. Others yearned for adventure.

The pope, too, had mixed motives. Urban hoped to increase his power in Europe and perhaps heal the split between the Roman and Byzantine churches. (See page 242.) He also saw lands in the Middle East as an outlet for Europe's growing population. Finally, he hoped that the Crusades would set Christian knights to fighting Muslims instead of one another.

**Massacre in Jerusalem.** For 200 years, crusaders marched, fought, and for a time occupied parts of Palestine. Only the First Crusade came close to achieving its goals. After a long,

# Crusades

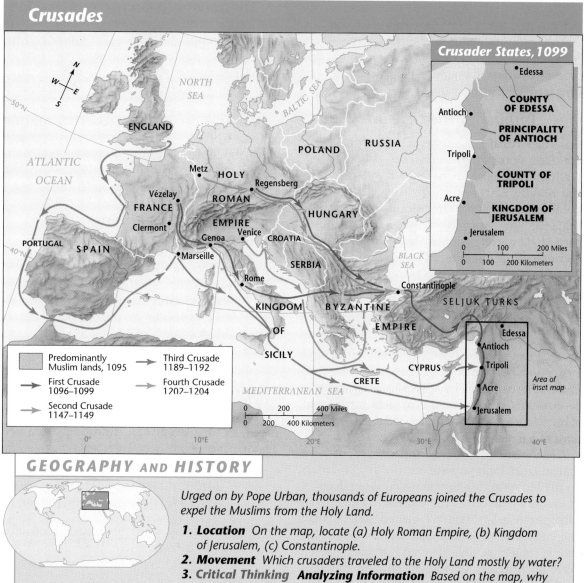

## Crusader States, 1099

- Edessa — **COUNTY OF EDESSA**
- Antioch — **PRINCIPALITY OF ANTIOCH**
- Tripoli — **COUNTY OF TRIPOLI**
- Acre
- **KINGDOM OF JERUSALEM**
- Jerusalem

0    100    200 Miles
0    100    200 Kilometers

**Legend:**
- Predominantly Muslim lands, 1095
- First Crusade 1096–1099
- Second Crusade 1147–1149
- Third Crusade 1189–1192
- Fourth Crusade 1202–1204

0    200    400 Miles
0    200    400 Kilometers

## GEOGRAPHY AND HISTORY

*Urged on by Pope Urban, thousands of Europeans joined the Crusades to expel the Muslims from the Holy Land.*

1. **Location** On the map, locate (a) Holy Roman Empire, (b) Kingdom of Jerusalem, (c) Constantinople.
2. **Movement** Which crusaders traveled to the Holy Land mostly by water?
3. **Critical Thinking** *Analyzing Information* Based on the map, why would it be difficult for Europeans to defend the Crusader States?

---

bloody campaign, Christian knights captured Jerusalem in 1099. They capped their victory with a massacre of Muslim and Jewish residents of the city.

**Later crusades.** The crusaders divided the captured lands into four small states. (See the map above.) The Muslims repeatedly sought to destroy these Christian kingdoms, prompting Europeans to launch new crusades. By 1187, Jerusalem had fallen to the able Muslim leader Salah al-Din, known to Europeans as Saladin. On the Third Crusade, Europeans tried but failed to retake Jerusalem. After negotiations, though, Saladin did reopen the holy city to Christian pilgrims.

Europeans also mounted crusades against other Muslim lands, especially in North Africa. All ended in defeat. During the Fourth Crusade, the crusaders were diverted from fighting Muslims to fighting Christians. After helping Venetian merchants defeat their Byzantine trade rivals in 1204, crusaders captured and looted Constantinople, the capital of the Byzantine empire itself!

Muslim armies meanwhile overran the crusader states. By 1291, they captured the last Christian outpost, the port city of Acre. As in Jerusalem 200 years earlier, the victors massacred their defeated enemies. This time, the victims were Christians.

## Impact of the Crusades

The Crusades failed in their chief goal—the conquest of the Holy Land. They also left a bitter legacy of religious hatred behind them. In the Middle East, both Christians and Muslims committed appalling atrocities in the name of religion. In Europe, crusaders sometimes turned their religious fury against Jews, massacring entire communities.

The Crusades did have some positive effects, however. Beginning just as Europe was emerging from the Middle Ages, they helped to quicken the pace of changes already underway.

**Increased trade.** Even before the Crusades, Europeans had developed a taste for luxury goods that merchants brought from the Byzantine empire. The Crusades increased the level of trade. Returning crusaders introduced fabrics, spices, and perfumes from the Middle East to a larger market.

Merchants in Venice and other northern Italian cities built large fleets to carry crusaders to the Holy Land. They later used those fleets to open new markets in the crusader states. Even after the Muslims had recaptured Acre, Italian merchants kept these trade routes open. Our words *sugar, cotton, rice,* and *muslin,* which were borrowed from Arabic, show the range of trade goods involved.

**The Church.** Enthusiasm for the Crusades brought papal power to its greatest height. This period of enhanced prestige was short-lived, however. As we have seen, popes were soon involved in bitter clashes with feudal monarchs. Also, the Crusades did not end the split between the Roman and Byzantine churches. In fact, Byzantine resentment against the West hardened as a result of the Fourth Crusade.

**Feudal rulers.** The Crusades also helped to increase the power of feudal monarchs. Rulers won new rights to levy taxes in order to support the Crusades. Some rulers, including the French king Louis IX, led crusades, which added greatly to their prestige.

**The money economy and serfdom.** The Crusades further encouraged the growth of a money economy. To finance a journey to the Holy Land, nobles needed money. They allowed peasants to pay rents in money rather than grain or labor, which helped undermine serfdom.

**A wider world view.** Contacts with the Muslim world led Christians to realize that millions of people lived in regions they had never known existed. Soon a few curious Europeans even visited far-off places like India and China.

In 1271, a young Venetian, Marco Polo, set out for China with his merchant father and uncle. After more than 20 years there, Polo returned to Venice, filled with stories about the many wonders of Chinese civilization. Unbelieving Europeans called Polo the "prince of liars," totally rejecting what they saw as incredible tales of government mail service and of burning black stones (coal) used to heat homes.

The experiences of crusaders and of travelers like Marco Polo expanded European horizons. They brought Europe into a wider world from which it had been cut off since the fall of Rome. By the 1400s, a desire to trade directly with India and China would lead Europeans to a new age of exploration.

## The Crusading Spirit and the Reconquista

The crusading spirit continued long after the European defeat at Acre. It flourished especially in Spain, where Christian warriors had been battling Muslims for centuries.

Muslims had conquered most of Spain in the 700s and carried Islamic civilization there. (See Chapter 11.) Several tiny Christian kingdoms survived in the north, however. As they slowly expanded their borders, they sought to take over Muslim lands. Their campaign to drive the Muslims from Spain became known as the Reconquista, or "reconquest."

**ISSUES For TODAY**

After years of isolation, Western Europeans began to renew contacts with the outside world. What effects does contact between cultures produce?

**Marco Polo in China** *Marco Polo served as an official of Kublai Khan, the ruler of China. He traveled throughout China and also visited Persia, Burma, Sumatra, and India. Polo's story kindled the European imagination and encouraged others to travel and explore.* **Economics and Technology** *How does this illustration portray China as a land of great wealth?*

**Christian advances.** Efforts by Christian warriors to expel the Muslims began in the 700s. Their first real success did not come, however, until 1085, when they recaptured the city of Toledo. During the next 200 years, Christian forces pushed slowly and steadily southward. By 1300, Christians controlled the entire Iberian Peninsula except for Granada. Muslim influences remained strong, though, and helped shape the arts and literature of Christian Spain.

**Ferdinand and Isabella.** In 1469, Isabella of Castile married Ferdinand of Aragon. This marriage between the rulers of two powerful kingdoms opened the way for a unified state. Using their combined forces, the two monarchs made a final push against the Muslim stronghold of Granada. In 1492, Granada fell. The Reconquista was complete.

Isabella and Ferdinand tried to impose unity on their diverse peoples. They joined forces with townspeople against powerful nobles. Isabella was determined to bring religious as well as political unity to Spain.

Under Muslim rule, Spain had enjoyed a tradition of religious toleration. Christians, Jews, and Muslims lived there in relative peace. Isabella ended that policy of toleration. Aided by the Inquisition, a Church court set up to try people accused of heresy, Isabella launched a brutal crusade against Jews and Muslims. Often, those who refused to convert to Christianity were burned at the stake.

More than 150,000 people fled into exile. The queen achieved religious unity but at a high price. Her policy destroyed two skilled, educated groups that had contributed much to Spain's economy and culture.

## SECTION 3 REVIEW

1. **Identify** (a) Crusades, (b) Council of Clermont, (c) Saladin, (d) Reconquista, (e) Isabella, (f) Ferdinand, (g) Inquisition.
2. What advanced civilizations flourished around the world at the time of the First Crusade?
3. (a) Why did Europeans join the Crusades? (b) What were three results of the Crusades?
4. How did Spain achieve political and religious unity?
5. *Critical Thinking* **Analyzing Information** How did the Crusades reflect the growing strength of medieval Europe?
6. *ACTIVITY* Write two articles reporting on the First Crusade: one from the point of view of a Christian knight, another from the point of view of a Muslim living in Jerusalem.

# 4 Learning, Literature, and the Arts

## Guide for Reading

- Why did a revival of learning occur in the High Middle Ages?

- How did literature reflect the changing culture of medieval Europe?

- What styles of architecture emerged in the High Middle Ages?

- **Vocabulary** *theology, scholasticism, vernacular*

By the 1100s, Europe was experiencing dynamic changes. No longer was everyone preoccupied with the daily struggle to survive. Improvements in agriculture were creating a steadier food supply. The revival of trade and growth of towns were signs of increased prosperity. Within the towns and cities of medieval Europe, a few people were acquiring wealth. In time, towns contributed a vital spark that ignited the cultural flowering of the High Middle Ages.

## Medieval Universities

As economic and political conditions improved in the High Middle Ages, the need for education expanded. The Church wanted better-educated clergy. Royal rulers also needed literate men for their growing bureaucracies. By getting an education, the sons of wealthy townspeople might hope to qualify for high jobs in the Church or royal governments.

**Academic guilds.** By the 1100s, schools had sprung up around the great cathedrals to train the clergy. Some of these cathedral schools evolved into the first universities. They were organized like guilds with charters to protect the rights of members and set standards for training.

Salerno and Bologna in Italy boasted the first universities. Paris and Oxford soon had theirs. In the 1200s, other cities rushed to organize universities. Students often traveled from one university to another. They might study law in

***Students in Class*** *Early universities were modeled on medieval trade guilds. In northern Europe, teachers acted as the guild masters, setting the term of study and establishing conditions for receiving a degree. In the schools of Italy, students ran the first guilds. They required teachers to start and finish lectures on time and fined them if they missed class or skipped material.* **Continuity and Change** *How does the curriculum of medieval universities compare to courses of study today?*

Bologna, medicine in Montpellier, and theology, or religion, in Paris.

**Student life.** University life offered few comforts. A bell wakened students at about 5 A.M. for prayers. Students then attended classes until 10 A.M., when they had their first meal of the day—perhaps a bit of beef and soup mixed with oatmeal. Afternoon classes continued until 5 P.M. Students ate a light supper and then studied until time for bed.

Since medieval universities did not have permanent buildings, classes were held in rented rooms or in the choir loft of a church. Students sat for hours on hard benches as the teacher dictated and then explained Latin texts. Students were expected to memorize what they heard.

A program of study covered the seven liberal arts: arithmetic, geometry, astronomy, music, grammar, rhetoric, and logic. To show they had mastered a subject, students took an oral exam. Earning a degree as a bachelor of arts took between three and six years. Only after several more years of study could a man qualify to become a master of arts and a teacher.

Women were not allowed to attend the universities. This exclusion seriously affected their lives. Without a university education, they could not become doctors, lawyers, administrators, church officials, or professors. They were also deprived of the mental stimulation that was an important part of university life.

## Europeans Acquire "New" Learning

Universities received a further boost from an explosion of knowledge that reached Europe in the High Middle Ages. Many of the "new" ideas had originated in ancient Greece but had been lost to Western Europeans after the fall of Rome.

In the Middle East, Muslim scholars had translated the works of Aristotle and other Greek thinkers into Arabic, and their texts had spread across the Muslim world. In Muslim Spain, Jewish scholars translated these works into Latin, the language of Christian European scholars.

**The challenge of Aristotle.** By the 1100s, these new translations were seeping into Western Europe. There they set off a revolution in the world of learning. The writings of the ancient Greeks posed a challenge to Christian scholars. Aristotle taught that people should use reason to discover basic truths. Christians, however, accepted many ideas on faith. They believed that the Church was the final authority on all questions. How could they use the logic of Aristotle without undermining their Christian faith?

Christian scholars, known as scholastics, tried to resolve the conflict between faith and reason. Their method, known as scholasticism, used reason to support Christian beliefs. Scholastics studied the works of the Muslim philosopher Averröes (ah VEHR oh eez) and the Jewish rabbi Maimonides (mī MAHN uh deez).

These thinkers, too, used logic to resolve the conflict between faith and reason.

**Thomas Aquinas.** The writings of these thinkers influenced the scholastic Thomas Aquinas (uh KWĪ nuhs). In a monumental work, *Summa Theologica*, Aquinas examined Christian teachings in the light of reason. Faith and reason, he concluded, existed in harmony. Both led to the same truth, that God ruled over an orderly universe. He thus brought together Christian faith and classical Greek philosophy.

**Science and mathematics.** Works of science, translated from Arabic and Greek, also reached Europe from Spain and the Byzantine empire. Christian scholars studied Hippocrates on medicine and Euclid on geometry, along with works by Arab scientists. They saw, too, how Aristotle had used observation and experimentation to study the physical world.

Yet science made little real progress in the Middle Ages because most scholars still believed that all true knowledge must fit with Church teachings. It would take many centuries before Christian thinkers changed the way they viewed the physical world. (See page 364.)

In mathematics, as we have seen, Europeans adopted Hindu-Arabic numerals. This system was much easier to use than the cumbersome system of Roman numerals that had been traditional throughout Europe for centuries. In time, Arabic numerals allowed both scientists and mathematicians to make extraordinary advances in their fields.

▲ *Performing surgery*

## Education for Women

Few women received a good education. An exception was Christine de Pizan (duh pee ZAHN), an Italian-born woman who came to live in the French court. De Pizan was married at 15, but her husband died before she was 25. Left with three children, De Pizan earned her living as a writer, an unusual occupation for a woman of that time.

De Pizan used her pen to examine the achievements of women. In *The City of Ladies*, she questions several imaginary characters about men's negative views of women. She asks Lady Reason, for example, whether women are less capable of learning and understanding, as men insist. Lady Reason replies:

> **66** If it were customary to send daughters to school like sons, and if they were then taught the same subjects, they would learn as thoroughly and understand the subtleties of all arts and sciences as well as sons. **99**

Still, men continued to look on educated women as oddities. Women, they felt, should pursue their "natural" gifts at home, raising children, managing the household, and doing needlework, and leave books and writing to men.

## Medieval Literature

While Latin was the language of scholars and churchmen, new writings began to appear in the vernacular, or the everyday languages of ordinary people, such as French, German, and Italian. These writings captured the spirit of the High Middle Ages. Medieval literature included epics about feudal warriors and tales of the common people.

**Heroic epics.** Across Europe, people began writing down oral traditions in the vernacular. French pilgrims traveling to holy sites loved to hear the *chansons de geste*, or "songs of heroic deeds." The most popular was the *Song of Roland*, which praises the courage of one of Charlemagne's knights who died while on a military campaign in Muslim Spain. A true feudal hero, Roland loyally sacrifices his life out of a sense of honor.

Spain's great epic, *Poem of the Cid*, also involves conflict with Islam. The Cid was Rodrigo Díaz, a bold and fiery Christian lord who battled Muslims in Spain. Calling to his warriors, he surges into battle full of zeal:

> **66** There are three hundred lances that each a pennant bears.
> At one blow every man of them his Moor has slaughtered there,
> And when they wheeled to charge anew as many more were slain,
> You might see great clumps of lances lowered and raised again. . . .
> Cried the Moor "Muhammed!" The Christians shouted on St. James of Grace,
> On the field Moors thirteen hundred were slain in little space. **99**

**Dante's journey.** "In the middle of the journey of life, I found myself in a dark wood, where the straight way was lost." So begins the *Divine Comedy* by the famed Italian poet Dante Alighieri (DAHN tay al lee GYEH ree). The poem takes the reader on an imaginary journey into hell and purgatory, where souls await forgiveness. Finally, Dante describes a vision of heaven.

"Abandon all hope, all ye that enter here" is the warning Dante receives as he approaches hell. There, he talks with people from history who tell how they earned a place in hell. Humor, tragedy, and the endless medieval quest for religious understanding are all ingredients in Dante's poem.

**Chaucer's wit.** In *The Canterbury Tales*, Geoffrey Chaucer follows a band of English pilgrims traveling to Thomas Becket's tomb. In brilliant word portraits, he sketches a range of characters, including a knight, a plowman, a merchant, a miller, a monk, a nun, and the five-times-widowed "wife of Bath." Each character

**GLOBAL CONNECTIONS**

Medieval poets often accompanied their recitations on the lute, a stringed instrument based on an Arab instrument called the al-'ud. The lute first arrived in Europe when Christians copied the instrument from their Islamic neighbors to the south.

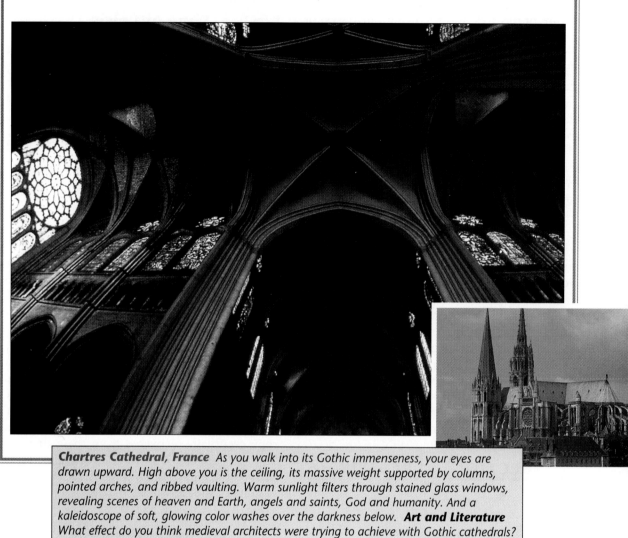

**Chartres Cathedral, France** *As you walk into its Gothic immenseness, your eyes are drawn upward. High above you is the ceiling, its massive weight supported by columns, pointed arches, and ribbed vaulting. Warm sunlight filters through stained glass windows, revealing scenes of heaven and Earth, angels and saints, God and humanity. And a kaleidoscope of soft, glowing color washes over the darkness below.* **Art and Literature** *What effect do you think medieval architects were trying to achieve with Gothic cathedrals? Did they succeed? Explain.*

tells a story. Whether funny, romantic, or bawdy, each tale adds to our picture of medieval life. (★ See *Skills for Success,* page 234.)

### Splendors in Stone

"In the Middle Ages," wrote French author Victor Hugo, "men had no great thought that they did not write down in stone." With riches from trade and commerce, townspeople, nobles, and monarchs indulged in a flurry of building. Their greatest achievements were the towering stone cathedrals that served as symbols of their wealth and religious devotion.

**Romanesque strength.** About 1000, monasteries and towns built solid stone churches that reflected Roman influences. These Romanesque churches looked like fortresses with thick walls and towers. Their roofs were so heavy that builders cut only tiny slits of windows in the walls for fear of weakening the supports. As a result, these massive structures were only dimly lit.

**Gothic grace.** About 1140, Abbot Suger wanted to build a new abbey church at St. Denis near Paris. He hoped that it "would shine with wonderful and uninterrupted light." Urged on by the abbot, builders developed what became known as the Gothic style of architecture. A key feature of this style was the flying buttresses, or stone supports that stood outside the church. These supports allowed builders to construct higher walls and leave space for huge stained-glass windows.

The new Gothic churches soared to incredible heights. Their graceful spires, lofty ceilings, and enormous windows carried the eye upward to the heavens. "Since their brilliance lets the splendor of the True Light pass into the church," declared a medieval visitor, "they enlighten those inside."

Soon cities all over Europe were competing to build grander, taller cathedrals. The faithful contributed money, labor, and skills to help build these monuments "to the greater glory of God."

**"Bibles in stone."** As churches rose, stonemasons carved sculptures to decorate them inside and out. At the same time, skilled crafts-workers, members of a guild, created the brilliant stained-glass windows that added to the splendor of medieval churches. Carvings and stained glass portrayed stories from the Bible and served as a religious education to the people, most of whom were illiterate.

## SECTION *4* REVIEW

1. **Identify** (a) Thomas Aquinas, (b) Christine de Pizan, (c) *Song of Roland,* (d) *Poem of the Cid,* (e) Dante, (f) Chaucer.
2. **Define** (a) theology, (b) scholasticism, (c) vernacular.
3. How did new knowledge pose a challenge to Christian scholars?
4. What were two kinds of vernacular literature that developed in the High Middle Ages?
5. What were the characteristics of (a) Romanesque architecture, (b) Gothic architecture?
6. *Critical Thinking* **Analyzing Information** Why do you think Gothic churches are sometimes called "Bibles in stone"?
7. *ACTIVITY* Solve this problem using Roman numerals: MCMLXXX + MMCCCLX. Then, translate and solve the problem using Arabic numerals. How do you think the introduction of Arabic numerals might have affected mathematics in Western Europe?

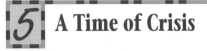

# 5 A Time of Crisis

## Guide for Reading

- Why was the late Middle Ages a time of decline?
- What challenges did the Church face in the late Middle Ages?
- Why did Joan of Arc become a national hero in France?

For Europeans in the late Middle Ages, the "Four Horsemen of the Apocalypse" were a fearful sight. These dreaded riders, whose images were widely portrayed on the walls of churches, symbolized famine, disease, war, and death. Their appearance, people believed, signaled the end of the world.

To Europeans in the mid-1300s, the end of the world indeed seemed to have come. The evils embodied by the Four Horsemen swept over the region. First, widespread crop failures brought famine, malnutrition, and starvation. Then plague and war deepened the crisis. Europe eventually recovered from these disasters. Still the upheavals of the 1300s and 1400s marked the end of the Middle Ages and the beginning of the early modern age.

### *The Black Death*

In the autumn of 1347, a fleet of Genoese trading ships, loaded with grain, left the Black Sea port of Caffa and sailed for Messina, Sicily. By mid-voyage, sailors were falling sick and dying. Soon after the ships tied up at Messina, townspeople, too, fell sick and died. A medieval chronicler reported:

66Seeing what a calamity of sudden death had come to them by the arrival of the Genoese, the people of Messina drove them in all haste from their city and port. But the sickness remained and a terrible mortality ensued.99

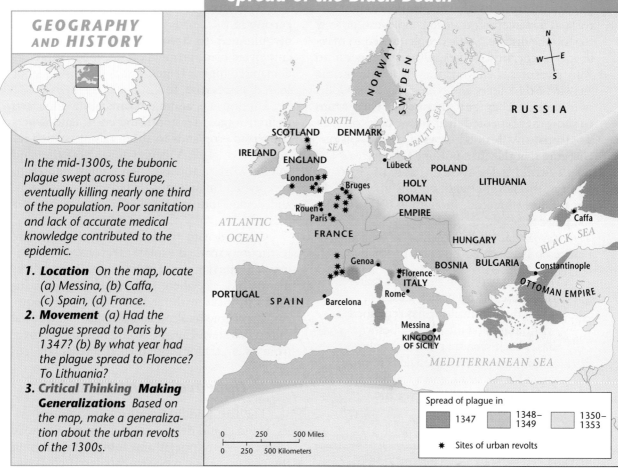

### GEOGRAPHY AND HISTORY

In the mid-1300s, the bubonic plague swept across Europe, eventually killing nearly one third of the population. Poor sanitation and lack of accurate medical knowledge contributed to the epidemic.

1. **Location** On the map, locate (a) Messina, (b) Caffa, (c) Spain, (d) France.
2. **Movement** (a) Had the plague spread to Paris by 1347? (b) By what year had the plague spread to Florence? To Lithuania?
3. **Critical Thinking** **Making Generalizations** Based on the map, make a generalization about the urban revolts of the 1300s.

Spread of plague in
1347 | 1348–1349 | 1350–1353

* Sites of urban revolts

Within months, the disease that Europeans called the Black Death was raging through Italy. By 1348, it had reached Spain and France. From there, it ravaged the rest of Europe. One in three people died, worse than any war in history.

**A global epidemic.** The sickness was the bubonic plague, a disease spread by fleas on rats. Bubonic plague had broken out before in Europe, Asia, and North Africa but had died down. One strain, though, had survived in the Gobi Desert of Mongolia. In the 1200s, Mongol armies conquered China and much of Asia, probably setting off the new outbreak.

In the premodern world, rats infested ships, towns, and even the homes of the rich and powerful, so no one took any notice of them. In the early 1300s, rats scurrying through crowded Chinese cities spread the plague, which killed about 35 million people there.

Fleas jumped from those rats to infest the clothes and packs of traders traveling west. As a result, the disease spread from Asia to the Middle East. Terrible reports reached Europe: "India was depopulated," wrote a chronicler. "Tartary, Mesopotamia, Syria, and Armenia were covered with dead bodies. The Kurds fled in vain to the mountains." In Cairo, one of the world's largest cities, the plague at its peak killed about 7,000 people a day.

**A terrible death.** The disease struck with stunning speed. "People lay ill little more than two or three days," wrote a French friar, Jean de Venette. "He who was well one day was dead the next." A few victims survived. Most did not.

Unsanitary conditions in towns and homes guaranteed that the disease would spread. Unaware of what a flea bite might mean, people paid little attention until they noticed the swellings and black bruises on their skin that promised death. Victims suffered heavy sweats and convulsive coughing. They spat blood, stank terribly, and died in agony.

*Chapter 9* 229

**Social upheaval.** The plague brought terror and bewilderment, since people had no way to stop the disease. Some people turned to magic and witchcraft for cures. Others plunged into wild pleasures, believing they would soon die anyway. Still others saw the plague as God's punishment. They beat themselves with whips to show they repented their sins.

Christians blamed Jews for the plague, charging that they had poisoned the wells. "The whole world," De Venette noted, "rose up against [the Jews] cruelly on this account." In the resulting hysteria, thousands of Jews were slaughtered.

Normal life broke down. The Italian poet Francesco Petrarch wrote to his brother:

> 66How will people in the future believe that there has been such a time . . . when the whole globe has remained without inhabitants? When before has it been seen that houses are left vacant, cities deserted, fields are too small for the dead, and a fearful and universal solitude [lay] over the whole Earth?99

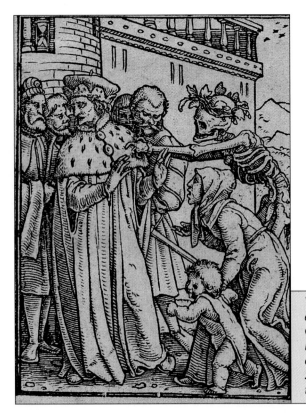

**Economic results.** As the plague kept recurring in the late 1300s, the European economy plunged to a low ebb. As workers and employers died, production declined. Survivors demanded higher wages, but as the cost of labor soared, prices rose, too.

Landowners and merchants pushed for laws to limit wages. To stop rising costs, landowners converted croplands to sheep raising, which required less labor. Villagers forced off the land sought work in towns. There, guilds refused to accept new members, limited apprenticeships, and denied journeymen the chance to become masters.

Coupled with the fear of the plague, these restrictions sparked explosive revolts. Bitter, angry peasants rampaged in England, France, Germany, and elsewhere. In cities, too, artisans fought, usually without success, for more power. The plague had spread both death and social unrest. Western Europe would not fully recover from its effects for more than 100 years. ▨

## Upheaval in the Church

The late Middle Ages brought spiritual crisis, scandal, and division to the Roman Catholic Church. Many priests and monks died during the plague. Their replacements faced challenging questions. "Why did God spare some and kill others?" asked survivors. The sacraments offered little comfort to people rocked by the fear of sudden death.

**Divisions within the Catholic Church.** The Church was unable to provide the strong leadership needed in this desperate time. In 1309, Pope Clement V had moved the papal court to Avignon on the border of southern France. (See page 214.) There it remained for about 70 years under French domination. This period is often called the Babylonian Captivity of the Church, referring to the time when the ancient Hebrews were held captive in Babylon.

*The Dance of Death* *The scene at left is from a set of engravings depicting the terror of the plague, by the German artist Hans Holbein, the Younger. The Black Death made no distinctions, taking men, women, and children of all backgrounds and classes.* **Political and Social Systems** *What social class is Death visiting in this engraving?*

In Avignon, popes reigned over a lavish court. Critics lashed out against the worldly, pleasure-loving papacy, and anticlergy sentiment grew. Within the Church itself, reformers tried to end the "captivity."

In 1378, reformers elected their own pope to rule from Rome. French cardinals responded by choosing a rival pope. For decades, two and sometimes even three popes claimed to be the true "vicar of Christ." Not until 1417 did a Church council at Constance finally end the crisis.

**New heresies.** With its moral authority weakened, the Church faced still more problems. Popular preachers challenged its power. In England, John Wycliffe, an Oxford professor, attacked Church corruption.

Wycliffe insisted that the Bible, not the Church, was the source of all Christian truth. He began translating the Bible into English so that people could read it themselves rather than rely on the clergy to read it. Czech students at Oxford carried Wycliffe's ideas to Bohemia— what is today the Czech Republic. There, Jan Hus led the call for reforms.

The Church responded by persecuting Wycliffe and his followers and suppressing the Hussites. Hus was tried for heresy and burned at the stake in 1415. The ideas of Wycliffe and Hus survived, however. A century later, other reformers took up the same demands.

## The Hundred Years' War

On top of the disasters of famine, plague, and economic decline came a long, destructive war. Between 1337 and 1453, England and France fought a series of conflicts, known as the Hundred Years' War. The fighting devastated France and drained England.

As you have read, English rulers had battled for centuries to hold onto the French lands of their Norman ancestors. French kings, for their part, were intent on extending their own power in France. When Edward III of England claimed the French crown in 1337, war erupted anew between these rival powers. Once fighting started, economic rivalry and a growing sense of national pride made it hard for either side to give up the struggle.

**English victories.** At first, the English won a string of victories—at Crécy in 1346,

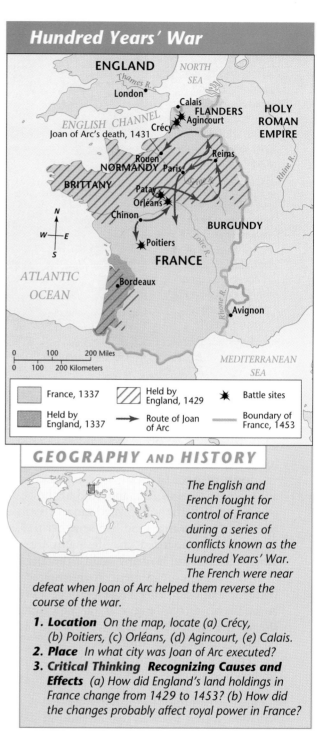

### Hundred Years' War

**Map legend:**
- France, 1337
- Held by England, 1337
- Held by England, 1429
- Route of Joan of Arc
- Battle sites
- Boundary of France, 1453

**GEOGRAPHY AND HISTORY**

The English and French fought for control of France during a series of conflicts known as the Hundred Years' War. The French were near defeat when Joan of Arc helped them reverse the course of the war.

1. **Location** On the map, locate (a) Crécy, (b) Poitiers, (c) Orléans, (d) Agincourt, (e) Calais.
2. **Place** In what city was Joan of Arc executed?
3. **Critical Thinking** *Recognizing Causes and Effects* (a) How did England's land holdings in France change from 1429 to 1453? (b) How did the changes probably affect royal power in France?

Poitiers 10 years later, and Agincourt in 1415. They owed their success not to braver or more skillful knights but to the longbow wielded by English archers. This powerful new weapon was six feet long and took years to master. But it could discharge three arrows in the time a French archer with his crossbow fired just one. And its arrows pierced all but the heaviest armor.

**Joan of Arc**
*Astonished by Joan's victories, English leaders claimed that she was aided by supernatural forces. Officials at her trial made 70 charges against her, including heresy and witchcraft. Here, Joan rallies her troops as they lay siege to the city of Paris.* **Impact of the Individual** *What effect do you think Joan's execution had on the morale of French soldiers?*

The English victories took a heavy toll on French morale. England, it seemed, was likely to bring all of France under its control. Then, in what seemed to the French a miracle, their fortunes were reversed.

**Joan of Arc.** In 1429, a 17-year-old peasant woman, Joan of Arc, appeared at the court of Charles VII, the uncrowned king of France. She told Charles that God had sent her to save France. She convinced the desperate French king to let her lead his army against the English.

To Charles's amazement, Joan inspired the battered and despairing French troops to fight anew. In an astonishing year of campaigning, she led the French to several victories and planted the seeds for future triumphs.

The poet Christine de Pizan honored Joan's bravery and success:

> **❝**Ah, what honor to the feminine sex!
> Which God so loved that he showed
> A way to this great people
> By which the kingdom, once lost,
> Was recovered by a woman,
> A thing that men could not do.**❞**

Joan paid for success with her life. She was taken captive by allies of the English and turned over to her enemies for trial. The English wanted to discredit her, and they had her tried for witchcraft. She was convicted and burned at the stake. That action, however, only strengthened her value to the French, who saw her as a martyr. Much later, the Church declared her a saint.

**Outcomes.** After Joan's death, the French took the offensive. With a powerful new weapon, the cannon, they attacked English-held castles. By 1453, the English held only the port of Calais in northwestern France.

In the end, the Hundred Years' War set France and England on different paths. The war created a growing sense of national feeling in France and allowed French kings to expand their power. During the war, English rulers turned repeatedly to Parliament for funds, which helped that body win the "power of the purse." England ended up losing its French lands, but that setback was not as disastrous for them as it appeared in 1453. With their dreams of a continental empire shattered, English rulers began looking at new trading ventures overseas.

## Looking Ahead

The Hundred Years' War brought many changes to the late medieval world. The longbow and cannon gave common soldiers a new importance on the battlefield and undermined the value of armored knights on horseback. Although neither nobles nor commoners knew it

# CAUSE AND EFFECT

### Long-Term Causes

Growth of strong monarchs
Growth of towns and cities
Growth of representative bodies
Crusades
Increased trade
Population decline

### Immediate Causes

Economic revival
New technology and agricultural productivity
Development of universities
Wider world view

## WESTERN EUROPEAN EMERGENCE FROM ISOLATION

### Immediate Effects

Population growth
End of feudalism
Centralized monarchies
Growth of Italian trading centers
Increased productivity

### Long-Term Effects

Renaissance
Age of Exploration
Scientific Revolution
Western European colonies in Asia, Africa,
   and the Americas

### Connections Today

Growth of strong central governments
Spread of representative government
Capitalism and powerful business classes
Influence of Western European culture around
   the world
Influence of technology on everyday life

*Interpreting a Chart  During the late Middle Ages, the chaos that had swept Europe for several hundred years gave way to an orderly society. As conditions improved, Europeans began to take a broader view of the world.  ■  Select two long-term causes from the chart at left. Explain how they contributed to Western Europe's eventual emergence from isolation.*

then, feudal society was changing. Knights and castles were doomed to disappear. Strong monarchs needed large armies, not feudal vassals, to fight their wars.

In the 1400s, as Europe recovered from the Black Death, other changes occurred. The population expanded and manufacturing grew. These changes, in turn, led to increased trade. Italian cities flourished as centers of shipping. They sent European cloth to the Middle East in exchange for spices, sugar, and cotton. Europeans developed new technologies. German miners, for example, used water power to crush ore and built blast furnaces to make cast iron.

The recovery of the late Middle Ages set the stage for further changes during the Renaissance, Reformation, and Age of Exploration, which you will read about in Unit 4. As Europe grew stronger, it would take a more prominent role on the global stage.

## SECTION 5 REVIEW

1. **Identify**  (a) bubonic plague, (b) Babylonian Captivity, (c) John Wycliffe, (d) Jan Hus, (e) Hundred Years' War, (f) Joan of Arc, (g) Charles VII.
2. What were three effects of the Black Death?
3. Why did reformers criticize the Church in the late 1300s?
4. How did new technologies affect fighting during the Hundred Years' War?
5. *Critical Thinking*  **Comparing**  Compare the effects of the Hundred Years' War in France and in England.
6. *ACTIVITY*  Imagine that you lived in Western Europe at the time of the Black Death. Write several diary entries that reflect what life was like during the plague years.

# Skills for Success

## Analyzing Literature as Historical Evidence

Works of literature often contain valuable information about the period in which they were written. Geoffrey Chaucer wrote *The Canterbury Tales* in the late 1300s. In it, he follows the adventures of a group of English pilgrims. In the excerpt below, he introduces the pilgrims.

Read the excerpt. Then, use the following steps to analyze it as a historical source.

**1 Identify the source.** (a) What is the title of the work? (b) Who wrote it? (c) When was it written?

**2 Define unfamiliar words and terms.** Use a dictionary or context clues to find out the meanings of the following: (a) uncloistered, (b) motley, (c) tithe.

**3 Study the content of the work.** (a) Who are some of the people that went on the pilgrimage? (b) How does the narrator describe the Knight? (c) Was the Merchant a successful businessman? (d) How does the narrator describe the Plowman?

**4 Analyze the source as historical evidence.** (a) How do the various members of the group make a living? (b) What was the author's view of the Monk? (c) How did it compare with his view of the Parson? (d) Give examples from the excerpt to show that religion and the Church were important to life in the Middle Ages.

*Beyond the Classroom* Choose a work of literature that you have read this year in English class or on your own. Follow the steps above to analyze it as historical evidence.

---

66 There was a KNIGHT, a most distinguished man,
Who from the day on which he first began
To ride abroad had followed chivalry,
Truth, honor, generousness and courtesy.
He had done nobly in his sovereign's war
And ridden into battle, no man more,
As well in Christian as heathen places,
And ever honored for his noble graces. . . .

A MONK there was, one of the finest sort
Who rode the country; hunting was his sport. . . .
He did not rate that text at a plucked hen
Which says that hunters are not holy men
And that a monk uncloistered is a mere
Fish out of water, flapping on the pier. . . .

There was a MERCHANT with a forking beard
And motley dress; high on his horse he sat, . . .
This estimable Merchant so had set
His wits to work, none knew he was in debt,
He was so stately in negotiation,
Loan bargain and commercial obligation. . . .

A holy-minded man of good renown
There was, and poor, the PARSON to a town.
Yet he was rich in holy thought and work.
He also was a learned man, a clerk,
Who truly knew Christ's gospel and would preach it
Devoutly to parishioners and teach it. . . .

He much disliked extorting tithe or fee,
Nay rather preferred beyond a doubt
Giving to poor parishioners round about
From his own goods and Easter offerings. . . .

There was a PLOWMAN with him there, his brother. . . .
He was an honest worker, good and true, . . .
For steadily about his work he went
To thrash his corn, to dig or to manure
Or make a ditch; and he would help the poor
For love of Christ and never take a penny
If he could help it, and, as prompt as any,
He paid his tithes in full when they were due
On what he owned, and on his earnings too. 99

## Building Vocabulary

Select *five* vocabulary words from the chapter. Write each word on a separate slip of paper. Then, write the definition for each word on other slips of paper. Scramble the slips and exchange them with another student. Match the words with their definitions, and then check each other's results.

## Reviewing Chapter Themes

1. **Political and Social Systems**  List four goals of medieval monarchs. Then, choose one monarch and explain how he furthered one of those goals.
2. **Global Interaction**  (a) How did the Crusades stimulate a renewed European interest in the larger world? (b) How did the crusading spirit affect Spain?
3. **Art and Literature**  Describe three developments that contributed to the flowering of medieval culture.
4. **Religions and Value Systems**  (a) How did Aristotle's work challenge medieval thinkers? (b) How did Thomas Aquinas resolve differences between faith and reason?
5. **Continuity and Change**  (a) Why were the late Middle Ages a period of decline in Europe? (b) What signs of revival appeared at the end of this period?

## Thinking Critically

1. **Defending a Position**  Review the conflict between Pope Gregory VII and the Holy Roman emperor Henry IV. Then, cite three arguments that each man might have given to defend his position.
2. **Drawing Conclusions**  As you have read, medieval Europeans devoted enormous amounts of time and money to building great stone cathedrals. Based on this information, what can you conclude about the values of medieval Europeans?
3. **Linking Past and Present**  Describe the reaction of Americans to the outbreak and spread of the AIDS virus. (a) How is it similar to the reaction of medieval Europeans to the Black Death? (b) How is it different?

4. **Recognizing Causes and Effects**  Construct a cause-and-effect chart for the Crusades. The chart should include both immediate and long-term effects. (★ See *Skills for Success*, page 18.)
5. **Analyzing Information**  Study the following excerpt from *Sayings of the Pope*, written in 1075. "The [pope] alone is properly called universal. He alone may depose bishops and reinstate them. . . . He may depose emperors." (a) What does this statement tell you about the way medieval popes viewed their role? (b) How do you think secular rulers might have responded to this view?
6. **Synthesizing Information**  Based on your readings in Chapters 8 and 9, make a chart showing the main political, economic, social, and religious developments of the early Middle Ages and the High Middle Ages. Next to each item, explain its importance. (★ See *Skills for Success*, page 896.)

### For Your Portfolio

Several historical figures discussed in this chapter have been featured as characters in well-known stories or plays. For example, the English playwright T. S. Eliot wrote about Thomas Becket in *Murder in the Cathedral*. Another English dramatist, George Bernard Shaw, told the story of Joan of Arc in *Saint Joan*. And the American author Howard Pyle included King John in his children's book *The Merry Adventures of Robin Hood*.

1. Choose one of the historical figures discussed in the chapter, such as Charlemagne, Hugh Capet, Philip IV, Saint Louis, Pope Gregory, or Christine de Pizan.
2. Research to find out about the life of the person you selected.
3. Use your research to create a dramatic scene or a short story about an event in the life of your character. You might read one of the works mentioned above for ideas about how to blend history with literature.
4. When you have completed your project, answer the following questions: (a) Why was the person you chose significant? (b) How were the problems your character faced unique? (c) Do you admire the person you chose? Why or why not?

# The Byzantine Empire and Russia

(330–1613)

## CHAPTER OUTLINE

1  The Byzantine Empire
2  The Rise of Russia
3  Shaping Eastern Europe

Prince Vladimir of Kiev was troubled. All his life, he had been loyal to the ancient Russian gods. He had dedicated wooden statues to the god of cattle and the god of the winds. But now he had heard of people who worshiped a single, all-powerful God. Should he abandon his traditional gods in favor of the God of the Jews, Christians, and Muslims? He sent agents to other lands to find out about these religions.

The ruler of the nearby Khazars had converted to Judaism. But, learning that Jews had been scattered across the Earth, Vladimir wondered if Judaism had enough worldly power. He rejected Islam because pork and alcohol were forbidden to Muslims. Roman Catholicism lost its appeal when Vladimir learned that the pope claimed authority over kings. Besides, Vladimir's agents reported that churches in Germany had little splendor.

Finally, Vladimir examined Greek Orthodox Christianity, the religion of the Byzantine empire to the south. When his agents returned from Constantinople, the Byzantine capital, they praised its glorious churches:

> 66We knew not whether we were in heaven or Earth. For on Earth there is no such splendor or such beauty, and we are at a loss how to describe it. We only know that God dwells there.99

Another agent reminded Vladimir, "If the Greek faith were evil, it would not have been adopted by your grandmother Olga, who was wiser than all others." Convinced, Vladimir and all his nobles tore down their wooden idols and converted to Orthodox Christianity in 998.

This story from Russia's earliest written history, *The Primary Chronicle,* mixes legend with truth. Still, Vladimir's conversion did mark a turning point in Russian history. It linked Russia to the Byzantine empire and to the cultural heritage of the eastern Roman empire.

As you have seen, the collapse of Rome left Europe divided. To the west, medieval civilization emerged. To the east, the Roman empire survived as the Byzantine empire. Byzantine civilization later influenced Eastern Europe, bringing Greek culture as well as Eastern Orthodox Christianity to the Slavic peoples.

FOCUS ON these questions as you read:

■ **Continuity and Change**
How did the Byzantine empire preserve the political and cultural heritage of Rome?

■ **Religions and Value Systems**
Why did a new form of Christianity emerge in the Byzantine empire and Russia?

■ **Political and Social Systems**
How did the rulers of Moscow build a powerful centralized Russian state?

■ **Diversity**
What peoples and cultural traditions shaped the Slavic kingdoms of Eastern Europe?

## TIME AND PLACE

**A Monument to Byzantine Glory** *The Byzantine emperor Justinian built the Church of Hagia Sophia, or "Holy Wisdom," as part of his plan to restore the glory of Rome. Located in the city of Constantinople (present-day Istanbul), it was the largest religious structure of its day. Murals, mosaics, and sculptures adorned almost every surface of its magnificent interior.* **Continuity and Change** *What architectural features did Hagia Sophia share with earlier Roman structures?*

## HUMANITIES LINK

*Art History* Icon of Christ and St. Maenas (page 243).
*Literature* In this chapter, you will encounter passages from the following works of literature: *The Primary Chronicle* (page 236); Procopius, *Secret History* (pages 240–241).

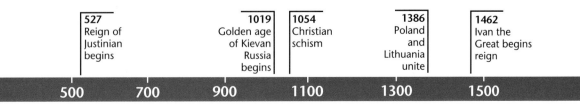

| 527 Reign of Justinian begins | 1019 Golden age of Kievan Russia begins | 1054 Christian schism | 1386 Poland and Lithuania unite | 1462 Ivan the Great begins reign |
|---|---|---|---|---|

500    700    900    1100    1300    1500

# 1 The Byzantine Empire

## Guide for Reading

■ What were the emperor Justinian's achievements?

■ Why was the Byzantine empire able to survive for so long?

■ How did the Byzantine empire influence later civilizations?

■ **Vocabulary** *autocrat, patriarch, icon, schism*

The teeming bazaars of Constantinople awed visitors. Rabbi Benjamin of Tudela, a Spanish traveler, saw merchants there from all over the Middle East, from Egypt—even from as far away as Russia and Hungary. "The city's daily income," he noted, "what with rent from shops and markets and taxes levied on merchants coming by sea and by land, reaches 20,000 gold pieces."

During the early Middle Ages, as the cities of the western Roman empire crumbled into ruin, Constantinople prospered. With its high walls and golden domes, it stood as the proud capital of the mighty Byzantine empire.

## Heir to Rome

You will recall that, as German invaders pounded the Roman empire in the west, emperors shifted their base to the eastern Mediterranean. By 330, the emperor Constantine had rebuilt the Greek city of Byzantium, renaming it Constantinople. From this "New Rome," roads fanned out from the Balkans to the Middle East and North Africa. In time, the eastern Roman empire became known as the Byzantine empire.

**Constantinople.** The vital center of the empire was Constantinople. Constantine had located his capital wisely on the shores of the Bosporus, a strait that linked the Mediterranean and Black seas. The city had an excellent harbor and was guarded on three sides by water. Later emperors built an elaborate system of land and sea walls to bolster its defenses.

Equally important, Constantinople commanded the key trade routes linking Europe and Asia. For centuries, the city's favorable location made it Europe's busiest marketplace. There, merchants sold silks from China, wheat from Egypt, gems from India, spices from Southeast Asia, slaves from Western Europe, and furs from the Viking lands in the north.

At the center of the city, Byzantine emperors and empresses lived in glittering splendor. Dressed in luxurious silk, they attended chariot races at the Hippodrome, an arena built by a Roman emperor in the 200s. Crowds cheered wildly as rival charioteers careened their vehicles around and around. The spectacle was another reminder of the city's glorious Roman heritage.

**A blending of cultures.** After rising to spectacular heights, the Byzantine empire eventually declined to a small area around Constantinople itself. Yet it was still in existence nearly 1,000 years after the fall of the western Roman empire. As the heir to Rome, it promoted a brilliant civilization that blended ancient Greek, Roman, and Christian influences with other traditions of the Mediterranean world.

## The Age of Justinian

The Byzantine empire reached its greatest size under the emperor Justinian, who ruled from 527 to 565. Justinian was determined to revive the grandeur of ancient Rome by recovering the western provinces that had been overrun by Germanic invaders. He spared no expense to achieve that dream.

Led by the brilliant general Belisarius, Byzantine armies reconquered North Africa, Italy, and southern Spain. The endless campaigns left Italy a bleeding ruin. The fighting

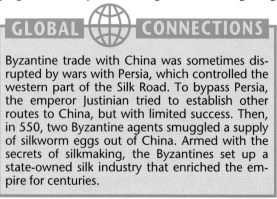

**GLOBAL CONNECTIONS**

Byzantine trade with China was sometimes disrupted by wars with Persia, which controlled the western part of the Silk Road. To bypass Persia, the emperor Justinian tried to establish other routes to China, but with limited success. Then, in 550, two Byzantine agents smuggled a supply of silkworm eggs out of China. Armed with the secrets of silkmaking, the Byzantines set up a state-owned silk industry that enriched the empire for centuries.

also exhausted Justinian's treasury and weakened his defenses in the east. In the end, the costly victories were temporary. Justinian's successors lost the bitterly contested lands in the west.

**Hagia Sophia.** Justinian left a more lasting monument in his buildings. To restore Roman glory, he launched a program to beautify Constantinople. His great triumph was the church of Hagia Sophia ("Holy Wisdom"). Its immense, arching dome improved on earlier Roman buildings. (See the picture on page 237.) The interior glowed with colored marble and with stunning silk curtains embroidered by local women.

Seeing this awesome church, the emperor recalled the temple King Solomon had built in Jerusalem. "Glory to God who has judged me worthy of accomplishing such a work as this!" Justinian exclaimed. "O Solomon, I have surpassed you!"

**Code of laws.** Justinian is best remembered for his reform of the law. Early in his reign, he set up a commission to collect, revise, and organize all the laws of ancient Rome. The result was the *Corpus Juris Civilis,* "Body of Civil Law," popularly known as Justinian's Code. This massive collection included laws passed by Roman assemblies or decreed by Roman emperors, as well as the legal writings of Roman judges and a handbook for students.

Justinian's Code had an impact far beyond the Byzantine empire. By the 1100s, it had reached Western Europe. There, both the Roman Catholic Church and medieval monarchs modeled their laws on its principles. The code thus preserved and transmitted the heritage of Roman law. Centuries later, the code also guided legal thinkers who began to put together the international law in use today.

**Absolute power.** To Justinian, the law was a means to unite the empire. Yet he himself was an autocrat, or sole ruler with complete authority. Like earlier Roman emperors, he had a large bureaucracy to carry out orders. Taxes from trade and industry enabled him to maintain a strong military and project Byzantine power abroad.

The emperor also had power over the Church. He was deemed Christ's co-ruler on Earth. As a Byzantine official wrote, "The em-

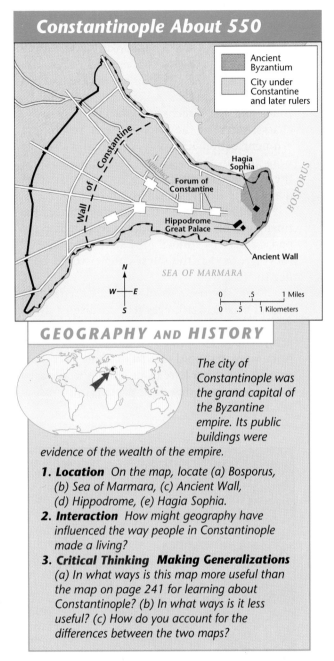

**Constantinople About 550**

Ancient Byzantium

City under Constantine and later rulers

Hagia Sophia

Forum of Constantine

Hippodrome
Great Palace

Ancient Wall

Wall of Constantine

Aqueduct

BOSPORUS

SEA OF MARMARA

N
W—E
S

0 .5 1 Miles
0 .5 1 Kilometers

**GEOGRAPHY AND HISTORY**

The city of Constantinople was the grand capital of the Byzantine empire. Its public buildings were evidence of the wealth of the empire.

1. **Location** On the map, locate (a) Bosporus, (b) Sea of Marmara, (c) Ancient Wall, (d) Hippodrome, (e) Hagia Sophia.
2. **Interaction** How might geography have influenced the way people in Constantinople made a living?
3. **Critical Thinking Making Generalizations** (a) In what ways is this map more useful than the map on page 241 for learning about Constantinople? (b) In what ways is it less useful? (c) How do you account for the differences between the two maps?

peror is equal to all men in the nature of his body, but in the authority of his rank he is similar to God, who rules all." Unlike feudal monarchs in Western Europe, he combined both political power and spiritual authority.

Powerful though he was, Justinian might never have achieved his goals without the help of his wife, Theodora. The empress did more than offer advice and influence policy. In 532, her firmness helped save the throne itself.

### Empress With an Iron Will

Justinian's court was in an uproar. A few days earlier, rioting had broken out between the Blues and the Greens, supporters of two rival chariot racers at the Hippodrome. Severe government action had only caused the two factions to join forces against the emperor. Now, the riot was turning into a revolt, with rebels demanding that Justinian give up the throne.

As rebels stormed the imperial palace, Justinian and his advisers huddled inside. The emperor asked his council for advice. One and all, they agreed that the safest course would be to flee the city.

Then, up rose a small woman of regal bearing. Her large, dark eyes flashed disgust at the cowardly advice of the council. Firmly, the empress Theodora spoke her mind. "Whether or not a woman should give an example of courage to men, is neither here nor there," she declared. "At a moment of desperate danger, one must do what one can."

**An ambitious woman.** Who was this woman whose words silenced the imperial council? Theodora had risen from humble beginnings. Her father was a bear keeper for the Hippodrome. At an early age, she herself became an actress, considered a lowly occupation. Charming, graceful, and intelligent, she led an adventurous life, traveling to Syria and Egypt. In her twenties, she settled in Constantinople, where she caught Justinian's eye. They wed in 525. Two years later, when he succeeded to the throne, she was crowned empress.

Theodora proved a shrewd, tough politician who did not hesitate to challenge the emperor's orders and pursue her own policies. She took a hand in diplomacy, trying to persuade the Persians to abide by a peace treaty. She moved quickly to help residents of Antioch after their city was destroyed in an earthquake. In addition, she championed the rights of women and set up hospitals for the poor.

At the same time, Theodora could be ruthless in pursuit of her goals. The Byzantine historian Procopius, in his *Secret History,* painted the empress as an evil, scheming monster. Those who opposed her might find themselves tossed out of office. Worse, they might disappear into her secret dungeons deep within the palace—never to be seen again.

**Theodora stands firm.** Now, with revolt threatening her husband's crown and her own, Theodora needed every ounce of her iron will. To her, the idea of fleeing was unthinkable. Without hesitation, she addressed Justinian and the council:

> 66If flight were the only means of safety, still I would not flee. Those who have worn the crown should never survive its loss. . . . Emperor, if you wish to flee, well and good, you have

*An Influential Empress* Theodora, seen in this mosaic carrying a church offering, encouraged her husband, Justinian, to protect women's rights. During their reign, new laws outlawed wife beating, enabled abused wives to sue for divorce, and permitted women to own property. *Impact of the Individual* How does this mosaic emphasize the majesty and power of Theodora?

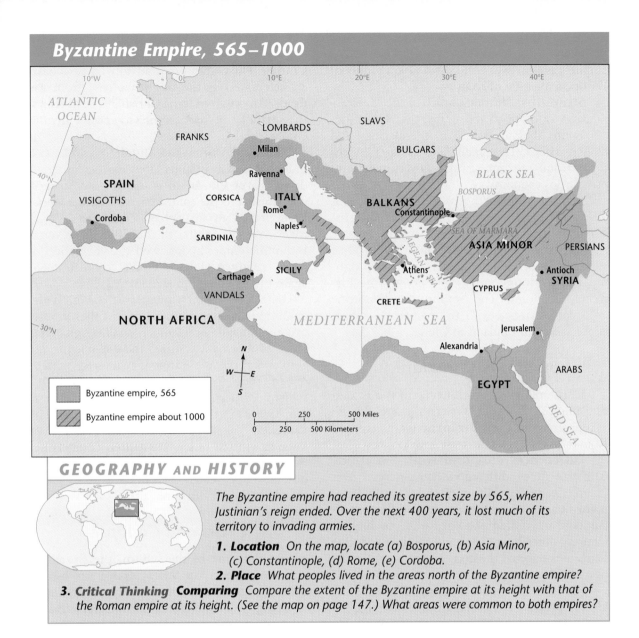

## Byzantine Empire, 565–1000

ATLANTIC OCEAN

FRANKS

LOMBARDS

SLAVS

SPAIN
VISIGOTHS
• Cordoba

CORSICA

Milan •

Ravenna •

ITALY
Rome •
Naples •

BULGARS

BLACK SEA

BOSPORUS

BALKANS
Constantinople •

SEA OF MARMARA

ASIA MINOR

PERSIANS

SARDINIA

Carthage •

SICILY

AEGEAN SEA

Athens •

CYPRUS

• Antioch
SYRIA

VANDALS

CRETE

MEDITERRANEAN SEA

Jerusalem •

NORTH AFRICA

Alexandria •

ARABS

EGYPT

RED SEA

N
W—E
S

Byzantine empire, 565

Byzantine empire about 1000

0     250     500 Miles
0   250   500 Kilometers

### GEOGRAPHY AND HISTORY

The Byzantine empire had reached its greatest size by 565, when Justinian's reign ended. Over the next 400 years, it lost much of its territory to invading armies.

**1. Location** On the map, locate (a) Bosporus, (b) Asia Minor, (c) Constantinople, (d) Rome, (e) Cordoba.
**2. Place** What peoples lived in the areas north of the Byzantine empire?
**3. Critical Thinking Comparing** Compare the extent of the Byzantine empire at its height with that of the Roman empire at its height. (See the map on page 147.) What areas were common to both empires?

the money, the ships are ready, the sea is clear. But I shall stay. I accept the ancient proverb: Royal purple is the best burial sheet. **99**

Her strong words fired Justinian's resolve. He rallied his supporters and moved to crush the revolt. Within days, the emperor's armies trapped 30,000 rioters in the Hippodrome and killed them all.

By her coolness and energy, Theodora had proven her value as adviser and co-ruler to Justinian. When she died of cancer in 548, he was shattered. Although he ruled for another 17 years, the most glorious days of his reign ended with Theodora's death. ▪

## Changing Fortunes of Empire

The fortunes of the Byzantine empire rose and fell in the centuries after Justinian. Time and again, its skilled forces held off foreign enemies. The empire withstood attacks by Persians, Slavs, Arabs, Vikings, Mongols, and Turks.

**A buffer to invaders.** During the early Middle Ages, the Byzantine empire served as a buffer, protecting Western Europe from the harshest onslaught of invaders from the east. In the 600s and 700s, Arab armies overran the wealthy Byzantine provinces of Egypt and Syria before advancing on Constantinople. The city held out, eventually turning back the attackers. By resisting the Arab advance, the Byzantine empire gave the weak and divided kingdoms of Europe a measure of security.

**Strengths.** Although much of the Mediterranean world fell to the Arabs, the Byzantines held onto their heartland in the Balkans and in Asia Minor. The empire's greatest strengths came from a strong central government and prosperous economy.

Peasants formed the backbone of the empire, working the land, paying taxes, and providing soldiers for the military. In the cities of the empire, trade and industry flourished. While Western Europe was reduced to a barter economy, the Byzantine empire preserved a healthy money economy. The bezant, the Byzantine gold coin stamped with the emperor's image, circulated from England to China.

## Byzantine Christianity

Christianity was as influential in the Byzantine empire as it was in Western Europe. But divisions grew between Byzantine Christians and Roman Catholics to the west.

**Differences east and west.** Since early Christian times, differences had emerged over Church leadership. Although the Byzantine emperor was not a priest, he controlled Church affairs and appointed the patriarch, or highest Church official, in Constantinople. Byzantine Christians rejected the pope's claim to authority over all Christians.

Further differences developed over time. Unlike priests in Western Europe, the Byzantine clergy retained their right to marry. Greek, not Latin, was the language of the Byzantine Church. The chief Byzantine holy day was Easter, celebrated as the day Jesus rose from the dead. Among western Christians, Christmas, the birthday of Jesus, came to receive greater emphasis.

**Schism.** During the Middle Ages, the two branches of Christianity drew farther apart. A dispute over the use of icons, or holy images, contributed to the split. Many Byzantine Christians prayed to images of Christ, the Virgin Mary, and the saints. In the 700s, however, a Byzantine emperor outlawed the veneration of icons, saying it violated God's commandment against worshiping "graven images."

The ban set off violent battles within the empire. The pope took a hand in the dispute, excommunicating the emperor. Although a later empress eventually restored the use of icons, the conflict left great resentment against the pope.

In 1054, other controversies provoked a schism, or permanent split, between the Eastern (Greek) Orthodox and the Roman Catholic churches. The pope and the patriarch excommunicated each other. Thereafter, contacts between the two churches were guarded and distant. They treated each other as rivals rather than branches of the same faith.

## Crisis and Collapse

By the time of the schism, the Byzantine empire was declining. Struggles over succession, court intrigues, and constant wars undermined its strength. As in Western Europe, powerful local lords gained control of large areas. As the empire faltered, its enemies advanced. The Nor-

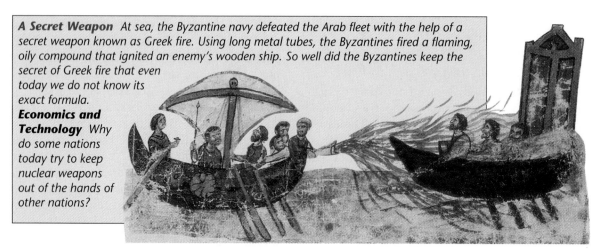

**A Secret Weapon** At sea, the Byzantine navy defeated the Arab fleet with the help of a secret weapon known as Greek fire. Using long metal tubes, the Byzantines fired a flaming, oily compound that ignited an enemy's wooden ship. So well did the Byzantines keep the secret of Greek fire that even today we do not know its exact formula. **Economics and Technology** Why do some nations today try to keep nuclear weapons out of the hands of other nations?

mans conquered southern Italy. Even more serious, the Seljuk Turks advanced across Asia Minor. A nomadic people out of central Asia, the Seljuks had converted to Islam in their migrations westward.

**The Crusades.** In the 1090s, the Byzantine emperor called for western help to fight the Seljuks, resulting in the First Crusade. (See page 220.) During later crusades, however, trade rivalry sparked violence between the Byzantine empire and Venice. Venetian merchants convinced knights on the Fourth Crusade to attack Constantinople in 1204. For three days, crusaders burned and plundered the city, sending much treasure west.

For 50 years, western Christians ruled Constantinople. Although a Byzantine emperor reclaimed the capital in the 1260s, the empire never recovered. Venetian merchants gained control of Byzantine trade, draining the wealth of the empire. More threatening, the Ottoman Turks overran most of Asia Minor and the Balkans, as you will read in Chapter 11.

**The end of an empire.** In 1453, Ottoman forces surrounded Constantinople. After a siege lasting two months, they stormed the broken walls. When the last Byzantine emperor was offered safe passage, he replied, "God forbid that I should live an emperor without an empire." He chose instead to die fighting.

The Ottoman ruler Muhammad II entered the city in triumph and renamed it Istanbul. The ancient Christian city became the capital of the Ottoman empire. Hagia Sophia was turned into an Islamic house of worship, and Istanbul soon emerged as a great center of Muslim culture.

## The Byzantine Heritage

Although Byzantine power had faded long before, the fall of Constantinople marked the end of an era. To Europeans, the empire had stood for centuries as the enduring symbol of Roman civilization. Throughout the Middle Ages, Byzantine influence radiated across Eu-

*Icon of Christ and St. Maenas* Painted in the 500s, this early Byzantine icon already displays the style of thousands of later icons. The holy figures stare directly outward, inviting the viewer into a personal relationship. Through a stained glass effect, light seems to shine through the painting. The background, halos, and the figures themselves seem to glow because the artist painted upon a background of reflecting gold paint. **Art and Literature** Why do you think most icons were done in the same traditional style?

rope. Even the Ottoman conquerors adapted features of Byzantine government, social life, and architecture.

What was the Byzantine heritage? For 1,000 years, the Byzantines built on the culture of the Hellenistic world. Byzantine civilization blended Christian beliefs with Greek science, philosophy, arts, and literature. The Byzantines also extended Roman achievements in engineering and law.

**Arts.** Byzantine artists made unique contributions, especially in religious art and architecture, that influenced western styles from the Middle Ages to the present. Icons, designed to evoke the presence of God, gave viewers a sense of personal contact with the sacred. Mosaics brought scenes from the Bible to glowing life. In architecture, Byzantine palaces and churches blended Greek, Roman, Persian, and other Middle Eastern styles.

**The world of learning.** Byzantine scholars preserved the classic works of ancient Greece. In addition, they produced their own books, especially histories.

Like the Greek historians Herodotus and Thucydides, Byzantine historians were mostly concerned with writing about their own times. Procopius, an adviser to the general Belisarius, chronicled the Byzantine campaign against Persia. As you have read, he also wrote a *Secret History* that savagely criticized Justinian and Theodora.

Anna Comnena is considered by many scholars to be the western world's first important female historian. In the *Alexiad,* she analyzed the reign of her father, Emperor Alexius I. Comnena's book portrayed Latin crusaders as greedy barbarians.

As the empire tottered in the 1400s, Greek scholars left Constantinople to teach at Italian universities. They took valuable Greek manuscripts to the West, along with their knowledge of Greek and Byzantine culture. The work of these scholars contributed to the European cultural flowering known as the Renaissance. (See Chapter 14.)

## SECTION 1 REVIEW

1. **Identify** (a) Hagia Sophia, (b) *Corpus Juris Civilis,* (c) Theodora, (d) Procopius, (e) Anna Comnena.
2. **Define** (a) autocrat, (b) patriarch, (c) icon, (d) schism.
3. Choose two accomplishments of Justinian and explain the importance of each.
4. How did location contribute to the strength of the Byzantine empire?
5. Describe the legacy of Byzantine civilization.
6. *Critical Thinking* **Analyzing Information** Reread Theodora's speech on pages 240–241. What do her words suggest about her character and goals?
7. *ACTIVITY* Create a chart illustrating some of the differences between Roman Catholic and Byzantine Christianity.

# 2 The Rise of Russia

## Guide for Reading

- What traditions influenced early Russia?
- How did the princes of Moscow become czars of Russia?
- What kind of government did Russian rulers develop?
- **Vocabulary** *boyar, czar*

In Russia, a patriotic monk saw a special meaning in the fall of Constantinople. The prince of Moscow, he declared, had inherited the mantle of the Roman and Byzantine emperors:

66The first Rome collapsed owing to its heresies. The second Rome fell victim to the Turks, but a new and third Rome has sprung up in the north, illuminating the whole universe like a sun.99

Moscow had reason to claim itself heir to the Byzantine empire. Over many centuries, Byzantine culture greatly influenced the development of Russian society.

## *Geography: The Russian Land*

Today, Russia is the largest nation in the world. Its early history, however, began in the fertile area of present-day Ukraine. In the later Middle Ages, its political center shifted northward to the city of Moscow. From there, Russia created a huge empire that extended from Eastern Europe across Asia to the Pacific.

Russia lies on the vast Eurasian plain that reaches from Europe to the borders of China. Although mapmakers use the Ural Mountains to mark the boundary between Europe and Asia, these ancient mountains were long ago worn away to wooded hills. They posed no obstacle to the movement of peoples.

**Regions.** Three broad zones with different climates and resources helped shape early Russian life. The northern forests supplied lumber for building and fuel. Fur-bearing animals attracted hunters, but poor soil and a cold, snowy climate hindered farming. Farther south, a band of fertile land attracted early farmers. This region was home to Russia's first civilization.

A third region, the southern steppe, is an open, treeless grassland. It offered splendid pasture for the herds and horses of nomadic people. With no natural barriers, the steppe was a great highway, along which streams of nomads migrated from Asia into Europe.

**Rivers.** Russia's network of rivers provided transportation for both people and goods. The Dnieper (NEE puhr) and Volga rivers became productive trade routes. Major rivers ran from north to south, linking the Russians early on to the advanced Byzantine world in the south.

### Growth of Kiev

During Roman times, the Slavs expanded into southern Russia. Like the Germanic peoples who pushed into Western Europe, the Slavs had no political organization more complex than the clan. They lived in small villages, farmed, and traded along the rivers connecting the Baltic in the north to the Black Sea.

**The Varangians.** In the 700s and 800s, the Vikings steered their long ships out of Scandinavia. These expert sailors were as much at home on Russian rivers as on the stormy Atlantic. The Vikings, called Varangians by later Russians, worked their way south along the rivers, trading with and collecting tribute from the Slavs. They also conducted a thriving trade with Constantinople.

Located at the heart of this vital trade network, the city of Kiev would become the center of the first Russian state. Within a few generations, the Varangians who had settled among the Slavs were absorbed into the local culture. Viking names like Helga and Waldemar became the Slavic names Olga and Vladimir.

**Byzantine influences.** Trade had already brought Kiev into the Byzantine sphere of influence. Constantinople later sent Christian

missionaries to convert the Slavs. About 863, two Greek monks, Cyril and Methodius, adapted the Greek alphabet so they could translate the Bible into Slavic languages. This Cyrillic (suh RIHL ihk) alphabet became the written script used in Russia and Ukraine to the present.

In 957, Olga, the reigning princess of Kiev, converted to Byzantine Christianity. But it was not until the reign of her grandson Vladimir that the new religion spread widely. (See page 236.) After his conversion, Vladimir married the sister of a Byzantine emperor. Soon Greek priests arrived in Kiev to preside over the mass baptisms organized by the prince.

With Byzantine Christianity came many changes. The Russians acquired a written language, and a class of educated Russian priests emerged. Russians adapted Byzantine religious art, music, and architecture. Byzantine domes capped with colorful, carved "helmets" became the onion domes of Russian churches.

Byzantine Christianity set the patterns for close ties between Church and state. Russian rulers, like the Byzantine emperor, eventually controlled the Church, making it dependent on them for support. The Russian Orthodox Church would long remain a pillar of state power.

**Yaroslav.** Kiev enjoyed its golden age under Yaroslav the Wise, who ruled from 1019 to 1054. To improve justice, he issued a written law code. A scholar, he translated Greek works into his language. He arranged marriages between his children and the royal families of Western Europe.

Kiev declined in the 1100s as rival families battled for the throne. Also, Russian trading cities were hurt because Byzantine prosperity faded. As Russian princes continued to squabble among themselves, Mongol invaders from central Asia struck the final blow.

## The Mongol Conquest

In the early 1200s, a young leader united the nomadic Mongols of central Asia. As his mounted bowmen overran lands from China to Eastern Europe, he took the title Genghiz Khan (GEHNG gihz KAHN), "World Emperor." You will read more about the Mongols (called Tatars by the Russians) in Chapter 13. Here, we will look at their impact on Russia.

**The Golden Horde.** Between 1236 and 1241, Batu, the grandson of Genghiz, led Mongol armies into Russia. Known as the Golden Horde, from the color of their tents, they looted and burned Kiev and other Russian towns. So many inhabitants were killed, declared a Russian historian, that "no eye remained to weep for the dead." From their capital on the Volga River, the Golden Horde ruled Russia for the next 240 years.

The Mongols, while fierce conquerors, were generally tolerant rulers. They demanded regular payments of heavy tribute, and Russian princes had to acknowledge the Mongols as their overlords. But as long as the tribute was paid, the Mongols left Russian princes to rule without much interference.

**Mongol influences.** Historians have long debated how Mongol rule affected Russia. Peasants felt the burden of heavy taxes. Some fled to remote regions, while others sought protection from Mongol raids by becoming serfs of Russian nobles. Even though the Golden Horde converted to Islam, the Mongols tolerated the Russian Orthodox Church, which grew more powerful during this period. The Mongol conquest brought peace to the huge swath of land between China and Eastern Europe, and Russian merchants benefited from new trade routes across this region.

During the period of Mongol rule, Russians adopted the practice of isolating upper-class women in separate quarters. Beginning in the 1200s, women became totally subject to male authority in the household. Husbands could even sell their wives into slavery to pay family debts.

The absolute power of the Mongols served as a model for later Russian rulers. Russian princes came to develop a strong desire to centralize their own power without interference from nobles, the clergy, or wealthy merchants. Perhaps most important, Mongol rule cut Russia off from contacts with Western Europe at a time when Europeans were making rapid advances in the arts and sciences.

## Moscow Takes the Lead

During the Mongol period, the princes of Moscow steadily increased their power. Their success was due in part to the city's location near important river trade routes. They also used their position as tribute collectors for the Mongols to subdue neighboring towns. When the head of the Russian Orthodox Church made Moscow his capital, the city became Russia's spiritual center as well.

As Mongol power declined, the princes of Moscow took on a new role as patriotic defenders of Russia against foreign rule. In 1380, they rallied other Russians and defeated the Golden Horde at the battle of Kulikovo. Although the Mongols continued their terrifying raids, their strength was much reduced.

**Ivan the Great.** The driving force behind Moscow's rising power was Ivan III, known as Ivan the Great. Between 1462 and 1505, he brought much of northern Russia under his rule. He also recovered Russian territories that had fallen into the hands of neighboring Slavic states.

Ivan built the framework for absolute rule. He tried to limit the power of the boyars, or great landowning nobles. After his marriage to Sophia-Zoë Paleologus, niece of the last Byzantine emperor, he adopted Byzantine court rituals. Like the Byzantine emperors, he used the double-headed eagle as his symbol. Ivan and his successors took the title czar, the Russian word for Caesar. "The czar," claimed Ivan, "is in nature like all men, but in authority he is like the highest God."

**Ivan the Terrible.** Ivan IV, grandson of Ivan the Great, further centralized royal power. He undercut the privileges of the old boyar families and granted land to nobles in exchange for military or other service. At a time when the manor system had faded in Western Europe, Ivan IV introduced new laws that tied Russian serfs to the land.

About 1560, Ivan IV became increasingly unstable, trusting no one and subject to violent fits of rage. In a moment of madness, he killed his own son. He organized the *oprichniki* (aw PREECH nee kee), agents of terror who enforced the czar's will. Dressed in black robes and

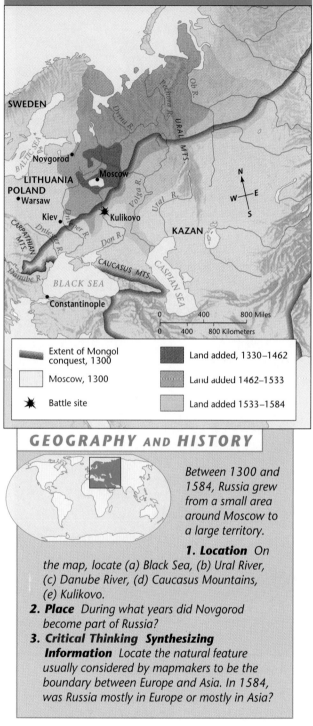

## Growth of Russia, 1300–1584

**Extent of Mongol conquest, 1300**

**Moscow, 1300**

**★ Battle site**

**Land added, 1330–1462**

**Land added 1462–1533**

**Land added 1533–1584**

## GEOGRAPHY AND HISTORY

Between 1300 and 1584, Russia grew from a small area around Moscow to a large territory.

1. **Location** On the map, locate (a) Black Sea, (b) Ural River, (c) Danube River, (d) Caucasus Mountains, (e) Kulikovo.
2. **Place** During what years did Novgorod become part of Russia?
3. **Critical Thinking Synthesizing Information** Locate the natural feature usually considered by mapmakers to be the boundary between Europe and Asia. In 1584, was Russia mostly in Europe or mostly in Asia?

**ISSUES For TODAY**

Russian princes were strongly influenced by the Byzantine tradition of autocratic rule. What advantages and disadvantages may result when a government is dominated by a single powerful individual?

mounted on black horses, they slaughtered rebellious boyars and sacked towns suspected of disloyalty. Their saddles were decorated with a dog's head and a broom, symbols of their constant watchfulness to sweep away their master's enemies.

**Ivan the Terrible** *This painting of Ivan IV, done some 300 years after his death, shows how his reputation as a harsh ruler survived the centuries. Yet the czar was a man of interesting contrasts. He was a devout member of the Orthodox Church and composed original prayers and church music. He once sent the names of 3,000 of his victims to various monasteries, directing the monks to pray for their souls.* **Impact of the Individual** *What aspect of Ivan's character did the artist emphasize in this portrait? Explain.*

The czar's awesome power, and the ways he used it, earned him the title "Ivan the Terrible." When he died in 1584, he left a wounded land seething with rebellion. But he had introduced Russia to a tradition of extreme absolute power.

**Looking ahead.** Disputes over succession, peasant uprisings, and foreign invasions soon plunged Russia into a period of disorder. This "Time of Troubles" lasted from 1604 to 1613. Finally, the *zemsky sobor* (ZEHM skee suh BAWR), an assembly of clergy, nobles, and townsmen, chose a new czar, 17-year-old Michael Romanov. His reign established the Romanov dynasty, which would rule Russia until 1917.

In the 1600s, Russia was an emerging power. Like monarchs in France or Spain, the czars expanded national borders and centralized royal control. But Russia developed along far different lines. Byzantine influences had helped establish a strong tradition of autocratic rule. Later Russian rulers were generally more autocratic than western kings and queens. Authoritarian leaders, from Peter the Great and Catherine the Great to Joseph Stalin, would shape Russian history down to this century.

## SECTION 2 REVIEW

1. **Identify** (a) Cyril and Methodius, (b) Vladimir, (c) Yaroslav, (d) Genghiz Khan, (e) Time of Troubles, (f) Michael Romanov.
2. **Define** (a) boyar, (b) czar.
3. Describe one way each of the following groups influenced Russia's development: (a) Slavs, (b) Varangians, (c) Byzantines, (d) Mongols.
4. How did the center of power in Russia shift to Moscow?
5. What methods did Ivan III and Ivan IV use to centralize their power?
6. *Critical Thinking* **Recognizing Points of View** Supporters of Ivan III called Moscow "the third Rome." (a) Why do you think they wanted to compare Moscow to Rome? (b) Do you agree that Moscow was truly the heir to Rome? Why or why not?
7. *ACTIVITY* Organize a debate on the following statement: "The only way to ensure absolute power is through the use of terror."

# Shaping Eastern Europe

## Guide for Reading

- Why did Eastern Europe develop diverse cultural traditions?

- What traditions shaped Eastern Europe in the Middle Ages?

- What threats did Eastern European kingdoms face?

- **Vocabulary** *ethnic group*

Many times in our century, people have opened their newspapers to find the news dominated by turbulent events in Eastern Europe. In 1914, a political assassination by Serbian nationalists triggered World War I. In 1938 and 1939, German aggression in Czechoslovakia and Poland sparked World War II. In 1989, revolts in Eastern European nations helped topple the Soviet empire. In the 1990s, the Balkans were again torn apart by war as rival national groups clashed in Bosnia.

The roots of such conflicts lie deep in the history of the region. As you will see, it has often been a history marked by war, revolution, and foreign conquest.

## *Geography: Eastern Europe*

The region known as Eastern Europe is a wide swath of territory lying between German-speaking Central Europe to the west and the largest Slavic nation, Russia, to the east. Many peoples, many nations have flourished in the area over the centuries. We will now look at the diverse geography and patterns of settlement that have shaped the region.

**A diverse region.** To get a sense of the geography of Eastern Europe, look at the map on page 187. Traveling from north to south, your eye will pass from the chilly waters of the Baltic Sea, down across the plains of Poland, then through the mountainous Balkans. The Balkan Peninsula, a roughly triangular arm of land, juts southward into the warm Mediterranean.

Several geographic features influenced developments in Eastern Europe. Much of the region lies on the great European plain that links up with the steppes of southern Russia. As in Russia, nomadic peoples migrated across the steppe from Asia. The pressure of these migrations created frequent turmoil and slowed the growth of prosperous, stable states.

The main rivers of Eastern Europe, like the Danube or the Vistula, flow either into the Black Sea or into the Baltic. Goods and cultural influences traveled along these river routes. As a result, the Balkans in the south felt the impact of the Byzantine empire and later the Muslim Ottoman empire. By contrast, the northern regions bordering Germany and the Baltic Sea forged closer links to Western Europe.

**A mix of peoples.** Many groups settled in Eastern Europe. In the early Middle Ages, the Slavs spread out from a central heartland in Russia. The West Slavs filtered into what is today Poland and the Czech and Slovak republics. The South Slavs descended into the Balkans and became the ancestors of the Serbs, Croats, and Slovenes.

The Balkans were peopled by other ethnic groups as well. An ethnic group is a large group of people who share the same language and cultural heritage. Waves of Asian peoples migrated into Eastern Europe, among them the Huns, Avars, Bulgars, Khazars, and Magyars. Vikings and other Germanic people added to the mix. The result is a region of many peoples, languages, and cultural traditions.

Powerful neighboring states exercised strong cultural influences on Eastern Europe, adding further to the diversity. From the south, Byzantine missionaries carried Eastern Orthodox Christianity, as well as Byzantine culture, throughout the Balkans. At the same time, German knights and missionaries from the West spread Roman Catholic Christianity to Poland, Hungary, the Czech area, and the western Balkans. In the 1300s, the Ottomans invaded the Balkans, spreading Islam into pockets of that area. As Russian power grew, its influence also radiated to Eastern Europe.

**Jewish settlements.** In the late Middle Ages, Eastern Europe was a refuge for many Jewish settlers. Western European Christians launched brutal attacks on Jewish communities during the Crusades and the Black Death. To escape persecution, hundreds of Jews fled east.

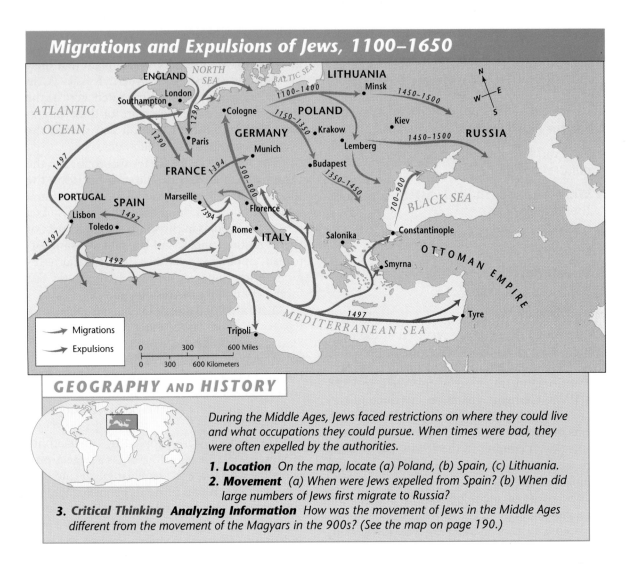

## Migrations and Expulsions of Jews, 1100–1650

GEOGRAPHY AND HISTORY

During the Middle Ages, Jews faced restrictions on where they could live and what occupations they could pursue. When times were bad, they were often expelled by the authorities.

1. **Location** On the map, locate (a) Poland, (b) Spain, (c) Lithuania.
2. **Movement** (a) When were Jews expelled from Spain? (b) When did large numbers of Jews first migrate to Russia?
3. **Critical Thinking** **Analyzing Information** How was the movement of Jews in the Middle Ages different from the movement of the Magyars in the 900s? (See the map on page 190.)

As monarchs centralized power in England, France, and Spain, they expelled Jews from their lands, and these groups, too, migrated eastward.

In the 1300s, Polish kings followed a policy of toleration toward Jews. As a result, Jewish villages sprang up in Poland and other sparsely populated areas of Eastern Europe. Jewish peasants and scholars contributed to the economic and cultural development of Poland during this period.

### Early Kingdoms

During the Middle Ages, Eastern Europe included many kingdoms, duchies (lands ruled by dukes), and principalities (lands ruled by princes). Wars constantly shifted boundaries. Sometimes, strong empires absorbed national groups. Alliances or royal marriages bound others together for a time. To get a sense of these shifting fortunes, we will look at the kingdoms of Poland, Hungary, and Serbia.

**Poland.** Western missionaries brought Roman Catholicism to the West Slavs of Poland in the 900s. A century later, the first Polish king was crowned. To survive, the new kingdom often had to battle German, Russian, and Mongol forces.

Poland's greatest age came after its queen Jadwiga (yahd VEE gah) married Duke Wladyslav Jagiello (vwah DIHS wahv  yahg YEH loh) of Lithuania in 1386. Under the Jagiello dynasty, Poland-Lithuania controlled the largest state in Europe, an empire stretching from the Baltic to the Black Sea. Jadwiga patronized the fine university at the city of Cracow, which became a major center of science and the arts.

Unlike Russia or Western Europe, where monarchs limited the power of nobles, Polish nobles gradually gained power at the expense of the monarch. They met in a diet, or assembly, where the vote of a single noble was enough to block the passage of a law. This *liberum veto,* or "free veto," made it hard for the government to take decisive action.

Without a strong central government, Poland declined in the 1600s. It enjoyed a final moment of glory in 1683 when the Polish king Jan Sobieski (YAHN saw BYEH skee) broke the Ottoman siege of Vienna, Austria. In the next century, however, Poland disappeared from the map entirely, gobbled up by ambitious neighbors. (See page 443.)

**Hungary.** Hungary was settled by the Magyars who had raided Europe from the Asian steppes in the century after Charlemagne. About 970, the Magyars adopted Roman Catholic Christianity. Traditionally, Hungarians credit Stephen I with converting the entire country when he was crowned Hungary's first Christian king on Christmas Day in 1000.

Hungary was larger in the Middle Ages than it is today. Its rulers controlled present-day Slovakia, Croatia, and parts of Romania. Like King John of England, though, the Hungarian king was forced to sign a charter recognizing the rights of his nobles. Known as the Golden Bull of 1222, it strictly limited royal power.

The Mongols overran Hungary in 1241, killing about half its population. They soon withdrew, so their invasion did not have the same impact as it had on Russia. The expansion of the Ottoman Turks, though, did end Hungarian independence in 1526. Later, the Austrian Hapsburgs replaced the Ottomans as rulers of Hungary.

**Serbia.** During the 600s, South Slavs settled the mountainous Balkans. Serbs, Croats, Slovenes, and other Slavic peoples in the Balkans had different histories during the Middle Ages. The Serbs accepted Orthodox Christianity. By the late 1100s, they had set up their own state, which reached its height under Stefan Dušan (STEH fahn DOO shahn). He battled the Byzantine empire and conquered Macedonia in the 1300s. Yet Stefan encouraged Byzantine culture and even modeled his law code on that of Justinian.

Stefan's successors lacked his political gifts, and Serbia could not withstand the Ottoman advance. At the battle of Kosovo in 1389, Serbs fought to the death, a memory still honored by their descendants. During almost 500 years of Ottoman rule, Serbs preserved a sense of their own identity.

**Looking ahead.** Migration, conquest, dynastic marriages, and missionary activity helped produce a tangle of overlapping claims to territories in Eastern Europe. In early modern times, large empires swallowed up much of the region. Yet whenever they had a chance, the peoples of Eastern Europe tried to recover their independence. In later chapters, we will see how the desire to rebuild separate states repeatedly ignited new turmoils.

## SECTION 3 REVIEW

1. **Identify** (a) Jadwiga, (b) *liberum veto,* (c) Jan Sobieski, (d) Golden Bull of 1222, (e) Stefan Dušan.
2. **Define** ethnic group.
3. How did Eastern Europe become home to many ethnic groups?
4. What religions were introduced into Eastern Europe?
5. *Critical Thinking* **Comparing** (a) How were the histories of Poland, Hungary, and Serbia similar? (b) How were their histories different?
6. *ACTIVITY* Create flashcards for *six* of the diverse groups that settled in or influenced Eastern Europe. On one side of each card, write the name of the group. On the other side, write a sentence describing one way that group affected developments in Eastern Europe. Use the flashcards to quiz other students.

▲ *A battle between Hungarian and Mongol troops*

# Skills for Success

## Organizing Your Writing

In the Skills for Success in Chapter 3, you learned about the writing process. (See page 66.) During the prewriting stage of a writing assignment, you must organize your ideas in a way that will make your writing clear and convincing. For example, if you were describing a sequence of events, you would probably use a chronological order, listing events in the order in which they happened. If you were listing facts that all supported the same basic idea, you might arrange them from the most important to the least important, or from the least important to the most important. Here, we will look at two of the most common forms of organization: *cause-and-effect* and *comparison-and-contrast.*

A cause-and-effect organization is useful if you are writing about why an event or development happened or what impact or result an event or development had. To locate cause-and-effect relationships in your reading, look for words such as *because, as a result, consequently,* and *thus.*

When you compare events or developments, you show how they are the same. When you contrast elements, you show how they are different. Skim your reading for words that are frequently used to compare and contrast, such as *like, unlike, but, besides, in addition, however, also, too,* and *as well as.*

Imagine that you are writing essays based on the two questions below. Read the questions. Then, use the following steps to organize your writing.

**1** **Identify the best method for organizing your writing.** Decide whether you are being asked about a cause-and-effect relationship or a comparison-and-contrast relationship. (a) What kind of organization would you choose to write an answer to question A? (b) What

kind of organization would you choose to write an answer to question B?

**2** **Arrange useful information into a prewriting chart or list.** (a) List some of the causes of the decline of the Byzantine empire. (b) Prepare a chart outlining some similarities and differences between Russia and the Byzantine empire. Use headings such as Political System or Economy. What other headings can you add to the chart? What similarities or differences would you include on the chart?

**3** **Draw conclusions that can be used as a thesis statement.** A thesis statement presents the main point in your writing, in the same way that a topic sentence presents the main idea in a paragraph. (a) What conclusions can you draw about the chief causes of the fall of the Byzantine empire? Write your conclusions in the form of a thesis statement. (b) What conclusions can you draw about the chief similarities and differences between the Byzantine empire and Russia? Write your conclusions in the form of a thesis statement.

**4** **Write an answer to the question based on your thesis statement.** Which details from your prewriting chart or list support your thesis statement for question A? For question B?

### Beyond the Classroom
Plan and organize a short paper describing the effects of one action you have taken or decision you have made. Make a list of the effects of that action. Then, organize the list based on order of importance, chronological order (how one effect led to another), or in some other way. Finally, write a thesis statement based on your list.

---

Question A. What events or developments led to the decline of the Byzantine empire?

Question B. How were Russia and the Byzantine empire similar? How were they different?

---

## Building Vocabulary

(a) Classify each of the vocabulary words introduced in this chapter under one of the following themes: Religions and Value Systems, Political and Social Systems, Diversity. (b) Choose *one* word in each category and write a sentence explaining how that word relates to the theme.

## Reviewing Chapter Themes

1. **Continuity and Change** (a) How did the Byzantine empire preserve the heritage of the Roman empire? (b) What regions were influenced by Byzantine civilization? In what ways? Give three examples.
2. **Religions and Value Systems** (a) What were the features of Greek Orthodox Christianity as it developed in the Byzantine empire? (b) How did conflict arise between the Orthodox Church and the Roman Catholic Church of Western Europe?
3. **Political and Social Systems** (a) Describe how Russia became a powerful centralized state with an autocratic monarchy. (b) How did the monarchies of Poland and Hungary differ from that of Russia?
4. **Diversity** Describe how the following groups came to Eastern Europe and the role played by each in the history of the region: (a) Slavs, (b) Magyars, (c) Jews.

## Thinking Critically

1. **Recognizing Points of View** Justinian and Theodora have been both condemned and admired by historians. (a) Why do you think a contemporary Byzantine historian like Procopius might have been critical of the emperor and empress? (b) What factors might influence later historians to have different views of such historical figures? (★ See *Skills for Success*, page 280.)
2. **Drawing Conclusions** How might European history have been different if the Byzantine empire had fallen after the death of Justinian?
3. **Defending a Position** Autocratic rule helped the princes of Moscow and the czars of Russia create a strong, central state. Do you think that great accomplishments can justify autocratic rule? Why or why not?

4. **Linking Past and Present** (a) How have long-standing ethnic differences in Eastern Europe influenced events in our own time? (b) Do you think long-standing ethnic differences have played a similar role in the development of modern American society? Explain.
5. **Synthesizing Information** (a) Using information from this chapter and Chapters 8 and 9, construct a time line showing events in both Western and Eastern Europe during the Middle Ages. (b) List three events that affected both regions during this period. (c) Based on your time line, make one generalization about political, cultural, or religious developments in the two regions of Europe. (★ See *Skills for Success*, page 896.)

### For Your Portfolio

Imagine that you and a classmate are art historians. A local museum has asked you to give a lecture about political and religious influences on the arts of either the Byzantine empire or Russia.

1. With your partner, review the information covered in this chapter. List any information given about links between the arts, politics, and religion. Make notes about areas for further research.
2. Decide on one form of art you want to focus on in your lecture. You might concentrate on architecture (including such buildings as Hagia Sophia or the Kremlin); on one of the visual arts (such as icons, mosaics, or frescoes); or on one of the decorative arts (such as illuminated manuscripts, textiles, ivory carvings, or religious artifacts).
3. Find examples of pictures that you can use to illustrate your lecture. Consult art books, art magazines, or museum catalogs in your local library. (You might also be able to get help at a local museum if there is one in your area.)
4. Outline your talk and organize the pictures to go with it. Then, write up your talk on index cards. Describe each picture and explain how it reflects religious and/or political themes.
5. Present your lecture and illustrations to the class. Be prepared to answer questions.

# The Muslim World

## (622–1650)

## CHAPTER OUTLINE

1 **Rise of Islam**
2 **Islam Spreads**
3 **Golden Age of Muslim Civilization**
4 **Muslims in India**
5 **The Ottoman and Safavid Empires**

The opportunity seemed perfect. In 1333, the sultan of Delhi wanted to hire educated foreigners to carry out his policies. Ibn Battuta (IHB uhn bat TOO tah), a scholar visiting India from Morocco, wanted a job. Still, he was nervous when he first met the sultan. Depending on the ruler's response, he could expect either great riches or instant dismissal. He recalled:

> 66I approached the sultan, who took my hand and shook it, and continuing to hold it addressed me most kindly, saying in Persian, 'This is a blessing; your arrival is blessed; be at ease, I shall be compassionate to you and give you such favors that your fellow country-men will hear of it and come to join you.' . . . Every time he said any en-couraging word I kissed his hand, until I had kissed it seven times.99

Ibn Battuta got the job and became a judge in the sultan's court.

Ibn Battuta was the greatest traveler of his day. By the time he reached India, he had al-ready visited Egypt, the Middle East, the east-ern coast of Africa, Asia Minor, Constantinople, and Central Asia. After eight years in India, he sailed on to Southeast Asia and China. Still later, he crossed the Sahara to tour West Africa. In all, he logged about 75,000 miles (120,700 km).

As far away as his travels took him, he rarely set foot outside what Muslims called the *Dar al-Islam,* or the "Abode of Islam." In Ibn Battuta's day, Muslim traditions linked lands from North Africa to Southeast Asia.

In 622, a major religion, Islam, emerged in Arabia. Within a few years, Arabs spread Islam across a huge empire. Although the Arab em-pire eventually broke apart, Islam continued to spread, creating shared traditions among diverse peoples. The Dar al-Islam also opened routes for the transfer of goods, ideas, and technolo-gies. Muslim civilization was thus the world's first multiregional civilization. It blended ele-ments from many cultures and pointed toward a global civilization to come.

**FOCUS ON** these questions as you read:

■ **Religions and Value Systems**
What are the central religious and moral teachings of Islam?

■ **Diversity**
How did Muslim rulers deal with the wide diversity among the peoples that they ruled?

■ **Global Interaction**
How did Muslim civilization create links among three continents?

■ **Art and Literature**
What artistic and literary traditions flour-ished in the Muslim world?

## TIME AND PLACE

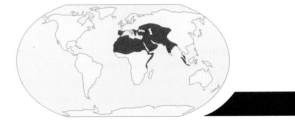

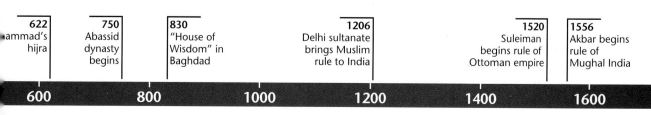

**Pages From a Sacred Book** *Muslim artists illuminated pages of the Quran with exquisite calligraphy and artwork. According to Muslim teachings, the Quran contains the true word of God, revealed to the prophet Muhammad. Muslims throughout the world study classical Arabic in order to read the Quran in its most sacred form.* **Diversity** *What languages had special importance for medieval Christians?*

## HUMANITIES LINK

***Art History*** Persian decorated tile (page 279).

***Literature*** In this chapter, you will encounter passages from the following works of literature: the Quran (pages 256 and 257); Rabiah al-Adawiyya, "Oh my Lord, if I worship Thee from fear of Hell" (page 263); Omar Khayyám, *The Rubáiyát* (page 270); Baki, "Will not the King awake from sleep?" (page 278).

| 622 | 750 | 830 | 1206 | 1520 | 1556 |
|---|---|---|---|---|---|
| ammad's hijra | Abassid dynasty begins | "House of Wisdom" in Baghdad | Delhi sultanate brings Muslim rule to India | Suleiman begins rule of Ottoman empire | Akbar begins rule of Mughal India |

| 600 | 800 | 1000 | 1200 | 1400 | 1600 |

# 1 Rise of Islam

## Guide for Reading

- How did Muhammad become the prophet of Islam?

- What are the basic teachings of Islam?

- How did Islamic teachings help shape the lives of believers?

- **Vocabulary** *hijra, caliph, mosque, hajj*

In the Arabian town of Mecca, the marketplace echoed with the bargaining and bustle of business as usual. One corner, though, was hushed. There, a husky, black-bearded man was speaking to a handful of followers:

> 66In the name of God, the Compassionate, the Merciful,
> Praise be to God, Lord of the Universe,
> The Compassionate, the Merciful,
> Sovereign of the Day of Judgment!
> You alone we worship, and to You alone we turn for help.99

Some bowed their heads, moved by the beauty of Muhammad's words. His wife, Khadija (kah DEE jah), a respected merchant, had fully accepted her husband's vision. But many had their doubts. Muhammad had once been a good merchant himself. Surely, they thought, he was now mad.

In years to come, Muhammad would be recognized by millions of Muslims as the Prophet. His followers would carry the message of Islam to people on three continents and set off one of the most powerful forces in world history.

## Oasis Towns and Desert Life

Islam appeared in the Arabian Peninsula, part of southwestern Asia. (See the map on page 261). The peninsula is mostly desert, but farming is possible in scattered oases and other areas where there is enough water for irrigation.

**Bedouins.** Many Arab clans occupied the region at the time of Muhammad. Nomadic herders, called Bedouins (BEHD oo ihnz), adapted to the conditions of the desert. Using camels, they crossed and recrossed long stretches of blistering, sandy desert in search of seasonal pasturelands. In this rugged environment, the Bedouins developed a strong tradition of hospitality and generosity toward travelers. At the same time, they acquired a strong sense of clan solidarity. Raids on scarce grazing territories led to frequent warfare. The Bedouins would form the backbone of the armies that conquered a huge empire in the 600s and 700s.

**Mecca.** Bedouins regularly traded with other Arabs who had settled in oasis towns like Mecca in western Arabia. This trade helped support a thriving economy. Mecca was a bustling market town at the crossroads of two main caravan routes. One route linked southern Arabia to India and to Syria and Palestine on the Mediterranean coast. The other route crossed from Mesopotamia to eastern Africa. Silks, spices, and other luxuries passed through the bazaars of Mecca.

Mecca was also a thriving pilgrimage center. Arabs came to pray at the Kaaba, an ancient shrine that Muslims today believe was built by the prophet Abraham. In Muhammed's time, though, the Kaaba housed statues of many local gods and goddesses. The pilgrim traffic brought good profits to the local merchants.

## The Prophet Muhammad

Muhammad was born in Mecca about 570. Orphaned at an early age, he was raised by an uncle. In his youth, he worked as a shepherd among the Bedouins. Later, he led caravans across the desert and became a successful merchant. When he was about 25, Muhammad married Khadija, a wealthy older widow, who ran a prosperous caravan business. By all accounts, he was a devoted husband and a loving father to his daughters.

**Muhammad's vision.** Troubled by the idol worship of the Arabs and by the moral ills of society, Muhammad often went to a lonely desert cave to pray and meditate. There, when he was about 40, he heard a voice saying, "Proclaim." According to Muslim belief, the voice was that of the angel Gabriel.

"What shall I proclaim?" asked Muhammad doubtfully. The voice replied:

**❝**Proclaim—in the name of your God, the Creator,
Who created man from a clot of congealed blood.
Proclaim! Your God is most generous,
He who has taught man by the pen things they knew not.**❞**

The vision left Muhammad terrified and puzzled. How could he, an illiterate merchant, become the messenger of God? But Khadija encouraged him to accept the call. She became the first convert to the faith called Islam, from the Arabic word for "submission." Muhammad devoted the rest of his life to spreading Islam. He urged people to give up their false gods and submit to the one true God.

**The hijra.** At first, few people listened to Muhammad. His rejection of the traditional Arab gods angered Meccan merchants who feared neglecting their idols and disrupting the pilgrim trade. In 622, faced with the threat of murder, Muhammad and his followers left Mecca for Yathrib, a journey known as the hijra. Later, Yathrib was renamed Medina, or "city of the Prophet," and 622 became the first year of the Muslim calendar.*

The hijra was a turning point for Islam. In Medina, Muhammad was welcomed by Muslim converts as ruler and lawgiver as well as God's prophet. As his reputation grew, thousands of Arabs adopted Islam. From Medina, Muslims launched attacks on Meccan caravans and defeated the Meccans in battle. Finally, in 630, Muhammad returned in triumph to Mecca, where he destroyed the idols in the Kaaba.

**Death of the Prophet.** In the next two years, Muhammad worked to unite the Arabs. His death in 632 plunged his followers into grief. Abu Bakr, an early convert to Islam, sternly told the faithful, "If you worship Muhammad, Muhammad is dead. If you worship God, God is alive."

Islam survived the death of its prophet. Abu Bakr was elected the first caliph, or successor to Muhammad. As you will read, under the caliphs, the message of Islam quickly spread far beyond Arabia.

---

*The Muslim calendar uses A.H. for dates after the hijra. However, this chapter, like the rest of the book, will continue to use dates based on the Christian Era calendar.

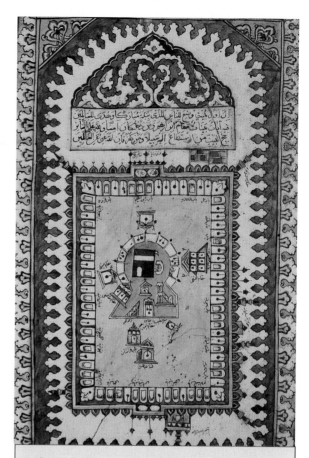

**A Shrine in Mecca** This ceramic tile shows the Kaaba, the most revered shrine in the holy city of Mecca. The Kaaba, a cubelike black structure, is located at the center. The surrounding courtyard can hold as many as 300,000 people. Today, as in the past, Muslim pilgrims from all over the world gather at the Kaaba to worship God and honor the prophet Muhammad. **Religions and Value Systems** Why does Mecca hold special importance to Muslims?

## The Message of Islam

Like Judaism and Christianity, Islam is based on strict monotheism. Muslims believe in one all-powerful, compassionate God, whose name in Arabic is Allah. Islam also teaches that people are responsible for their own actions. "Whoever strays bears the full responsibility for straying," states the Quran (ku RAHN), the sacred text of Islam. Each individual will stand before God on the final judgment day and, depending on his or her actions, face either eternal punishment in hell or eternal bliss in paradise. Muslims recognize no official priests who mediate between the people and God.

**Five Pillars.** All Muslims accept five basic duties, known as the Five Pillars of Islam. The first is a declaration of faith. "There is no god but God, Muhammad is the messenger of God." Muslims believe that God had sent other prophets, including Abraham, Moses, and Jesus, but that Muhammad was the last and greatest prophet.

The second pillar is daily prayer. After a ritual washing, Muslims face the holy city of Mecca to pray. Although Muslims may pray anywhere, they often gather in houses of worship called *masjids* or mosques. The third pillar is giving charity to the poor. The fourth is fasting from sunrise to sunset during the holy month of Ramadan. The fifth pillar is the hajj, or pilgrimage to Mecca. All Muslims who are able are expected to visit the Kaaba at least once. Pilgrims wear simple clothes so that all stand as equals before God.

Some Muslims look on jihad (jee HAHD), or effort in God's service, as another duty. Jihad has often been mistakenly translated simply as "holy war." In fact, it may include acts of charity or an inner struggle to achieve spiritual peace, as well as any battle in defense of Islam.

**The Quran.** To Muslims, the Quran contains the sacred word of God as revealed to Muhammad. It is the final authority on all matters. The Quran not only teaches about God, but also provides a complete guide to life. Its ethical standards emphasize honesty, generosity, and social justice. It sets harsh penalties for crimes such as stealing or murder.

Muslims believe that, in its original Arabic form, the Quran is the "inimitable" word of God. Because the meaning and beauty of the Quran reside in its original language, converts to Islam learn Arabic. This shared language has helped unite Muslims from many regions.

**Sharia.** Over time, Muslim scholars developed an immense body of law interpreting the Quran and applying its teachings to daily life. This Islamic system of law, the Sharia, regulates moral conduct, family life, business practices, government, and others aspects of a Muslim community. Like the Quran, the Sharia helped unite the many peoples who converted to Islam.

Unlike the law codes that evolved in the west, the Sharia does not separate religious matters from criminal or civil law. It applies the Quran to all legal situations. Thus, Islam became both a religion and a way of life.

**"People of the Book."** As you have seen, Muslims believe in the same God as Jews and Christians, recognize many of the same prophets, and accept the idea of heaven and hell. The Quran teaches that, while Islam was God's final and complete revelation, the Torah and Bible contained partial revelation from God. To Muslims, Jews and Christians are "People of the Book," spiritually superior to polytheistic idol worshipers. Although some later Muslims overlooked Muhammad's principle of tolerance, in general, the People of the Book enjoyed religious freedom in early Muslim societies.

## Women in Early Muslim Society

Before Islam, the position of women in Arab society varied. In some communities, women took a hand in many activities, including religion, trade, and warfare. Khadija, for example, owned her own business and as a widow chose to remarry. Most women, however, were under the control of a male guardian and could not inherit property. Among a few tribes, unwanted daughters were sometimes killed at birth.

**Rights.** Islam affirmed the spiritual equality of women and men. "Whoever does right, whether male or female," states the Quran, "and is a believer, all such will enter the Garden." The Quran prohibited the killing of daughters and ensured protection for widows. Inheritance laws guaranteed a woman a share of her parents' or husband's property. Muslim women had to consent freely to marriage and had the right to divorce, although it was harder for a woman to get a divorce than for a man. Muslim women also had the right to an education. In the early days of Islam, some Arab women participated actively in public life.

Though spiritually equal, men and women had different roles and rights. For example, the amount of an inheritance given to a daughter was less than that given to a son. The Quran

**ISSUES**
*For*
**TODAY**

For the devout Muslim, Islamic teachings guide every aspect of life. How can religious beliefs and values influence the way of life of a society?

# World Religions

| Religion | Origins | Holy Books | Major Beliefs | Connections Today |
|---|---|---|---|---|
| **Hinduism** | Prehistoric India | The Vedas are considered most sacred. | One God who can take many forms; goal: to achieve moksha; reincarnation; nonviolence | About 750 million Hindus in India and Indian communities around the world |
| **Judaism** | Palestine (around 2000 B.C.) | The Torah | One God; Ten Commandments; the Torah as God's revelation and the plan for proper living | About 18 million Jews in the world, most of whom live in the United States or Israel |
| **Buddhism** | Northern India (500s B.C.) | The Tripitaka | Four Noble Truths; the Eightfold Path; goal: to reach nirvana | About 335 million Theravada and Mahayana Buddhists, mostly in Southeast Asia and East Asia |
| **Daoism** | China (500s B.C.) | Tao Te Ching Chuang Tze | Natural spontaneity; desire for harmony; sense of the absurd | Possibly as many as 480 million Daoists, mostly in China |
| **Christianity** | Palestine (A.D. 30) | The Bible | One God; Jesus, son of God and redeemer of humankind | About 1.8 billion Roman Catholics, Protestants, and Eastern Orthodox Christians around the world |
| **Islam** | Arabia (A.D. 622) | The Quran | One all-powerful, compassionate God; Muhammad was prophet of Islam; Five Pillars of Islam | More than 1 billion Muslims worldwide, mostly in Asia and Africa |

Hundreds of millions of people practice local traditions that go back hundreds of thousands of years. These include Shinto in Japan and a variety of practices among Native Americans, Africans, and Pacific islanders.

*Interpreting a Chart* Muhammad began preaching the message of Islam at a time when Hinduism, Buddhism, and Christianity already dominated much of the world. Today, these four religions are the most widely practiced religions in the world. ■ Which religions on this chart emerged in Asia? How does Muhammad's role in Islam differ from Jesus Christ's role in Christianity?

permitted a man to have up to four wives if he treated them all justly. Still, few men could afford to support more than one wife.

**Changes.** As Islam spread, Arabs sometimes absorbed attitudes from the non-Arab peoples they conquered. In Persia and Byzantine lands, for example, Arabs adopted the practice of veiling women and secluding them in a separate part of the home. Muslims called the women's quarters the harem because it was *haram*, or forbidden, to violate it. The harem was the center of activity where women planned and carried out the indoor life of the family.

In many cities, upper-class women in particular faced restrictions. Secluded in their quarters, they were waited on by women servants and seldom ventured out. An Egyptian judge of the 1300s stated that "a woman should leave her home on three occasions only: when she is conducted to the house of her bridegroom, when her parents die, and when she goes to her own grave."

Still, as in other cultures, women's lives varied greatly according to region and class. Veiling and seclusion were not so strictly followed among lower-class city women. In rural areas, peasant women continued to contribute to the economy in many ways.

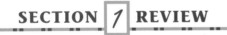

## SECTION 1 REVIEW

1. **Identify** (a) Mecca, (b) Kaaba, (c) Khadija, (d) Quran, (e) Sharia, (f) People of the Book.
2. **Define** (a) hijra, (b) caliph, (c) mosque, (d) hajj.
3. How did Muhammad become the prophet of Islam?
4. (a) What are the Five Pillars of Islam? (b) How do they help unite Muslims?
5. How do the Quran and Sharia guide the lives of Muslim men and women?
6. *Critical Thinking* **Analyzing Information** Reread Abu Bakr's words about the death of Muhammad on page 257. (a) Restate his main point in your own words. (b) Why do you think he made this statement?
7. *ACTIVITY* Organize a debate around the following statement: "By and large, Arab women benefited from the rise of Islam."

# 2 Islam Spreads

## Guide for Reading

- How did Islam spread rapidly over a wide area?
- What divisions emerged within Islam?
- Why did the Arab empire decline?
- **Vocabulary** *minaret, sultan*

Every day, more Arabs joined the forces of Amr ibn-al-As as he rode toward Alexandria, gateway to the fertile Nile Valley. The city was a Byzantine stronghold. After a year's siege, Alexandria fell. Amr told his victorious army:

66The Nile floods have fallen, the spring grazing is good. There is milk for the lambs and the kids. Go out with God's blessing and enjoy the land, its milk, its flocks, and its herds. And take good care of your neighbors.99

Inspired by the teachings of Muhammad, Arab armies surged across the Byzantine and Persian empires. In a stunningly short time, an Arabic empire reached from the Atlantic to the borders of India.

## *The Age of Conquest*

When Muhammad died, Abu Bakr faced an immediate crisis. The loyalty of some Arab tribal leaders had been dependent on Muhammad's personal command. They now withdrew their loyalty for the Muslim state. Abu Bakr's most important contribution was to reunify the Arabs on a firmer base of loyalty to Islam itself. The reunited forces then embarked on a remarkable military campaign.

**From victory to victory.** Under the first four caliphs, Arab armies marched from victory to victory. They conquered great chunks of the Byzantine empire, including the provinces of Syria and Palestine with the cities of Damascus and Jerusalem. Next, they rapidly demolished the Persian empire. The Arabs then swept into Egypt.

## Spread of Islam

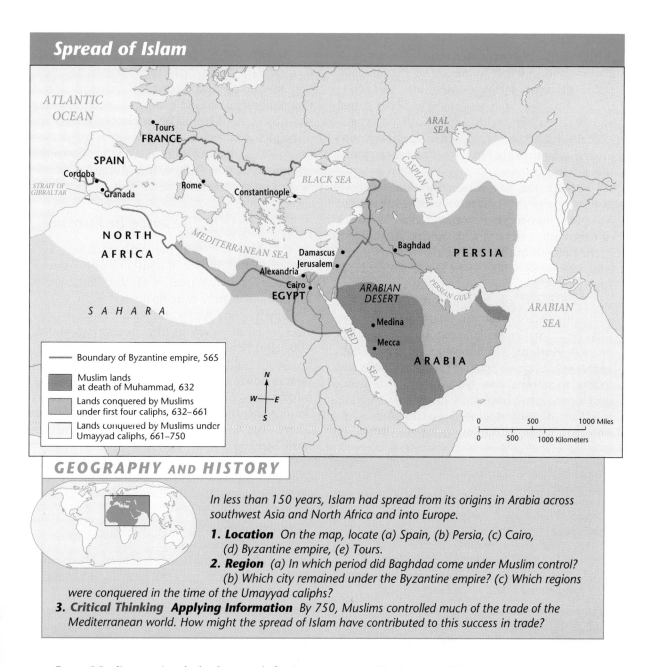

Boundary of Byzantine empire, 565

Muslim lands
at death of Muhammad, 632

Lands conquered by Muslims
under first four caliphs, 632–661

Lands conquered by Muslims under
Umayyad caliphs, 661–750

### GEOGRAPHY AND HISTORY

*In less than 150 years, Islam had spread from its origins in Arabia across southwest Asia and North Africa and into Europe.*

1. **Location**  On the map, locate (a) Spain, (b) Persia, (c) Cairo, (d) Byzantine empire, (e) Tours.
2. **Region**  (a) In which period did Baghdad come under Muslim control? (b) Which city remained under the Byzantine empire? (c) Which regions were conquered in the time of the Umayyad caliphs?
3. **Critical Thinking  Applying Information**  By 750, Muslims controlled much of the trade of the Mediterranean world. How might the spread of Islam have contributed to this success in trade?

Later Muslim armies dashed west, defeating Byzantine forces across North Africa. In 711, they crossed the Strait of Gibraltar into Spain and pushed up the peninsula into France. At the other end of the Mediterranean, they crossed the Bosporus to besiege the Byzantine capital of Constantinople.

The breathtaking swiftness of the Arab conquests did not slow down until nearly 100 years after Muhammad's death. In 718, the Arabs abandoned the siege of Constantinople. (As you read in Chapter 10, not until 1453 did Constantinople fall to another Muslim people, the Ottoman Turks.) In 732, the Arab push into Europe was turned back at the battle of Tours in France.

Still, Muslim and Christian forces would continue to contend in Spain for centuries. Later waves of conquest would also expand the Muslim zone much farther, especially in Asia and Africa. (See Chapters 12 and 13.)

**Reasons for success.** Why did the Arabs have such an astonishing series of victories? One reason was the weakness of the Byzantine and Persian empires. These longtime rivals had fought each other to exhaustion. Many people in the Fertile Crescent welcomed the Arabs as liberators from harsh Byzantine or Persian rule. Bold, efficient fighting methods also contributed to the Arab success. The Arab camel and horse cavalry, with generations of experience in desert warfare, mounted aggressive and mobile offensives that overwhelmed more traditional armies.

Perhaps the key reason for Arab success, however, was the common faith Muhammad had given his people. Islam welded a patchwork of tribes into a determined, unified state. Belief in the holiness of their faith and certainty of paradise for those who fell in battle spurred the Arab armies to victory.

**Treatment of conquered people.** The advancing Arabs brought many people under their rule. Muslim leaders imposed a special tax on non-Muslims, but allowed Christians, Jews, and Zoroastrians to practice their own faiths and follow their own laws. As Muslim civilization developed, many Jews and Christians played key roles as officials, doctors, and translators. In time, many non-Muslims converted to Islam.

*Great Mosque of Cordoba   The interior of this Spanish mosque seems like a dense forest of columns. The columns support two levels of decorated horseshoe arches that in turn support the roof above. After retaking the city of Cordoba in 1236, Christians converted the mosque into a cathedral.* **Global Interaction** *What earlier civilizations used columns and arches and influenced the development of Muslim architecture?*

Many nomadic people of North Africa and Central Asia chose Islam immediately. Its message was simple and direct, and they saw its triumph as a sign of God's favor. Moreover, Islam had no religious hierarchy or class of priests. In principle, it emphasized the equality of all believers, regardless of race, sex, class, or wealth. In later centuries, Turkish and Mongol converts helped spread Islam far across Asia.

## The Muslim Presence in Europe

As you have read, the Arab conquests extended to the fringes of southern and western Europe. The major areas of Muslim influence in Europe at this time were Spain and Sicily.

**Spain.** The Arabs and their North African allies overran Spain at the beginning of the 700s. But rivalries among princes divided Muslim Spain politically. Spanish Christian counterattacks slowly reclaimed the peninsula, gradually pushing the Moors, as Christians called North African Muslims, back into southern Spain. There, the Muslim presence remained strong until 1492. (See Chapter 9.)

For centuries, Spain was one of the most brilliant corners of the Muslim world. Princes encouraged poetry, the arts, and scholarship. At great centers of learning such as the city of Cordoba, rulers employed Jewish officials and welcomed Christian students to absorb Greek ideas at the feet of Muslim teachers. The beauty of the royal courts may still be seen today in the

Alhambra, a Muslim palace in Granada, with its elaborately decorated halls and columns, its courtyards, gardens, and reflecting pools.

**Sicily.** During the early Middle Ages, when Europe was weak, the Arabs seized control of Sicily and a number of other Mediterranean islands. The Arab presence was much briefer in Sicily than in Spain. Europeans soon regained the lost lands. Although Sicily was now ruled by knights from Normandy, it remained strongly Arabic in culture. Muslim officials, merchants, and farmers gave the island good government and a flourishing economy. Arab poets, philosophers, and scientists enriched the courts of Norman kings.

## Movements Within Islam

Not long after Muhammad's death, divisions arose within Islam over his successor. The split between Sunni (SOO nee) and Shiite (SHEE ite) Muslims had a profound impact on later Islamic history.

**Rival factions.** The Sunnis felt that the caliph should be chosen by leaders of the Muslim community. Although the Sunnis agreed that the caliph should be a pious Muslim, they viewed him simply as a leader, not as a religious authority.

The Shiites, on the other hand, argued that the only true successors to the Prophet were descendants of Muhammad's daughter and son-in-law, Fatima and Ali. The Shiites believed that the descendants of the Prophet were divinely inspired. The Sunnis believed that inspiration came from the example of Muhammad as recorded by his early followers.

Ali became the fourth caliph, but he was assassinated in 661 in a struggle for leadership. Later his son, too, was killed. Many other Shiites died in battle against Sunnis, trying to install their candidates for caliph. Shiites grew to admire martyrdom as a demonstration of their faith.

Like the schism between Roman Catholic and Eastern Orthodox Christians, the division between Sunni and Shiite Muslims has survived for more than 1,300 years. Members of both branches believe in the one true God, look to the Quran for guidance, and make the hajj to Mecca. But numerous differences have emerged

**Sufi Preaching** *This Persian manuscript shows a group of Muslims listening reverently to the words of a visiting Sufi. Older men sit nearest to the teacher, while younger men listen from the sidelines. Women and children occupy a gallery of their own.*
**Religions and Value Systems** *Based on what you have read, what kind of message do you think this Sufi might be preaching?*

in such areas as religious practice, law, and daily life. Traditionally, Sunnis have been the majority branch within Islam. Today, about 90 percent of Muslims are Sunnis. Most Shiites live in Iran, Lebanon, Iraq, and Yemen. The Shiite movement itself has split into several different factions.

**Sufi.** A third tradition emerged with the Sufis, Muslim mystics who sought communion with God through meditation, fasting, and other rituals. Sufis were respected for their piety and miraculous powers. One of the earliest Sufis, Rabiah al-Adawiyya (RAHB ee ah al a da WEE ah), rejected marriage and devoted her life to prayer. In her poetry, she urged Muslims to worship God selflessly, without hope of reward:

> **❝**Oh my Lord, if I worship Thee from
>     fear of Hell, burn me in Hell,
> And if I worship Thee in hope of
>     Paradise, exclude me from Paradise
> But if I worship Thee for Thine own
>     sake,
> Then withhold not from me Thine
>     eternal beauty.**❞**

Like Christian monks and nuns, some Sufis helped spread Islam through missionary work.

They carried the faith to remote villages, where they blended local traditions and beliefs into Muslim culture.

## The Arab Empire

After the death of Ali, the Umayyad (oh MĪ ad) family set up a dynasty that ruled the Islamic world until 750. From their capital at Damascus in Syria, they directed the spectacular conquests that carried Islam from the Atlantic to the Indus Valley.

**Umayyads.** Even as victories expanded the Arab empire, the Umayyads faced numerous problems. First, they had to adapt from desert life to ruling large cities and huge territories. To govern their empire, the Umayyads often relied on local officials, including educated Jews, Greeks, and Persians. As a result, Byzantine and Persian traditions of government influenced Arab rulers.

While conquests continued, vast wealth flowed into Umayyad hands. When conquests slowed in the 700s, economic tensions increased between wealthy Arabs and those who had less. Many Muslims criticized the court at Damascus for abandoning the simple ways of the early caliphs. Shiites hated the Umayyads because they had defeated Ali and killed his son, dishonoring the Prophet's family. Unrest also festered among non-Arab converts to Islam, who under the Umayyads had fewer rights than Arabs.

**Abbassids.** Discontented Muslims found a leader in Abu al-Abbas, who captured Damascus in 750. Soon after, one of his generals invited members of the defeated Umayyad family to a banquet—and killed them all. Only one Umayyad escaped to Spain, where he set up an independent caliphate at Cordoba. Abu al-Abbas then founded the Abbassid dynasty, which lasted until 1258.

The Abbassid dynasty ended Arab dominance and helped make Islam a truly universal religion. Under the early Abbassids, the empire of the caliphs reached its greatest wealth and power, and Islamic civilization enjoyed a golden age.

**"City of Peace."** The Abbassid caliph al-Mansur chose as the site of his new capital Baghdad, a small market town in present-day Iraq. He noted that the location offered many strategic advantages:

> **"**It is an excellent military camp. Besides here is the Tigris to put us in touch with lands as far as China and bring us all that the seas yield.**"**

Under the Abbassids, Baghdad exceeded Constantinople in size and wealth.

In Baghdad, Persian traditions strongly influenced Arab life, but Islam remained the religion and Arabic the language of the empire. Poets, scholars, philosophers, and entertainers from all over the Muslim world flocked to the Abbassid court. Visitors no doubt felt that Baghdad deserved its title "City of Peace, Gift of God, Paradise on Earth."

Many gardens, dotted with fabulous fountains, gleamed in the sunlight. Above the streets loomed domes and minarets, the slender towers of mosques, from which the *muezzin,* or crier, called the faithful to prayer. In busy market courtyards, merchants sold goods from Africa, Asia, and Europe. The palace of the caliph echoed with the music of flutes, cymbals, and tambourines, and the voices of female singers.

**Harun al-Rashid.** From 786 to 809, the caliph Harun al-Rashid ruled an empire larger than that of his European contemporary Charlemagne. For centuries, in both Europe and the Muslim world, Harun was seen as a model ruler and as a symbol of wealth and splendor.

Many stories and legends recall Harun's fabulous wealth and his generous support of the arts. One story tells how Harun was struck by the beauty of some verses. He ordered his treasurer to pay the poet 10,000 dirhams—a vast sum of money.

The poet was overwhelmed. Bowing low, he stammered, "O prince of the faithful, your words of praise are better than my verse."

**GLOBAL CONNECTIONS**

Harun's court at Baghdad enjoyed friendly relations with Charlemagne's court at Aachen. Harun hoped that the Frankish king might join him in an alliance against the rival Umayyad caliphate in Spain. To that end, Harun sent Charlemagne a number of fabulous gifts, including a mechanical clock and an elephant. According to some reports, Harun also sent a chess set—perhaps the first one ever seen in Western Europe.

Delighted, the caliph again turned to his treasurer. "O Fadhl," he ordered, "give him another 100,000." The caliph would hardly miss such sums. At his death, he had an estimated billion dirhams in cash plus large stores of jewels, gold, and other treasure.

## Decline of the Caliphate

Starting about 850, Abbassid control over the Arab empire fragmented. In Spain, Egypt, and elsewhere, independent dynasties ruled separate Muslim states. Cairo and Cordoba in Spain flourished as centers of religion, scholarship, and trade.

As the caliph's power faded, civil wars erupted, and Shiite rulers took over parts of the empire. Between 900 and 1400, a series of invasions added to the chaos.

**Seljuks.** In the 900s, the Seljuk Turks migrated into the Middle East from Central Asia. They adopted Islam and built a large empire across the Fertile Crescent. By 1055, a Seljuk sultan, or authority, controlled Baghdad, but he left the Abbassid caliph as a figurehead.

As the Seljuks pushed into Asia Minor, they threatened the Byzantine empire. As you read in Chapter 9, stories of Seljuk interference with Christian pilgrims traveling to Jerusalem led Pope Urban II to preach the First Crusade in 1095.

**The Crusaders.** In 1099, after a long and bloody siege, Christian crusaders captured Jerusalem, a city holy to Christians, Muslims, and Jews. For 200 years, the city passed back and forth between Muslims and Christians. The Muslim general Salah al-Din, or Saladin, ousted Christians from Jerusalem in 1187. They regained it after his death, holding it until 1244.

Christians also ruled a few tiny states in Palestine, but they were eventually expelled. In the long term, the Crusades had a much greater impact on Europe than on the Muslim world. (★ See *Skills for Success,* page 280.)

**Mongols.** In 1216, Genghiz Khan led the Mongols out of Central Asia across Persia and Mesopotamia. Mongol armies returned again and again. In 1258, Hulagu, grandson of Genghiz, burned and looted Baghdad, killing the last Abbassid caliph. Later, the Mongols adopted Islam. (You will read more about the Mongols in Chapter 13.)

# CAUSE AND EFFECT

### Long-Term Causes

Weakness of Byzantine and Persian empires
Economic and social changes in Arabia

### Immediate Causes

Tribes of Arabia unified by Islam around a central message
Wide acceptance of religious message of Islam
Easy acceptance of social ideas of Islam, such as equality among believers

## SPREAD OF ISLAM

### Immediate Effects

Islam spreads from the Atlantic coast to the Indus Valley
Centers of learning flourish in Cairo, Cordoba, and elsewhere

### Long-Term Effects

Muslim civilization emerges
Linking of Europe, Asia, and Africa through Muslim trade network
Arabic becomes shared language of Muslims
Split between Sunnis and Shiites

### Connections Today

Islam is religion of nearly one fifth of world population
Millions of Muslims make pilgrimages to Mecca
Arabic is among the most widely known languages in the world

*Interpreting a Chart* Islam spread most dramatically in the centuries immediately following the hijra. Religion, politics, and culture all played a role in its rapid rise. ■ How does the spread of Islam help explain the wide knowledge of Arabic in today's world?

In the late 1300s, another Mongol leader, Timur the Lame, or Tamerlane, led his armies into the Middle East. Though himself a Muslim, Tamerlane's ambitions led him to conquer Muslim as well as non-Muslim lands. His armies overran Persia and Mesopotamia before invading Russia and India.

**Looking ahead.** As the 1200s drew to a close, the Arab empire had fragmented and fallen. Independent Muslim caliphates and states were scattered across North Africa and Spain, while a Mongol khan ruled the Muslim Middle East. After five centuries, the Dar al-Islam was as politically divided as the Christian world.

Even though the empire crumbled, Islam continued to link diverse people across an enormous area. In the future, other great Muslim empires would arise in the Middle East and India. Muslims also benefited from an advanced civilization that had taken root under the Abbassids. In the next section, you will read about the achievements of this Muslim civilization.

## SECTION 2 REVIEW

1. **Identify** (a) Fatima and Ali, (b) Sufi, (c) Rabiah al-Adawiyya, (d) Umayyads, (e) Abu al-Abbas, (f) Harun al-Rashid, (g) Tamerlane.
2. **Define** (a) minaret, (b) sultan.
3. (a) What areas did Arab armies conquer? (b) Give three reasons for the rapid success of the Arab conquests.
4. What issues divided Sunni Muslims and Shiite Muslims?
5. (a) How did divisions within the Arab empire lead to the emergence of the Abbassid dynasty? (b) Why did the empire eventually break up?
6. *Critical Thinking* **Drawing Conclusions** Muhammad said, "Know ye that every Muslim is a brother to every other Muslim and that ye are now one brotherhood." How might this idea have increased the appeal of Islam to conquered peoples?
7. *ACTIVITY* Imagine that you are a Bedouin who is visiting Baghdad for the first time during the reign of Harun al-Rashid. Record in your diary how city life differs from nomadic life in the desert.

## 3 Golden Age of Muslim Civilization

### Guide for Reading

■ What were the economic strengths of the Muslim world?

■ What traditions influenced Muslim arts and literature?

■ What advances did Muslims make in the sciences?

One night, Caliph al-Mamun had a vivid dream. There in his chambers he came upon a balding, blue-eyed stranger sitting on the low couch.

"Who are you?" the caliph demanded.

"Aristotle," the man replied.

The caliph was delighted. He plied the great Greek philosopher with questions about ethics, reason, and religion.

Although al-Mamun soon awoke, his dream inspired him to action. He had scholars collect and translate the great works of the classical world into Arabic. By 830, the caliph had set up the "House of Wisdom," a library and university in Baghdad.

Under the Abbassids, Islam absorbed traditions from many cultures. In the process, a vital new civilization rose that flourished in cities from Damascus to Cairo to Cordoba and later to Delhi in India. The great works produced by scholars of the Abbassid golden age shaped the Muslim world just as Greek and Roman classics shaped western culture.

### Society and the Economy

The Muslim empire united people from diverse cultures, including Arabs, Persians, Egyptians and other Africans, and Europeans. Later, Mongols, Turks, Indians, and people in Southeast Asia declared their faith in Islam. In time, Muslim civilization absorbed and blended many traditions.

**Social classes.** Muslim society was more open than that of medieval Europe. Although Arabs had held themselves apart from non-Arab

## Going Shopping

Some complain that the marketplace is loud, busy, crowded. But for merchants selling their wares, shoppers looking for bargains, and people who just want to be with people, this is the place to be.

**Linking Past and Present** What advantages does an enclosed mall have over an open-air marketplace? Why are some open-air markets still popular?

**PAST** *Muslim bazaars, or marketplaces, sold local goods as well as imports made available by a vast trading network. In major cities, such as Baghdad and Istanbul, the bazaar consisted of miles of streets enclosed by a roof. In this illustration, we see, from left to right, a jeweler, a druggist, a butcher, and a baker.*

**PRESENT** *The giant, multilevel, indoor mall is a modern version of the bazaar. Within its great expanse, you may shop, dine, see a movie, or perhaps even ice skate.*

Muslims at first, that distinction faded under the Abbassids. People could move up in society, especially through religious, scholarly, or military achievements.

As in Greece and Rome, slavery was common in the cities of the Muslim world. Slaves were brought from conquered lands in Spain, Greece, Africa, India, and Central Asia. Muslims could not be enslaved. If non-Muslim slaves converted to Islam, they did not automatically become free, but their children did. A female slave who married her owner also gained freedom.

Most slaves worked as household servants. Some were skilled artisans. The Abbassids used slave-soldiers who fought loyally for the caliph. Slaves of rulers sometimes rose to high positions in government, and a number of caliphs were the sons of slave mothers. Islamic law encouraged the freeing of slaves. Many slaves bought their freedom, often with the help of charitable donations or even state funds.

**An international trade network.** Merchants were honored in the Muslim world, in part because Muhammad had been a merchant.

A traditional collection of deeds and sayings of the Prophet stated:

> 66The honest, truthful Muslim merchant will stand with the martyrs on the Day of Judgment. I commend the merchants to you, for they are the couriers of the horizon and God's trusted servants on Earth. . . . If God permitted the inhabitants of Paradise to trade, they would deal in cloth and perfume.99

Between 750 and 1350, merchants built a vast trading network across the Muslim world and beyond, spreading Islam peacefully in their wake. Camel caravans crossed the Sahara into West Africa. Muslim traders traveled the Silk Road from China. Monsoon winds carried Arab ships from East Africa to India. Everywhere Muslim traders bought and exchanged goods, creating great fortunes for the most successful.

Trade spread both products and technologies. As you have read, Arab merchants brought Arabic numerals from India to the western world. Arabs also carried sugar from India and papermaking from China. A common language and religion helped this global exchange to grow and thrive.

Extensive trade and a prosperous money economy led Muslims to pioneer new ways of doing business. They set up partnerships, bought and sold on credit, and formed banks to change currency. To make the transfer of money easier, Muslims invented the ancestors of today's bank checks. We get our word *check* from the Arabic word *sakk*.

**Manufacturing.** As in medieval Europe, handicraft manufacturing in Muslim cities was typically organized by guilds. The heads of the guilds, chosen by their members, often had the authority to regulate prices, weights and measures, methods of production, and the quality of the product. Most labor was done by wage workers.

Across the Muslim world, artisans produced a wealth of fine goods. Steel swords from Damascus, leather goods from Cordoba, cotton textiles from Egypt, and carpets from Persia were highly valued. Workshops also turned out fine glassware, furniture, and tapestries.

**Agriculture.** Outside the cities, agriculture flourished across a wide variety of climates and landforms. Muslim farmers cultivated sugar cane, cotton, dyes, medicinal herbs, fruits, vegetables, and flowers that were bought and sold in world markets.

The more arid regions of the Muslim world were basically divided into two kinds of land, "the desert and the sown." Small farming communities faced a constant scarcity of water. To improve farm output, the Abbassids organized massive irrigation projects and drained swamplands between the Tigris and Euphrates. Farmers in Mesopotamia, Egypt, and the Mediterranean coast produced grain, olives, dates, and other crops.

The deserts continued to support independent nomads who lived by herding. Still, nomads and farmers shared economic ties. Nomads bought dates and grain from settled peoples, while farming populations acquired meat, wool, and hides from the nomads.

## Muslim Art

As in Christian Europe and Hindu India, religion shaped the arts of the Islamic world. Muslim artists also drew on the technical skills and styles of the many peoples with whom they came in contact.

**Design and decoration.** Because the Quran strictly banned the worship of idols, Muslim religious leaders forbade artists to portray God or human figures in religious art. The walls and ceilings of mosques were decorated with elaborate abstract and geometric patterns. The arabesque, an intricate design composed of curved lines that suggest floral shapes, appeared in rugs, textiles, and glassware. Muslim artists also perfected skills in calligraphy. They worked the flowing Arabic script, especially verses from the Quran,

▲ Bronze griffin

**Dome of the Rock** *Jerusalem is a holy city for Muslims, Christians, and Jews. The most revered Muslim site in Jerusalem is the Dome of the Rock. It was built in the 600s over a rock where Muslims believed Muhammad ascended into Heaven, and where Jews believed Abraham offered his son Isaac to God.* **Continuity and Change** *Why are Jews, Muslims, and Christians all familiar with the story of Abraham?*

into decorations on buildings and objects of art. (See the picture on page 255.)

In nonreligious art, some Muslim artists did paint human and animal figures. Arabic scientific works were often lavishly illustrated. Literary works and luxury objects sometimes showed stylized figures. In later periods, Persian, Turkish, and Indian artists excelled at painting miniatures to illustrate books of poems and fables.

**Architecture.** Muslim architects adapted the domes and arches of Byzantine buildings to new uses. In Jerusalem, they built the Dome of the Rock, a great shrine capped with a magnificent dome. Domed mosques and high minarets dominated Muslim cities in the same way that cathedral spires dominated medieval Christian cities. Outside many mosques lay large courtyards, with fountains where the faithful performed ceremonial washing before prayer.

## Literature

The great work of Islamic literature was the poetic Quran itself. Scholars studied the sacred words of the Quran in Arabic and then produced their own works interpreting its meaning.

**Poetry.** Long before Muhammad, Arabs had a rich tradition of oral poetry, which helped bring the various Arab groups together as one culture. In musical verses, Bedouin poets chanted the dangers of desert journeys, the joys of battle, or the glories of their clans. Their most important themes, chivalry and the romance of nomadic life, recurred in Arab poetry throughout the centuries. Through Muslim Spain, these traditions came to influence medieval European literature and music.

Later Arab poets developed elaborate formal rules for writing poetry and explored both religious and worldly themes. As you have read, the poems of Rabiah al-Adawiyya expressed Sufi mysticism. Other poets praised important leaders, described the lavish lives of the wealthy, sang of the joys and sorrows of love, or conveyed nuggets of wisdom.

Persian Muslims also had a fine poetic tradition. Firdawsi (fihr DOW see) wrote in Persian using Arabic script. His masterpiece, the *Shah-namah,* or *King's Book of Kings,* tells the history of Persia in 60,000 verses. Omar Khayyám (kī YAHM), famous in the Muslim world as a scholar and astronomer, is best known to westerners for *The Rubáiyát* (ROO bī yaht). In this collection of four-line poems, he meditates on fate and the fleeting nature of life:

   **❝**The Moving Finger writes; and having
     writ,
    Moves on; nor all your Piety nor Wit
    Shall lure it back to cancel half a line,
    Nor all your Tears wash out a word of
    it.**❞**

**Tales.** Arab writers prized the art of storytelling. Across their empire, they gathered and adapted stories from Indian, Persian, Greek, Jewish, Egyptian, and Turkish sources. The best-known collection is *The Thousand and One Nights,* a group of tales narrated by the fictional princess Scheherezade (shu hehr uh ZAH duh). They include romances, fables, adventures, and humorous anecdotes, many set in the Baghdad of Harun al-Rashid. Later versions filtered into Europe, where millions of children thrilled to "Aladdin and His Magic Lamp" or "Ali Baba and the Forty Thieves."

## *The World of Learning*

"Seek knowledge even as far as China," declared Muhammad. Although he could not read and write, his respect for learning set the tone for Muslim civilization. Al-Mamun and later caliphs made Baghdad into the greatest Muslim center of learning. Its vast libraries attracted a galaxy of scholars, who were well paid and highly respected. Other cities, like Cairo, Bukhara, Timbuktu, and Cordoba, had their own centers of learning.

**Philosophy.** Muslim scholars translated the works of the Greek philosophers, as well as many Hindu and Buddhist texts. Like later Christian thinkers in Europe, Muslim scholars tried to harmonize Greek ideas about reason with religious beliefs based on divine revelation. In Cordoba, the philosopher Ibn Rushd—known in Europe as Averroës—put all knowledge to the test of reason. His writings on Aristotle were translated into Latin and influenced Christian scholastics in medieval Europe. Ibn Khaldun set standards for the scientific study of history. He stressed the importance of studying the causes of events.

**Mathematics.** Muslim scholars studied both Indian and Greek mathematics before making their original contributions. The greatest Muslim mathematician was al-Khwarizmi (ahl kwah REEZ mee). His work pioneered the study of algebra (from the Arabic word *al-jabr*). In the 800s, he wrote a book that was later translated into Latin and became a standard mathematics textbook in Europe.

**Astronomy.** Like many scholars of the time, al-Khwarizmi made contributions in other fields. He developed a set of astronomical tables based on Greek and Indian discoveries. At observatories from Baghdad to Central Asia, Muslim astronomers studied eclipses, observed the Earth's rotation, and calculated the circumference of the Earth to within a few thousand feet. The work of Muslim astronomers and navigators helped pave the way for later explorers like Christopher Columbus.

## *Masters of Medicine*

If you had been on the streets of Baghdad one day in the early 900s, you might have seen a puzzling sight. A well-dressed man was traveling through the city, pausing at various locations. Wherever he stopped, he hung up a piece of raw meat, then moved on. You might have been even more puzzled to learn that the man was

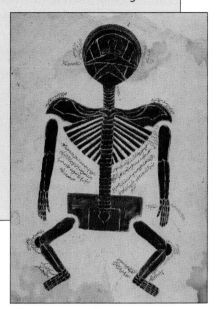

Muhammad al-Razi—the most respected doctor in the city.

In fact, al-Razi was engaged in serious environmental research. He had been given the task of choosing the site for a new hospital. But how could he determine the healthiest location? By carefully observing the pieces of raw meat, al-Razi found his answer. He advised that the hospital be built at the place where the meat rotted most slowly!

**The Muslim medical world.** Building on the knowledge of Greeks, Muslims made remarkable advances in medicine and public health. Under the caliphs, physicians and pharmacists had to pass a test before they could practice. The government set up hospitals, with separate wards for women. Injured people could get quick treatment at a department similar to today's emergency room. Physicians traveled to rural areas to provide health care to those who could not get to a city, while others regularly visited jails.

As you have seen, one of the most original medical thinkers was al-Razi, head physician at Baghdad's chief hospital. He wrote many books on medicine, including a pioneering study of measles and smallpox. He also challenged accepted medical practices. Treat the mind as well as the body, he advised young doctors. If a doc-

tor made hopeful comments, he taught, patients would recover all the faster.

Equally famous was the Persian physician Ibn Sina, known in Europe as Avicenna. By the age of 16, he was already a doctor to the Persian nobility. His great work was the *Canon on Medicine,* a huge encyclopedia of what the Greeks, the Arabs, and he himself had learned about the diagnosis and treatment of disease. The book includes a list of more than 4,000 prescriptions, made with such ingredients as mercury from Spain, myrrh from East Africa, and camphor from India.

Behind these two great names stood dozens of others. Muslim eye surgeons developed a way to treat cataracts, drawing fluid out of the lenses with a hollow needle. For centuries, surgeons around the world used this method to save patients' eyesight. Arab pharmacists were the first to mix bitter medicines into sweet-tasting syrups and gums.

**Knowledge moves west.** A story from the Crusades illustrates the vast difference in medical knowledge between Arab and European doctors at that time. A French knight in Syria, who had severely wounded his leg, came under the care of a Lebanese doctor. Using herbs and oils, the doctor was able to ease the leg's infection.

Suddenly, a French doctor arrived on the scene and demanded to take over the treatment. The Lebanese doctor reported what happened next:

66 The French doctor then said to the knight, 'Which would thou prefer, living with one leg or dying with two?' The latter replied, 'Living with one leg.' The physician said, 'Bring me a strong knight and a sharp ax.' A knight came with the ax. . . . Then the physician laid the leg of the patient on a block of wood and bade the knight strike his leg with the ax and chop it off at one blow. Accordingly he struck it— while I was looking on—one blow, but the leg was not severed. He dealt another blow, upon which . . . the patient died on the spot. 99

In time, however, European physicians began to attend Muslim universities in Spain and translate Arabic medical texts. For 500 years, the works of Avicenna and al-Razi became the standard medical textbooks at European schools. ◾

## SECTION 3 REVIEW

1. **Identify** (a) Dome of the Rock, (b) Omar Khayyám, (c) *The Thousand and One Nights*, (d) Averroës, (e) Muhammad al-Razi, (f) Avicenna.
2. (a) Why did trade flourish across the Muslim world? (b) How did new business methods encourage trade?
3. How did the teachings of Islam influence the arts?
4. Describe one advance made by Muslim civilization in each of the following areas: (a) mathematics, (b) astronomy, (c) medicine.
5. *Critical Thinking* **Applying Information** Muhammad taught that "the ink of the scholar is holier than the blood of the martyr." (a) What do you think he meant? (b) How might this attitude have contributed to the development of Muslim civilization?
6. *ACTIVITY* Examine the examples of Arabic calligraphy on page 255. Then, write your own first name in a similar style.

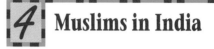

## 4 Muslims in India

### Guide for Reading

■ What impact did the Muslim invasions have on India?

■ How did Muslim and Hindu traditions clash and blend?

■ How did Akbar strengthen Mughal rule?

The whole of India is full of gold and jewels," advisers told Sultan Mahmud of Ghazni. "And since the inhabitants are chiefly infidels and idolators, by the order of God and his Prophet, it is right for us to conquer them." In 1001, Mahmud led his armies into northern India. Smashing and looting Hindu temples, he used the fabulous riches of India to turn his capital into a great Muslim center. Later Muslim invaders did more than loot and destroy. They built a dazzling new Muslim empire in India.

The arrival of Islam brought changes to India as great as those caused by the Aryan migrations 2,000 years earlier. As Muslims mingled with Indians, each civilization absorbed elements from the other.

### The Muslim Advance

As you read in Chapter 4, the Gupta empire fell about 550. India again fragmented into many local kingdoms. In the age-old pattern, rival princes battled for control of the northern plain. Despite power struggles, Indian culture flourished. Hindu and Buddhist rulers spent huge sums to build and decorate magnificent temples. Trade networks linked India to the Middle East, Southeast Asia, and China.

Although Arab armies conquered the Indus Valley in 711, they advanced no farther into the subcontinent. Then about 1000, Turkish converts to Islam pushed into India. At first, they were adventurers like Mahmud, who pillaged much of the north. In the late 1100s, though, the sultan of Ghur defeated Hindu armies across the northern plain. He made Delhi his capital. From there, his successors organized the Delhi sultanate, which lasted from 1206 to 1526. The Delhi sultanate marked the beginning of Muslim rule in northern India.

Why did the Muslim invaders triumph? They won on the battlefield in part because Turkish mounted archers had far greater mobility than Hindu forces, who rode slow-moving war elephants. Then, too, Hindu princes wasted their resources battling one another instead of uniting against a common enemy. In some places, large numbers of Hindus, especially from low castes, converted to Islam.

## Delhi Sultanate

Muslim rule brought changes to Indian government and society. Sultans expanded their power over much of India, introducing Muslim traditions of government. Many Turks, Persians, and Arabs migrated to India to serve as soldiers or officials. Trade between India and the Muslim world increased. During the Mongol raids of the 1200s, many scholars and adventurers fled from Baghdad to India, bringing Persian and Greek learning. The newcomers helped create a brilliant civilization at Delhi, where Persian art and architecture flourished.

In 1398, Tamerlane invaded India. He plundered the northern plain and smashed into Delhi. "Not a bird on the wing moved," reported stunned survivors. Tens of thousands of artisans were enslaved and marched off to build Tamerlane's capital at Samarkand. Delhi, an empty shell, slowly recovered. But the sultans no longer controlled a large empire, and northern India again fragmented, this time into rival Hindu and Muslim states.

## Meeting of Two Cultures

At its worst, the Muslim conquest of northern India inflicted disaster on Hindus and Buddhists. The widespread destruction of Buddhist monasteries contributed to the drastic decline of Buddhism as a major religion in India. During the most violent onslaughts, many Hindus were killed. Others may have converted to escape death. In time, though, relations became more peaceful.

**Hindu-Muslim differences.** The Muslim advance brought two utterly different religions

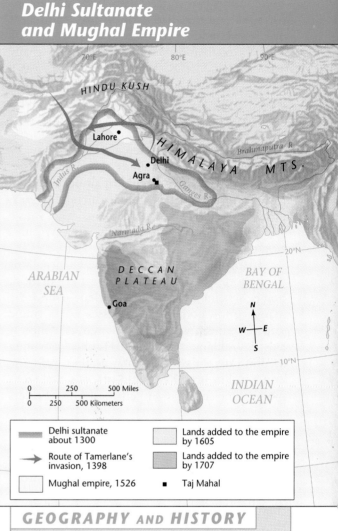

**Delhi Sultanate and Mughal Empire**

Legend:
- Delhi sultanate about 1300
- Route of Tamerlane's invasion, 1398
- Mughal empire, 1526
- Lands added to the empire by 1605
- Lands added to the empire by 1707
- ■ Taj Mahal

## GEOGRAPHY *AND* HISTORY

*Two Muslim dynasties ruled much of the Indian subcontinent. The Delhi sultanate, founded in 1206, was a powerful presence in northern India for more than 300 years. It was replaced by the Mughal dynasty in 1526.*

1. **Location** On the map, locate (a) Delhi, (b) Hindu Kush, (c) Ganges River, (d) Taj Mahal.
2. **Movement** Describe Tamerlane's invasion route into India in 1398.
3. **Critical Thinking** **Linking Past and Present** Use the map on page 988 to name the present-day countries that now occupy the land of the Mughal empire.

and cultures face to face. Hinduism was an ancient religion that had evolved over thousands of years. Hindus recognized many sacred texts and prayed before statues representing many gods and goddesses. Islam, by contrast, was a newer faith with a single sacred text. Muslims were devout monotheists who saw the statues and carvings in Hindu temples as an offense to the one true God.

Hindus accepted differences in caste status and honored Brahmans as a priestly caste. Muslims taught the equality of all believers before God and had no religious hierarchy. Hindus celebrated religious occasions with music and dance, a practice that many strict Muslims condemned.

**Interactions.** Eventually, the Delhi sultans grew more tolerant of their subject population. Some Muslim scholars argued that behind the many Hindu gods and goddesses was a single god. Hinduism was thus accepted as a monotheistic religion. Although Hindus remained second-class citizens, as long as they paid the non-Muslim tax, they could practice their religion. Some sultans even left local Hindu rulers in place.

During the Delhi sultanate, a growing number of Hindus converted to Islam. Some lower-caste Hindus preferred Islam because it rejected the caste system. Other converts came from higher castes but chose to accept Islam because they accepted its monotheistic beliefs or because they served in the Muslim government. Indian merchants were attracted to Islam in part because of the strong trade network across Muslim lands.

**Cultural blending.** During this period, too, Indian Muslims absorbed elements of Hindu culture, such as marriage customs and caste ideas. A new language, Urdu, evolved as a marriage of Persian, Arabic, and Hindi. Local artisans applied Persian art styles to Indian subjects.

An Indian holy man, Nanak, sought to blend Muslim monotheism and Hindu beliefs. He preached "the unity of God, the brotherhood of man, the rejection of caste, and the futility of idol worship." His teachings led to the rise of a new religion, Sikhism (SEEK iz uhm), in northern India. The Sikhs later organized into military forces that clashed with the powerful Mughal rulers of India.

## Mughal India

In 1526, Turkish and Mongol invaders again poured through the mountain passes in India. At their head rode Babur (BAH buhr), who claimed descent from Genghiz Khan and Tamerlane. "I placed my foot in the stirrup of resolution and my hands on the reins of confidence in God," recalled Babur in his memoirs. Just north of Delhi, Babur met a huge army led by the sultan Ibrahim. Babur's force was small but had cannons, which he put to good use.

In no time, Babur swept away the remnants of the Delhi sultanate and set up the Mughal dynasty, which ruled from 1526 to 1857. (*Mughal* is the Persian word for Mongol.) Babur and his heirs conquered an empire that stretched from the Himalayas to the Deccan.

**Akbar the Great.** The chief builder of the Mughal empire was Babur's grandson Akbar. During his long reign, from 1556 to 1605, he created a strong central government on the subcontinent, earning the title Akbar the Great.

Akbar was a leader of unusual abilities. Although a Muslim, he won the support of Hindu subjects through his policy of toleration. He opened government jobs to Hindus of all castes and treated Hindu princes as his partners in ruling the vast empire. He ended the tax on non-Muslims and himself married a Hindu princess.

Akbar could not read and write, but consulted leaders of many faiths, including Muslims, Hindus, Buddhists, and Christians. Like Asoka (see page 83), he hoped to promote religious harmony through tolerance:

&&O God, in every temple I see people
that seek You. In every language I hear
spoken, people praise you. If it be a
mosque, people murmur the holy
prayer. If it be a Christian church, they
ring the bell for love of You. . . .
It is You whom I seek from temple to
temple.99

By recognizing India's diversity, Akbar placed Mughal power on a firm footing. (■ See *You Decide,* "Does Diversity Strengthen or Weaken a Society?" pages 338–339.)

Akbar strengthened his empire in other ways. To improve government, he used paid officials in place of hereditary officeholders. He

**Akbar the Great**
Despite his power and rank, Akbar tried to keep in touch with all the people of his empire. Hindus and Muslims, rich and poor, men and women, were all welcome to present petitions to him at his court. Here, Akbar enjoys an evening's entertainment of music and dance. **Impact of the Individual** What might have occurred in India if Akbar's policies had been less tolerant?

modernized the army, encouraged international trade, and introduced land reforms.

**Akbar's successors.** Akbar's son Jahangir (juh hahn GIR) was a weaker ruler than his father. He left most details of government in the hands of his wife, Nur Jahan. Fortunately, she was an able leader whose shrewd political judgment was matched only by her love of poetry and royal sports. She was the most powerful woman in Indian history until this century.

The high point of Mughal literature, art, and architecture came with the reign of Shah Jahan, Akbar's grandson. When his wife, Mumtaz Mahal, died at age 39, after giving birth to her fourteenth child, Shah Jahan was distraught. "Empire has no sweetness," he cried, "life itself has no relish left for me now." He then had a stunning tomb built for her, the Taj Mahal (TAHZH muh HAHL). It was designed in Persian style, with spectacular white domes and graceful minarets mirrored in clear blue reflecting pools. Verses from the Quran adorn its walls. The Taj Mahal stands as perhaps the greatest monument of the Mughal empire.

**Decline.** In the late 1600s, the emperor Aurangzeb resumed persecution of Hindus.

Economic hardships increased under heavy taxes, and discontent sparked revolts against Mughal rule. Against this background, as you will read, European traders began to mobilize against the once-powerful Mughal empire.

## SECTION 4 REVIEW

1. **Identify** (a) Urdu, (b) Sikhism, (c) Babur, (d) Nur Jahan, (e) Taj Mahal.
2. (a) Describe the stages by which Muslims advanced into India. (b) Why were they able to conquer the subcontinent?
3. How did relations between Hindus and Muslims evolve over time?
4. What policies did Akbar follow to strengthen his empire?
5. *Critical Thinking* **Applying Information** How does the history of Muslims in India illustrate the process of cultural diffusion? (See page 17.)
6. *ACTIVITY* Using information in this chapter and Chapter 4, create a chart listing differences between Islam and Hinduism.

# The Ottoman and Safavid Empires

## Guide for Reading

- How did the Ottomans and Safavids build powerful, prosperous empires?

- How did Muslim traditions influence these empires?

- Why did culture flourish under the Ottomans and Safavids?

- **Vocabulary** *millet*

While the Mughals ruled India, two other dynasties, the Ottomans and Safavids, dominated the Middle East and parts of Eastern Europe. All three empires owed much of their success to new weapons. In 1453, Ottoman cannons blasted gaps in the great defensive walls of Constantinople. Later, muskets made a new kind of army possible, giving firepower to ordinary foot soldiers and reducing the importance of mounted warriors.

The new military technology helped the Ottomans and Safavids create strong central governments. As a result, this period from about 1450 to 1650 is sometimes called "the age of gunpowder empires."

## The Ottoman Advance

The Ottomans were yet another Turkish-speaking nomadic people who had migrated from Central Asia into northwestern Asia Minor. In the 1300s, they expanded across Asia Minor and into the Balkans. Their growing forces threatened the crumbling Byzantine empire. In 1453, Muhammad II captured Constantinople, which he renamed Istanbul.

In the next 200 years, the Ottoman empire continued to expand. At its height it stretched from Hungary to Arabia and Mesopotamia and across North Africa. In 1529 and 1683, Ottoman armies besieged Vienna, sending waves of fear through Western Europe. Although they failed to take Vienna, the Ottomans ruled the largest, most powerful empire in both Europe and the Middle East for centuries.

## Ottoman Culture

The Ottoman empire enjoyed its golden age under the sultan Suleiman (SOO lay mahn), who ruled from 1520 to 1566. Called Suleiman the Magnificent by westerners, he was known to his people as the "Lawgiver."

A brilliant general and wise ruler, Suleiman modernized the army and conquered many new lands. He strengthened the government of the rapidly growing empire and improved its system of justice. As sultan, Suleiman had absolute power, but he ruled with the help of a grand vizier and a divan, or council. A huge bureaucracy supervised the business of government, and the powerful military kept the peace. As in other Islamic states, Ottoman law was based on the Sharia, supplemented by royal edicts. Government officials worked closely with religious scholars who interpreted the law.

**Social organization.** The Ottomans divided their subjects into four classes, each with its appointed role. At the top were "men of the pen"—such as scientists, lawyers, judges, and poets— and "men of the sword," soldiers who guarded the sultan and defended the state. Below them were "men of negotiation"—such as merchants, tax collectors, and artisans, who carried out trade and production—and "men of husbandry," farmers and herders who fed the community.

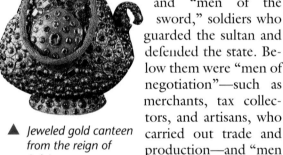

▲ *Jeweled gold canteen from the reign of Suleiman*

The Ottomans ruled diverse peoples who had many religions. The men of the sword and men of the pen were almost all Muslims, while the other classes included non-Muslims as well. Non-Muslims were organized into millets, or religious communities. These included Greek Christians, Armenian Christians, and Jews. Each millet had its own religious leaders who were responsible for education and some legal matters.

**Janissaries.** Like earlier Muslim empires, the Ottomans recruited officers for the army and government from among the huge populations of conquered peoples in their empire. The

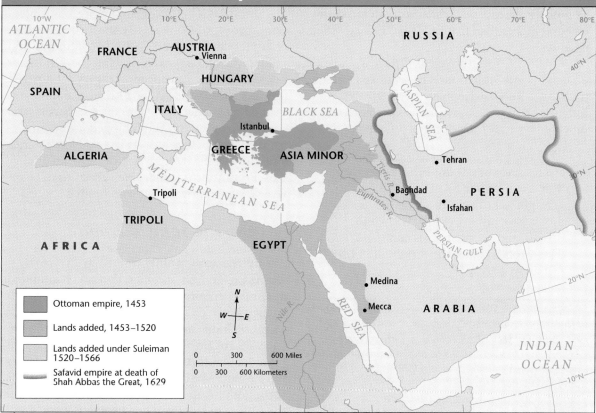

## Ottoman and Safavid Empires

**Legend:**
- Ottoman empire, 1453
- Lands added, 1453–1520
- Lands added under Suleiman 1520–1566
- Safavid empire at death of Shah Abbas the Great, 1629

0    300    600 Miles
0    300    600 Kilometers

## GEOGRAPHY AND HISTORY

At its height, the Ottoman empire covered vast lands in Europe, Africa, and Asia. During the same period, the Safavids controlled most of present-day Iran.

**1. Location** On the map, locate (a) Black Sea, (b) Nile River, (c) Istanbul, (d) Baghdad, (e) Arabia.

**2. Region** (a) Into what regions did the Ottoman empire expand under Suleiman? (b) What region did the Safavids control in 1629?

**3. Critical Thinking Recognizing Points of View** How do you think Russians probably felt about the growth and expansion of the Ottoman empire?

Ottomans levied a "tax" on Christian families in the Balkans, requiring them to turn over young sons to the government.

The boys were converted to Islam and put into rigorous military training at the palace school. The best soldiers won a prized place in the janissaries, the elite force of the Ottoman army. The brightest students received special education to become officials and might serve as judges, poets, or even grand vizier.

As boys were recruited into the janissaries, so non-Muslim girls were sought to act as slaves in the households of the wealthy. Most female slaves were from Eastern Europe. (The word *slave* is derived from Slav.) Slaves were accepted as members of the household and often became free on the death of their masters.

**The arts and literature.** The arts blossomed under Suleiman. Influenced by Persian artistic styles, Ottoman painters produced magnificently detailed miniatures and illuminated manuscripts. The royal architect Sinan, a janissary military engineer, designed hundreds of mosques and palaces. He compared his most famous building, the Selimiye Mosque at Edirne, to the greatest church of the Byzantine empire: "With God's help and the Sultan's mercy," Sinan wrote, "I have succeeded in building a dome for the mosque which is greater in diameter and higher than that of Hagia Sophia." (See page 237.)

Literature, too, thrived as Ottomans adapted Persian and Arab models to produce works in their own Turkish language. The greatest Ottoman poet was Baki, whose masterpiece was a moving lament for the death of Suleiman:

> 66 Will not the King awake from sleep?
>     The dawn of day has broken.
> Will not he come forth from his tent
>     bright as heaven's display?
> Long have our eyes looked down the
>     road, and yet no news is come
> From yonder land, the threshold of his
>     majesty's array. 99

**A Magnificent Sultan** *Europeans dubbed Suleiman "the Magnificent" largely because of the splendor of his court. But they also admired his virtues as a ruler. "The Sultan himself assigns to all their duties and offices," noted a Flemish visitor, "and in doing so pays no attention to wealth or the empty claims of rank. He only considers merit. Thus, offices are filled by men capable of performing them."* **Impact of the Individual** *By what title was Suleiman known to his own subjects? How did he earn this title?*

**Decline.** The Ottoman empire was a powerful force for 500 years. By the 1700s, however, European advances in both commerce and military technology were leaving the Ottomans behind. While European industry and trade pressed ahead, the aging Ottoman empire remained dependent on agriculture. Russia and other European powers chipped away at Ottoman lands, while local rulers in North Africa and elsewhere broke away from Ottoman control. From time to time, able sultans tried to revive Ottoman power, but with limited success.

## The Safavid Empire

By the early 1500s, the Safavids (sah FAH weedz), a Turkish-speaking dynasty, had united a strong empire in present-day Iran. Sandwiched between two other expansionist powers, Mughal India and the Ottoman empire, the Safavids engaged in frequent warfare. Religion played a major role in the conflict. The Safavids were Shiite Muslims who enforced their beliefs throughout Iran and found sympathizers within the Ottoman empire. The Ottomans were Sunni Muslims who despised the Shiites as heretics.

**Abbas the Great.** The outstanding Safavid ruler, Shah Abbas the Great, revived the glory of ancient Persia. From 1588 to 1629, he centralized the government and created a powerful military force modeled on the Ottoman janissaries. Abbas used a mixture of force and diplomacy against the Ottomans. He also sought alliances with European states who had reason to fear Ottoman power.

To strengthen the economy, Abbas reduced taxes on farmers and herders and encouraged the growth of industries. While earlier Safavids had imposed their faith on the empire, Abbas tolerated non-Muslims and valued their economic contributions. He wanted to make his new capital at Isfahan (is fuh HAHN) a center of the international silk trade. Because the trade was controlled by Armenians, Abbas had thousands of Armenians brought to Isfahan. Even though they were Christians, he had a settlement built for them just outside the capital, where they could govern themselves.

Under Abbas, Isfahan flourished as a center of Persian culture. He welcomed artists, poets, and scholars to the court. Palace workshops

**Persian Decorated Tile** *The mihrab, or niche, of a mosque indicates the direction of Mecca, the focal point for Muslim prayer. This mihrab from the Safavid city of Isfahan consists of ceramic tiles fitted together to form geometric designs, floral patterns, and beautiful calligraphy. The geometric design symbolizes the logic and perfect order of God's creations.* **Art and Literature** *How does this mosaic differ from the Byzantine mosaic on page 240? What religious beliefs or customs explain these differences?*

produced magnificent porcelains, clothes, and rugs. Women and men wove intricately designed flowers and animals into marvelous garden scenes.

Abbas liked to walk the streets of Isfahan in disguise, mingling with the crowds in bazaars. Amid the cries of street vendors and swarms of traders and customers, he asked people about their problems. If he heard stories of corruption, he punished the guilty.

**Decline.** Safavid glory slowly faded after the death of the Shah Abbas, though the dynasty held onto power until 1722. In the late 1700s, a new dynasty, the Qajars (kah JAHRZ), won control of Iran. They made Tehran their capital and ruled until 1925. Still, the Safavids had left a lasting legacy. They planted Shiite traditions firmly in Iran and gave Persians a strong sense of their own identity.

## Looking Ahead

By 1500, Islam had become the dominant faith across a large part of the world from West Africa to Southeast Asia. Islam was not a regional culture like Christian Europe, but an international culture reaching across three continents. An extraordinary diversity of peoples—Arabs, Berbers, Turks, Persians, Slavs, Mongols, Indians, and many others—answered the muezzin's call to prayer each day. This vast world was not politically united, but the Quran, the Sharia, and a network of cultural and economic ties linked Muslims across the Dar al-Islam.

Three large states dominated the Muslim world in the 1500s. The Ottomans, the Safavids, and the Mughals were reaching their peak of power. At the same time, however, the nations of Europe were undergoing a period of dynamic growth. Several of these nations would soon challenge Muslim power.

## SECTION 5 REVIEW

1. **Identify** (a) janissaries, (b) Sinan, (c) Baki, (d) Isfahan.
2. **Define** millet.
3. How did the Ottomans govern a large and diverse empire?
4. Why were the Safavids and Ottomans often at war?
5. Describe one way the arts flourished under each of the following rulers: (a) Suleiman, (b) Shah Abbas.
6. *Critical Thinking* **Linking Past and Present** (a) How did the introduction of cannons and muskets affect the growth of the Ottoman and Safavid empires? (b) What changes in military technology have shaped today's world?
7. *ACTIVITY* Design a banner or write a motto that might have been used by one of the four social classes in the Ottoman empire.

# Skills for Success

**Critical Thinking** | **Writing and Researching** | **Maps, Charts, and Graphs** | **Speaking and Listening**

## Recognizing Points of View

Point of view influences the way a person describes events. For example, a person who is opposed to war of any kind can observe a battle and see only a senseless loss of life. A military veteran who observes the same battle may focus on the strategic movement of the troops and the heroic acts of soldiers. Historians must be aware that their individual points of view may affect their accounts.

The excerpts below are from two accounts of the First Crusade. In the first, Fulcher of Chartres, a Christian chronicler, describes the crusaders' capture of the city of Antioch in southern Turkey. In the second, the Muslim historian Ibn al-Athir describes the same event. Read their accounts, then answer the following questions.

**1** **Study the contents of each source.** (a) According to both accounts, how did the Franks gain entry into Antioch? (b) List three other points on which the two writers agree.

**2** **Analyze the points of view.** (a) Why does Fulcher refer to the capture of Antioch as a "return"? (b) Why does al-Athir refer to the Muslims as "defenders"? (c) How do the two accounts differ in their treatment of Ruzbih? (d) Give two other examples of how the words each writer uses suggest his point of view. (e) Why do the two writers give different dates for the event?

**3** **Evaluate the usefulness of the sources.** (a) Do you think that these excerpts are reliable sources of information about the Crusades? Explain. (b) Taken together, what do these two readings suggest about the Crusades?

*Beyond the Classroom* The editorial section of a newspaper is where the paper's staff and readers express their views on current events. Locate two pieces that express different views of a similar event. List information that both writers agree on and identify each writer's point of view.

---

**Fulcher of Chartres:**

66 From this month of October, the siege of the city continued throughout the following winter and spring until the month of June 1098. . . . God appeared to a certain Turk predestined by His grace and said to him, 'Arise, you who sleep! I command you to return the city to the Christians.' . . . The Turk, no longer doubting, secretly made a plot with our men by which they should obtain the city.

"On the appointed night, the Turk admitted over the wall twenty of our men by means of rope ladders. At once, without delay, the gate was opened. The Franks, who were ready, entered the city. Forty more of our soldiers who had already entered by means of the ropes slew sixty Turks whom they found guarding the towers. Then all the Franks shouted together in a loud voice, 'God wills it! God wills it!' For this was our signal cry when we were about to accomplish any good enterprise. 99

**Ibn al-Athir:**

66 After the siege had been going on for a long time, the Franks made a deal with one of the men who were responsible for the towers. He was an armor-maker called Ruzbih whom they bribed with a fortune in money and lands. He worked in the tower that stood over the river bed, where the river flowed out of the city into the valley. The Franks sealed their pact with the armor-maker, God curse him! and made their way to the water gate. They opened it and entered the city. Another gang of them climbed the tower with ropes. At dawn, when more than 500 of them were in the city and the defenders were worn out after the night watch, they sounded their trumpets. . . . They entered the city by the gates and sacked it, slaughtering all the Muslims they found there. This happened in 491. 99

# CHAPTER 11 REVIEW

## Building Vocabulary

Choose *four* vocabulary words from this chapter. Then, write a sentence for each word in which you define the word and describe its relation to the beliefs and practices of Islam.

## Reviewing Chapter Themes

1. **Religions and Value Systems** Describe the importance of each of the following to Muslims: (a) the Five Pillars of Islam, (b) the Quran, (c) the Sharia.
2. **Diversity** Describe how *two* of the following dealt with the diverse peoples within their empires: (a) the caliphs, (b) the Mughals, (c) the Ottomans.
3. **Global Interaction** (a) How was Islamic civilization more global than earlier empires? (b) Give two examples of interaction across different parts of the Muslim world.
4. **Art and Literature** (a) Why did Muslim artists develop skills in design and calligraphy? (b) What religious and secular traditions influenced Muslim literature?

## Thinking Critically

1. **Comparing** Review the discussion of the schism in the Christian church on page 242. (a) How was the break between Sunni and Shiite Muslims similar to the schism between Roman Catholic and Orthodox Christians? (b) As you have read, Buddhism also split into two schools. What kinds of issues might cause religions to divide?
2. **Analyzing Literature** A Muslim woman poet wrote, "Under my veil is kingly power . . . / I withhold the beauty of my shadow / From the sun that gads about in the marketplace." (a) What practices is this poet describing? (b) What is her attitude toward these practices? (★ See *Skills for Success*, page 234.)
3. **Recognizing Points of View** "If God gives us the grace to drive His enemies from Jerusalem what happiness will be ours!" Do you think these words express the point of view of a crusader or of a Muslim? Explain. (★ See *Skills for Success*, page 280.)

4. **Linking Past and Present** (a) What Muslim business techniques are still in use today? (b) Why is buying and selling on credit essential to business transactions?
5. **Applying Information** "If men walk in the way of God's will," declared Akbar, "interference with them would be unfair." How did Akbar's policies reflect this idea?
6. **Synthesizing Information** The Arab, Ottoman, and Safavid empires all declined after periods of strength. Review what you have read about other empires in Egypt, India, China, and Rome. (a) What forces tend to strengthen an empire? (b) What forces tend to make an empire decline? (★ See *Skills for Success*, page 896.)

### For Your Portfolio

You and a small crew of other classmates are making a travel documentary based on the journeys of the Moroccan Muslim scholar Ibn Battuta in the 1300s. In this assignment, you will write the narration for the documentary and identify scenes to be filmed.

1. Begin by rereading the introduction to this chapter on page 254. Make a list of the places visited by Ibn Battuta during his travels throughout the world.
2. Use library resources to do further research on the life and travels of Ibn Battuta. Look for more details about the places he visited and his experiences in each place. (For an interesting comparison, you might also read *In an Ancient Land*, a book by Amitav Ghosh about another traveler of this period.)
3. Look for pictures, charts, and maps to include in your documentary. If necessary, create your own map of Ibn Battuta's travels.
4. Make an outline for your documentary, indicating the topics you want to cover. (You might also include some incidents that could be dramatized.) Then, write the narration that will go with your documentary. Include comments about what the travels of Ibn Battuta show us about the Muslim world of his time.
5. Present the visuals and commentary for your documentary to the class. Follow up by discussing the importance of the Dar al-Islam in spreading ideas, goods, and technologies.

# Kingdoms and Trading States of Africa

## (750 B.C.–A.D. 1586)

## CHAPTER OUTLINE

1 Early Civilizations of Africa
2 Kingdoms of West Africa
3 Trade Routes of East Africa
4 Many Peoples, Many Traditions

Today, nothing remains of Kumbi Saleh but ruins in the Saharan sands. In the mid-1000s, however, the city was the capital of the wealthy West African kingdom of ancient Ghana. In his *Book of Roads and Kingdoms,* the Spanish Arab historian al-Bakri described the splendors of Kumbi Saleh. Although the Muslim writer had not visited Ghana himself, he had collected information from traders who had.

Kumbi Saleh was made up of two separate walled towns, some six miles apart. The first town was dominated by the royal palace, surrounded by a complex of domed buildings. Here, the king of Ghana sat in regal splendor, adorned in necklaces and bracelets. "And when he sits before the people," noted al-Bakri, "he puts on a high cap decorated with gold and wrapped in turbans of fine cotton." Al-Bakri then described the elaborate ceremonies when the king dispensed justice:

66When he gives audience to his people,
to listen to their complaints and set
them to rights, he sits in a pavilion
around which stand his horses adorned
in cloth of gold. Behind him on his
right hand are the sons of the princes
of his empire, splendidly clad and
with gold braided into their hair. . . .
The beginning of the audience is announced by the beating of a kind of
drum which they call *deba,* made of a
long piece of hollowed wood.99

In the second town, prosperous Muslim merchants from north of the Sahara lived in luxurious stone buildings. Lured by the gold wealth of Ghana, these merchants helped make Kumbi Saleh a bustling center of trade. As Muslims, they also helped spread their Islamic faith to West Africa. The Muslim quarter housed 12 separate mosques.

By the time Ghana reached its peak, the vast continent of Africa had already been home to a number of other civilizations. In some regions, major political powers rose despite geographic obstacles, such as poor soil or harsh climates. From the time of ancient Egypt, trade and other contacts linked parts of Africa to Europe, the Middle East, India, and other parts of Asia.

FOCUS ON these questions as you read:

■ **Geography and History**
How did geography both help and hinder the peoples of Africa?

■ **Diversity**
What conditions contributed to the development of varied cultures in Africa?

■ **Global Interaction**
How were parts of Africa tied into major trading networks?

■ **Art and Literature**
What literary and artistic traditions developed in Africa?

## TIME AND PLACE

*African Masks* In Africa, as elsewhere, people believed that art played a vital role in society, especially when combined with music and dance. Elaborate masks, like the ones shown here, were used in political, religious, and social ceremonies. **Art and Literature** Compare these masks to the Greek sculptures on page 103. How do the artists' styles differ?

## HUMANITIES LINK

*Art History* Benin bronze sculpture (page 293).
*Literature* In this chapter, you will encounter passages from the following works of literature: al-Bakri, *Book of Roads and Kingdoms* (page 282); Leo Africanus, *The History and Description of Africa* (page 289); *The Glory of Kings* (page 294); Yoruba riddles (page 301); *Sundiata* (pages 302–303).

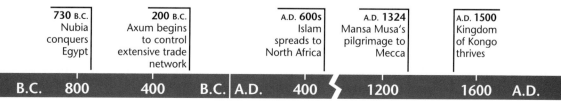

| **730 B.C.** Nubia conquers Egypt | **200 B.C.** Axum begins to control extensive trade network | **A.D. 600s** Islam spreads to North Africa | **A.D. 1324** Mansa Musa's pilgrimage to Mecca | **A.D. 1500** Kingdom of Kongo thrives |

| B.C. | 800 | 400 | B.C. | A.D. | 400 | 1200 | 1600 | A.D. |

# Early Civilizations of Africa

## Guide for Reading

■ What geographic features have influenced African life?

■ What were the achievements of Nubian civilization?

■ What early civilizations influenced North Africa?

■ **Vocabulary** *savanna, desertification*

As the sun rose above the east bank of the Nile, workers hurried to the construction site. They had only a few hours to work in comfort before the sun turned the desert into a furnace. Still, as long as King Taharqa (tuh HAHR kuh) was determined to restore Egyptian monuments and beautify his own kingdom of Nubia, their work would continue.

An ancient inscription explains how Taharqa's artisans and architects renovated an old mud-brick temple and turned it into a spectacular monument. Set amid an artificial lake and gardens, the monument was "built of good white sandstone, excellent, hard, . . . the house being of gold, the columns of gold, the inlays thereof being of silver."

About 680 B.C., Taharqa commanded the Nile Valley from Nubia to the Mediterranean. By that time, Nubia was already 3,000 years old. Along with Egypt, it stood as one of the world's early civilizations.

## Geography: The Continent of Africa

After Asia, Africa is the second largest continent, covering one fifth of all the Earth's land surface. Its geography is immensely varied, but certain features have had a major impact on its development.

**Climate zones.** Many outsiders, misled by movies, imagine Africa as a continent covered with thick jungles. In fact, tropical rain forests cover less than five percent of the land, mostly along the Equator. (See the map opposite.) Thick trees and roots make this region unsuitable for farming.

Africa's largest and most populated climate zone is the savanna, or grassy plains, which stretches north and south of the forest zone. The savanna generally has good soil and enough rainfall to support farming, but irregular patterns of rainfall sometimes cause long, deadly droughts. In parts of the savanna, the tsetse fly infects people and cattle with sleeping sickness. But in other parts of the savanna, cattle herding is a common occupation.

The savanna belts trail off into increasingly dry steppe zones and then into two major deserts. The blistering Sahara in the north is the world's largest desert. Although the Sahara did become a highway for migration and trade, its size and harsh terrain limited movement. The Kalahari and Namib in the south are smaller but equally forbidding.

Along the Mediterranean coast of North Africa and at the tip of southern Africa lie areas of fertile farmland. As you have read, the fertile Nile River valley offered a favorable environment to early farmers.

**Movement.** In addition to deserts and rain forests, other geographic features have acted as barriers to easy movement of people and goods. Although Africa is surrounded by oceans and seas, it has few good natural harbors. In addition, much of the interior is a high plateau. As rivers flow down to the coast, they cascade through a series of rapids and cataracts that hinder travel between the coast and the interior. Within the interior, though, the same rivers—including the Zambezi, Congo, and Niger—serve as open highways.

Despite geographic barriers, people did migrate, both within Africa and to neighboring continents. Like the rivers, the Great Rift Valley of East Africa served as an interior corridor. People also traveled across the savanna lands. The Red Sea and Indian Ocean linked East Africa to the Middle East and other Asian lands, while North Africa formed the southern rim of the Mediterranean world.

**Resources.** Since ancient times, Africa's mineral wealth has spurred trade among various regions. Salt, iron, gold, and copper were important commodities in early trade networks. In

# Geography of Africa

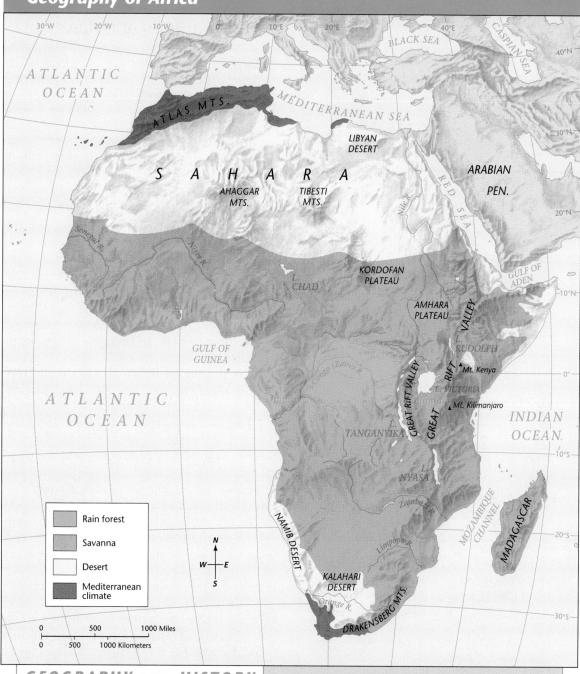

ATLANTIC OCEAN

MEDITERRANEAN SEA

BLACK SEA

CASPIAN SEA

ATLAS MTS.

LIBYAN DESERT

S A H A R A

ARABIAN PEN.

AHAGGAR MTS.

TIBESTI MTS.

Nile R.

RED SEA

Senegal R.

Niger R.

L. CHAD

KORDOFAN PLATEAU

GULF OF ADEN

AMHARA PLATEAU

GULF OF GUINEA

Congo (Zaire) R.

GREAT RIFT VALLEY

GREAT RIFT VALLEY

L. RUDOLPH

Mt. Kenya

L. VICTORIA

Mt. Kilimanjaro

ATLANTIC OCEAN

INDIAN OCEAN

L. TANGANYIKA

L. NYASA

Zambezi R.

MOZAMBIQUE CHANNEL

MADAGASCAR

NAMIB DESERT

Limpopo R.

KALAHARI DESERT

Orange R.

DRAKENSBERG MTS.

**Legend:**
- Rain forest
- Savanna
- Desert
- Mediterranean climate

N
W—E
S

| 0 | 500 | 1000 Miles |
| 0 | 500 | 1000 Kilometers |

## GEOGRAPHY AND HISTORY

Africa is the second largest continent in the world. Stretching more than 5,000 miles from north to south, the continent has widely varied terrains and climates.

**1. Location** On the map, locate (a) Congo River, (b) Sahara, (c) Great Rift Valley, (d) Mount Kilimanjaro, (e) Atlas Mountains, (f) Namib Desert, (g) Kalahari Desert.

**2. Interaction** Which type of climate zone might be most attractive for people to live in? Why?

**3. Critical Thinking  Applying Information** Why do you think the climate in most of Africa is warm throughout the year?

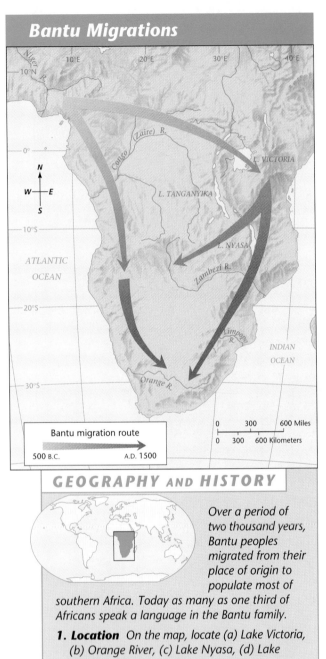

## Bantu Migrations

N
W E
S

ATLANTIC OCEAN

INDIAN OCEAN

Bantu migration route

500 B.C. ————————→ A.D. 1500

0    300    600 Miles
0    300    600 Kilometers

## GEOGRAPHY AND HISTORY

Over a period of two thousand years, Bantu peoples migrated from their place of origin to populate most of southern Africa. Today as many as one third of Africans speak a language in the Bantu family.

1. **Location** On the map, locate (a) Lake Victoria, (b) Orange River, (c) Lake Nyasa, (d) Lake Tanganyika.
2. **Movement** (a) Where did Bantu peoples originate? (b) Approximately when did Bantu peoples reach the Orange River?
3. **Critical Thinking Solving Problems** How have scientists learned about the Bantu migrations?

the 1800s, desire for gold and diamonds was one cause that led Europeans to seek control of territories in Africa. More recently, nations such as Nigeria and Angola have exported large quantities of oil.

## Migration of Peoples

Archaeologists have uncovered evidence to pinpoint the Great Rift Valley of East Africa as the home of the earliest people. (See pages 8–9.) Gradually, their descendants spread to almost every corner of the Earth.

**Stone Age cultures.** In Africa, as elsewhere, Paleolithic people developed skills as hunters and food gatherers. By 5500 B.C., Neolithic farmers had learned to cultivate the Nile Valley and to domesticate animals. These early farmers settled into permanent villages that eventually supported the great civilization of ancient Egypt. (See Chapter 2.)

Farming spread across North Africa. Neolithic villages even appeared in the Sahara region, which at that time was a well-watered zone. Ancient rock paintings show a Sahara full of forests and rivers. In these paintings, people wear clothes similar to those worn by groups such as the Fulani today. Women tend crops, cook, and help move camp. Men hunt, herd the cattle, and defend the community.

**The Sahara dries out.** About 2500 B.C., however, a climate change slowly dried out the Sahara. As the land became parched, the desert spread. This process of desertification has continued to the present, devouring thousands of acres of cropland and pastureland each year.

As the region dried, people retreated. Some moved north to the Mediterranean coast. Mingling with local people, they became the ancestors of the Berbers who live there today. Others migrated south to the savanna or rain forests.

**The Bantu migrations.** Over thousands of years, other migrations contributed to the rich diversity of African peoples and cultures. Scholars have been able to trace these migrations by studying language patterns. They have learned that West African farmers and herders migrated to the south and east between about A.D. 500 and 1500. Wherever they settled, they spread their skills in farming and ironworking. Like the Indo-European peoples who migrated across Europe and Asia, these West African peoples spoke a variety of languages that derived from a common root language. (See Chapter 3.) We call this African root language Bantu.

Bantu peoples met, and often displaced, earlier groups. In central and southern Africa, for example, they forced the Khoisan (KOI sahn) into less-desirable areas, such as the Zaire rain forest or the Kalahari desert. On the east coast of Africa, Bantu-speaking peoples encountered migrants from Asia.

As people migrated across Africa, they adapted to its many climates and developed a diversity of cultures. While some were nomadic cattle herders, others cultivated grain or root crops. In several regions, farming people built great empires, as you will read.

## The Nile Kingdom of Nubia

While Egyptian civilization was developing, another African civilization took shape on a wide band of fertile land among the cataracts of the upper Nile. The ancient kingdom of Nubia, also called Kush, was located in present-day Sudan. Archaeologists and historians have just begun to document the shifting tides of Nubia's 4,000-year history.

**Nubia and Egypt.** From time to time, ambitious Egyptian pharaohs subdued Nubia, but the Nubians always regained their independence. As a result of conquest and trade, Nubian rulers adopted many Egyptian traditions. They built palaces and pyramids modeled on Egyptian styles. They used Egyptian titles and worshiped deities like Amon-Re and Isis.

About 750 B.C., as you have read, the Nubian king Piankhi (pee AHNG kee) conquered Egypt. "Raging like a panther," he defeated his enemies "like a cloud burst," according to an inscription. For a century, Nubian kings like Taharqa ruled Egypt. But Taharqa's armies could not match the iron weapons of the invading Assyrians. Forced to retreat from Egypt, the Nubians returned south.

◀ King Taharqa

**The furnaces of Meroë.** By 500 B.C., Nubian rulers moved their capital to Meroë (MEHR uh wee). Meroë commanded both the north-south Nile routes and the east-west route from the Red Sea into the savanna. Along this wide trade network, Nubia sent gold, ivory, animal skins, perfumes, and slaves to the Mediterranean world and the Middle East.

Equally important, Meroë was rich in iron ore. Its furnaces, fueled by large quantities of timber, produced iron for tools and weapons. Trade may have spread iron technology across the savanna lands into West Africa. Today, giant heaps of iron waste remain as evidence of the prosperous iron industry of ancient Meroë.

**Splendors and decline.** Although Nubia absorbed much from Egypt, it later followed an independent course. Nubians worshiped their own gods including Apedemak, a lion-headed warrior god. At Meroë, artistic styles reflected a greater sense of freedom than Egyptian styles. Nubians also created their own system of writing, using an alphabet instead of hieroglyphics. Unfortunately, the Nubian alphabet has yet to be deciphered.

After the joint reign of King Natakamani and Queen Amanitere in the first century A.D., Nubia's golden age dimmed. Desertification may have engulfed Nubian farmlands. Finally, about A.D. 350, armies from the kingdom of Axum on the Red Sea overwhelmed Nubia. King Ezana of Axum boasted:

❝I burnt their towns, both those built of brick and those built of reeds, and my army carried off their food and copper and iron . . . and destroyed the statues in their temples.❞

As you will read later, Axum would make its own mark on this region beyond the Nile.

## North Africa in the Ancient World

Early African civilizations had strong ties to the Mediterranean world. Trade linked Egypt with Greece and Mesopotamia. Later, Egypt was ruled, in turn, by the Greeks and Romans. These powers also knew of the rich civilization that lay south of Egypt and valued Nubian exports. Over time, however, Nubia lost touch with the Mediterranean world.

**Ships of the Desert** With the help of camels, merchants and warriors overcame the obstacles of the Sahara. Camel caravans, like those that still traverse the Sahara today, also helped Islam spread across North Africa. **Geography and History** What other domesticated animals are well suited for travel in a particular environment? Explain.

**Carthage.** At the opposite end of the Mediterranean, Carthage rose as a great North African power. Like Nubia, its wealth came from trade. Founded by Phoenician traders, Carthage came to dominate the western Mediterranean. Between 800 B.C. and 146 B.C., it forged an empire that stretched from the Maghreb (present-day Tunisia, Algeria, and Morocco) to southern Spain and Sicily, as well as outposts in England, France, and possibly West Africa.

As Rome expanded, territorial and trade rivalries erupted between the two powers. Despite the efforts of Hannibal, Rome eventually crushed Carthage. (See pages 132–133).

**Roman rule.** The Romans built roads, dams, aqueducts, and cities across North Africa. They developed its farmlands to harvest bumper crops of grain, fruit, and other foods. From North Africa, they imported lions and other fierce animals to Rome to do battle with gladiators. North Africa also provided soldiers for the Roman army. One of them, Septimius Severus, later became emperor of Rome.

Under Roman rule, Christianity spread to the cities of North Africa. St. Augustine, the most influential Christian thinker of the late Roman empire, was born in present-day Algeria. From 395 to 430, Augustine was bishop of Hippo, a city near the ruins of ancient Carthage.

**The camel revolutionizes trade.** By A.D. 200, camels had been brought to North Africa from Asia. These hardy "ships of the desert" revolutionized trade across the Sahara. Although daring traders had earlier made the difficult desert crossing in horse-drawn chariots, camel caravans created new trade networks. Camels could carry loads of up to 500 pounds and could plod 20 or 30 miles a day, often without water. The caravan brought great profits to merchants on both sides of the Sahara.

**Spread of Islam.** Further changes came in the 600s, when Arab armies carried Islam into North Africa. At first, the Arabs occupied the cities and battled the Berbers in the desert. In time, however, Berbers and Arabs joined forces to conquer Spain. Islam replaced Christianity as the dominant religion of North Africa, and Arabic replaced Latin as its language.

North Africa benefited from the blossoming of Muslim civilization. Cities like Cairo, Fez, and Marrakesh were famed for their mosques and libraries. Linked into a global trade network, North African ports did a busy trade in grain, wine, fruit, ivory, and gold. Along with their goods, Muslim traders from North Africa carried Islam into West Africa.

## SECTION 1 REVIEW

1. **Identify** (a) Bantu, (b) Piankhi, (c) Taharqa, (d) Meroë, (e) St. Augustine.
2. **Define** (a) savanna, (b) desertification.
3. (a) What barriers to movement did the geography of Africa pose? (b) Describe two examples of migration in Africa.
4. How did Nubian civilization prosper?
5. Describe one way each of the following influenced North Africa: (a) the growth of the Roman empire, (b) the spread of Islam.
6. *Critical Thinking* **Linking Past and Present** (a) What effects did desertification have on African peoples? (b) How might life in the United States be affected if well-watered areas began to turn into desert today?
7. *ACTIVITY* Imagine that you are a merchant preparing to embark on a camel caravan across the Sahara. Write a diary entry describing your feelings about the journey.

# 2 Kingdoms of West Africa

## Guide for Reading

- What role did resources and trade play in West Africa?

- How did West African rulers build powerful kingdoms?

- How did Islam influence the peoples of West Africa?

In the early 1500s, the scholar Hassan ibn Muhammad—known in the West as Leo Africanus—described the commercial wealth and bustling markets of the West African city of Timbuktu:

&&Here are shops of artisans and merchants, and especially such as weave linen and cotton cloth. And here do the merchants of North Africa bring the cloth of Europe. All the women of this region, except the maid-servants, go with their faces covered and sell all the necessary foods.&&

Timbuktu stood at one end of a trade network that reached north to Cairo and then across the Mediterranean Sea to Italy. Between about 800 and 1600, several powerful kingdoms won control of the prosperous Sahara trade. Among the richest West African states were Ghana, Mali, and Songhai.

## The West African Landscape

As the Sahara dried out, you will recall, some Neolithic people migrated southward into the western savanna. There, farmers grew beans, melons, and a wide variety of cereal grains. Men cleared the land and prepared the fields for planting, while women did most of the weeding, transplanting, threshing, and grinding of the grain.

By A.D. 100, settled farming villages were expanding, especially along the Senegal and Niger rivers and around Lake Chad. In time, some villages grew into towns with local rulers, creating larger political units.

**Trading patterns.** Villagers traded any surplus food they produced. Gradually, a trade network linked the savanna to forest lands in the south and then funneled goods across the Sahara to the Mediterranean and Middle East. From West Africa, caravans crossed the Sahara carrying leather goods, kola nuts, cotton cloth, and slaves. From North Africa, Arab and Berber merchants brought silk, steel, Venetian glass beads, and horses.

**Gold for salt.** Two products, gold and salt, dominated the Sahara trade. Gold was plentiful in present-day Ghana, Nigeria, and Senegal. Men dug the gold-bearing soil from pits. Then, women washed the soil to extract the gold dust. The precious metal was stuffed into hollow feather quills for safe travel to the markets of North Africa and Europe.

In return, West Africans received an equally valuable commodity, salt. People need salt in their diet to prevent dehydration, especially in hot, tropical areas.

The Sahara had an abundance of salt. In fact, at Taghaza in the central Sahara, people even built homes of salt blocks. But in the savanna, several hundred miles south, salt was scarce. A block of salt was easily worth its weight in gold.

▲ *West African gold*

As farming and trade prospered, cities developed on the northern edges of the savanna. Strong monarchs gained control of the most profitable trade routes.

## Gold Wealth of Ghana

By A.D. 800, the rulers of the Soninke people had united many farming villages to create the kingdom of Ghana.* Ghana was located in the broad "V" made by the Niger and Senegal rivers. (See the map on page 295.) From there, the king controlled gold-salt trade routes across

---

*Ghana, meaning ruler, was the name used for the kingdom by Arab traders. The modern nation of Ghana is not located on the site of the ancient kingdom, but several hundred miles to the south.

West Africa. The two streams of trade met in the marketplaces of Ghana, where the king collected tolls on all goods entering or leaving his land. So great was the flow of gold that Arab writers called Ghana "land of gold."

**King and court.** As you read, the king of Ghana presided over elaborate ceremonies at his court in Kumbi Saleh. To the people, he was a semi-divine figure who dispensed justice and kept order. According to al-Bakri, the king had a huge army of foot soldiers as well as a small, well-trained cavalry.

Women in Ghana had a high status and played an active role in the economic life of the empire. Some held positions in the government. The ruler himself inherited the throne through his mother, the previous king's sister.

**Influence of Islam.** Muslim merchants formed their own settled communities throughout the kingdom. Islam spread slowly at first. The king employed Muslims as counselors and officials, gradually absorbing Muslim military technology and ideas about government. Muslims also introduced their written language, coinage, business methods, and styles of architecture. In time, a few city dwellers adopted Islam, but most Soninke continued to follow their own traditional beliefs.

About 1050, however, the Almoravids (al MOR uh veedz), pious Muslims of North Africa, launched a campaign to spread their form of Islam. After conquering the Maghreb and Spain, they pressed south across the Sahara. They overwhelmed Ghana, whose rulers may have converted to Islam. In the end, though, the Almoravids were unable to maintain control over such a distant land. Ghana survived, but its empire declined in the late 1100s. In time it was swallowed up by a rising new power, the West African kingdom of Mali.

## Mali: Where the King Dwells

Amid the turmoil of Ghana's collapse, the Mandinke people on the upper Niger suffered a bitter defeat by a rival leader. Their king and all but one of his sons were executed. According to tradition, the survivor was Sundiata, a sickly boy regarded as too weak to be a threat. But Sundiata grew up to be a brilliant military leader. By 1250, he had crushed his enemies, won control

of the gold trade routes, and founded the empire of Mali. (📖 See *World Literature*, "Sundiata," pages 302–303.)

*Mali* is an Arab version of the Mandinke word meaning "where the king dwells." Sundiata and succeeding *mansas*, or kings, expanded their influence over both the gold-mining regions to the south and the salt supplies of Taghaza. Where caravan routes crossed, towns like Timbuktu mushroomed into great trading cities.

The greatest emperor of Mali was Mansa Musa (MAHN sah MOO sah), who came to the throne in about 1312. Musa expanded Mali's borders westward to the Atlantic Ocean and pushed northward to conquer many Berber cities. During Mansa Musa's 25-year reign, he worked to ensure peace and order in his empire. "There is complete and general safety throughout the land," commented Ibn Battuta when he visited Mali. "The traveler here has no more reason to fear thieves than the man who stays at home."

Musa converted to Islam and based his system of justice on the Quran. At the same time, he did not adopt all customs associated with some nearby Muslim societies. For example, women in Mali wore no veils and were not secluded within the home.

In 1324, Mansa Musa fulfilled one of the Five Pillars of Islam. Like all able Muslims, he made his pilgrimage to Mecca.

## The Emperor's Hajj

From the tall mosque in Cairo, the muezzin called faithful Egyptian Muslims to prayer. "*La ilaha illa Allah; Muhammadun rasulu Allah,*" he cried. "There is no God but God; Muhammad is the prophet of God." Today, a visitor from thousands of miles away also heard the muezzin's call. He was Mansa Musa, stopping at Egypt on his way to Mecca.

**A fabulous journey.** By the time he reached Cairo, the emperor had already made the difficult journey across the Sahara. He traveled in kingly style. Musa was accompanied by 500 slaves, each bearing a golden staff. His caravan boasted 100 camels heavily laden with gold.

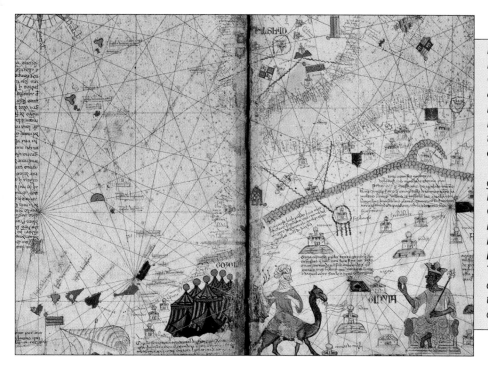

**Mansa Musa** *The mapmaker Abraham Cresque drew this map of West Africa for the king of France. It shows Mansa Musa on his throne holding symbols of power and wealth. "So abundant is the gold which is found in his country," noted Cresque, "that he is the richest and most noble king in all the land."* **Economics and Technology** *How does the map indicate the economic prosperity of West Africa?*

Egyptians were awed by this fabulous display of wealth. Nor was Musa stingy about sharing it. One witness reported:

> 66This man spread upon Cairo the flood of his generosity: there was no person, officer of the court, or holder of any office of the Sultanate who did not receive a sum of gold from him. The people of Cairo earned incalculable sums from him, whether by buying and selling or by gifts.99

In fact, the emperor and his servants spent so lavishly that the value of gold in Cairo dropped for more than 10 years!

Musa had one moment of tension during his stopover in Cairo. An Egyptian official requested that the emperor visit the palace of the sultan. Musa balked, however, at kissing the ground before the sultan's feet. The emperor finally did agree to the custom, but said, "I will prostrate myself before God who created me and brought me into the world."

Musa at length resumed his journey to Arabia. Finally, the caravan reached Mecca. Like other pilgrims, he visited the Kaaba and prayed humbly in the city most sacred to Muslims. Then he made the long journey back across the Sahara to Mali. The hajj had taken over a year.

**Results of the hajj.** Through his pilgrimage, Mansa Musa showed his devotion to Islam. At the same time, he forged new trading and diplomatic ties with Muslim states such as Egypt and Morocco. Musa also returned home with scholars and artists, like as-Sahili, a poet and architect from Spain. The newcomers introduced Arab styles in the palaces and mosques of Mali.

As a result of Musa's pilgrimage, word of Mali's enormous wealth spread across the Muslim world and filtered into Europe. The news sparked the interest of European rulers in African gold, especially since they had recently begun to use gold coins.

In 1375, Abraham Cresque, a French Jewish mapmaker, included a picture of Mansa Musa on a map of West Africa. It shows the ruler wearing a gold crown and holding a solid gold nugget in one hand. To this day, that image, along with the eyewitness reports of Mansa Musa's pilgrimage, still stands as a glowing symbol of the splendors of Mali. ▪

## A New Empire in the Grasslands

In the 1400s, disputes over succession weakened Mali. Subject peoples broke away, and the empire shriveled. By 1450, the wealthy trading city of Gao (GOW) had emerged as the capital of a new West African kingdom, Songhai (SAWNG hī).

**Two great leaders.** Songhai grew up on the bend of the Niger River in present-day Niger and Burkina Faso. Between 1464 and 1492, the soldier-king Sonni Ali used his powerful army to forge the largest state that had ever existed in West Africa. Sonni Ali brought key trade routes and wealthy cities like Timbuktu under his control. Unlike the rulers of Mali, he did not adhere to the practices of Islam. Instead, he followed traditional religious beliefs.

Soon after Sonni Ali's death, though, the emperor Askia Muhammad set up a Muslim dynasty. He further expanded the territory of Songhai and improved the government. He set up a bureaucracy with separate departments for farming, army, and the treasury. The king appointed officials to supervise each of these departments.

Like Mansa Musa, Askia Muhammad made a pilgrimage to Mecca that led to increased ties with the Muslim world. Scholars and poets from Muslim lands flocked to his court at Gao. In towns and cities across Songhai, Askia Muhammad built mosques and opened schools for the study of the Quran.

**Timbuktu.** By the 1400s, Timbuktu had become a leading center of learning. The city drew some of the best scholars from all over the Muslim world. Hassan ibn Muhammad described the city's intellectual life:

> 66Here are great store of doctors, judges, . . . and other learned men, that are bountifully maintained at the king's cost and charges. And hither are brought various manuscripts of books from North Africa, which are sold for more money than any other merchandise.99

**Invaders from the north.** Songhai prospered until about 1586, when disputes over succession led to civil war. Soon after, the ruler of Morocco sent his armies south to seize the West African gold mines. The invaders used gunpowder weapons to defeat the disunited forces of Songhai.

Like the Almoravids in Ghana, however, the Moroccans were not able to rule an empire across the Sahara. With the downfall of Songhai, this part of West Africa splintered into many small kingdoms.

## Other Kingdoms of West Africa

In the period from 500 to 1500, other kingdoms flourished in various parts of West Africa. The fertile northern lands of modern-day Nigeria were home to the Hausa people, who had probably migrated there when the Sahara dried out. They were both successful farmers and traders.

**Walled towns of the Hausa.** By the 1300s, the Hausa had built a number of clay-walled cities. While these city-states remained independent of one another, in time they expanded into thriving commercial centers. In the cities, cotton weavers and dyers, leatherworkers, and other artisans produced goods for sale. Merchants traded with Arab and Berber caravans from north of the Sahara. Hausa goods were sold as far away as North Africa and southern Europe.

Kano was the most prosperous Hausa city-state. Its walls, 14 miles in circumference, housed a population of more than 30,000 people. Kano's greatest king, Muhammad Rumfa, was a Muslim, as were many merchants and officials. The Hausa developed a written language based on Arabic.

Many Hausa rulers were women, such as Amina of the city-state of Zaria. In the 1500s, she conquered Kano and expanded the boundary of Zaria as far as the Niger River. Under Amina, the Hausa came to dominate Saharan trade routes.

**The forest kingdom of Benin.** South of the savanna, Benin (beh NIN) rose in the rain forests of the Guinea coast. The forest peoples carved out farming villages and traded pepper, ivory, and later slaves to their neighbors in the savanna.

The rulers of Benin organized their kingdom in the 1300s, probably building on the achievements of earlier forest cultures. An *oba*, or king, was both a political and religious leader. Still, much power was spread among other figures, including the queen mother and a council of hereditary chiefs. A three-mile-long wall surrounded the capital, Benin City. Its broad avenues were dotted with tidy homes and a great palace.

The palace, in particular, was decorated with elaborate brass plaques and sculptures. Accord-

# ART HISTORY

**Benin Bronze Sculpture** *This bronze from the forest kingdom of Benin shows a powerful queen mother surrounded by attendants. Benin artisans used a lost-wax process to create sculptures of bronze and brass. In this process, the sculptor formed a wax model encased within a clay shell. Molten metal was then poured into the clay shell. The melting wax ran out and was replaced with the finished metal sculpture.* **Art and Literature** *What does this sculpture suggest about the importance of the queen mother in Benin?*

ing to tradition, artisans from Ife (EE fee), an earlier forest society, had taught the people of Benin how to cast bronze and brass. Benin sculptors developed their own unique style for representing the human face and form. Their works depicted warriors armed for battle, queen mothers with upswept hairstyles, and the oba himself.

**Looking ahead.** Later Benin bronze works showed helmeted and bearded Portuguese merchants. These newcomers began to arrive in growing numbers in the 1500s. At first, Benin benefited from the new trade with European countries. However, as you will read in Chapter 16, increasing contacts with Europe opened the door to a booming slave trade that would have far-reaching consequences for all of West Africa.

## SECTION 2 REVIEW

1. **Identify** (a) Almoravids, (b) Sundiata, (c) Sonni Ali, (d) Askia Muhammad.
2. How did the gold-salt trade develop between West Africa and North Africa?
3. How did the arrival of Muslim traders affect West Africa?
4. How did the Hausa states differ from kingdoms such as Mali or Songhai?
5. *Critical Thinking* **Recognizing Causes and Effects** (a) Describe two short-term effects of Mansa Musa's hajj. (b) What do you think was the most important long-term effect?
6. *ACTIVITY* Write an art review comparing the Benin bronze above to a piece of sculpture from an earlier chapter.

# Trade Routes of East Africa

## Guide for Reading

■ How did the kingdom of Axum emerge as a prosperous state?

■ What religious traditions influenced East Africa?

■ What trade networks linked East Africa to other regions?

According to Ethiopian tradition, the first emperor of Ethiopia was the son of the Hebrew king Solomon and Makeda, the Queen of Sheba. The ancient chronicle *The Glory of Kings* tells how Makeda journeys to Jerusalem after hearing of Solomon's wisdom. "Learning is better than treasures of silver and gold," she says. The queen spends six months at Solomon's court, gathering knowledge to bring back to her people.

When Makeda is about to return to Sheba, Solomon gives her a ring and a blessing:

66May the peace of God be with thee. While I was sleeping . . . I had a vision. The sun which before my eyes was shining upon Israel, moved away. It went and soared above Ethiopia. It remained there. Who knows but that thy country may be blessed because of thee? Above all keep the truth which I have brought thee. Worship God.99

The East African kingdom of Ethiopia had proud roots in Jewish and Christian tradition. In later centuries, when other African kingdoms were coming under the influence of Islam, Ethiopia remained a center of Christianity.

## Axum and Its Successors

About A.D. 350, you will recall, King Ezana of Axum conquered and absorbed the ancient kingdom of Nubia. Located southeast of Nubia, Axum extended from the mountains of modern Ethiopia to the sun-bleached shores of the Red Sea. The peoples of Axum were descended from African farmers and from traders who had immigrated from Arabia. This merging of cultures introduced Hebrew religious traditions to Axum. It also gave rise to a unique written and spoken language, Geez.

**Trade.** The kingdom of Axum profited from the strategic location of its two main cities, the port of Adulis on the Red Sea and the upland capital city of Axum. From about 200 B.C. to A.D. 400, Axumites commanded a triangular trade network linking Africa, India, and the Mediterranean world.

Products from the African interior such as ivory, hides, rhinoceros horn, and gold passed through the city of Axum. To Adulis came ships carrying goods from farther down the coast of East Africa, or from India across the Indian Ocean. These goods would then flow north up the Red Sea to the Mediterranean, to the Middle East, Greece, Rome, and beyond.

**Christian converts.** In these great centers of international trade, Greek, Egyptian, Arab, and Jewish merchants mingled with African, Indian, and other traders. As elsewhere, ideas spread along with goods. The powerful king Ezana converted to Christianity in the 300s. As the new religion took root among the people, Christian churches replaced older temples.

At first, Christianity strengthened ties between Axum and the Mediterranean world.

▲ *Ethiopian rock church*

Then in the 600s, Islam came to dominate North Africa, leaving Axum an isolated island of Christianity. Weakened by civil war and cut off from its harbors, Axum slowly declined.

**Ethiopia, a Christian outpost.** Though Axum faded, its legacy survived among people of the interior uplands. The Axumites became the ancestors of the present-day Ethiopians, who maintained their independence through the centuries. Their survival was due in part to the unifying power of their Christian faith, which gave them a unique sense of their own identity. Geography helped, too, by providing the protection of rugged, mountainous terrain.

In the early 1200s, King Lalibela had a dozen churches carved into the mountains. (See the picture on page 294.) Ethiopian chronicles affirmed that the builders had divine help:

❝Angels joined the workers, the quarry men, the stone cutters, and the laborers. The angels worked with them by day and by themselves at night. The men . . . doubted whether the angels were doing this work because they could not see them, but Lalibela knew, because the angels, who understood his virtue, did not hide from him.❞

Over the centuries, Ethiopian Christians absorbed many traditions. They adapted traditional East African drum music and dances that are still used in church services today. They also observed Jewish holidays and dietary laws. (A separate group of Ethiopian Jews, the Falasha, survived in the mountains of Ethiopia until recent years.) Until the fall of the last emperor in 1974, Ethiopian rulers claimed descent from Solomon.

## East African City-States

While Axum declined, a string of commercial cities gradually rose along the East African coast. Since ancient times, Phoenician, Greek, Roman, and Indian traders had visited this coast. In the A.D. 600s, Arab and Persian merchants set up Muslim communities under the protection of local African rulers. Later, Bantu-speaking peoples migrated into the region and adopted Islam. Other waves of Asian immigrants from as far away as Indonesia added to the rich cultural mix.

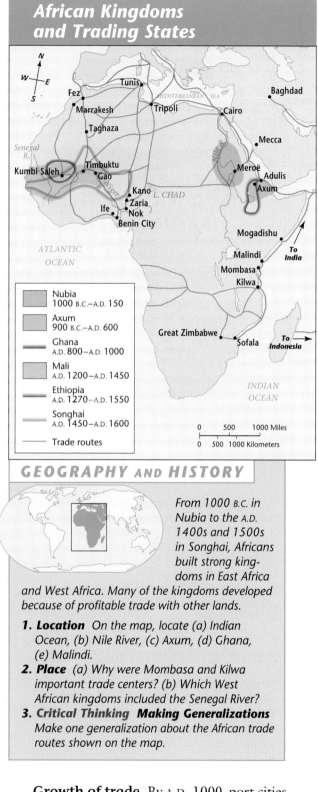

## African Kingdoms and Trading States

**Key:**
- Nubia 1000 B.C.–A.D. 150
- Axum 900 B.C.–A.D. 600
- Ghana A.D. 800–A.D. 1000
- Mali A.D. 1200–A.D. 1450
- Ethiopia A.D. 1270–A.D. 1550
- Songhai A.D. 1450–A.D. 1600
- Trade routes

0  500  1000 Miles
0  500  1000 Kilometers

**GEOGRAPHY AND HISTORY**

From 1000 B.C. in Nubia to the A.D. 1400s and 1500s in Songhai, Africans built strong kingdoms in East Africa and West Africa. Many of the kingdoms developed because of profitable trade with other lands.

1. **Location** On the map, locate (a) Indian Ocean, (b) Nile River, (c) Axum, (d) Ghana, (e) Malindi.
2. **Place** (a) Why were Mombasa and Kilwa important trade centers? (b) Which West African kingdoms included the Senegal River?
3. **Critical Thinking** *Making Generalizations* Make one generalization about the African trade routes shown on the map.

**Growth of trade.** By A.D. 1000, port cities like Mogadishu (mahg uh DIHSH oo), Kilwa, and Sofala, and offshore islands like Zanzibar, were thriving from trade across the Indian

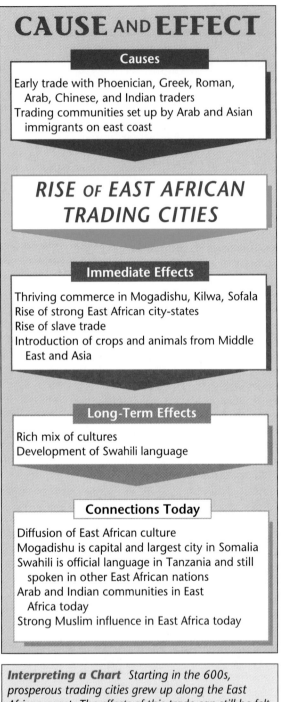

# CAUSE AND EFFECT

### Causes

Early trade with Phoenician, Greek, Roman, Arab, Chinese, and Indian traders

Trading communities set up by Arab and Asian immigrants on east coast

## RISE OF EAST AFRICAN TRADING CITIES

### Immediate Effects

Thriving commerce in Mogadishu, Kilwa, Sofala

Rise of strong East African city-states

Rise of slave trade

Introduction of crops and animals from Middle East and Asia

### Long-Term Effects

Rich mix of cultures

Development of Swahili language

### Connections Today

Diffusion of East African culture

Mogadishu is capital and largest city in Somalia

Swahili is official language in Tanzania and still spoken in other East African nations

Arab and Indian communities in East Africa today

Strong Muslim influence in East Africa today

**Interpreting a Chart** *Starting in the 600s, prosperous trading cities grew up along the East African coast. The effects of this trade can still be felt in Africa.* ■ *Why are there Arab and Indian communities in East Africa today?*

Trade helped local rulers build strong city-states. A Muslim visitor described Kilwa as "one of the most beautiful and well-constructed towns in the world." Its royal palace, built of coral and cut stone, stood on a high cliff overlooking the city. In the marketplace of Kilwa, merchants offered goods from both inland and coastal regions. A thriving slave trade also developed. Thousands of Africans were seized as slaves inland and sold to Persian traders.

**A blend of cultures.** International trade created a rich and varied mix of cultures in the East African city-states. Bantu-speaking Africans mingled in the streets with traders from Arabia and Southeast Asia. With the spread of Islam, Middle Eastern influences grew stronger. Marriages between African women and non-African Muslim men furthered the spread of Muslim culture. A wife's property rights allowed her husband to settle and own land. Their children often gained positions of leadership.

Eventually, the blend of cultures gave rise to a new language, Swahili. Swahili fused many Arabic words onto a Bantu base and was written in Arabic script.

## The Stones of Great Zimbabwe

To the south and inland from the coastal city-states, massive stone ruins sprawl across rocky hilltops near the great bend in the Limpopo River. Looming walls, a great palace, and cone-shaped towers testify to the powerful and prosperous capital of a great inland empire. Today, these impressive ruins are known as Great Zimbabwe, which means "great stone buildings."

Europeans who came upon these ruins in the 1800s thought they were the work of the ancient Phoenicians. In fact, the builders were a succession of Bantu-speaking peoples who settled in the region between 900 and 1500. The newcomers brought improved farming skills, iron, and mining methods. On the relatively fer-

Ocean. Riding the monsoon winds, merchant vessels sailed northeast to India between April and August, and returned to East Africa between December and March.

**ISSUES** *For* **TODAY** Trading patterns encouraged a blending of diverse cultures in the city-states of coastal East Africa. How can economic links lead to cultural diffusion?

tile land, they produced enough food to support a growing population.

**Economy and government.** We know little about how this civilization developed, but it probably reached its height about 1300. By then, it had tapped nearby gold resources and created profitable commercial links with coastal cities like Sofala. Archaeologists have found beads from India and porcelain from China, showing that Great Zimbabwe was part of a trade network that reached across the Indian Ocean.

Very little is known about the government in Great Zimbabwe. Scholars have suggested, however, that the ruler of Great Zimbabwe was a god-king who presided over a large court. He may have shared authority with a powerful queen mother and nine queens, each of whom had her own court. A central bureaucracy ruled an inner ring of provinces, while appointed governors had authority in more distant villages.

**Decline.** By 1500, Zimbabwe was in decline. Some scholars suggest that overfarming had exhausted the soil. Civil war and dwindling trade probably contributed to the breakup of Zimbabwe. By then, Portuguese traders were pushing inland to find the source of gold that reached the coast. They failed to discover the gold mines, and their intrusion helped undermine later small states that formed in the region.

## SECTION 3 REVIEW

1. **Identify** (a) Queen of Sheba, (b) Ezana, (c) Geez, (d) Lalibela, (e) Swahili.
2. Why was Axum a key trading center for three continents?
3. What religious traditions came together in Ethiopia?
4. What evidence suggests that Great Zimbabwe was a center of trade?
5. *Critical Thinking* **Analyzing Information** (a) Why did Ethiopia become increasingly isolated over the centuries? (b) What might have helped it survive as an independent kingdom?
6. *ACTIVITY* Create a map showing trade networks and goods exchanged between East Africa, Asia, and the Middle East.

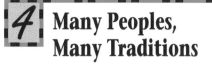

# 4 Many Peoples, Many Traditions

## Guide for Reading

- How did African peoples adapt to different environments?
- What bonds held African societies together?
- How did art and literature strengthen African societies?
- **Vocabulary** *slash-and-burn agriculture, nuclear family, patrilineal, matrilineal, lineage, griot*

At harvest time, the Kikuyu (kee KOO yoo) people of East Africa offered an ancient prayer of thanksgiving to their traditional gods:

66Mwene-Nyaga, you who have brought us rain and have given us good harvest, let people eat grain of this harvest calmly and peacefully. . . . Guard us against illness of people or our herds and flocks so that we may enjoy this season's harvest in peace.99

In West African mosques, Muslims recited a different prayer: "Praise be to God, Lord of the Universe, the Compassionate, the Merciful."

Differing religious traditions contributed to the diversity of the vast continent of Africa. At the same time, they also formed bonds that held individual societies together.

## Adapting to the Land

Bantu peoples, you will recall, gradually migrated across Africa, bringing farming skills and knowledge of ironworking to its many regions. Wherever they settled, they adapted to local environments and absorbed ideas from the peoples they encountered. Trade or other contacts brought additional changes. As a result, the ways of life of African societies varied greatly from place to place.

**Hunters and food gatherers.** The great Bantu migrations pushed the earliest hunting and food-gathering peoples of Africa to fringe areas. The Khoisan people, for example, adapted to the harsh desert conditions of the Kalahari by gathering edible roots and herbs and hunting small game.

Because food was scarce, these hunting-gathering people lived in small bands numbering only about 20 or 30. Their knowledge of the natural world, however, was unmatched by city dwellers or farming villagers. They could track animals across long distances and could identify the food and healing properties of many different plants.

**Herding and fishing.** In parts of the savanna free from the tsetse fly, some peoples raised herds of cattle. Because of limited grass for grazing, these societies were often nomadic. In general, the men herded and hunted, while the women raised food in small gardens. To protect their herds against raiders, these societies perfected skills in warfare.

Along the coasts and rivers, fish was the basic food source for some people. Most fishing peoples used nets. They traded any surplus fish for grain, animal skins, and other products made by people who lived inland. Some fishing areas had enough food resources to support large populations.

**Settled farming societies.** Farming communities raised a variety of crops from grains to root crops like yams or tree crops like bananas. Most farming peoples practiced a method that is today called slash-and-burn agriculture. They cleared forest and brush land with iron axes and hoes, then burned the remains, using the ash for fertilizer. Because the land lost its fertility within a few years, villagers would move on to clear other land. Eventually, after giving the soil time to renew its fertility, they might return to the abandoned fields.

## Forms of Village Government

Farming peoples generally lived in tightknit communities and helped one another in tasks such as clearing the land, planting, and harvesting. Both men and women planted, but usually were responsible for different crops. Political patterns varied, depending in part on the size of the communities that the land could support. However, village governments often had similar features.

**Sharing power.** In these pre-urban societies, power was usually shared among a number of people rather than centralized in the hands of a single leader. In some villages, a chief had a good deal of authority, but in many others, elders made the major decisions. Sometimes, older men would supervise religious ceremonies, while younger men made decisions about war. In some places, especially in parts of West Africa, women took the dominant role in the marketplace or acted as official peacemakers in the village.

Villages often made decisions by a process known as consensus. In open discussions, people whose opinions were valued voiced their views before a general agreement was reached. The opinions of older women and men usually held the greatest weight. People also exercised authority as members of village associations. For example, religious and market associations gave women a way to voice their concerns about village matters.

Villages that were ruled by a larger kingdom like Songhai had to obey decisions made at a distant court. These villagers, like those in China or India, had to pay taxes and provide soldiers to the central government.

**The kingdom of Kongo.** The kingdom of Kongo, which flourished about 1500 in the forest zone of present-day Zaire, illustrates one form of government organization. It consisted of many villages grouped into districts and provinces and governed by officials appointed by the king. Each village had its own chief, a man chosen on the basis of the descent of his mother's family.

In theory, the king of Kongo had absolute power. In fact, that power was limited. The king was chosen by a board of electors and had to govern according to traditional laws. Unlike rulers of West African states, who maintained strong standing armies, kings of Kongo depended on a system of military service that called upon men to fight only in times of need. Through local governors, the king collected taxes either in goods or in cowrie shells, a common African currency.

The organization of Kongo was just one type of African government. In many regions, people belonged to small local societies without a centralized government.

## Family Patterns

In Africa, as elsewhere, the family was the basic unit of society. Patterns of family life varied. In hunting and gathering societies, for example, the nuclear family was typical, with parents and children living and working together as a unit. In other African communities, people lived in joint families. Several generations shared the same complex of houses.

**Lines of descent.** Family organization varied in other ways as well. Some families were patrilineal, that is, important kinship ties, such as inheritance and residence, were passed through the father's side. Other families were matrilineal, with inheritance and descent traced through the mother's side. In a patrilineal culture, a bride would move to her husband's village and become part of his family. In a matrilineal culture, the husband joined his wife's family in her village.

Matrilineal cultures also forged strong ties between brothers and sisters. Brothers were expected to protect their sisters, while sisters made their sons available to help their brothers when ever needed.

**Wider ties.** Each family belonged to a lineage, or group of households who claimed a common ancestor. Several lineages formed a clan that traced its descent to an even more remote and often legendary ancestor. Belonging to a particular family, lineage, or clan gave people a strong sense of community values. Elders taught both girls and boys their special roles in the community along with their clan's history and religious beliefs.

An individual's place in society was also determined by a system of age grades. An age grade included all girls or boys born in the same year. Each age grade had particular responsibilities and privileges. In the older age grades, children began to take part in village activities, which created social ties beyond the family.

## Religious Beliefs

Across Africa, religious beliefs were varied and complex. Like Hindus or ancient Greeks and Romans, village Africans worshiped many gods and goddesses. Along with all ancient peoples, they identified the forces of nature with divine spirits and tried to influence those forces

*Village Life* This sculpted panel depicts people at work in an agricultural village. For most Africans, the activities of daily life revolved around family and community. Each individual was expected to help provide for the needs of the group. **Economics and Technology** What economic activities are depicted in this sculpture?

## Traditions in Fabric

The color, weave, and pattern of a fabric often reveals its cultural origin. From the tartan plaids of Scotland to the colorful batiks of Indonesia, these unique styles form part of a cultural heritage that has been passed from generation to generation.

**Linking Past and Present**  Why do you think clothing in kente patterns has become popular in the United States?

**PAST**  *The sample of kente cloth below was produced by the Ashanti people of West Africa. The beautiful fabric is typically made of silk, with woven strips of multicolored design. Ashanti kings and chieftains wore kente as a symbol of their power and prestige.*

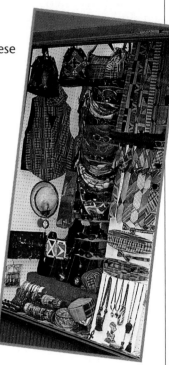

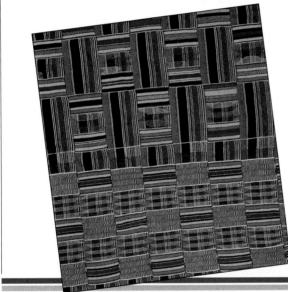

**PRESENT**  *This New York shop has an interesting collection of African wares. Customers may purchase American-style ties, belts, and other clothing in a variety of traditional African patterns.*

through the rituals and ceremonies that they practiced.

Village elders called upon certain spirits to bring rain or good harvests. To cure illnesses or other troubles, specially trained healers mingled their skills in herbal medicine with prayers to the gods. Diviners sought advice about the future from the spirit world.

Many African peoples believed that a single, unknowable supreme being stood above all the other gods and goddesses. This supreme being was the creator and ruler of the universe and was helped by the lesser spirits, who were closer to the people. Like the Chinese, many African peoples believed that the spirits of their ancestors were present on Earth. Just as Christians in me-

dieval Europe called on the saints for help, people in Africa turned to the spirits of their departed ancestors.

Christianity and Islam, as you have seen, influenced peoples in some parts of Africa. Converts often associated the God of Christians and Muslims with their traditional supreme being. In this way, Christianity and Islam absorbed many local practices and beliefs.

### African Arts

In art and architecture, African traditions extend far back in time to the ancient rock paintings of the Sahara. The pyramids of Egypt and Nubia, the rock churches of Ethiopia, and the stones of Great Zimbabwe bear lasting witness to the creative power of these early civilizations. Sadly, many wooden buildings and works of art have not survived the ages.

African artists created works in ivory, wood, and bronze. Sometimes, their work was decorative. Artisans wove and dyed cloth, inscribed jugs and bowls, and shaped bracelets and neck ornaments simply to beautify them. Much art, though, served social and religious purposes.

Art strengthened bonds within the community and linked both the makers and the users of the work. Patterns used to decorate textiles, baskets, swords, and other objects had important meanings. Often, they identified an object as the work of a particular clan or possession of royalty. Boldly patterned kente cloth was once worn only by West African rulers or members of the royal family.

In Africa, as elsewhere, much art was closely tied to religion. Statues and other objects were used in religious ceremonies. In many rituals, leaders wore impressively carved wooden masks decorated with cowrie shells or grass. Once the mask was in place, both the wearer and the viewers could feel the presence of the spiritual force it represented. As you will read, the stylized forms of African masks and other works had a dramatic influence on the development of modern art in the western world.

### Literary Traditions

African societies preserved their histories and values through both oral and written literature. Ancient Egypt, Nubia, and Axum left written records of their past. Later, Arabic provided a common written language for peoples in parts of Africa influenced by Islam. African Muslim scholars gathered in cities like Timbuktu and Kilwa as well as in Cairo and other North African centers. Documents in Arabic offer invaluable evidence about law, religion, and history.

Oral traditions date back many centuries. In West Africa, griots (GREE ohs), or professional poets, recited ancient stories. They preserved both histories and traditional folk tales in the same way that the epics of Homer or Aryan India were passed orally from generation to generation.

Griots often used riddles to sharpen the wits of the audience. The following traditional riddles have been handed down by the Yoruba people of present-day Nigeria:

> **66**We call the dead—they answer.
>   We call the living—they do not answer.
>
> Two tiny birds
> Jump over two hundred trees.**99**

The answer to the first riddle is "leaves." Dead leaves make noise when stepped on, but fresh ones do not. The second riddle refers to the eyes, which can see over long distances.

Histories praised the heroic deeds of famous ancestors or kings. Folk tales, which blended fanciful stories with humor and sophisticated word play, taught important moral lessons. Oral literature, like religion and art, thus fostered a sense of community and common values among peoples of Africa.

## SECTION 4 REVIEW

1. **Define** (a) slash-and-burn agriculture, (b) nuclear family, (c) patrilineal, (d) matrilineal, (e) lineage, (f) griot.
2. Describe three types of African society.
3. (a) How did family patterns vary across Africa? (b) How did the age-grade system strengthen community ties?
4. How was art connected to religion in African cultures?
5. *Critical Thinking* **Analyzing Information** How might a matrilineal line of descent allow women to excercise greater authority in village affairs?
6. *ACTIVITY* Using the Yoruba riddles on this page as a model, create three riddles about the world around you.

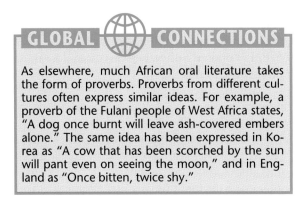

**GLOBAL CONNECTIONS**

As elsewhere, much African oral literature takes the form of proverbs. Proverbs from different cultures often express similar ideas. For example, a proverb of the Fulani people of West Africa states, "A dog once burnt will leave ash-covered embers alone." The same idea has been expressed in Korea as "A cow that has been scorched by the sun will pant even on seeing the moon," and in England as "Once bitten, twice shy."

# World Literature

## Sundiata

**Introduction** *The epic of Sundiata, founder of Mali, is part of Africa's long tradition of oral literature. Like the* Mahabharata *in India or the* Iliad *in Greece, the* Sundiata *epic was passed down from memory for many centuries before being written down. This version was translated in the 1960s by Djibril Tamsir Niane, who heard the tale from a griot.*

*The epic recounts the efforts of young Sundiata to reclaim his father's kingdom from his enemy Soumaoro (soo mah AWR oh), king of Sosso. In it, details of battle are mixed with praise of Sundiata's courage, his distinguished ancestors, and his supernatural powers. In the following passage, Sundiata and Soumaoro confront each other on the eve of the final battle.*

Sundiata went and pitched camp at Dayala in the valley of the Niger. Now it was he who was blocking Soumaoro's road to the south. . . .

Soumaoro advanced as far as Krina, near the village of Dayala on the Niger, and decided to assert his rights before joining battle. Soumaoro knew that Sundiata also was a sorcerer, so, instead of sending an embassy, he committed his words to one of his owls. The night bird came and perched on the roof of Sundiata's tent and spoke. Sundiata in his turn sent his own to Soumaoro. Here is the dialogue of the sorcerer kings:

"Stop, young man. Henceforth I am the king of Mali. If you want peace, return to where you came from," said Soumaoro.

"I am coming back, Soumaoro, to recapture my kingdom. If you want peace you will make amends to my allies and return to Sosso where you are the king."

"I am king of Mali by force of arms. My rights have been established by conquest."

"Then I will take Mali from you by force of arms and chase you from my kingdom."

"Know, then, that I am the wild yam of the rocks; nothing will make me leave Mali."

"Know, also that I have in my camp seven master smiths who will shatter the rocks. Then, yam, I will eat you."

"I am the poisonous mushroom that makes the fearless ill."

"As for me, I am the ravenous rooster, the poison does not matter to me."

"Behave yourself, little boy, or you will burn your foot, for I am the red-hot cinder."

"But me, I am the rain that extinguishes the cinder; I am the boisterous torrent that will carry you off."

"I am the mighty silk-cotton tree that looks from on high on the tops of other trees."

"And I, I am the strangling creeper that climbs to the top of the forest giant."

"Enough of this argument. You shall not have Mali."

"Know that there is not room for two kings on the same skin, Soumaoro; you will let me have your place."

"Very well, since you want war I will wage war against you, but I would have you know that I have killed nine kings. . . ."

"Prepare yourself, Soumaoro, for it will be long before the calamity that is going to crash down upon you and yours comes to an end."

Thus Sundiata and Soumaoro spoke together. After the war of mouths, swords had to decide the issue. . . .

In the evening, to raise the men's spirits, Sundiata gave a great feast, for he was anxious that his men should wake up happy in the morning. . . . Sundiata's griot, in front of the whole army, called to mind the history of old Mali. He praised Sundiata, seated amidst his lieutenants, in this manner:

"Now I address myself to you, Sundiata, I speak to you king of Mali, to whom dethroned monarchs flock. The time foretold to you is now coming. Sundiata, kingdoms and empires are in the likeness of man; like him they are born, they grow and disappear. Each king embodies one moment of that life. Formerly, the

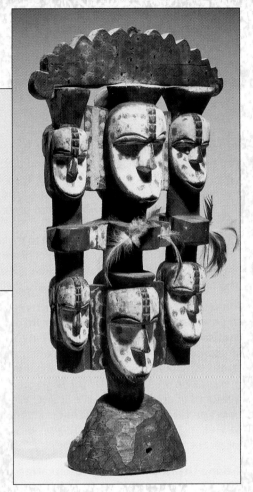

**Ceremonial Headdress** *Veneration of ancestors played an important role in many traditional African religions. In the* Sundiata *epic, the griot takes great pains to recount the king's exalted ancestry. Elsewhere in West Africa, headdresses like the one at the right were used in religious ceremonies. Through dance and ritual, the people thanked ancestors for successful harvests and honored great warriors of the past.* **Religions and Value Systems** *Name another culture in which veneration of ancestors played an important role.*

kings of Ghana extended their kingdom over all the lands, but the circle has closed and the kings of Ghana are nothing more than petty princes in a desolate land. Today, another kingdom looms up, powerful, the kingdom of Sosso. Humbled kings have brought their tribute to Sosso, Soumaoro's arrogance knows no more bounds and his cruelty is equal to his ambition. . . . The kingdom of Sosso is but the growth of yesterday, whereas that of Mali dates from ancient times. Each kingdom has its childhood, but Soumaoro wants to force the pace, and so Sosso will collapse under him like a horse worn out beneath its rider. . . .

"You are the outgrowth of Mali just as the silk-cotton tree is the growth of the earth, born of deep and mighty roots. To face the tempest the tree must have long roots and gnarled branches. . . . You are the son of Nare Maghan, but you are also the son of your mother Sogolon, the buffalo-woman, before whom powerless sorcerers shrank in fear. You have the strength and majesty of the lion, you have the might of the buffalo. . . .

"Tomorrow, allow me to sing the 'Song of the Vultures' over the bodies of the thousands of Sossos whom your sword will have laid low before evening."

Source: D. T. Niane, *Sundiata: An Epic of Old Mali* (Harlow, England: Longman Group Ltd., 1965).

## Thinking About Literature

1. **Vocabulary** Use the dictionary to find the meanings of the following words: embassy, amends, ravenous, boisterous, torrent, embodies, tempest.
2. (a) How do Sundiata and Soumaoro conduct their war of words on the eve of the battle? (b) Describe the nature of their conversation.
3. (a) What does Sundiata's griot say about the nature of empires? (b) Why does he predict that Soumaoro is doomed to failure? (c) What importance does the griot give to Sundiata's ancestry?
4. *Critical Thinking* **Drawing Conclusions** People went to great pains to memorize lengthy epics like *Sundiata,* the *Mahabharata,* and the *Iliad.* Why do you think they felt it was important to pass down these stories?

# Skills for Success

## Making Presentations

Effective presentations are the result of good planning. Before you go before a group of people to present information, you must spend time organizing your information, deciding how best to present it, and practicing the presentation aloud.

Imagine that you have been assigned to make a presentation on African arts to a group of history students in a lower grade. The following steps can help you prepare your presentation more effectively.

**1 Make a list of questions to be answered in your presentation and gather information to answer them.** (a) Look at the list of possible questions below. Which of these questions should you try to answer in your presentation on African arts? (b) What other questions might you add to the list? (c) What pages of this textbook provide information on African arts? (d) Where else could you look to locate such information?

**2 Define the goal of your presentation and identify your audience.** A presentation can have several goals. For example, your main goal could be to present a point of view, to persuade, to entertain, or to inform. Your approach to the topic will depend on the attitudes, interests, and knowledge of your audience. (a) What do you think would be the main goal of your presentation on African arts? (b) Who is your audience? How much do you think they know about art? About Africa? How much interest do you think they would have in the topic? (c) How might the answers to these questions affect your presentation? (d) How would your approach be different if you were making the presentation to a group of art students from your own class?

**3 Prepare an outline and a list of key words to guide you during the presentation.** Look back at your list of questions and arrange them in order. Then, jot down key words that will help you remember what you want to say. Choose visual aids that you could

use to illustrate your presentation. (a) Which question should you answer first during your presentation? Why? (b) Which question should you answer last? Why? (c) What key words would help you remember the answers to these questions? (d) Why should you avoid writing out your entire presentation and then reading it to your audience? (e) What pictures in this chapter could you use to illustrate your presentation?

**4 Practice your presentation aloud.** As you practice, time yourself and evaluate your delivery. Check that you are speaking clearly, that you are not speaking too fast or too slowly, and that you are keeping your audience in mind. (a) Why is it important to time your presentation? (b) What are the dangers of speaking too quickly? Too slowly?

*Beyond the Classroom* Imagine that a church or community group has asked you to make a presentation about one of your hobbies. Choose a topic. Write down five questions you would address in your presentation. Next to each question, jot down key words to help you remember what you plan to say. Make a list of five visuals that you could use in your presentation.

---

*Possible Questions to Be Answered in the Presentation*

**A.** What materials did African artists use?

**B.** Why did Nubian rulers move their capital to Meroë?

**C.** What was the purpose behind much early African art?

**D.** What skills did artisans of Benin develop?

**E.** How did the camel revolutionize trade in Africa?

**F.** How did African art influence the development of modern art?

**G.** What are the unique qualities of African art?

**H.** What family patterns were found in African societies?

**I.** Why is it worthwhile to learn about the art of Africa?

---

## Building Vocabulary

Write sentences using *five* of the vocabulary words from this chapter, leaving blanks where the vocabulary words would go. Exchange your sentences with another student and fill in the blanks on each other's lists.

## Reviewing Chapter Themes

1. **Geography and History** Describe the role of each of the following in the development of African societies and ways of life: (a) the Sahara, (b) the savanna, (c) surrounding oceans and seas.
2. **Diversity** (a) How did the Bantu migrations contribute to the diversity of African cultures? (b) Why did East Africa become a cultural mixing ground? (c) Describe how two languages of Africa developed.
3. **Global Interaction** (a) Why did powerful trading empires emerge in West Africa? (b) How did the spread of Islam influence the development of these kingdoms?
4. **Art and Literature** What purposes did the arts and literature serve in African cultures? Use one example shown or discussed in the chapter to illustrate your answer.

## Thinking Critically

1. **Analyzing Fine Art** Compare the pictures on pages 24 and 287. (a) What similarities in style can you see? (b) Based on what you have read, how would you account for these similarities? (★ See *Skills for Success,* page 368.)
2. **Linking Past and Present** Most modern African nations regained their independence from European rule between 1957 and 1979. (a) Look at the map of modern Africa on page 986. Which nations took their names from ancient African kingdoms? (b) Why do you think these nations chose these names?
3. **Analyzing Information** Reread the selection from *The Glory of Kings* on page 294. (a) What reason does Makeda give for going to Jerusalem? (b) According to Solomon, what is the great lesson he has taught Makeda? What prediction does he make? (c) Why do you think the

Queen of Sheba has been honored in Ethiopia? (d) Would you consider *The Glory of Kings* a reliable source of historical information? Why or why not?
4. **Predicting Consequences** (a) Describe the process of slash-and-burn agriculture. (b) What might be some dangers of the extensive use of slash-and-burn methods? (★ See *Skills for Success,* page 974.)
5. **Drawing Conclusions** From what you have learned about African religions, why do you think many Africans found it easy to accept the monotheism of Christianity or Islam?
6. **Comparing** (a) Describe three traditions that created social bonds in African communities. (b) How are these traditions similar to the traditions that create social bonds in your community? How are they different?

### *For Your Portfolio*

Your local library is hosting an international literature festival. As an African griot, you have been asked to recite a traditional tale from an African culture.

1. Begin your preparation by reviewing the section titled Literary Traditions on page 301.
2. Use resources at the public or school library to find a traditional African folk tale or historical event that you might retell. For example, you might use one of the Anansi stories. Or you might use a Cinderella tale such as the one from Zimbabwe retold in *Mufaro's Beautiful Daughters* by John Steptoe. Learn what you can about the background of the story you choose.
3. Read the tale or history several times until you are familiar with it and can retell it in your own words. Practice telling the tale aloud, using different voices, facial expressions, and gestures to make it come alive.
4. Prepare an introduction to your presentation in which you explain the origin and significance of your story. Be sure to identify which African people originated the tale and be able to show on a map where they lived. You might want to include a riddle or two as authentic griots did.
5. Introduce your story to the class and then recite it. Be prepared to explain any special customs or terms that appear in the tale.

# Spread of Civilizations
# in East Asia

## (500–1603)

## CHAPTER OUTLINE

1  Two Golden Ages of China
2  The Mongol and Ming Empires
3  Korea and Its Traditions
4  An Island Empire Emerges
5  Japan's Feudal Age

Many people in China distrusted the empress Wu Zhao (WOO JOW). From humble beginnings, she had risen to a position of influence with the emperor. After his death, she had ruthlessly taken power into her own hands, even unseating her own sons. No other woman had ever dared to assume the title of emperor!

Now, rival princes and Confucian scholars were raising the banner of revolt against her. Lo Binwang, a respected poet, wrote a declaration condemning the empress as a "vile character." He issued a fiery call to arms:

❝Rise, rise, all men! . . . Are your hearts dead? Does not the royal will still ring in your ears? Consider, the orphans of our emperor are left helpless and defenseless while their father's grave is hardly dry!❞

Soon, the declaration came to the attention of Wu Zhao herself. "Who wrote it?" she demanded angrily.

"Lo Binwang," replied her chief ministers. Surely, they thought, the poet would now feel Wu Zhao's wrath.

Surprisingly, the empress did not direct her anger at Lo Binwang. Rather, she berated her own ministers. Why had they failed to bring such a talented writer into her service? Like other educated Chinese, Wu prized a skilled and brilliant writer, no matter what side he was on.

In the late 600s, Wu Zhao became the only woman to rule China in her own name. Like many other rulers, she won power by combining political skill with ruthlessness. Many Chinese historians saw her as an evil adventurer. Others praised her for supporting Buddhism and recruiting able officials regardless of social standing. Her strong rule helped guide China through one of its most brilliant periods.

After the 500s, China again emerged as a united empire. "Barbarians" on the fringes of the Middle Kingdom admired and copied Chinese civilization. As a result, Chinese culture spread to neighboring lands. While Korea and Japan adopted much from China, they reshaped these traditions to fit their own distinct patterns of civilization.

**FOCUS ON** these questions as you read:

■ **Continuity and Change**
What traditions helped preserve Chinese civilization despite the rise and fall of dynasties?

■ **Global Interaction**
How did Chinese civilization come to influence people in Korea and Japan?

■ **Political and Social Systems**
How did Japan develop into a feudal society?

■ **Art and Literature**
What distinct literary and artistic traditions emerged in China and Japan?

## TIME AND PLACE

*An Enlightened Ruler* Emperors of the Tang dynasty helped create a golden age in China. This picture shows Ming Huang, or "Enlightened Emperor," on horseback. His achievements included reforming the political bureaucracy, restoring the canal system, and strengthening border defenses. He also established several music academies and supported the work of painters and writers. **Impact of the Individual** Why do you think this ruler was called "Enlightened Emperor"?

## HUMANITIES LINK

**Art History** Li Ching, *Buddhist Temple in the Hills After Rain* (page 313).
**Literature** In this chapter, you will encounter passages from the following works of literature: Li Bo, "Beside my bed the bright moonbeams glimmer" (page 313); Li Qingzhao, "Year after year I have watched" (page 313); Marco Polo, *A Description of the World* (page 317); *Songs of the Flying Dragons* (page 322); Sei Shonagon, *The Pillow Book*, (page 326); Sogi, "To live in the world" (page 327); Kenko, *Essays in Idleness* (page 330).

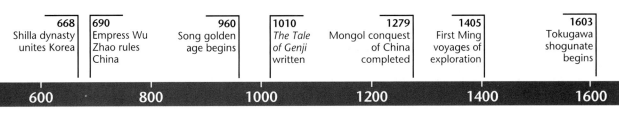

| **668**<br>Shilla dynasty<br>unites Korea | **690**<br>Empress Wu<br>Zhao rules<br>China | **960**<br>Song golden<br>age begins | **1010**<br>*The Tale<br>of Genji*<br>written | **1279**<br>Mongol conquest<br>of China<br>completed | **1405**<br>First Ming<br>voyages of<br>exploration | **1603**<br>Tokugawa<br>shogunate<br>begins |

| 600 | 800 | 1000 | 1200 | 1400 | 1600 |

# 1 Two Golden Ages of China

## Guide for Reading

- How did the Tang and Song dynasties restore Chinese culture and prosperity?

- How did social patterns reflect Confucian traditions?

- What were the artistic achievements of Tang and Song China?

- **Vocabulary** *tributary state, pagoda*

Slowly the artisan inscribed the Chinese characters onto a wood block. He carefully cut away the spaces between each one. One slip of the knife and the page would be ruined. With a brush, he then stroked velvety black ink onto the characters. Finally, he pressed a sheet of paper against the inked block. When he pulled it away, he had a beautifully printed page ready for binding.

The job required special attention because it was an important government order. In 932, the emperor asked for a printed copy of the Confucian classics. Using this system of woodblock printing, it would take 20 years to print all 130 volumes.

Woodblock printing was just one of the many significant inventions created in China between the 600s and 1200s. At a time when Europe was fragmented into many small feudal kingdoms, China remained a unified state under two powerful dynasties.

▲ *Emperor Tang Taizong*

## The Brilliant Tang

After the Han dynasty collapsed in 220, China remained a divided land for nearly 400 years. During this period, however, China escaped the grim decay that disrupted Western Europe after the fall of Rome. Farm production expanded and technology slowly improved. Buddhism spread, while learning and the arts continued. Even Chinese cities survived. Although invaders stormed northern China, they would often adopt Chinese civilization rather than demolish it.

Meanwhile, various Chinese dynasties rose and fell in the south. Despite frequent warfare, China's impulse toward unity and the old Confucian order remained strong. During the brief Sui dynasty (589–618), Emperor Sui Wendi reconquered most Han territory and reunited the north and south. But the Middle Kingdom was not restored to its earlier glory until the rule of the Tang (618–907) and, later, the Song (960–1279) dynasties.

**Building the Tang empire.** The first two Tang emperors were father and son, but the son was the driving force behind the dynasty. The father, Li Yuan, was a leading general under the Sui dynasty. When the Sui began to crumble, his ambitious son Li Shimin urged him to lead a revolt. Though only 16 years old, Li Shimin was already a war hero. Father and son crushed all rivals and firmly established the Tang dynasty.

Eight years later, Li Shimin compelled his aging father to step down and mounted the throne himself, taking the name Tang Taizong. Brilliant general, government reformer, famous historian, and master of the calligraphy brush, Tang Taizong would become the most admired of all Chinese emperors.

The Tang dynasty carried empire building to greater heights, conquering territories deep into Central Asia as far as present-day Afghanistan. Chinese armies forced the neighboring lands of Vietnam, Tibet, and Korea to become tributary states. That is, while these states remained independent, their rulers had to acknowledge Chinese supremacy and send regular tribute to the Tang emperor.

The size, wealth, and advanced civilization of Tang China deeply impressed nearby peoples. As you will read, students from Korea and Japan traveled to the Tang capital of Changan to learn about Chinese government, law, and arts.

**Government and the economy.** Tang rulers, such as Empress Wu Zhao, restored the Han system of uniform government throughout

**Porcelain Art** *Most ceramics from the Tang period, like these figures, have been found in tombs. Chinese artisans made porcelain by mixing a pure white clay called kaolin with a special mineral called china stone. They then baked the clay in kilns at temperatures exceeding 2,200° Fahrenheit.* **Economics and Technology** *Why do you think Chinese porcelain has been highly prized throughout the world?*

China. They rebuilt the bureaucracy and enlarged the civil service system to recruit talented officials trained in Confucian philosophy. They also set up schools to prepare male students for the exams and developed a flexible new law code.

Under a system of land reform, the Tang emperors redistributed land to peasants. This policy weakened the power of large landowners. At the same time, it increased government revenues, since the peasants could now pay taxes.

Under the Tang, a system of canals encouraged internal trade and transportation. The largest of these, the Grand Canal, linked the Hwang He and Yangzi rivers. As a result, food from farming regions in the south could be sent by water to the capital in the north. At the time, the Grand Canal was the longest waterway ever dug by human labor.

**Decline.** Like earlier dynasties, the Tang eventually weakened. Later Tang emperors lost China's northwestern territories in Central Asia to the Arabs. Government corruption, crushing taxes, drought, famine, and rebellions all contributed to the downward swing of the dynastic cycle. (See page 62.) In 907, a rebel general overthrew the last Tang emperor. This time, however, the chaos following the collapse of a dynasty did not last long.

## Prosperity Under the Song

In 960, a scholarly general, Zhao Kuangyin (JOW koo awng YEEN), reunited much of China and founded the Song dynasty. The Song ruled 319 years, slightly longer than the Tang, However, the Song controlled less territory than the Tang had. In addition, the Song faced the constant threat of invaders in the north. In the early 1100s, the battered Song retreated south of the Hwang He River. There, the Southern Song ruled for another 150 years from their new capital at Hangzhou (HAHNG JOH).

Despite military setbacks, the Song period was a golden age. Chinese wealth and culture dominated East Asia even when its armies did not. Under the Song, the Chinese economy expanded. The center of farming shifted from the millet and wheat-growing north to the rice paddies of the Yangzi and south. There, new strains of rice and improved irrigation methods helped peasants produce two rice crops a year. The rise in productivity created surpluses, allowing more people to pursue commerce, learning, or the arts.

Under the Song, as under the Tang, foreign trade flourished. Merchants arrived by land and sea from India, Persia, and the Middle East. The

## Science and Technology of Tang and Song China

| Invention | Description | Diffusion | Connections Today |
|---|---|---|---|
| **Mechanical clock** 700s | Chinese learned of water-powered clocks from Middle Easterners. Mechanical clocks used a complex series of wheels, shafts, and pins, turning at a steady rate, to tell exact time. | In early 1300s, European traders carried Chinese mechanical clocks westward. | Mechanical clocks have been largely replaced by quartz-crystal clocks. Today very accurate atomic clocks use steady frequency of energy changes in atoms to tell exact time. |
| **Gunpowder** 850 | Made from mixture of saltpeter, sulfur, and charcoal, all found in abundance in China; used first in fireworks, later in weapons. | Knowledge of gunpowder and its ingredients, carried by Arab traders, reached Europe in the late 1200s. | Gunpowder is still used today with much the same formula to make deadly weapons and brilliant fireworks. |
| **Smallpox vaccine** 900s | Small amounts of smallpox virus given to patients; the patient's own immune system then created antibodies to fight the disease; became widely used in China in the 1500s. | Idea spread to Turkish regions in the 1600s, where Europeans learned of it. | Led to later vaccines and to the science of immunology. |
| **Block printing**, 700s **Movable type**, 1040s | Based on earlier techniques such as seals (first used in the Middle East). In block printing, a full page of characters was carved onto a wooden block. Movable type was made up of pre-cut characters that were combined to form a page. | Printing spread to Korea; later carried to Japan by Buddhist monks. May have spread to Europe with Mongol armies. | Block printing today is used mainly for book illustrations and decorative arts. Movable type is being replaced by faster electronic typesetting, which is done by computer. |
| **Spinning wheel** 1000s | A belt turned a large wheel, which then turned a spindle on which thread was wound. | Probably spread to Europe by Italians who traveled to China during Mongol dynasty. | Spindles and wheels are still used in high-speed machinery to mass produce yarn and thread. |

*Interpreting a Chart* *The Tang and Song periods were golden ages, not only for the arts, but for science and technology as well. In addition to the developments shown on this chart, the Chinese also introduced paper money and pioneered the use of arches in bridge building. Many inventions traveled westward only after many centuries.* ■ *Which of the advances on this chart do you think probably had the greatest impact on history? Explain.*

Chinese built better ships, and their merchants carried goods to Southeast Asia in exchange for spices and special woods. Song porcelain has been found as far away as East Africa. To improve trade, the government issued paper money. China's cities, which had been mainly centers of government, now prospered as centers of trade. Several cities boasted populations over one million.

## Three Levels of Chinese Society

Under the Tang and Song, China was a well-ordered society. The emperor ruled over a splendid court filled with aristocratic families. The court stood at the center of a huge bureaucracy from which officials fanned out to every province and county in China.

**Gentry.** The two main classes of Chinese society were the gentry and the peasantry. The gentry were wealthy landowners. They valued scholarship more than physical labor. Most scholar-officials at court came from this class because they alone could afford to spend years studying the Confucian classics. Only a few lucky men passed the grueling civil service exam and won the most honored positions in government. (See Chapter 4.) When not in government service, the gentry often served in the provinces as allies of the emperor's officials.

The Song scholar-gentry supported a revival of Confucian thought, searching out old Confucian texts. New schools of thinkers reinterpreted Confucian ideas that emphasized social order based on duty, rank, and proper behavior. This Confucian revival stressed traditions of the past. Although corruption and greed existed among civil servants, the ideal Confucian official was a wise, kind, selfless, virtuous scholar who knew how to ensure harmony in society.

**Peasants.** Most Chinese were peasants who worked the land, living on what they produced. Drought and famine were a constant threat, but better tools and new crops did improve the lives of many peasants. To add to their income, some families produced handicrafts such as baskets or embroidery. They carried these products to nearby market towns to sell or trade for salt, tea, or iron tools.

Peasants lived in small, largely self-sufficient villages that managed their own affairs. "Heaven is high," noted one Chinese saying, "and the emperor far away." Peasants relied on one another rather than on the government. When disputes arose, a village leader and council of elders put pressure on the parties to resolve the problem. Only when these efforts failed did villagers take their disputes to the emperor's county representative.

Although the joint family was the ideal, few peasants could support several generations within a household. Still, both peasants and gentry valued family ties. They conducted ceremonies to consult the spirits of their ancestors for help with family problems.

In China, even peasants could move up in society through education and government service. If a bright peasant boy received an education and passed the civil service examinations, both he and his family rose in status.

**Merchants: prosperous but lowly.** In market towns and cities, some merchants acquired vast wealth. Still, according to Confucian tradition, merchants had an even lower social status than peasants because their riches came from the labor of others. An ambitious merchant therefore might buy land and educate at least one son to enter the ranks of the scholar-gentry.

The Confucian attitude toward merchants affected economic policy. Some rulers favored trade and commerce but sought to control it. They often restricted where foreign merchants could live and even limited the activities of private traders. Despite restrictions, Chinese trade flourished during Song times.

## Status of Women

Women seem to have had higher status in Tang and early Song times than they did later. Within the home, women were called upon to run family affairs. Wives and mothers-in-law had great authority and managed family finances, discipline, and servants. Still, within families, boys were valued more highly than girls were. To eliminate conflict within families, judges ruled that when a young woman married, she must completely become a part of her husband's family. She no longer could keep her dowry and could never remarry.

Women's subordinate position was reinforced in late Song times when the custom of

footbinding emerged. The practice probably began at the imperial court. The feet of young girls were bound with long strips of cloth, producing a lily-shaped foot about half the size of a foot that was allowed to grow normally. Tiny feet and a stilted walk became a symbol of female nobility and beauty. Footbinding was intensely painful, yet the custom survived because parents feared that a daughter with large feet would be unable to find a good husband. Eventually, the custom spread from the wealthy to the lower classes. Peasant families hoped that attractive daughters with lily feet would be able to marry into the gentry.

Not every girl in China had her feet bound. Peasants who relied on their daughters for field labor did not accept the practice, nor did some peoples like the Hakka of the southeastern mountains. Still, most women came to accept footbinding as a rite of passage. By making it impossible for women to leave home without assistance, the custom of footbinding reinforced the Confucian belief that women were "inside" people who did not do any outside work.

## A Flood of Literature

Prose and poetry flowed from the brushes of Tang and Song writers. Scholars produced works on philosophy, religion, and history. Short stories that often mixed fantasy, romance, and adventure made their first appearance in Chinese literature.

Still, among the gentry, poetry was the most respected form of Chinese literature. Confucian scholars were expected to master the skills of poetry. We know the names of some 200 major and 400 minor Tang and Song poets. Their works touched on Buddhist and Daoist themes as well as on social issues. Many poems reflected on the shortness of life and the immensity of the universe.

Probably the greatest Tang poet was Li Bo (LEE BOW). A zestful lover of life and freedom, he spent most of his life moving from place to place. He wrote some 2,000 poems celebrating harmony with nature or lamenting the passage of time. In one poem, he wrote of old memories:

> **66**Beside my bed the bright moonbeams
>     glimmer
> Almost like frost on the floor.
> Rising up, I gaze at the mountains
>     bathed in moonlight:
> Lying back, I think of my old home.**99**

A popular legend says that Li Bo drowned when he tried to embrace the reflection of the moon in a lake.

More realistic and less romantic were the poems of Li Bo's close friend Du Fu. His verses described the horrors of war or condemned the lavishness of the court. A later poet was Li Qingzhao (LEE CHING jow). The educated daughter of scholars, she wrote at a time when invasion threatened the Song dynasty. In this poem, Li Qingzhao describes the experience of women left behind when a loved one must go off to war:

> **66**Year after year I have watched
> My jade mirror. Now my rouge
> And creams sicken me.
> One more
> Year that he has not come back.
> My flesh shakes when a letter
> Comes from South of the River.**99**

## Achievements in the Arts

A prosperous economy supported the rich culture of Tang and Song China. The splendid palaces of the emperors were long ago destroyed, but statues, paintings, and ceramics have survived.

**Landscapes.** Along with poetry, painting and calligraphy were essential skills for the scholar-gentry. In both of these arts they sought balance and harmony through the mastery of simple strokes and lines. The Song period saw the triumph of Chinese landscape painting. Steeped in the Daoist tradition, painters sought to capture the spiritual essence of the natural world. "When you are planning to paint," instructed a Song artist, "you must always create a harmonious relationship between heaven and earth." (See the picture at right.)

Misty mountains and delicate bamboo forests dominated Chinese landscapes. Yet Chinese painters also produced realistic, vivid

### ART HISTORY

***Buddhist Temple in the Hills After Rain*** *This painting is believed to be the work of the Song artist Li Ching. Landscapes of the Song period were influenced by Confucianism, Daoism, and Buddhism. A landscape represented nature as a whole, while mountains and water had special symbolic meaning. Color was unimportant because the artist's goal was not to reproduce a realistic scene, but to convey a feeling. One artist explained, "Outwardly, nature has been my teacher, but inwardly I follow the springs of inspiration in my heart."* **Art and Literature** *Explain the meaning of this quotation.*

portraits of emperors, like those on pages 307 and 308. Other painters created lively scenes of city life.

**Sculpture and architecture.** Buddhist themes dominated sculpture and influenced Chinese architecture. Sculptors created striking statues of the Buddha. In fact, these statues created such a strong impression that, today, many people picture the Buddha as a Chinese god rather than an Indian holy man. In China, the Indian stupa evolved into the graceful pagoda, a multistoried temple with eaves that curved up at the corners.

**Porcelain.** The Chinese perfected skills in making porcelain, a shiny, hard pottery, that was prized as the finest in the world. (See the picture on page 309.) They developed beautiful glazes to decorate vases, tea services, and other objects that westerners would later call "chinaware." Artists also produced porcelain figures of neighing camels, elegant court ladies playing polo, and bearded foreigners fresh from their travels on the Silk Road.

## SECTION 1 REVIEW

1. **Identify** (a) Sui Wendi, (b) Tang Taizong, (c) Wu Zhao, (d) Grand Canal, (e) Zhao Kuangyin, (f) Li Bo.
2. **Define** (a) tributary state, (b) pagoda.
3. How did the rise of the Tang and Song dynasties benefit China?
4. (a) Describe the social structure of China under the Tang and Song dynasties. (b) Why did merchants have such a low status in the Chinese social system?
5. (a) What ideas and traditions shaped Chinese painting? (b) What themes did Chinese poets address?
6. *Critical Thinking* **Applying Information** "Distant water cannot put out a nearby fire." How does this saying reflect the nature of village government under the Tang and Song dynasties?
7. *ACTIVITY* Imagine that you are a young girl or the parent of a young girl in late Song China. Write a letter or poem in which you express your feelings about the custom of footbinding.

## 2 The Mongol and Ming Empires

### Guide for Reading

■ How did the Mongols create a world empire?

■ What was the legacy of the Mongol conquest?

■ How did Ming rulers reassert Chinese greatness?

In the early 1200s, the Song were threatened by a new wave of invaders from the north. You have already met the leader of this invasion. He was the brilliant Mongol chieftain Genghiz Khan, who now turned his attention to subduing China.

### *The Mighty Mongol War Machine*

Genghiz Khan was born Temujin, or Iron-smith, in 1162. According to Mongol tradition, he was marked for greatness from the moment of his birth. His mother had been shocked to see her newborn baby holding a clump of blood in his hand. His father, a minor chief, quickly consulted a Mongol holy man. "This child," predicted the seer, "will rule the world." The prediction was not far wrong.

**Early years.** When Temujin was born, the Mongols were a nomadic people who grazed their horses and sheep on the steppe grasslands of Central Asia. While he was still a boy, his father was poisoned by a rival clan. Unprepared to lead his father's armies, Temujin suffered major disasters in battle. At the age of 15, he was taken prisoner. For the rest of his life, he never forgot the humiliation of being locked in a wooden collar and paraded before his enemies.

Escaping to the mountains, the youth wandered as an outcast among drifting clans. As he grew up, he acquired a reputation for courage and a genius for military leadership. He first took revenge on the clan that had enslaved him. Then, before the age of 45, he was elected

**Ready for Battle**
Mongol warriors carried two bows—one for short-range firing and another for long-range. Other weapons included small swords, javelins, and hooked lances for dragging enemy soldiers off their saddles. Leather stirrups, like the ones shown here, helped warriors stay on horseback while engaged in combat. **Diversity** Can you name another people whose warriors relied on skillful archery and horsemanship?

supreme ruler of all the Mongols. He was now known as Genghiz Khan, "World Emperor."

**Mongols in battle.** Genghiz Khan imposed strict military discipline and demanded absolute loyalty. Under his inspired leadership, Mongol armies swept to triumph. They were tough, skilled warriors who lived in the saddles of their shaggy ponies. They could travel for days at a time, eating only a few handfuls of grain and drinking mare's milk.

These highly trained, mobile armies were possibly the most skilled horsemen in the world. A later observer described the Mongols battle tactics:

66They keep hovering about the enemy, discharging their arrows first from one side and then from the other, occasionally pretending to flee, and during their flight shooting arrows backwards at their pursuers. . . . In this sort of warfare the adversary imagines he has gained a victory, when in fact he has lost the battle; for the Mongols . . . wheel about, and renewing the fight,

overpower his remaining troops. . . . Their horses are so well broken-in to quick changes of movement, that upon the signal given, they instantly turn in any direction, and by these rapid maneuvers many victories have been obtained.99

Mongol women were also great riders and fighters. Some women commanded their own military forces. Mostly, though, they took the responsibility of managing the needs of the camp, leaving the entire male population free for warfare.

As terrifying as the Mongol armies was Genghiz Khan's reputation for fierceness. He told his troops:

66The greatest joy is to conquer one's enemies, to pursue them, to seize their belongings, to see their families in tears, to ride their horses.99

Yet he could also be a generous victor. Once, an enemy soldier, standing alone against the advancing Mongols, shot Genghiz's horse out from under him. Genghiz not only spared the man's life, but rewarded his bravery by offering him a high post in the Mongol army.

**On to China.** As Mongol armies advanced into China, they faced the problem of attacking walled cities. They turned to Chinese and Turkish military experts to teach them to use cannon and other new weapons. Both the Mongols and Chinese launched missiles against each other from metal tubes filled with gunpowder. This use of cannon in warfare would soon spread westward to Europe.

Genghiz Khan did not live to complete the conquest of China. Still, before he died in 1227, he had shattered the settled lives of peoples across Eurasia and become the world's most successful conqueror. The domain of the "World Emperor" was indeed the largest the world had yet seen. ◼

### Effects of Mongol Domination

The heirs of Genghiz Khan continued to expand the Mongol empire. For the next 150 years, they dominated much of Asia. Their furious assaults toppled empires and spread destruction from southern Russia through Muslim lands in the Middle East to China. In China, the Mongols devastated the flourishing province of Sichuan (SECH WAHN) and annihilated its great capital city of Chengdu.

Once conquest was completed, though, the Mongols were not oppressive rulers. Often, they allowed conquered people to live much as they had before—as long as they regularly paid their tribute to the Mongols.

Genghiz Khan had set an example for his successors by ruling conquered lands with tolerance and justice. Although the Mongol warrior had no use for city life, he had respect for scholars, artists, and artisans. He listened to the ideas of Confucian and Muslim scholars, Buddhist monks, Christians, Jews, and Zoroastrians.

In the 1200s and 1300s, the sons and grandsons of Genghiz Khan established peace and order within their domains. Political stability set the stage for economic growth. Under the protection of the Mongols, who now controlled the great Silk Road, trade flourished across Eurasia. A contemporary noted that Mongol rule meant that people "enjoyed such a peace that a man might have journeyed from the land of sunrise to the land of sunset with a golden platter upon his head without suffering the least violence from anyone."

Cultural exchanges increased as foods, tools, inventions, and ideas spread along the trade routes. From China, the use of windmills and gunpowder moved westward. Techniques of papermaking reached the Middle East, while crops and trees from the Middle East were carried into East Asia.

### The Yuan: A Foreign Dynasty

Although Genghiz Khan had subdued northern China, the Mongols needed nearly 70 more years to conquer the south. Genghiz Khan's grandson, Kublai (KOO blī), finally toppled the last Song emperor in 1279. From his capital at Cambulac, present-day Beijing, Kublai Khan ruled all China as well as Korea, Tibet, and Vietnam.

**Government.** Kublai Khan tried to keep the Mongols from being absorbed into Chinese civilizations as other conquerors of China had been. He decreed that only Mongols could serve in the military. He also reserved the highest government jobs for Mongols or other non-Chinese officials whom he employed. Still, because the Mongols were too few to control so vast an empire, Kublai allowed Chinese officials to continue to rule the provinces.

Under Mongol rule, an uneasy mix of Chinese and foreign ways developed. Kublai adopted a Chinese name for his dynasty, the Yuan (yoo AHN), and turned Cambulac into a Chinese walled city. At the same time, he had Arab architects design his palace, and many rooms reflected Mongol steppe dwellings.

Kublai Khan was an able though demanding ruler. He rebuilt and extended the Grand Canal to his new capital, but at a terrible cost in human lives. He welcomed many foreigners to his court, including the African Muslim world traveler Ibn Battuta. (See page 254.)

**A western visitor.** The Italian merchant Marco Polo was one of many visitors to China during the Yuan dynasty. In 1271, he left Venice with his father and uncle, eventually reaching China by way of Persia and Central Asia. He spent 17 years in Kublai's service before he re-

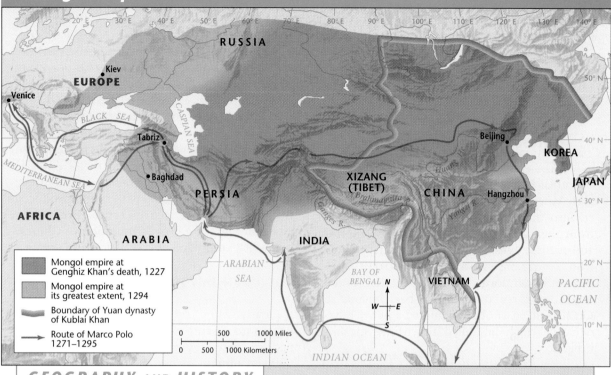

Map legend:
- Mongol empire at Genghiz Khan's death, 1227
- Mongol empire at its greatest extent, 1294
- Boundary of Yuan dynasty of Kublai Khan
- Route of Marco Polo 1271–1295

## GEOGRAPHY AND HISTORY

At its height, the Mongol empire was the largest in the world. One result of the Mongol conquest of China was increased contact between China and the western world. Marco Polo's visit to China also spurred cultural exchanges.

1. **Location** On the map, locate (a) Beijing, (b) Indian Ocean, (c) Hangzhou, (d) Venice.
2. **Region** Compare the extent of the Mongol empire in 1227 to the extent of the empire in 1294.
3. **Critical Thinking** **Linking Past and Present** Look at the Atlas maps on pages 988 and 990. Identify the present-day countries through which Marco Polo would have to travel if he made his journey to Asia today.

turned to Venice by sea, visiting Southeast Asia and India.

In *A Description of the World,* Marco Polo left a vivid account of the wealth and splendor of China. Here, he describes the royal palace of Kublai Khan:

66The palace itself has a very high roof. Inside, the walls of the halls and chambers are all covered with gold and silver and decorated with pictures of dragons and birds and horsemen and various breeds of beasts and scenes of battle. The ceiling is similarly adorned, so that there is nothing to be seen anywhere but gold and pictures. The hall is so vast and so wide that a meal might well be served there for more than 6,000 men.99

Polo also described the efficient royal mail system, with couriers riding swift ponies along the empire's well-kept roads. Furthermore, he reported, the city of Hangzhou was 10 or 12 times the size of Venice, one of Italy's richest city-states.

As you read, Marco Polo's book astonished readers in medieval Europe. In the next centuries, Polo's reports sparked European interest in the riches of Asia.

**Other contacts.** As long as the Mongol empire prospered, contacts between Europe and Asia continued. The Mongols tolerated a variety of beliefs. The pope sent Christian priests to Beijing, while Muslims set up their own communities in China. Meanwhile, some Chinese products moved toward Europe. They included gunpowder, porcelain, and playing cards.

## *The Ming: Restoring Chinese Rule*

The Yuan dynasty declined after the death of Kublai Khan. Most Chinese despised the foreign Mongol rulers. Confucian scholars retreated into their own world, seeing little to gain from the barbarians. Heavy taxes, corruption, and natural disasters led to frequent uprisings. Zhu Yuanzhang (DZOO yoo ahn DZUHNG), a peasant leader, forged a rebel army that toppled the Mongols and pushed them back beyond the Great Wall. In 1368, he founded a new Chinese dynasty, which he called the Ming, meaning brilliant.

Early Ming rulers sought to reassert Chinese greatness after years of foreign rule. The Ming restored the civil service system, and Confucian learning again became the road to success. The civil service exams became more rigorous than ever. A board of censors watched over the bureaucracy, rooting out corruption and disloyalty.

**Economic revival.** Economically, Ming China was immensely productive. The fertile, well-irrigated plains of eastern China supported a population of more than 100 million. In the Yangzi Valley, peasants produced huge rice crops. Better methods of fertilizing helped to improve farming. In the 1500s, new crops reached China from the Americas, especially corn and sweet potatoes. (See Chapter 16.)

▲ *Ming porcelain jar*

Chinese cities were home to many industries, including porcelain, paper, and tools. The Ming repaired the extensive canal system that linked various regions and made trade easier. New technologies increased output in manufacturing. Better methods of printing, for example, led to the production of a flood of books.

**Cultural flowering.** Ming China also saw a revival of arts and literature. Ming artists developed their own styles of landscape painting and created brilliant blue and white porcelain. Ming vases were among the most valuable and popular products exported to the West.

While Confucian scholars continued to produce classical poetry, new forms of popular literature began to emerge. Ming writers composed popular novels, including *The Water Margin*, about an outlaw gang that tries to end injustice by corrupt officials. Ming writers also produced the world's first detective stories. Performing artists developed a popular tradition of Chinese opera that combined music, dance, and drama.

## *China and the World*

Early Ming rulers proudly sent Chinese fleets into distant waters. The most extraordinary of these ventures were the voyages of the Chinese admiral Zheng He (DZUHNG HEH).

**The voyages of Zheng He.** In 1405, Zheng He departed at the head of a fleet of 62 huge ships and hundreds of smaller ones, carrying a crew of more than 25,000 sailors. The largest ships measured 400 feet long. Zheng He's goal was to promote trade and collect tribute from lesser powers across the "western seas."

During seven expeditions between 1405 and 1433, Zheng He explored the coasts of Southeast Asia and India and the entrances to the Red Sea and the Persian Gulf. He dropped anchor and visited many ports in East Africa, returning home with new and unfamiliar animals for the imperial zoo. One of these creatures the Chinese identified as a *qilin*, a legendary beast whose appearance was a sign of Heaven's favor. People flocked to marvel at this 15-foot-tall creature with the body of a deer, the tail of an ox, and red spots—a giraffe.

In the wake of the voyages, Chinese merchants settled in Southeast Asian and Indian trading centers. The voyages also showed local rulers the power and strength of the Middle Kingdom. Many acknowledged the supremacy of the Chinese empire.

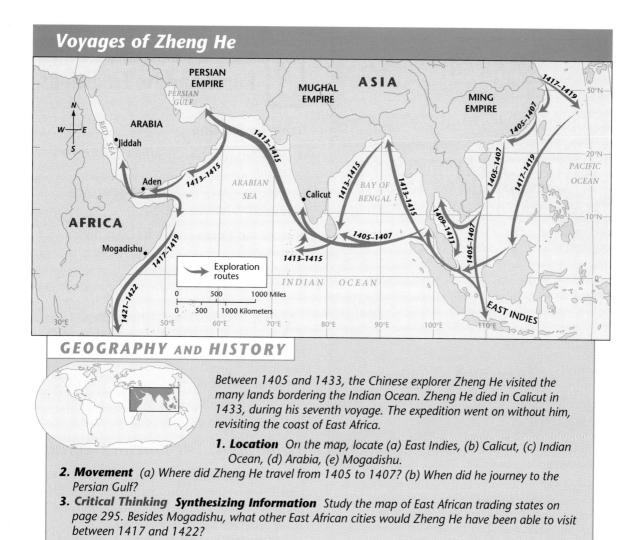

## Voyages of Zheng He

**GEOGRAPHY** *AND* **HISTORY**

Between 1405 and 1433, the Chinese explorer Zheng He visited the many lands bordering the Indian Ocean. Zheng He died in Calicut in 1433, during his seventh voyage. The expedition went on without him, revisiting the coast of East Africa.

1. **Location** On the map, locate (a) East Indies, (b) Calicut, (c) Indian Ocean, (d) Arabia, (e) Mogadishu.
2. **Movement** (a) Where did Zheng He travel from 1405 to 1407? (b) When did he journey to the Persian Gulf?
3. **Critical Thinking** **Synthesizing Information** Study the map of East African trading states on page 295. Besides Mogadishu, what other East African cities would Zheng He have been able to visit between 1417 and 1422?

---

The Chinese proudly proclaimed that the Ming had unified the "seas and continents":

> 66The countries beyond the horizon and from the ends of the Earth have all become subjects. . . . We have crossed immense water spaces and have seen huge waves like mountains rising sky-high, and we have set eyes on barbarian regions far away . . . while our sails loftily unfurled like clouds day and night continued their course, crossing those savage waves as if we were walking on a public highway.99

**Turning inward.** In 1433, the year Zheng He died, the Ming emperor suddenly banned the building of seagoing ships. Later, ships with more than two masts were forbidden. Zheng He's huge ships were retired and rotted away.

Why did China, with its advanced naval technology, turn its back on overseas exploration? The fleets were costly and did not produce any profits. Also, Confucian scholars at court had little interest in overseas ventures. To them, Chinese civilization was the most successful in the world. They wanted to preserve its ancient traditions, which they saw as the source of stability. In fact, such rigid loyalty to tradition would eventually weaken China.

Less than 60 years after China halted overseas expeditions, the explorer Christopher Columbus would sail west from Spain in search of a sea route to Asia. As you will see, this voyage made Spain a major power and had a dramatic impact on the entire world. We can only wonder how the course of history might have changed if the Chinese had continued the explorations they had begun under the Ming.

*Forbidden!* *Ming rulers built the Forbidden City, a complex of royal buildings deep within Beijing. The dragon ramp, shown here, led to the Hall of Supreme Harmony, where the emperor received the few foreigners who were allowed inside.* **Political and Social Systems** *What does the Forbidden City suggest about the position of the Ming emperor?*

## SECTION  REVIEW

1. **Identify** (a) Kublai Khan, (b) Marco Polo, (c) Zheng He.
2. Why were the Mongols successful warriors?
3. How did the Mongol conquests promote trade and cultural exchanges?
4. How did the Ming emperors try to restore Chinese culture?
5. *Critical Thinking* **Making Inferences** What does Marco Polo's awe at the glories of China suggest about the differences between China and Europe at that time?
6. *ACTIVITY* Organize a debate between Confucian scholars who want to end overseas voyages and court supporters of Zheng He.

 **Korea and Its Traditions**

### Guide for Reading

■ How did geography affect the Korean peninsula?

■ What Chinese traditions influenced Korea?

■ How did Korea shape its own distinct culture?

■ **Vocabulary** *hangul*

As early as Han times, China extended its influence to a ring of states and peoples on the borders of the Middle Kingdom. To the northeast, Korea lay within the Chinese zone of influence. While Korea absorbed many Chinese traditions over the centuries, it also maintained its own identity.

### *Geography: The Korean Peninsula*

Korea is located on a peninsula that juts south from the Asian mainland with its tip pointing toward Japan. Mountains and the Yalu River separate Korea from China.

**Mountains and seas.** An early visitor once compared Korea's landscape to "a sea in a heavy gale." Low but steep mountains cover nearly 70 percent of the Korean peninsula. The most important range, the T'aebaek (TEH BEHK), runs from the north to the south along the eastern coast, with smaller chains branching off to form hilly areas. Since farming is difficult on the mountains, most people live along the western coastal plains, Korea's major farming region.

Korea has a 5,400-mile (8,700-km) coastline with hundreds of good harbors. In addition, the offshore waters feature thousands of islands. Since earliest times, Koreans have depended upon seafood for most of the protein in their diet. Today, South Korea has the third largest fishing industry in the world.

**The impact of location.** Korea's location on China's doorstep has played a key role in its development. From its powerful mainland neighbor, Korea received many cultural and

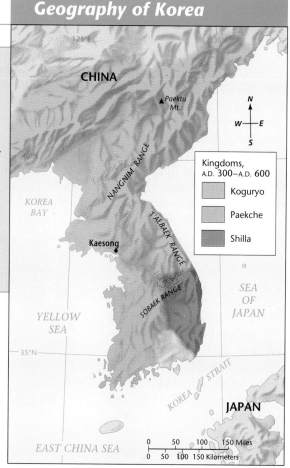

Korea occupies a peninsula jutting south from China toward the islands of Japan. In ancient times it was divided into three kingdoms whose territory extended into present-day China.

1. **Location** On the map, locate (a) Yalu River, (b) Han River, (c) T'aebaek range, (d) Korea Strait.
2. **Region** Why do most Koreans live along the western coastal plains?
3. **Critical Thinking** *Analyzing Information* How might the physical features of Korea have made it difficult to unite the people?

technological influences. At times, China extended political control over the peninsula. Throughout its history, Korea has also served as a cultural bridge linking China and Japan. From early times, Koreans adapted and transformed Chinese traditions before passing them on to Japan.

Despite the strong ties, the Korean language is unrelated to Chinese. The earliest Koreans probably migrated eastward from Siberia and northern Manchuria during the Stone Age. They evolved their own ways of life before the first wave of Chinese influence reached the peninsula during the Han dynasty. In 108 B.C., the Han emperor Wudi invaded Korea and set up a military colony there. From this outpost, Confucian traditions and Chinese ideas about government, as well as Chinese writing and farming methods, spread to Korea.

## Korea United

Between about A.D. 300 and 600, powerful local rulers forged three separate kingdoms: Koguryo (KOH GUH REE OH) in the north, Paekche (PEHK CHEH) in the southwest, and Shilla (SHIL LAH) in the southeast. Although they shared the same language and cultural background, the three kingdoms often warred with each other or with China. Still, Chinese influences continued to arrive. Missionaries spread

Mahayana Buddhism, which took root among the rulers and nobles. Korean monks then traveled to China and India to learn more about Buddhism. They brought home the arts and learning of China.

In 668, with the support of the Tang empress Wu Zhao, the Shilla dynasty united the Korean peninsula. Unlike China, Korea had only three dynasties. The Shilla ruled from 668 to 918, the Koryo (KOR EE OH) from 918 to 1392, and the Choson (CHOH SUHN) or Yi from 1392 to 1910.

**Adapting Chinese influences.** Under the Shilla dynasty, Korea became a tributary state, acknowledging Chinese overlordship but preserving its independence. Over the centuries, Korea came to see its relationship to China in Confucian terms, as that of a younger brother who owed respect and loyalty to an older brother. Koreans also adopted the Confucian emphasis on the family as the foundation of the state.

Women's public roles were restricted, and their position within the family became subordinate to the male head of the household.

At the same time, Koreans adapted and modified Chinese ideas. For example, they adapted the Chinese civil service examination to reflect their own system of inherited ranks. In China, even a peasant could win political influence by passing the exam. In Korea, only aristocrats were permitted to take the test.

**The Koryo dynasty.** During the Koryo age, Buddhism reached its greatest influence in Korea. Korean scholars wrote histories and poems based on Chinese models, while artists created landscape paintings following Chinese principles. The Koryo dynasty built their capital at Kaesong (KEH SUNG) following the plan of the Tang capital at Changan.

Koreans used woodblock printing from China to produce a flood of Buddhist texts. Later, Korean inventors made movable metal type to print large numbers of books. Koreans improved on other Chinese inventions. They learned to make porcelain from China, but then perfected techniques of making celadon ware with an unusual blue-green glaze. Korean celadon vases and jars were prized throughout Asia. In the 1200s, when the Mongols overran Korea and destroyed many industries, the secret of making celadon was lost forever.

▲ *Celadon pitcher*

## *Choson: The Longest Dynasty*

The Mongols occupied Korea until the 1350s. In 1392, the brilliant Korean general Yi Song-gye (EE SUNG KEH) set up the Choson dynasty. In *Songs of the Flying Dragons*, Korea's leading poets held Yi up as a model of virtue and wisdom for future rulers:

66When you have men at your beck and
    call,
When you punish men and sentence
    them,
Remember, my Lord,
His mercy and temperance.

If you are unaware of people's sorrow,
Heaven will abandon you.
Remember, my Lord,
His labor and love.99

Yi reduced Buddhist influence and set up a government based upon Confucian principles. Within a few generations, Confucianism had made a deep impact on Korean life.

**Hangul.** Despite Chinese influence, Korea preserved its distinct identity. In 1443, King Sejong (SEH JONG) decided to replace the Chinese system of writing. "The language of this land," he noted, "is different from China's." He had experts develop hangul, an alphabet using symbols to represent the sounds of spoken Korean.

Although Confucian scholars rejected hangul at the outset, its use quickly spread. Hangul was easier for Koreans to use than the thousands of characters of written Chinese. Its use led to an extremely high literacy rate.

**Looking ahead.** In the 1590s, the ambitious ruler of Japan decided to invade the Asian mainland by way of Korea. The Korean admiral Yi Sun-shin used metal-plated "turtle boats" to beat back the invaders. The Koreans sought Chinese help, and after six years of war, the Japanese gave up their quest. As the Japanese withdrew from Korea, though, they carried off many Korean artisans who took their skills to Japan.

## SECTION 3 REVIEW

1. **Identify** (a) Shilla, (b) Koryo, (c) Choson, (d) Yi Song-gye, (e) Sejong.
2. **Define** hangul.
3. How did location influence the development of Korean civilization?
4. Give two examples of how Koreans adapted or modified Chinese ideas.
5. *Critical Thinking* **Analyzing Information** Today, South Korea observes Hangul Day as a national holiday. Why do you think Koreans celebrate the creation of their alphabet?
6. *ACTIVITY* Draw a poster expressing the relationship between Korea and China during the Shilla, Koryo, or Choson dynasty.

# 4 An Island Empire Emerges

## Guide for Reading

- What geographic features influenced the early development of Japan?
- How did Chinese civilization influence Japan?
- What cultural traditions emerged at the Heian court?
- **Vocabulary** *archipelago, kami, kana*

**P**rince Shotoku of Japan's ruling Yamato clan wanted to create an orderly society. In 604, he completed a document that outlined ideals of behavior he felt should be followed, not only at the royal court, but throughout Japan. The prince wrote:

> 66Harmony should be valued and quarrels should be avoided. Everyone has his biases, and few men are far-sighted. Therefore some disobey their lords and fathers and keep up feuds with their neighbors. But when the superiors are in harmony with each other and inferiors are friendly, then affairs are discussed quietly and the right view of matters prevails. 99

Shotoku was strongly influenced by Confucian ideas about social order. He was a devout Buddhist and an energetic student of Chinese thought.

Like Korea, Japan felt the powerful influence of Chinese civilization early in its history. At the same time, the Japanese continued to maintain their own distinct culture.

## Geography: Japan, a Land Apart

Japan is located on an archipelago (ahr kuh PEHL uh goh), or chain of islands, about 100 miles (161 km) off the Asian mainland. Its four main islands—Hokkaido (hoh KĪ doh), Honshu (hahn SHOO), Kyushu (kee OO shoo), and Shikoku (shee KOH koo)—lie to the east of the Korean peninsula.

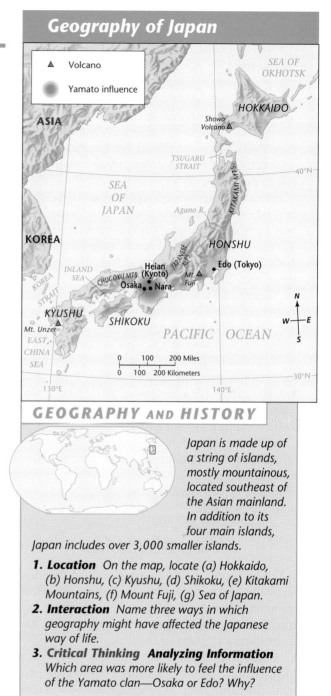

## Geography of Japan

- ▲ Volcano
- ● Yamato influence

### GEOGRAPHY AND HISTORY

Japan is made up of a string of islands, mostly mountainous, located southeast of the Asian mainland. In addition to its four main islands, Japan includes over 3,000 smaller islands.

1. **Location** On the map, locate (a) Hokkaido, (b) Honshu, (c) Kyushu, (d) Shikoku, (e) Kitakami Mountains, (f) Mount Fuji, (g) Sea of Japan.
2. **Interaction** Name three ways in which geography might have affected the Japanese way of life.
3. **Critical Thinking** **Analyzing Information** Which area was more likely to feel the influence of the Yamato clan—Osaka or Edo? Why?

**Land and sea.** Japan is about the size of Montana, but four fifths of its land is too mountainous to farm. As a result, most people settled in narrow river valleys and along the coastal plains. A mild climate and sufficient rainfall, however, helped Japanese farmers make the most of the limited arable land. As in ancient Greece, the mountainous terrain at first was an obstacle to unity.

The surrounding seas have both protected and isolated Japan. While it was close enough to the mainland to learn from Korea and China, Japan was too far away for China to conquer. The Japanese thus had greater freedom to accept or reject Chinese influences than did other East Asian lands. At times, the Japanese sealed themselves off from foreign influences, choosing to go their own way.

The seas that helped Japan preserve its identity also served as trade routes. The Inland Sea was an especially important link between various Japanese islands. The seas also offered plentiful food resources. The Japanese, like the Koreans, developed a thriving fishing industry.

**Ring of Fire.** Japan lies in a Pacific region known as the Ring of Fire, which also includes the Philippines, Indonesia, and parts of Australia and South America. This region is subject to frequent earthquakes and volcanoes. Violent underwater earthquakes can launch killer tidal waves, called tsunami (tsoo NAH mee), that sweep over the islands without warning, wiping out everything in their path.

The Japanese came to fear and respect the dramatic forces of nature. Today, as in the past, soaring Mount Fuji, with its snow-capped volcanic crater, is a sacred symbol of the beauty and majesty of nature.

## Early Traditions

The people we know today as the Japanese probably migrated from the Asian mainland more than 2,000 years ago. They slowly pushed the earlier inhabitants, the Ainu, onto the northernmost island of Hokkaido.

**Yamato clan.** Early Japanese society was divided into uji, or clans. Each uji had its own chief and a special god or goddess who was seen as the clan's original ancestor. Some clan leaders were women, suggesting that women held a respected position in society.

By about A.D. 500, the Yamato clan came to dominate a corner of Honshu, the largest Japanese island. For the next 1,000 years, the Yamato Plain—home to the present-day cities of Nara, Kyoto, and Osaka—was the heartland of Japanese government. The Yamato set up Japan's first and only dynasty. They claimed direct descent from the sun goddess, Amaterasu.

The rising sun, therefore, become their symbol. Later Japanese emperors were revered as living gods. While this is no longer the case, the current Japanese emperor still traces his roots to the Yamato clan.

**Shinto.** The kami, or clan gods and goddesses, were generally nature spirits. This worship of the forces of nature became known as Shinto, meaning "the way of the gods." Shinto never evolved into an international religion like Christianity, Buddhism, or Islam. Still, its traditions have survived to the present day. Hundreds of Shinto shrines dot the Japanese countryside. These Shinto shrines are dedicated to special sites or objects such as mountains or waterfalls, ancient gnarled trees, or even oddly shaped rocks.

**The Korean bridge.** The Japanese language is distantly related to Korean but completely different from Chinese. During the early centuries A.D., Japan and Korea were in continuous contact with each other. Korean artisans and metalworkers settled in Japan, bringing sophisticated skills and technology. Japanese and Korean warriors crossed the sea in both directions to attack each other's strongholds. Some of the leading families at the Yamato court claimed Korean ancestors.

By about A.D. 500, missionaries from Korea had introduced Buddhism to Japan. With it came knowledge of Chinese writing and culture. This opening sparked a sudden surge of Japanese interest in Chinese civilization.

## Japan Looks to China

In the early 600s, Prince Shotoku, a member of the Yamato ruling family, decided to learn about China directly instead of through Korean sources. He sent young Japanese nobles to study in China. Over the next 200 years, many students, monks, traders, and officials would visit the great court of Changan during the heyday of the Tang dynasty.

**ISSUES** *For* **TODAY**

Both Korea and Japan were part of China's "sphere of influence"—the region dominated by Chinese civilization. How can a powerful nation exert influence on its neighbors?

**Imported from Tang China.** Each mission spent a year or more in China—negotiating, trading, but above all studying. They returned to Japan eager to spread Chinese thought, technology, and arts. Equally important, they imported Chinese ideas about government. Like the Chinese emperor, Japanese rulers adopted the title "Heavenly Emperor" and claimed absolute power. They strengthened the central government, set up a bureaucracy, and adopted a law code similar to that of China.

In 710, the Japanese emperor built a new capital at Nara, modeled on the Tang capital at Changan. There, nobles spoke Chinese and dressed in Chinese fashion. Their cooks had to learn to cook Chinese dishes and served food on Chinese-style pottery. Tea drinking and the tea ceremony were imported from China. Japanese officials and scholars used Chinese characters to write official histories. Tang music and dances became very popular, as did gardens designed along Chinese lines.

Most changes affected only a small number of people at the court. Although Japan set up a bureaucracy like China's, it had little real authority beyond the court. In the countryside, the old clans remained strong.

As Buddhism spread, the Japanese adopted pagoda architecture. Buddhist monasteries grew rich and powerful. Confucian ideas and ethics also took root. They included the emphasis on filial piety, the relationships between superior and inferior, and respect for learning.

**Selective borrowing.** After the first enthusiasm for everything Chinese died down, the Japanese became more selective. They kept some Chinese ways but discarded or modified others. Japan, for example, never accepted the Chinese civil service examination to choose officials based on merit. Instead, they maintained their tradition of inherited status through family position. In the end, officials were the educated sons of nobles.

By the 800s, as Tang China began to decline, the Japanese court turned away from its model. After absorbing all they could from China, the Japanese spent the next 400 years digesting and modifying these cultural acquisitions to produce their own unique civilization. The Japanese asserted their identity by revising the Chinese system of writing and adding kana, or

**Divine Protector** *In the 700s, Emperor Shōmu ordered Buddhist monasteries and temples to be built throughout Japan. This statue of a warrior god protected a Buddhist temple from evil spirits.* **Global Interaction** *How was Buddhism introduced into Japan?*

phonetic symbols representing syllables. Japanese artists developed their own styles.

## The Heian Period

This blend of cultures occurred from 794 to 1185. During this time, the imperial capital was in Heian (hay AHN), present-day Kyoto. There, wealthy court families like the Fujiwara wielded real power, while emperors performed traditional religious ceremonies. The Fujiwara married their daughters to the heir to the throne, thus ensuring their authority.

**An elegant court.** At court a sophisticated culture blossomed. Noblewomen and noblemen lived in a fairy-tale atmosphere of beautiful pavilions, gardens, and lotus pools. Elaborate rules of etiquette governed court ceremony. Courtiers dressed with extraordinary care in delicate, multicolored silk. Draping one's sleeve out a carriage window was a fine art.

**Poet of the Heian Court** Lady Komachi, captured here in ink and color on paper, is one of 36 men and women considered to be the classical poets of the Heian period. Draped about her are layer upon layer of extravagant robes. Upper-class women of the time customarily powdered their faces, blackened their teeth, and wore as many as 25 layers of robes. **Art and Literature** Why do you think poets were highly honored at the Heian court?

Although men at court still studied Chinese, women were forbidden to learn the language. Still, it was Heian women who produced the most important works of Japanese literature using the new kana. Sei Shonagon, a lady-in-waiting to the empress in the late 900s, wrote *The Pillow Book*. In a series of anecdotes and personal observations, Shonagon gives vivid details of court manners, decor, and dress. In one section, she lists some pet peeves about court life:

❝One is in a hurry to leave, but one's visitor keeps chattering away. If it is someone of no importance, one can get rid of him by saying, 'You must tell me all about it next time.' But should it be the sort of visitor who commands one's best behavior, the situation is hateful indeed.❞

**Lady Murasaki.** The best-known Heian writer was Shonagon's rival, Murasaki Shikibu. Her monumental work, *The Tale of Genji,* is considered the world's first novel. Composed about 1010, it recounts the lives and loves of the fictional Prince Genji and his son.

In one scene, Prince Genji moves with ease through the festivities at an elaborate "Chinese banquet." After dinner "under the great cherry tree of the Southern court," the entertainment begins. Genji performs skillfully on the "thirteen stringed zither" and does the Wave Dance. But the main event is a Chinese poetry contest, which Murasaki describes in elaborate detail.

The Heian romances are haunted by a sense that beauty and love are soon gone. Perhaps this feeling of melancholy was prophetic. Outside the walls of the court, clouds of rebellion and civil war were gathering.

## SECTION 4 REVIEW

1. **Identify** (a) Ring of Fire, (b) Yamato clan, (c) Amaterasu, (d) Shinto, (e) Shotoku, (f) Sei Shonagon, (g) Murasaki Shikibu.
2. **Define** (a) archipelago, (b) kami, (c) kana.
3. Describe two ways geography affected Japan.
4. (a) What aspects of Japanese life were influenced by China? (b) How did the Japanese preserve their own culture?
5. How did women influence culture at the Heian court?
6. *Critical Thinking* **Comparing** How was the Japanese development of kana similar to the Korean development of hangul?
7. *ACTIVITY* Create your own list of three dislikes written in the style of Sei Shonagon's *Pillow Book.*

# 5 Japan's Feudal Age

## Guide for Reading

- How did feudalism develop in Japan?
- What changes took place under the Tokugawa shoguns?
- What cultural traditions emerged in feudal Japan?
- **Vocabulary** *shogun, daimyo, samurai, bushido, kabuki, haiku*

❝To live in the world
 Is sad enough without this rain
 Pounding on my shelter.❞

In this verse, the poet Sogi reveals a sense of uncertainty and despair. The 1400s, when Sogi lived, were a time of political intrigue, rebellions, and war in Japan. Yet, despite centuries of turmoil, Japanese culture blossomed.

## Age of the Samurai

While the emperor presided over the splendid court at Heian, rival clans battled for control of the countryside. Local warlords and even Buddhist temples formed armed bands loyal to them rather than to the central government. As these armies struggled for power, Japan evolved a feudal system. As in the feudal world of medieval Europe, a warrior aristocracy dominated Japanese society.

**Feudal society.** In theory, the emperor headed Japanese society. In fact, he was a powerless, though revered, figurehead. Real power lay in the hands of the shogun, or supreme military commander. Yoritomo Minamoto was appointed shogun in 1192. He set up the Kamakura shogunate, the first of three military dynasties that ruled Japan for almost 700 years.

Often the shogun controlled only a small part of Japan. He distributed lands to vassal lords who agreed to support him with their armies in time of need. These great warrior lords were later called daimyo (DĪ myoh). They, in turn, granted land to lesser warriors called samurai, meaning "those who serve." Samurai were the fighting aristocracy of a war-torn land. (★ See *Skills for Success,* page 332.)

**Bushido.** Like medieval Christian knights, samurai were heavily armed and trained in the skills of fighting. They also developed their own code of values. Known as bushido (BOO shee doh), or the way of the warrior, the code emphasized honor, bravery, and absolute loyalty to one's lord.

The true samurai had no fear of death. "If you think of saving your life," it was said, "you had better not go to war at all." Samurai prepared for hardship by going hungry or walking barefoot in the snow. A samurai who betrayed the code of bushido was expected to commit *seppuku* (seh POO koo), or ritual suicide, rather than live without honor.

**Women.** During the age of the samurai, the position of women declined steadily. At first, some women in feudal society trained in the military arts or supervised their family's estates. A few even became legendary warriors. As fighting increased, though, inheritance was limited to sons. Unlike the European ideal of chivalry, though, the samurai code did not set women on a pedestal. Instead, the wife of a warrior had to accept the same hardships as her husband and owed the same loyalty to his overlord.

**Mongol invasions.** During the feudal age, most fighting took place between rival warlords, but the Mongol conquest of China and Korea also threatened Japan. When the Japanese refused to accept Mongol rule, Kublai Khan launched an invasion from Korea in 1274. After a fleet carrying 30,000 troops arrived, a typhoon wrecked many Mongol ships.

In 1281, the Mongols landed an even larger invasion force, but again a typhoon destroyed

**GLOBAL CONNECTIONS**

Samurai were trained, not only in swordsmanship and archery, but in techniques of combat without weapons. These "martial arts" probably originated among Buddhist monks in India and Tibet. They gradually spread to China, then to Korea, and finally to Japan, with each culture developing its own unique versions. In recent years, Japanese karate and Korean tae kwon do have become increasingly popular in the United States and other western countries.

**Armorers at Work** Japanese artisans constructed armor and weapons for samurai warriors. Unlike the solid steel plates used by European knights, a samurai's armor consisted of thin strips of steel held together by brightly colored silk cords. **Diversity** Compare the armor of a samurai with that of the European knight on page 193. What were the advantages and disadvantages of each type of armor?

much of the Mongol fleet. The Japanese credited their miraculous delivery to the *kamikaze,* (kah mih KAH zee), or divine winds. The Mongol failure reinforced the Japanese sense that they were a people set apart who enjoyed the special protection of the gods.

## Order and Unity Under the Tokugawas

The Kamakura shogunate crumbled in the aftermath of the Mongol invasions. A new dynasty took power in 1338, but the level of warfare increased after 1450. To defend their castles, daimyo armed peasants as well as samurai, which led to even more ruthless fighting.

Gradually, several powerful warriors united large parts of Japan. By 1590, the brilliant general Toyotomi Hideyoshi (hee day HOH shee), a commoner by birth, had brought most of Japan under his control. He then tried, but failed, to conquer Korea and China. After his death in 1598, the ambitious daimyo Tokugawa Ieyasu (toh kuh GAH wah ee YAY yah soo) defeated all rivals for power. In 1603, he founded the Tokugawa shogunate, which ruled Japan until 1868.

**Centralized feudalism.** The Tokugawa shoguns were determined to end feudal warfare. They kept the outward forms of feudal society but imposed central government control on all Japan. For this reason, their system of government is called centralized feudalism.

The Tokugawas created a unified, orderly society. To control the daimyo, they required these great lords to live in the shogun's capital at Edo (Tokyo) every other year. A daimyo's wife and children had to remain in Edo full time, giving the shogun a check on the entire family. The shogun also forbade daimyo to repair their castles or marry without permission.

New laws fixed the old social order rigidly in place and upheld a strict moral code. Only samurai were allowed to serve in the military or hold government jobs. They were expected to follow the traditions of bushido. Peasants had to remain on the land. Lower classes were forbidden to wear luxuries such as silk clothing. Women, too, faced greater restrictions under the Tokugawas. One government decree sent to all villages stated:

66The husband must work in the fields, the wife must work at the loom. Both must do night work. However good-looking a wife may be, if she neglects her household duties by drinking tea or sightseeing or rambling on the hillsides, she must be divorced.99

**Economic growth.** While the shoguns tried to hold back social change, the Japanese economy grew by leaps and bounds. With peace restored to the countryside, agriculture improved and expanded. New seeds, tools, and the use of fertilizer led to greater output of crops.

Food surpluses supported rapid population growth. Towns sprang up around the castles of daimyo. Edo grew into a booming city, where artisans and merchants flocked to supply the needs of the daimyo and their families.

Trade flourished within Japan. New roads linked castle towns and Edo. Each year, daimyo and their servants traveled to and from the capital, creating a demand for food and services along the route. In the cities, a wealthy merchant class emerged. In accordance with Confucian tradition, merchants had low status. Still, Japanese merchants gained influence by lending money to daimyo and samurai. Some merchants further improved their social position by marrying their daughters into the samurai class.

## Zen Buddhism

During Japan's feudal age, a Buddhist sect from China won widespread acceptance among samurai. Known in Japan as Zen, it emphasized meditation and devotion to duty. Zen had seemingly contradictory traditions. Zen monks were great scholars, yet they valued the uncluttered mind and stressed the importance of reaching a moment of "non-knowing." Zen stressed compassion for all, yet samurai fought to kill. In Zen monasteries, monks sought to experience absolute freedom, yet rigid rules gave the master complete authority over his students.

Zen beliefs shaped Japanese life in many ways. At Zen monasteries, upper-class men learned to express devotion to nature in such activities as landscape gardening. Zen Buddhists believed that people could seek enlightenment, not only through meditation, but through the precise performance of everyday tasks. For example, the elaborate rituals of the tea ceremony reflected Zen values of peace, simplicity, and love

*Harmony With Nature* This temple, named the Silver Pavilion, was a Zen monastery and a peaceful retreat for visiting shoguns. Zen monks served as advisers to shoguns and were the leading scholars and artists of their day. **Religions and Value Systems** How does the setting of this temple reflect Zen values?

of beauty. (See the chart below.) Zen reverence for nature also influenced the development of fine landscape paintings.

## Changing Artistic Traditions

Cities such as Edo and Osaka were home to an explosion in the arts and theater. At stylish entertainment quarters, sophisticated nobles mixed with the urban middle class. Urban culture emphasized luxuries and pleasures and differed from the feudal culture that had dominated Japan for centuries.

**Theater.** In the 1300s, feudal culture had produced Nō plays performed on a square wooden stage without scenery. Men wore elegant carved masks while a chorus chanted important lines to musical accompaniment. The action was slow. Each movement had a special meaning. Many Nō plays presented Zen Buddhist themes, emphasizing the need to renounce selfish desires. Others recounted fairy tales or the struggles between powerful lords.

In the 1600s, towns gave rise to a new form of drama, kabuki (kuh BOO kee). Kabuki was influenced by Nō plays, but it was less refined and included comedy or melodrama in portraying family or historical events. Dressed in colorful costumes, actors used lively and exaggerated movements to convey action. Kabuki was originated by an actress and temple dancer named Okuni, who became famous for her performance of warrior roles. However, women were soon banned from performing on stage.

**Literature.** The feudal age produced stories like the *Tale of the Heike* about a violent conflict between two families. Another important prose work of the feudal period was *Essays in Idleness,* a loosely organized collection of 243 short essays by a Zen Buddhist priest named Kenko. In one essay, Kenko wrote of the fleeting nature of worldly things:

**66**If we were never to fade away . . . , but linger on forever in the world, how things would lose their power to move us! The most precious thing in life is its uncertainty. What a wonderfully unhurried feeling it is to live even a single year in perfect serenity! If that is not enough for you, you might live a thousand years and still feel it was but a single night's dream.**99**

The Japanese adapted Chinese poetry models, creating miniature poems, called haiku. In only three lines—totaling 17 syllables in the Japanese language—these tiny word pictures express a feeling, thought, or idea. The poem by Sogi on page 327 is an example of haiku.

**Arts.** Japanese paintings often reflected the influence of Chinese landscape paintings. Yet Japanese artists developed their own styles. On magnificent scrolls, artists boldly re-created historical events, such as the Mongol invasions.

In the 1600s, the vigorous urban culture produced a flood of colorful woodblock prints to satisfy middle-class tastes. Some woodblock

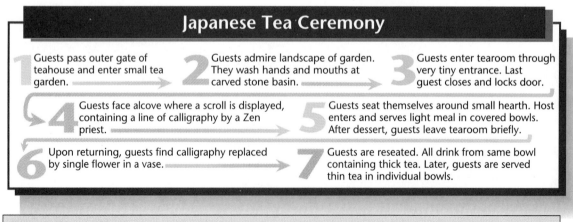

## Japanese Tea Ceremony

**1** Guests pass outer gate of teahouse and enter small tea garden.

**2** Guests admire landscape of garden. They wash hands and mouths at carved stone basin.

**3** Guests enter tearoom through very tiny entrance. Last guest closes and locks door.

**4** Guests face alcove where a scroll is displayed, containing a line of calligraphy by a Zen priest.

**5** Guests seat themselves around small hearth. Host enters and serves light meal in covered bowls. After dessert, guests leave tearoom briefly.

**6** Upon returning, guests find calligraphy replaced by single flower in a vase.

**7** Guests are reseated. All drink from same bowl containing thick tea. Later, guests are served thin tea in individual bowls.

*Interpreting a Chart* The chart above illustrates the steps of the Japanese tea ceremony, or chanoyu. By following a precise series of rituals, guests tried to leave the outside world behind. The complete ceremony could take up to four hours. ■ At what point is tea actually served? How might this ceremony give a sense of relief from everyday anxieties?

# PARALLELS THROUGH TIME

## Musical Theater

Music, drama, and spectacle have had a long and successful partnership on the stage. When acting, singing, and dancing are combined with imaginative costumes and striking stage sets, the result is usually unbeatable entertainment.

**Linking Past and Present**  What different types of musical theater entertain people today?

**PAST**  *In the towns of Tokugawa Japan, audiences attended kabuki programs that ran from morning till night. Kabuki captivated its fans with sensational plots, realistic dialogue, acrobatics, and swordplay. In both dramas and comedies, actors wore elaborate costumes and makeup as they told their stories through music and dance.*

**PRESENT**  *Musical theater remains a popular art form in many cultures today. A summer evening is the perfect time to enjoy an Italian opera in the open air.*

---

artists produced humorous prints. Their fresh colors and simple lines give us a strong sense of the pleasures of town life in Japan.

### Looking Ahead

The Tokugawa shogunate brought peace and stability to Japan. Trade flourished, merchants prospered, and prosperity contributed to a flowering of culture. Still, the shoguns were extremely conservative. They tried to preserve samurai virtues and ancient beliefs.

In the 1500s, Japan faced a new wave of foreign influence. The shogun at first welcomed the outsiders, then moved to sever foreign ties. In Chapter 15, you will read about Japan's uneasy relationship with an expanding Europe.

## SECTION 5 REVIEW

1. **Identify** (a) Yoritomo Minamoto, (b) Toyotomi Hideyoshi, (c) Tokugawa Ieyasu, (d) Zen.
2. **Define** (a) shogun, (b) daimyo, (c) samurai, (d) bushido, (e) kabuki, (f) haiku.
3. (a) Who held the most power in feudal Japan? (b) What values did bushido emphasize?
4. Describe three results of centralized feudalism.
5. How did the growth of towns influence Japanese arts and literature?
6. *Critical Thinking* **Analyzing Information** Why do you think the Tokugawas wanted to restrict the role of women?
7. *ACTIVITY* Write a haiku describing an aspect of the world around you.

# Skills for Success

## Interpreting a Chart

A chart provides a great deal of information in a simple, easy-to-follow form. One common type of chart is a flowchart, which illustrates complex processes or procedures step by step. The chart on page 330 is an example of a flowchart. Another type of chart is an organizational chart, which shows the basic structure of an organization or society. Lines and arrows show relationships among people or groups within the organization. Reading the information and examining the images in sequence can give you a clearer picture of the entire organization.

The chart on the right illustrates the social levels of feudal society in Japan. Study the chart and then answer the questions below.

**1** **Identify the parts of the chart.** (a) What is the title of the chart? (b) What does each level of the chart show? (c) What do the black lines show?

**2** **Practice reading the chart.** (a) Who occupied the highest position in Japanese feudal society? How does the chart show this? (b) What is the relationship between the shogun and the daimyo? Between the daimyo and the samurai? (c) Who had a more respected status in feudal society: peasants or merchants? How does the chart show this? (d) Why does the chart show no lines connecting the peasants, artisans, and merchants?

**3** **Draw conclusions based on the information shown on the chart.** (a) Based on this chart, what words would you use to describe Japanese feudal society? (b) What does this chart imply about the relationship between the emperor and the majority of people? (c) Compare this chart to the one on page 192. Based on these charts, how was Japanese feudalism similar to European feudalism?

***Beyond the Classroom*** Create an organizational chart for a group to which you or someone you know belongs. You might choose the student government of your school, an after-school job, or a school, community, or church group to which you belong. Make sure your chart clearly indicates levels of authority, as well as relationships among individuals or groups. How might such a chart be useful?

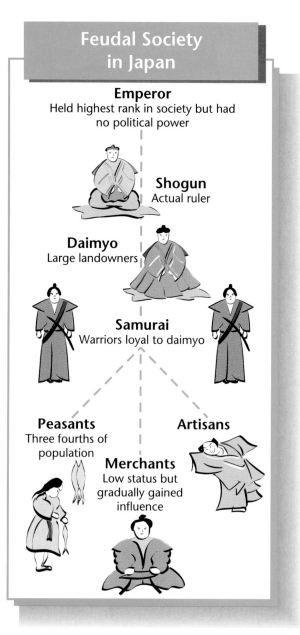

### Feudal Society in Japan

**Emperor**
Held highest rank in society but had no political power

**Shogun**
Actual ruler

**Daimyo**
Large landowners

**Samurai**
Warriors loyal to daimyo

**Peasants**
Three fourths of population

**Artisans**

**Merchants**
Low status but gradually gained influence

## Building Vocabulary

Review the vocabulary words in this chapter. Then, use *seven* of these vocabulary words and their definitions to create a matching quiz. Exchange quizzes with another student. Check each other's answers when you are finished.

## Reviewing Chapter Themes

1. **Continuity and Change**  Describe one effect of each of the following on China: (a) the rise of the Tang dynasty, (b) the Mongol invasion, (c) the expulsion of the Mongols.
2. **Global Interaction**  (a) How did Confucianism and Buddhism spread from China across a wide area of East Asia? (b) Give two examples of how Korea and Japan maintained their own identities.
3. **Political and Social Systems**  (a) How was early Japanese feudal society organized? (b) How did feudalism change under the Tokugawas?
4. **Art and Literature**  (a) What traditions influenced the development of Chinese poetry? (b) In Japan, how did the arts of the merchant class in the towns differ from those of military feudal culture?

## Thinking Critically

1. **Applying Information**  Using the information in this chapter and in Chapters 3 and 4, construct a time chart of major Chinese dynasties. (a) What dynasties are included? (b) When did each one rise and fall? (c) What periods fall between major dynasties? (d) Based on this chart, make one generalization about the history of dynasties in China.
2. **Comparing**  (a) How did the custom of footbinding restrict the lives of upper-class women in China? (b) How was it similar to restrictions placed upon women in other cultures you have read about?
3. **Synthesizing Information**  Review what you have read about the Mongol empire in this chapter and in Chapters 10 and 11. (a) How was the Mongol period both destructive and constructive? (b) What do you think were the three greatest effects of the Mongol conquests across

East Asia, Russia, and the Muslim world? (★ See *Skills for Success*, page 896.)
4. **Analyzing Fine Art**  Locate three examples of porcelain in this chapter. (a) During what period was each piece made? (b) Compare the Tang figures with the Han pottery on page 93. How do they show advances in pottery techniques? (c) Based on your reading, how did celadon combine Chinese and Korean influences? (★ See *Skills for Success*, page 368.)
5. **Drawing Conclusions**  (a) Describe the Japanese practice of selective borrowing from China. (b) How have Americans borrowed from other cultures? Give two examples. (c) What are the benefits and disadvantages of taking ideas from other cultures?
6. **Linking Past and Present**  Review the chart showing the Japanese tea ceremony on page 330. (a) How did the ceremony reflect Zen values? (b) Are there any activities in our society today that follow a clearly defined ritual? If so, what values do these rituals reflect?

### *For Your Portfolio*

An educational publisher has asked you and two partners to create a chart to accompany one of its history books. The chart will show areas of cultural diffusion among China, Japan, and Korea.

1. Begin by reviewing the material in this chapter. Make notes as you read. Identify the cultural areas you will need to do further research on.
2. Brainstorm ways to organize your chart. For example, you might put China in the middle with Japan and Korea on either side. Decide what headings to include on the chart. Some possibilities are: language, literature, architecture, arts, customs, technology, ideas and philosophy, fashion, food, government, religion.
3. Use the resources at the library to add to your information on each cultural area. Remember to consult sources about each of the three cultures.
4. Create your chart. You might consider using illustrations as well as color-coded headings or arrows. (It might also be useful to make a sketch of the chart beforehand.)
5. Display your finished chart in the classroom. Be prepared to discuss how cultural influences moved from one country to another.

# Unit-in-Brief

## Regional Civilizations

### Chapter 8    The Rise of Europe
(500–1300)

From 500 to 1000, Europe was a fragmented, largely isolated region. Feudalism, the manor economy, and the Roman Catholic Church were dominant forces during the early Middle Ages.

- Between 400 and 700, Germanic invaders carved Europe up into small kingdoms.
- In the 800s, Charlemagne temporarily reunited much of Europe. He revived learning and furthered the blending of German, Roman, and Christian traditions.
- Feudalism, based on mutual obligations among lords and vassals, gave a strict order to medieval society.
- The Church governed the spiritual lives of Christians and was the most powerful secular force in medieval Europe.
- By the 1000s, advances in agriculture and commerce spurred economic revival.

### Chapter 9    The High Middle Ages
(1050–1450)

During the High Middle Ages, economic conditions improved and learning and the arts flourished. At the same time, feudal monarchs moved to centralize their power, building a framework for the modern nation-state.

- In England and France, long-lasting traditions of royal government evolved.
- In the Holy Roman Empire, conflicts erupted between popes and secular rulers.

- European contacts with the Middle East during the Crusades revived interest in trade and exploration.
- Beginning in the 1300s, famine, plague, and war marked the decline of medieval Europe.

### Chapter 10    The Byzantine Empire and Russia
(330–1613)

After the fall of Rome, the Greco-Roman heritage survived in the Byzantine empire. Byzantine civilization shaped the developing cultures of Russia and Eastern Europe.

- The Byzantine empire served as a center of world trade and a buffer between Western Europe and the Arab empire.
- Traders and missionaries carried Byzantine culture and Eastern Orthodox Christianity to Russia and Eastern Europe.
- Czars Ivan III and Ivan IV expanded the Russian empire and laid the foundation for extreme absolute power.
- Invasions and migrations created a mix of ethnic and religious groups in Eastern Europe.

## Chapter 11 The Muslim World
### (622–1650)

The religion of Islam emerged on the Arabian peninsula in the 600s. Muslim civilization eventually created cultural ties among diverse peoples across three continents.

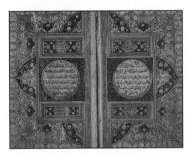

- Muhammad was the prophet of Islam, a monotheistic religion. Through the Quran, the Five Pillars, and the Sharia, Islam was both a religion and a way of life.
- The Arab empire was ruled by several powerful caliphates. After 850, they were replaced by independent dynasties ruling separate Muslim states.
- Learning, literature, science, medicine, and trade flourished during the golden age of Muslim civilization.
- By the 1500s, the Mughals, Ottomans, and Safavids dominated the Muslim world with powerful empires in India, Eastern Europe, and the Middle East.

## Chapter 12 Kingdoms and Trading States of Africa
### (750 B.C.– A.D. 1586)

Despite geographic barriers, many civilizations rose and flourished in Africa. Kingdoms in the west and city-states in the east became important commercial and political centers.

- The Bantu migrations, contacts with Greece and Rome, and the spread of Islam contributed to Africa's diversity.
- Between 800 and 1600, a succession of powerful West African kingdoms controlled the rich Sahara trade route.
- Indian Ocean trade routes led to the growth of prosperous city-states along the East African coast.
- Art and oral literature fostered common values and a sense of community among the peoples of Africa.

## Chapter 13 Spread of Civilizations in East Asia
### (500–1603)

After 400 years of fragmentation, China re-emerged as a united empire and the most powerful force in East Asia. While Korea and Japan were heavily influenced by Chinese civilization, each maintained its own identity.

- China expanded and prospered under the powerful Tang and Song dynasties.
- During the 1200s and 1300s, the Mongols ruled much of Asia. After the fall of the Mongols, the Ming restored Chinese culture and later imposed a policy of isolation.
- While maintaining its own identity, Korea served as a cultural bridge linking China and Japan.
- The seas allowed Japan to preserve its unique culture while selectively borrowing religious, political, and artistic traditions from China.
- During the 1100s, Japan created a feudal society that was ruled by powerful military lords.

# A Global View

## How Did Regional Civilizations Expand the Scope of World History?

During the period of roughly a thousand years from 500 to 1500, sprawling regional civilizations came to dominate much of the world. Extending beyond the borders of any single empire, regional civilizations linked diverse nations within a shared culture.

### Shared Cultures

Sometimes regional civilizations were based on a common religion that spread to a number of neighboring countries. Sometimes a powerful empire would influence its neighbors until they all shared a common regional culture. Sometimes geographic features, such as grassy plains or mountains, influenced all the people who lived there, producing a single regional style of civilization.

Important regional civilizations between 500 and 1500 included Christian Europe, the Muslim zone of Eurasia and North Africa, the trading states of Africa south of the Sahara, and the Chinese sphere of influence in East Asia.

### Christendom and Islam

Two of the major regional civilizations that took shape during this period were based on a common religion. These were the civilizations of the Christian and Muslim zones.

Within each of these regions, diverse peoples shared powerful religious beliefs. Christians and Muslims also felt a duty to spread their religions, and the civilizations that went with them, to neighboring peoples. Both these crusading faiths thus brought cultural unity to many peoples and nations.

Christianity had already spread around the Mediterranean and westward across Europe in Roman times. During the Middle Ages, the Christian religion and related institutions spread across Eastern Europe as well. Influential medieval institutions included feudalism, the manor system, and the medieval Christian churches—Roman Catholic in the West and Greek Orthodox in the East.

The Prophet Muhammad proclaimed the Muslim faith in

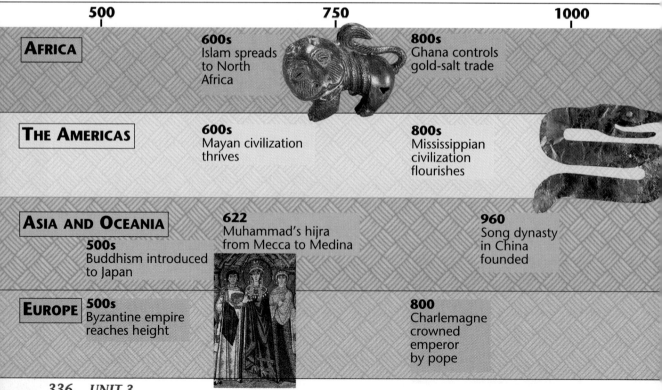

| | 500 | 750 | 1000 |
|---|---|---|---|
| **AFRICA** | | **600s** Islam spreads to North Africa | **800s** Ghana controls gold-salt trade |
| **THE AMERICAS** | | **600s** Mayan civilization thrives | **800s** Mississippian civilization flourishes |
| **ASIA AND OCEANIA** | **500s** Buddhism introduced to Japan | **622** Muhammad's hijra from Mecca to Medina | **960** Song dynasty in China founded |
| **EUROPE** | **500s** Byzantine empire reaches height | | **800** Charlemagne crowned emperor by pope |

the 600s. Believers spread Islam far across North Africa, western Asia, and even parts of southern Europe. With the religion came literacy, cities, long-distance trade, and developments in philosophy and art. Islam thus shaped the culture of many peoples, from Muhammad's own Arabian neighbors to the nomads of the Eurasian steppes, from the kingdoms of western Africa to India and Southeast Asia.

## Africa and Asia

Other regions of Africa and Asia saw the rise of other kinds of regional civilizations during this period. Across Africa, geography and trade linked many peoples, while in East Asia the influence of China imposed a common culture on a wide region.

In West Africa, peoples of the grasslands built a series of similar kingdoms and empires. All profited greatly from their commercial ties to Muslim traders from the north and the gold mines of the Guinea coast to the south. On the other side of the continent, African rulers and Muslim merchants from the north constructed a string of commercial city-states down the East African coast. These coastal trading cities linked India and China to inner Africa and the Mediterranean.

In East Asia, China's looming power continued to influence surrounding states, especially Korea and Japan. From the Chinese empire, the Japanese and Korean peoples adapted Confucian philosophy, belief in divine emperors, and the Chinese version of Buddhism, among other things. A common civilization, often described as Confucian, thus united this vast region.

## Looking Ahead

Regional civilizations were a step beyond kingdoms and empires. They brought common economic and cultural characteristics to regions that were still too large for political unification. Next, regional civilizations headed toward global interdependence. This step would be taken only after European expansion began in 1492.

**ACTIVITY** Choose two events and two pictures from the time line below. For each, write a sentence explaining how it relates to the themes expressed in the Global View essay.

| **1000** | **1250** | **1500** |
|---|---|---|
| **1000** East African trading cities prosper | **1250** Empire of Mali reaches height | **1500** Kongo kingdom flourishes |
| **1000s** Anasazis build pueblo towns | **1438** Incan empire founded | **1500** Aztec empire reaches height |
| **1206** Delhi Sultanate founded | **1368** Ming dynasty ends Mongol rule | **1520** Reign of Suleiman begins |
| **1066** Normans conquer Britain | **1215** English Magna Carta signed | **1389** Ottomans defeat Serbs at Kosovo | **1462** Reign of Ivan the Great begins |

# You Decide

## Exploring Global Issues

### Does Diversity Strengthen or Weaken a Society?

"India has not ever been an easy country to understand," commented Indian prime minister Indira Gandhi in the 1970s. "Perhaps it is too deep, contradictory, and diverse." Many earlier rulers might have agreed with her. Although the Mughal emperor Akbar was able to strengthen his rule by accepting India's many religions, other leaders found diversity a daunting challenge and a threat to national unity.

Today, with modern technology bringing people together at a faster rate than ever before, questions remain. Should a nation encourage diversity? Or can lack of unity weaken the fabric of a society? To begin your own investigation, examine these viewpoints.

**ITALY**

**1835**

Giuseppe Mazzini, who led a movement to unite Italy into a single state, defined the ties that bind a nation:

> **"**A nation is an association of those who are brought together by language, by given geographical conditions, or by the role assigned them by history, who acknowledge the same principles and who march together to the conquest of a single definite goal under the rule of a common body of law. . . . It is necessary that [a nation's] ideas be shown to other lands in their beauty and purity, free from any alien mixture.**"**

**MEXICO**

**1853**

Lucas Alamán, a conservative leader, believed that religious unity was vital to his recently independent nation:

> **"**First and foremost is the need to preserve the Catholic religion, because we believe in it and because . . . we consider it to be the only common bond that links all Mexicans when all the others have been broken.**"**

**ARGENTINA**

**1925**

The cultures of many Latin American nations blend Native American, European, and African influences. Several paintings by Pedro Figari, including this one, *Creole Dance,* celebrate the richness of this heritage. ▶

## EGYPT
### 1933

Taha Husayn, a respected scholar, pointed out that his nation's culture was a blend of three distinct traditions. The first came from ancient Egypt, the second from Arabian Muslims:

> **"**As for the third element, it is the foreign element which has always influenced Egyptian life, and will always do so. It is what has come to Egypt from its contacts with the civilized peoples in the east and west . . . Greeks, and Romans, Jews and Phoenicians in ancient times, Arabs, Turks and Crusaders in the Middle Ages, Europe and America in the modern age. . . . I should like Egyptian education to be firmly based on a certain harmony between these three elements.**"**

## UNITED STATES
### 1935

Anthropologist Margaret Mead based her views on her observations of both American and Pacific island societies:

> **"**If we are to achieve a richer culture, rich in contrasting values, we must recognize the whole gamut of human potentialities, and so weave a less arbitrary social fabric, one in which each diverse human gift will find a fitting place.**"**

"CANADA IS MADE UP OF TWO DISTINCT NATIONS, JUST LIKE TWO TRAINS ON PARALLEL TRACKS THAT WILL NEVER MEET"—PREMIER RENE LEVESQUE

## CANADA
### 1980s

This cartoon comments on long-standing tensions between French-speaking Canadians and those who speak English. Rene Levesque was a leader who called for French Quebec to break away from the rest of Canada. ▷

---

### COMPARING VIEWPOINTS

1. Do you think Alamán would agree with Akbar's religious policies? Explain.
2. How does Mazzini's view of what strengthens a society differ from Mead's?
3. What is Husayn's attitude toward cultural diversity? Which other viewpoints here seem closest to his?
4. Which of the quotations or pictures here suggest that diversity can be dangerous to a society? In what way?

### YOUR INVESTIGATION

**ACTIVITY**

1. Find out more about one of the viewpoints above or another viewpoint related to this topic. You might investigate:

- ▇ The attitude toward diversity in a single-culture society such as Japan or Korea.
- ▇ The ideas of nationalist leaders of the 1800s in Germany, Italy, Greece, Ireland, and other European countries.
- ▇ The contributions of immigrants to the development of the United States or Canada.
- ▇ The effects of ethnic or religious conflicts on a nation such as Yugoslavia, Nigeria, or Lebanon.
- ▇ Recent debates about multiculturalism or immigration policy in the United States.

2. Decide which viewpoint you agree with most closely and express it in your own way. You may do so in an essay, a cartoon, a poem, a drawing or painting, a song, a skit, a video, or some other way.

# EARLY MODERN TIMES

**Art and Literature**

2  *In the forest kingdom of Benin, artisans developed skills for casting superb bronze and brass pieces. This hip plate shows three Benin warriors.*

*ATLANTIC OCEAN*

Tenochtitlán

**Impact of the Individual**

1  *Atahualpa was the last of the mighty Incan god-kings. He seized power from his brother in 1532 but was unable to withstand a threat from Spanish invaders.*

*PACIFIC OCEAN*

Cuzco        1

N
W — E
S

**Global Interaction**

3  *By 1500, European explorers were navigating the world's oceans. This cup honored Sir Francis Drake's feat of sailing around the globe from 1577 to 1580.*

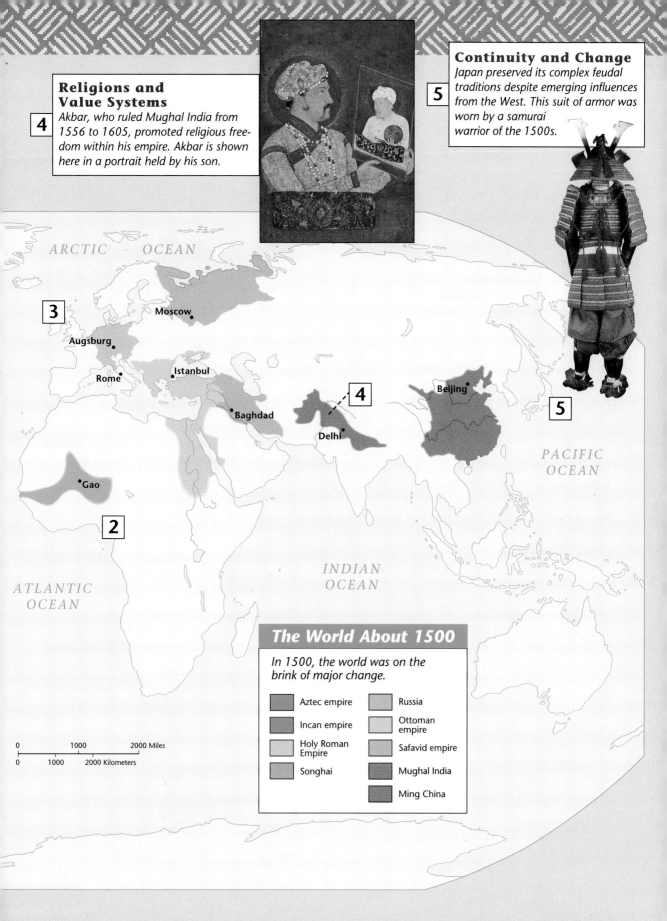

### Religions and Value Systems

**4** Akbar, who ruled Mughal India from 1556 to 1605, promoted religious freedom within his empire. Akbar is shown here in a portrait held by his son.

### Continuity and Change

**5** Japan preserved its complex feudal traditions despite emerging influences from the West. This suit of armor was worn by a samurai warrior of the 1500s.

ARCTIC OCEAN

**3**

Moscow

Augsburg

Rome

Istanbul

Baghdad

**4**

Delhi

Beijing

**5**

PACIFIC OCEAN

Gao

**2**

ATLANTIC OCEAN

INDIAN OCEAN

0    1000    2000 Miles
0    1000    2000 Kilometers

## The World About 1500

In 1500, the world was on the brink of major change.

| | |
|---|---|
| Aztec empire | Russia |
| Incan empire | Ottoman empire |
| Holy Roman Empire | Safavid empire |
| Songhai | Mughal India |
| Ming China | |

# The Renaissance and Reformation

## (1300–1600)

## CHAPTER OUTLINE

1  **The Renaissance in Italy**
2  **The Renaissance Moves North**
3  **The Protestant Reformation**
4  **Reformation Ideas Spread**
5  **The Scientific Revolution**

Michelangelo rushed from the Vatican. He yanked tight the straps of his saddle and flung himself onto his horse. No one treated him like that, he swore silently. Not even the pope!

Within moments, Michelangelo was galloping out Rome's northern gate, homeward bound toward Florence. As he rode, the great artist thought about the scene that had just ended in the Vatican. He could not believe that Pope Julius II had rejected the project they had planned so carefully for years. Even more humiliating, the pope had had Michelangelo thrown out by a groom!

Before long, the pope and the artist forgot their quarrel, and Julius set Michelangelo to work on an even greater project. He would create a huge mural to decorate the ceiling of the Sistine Chapel in the Vatican.

It was an enormous task. For four years, Michelangelo lay on his back on a wooden platform suspended just a few inches below the chapel ceiling. Paint dripping in his face, he painstakingly illustrated the biblical history of the world, from the Creation to the Flood. In a poem, the artist later described his ordeal:

66My stomach is thrust toward my chin,
   My beard curls up toward the sky,
   My head leans right over onto my
      back . . .
   The brush endlessly dripping onto
      my face . . .
   I am bent as a Syrian bow.99

Michelangelo was one of the towering geniuses of the Renaissance, the great period of cultural rebirth that transformed Europe between the 1300s and the 1500s. The Renaissance began in northern Italy and spread throughout Europe. It ushered in a golden age in the arts and literature and a revolution in the sciences. At the same time, divisions within the Church shattered Christian unity in the West.

**FOCUS ON** these themes as you read:

■ **Art and Literature**
How did the rediscovery of classical models influence the arts and literature of the Renaissance?

■ **Religions and Value Systems**
How did discontent with the Church lead to the Protestant Reformation?

■ **Impact of the Individual**
How did the Renaissance create a new emphasis on individual achievement?

■ **Economics and Technology**
What influence did the new technology of printing have on European life and culture?

■ **Continuity and Change**
How did the Scientific Revolution transform the way people viewed the physical world?

## TIME AND PLACE

*A Golden Age in the Arts* During the Renaissance, the rulers of Italy's many states supported the work of hundreds of artists. This family portrait by Andrea Mantegna was commissioned by the Gonzagas, rulers of Mantua in northern Italy. The Gonzagas hoped that Mantegna would make their city a leading center of the arts. **Continuity and Change** How are artists supported in our society?

## HUMANITIES LINK

*Art History* Raphael, *The Marriage of the Virgin* (page 346).
*Literature* In this chapter, you will encounter passages from the following works of literature: Michelangelo, "My stomach is thrust toward my chin" (page 342); Niccolò Machiavelli, *The Prince* (page 349); William Shakespeare, *Hamlet* (page 352); Alexander Pope, *Epitaphs: Intended for Sir Isaac Newton* (page 366).

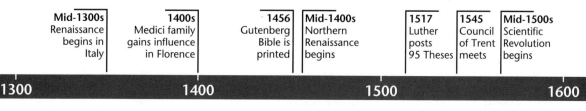

| Mid-1300s Renaissance begins in Italy | 1400s Medici family gains influence in Florence | 1456 Gutenberg Bible is printed | Mid-1400s Northern Renaissance begins | 1517 Luther posts 95 Theses | 1545 Council of Trent meets | Mid-1500s Scientific Revolution begins |
|---|---|---|---|---|---|---|

| 1300 | 1400 | 1500 | 1600 |
|---|---|---|---|

# 1  The Renaissance in Italy

## Guide for Reading

- How did the Renaissance differ from the Middle Ages?
- Why did the Renaissance begin in Italy?
- What ideas influenced Renaissance scholars, artists, and writers?
- **Vocabulary** *patron, humanism, perspective*

The philosopher Marsilio Ficino smiled with pleasure as he watched the sun cast a golden glow over his native city of Florence. To Ficino, this glow symbolized the revival of art and thought that was taking place in Italy. Dipping his pen in ink, he began to write. "This century," he wrote, "like a golden age has restored to light the liberal arts, which were almost extinct: grammar, poetry, rhetoric, painting, sculpture, architecture, music." What a glorious time to be alive, he thought.

As Ficino recognized, a new age had dawned in Western Europe in the 1300s and 1400s. Europeans called it the Renaissance, meaning "rebirth."

## What Was the Renaissance?

The Renaissance was a time of creativity and change in many areas—political, social, economic, and cultural. Perhaps most important, however, were the changes that took place in the way people viewed themselves and their world. Spurred by a reawakened interest in classical learning, especially the culture of ancient Rome, creative Renaissance minds set out to transform their own age. Their era, they felt, was a time of rebirth after the disorder and disunity of the medieval world.

But Renaissance Europe did not really break completely with its medieval past. After all, the Middle Ages had preserved much of the classical heritage. Latin had survived as the language of the Church and of educated people. And the mathematics of Euclid, the astronomy of Ptolemy, and the works of Aristotle were well known to late medieval scholars.

Yet the Renaissance did produce new attitudes toward culture and learning. Unlike medieval scholars, who debated the nature of life after death, Renaissance thinkers were eager to explore the richness and variety of human experience in the here and now. At the same time, there was a new emphasis on individual achievement. Indeed, the Renaissance ideal was the person with talent in many fields.

*Jewel of the Renaissance  Florence, situated along the banks of the Arno River, was one of the richest and most beautiful cities of Italy. Its rulers used their wealth to attract the best artists and writers of the time, and Florence came to symbolize the creative spirit of the Renaissance.* **Geography and History** *Why was location on a body of water important for early cities?*

The Renaissance supported a spirit of adventure and a wide-ranging curiosity that led people to explore new worlds. Columbus, who sailed to the Americas in 1492, represented that spirit. So did Nicolaus Copernicus, the scientist who revolutionized the way people viewed the universe. Renaissance writers and artists, eager to experiment with new forms, were also products of that adventurous spirit.

## Italian Beginnings

The Renaissance began in Italy in the mid-1300s, then spread north to the rest of Europe. It reached its height in the 1500s. Italy was the birthplace of the Renaissance for several reasons.

**Why Italy?** As you have read, the Renaissance was marked by a reawakened interest in the culture of ancient Rome. Since Italy was the center of ancient Roman history, it was only natural for this reawakening to start there. Architectural remains, antique statues, coins and inscriptions—all were visible reminders to Italians of the "glory that was Rome."

Italy differed from the rest of Europe in another important way. Italy's cities had survived the Middle Ages. In the north, city-states like Florence, Milan, Venice, and Genoa grew into prosperous centers of trade and manufacturing. Rome, in central Italy, and Naples in the south, along with a number of smaller city-states, also contributed to the Renaissance cultural revival.

A wealthy and powerful merchant class in these city-states further promoted the cultural rebirth. These merchants exerted both political and economic leadership, and their attitudes and interests helped to shape the Italian Renaissance. They stressed education and individual achievement. They also spent lavishly to support the arts.

**Florence and the Medicis.** Florence, perhaps more than any other city, came to symbolize the Italian Renaissance. Like ancient Athens, it produced a dazzling number of gifted poets, artists, architects, scholars, and scientists in a short space of time.

In the 1400s, the Medici (MEH dee chee) family of Florence organized a banking business. The business prospered, and the family expanded into wool manufacturing, mining, and other ventures. Soon, the Medicis ranked among the

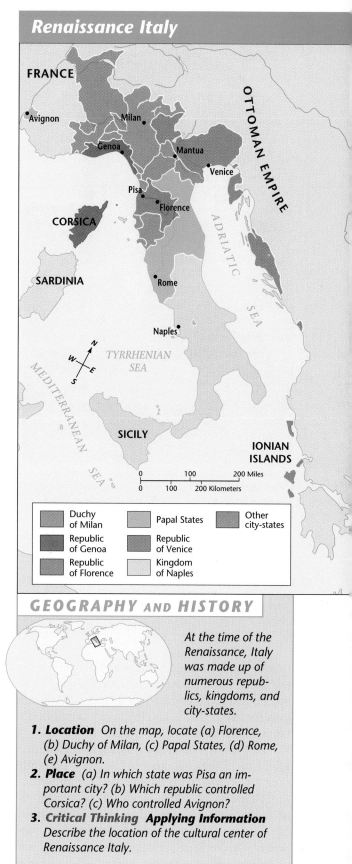

**Renaissance Italy**

Duchy of Milan
Republic of Genoa
Republic of Florence
Papal States
Republic of Venice
Kingdom of Naples
Other city-states

GEOGRAPHY AND HISTORY

At the time of the Renaissance, Italy was made up of numerous republics, kingdoms, and city-states.

1. **Location** On the map, locate (a) Florence, (b) Duchy of Milan, (c) Papal States, (d) Rome, (e) Avignon.
2. **Place** (a) In which state was Pisa an important city? (b) Which republic controlled Corsica? (c) Who controlled Avignon?
3. **Critical Thinking** **Applying Information** Describe the location of the cultural center of Renaissance Italy.

**The Marriage of the Virgin** *In this painting, we see Raphael's skillful use of perspective and color and his knowledge of human anatomy. Raphael creates perspective with the pavement grid, which leads the viewer's eye through the open church doors to the landscape beyond. With its dome, columns, and arches, the church building is typically classical in style.* **Art and Literature** *Compare this painting to the medieval painting on page 232. What differences in style do you see?*

richest merchants and bankers in Europe. Money translated into cultural and political power. Cosimo de' Medici gained control of the Florentine government in 1434, and the family continued as uncrowned rulers of the city for many years.

Best known of all the Medicis was Cosimo's grandson Lorenzo, known as "the Magnificent." Lorenzo, who died in 1492, represented the Renaissance ideal. A clever politician, he held Florence together during difficult times. He was also a generous patron, or financial supporter, of the arts. Under Lorenzo, poets and philosophers frequently visited the Medici palace. Artists like Michelangelo learned their craft by sketching ancient Roman statues collected in the Medici gardens. Lorenzo was himself a poet, and some of his works are still featured in collections of Italian verse.

## Humanism

At the heart of the Italian Renaissance was an intellectual movement known as humanism. Based on the study of classical culture, humanism focused on worldly subjects rather than on the religious issues that had occupied medieval thinkers. Humanist scholars hoped to use the wisdom of the ancients to increase their understanding of their own times.

Humanists believed that education should stimulate the individual's creative powers. They returned to the *studia humanitas,* or humanities, the subjects taught in ancient Greek and Roman schools. The main areas of study were grammar, rhetoric, poetry, and history, based on Greek and Roman texts. Humanists did not accept the classical texts without question, however. Rather, they studied the ancient authorities in light of their own experiences.

**Petrarch.** Francesco Petrarch (PEE trahrk), a Florentine who lived from 1304 to 1374, was an early Renaissance humanist. In monasteries and churches, he hunted down and assembled a library of Greek and Roman manuscripts. Through his efforts, as well as the efforts of others encouraged by his example, the speeches of Cicero, the poems of Homer and Virgil, and Livy's *History of Rome* again became known to Western Europeans.

Petrarch also wrote literature of his own. His *Sonnets to Laura,* love poems written in the vernacular and inspired by a woman he knew only from a distance, greatly influenced other writers of his time.

## A Golden Age in the Arts

The Renaissance reached its most glorious expression in its paintings, sculpture, and architecture. Wealthy patrons played a major role in this artistic flowering. Popes and princes supported the work of hundreds of artists. Wealthy and powerful women such as Isabella d'Este of Mantua were important patrons of the arts as well.

Renaissance art reflected humanist concerns. Like artists of the Middle Ages, Renaissance artists portrayed religious figures such as Mary, Jesus, and the saints. However, they often set these figures against Greek or Roman backgrounds. Painters also produced portraits of well-known figures of the day, reflecting the humanist interest in individual achievement.

Renaissance artists studied ancient Greek and Roman works and revived many classical forms. The sculptor Donatello, for example, created a life-size statue of a soldier on horseback. It was the first such figure done since ancient times.

Roman art had been very realistic, and Renaissance painters developed new techniques for representing both humans and landscapes in a realistic way. Renaissance artists learned the rules of perspective. By making distant objects smaller than those close to the viewer, artists could paint scenes that appeared three-dimensional. They also used shading to make objects look round and real. Renaissance artists studied human anatomy and drew from live models. This made it possible for them to portray the human body more accurately than medieval artists had done.

**The genius of Leonardo.** Florence was home to many outstanding painters and sculptors. One of the most brilliant was Leonardo da Vinci (DAH VIHN chee), who was born in 1452. His exploring mind and endless curiosity fed a genius for invention. Today, people admire Leonardo's paintings for their freshness and realism. Most popular is *Mona Lisa,* a portrait of a woman whose mysterious smile has baffled viewers for centuries.

To produce his masterpieces, Leonardo made sketches of nature and of models in his studio. He even dissected corpses to learn how bones and muscles work. "Indicate which are the muscles and which the tendons, which become prominent or retreat in the different movements of each limb," he wrote in his notebook.

Leonardo thought of himself as an artist, but his talents and accomplishments ranged over many areas. His interests extended to botany, anatomy, optics, music, architecture, and engineering. He made sketches for flying machines and undersea boats centuries before the first airplane or submarine was actually built.

**Michelangelo.** Like Leonardo, Michelangelo was a many-sided genius—sculptor, engineer, painter, architect, and poet. As a young man, he shaped stone into masterpieces like the *Pietà,* which captures the sorrow of Mary as she cradles the dead Christ on her knees. *David,* Michelangelo's statue of the biblical shepherd who killed the giant Goliath, recalls the harmony and grace of ancient Greek tradition.

**Raphael.** A few years younger than Leonardo and Michelangelo, Raphael (RAF ee uhl) studied the works of those great masters. His paintings blend Christian and classical styles. One of his well-known works, *School of Athens,* pictures an imaginary gathering of great thinkers and scientists, including Plato, Aristotle, Socrates, and even the Arab philosopher Averroës. In typical Renaissance fashion, Raphael includes the faces of Michelangelo, Leonardo, and himself in the assembled group.

*Michelangelo's Moses* Michelangelo sculpted this huge statue of the prophet Moses for the tomb of Pope Julius II. Standing almost eight feet tall, the monumental sculpture took years to complete. After it was finally set up, the artist lamented, "I lost all my youth in bondage to this tomb." **Art and Literature** How does the sculpture reflect Michelangelo's attention to anatomical detail?

Raphael is probably best known, however, for his tender portrayals of the madonna, the mother of Christ.

**Women artists.** Some women overcame the limits on education and training to become professional artists. Sometimes, these women kept their work secret, allowing their husbands to pass it off as their own.

A few women artists did gain acceptance. In the 1500s, Sofonisba Anguissola (soh foh NIHZ bah ahn gwee SOH lah), an Italian noblewoman, won fame as a portrait painter. One of her works, *The Artist's Sisters Playing Chess,* earned her an invitation to become court painter to King Philip II of Spain. In the 1600s, Artemisia Gentileschi (ahr teh MEE zee uh jehn tee LEHS kee) created bold paintings of dramatic realism. In *Judith and the Maidservant,* she depicts the nobility of the biblical heroine Judith, who saved Israel from an invading army by killing the enemy leader.

**Architecture.** Renaissance architects rejected the Gothic style of the late Middle Ages as cluttered and disorderly. Instead, they adopted the columns, arches, and domes that had been favored by the Greeks and Romans. For the cathedral in Florence, Filippo Brunelleschi (broo nehl LEHS kee) created a magnificent dome, which he modeled on the dome of the Parthenon in Rome. Equally famous is Michelangelo's design for the dome of St. Peter's Church in Rome. It served as a model for many later buildings, including the United States Capitol in Washington, D.C.

## *Writings for the New Age*

Poets, artists, and scholars mingled with politicians at the courts of Renaissance rulers. A literature of "how-to" books sprang up to help ambitious men and women who wanted to rise in the Renaissance world.

**Castiglione's ideal courtier.** The most widely read of these books was *The Book of the Courtier* by Baldassare Castiglione (bahl dahs SAHR ray kahs steel YOHN ay). Castiglione's ideal courtier was a well-educated, well-mannered aristocrat who has mastered many fields, from poetry to music to sports.

The ideal differed for men and women. The ideal man, wrote Castiglione, is athletic but not overactive. He is good at games, but not a gambler. He plays a musical instrument and knows literature and history but is not arrogant. The ideal woman offers a balance to men. She is graceful and kind, lively but reserved. She is pure but not prudish. She is beautiful, "for outer beauty," wrote Castiglione, "is the true sign of inner goodness."

**Machiavelli's advice.** Niccolò Machiavelli (mahk ee uh VEHL ee) wrote a different kind of handbook. Machiavelli had served Florence as a diplomat and had observed kings and princes in foreign courts. He also had studied ancient Roman history. In *The Prince,* published in 1513, Machiavelli combined his personal experience of politics with his knowledge of the past to offer a guide to rulers on how to gain and maintain power.

*The Prince* did not discuss leadership in terms of high ideals. Instead, Machiavelli took a look at real rulers in an age of ruthless power politics. He stressed that the end justifies the

**The Renaissance Prince** *The most important personality trait of a successful ruler, said Machiavelli in* The Prince, *was the ability to instill fear in his subjects. Machiavelli dedicated his handbook of princely behavior to Lorenzo de' Medici of Florence, shown here.* **Continuity and Change** *What personality trait do you think is most important for rulers today?*

means. He urged rulers to use whatever methods were necessary to achieve their goals. On the issue of honesty in government, for example, he taught that results were more important than promises. He wrote:

66How praiseworthy it is for a prince to keep his word and live with integrity rather than craftiness, everyone understands; yet . . . those princes have accomplished most who paid little heed to keeping their promises, but who knew how craftily to manipulate the minds of men.99

Machiavelli saw himself as an enemy of oppression and corruption. But critics attacked his cynical advice, claiming that he was inspired by the devil. Later students of government, however, argued that he provided a realistic look at politics. His work continues to spark debate because it raises important ethical questions about the nature of government.

## SECTION 1 REVIEW

1. **Identify** (a) Lorenzo de' Medici, (b) Francesco Petrarch, (c) Leonardo da Vinci, (d) Michelangelo, (e) Raphael, (f) Sofonisba Anguissola, (g) Filippo Brunelleschi, (h) Baldassare Castiglione, (i) Niccolò Machiavelli.
2. **Define** (a) patron, (b) humanism, (c) perspective.
3. Describe three ways in which the Renaissance differed from the Middle Ages.
4. What conditions in Italy contributed to the Renaissance?
5. How did Renaissance art reflect humanist concerns?
6. *Critical Thinking* **Linking Past and Present** In *The Prince,* Machiavelli wrote that "It is much safer to be feared than loved." (a) What did he mean by that? (b) Do you think a ruler today would be wise to follow that advice? Why or why not?
7. *ACTIVITY* Create a cover for a magazine about the Italian Renaissance. Then, write a short "Letter from the Publisher" in which you summarize the most important features of the Italian Renaissance.

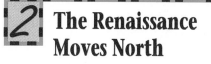

# 2 The Renaissance Moves North

## Guide for Reading

■ Why was the Renaissance delayed in northern Europe?

■ How did individual artists and writers contribute to the northern Renaissance?

■ What themes did northern humanists explore?

■ How did the printing press transform Europe?

In the mid-1300s, Europe was ravaged by the Black Death. (See page 228.) The plague reduced the population by one third and brought the economy to a standstill. Italy recovered fairly quickly and was soon the center of the creative upsurge known as the Renaissance. In northern Europe, recovery was delayed for nearly 100 years. Only after 1450 did the north enjoy the economic growth that had earlier supported the Renaissance in Italy.

## *Artists of the Northern Renaissance*

The northern Renaissance began in the 1400s in the prosperous cities of Flanders, a region that included parts of what is today northern France, Belgium, and the Netherlands. Spain, France, Germany, and England enjoyed their great cultural rebirth 100 years later, in the 1500s.

**A "German Leonardo."** Albrecht Dürer traveled to Italy in 1494 to study the techniques of the Italian masters. Returning home, he employed these methods in paintings, engravings, and prints that portray the religious upheaval of his age. Through these works as well as through essays, Dürer helped to spread Italian Renaissance ideas in his homeland.

Dürer had a keen and inquiring mind. Because of his wide-ranging interests, which extended far beyond art, he is sometimes called the "German Leonardo."

**Peasant Dance** *Though a highly educated city dweller, Pieter Bruegel earned the nickname "peasant Bruegel" from his paintings. He painted farm people, exploring their everyday lives and customs. The villagers in this lively scene are engaged in a variety of festive activities.* **Art and Literature** *How would Bruegel's paintings be valuable to historians?*

**Flemish painters.** Among the many talented artists of Flanders in the 1400s, Jan and Hubert van Eyck (VAN ĪK) stand out. Their portrayals of townspeople as well as their religious scenes abound in rich details that add to the realism of their art. The van Eycks also developed oil paint. Northern artists used this new medium to produce strong colors and a hard surface that could survive the centuries.

A leading Flemish artist of the 1500s was Pieter Bruegel (PEE tuhr BROY guhl). Bruegel used vibrant colors to portray lively scenes of peasant life. Bruegel's work influenced later Flemish artists, who painted scenes of daily life rather than religious or classical themes.

In the 1600s, Peter Paul Rubens created a larger and lusher style of Flemish painting. His work blended the realistic tradition of Flemish painters like Bruegel with the classical themes and artistic freedom of the Italian Renaissance. Many of his enormous paintings portray pagan figures from the classical past. Rubens, who spoke six languages, enjoyed a successful career as a diplomat as well as a painter.

## Northern Humanists

Like Italian humanists, northern European humanist scholars stressed education and a revival of classical learning. At the same time, however, they emphasized religious themes. They believed that the revival of ancient learning should be used to bring about religious and moral reform.

**Erasmus.** The great Dutch humanist Desiderius Erasmus used his knowledge of classical languages to produce a new Greek edition of the New Testament. He also created a much-improved Latin translation of the entire Bible. At the same time, he called for a translation of the Bible into the everyday language of the people. He wrote:

❝I disagree very much with those who are unwilling that Holy Scripture, translated into the vernacular, be read by the uneducated . . . as if the strength of the Christian religion consisted in the ignorance of it.❞

**Erasmus** As priest and humanist scholar, Erasmus criticized abuses in the Church. He boldly advised popes to "lose all that wealth and honor, all those possessions, triumphal processions, offices, dispensations, tributes, and indulgences." He urged them instead to imitate the life of Christ. **Impact of the Individual** How did humanism cause conflict within the Church?

Erasmus used his pen to call for reforms in the Church. He challenged the worldliness of Church practices and urged a return to early Christian traditions. In his best-known work, *The Praise of Folly,* he uses humor to expose the ignorant and immoral behavior of many people of his day, including the clergy. A Christian thinker, he taught that an individual's chief duties are to be open-minded and of good will toward others.

**Sir Thomas More.** Erasmus's friend the English humanist Sir Thomas More also used his pen to press for social and economic reform. In *Utopia,* More describes an ideal society, where men and women live in peace and harmony. Private property does not exist in More's utopia. No one is idle, all are educated, and justice is used to end crime rather than to eliminate the criminal. More, an English judge, was later put to death when he refused to support King Henry VIII in a controversy with the pope. (See pages 358–359.)

## Literature of the Northern Renaissance

While Erasmus and More wrote mostly in Latin, many northern writers used the modern languages of their countries. In towns and cities, the middle class formed a demanding new audience for works in the vernacular. The middle class particularly enjoyed dramatic tales and comedies.

**Rabelais.** The French humanist François Rabelais had a varied career as a monk, physician, Greek scholar, and author. In the novel *Gargantua and Pantagruel,* written in French, he chronicles the adventures of two gentle giants, Gargantua and his son, Pantagruel. On the surface, Rabelais's book is a comic adventure of travel and war. But Rabelais uses his characters to offer opinions on a wide variety of serious subjects, such as education and religion.

**Shakespeare.** The towering figure of Renaissance literature was the English poet and playwright William Shakespeare. Between 1590 and 1613, he wrote 37 plays that are still performed around the world.

Shakespeare's comedies, such as *A Midsummer Night's Dream,* laugh at the follies and joys of young people in love. His history plays, such as *Richard III,* chronicle the power struggles of English kings. His tragedies show human beings crushed by powerful forces or their own weakness. In *Romeo and Juliet,* two teenagers fall victim to an old family feud. In *Othello,* a noble warrior is driven mad by jealousy, while *Macbeth* depicts an ambitious couple whose desire for political power leads them to commit murder.

Shakespeare's love of words vastly enriched the English language. More than 1,700 words appeared for the first time in his works, including *bedroom, lonely, generous, gloomy, heartsick, hurry,* and *sneak.* Also, many lines from Shakespeare's plays are still quoted today. For example, in *Hamlet,* a father gives the following advice to his son:

**66**To thine own self be true,
And it must follow as the night the day
Thou canst not then be false to any man.**99**

## The Printing Press

People have always sought better, faster, and easier ways to communicate with one another. Early civilizations transformed communication by developing writing systems. Hundred of years later, the development of the printing press began another communications revolution.

**Linking Past and Present** How is computer technology revolutionizing the way we communicate today?

**PAST** In this early print shop, the workers at left set type into adjustable molds. At center, the type is inked and a sheet of paper placed over it. Finally, the worker at right uses a screw to lower and press a metal platen onto the type, thus creating the printed page.

**PRESENT**

High-speed automation, combined with the latest in computer technology, drives the presses in modern printing plants.

**Cervantes.** The Renaissance in Spain in the early 1600s produced its own great works. Best known is *Don Quixote* (DAHN kee HOH tay), by Miguel de Cervantes (suhr VAN teez), an entertaining tale that mocks romantic notions of medieval chivalry. (See page 193.)

The novel follows the adventures of Don Quixote, a foolish but idealistic knight, and his faithful servant, Sancho Panza. Quixote imagines himself involved in one dangerous adventure after another. Panza tries without success to convince the knight that the "castles" he sees are really humble inns and the "jousting knights" that he tries to fight are in fact windmills. Quixote, however, is unable to understand the modern world, which requires the skills of practical men like Sancho Panza rather than those of romantic and battle-ready knights.

### The Printing Revolution

The great works of Renaissance literature reached a large audience. The reason for this was a crucial breakthrough in technology—the development of printing in Europe.

**The technology.** The Chinese had learned to make paper and had printed books centuries earlier. By 1300, methods of papermaking had reached Europe. By the 1400s, German engravers had developed movable type. At last, in 1456, Johann Gutenberg of Mainz, Germany, printed a complete edition of the Bible using movable metal type. With the Gutenberg Bible, the European age of printing had begun.

Printing presses sprang up in Italy, Germany, the Netherlands, and England. By 1500, they had turned out more than 20 million volumes. In the next century, between 150 and 200 million books went into circulation.

**Impact.** The printing revolution brought immense changes. Books printed with movable type on rag paper were cheaper and easier to produce than hand-copied works. As books became more readily available, more people learned to read and write. They also gained access to a broad range of knowledge as presses churned out books on topics from medicine and law to astrology, mining, and geography.

Printing influenced both religious and secular thought. "The preaching of sermons is speaking to a few of mankind," noted an English author, "but printing books is talking to the whole world." With printed books, educated Europeans were exposed to new ideas that greatly expanded their horizons.

The new presses contributed to the religious turmoil that engulfed Europe in the 1500s. (See Section 3.) By then, many Christians could read the Bible for themselves. As a result, the ideas of religious reformers spread faster and to a larger audience than ever before.

## SECTION 2 REVIEW

1. **Identify** (a) Jan and Hubert van Eyck, (b) Albrecht Dürer, (c) Pieter Bruegel, (d) Peter Paul Rubens, (e) William Shakespeare, (f) Johann Gutenberg.
2. Why did the northern Renaissance take place nearly 100 years after the Renaissance in Italy?
3. What role did Dürer play in the spread of Renaissance ideas?
4. (a) What issues did Erasmus raise in his writings? (b) What themes did Thomas More explore in *Utopia?*
5. What were three effects of the printing revolution?
6. *Critical Thinking* **Recognizing Causes and Effects** Why do you think the cultural flowering of the Renaissance did not begin until after economic growth had taken place?
7. *ACTIVITY* Shakespeare invented new words by combining two existing words. Examples of these compound words are *eyesore, heartsick, hot-blooded, leapfrog,* and *tonguetied.* Look up definitions of these words. Then, create five compound words of your own.

## 3 The Protestant Reformation

### Guide for Reading

■ Why did the Church face widespread criticism?

■ How did Martin Luther challenge the Church?

■ What role did John Calvin play in the Reformation?

■ **Vocabulary** *indulgence, recant, predestination, theocracy*

During the Renaissance, the Roman Catholic Church fell on troubled times. Christians from all levels of society grew impatient with the corruption of the clergy and the worldliness of the Church. In the words of one unhappy peasant, "Instead of saving the souls of the dead and sending them to Heaven, [the clergy] gorge themselves at banquets after funerals. . . . They are wicked wolves! They would like to devour us all, dead or alive."

From such bitterness sprang new calls for reform. During the Middle Ages, the Church had renewed itself from within. (See pages 230–231.) In the 1500s, however, the movement for reform unleashed forces that shattered Christian unity in Europe. This reform movement is known as the Protestant Reformation.

### Abuses in the Church

Beginning in the late Middle Ages, the Church had become increasingly caught up in worldly affairs. Popes competed with Italian princes for political power. They fought long wars to protect the Papal States against invasions by secular rulers. They intrigued against powerful monarchs who tried to seize control of the Church within their lands.

During the Renaissance, popes, like other Renaissance rulers, maintained a lavish lifestyle. When Leo X, a son of Lorenzo the Magnificent, was elected pope, he is said to have exclaimed:

"God has given us the papacy—let us enjoy it!" Like wealthy merchants, popes, too, were patrons of the arts. They hired painters and sculptors to beautify churches and spent vast sums to rebuild the cathedral of St. Peter's at Rome.

To finance such projects, the Church increased fees for religious services like marriages and baptisms. It also promoted the sale of indulgences. An indulgence was a pardon for sins committed during a person's lifetime. In the Middle Ages, the Church had granted indulgences only for good deeds, such as going on a crusade. By the late 1400s, however, an indulgence could be obtained in exchange for a money gift to the Church.

Many Christians protested such practices. In northern Europe, especially, religious piety deepened even as interest in secular things was growing. Christian humanists such as Erasmus urged a return to the simple ways of the early Christian Church. They stressed Bible study, exposed Church abuses, and rejected Church pomp and ceremony.

## Luther's Protest

Protests against Church abuses continued to grow. In 1517, these protests erupted into a full-scale revolt. The man who triggered the revolt was a German monk and professor of theology named Martin Luther.

The son of a middle-class German family, Luther had been slated by his father for a career as a lawyer. As a youth, however, he had a powerful religious experience that changed his life. One day, during a violent storm, Luther was knocked to the ground by lightning. Terrified, he cried out to St. Anne for help. He promised to become a monk if he were spared.

True to his word, Luther entered a monastery. There, he prayed and fasted and tried to lead a holy life. Still, he suffered from doubts. He believed he was a sinner, doomed to eternal damnation. He also grew increasingly disillusioned with what he saw as the corruption and worldliness of the Church. At last, an incident in his native town of Wittenberg prompted him to act.

**Attack on indulgences.** In 1517, a German priest named Johann Tetzel set up a pulpit on the outskirts of Wittenberg. With the approval of the pope, he sold indulgences to any Christian who contributed money for the new Cathedral of St. Peter in Rome. Tetzel claimed that purchase of these indulgences would assure the entrance into heaven not only of the purchasers but of their dead relatives as well. "Don't you hear the voices of your dead parents and other relatives crying out?" he demanded. " 'Have mercy on us, for we suffer great torment from which you can release us with a few [pennies].' "

To a pious man like Martin Luther, "indulgence salesman" Tetzel was the final insult. It made Luther furious to see people paying for indulgences instead of seeking true repentance.

He jeered that Tetzel's favorite jingle was, "As soon as the coin in the coffer rings, a soul from purgatory springs!"

The outraged Luther drew up his 95 Theses, a list of arguments against indulgences. In accordance with the custom of the time, he posted the list on the door of Wittenberg's All Saints Church. Among other things, he argued that indulgences had no basis in the Bible, that the pope had no authority to release souls from purgatory, and that Christians could be saved only through faith.

**Martin Luther versus the Church.** Almost overnight, copies of Luther's 95 Theses were printed and distributed across Europe, where they stirred up furious debate. The Church tried to persuade Luther to recant, or give up his views. Luther refused. Instead, he developed even more radical new doctrines. Before long, he was urging Christians to reject what he saw as the tyranny of Rome. Since the Church would not reform itself, he wrote, it must be reformed by secular authorities.

In 1521, the pope excommunicated Luther. Later that year, the new Holy Roman emperor, Charles V, summoned Luther to the diet, or assembly of German princes, at Worms. Luther went, expecting to defend his writings. Instead, the emperor simply ordered him to give them up. Luther refused:

> 66I cannot and will not recant anything, for to go against conscience is neither right nor safe. . . . Here I stand. I cannot do otherwise.99

Charles declared Luther an outlaw, making it a crime for anyone in the empire to give him food or shelter. Luther had many powerful supporters, however. One of these, Prince Frederick of Saxony, hid him at a castle in Wartburg. Luther remained in hiding for nearly a year. Throughout Germany, in the meantime, thousands hailed him as a hero. They accepted his teachings and, following his lead, renounced the authority of the pope.

**Luther's teachings.** At the heart of Luther's teachings were several beliefs. First, he argued that salvation could be achieved through faith alone. He thus rejected the Church doctrine that good deeds were necessary for salvation.

Second, Luther declared that the Bible was the sole source of religious truth. He denied other traditional authorities, such as Church councils or the pope.

Third, Luther rejected the idea that priests and the Church hierarchy had special powers. He talked, instead, of the "priesthood of all believers." All Christians, he said, had equal access to God through faith and the Bible. Luther translated the Bible into the German vernacular so that ordinary people could study it by themselves. Every town, he said, should have a school so that girls and boys could learn to read the Bible.

Luther called for other practices of the Catholic Church to be modified. He rejected five of the seven sacraments because the Bible did not mention them. He banned indulgences,

**German Bible** *Before the Reformation, few people could read the Bible, which was in Latin. Then Martin Luther translated the Bible into German. The translation was a bestseller, and before long a half million copies were in print. Here, Luther's image appears on a 1574 edition of the Bible.* **Religions and Value Systems** *What effect do you think the Reformation had on literacy? Explain.*

confession, pilgrimages, and prayers to saints. He abolished the elaborate ritual of the Catholic mass and instead emphasized the sermon. And he permitted the clergy to marry. These, and other changes, were adopted by the Lutheran churches set up by Luther's followers.

## Spread of Lutheran Ideas

Luther's ideas found a fertile field in northern Germany and Scandinavia. While the new printing presses spread Luther's writings, fiery preachers denounced Church abuses. By 1530, the Lutherans were using a new name, *Protestant,* for all those who "protested" papal authority.

**Widespread support.** Why did Lutheranism win widespread support? Many of the clergy saw Luther's reforms as the answer to corruption in the Roman Catholic Church. A number of German princes, however, embraced Lutheran beliefs for more selfish reasons. Some saw Lutheranism as a way to throw off the rule of both the Church and the Holy Roman emperor. Others welcomed a chance to seize Church property in their territory. Still other Germans supported Luther because of feelings of national loyalty. They were tired of seeing German money used to build Roman churches or line the pockets of Italian churchmen.

**The Peasants' Revolt.** The peasants also took up Luther's banner. They hoped to gain his support for social and economic change as well as religious reform.

In 1524, a Peasants' Revolt erupted across Germany. The rebels demanded an end to serfdom. They also demanded other changes in their harsh lives. As the revolt grew more violent, Luther denounced it. He did not see himself as a social reformer. In fact, he urged nobles to suppress the rebellion. They did so, with great brutality, killing between 70,000 and 100,000 people and leaving 50,000 more homeless.

**The Peace of Augsburg.** During the 1530s and 1540s, the Holy Roman emperor Charles V tried to force Lutheran princes back into the Catholic Church. He had little success. Finally, Charles and the princes reached a settlement. The Peace of Augsburg, signed in 1555, allowed each prince to decide which religion—Catholic or Lutheran—would be followed in his lands. Most northern German states chose Lutheranism. The south remained largely Catholic.

**Civil War in France** *The conflict between French Catholics and Protestants resulted in numerous atrocities. On St. Bartholomew's Day in 1572, Catholics massacred thousands of Huguenots in Paris. In this illustration, Huguenots destroy and loot a Catholic church.* **Continuity and Change** *Do religious conflicts still occur today? Explain.*

## John Calvin

The most important reformer to follow Martin Luther was John Calvin. Calvin had a logical, razor-sharp mind, and his ideas had a profound effect on the direction of the Protestant Reformation.

**Teachings.** Calvin was born in France and trained as a priest and lawyer. In 1536, Calvin published the *Institutes of the Christian Religion*. In this book, which was read by Protestants everywhere, he set forth his religious beliefs. He also provided advice on how to organize and run a Protestant church.

Like Luther, Calvin believed that salvation was gained through faith alone. He, too, regarded the Bible as the only source of religious truth. But Calvin put forth a number of ideas of his own.

Calvin taught that God was all powerful and that humans were by nature sinful. God alone, he said, decided whether an individual achieved eternal life.

Calvin preached predestination, the idea that God had long ago determined who would gain salvation. To Calvinists, the world was divided into two kinds of people—saints and sinners. Calvinists tried to live like saints, believing that only those who were saved could live truly Christian lives.

**Calvin's Geneva.** In 1541, Protestants in the city-state of Geneva in Switzerland asked Calvin to lead their community. In keeping with his teachings, Calvin set up a theocracy, or government run by church leaders.

Calvin's followers in Geneva came to see themselves as the new "chosen people." They were crusaders in a religious revolution whose job it was to build a truly Christian society. Calvinists stressed hard work, discipline, thrift, honesty, and morality. Citizens faced fines or other harsher punishments for offenses such as fighting, swearing, laughing in church, and dancing. Calvin closed theaters and frowned on elaborate dress. To many Protestants, this emphasis on strict morality made Calvinist Geneva seem a model community.

Like Luther, Calvin believed in religious education for girls as well as boys. Women, he felt, should read the Bible—in private. He also allowed them to sing in church, a practice that earned him criticism from some church leaders.

**Spread of Calvinism.** Reformers from all over Europe visited Geneva and then returned home to spread Calvin's ideas. By the late 1500s, they had planted Calvinism in Germany, France, the Netherlands, England, and Scotland. This new challenge to the Catholic Church set off bloody wars of religion across Europe.

In Germany, Calvinists faced opposition from Lutherans as well as from Catholics. In France, wars raged between French Calvinists, called Huguenots, and Catholics in the late 1500s. Calvinists in the Netherlands organized the Dutch Reformed Church. To avoid persecution, "field preachers" gave sermons in the countryside, away from the eyes of town authorities.

In Scotland, a Calvinist preacher named John Knox led a religious rebellion. He declared that "right religion takes neither [its origin] nor authority from worldly princes, but from the eternal God alone." Under Knox, Scottish Protestants overthrew their Catholic queen. They then set up the Scottish Presbyterian Church.

## SECTION 3 REVIEW

1. **Identify** (a) Protestant Reformation, (b) Martin Luther, (c) Peace of Augsburg, (d) John Calvin, (e) Huguenot, (f) John Knox.
2. **Define** (a) indulgence, (b) recant, (c) predestination, (d) theocracy.
3. Why did many Christians feel that the Church needed to be reformed?
4. (a) How did Luther's ideas about Christianity differ from those of the Catholic Church? (b) Why did Luther's ideas gain widespread support?
5. (a) Identify five ideas taught by Calvin. (b) Which of these ideas were different from Luther's?
6. *Critical Thinking* **Synthesizing Information** How did the Reformation reflect humanist ideas?
7. *ACTIVITY* Make a concept map comparing the basic teachings of Roman Catholicism, Lutheranism, and Calvinism.

# 4 Reformation Ideas Spread

## Guide for Reading

■ Why did England form a new Church?

■ How did the Catholic Church reform itself?

■ What were the results of the Reformation?

■ **Vocabulary** *annul, ghetto*

Henry III, the Catholic king of France, was deeply disturbed the Calvinist reformers in Geneva. "It have been a good thing," he wrote, "if the city of Geneva were long ago reduced to ashes, because of the evil doctrine which has been sown from that city throughout Christendom."

Henry was not alone in his resentment. Throughout Europe, Catholic monarchs and the Catholic Church fought back against the Protestant challenge. They also took steps to reform the Church and to restore its spiritual leadership of the Christian world.

## Radical Reformers

As the Reformation continued, hundreds of new Protestant sects sprang up. These sects often had ideas that were even more radical than those of Luther and Calvin. A number of groups, for example, rejected infant baptism. Infants, they argued, are too young to understand what it means to accept the Christian faith. Only adults, they felt, should receive the sacrament of baptism. Because of this belief, these groups were known as Anabaptists.

Some Anabaptists sought radical social change, as well. Some called for the abolition of private property. Others wanted to speed up the coming of God's day of judgment, by violent means if necessary. When a group of radical Anabaptists took over the city of Munster in Germany, even Luther advised his supporters to join Catholics in suppressing the threat to the traditional order.

Most Anabaptists, however, were peaceful women and men. In an age of intolerance, they called for religious toleration and separation of church and state. Despite the harsh persecution they suffered, these groups influenced Protestant thinking in many countries. Today, Protestant denominations such as Baptists, Quakers, Mennonites, and Amish all trace their ancestry to the Anabaptists.

## The English Reformation

In England, religious leaders such as John Wycliffe had called for Church reform as early as the 1300s. (See page 231.) By the 1520s, even some English clergy were toying with Protestant ideas. The final break with the Catholic Church, however, was the work not of religious leaders but of the English king Henry VIII. For political reasons, Henry wanted to end papal control over the English church.

**Seeking an annulment.** At first, Henry VIII stood firmly against the Protestant revolt. The pope even awarded him the title "Defender of the Faith" for a pamphlet that he wrote denouncing Luther. In 1527, however, an issue arose that set Henry at odds with the Church.

After 18 years of marriage, Henry and his wife, Catherine of Aragon, had only one surviving child, a daughter named Mary Tudor. Henry felt that England's stability depended on his having a male heir to succeed him. He decided to remarry, hoping that a new wife would bear him a son. Since Church law does not permit divorce, he asked the pope to annul, or cancel, his marriage to Catherine.

**Break with Rome.** Popes had freed rulers from marriages before. But the current pope did not want to offend the powerful Holy Roman emperor Charles V, Catherine of Aragon's nephew. He therefore refused Henry's request.

Henry was furious. Spurred on by his advisers, many of whom leaned toward the new Protestant teachings, he decided on a course of action. First, he would stir up English feelings against the pope. Second, he would take over the English church.

Acting through Parliament, Henry had a series of laws passed. They took the English Church from the pope's control and placed it under Henry's rule. The most notable of these laws, the Act of Supremacy passed in 1534, made Henry "the only supreme head on Earth of the Church of England."

At the same time, Henry appointed Thomas Cranmer archbishop. Cranmer annulled the king's marriage to Catherine. Henry then wed Anne Boleyn, Catherine's lady-in-waiting. Anne bore him a second daughter, Elizabeth. In the years that followed, Henry married four more times but had only one son, Edward.

**The Church of England.** Between 1536 and 1540, Henry shut down all convents and monasteries in England and seized their lands. This move brought new wealth to the royal exchequer. Henry shrewdly offered aristocrats and others of high standing a share of the gains, thereby securing their support for the Anglican Church, as the new Church of England was called.

But Henry was not a religious radical. Aside from making himself head of the Anglican Church and allowing the use of the English Bible, he kept most Catholic forms of worship.

When Henry died in 1547 and his 10-year-old son, Edward VI, inherited the throne, religious turmoil swept England. The young king was dominated by devout Protestants who pushed for Calvinist reforms. Thomas Cranmer drew up the *Book of Common Prayer.* It imposed a moderate form of Protestant service but preserved many Catholic doctrines. Even so, the changes sparked violence.

When Edward died in his teens, his half-sister Mary Tudor, inherited the throne. A pious Catholic, Mary was determined to make England Catholic again. She failed, but not before hundreds of Protestants had died at the stake. After Mary's death, her Protestant half-sister, Elizabeth I, became queen. Under her skillful rule, unity was restored and England became firmly established as a Protestant land.

## Elizabeth I Restores Unity to England

Mary Tudor was 17 years old when Elizabeth I was born. At court, Mary treated her young half-sister kindly, frequently giving her gifts when she was a "good girl." When

*Queen Elizabeth I  Though regal and often aloof, Elizabeth I took pains to court her subjects. On trips through the countryside, the royal coach often stopped so that she could thank the crowds for their loyalty. A noble she had once imprisoned later remarked: "If ever a person had the gift or the style to win the hearts of the people, it was this Queen."* **Impact of the Individual**  *In what way was Elizabeth a successful politician?*

Mary became queen, however, kindness was replaced by fear. Elizabeth, Mary realized, possessed two qualities that made her dangerous to an unpopular Catholic queen. Elizabeth was Protestant and popular.

**Imprisoned in the Tower.** In January 1554, barely six months after Mary ascended to the throne, a plot against her was uncovered. Although she had no proof, Mary was convinced that Elizabeth was involved. She had Elizabeth arrested and imprisoned in the Tower of London.

For two months, Elizabeth waited in terror. Her own mother, Anne Boleyn, had gone to her death from the Tower, as had many other innocent victims. Would the same thing happen to her? she wondered.

Early in May, soldiers appeared. Their orders were to remove Elizabeth to the queen's manor house in the distant town of Woodstock. They assured her that there was no cause for alarm. The frightened Elizabeth, however, did not believe them. Once she was away from London, she was sure, she would be murdered.

Elizabeth's unjust imprisonment in the Tower had made her even more popular with the people. Eager crowds turned out to greet her during the four-day journey from London to Woodstock. In villages all along the route, countryfolk pressed forward to catch a glimpse of the princess and to offer her cakes and other sweets. Church bells rang to pay her homage, and onlookers cried out "God save your Grace!" as she passed.

**Confined at Woodstock.** At Woodstock, Elizabeth was lodged in the gatehouse, a shabby building of four rooms. Her servants were replaced by members of Queen Mary's household, and she could not talk to strangers unless a guard was present. She was not allowed paper, pen, and ink. Any books she received were first sent to London to be examined by the queen and her council for secret messages.

Mary kept Elizabeth at Woodstock for nearly a year. At last, in April 1555, she allowed her to return to court. Shortly after, Elizabeth retired to the country, where she lived until Mary's death in 1558 made her queen.

**A policy of religious compromise.** As queen, Elizabeth adopted a policy of religious compromise. She moved cautiously at first but gradually enforced reforms that she felt both moderate Catholics and Protestants could accept. She attacked anyone—Catholic or Protestant—who defied her.

▲ The Lord's Prayer

Under Elizabeth, English replaced Latin as the language of the Anglican Church service. The *Book of Common Prayer* was restored, although it was revised to make it more acceptable to Catholics. A lot of the pomp and ceremony of Catholic ritual, including the robes of the clergy, was retained. The Catholic hierarchy of bishops and archbishops was also kept, although Elizabeth acted quickly to reaffirm that the monarch was at the head of the Anglican Church.

Even though she preserved many traditional Catholic ideas, Elizabeth firmly established England as a Protestant nation. After her death, England again faced religious storms. But during her long and skillful reign, England escaped the kinds of religious wars that tore apart other European states during the 1500s. ◾

## The Catholic Reformation

As the Protestant Reformation swept across northern Europe, a vigorous reform movement took hold within the Catholic Church. The leader of this movement, known as the Catholic Reformation, was Pope Paul III. During the 1530s and 1540s, he set out to revive the moral authority of the Church and roll back the Protestant tide. To end corruption within the papacy itself, he appointed reformers to key posts. They and their successors guided the Catholic Reformation for the rest of the century.

**Council of Trent.** To establish the direction that reform should take, the pope called the Council of Trent in 1545. It met off and on for almost 20 years. The council reaffirmed traditional Catholic views, which Protestants had challenged. Salvation comes through faith *and* good works, it declared. The Bible, while a major source of religious truth, is not the *only* source.

The council also took steps to end abuses in the Church. It provided stiff penalties for worldliness and corruption among the clergy. It also established new schools to create a better-educated clergy who could challenge Protestant teachings.

**The Inquisition.** To deal with the Protestant threat more directly, Pope Paul strengthened the Inquisition. As you have read, the Inquisition was a Church court set up to root out heresies during the Middle Ages. The Inquisition used secret testimony, torture, and execution to stamp out heresy. It also prepared the Index of Forbidden Books, a list of works considered too immoral or irreligious for Catholics to read. Included on the Index were books by Luther and Calvin.

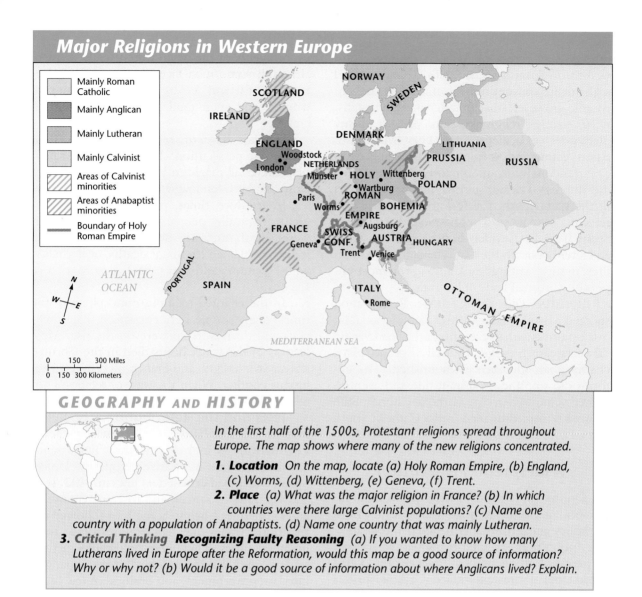

## Major Religions in Western Europe

**Legend:**
- Mainly Roman Catholic
- Mainly Anglican
- Mainly Lutheran
- Mainly Calvinist
- Areas of Calvinist minorities
- Areas of Anabaptist minorities
- Boundary of Holy Roman Empire

NORWAY, SCOTLAND, IRELAND, SWEDEN, ENGLAND, DENMARK, LITHUANIA, Woodstock, London, NETHERLANDS, PRUSSIA, RUSSIA, Münster, HOLY, Wittenberg, POLAND, Paris, Wartburg, ROMAN, BOHEMIA, Worms, EMPIRE, FRANCE, Augsburg, SWISS, AUSTRIA, HUNGARY, Geneva, CONF., Trent, Venice, ATLANTIC OCEAN, PORTUGAL, SPAIN, ITALY, Rome, OTTOMAN EMPIRE, MEDITERRANEAN SEA

N W E S

0   150   300 Miles
0   150   300 Kilometers

## GEOGRAPHY AND HISTORY

In the first half of the 1500s, Protestant religions spread throughout Europe. The map shows where many of the new religions concentrated.

1. **Location** On the map, locate (a) Holy Roman Empire, (b) England, (c) Worms, (d) Wittenberg, (e) Geneva, (f) Trent.
2. **Place** (a) What was the major religion in France? (b) In which countries were there large Calvinist populations? (c) Name one country with a population of Anabaptists. (d) Name one country that was mainly Lutheran.
3. **Critical Thinking** **Recognizing Faulty Reasoning** (a) If you wanted to know how many Lutherans lived in Europe after the Reformation, would this map be a good source of information? Why or why not? (b) Would it be a good source of information about where Anglicans lived? Explain.

**Ignatius of Loyola.** In 1540, the pope recognized a new religious order, the Society of Jesus, or Jesuits. Founded by Ignatius of Loyola, the Jesuit order was determined to combat heresy and spread the Catholic faith.

Ignatius was a Spanish knight raised in the crusading tradition. His military career ended abruptly when his leg was shattered in battle. During a long and painful recovery, he found comfort in reading about Christian saints who had overcome mental and physical torture. He decided to become a "soldier of God."

Ignatius drew up a strict program for the Jesuits. It included spiritual and moral discipline, rigorous religious training, and absolute obedience to the Church. Led by Ignatius, the

Jesuits embarked on a crusade to defend and spread the Catholic faith throughout the world.

To further the Catholic cause, Jesuits became advisers to Catholic rulers, helping them combat heresy in their lands. They set up schools that taught humanist and Catholic beliefs and enforced discipline and obedience. Daring Jesuits slipped into Protestant lands in disguise to minister to the spiritual needs of Catholics. Jesuit missionaries spread their Catholic faith to distant lands, including Asia, Africa, and the Americas.

**St. Teresa of Avila.** As the Catholic Reformation spread across Europe, many Catholics experienced renewed feelings of intense faith. One woman who symbolized this religious renewal was Teresa of Avila. A daughter of a well-to-do Spanish noble family, Teresa entered a Carmelite convent in her youth. The convent routine, however, was not strict enough to satisfy her strongly religious nature. She set up her own order of Carmelite nuns. They lived in isolation, eating and sleeping very little and dedicating themselves to prayer and meditation.

Impressed by her spiritual life, her superiors in the Church asked Teresa to reorganize and reform convents and monasteries throughout Spain. Teresa was widely honored for her work, and after her death the Church made her a saint. Her mystical writings rank among the most important Christian texts of her time.

**Results.** Did the Catholic Reformation succeed? By the late 1500s, Rome was a far more pious city than the one Luther had visited 70 years earlier. Across Catholic Europe, piety, charity, and religious art flourished. The reforms did stop the Protestant tide and even returned some areas to the Catholic Church. Still, Europe remained divided into a Catholic south and a Protestant north.

## Widespread Persecution

During this period of heightened religious passion, persecution was widespread. Both Catholics and Protestants fostered intolerance. The Inquisition executed many people accused of heresy. Catholic mobs attacked and killed Protestants. Protestants killed Catholic priests and destroyed Catholic churches. Both Catholics and Protestants persecuted radical sects like the Anabaptists.

**Witch hunts.** Almost certainly, the religious fervor of the times contributed to a wave of witch hunting. Those accused of being witch-

es, or agents of the devil, were usually women, although some men faced similar attacks. Between 1450 and 1750, tens of thousands of women and men died in the witch-hunting craze.

Scholars have offered various reasons for this savage persecution. At the time, most people believed in magic and spirits. They also saw a close link between magic and heresy.

In troubled times, people look for scapegoats. Typically, people accused of witchcraft were social outcasts—beggars, poor widows, midwives blamed for infant deaths, or herbalists whose potions and cures were seen as gifts of the devil.

In the charged religious atmosphere of the times, many people were convinced that witchcraft and devil worship were on the rise. Most victims of the witch hunts died in the German states, Switzerland, and France, all centers of religious conflict. When the wars of religion ended, the persecution of witches also declined.

**Jews and the Reformation.** The Reformation brought hard times to Europe's Jews. For many Jews in Italy, the early Renaissance had been a time of relative prosperity. Unlike Spain, which had expelled its Jews in 1492, Italy allowed Jews to remain and to enjoy economic and cultural well-being. Some Jews followed the traditional trades they had been restricted to in medieval times. They were goldsmiths, artists, traders, and moneylenders. Others expanded into law, government, and business. A few highly educated Jews served as advisers to powerful rulers.

Yet the pressure remained strong on Jews to convert. By 1516, Jews in Venice had to live in a separate quarter of the city, known as the ghetto. Other Italian cities set up walled ghettos for Jews.

Humanist scholars like Erasmus had sympathy for Jews. At first, Luther hoped that Jews would be converted to his teachings. When they were not, he called for them to be expelled from Christian lands and for their synagogues and books to be burned.

During the Reformation, restrictions on Jews increased. Some German princes expelled Jews from their lands. All German states confined Jews to ghettos or required them to wear a yellow badge if they traveled outside the ghetto.

# CAUSE AND EFFECT

## Long-Term Causes

Roman Catholic Church becomes more worldly
Humanists urge return to simple religion
Strong national monarchs emerge

## Immediate Causes

Johann Tetzel sells indulgences in Wittenberg
Martin Luther posts 95 Theses
Luther translates the Bible into German
Printing press allows spread of reform ideas
Calvin and other reformers preach against
    Roman Catholic traditions
Luther calls for Jews to be expelled from
    Christian lands

## PROTESTANT REFORMATION

## Immediate Effects

Peasants' Revolt
Founding of Lutheran, Calvinist, Anglican,
    Presbyterian, and other Protestant churches
Weakening of Holy Roman emperor

## Long-Term Effects

Religious wars in Europe for more than 100
    years
Catholic Reformation
Strengthening of the Inquisition
Jewish migration to Eastern Europe
Increased anti-Semitism

## Connections Today

About one fourth of Christians are Protestant
Religious conflict in Northern Ireland

*Interpreting a Chart  The Protestant Reformation brought sweeping changes to Western Europe. ■ How did Johann Tetzel's sale of indulgences contribute to the onset of the Reformation? Identify one effect of the Protestant Reformation that you see today.*

In the 1550s, Pope Paul IV reversed the lenient policy of Renaissance popes and restricted Jewish activity. Even Emperor Charles V, who had supported tolerance of Jews in the Holy Roman Empire, banned the migration of Jews to his colonies in the Americas. After 1550, many Jews migrated to Poland-Lithuania and to parts of the Ottoman empire, where they were allowed to prosper. Dutch Calvinists also tolerated Jews, taking in families who were driven out of Portugal and Spain.

## Looking Ahead

The upheavals of the Catholic and Protestant reformations sparked wars of religion in Europe until the mid-1600s. At that time, issues of religion began to give way to issues of national power. As you will read in Chapter 17, Catholic and Protestant rulers of the mid-1600s often made decisions based on political interests rather than for purely religious reasons.

## SECTION 4 REVIEW

1. **Identify** (a) Anabaptists, (b) Henry VIII, (c) Mary Tudor, (d) *Book of Common Prayer,* (e) Elizabeth I, (f) Catholic Reformation, (g) Council of Trent, (h) Inquisition, (i) Jesuits, (j) St. Teresa of Avila.
2. **Define** (a) annul, (b) ghetto.
3. (a) Describe the steps by which England became a Protestant country. (b) How did England's experience differ from that of the German states?
4. (a) What were the goals of the Catholic Reformation? (b) Did it succeed? Explain your answer.
5. (a) Why did persecution increase during the Reformation? (b) Which groups faced the greatest persecution?
6. *Critical Thinking* **Recognizing Causes and Effects** If the Catholic Church had undertaken reform earlier, do you think that the Protestant Reformation would have occurred? Explain.
7. *ACTIVITY* Prepare a script for a TV news program reporting on King Henry VIII's break with the Catholic Church.

# The Scientific Revolution

## Guide for Reading

- How did astronomers change the way people viewed the universe?

- What was the new scientific method?

- How did Newton's work link physics and astronomy?

- What advances were made in chemistry and medicine?

- **Vocabulary** *heliocentric, gravity*

Both the Renaissance and the Reformation looked to the past for models. Humanists turned to ancient classical ideas. Religious reformers looked to the Bible and early Christian times for inspiration. The profound change that took place in science beginning in the mid-1500s, by contrast, pointed ahead, toward a future shaped by a new way of thinking about the physical universe. We call that historic change the Scientific Revolution.

## Changing Views of the World

Until the mid-1500s, European scholars accepted the idea of the ancient Greek astronomer Ptolemy that the Earth was the center of the universe. They accepted this view because it seemed to agree with common sense. It also followed the teachings of the Church. In the 1500s and 1600s, some startling discoveries radically changed the way Europeans viewed the physical world.

**A revolutionary theory.** In 1543, Polish scholar Nicolaus Copernicus (koh PERnuh kuhs) published *On the Revolutions of the Heavenly Spheres*. In it, he proposed a heliocentric, or sun-centered, model of the universe. The sun, he said, stood at the center of the universe. The Earth, he went on, was just one of several planets that revolved around the sun.

Most experts rejected this revolutionary theory, which contradicted both Church teachings and the teachings of Ptolemy. In Europe at the time, all scientific knowledge and many religious teachings were based on the arguments developed by classical thinkers. If Ptolemy's reasoning about the planets was wrong, they believed, then the whole system of human knowledge would also have to be questioned.

Then, in the late 1500s, the Danish astronomer Tycho Brahe (TEE koh BRAH uh) provided evidence that supported Copernicus's theory. Brahe set up an astronomical observatory. Every night for years, he carefully observed the sky, accumulating data about the movement of the heavenly bodies.

After Brahe's death, his assistant, the brilliant German astronomer and mathematician Johannes Kepler, used Brahe's data to calculate

*A Home Devoted to Science* Tycho Brahe named his unique home Uraniburg, or Heavenly City. It consisted of a castle, library, laboratory, observatories, and a shop for making instruments. There, Brahe and his students made observations and developed instruments that were more accurate than any previous work. *Economics and Technology* Besides science, what other academic subject is useful to astronomers?

the orbits of the planets revolving around the sun. His calculations supported Copernicus's heliocentric view. At the same time, however, they showed that the planets did not move in perfect circles, as both Ptolemy and Copernicus believed, but in another kind of orbit called an ellipse.

**"It does move."** Scientists of many lands built on the foundations laid by Copernicus and Kepler. In Italy, Galileo Galilei used technology developed by a Dutch lens grinder to assemble an astronomical telescope. With this instrument, he became the first person to see the mountains on the moon and sunspots. He also observed the four moons of Jupiter moving slowly around that planet—exactly, he realized, the way Copernicus said that the Earth moved around the sun.

Galileo's discoveries caused an uproar. Other scholars attacked him because his observations contradicted ancient views about the world. The Church condemned him because his ideas challenged the Christian teaching that the heavens were fixed, unmoving, and perfect.

In 1633, Galileo was brought to trial before the Inquisition. Threatened with death unless he withdrew his "heresies," Galileo agreed to publicly state that the Earth stood motionless at the center of the universe. "Nevertheless," he is said to have muttered as he left the court, "it does move."

**ISSUES** *For* **TODAY** Artists, writers, scholars, and scientists of the Renaissance and Reformation transformed the world with their revolutionary new ideas. What are some consequences of challenging accepted ways of thinking?

**The new scientific method.** Despite the opposition of religious authorities, by the early 1600s a new approach to science had emerged. Unlike most earlier approaches, it started not with Aristotle or Ptolemy or even the Bible but with observation and experimentation. Complex mathematical calculations were used to convert the observations and experiments into scientific laws. In time, this approach became known as the scientific method.

## Newton Ties It All Together

As a student at Cambridge University in England, Isaac Newton devoured the works of the leading scientists of his day. By age 24, he had developed a brilliant theory to explain why the planets moved as they did. According to one story, Newton was sitting in a garden when an apple fell from a tree. He wondered whether the force that pulled that apple to the Earth might not also control the movements of planets in space.

In the next 20 years, Newton perfected his theory. Using mathematics, he showed that a single force keeps the planets in their orbits around the sun. He called this force gravity.

In 1687, Newton published *Mathematical Principles of Natural Philosophy*, explaining the law of gravity and other workings of the universe. Nature, argued Newton, follows uniform laws. All motion in the universe can be measured and described mathematically.

To many, Newton's work seemed to link physics and astronomy, to bind the new science together as gravity itself held the universe together. English poet Alexander Pope caught the spirit of what would later be called the Newtonian revolution in these lines:

> **66**Nature and Nature's Laws lay hid in night,
>    God said, Let Newton be! and all was light.**99**

For over 200 years, Newton's laws held fast, until a revolution in physics in the early 1900s once more transformed the way people view the universe.

## More Scientific Advances

The 1500s and 1600s saw change in areas other than astronomy. Among the most important breakthroughs were those that occurred in chemistry and medicine.

**Chemistry.** Chemistry slowly freed itself from the magical notions of alchemy. Alchemists optimistically believed it was possible to transform ordinary metals into gold.

In the 1600s, Robert Boyle distinguished between individual elements and chemical compounds. He also explained the effect of temperature and pressure on gases. Boyle's work opened the way to modern chemical analysis of the composition of matter.

**Medicine.** Medieval physicians relied on the ancient works of Galen. Galen, however, had made many errors, in part because he had limited knowledge of human anatomy. During the Renaissance, artists like Leonardo da Vinci, as well as physicians, made new efforts to study the human body. In 1543, Andreas Vesalius published *On the Structure of the Human Body*, the first accurate and detailed study of human anatomy. Vesalius's careful and clear drawings corrected errors inherited from ancient classical authorities.

A French physician, Ambroise Paré, developed a new and more effective ointment for

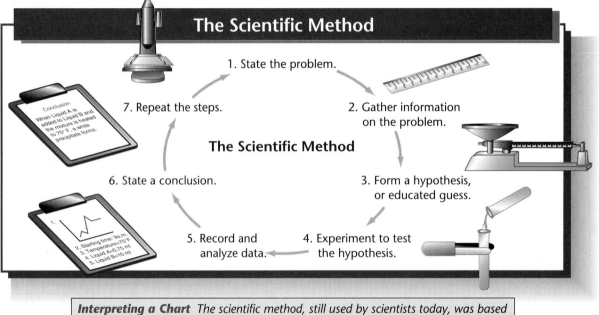

### The Scientific Method

1. State the problem.
2. Gather information on the problem.
3. Form a hypothesis, or educated guess.
4. Experiment to test the hypothesis.
5. Record and analyze data.
6. State a conclusion.
7. Repeat the steps.

**The Scientific Method**

Conclusion
When Liquid A is added to Liquid B and the mixture is heated to 75° F, a white precipitate forms.

2. Starting time: 9 a.m.
3. Temperature: 75°F
4. Liquid A: 75 ml
5. Liquid B: 10 ml

*Interpreting a Chart* The scientific method, still used by scientists today, was based on a new way of thinking. For the first time, scientists relied on objective data that they collected and measured, rather than on subjective observation. After reaching a conclusion, followers of the scientific method repeated their work at least once—and usually many times—to make sure that their findings were correct. ■ Why do you think it is important for scientists to repeat their work, as shown in Step 7?

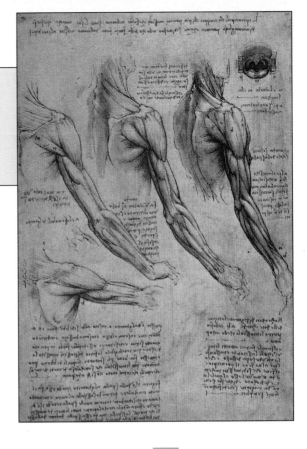

**Human Anatomy** *Leonardo da Vinci's drawings of human anatomy were based on dissections of more than 30 cadavers. He traced the circulatory, nervous, muscular, and skeletal systems with fair accuracy.* **Continuity and Change** *How would the practice of medicine be affected today if physicians did not have accurate knowledge of anatomy?*

preventing infection. He also developed a technique for closing wounds with stitches.

In the early 1600s, William Harvey, an English scholar, described the circulation of the blood for the first time. He showed how the heart serves as a pump to force blood through veins and arteries. These pioneering scientists opened the way for further advances.

## Bacon and Descartes

The new scientific method was really a revolution in thought. Two giants of this revolution were the Englishman Francis Bacon and the Frenchman René Descartes (ruh NAY day KAHRT). Each devoted himself to the problem of knowledge.

Both Bacon and Descartes rejected Aristotle's scientific assumptions. They also challenged the scholarly traditions of the medieval universities that sought to make the physical world fit in with the teachings of the Church. Both argued that truth is not known at the beginning of inquiry but at the end, after a long process of investigation.

Bacon and Descartes differed in their methods, however. Bacon stressed experiment and observation. He wanted science to make life better for people by leading to practical technologies. Descartes emphasized human reasoning as the best road to understanding. His *Discourse on Method* begins with the statement: "I think, therefore I am." Through reason, he argued, rather than traditional sources of knowledge, people could discover basic truths.

Thinkers like Bacon and Descartes helped bring the scientific method to the pursuit of all knowledge. They also spread the idea of the possibility of human progress. With their pioneering approaches, they opened the way to the Enlightenment of the 1700s. (See Chapter 18.)

## SECTION 5 REVIEW

1. **Identify** (a) Nicolaus Copernicus, (b) Tycho Brahe, (c) Johannes Kepler, (d) Galileo Galilei, (e) Andreas Vesalius, (f) William Harvey, (g) René Descartes.
2. **Define** (a) heliocentric, (b) gravity.
3. Why did each of the following challenge the heliocentric theory: (a) scholars, (b) the Church?
4. How did the new scientific method that was developed in the 1500s and 1600s differ from the traditional approach to science?
5. How did Newton explain the workings of the universe?
6. Identify three advances in medicine during the 1500s and 1600s.
7. *Critical Thinking* **Applying Information** Identify three ways in which your life would be different if the Scientific Revolution had not occurred.
8. *ACTIVITY* Review the material on Galileo Galilei on page 365. Then, with some of your classmates reenact Galileo's trial before the Inquisition.

# Skills for Success

## Analyzing Fine Art

Works of fine art, such as paintings and sculptures, can be a valuable source of historical information. Portraits may show us what famous people looked like. Religious paintings and statues suggest a culture's beliefs and values. Scenes of everyday life give details about what people wore, where they lived, or what they did for work and play. Works of art also show the kinds of technologies and materials that were available to the artist.

As with written sources, a historian must determine the reliability of an artwork. For example, a painter might have tried to flatter the king who was paying for a portrait by making him look more attractive or imposing than he was in real life. Or one painting may idealize the pleasures of city life, while another may stress its harshness, depending on the artist's point of view.

At right is a section of a large painting called *Children's Games*, by Pieter Bruegel. (See page 350.) Study the painting and answer the following questions.

**1** **Identify the work of art and the artist.** (a) What is the title of the painting? (b) Who was the artist? (c) When and where did he live?

**2** **Analyze the information in the art work.** (a) What is the subject of the painting? (b) Identify or describe three of the games shown. (c) Does Bruegel suggest any differences between the way boys and girls played? Explain. (d) What do you think is the social class of these children? How do you know?

**3** **Draw conclusions based on the work of art.** (a) In what ways is the scene in the painting realistic? In what ways is it not realistic? (b) Would you consider this painting a reliable source of information? Explain. (c) What kinds of information about children did Bruegel leave out? (d) Based on this painting, compare children's games in Bruegel's time with children's games today.

*Beyond the Classroom*  Locate a recent painting that you think presents a realistic view of modern American life. (The artist could be either a professional artist or a fellow student.) Identify the subject of the painting and determine the artist's point of view. Then, explain what kinds of information the painting could provide future generations about American life today.

## Building Vocabulary

Review the vocabulary words in this chapter. Then, use *ten* of these words to create a crossword puzzle. Exchange puzzles with a classmate. Complete the puzzles and then check each other's answers.

## Reviewing Chapter Themes

1. **Art and Literature** Describe the contributions that Renaissance artists made in each of the following areas: (a) painting, (b) sculpture, (c) architecture.
2. **Religions and Value Systems** (a) Why were many Europeans discontented with the Catholic Church? (b) What reforms did Luther introduce? (c) What reforms did Calvin introduce?
3. **Impact of the Individual** Describe three examples of individual achievement during the Renaissance.
4. **Economics and Technology** (a) How did Europeans learn about the technology of printing? (b) How did the spread of printing affect people's lives?
5. **Continuity and Change** How did each of the following contribute to the Scientific Revolution: (a) Nicolaus Copernicus, (b) Galileo Galilei, (c) Isaac Newton?

## Thinking Critically

1. **Making Inferences** Why might powerful rulers and wealthy business people choose to become patrons of the arts during the Renaissance?
2. **Analyzing Information** How did Renaissance ideas about life differ from those of the Middle Ages?
3. **Linking Past and Present** Renaissance writers published many books on how men and women should behave. (a) Describe one piece of advice that people today give to girls that they do not give to boys. (b) Describe one piece of advice they give only to boys. (c) How do you account for the difference?
4. **Comparing** (a) Compare and contrast the Renaissance in Italy with the Renaissance in northern Europe. (b) How would you account for the differences?

5. **Analyzing Information** Why do you think Luther's teachings caused a split in the Catholic Church when earlier reform movements did not?
6. **Recognizing Causes and Effects** (a) How did England become a Protestant nation? (b) Why did England escape the kinds of religious wars that tore apart other European nations? (★ See *Skills for Success*, page 18.)
7. **Recognizing Points of View** Protestants called the reform movement that took hold in the Catholic Church the Counter-Reformation. Catholics called it the Catholic Reformation. How do the terms reflect the different points of view of the two groups? (★ See *Skills for Success*, page 280.)
8. **Linking Past and Present** Modern scientists refer to the discoveries of Copernicus as the Copernican Revolution. Why do you think they use that term?

### For Your Portfolio

Imagine that you are a member of a book discussion group. At each meeting the members gather to discuss and review a book. The upcoming topic is the Renaissance and Reformation, and it is your turn to give the review.

1. Start by making a list of the books mentioned in this chapter. You might also research other titles at the library or confer with your English teacher.
2. Decide whether you wish to read fiction or nonfiction. Preview two or three books at the library before selecting one to read.
3. Make notes as you read so that you can begin your review with a brief summary and can address these questions: What point or points is the author making? How do these ideas or stories reflect the period in which they were written? How did they contribute to the growth of knowledge and the cultural rebirth that marked the Renaissance, or the arguments that spurred the Reformation?
4. After writing your review, prepare to present it to your group. Be ready to defend your point of view with examples from the book you read.

# The First Global Age: Europe and Asia

## (1415–1796)

## CHAPTER OUTLINE

In early July 1511, Portuguese naval commander Afonso de Albuquerque (ahl boo KEHR kuh) ordered his fleet to drop anchor off Malacca. Malacca was a rich trading port that controlled the sea route linking India, Southeast Asia, and China. To announce his arrival, Albuquerque fired a cannon salute and sounded trumpets.

The sultan of Malacca sent a message to the Portuguese. "Have you come in peace or in war?"

"Peace," replied Albuquerque. His true goal, however, was not peace, but conquest. He was determined to defeat the Muslim rulers who controlled the rich Indian Ocean spice trade and to build a Portuguese trading empire in Asia.

The fleet remained at anchor for several weeks. Then, on July 25, Albuquerque gave the order to open fire. An observer described the bombardment of Malacca:

66[The cannonballs] came like rain, and the noise of the cannon was as the noise of thunder in the heavens and the flashes of fire of their guns were like flashes of lightning in the sky. And the noise of their guns was like that of groundnuts popping in the frying pan.99

The Portuguese took the city, killing its inhabitants and seizing its wealth. On the ruins of a mosque, Albuquerque built a fort. The sultan had fled, thinking the invaders would loot and leave. But when he heard about the fort, he realized that the Portuguese had come to stay.

Portugal was the first European power to gain a foothold in Asia. In the early 1500s, European nations explored the seas beyond Europe, hunting for an all-water trade route to Asia. In the process, they encountered two previously unknown continents, the Americas.

Although Europeans mastered the seas, they could transport few soldiers to face the mighty empires of Asia. In the 1600s, however, European strength increased and older Asian empires declined. In this chapter and the next, you will see how Europeans ushered in the first global age, bringing together many peoples and civilizations for the first time.

**FOCUS ON** these questions as you read:

- **Economics and Technology**
  How did technology help Europeans explore the seas and build trading empires in Asia?

- **Diversity**
  What patterns of civilizations emerged in Southeast Asia?

- **Global Interaction**
  What new global patterns resulted from the European age of exploration?

- **Continuity and Change**
  How did the first global age affect the civilizations of Asia?

## TIME AND PLACE

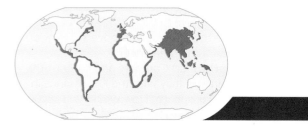

*Global Trade Network* Through trade with India and East Asia, European states grew wealthy and powerful. This painting shows the busy port city of Lisbon, capital of Portugal and the home port of a global trade network. During the 1500s, Portugal used military force to gain control of trade routes on the Indian Ocean. **Global Interaction** How are these Portuguese ships equipped for military conquest?

## HUMANITIES LINK

*Art History* Japanese screen painting (page 389).
*Literature* In this chapter, you will encounter passages from the following works of literature: "All the male heroes bowed their heads" (page 381); Pak Chi-won, "The Story of Ho" (page 388).

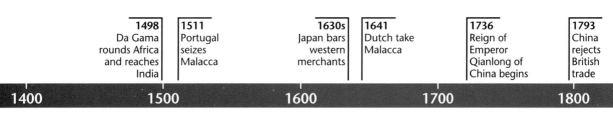

| 1498 | 1511 | 1630s | 1641 | 1736 | 1793 |
|---|---|---|---|---|---|
| Da Gama rounds Africa and reaches India | Portugal seizes Malacca | Japan bars western merchants | Dutch take Malacca | Reign of Emperor Qianlong of China begins | China rejects British trade |

| 1400 | 1500 | 1600 | 1700 | 1800 |

# 1 The Search for Spices

## Guide for Reading

- Why did European nations send explorers across the oceans?

- How did technology aid European sailors?

- What countries led the way in overseas exploration?

- **Vocabulary** *cartographer, astrolabe, caravel, circumnavigate*

Today, we take pepper for granted. To Europeans of past ages, though, this spice was as valuable as gold. Ancient Romans paid as much as $125 for 12 ounces (340 g) of pepper. During the Middle Ages, the pepper in your local supermarket could have paid a year's rent. The price was measured in more than just money. As pepper traveled from Asia to Europe, each cargo cost an estimated 1,000 lives.

By the late 1400s, the desire to share in the rich spice trade of the East spurred Europeans to explore the oceans. In the hope of enormous reward, sailors risked death on long sea voyages in tiny wooden ships.

## Europeans Take to the Seas

Europeans had traded with Asia long before the Renaissance. During the Middle Ages, the Crusades introduced Europeans to many luxury goods from Asia. Later, when the Mongol empire united much of Asia in the 1200s and 1300s, Asian goods flowed to Europe along complex overland trade routes. Marco Polo's tales of Chinese wealth and splendor fascinated Europeans.

The Black Death and the breakup of the Mongol empire disrupted Asian trade routes. By the 1400s, though, Europe was recovering from the plague. As its population increased, so, too, did the demand for Asian goods. The most valued trade items were spices, such as cloves, cinnamon—and, especially, pepper. In the days before refrigeration, meat spoiled quickly. People used spices to preserve food and to add flavor to dried and salted meat. Spices were also used to make medicines and perfumes. The major source of spices was the Moluccas, an island chain in present-day Indonesia, which Europeans called the Spice Islands.

**Motives.** In the 1400s, Muslim and Italian merchants controlled most trade between Asia and Europe. Muslim traders brought spices and other prized goods to eastern Mediterranean ports in Egypt, Syria, and Turkey. From there, traders from Venice and other Italian cities carried the precious cargoes to European markets. Each time goods passed from one trader to another, the prices increased. Europeans wanted to cut out the Muslim and Italian middlemen and gain direct access to the riches of Asia. To do so, the Atlantic powers—first Portugal, then Spain—sought a new route to Asia that bypassed the Mediterranean.

Many sailors hoped to get rich by trading in spices or conquering rich lands. Yet the desire for wealth was not the only motive that lured men to sea. Some voyagers were still fired by the centuries-old desire to crusade against the Muslims. During the Catholic Reformation, missionaries and soldiers set out overseas to win new converts to Christianity. The Renaissance spirit of inquiry fired people's desire to learn more about the lands beyond Europe.

**Improved technology.** Several improvements in technology helped Europeans conquer the vast oceans of the world. Cartographers, or mapmakers, created more accurate maps and sea charts. European sailors also learned to use the astrolabe, an instrument developed by the ancient Greeks and perfected by the Arabs, to determine their latitude at sea. The chart on the next page shows some of the other technological advances that helped navigators chart long sea voyages.

Along with more reliable navigational tools, Europeans designed larger and better ships. The Portuguese developed the caravel, which combined the square sails of European ships with Arab lateen, or triangular, sails. Caravels also adapted the sternpost rudder and numerous masts of Chinese ships. The new rigging made it easier to sail across or even into the wind. Finally, European ships added more armaments, including sturdier cannons.

# Technology of Ocean Navigation

| Device or Improvement | Description | Importance at the Time | Connections Today |
|---|---|---|---|
| **Magnetic compass** (around 1000) | A device for determining direction. A magnetic needle, floating in a dish of liquid, pointed north-south, allowing sailors to determine the direction of the ship. | Made it possible to find direction at sea, but was not very accurate; magnetic compass pointed northward but not to actual North Pole; iron in a ship could cause false readings. | Limits of magnetic compass led to development of the gyrocompass, which is not affected by magnetic force or gravity. Today it is used in ships, aircraft, and spacecraft. |
| **Astrolabe** (late 1400s) | A device used to measure the angles of the sun and stars above the horizon. It was difficult to use accurately in rough seas. | Improvement over the former method of measuring the altitude of the sun or stars as so many "hand widths" above the horizon. | Its weaknesses led to the development of the more accurate sextant. |
| **Mercator projection** (1569) | Map projection that shows latitude and longitude as straight lines; shapes are accurate, but size is distorted the farther one moves from the equator. | Excellent map for navigators because it showed true directions of places in relation to each other. | One of the most common types of map projections, even today. (See, for example, the map on page 995.) |
| **Sextant** (forerunner, about 1500; first sextant, 1730) | Device for determining the altitude of the sun or stars. By comparing this altitude at different degrees of latitude, the navigator could find the latitude of the ship. | Improvement over the astrolabe because the movements of the ship did not affect the reading so much and the user did not have to look directly into the sun. | The sextant, with only slight variations, was widely used until the mid-1900s. Since World War II, other inventions, such as radar, have taken its place. |

*Interpreting a Chart* Today, space travel would be unthinkable without the computer and the radio. In the 1400s, ocean travel would have been unthinkable without the compass and the astrolabe. Such technology allowed ships to navigate on the open seas, far out of sight of land. ■ *Why was the Mercator projection an important contribution to navigation? How was navigation linked to astronomy?*

## Portuguese Pioneers

Portugal, a small nation on the western edge of Spain, led the way in exploration. As in Spain, Christian knights in Portugal had fought off Muslim rule. By the 1400s, Portugal was strong and stable enough to expand into Muslim North Africa. In 1415, the Portuguese seized Ceuta (SAY oo tah) on the North African coast. The victory sparked the imagination of Prince Henry, known to history as Henry the Navigator.

**Mapping the coast of Africa.** Prince Henry embodied the crusading drive and the new spirit of exploration. He had heard tales of a mysterious but very rich Christian African ruler, Prester John. Henry hoped to form an alliance with Prester John against the Muslims. He also wanted to find the source of African gold.

At Sagres in southern Portugal, Henry gathered scientists, cartographers, and other experts. They redesigned ships, prepared maps, and trained captains and crews for long voyages. Henry then sent out ships that slowly worked their way south to explore the coast of West Africa.

Henry died in 1460, but the Portuguese continued their quest. In 1488, Bartholomeu Dias rounded the southern tip of Africa after being blown off course by a violent storm. Despite the turbulent seas, the tip became known as the Cape of Good Hope because it opened the way for a sea route to Asia.

**On to India.** In 1497, Vasco da Gama led four ships around the Cape of Good Hope. As he sailed up the coast of East Africa, he took on an Indian pilot who guided him across the Indian Ocean. After a 10-month voyage, Da Gama finally reached the great spice port of Calicut on the west coast of India.

The long voyage home took a heavy toll. The Portuguese lost half their ships. Many sailors died of hunger, thirst, and scurvy, a disease caused by the lack of vitamin C during months at sea. An officer wrote:

66All our people suffered from their gums, which grew over their teeth so that they could not eat. Their legs swelled, and other parts of the body, and these swellings spread until the sufferer died.99

Still, the venture proved highly profitable to the survivors. In India, Da Gama had acquired a cargo of spices that he sold at a profit of 3,000 percent.

Da Gama quickly outfitted a new fleet. In 1502, he forced a treaty of friendship on the Hindu ruler of Calicut. Da Gama then left Portuguese merchants there to buy spices when prices were low and to keep them stored near the dock until the next fleet could return to pick them up. As you will read, the Portuguese would soon seize key outposts around the Indian Ocean to create a vast trading empire.

## Spain Enters the Race

The profitable Portuguese voyages spurred other European nations to seek a sea route to Asia. In the 1480s, an Italian navigator from the port of Genoa, Christopher Columbus, sought Portuguese backing for his own plan. He wanted to reach the Indies* by sailing west across the Atlantic. Like most educated Europeans, Columbus knew that the Earth was a sphere. A few weeks sailing west, he reasoned, would bring a ship to eastern Asia.

Although his plan made sense, Columbus made two errors. First, he greatly underestimated the circumference of the Earth. Second, he had no idea that two continents, North and South America, lay in his path.

**Voyages of Columbus.** In 1492, Columbus finally convinced Ferdinand and Isabella of Spain to finance his "enterprise of the Indies." That year, the Catholic rulers had driven the Muslims from their last stronghold in Spain. To strengthen the power of their new monarchy, they sought new sources of wealth. Like the Portuguese, the Spanish hoped to bypass the Muslim-Italian monopoly on the spice trade. Queen Isabella was also anxious to spread Christianity among the people of Asia.

On August 3, 1492, Columbus sailed west with three small ships, the *Pinta,* the *Niña,* and the *Santa María.* He carried a letter to the ruler of China and took along an interpreter who spoke Arabic. With good weather and a favorable wind, his voyage was much shorter than Da Gama's would be. Still, the crew grew anxious as provisions ran low and no land came into sight. Finally, on October 12, a lookout yelled, "Land! Land!" The tiny fleet dropped anchor in the Caribbean Sea, off what were probably the Bahamas.

Columbus spent several months cruising the islands of the Caribbean, searching for China and Japan. Since he thought he had reached the Indies, he called the people of the region Indians. In 1493, he returned to Spain to a hero's welcome. In three later voyages, Columbus remained convinced he had reached islands off the coast of East Asia. Before long, though, other

---

*The Indies, or East Indies, was the European name for a group of islands in Southeast Asia. Today, they are a part of Indonesia.

Europeans realized that he had found a route to a continent previously unknown to them.

**Line of Demarcation.** Spain and Portugal pressed rival claims to the islands Columbus explored. In 1493, Pope Alexander VI stepped in to keep the peace. He set a Line of Demarcation that divided the non-European world into two zones. Spain had the right to trade and explore lands west of the line. Portugal had the same rights east of the line. The next year, in the Treaty of Tordesillas (tor day SEE yahs), the two countries moved the line.

In 1500, the Portuguese captain Pedro Alvarez Cabral was blown off course as he sailed around Africa. Landing in Brazil, which lay east of the Line of Demarcation, he claimed it for Portugal. In the next chapter, you will read about the effects of these Spanish and Portuguese claims.

**Naming the "New World."** In 1507, a German cartographer read reports about the "New World" by an Italian sailor, Amerigo Vespucci. The mapmaker labeled the region America and the name stuck. The islands Columbus had explored in the Caribbean became known as the West Indies.

Europeans continued to seek routes around or through the Americas to Asia. In 1513, the Spanish adventurer Vasco Nuñez de Balboa, with the help of Native Americans, hacked a passage through the tropical forests of Panama. From a ridge on the west coast, he gazed at a huge body of water that he called the South Sea. Before long, another hardy explorer, Ferdinand Magellan, would rename it the Mar Pacifico, the Pacific (peaceful) Ocean.

## The Quest for El Paso

A minor Portuguese noble, Magellan was only 19 when Vasco da Gama returned from his historic voyage to India. By 1511, Magellan himself had sailed around Africa to the East Indies and joined Afonso de Albuquerque in the attack on Malacca. Magellan slowly became convinced that he could find *El Paso,* a sea route through the Americas to the Indies. After Magellan had a falling out with the king of Portugal, he convinced King Charles of Spain to finance his voyage.

**A bold plan.** Magellan recruited sailors for a two-year voyage, but would not reveal their destination. Adventurous crew members signed on from many European nations—Spain, Portugal, the German states, the Netherlands—as well as from Africa and Southeast Asia. Among Magellan's recruits was an Italian adventurer, Antonio Pigafetta, whose journal gives us a fascinating record of the voyage.

Onto five ships Magellan loaded two years' worth of stores, including 10 tons of biscuits, 6,000 pounds of salt beef and pork, dried beans, flour, water, and wine, plus lumber, weapons, and gunpowder. He added mirrors, fishhooks, cloth, and knives as trade goods. Finally, on September 20, 1519, the ships sailed from Spain toward the "bottom of the world."

**Perils at sea.** As they sailed south and west, discontent surfaced. Magellan had to put down more than one mutiny. In October, storms lashed the ships. "We went up and down

*Fear of the Unknown* It took courage to volunteer for a long voyage. Popular tales warned that the oceans were full of dragons, sea serpents, and other monsters. This 1550 drawing contrasts the tame animals of the land with the fearsome creatures of the sea.
**Continuity and Change** In popular fiction today, what unexplored regions are sometimes populated by monsters?

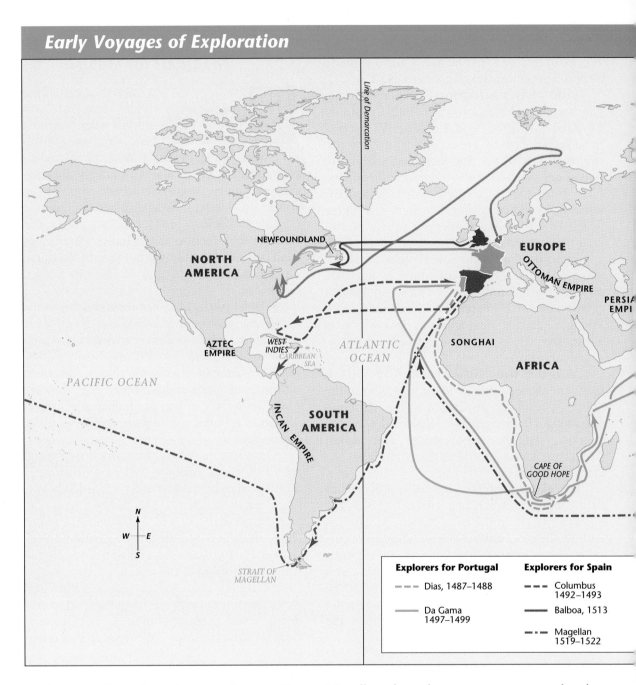

**Explorers for Portugal**

- - - - Dias, 1487–1488

———— Da Gama
1497–1499

**Explorers for Spain**

- - - - Columbus
1492–1493

———— Balboa, 1513

—·—·— Magellan
1519–1522

in the sea until good weather came," wrote Pigafetta. Then the fleet was becalmed for weeks. Food rotted in the tropical heat.

Finally, the fleet reached the coast of South America. Slowly, they explored each bay, hoping that one would lead to the Pacific. When another mutiny erupted, Magellan left the traitors on a barren part of the coast and sailed away, ignoring their cries for mercy.

In November 1520, more than a year after leaving Spain, Magellan's ships entered a bay at the southern tip of South America. Amid brutal storms, rushing tides, and unpredictable winds,

Magellan charted a tortuous passage that became known as the Strait of Magellan. "I think that there is not in the world a more beautiful country, or better strait than this one," wrote Pigafetta.

The ships emerged from this lashing into the calm Pacific Ocean. Although many wanted to return to Spain the way they had come, Magellan insisted they push on across the Pacific to the East Indies. Three more weeks, he thought, would bring them to the Spice Islands.

**Violence and bloodshed.** Like Columbus, Magellan had miscalculated. The Pacific

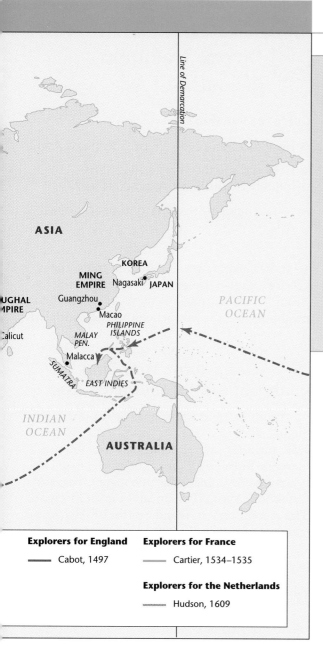

Line of Demarcation

ASIA

KOREA

MING EMPIRE    Nagasaki  JAPAN

UGHAL MPIRE    Guangzhou

Macao
PHILIPPINE
MALAY  ISLANDS
PEN.
Malacca

Calicut

PACIFIC OCEAN

SUMATRA

EAST INDIES

INDIAN OCEAN

AUSTRALIA

**Explorers for England**
—— Cabot, 1497

**Explorers for France**
—— Cartier, 1534–1535

**Explorers for the Netherlands**
∿∿∿ Hudson, 1609

*Beginning in the later 1400s, European nations sent explorers across the oceans in search of riches. Many explorers sought a northwest passage around the Americas, but none succeeded in finding one.*

1. **Location**  On the map, locate (a) Cape of Good Hope, (b) East Indies, (c) West Indies, (d) Europe, (e) Incan empire.
2. **Movement**  (a) For which country did Balboa sail? Cartier? (b) Which lands did Cabot explore? Da Gama? (c) Which explorers were probably looking for the northwest passage?
3. **Critical Thinking**  **Applying Information**  Why does the Line of Demarcation appear to be two lines on the map?

was much wider than he imagined. Pigafetta described their terrible hardships:

66We remained 3 months and 20 days without taking in provisions or other refreshments and ate only old biscuit reduced to powder, full of grubs and stinking from the dirt which rats had made on it. We drank water that was yellow and stinking. We also ate the ox hides from under the mainyard which we softened by soaking in seawater for several days.99

Soon, there was an outbreak of scurvy, which killed 19 crew members. Finally in March 1521, the fleet anchored off the Philippines. It had crossed the Pacific Ocean.

**Around the world.** Magellan won many converts to Christianity among the Filipinos, but he unfortunately made the mistake of getting involved in local politics. In a minor battle with one ruler, he found himself trapped. He died fighting to save his comrades. "Thus we lost our mirror, light, comfort and true guide," mourned Pigafetta.

After further battles and disasters, 18 half-dead sailors aboard a single ship completed the voyage. On September 8, 1522, more than three years after setting out, they anchored off Seville. The survivors, including Pigafetta, "went in shirts and barefoot" to give thanks at a nearby shrine. This ragged band were hailed as the first people to circumnavigate, or sail around, the world. ■

## The Search Continues

"I believe that never more will any man undertake to make such a voyage," predicted Pigafetta. But he was wrong. Although Spain and Portugal had divided the world between themselves, English, Dutch, and French explorers searched the coast of North America for a northwest passage to Asia.

**Seeking a northwest passage.** In 1497, King Henry VII of England had already sent a Venetian navigator named John Cabot (Giovanni Caboto) to seek a more northerly route than the one Columbus had charted. Cabot found rich fishing grounds off Newfoundland, which he claimed for England. Later the French captain Jacques Cartier explored the St. Lawrence River, while Henry Hudson, sailing for the Dutch, explored the Hudson River. Neither found the hoped-for passage to Asia, though.

The search for a northwest passage continued for centuries. In the meantime, bold sailors like Francis Drake followed Magellan's course around the stormy tip of South America.

**Looking ahead.** The European age of exploration marked the beginning of a period of growing global interdependence that has continued to the present day. Yet the activities of European explorers brought tragedy as well as triumph. In Chapter 16, you will read about the impact of European expansion on peoples of the Americas and West Africa.

The immediate impact of European exploration, though, was felt in Asia. When European fleets sailed toward Southeast Asia, they entered a world that had long ago developed its own cultures and trading patterns.

## SECTION 1 REVIEW

1. **Identify** (a) Prince Henry the Navigator, (b) Vasco da Gama, (c) Christopher Columbus, (d) Treaty of Tordesillas, (e) Vasco Nuñez de Balboa, (f) Ferdinand Magellan.
2. **Define** (a) cartographer, (b) astrolabe, (c) caravel, (d) circumnavigate.
3. Why did European nations seek a sea route to Asia?
4. Describe how each of the following countries contributed to the conquest of the world's oceans: (a) Portugal, (b) Spain.
5. *Critical Thinking* **Making Decisions** What pros and cons would you weigh if you were a sailor trying to decide whether to sign on with Da Gama, Columbus, or Magellan?
6. *ACTIVITY* Write a proclamation or design a poster that Prince Henry might have issued to attract navigators, sailors, and other experts to his sailing school at Sagres.

## 2 Diverse Traditions of Southeast Asia

### Guide for Reading

■ How did trade help shape Southeast Asia?

■ How did neighboring civilizations influence Southeast Asian cultures?

■ What major states emerged in Southeast Asia?

Sandwiched between China and India, the region known today as Southeast Asia was strongly influenced by these two powerful neighbors. Yet the distinct cultures of Southeast Asia retained their own unique identities.

### Geography: Mainland and Islands of Southeast Asia

Southeast Asia is made up of two major regions. The first region, mainland Southeast Asia, includes several peninsulas that jut south between India and China. Today, the mainland is home to Myanmar (MEE uhn mahr), Thailand, Cambodia, Laos, Vietnam, and part of Malaysia. The second region, island Southeast Asia, consists of more than 20,000 islands scattered between the Indian Ocean and the South China Sea. It includes the present-day nations of Indonesia, Singapore, Brunei (bru NĪ), and the Philippines.

**Location.** The mainland is separated from the rest of Asia by mountains and high plateaus. Still, traders and invaders did push overland into the region. The mountains also separated the four main river valleys of Southeast Asia—the Irrawaddy (ihr uh WAHD ee), Chao Phraya, Mekong, and Red. As elsewhere, the earliest civilizations emerged in these fertile river valleys.

Island Southeast Asia has long been of strategic importance. All seaborne trade between China and India had to pass through either the Malacca or Sunda straits. Whoever commanded the straits controlled rich trade routes. As you will read, the movements of people and goods between India and China would greatly influence Southeast Asia.

**Growing Rice** *In the river valleys and deltas of Southeast Asia, farmers have relied on rice as their staple crop. In fact, in several languages, the words for rice and for food are the same. Rice grows in padis, fields that are flooded by irrigation or heavy rains. These Vietnamese padis are flooded by the Mekong River.* **Geography and History** *What type of climate is needed for rice farming?*

**Trade routes in the southern seas.** The monsoons, or seasonal winds, shaped trading patterns in the "southern seas." Ships traveled northeast in summer and southwest in winter. Between seasons, while waiting for the winds to shift, merchants harbored their vessels in Southeast Asian ports, which became important centers of trade and culture. By the time of the Han empire, an international trade network linked East Africa and the Middle East to India, Southeast Asia, and China.

The key products of Southeast Asia were spices. In coastal towns from India to Southeast Asia, merchants bought and sold cloves, nutmeg, ginger, pepper, and other spices. Only a fraction of the spices traded in the region was destined for markets in Europe. Most cargoes went to East Asia, the Middle East, and East Africa.

**Early traditions.** The peoples of Southeast Asia developed their own cultures before Indian or Chinese influences shaped the region. At Bang Chiang in Thailand, archaeologists have found jars and even bronze bracelets at least 5,000 years old. This evidence is challenging old theories about when civilization began in the region.

Over the centuries, diverse ethnic groups speaking many languages settled in Southeast Asia. In isolated villages, they followed their own religious and cultural patterns. Many societies were built around the nuclear family rather than the joint families common in India and China.

Women had greater equality in Southeast Asia than elsewhere in Asia. Female merchants took part in the spice trade, gaining fame for their skill in bargaining, finance, and languages. In some port cities, they gained enough wealth and influence to become rulers. Matrilineal descent was an accepted custom in Southeast Asia, and women also had some freedom in choosing or divorcing marriage partners. Even after Indian and Chinese influences arrived, women retained their traditional rights.

## Impact of India

Indian merchants and Hindu priests filtered into Southeast Asia, slowly spreading their culture. Later, Buddhist monks and scholars introduced Theravada beliefs. Following the path of trade and religion came the influence of Sanskrit writing, Indian law, government, art, architecture, and farming.

**Increasing contacts.** In the early centuries A.D., Indian traders settled in port cities in growing numbers. They gave presents to local rulers and married into influential families. Trade brought prosperity as merchants exchanged Indian cottons, jewels, and perfume for raw materials such as timber, spices, and gold.

In time, local Indian families exercised considerable power. Also, people from Southeast Asia visited India as pilgrims or students. As these contacts increased, Indian beliefs and ideas won widespread acceptance. Indian influence reached its peak between 500 and 1000.

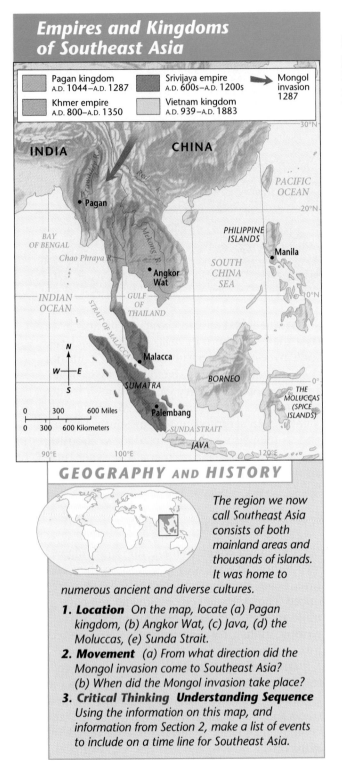

## Empires and Kingdoms of Southeast Asia

**Pagan kingdom** A.D. 1044–A.D. 1287

**Khmer empire** A.D. 800–A.D. 1350

**Srivijaya empire** A.D. 600s–A.D. 1200s

**Vietnam kingdom** A.D. 939–A.D. 1883

→ **Mongol invasion 1287**

### GEOGRAPHY AND HISTORY

*The region we now call Southeast Asia consists of both mainland areas and thousands of islands. It was home to numerous ancient and diverse cultures.*

1. **Location** On the map, locate (a) Pagan kingdom, (b) Angkor Wat, (c) Java, (d) the Moluccas, (e) Sunda Strait.
2. **Movement** (a) From what direction did the Mongol invasion come to Southeast Asia? (b) When did the Mongol invasion take place?
3. **Critical Thinking** **Understanding Sequence** Using the information on this map, and information from Section 2, make a list of events to include on a time line for Southeast Asia.

islands of Indonesia and as far east as the Philippines.* Arab merchants, too, spread the new faith. The prevalence of Islam in lands surrounding the Indian Ocean helped create a stable, thriving trade network.

## New Kingdoms and Empires

The blending of Indian influences with traditional ways produced a series of kingdoms and empires in Southeast Asia. Some of these states rivaled those of India.

**Pagan.** The kingdom of Pagan (pah GAHN) arose in the fertile rice-growing Irrawaddy Valley in present-day Myanmar. In 1044, King Anawrata (ah nuh RAH tuh) united the region. He is credited with bringing Buddhism to the Burman people. Although Buddhism had reached nearby cultures long before, Anawrata made Pagan a major Buddhist center. He filled his capital city with magnificent stupas and shrines at about the same time that people in medieval Europe were beginning to build Gothic cathedrals.

Pagan flourished for some 200 years after Anawrata's death, but fell in 1287 to conquering Mongols. When the Burmans finally threw off foreign rule to become masters of their own fate, they looked back with pride to the great days of Pagan.

**The Khmer empire.** Indian influences also helped shape the Khmer (kuh MEHR) empire that reached its peak between 800 and 1350. Its greatest rulers controlled much of present-day Cambodia, Thailand, and Malaysia. During its centuries of splendor, the Khmer people adapted Indian writing, mathematics, architecture, and art. Khmer rulers became pious Hindus. Like the princes and emperors of India, they saw themselves as god-kings. Most ordinary people, however, preferred Buddhism.

In the 1100s, King Suryavarman II built the great temple complex at Angkor Wat. The ruins that survive today, though overgrown with jungle and pocked by the bullets of recent wars, are among the most impressive in the world. Hundreds of carved figures tell Hindu myths and glorify the king. Although the images of Vishnu,

**Islam.** Long after Hinduism and Buddhism took root in Southeast Asia, Indians carried a third religion, Islam, into the region. By the 1200s, Muslims ruled northern India. (See Chapter 11.) From there, traders spread both Islamic beliefs and civilization throughout the

---

*Today, Indonesia has the largest Muslim population of any nation in the world.

▲ Temple at Angkor Wat

Shiva, and the Buddha reflect strong Indian influence, the style is uniquely Khmer.

**Srivijaya.** The trading empire of Srivijaya (shree vah JĪ yah), in Indonesia, flourished from the 600s to the 1200s. Srivijaya controlled the Malacca Strait. Both Hinduism and Buddhism reached this island empire. As elsewhere in Southeast Asia, however, the local people often blended Indian beliefs into their own forms of worship, based on nature spirits.

Later, Islam spread to Sumatra, Java, and other islands. Local rulers adopted the new religion, which cemented commercial links with other Muslim trading centers around the Indian Ocean.

## Vietnam Emerges

In most of Southeast Asia, Indian influence outweighed Chinese influence. Indian traditions spread mostly through trade. China, however, sent military forces to conquer neighboring Annam, what is today northern Vietnam.

The heart of northern Vietnam was the Red River delta around present-day Hanoi. There, the river irrigated fertile rice padis, which fed a growing population. The Vietnamese had their own culture. As elsewhere in Southeast Asia, women often held positions of authority.

**Chinese domination.** In 111 B.C., Han armies conquered the region. China remained in control for 1,000 years. During that time, the Vietnamese absorbed Confucian ideas. They adopted the Chinese civil service system and built a government bureaucracy similar to China's. Vietnamese nobles learned to speak and read Chinese. Unlike the rest of Southeast Asia, where Theravada Buddhism had the strongest impact, Vietnam adopted Mahayana beliefs from China. Daoism also helped shape Vietnamese society.

**Resistance.** Despite these powerful Chinese influences, the Vietnamese preserved a strong sense of their separate identity. In A.D. 39, two noble sisters, Trung Trac and Trung Nhi, led an uprising that drove the Chinese occupiers from the land. Trung Trac set up a royal court in Melinh. She rejected Chinese influence and tried to restore a simpler form of government according to ancient Vietnamese traditions. She also abolished the hated tribute taxes that had been imposed by the Chinese.

A Han general soon crushed the revolt, but the Trung sisters refused to surrender. To this day, they are remembered as great martyrs and heroes. A Vietnamese poet of the 1400s wrote:

> 66All the male heroes bowed their heads in submission;
> Only the two sisters proudly stood up to avenge their country.99

Finally in 939, as the Tang dynasty collapsed in China, Vietnam was able to break free from Chinese rule. The Vietnamese turned back repeated Chinese efforts to reconquer their land, but did remain a tributary state of China. Ties between the two countries remained so strong that, while China was the "large dragon" of East Asia, Vietnam became known as the "smaller dragon."

## SECTION 2 REVIEW

1. **Identify** (a) Pagan, (b) Anawrata, (c) Khmer, (d) Suryavarman II, (e) Trung sisters.
2. How did an international trade network emerge in the Indian Ocean?
3. What outside religious beliefs influenced the peoples of Southeast Asia?
4. Describe the relationship between Vietnam and China.
5. *Critical Thinking* **Analyzing Information** Women had an inferior social status in both India and China. Why do you think Southeast Asian women retained their equality despite Indian and Chinese influence?
6. *ACTIVITY* Create a map showing foreign influences in Southeast Asia. First, draw or trace an outline map of the region. Use arrows to show the origins and direction of influences—blue arrows for trade routes, red arrows for invasion routes. Then, show what products or ideas traveled along these routes.

# 3 European Footholds in Southeast Asia and India

## Guide for Reading

- How did Portugal build a trading empire in Southeast Asia?
- How did the Dutch become a leading commercial power?
- Why were Europeans able to extend their influence in India after 1700?

- **Vocabulary** *sepoy, raj*

When the Portuguese arrived in the Indian Ocean, their ships were small in size and number, but they had one great advantage. The firepower of their shipboard cannons was unmatched. When the Portuguese first reached Colombo in present-day Sri Lanka, witnesses reported that they had "guns with a noise like thunder and a ball from one of them, after traversing a league, will break a castle of marble." In time, their firepower helped the newcomers win control of the existing Indian Ocean trade network.

## Portugal's Empire in the East

After Vasco da Gama's voyage, the Portuguese burst into the Indian Ocean. In 1510, they seized the island of Goa off the coast of India, making it their major base. Afonso de Albuquerque then moved to end Muslim power and make the Indian Ocean a "Portuguese lake."

**Trading outposts.** Albuquerque burned coastal towns and crushed Arab fleets at sea. The Portuguese attacked Aden, at the entrance to the Red Sea, and took Ormuz, gateway to the Persian Gulf. The richest prize, though, was the port of Malacca, as Albuquerque knew:

> 66 If we take this trade of Malacca away from them, Cairo and Mecca will be entirely ruined, and Venice will receive no spiceries unless her merchants go to buy them in Portugal. 99

In 1511, Albuquerque was successful in taking Malacca. The Portuguese massacre of the city's Muslims made the Europeans hated and feared.

In less than 50 years, the Portuguese had military and trading outposts rimming the southern seas. They seized cities on the east coast of Africa so they could resupply and repair their ships traveling to and from the Indies. For most of the 1500s, Portugal controlled the spice trade between Europe and Asia.

**Matchmaking in Goa** In this 1628 painting, two Indian women welcome a Portuguese settler. Many Portuguese men married local women who converted to Christianity. Their children formed the base of a new colonial society. Goa remained under Portuguese control until 1961. **Global Interaction** Why did the Portuguese seize control of Goa?

## Endangered Species

In the fragile balance of nature, each plant and animal is especially suited to conditions in its environment. Sudden changes to that environment may threaten the survival of an entire species. In fact, scientists estimate that 99 percent of all species that ever existed—including the giant dinosaurs and the woolly mammoth—are already extinct!

**Linking Past and Present** Why do many individuals and governments today try to protect endangered species?

**PAST** The flightless dodo bird (left) once thrived on an island in the Indian Ocean. But when the Portuguese and Dutch arrived in the 1500s, they found the placid dodo very easy to hunt. Also, the newcomers introduced rats, pigs, and dogs that ate countless dodo eggs. Within 200 years, the dodo bird was extinct.

**PRESENT** Today, world organizations keep careful track of endangered species, such as the Galapagos penguin (left) and the scarlet macaw (above). To protect them and their environment, conservationists try to limit hunting and control the introduction of new species.

**Impact.** Despite their sea power, the Portuguese remained on the fringe of Asian trade. They had neither the strength nor the resources to conquer much territory on land. In India and China, where they faced far stronger empires, they merely sought permission to trade.

The intolerance of Portuguese missionaries caused resentment. In Goa, they attacked Muslims, destroyed Hindu temples, and introduced the Inquisition. Portuguese ships even sank Muslim pilgrim ships on their way to Mecca. While the Portuguese disrupted some older trade patterns, exchanges continued among Asians. Some bypassed Portuguese-controlled towns. Others traded with the newcomers.

In the late 1500s, Portuguese power declined overseas. By the early 1600s, other Europeans were vying to replace the Portuguese.

### Rise of the Dutch

The Dutch were the first Europeans to challenge Portuguese domination in Asia. The land we know today as the Netherlands included a group of provinces and prosperous cities on the North Sea. The region had long been a center of handicrafts and trade. Through royal marriages, it fell under Spanish rule in the early 1500s. Later, the Protestant northern provinces won independence. (See Chapter 17.)

**Sea power.** In 1599, a Dutch fleet returned to Amsterdam from Asia after more than a year's absence. It carried thousands of pounds of pepper and cloves, along with other spices. Church bells rang to celebrate this "Happy Return." Those who had invested in the venture received 100 percent profit. The success of this voyage led to a frenzy of overseas activity.

By the late 1500s, their warships and trading vessels put the Dutch in the forefront of European commerce. They used their sea power to set up colonies and trading posts around the world. Like the Portuguese, the Dutch wanted to profit from the spice trade. They charted routes to bypass sea lanes under Portuguese control. At the southwestern tip of Africa, the Dutch built the Cape Town settlement, where they could repair and resupply their ships.

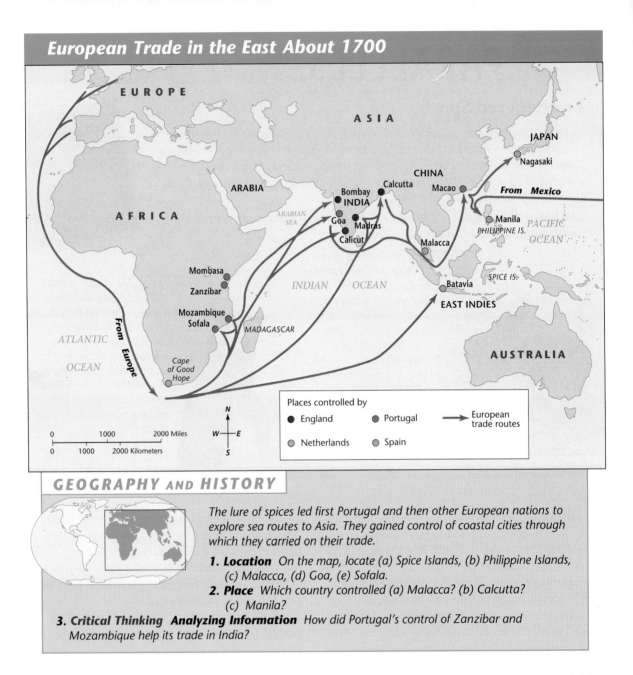

## European Trade in the East About 1700

Places controlled by
- England
- Netherlands
- Portugal
- Spain

→ European trade routes

N W E S

0 1000 2000 Miles
0 1000 2000 Kilometers

### GEOGRAPHY AND HISTORY

*The lure of spices led first Portugal and then other European nations to explore sea routes to Asia. They gained control of coastal cities through which they carried on their trade.*

**1. Location** On the map, locate (a) Spice Islands, (b) Philippine Islands, (c) Malacca, (d) Goa, (e) Sofala.

**2. Place** Which country controlled (a) Malacca? (b) Calcutta? (c) Manila?

**3. Critical Thinking** **Analyzing Information** How did Portugal's control of Zanzibar and Mozambique help its trade in India?

**Dutch dominance.** In 1602, a group of wealthy Dutch merchants formed the Dutch East India Company. In the next decades, the Dutch strove to make themselves the major European power in the east. In 1641, they captured Malacca from the Portuguese and opened trade with China. Before long, they were able to enforce a monopoly in the Spice Islands, controlling shipments to Europe as well as much of the trade within Southeast Asia.

The Dutch, like the Portuguese, used military force to further their trading goals. At the same time, they forged closer ties with local rulers than the Portuguese had. The Dutch generally avoided aggressive missionary activities. Many Dutch merchants married Asian women.

Trade brought the Dutch enormous wealth. At home, Dutch merchants built tall mansions along the canals of Amsterdam and hired artists like Rembrandt to paint their portraits. In the 1700s, however, the growing power of England and France contributed to a decline in the Dutch overseas trading empire.

### Spain Seizes the Philippines

While the Portuguese and Dutch set up bases on the fringes of Asia, Spain took over the

Philippines. Magellan claimed the archipelago for Spain in 1521. Within about 50 years, Spain had conquered and colonized the islands. They were then named for the Spanish king Philip II. Unlike most other peoples of Southeast Asia, the Filipinos were not united. As a result, they could be more easily conquered.

In the spirit of the Catholic Reformation, Spanish priests set out to convert the Filipino people to the Christian religion. Later, missionaries moved on from the Philippines to spread Catholic teachings in East Asia.

The Philippines became a key link in Spain's overseas trading empire. The Spanish shipped silver mined in Mexico and Peru across the Pacific to the Philippines. From there, they used it to buy goods in China. In this way, large quantities of American silver flowed into the trade networks of East Asia.

## Mughal India and European Traders

Before the 1700s, European traders made very little impression on India, which was enjoying one of its greatest periods of strength and prosperity. In 1526, Babur had founded the Mughal dynasty. It achieved its peak under his grandson Akbar. (See Chapter 11.) European merchants, who had reached India before the rise of the Mughals, were dazzled by India's splendid court and its many luxury goods. There seemed little that Europeans could offer of value to the Mughals.

**Industry and commerce.** Besides producing spices, Hindu and Muslim families across India presided over vigorous handicraft and shipbuilding industries. India was the world leader in textile manufacturing. It exported large quantities of silk and cotton, from sheer muslins to elaborate chintzes.

The Mughal empire was larger, richer, and more powerful than any in Europe. When Europeans sought trading rights, the emperors saw

**A Prized Import** *Indian artisans created products like this hand-painted cotton wall hanging for European markets. Indian cottons became so popular in England that, to protect the British textile industry, Parliament tried to ban them.* **Global Interaction** *How does this wall hanging reflect both Indian and European culture?*

no threat in granting such concessions. The Portuguese and later the Dutch, English, and French built forts and warehouses in coastal towns. There they bought and shipped cargoes to Europe.

**Turmoil and decline.** When Akbar's successors ended his policy of religious toleration, conflicts rekindled between Hindu and Muslim princes. Civil war drained Mughal resources. Rulers then increased taxes, sparking peasant rebellions. An Indian historian at the time noted:

> 66Tax collectors have become a scourge for the peasants. . . . Many townships that used to yield full revenue have, owing to the oppression of officials, been so far ruined and devastated that they have become forests infested by tigers and lions.99

Several weak rulers held the throne in the early 1700s. Corruption became widespread, and the central government collapsed.

**ISSUES** *For* **TODAY** The desire to dominate the spice trade led Europeans on a course of exploration and conquest. How can control of major resources influence political developments?

**British-French rivalry.** As Mughal power faltered, French and English traders played off rival Indian princes against each other. The British and French East India companies made alliances with local officials and independent rajahs. Each company organized its own army of sepoys, or Indian troops. Well trained and disciplined, sepoy regiments helped keep order in areas ruled by the companies.

By the mid-1700s, the British and the French were locked in a global power struggle. In 1756, war between Britain and France erupted in Europe, and fighting soon spread to their lands overseas.

In India, Robert Clive, an agent of the British East India Company, used an army of British troops and sepoys to drive the French from their trading posts. The Company then forced the Mughal emperor to recognize its right to collect taxes in Bengal in the northeast. By the late 1700s, the Company had become the real ruler of Bengal. With its great wealth, the Company built forts and raised armies to spread its influence into other parts of India.

The Company often gained its ends, not only by military force, but by winning the backing of local Indian rulers. The activities of the British East India Company set the stage for the expanding British raj, or rule, to come.

## SECTION 3 REVIEW

1. **Identify** (a) Afonso de Albuquerque, (b) Robert Clive.
2. **Define** (a) sepoy, (b) raj.
3. How did Portugal gain control of the spice trade?
4. How did the Dutch replace the Portuguese as the major European trading power in Asia?
5. (a) Why did Mughal power decline? (b) How did the decline help France and Britain?
6. *Critical Thinking* **Analyzing Information** How did European powers build on existing trade networks in the Indian Ocean?
7. *ACTIVITY* "Whoever is head of Malacca has his hand on the throat of Venice," noted Portuguese naval commander Afonso de Albuquerque. Draw a cartoon showing what he meant by this.

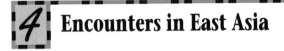

# 4 Encounters in East Asia

## Guide for Reading

■ How did shifts in power affect China and its relations with European powers?

■ Why did Korea become the Hermit Kingdom?

■ What policy did Tokugawa shoguns take toward foreigners?

The Europeans who reached Asia in the 1500s often made a poor impression on their hosts. The Italian traveler Niccoló Manucci told how Asians thought that Europeans "have no polite manners, that they are ignorant, wanting in ordered life, and very dirty."

Europeans, by contrast, wrote enthusiastically about China. In 1590, a visitor described Chinese artisans "cleverly making devices out of gold, silver and other metals." He was also impressed with their industries:

66 Their industry appears in the making of guns and gunpowder, whereof there are many rare fireworks. To these may be added the art of printing. Although their letters are many and most difficult . . . they daily publish huge multitudes of books.99

Portuguese ships first reached China by way of the South China Sea during the Ming dynasty. To the Chinese, the Portuguese were "southern barbarians" who, like other foreigners, lacked the civilized ways of the Middle Kingdom.

## European Trade With China

The Ming dynasty, you will recall, ended its overseas explorations in the mid-1400s. Confucian officials had little use for foreigners. "Since our empire owns the world," said a Ming document, "there is no country on this or other sides of the seas which does not submit to us."

**Limits on foreign trade.** Portuguese traders reached China by sea in 1514. To the Chinese, the newcomers had little to offer in exchange for silks and porcelains. European textiles, metalwork, and other goods were inferior to Chinese products. The Chinese therefore demanded payment in gold or silver.

The Ming eventually allowed the Portuguese a trading post at Macao, near Canton, present-day Guangzhou (gwahng JOH). Later, they let Dutch, English, and other Europeans trade with Chinese merchants but under strict limits. Foreigners could trade only at Canton under the supervision of imperial officials. When each year's trading season ended, they had to sail away. Europeans tried, without success, to break these restrictions.

**Matteo Ricci.** A few European scholars, like the brilliant Jesuit priest Matteo Ricci, did make a positive impression on Ming China. In the 1580s, Ricci learned to speak Chinese and adopted Chinese dress. His goal was to convert upper-class Chinese to Christianity. He hoped that they, in turn, would spread Christian teachings to the rest of China.

▲ *Chinese fan showing foreign flags in Canton*

Ricci won friends among the scholar-gentry by sharing his knowledge of the arts and sciences of Renaissance Europe. The Chinese were fascinated by new European technologies, including maps. They were also open to European discoveries in astronomy and mathematics. While Chinese rulers welcomed Ricci and other Jesuits for their learning, the priests had little success spreading their religious beliefs.

## The Manchu Conquest

In the early 1600s, the aging Ming dynasty decayed. Revolts erupted, and Manchu invaders pushed through the Great Wall. The Manchus ruled a region in the northeast that had long been influenced by Chinese civilization. In 1644, victorious Manchu armies seized Beijing and made it their capital.

**Qing rule.** The Manchus set up a new dynasty called the Qing (CHIHNG), meaning "pure." To preserve their distinct identity, the Manchus barred intermarriage between Manchus and Chinese. Manchu women were forbidden to follow the traditional Chinese practice of footbinding. Still, the Manchus won the support of the Chinese scholar-gentry because they adopted the Confucian system of government. For each top government position, the Qing chose two people, one Manchu and one Chinese. Local government remained in the hands of the Chinese, but Manchu troops stationed across the empire ensured loyalty.

Two rulers oversaw the most brilliant age of the Qing. Kangxi (kahng SHEE), who ruled from 1661 to 1722, was an able administrator and military leader. He extended Chinese power into Central Asia and promoted Chinese culture. Kangxi's grandson Qianlong (chyehn LOHNG) had an equally successful reign from 1736 to 1796. He expanded the borders to rule the largest area in Chinese history. Qianlong retired after 60 years because he did not want to rule longer than his grandfather had.

**Prosperity.** The Chinese economy expanded under both emperors. New crops from the Americas, such as potatoes and corn, boosted farm output, which contributed to a population boom. China's population rose from 140 million in 1740 to over 300 million by 1800. Peace and prosperity contributed to further growth in handicraft industries, including silk, cotton, and porcelain. Internal trade grew, as did the demand for Chinese goods from all over the world.

**Response to westerners.** The Qing maintained the Ming policy of restricting foreign traders. Still, Europeans kept pressing to open up new cities to trade. In 1793, Lord Macartney arrived in China at the head of a British diplomatic mission. He brought samples of British-made goods to show the Chinese the advantages of trade with westerners. The Chinese thought the goods were gifts offered as tribute to the emperor and looked on them as rather crude products.

Further misunderstandings followed. The Chinese told Macartney he would have to perform the traditional kowtow, touching his head to the ground to show respect to the emperor. Macartney refused. He also offended the Chinese by speaking of the natural superiority of the English. The negotiations faltered. In the end, Qianlong did receive Macartney, but the meeting accomplished nothing. Later, in a letter to King George III of Britain, Qianlong rejected the request for trading rights. ( ★ See *Skills for Success,* page 390.)

At the time, Qianlong's attitude seemed justified by China's successes. After all, he already ruled the world's greatest empire. In the long run, however, his policy proved disastrous. Even then, there was much the Chinese could have learned from the West. In the 1800s, China would learn about western advances—especially in military technology—the hard way.

## The Hermit Kingdom

Like China, Korea restricted outside contacts in the 1500s and 1600s. Earlier, Korean traders had far-ranging contacts across East Asia. A Korean map from the 1300s accurately outlines lands from Japan to the Mediterranean. Koreans probably acquired this knowledge from Arab traders who had visited Korea.

The Choson dynasty, you will recall, firmly embraced Confucian ethics and ideas. Like the Chinese, Koreans felt that Confucian learning was the most advanced in the world. The low status of merchants in Confucianism also led Koreans to look down on foreign traders.

Two other events led the Koreans to turn inward. The Japanese invasion in the 1590s devastated the land of Korea. Then in 1636, the Manchus conquered Korea before overrunning Ming China. When the Manchus set up the Qing dynasty in China, Korea became a tributary state, forced to acknowledge Chinese supremacy. The two invasions left Korea feeling like "a shrimp among whales."

In response, the Koreans chose isolation, excluding all foreigners except the Chinese and a few Japanese. When European sailors were shipwrecked on Korean shores, they were imprisoned. As a result, Korea became known as the Hermit Kingdom.

Even though Korea had few contacts with the world for about 250 years, this period was a great age for Korean arts and literature. In one satirical tale, "The Story of Ho," Pak Chi-won describes a poor scholar who breaks with tradition by becoming a merchant. Here, Master Ho describes doing business in an isolated country:

66 Our country has no trade with other countries, and . . . everything we use is produced and consumed in the same province. . . . With ten thousand yang, you can buy just about all of one particular item produced in the country. You can buy the whole lot, whether you load it on a cart or on a boat. 99

## Tokugawa Shoguns and Foreign Traders

Unlike the Chinese or Koreans, the Japanese at first welcomed western traders. In 1543, the Portuguese reached Japan. Later came the Spanish, Dutch, and English. They arrived at the turbulent time when strong daimyo were struggling for power. The Japanese quickly acquired western firearms and built castles modeled on European designs. In fact, the new weapons may have helped the Tokugawa shoguns centralize power and impose order.

**Spread of Christianity.** Japan was much more open to European missionaries than China. Jesuits, like the Spanish priest Francis Xavier, found the Japanese curious and eager to learn about Christianity. A growing number of Japanese adopted the new faith. As a missionary reported, some Japanese "hang a crucifix from their shoulders or waist . . . some, who are especially kindly disposed, have memorized the *Our Father* and the *Hail Mary,* and recite them as they walk in the streets."

**Closing the door.** The Tokugawa shoguns, however, became increasingly hostile

**GLOBAL CONNECTIONS**

Qianlong was also disturbed by word of the French Revolution, which had begun in 1789. French revolutionaries spread ideas about liberty and equality and eventually toppled the monarchy. Even worse, the king of France was beheaded not long before Macartney's visit. This news confirmed Qianlong's desire to remain aloof from the West.

**Japanese Screen Painting** *Shoguns and daimyos filled their castles with brilliant, multi-paneled screen paintings. Many screens depicted the beauties of nature. Others portrayed scenes of everyday life, including a popular series of "Southern Barbarian" screens. This screen depicts the activities of Japanese and Portuguese seafarers aboard a large ship.* **Art and Literature** *How did the artist create a sense of motion?*

toward foreigners. After learning how Spain had seized the Philippines, they may have seen the newcomers as agents of an invading force. In addition, Japanese officials disliked the intrigues and competition among Christian missionaries. They also suspected that Japanese Christians—who may have numbered 300,000—owed their allegiance to a foreign power, the pope.

In response, the Tokugawas expelled foreign missionaries. They brutally persecuted Japanese Christians, killing many thousands. The few Christians who survived practiced their religion in secret for the next 200 years.

By 1638, the Tokugawas had barred all western merchants and forbidden Japanese to travel abroad. They outlawed the building of large ships, thereby ending foreign trade. To keep informed about world events, they permitted just one or two Dutch ships each year to trade at a small island in Nagasaki harbor. Through this tiny gateway, the Japanese did learn about some foreign ideas. They studied Dutch medical texts, for example, which they found to be more accurate than Chinese ones.

**Looking ahead.** Japan maintained its policy of strict isolation for more than 200 years. During this time, internal trade boomed. Cities grew in size and importance. By the late 1700s, Edo (present-day Tokyo) had a million inhabitants, more than either London or Paris.

In 1853, Japan was forced to reopen contacts with the western world. Renewed relations unleashed an extraordinary period of change that helped Japan emerge as a major world power. (See Chapter 26.)

## SECTION 4 REVIEW

1. **Identify** (a) Matteo Ricci, (b) Manchus, (c) Kangxi, (d) Qianlong, (e) Hermit Kingdom.
2. (a) How was economic prosperity reflected in Qing China? (b) How did the Qing restrict foreign trade?
3. Why did Korea pursue a policy of isolation?
4. Why did the Tokugawa policy toward foreigners change over time?
5. *Critical Thinking* **Linking Past and Present** Why are some Americans today in favor of limiting ties to foreign countries?
6. *ACTIVITY* Write a dialogue between two officials in China, Korea, or Japan. One official should express a willingness to establish relations with European powers. The other should argue in favor of a policy of isolation.

# Skills for Success

**Critical Thinking**

**Writing and Researching**

**Maps, Charts, and Graphs**

**Speaking and Listening**

## Recognizing Bias

A critical reader of primary sources must be able to detect bias. **Bias** is a prejudice for or against someone or something. One form of bias, cultural bias, is directed toward people of another culture. Personal experience can also lead to bias.

As cultures came into closer contact during the first global age, both Europeans and Asians exhibited cultural biases. As you have read, many Asians viewed Europeans as dirty, ignorant, and rude in manner. In the same way, many Europeans considered themselves more civilized than the peoples of Asia. Europeans routinely referred to Hindus and Buddhists as "heathens" or "idolaters."

The first reading below is from Qianlong's letter to King George III. (See page 388.) The second is from a later analysis of China by Lord Macartney. Read both excerpts and answer the following questions.

**1** **Identify the source of the writing.**
(a) What was Qianlong's cultural background?
(b) What led him to write this letter? (c) What was Macartney's cultural background? (d) What was his relationship to Qianlong?

**2** **Look for evidence of bias.** (a) What words does Qianlong use to describe the English? (b) What words does he use to describe the Chinese? (c) How does Macartney refer to Qianlong? (d) What seems to be his general attitude toward China? How can you tell?

**3** **Draw conclusions.** (a) What cultural attitudes influenced Qianlong's viewpoint? (b) Do you think bias led him to misinterpret King George's motives? Explain. (c) How may Macartney's personal experiences have colored his opinions?

***Beyond the Classroom*** Look for a newspaper or magazine article, television program, or movie that presents images of people of other cultures. Write a paragraph describing the image presented and discuss whether you think the source exhibits a cultural bias.

---

### Emperor Qianlong

❝You, O King, from afar have yearned after the blessings of our civilization, and in your eagerness to come into touch with our converting influence have sent an Embassy across the sea bearing a letter. I have already taken note of your respectful spirit of submission. . . .

Before now, all European nations, including your own country's barbarian merchants, have carried on their trade with our Celestial Empire at Canton. Such has been the procedure for many years, although our Celestial Empire possesses all things in abundance and lacks no product within its own borders. There was therefore no need to import the manufactures of outside barbarians. . . .

Your Ambassador has put forward requests which completely fail to recognize the Throne's principle to 'treat strangers from afar with indulgence,' and to exercise a pacifying control over barbarian tribes the world over. . . . Nevertheless, I do not forget the lonely remoteness of your island, cut off from the world by intervening wastes of sea, nor do I overlook your excusable ignorance of the customs of our Celestial Empire. I have therefore commanded my minister to enlighten your Ambassador on the subject.❞

### Lord Macartney

❝The empire of China is an old first-rate [warship], which a succession of vigilant officers has continued to keep afloat for these 150 years past, and have overawed their neighbors merely by her bulk and appearance. But whenever an insufficient man happens to have command on deck, [goodbye] to the discipline and safety of the ship. She may perhaps not sink outright. She may drift for a time as a wreck, and then be dashed to pieces on the shore. But she can never be rebuilt.❞

## Building Vocabulary

Write sentences using *four* of the vocabulary words from this chapter, leaving blanks where the vocabulary words would go. Exchange your sentences with another student and fill in the blanks on each other's lists.

## Reviewing Chapter Themes

1. **Economics and Technology** Describe three ways that new inventions or knowledge made possible the European age of exploration and expansion.
2. **Diversity** (a) Describe three ways that India influenced the development of civilizations of Southeast Asia. (b) How did Vietnam retain its distinct culture despite Chinese dominance?
3. **Global Interaction** (a) What trade networks existed in Asia before the 1500s? (b) Why were Europeans anxious to take part in Asian trade? (c) Describe how two European powers gained a foothold in India and Southeast Asia.
4. **Continuity and Change** (a) Describe two effects of the Manchu conquest on Chinese traditions. (b) How did either China, Japan, or Korea try to preserve its way of life after the arrival of Europeans?

## Thinking Critically

1. **Linking Past and Present** (a) Why were spices such valued trading goods in the 1400s? (b) What goods and resources play a similar role in the world economy today?
2. **Recognizing Points of View** Many people have admired explorers such as Christopher Columbus and Vasco da Gama as bold adventurers. Others have condemned them as vicious conquerors. (a) Who do you think might hold each of these viewpoints? (b) What evidence can be given to support each opinion? ( ★ See *Skills for Success*, page 280.)
3. **Comparing** Review Section 3 of Chapter 13. How was Vietnam's relationship to China similar to that of Korea? How was it different?
4. **Recognizing Bias** Tomé Pires, a Portuguese trader, described merchants of northwest India: "All the trade is in the hands of the heathen. . . .

They are diligent, quick men in trade. They do their accounts with figures like ours and with our very writing." (a) What does Pires disapprove of about the Indian merchants? (b) What does he admire about them? (c) How do you think Pires's background and profession influenced his judgment? (d) Do you think Pires was aware that the numerals used in Europe originally came from India? Explain. ( ★ See *Skills for Success*, page 390.)
5. **Analyzing Information** How did European encounters with India, China, and Japan link economic, religious, and political activity? Give two examples.
6. **Identifying Alternatives** (a) Describe the policy the Tokugawa shoguns followed toward foreign merchants after 1638. (b) What other policies might they have followed instead? ( ★ See *Skills for Success*, page 654.)

## *For Your Portfolio*

During the first global age, European explorers, traders, missionaries, and officials made contact with many regions of the world. These travelers usually knew very little about the peoples they encountered. Your objective is to advise them about the customs and cultures of the lands they will visit.

1. Choose one of the following European countries: Portugal, Spain, France, England, or the Netherlands. Then, choose a land in Asia where people from that nation explored, traded, or conquered. Possible places include Malacca, Goa, India, China, or Japan.
2. Use library resources to learn about the region of Asia you have chosen. You might pay particular attention to such topics as social customs, religious beliefs, and trading practices.
3. Write an advice column for Europeans who come to this land. Explain what they might encounter that will appear unfamiliar to them. Explain why different customs are followed and what they mean.
4. Share your advice column with members of your class. Discuss the following questions: (a) Why were the Europeans so ignorant of other lands? (b) How did their lack of information cause problems? (c) Do similar problems still occur today? Why or why not?

# The First Global Age: Europe, the Americas, and Africa

## (1492–1750)

## CHAPTER OUTLINE

The Indians assembled on the beach, as the strangers from across the sea had asked them to do. They listened silently as the young Spanish captain read the *Requerimiento,* or "Requisition." This document, drafted in Spain, claimed the Indians' land for the Spanish king and queen, as earthly representatives of the Catholic Church. If the Indians accepted the authority of these rulers, the document stated, "all would be well." If they did not, punishment would be swift and severe:

> 66If you do not do this, . . . we shall take you and your wives and your children, and make slaves of them. . . . We shall take away your goods, and shall do you all the mischief and damage that we can, as to vassals who do not obey, and refuse to receive their lord.99

Scenes such as this were repeated across South America and the Caribbean in the early 1500s. A flood of Spanish explorers, settlers, and missionaries had followed Columbus to the Americas. Wherever they went, they claimed the land and its people for their king and Church. If native peoples resisted, the invaders imposed their will by force. As loyal Christians, they believed, it was not only their right but their *duty* to bring their civilization to the Indians.

The Spanish were the first Europeans to arrive in the Americas. Their early encounters with the native population set a pattern of interaction that would continue in the centuries to come. At the same time, Spanish explorations and colonization set in motion the modern global age. Not only did they bring into contact the peoples of Africa, Europe, and the Americas, but they began an exchange of plants, animals, institutions, values, and ideas that affects the world to this day.

**FOCUS ON** these questions as you read:

- **Economics and Technology**
  How did the winning of overseas empires affect the economy of Europe?

- **Global Interaction**
  What global exchanges occurred as a result of European expansion overseas?

- **Political and Social Systems**
  How were the governments of the Spanish, French, and English colonies similar? How were they different?

- **Diversity**
  How were different cultures around the world brought into contact during the 1500s and 1600s?

- **Religions and Value Systems**
  What role did Christian values and teachings play in the European colonization of the Americas?

## TIME AND PLACE

*A First Encounter* This early encounter between the Spanish conqueror Hernan Cortés and the Aztecs of Mexico was friendly. Cortés, however, later conquered the Aztecs and seized their empire. Encounters among the peoples of Europe, Africa, and the Americas sometimes resulted in peaceful exchanges but other times led to turbulence and conflict. **Art and Literature** How did the artist suggest Cortés's violent intentions?

## HUMANITIES LINK

*Art History* Gold ritual ornament (page 395).
*Literature* In this chapter, you will encounter a passage from the following works of literature: Aztec poet, "And all this happened to us" (page 395); Carlos de Sigüenza y Góngora, *The Misadventures of Alonso Ramírez* (pages 416–417).

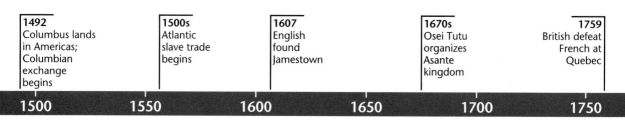

| 1492 | 1500s | 1607 | 1670s | 1759 |
|---|---|---|---|---|
| Columbus lands in Americas; Columbian exchange begins | Atlantic slave trade begins | English found Jamestown | Osei Tutu organizes Asante kingdom | British defeat French at Quebec |

1500    1550    1600    1650    1700    1750

# 1 Conquest in the Americas

## Guide for Reading

- Why did Spanish explorers travel to the Americas?

- Why were the Spanish able to conquer the Aztec and Incan empires?

- What were the results of the first encounters between the Spanish and Native Americans?

- **Vocabulary** *conquistador*

The Spanish soldiers who reached the Aztec capital of Tenochtitlán in 1519 were astonished by its size and splendor. From the emperor's palace, one soldier wrote, "we had a clear view of the three causeways by which Mexico communicated with the land, and of the aqueduct . . . which supplied the city with the finest water." They also saw the majestic temples "of the nearby cities, built in the form of towers and fortresses, . . . and others . . . all whitewashed, and wonderfully brilliant."

Within a few years, the Spanish had captured and destroyed the Aztec capital. In its place, they built a new city that became the heart of the Spanish empire in the Americas.

## First Encounters

In 1492, Christopher Columbus landed in the islands that are now called the West Indies, in the Caribbean. There, he encountered the Taíno people. The Taínos lived in villages and grew corn, yams, and cotton, which they wove into cloth. They were friendly and generous toward the Spanish. Columbus reported that "they invite you to share anything they possess, and show as much love as if their hearts went with it." He further noted "how easy it would be to convert these people [to Christianity]— and to make them work for us."

Friendly relations soon evaporated. Streams of Spanish conquistadors (kahn KEES tuh dohrz), or conquerors, followed in the wake of Columbus. They settled on the islands of Hispaniola (now the Dominican Republic and Haiti), Cuba, and Puerto Rico. They seized the gold ornaments worn by the Taínos, then enslaved them to make them pan for more gold. At the same time, the newcomers forced the Taínos to convert to Christianity. Those who resisted were treated cruelly.

Meanwhile, a deadly but invisible invader was at work—disease. Europeans unknowingly carried diseases such as smallpox, measles, and influenza to which Native Americans had no immunity. These diseases spread rapidly and wiped out village after village. As a result, the Native American population of the Caribbean islands declined by as much as 90 percent in the 1500s. This cycle of disease and death was repeated in many other places across the Western Hemisphere.

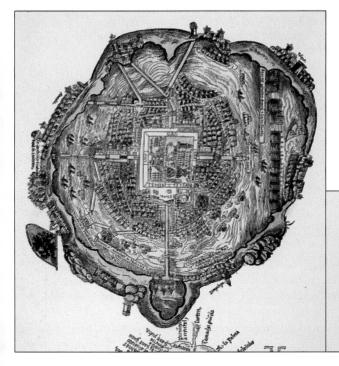

*Tenochtitlán* Shortly after his arrival in Mexico, Cortés sent this map of Tenochtitlán, the Aztec capital, to the Spanish king. As the map shows, the city was built on an island in the middle of a lake and connected to the mainland by broad wooden causeways, or bridges. Four major roads divided the city into quarters and led to a central plaza dominated by massive temples to the Aztec gods. **Economics and Technology** How do you think the causeways served as a defense against invaders?

## The Conquistadors

From Cuba, Spanish explorers probed the coasts of the Americas. They spread stories of empires rich in gold. Attracted by the promise of riches as well as by religious zeal, a flood of adventurers soon followed. Bernal Diaz del Castillo, a Spanish soldier, later noted:

66[The conquistadors acted] in the service of God and his Majesty, and to give light to those who sat in darkness, and also to acquire that wealth that most men covet.99

**Cortés in Mexico.** Among the earliest conquistadors was Hernan Cortés. Cortés landed on the coast of Mexico in 1519 with about 600 men, 16 horses, and a few cannons. As he headed inland toward Tenochtitlán, he was helped by Malinche (mah LIHN chay), a young Indian woman who served as his translator and adviser. The Spanish called her Doña Marina. Malinche knew both the Mayan and Aztec languages, and she learned Spanish quickly.

From Malinche, Cortés learned that many conquered peoples hated their Aztec overlords. The Aztecs, you will recall, sacrificed thousands of captives to their gods each year. Malinche helped Cortés arrange alliances with these discontented groups.

**Moctezuma's dilemma.** Meanwhile, in Tenochtitlán, messengers brought word about the newcomers to the Aztec emperor Moctezuma. The Aztec ruler hesitated. Was it possible that the leader of the pale-skinned, bearded strangers was Quetzalcoatl, the god-king who had long ago vowed to return from the east? To be safe, Moctezuma sent gifts of gold, silver, and precious stones. At the same time, he urged the strangers not to continue to Tenochtitlán.

Cortés had no intention of turning back. Fighting and negotiating by turns, he and his men advanced steadily inland toward the capital. At last, they arrived in Tenochtitlán, where they were dazzled by the grandeur of the city and by the gold in its temples.

**Fall of Tenochtitlán.** Moctezuma welcomed Cortés to his capital. However, relations between the Aztecs and Spaniards soon grew strained, and the Aztecs drove the Spanish from the city. Moctezuma was killed in the fighting.

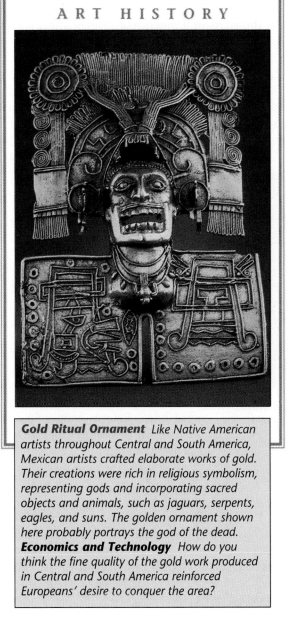

ART HISTORY

***Gold Ritual Ornament*** *Like Native American artists throughout Central and South America, Mexican artists crafted elaborate works of gold. Their creations were rich in religious symbolism, representing gods and incorporating sacred objects and animals, such as jaguars, serpents, eagles, and suns. The golden ornament shown here probably portrays the god of the dead.* ***Economics and Technology*** *How do you think the fine quality of the gold work produced in Central and South America reinforced Europeans' desire to conquer the area?*

Cortés retreated to the coast to plan an assault. In 1521, in a brutal struggle, Cortés and his Indian allies captured and demolished Tenochtitlán. An unknown Aztec lamented:

66And all this happened to us
We saw it,
We are amazed
With this lamentable and sad fortune,
We see ourselves anguished.
Broken spears lie in the road;
We have torn our hair with grief.
The houses are roofless now, and their
walls are red with blood.99

On the ruins of Tenochtitlán, the Spanish later built Mexico City. From this new capital, Spanish forces marched out to conquer an empire across Mexico and Central America.

**Pizarro in Peru.** Cortés's success inspired other adventurers. Among them was Francisco Pizarro. He arrived in Peru in 1532, just after the Incan ruler Atahualpa (ah tah WAHL pah) won the throne from his brother in a bloody civil war. (See Chapter 7.)

Helped by Indian allies, Pizarro captured Atahualpa after slaughtering thousands of his followers. The Spanish demanded a huge ransom in return for the ruler's freedom. Although the Incas paid the ransom, the Spanish killed Atahualpa anyway.

Despite continuing resistance, the invaders overran the Incan heartland. From Peru, Spanish forces surged across lands once ruled by the Incas in Ecuador and Chile. Before long, Spain added much of South America to its growing empire.

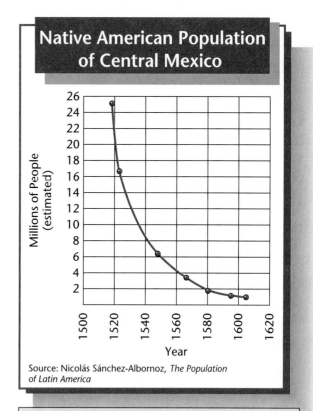

▲ *Francisco Pizarro*

### Reasons for Victory

Why did the mighty Aztecs and Incas fall so rapidly? How was it possible for a few hundred European soldiers to overrun huge Native American empires with populations in the millions? Several reasons explain the amazing successes of the Spanish.

1. Superior military technology was a key factor. The Spaniards' horses frightened some Indians, who had never seen animals like these. Spanish muskets and cannons—weapons of "fire and thunder"—terrorized Indian soldiers, while metal helmets and armor protected the Spanish from the Indians' arrows and spears.

2. Division and discontent among the Indians aided the Spanish. The Aztecs and Incas had defeated many rival groups to forge their empires. The Spanish played on old hatreds to make allies. In fact, Indian warriors provided Cortés and Pizarro with much of their fighting power.

3. Disease brought by the Europeans weakened the Aztecs and Incas. As tens of thousands of Indians died, the bewildered and demoralized survivors felt that their gods had deserted them. The Spanish seemed almost immune to the same diseases, which supported the idea that the gods of the conquerors were more powerful.

4. Many Indians believed that the disasters they suffered marked the end of the world. To the Aztecs, the destruction of Tenochtitlán signaled the end of the reign of the sun god. (See page 158.) "Let us die, then," the Aztecs lamented, "for our gods are already dead."

**Ongoing resistance.** As the pattern of disease and conquest was repeated across the Americas, Native Americans continued to resist the invaders. For years, Mayas in the Yucatan re-

**Native American Population of Central Mexico**

Source: Nicolás Sánchez-Albornoz, *The Population of Latin America*

*Interpreting a Chart* Disease and conquest combined to drastically reduce the Native American population. This graph shows what happened to central Mexico's Native Americans after the arrival of the Spanish in 1519. ■ How many Native Americans lived in central Mexico in 1519? How many lived there in 1605?

gion of Central America fought Spanish rule. Long after the death of Atahualpa, revolts erupted among the Incas.

Resistance did not always take the form of military action. Throughout the Americas, Indians resisted Europeans by preserving aspects of their own culture—language, religious traditions, foods, clothing, and skills such as weaving and pottery.

## Looking Ahead

Spanish conquests in the Americas would bring changes to peoples and cultures around the world. An immediate result was the flow of treasure from the Americas to Spain. The Spanish melted down gold and silver statues and ornaments taken from the Aztecs and Incas. When they depleted these sources, they forced Native Americans to mine silver from rich lodes in Peru and Mexico.

In the 1500s and early 1600s, treasure fleets sailed each year to Spain or the Spanish Philippines loaded with gold and silver. As you will read, this flood of wealth created both benefits and problems for the economy of Europe.

## SECTION 1 REVIEW

1. **Identify** (a) Taínos, (b) Hernan Cortés, (c) Malinche, (d) Moctezuma, (e) Francisco Pizarro, (f) Atahualpa.
2. **Define** conquistador.
3. Describe the motives of the Spanish conquistadors.
4. (a) How did divisions within the Aztec and Incan empires help the Spanish? (b) What other reasons explain the rapid conquest of the Spanish invasion?
5. What were the effects of the Spanish conquest of the Americas?
6. *Critical Thinking* **Comparing** Compare the Spanish conquest of the Americas with the Reconquista or the Crusades. (a) How were they similar? (b) How were they different?
7. *ACTIVITY* Write a song about Cortés's arrival in Mexico from either the Aztec or Spanish point of view.

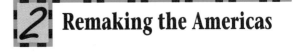

# 2 Remaking the Americas

## Guide for Reading

■ How did Spain govern its American empire?

■ Why did the Spanish bring enslaved Africans to the Americas?

■ What new social structure emerged in Spanish America?

■ How did cultural blending reshape the Americas after 1492?

■ **Vocabulary** *viceroy, plantation, encomienda, peon, peninsular, creole, mestizo, mulatto*

In order to build an American empire, the Spanish set out to impose their culture, language, religion, and way of life on millions of subjects. It was simple to erect new Spanish-style cities on top of the ruins of conquered Indian capitals. "Christianizing" Native Americans, on the other hand, turned out to be a little more complex. From the first, Christian Europeans had much to learn from the peoples that they conquered. In the end, a new culture emerged that reflected both European and Native American traditions.

## Ruling the Spanish Empire

In the 1500s, Spain claimed a vast empire stretching from California to South America. In time, it divided these lands into five provinces. The most important were New Spain (Mexico) and Peru.

Spain was determined to maintain strict control over its empire. To achieve this goal, the king set up the Council of the Indies to pass laws for the colonies. He also appointed viceroys, or representatives who ruled in his name, in each province. Lesser officials and *audiencias,* or advisory councils of Spanish settlers, helped the viceroy rule. The Council of the Indies in Spain closely monitored these colonial officials to make sure they did not overstep their bounds.

**The Catholic Church.** To Spain, winning souls for Christianity was as important as gaining land. The Catholic Church played a key role in the colonies, working hand in hand with the government. Church leaders often served as royal officials and helped to regulate the activities of Spanish settlers. As Spain's American empire expanded, Church authority expanded along with it.

Franciscan, Jesuit, and other missionaries baptized thousands of Native Americans. In frontier regions, they built mission churches and worked to turn new converts into loyal subjects of the Catholic king of Spain. They emphasized the superiority of European culture over Native American traditions. They also introduced western clothing, the Spanish language, and new crafts such as carpentry and locksmithing.

**Economy.** To make the empire profitable, Spain closely controlled its economic activities, especially trade. Colonists could export raw materials only to Spain and could buy only Spanish manufactured goods. Laws forbade colonists from trading with other European nations or even with other Spanish colonies. The most valuable resources shipped from Spanish America were silver and gold.

*A Mission Church* Priests set up missions throughout New Spain. They encouraged Native Americans to live in the missions, where they could learn the Christian faith. Nearby forts protected the missions as well as neighboring mines and ranches. **Political and Social Systems** Why do you think Spanish missions needed military protection?

Sugar cane was introduced into the West Indies and elsewhere and quickly became a profitable resource. The cane was refined into sugar, molasses, and rum. Sugar cane, however, had to be grown on **plantations,** large estates run by an owner or the owner's overseer. Finding the large numbers of workers needed to make the plantations profitable was a major problem.

At first, Spanish monarchs granted the conquistadors **encomiendas,** the right to demand labor or tribute from Native Americans in a particular area. The conquistadors used this system to enslave Native Americans under the most brutal conditions. Those who resisted were hunted down and killed. Disease, starvation, and cruel treatment caused catastrophic declines in the population.

**Bartolomé de las Casas.** A few bold priests, like Bartolomé de las Casas, condemned the evils of the encomienda system. In vivid reports to Spain, Las Casas detailed the horrors that Spanish rule had brought to Native Americans and pleaded with the king to end the abuse.

Prodded by Las Casas, Spain passed the New Laws of the Indies in 1542 forbidding enslavement of Native Americans. The laws were meant to end abuses against Native Americans, but Spain was too far away to enforce them. Many Native Americans were forced to become **peons,** workers forced to labor for a landlord in order to pay off a debt. Landlords advanced them food, tools, or seeds, creating debts that workers could never pay off in their lifetime.

**Workers from Africa.** To fill the labor shortage, Las Casas urged colonists to import workers from Africa. Africans were immune to tropical diseases, he said, and had useful skills in farming, mining, and metalworking. Las Casas later regretted that advice because it furthered the brutal African slave trade. Colonists had begun bringing Africans to the Americas as early as 1502.

As demand for sugar products skyrocketed, the settlers imported millions of Africans. The newcomers were forced to work as field hands, miners, or servants in the houses of wealthy landowners. Others became peddlers, skilled artisans, artists, and mechanics.

In time, Africans and their American-born descendants greatly outnumbered European settlers in the West Indies and parts of South America. Often, they resisted slavery by rebelling or running away. In the cities, some enslaved Africans earned enough money to buy their freedom.

## Social Classes

In Spanish America, the unique mix of peoples gave rise to a new social structure. At the top of colonial society were peninsulares, people born in Spain. (The term *peninsular* referred to the Iberian Peninsula, on which Spain is located.) Peninsulares filled the highest positions in both colonial governments and the Catholic Church. Next came creoles, American-born descendents of Spanish settlers. Creoles owned most of the plantations, ranches, and mines.

Other social groups reflected the mixing of populations. They included mestizos, people of Native American and European descent, and mulattoes, people of African and European descent. At the bottom of society, Native Americans and people of African descent formed the lowest social classes.

## Colonial Culture

Over the centuries, the Spanish colonies developed a unique culture. It combined European, Native American, and African traditions.

**Cities.** Spanish settlers preferred to live in towns and cities. Mexico City grew so quickly that by 1550 it was the largest Spanish-speaking city in the world.

Colonial cities were centers of government, commerce, and European culture. Around the central plaza, or square, stood government buildings and a Spanish-style church. Broad avenues and public monuments symbolized European power and wealth. Cities were also centers of intellectual and cultural life. Architecture and painting as well as poetry and the exchange of ideas flourished.

**Education.** To meet the Church's need for educated priests, the colonies built universities. The University of Mexico was established as early as 1551. A dozen Spanish American universities were busy educating young men long before Harvard, the first North American university, was founded in 1636.

**A New Society** The social structure of Spain's American empire reflected its unique blend of people. This portrait depicts a Spanish man, his Mexican wife, and their young daughter, a mestizo. **Diversity** What were the social classes of New Spain?

Women wishing an education might enter a convent. One such woman was Sor Juana Inés de la Cruz. Refused admission to the University of Mexico because she was a girl, Juana entered a convent at the age of 16. There, she devoted herself to study and the writing of poetry. She earned a reputation as one of the greatest lyric poets ever to write in the Spanish language.

**Cultural blending.** Although Spanish culture was dominant in the cities, the blending of diverse traditions changed peoples' lives throughout the Americas. Settlers learned Native American styles of building, ate foods native to the Americas, and traveled in Indian-style canoes. Indian artistic styles influenced the newcomers. At the same time, settlers taught their religion to Native Americans. They also introduced animals, especially the horse, that transformed the lives of many Native Americans.

Africans contributed to this cultural mix with their farming methods, cooking styles, and crops, including okra and palm oil. African drama, dance, and song heightened Christian worship services. In Cuba, Haiti, and elsewhere, Africans forged new religions that blended African and Christian beliefs.

## The Portuguese in Brazil

A large area of South America remained outside the Spanish empire. By the Treaty of Tordesillas in 1494, Portugal claimed Brazil. (See the map on page 402.) Portugal issued grants of land to Portuguese nobles, who agreed to develop them and share profits with the crown. Landowners sent settlers to build towns, plantations, and churches.

Unlike Spain's American lands, Brazil offered no instant wealth from silver or gold. Early settlers clung to the coast, where they cut and exported brazilwood, used to produce a precious dye. Before long, they turned to plantation agriculture and cattle raising. They forced Indians and Africans to clear land for sugar plantations. As many as five million Africans were sent to Brazil.

The thickly forested Amazon basin remained largely unexplored by settlers. However, ruthless adventurers slowly pushed inland. They attacked and enslaved Native American peoples and claimed for themselves land for immense cattle ranches. Some even discovered gold.

As in Spanish America, a new culture emerged in Brazil that blended European, Native American, and African patterns. European culture dominated the upper and middle classes, but Native American and African influences left their mark. Portuguese settlers, for example, eagerly adopted Indian hammocks. A settler expressed his enthusiasm:

66Would you believe that a man could sleep suspended in a net in the air like a bunch of hanging grapes? Here it is a common thing . . . I tried it and will never again be able to sleep in a bed, so comfortable is the rest one gets in the net.99

## Challenging Spanish Power

In the 1500s, the wealth of the Americas helped make Spain the most powerful country in Europe. As you have read, Spain controlled all trade with its American colonies. That policy annoyed other Europeans. Many English and Dutch agreed with the French king Francis I, who declared that "I should like to see Adam's will, wherein he divided the Earth between Spain and Portugal." Smugglers soon did a flourishing business with Spanish colonists.

Spanish treasure fleets also offered a tempting target to Dutch, English, and French pirates. Their ships nested among the Caribbean islands ready to pounce on Spanish galleons. Some pirates, called privateers, operated with the approval of European governments. England's Queen Elizabeth, for example, knighted Francis Drake for his daring raids on Spanish treasure ships. (📖 See *World Literature*, "The Misadventures of Alonso Ramírez," page 416.)

Like the Spanish, the Dutch, English, and French hunted for rich gold empires in the Americas and for a northwest passage around North America to Asia. In doing so, they explored the coasts and planted settlements in North America. (See Chapter 15.)

## SECTION 2 REVIEW

1. **Identify** (a) Council of the Indies, (b) Bartolomé de las Casas, (c) New Laws of the Indies, (d) Sor Juana Inés de la Cruz.
2. **Define** (a) viceroy, (b) plantation, (c) encomienda, (d) peon, (e) peninsular, (f) creole, (g) mestizo, (h) mulatto.
3. (a) Describe how Spain controlled its American empire. (b) What role did the Catholic Church play in the empire?
4. (a) Why did Las Casas urge Spanish settlers to import workers from Africa? (b) What labor did enslaved Africans perform in the colonies?
5. How did the mix of peoples in Spanish America result in a new social structure?
6. Give three examples of cultural blending in Spain's American empire.
7. *Critical Thinking* **Making Decisions** The Spanish tried to fill their need for labor by enslaving first Native Americans and then Africans. How would you have solved the problem of a dependable labor supply without the use of slavery?
8. *ACTIVITY* Review what you have read about Spanish treatment of Native Americans, on page 398. Then, design a poster to rouse public opinion in Spain to protect the Indians.

# 3 Struggle for North America

## Guide for Reading

- What problems did settlers in New France face?

- What traditions of government evolved in the English colonies?

- How did the Treaty of Paris of 1763 affect North America?

- How did Native American traditions influence European colonists?

In the 1500s and 1600s, other European powers moved into the Americas and began building settlements. France, the Netherlands, England, and Sweden joined Spain in claiming parts of North America.

At first, the Europeans were disappointed. North America did not yield gold treasure or offer a water passage to Asia, as they had hoped. Before long, though, the English and French were turning large profits by growing tobacco in Virginia, fishing off the North Atlantic coast, and trading fur from New England to Canada.

By 1700, France and England controlled large parts of North America. As their colonies grew, they developed their own governments, different from each other and from that of Spanish America.

## Building New France

By the early 1500s, French fishing ships were crossing the Atlantic each year to harvest rich catches of cod off Newfoundland, Canada. Distracted by wars at home, though, French rulers at first paid little attention to Canada—New France, as they called it. Only in 1608 did Samuel de Champlain build the first permanent French settlement in Quebec. Jesuits and other

**Settlers in New France** This illustrated map depicts French settlers arriving in New France. Does the map seem confusing? Try turning it upside down. You should now recognize eastern North America, from the Florida peninsula in the south to Canada in the north. **Geography and History** Why do you think the French mapmaker drew this map "upside down"?

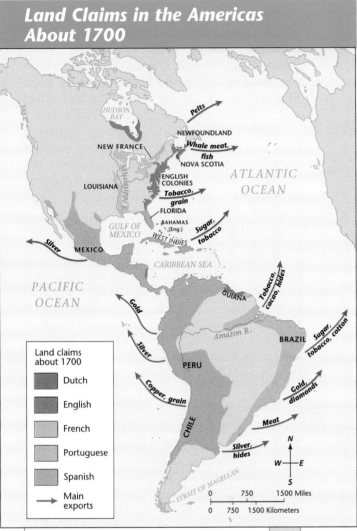

## Land Claims in the Americas About 1700

HUDSON BAY

Pelts

NEWFOUNDLAND

NEW FRANCE

Whale meat, fish

NOVA SCOTIA

ENGLISH COLONIES

Tobacco, grain

FLORIDA

LOUISIANA

Mississippi

ATLANTIC OCEAN

GULF OF MEXICO

BAHAMAS (Eng.)

WEST INDIES

Sugar, tobacco

Silver

MEXICO

CARIBBEAN SEA

PACIFIC OCEAN

GUIANA

Tobacco, cacao, hides

Amazon R.

BRAZIL

Sugar, tobacco, cotton

Gold

Silver

PERU

Copper, grain

Gold, diamonds

CHILE

Meat

Silver, hides

STRAIT OF MAGELLAN

N
W   E
S

0    750    1500 Miles
0  750  1500 Kilometers

**Land claims about 1700**

- Dutch
- English
- French
- Portuguese
- Spanish
- → Main exports

### GEOGRAPHY AND HISTORY

By the 1700s, European nations had claimed vast stretches of land in both North and South America. They used their American colonies as a steady source of raw materials for making manufactured goods.

1. **Location** On the map, locate (a) New France, (b) Louisiana, (c) Mexico, (d) Peru, (e) Brazil, (f) Chile.
2. **Movement** (a) Which raw materials were exported from the West Indies? (b) From Mexico?
3. **Critical Thinking Synthesizing Information** Based on the map and what you have read, to which European country did Brazil probably send its raw materials? Explain.

missionaries soon followed. They advanced into the wilderness, converting Native Americans to Christianity.

**Slow growth.** Helped by Native American allies, French fur traders traveled inland, claiming vast territory. France's American empire reached from Quebec to the Great Lakes and down the Mississippi to Louisiana and the Gulf of Mexico. (See the map at left.)

The population of New France grew slowly. Wealthy landlords owned huge tracts along the St. Lawrence River. They sought settlers to farm the land, but the harsh Canadian climate attracted few French peasants.

Many who went to New France soon abandoned farming in favor of fur trapping and trading. They faced a hard life in the wilderness, but the soaring European demand for fur ensured good prices. Fur traders and trappers learned survival and trapping skills from Native Americans. Many married Native American women. Fishing, too, supported settlers who lived in coastal villages and exported cod and other fish to Europe.

**Government policy.** In the late 1600s, the French king Louis XIV set out to strengthen royal power and boost tax revenues from his overseas empire. He appointed officials to oversee justice and economic activities in New France. He also sent more settlers and soldiers to North America. He even paid for unmarried women to travel to New France, where they might find husbands and help build new communities. The Catholic Louis, however, prohibited Protestants from settling in New France.

By the early 1700s, French forts, missions, and trading posts stretched from Quebec to Louisiana. Yet the population of New France remained small compared to that of the 13 English colonies expanding along the Atlantic coast.

## The 13 English Colonies

The English built their first permanent colony at Jamestown, Virginia, in 1607. Its early years were filled with disaster. Many settlers died of starvation and disease. The rest survived with the help of friendly Native Americans. The colony finally made headway when the settlers started to grow and export tobacco, a crop they learned about from the Indians.

In 1620, other English settlers, the Pilgrims,* landed at Plymouth, Massachusetts. They were seeking religious freedom, rather than commercial profit. Before coming ashore, they signed the Mayflower Compact, in which they set out guidelines for governing their North American colony. It read:

66We, whose names are underwritten . . . having undertaken for the Glory of God, and Advancement of the Christian Faith . . . a voyage to plant [a] colony in the [Americas] . . . do enact, constitute, and frame, such just and equal Laws . . . as shall be thought most [fitting] and convenient for the general Good of the Colony.99

Today, we see this document as an important early step toward self-government.

Many Pilgrims died in the early years. Local Indians, however, taught them to grow corn and helped them survive in the new land. Soon, a new wave of Puritan immigrants arrived to establish the Massachusetts Bay Colony.

**Growth.** In the 1600s and 1700s, other groups and individuals founded colonies. Some, like Virginia, were commercial ventures, organized for profit. Others, like Massachusetts, Pennsylvania, and Maryland, were set up as havens for persecuted religious groups.

Geographic conditions helped shape different ways of life in the New England, middle, and southern colonies. In New England, many settlers were farmers who transferred to North America the village life they had enjoyed in England. In parts of the South, a plantation economy emerged.

Like New Spain, the English colonies needed workers to clear land and raise crops. A growing number of Africans were brought to the colonies and sold as slaves. In several mainland colonies, enslaved Africans and their descendants outnumbered Europeans.

---

*Pilgrims were a band of English Puritans, a Protestant group, who rejected the practices of the official Church of England. (See page 359.)

**Government.** Like the rulers of Spain and France, English monarchs asserted control over their American colonies. They appointed royal governors to oversee colonial affairs and had Parliament pass laws to regulate colonial trade. Yet compared to settlers in the Spanish and French colonies, English colonists enjoyed a large degree of self-government. Each colony had its own representative assembly elected by propertied men. The assemblies advised the royal governor and made decisions on local issues.

The tradition of consulting representative assemblies grew out of the English experience. (See page 212.) Beginning in the 1200s, Parliament had played an increasingly important role in English affairs. Slowly, too, English citizens had gained certain legal and political rights. England's American colonists expected to enjoy the same rights. When colonists later protested British policies in North America, they saw themselves as "freeborn Englishmen" defending their traditional rights.

## Caught Up in Global Power Struggles

By the 1600s, Spain, France, England, and the Netherlands were competing for trade and colonies around the world. All four nations had colonies in North America, where they often fought for territory. After several naval wars with the Netherlands, the English seized the Dutch colony of New Netherland in 1664 and renamed it New York. English settlers in Georgia clashed with the Spanish in nearby Florida.

Competition was also fierce in the Caribbean region. The Dutch brought sugar production to the Caribbean from Brazil and made it a big business. The French acquired Haiti, the richest of the sugar colonies, as well as Guadaloupe and Martinique. The English took Barbados and Jamaica. In the late 1600s, the French and English Caribbean islands, worked

**ISSUES** *For* **TODAY** Compared to the Spanish and French colonies, the 13 English colonies enjoyed a large degree of self-government. How are people's lives affected by the form of government under which they live?

Quebec and then Montreal. Though the war dragged on until 1763, the British had won control of Canada.

**The peace treaty.** By the Treaty of Paris that ended the war, France ceded Canada and its lands east of the Mississippi River to Britain. As you have read, the British also forced the French out of India. The French, however, regained the rich sugar-producing islands in the Caribbean and the slave-trading outposts in Africa that the British had seized during the war.

The peace treaty ensured British dominance in North America. Yet thousands of French settlers remained in Canada and Louisiana. French culture continues to shape both areas to the present day.

## Impact on Native Americans

As in Spanish America, the arrival of European settlers in North America had a profound impact on Native Americans. Some Native Americans traded or formed alliances with the newcomers. In the West, as we will see, the arrival of the horse transformed the lifestyle of buffalo-hunting Indians.

Frequently, however, clashes erupted. As settlers claimed more land, Native Americans resisted their advance. Bitter fighting resulted. In the end, superior weapons helped the English to victory. Year by year, the flood of new settlers pushed the frontier—and the Indians—slowly westward.

**Disease.** As elsewhere, the Native American population of North America plummeted. Disease weakened or killed large numbers. In 1608, an estimated 30,000 Algonquians lived in Virginia. By 1670, only 2,000 remained.

In New England, diseases brought by European fishing fleets wiped out entire Indian villages even before the European settlers arrived. A Pilgrim noted that Indians "had been melted

by enslaved Africans, surpassed Brazil as the world's largest exporter of sugar. Shortly after, these little islands had surpassed the whole of North America in exports to Europe.

**British-French rivalry.** By the 1700s, Britain and France had emerged as bitter rivals for power around the globe. Their clashes in Europe often ignited conflicts in the Caribbean, North America, and India. The struggle came to a head when the Seven Years' War erupted in Europe in 1756. The war soon spread to India and North America. In the English colonies, it was called the French and Indian War.

Although France held more territory in North America, the British colonies had more people. Trappers, traders, and farmers from the English colonies were pushing west into the Ohio Valley, a region claimed by France. The French, who had forged alliances with the Indians, fought to oust the intruders.

During the war, a combined force of British soldiers and colonial troops launched a series of campaigns against the French in Canada and on the Ohio frontier. In 1759, the British captured

down by . . . disease, whereof nine-tenths of them have died."

**Legacy.** While encounters with Europeans often brought disaster to Native American societies, the Indian way of life helped shape the emerging new culture of North America. Settlers adopted Native American technologies. From Indians, they learned to grow corn, beans, squash, and tomatoes and to hunt and trap forest animals. Today's Thanksgiving menu of turkey and pumpkin pie reflects Indian foods.

On the frontier, some colonists adopted Indian clothing. "It is not uncommon to see a Frenchman wearing Indian moccasins and leggings," observed a visitor to New France. At the same time, though, he might also sport "a fine ruffled shirt and a laced waistcoat."

Trails blazed by Indians became highways for settlers moving west. Across the continent, rivers like the Mississippi and mountains like the Appalachians bear Indian names. Some Europeans came to respect Native American medical knowledge. Today, many people are taking a new look at Indian religious traditions that stress respect for the natural environment.

## SECTION 3 REVIEW

1. **Identify** (a) Samuel de Champlain, (b) Louis XIV, (c) Jamestown, (d) Pilgrims, (e) Mayflower Compact, (f) French and Indian War, (g) Treaty of Paris.
2. (a) Why did New France have a hard time attracting settlers? (b) What economic activities were profitable in New France?
3. What motives brought English settlers to North America?
4. (a) What European countries competed for power in North America? (b) How did Britain come to dominate the continent?
5. Describe three ways in which Native Americans influenced the emerging new culture of North America.
6. *Critical Thinking* **Synthesizing Information** Compare New France and the 13 English colonies in terms of (a) population, (b) size, and (c) government.
7. *ACTIVITY* Create a brochure to attract settlers to New France.

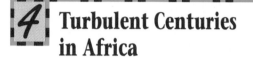

# 4 Turbulent Centuries in Africa

## Guide for Reading

- What were the results of early encounters between Europeans and Africans?
- How did the Atlantic slave trade affect Africa?
- What kingdoms emerged in West Africa in the early modern age?
- What groups battled for power in southern Africa?

The first encounters between Europeans and Africans took place in the 1400s. By then, as you have read, diverse societies had emerged in Africa, and Islam, spread by Muslim traders, had become an important force on the continent. Europeans brought new influences to Africa. At the same time, the contact caused people and products from Africa to become part of the international exchanges that marked this first global age.

## *European Outposts in Africa*

In the 1400s, Portuguese ships explored the coast of West Africa, looking for a sea route to India. They built a string of small forts along the West African coast to trade for gold, collect food and water, and repair their ships. African rulers set the terms of trade.

The Portuguese lacked the power or resources to push into the African interior. They did, however, attack the coastal cities of East Africa, such as Mombasa and Malindi, which were hubs of international trade. (See Chapter 12.) With muskets and cannons blazing, they expelled the Arabs who controlled the East African trade and took over this commerce for themselves.

The Portuguese, however, gained little profit from their victories. Trade between the interior and the coast soon dwindled. By 1600, the once prosperous East African coastal cities had sunk into poverty.

**West African Carving**
West African artists produced many fine carvings. This ivory salt cellar depicts Portuguese soldiers of the 1500s.
**Art and Literature**
Whom do you think the artist created the salt cellar for? Explain.

Other Europeans soon followed the Portuguese into Africa. The Dutch, the English, and the French established forts along the western coast of Africa. Like the Portuguese, they exchanged muskets, tools, and cloth for gold, ivory, hides, and slaves.

## The Atlantic Slave Trade

In the 1500s, Europeans began to view slaves as the most important item of African trade. Slavery had existed in Africa, as elsewhere around the world, since ancient times. Egyptians, Greeks, Romans, Persians, Indians, and Aztecs often enslaved defeated foes. Our word *slave* comes from the large number of Slavs, taken from southern Russia, to work as unpaid laborers in Roman times.

The Arab empire also used slave labor, often captives taken from Africa. In the Middle East, many enslaved Africans worked on farming estates or large-scale irrigation projects. Others became artisans, soldiers, or merchants. Some rose to prominence in the Muslim world even though they were officially slaves.

**European slave traders in Africa.** The Atlantic slave trade began in the 1500s, to fill the need for labor in Spain's American empire. In the next 300 years, it grew into a huge and profitable business. Each year, traders shipped tens of thousands of enslaved Africans across the Atlantic to work on tobacco and sugar plantations in the Americas.

Europeans seldom took part in slave raids. Instead, they relied on African traders to bring captives from the interior to coastal trading posts. There, the captives were exchanged for textiles, metalwork, rum, tobacco, weapons, and gunpowder.

**Horrors of the Middle Passage.** Once purchased, Africans were packed below the decks of slave ships. For enslaved Africans, the Middle Passage,* as Europeans called the voyage, was a horror. Hundreds of men, women, and children were crammed into a single vessel. Slave ships became "floating coffins" on which up to half the Africans on board died from disease or brutal mistreatment. Sometimes, enslaved Africans committed suicide by leaping overboard. Others tried to seize control of the ship and return to Africa.

## African Leaders Resist

Some African leaders tried to slow down the transatlantic slave trade or even to stop it altogether. They used different forms of resistance. But in the end, the system that supported the trade was simply too strong for them to resist. The efforts of two of these leaders are recounted below.

**King Affonso speaks out.** An early voice raised against the slave trade was that of Affonso I, ruler of Kongo in west-central Africa. Affonso had been born Nzinga Mbemba (uhn ZIHN gah uhm BEHM bah). As a young man, he was tutored by Portuguese missionaries, who baptized him in 1491 with the Christian name Affonso.

Impressed by his early contacts with the Portuguese, Affonso dreamed of building a modern Christian state in Kongo. After becoming king in 1505, he called on Portuguese missionaries, teachers, and technical experts to help

---

*The Middle Passage was part of a three-legged trade network that sent raw materials from the Americas to Europe, slaves from Africa to the Americas, and manufactured goods from Europe to Africa.

him develop Kongo. He sent his sons to Portugal to be educated in Christian ways.

Soon, however, Affonso grew worried. Each year, more and more Portuguese arrived in Kongo to buy slaves. They offered such high prices that government officials and local chiefs were eager to become involved in the business. Even Christian missionaries began to buy and sell Africans. In 1526, Affonso wrote in dismay to the king of Portugal:

> **66**Merchants are taking every day our natives, sons of the land and sons of our nobles and vassals and our relatives, because the thieves and men of bad conscience . . . grab them and get them to be sold. . . . Our country is being completely depopulated.**99**

Affonso insisted that "it is our will that in these Kingdoms there should not be any trade of slaves nor outlet for them." Kongo, he stated, could benefit from contacts with Europe, but the trade in human lives was evil. His appeal failed, and the slave trade continued.

**The almamy passes a law.** In the late 1700s, another African ruler, the almamy of Futa Toro in northern Senegal, tried to halt the slave trade in his lands. Unfortunately, he enjoyed no more success than Affonso had 200 years earlier.

Since the 1500s, French sea captains had bought slaves from traders in Futa Toro. The almamy decided to put a stop to this practice. In 1788, he passed a law forbidding anyone to transport slaves through Futa Toro for sale abroad.

The sea captains were furious. They protested to the almamy and requested him to repeal the law. The almamy refused. He returned the presents the captains had sent him in hopes of winning him over to their cause. "All the riches in the world would not make me change my mind," he said.

The almamy's victory was short-lived, however. The inland slave traders simply worked out another route for bringing their captives to the coast. Weighing anchor, the French captains sailed to this new market. There, they supplied

*A Profitable Business* From walled compounds in this thriving West African town, Portuguese, French, English, and Dutch traders competed for shares in the highly profitable slave trade. African merchants who supplied them with slaves made large profits, too. King Affonso I of Kongo could not end the slave trade because he could not end African and European greed. **Global Interaction** Why did the Atlantic slave trade become important?

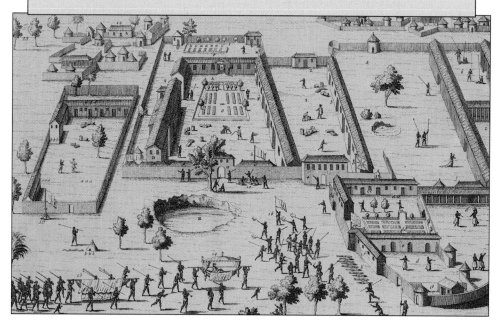

# African Slave Trade

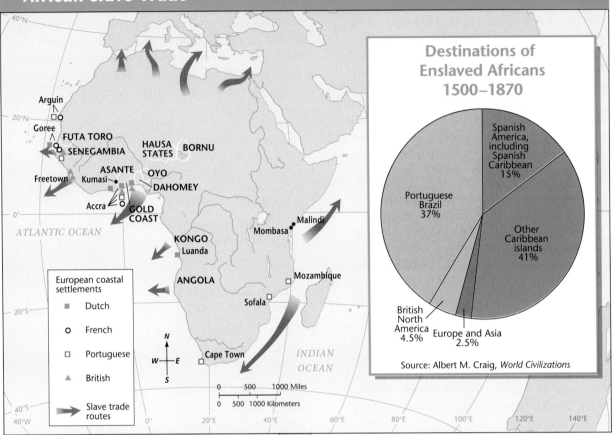

**Destinations of Enslaved Africans 1500–1870**

- Spanish America, including Spanish Caribbean 15%
- Other Caribbean islands 41%
- Europe and Asia 2.5%
- British North America 4.5%
- Portuguese Brazil 37%

Source: Albert M. Craig, *World Civilizations*

**European coastal settlements**
- ■ Dutch
- ○ French
- □ Portuguese
- ▲ British
- ➤ Slave trade routes

## GEOGRAPHY AND HISTORY

From bases along the coasts of Africa, European ships carried millions of enslaved Africans to be sold in markets in Europe, Asia, and the Americas.

1. **Location** On the map, locate (a) Accra, (b) Futa Toro, (c) Kongo, (d) Bornu, (e) Malindi.
2. **Place** (a) Name one trading settlement set up by the French. (b) Name one settlement set up by the British.
3. **Critical Thinking** *Analyzing Information* Many slaves who were first shipped to the Caribbean were later sold to slaveholders in British North America. How might this fact affect your analysis of the information on the circle graph about the proportion of slaves in British North America?

themselves with the slaves that the almamy had prevented them from buying in Senegal. There was no way the almamy could stop them. ■

## Impact of the Atlantic Slave Trade

Historians are still debating the number of Africans who were affected by the Atlantic slave trade. In the 1500s, they estimate, about 2,000 enslaved Africans were sent to the Americas each year. In the 1780s, when the slave trade was at its peak, that number topped 80,000 a year. By the 1800s, when the overseas slave trade was finally stopped, an estimated 11 million enslaved Africans had reached the Americas. Another two million probably died under the brutal conditions of the voyage between Africa and the Americas.

The slave trade had other results, too. One of the most important was the loss of countless numbers of young women and men from West Africa. The region as a whole recovered from this population drain. But with their youth captured, some societies and small states disappeared forever. At the same time, there was a rise of new African states whose way of life depended on the slave trade.

## Rise of New States

Among the large states that rose in West Africa in the 1600s and 1700s were Oyo, Bornu, and Dahomey. Another state, the Asante kingdom, emerged in the area occupied by modern Ghana.

**The Asante kingdom.** In the late 1600s, an able military leader, Osei Tutu, won control of the trading city of Kumasi. From there, he conquered neighboring peoples and organized the Asante kingdom. Osei Tutu claimed to rule by divine right. Leading chiefs served as a council of advisers but were subject to the royal will.

Officials chosen by merit rather than birth supervised an efficient bureaucracy. They managed the royal monopolies over gold mining and the slave trade. The Asante traded with Europeans on the coast, exchanging gold and slaves for firearms. But they shrewdly played off rival Europeans against each other to protect their own interests.

**Islamic crusades.** In the 1700s and early 1800s, an Islamic revival spread across West Africa. It began among the Fulani people in northern Nigeria.

The Fulani scholar and preacher Usman dan Fodio denounced the corruption of the local Hausa rulers, who were Muslim in name only. He called for social and religious reforms based on the Sharia, or Islamic law. In the early 1800s, Usman inspired Fulani herders and Hausa townspeople to rise up against their rulers.

Usman and his successors set up a powerful Islamic state. Under their rule, literacy increased, local wars quieted, and trade improved. Their success inspired other Muslim reform movements in West Africa. Between about 1780 and 1880, more than a dozen Islamic leaders rose to power, replacing old rulers or founding new states in the western Sudan.

## Conflicts in Southern Africa

Over many centuries, you will recall, Bantu-speaking peoples had migrated into southern Africa. (See Chapter 12.) In 1652, Dutch immigrants also arrived in the region. They built Cape Town to supply ships sailing to or from the East Indies. Dutch farmers, called Boers, settled around Cape Town. Over time, they ousted or enslaved the Khoisan herders who lived there. The Boers held to a Calvinist belief that they were the elect of God and looked on Africans as inferiors.

In the 1700s, Dutch herders and ivory hunters began to push north. As they did, they battled powerful African groups like the Zulus.

**Shaka.** The Zulus had migrated into southern Africa in the 1500s. In the early 1800s, they emerged as a major force under a ruthless and brilliant leader, Shaka. He built on the successes of earlier leaders who had begun to organize young fighters into permanent regiments.

Between 1818 and 1828, Shaka waged relentless war and conquered many nearby peoples.

**Asante Power** *The Asantes traded gold and slaves for European guns. With the help of these weapons, they built a large and powerful kingdom. Here, an Asante warrior stands guard before the royal armory in the palace.* **Economics and Technology** *How do you think the Asantes would respond to movements to end the slave trade? Explain.*

He absorbed their young men and women into Zulu regiments. By encouraging rival groups to forget their differences, he cemented a growing pride in the Zulu kingdom.

Shaka's wars disrupted life across southern Africa. Groups driven from their homelands by the Zulus adopted Shaka's tactics. They then migrated north, conquering still other peoples and creating their own powerful states.

Later Shaka's half-brother took over the Zulu kingdom. About this time, the Zulus faced a new threat, the arrival of well-armed, mounted Boers migrating north from the Cape Colony.

**Boers versus Zulus.** In 1806, the Cape Colony had passed from the Dutch to the British. Many Boers resented British laws that abolished slavery and otherwise interfered in their way of life. To escape British rule, they loaded their goods into covered wagons and started north. In the late 1830s, several thousand Boer families joined this "Great Trek."

As they traveled northward, the Boers came into contact with the Zulus. Fighting quickly broke out. At first, Zulu regiments held their own. But in the end, Zulu spears could not hold back Boers armed with guns. The struggle for control of the land would rage until the end of the century, as you will read in Chapter 25.

## SECTION 4 REVIEW

1. **Identify** (a) Middle Passage, (b) Asante, (c) Usman dan Fodio, (d) Boer, (e) Shaka.
2. Describe the early contacts between Europeans and Africans in the 1500s.
3. (a) Why did the Atlantic slave trade prosper? (b) What effects did it have on Africa?
4. What steps did the Asante ruler take to ensure his power?
5. How did southern Africa become a battleground for various groups?
6. *Critical Thinking* **Solving Problems** (a) What kinds of information would historians need to determine the number of Africans involved in the slave trade? (b) Why might they have trouble finding this information?
7. *ACTIVITY* Write five questions that could be used to review the content of this section. Then, write answers to the questions.

# 5 Changes in Europe

## Guide for Reading

- How did European explorations lead to a global exchange?
- What economic changes occurred in Europe in the 1500s and 1600s?
- What social changes took place in Europe during the 1500s and 1600s?
- **Vocabulary** *inflation, capitalism, entrepreneur, joint stock company, mercantilism, tariff*

In 1570, Joseph de Acosta visited the Americas. He wrote in amazement about the many strange forms of life that he saw there:

66[There are] a thousand different kinds of birds and beasts of the forest, which have never been known, neither in shape nor name; and whereof there is no mention made, neither among the Latins nor Greeks, nor any other nations of the world.99

To Europeans like Acosta, the Americas were so different that they believed they were a "new world." Acosta, a clergyman, even wondered if God had created the Americas at a different time from the rest of the globe.

European explorations between 1500 and 1700 brought major changes to the world. You have already seen how the arrival of Europeans affected peoples in Asia, Africa, and the Americas. Here, we will look at the impact that these explorations had on Europe itself.

## A Global Exchange

When Columbus returned to Spain in March 1493, he brought with him "new" plants and animals that he had found in the Americas. He also brought back a group of Taínos, people from the West Indies. Later that year, Columbus returned to the Americas. With him were some 1,200 settlers and a collection of European animals and plants, including horses, cows, pigs, wheat, barley, and sugar cane. In this way, Columbus began a vast global exchange that would have a profound effect on the world. In addition to people, plants, and animals, it included technology and even disease. Because this global exchange began with Columbus, we call it the Columbian exchange.

**New foods.** From the Americas, Europeans brought home a long list of foods. Tomatoes, sweet potatoes, pumpkins, squash, beans, manioc (a root vegetable), pineapples, and peppers enriched the diet of Europeans. Tobacco and chocolate also made the voyage east to Europe. Perhaps the most important foods from the Americas, however, were corn and the potato. Easy to grow, the potato helped feed Europe's rapidly growing population. Corn spread all across Europe and to Africa and Asia, as well.

At the same time, Europeans carried a wide variety of plants and animals to the Americas. Foods included wheat, melons, and grapes from Europe itself, and bananas, coconut palms, coffee, and sugar cane from Africa and Asia. Cattle, pigs, goats, and chickens, unknown before the European encounter, added protein to the Native American diet. Horses and donkeys introduced by the Europeans also changed the lives

▲ *Pumpkin and pineapple: foods from the Americas*

of Native Americans. The horse, for example, gave the nomadic peoples of western North America a new, more effective way to hunt buffalo.

**Impact on population.** The transfer of food crops from continent to continent took time. By the 1700s, however, corn, potatoes, manioc, beans, and tomatoes were contributing to population growth around the world, from Europe to West Africa to China. While other factors help account for the population explosion that began at this time, new food crops from the Americas were probably a key cause.

**Migration of people and ideas.** The Columbian exchange sparked the migration of millions of people. Each year, shiploads of European settlers sailed to the Americas. Europeans also settled on the fringes of Africa and Asia. As you have read, the Atlantic slave trade forcibly brought millions of Africans to the Americas. The Native American population, as we have seen, declined drastically in the early years of the western invasion.

The vast movement of peoples led to the transfer of ideas and technologies. Europeans and Africans brought to the Americas their beliefs and customs. In Europe and elsewhere, people adapted customs and inventions from distant lands. Language also traveled. Words such as *pajama* (from India) or *hammock* and *canoe* (from the Americas) entered European languages as evidence of the exchange.

## A Commercial Revolution

The opening of direct links with Asia, Africa, and the Americas had far-reaching consequences for Europeans. Their conquest of empires in the Americas and increased trade with Asia contributed to dramatic economic changes. Among them were an upsurge in prices, known as the price revolution, and the rise of modern capitalism.

**The price revolution.** In the early modern age, prices began to rise in parts of Europe.

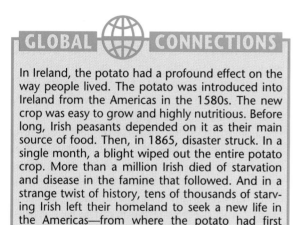

**GLOBAL CONNECTIONS**

In Ireland, the potato had a profound effect on the way people lived. The potato was introduced into Ireland from the Americas in the 1580s. The new crop was easy to grow and highly nutritious. Before long, Irish peasants depended on it as their main source of food. Then, in 1865, disaster struck. In a single month, a blight wiped out the entire potato crop. More than a million Irish died of starvation and disease in the famine that followed. And in a strange twist of history, tens of thousands of starving Irish left their homeland to seek a new life in the Americas—from where the potato had first come.

# CAUSE AND EFFECT

## Long-Term Causes

Scientific Revolution
Europeans search for a sea route to Asia

## Immediate Causes

Columbus and other Europeans arrive in the Americas
Europeans bring new plants, animals, and diseases to the Americas
Europeans encounter new plants and animals in the Americas

## COLUMBIAN EXCHANGE

## Immediate Effects

Spanish defeat Aztec and Incan empires
Millions of Native Americans die from "European" diseases
Enslaved Africans are sent to the Americas
American foods, including corn and potatoes, are introduced into Europe

## Long-Term Effects

Spread of items such as horses, corn, potatoes, and sugar around the world
Population growth in Europe, Africa, and Asia
Exchange of ideas, technology, arts, and language between Europe and the Americas
Population migration from Europe to the Americas
Growth of capitalism

## Connections Today

A multicultural society in the United States
Worldwide reliance on staples such as corn and potatoes

**Interpreting a Chart** *The arrival of Columbus in the Americas set off a global exchange of people, goods, and ideas that has continued to this day.* ■ *Based on the chart, name one immediate and one long-term effect of the Columbian exchange. What effects of the Columbian exchange can you see in your life?*

The economic cycle that involves a rise in prices linked to a sharp increase in the amount of money available is today called inflation.

One cause of European inflation was the increase in population. As the population grew, the demand for goods and services rose. Because goods were scarce, sellers could raise their prices.

Inflation was also fueled by an increased flow of silver and gold. By the mid-1500s, tons of these precious metals were flowing into Europe from the Americas. Rulers used much of the silver and gold to make coins. The increased money in circulation, combined with the scarcity of goods, caused prices to rise.

**Growth of capitalism.** Expanded trade and the push for overseas empires spurred the growth of European capitalism, the investment of money to make a profit. Entrepreneurs, or enterprising merchants, organized, managed, and assumed the risks of doing business. They hired workers and paid for raw materials, transport, and other costs of production.

As trade increased, entrepreneurs sought to expand into overseas ventures. Such ventures were risky. Capitalist investors were more willing to take the risks when demand and prices were high. Thus, the price revolution of the early modern age gave a boost to capitalism.

Entrepreneurs and capitalists made up a new business class devoted to the goal of making profits. Together, they helped change the local European economy into an international trading system.

**New business methods.** Early capitalists discovered new ways to create wealth. From the Arabs, they adapted methods of bookkeeping to show profits and losses from their ventures. During the late Middle Ages, as you have read, banks sprang up, allowing wealthy merchants to lend money at interest. Capitalists also developed insurance to reduce the risk of financial disaster in dangerous ventures.

The joint stock company, also developed in late medieval times, grew in importance. It allowed people to pool large amounts of capital needed for overseas ventures. As you have read, East India companies were founded in England, France, and the Netherlands in the early 1600s. With government approval, these companies invested in trading ventures around the world.

# PARALLELS THROUGH TIME

## Making a Profit

In a capitalist market system, almost anything can be traded. If demand is great, prices rise dramatically and traders earn amazing profits. When demand falls, however, traders can be completely wiped out. The trick is knowing when to buy and when to sell.

**Linking Past and Present** How would supply and demand affect price?

**PAST** *For Europeans of the 1600s, the tulip was a luxury item. In the Netherlands, the enormous demand for tulips attracted numerous profit-seeking investors and led to a buying frenzy that became known as* tulipomania. *At first, tulip prices skyrocketed. But a bust soon followed. Prices—and the dreams of many investors—crashed.*

**PRESENT** *Today, many young people collect baseball cards. For those who are lucky, an initial purchase price of a few dollars may result in a handsome profit in the future.*

---

**Bypassing the guilds.** The growing demand for goods led merchants to find ways to increase production. Traditionally, guilds controlled the manufacture of goods. But guild masters often ran small-scale businesses without the capital to produce for large markets. They also had strict rules regulating quality, prices, and working conditions.

Enterprising capitalists devised a way to bypass the guilds. The putting out system, as it was called, was first used to produce textiles but later spread to other industries. Under the putting out system, a merchant capitalist distributed raw wool to peasant cottages. Cottagers spun the wool into thread and then wove the thread into cloth. Merchants bought the wool cloth from the peasants and sent it to the

city for finishing and dyeing. Finally, the merchants sold the finished product for a profit.

The putting out system separated capital and labor for the first time. From this system controlled by merchants, the next step would be the capitalist-owned factories of the Industrial Revolution. (See Chapter 20.)

## A New Economic Policy

European monarchs enjoyed the benefits of the commercial revolution. In the fierce competition for trade and empire, they adopted a new policy, known as mercantilism, aimed at strengthening their national economies.

**Foreign trade.** Mercantilists supported several basic ideas. They believed that a nation's real wealth was measured in its gold and silver treasure. To build its supply of gold and silver, they said, a nation must export more goods than it imported. Thomas Mun, an eager spokesman for mercantilism, endorsed this idea:

66 The ordinary means . . . to increase our wealth and treasure is by foreign trade, wherein we must ever observe this rule: to sell more to strangers [foreigners] yearly than we consume of theirs in value. 99

**The role of colonies.** Overseas empires were central to the mercantile system. Colonies, said mercantilists, existed for the benefit of the parent country. They should provide resources and raw materials not available in Europe. In turn, they should enrich a parent country by serving as a market for its manufactured goods.

To achieve these goals, European powers passed strict laws regulating trade with their colonies. Colonists could not set up industries to manufacture goods or buy goods from a foreign country. Also, only ships from the parent country or the colonies themselves could be used to send goods in or out of the colonies.

**Increasing national wealth.** Mercantilists urged rulers to adopt other policies to increase government revenues. To boost production, governments cleared wasteland, exploited mineral and timber resources, drained swamps, built roads and canals, and backed new industries. They imposed a single national currency and established standard weights and measures.

Governments also sold monopolies, or the right to operate without competition, to large producers in certain industries as well as to big overseas trading companies. Finally, governments imposed tariffs, or taxes on imported goods, to protect local industries from foreign competition.

## The Lives of Ordinary People

How did these economic changes affect the average European? In general, their impact depended on a person's social class. The price revolution, for example, hurt nobles. Their wealth was in land, and they had trouble raising money to pay higher costs for stylish clothing, fancy foods, and other luxuries. Some had to sell off land, which in turn reduced their income. Merchants, however, who invested in overseas ventures acquired wealth. Yet in towns and cities the wages of hired workers did not keep up with inflation, creating poverty and discontent.

**Peasants.** Most Europeans were still peasants. Europe's growing involvement in the world had little immediate effect on their lives. Changes took generations, even centuries, to be felt.

Like their medieval ancestors, peasants in the 1500s and 1600s struggled through harvests, survived wars, and did their best to enjoy whatever leisure time they had. Tradition-bound peasants were often reluctant to grow foods brought from the Americas. Only in the late 1700s did German peasants begin to raise potatoes. Even then, many complained that these strange-looking tubers tasted terrible.

**Growing cities.** Within Europe's growing cities, there were great differences in wealth and power. Successful merchants dominated city life. Guilds, too, remained powerful. And as trade grew, another group—lawyers—gained importance for their skills in writing contracts.

Middle-class families enjoyed a comfortable life. They lived in fine homes and dressed in fine clothing. Servants cooked, cleaned, and waited on them. Other city residents, such as journeymen and other laborers, were not so lucky, often living in crowded quarters on the edge of poverty.

**Family.** Noble households, which had once numbered in the hundreds and included immediate and distant relatives as well as unrelated members of the court, grew smaller. Among other classes, the nuclear family made up of parents and children had long been the usual family unit.

Among middle-class families, parents took great care to plan for their children's education, careers, and marriages. They arranged marriages with an eye to financial and social advantages.

**Women.** European families were patriarchal, with the husband and father responsible for the behavior of his wife and children. A woman's chief roles were as wife and mother. Society stressed such womanly virtues as modesty, household economy, obedience, and caring for her family.

**Sharing the Work** In this Dutch painting from the 1600s, men, women, and children work together spinning and weaving wool. Most women learned to weave at home, and their work skills were highly valued in a weaver's shop. **Economics and Technology** How does this painting convey a sense of economic prosperity?

Middle-class women might help their husbands in a family business, although guilds increasingly pushed women out of many trades. Peasant women worked alongside their husbands in the fields. In towns, young girls and married women alike worked as servants.

Women had almost no property or legal rights. Very slowly after the 1600s, that situation changed. A few women from well-to-do families acquired an education. In England, several women became playwrights. Katherine Boyle, sister of the English chemist Robert Boyle, took an active role in the "new science" of the period.

### Looking Ahead

In the 1500s and 1600s, Europe emerged as a powerful new force on the world scene. The voyages of exploration marked the beginning of what would become European domination of the globe. In the centuries ahead, competition for empire would spark wars in Europe and on other continents.

European expansion would spread goods and other changes throughout the world. It would also revolutionize the European economy and transform its society. The concept of "the West" itself emerged as European settlers transplanted their culture to the Americas and, later, to Australia and New Zealand.

For centuries, most Europeans knew little or nothing about the other parts of the globe. Exposure to different cultures was both unsettling and stimulating. As their horizons broadened, they had to reexamine old beliefs and customs. Educated Europeans studied the geography, histories, and cultures of other worlds, which they in turn used to create a new world of ideas.

## SECTION 5 REVIEW

1. **Identify** (a) Columbian exchange, (b) putting out system.
2. **Define** (a) inflation, (b) capitalism, (c) entrepreneur, (d) joint stock company, (e) mercantilism, (f) tariff.
3. How did the voyages of Columbus lead to global exchanges of goods and ideas?
4. Explain how each of the following contributed to economic changes in Europe in the 1500s and 1600s: (a) the price revolution, (b) capitalism, (c) mercantilism.
5. Choose one social group. Explain how the lives of that group changed during the 1500s and 1600s.
6. *Critical Thinking* **Applying Information** "The treasure which is brought into the realm by the balance of our foreign trade is that money which only does abide with us, and by which we are enriched." How does this statement reflect mercantilist thinking?
7. *ACTIVITY* Create an illustrated map of the world showing the movement of items in the Columbian exchange.

# World Literature
## The Misadventures of Alonso Ramírez
### Carlos de Sigüenza y Góngora

**Introduction**  *One of the most noted scholars of colonial Mexico was Carlos de Sigüenza y Góngora (see GWEHN sah EE GOHN goh rah), a Jesuit priest, poet, and scientist. In 1690, he published* The Misadventures of Alonso Ramírez, *one of the first and finest seagoing adventure stories of the new global age.*

*There was a real sailor named Alonso Ramírez. He told his life story to Sigüenza y Góngora, who turned it into an exciting narrative filled with pirates, exotic places, and daring exploits. The action moves from South America to Southeast Asia and India to the Caribbean. Here, Ramírez describes being kidnapped by a band of English pirates.*

Before setting sail they put my 25 men on board the flagship. It was commanded by an Englishman called Master Bel. It had 80 men, 24 pieces of artillery, and 8 stone mortars all bronze. Captain Donkin was master of the second ship, and he had 70 men, 20 pieces of artillery, and 8 stone mortars. In both there were a great many shotguns, cutlasses, axes, grenades, and pots full of various foul-smelling ingredients besides grappling irons. . . .

Turning the ships toward Caponiz with mine in tow, they began with pistols and cutlasses in hand to examine me again and even to torture me. . . .

They put me and [a] companion in the hold, where we could hear above much shouting and the report of a blunderbuss. I noticed the blood on the deck after they let us out, and showing it to me they said it was that of one of my men who had died and that the same thing would happen to me if I did not respond properly to questioning. I told them humbly that they could do what they wanted with me because I had nothing to add to what I had already said.

Careful then to find out which of my companions had died, I checked and found the number the same as before, which puzzled me. I found out much later that what I had seen was the blood of a dog and that the whole episode had been feigned.

Not satisfied with what I had said, they began asking questions again in a solicitous manner of my Indian boatswain . . . and they discovered from him that there was a village and prison on the island of Caponiz. . . .

They anchored off land from a direction where they expected no trouble from the islanders. . . . Arming their canoes with sufficient men they made for land and found the inhabitants friendly. They told the islanders they only wished a safe harbor for the ships so as to add provisions and fruit, which they lacked.

Either through fear or for other motives which I did not learn about, the poor islanders agreed to this. They received clothes which had been stolen in return for pitch, fat, salted turtle meat, and other items. . . .

[*After a four-month stay, the pirates decide to leave the island.*]

Consulting over the price they should give the islanders for their hospitality, they settled it the same day they set sail by attacking at dawn those who were sleeping without precautions, and putting everyone to the knife. . . . Setting fire to the village and then hoisting colors, they boarded their ships with great rejoicing. . . .

[*The pirates sail to the port of Cicudana on the island of Borneo.*]

The pirates set to work in their canoes to sound the river bar, not only to see if larger ships might enter but to plan an attack. They were interrupted in this by a coastal sampan in which were representatives of the authorities of the place, who had come to reconnoiter. The pirates answered that they were from the

**A Pirate Raid** Some pirates, such as England's Sir Francis Drake, operated with the approval of European governments. Here, Drake leads his fleet on a raid of the Spanish settlement of Santo Domingo. **Political and Social Systems** Why do you think England's Queen Elizabeth encouraged Drake's raids on the Spanish?

English nation and were loaded with noble and exquisite goods to be exchanged for diamonds.

As they had received friendly treatment from this nation and saw rich samples from the ships captured [earlier], they granted a license to trade. They gave a generous gift to the governor and received permission to go up river to the town, a fourth of a league from the sea, whenever they wished.

During the three days we were there, our captors found the place to be undefended and open on all sides. Telling the Cicudanes that they could not stay for long and that they should collect their diamonds in the governor's house, where there would be a fair, they left us on board under guard and went up river at midnight well armed. They attacked the village by surprise, advancing first on the governor's house. There they sacked the building for the diamonds and other precious stones gathered there and then proceeded to do the same with other houses, which they put to the torch together with some boats they found there.

On board we could hear the clamor of the village and the shots; the mortality, as they bragged later, was considerable. This detestable treachery being carried out without injury to themselves, they brought the governor as a prisoner together with other leaders on board

with great speed, and raising the anchor they sped away. Never has there been pillage to compare to this in the high price received for so little effort. Who can say what it was worth? I saw Captain Bel with the crown of his hat heaped full of diamonds.

Source: Carlos de Sigüenza y Góngora, *The Misadventures of Alonso Ramírez*, translated by Edwin H. Pleasants (New York: The Borzoi Anthology of Latin American Literature, Volume 1, 1977).

## Thinking About Literature

1. **Vocabulary** Use the dictionary to find the meanings of the following words: blunderbuss, feign, solicitous, sampan, reconnoiter, sack, mortality, pillage.
2. (a) What words does the narrator use to describe the English pirates? (b) Describe one example he gives to show their treachery.
3. How does this selection illustrate global interaction? Give three examples.
4. *Critical Thinking* **Linking Past and Present** Today, people continue to be fascinated by stories of pirates. (a) How is Sigüenza y Góngora's picture of pirates similar to that found in popular literature, movies, or television programs today? (b) Do you think this is an accurate picture of pirates? Explain.

# Skills for Success

Critical Thinking

Writing and Researching

Maps, Charts, and Graphs

Speaking and Listening

## Using a Computerized Card Catalog

Computerized card catalogs use a system of menus and prompts to help you locate information. The screens below are examples of what you will see when you use a computerized card catalog. Follow the directions to research the slave trade.

**1** **Start your search.** When you begin, the computer will present you with a list of options. Look at Screen 1 below. (a) What would you type to find information about the slave trade? (b) What would you type to find books by Bartolomé de las Casas? (c) What would you type to find out if the library owns the book *Human Cargo: The Story of the Atlantic Slave Trade*?

**2** **Narrow your search.** Study Screen 2. (a) How many books does the library have on the slave trade in West Africa? (b) Which number would you type if your topic is the Atlantic slave trade?

**3** **Select the books that relate to your topic.** Scan the list of books on Screen 3. Imagine you are writing a report about personal experiences of Africans in the Atlantic slave trade. (a) Which title would you select? (b) What number would you type to find out more about that title?

**4** **Locate the books you need.** Study Screen 4. (a) What is the call number of the book you selected? (b) Is the book on the library shelves? How do you know?

**Beyond the Classroom** Identify a topic in this chapter that you would like to learn more about. Then, use the computerized card catalog in the local library to locate two books on your topic.

---

### Screen 1

You may search the catalog by one of the following:

    A = Author
    T = Title
    S = Subject

Enter your search below:

>> S = slave trade

### Screen 2

Your search: S = slave trade

| Line # | # of Titles | ------------Subjects------------- |
|--------|-------------|-----------------------------------|
| 1 | 3 | Slave trade -- Atlantic |
| 2 | 7 | Slave trade -- West Africa |
| 3 | 1 | Slave traders -- Fiction |

Enter line # to see works associated with your search.

>> 1

### Screen 3

Your search: S = Slave trade -- Atlantic

| Line # | --Author----- | ----------Title-------------------- |
|--------|---------------|-------------------------------------|
| 1 | Conneau, Theophile | Captain Canot, an African slaver. |
| 2 | Howard, Thomas | Black voyage: eyewitness accounts of the Atlantic slave trade. |
| 3 | Pescatello, Ann | The African in Latin America. |

Enter line # to see more information
>> 2

### Screen 4

(Record 2 of 3)

AUTHOR:    Howard, Thomas

TITLE:       Black voyage: eyewitness accounts of the Atlantic slave trade.

PUBLISHER: Little, Brown (1971)

Call Number: 380.1 H    Status: Checked in

>>                          Enter ? for HELP

# CHAPTER 16 REVIEW

## Building Vocabulary

Review the vocabulary words in this chapter. Then, use *ten* of these words to create a crossword puzzle. Exchange puzzles with a classmate. Complete the puzzles and then check each other's answers.

## Reviewing Chapter Themes

1. **Economics and Technology** (a) Describe three major economic changes that the conquest of empires in the Americas and increased trade with Asia produced in Europe. (b) What was mercantilism? (c) What political policies did European nations adopt as a result of mercantilism?
2. **Global Interaction** How did European overseas expansion affect the peoples of Africa?
3. **Political and Social Systems** How did each of the following nations govern their overseas colonies: (a) Spain, (b) France, (c) England?
4. **Diversity** How did Native Americans contribute to the success of European colonies in the Americas?
5. **Religions and Value Systems** What role did religion play in the founding of (a) New Spain, (b) the 13 English colonies?

## Thinking Critically

1. **Analyzing Information** When Cortés arrived in Mexico, he sent Moctezuma a helmet and asked for it to be returned filled with gold. Moctezuma did as Cortés asked. A Spanish historian later wrote, "This act cost Moctezuma his life." What do you think he meant by this statement?
2. **Comparing** Compare the impact of the Spanish in the Americas to that of the Portuguese in Asia in the 1500s. How do you account for the differences?
3. **Synthesizing Information** Based on your reading in this chapter and in Chapter 15, give examples of aggressive expansion on the part of European merchants and rulers. ( ★ See *Skills for Success*, page 896.)
4. **Linking Past and Present** How might your life be different if France had defeated England in the Seven Years' War?
5. **Recognizing Points of View** How might each of the following people have viewed European explorations in the 1500s and 1600s: (a) a Spaniard, (b) a Native American, (c) an African? ( ★ See *Skills for Success*, page 280.)
6. **Recognizing Causes and Effects** (a) What were three causes of the expansion of the Atlantic slave trade? (b) What were three immediate effects of the slave trade on Africa? (c) What do you think might be some long-term effects of the slave trade on Africa's future development? Explain. ( ★ See *Skills for Success*, page 18.)
7. **Applying Information** (a) Describe three kinds of exchanges that occurred as a result of European explorations. (b) Do you think the benefits of these exchanges outweighed the disadvantages? Explain.
8. **Analyzing Information** How might mercantilism encourage economic warfare among nations?

## *For Your Portfolio*

A manufacturer has asked you to develop an educational board game. Assemble a team of workers to carry out this project. The game will focus on European activities in the Americas and Africa during the first global age.

1. Begin by analyzing a few board games to see how they are laid out and played. Then, decide on a format for your game.
2. Review the chapter to make a list of facts you will use in your game. Use library sources to research additional material. You might base your game on the entire chapter or focus on a single area. Whichever you decide, however, keep in mind that your game is an educational one. It should inform as well as challenge players.
3. Write and design your game. You may want to assign some members of the team to work on the board configuration, while others fashion the pieces, write any necessary cards, and develop the rules.
4. Play your game to see if it works. Make adjustments as necessary.
5. Share your game with the class. Have players list at least three new facts or ideas they learn from the game.

# The Age of Absolutism

## (1550–1800)

## CHAPTER OUTLINE

"I have had an idea that will . . . give much pleasure to the people here, particularly the Queens," wrote Louis XIV, the young king of France. His plan was to throw a grand party where each guest would receive a lottery ticket for a prize of jewelry—and every ticket would be a winner.

Louis's party quickly grew into a more elaborate affair called "The Pleasures of the Enchanted Isle." Some 600 noble guests flocked to the royal palace at Versailles (ver sī) for three days of pageants, sports, ballets, dances, plays, and music. On the first day, courtiers costumed as medieval knights staged a tournament:

❝All knights, with their helmets covered in plumes of different colors and their tournament cloaks, gathered round the tournament barriers making an enchanting scene.❞

Later they feasted on 100 sumptuous dishes. As darkness fell, flaming torches and costumed dancers created a magical evening.

Day two featured an opera and a comedy by France's leading playwright. The king himself performed in a ballet with "incredible agility and grace." Day three ended with fireworks and music along the river. The magnificent entertainment stretched from three days to a week. At last, the costumed gods, goddesses, knights, and ladies were transformed back into French courtiers. But the extravaganza was only the first of many. The elegance of the French court became the talk of European ruling circles.

Louis XIV was more than a lavish party giver. In this chapter, you will see that he and other European monarchs created ever more powerful nations in the 1500s and 1600s. They built up their state bureaucracies and equipped powerful armies. They ensured loyalty to the crown and used their growing resources for bold ventures at home and overseas. While Spain, Portugal, and the Netherlands quickly took the lead in acquiring overseas empire, France and Britain surpassed them in the 1600s and 1700s. As they did so, the center of world civilization shifted to Europe.

**FOCUS ON** these questions as you read:

- **Political and Social Systems**
  How did absolute monarchs centralize their power?

- **Impact of the Individual**
  What role did individual rulers such as Louis XIV of France and Peter the Great of Russia play in shaping their nations?

- **Continuity and Change**
  How did struggles between monarchs and Parliament affect the development of Britain?

- **Art and Literature**
  How did European monarchs contribute to cultural flowering within their countries?

## TIME AND PLACE

**The Palace at Versailles** From 1669 to 1685, Louis XIV had the vast palace of Versailles built about 10 miles from Paris. More than a cluster of luxurious buildings, the palace was an advertisement for the French monarchy. Versailles dazzled rulers in Europe and beyond, and kings from Morocco to Russia tried to imitate its splendor. **Political and Social Systems** Unlike medieval castles, Versailles was not protected by walls or moats. What does this suggest about France under Louis XIV?

## HUMANITIES LINK

*Art History* Salon de la Guerre, Versailles (page 429).
*Literature* In this chapter, you will encounter passages from the following works of literature: Miguel de Cervantes, *Don Quixote* (page 425); Jacques Bossuet, *Universal History* (page 427); John Evelyn, Diary (pages 434–435); Jacob von Grimmelshausen, *Simplicissimus* (page 436); Alexander Pushkin, *The Bronze Horseman* (page 441).

| 1556 | 1642 | 1685 | 1697 | 1756 | 1795 |
|------|------|------|------|------|------|
| Hapsburg empire divided; Philip II begins rule of Spain | English civil war begins | Louis XIV revokes Edict of Nantes | Peter the Great tours Western Europe | Seven Years' War begins | Third partition of Poland |

| 1550 | 1600 | 1650 | 1700 | 1750 | 1800 |

# 1 Extending Spanish Power

## Guide for Reading

- How did Philip II use royal power?
- How did the arts flourish during Spain's golden age?
- Why did the Spanish economy decline in the 1600s?
- **Vocabulary** *absolute monarch, divine right*

66 On 22 March 1595, ships from the Indies . . . began to discharge and deposit with the Chamber of Commerce 332 cartloads of silver, gold, and pearls of great value. On 8 April, 103 cartloads of silver and gold were unloaded. 99

In the 1500s, wealth from the Americas helped make Spain the most powerful state in Europe. American gold also paved the way for a golden age of literature and art. Yet the flood of gold and silver would eventually contribute to an economic decline.

## Spain and the Hapsburg Empire

In the 1500s, Spain emerged as the first modern European power. Under Isabella and Ferdinand, Spain had expelled the last Muslim rulers and enforced religious unity. In 1492, Isabella financed Columbus's voyage, leading to the Spanish conquest of the Americas.

**Wearing two crowns.** The next monarch, Charles V,* ruled an even larger empire from 1519 to 1556. A grandson of Ferdinand and Isabella, Charles was also heir to the Hapsburgs, the Austrian rulers of the Holy Roman Empire and the Netherlands.

Ruling two empires involved Charles in constant warfare. He continued a long Hapsburg struggle with France over rival claims in Italy. As a devout Catholic, he also fought to sup-

---
*Within Spain, the king was known as Charles I. However, historians usually refer to him by his Hapsburg title, Charles V.

press the Protestant movement in the German states. After years of religious warfare, however, Charles was forced to allow the German princes to make their own choice of religions. (See page 437.)

His greatest foe was the Ottoman empire. Under Suleiman, Ottoman forces advanced across central Europe to the walls of Vienna, Austria. (See page 276.) Although Austria held firm, the Ottomans occupied much of Hungary. Ottoman naval forces also challenged Spanish power in the Mediterranean.

**An empire divided.** Perhaps the Hapsburg empire was too scattered and diverse for any one person to rule. Exhausted and disillusioned, Charles V gave up his titles and entered a monastery in 1556. He divided his empire, leaving the Hapsburg lands in central Europe to his brother Ferdinand, who became Holy Roman emperor. He gave Spain, the Netherlands, southern Italy, and the huge Spanish overseas empire to his 29-year-old son Philip.

## An Imposing Monarch

Like his father, King Philip II was hardworking, devout, and ambitious. During his long reign from 1556 to 1598, he sought to expand Spanish influence, strengthen the Catholic Church, and make his own power absolute. Thanks in part to silver from the Americas, he made Spain the foremost power in Europe.

**A tireless worker.** Unlike many other monarchs, Philip devoted much time to government work. He seldom hunted, never jousted, and lived as sparsely as a monk. His isolated, somber palace outside Madrid reflected Philip's character. Called the Escorial (ehs KOHR ee uhl), it served as a church, a residence, and a tomb for members of the royal family.

"It is best to keep an eye on everything," Philip often said. He plowed through a mountain of paperwork each day, making notes on even the most trivial matters. Once the Spanish ambassador to England wrote about a new kind of insect he had seen in London. "Probably fleas," Philip scribbled on the letter.

**King by divine right.** Like Ferdinand and Isabella, Philip further centralized royal power, making all parts of the government responsible to him. He became an absolute monarch, a

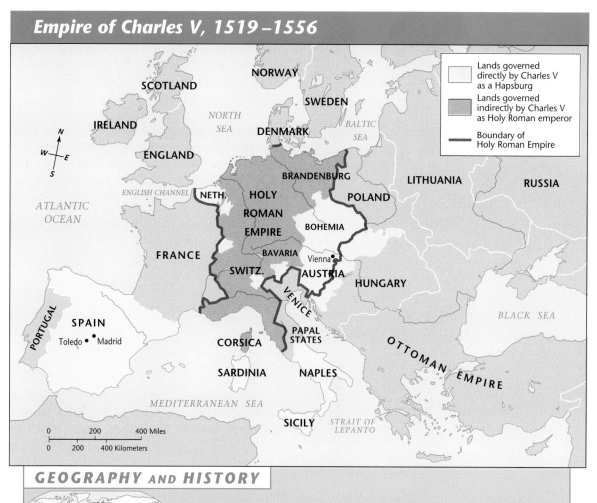

## Empire of Charles V, 1519–1556

**Legend:**
- Lands governed directly by Charles V as a Hapsburg
- Lands governed indirectly by Charles V as Holy Roman emperor
- Boundary of Holy Roman Empire

NORWAY
SCOTLAND
SWEDEN
IRELAND
*NORTH SEA*
DENMARK
*BALTIC SEA*
ENGLAND
BRANDENBURG
LITHUANIA
RUSSIA
*ENGLISH CHANNEL*
NETH.
HOLY ROMAN EMPIRE
POLAND
*ATLANTIC OCEAN*
BOHEMIA
FRANCE
BAVARIA
Vienna
SWITZ.
AUSTRIA
HUNGARY
VENICE
PORTUGAL
SPAIN
Toledo • Madrid
CORSICA
PAPAL STATES
*BLACK SEA*
OTTOMAN EMPIRE
SARDINIA
NAPLES
*MEDITERRANEAN SEA*
SICILY
*STRAIT OF LEPANTO*

0    200    400 Miles
0    200    400 Kilometers

### GEOGRAPHY AND HISTORY

For 37 years, Charles V tried to juggle the enormous responsibilities of his far-flung empire. Finally, in 1556 he retired, dividing his empire between his son and his brother.

1. **Location** On the map, locate (a) Holy Roman Empire, (b) Spain, (c) Ottoman empire, (d) Russia.
2. **Region** (a) Why does the map show the parts of Charles V's empire in two different colors? (b) Name two places that Charles V governed directly.
3. **Critical Thinking Identifying Main Ideas** What is the main idea of this map? How can you tell what the main idea is?

ruler with complete authority over the government and the lives of the people. Like other European rulers, Philip believed that he ruled by *divine right.* That is, he believed that his authority to rule came directly from God.

Partly as a result of the concept of divine right, Philip saw himself as the guardian of the Catholic Church. The great undertaking of his life was to defend the Catholic Reformation and turn back the Protestant tide in Europe. Within his own lands, he enforced religious unity, turning the Inquisition against Protestants and other people considered to be heretics.

## The Wars of Philip II

Philip fought many wars as he advanced Spanish Catholic power throughout the world. At the battle of Lepanto in 1571, Spain and its Italian allies soundly defeated an Ottoman fleet in the Mediterranean. Although Christians hailed this as a great victory, the Ottomans remained a major power in the Mediterranean for centuries.

**Revolt in the Netherlands.** During the last half of his reign, Philip battled Protestant rebels in the Netherlands. At the time, the region

**A Religious King** *This sculpture from the tomb of Philip II shows the Spanish king with members of his family. Philip was a devout Catholic. Yet his desire to rule as an absolute monarch often led him to meddle in Church policy. He even went so far as to tell Spanish bishops what they should wear!* **Impact of the Individual** *How does this sculpture suggest the seriousness and religious faith of Philip II?*

included 17 provinces that are today Belgium, the Netherlands, and Luxembourg. It was the richest part of Philip's empire. Protestants in the Netherlands resisted Philip's efforts to crush their faith. Both Protestant and Catholic subjects also opposed burdensome taxes and autocratic Spanish rule, which threatened their traditions of local self-government.

In the 1560s, riots against the Inquisition sparked a general uprising in the Netherlands. Savage fighting raged for decades. In 1581, the northern, largely Protestant provinces declared independence and became known as the Dutch Netherlands. They did not gain official recognition, however, until 1648. The southern, mostly Catholic provinces remained part of the Spanish empire.

**The Armada sails.** By the 1580s, Philip saw England's Queen Elizabeth I as his chief Protestant enemy. First secretly, then openly, Elizabeth had supported the Dutch against Spain. She even encouraged English captains, known as Sea Dogs, to plunder Spanish treasure

ships. Francis Drake, the most daring Sea Dog, looted Spanish cities in the Americas. To Philip's dismay, instead of punishing the pirate, Elizabeth made him a knight!

To end English attacks and subdue the Dutch, Philip prepared a huge armada, or fleet, to carry a Spanish invasion force to England. In 1588, the Armada sailed with more than 130 ships, 20,000 men, and 2,400 pieces of artillery. A Spanish commander confidently predicted:

“It is well known that we fight in God's cause. So, when we meet the English, God will surely arrange matters so that we can grapple and board them, either by sending some strange freak of weather or, more likely, just by depriving the English of their wits. If we can come to close quarters, Spanish valor and Spanish steel . . . will make our victory certain.”

The "strange freak of weather," however, favored the other side. In the English Channel, lumbering Spanish ships took losses from the lighter, faster English ships. Suddenly, a savage storm blew up, scattering the Armada. After further disasters at sea, the tattered remnants limped home in defeat.

While the defeat of the Spanish Armada ended Philip's plan to invade England, it had little short-term effect on his power. In the long term, however, Spain's naval superiority did dwindle. In the 1600s and 1700s, Dutch, English, and French fleets challenged—and surpassed—Spanish power in Europe and around the world.

## The Golden Century

The century from 1550 to 1650 is often called Spain's *siglo de oro,* or "golden century," for the brilliance of its arts and literature. Philip II was a patron of the arts and also founded academies of science and mathematics.

**Painters.** Among the famous painters of this period was El Greco, meaning "the Greek." Born on the Greek island of Crete, El Greco had studied in Renaissance Italy before settling in Spain. He produced haunting religious pictures and striking portraits of Spanish nobles, done in a dramatically elongated style.

El Greco's use of vibrant colors influenced the work of Diego Velázquez (vuhl LAHS kehs), court painter to King Philip IV. Velázquez is perhaps best known for his portraits of Spanish royalty. In one painting, *The Maids of Honor*, he shows himself in the act of painting the portraits of several young girls.

**Writers.** Spain's golden century produced outstanding writers like Lope de Vega. A peasant by birth, he wrote more than 1,500 plays, including witty comedies and action-packed romances.

Miguel de Cervantes (suhr VAN tayz) wrote *Don Quixote* (dahn kee HOHT ee), the first modern novel in Europe. It pokes fun at medieval tales of chivalry. Dressed in rusty armor, the madman Don Quixote rides out on his broken-down plowhorse in search of adventure. He battles a windmill, which he thinks is a giant, and mistakes two flocks of sheep for opposing armies. Don Quixote's companion, Sancho Panza, a practical-minded peasant, expresses doubt about their quest:

66 'What I can gather clearly from all this is that those adventures that we are after will bring us in the end so many misadventures that we won't know our right foot from our left. The best and wisest thing for us to do, in my humble opinion, is to go back to our village, now that it's reaping time, and look after our own affairs. . . .'

'How little you know of knighthood, Sancho,' answered Don Quixote. 'Be quiet and have patience, for a day will come when you will see with your own eyes how fine a thing it is to follow this profession. . . . What greater contentment can the world offer, or what pleasure can equal that of winning a battle and triumphing over one's enemy?' 99

*Don Quixote* mocked the traditions of Spain's feudal past. Yet Cervantes admired both the unromantic realism of Sancho and the foolish yet heroic idealism of Don Quixote.

# PARALLELS THROUGH TIME

## "Living" Dolls
Mechanical dolls have fascinated people for centuries. Whether wound by key or powered by batteries, they give the magical illusion that an inanimate object has come to life.

**Linking Past and Present**   Give other examples of how technology has affected the way children and adults play.

**PAST**  *Mechanical dolls were once the playthings of aristocrats. This elegant lady of the Spanish court was made in the late 1500s. She could walk, turn her head, and strum the cittern, a musical instrument related to the guitar.*

**PRESENT**  *Computer technology has produced dolls that tell stories, imitate voices, and perform a wide range of actions. A remote control can make this Jennie Gymnast™ doll do splits, headstands, and leg kicks.*

## Economic Decline

In the 1600s, Spanish power slowly declined. The successors of Philip II were less able rulers than he. Economic problems were also partly to blame.

Costly overseas wars drained wealth out of Spain almost as fast as it came in. Then, too, treasure from the Americas led Spain to neglect farming and commerce. The government heavily taxed the small middle class, weakening a group that in other European nations supported royal power. The expulsion of Muslims and Jews from Spain deprived the economy of many skilled artisans and merchants. Finally, American gold and silver led to soaring inflation, with prices rising much higher in Spain than elsewhere in Europe.

Even though Spain still ruled a huge colonial empire, its strength slipped away. By the late 1600s, France had replaced Spain as the most powerful European nation.

## SECTION 1 REVIEW

1. **Identify** (a) Hapsburgs, (b) *siglo de oro*, (c) El Greco, (d) Diego Velázquez, (e) Miguel de Cervantes.
2. **Define** (a) absolute monarch, (b) divine right.
3. (a) Describe three ways in which Philip II ensured absolute power. (b) How did he try to further Catholicism?
4. Why was the period from 1550 to 1650 Spain's golden age?
5. Explain three reasons why Spanish power and prosperity declined.
6. *Critical Thinking* **Recognizing Points of View** The English referred to the storm that battered the Spanish Armada as "the Protestant wind." (a) What does this nickname mean? (b) What might the Spanish have called it?
7. *ACTIVITY* Imagine that you are Charles V shortly after you have given up your throne and divided your empire. Write a letter to Philip II in which you explain the reasons for your actions and give one piece of advice about being king.

# 2 France Under Louis XIV

## Guide for Reading

- How did wars of religion divide France?
- How did French rulers become absolute monarchs?
- What were the results of the reign of Louis XIV?
- **Vocabulary** *intendant, balance of power*

Louis XIV was an expert on power. He even wrote a book teaching his heir how to rule:

66 Consider the king in his workchamber. From it goes forth the orders that make magistrates and captains, citizens and soldiers, provinces, navies, and armies act together. He is the image of God, who from His throne in highest heaven makes all the world go. 99

By the late 1600s, Louis had become absolute monarch as well as the most powerful ruler in Europe. Yet, just 100 years earlier, France had been caught in terrible turmoil.

## Rebuilding France

From the 1560s to the 1590s, religious wars between Huguenots (French Protestants) and the Catholic majority tore France apart. Leaders on both sides used the strife to further their own ambitions. Two of the noble families, the Catholic Guises and the Protestant Bourbons, hoped to replace the declining Valois dynasty on the throne.

Each side committed terrible atrocities. The worst began on St. Bartholomew's Day, August 24, 1572. As Huguenot and Catholic nobles gathered to celebrate a royal wedding, violence erupted that led to the massacre of 3,000 Huguenots. In the next few days, thousands more were slaughtered. For many, the St. Bartholomew's Day Massacre symbolized the complete breakdown of order in France.

**Henry IV.** In 1589, a Bourbon prince and Huguenot leader, Henry of Navarre, inherited the French throne as Henry IV. Knowing that a

Protestant would face severe problems ruling a largely Catholic land, he became Catholic. "Paris is well worth a Mass," he is supposed to have said. To protect Protestants, however, he issued the Edict of Nantes in 1598. It granted the Huguenots religious toleration and let them fortify their own towns and cities.

Henry IV then set out to heal his shattered land. His goal, he said, was not the victory of one sect over another, but "a chicken in every pot"—a good Sunday dinner for every peasant. Under Henry, the government reached into every area of life. Royal officials administered justice, improved roads, built bridges, and revived agriculture. By building the royal bureaucracy and reducing the influence of nobles, Henry laid the foundations for royal absolutism.

**Richelieu.** When Henry IV fell victim to an assassin in 1610, his nine-year-old son, Louis XIII, inherited the throne. For a time, nobles reasserted their power. Then, in 1624, Louis XIII appointed Cardinal Armand Richelieu (RIHSH uh loo) as his chief minister. This cunning, capable leader spent the next 18 years strengthening the central government.

Richelieu was determined to destroy the power of the nobles and the Huguenots, two groups that did not bow down to royal authority. He defeated the private armies of the nobles and destroyed their fortified castles. While reducing their independence, Richelieu tied the nobles to the king by giving them high posts at court or in the royal army. At the same time, he smashed the walled cities of the Huguenots and outlawed their armies. Yet he allowed them to continue to practice their religion.

Richelieu handpicked his able successor, Cardinal Jules Mazarin. When five-year-old

▲ *Cardinal Richelieu*

Louis XIV inherited the throne in 1643, the year after Richelieu's death, Mazarin was in place to serve as the young king's chief minister. Like Richelieu, Mazarin worked tirelessly to extend royal power.

## *From Boy King to Sun King*

Soon after Louis XIV became king, disorder again swept France. In an uprising called the Fronde, nobles, merchants, peasants, and the urban poor rebelled, each group for its own reasons. On one occasion, rioters drove the boy king from his palace. It was an experience Louis would never forget.

When Mazarin died in 1661, Louis resolved to take over the government himself. "I have been pleased to entrust the government of my affairs to the late Cardinal," he declared. "It is now time that I govern them myself."

**"I am the state."** Like his great-grandfather Philip II of Spain, Louis believed in divine right. He took the sun as the symbol of his power. Like the sun that stands at the center of the solar system, the Sun King was the center of the French nation. Louis is often quoted as saying, *"L'etat, c'est moi"*—"I am the state."

Bishop Jacques Bossuet (bah soo WAY), a court preacher and tutor to Louis's son, summed up the theory of divine right in his *Universal History*. As God's representative on Earth, wrote Bossuet, the king was entitled to unquestioning obedience. The king himself was responsible only to God:

66The royal power is absolute. . . . Without this absolute authority the king could neither do good nor repress evil. It is necessary that his power be such that no one can escape him.99

Not once during his reign did Louis XIV call a meeting of the Estates General. (See page 214.) In fact, the Estates General did not meet between 1614 and 1789. Thus, unlike the English Parliament, the Estates General played no role in checking royal power.

**The business of government.** Like Philip II, Louis spent many hours each day attending to government affairs. To strengthen the state, he followed the policies of Richelieu. He expanded the bureaucracy and appointed intendants, royal officials who collected taxes, recruited soldiers, and carried out his policies in the provinces. The office of intendant and other government jobs often went to wealthy middle-class men. In this way, Louis cemented ties between the middle class and the monarchy.

Under Louis XIV, the French army became the strongest in Europe. The state paid, fed, trained, and supplied up to 300,000 soldiers. Louis used this highly disciplined army to enforce his policies at home and abroad.

**Colbert and the French economy.** Louis found an expert organizer in his chief finance minister, Jean Baptiste Colbert (kohl BEHR). Colbert followed mercantilist policies to bolster the economy and promote trade.

Colbert had new lands cleared for farming, encouraged mining and other basic industries, and built up luxury trades such as lacemaking. To protect French manufacturers, he put high tariffs on imported goods. He also encouraged overseas colonies, such as New France in North America, and regulated trade with the colonies to enrich the royal treasury.

Colbert's policies helped make France the wealthiest state in Europe. Yet Louis XIV was often short of cash. Not even the financial genius of Colbert could produce enough income to support the huge costs of Louis's court or pay for his many foreign wars.

## The Splendor of Versailles

In the countryside near Paris, Louis XIV turned a royal hunting lodge into the immense palace of Versailles. He spared no expense to make Versailles the most magnificent building in Europe. Its halls and salons displayed the finest paintings and statues, glittering chandeliers and mirrors. In the royal gardens, millions of flowers, plants, trees, and fountains were set out in precise geometric patterns.

Versailles became the perfect symbol of the Sun King's wealth and power. As both the king's home and the seat of government, it housed at least 10,000 people, from nobles and officials to servants.

**Ceremonies of daily life.** Louis XIV perfected elaborate ceremonies that emphasized his own importance. Each day began with "*la levée*," the king's rising, a major court occasion. High-ranking nobles competed for the honor of holding the royal wash basin or handing the king his diamond buckle shoes. At night the ceremony was repeated in reverse. Wives of nobles vied to attend upon women of the royal family.

Such ceremonies served another purpose. French nobles were descendants of the feudal lords who held power in medieval times. Left at their estates, these nobles were a threat to the power of the monarchy. By luring nobles to Versailles, Louis turned them into courtiers angling for privileges rather than warriors battling for power. Louis carefully protected their prestige and left them free from paying taxes.

**Cultural flowering.** The king, along with wealthy residents of Versailles and Paris, supported a "splendid century" of the arts. The king sponsored musical entertainments and commissioned plays by the best writers. Women of the court acted, played music, and danced in pageants.

The age of Louis XIV was the classical age of French drama. Jean Racine (rah SEEN) wrote tragedies based on ancient Greek myths. The

*The King Dances* The French nobles at Versailles put on plays and other entertainments. Often, the king himself took part. Here, Louis XIV performs in a ballet for an audience of courtiers. ***Political and Social Systems*** How did Louis's costume reinforce his image as king?

**Salon de la Guerre, Versailles** *The Salon de la Guerre, or Hall of War, is a dazzling example of an ornate artistic style called baroque. The hall is decorated with gilded bronze, carved marble, crystal, and mirrors. Oil paintings depict war through the ages. The oval sculpture in the center of the room shows Louis XIV as the Roman god of war.* **Art and Literature** *How do the images in the Salon de la Guerre glorify Louis XIV?*

actor-playwright Molière (mohl YAIR) turned out comedies such as *The Miser* that poked fun at French society to the delight of both middle-class citizens and sophisticated courtiers.

In painting, music, architecture, and decorative arts, French styles became the model for all Europe. A new form of dance drama, ballet, gained its first great popularity at the French court. As a leading patron of culture, Louis sponsored the French Academies, which set high standards for both the arts and sciences.

## Successes and Failures

Louis XIV ruled France for 72 years, longer than any other monarch. During that time, French culture, manners, and customs replaced those of Renaissance Italy as the standard for European taste. In both foreign and domestic affairs, however, many of Louis's policies were costly failures.

**The wars of Louis XIV.** Louis XIV poured vast resources into wars to expand French borders and dominate Europe. At first, he did gain some territory. His later wars were disastrous, though, because rival rulers joined forces to check French ambitions. Led by the Dutch or the English, these alliances fought to maintain the balance of power, a distribution of military and economic power that would prevent any one nation from dominating Europe.

In 1700, Louis's grandson Philip V inherited the throne of Spain. Louis declared that France and Spain "must regard themselves as one." But neighboring powers led by England were determined to prevent this union. The War of the Spanish Succession dragged on until 1713, when an exhausted France signed the Treaty of Utrecht. Philip remained on the Spanish throne, but France agreed never to unite the two crowns.

**Persecution of Huguenots.** Perhaps Louis's most costly blunder was his treatment of the Huguenots. He saw the Protestant minority as a threat to religious and political unity. In 1685, he revoked the Edict of Nantes. Facing persecution, more than 100,000 Huguenots fled France. Huguenots, however, had been among the most hard-working and prosperous of Louis's subjects. Their loss was thus a serious blow to the French economy, just as the expulsion of Muslims and Jews had hurt Spain.

**Looking ahead.** Louis outlived his sons and grandsons. When he died in 1715, his five-year-old great-grandson inherited the throne as Louis XV. Although France was then the strongest state in Europe, years of warfare had drained the treasury. The prosperity nurtured by Colbert evaporated under the burden of bad harvests, heavy taxes, and other problems.

Louis XV was far too weak a king to deal with such problems. He neglected his duties and filled his hours with dances, hunting, and other pleasures. Meanwhile, the need for reform was growing, and he knew it. He used to quote an old French proverb, "After us, the deluge." As you will read in Chapter 19, the deluge came during the reign of the next king.

## SECTION 2 REVIEW

1. **Identify** (a) St. Bartholomew's Day Massacre, (b) Edict of Nantes, (c) Fronde, (d) Versailles, (e) Molière, (f) War of the Spanish Succession.
2. **Define** (a) intendant, (b) balance of power.
3. (a) What were the effects of the French wars of religion? (b) How did Henry IV rebuild French unity?
4. Describe one way each of the following strengthened the power of the French monarchy: (a) Richelieu, (b) Louis XIV, (c) Colbert.
5. *Critical Thinking* **Applying Information** On his deathbed, Louis XIV told his heir, "I have loved war too well; do not copy me in this, nor in the lavish expenditures I have made." Why do you think Louis gave this advice?
6. *ACTIVITY* Imagine that your school is putting on a play about Louis XIV set at Versailles. You have been asked to design the set. Make a list of furniture, paintings, and other items you would want to include in the set.

## 3 Triumph of Parliament in England

### Guide for Reading

- What issues divided the Stuart kings and Parliament?
- What were the causes and results of the English Civil War?
- How did the Glorious Revolution ensure the rule of law?
- **Vocabulary** *limited monarchy, habeas corpus*

"The most high and absolute power in the realm consists in the Parliament," wrote an English statesman in the 1560s. He was voicing a tradition that had roots in the Middle Ages. But in 1603, a monarch with far different ideas took the throne. "Kings are called gods," declared James I, "because they sit upon God's throne on Earth." Before long, the new king found himself on a collision course with Parliament.

In the 1600s, while Louis XIV perfected royal absolutism in France, England developed in a different direction. In this section, we will look at why and how the English Parliament asserted itself against royal power.

### The Tudors and Parliament

From 1485 to 1603, England was ruled by the Tudor dynasty. Although the Tudors believed in divine right, they shrewdly recognized the value of good relations with Parliament. When Henry VIII broke with the Roman Catholic Church, he turned to Parliament to legalize his actions. Parliament approved the Act of Supremacy, making him head of the Church of England, and voted on his seizure of monastery lands. (See Chapter 14.)

A constant need for money also led Henry to consult Parliament frequently. Although he had inherited a bulging treasury, he quickly used up his funds fighting overseas wars. To levy new taxes, the king had to seek the approval of Parliament. Members of Parliament tended to vote as Henry's agents instructed. Still, they got used to being consulted on important matters.

Like her father, Elizabeth I both consulted Parliament and controlled it with a firm hand. Her advisers conveyed Elizabeth's wishes to Parliament and forbade discussion of certain subjects, such as foreign policy or the queen's marriage. Her skill in handling Parliament helped make "Good Queen Bess" a popular and successful ruler.

## The Early Stuarts

In 1603, after a 45-year reign, Elizabeth died without a direct heir. The throne passed to her relatives the Stuarts, the ruling family of Scotland. The Stuarts were neither as popular as the Tudors nor as skillful in dealing with Parliament. They also inherited problems that Henry and Elizabeth had long suppressed. The result was a "century of revolution" that pitted the Stuart monarchs against Parliament.

**A New English Bible**
In 1604, James I asked a group of scholars to translate the Bible from Greek and Hebrew into English. For seven years, the committee worked on what we now call the "King James" Bible. Written in the rich language of the age of Shakespeare, it is still the best-known English version of the Bible. **Religions and Value Systems** Why would English Protestants favor an English translation of the Bible?

**The royal challenge.** James I, the first Stuart monarch, had agreed to rule according to English laws and customs. Soon, however, he was lecturing Parliament about divine right. "I will not be content that my power be disputed upon," he declared.

James repeatedly clashed with Parliament over money and foreign policy. He needed funds to finance his lavish court and wage wars. When members wanted to discuss foreign policy before voting funds, James dissolved Parliament and collected taxes on his own. Leaders in the House of Commons fiercely resisted the king's claim to absolute power.

James also found himself embroiled in religious disputes. At that time, English Protestants called Puritans were pressing to "purify" the Church of England of Catholic practices. Puritans wanted simpler services and a more democratic church without powerful bishops. James rejected their demands. As Puritans pushed harder for change, the king warned, "I will make them conform themselves or I will harry them out of this land or else do worse."

**Parliament responds.** Charles I inherited the throne in 1625. Like his father, Charles behaved like an absolute monarch. He imprisoned foes without trial and squeezed the nation for money. By 1628, though, his need to raise taxes forced Charles to summon Parliament. Before voting any funds, Parliament insisted that Charles sign the Petition of Right. It prohibited the king from raising taxes without the consent of Parliament or imprisoning anyone without just cause.

Charles did sign the petition, but he then dissolved Parliament in 1629. For 11 years, he ignored the petition and ruled without Parliament. During that time, he created bitter enemies, especially among Puritans. His Archbishop of Canterbury, William Laud, tried to force all clergy to follow strict Anglican rules, dismissing or imprisoning any who resisted. Many people felt that the archbishop was trying to revive Catholic practices.

In 1637, Charles and Laud tried to impose the Anglican prayer book on Scotland. The Calvinist Scots revolted. To get funds to suppress the Scottish rebellion, Charles finally had to summon Parliament in 1640. When it met, however, Parliament launched its own revolt.

**The Long Parliament.** The Parliament that Charles I summoned became known as the Long Parliament because it lasted on and off until 1653. Its actions triggered the greatest political revolution in English history. In a mounting struggle with the king, Parliament tried and finally executed his chief ministers, including Archbishop Laud. It further declared that the Parliament could not be dissolved without its consent and called for the abolition of bishops.

Charles lashed back. In 1642, he led troops into the House of Commons to arrest its most radical leaders. They escaped through a back door and soon raised their own army. The clash between them now moved to the battlefield.

## The English Civil War

The civil war that followed lasted from 1642 to 1649. Like the Fronde that occurred about the same time in France, it posed a major challenge to the rise of absolute monarchs. But while the forces of royal power won in France, in England the forces of revolution triumphed.

**Cavaliers and Roundheads.** At first, the odds seemed to favor the Cavaliers, or supporters of Charles I. Many Cavaliers were wealthy nobles, proud of their plumed hats and fashionably long hair. Well trained in dueling and warfare, the Cavaliers expected a quick victory. But their foes proved to be tough fighters having the courage of their convictions. The forces of Parliament were composed of country gentry, town-dwelling manufacturers, and Puritan clergy. They were called Roundheads because their hair was cut close around their heads.

The Roundheads found a leader of genius in Oliver Cromwell. A Puritan member of the lesser gentry, Cromwell was a skilled general. He organized the "New Model Army" for Parliament into a disciplined fighting force. Inspired by Puritan chaplains, Cromwell's army defeated the Cavaliers in a series of decisive bat-

> **A Roundhead Victory** The Battle of Marston Moor, fought in 1644, was a turning point in the English Civil War. Cromwell, seen here on his horse, was wounded in the neck early in the battle. However, he rallied his troops for a second attack and finally defeated the forces of King Charles I. **Continuity and Change** How would a modern battle scene differ from this one?

tles. By 1647, the king was in the hands of parliamentary forces.

**Execution of a king.** Eventually, Parliament set up a court to put the king on trial. It found him guilty and condemned him to death as "a tyrant, traitor, murderer, and public enemy." On a cold January day in 1649, Charles I stood on a scaffold surrounded by his foes. "I am a martyr of the people," he declared.

Showing no fear, the king told the executioner that he himself would give the sign for him to strike. After a brief prayer, Charles knelt and placed his neck on the block. Silence gripped the crowd as the executioner raised his ax. On the agreed signal, he severed the king's head with a single stroke.

The execution sent shock waves throughout Europe. In the past, kings had occasionally been murdered by rivals or died on the battlefield. But for the first time, a ruling monarch had been tried and executed by his own people. The parliamentary forces had sent a clear signal that, in England, no ruler could claim absolute power and ignore the rule of law.

## The Kingless Decade

After the execution of Charles I, the House of Commons abolished the monarchy, the House of Lords, and the official Church of England. It declared England a republic, known as the Commonwealth, under the leadership of Oliver Cromwell.

**Rebels in Ireland.** The new republic faced many problems. Supporters of Charles II, the uncrowned heir to the throne, attacked England by way of Ireland and Scotland. Cromwell led forces into Ireland to crush the uprising. He then took stern measures against the Irish Catholic majority. In 1652, Parliament passed a law exiling most Catholics to barren land in the west of Ireland. Anyone found disobeying the order could be killed on sight.

**The Levellers.** Squabbles also splintered forces within the Commonwealth. One group, called Levellers, thought that poor men should have as much say in government as the gentry, lawyers, and other leading citizens. "I think that the poorest He that is in England hath a life to live as well as the greatest He," wrote one Leveller:

❝Every man that is to live under a government ought first by his own consent to put himself under that government.❞

Such ideas horrified the gentry, who dominated Parliament. Cromwell and his generals suppressed the Levellers, as well as more radical groups who threatened property ownership. As the challenges to order grew, Cromwell took the title Lord Protector in 1653. From then on, he ruled through the army.

## Life in the Commonwealth

In the 1650s, Parliament enacted a series of laws designed to make sure that Sunday was set aside for religious observance. Anyone over the age of 14 who was caught "profaning the Lord's Day" could be fined, including

❝Every person being in any tavern, tobacco-house, cellar or shop; . . . every person dancing or profanely singing or playing upon musical instruments; . . . all tailors fitting or going to fit any wearing apparel; and barbers trimming upon the day aforesaid.❞

Under the Commonwealth, Puritan preachers tried to root out godlessness and impose a "rule of saints." The English Civil War thus ushered in a social revolution as well as a political one.

**Puritan morality.** To the Puritans, theaters were "spectacles of pleasure too commonly expressing mirth and levity." So, like Calvin in Geneva, Cromwell closed all theaters. Puritans also frowned on lewd dancing, raged against taverns and gambling, and cut down Maypoles. Yet Puritans enjoyed many types of entertainment. While they banned music in churches, they played music at home and even joined in modest dancing.

Although Cromwell could not accept open Catholic worship, he believed in religious freedom for other Protestant groups. "What greater hypocrisy," Cromwell demanded, "than for those who were oppressed by the bishops to become the greatest oppressors themselves, so

The Orthodox true Minister,    the Seducer and false Prophet.

soon as their yoke was removed?" He even welcomed Jews back to England, after more than 350 years of exile.

**Schooling.** Puritans felt that every Christian, rich and poor, must be able to read the Bible. To spread religious knowledge, they encouraged education for all people. (■ See *You Decide*, What Is the Goal of Education? pages 450–451.)

By mid-century, families from all classes were sending their children to school, girls as well as boys. Students learned the alphabet from hornbooks, paddle-shaped pieces of wood with letters and words carved on them. A popular rhyme taught the alphabet through moral lessons and references to the Bible:

> **"A**  In **A**dam's fall,
>     We sinned all.
>
> **B**  Thy life to mend,
>     This **B**ook [the Bible] attend. . . .
>
> **F**  The idle **F**ool
>     Is whipt at School.**"**

**Women.** Puritans pushed for changes in marriage to ensure greater fidelity. In addition to marriages based on business interests, they encouraged marriages based on love. As in the past, women were seen mainly as caretakers of the family, subordinate to men.

Despite their lower status, some women sought new liberties. Female Levellers asserted their right to petition Parliament. "Have we not an equal interest with the men of this nation in those liberties and securities contained in the . . . laws of the land?" they asked.

Among some radical Protestant groups, women even preached sermons. Katherine Chidley, an outspoken writer on religious matters, asserted that a husband had authority over a wife "in bodily and civil respects, but not to be a Lord over her conscience."

Still, whenever women took a public role, most men were horrified. A popular rhyme warned, "When women preach and cobblers pray / The fiends in hell make holiday."

**End of the Commonwealth.** Soon after Cromwell's death in 1658, the Puritans lost their grip on England. Many people were tired of military rule and strict Puritan ways. In 1660, a newly elected Parliament invited Charles II to return to England from exile.

The Puritan experiment ended in the restoration of the monarchy. Yet Puritan ideas about morality, government, equality, and education lasted. Years later, they would play an important role in shaping the United States of America. ◼

## The Stuarts Restored

In late May 1660, cheering crowds welcomed Charles II back to London. John Evelyn wrote in his diary:

> **"**This day came his Majesty, Charles the Second to London, after a sad and long

exile. . . . This was also his birthday, and with a triumph of above 20,000 horse and foot [soldiers], branding their swords, and shouting with inexpressible joy; the ways strewd with flowers, the bells ringing, the streets hung with tapestry. **99**

With his charm and flashing wit, young Charles II was a popular ruler. He reopened theaters and taverns and presided over a lively court in the manner of Louis XIV. Charles restored the official Church of England, but tolerated other Protestants such as Presbyterians, Quakers, and Baptists.

Although Charles accepted the Petition of Right, he shared his father's faith in absolute monarchy and secretly had Catholic sympathies. Still, he shrewdly avoided his father's mistakes in dealing with Parliament.

Charles's brother James II inherited the throne in 1685. Unlike Charles, James flaunted his Catholic faith. He further angered his subjects by suspending laws at whim and appointing Catholics to high office. Many feared that James would restore the Roman Catholic Church. In 1688, alarmed parliamentary leaders invited James's Protestant daughter, Mary, and her Dutch Protestant husband, William III of Orange, to become rulers of England.

## The Glorious Revolution

When William and Mary landed with their army late in 1688, James II fled to France. This bloodless overthrow of a king became known as the Glorious Revolution. Before they could be crowned, however, William and Mary had to accept several acts passed by Parliament that became known as the English Bill of Rights.

**Limits on royal power.** The Bill of Rights ensured the superiority of Parliament over the monarchy. It required the monarch to summon Parliament regularly and gave the House of Commons the "power of the purse." A king or queen could no longer interfere in Parliamentary debates or suspend laws. The bill also barred any Catholic from sitting on the throne. Under the Bill of Rights, England became a limited monarchy, a government in which a constitution or legislative body limits the monarch's powers.

The Bill of Rights formally restated the traditional rights of English citizens, such as trial by jury. It abolished excessive fines and cruel or unjust punishment. It also affirmed the principle of habeas corpus. That is, no person could be held in prison without first being charged with a specific crime. Later, the Toleration Act of 1689 granted limited toleration to Puritans, Quakers, and other Protestant dissenters, though not yet to Catholics. Still, only members of the Church of England could hold public office.

**Looking ahead.** What the Glorious Revolution accomplished was not democracy, but the beginnings of constitutional monarchy. English rulers still had much power, but they had to obey the law and govern in partnership with Parliament. In the age of absolute monarchy elsewhere in Europe, a limited monarchy in England was radical enough.

## SECTION 3 REVIEW

1. **Identify** (a) Petition of Right, (b) Cavalier, (c) Roundhead, (d) Oliver Cromwell, (e) Leveller, (f) Bill of Rights.
2. **Define** (a) limited monarchy, (b) habeas corpus.
3. (a) How did the Tudors handle Parliament? (b) Why did the Stuarts clash with Parliament?
4. (a) Explain two causes of the English Civil War. (b) Why did many people welcome the return of the monarchy?
5. Describe two results of the Glorious Revolution.
6. *Critical Thinking* **Analyzing Information** (a) How might Puritan teachings have led some women to seek greater liberties? (b) Why do you think many men were upset by the idea of women speaking in public?
7. *ACTIVITY* Draw a political cartoon about the execution of Charles I from the point of view of either a Roundhead or a Cavalier.

**ISSUES** *For* **TODAY** While Louis XIV strengthened absolute power in France, the Stuarts were unable to do the same in England. How do leaders achieve and maintain power?

# 4 Rise of Austria and Prussia

## Guide for Reading

- What were the results of the Thirty Years' War?

- How did Austria and Prussia emerge as great powers?

- How did the balance of power affect European diplomacy?

Year after year, war ravaged the German states of central Europe. Bodies of victims littered fields and roads. "God send that there may be peace again," prayed a German peasant in 1638. But peace never lasted long. As the Thirty Years' War dragged on, almost every European power was sucked into the conflict.

Finally, two great German-speaking powers, Austria and Prussia, rose out of the ashes. Like Louis XIV in France, their rulers perfected skills as absolute monarchs.

## The Thirty Years' War

The French philosopher Voltaire noted that, by early modern times, the Holy Roman Empire was neither holy, nor Roman, nor an empire. It was a patchwork of several hundred small, separate states that paid little heed to the emperor. Religion further divided the German states. The north was largely Protestant, while the south was Catholic. This power vacuum sparked the Thirty Years' War.

**The war begins.** The war had both religious and political causes. It began as a local conflict in Bohemia, the present-day Czech Republic. Ferdinand, the Hapsburg king of Bohemia, sought to suppress Protestants and to assert royal power over local nobles. In May 1618, rebellious Protestant noblemen tossed two royal officials out of a castle window in Prague. This act signaled the start of a general revolt, which Ferdinand* moved quickly to sup-

---

*The following year, Ferdinand was elected Holy Roman emperor and became known as Ferdinand II.

press. The conflict widened as both sides sought allies.

With the support of Spain, Poland, and other Catholic states, Ferdinand tried to roll back the Reformation. At first, he defeated the Bohemians and their Protestant allies. Alarmed by the Hapsburg victories, Protestant powers like the Netherlands and Sweden sent troops into Germany.

What began as a local religious struggle blazed into a European conflict. Before long, political motives outweighed religious issues. Catholic and Protestant rulers shifted alliances to suit their own interests. At one point, Catholic France led by Cardinal Richelieu joined Lutheran Sweden against the Catholic Hapsburgs of Austria.

**"God have pity on us."** The fighting took a brutal toll. Roving armies of mercenaries burned villages and sacked cities. "We have had blue coats and red coats and now come the yellow coats," cried the citizens of one German town. "God have pity on us." Soldiers destroyed crops and homes and killed without mercy. Jacob von Grimmelshausen captured the nightmare violence in his novel *Simplicissimus.* At one point, he describes the plunder of a fictional village by marauding soldiers:

> 66For one of [the peasants] they had taken they thrust into the baking oven and there lit a fire under him, although he had as yet confessed to no crime; as for another, they put a cord around his head and twisted it so tight with a piece of wood that the blood gushed from his mouth and nose and ears. In a word each had his own device to torture the peasants, and each peasant his several tortures.99

Murder and torture were followed by famine and disease. Wolves, not seen in settled areas since the Middle Ages, stalked the deserted streets of once-bustling villages. Perhaps one third of the population of the German states died in the Thirty Years' War.

**Peace at last.** Finally, in 1648, the exhausted combatants accepted a series of treaties, known as the Peace of Westphalia. Because so many powers had been involved in the conflict, the war ended with a general European peace

*The horrors of the Thirty Years' War finally ended with a series of treaties called the Peace of Westphalia. The map shows who controlled various European lands after the treaties went into effect.*

**1. Location** On the map, locate (a) Poland, (b) Sweden, (c) Spanish Netherlands, (d) Westphalia.

**2. Place** (a) In 1648, who controlled Bohemia? (b) What country separated the two parts of Prussia? (c) What lands did the Spanish Hapsburgs control?

**3. Critical Thinking Drawing Conclusions** How can you tell from the map that the Holy Roman Empire was not a strong, unified state?

and an attempt to settle other international problems as well.

France emerged a clear winner, gaining territory on both its Spanish and German frontiers. The Hapsburgs were big losers because they had to accept the almost total independence of all the princes of the Holy Roman Empire. The Netherlands and the Swiss Federation (present-day Switzerland) won recognition as independent states.

The Thirty Years' War left Germany divided into more than 360 separate states, "one for every day of the year." These states still formally acknowledged the leadership of the Holy Ro-

man emperor. Yet each state had its own government, coinage, state church, armed forces, and foreign policy. Germany, potentially the most powerful nation in Europe, thus remained fragmented for another 200 years.

## Hapsburg Austria

Though weakened by war, the Hapsburgs still wanted to create a strong united state. They kept the title of Holy Roman emperors, but focused their attention on expanding their own lands. To Austria, they added Bohemia, Hungary, and, later, parts of Poland and Italy.

**Unity and diversity.** Uniting these lands proved difficult. Divided by geography, they also included diverse peoples and cultures. By the 1700s, the Hapsburg empire included Germans, Magyars, Slavs, and others. Its people spoke many languages, including Czech, Hungarian, Polish, and Italian. In many parts of the empire, people had their own laws, assemblies, and customs.

The Hapsburgs succeeded in exerting some control over these diverse peoples. They sent German-speaking officials to Bohemia and Hungary and settled Austrians on confiscated lands in these provinces. The Hapsburgs also put down revolts in both Bohemia and Hungary. Still, the Hapsburg empire never developed a centralized system like that of France.

**Maria Theresa.** In the early 1700s, the emperor Charles VI faced a new crisis. He had no son. His daughter, Maria Theresa, was intelligent and capable, but no woman had yet ruled Hapsburg lands in her own name. Charles persuaded other European rulers to recognize his daughter's right to succeed him. When he died, however, many ignored their pledge. Maria Theresa later recalled:

> **❝**I found myself . . . without money, without credit, without army, without experience and knowledge of my own, and finally also without any counsel, because each one of them first wanted to wait and see what would develop.**❞**

The greatest threat came in 1740, when Frederick II of Prussia seized the rich Hapsburg province of Silesia. Maria Theresa set off for Hungary to appeal for military help. The Hungarians were ordinarily unfriendly to the Hapsburgs. But she made a dramatic plea before an assembly of Hungarian nobles. According to one account, the nobles rose to their feet and shouted, "Our lives and blood for your Majesty! We will die for our monarch, Maria Theresa!" She eventually got further help from Britain and Russia.

During the eight-year War of the Austrian Succession, Maria Theresa failed to push Frederick out of Silesia. Still, she did preserve her empire and win the support of most of her people. Equally important, she strengthened Hapsburg power by reorganizing the bureaucracy and improving tax collection. She even forced nobles and clergy to pay taxes and tried to ease the burden of taxes and labor services on peasants. Many of her reforms were later extended by her son and successor, Joseph II. (See Chapter 18.)

*A Large Royal Family* Maria Theresa had one thing in common with most women of her day—her duties included motherhood. During her reign, she gave birth to 11 daughters and 5 sons. When her oldest son became Emperor Joseph II, she often quarreled with him about state policy. Another child, Marie Antoinette, married the king of France. *Political and Social Systems* Why are family ties important in a monarchy?

## Prussia: Out of the Ashes

While Austria was molding a strong Catholic state, Prussia emerged as a new Protestant power. In the 1600s, the Hohenzollern (HOH uhn tsahl ern) family ruled scattered lands across north Germany. After the Peace of Westphalia, ambitious Hohenzollern rulers united their lands by taking over the states between them. Like absolute rulers elsewhere, they imposed royal power on all their subjects and reduced the independence of their nobles, called Junkers (YOON kerz).

To achieve their goals, Prussian rulers set up an efficient bureaucracy and forged one of the best-trained armies in Europe. Great emphasis was put on military values. A Prussian military leader boasted, "Prussia is not a state which possesses an army, but an army which possesses a state." The Hohenzollerns won the loyalty of the Junkers by giving them positions in the army and government. By 1740, Prussia was strong enough to challenge its rival Austria.

**Frederick II.** That year, young Frederick II inherited the Prussian throne. His father, Frederick William, had made sure that, from an early age, Frederick was trained in the art of war:

> 66His tutor must take the greatest pains to imbue my son with a sincere love for the soldier's profession and to impress upon him that nothing else in the world can confer upon a prince such fame and honor as the sword.99

In fact, young Frederick preferred playing the flute and writing poetry. Frederick William despised these pursuits and treated the young prince so badly that he decided to flee the country. Discovering these plans, Frederick William put his son in solitary confinement. A friend who had helped Frederick was beheaded while the 18-year-old prince was forced to watch.

**Military successes.** Frederick's harsh military training did have an effect. As king, Frederick II lost no time in using his army. As you read, he boldly seized mineral-rich Silesia from Austria, sparking the War of the Austrian Succession.

In several later wars, Frederick made brilliant use of his disciplined army, forcing all to accept Prussia as a great power. His exploits earned him the name Frederick the Great.

## Keeping the Balance of Power

By 1750, the great powers of Europe included Austria, Prussia, France, England, and Russia. They formed various alliances to maintain the balance of power. As you have seen, early in the century, the Dutch and English combined to check the aggressive ambitions of Louis XIV. At times, the great powers switched partners, but two rivalries persisted. Prussia battled Austria for control of the German states, while Britain and France competed for overseas empire.

Sometimes, rivals went to war to maintain the balance of power. In the 1700s, those wars ignited worldwide conflict. The Seven Years' War, which lasted from 1756 to 1763, was fought on three continents. Prussia, Austria, Russia, France and Britain battled in Europe. As you read, Britain and France also fought in India and in North America, where the conflict was known as the French and Indian War. The Treaty of Paris ending the war gave Britain a huge empire.

## SECTION 4 REVIEW

1. **Identify** (a) Peace of Westphalia, (b) Maria Theresa, (c) Frederick the Great, (d) Seven Years' War.
2. How did the Thirty Years' War affect the German states?
3. (a) What two major powers emerged at the end of the Thirty Years' War? (b) How were their goals similar or different?
4. (a) Why did European nations want to maintain a balance of power? (b) What methods did they use?
5. *Critical Thinking* **Linking Past and Present** Westphalia was the first modern peace conference. (a) Why do you think such a peace conference had to be devised? (b) How do warring nations try to settle their disputes today?
6. *ACTIVITY* Both Louis XIV and Frederick William wrote instructions for training their sons. With a partner, create your own list of rules for a successful absolute monarch in the 1600s and 1700s.

# 5 Absolute Monarchy in Russia

## Guide for Reading

- How did Peter the Great strengthen Russia?
- What were the goals of Russian foreign policy?
- What were the results of the partition of Poland?

In the early 1600s, Russia was still a medieval state, untouched by the Renaissance and largely isolated from Western Europe. The "Time of Troubles" had plunged the state into a period of disorder and foreign invasions. (See page 248.) The election of the first Romanov czar in 1613 restored a measure of order. Not until 1682, however, did a czar emerge who was strong enough to regain the absolute power of earlier czars. He was Peter the Great, who pushed Russia on the road to becoming a great modern power.

## Peter the Great

Peter, just 10 years old when he came to the throne, did not take control of the government until 1689. The young czar was a striking figure, nearly seven feet tall, with a booming laugh and a furious temper. Though he was not well educated, Peter was immensely curious. He spent hours in the "German quarter," the Moscow suburb where many Dutch, Scottish, English, and other foreign artisans and soldiers lived. There, he heard of the advanced technology that was helping Western European monarchs forge powerful empires.

**Journey to the West.** In 1697, Peter set out to study western technology for himself.

He spent hours walking the streets of European cities, noting the manners and homes of the people. He visited factories and art galleries, learned anatomy from a doctor, and had a dentist teach him how to pull teeth. Disguised in shabby clothes, he even worked for a time as a carpenter in a Dutch shipyard. In England, Peter was impressed by Parliament. "It is good," he said, "to hear subjects speaking truthfully and openly to their king."

Returning to Russia, Peter brought along a group of technical experts, teachers, soldiers, and nobles he had recruited in the West. He then began to reshape Russia in his large, callused hands. But convincing fellow Russians to modernize proved difficult. To impose his will, Peter became the most autocratic of Europe's absolute monarchs.

**Autocrat and reformer.** Peter was determined to centralize royal power. He brought all Russians under his control, including the Russian Orthodox Church. He forced the haughty boyars to serve the state in civilian or military jobs.

Under Peter, serfdom spread in Russia, long after it had died out in Western Europe. By tying peasants to land given to nobles, he ensured that nobles could serve the state. Further, he forced some serfs to become soldiers or labor on roads, canals, and other government projects.

Using autocratic methods, Peter pushed through social and economic reforms. He imported western technology, improved education, simplified the Russian alphabet, and set up academies for the study of mathematics, science, and engineering. To pay for his reforms, he adopted mercantilist policies and encouraged exports. He improved the waterways and canals, developed mining and textiles, and backed new trading companies.

Some changes had a symbolic meaning. After returning from the West, Peter insisted that noblemen shave their beards and replace their old-fashioned robes with Western European clothes. To

◀ Peter the Great

*Off With Their Beards!* This famous cartoon shows Peter the Great shearing the beard off a protesting Russian boyar. To encourage men to shave, Peter imposed a tax on beards in 1705. The "beard license" at right was proof that its bearer had paid the tax and did not need to shave. **Continuity and Change** Why did Peter want noblemen to shave off their beards?

end the practice of secluding women, he held grand parties at which upper-class women and men were expected to dance together. Russian nobles resisted this radical mixing of the sexes in public.

Peter had no mercy for any who resisted the new order. When elite palace guards revolted, he had over 1,000 tortured and executed. As an example of his power, he left their rotting corpses outside the palace walls for months.

## Russian Expansion

From his earliest days as czar, Peter worked to build Russian military power. He created the largest standing army in Europe and set out to extend Russian borders.

**Search for a warm-water port.** In 1700, Peter began a long war against Sweden, Russia's northwestern neighbor that dominated the Baltic region. After early setbacks, Peter eventually rebuilt his army, pushed the Swedes back, and won land along the Baltic. However, Baltic seaports were frozen over in the winter. Peter therefore turned south, seeking a warm-water port that would allow Russia to trade with the West all year long.

The nearest warm-water coast was that of the Black Sea. Peter fought the Ottoman Turks to recover Russian lands north of the Black Sea. Though Peter failed in this effort, the later Russian empress Catherine the Great succeeded before the century was over.

**Peter's city.** The great symbol of Peter's desire to forge a modern Russia was his new capital city, St. Petersburg. Seeking to open a "window on the West," he located the city on the swampy shores of the Neva River near the Baltic coast. He forced tens of thousands of serfs to drain the swamps. Many thousands died, but Peter got his city. He then invited Italian architects and artisans to design great palaces in western style.

A hundred years later, Russia's best-known poet, Alexander Pushkin, wrote *The Bronze Horseman*. Pushkin portrays Peter as a larger-than-life ruler who is determined to tame nature at whatever cost:

> **❝**Here, Swede, beware. Soon by our labor
> Here a new city shall be wrought,
> Defiance to the haughty neighbor.
> Here we at Nature's own behest
> Shall break a window to the West,
> Stand planted on the ocean level;
> Here flags of foreign nations all
> By waters new to them will call
> And unencumbered we shall revel.**❞**

**Toward the Pacific.** Russian traders and raiders also blazed trails across Siberia to the Pacific. Under Peter, Russia signed a treaty with Qing China, defining their common border in the east. In the early 1700s, Peter hired the Danish navigator Vitus Bering to explore what became known as the Bering Strait between

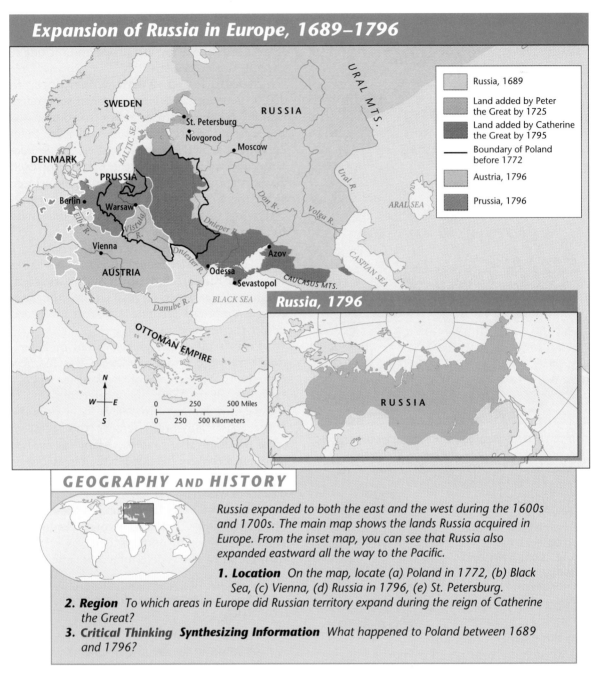

## Expansion of Russia in Europe, 1689–1796

**Legend:**
- Russia, 1689
- Land added by Peter the Great by 1725
- Land added by Catherine the Great by 1795
- Boundary of Poland before 1772
- Austria, 1796
- Prussia, 1796

*Russia, 1796*

### GEOGRAPHY AND HISTORY

*Russia expanded to both the east and the west during the 1600s and 1700s. The main map shows the lands Russia acquired in Europe. From the inset map, you can see that Russia also expanded eastward all the way to the Pacific.*

1. **Location** On the map, locate (a) Poland in 1772, (b) Black Sea, (c) Vienna, (d) Russia in 1796, (e) St. Petersburg.
2. **Region** To which areas in Europe did Russian territory expand during the reign of Catherine the Great?
3. **Critical Thinking** **Synthesizing Information** What happened to Poland between 1689 and 1796?

Siberia and Alaska. Russian pioneers crossed into Alaska and migrated as far south as California. Few Russians moved east of the Ural Mountains at this time, but on a map, Russia was already the largest country in the world, as it still is today.

**Peter's legacy.** When Peter died in 1725, he left a mixed legacy. He had expanded Russian territory, gained ports on the Baltic Sea, and created a mighty army. Yet many reforms died with him. Nobles, for example, soon ignored his policy of service to the state.

Like earlier czars, Peter the Great had brandished terror to enforce his absolute power. His policies contributed to the growth of serfdom, which only served to widen the gap between Russia and the West that Peter had sought to narrow.

### Catherine the Great

Peter's immediate successors were ineffective rulers. Russian nobles quickly reasserted their independence. Then a new monarch took the reins of power firmly in hand. She became known to history as Catherine the Great.

**Absolute rule.** A German princess by birth, Catherine had come to Russia at the age of 15 to wed the heir to the Russian throne. She learned Russian, embraced the Russian Orthodox faith, and won the loyalty of the people. In 1762, her mentally unstable husband, Czar Peter III, was murdered by a group of Russian army officers. Whether or not Catherine was involved in the plot, she certainly benefited. With their support, she ascended the Russian throne herself.

Catherine proved to be an efficient, energetic empress. She reorganized the provincial government, codified laws, and began state-sponsored education for boys and girls. Like Peter the Great, she embraced western ideas. At court, she encouraged French language and customs, wrote histories and plays, and organized court performances. As you will read in the next chapter, she was also a serious student of the French thinkers who led the movement known as the Enlightenment.

Like other absolute monarchs, Catherine could be ruthless. She granted Russian nobles important rights, such as exemption from taxes, but also let them increase their stranglehold on the peasants. When peasants rebelled against the harsh burdens of serfdom, Catherine took firm action to repress them.

Catherine was determined to expand Russia's borders. After a war against the Ottoman empire, she achieved the Russian dream of a warm-water port on the Black Sea. She also took steps to seize territory from neighboring Poland.

**Partition of Poland.** As you read in Chapter 10, Poland had once been a great European power. However, Polish rulers were un-able to centralize their power or diminish the influence of the Polish nobility. The divided Polish government was ill prepared to stand up to the increasing might of its neighbors Russia, Prussia, and Austria.

In the 1770s, Catherine the Great, Frederick the Great, and Emperor Joseph II of Austria hungrily eyed Poland. To avoid fighting each other, the three monarchs agreed to partition, or divide up, Poland. Poland was partitioned three times, first in the 1770s, then twice in the 1790s. By the time Austria, Prussia, and Russia had taken their final slice in 1795, the independent kingdom of Poland had vanished from the map. Not until 1918 would a free Polish state reappear.

## Looking Ahead

By the mid-1700s, absolute monarchs ruled four of the five major European powers. Britain, with its strong Parliament, was the only exception. But new ideas would soon shatter the French monarchy, upset the balance of power, and revolutionize European societies. In the next chapters, you will read about how the Enlightenment, the French Revolution, the rise of Napoleon Bonaparte, and the Industrial Revolution would transform Europe.

## SECTION 5 REVIEW

1. **Identify** (a) St. Petersburg, (b) Vitus Bering, (c) Catherine the Great.
2. (a) List three goals of Peter the Great. (b) Explain one reform that Peter undertook to achieve each goal.
3. Why did Russian rulers seek to expand their territory in the 1700s?
4. How did Poland disappear as an independent state in the late 1700s?
5. *Critical Thinking* **Comparing** Compare the goals and policies of Peter the Great to those of *one* of the following: (a) Louis XIV, (b) Frederick II, (c) Maria Theresa.
6. *ACTIVITY* Imagine that Peter the Great wanted to learn about the latest technology and ways of life in the United States today. Draw up a list of the people he should meet and the places he should visit.

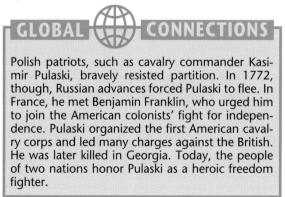

**GLOBAL CONNECTIONS**

Polish patriots, such as cavalry commander Kasimir Pulaski, bravely resisted partition. In 1772, though, Russian advances forced Pulaski to flee. In France, he met Benjamin Franklin, who urged him to join the American colonists' fight for independence. Pulaski organized the first American cavalry corps and led many charges against the British. He was later killed in Georgia. Today, the people of two nations honor Pulaski as a heroic freedom fighter.

# Skills for Success

| Critical Thinking | Writing and Researching | Maps, Charts, and Graphs | Speaking and Listening |

## Interviewing

You have seen how historians use firsthand accounts, such as letters, diaries, and autobiographies, to gain information about the life and people of an earlier era. In recent years, interviewing has become an increasingly more common method of gathering firsthand information. Interviewers may choose to focus on a single subject, such as a leading politician or a movie star. Other interviewers may compile the recollections of a large number of people, both famous and ordinary, about a time period or event. Such a collection of remembrances is referred to as an **oral history.**

Before interviewers begin asking questions, they need to be well informed about the topic. To begin, they need to find out answers to basic questions such as what, when, and why. Once the interview begins, the interviewer tries to go into greater depth and get as thorough information as possible. To do this, interviewers should avoid questions that can be answered by a simple yes or no. If the subject's answers are incomplete, interviewers must also be prepared with follow-up questions that probe the topic more deeply.

Preparing imaginary interviews with historical figures is a good way to practice interviewing skills. The interview questions listed below are some possible questions an interviewer who lived in the 1600s might have asked Louis XIV.

**1 Prepare a list of questions in advance of the interview.** (a) Is question E or F a better question to ask about the Huguenots? Why? (b) Would it be good interviewing technique to ask question C? Why or why not? (c) What question would you add to this list that you would like Louis XIV to answer?

**2 Organize the questions in a logical progression.** (a) Should question C come before or after question D? Why? (b) Which questions deal with the king's policies? Which deal with his personal tastes and feelings? (c) Which question would you use as your closing question—A, F, H, or J? Explain.

**3 Anticipate responses and prepare questions for follow-up.** (a) How would you expect Louis XIV to answer question F? (b) What would be a good follow-up question to this answer? (c) How would you expect the king to answer question H? (d) What would be a good follow-up question to this answer?

**4 Listen carefully and record the answers during the interview.** (a) Why is it important to listen carefully during an interview? (b) Why is it important to record answers during the interview instead of after it is over?

***Beyond the Classroom*** Choose a person you know whom you would like to interview. Prepare for the interview following the steps above, and then hold and record the interview. Provide your classmates with a summary of the interview and what you learned from it.

---

*Interview Questions*

A. What do you consider to be your greatest accomplishment and why?
B. What do you consider to be your greatest disappointment and why?
C. When did you first come to power?
D. What did it feel like to assume the leadership of your nation at such a young age?
E. As a Christian, how can you justify the persecution of the Huguenots?
F. Why did you revoke the Edict of Nantes and resume the older state policy against the Huguenots?
G. Did you know that France's wars have left the nation deeply in debt?
H. What do you propose to do about France's debt problems?
I. Who do you think are France's greatest painters and writers today? Why?
J. What do you like best about the palace of Versailles? Why?

## Building Vocabulary

Choose *four* vocabulary words from this chapter. Then, write a sentence for each word in which you define the word and describe its relation to the political system of one of the major European powers.

## Reviewing Chapter Themes

1. **Political and Social Systems** (a) Describe the system of absolute monarchy that emerged in Spain and France. (b) How did the idea of divine right support the power of the absolute monarch? (c) Why did absolute monarchs work to limit the power of nobles?
2. **Impact of the Individual** Choose *two* of the following monarchs: Philip II, Louis XIV, Maria Theresa, Frederick the Great, Peter the Great, Catherine the Great. (a) List the chief goals of each of the monarchs you have chosen. (b) Describe one action each monarch took to centralize his or her power. (c) Describe how each monarch tried to increase the power of his or her nation in the world.
3. **Art and Literature** Describe three ways that Louis XIV and his court at Versailles influenced the arts.
4. **Continuity and Change** Describe the impact of *two* of the following on the British system of government: (a) the reign of the Tudors, (b) the reign of James I, (c) the English Civil War, (d) the Glorious Revolution.

## Thinking Critically

1. **Understanding Sequence** Create a time line showing key events in Spain's history between the rise of Ferdinand and Isabella and the end of the golden age. Use events from this chapter and from Chapters 9, 15, and 16.
2. **Comparing** Review pages 328–329. How were the methods used by European monarchs to centralize their power similar to the methods used by the Tokugawa shoguns to centralize power in Japan?
3. **Analyzing Primary Sources** Bishop Bossuet wrote, "Let God take away his hand and the world will fall back into nothingness; let authority fail in the kingdom, and total confusion will result." (a) According to Bossuet, what is the benefit of absolute monarchy? (b) What assumption does he make about the source of royal power? (c) How might the history of France in the late 1500s have influenced Bossuet's viewpoint? (d) Do you agree or disagree with his conclusion? Explain. (★ See *Skills for Success,* page 154).
4. **Linking Past and Present** Which aspects of Commonwealth society are part of American society today? Which are not?
5. **Recognizing Points of View** How might each of the following have viewed the reign of Peter the Great: (a) a boyar, (b) a serf, (c) a visitor from Western Europe, (d) Catherine the Great? (★ See *Skills for Success,* page 280.)
6. **Recognizing Causes and Effects** Review the discussion of the kingdom of Poland in Chapter 10. (a) What were the immediate causes of the partition of Poland? (b) What do you think were the long-term causes? (★ See *Skills for Success,* page 18.)

## *For Your Portfolio*

Imagine that you are a European diplomat some time between 1550 and 1800. Several well-known European rulers are attending a large conference. You have been asked to give a brief speech introducing one of them to the assembled crowd.

1. Start by listing important European rulers and the lands they ruled. Choose the ruler you will introduce. (Remember, not all of the rulers studied in this chapter lived at the same time.)
2. Use the chapter text and additional resources to learn as much as you can about the ruler you have chosen. Research facts about this person's character, experience, ambitions, philosophy of government, and nation. Find at least one high-interest anecdote that you can include in your introduction.
3. Write your speech. Include the ruler's key accomplishments and explain why he or she is influential. You might also predict what this person's role in history will be.
4. Give your introduction to the class. Afterward, discuss why you think this ruler was or was not a positive force in the development of his or her nation.

# Unit-in-Brief

## Early Modern Times

**Chapter 14** The Renaissance
and Reformation
(1300–1600)

Between the 1300s and 1500s, Europe experienced a period of cultural rebirth known as the Renaissance. During the same period, the Protestant Reformation and the Scientific Revolution reshaped European civilization.

- Beginning in Italy and later spreading to northern Europe, the Renaissance reached its most glorious expression in painting, sculpture, and architecture.
- The intellectual movement known as humanism stressed the study of classical Greek and Roman cultures and the development of the individual.
- Reformers like Martin Luther and John Calvin challenged Church corruption and eventually broke away from the Church entirely.
- In response to the Protestant Reformation, the Catholic Church undertook its own vigorous reform movement.
- Religious fervor led to widespread intolerance and persecution by both Protestants and Catholics.
- During the Scientific Revolution, startling discoveries by individuals such as Copernicus, Newton, and Galileo changed the way Europeans viewed the physical world.

**Chapter 15** The First Global Age:
Europe and Asia
(1415–1796)

Beginning in the 1500s, European powers gradually built trading empires in Asia. Thus began a period of increasing global interdependence that has continued to the present day.

- Improvements in technology helped European explorers navigate the vast oceans of the world.
- In his search for a sea route to Asia, Christopher Columbus came upon the Americas, two continents previously unknown to Europeans.
- While strongly influenced by China and India, the nations of Southeast Asia retained their own unique cultural identities.
- The desire for spices led Europeans to seek control of the Indian Ocean trade network.
- By the late 1500s, the Dutch replaced the Portuguese as the major European power in Asia. In the 1700s, England and France vied for dominance.

- During the 1500s and 1600s, China and Korea restricted contact with the outside world.
- While the Japanese initially welcomed western traders, they later adopted a similar policy of isolation.

## Chapter 16   The First Global Age: Europe, the Americas, and Africa
### (1492–1750)

During the age of exploration, European powers built colonial empires in the Americas. New patterns of conquest and global exchange had an enormous impact on the civilizations of Africa as well.

- Spanish conquistadors vanquished the Aztec and Incan civilizations and set up a vast empire in the Americas.
- By the 1600s, Spain, France, England, and the Netherlands were competing for trade and colonies.
- The arrival of European settlers in North America brought disaster to Native Americans.
- Beginning in the 1400s, Europeans began establishing trading outposts in Africa.
- Millions of slaves were imported from Africa to meet labor needs in American colonies. The slave trade led to the fall of some African states and the rise of others.
- The Columbian Exchange was a vast global interchange of people, animals, culture, ideas, and technology.

- Beginning in the 1500s, Europe experienced a commercial revolution that brought about dramatic economic changes, including the rise of capitalism.

## Chapter 17   The Age of Absolutism
### (1550–1800)

During the 1500s and 1600s, European monarchs struggled to centralize their power. As they vied for the lead in overseas empire, the center of world civilization shifted to Europe.

- During the 1500s, wealth from the Americas helped make Spain the most powerful nation in Europe.
- Following a period of religious and social turmoil, Louis XIV achieved royal absolutism and helped France become the most powerful nation in Europe in the 1600s.
- Despite efforts at absolutism by several English monarchs, Parliament successfully asserted itself against royal power.
- The Thirty Years' War involved most of Europe. After the Peace of Westphalia, Prussia emerged as a new Protestant power.
- The Hapsburgs expanded Austrian territory but were unable to develop a strong centralized system.
- Peter the Great of Russia centralized royal power, embarked on a program of modernization, and sought to expand Russian territory from Europe to the Pacific.

# A Global View

## How Did Changes in Western Europe Help Bring About the First Global Age?

Between the 1300s and the 1600s, Europe moved out of the medieval period of relative isolation. European nations extended their economic links—and, sometimes, their military might—around the world. For these and other reasons, many historians consider this period to be the birth of the modern age.

### Rebirth and Reform

The Renaissance was truly a "rebirth" of western culture. Great artists like Michelangelo and writers like Shakespeare created modern styles in the arts. During the Reformation, religious reformers like Luther and Calvin founded the modern Protestant churches. Con-flicts between Catholic and Protestant nations would shape European politics for centuries.

Finally, the Scientific Revolution began the exploration of the physical universe by the methods of modern science. Scientists from Copernicus to Newton formulated numerous scientific laws for the first time.

### Western Empires

While these changes in western culture were going on, Europeans also embarked upon an unprecedented surge of empire building. Equipped with new ships, navigational aids, and gunpowder weapons, European soldiers, traders, and missionaries spread western power around the world.

The first target of European empire builders was Asia, Europe's longtime trading partner. During the 1500s and 1600s, Europeans established scattered trading posts and colonies in India, Southeast Asia, and beyond. They brought back profitable cargoes of spices, silks, and other valuable Asian goods.

At the same time, Europeans also established a presence in Africa and the Americas. Spanish conquistadors, followed by settlers from Portugal, the Netherlands, France, and England, conquered much of the so-called New World—South America, the Caribbean islands, and North America.

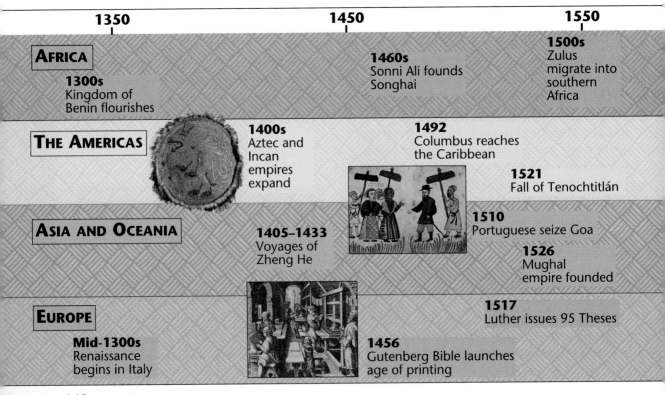

**1350**    **1450**    **1550**

**AFRICA**

**1300s**
Kingdom of Benin flourishes

**1460s**
Sonni Ali founds Songhai

**1500s**
Zulus migrate into southern Africa

**THE AMERICAS**

**1400s**
Aztec and Incan empires expand

**1492**
Columbus reaches the Caribbean

**1521**
Fall of Tenochtitlán

**ASIA AND OCEANIA**

**1405–1433**
Voyages of Zheng He

**1510**
Portuguese seize Goa

**1526**
Mughal empire founded

**EUROPE**

**Mid-1300s**
Renaissance begins in Italy

**1456**
Gutenberg Bible launches age of printing

**1517**
Luther issues 95 Theses

These colonists shipped home gold, silver, sugar, tobacco, and other commodities.

Western people first settled on the coasts of Africa to establish way stations on the new sea route to Asia. To get laborers for their American plantations and mines, however, Europeans soon developed a brutal but lucrative trade in African slaves. The slave trade added very substantially to the working population of the Americas but cost Africa millions of human beings.

## Powerful Kings and Queens

While these empires were growing overseas, the modern system of great powers was evolving in Europe itself. France became Europe's superpower in the 1600s. Louis XIV, the "Sun King," served as a model of absolute royal power. England in the 1600s, by contrast, provided an early example of more democratic rule as Parliament limited the power of monarchs.

Farther east, three states—Austria, Prussia, and Russia—emerged as great modern powers in the 1700s. The Russia of Peter the Great and the Prussia of Frederick the Great particularly emphasized strong bureaucracies and armies as instruments of royal power.

## Looking Ahead

All these trends and developments had great significance for the future. Reformed religion and Renaissance art would continue to shape the cultural experience of Europeans for centuries. The Scientific Revolution, combined with the later rise of industry, would give human beings unprecedented understanding of the world they lived in.

The European great power system would build the empires and fight the wars of later centuries. Modern democratic and bureaucratic governments would grow from these early modern nation states. And the global connections first forged by European empire builders would evolve into the modern world, where people are linked by trade, travel, and international organizations.

**ACTIVITY** Choose two events and two pictures from the time line below. For each, write a sentence explaining how it relates to the themes expressed in the Global View essay.

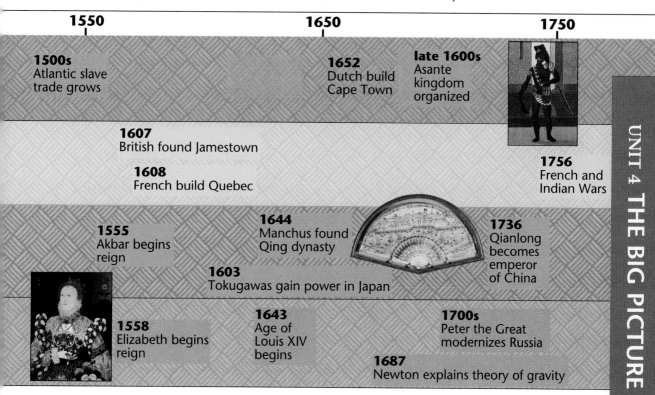

**1550**

**1650**

**1750**

**1500s**
Atlantic slave trade grows

**1652**
Dutch build Cape Town

**late 1600s**
Asante kingdom organized

**1607**
British found Jamestown

**1756**
French and Indian Wars

**1608**
French build Quebec

**1555**
Akbar begins reign

**1644**
Manchus found Qing dynasty

**1736**
Qianlong becomes emperor of China

**1603**
Tokugawas gain power in Japan

**1558**
Elizabeth begins reign

**1643**
Age of Louis XIV begins

**1700s**
Peter the Great modernizes Russia

**1687**
Newton explains theory of gravity

# *You Decide*

## Exploring Global Issues

### *What Is the Goal of Education?*

Like other Puritans, writer John Milton valued education. He supported a curriculum that included Greek and Latin, politics and music—even "all the locks and grips of wrestling." But he also believed that the final purpose of education was to gain knowledge of God and "out of that knowledge to love Him, to imitate Him, to be like Him."

Today, the idea of education for all is widely accepted, but educators still debate the final purpose. To begin your investigation, examine these viewpoints.

**GREECE**

**450 B.C.**

This vase painting, *Instruction in Music and Grammar at an Attic School,* illustrates the classical ideal that education should teach all arts for the development of well-rounded citizens. ▶

**FRANCE**

**1762**

Jean-Jacques Rousseau, an influential philosopher, summed up his ideas about education in his book *Emile:*

❝All men being equal, their common vocation is the profession of humanity. . . . It matters little to me, whether my pupil be designed for the army, the bar, or the pulpit. . . . To live is the profession I would teach him.❞

**CUBA**

**1883**

José Martí, a poet and political leader, turned away from classical ideas about what should be taught:

❝The schools teach classes in ancient geography, rules of rhetoric, and similar things of long ago, but in their place there should be courses in health; advice on hygiene; practical counseling; clear and simple studies of the human body, its parts, functions, ways of adjusting one to the other, economizing one's strength, and directing it well so that there will be no reason to restore it later.❞

**BRITAIN**

**1944**

Sir William Beveridge, a leading economist, argued that education was vital to a democracy:

❝Ignorance is an evil weed, which dictators may cultivate among their dupes, but which no democracy can afford amongst its citizens.❞

Virginia Gildersleeve, dean of Barnard College, summed up her ideas about a well-rounded education:

66The ability to think straight, some knowledge of the past, some vision of the future, some skill to do useful service, some urge to fit that service into the well-being of the community—those are the most vital things education must try to produce.99

NIGERIA
1960s

After gaining independence, many African nations set up educational systems that stressed the skills needed to modernize, such as engineering or agriculture. Here, a botany student learns about plant chemistry. ▶

JAPAN
1980s

Jiro Nagai, a professor of education, listed the goals of modern Japanese schooling:

66Citizenship education should produce citizens who (1) realize that the dignity of the individual and respect for human rights form the basis of a democratic social life; (2) have a deep love and awareness of their own nation and culture . . . ; (3) have a spirit of international understanding and cooperation. Schools in Japan are expected to develop such qualities in the nation's younger generation.99

## COMPARING VIEWPOINTS

1. Which of these viewpoints focus mainly on the needs of the individual student? Which focus on the needs of the community?
2. Which of the two pictures better illustrates Martí's point of view? Which of the pictures represents an opposing idea? Explain.
3. Which of these viewpoints seems closest to the educational goals of your own school?

## YOUR INVESTIGATION

**ACTIVITY**

1. Find out more about other viewpoints related to this topic. You might investigate one or more of the following:
- The educational and civil service system in Confucian China.
- The goals of the traditional age-grade system shared by many African cultures.
- The work of an educational reformer, such as Friedrich Froebel of Germany, George Dewey of the United States, or Maria Montessori of Italy.
- The educational system of a totalitarian state, such as Nazi Germany or the Soviet Union under Stalin.
- Current debates in the United States over "tech-prep" education or the teaching of values in schools.

2. Decide which viewpoint you agree with most closely and express it in your own way. You may do so in an essay, a cartoon, a poem, a drawing or painting, a song, a skit, a video, or some other way.

UNIT 4 THE BIG PICTURE

# ENLIGHTENMENT AND REVOLUTION

## Global Interaction

2 From 1756 to 1763, Britain and France fought for empire in Europe, North America, and Asia. As a result of the Seven Years' War, Britain won control of Canada.

NORTH AMERICA

2

1

ATLANTIC OCEAN

PACIFIC OCEAN

SOUTH AMERICA

## Political and Social Systems

1 Colonial Latin America developed a rigid social hierarchy. This painting shows members of different Mexican social classes during the later colonial period.

N
W   E
S

## Continuity and Change

3 The Atlantic slave trade led to the decline of some West African kingdoms and the rise of others. This helmet is from the Asante kingdom, which flourished in the 1700s.

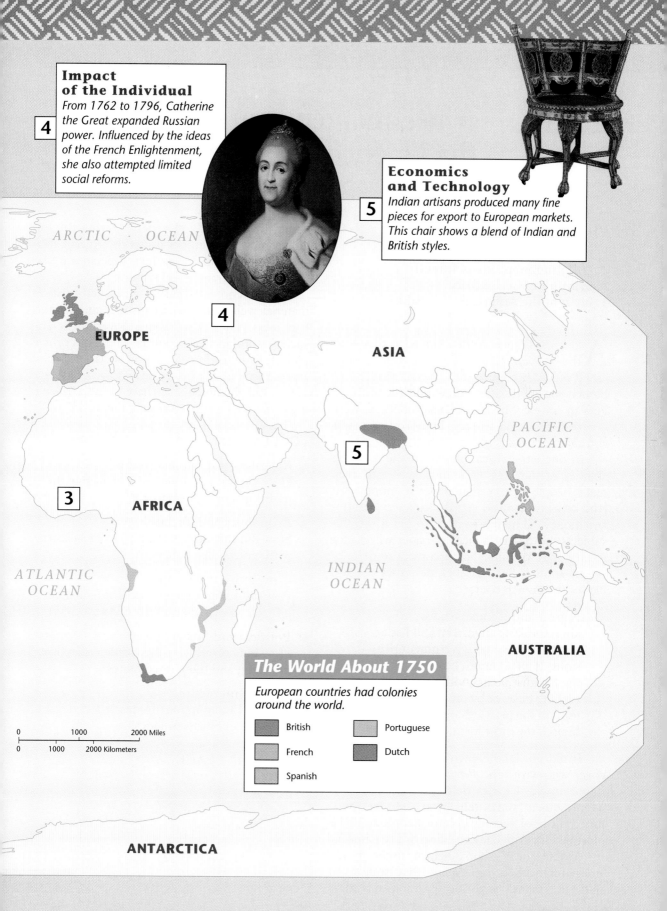

## Impact of the Individual

**4**

From 1762 to 1796, Catherine the Great expanded Russian power. Influenced by the ideas of the French Enlightenment, she also attempted limited social reforms.

## Economics and Technology

**5**

Indian artisans produced many fine pieces for export to European markets. This chair shows a blend of Indian and British styles.

ARCTIC OCEAN

EUROPE

**4**

ASIA

PACIFIC OCEAN

**3**

AFRICA

**5**

ATLANTIC OCEAN

INDIAN OCEAN

AUSTRALIA

### The World About 1750

European countries had colonies around the world.

- British
- French
- Spanish
- Portuguese
- Dutch

0   1000   2000 Miles
0   1000   2000 Kilometers

ANTARCTICA

# The Enlightenment and the American Revolution

## (1715–1800)

## CHAPTER OUTLINE

1 **Philosophy in the Age of Reason**
2 **Enlightenment Ideas Spread**
3 **Britain at Mid-Century**
4 **Birth of the American Republic**

All across France, readers smiled as they read the *Persian Letters*. This collection, published in 1721, commented on many aspects of French society. Readers knew that the authors, Persian travelers named Usbek and Rica, were not real. Still, the writers' humorous remarks and sharp criticisms of France hit home.

In one letter, Rica reports on the amazing abilities of the king of France, who can even make people believe that paper is money: "If [the king] is involved in a difficult war without any money, all he has to do is to get it into his subjects' heads that a piece of paper will do for money, they are immediately convinced of it."

In another letter, Usbek describes the nobles of the French court:

66A great lord is a man who sees the king, speaks to ministers, and has ancestors, debts, and government pensions. If, in addition, he can conceal the fact that he has nothing to do by looking busy, or by pretending to be fond of the pleasures of life, he thinks himself the most fortunate of men.99

It did not take French readers long to discover who wrote the *Persian Letters*. He was a minor noble, Charles de Secondat, Baron de Montesquieu (MAHN tehs kyoo). He had published the book secretly because people could be punished for criticizing the king or the Church.

Montesquieu's book helped usher in the Enlightenment, a movement that sought to shine the "light" of reason on traditional ideas about government and society. During the Enlightenment, sometimes called the Age of Reason, thinkers fought against superstition, ignorance, intolerance, and tyranny.

Enlightenment thinkers promoted goals of material well-being, social justice, and worldly happiness. Their ideas about government and society stood in sharp contrast to the old principles of divine-right rule, a rigid social hierarchy, and the promise of a better life in heaven. Since the 1700s, Enlightenment ideas have spread, challenging established traditions around the world.

**FOCUS ON** these questions as you read:

- **Religions and Value Systems**
  How did the Enlightenment challenge the traditional order in Europe?

- **Economics and Technology**
  How did the ideas of the physiocrats clash with mercantilist policy?

- **Continuity and Change**
  Why did Enlightenment ideas at first affect only the upper levels of European society?

- **Political and Social Systems**
  How did constitutional government evolve in Britain and the United States?

- **Global Interaction**
  How did Enlightenment ideas affect developments in North America?

## TIME AND PLACE

*A New View of the World* The first balloon flights in the late 1700s caused a sensation. By conquering gravity, balloons not only gave people a new perspective on the world but also inspired a new faith in the power of human reason. In this way, they are a perfect symbol for the European Age of Enlightenment, during which they were invented. **Economics and Technology** How would balloon flights provide a new perspective on the world?

## HUMANITIES LINK
*Art History* Jean-Antoine Houdon, *Voltaire* (page 457).
*Literature* In this chapter, you will encounter passages from the following works of literature: Baron de Montesquieu, *Persian Letters* (page 454); Alexander Pope, "Essay on Man" (page 456); Fanny Burney, *Evelina* (pages 474–475).

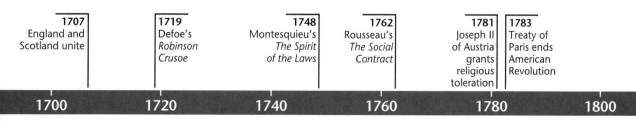

| 1707 England and Scotland unite | 1719 Defoe's *Robinson Crusoe* | 1748 Montesquieu's *The Spirit of the Laws* | 1762 Rousseau's *The Social Contract* | 1781 Joseph II of Austria grants religious toleration | 1783 Treaty of Paris ends American Revolution |
|---|---|---|---|---|---|

| 1700 | 1720 | 1740 | 1760 | 1780 | 1800 |

# 1 Philosophy in the Age of Reason

## Guide for Reading

- How was the Enlightenment linked to the Scientific Revolution?

- What ideas about government emerged during the Enlightenment?

- What economic ideas did Enlightenment thinkers support?

- **Vocabulary** *natural laws, social contract, natural rights, philosophe, physiocrat, laissez faire, free market*

66Go, wondrous creature! mount where
    Science guides;
  Go, measure earth, weigh air, and state
    the tides;
  Instruct the planets in what orbs to run,
  Correct old Time, and regulate the
    sun.99

Those lines by the English poet Alexander Pope celebrated the successes of humans—the "wondrous creature"—in the Scientific Revolution. By the early 1700s, European thinkers felt that nothing was beyond the reach of the human mind. Using the methods of modern science, reformers set out to study human behavior and solve the problems of society.

## A World of Progress and Reason

The Enlightenment grew out of the Scientific Revolution of the 1500s and 1600s, with its amazing discoveries by thinkers like Copernicus and Newton. (See pages 364–367.) In the 1700s, other scientists expanded European knowledge. Joseph Priestley and Antoine Lavoisier (ahn TWAHN lah vwah ZYAY), for example, built the framework for modern chemistry. Edward Jenner developed a vaccine against smallpox, a disease whose path of death spanned the centuries.

Scientific successes created great confidence in the power of reason. If people used reason to find laws that governed the physical world, why not use reason to discover natural laws—laws that govern human nature? By applying scientific knowledge, inventors changed peoples' lives. Why not apply natural laws to change human society? Through the use of reason, insisted Enlightenment thinkers, they could solve every social, political, and economic problem. Heaven could be achieved here on Earth.

## Two Views of the Social Contract

In the 1600s, two English thinkers, Thomas Hobbes and John Locke, set forth ideas that were to become key to the Enlightenment. Both men lived through the upheavals that shook England early in the century. (See Chapter 17.) Yet they came to very different conclusions about human nature and the purpose and nature of government.

**"Nasty, brutish, and short."** Thomas Hobbes set out his ideas in a work titled *Leviathan.* Hobbes argued that people were naturally cruel, greedy, and selfish. If not strictly controlled, they would fight, rob, and oppress one another. Life in the "state of nature"—without laws or other control—would be "solitary, poor, nasty, brutish, and short."

To escape that "brutish" life, said Hobbes, people entered into a social contract, an agreement by which they gave up the state of nature for an organized society. Hobbes believed that only a powerful government could ensure an orderly society. Such a government was an absolute monarchy, which could impose order and compel obedience. Not surprisingly, Hobbes had supported the Stuart kings in their struggle against Parliament.

**Natural rights.** John Locke had a more optimistic view of human nature. People were basically reasonable and moral, he said. Further,

**GLOBAL CONNECTIONS**

Growing knowledge of other cultures enriched western thought. Enlightenment thinkers were drawn to the sages of China and the gurus, or religious thinkers of India, as well as to Greek and Roman philosophers. Some saw Native American sachems, or wisemen, as great sources of wisdom, closer to nature and natural truths than western thinkers.

they had natural rights, or rights that belonged to all humans from birth. These included the right to life, liberty, and property.

In *Two Treatises of Government,* Locke argued that people formed governments to protect their natural rights. The best kind of government, he said, had limited power and was accepted by all citizens. Thus, unlike Hobbes, Locke rejected absolute monarchy and sided with Parliament in its struggle against the Stuarts.

Locke then set out a radical idea. A government, he said, has an obligation to those it governs. If a government fails its obligations or violates people's natural rights, the people have the right to overthrow the government. This right to revolution would echo through Europe, in Britain's North American colonies, and around the world in the centuries that followed.

## *Montesquieu's* Spirit of the Laws

In the 1700s, France saw a flowering of Enlightenment thought. An early and influential thinker was the Baron de Montesquieu. Montesquieu studied the governments of Europe, from Italy to England. He read all he could about ancient and medieval Europe and learned about Chinese and Native American cultures. His sharp criticism of absolute monarchy opened the doors for later debate.

In 1748, Montesquieu published *The Spirit of the Laws.* In it, he discussed governments throughout history and wrote admiringly about Britain's limited monarchy. Montesquieu felt that the British had protected themselves against tyranny by dividing the functions and powers of government among three separate branches: the legislature, executive, and judiciary. (In fact, Montesquieu had misunderstood the British system, which did not separate powers in this way.) To him, the separation of powers was the best way to protect liberty.

Montesquieu also felt that each branch of government could serve as a check on the other two, an idea that we call checks and balances. Some 40 years after Montesquieu's book appeared in France, the ideas of separation of powers and checks and balances in government were written into the Constitution of the United States. (See page 473.)

***Voltaire*** *Jean-Antoine Houdon, who lived from 1741 to 1828, was the greatest sculptor of his time. His work combined classical dignity with precise realism. In this statue, even though Voltaire is shown in the robes of ancient Rome, his face is starkly realistic. Houdon makes no effort to hide the ravages of old age on the features of the philosopher, who was 84 years old at the time the sculpture was begun.* **Art and Literature** *Look at the pictures on page 103. How do you think a classical Greek sculpture of Voltaire might differ from this one by Houdon? Explain.*

## *The World of the Philosophes*

In France, a group of Enlightenment thinkers applied the methods of science to better understand and improve society. These thinkers were called philosophes, which means "lovers of wisdom."

**Voltaire defends freedom of thought.** Probably the most famous philosophe was François-Marie Arouet, who took the name Voltaire. "My trade," said Voltaire, "is to say what I think," and he did so throughout his long, controversial life. Voltaire used biting wit as a weapon to expose the abuses of his day. He targeted corrupt officials and idle aristocrats. Barbs flew from his pen against inequality, injustice, and superstition. He detested the slave trade and deplored religious prejudice.

Voltaire's outspoken attacks offended the government and the Catholic Church. He was imprisoned and forced into exile. He saw his books censored and burned, but he continued to defend freedom of speech. "I do not agree with a word that you say," he supposedly declared, "but I will defend to the death your right to say it." (■ See *You Decide*, "What Limits Should There Be on Freedom of Speech?" pages 550–551.)

**The Encyclopedia.** Another philosophe, Denis Diderot (dee DROH), labored some 25 years to produce a 28-volume *Encyclopedia*. As the editor of this huge work, Diderot did more than just gather articles on human knowledge. His purpose was "to change the general way of thinking" by explaining the new thinking on government, philosophy, and religion. Diderot's *Encyclopedia* included articles by leading thinkers of the day, including Montesquieu and Voltaire.

▲ *Diderot's* Encyclopedia

In their *Encyclopedia* articles, the philosophes denounced slavery, praised freedom of expression, and urged education for all. They attacked divine-right theory and traditional religions. Critics raised an outcry. The French government argued that the *Encyclopedia* was an attack on public morals, while the pope threatened to excommunicate Catholics who bought or read the volumes.

Despite efforts to ban the *Encyclopedia*, as many as 20,000 copies were printed between 1751 and 1789. This work did much to shape French public opinion in the mid-1700s. When translated into other languages, it helped spread Enlightenment ideas across Europe and into the Americas.

## Rousseau: A Controversial Figure

The most controversial philosophe was Jean-Jacques Rousseau (ZHAHN ZHAHK roo SOH). Rousseau was a strange, difficult man. Coming from a poor family, he never felt comfortable in the glittering social world of Enlightenment thinkers.

Rousseau believed that people in their natural state were basically good. This natural innocence, he felt, was corrupted by the evils of society, especially the unequal distribution of property. This view was later adopted by many reformers and revolutionaries.

In 1762, Rousseau set forth his ideas about government and society in *The Social Contract*. It begins: "Man is born free, and everywhere he is in chains." The chains, says Rousseau, are those of society, which controls the way people behave. He argues, however, that some social controls—control by a freely formed government, for example—are good, not evil. In consenting to form a government, he says, individuals choose to give up their self-interest in favor of the common good. Although people surrender their rights, they retain their freedom because the government is based on the consent of the governed.

Rousseau put his faith in the "general will"—the will of the majority. The majority should always work for the common good, he said. Even those who resist should be compelled to accept the general will—they must "be forced to be free." Thus, unlike many Enlightenment thinkers who put the individual first, Rousseau felt that the individual should be subordinate to the community.

Rousseau has influenced political and social thinkers for more than 200 years. Woven through his work is a hatred of political and economic oppression. His ideas would help fan the flames of revolt in centuries to come.

## Limited "Natural Rights" for Women

The Enlightenment slogan "free and equal" did not apply to women. Women did have "natural rights," said the philosophes. But unlike the natural rights of men, these rights were limited to the areas of home and family.

# European Political Thinkers

| Thinker | Major Ideas | Quotation | Connections Today |
|---|---|---|---|
| **Thomas Hobbes** *Leviathan* (1651)  | People are driven by selfishness and greed. To avoid chaos, they give up their freedom to a government that will ensure order. Such a government must be strong and able to suppress rebellion. | "The condition of man [in the state of nature] . . . is a condition of war of everyone against everyone." | Hobbes's ideas have been used to justify absolute power. To some people today, Hobbes presents a bleak but true view of how people and governments behave. |
| **John Locke** *Two Treatises of Government* (1690) 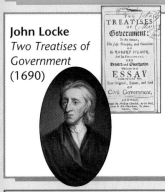 | People have a natural right to life, liberty, and property. Rulers have a responsibility to protect those rights. People have the right to change a government that fails to do so. | "Men being . . . by nature all free, equal, and independent, no one can be put out of this estate and subjected to the political power of another without his own consent." | Locke's ideas influenced authors of U.S. Declaration of Independence and French revolutionaries in the 1790s. Later, people extended his ideas to include equality for women and others. |
| **Baron de Montesquieu** *The Spirit of the Laws* (1748) | The powers of government should be separated into executive, legislative, and judicial branches, to prevent any one group from gaining too much power. | "In order to have . . . liberty, it is necessary that government be set up so that one man need not be afraid of another." | His ideas about separation of powers greatly influenced framers of U.S. Constitution. |
| **Jean-Jacques Rousseau** *The Social Contract* (1762)  | People are basically good but become corrupted by society. In an ideal society, people would make the laws and would obey them willingly. | "Only the general will can direct the energies of the state in a manner appropriate to the end for which it was founded, i.e., the common good." | Rousseau has been hailed as a champion of democracy for his idea that political authority lies with the people. But dictators have used his ideas about the "common good" to justify their programs. |

*Interpreting a Chart* Political and social philosophers thrived in Enlightenment Europe. Their ideas had a major impact throughout the world of their time and continue to influence developments today. ■ Why did Montesquieu recommend separation of powers of government? How might Rousseau's ideas be used to justify dictatorship?

By the mid-1700s, a small but growing number of women protested this view. They questioned the notion that women were by nature inferior to men and that men's domination of women was therefore part of "nature's plan." Germaine de Staël in France and Catharine Macaulay and Mary Wollstonecraft in England argued that women had been excluded from the social contract itself. Their arguments were ridiculed and often sharply condemned.

Wollstonecraft was the best known of the British female critics. She accepted that a woman's first duty was to be a good mother. At the same time, however, she felt that a woman should be able to decide what is in her own interest and should not be completely dependent on her husband. In 1792, Wollstonecraft published *A Vindication of the Rights of Woman*. In it, she called for the same education for girls and boys. Only education, she argued, could give women the tools they needed to participate equally with men in public life.

## New Economic Thinking

Other thinkers, the physiocrats, focused on economic reforms. Like the philosophes, physiocrats looked for natural laws to define a rational economic system.

**Laissez faire.** Physiocrats rejected mercantilism, which required government regulation to achieve a favorable balance of trade. Instead, they urged a policy of laissez faire (LEHS ay FAIR), allowing business to operate with little or no government interference. Unlike mercantilists, who called for acquiring gold and silver wealth through trade, the physiocrats claimed that real wealth came from making the land more productive. Extractive industries, they said, such as agriculture, mining, and logging, produced new wealth. While mercantilists had imposed tariffs, or taxes on foreign goods, to protect local manufacturing, physiocrats supported free trade and wanted to lift all tariffs.

**ISSUES** *For* **TODAY** Laissez-faire economists argue that society would be better off if the government allowed business and the marketplace to operate without interference. What is the proper role of government in a nation's economy?

**Adam Smith.** British economist Adam Smith greatly admired the physiocrats. In his influential work, *The Wealth of Nations*, he argued that the free market, the natural forces of supply and demand, should be allowed to operate and regulate business. He tried to show how manufacturing, trade, wages, profits, and economic growth were all linked to the forces of supply and demand. Wherever there is a demand for goods or services, he said, suppliers will seek to meet it. They do so because of the economic rewards they can get from fulfilling the demand. A strong supporter of laissez faire, Smith believed that the marketplace was better off without any government regulation. At the same time, however, he did believe that government had a duty to protect society, administer justice, and provide public works.

Adam Smith's ideas would gain increasing influence as the Industrial Revolution spread across Europe and beyond. His emphasis on the free market and the law of supply and demand would help to shape immensely productive economies in the 1800s and 1900s.

## SECTION 1 REVIEW

1. **Identify** (a) Thomas Hobbes, (b) John Locke, (c) Baron de Montesquieu, (d) Voltaire, (e) Denis Diderot, (f) Jean-Jacques Rousseau, (g) Mary Wollstonecraft, (h) *The Wealth of Nations.*
2. **Define** (a) natural laws, (b) social contract, (c) natural rights, (d) philosophe, (e) physiocrat, (f) laissez faire, (g) free market.
3. How did the successes of the Scientific Revolution influence Enlightenment thinkers?
4. Describe the government favored by each of the following: (a) Hobbes, (b) Locke.
5. How were the physiocrats different from the mercantilists?
6. *Critical Thinking* **Defending a Position** Rousseau put the "general will"—the common good—over the interest of the individual. Do you agree with that position? Why or why not?
7. *ACTIVITY* Create a cartoon to illustrate the ideas of one or more of the philosophes you read about in this section.

# 2 Enlightenment Ideas Spread

## Guide for Reading

- How did Enlightenment ideas pose a challenge to the established order?

- Why did some European rulers embrace Enlightenment ideas?

- What ideas influenced artists and writers of the Enlightenment?

- How did most people live during the Age of Reason?

- **Vocabulary** *salon, enlightened despot, baroque*

From France, Enlightenment ideas flowed across Europe, and beyond. Everywhere, thinkers examined traditional beliefs and customs in the light of reason and found them flawed. Even absolute monarchs experimented with Enlightenment ideas, although they drew back when it became clear that the changes called for by the philosophes might threaten the old order—that is, the established way of doing things.

## The Challenge of New Ideas

The ideas of the Enlightenment spread quickly through many levels of society. Educated people all over Europe eagerly read not only Diderot's *Encyclopedia* but also the small, cheap pamphlets that printers churned out on a broad range of issues. At the same time, middle-class men met to discuss the new ideas in the coffeehouses that were sprouting up in Europe's major cities.

**Achieving a just society.** As Enlightenment ideas spread, people began to challenge the old ways. More and more, they saw the need for reform to achieve a just society.

During the Middle Ages, most Europeans had accepted without question a society based on divine-right rule, a strict class system, and a belief in heavenly reward for earthly suffering. In the Age of Reason, such ideas seemed unscientific and irrational. A just society, Enlightenment thinkers taught, should ensure material well-being, social justice, and happiness in this world.

**Censorship.** Government and Church authorities felt they had a sacred duty to defend the old order. They believed the old order had been set up by God. To protect against the attacks of the Enlightenment, they waged a war of censorship, banning and burning books and imprisoning writers. Some writers avoided the censors by having their books printed in the few countries, like the Netherlands, that allowed

**Spreading Enlightenment Ideas** *Printing presses helped carry the ideas of the philosophes to a growing literate middle class. Booksellers offered not only Diderot's massive* Encyclopedia *but also cheaper books and pamphlets on a range of issues. Here, customers examine the wares in a local bookshop.* **Continuity and Change** *How are ideas spread today?*

**Salon de Madame Geoffrin** The salon of Madame Geoffrin attracted the leading artists, writers, and thinkers of the day. Through gatherings like these, women helped to shape the tastes and manners of the Enlightenment. **Political and Social Systems** Based on the painting, did more women or men attend Madame Geoffrin's salon? Why do you think this was so?

freedom of the press. Others published their books under a false name.

Writers like Montesquieu, Voltaire, and Rousseau sometimes disguised their ideas in works of fiction. You have already seen how Montesquieu mocked French society in the *Persian Letters*. The hero of Voltaire's humorous novel *Candide* travels across Europe and even to the Americas and the Middle East in search of "the best of all possible worlds." Voltaire slyly uses the tale to expose the corruption and hypocrisy of European society. Novels like *Candide* did not suggest specific reforms but did show readers the need for change.

### Salons

The new literature, the arts, science, and philosophy were regular topics of discussion in salons, informal social gatherings at which writers, artists, philosophers, and others exchanged ideas. The salon originated in the 1600s, when a group of noblewomen in Paris began inviting a few friends to their homes for poetry readings. Only the most witty, intelligent, and well-read people were invited to the salons.

By the 1700s, some middle-class women began holding salons. In the drawing rooms of these *salonières* (sah lohn YAIR), middle-class citizens could meet with the nobility on an equal footing to discuss and spread Enlightenment ideas.

### The Salon in the Rue Saint Honoré

In 1713, 14-year-old Marie-Thérèse Rodet was wed to François Geoffrin (zhehf RAN), 48. Everyone said it was a good match. Monsieur Geoffrin was a rich and well-respected manufacturer who would provide a comfortable life for his young wife.

The Geoffrins settled into a house on the Rue Saint Honoré (SAHN ahn oh RAY) in Paris. In the years that followed, Madame Geoffrin gave birth to two children and dutifully cared for her home and family. The pattern of her life seemed set forever—quiet and uneventful, without much intellectual excitement.

**A new world.** Then one day, a neighbor invited Madame Geoffrin to attend her salon. For the first time, the young woman heard the polished conversation of learned men and women. It opened the door to a new world.

Inspired, Madame Geoffrin eventually set up her own salon in the house on Rue Saint Honoré. She entertained poets and philosophers, artists and musicians. Her husband protested, but she would not give in. For years, he sat silent and ignored at the table while her guests dined and talked. One day, someone noticed that the old man was absent and inquired about him. "It was my husband," replied Madame Geoffrin. "He is dead."

**The *salonière*.** By 1750, Madame Geoffrin was a leading *salonière*. In her home, she brought together the brightest and most talented people of her day. On Mondays, Geoffrin welcomed artists and musicians. The young musical genius Wolfgang Amadeus Mozart played for her guests. On Wednesdays, philosophers and poets came for discussion and dispute. Diderot was a regular at the Wednesday dinners, and Madame Geoffrin donated large sums of money to support the *Encyclopedia*.

Even visiting monarchs paid their respects at what came to be called the "kingdom" of Rue Saint Honoré. Madame Geoffrin corresponded with Catherine II of Russia and Maria Theresa of Austria. Catherine was so eager to learn what was going on that she had spies report on the conversation at Geoffrin's salon.

**"Women ruled then."** *Salonières* like Madame Geoffrin were often not well educated themselves. They set up salons to learn from the conversations of educated men. The *salonières* were not intimidated by such men, however. While remaining gracious, they demanded high standards of discussion. Diderot commented:

66Women accustom us to discuss with charm and clearness the driest and thorniest subjects. . . . Hence we develop a particular method of explaining ourselves easily, and this method passes from conversation into style.99

By the end of the 1700s, the influence of women's salons had ended. Later, looking back, the celebrated court painter Elisabeth Vigée Lebrun observed: "Women ruled then." 

## Enlightened Despots

Discussions of Enlightenment theories also enlivened the courts of Europe. Philosophes tried to convince European rulers to adopt their ideas. If they could "enlighten" the ruling classes, they thought, they could bring about reform. Some monarchs did accept Enlightenment ideas. They became enlightened despots, or absolute rulers who used their power to bring about political and social change.

**Frederick the Great.** As king of Prussia from 1740 to 1786, Frederick II exerted extremely tight control over his subjects. Still, he saw himself as the "first servant of the state," with a duty to work for the common good.

Frederick admired Voltaire and lured him to Berlin to develop a Prussian academy of science. When the king was not busy fighting wars, he had swamps drained and forced peasants to grow new crops such as the potato. He also had seed and tools distributed to peasants who had suffered in Prussia's wars. He tolerated religious differences, welcoming victims of religious persecution. "In my kingdom," he said, "everyone can go to heaven in his own fashion."

Frederick's reforms were directed mainly at making the Prussian government more efficient. He reorganized the civil service and simplified laws. But a "rationalized" bureaucracy also meant a stronger monarchy—and more power for Frederick himself. (★ See *Skills for Success*, page 476.)

**Catherine the Great.** Catherine II of Russia read the works of the philosophes and exchanged letters with Voltaire and Diderot. She praised Voltaire as someone who had "fought the united enemies of humankind: superstition, fanaticism, ignorance, trickery."

Catherine, who became empress in 1762, experimented with Enlightenment ideas. Early in her reign, she made limited reforms in law and government. She granted nobles a charter of rights and spoke out against serfdom. Still, like Frederick in Prussia, Catherine intended to give up no power. When a serf revolt broke out, she ruthlessly suppressed it. She also allied herself with the Russian nobles who opposed change. In the end, Catherine's contribution to Russia was not reform but an expanded empire.

**Joseph II.** The most radical enlightened despot was the Hapsburg emperor Joseph II, son and successor of Maria Theresa. An eager student of the Enlightenment, Joseph traveled in disguise among his subjects to learn of their problems. His efforts to improve their lives won him the nickname the "peasant emperor."

Maria Theresa had begun to modernize Austria's government. Joseph continued her reforms. He chose talented middle-class officials rather than nobles to head departments and imposed a range of political and legal reforms. Despite opposition, he granted toleration to Protestants and Jews in his Catholic empire. He ended censorship and attempted to bring the

Catholic Church under royal control. He sold the property of many monasteries and convents, which he saw as unproductive, and used the proceeds to build hospitals. Joseph even abolished serfdom. Like many of his reforms, however, this measure was canceled after his death.

## The Arts and Literature

In the 1600s and 1700s, the arts evolved to meet changing tastes. As in earlier periods, artists and composers had to please their patrons, the men and women who commissioned works from them or gave them jobs.

**Courtly art.** In the age of Louis XIV, courtly art and architecture were either in classical style, in the Greek and Roman tradition, or in the grand, complex style known as baroque. (See the picture on page 429.) Baroque paintings were huge, colorful, and full of excitement. They glorified historic battles or the lives of saints. Such works matched the grandeur of European courts.

By the mid-1700s, architects and designers developed the rococo style. Unlike the heavy splendor of the baroque, rococo art was personal, refined, elegant, and charming. Furniture and tapestries featured delicate shells and flowers, as well as a European version of Chinese decorations. Portrait painters showed noble subjects in charming rural settings, surrounded by happy servants and pets.

**Middle-class audiences.** A new audience, the growing middle class, emerged with its own requirements. Successful merchants and town officials wanted their portraits painted, but without frills. They liked pictures of family life or realistic town or country scenes. Dutch painters such as Rembrandt van Rijn (REHM brant van RIN) conferred great dignity on merchants and other ordinary, middle-class subjects.

**Trends in music.** New kinds of musical entertainment evolved in the baroque era. Ballets and operas—plays set to music—were performed at royal courts. Before long, opera houses sprang up from Italy to England to amuse the paying public. The music of the period followed ordered, structured forms well suited to the Age of Reason.

Among the towering musical figures of the period was Johann Sebastian Bach. A devout German Lutheran, Bach wrote complex and beautiful religious works for organ and choirs. Another German-born composer, George Frederick Handel, spent much of his life in England. There, he wrote the *Water Music* and other pieces for King George I, as well as many operas. His most celebrated work, the *Messiah,* combines instruments and voices. Today, it is a standard at Christmas and Easter concerts.

In 1762, a six-year-old prodigy, Wolfgang Amadeus Mozart, burst onto the European scene to gain instant celebrity as a composer and performer. In his brief life, the young man from Salzburg composed an amazing variety of music with remarkable speed. His brilliant operas, graceful symphonies, and moving religious music helped define the new style of classical composition. At age 35, Mozart died in poverty, leaving a musical legacy that thrives today.

**The novel.** By the 1700s, literature developed new forms and a wide new audience. Middle-class readers, for example, liked stories about their own times told in plain prose. One result was an outpouring of novels, long works of prose fiction.

A number of English novelists created popular works. Daniel Defoe wrote *Robinson Crusoe,* an exciting tale about a sailor ship-

*Throwing a Kiss* These delicate porcelains in the rococo style that developed in the 1700s show an aristocratic couple flirting. The man wears a long Chinese-style robe, called a banyan, that was in fashion among the nobility at the time.
**Religions and Value Systems** What do the gestures of the two figures tell you about the manners of the aristocracy?

wrecked on a tropical island. Through hard work, his own wits, and the help of an islander whom he names Friday, Crusoe survives his ordeal. In *Pamela*, Samuel Richardson used a series of letters to tell a story about a servant girl. This technique was adopted by several other authors of the period. (📖 See *World Literature*, "Evelina," pages 474–475.)

### Lives of the Majority

Most Europeans were untouched by either courtly or middle-class culture. They remained what they had always been—peasants living in small rural villages. Their culture was based on centuries-old traditions that changed slowly.

**Conditions west and east.** Peasant life varied across Europe. Villages in Western Europe were relatively more prosperous than those in Eastern Europe. In the West, serfdom had largely disappeared. Instead, some peasants worked their own patches of land. Others were tenants of large landowners, paying a yearly rent for the land they farmed. Still others were day laborers who hired themselves out for the farm season.

In central and Eastern Europe, by contrast, serfdom was firmly rooted. In Russia, it spread and deepened in the 1700s. Peasants bound to the land owed labor services to their lords and could be bought and sold with the land. Russian landowners could also send serfs to labor in government mines or serve long terms as soldiers in the imperial armies.

**Old ways survive.** Despite advances, some echoes of serfdom survived in Western Europe. In France, peasants still had to provide free labor, repairing roads and bridges after the spring floods just as their ancestors had done. In England, country squires had the right to hunt foxes across the plowed and planted fields of their tenants.

By the late 1700s, radical ideas about equality and social justice seeped into peasant villages. While some peasants eagerly sought to topple the old order, others resisted efforts to bring about change. In the 1800s, war and political upheaval as well as changing economic conditions would transform peasant life in Europe.

## SECTION 2 REVIEW

1. **Identify** (a) *Candide*, (b) Joseph II, (c) Johann Sebastian Bach, (d) George Frederick Handel, (e) Wolfgang Amadeus Mozart, (f) Daniel Defoe.
2. **Define** (a) salon, (b) enlightened despot, (c) baroque.
3. (a) Describe three ways in which Enlightenment ideas spread. (b) Why did those ideas threaten the old order?
4. What were the goals of enlightened despots?
5. How did courtly tastes differ from middle-class tastes?
6. How did peasant life vary across Europe?
7. *Critical Thinking* **Analyzing Information** (a) What did Frederick II mean when he said, "In my kingdom, everyone can go to heaven in his own fashion"? (b) How did his actions reflect that idea?
8. *ACTIVITY* Imagine that you are living in Paris during the 1700s. Organize a salon to discuss a "just society." Be sure to include supporters of both the old order and Enlightenment ideas among your guests.

# Britain at Mid-Century

## Guide for Reading

- Why did Britain become a global power in the 1700s?

- What new political institutions emerged in Britain in the 1700s?

- What groups held political power in Britain?

- **Vocabulary** *constitutional government, prime minister*

> **66**Foreign trade is . . . the honor of the kingdom, the noble profession of the merchant, . . . the supply of our wants, the employment of our poor, the improvement of our lands, the nursery of our [sailors], the walls of the kingdom, the means of our treasure, the sinews of our wars, the terror of our enemies.**99**

With words like these, English advocates of mercantilism preached their cause in the mid-1600s. Over the next century, Britain embraced this doctrine and built a colonial and commercial empire that reached around the world. It replaced Spain as the most successful European empire builder and outstripped the Netherlands as the foremost European trading nation. At the same time, Britain developed a constitutional monarchy, a political system somewhere between the absolute monarchies of the European continent and later democratic governments.

## Global Expansion

Why did Britain, a small island kingdom on the edge of Europe, rise to global prominence in the 1700s? Here, we can look at only a few reasons for its success.

**Geography.** England's location made it well placed to control trade during the Renaissance. In the 1500s and 1600s, English merchants sent ships across the world's oceans and planted outposts in the West Indies, North America, and India. From these tiny settlements, England would eventually build a global empire.

**Success in war.** In the 1700s, Britain was generally on the winning side in European conflicts. Each victory brought valuable rewards. By the Treaty of Utrecht, France gave Britain Nova Scotia and Newfoundland in North America. (See page 429.) It also won a monopoly on the slave trade in Spanish America. The slave trade brought enormous wealth to British merchants, who invested their profits in other ventures. In 1763, the Treaty of Paris ending the Seven Years' War brought Britain all of French Canada. (See page 404.) The British East India Company pushed the French out of India.

Unlike its European rivals, Britain had no large standing army. Instead, it built up its fleet. By 1763, Britain had a more powerful navy than its greatest rival, France. With its superior naval power, it was well able to protect its growing empire and trade.

**A favorable business climate.** England offered a more favorable climate to business and commerce than its European rivals. Although

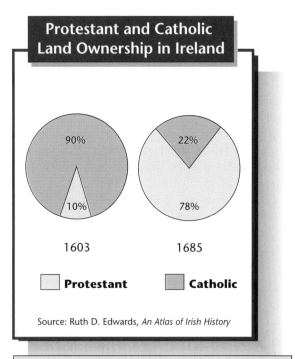

### Protestant and Catholic Land Ownership in Ireland

90% 10%
1603

22% 78%
1685

Protestant ☐     Catholic ☐

Source: Ruth D. Edwards, *An Atlas of Irish History*

---

*Interpreting a Chart* In the 1600s, England seized land from Irish Catholics and gave it to English and Scottish settlers, who were Protestants. By the end of the century, Protestants controlled most of Ireland.
■ What percentage of Ireland's land was owned by Catholics in 1603? In 1685?

**United Kingdom of Great Britain, 1707**

The Act of Union joined England and Scotland in the United Kingdom of Great Britain in 1707. The tiny kingdom of Wales had joined with England some 200 years earlier.

1. **Location** On the map, locate (a) Irish Sea, (b) Edinburgh, (c) London, (d) English Channel.
2. **Place** Which neighboring land was controlled by Britain but was not part of the United Kingdom in 1707?
3. **Critical Thinking** *Applying Information* How might it benefit England to join politically with its neighbors?

England followed mercantilist policies, it put fewer restrictions on trade than France did. Also, while British nobles, like most nobles in Europe, looked down on trade, some did engage in business activities.

**Union with Scotland.** At home, England grew by merging with neighboring Scotland. In 1707, the Act of Union united the two countries in the United Kingdom of Great Britain. The union brought economic advantages to both lands. It allowed trade to pass freely between England and Scotland, creating a larger market for farmers and manufacturers. Although many Scots resented the union, growing prosperity eventually made it more acceptable. The United Kingdom also included Wales.

**Ireland.** England had controlled Ireland since the 1100s. In the 1600s, English rulers tried to subdue Catholic Ireland by sending Protestants from England and Scotland to settle there. They gave Protestant settlers title to Irish Catholic lands.

The Irish fiercely resisted Protestant rule. When uprisings failed, repression increased. Catholics were forbidden to own weapons, marry non-Catholics, or serve as teachers.

## Growth of Constitutional Government

In the century after the Glorious Revolution (see page 435), three new political institutions arose in Britain: political parties, the cabinet, and the office of prime minister. The appearance of these institutions was part of the evolution of England's constitutional government—that is, a government whose power is defined and limited by law. Unlike the United States Constitution, which is a single written document, the British constitution is made up of all acts of Parliament over the centuries. It also includes documents such as the Magna Carta and Bill of Rights, as well as unwritten traditions that protect citizens' rights.

**Political parties.** Two political parties emerged in England in the late 1600s, Tories and Whigs. The conservative Tories were generally landed aristocrats who sought to preserve older traditions. They supported broad royal powers and a dominant Anglican Church. The Whigs backed the more liberal policies of the Glorious Revolution. They were more likely to reflect urban business interests, support religious toleration for Protestants, and favor Parliament over the crown. For much of the 1700s, the Whigs dominated Parliament.

*Chapter 18* **467**

# PARALLELS THROUGH TIME

## Political Campaigns

Wherever there have been elections, there have also been election campaigns. Throughout history, politicians eager to win office have done whatever they could to win votes.

**Linking Past and Present**  What methods do candidates use to win votes in the United States today? Do you think any of the same methods were used in England in the 1700s? Explain.

**PAST** *Only men who owned land could vote in England during the 1700s. Even so, elections were a time of bustling activity. In this painting by the great British artist William Hogarth, campaigners try to win votes for their candidates outside a tavern.*

**PRESENT** *In the United States today, political campaigns are elaborate affairs, and citizens participate in events like the convention (right) mainly through television. Candidates, such as Carol Moseley-Braun (far right), however, still go out to shake hands with their supporters.*

These early political parties were unlike the party organizations that we know today. They represented cliques among the rich, powerful men who served as members of Parliament. Linked by family ties or personal agreements, members pooled their votes to advance their common interests. The modern political party, representing groups of voters and with a distinct platform, did not appear until the 1800s.

**The cabinet system.** The cabinet was another new feature of government. In 1714, the British throne passed by hereditary right to a German Protestant prince. George I spoke no English and relied on the leaders in Parliament to help him rule. Under George I, and his German-born son George II, a handful of parliamentary advisers set policy. They were called the cabinet because they met in a small room, or "cabinet."

In time, the cabinet gained official status. It was made up of leaders of the majority party in the House of Commons. The cabinet remained in power so long as it enjoyed the support of the Commons. If the Commons voted against a cabinet decision, the cabinet resigned. This cabinet system (also called a parliamentary system) was later adopted by other countries in Europe and elsewhere around the world.

**The prime minister.** Heading the cabinet was the prime minister. The prime minister was the leader of the majority party in Parliament and in time the chief official of the British government. From 1721 to 1742, the able Whig leader Robert Walpole molded the cabinet into a unified body, requiring all members to agree on major issues. Although the title was not yet used, Walpole is often called Britain's first prime minister.

## Politics and Society

The age of Walpole was a time of peace and prosperity. But even as Parliament and the cabinet assumed new powers, British government was far from democratic. Rather, it was an oligarchy—as you recall, a government in which the ruling power belongs to a few people.

**The ruling elite.** In Britain as on the continent, landowning aristocrats were seen as the "natural" ruling class. The highest nobles held seats in the House of Lords. Other wealthy landowners, along with rich business leaders in the cities, controlled elections to the House of Commons. The right to vote was limited to a relatively few male property owners, and their votes were often openly bought.

**Other classes.** The lives of most people contrasted sharply with those of the ruling elite. The majority made a meager living from the land. In the 1700s, even that poor existence was threatened. Wealthy landowners bought up farms and took over common lands, evicting tenant farmers and small landowners. Many landless families drifted into towns, where they faced a harsh and desperate existence.

A small but growing middle class included successful merchants and manufacturers. They controlled affairs in the towns and cities. Some improved their social standing by marrying into the landed gentry. The middle class also produced talented inventors and entrepreneurs who helped usher in the Industrial Revolution. (See Chapter 20.)

## George III Reasserts Royal Power

In 1760, George III embarked on a 60-year reign. Unlike his father and grandfather, the new king was born in England. He spoke English and loved Britain. But George was eager to recover the powers the crown had lost. Following his mother's advice, "George, be a king!" he set out to reassert royal power. He wanted to end Whig domination, choose his own ministers, dissolve the cabinet system, and make the House of Commons follow his will.

**Personal rule.** Gradually, George found seats in Parliament for "the king's friends." Then, with their help, he set out to regain control of the government.

His troubles, however, began early in his reign. After the Seven Years' War, George and his ministers adopted a new policy: English colonists in North America must pay the costs of their own defense. When colonists protested, Parliament passed harsh measures to force them to obey. In 1775, these and other conflicts triggered the American Revolution—and disaster for Britain. (See Section 4.)

**Cabinet rule restored.** Britain's loss of its American colonies discredited the king. Increasingly, too, he suffered from bouts of mental illness. In the crisis of leadership that followed, cabinet rule was restored in 1788.

In the decades ahead, revolution engulfed France, and Napoleon Bonaparte's armies stormed across Europe, dragging Britain into long wars. During that time, the cabinet controlled the government. The British came to see the prime minister as their real political leader.

## SECTION 3 REVIEW

1. **Identify** (a) Act of Union, (b) Tories, (c) Whigs, (d) Robert Walpole, (e) George III.
2. **Define** (a) constitutional government, (b) prime minister.
3. How did each of the following contribute to Britain's rise to global prominence in the 1700s: (a) geography, (b) success in war, (c) attitudes toward business and commerce?
4. Who made up the ruling oligarchy in Britain?
5. *Critical Thinking* **Comparing** How does the parliamentary system of government that evolved in England differ from the modern American system of government?
6. *ACTIVITY* Make a diagram showing the relationship among the English crown, prime minister, cabinet, and Parliament.

# 4 Birth of the American Republic

## Guide for Reading

- How were the 13 English colonies part of a global empire?

- Why did colonists come to resent British rule?

- How did Enlightenment ideas influence Americans?

- What was the global impact of the American Revolution?

Early in 1776, English colonists in North America eagerly read the newly published *Common Sense*. The pamphlet called on them to declare their independence from Britain. Its author, Tom Paine, a recent immigrant from England, wrote with passion under the cool banner of reason. "In the following pages," he declared, "I offer nothing more than simple facts, plain arguments, and common sense."

In *Common Sense,* Paine echoed the themes of the Enlightenment. He rejected ancient prejudice and tyranny, while appealing to reason, natural laws, and the promise of freedom. He wrote:

> **66** 'Tis repugnant to reason, to the universal order of things, to all examples from former ages, to suppose that this Continent can long remain subject to any external power. **99**

Colonists hotly debated Paine's arguments. As resentment of British policies grew, however, many came to agree with his radical ideas. Soon, they set out on the dangerous and uncertain road that led to independence from British rule.

## The 13 English Colonies

By 1750, a string of 13 prosperous colonies stretched along the eastern coast of North America. They were part of Britain's growing empire. Colonial cities such as Boston, New York, and Philadelphia were busy centers of commerce linking North America, the West Indies, Africa, and Europe. Colonial shipyards produced many vessels used in that global trade.

Britain applied mercantilist policies to its colonies. In the 1600s, Parliament had passed the Navigation Acts to regulate colonial trade and manufacturing. For the most part, these acts were not rigorously enforced. Smuggling was common and was not considered a crime by the colonists.

By mid-century, too, the colonies were home to diverse religions and ethnic groups. Social distinctions were more blurred than in Europe, although government and society were dominated by wealthy landowners and merchants. In politics as in much else, there was a good deal of free discussion. Colonists felt entitled to the rights of English citizens, and their colonial assemblies exercised much control over local affairs.

Ways of life differed from New England to the southern colonies. Still, colonists shared common values, respect for individual enterprise, and a growing self-confidence. They also had an increasing sense of their own destiny separate from Britain.

## Growing Discontent

After 1763, relations between Britain and the 13 colonies grew strained. The Seven Years' War, called the French and Indian War in North America, had drained the British treasury. King George III and his ministers thought that the colonists should help pay for the war and for the troops still stationed on the frontier. Britain began to enforce the long-neglected laws regulating colonial trade, and Parliament passed new laws to raise taxes from the colonies.

The British measures were not burdensome. Still, colonists bitterly resented what they saw as an attack on their rights. "No taxation without representation," they protested. Since they had no representatives in Parliament, they believed, Parliament had no right to tax them. While Parliament did repeal some of the

*Teapot celebrating repeal of a British tax*

**Ben Franklin** *Enlightenment ideas influenced many American colonists, among them Benjamin Franklin. Franklin, a writer and scientist, was known in Europe as an American philosophe. Among his many practical inventions were the bifocal glasses, shown here.* **Global Interaction** *Franklin wrote, "Much of the strength and efficiency of any government, in procuring and securing happiness to the people, depends on [public] opinion." How does this statement reflect Enlightenment ideas?*

hated measures, in general, it asserted its right to tax.

**Early clashes.** A series of violent clashes intensified the crisis. In 1770, British soldiers in Boston opened fire on a crowd that was pelting them with stones and snowballs. Colonists called the death of five protesters the "Boston Massacre." In 1773, a handful of colonists staged the Boston Tea Party, hurling a cargo of recently arrived British tea into the harbor to protest a tax on tea. When Parliament passed harsh laws to punish Massachusetts, other colonies rallied to its support.

**Fighting begins.** In April 1775, the crisis exploded into war. The next month, as fighting spread, colonial leaders met in a Continental Congress to decide what action to take. Members included some extraordinary men: the radical yet fair-minded Boston lawyer John Adams, the Virginia planter and soldier George Washington, and such pillars of the American Enlightenment as Benjamin Franklin and Thomas Jefferson.

**Declaring independence.** The Congress set up a Continental Army, with George Washington in command. The following year, it took a momentous step, voting to declare independence from Britain. Young Thomas Jefferson drafted the Declaration of Independence, a document that clearly reflects the ideas of John Locke in lines such as these:

66We hold these truths to be self-evident, that all men are created equal, that they are endowed by their Creator with certain unalienable rights, that among these are life, liberty, and the pursuit of happiness. That to secure these rights, governments are instituted among men, deriving their just powers from the consent of the governed.99

The Declaration claimed that people had the right "to alter or abolish" unjust governments—a right to revolt. Jefferson carefully detailed the colonists' grievances against Britain. Because the king had trampled colonists' natural rights, he argued, the colonists had the right to rebel and set up a new government that would protect them. Aware of the risks involved, on July 4, 1776, American leaders adopted the Declaration, pledging "our lives, our fortunes, and our sacred honor" to the cause of the United States of America.

## The American Revolution

At first, the American cause looked bleak. The British had professional soldiers, a huge fleet, and plentiful money. They occupied most major American cities. Also, about a third of the colonists were Loyalists who supported Britain. Many others refused to fight for either side.

The Continental Congress had few military resources and little money to pay its soldiers. Still, colonists battling for independence had some advantages. They were fighting on their own ground for their farms and towns. Although the British held New York and Philadelphia, rebels controlled the countryside.

**The French alliance.** A turning point in the war came with the American triumph over

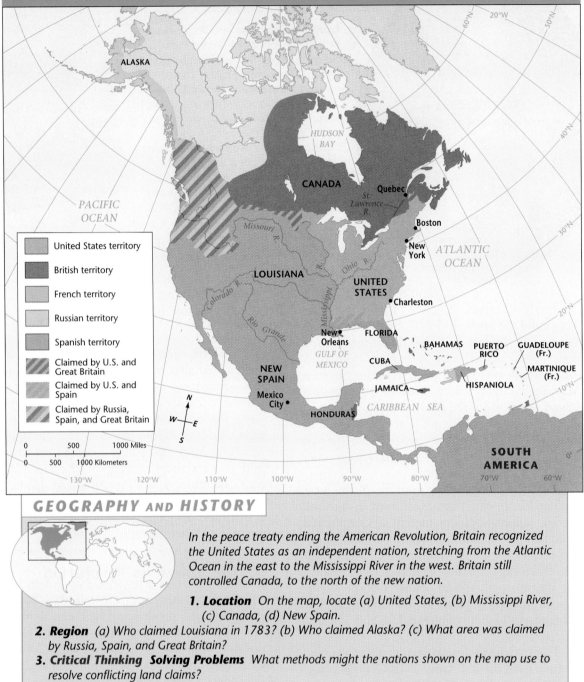

## North America, 1783

United States territory
British territory
French territory
Russian territory
Spanish territory
Claimed by U.S. and Great Britain
Claimed by U.S. and Spain
Claimed by Russia, Spain, and Great Britain

ALASKA

HUDSON BAY

PACIFIC OCEAN

CANADA

Quebec

St. Lawrence R.

Boston

New York

ATLANTIC OCEAN

Missouri R.

LOUISIANA

Ohio R.

UNITED STATES

Charleston

Colorado R.

Rio Grande

Mississippi R.

New Orleans

FLORIDA

GULF OF MEXICO

BAHAMAS

PUERTO RICO

GUADELOUPE (Fr.)

NEW SPAIN

CUBA

MARTINIQUE (Fr.)

Mexico City

JAMAICA

HISPANIOLA

HONDURAS

CARIBBEAN SEA

SOUTH AMERICA

N
W—E
S

0   500   1000 Miles
0   500   1000 Kilometers

130°W   120°W   110°W   100°W   90°W   80°W   70°W   60°W
20°W   50°N   60°N   40°N   30°N   20°N   10°N   0°

## GEOGRAPHY AND HISTORY

In the peace treaty ending the American Revolution, Britain recognized the United States as an independent nation, stretching from the Atlantic Ocean in the east to the Mississippi River in the west. Britain still controlled Canada, to the north of the new nation.

1. **Location** On the map, locate (a) United States, (b) Mississippi River, (c) Canada, (d) New Spain.
2. **Region** (a) Who claimed Louisiana in 1783? (b) Who claimed Alaska? (c) What area was claimed by Russia, Spain, and Great Britain?
3. **Critical Thinking** **Solving Problems** What methods might the nations shown on the map use to resolve conflicting land claims?

the British in 1777 at the Battle of Saratoga. The victory convinced France to join the Americans against its old rival, Britain. The alliance brought the Americans desperately needed supplies, trained soldiers, and French warships. Spurred by the French example, the Netherlands and Spain soon added their support.

Hard times continued, however. In the brutal winter of 1777–1778, Continental troops at Valley Forge suffered from cold, hunger, and disease. Through this crisis and others, George Washington proved a patient, courageous, and determined leader able to hold the ragged army together.

**Treaty of Paris.** Finally in 1781, with the help of the French fleet, Washington forced the surrender of a British army at Yorktown, Virginia. With that defeat, the British war effort crumbled. Two years later, American, British, and French negotiators signed the Treaty of Paris ending the war. In it, Britain recognized the independence of the United States of America. It also accepted the new nation's western frontier as the Mississippi River.

## A New Constitution

A national government set up by a document that Americans called the Articles of Confederation was too weak to rule the new United States effectively. To address this problem, the nation's leaders gathered once more in Philadelphia. During the hot summer of 1787, they hammered out the Constitution of the United States. This framework for a strong, flexible government has adapted to changing conditions for more than 200 years.

**The impact of Enlightenment ideas.** The framers of the Constitution had absorbed the ideas of Locke, Montesquieu, and Rousseau and had studied history. They saw government in terms of a social contract entered into by "We the People of the United States." They provided not only for an elective legislature but also for an elected president rather than a hereditary monarch.

The Constitution created a federal republic, with power divided between the federal, or national, government and the states. A central feature of the new federal government was the separation of powers among the legislative, executive, and judicial branches, an idea borrowed directly from Montesquieu. Within that structure, each branch of government was provided with checks and balances on the other branches.

The Bill of Rights, the first 10 amendments to the Constitution, recognized the idea that people had basic rights that the government must protect. They included freedom of religion, speech, and the press, as well as the rights to trial by jury and to private property.

**Limited freedom.** In 1789, the Constitution became law. It set up a representative government with an elected legislature to reflect the wishes of the governed.

Yet most Americans at the time did not have the right to vote. Only white men who met certain property requirements could vote. Women could not cast a ballot. Nor could African Americans—enslaved *or* free—or Native Americans. It would take many years of struggle before the right to vote and equal protection under the law were extended to all adult Americans.

**Global impact.** Despite its limits, the Constitution of the United States created the most liberal government of its day. From the start, the new republic shone as a symbol of freedom to European countries and to Latin America. Its Constitution would be copied or adapted by many lands throughout the world.

The Enlightenment ideals that had inspired American colonists brought changes in Europe, too. In France in 1789, a revolution in the name of liberty and equality toppled the monarchy. Before long, other Europeans took up the cry for freedom. By the mid-1800s, most absolute monarchs across Europe would see their powers greatly reduced.

## SECTION 4 REVIEW

1. **Identify** (a) Navigation Acts, (b) Continental Congress, (c) George Washington, (d) Thomas Jefferson, (e) Battle of Saratoga, (f) Treaty of Paris of 1783, (g) Bill of Rights.
2. What role did the 13 colonies have in the British empire?
3. Explain why conflict between the colonists and Britain increased after 1763.
4. Give two examples of how Enlightenment ideas were reflected in each of the following: (a) the Declaration of Independence, (b) the Constitution of the United States.
5. How did the ideals of the American Revolution influence other nations?
6. *Critical Thinking* **Analyzing Information** In your own words, describe the idea of separation of powers. Then, give two examples of how your life would be different if the Constitution did not provide for separation of powers.
7. *ACTIVITY* Write a storybook for young children describing the causes, main events, and effects of the American Revolution.

# World Literature

## Evelina

### Fanny Burney

**Introduction** *One of England's first female novelists was Fanny Burney. In 1778, she published* Evelina, or The History of a Young Lady's Entrance Into the World. *It tells the story of a 16-year-old woman who is sent from her small rural village to visit London. In a series of letters home, Evelina tells of her adventures in the city. The novel gives us an interesting picture of upper-middle-class life. In the following passage, Evelina describes going to her first dance in London.*

LETTER X
EVELINA TO THE REV. MR. VILLARS
*Monday, April 4*

We are to go this evening to a private ball, given by Mrs. Stanley, a very fashionable lady of Mrs. Mirvan's acquaintance.

We have been *a-shopping* as Mrs. Mirvan calls it, all this morning, to buy silks, caps, gauzes, and so forth.

The shops are really very entertaining, especially the [textile dealers]; there seem to be six or seven men belonging to each shop; and every one took care by bowing and smirking, to be noticed. We were conducted from one to another, and carried from room to room with so much ceremony, that at first I was almost afraid to go on.

I thought I should never have chosen a silk: for they produced so many, I knew not what to fix upon; and they recommended them all so strongly, that I fancy they thought I only wanted persuasion to buy everything they showed me. And, indeed, they took so much trouble, that I was almost ashamed I could not.

At the [hat shop], the ladies we met were so much dressed, that I should rather have imagined they were making visits than purchases. But what most diverted me was, that we were more frequently served by men than by women; and such men! so [fussy], so affected! they seemed to understand every part of a woman's dress better than we do ourselves. . . .

The dispatch with which they work in these great shops is amazing, for they have promised me a complete suit of linen [by] the evening.

I have just had my hair dressed. You can't think how oddly my head feels; full of powder and black pins, and a great cushion on the top of it. I believe you would hardly know me, for my face looks quite different to what it did before my hair was dressed. When I shall be able to make use of a comb for myself I cannot tell; for my hair is so much entangled, *frizzled* they call it, that I fear it will be very difficult.

I am half afraid of this ball tonight; for, you know, I have never danced but at school; however, Miss Mirvan says there is nothing in it. Yet, I wish it was over.

Adieu, my dear Sir, pray excuse the wretched stuff I write; perhaps I may improve by being in this town, and then my letters will be less unworthy your reading. Meantime, I am,

Your dutiful and affectionate,
EVELINA

P. S. Poor Miss Mirvan cannot wear one of the caps she made, because they dress her hair too large for them.


LETTER XI
EVELINA TO THE REV. MR. VILLARS
*Tuesday, April 5*

We passed a most extraordinary evening. A *private* ball this was called, so I expected to have seen about four or five couples; but Lord! my dear sir, I believe I saw half the world! Two very large rooms were full of company; in one were cards for the elderly ladies, and in the other were the dancers. My mamma Mirvan, for she always calls me her child, said she would sit with Maria and me till we were provided with partners, and then join the card-players.

**Rich Women and Poor** Lines between social classes were sharply drawn in London of the 1700s. Here, a wealthy Englishwoman and her daughters give money to a poor woman and her baby. **Diversity** How does clothing signal the difference between rich and poor in this painting?

The gentlemen, as they passed and repassed, looked as if they thought we were quite at their disposal, and only waiting for the honor of their commands; and they sauntered about, in a careless indolent manner, as if with a view to keep us in suspense. I don't speak of this in regard to Miss Mirvan and myself only, but to the ladies in general; and I thought it so provoking, that I determined in my own mind that, far from honoring such airs, I would rather not dance at all, than with anyone who would seem to think me ready to accept the first partner who would condescend to take me.

Not long after, a young man, who for some time looked at us with a kind of negligent impertinence, advanced on tiptoe towards me; he had a set smile on his face, and his dress was so foppish, that I really believed he even wished to be stared at; and yet he was very ugly.

Bowing almost to the ground with a sort of swing, and waving his hand, with the greatest conceit, after a short and silly pause, he said, "Madam—may I presume?"—and stopped, offering to take my hand. I drew it back, but could scarce forbear laughing. "Allow me, Madam," he continued, affectedly breaking off every half moment, "the honor and happiness—if I am not so unhappy as to address you too late—to have the happiness and honor—"

Again he would have taken my hand; but, bowing my head, I begged to be excused, and turned to Miss Mirvan to conceal my laughter.

He then desired to know if I had already engaged myself to [dance with] some more fortunate man? I said No, and that I believed I should not dance at all. He would keep himself, he told me, disengaged, in hopes I should relent; and then, uttering some ridiculous speeches of sorrow and disappointment, though his face still wore the same invariable smile, he retreated.

Source: Fanny Burney, *Evelina, or The History of a Young Lady's Entrance Into the World* (New York: W.W. Norton & Company, 1965).

## Thinking About Literature

1. **Vocabulary** Use the dictionary to find the meanings of the following words: saunter, dispatch, indolent, provoke, condescend, foppish.
2. (a) What preparations does Evelina make for the ball? (b) Describe three things that she finds surprising or amusing.
3. What annoys Evelina about the behavior of the men at the ball?
4. *Critical Thinking* **Linking Past and Present** (a) Based on the excerpts, do you think that *Evelina* reflected the experiences of most middle-class young women of the 1700s? (b) Why would Burney's novel appeal to these young women? (c) Do similar stories appeal to young women today? Explain.

# Skills for Success

## Distinguishing Facts From Opinions

When reading either primary or secondary sources, you must be able to distinguish facts from opinions. A fact is a statement that can be observed or proved by reliable sources. An opinion is a judgment that reflects a person's beliefs or feelings. It may or may not be provable.

The passage below is from a college textbook discussion of Frederick the Great. Read the passage. Then, answer the following questions.

**1** **Determine which statements are facts.**
(a) List three statements about Frederick's economic policies that appear to be facts. (b) List two statements about Frederick's religious policies that appear to be facts. (c) How might you prove that these statements are facts?

**2** **Determine which statements are opinions.**
(a) List three statements from the passage that are opinions. (b) How do you know they are opinions? (c) Are some of the opinions positive? Are some negative? Explain.

**3** **Determine how the writer uses facts to support his opinions.** (a) Does the author of the passage think that Frederick the Great was an enlightened despot? (b) What facts does he use to support his opinion? (c) Do you think that he is justified in drawing his conclusions based on the facts that he presents?

*Beyond the Classroom* Newspaper editorials often combine facts and opinions. Select an editorial from a recent newspaper. Circle the statements of fact with a red pen, and circle the statements of opinion with a black pen.

66 Viewed as a general, diplomat, and the master mechanic of Prussian administration, Frederick the Great was efficient and successful, but he was scarcely enlightened. His claim to be [an enlightened] despot must rise or fall on the record of his social and economic reforms.

No physiocrat could have done more than Frederick to improve Prussian agriculture. From England he imported clover, crop rotation, and the iron plow, which turned up the soil more effectively than the old wooden share. He drained the swamps of the lower Oder Valley, opened up farms in Silesia and elsewhere, and brought in 300,000 immigrants to populate the new lands. . . . He nursed along the admirable German tradition of scientific forestry, then in its infancy.

Frederick, however, was hostile to the doctrine of laissez faire and cut imports to the bone to save money for the support of the army. His mercantilism stimulated the growth of Prussian industry, particularly the textiles and metals needed by the army. But it also placed a staggering burden of taxation on his subjects and produced several economic absurdities. For instance, Frederick tried to make Prussia grow its own tobacco, for which the climate was not suited. . . .

Frederick prided himself on religious tolerance. He invited Jesuits to seek refuge in Prussia and protected the minority of Catholics in his predominantly Protestant kingdom. . . . He even boasted that he would build a mosque in Berlin if Muslims wanted to settle there. Yet the same Frederick . . . levied special heavy taxes on his Jewish subjects, and tried to exclude them from the professions and from the civil service.

Frederick rendered Prussians a great service by his judicial reforms. He reduced the use of torture. . . . Yet the same Frederick took a positively medieval view of the merits of [social class]. He did nothing to loosen the bonds of serfdom that still shackled much of the Prussian peasantry. . . .

He was an enlightened despot only so far as he could reconcile the [principles] of the Age of Reason with the [demands] of Prussian kingship. 99

Source: Crane Brinton et al., *Modern Civilization* (Englewood Cliffs, NJ: Prentice Hall, 1967).

## Building Vocabulary

Select *five* vocabulary words from the chapter. Write each word on a separate slip of paper. Then, write the definition for each word on other slips of paper. Scramble the slips and exchange them with another student. Match the words with their definitions, and then check each other's results.

## Reviewing Chapter Themes

1. **Religions and Value Systems** (a) How did Enlightenment thinkers want to reform society? (b) What groups felt challenged by their ideas? Why?
2. **Economics and Technology** (a) How did the physiocrats want to reform the economy? (b) What forces did they believe should be allowed to regulate business?
3. **Continuity and Change** Describe the lives of peasants in Western and Eastern Europe during the 1700s.
4. **Political and Social Systems** What was the role of each of the following in the evolution of constitutional government in Britain: (a) political parties, (b) the cabinet, (c) the office of prime minister?
5. **Global Interaction** (a) What ideas developed during the Enlightenment helped inspire England's American colonists to declare independence? (b) What Enlightenment ideas were reflected in the United States Constitution and the Bill of Rights?

## Thinking Critically

1. **Making Inferences** How did the Enlightenment bring together the ideas of the Renaissance and Reformation?
2. **Synthesizing Information** Write a sentence summarizing the major ideas of each of the following thinkers: (a) John Locke, (b) Baron de Montesquieu, (c) Voltaire, (d) Mary Wollstonecraft, (e) Adam Smith. ( ★ See *Skills for Success*, page 896.)
3. **Linking Past and Present** Today, we talk about human rights rather than natural rights. Describe a human rights issue that has recently been in the news.

4. **Applying Information** Which political thinker would have spoken about the state of nature as a "war against all"? Explain.
5. **Predicting Consequences** What do you think would be the effects of Britain's repression of Catholics in Ireland? ( ★ See *Skills for Success*, page 974.)
6. **Analyzing Information** (a) What ideas about government do you think English settlers brought with them to the Americas in the 1600s and 1700s? (b) How might those ideas have contributed to the outbreak of the American Revolution?
7. **Defending a Position** During the Revolution, Tom Paine used the following words to encourage the colonists during an especially grim time: "What we obtain too cheaply, we esteem too light; it is [costliness] only that gives everything its value." (a) What did he mean by this? (b) Do you agree or disagree? Give an example to defend your position.

## For Your Portfolio

Imagine that you live in Western Europe or North America during the Age of Enlightenment. Because it is such a remarkable period, you keep a diary to record your thoughts on the important ideas and events of the day. In this assignment, you will write a diary entry.

1. To begin, review the chapter and make a list of people, ideas, and events that you might comment on.
2. Choose the topic for your diary entry. You might write about publication of an influential book such as *Leviathan* by Thomas Hobbes or *A Vindication of the Rights of Woman* by Mary Wollstonecraft. You might also write about a salon, an art exhibit, or a concert by Bach, Handel, or Mozart. You might choose to reflect on politics and society in England or its American colonies during this period.
3. Use library resources to add to the information in the text.
4. Write your diary entry. Include as many details as you can to make it "authentic."
5. Share your diary with the class. Explain why you chose the topic you did.

# The French Revolution and Napoleon
## (1789–1815)

## CHAPTER OUTLINE

1 **On the Eve of Revolution**
2 **Creating a New France**
3 **Radical Days**
4 **The Age of Napoleon Begins**
5 **The End of an Era**

Rain pounded the Parisian suburb of Versailles on the morning of June 20, 1789. In the street, delegates to the National Assembly milled about outside their meeting hall. A notice on the door announced that King Louis XVI would speak to them on a future day. But why were the doors locked?

These middle-class men had been chosen as representatives to help the king solve France's financial crisis. But they had their own plans, too. They wanted sweeping reforms of a government sadly out of touch with its people. Already they had challenged the old order by insisting that nobles and clergy meet with them.

Perhaps that demand had pushed the king too far. Did the locked door mean that he was going to forbid them to meet altogether? The delegates stood in the rain, debating what to do next. One delegate suggested that they move their meeting to an indoor tennis court nearby.

They trooped off to the tennis court. Crowds of curious spectators pushed into the galleries. Jean-Joseph Mounier (moon YAY), a leading member of the Assembly, spoke up:

❝Let us swear to God and our country never to separate and to meet wherever circumstances might require until we have established a sound and just constitution.❞

As the delegates took the oath, the crowd in the gallery cheered. They sensed that they were witnessing a revolutionary moment.

The men who took the Tennis Court Oath were children of the Enlightenment who believed that the government could be rationally reformed. Like the delegates to the American Continental Congress in 1776, they pledged their lives to freeing their country from tyranny. They had no idea that they would help trigger an upheaval considerably more radical than the American Revolution. The French Revolution ultimately destroyed an absolute monarchy and disrupted a centuries-old social system.

Between 1789 and 1815, events in France upset the balance of power across all of Europe. Most historians see the French Revolution as a major turning point that helped usher in the modern era in European politics.

**FOCUS ON** these questions as you read:

■ **Religions and Value Systems**
What beliefs and attitudes inspired the leaders of the French Revolution?

■ **Political and Social Systems**
How did the French Revolution reshape social and political institutions?

■ **Impact of the Individual**
How did the rise of Napoleon Bonaparte create upheaval across Europe?

■ **Continuity and Change**
What were the temporary and lasting effects of the French Revolution?

## TIME AND PLACE

**Storming the Bastille** *For centuries, French kings jailed their enemies in the Bastille, an imposing fortress in Paris. Even the great philosopher Voltaire was once held there. Its heavy cannons, high towers, and thick walls symbolized the monarch's power. But on July 14, 1789, an angry mob seized the Bastille, shaking the monarchy to its roots.* **Political and Social Systems** *Compare this picture to the one on page 421. How do Versailles and the Bastille represent two sides of absolute monarchy?*

## HUMANITIES LINK

*Art History* Francisco Goya, *The Third of May, 1808* (page 500).

*Literature* In this chapter, you will encounter passages from the following works of literature: William Wordsworth, *The Prelude* (pages 488 and 492); Edmund Burke, *Reflections on the Revolution in France* (page 488); Olympe de Gouges, *Declaration of the Rights of Woman* (page 493).

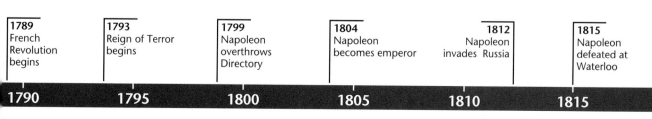

| 1789 French Revolution begins | 1793 Reign of Terror begins | 1799 Napoleon overthrows Directory | 1804 Napoleon becomes emperor | 1812 Napoleon invades Russia | 1815 Napoleon defeated at Waterloo |
|---|---|---|---|---|---|
| 1790 | 1795 | 1800 | 1805 | 1810 | 1815 |

## Guide for Reading

- What was the social structure of the old regime?

- Why did France face an economic crisis by 1789?

- Why did efforts at reform fail?

- **Vocabulary** *bourgeoisie, deficit spending*

On April 28, 1789, unrest exploded at the Réveillon (ray vay OHN) wallpaper factory in Paris. A rumor had spread that, though bread prices were soaring, the owner was planning to cut wages for his workers. Enraged workers then invaded the owner's home, leaving it in ruins.

Meanwhile, on the outskirts of the city, a group of nobles was enjoying an afternoon at the racetrack. Unaware of the trouble, they returned to Paris through the neighborhood of Réveillon's factory. An eyewitness told what happened as the aristocrats' carriages bumped through the streets:

66 A troop of men stopped the people returning from the races . . . asking them whether they were for the nobles or the Third Estate [the common people] . . . insulting those it thought noble. They forced the women from their carriages and made them shout: 'Long live the Third Estate!' 99

Though unpleasant, incidents like the Réveillon riots did not worry most aristocrats too much. Yes, France was facing a severe economic crisis. But a few financial reforms would certainly settle things. And rioters would get the hanging they deserved.

The nobles could not have been more wrong. The crisis went deeper than government finances. Reform would not be enough. By July, the hungry, unemployed, or poorly paid people of Paris had taken up arms. Their actions would push events further and faster than anyone could foresee.

## The Old Regime

In 1789, France, like the rest of Europe, still clung to an outdated social system that had emerged in the Middle Ages. Under this *ancien regime,* or old order, everyone in France belonged to one of three classes: the First Estate, made up of the clergy; the Second Estate, made up of the nobility; or the Third Estate, the vast majority of the population.

**The clergy.** In the Middle Ages, the Church had exerted great influence throughout Christian Europe. In 1789, the French clergy still enjoyed enormous wealth and privilege. They owned about 10 percent of the land, collected tithes, and paid no direct taxes to the state. High Church leaders such as bishops and abbots were usually nobles who lived very well. Parish priests, however, often came from humble origins and might be as poor as their peasant congregations.

The First Estate did provide social services. Nuns, monks, and priests ran schools, hospitals, and orphanages. But during the Enlightenment, philosophes targeted the Church for reform. They pointed to the idleness of some clergy, Church interference in politics, and its intolerance of dissent. In response, many clergy condemned the Enlightenment for undermining religion and moral order.

**Nobles.** The Second Estate was the titled nobility of French society. In the Middle Ages, noble knights had defended the land. In the 1600s, Richelieu and Louis XIV had crushed the nobles' military power but given them other rights—under strict royal control. Those rights included top jobs in government, the army, the courts, and the Church.

At Versailles, ambitious nobles vied for royal appointments, while idle courtiers enjoyed endless entertainments. Many nobles, however, lived far from the center of power. Though they owned land, they had little money income. As a result, they felt the pinch of trying to maintain their status in a period of rising prices.

Many nobles hated absolutism and resented the royal bureaucracy that employed middle-class men in positions once reserved for the aristocracy. They feared losing their traditional privileges, especially their freedom from paying taxes.

**The Third Estate.** In 1789, the Third Estate numbered about 27 million people, or 98 percent of the population. It was a diverse group. At the top sat the bourgeoisie (boor zhwah ZEE), or middle class. The bourgeoisie included the prosperous bankers, merchants, and manufacturers who propped up the French economy. It also included the officials who staffed the royal bureaucracy, as well as lawyers, doctors, journalists, professors, and skilled artisans.

The bulk of the Third Estate—9 out of 10 people in France—were rural peasants. Some were prosperous landowners who hired laborers to work for them. Others were tenant farmers or day laborers. Still others owed obligations to local nobles.

The poorest members of the Third Estate were city workers. They included apprentices, journeymen, and others who worked in industries such as printing or clothmaking. Many women and men earned a living as servants, stable hands, porters, construction workers, or street hawkers of everything from food to pots and pans. A large number were unemployed. To survive, some turned to begging or crime.

**Discontent.** From rich to poor, members of the Third Estate resented the privileges enjoyed by their social "betters." Wealthy bourgeois families could buy political office and even titles, but the best jobs were still reserved for nobles. Urban workers earned miserable wages. Even the smallest rise in the price of bread, their main food, might mean starvation.

Peasants were burdened by taxes on everything from land to soap to salt. Though technically free, many owed fees and services that dated to medieval times, such as the corvée (kohr VAY), unpaid labor to repair roads and bridges. Peasants were also incensed when nobles, hurt by rising prices, tried to reimpose old manor dues. Also, only nobles had the right to hunt game. Peasants were even forbidden to kill rabbits that ate their crops.

In towns and cities, Enlightenment ideas led people to question the ancien regime. Why, people demanded, should the first two estates have privileges at the expense of the majority? It did not meet the test of reason! Everywhere, the Third Estate called for the privileged classes to pay their share. In 1789, the Abbé Sieyès (syay

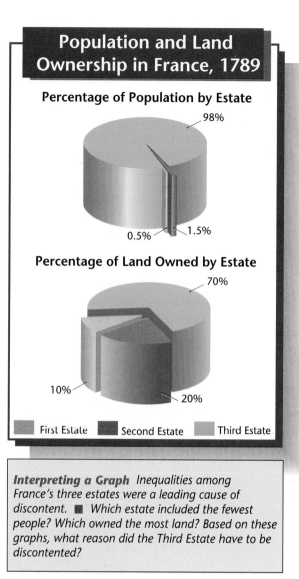

## Population and Land Ownership in France, 1789

**Percentage of Population by Estate**

98%

0.5%    1.5%

**Percentage of Land Owned by Estate**

70%

10%    20%

☐ First Estate   ■ Second Estate   ☐ Third Estate

*Interpreting a Graph* Inequalities among France's three estates were a leading cause of discontent. ■ Which estate included the fewest people? Which owned the most land? Based on these graphs, what reason did the Third Estate have to be discontented?

EHS), a member of the clergy, wrote a widely read pamphlet that asked:

66What is the Third Estate?
  EVERYTHING.
What has it been in the political order
  up to now? NOTHING.
What is it asking for? To become
  SOMETHING.99

## A Financial Crisis

Hand in hand with social unrest went a mushrooming financial crisis. The crisis was caused in part by years of deficit spending, that is, a government spending more money than it takes in. Louis XIV had left France deeply in debt. Wars like the Seven Years' War and the American Revolution strained the treasury even further. Costs generally had risen in the 1700s, and the lavish court soaked up millions. To bridge the gap between income and expenses, the government borrowed more and more money. By 1789, half its tax income went just to pay interest on this enormous debt.

To solve the financial crisis, the government would have to increase taxes, reduce expenses, or both. However, the nobles and clergy fiercely resisted any attempt to end their exemption from taxes.

**A crumbling economy.** Other economic woes added to the crisis. A general economic decline began in the 1770s. Then, in the late 1780s, bad harvests sent food prices soaring and brought hunger to poorer peasants and city dwellers.

Hard times and lack of food inflamed these people. In towns, people rioted, demanding bread. In the countryside, peasants began to attack the manor houses of the nobles. Arthur Young, an English visitor to France, witnessed the violence:

66 Everything conspires to render the present period in France critical: the [lack] of bread is terrible; accounts arrive every moment from the provinces of riots and disturbances, and calling in the military, to preserve the peace of the markets. 99

**Failure of reform.** The heirs of Louis XIV were not the right men to solve the crisis. Louis XV, who ruled from 1715 to 1774, pursued pleasure before serious business and ran up more debts. His grandson, Louis XVI, was well-meaning but weak and indecisive. He wisely chose Jacques Necker, a financial wizard, as an adviser. Necker urged the king to reduce court spending, reform government, and improve internal trade by abolishing tariffs that made trade costly. When Necker proposed taxing the First and Second estates, however, the nobles and high clergy forced the king to dismiss the would-be reformer.

As the crisis deepened, the pressure for reform mounted. Finally, the wealthy and powerful classes demanded that the king call the

**A Heavy Burden** In this cartoon, a priest and a nobleman stand on a stone that crushes a peasant. The words on the stone refer to taxes and other obligations that peasants traditionally owed to the government. **Political and Social Systems** What was the cartoonist saying about the relationship among France's three estates?

Estates General before making any changes. (See page 214.) French kings had not summoned the Estates General for 175 years, fearing that nobles would try to recover the feudal powers that they had lost under absolute rule. To reform-minded nobles, the Estates General seemed to offer a chance to carry out changes like the Glorious Revolution in England. It would establish a constitution to bring the absolute monarch under the control of the nobles and guarantee their privileges.

## The King Takes Action

As 1788 closed, France tottered on the verge of bankruptcy. Bread riots were spreading, and nobles, fearful of taxes, were denouncing royal tyranny. A baffled Louis XVI finally summoned the Estates General to meet at Versailles in May 1789.

**The cahiers.** In preparation, Louis had all three estates prepare *cahiers* (kah YAY), or notebooks, listing their grievances. Many cahiers called for reforms such as fairer taxes, freedom of the press, or regular meetings of the Estates General. In one town, shoemakers denounced regulations that made leather so expensive they could not afford to make shoes. Some peasants demanded the right to kill animals that were destroying their crops. Servant girls in the city of Toulouse demanded the right to leave service when they wanted and that "after a girl has served her master for many years, she receive some reward for her service."

The cahiers testified to boiling class resentments. One called tax collectors "bloodsuckers of the nation who drink the tears of the unfortunate from goblets of gold." Another one of the cahiers condemned the courts of nobles as "vampires pumping the last drop of blood" from the people. Another complained that "20 million must live on half the wealth of France while the clergy . . . devour the other half."

**The Tennis Court Oath.** Delegates to the Estates General from the Third Estate were elected, though only propertied men could vote. Thus, they were mostly lawyers, middle-class officials, and writers. They were familiar

▲ *Fan celebrating the Estates General*

with the writings of Voltaire, Rousseau, and other philosophes and with the complaints in the cahiers. They went to Versailles, not only to solve the national financial crisis, but also to insist on reform.

From the beginning, the Estates General was deadlocked over the issue of voting. Traditionally, each estate had met separately and voted as a group. This system always allowed the First and Second estates to outvote the Third Estate two to one. The Third Estate wanted all three orders to meet together.

After weeks of stalemate, delegates of the Third Estate took a daring step. Saying that they represented the people of France, they transformed themselves into the National Assembly. They then invited members of the other estates to help them shape a constitution. A few days later, as you have read, the National Assembly found itself locked out of its meeting place. In fact, workers were just preparing the hall for a royal speech, but many delegates believed that the king intended to send them home. They then took the famous Tennis Court Oath, vowing not to disband until they had drawn up a constitution for France.

When some reform-minded clergy and nobles joined the National Assembly, Louis XVI grudgingly had to accept it. At the same time, royal troops gathered around Versailles and Paris. Rumor held that the king would dissolve the Assembly.

The crisis deepened in early July. The king, who had brought back Necker to help with the financial crisis, again dismissed the popular minister. Food shortages were also getting worse because of a disastrous 1788 harvest.

## Storming the Bastille

On July 14, Paris seized the spotlight from the National Assembly meeting in Versailles. The streets buzzed with rumors that royal troops were going to occupy the capital. More than 800 Parisians assembled outside the Bastille, a grim medieval fortress used as a prison for political and other prisoners. The crowd was demanding weapons and gunpowder believed to be stored there.

The commander of the Bastille refused to open the gates and opened fire on the crowd. In the battle that followed, many people were killed. Finally, the enraged mob broke through the defenses. They killed the commander and five guards and released a handful of prisoners, but found no weapons.

When told of the attack, Louis XVI asked, "Is it a revolt?" "No, sire," replied a noble, "It is a revolution." The storming of the Bastille quickly became a symbol of the French Revolution. Supporters saw it as a blow to tyranny, a step toward freedom. Today, the French still celebrate July 14 as Bastille Day, the French national holiday.

## SECTION 1 REVIEW

1. **Identify** (a) Jacques Necker, (b) cahiers, (c) National Assembly, (d) Bastille.
2. **Define** (a) bourgeoisie, (b) deficit spending.
3. (a) Describe the three estates of French society. (b) Why were members of each estate discontented with conditions in 1789?
4. What were the causes of the financial crisis that gripped France?
5. (a) Why did Louis XVI call the Estates General in 1789? (b) What were the results of this decision?
6. *Critical Thinking* **Applying Information** A French lawyer of the day wrote that Louis XVI "was too well intentioned not to try to remedy abuses that had shocked him, but he possessed neither the character nor the talents to control an impetuous nation in a situation that cried out for reform." (a) How does this description apply to the king's actions in 1789? (b) Do you think Louis XVI could have prevented the outbreak of revolution? Why or why not?
7. *ACTIVITY* Imagine that you belong to one of the following groups in 1789 France: nobles, high clergy, parish priests, the bourgeoisie, peasants, city workers. With two partners, write a cahier describing what you think is the chief problem facing the nation.

 **Creating a New France**

### Guide for Reading

- How did popular uprisings contribute to the French Revolution?

- What political and social reforms emerged in the early stages of the revolution?

- How did people outside France respond to the revolution?

- **Vocabulary** *émigré, sans-culotte*

Excitement, wonder, and fear engulfed France as the revolution unfolded at home and spread abroad. Today, historians divide this revolutionary era into four phases. The moderate phase of the National Assembly (1789–1791) turned France into a constitutional monarchy. Then, a radical phase (1792–1794) of escalating violence led to a Reign of Terror. There followed a period of reaction against extremism, known as the Directory (1795–1799). Finally, the Age of Napoleon (1799–1815) consolidated many changes brought by the revolution. In this section, you will read about the moderate start of the French Revolution.

### Revolts in Paris and the Provinces

The political crisis of 1789 was punctuated by the worst famine in memory. Starving peasants roamed the countryside or flocked to the towns, where they swelled the ranks of the unemployed. As grain prices soared, even people with jobs had to spend up to 80 percent of their income on bread.

**The Great Fear.** In such desperate times, rumors ran wild, setting off what was later called the "Great Fear." Tales of marauders attacking villages and towns spread panic. Other rumors claimed that government troops were seizing peasant crops.

Inflamed by famine and fear, peasants unleashed their fury on nobles who were trying to reimpose medieval dues. Defiant peasants attacked the homes of nobles, burned old manor records, and stole grain from storehouses. The attacks died down after a time, but they demonstrated peasant anger with an unjust regime.

**Paris in arms.** Paris, too, was in turmoil. As the capital and chief city of France, it was the revolutionary center. Various factions competed for power. Moderates looked to the Marquis de Lafayette, the aristocratic "hero of two worlds" who had fought alongside George Washington in the American Revolution. Lafayette headed the National Guard, a largely middle-class militia organized in response to the arrival of royal troops in Paris. The Guard was the first group to don the tricolor, a red, white, and blue badge, which was eventually adopted as the national flag of France.

A more radical group, the Paris Commune, replaced the royalist government of the city. It could mobilize whole neighborhoods for protests or violent action to further the revolution. Newspapers and political clubs—many even more radical than the Commune—blossomed everywhere. Some demanded an end to monarchy and spread scandalous stories about the royal family and members of the court.

## Liberty, Equality, Fraternity

Peasant uprisings and the storming of the Bastille stampeded the National Assembly into action. On August 4, at a stormy all-night meeting, nobles in the National Assembly voted to end their privileges. They gave up their old manorial dues, their exclusive hunting rights, their special legal status, and their exemption from taxation.

**An end to special privilege.** "Feudalism is abolished," announced the weary delegates at 2 A.M. The president of the Assembly later wrote:

66 This has been a night for destruction and for public happiness. We may view this moment as the dawn of a new revolution, when all the burdens weighing on the people were abolished and France was truly reborn. 99

Were the votes on the night of August 4 voluntary? Contemporary observers and historians today note that the nobles gave up nothing that they had not already lost. In the months ahead, the National Assembly turned the reforms of

**Declaration of Rights** *The Marquis de Lafayette presented a first draft of the Declaration of the Rights of Man and the Citizen in July 1789. Lafayette had fought for American independence and was inspired by the ideals of the new United States. The final declaration, shown here, expresses the basic beliefs of the French Revolution in 17 articles.* **Religions and Value Systems** *How does this painting glorify the value of human rights?*

August 4 into law, meeting a key Enlightenment goal—the equality of all citizens before the law.

**Declaration of the Rights of Man.** In late August, as a first step toward writing a constitution, the Assembly issued the Declaration of the Rights of Man and the Citizen. The document was modeled in part on the American Declaration of Independence. All men, it announced, were "born and remain free and equal in rights." They enjoyed natural rights to "liberty, property, security, and resistance to oppression." Like Locke and the philosophes, it insisted that governments exist to protect the natural rights of citizens.

The Declaration further proclaimed that all male citizens were equal before the law. Each French man had an equal right to hold public office "with no distinction other than that of

**Sweet Dreams** *Lavish tapestries and glittering chandeliers adorned the bedchamber of Queen Marie Antoinette at Versailles. Tales of her extravagance inflamed public anger against the queen. She even had a mock peasant village built on the ground of Versailles so that she and her ladies-in-waiting could play at being milkmaids.* **Art and Literature** *Compare this picture to the one on page 429. How are these two rooms similar in style?*

their virtues and talents." In addition, the Declaration asserted freedom of religion and called for taxes to be levied according to ability to pay. Its principles were captured in the enduring slogan of the French Revolution, "Liberty, Equality, Fraternity."

Uncertain and hesitant, Louis XVI was slow to accept the reforms of the National Assembly. Parisians grew suspicious as more royal troops arrived. Nobles continued to enjoy gala banquets while people were starving. By autumn, anger again turned to action.

## Women March on Versailles

"Bread!" shouted the mob as it streamed down the road that led from Paris to Versailles. "Bread!" In a driving rainstorm, they marched the entire 12 miles (19 km). They wanted to see the king and would not take no for an answer.

Angry mobs were not a new sight in France. What surprised many observers, however, was that this mob was made up of thousands of women. On October 5, they showed themselves as determined as the men who had stormed the Bastille three months earlier.

A group of rough-spoken market women burst into the palace at Versailles. A duchess later recalled the scene:

66 The fishmonger women cried out that they wanted to speak to the king . . . and they could be calmed only by admitting a dozen of them to the presence of that unfortunate prince. His goodness disarmed them, and their opinions were so changed by the time they returned to their companions that they ran the risk of being the victims of their fury. 99

**"We'll wring her neck!"** Much of the crowd's anger was directed at the queen, Marie Antoinette. She was the daughter of Maria Theresa, the Hapsburg empress of Austria. (See Chapter 17.) Ever since Marie Antoinette had married Louis, she had come under attack for being frivolous and extravagant. She eventually grew more serious and even advised the king to compromise with moderate reformers. Still, she remained a source of scandal. Enemies accused her of immorality. Early in the revolution, the radical press spread the story that she had answered the cries of hungry people for bread by saying "Let them eat cake." Though the story was untrue, it helped inflame feelings against the queen.

"Death to the Austrian! We'll wring her neck!" shouted the women who stormed Versailles. "Tear out her heart, cut off her head, fry her liver and even then it won't be all over."

Lafayette and the National Guard eventually calmed the crowd. Still, the women would not leave Versailles until the king met their most important demand—to return with them to Paris. Not too happily, the king agreed.

**A triumphant procession.** The next morning, the crowd marched back to Paris, led by women perched on the barrels of seized cannon. They told bewildered spectators that they were bringing back to Paris "the baker, the baker's wife, and the baker's boy"—Louis XVI, Marie Antoinette, and their son. "Now we won't have to go so far/When we want to see our king," they sang. Crowds along the way cheered the king, who now wore the tricolor.

The royal family moved into the Tuileries (TWEE luh reez) palace. For the next three years, Louis was a virtual prisoner in his own capital.

---

**To Versailles!** As famine gripped Paris, poor mothers did not have enough food for their children. On October 5, 1789, thousands of women decided to bring Louis XVI to Paris, where he could no longer ignore their suffering. **Continuity and Change** Based on this painting, in what ways do you think the march challenged traditional roles of women?

---

The women of Paris would continue to take action during the revolution. Elisabeth Guenard, who sympathized with the royal cause, also understood what drove the women to Versailles. "You have to be a mother," she wrote, "and have heard your children ask for bread you cannot give them to know the level of despair to which this misfortune can bring you."

## A Time of Reform

The National Assembly soon followed the king to Paris. Its largely bourgeois members worked to draft a constitution and to solve the continuing financial crisis.

**Reorganizing the Church.** To pay off the huge government debt—much of it owed to the bourgeoisie—the Assembly voted to take over and sell Church lands. In an even more radical move, it put the French Catholic Church under state control. Under the Civil Constitution of the Clergy, issued in 1790, bishops and priests became elected, salaried officials. The Civil Constitution ended papal authority over the French Church and dissolved convents and monasteries.

Reaction was swift and angry. Many bishops and priests refused to accept the Civil Constitution. The pope condemned it. Large numbers of French peasants, who were basically conservative, also rejected the changes. When the government punished clergy who refused to

support the Civil Constitution, a huge gulf opened between revolutionaries in Paris and the peasantry in the provinces.

**A written constitution.** The National Assembly completed its main task by producing a constitution. The Constitution of 1791 set up a limited monarchy in place of the absolute monarchy that had ruled France for centuries. A new Legislative Assembly had the power to make laws, collect taxes, and decide on issues of war and peace. Lawmakers would be elected by tax-paying male citizens. Still, only about 50,000 men in a population of more than 27 million could qualify as candidates to run for the Assembly.

To make government more efficient, the constitution replaced the old provinces with 83 departments of roughly equal size. It abolished the old provincial courts and reformed laws. The middle-class framers of the constitution protected private property and supported free trade. They compensated nobles for land seized by the peasants, abolished guilds, and forbade city workers to organize labor unions.

To moderate reformers, the Constitution of 1791 seemed to complete the revolution. Reflecting Enlightenment goals, it ended Church interference in government and ensured equality before the law for all citizens. At the same time, it put power in the hands of men with the means and leisure to serve in government.

**The fateful flight.** Meanwhile, Marie Antoinette and others had been urging the king to escape their humiliating situation. In 1791, Louis finally gave in. One night in June, a large coach lumbered north from Paris toward the border. Inside sat the king disguised as a valet, the queen dressed as a governess, the royal children, and a loyal friend pretending to be their wealthy Russian employer.

When they stopped at a small town, a former soldier who had been stationed in Paris recognized Marie Antoinette. Louis's disguise was uncovered when someone held up the new revolutionary currency with the king's face on it.

The royal family was trundled back to Paris, to the insults of the crowds. The old shouts of "Long live the King!" were replaced by cries of "Long live the Nation!" To Parisians, the king's dash to the border showed he was a traitor to the revolution.

## Reaction Outside France

Events in France stirred debate all over Europe. Supporters of the Enlightenment applauded the reforms of the National Assembly. They saw the French experiment as the dawn of a new age for justice and equality. In his poem *The Prelude,* the English poet William Wordsworth later recalled how the start of the French Revolution stirred feelings of joy and hope:

> 66Bliss was it in that dawn to be alive,
>     But to be young was very Heaven!99

**Widespread fears.** European rulers and nobles, however, denounced the French Revolution. They increased border patrols, fearing the spread of the "French plague." Fueling those fears were the horror stories that were told by émigrés (EHM ih grayz)—nobles, clergy, and others who had fled revolutionary France. Émigrés reported attacks on their privileges, property, religion, and even their lives. "Enlightened" rulers turned against French ideas. Catherine the Great of Russia burned Voltaire's letters and locked up her critics.

In Britain, Edmund Burke, who had defended the American Revolution, bitterly condemned revolutionaries in Paris. In *Reflections on the Revolution in France,* he predicted all too accurately that the revolution would become more violent:

> 66Plots and assassinations will be anticipated by preventive murder and preventive confiscation. . . . When ancient opinions and rules of life are taken away, the loss cannot possibly be estimated. From that moment we have no compass to govern us.99

**Threats from abroad.** Louis XVI's failed flight brought further hostile rumblings from abroad. In August 1791, the king of Prussia and the emperor of Austria—who was Marie Antoinette's brother—issued the Declaration of Pilnitz. In it, they threatened to intervene if necessary to protect the French monarchy.

The declaration may have been mostly bluff. But revolutionaries in France took the threat seriously and prepared for war. The revolution was about to enter a new, more radical phase.

## War at Home and Abroad

In October 1791, the newly elected Legislative Assembly took office. Faced with crises at home and abroad, it would survive for less than a year. Economic problems fed renewed turmoil. Assignats, the revolutionary currency, dropped in value, which caused prices to rise rapidly. Uncertainty about prices led to hoarding and additional food shortages.

**The sans-culottes.** In Paris and other cities, working-class men and women, called sans-culottes* (sanz kyoo LAHTZ), pushed the revolution into more radical action. By 1791, many sans-culottes demanded a republic. They also wanted the government to guarantee them a living wage.

The sans-culottes found support among radical leaders in the Legislative Assembly, especially the Jacobins. A revolutionary political club, the Jacobins were mostly middle-class lawyers or intellectuals. They used pamphleteers and sympathetic newspaper editors to advance the republican cause.

**From right to left.** Within the Legislative Assembly, hostile factions feuded for power. Members with similar views sat together in the meeting hall. On the right sat those who felt reform had gone far enough or even wanted to turn the clock back to 1788. In the center sat supporters of moderate reform. On the left sat the Jacobins and other republicans who wanted to abolish the monarchy and pushed for other radical changes. This seating arrangement led to the modern use of the terms *right*, *center*, and *left* to describe similar political positions.

**War on tyranny.** Groups on the left soon held the upper hand. In April 1792, the war of words between French revolutionaries and European monarchs moved onto the battlefield. Eager to spread the revolution and destroy tyranny abroad, the Legislative Assembly declared war first on Austria, then on Prussia, Britain, and other states. The great powers expected to win an easy victory against France, a land divided by revolution. In fact, the fighting that began in 1792 lasted on and off until 1815.

---

*Sans-culottes* means "without culottes," the fancy knee-breeches worn by upper-class men. Shopkeepers, artisans, and other working-class men wore trousers, not culottes.

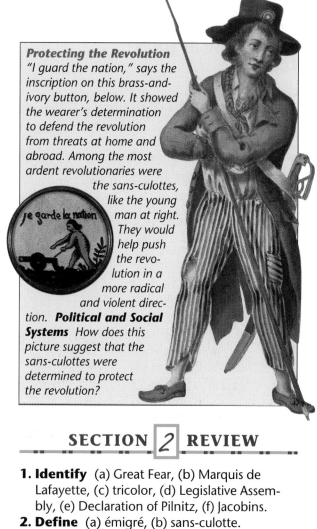

**Protecting the Revolution** "I guard the nation," says the inscription on this brass-and-ivory button, below. It showed the wearer's determination to defend the revolution from threats at home and abroad. Among the most ardent revolutionaries were the sans-culottes, like the young man at right. They would help push the revolution in a more radical and violent direction. **Political and Social Systems** How does this picture suggest that the sans-culottes were determined to protect the revolution?

*je garde la nation*

## SECTION 2 REVIEW

1. **Identify** (a) Great Fear, (b) Marquis de Lafayette, (c) tricolor, (d) Legislative Assembly, (e) Declaration of Pilnitz, (f) Jacobins.
2. **Define** (a) émigré, (b) sans-culotte.
3. What role did the people of Paris play in the French Revolution?
4. Describe two main ideas or reforms contained in each of the following: (a) the Declaration of the Rights of Man and the Citizen, (b) the Civil Constitution of the Clergy, (c) the Constitution of 1791.
5. (a) Why did some people outside France support the French Revolution? (b) Why did other people oppose it?
6. *Critical Thinking* **Comparing** Compare the women's march on Versailles to the storming of the Bastille in terms of goals and results.
7. *ACTIVITY* In a group of five or six students, write and perform a skit about *one* of the following events: the Great Fear; the night of August 4; the women's march on Versailles; the flight and capture of the royal family.

# Radical Days

## Guide for Reading

- Why did the revolution become more radical?

- What was the Reign of Terror?

- How did the French Revolution change daily life?

- **Vocabulary** *suffrage, nationalism*

Someone who had left Paris in 1791 and returned in 1793 could have gotten lost. Almost 4,000 streets had new names. Louis XV Square was renamed the Square of the Revolution. King-of-Sicily Street, named for the brother of Louis XVI, had become the Rights of Man Street.

Renaming streets was one way that Jacobins tried to wipe out all traces of the old order. In 1793, the revolution entered a radical phase. For a year, France experienced one of the bloodiest regimes in its history as determined leaders sought to extend and preserve the revolution.

## *Downfall of the Monarchy*

War heightened tensions in Paris, especially as dismal news arrived from the front. Well-trained Prussian forces were cutting down raw French recruits. Royalist officers deserted the French army, joining émigrés and others seeking to restore the king to power.

**Outbreaks of violence.** Battle disasters inflamed revolutionaries who thought the king was in league with the invaders. A crowd of Parisians invaded the Tuileries on August 10, 1792, and slaughtered the king's guards. The royal family fled to the Legislative Assembly.

A month later, citizens attacked the prisons that were holding nobles and priests accused of political offenses. These prisoners were killed, along with many ordinary criminals. Historians have disagreed about the people who carried out the "September massacres." Some call them "bloodthirsty savages," while others argue that they were patriots defending France from its enemies. In fact, most were ordinary citizens fired to fury by real and imagined grievances.

**The French Republic.** Backed by Paris crowds, radicals took control of the Assembly. Radicals called for the election of a new legislative body, the National Convention. Suffrage, the right to vote, was to be extended to all male citizens, not just to property owners.

The Convention that met in September 1792 was a more radical body than earlier assemblies. It voted to abolish the monarchy and declare France a republic. Deputies then drew up a new constitution for France. The Jacobins, who controlled the Convention, set out to erase all traces of the old order. They seized lands of nobles and abolished titles of nobility. All French men and women were called "Citizen." Louis XVI became Citizen Capet, from the dynasty that ruled France in the Middle Ages.

**Death of a king and queen.** The Convention also put Louis XVI on trial as a traitor to France. The king was convicted by a single vote and sentenced to death. On a foggy morning in January 1793, Louis mounted a scaffold in a public square in Paris. He tried to speak, but his words were drowned out by a roll of drums. Moments later, the king was beheaded.

In October, Marie Antoinette was also executed. The popular press celebrated her death. "The Widow Capet," however, showed great dignity as she went to her death. Their son, the uncrowned Louis XVII, died of unknown causes in the dungeons of the revolution.

## *The Convention Under Siege*

By early 1793, danger threatened France on all sides. The country was at war with much of Europe, including Britain, the Netherlands, Spain, and Prussia. In the Vendée (vahn DAY) region of western France, royalists and priests led peasants in a rebellion against the government. In Paris, the sans-culottes demanded relief from food shortages and rising prices. The Convention itself was bitterly divided between Jacobins and a rival group, the Girondins.

**ISSUES** *For* **TODAY**

A complex blend of ideas and conditions led to the overthrow of the French monarchy. What circumstances can lead to revolution?

## Portraits in Wax

The custom of making wax sculptures of famous people dates to Roman times. Today, wax museums such as the legendary Madame Tussaud's in London or the Hollywood Wax Museum in Los Angeles remain popular tourist attractions.

**Linking Past and Present**  Why do you think wax museums have fascinated people for centuries?

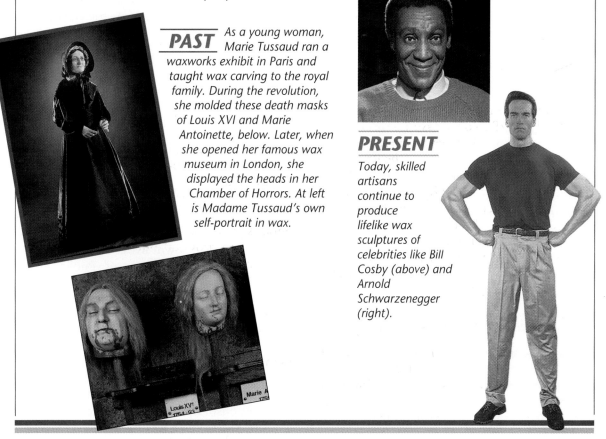

**PAST**  *As a young woman, Marie Tussaud ran a waxworks exhibit in Paris and taught wax carving to the royal family. During the revolution, she molded these death masks of Louis XVI and Marie Antoinette, below. Later, when she opened her famous wax museum in London, she displayed the heads in her Chamber of Horrors. At left is Madame Tussaud's own self-portrait in wax.*

**PRESENT**

*Today, skilled artisans continue to produce lifelike wax sculptures of celebrities like Bill Cosby (above) and Arnold Schwarzenegger (right).*

**Committee of Public Safety.** To deal with the threats to France, the Convention created the Committee of Public Safety. The 12-member committee had almost absolute power as it battled to save the revolution. It prepared France for all-out war, ordering all citizens to join the war effort:

66 Young men shall go to battle. Married men shall forge arms and transport provisions. Women shall make tents and clothing and serve in hospitals. Children will make lint from old linen. And old men shall be brought to public places to arouse the courage of soldiers. 99

Spurred by revolutionary fervor, French recruits marched off to defend the republic. Young officers developed effective new tactics to win battles with masses of ill-trained but patriotic forces. Soon, French armies overran the Netherlands and later invaded Italy. At home, they crushed peasant revolts. European monarchs shuddered as the revolutionaries carried "freedom fever" into conquered lands.

**Robespierre.** At home, the government battled counterrevolutionaries under the guiding hand of Maximilien Robespierre (ROHBZ pyair). Robespierre, a shrewd lawyer and politician, quickly rose to the leadership of the Committee of Public Safety. Among Jacobins, his selfless dedication to the revolution earned him the nickname "the incorruptible." Enemies called him a tyrant.

Robespierre had embraced Rousseau's idea of the general will. He promoted religious toleration and sought to abolish slavery. Though cold and humorless, he was popular with the sans-culottes, who hated the old regime as much as he. He believed that France could achieve a "republic of virtue" only through the use of terror. "Liberty cannot be secured," he cried, "unless criminals lose their heads."

**Reign of Terror.** Robespierre was a chief architect of the Reign of Terror, which lasted from about July 1793 to July 1794. Revolutionary courts conducted hasty trials. Spectators greeted death sentences with cries of "Hail the Republic!" or "Perish the traitors!"

Perhaps 40,000 people died during the Terror. About 15 percent were nobles and clergy. Another 15 percent were middle-class citizens, often moderates who had supported the revolution in 1789. The rest were peasants and sans-culottes involved in riots or revolts against the Republic. Many were executed, including victims of mistaken identity or false accusations by their neighbors. Many more were packed into hideous prisons, where deaths were common.

The engine of the Terror was the guillotine. Its fast-falling blade extinguished life instantly. A member of the legislature, Dr. Joseph Guillotin (GEE oh tan), had introduced it as a more humane method of beheading than the uncertain ax. But the guillotine quickly became a symbol of horror. William Wordsworth, who had welcomed the start of the revolution, turned in revulsion from the Terror:

> 66The Mother from the Cradle of her Babe,
> The Warrior from the Field, all perished, all,
> Friends, enemies, of all parties, ages, ranks,
> Head after head, and never heads enough
> For those that bade them fall.99

Within a year, though, the Reign of Terror consumed its own. Weary of bloodshed and fearing for their own lives, the Convention turned on the Committee of Public Safety. Once the heads of Robespierre and other radicals fell, executions slowed down dramatically.

## Reaction and the Directory

In reaction to the Terror, the revolution entered a third stage. Moving away from the excesses of the Convention, moderates produced another constitution, the third since 1789. The Constitution of 1795 set up a five-man Directory

---

**The Guillotine** *Early versions of the guillotine had been used for centuries. In the 1790s, though, it became a symbol of the Reign of Terror. Some people considered the guillotine humane because it worked swiftly and surely. Others were horrified because it made executions routine and simple, like a present-day assembly line.* **Economics and Technology** *What newer methods of capital punishment have been invented since the 1700s?*

and a two-house legislature elected by male citizens of property.

The Directory held power from 1795 to 1799. Weak but dictatorial, it faced growing discontent. Leaders lined their own pockets but failed to solve pressing problems. When rising bread prices stirred hungry sans-culottes to riot, the Directory quickly suppressed them.

As chaos threatened, politicians turned to a popular military hero, Napoleon Bonaparte. They planned to use him to advance their own goals—a bad miscalculation! Before long, Napoleon would outwit them all to become ruler of France.

## Women in the Revolution

As you have seen, women of all classes participated in the revolution from the very beginning. Working-class women demonstrated and fought in street battles. In Paris and elsewhere, women formed their own political clubs. A few, like Jeanne Roland, were noted leaders. Roland supported the revolution through her writings, her salon, and her influence on her husband, a government minister.

**Rights for women.** Many women were disappointed when the Declaration of the Rights of Man did not grant equal citizenship to women. Olympe de Gouges (oh LAMP duh GOOZH), a journalist, demanded equal rights in her *Declaration of the Rights of Woman*:

66Woman is born free and her rights are the same as those of man. . . . All citizens, be they men or women, being equal in the state's eyes, must be equally eligible for all public offices, positions, and jobs. . . . [Women] have the right to go to the scaffold; they must also have the right to go to parliament.99

Women did gain some rights. The government made divorce easier, a move aimed at weakening Church authority. It allowed women to inherit property, to undermine the tradition of nobles leaving large estates to their oldest sons. These reforms, like others, did not last long after Napoleon gained power.

**Setbacks.** As the revolution progressed, women's right to express their views in public came under fire. In 1793, a committee of the National Convention declared that women did not have "the moral and physical strength necessary to practice political rights." Women's revolutionary clubs were banned.

Among the many women who became victims of the Terror were republicans like Gouges and moderates like Roland. As she mounted the steps to the guillotine, Roland cried, "O liberty, what crimes are committed in your name!"

## Changes in Daily Life

By 1799, the 10-year-old French Revolution had dramatically changed France. It had dislodged the old social order, overthrown the monarchy, and brought the Church under state control.

New symbols such as the red "liberty caps" and the tricolor confirmed the liberty and equality of all male citizens. Elaborate fashions and powdered wigs gave way to the practical clothes and simple haircuts of the sans-culottes. To show their revolutionary spirit, enthusiastic parents gave their children names like Constitution, Republic, or August Tenth.

**Nationalism.** Revolution and war gave people a strong sense of national identity. In earlier times, people had felt loyalty to local authorities. As monarchs centralized power, loyalty shifted to the king or queen. Now, the government rallied sons and daughters of the revolution to defend the nation itself. Nationalism, an aggressive feeling of pride in and devotion to one's country, spread throughout France.

By 1793, France was a nation in arms. From the port city of Marseilles (mahr SAY), troops marched to a rousing new song:

66Come, children of the fatherland,
The glorious day has arrived.
Against us the bloody banner
Of tyranny is raised.
To arms, citizens!
Join the battalions.
Let us march, let us march!99

"La Marseillaise" (mahr say EHZ) would later become the French national anthem.

**Social reform.** Revolutionaries pushed for social reform, such as compulsory elementary education. The Convention set up state schools to replace religious ones and organized systems to help the poor or care for old soldiers and war widows. The government also abolished slavery in French West Indian colonies and extended religious toleration.

The Convention tried to de-Christianize France. It created a secular calendar with 1793 as the Year I of the new era of freedom. It banned many religious festivals, replacing them with secular celebrations. Huge public ceremonies boosted support for republican and nationalist ideals.

**The arts.** French arts moved toward a grand classical style that echoed the grandeur of ancient Rome. The leading artist of the period was Jacques Louis David (dah VEED). David immortalized such stirring events as the Tennis Court Oath and, later, the reign of Napoleon. (See the painting on page 495.) David's paintings helped shape the way future generations pictured the French Revolution.

## SECTION 3 REVIEW

1. **Identify** (a) Committee of Public Safety, (b) Maximilien Robespierre, (c) Directory, (d) Olympe de Gouges, (e) "La Marseillaise," (f) Jacques Louis David.
2. **Define** (a) suffrage, (b) nationalism.
3. (a) Why did revolutionaries fear that the revolution was in danger? (b) What was their response to that danger?
4. What were three results of the Reign of Terror?
5. Describe one effect of the French Revolution on each of the following: (a) daily life, (b) the arts, (c) the rights of women.
6. *Critical Thinking* **Defending a Position** Robespierre wrote, "Terror without virtue is fatal. Virtue without terror is powerless. Terror is nothing but prompt, severe, and unbending justice." Do you agree that the Reign of Terror was necessary to defend the republic? Why or why not?
7. *ACTIVITY* Create a poster that might have been used to support or oppose *one* of the following: the goals of the Jacobins; the execution of Louis XVI or Marie Antoinette; the policies of the Committee of Public Safety; French nationalism; equal rights for women.

# 4 The Age of Napoleon Begins

## Guide for Reading

■ How did Napoleon gain power?

■ What role did Napoleon play in furthering the French Revolution?

■ How did Napoleon build and defend his empire?

■ **Vocabulary** *plebiscite, annex, blockade*

66He was like an expert chess player, with the human race for an opponent, which he proposed to checkmate.99

Thus did Madame Germaine de Staël (STAHL), a celebrated writer and intellectual, describe Napoleon Bonaparte. Napoleon himself expressed a humbler view of his rise to power. "Nothing has been simpler than my elevation," he once observed. "It is owing to the peculiarities of the time."

From 1799 to 1815, Napoleon would dominate France and Europe. A hero to some, an evil force to others, he gave his name to the final phase of the revolution—the age of Napoleon.

## *The Man From Corsica*

Napoleon Buonaparte (as he once spelled his name) was born on the French-ruled island of Corsica in the Mediterranean. His family were minor nobles, but had little money. At age nine, he was sent to France to be trained for a military career. When the revolution broke out, he was an ambitious 20-year-old lieutenant, eager to make a name for himself.

Napoleon favored the Jacobins and republican rule. However, he found the conflicting ideas and clashing personalities of the revolution confusing. He wrote his brother in 1793:

66Since one must take sides, one might as well choose the side that is victorious, the side which devastates, loots, and burns. Considering the alternative, it is better to eat than be eaten.99

**Napoleon Crossing the Alps** *This portrait by Jacques Louis David glorifies Napoleon as a military hero. His fame as a general helped Napoleon become emperor. When a government is weak, he commented, the people look for a genius to save the country. Once they find him, "a great people, thronging around him, seems exultingly to proclaim, 'This is the man.'"* **Impact of the Individual** *Why do you think other French soldiers are barely visible in this painting?*

**Early successes.** During the turmoil of the revolution, he rose quickly in the army. In December 1793, he drove British forces out of the French port of Toulon (too LOHN). He then went on to win several dazzling victories against the Austrians, capturing most of northern Italy and forcing the Hapsburg emperor to make peace. Hoping to disrupt British trade with India, he led a colorful expedition to Egypt in 1798. The Egyptian campaign proved disastrous, but Napoleon managed to hide stories of the worst losses from his admirers in France.

Success fed his ambition. By 1799, he moved from victorious general to political leader. That year, he helped overthrow the weak Directory and set up a three-man governing board, the Consulate. Another constitution was drawn up, but Napoleon soon took the title First Consul. In 1802, he had himself named consul for life.

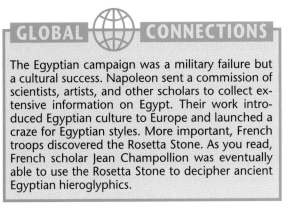

**GLOBAL CONNECTIONS**

The Egyptian campaign was a military failure but a cultural success. Napoleon sent a commission of scientists, artists, and other scholars to collect extensive information on Egypt. Their work introduced Egyptian culture to Europe and launched a craze for Egyptian styles. More important, French troops discovered the Rosetta Stone. As you read, French scholar Jean Champollion was eventually able to use the Rosetta Stone to decipher ancient Egyptian hieroglyphics.

**A self-made emperor.** Two years later, Napoleon had accumulated enough power into his hands to take the title Emperor of the French. He invited the pope to preside over his coronation at Notre Dame cathedral in Paris. During the ceremony, however, Napoleon took the crown from the pope's hands and placed it on his own head. By this action, Napoleon meant to show that he owed his throne to no one but himself.

Yet at each step on his rise to power, Napoleon had held a plebiscite (PLEHB ih sīt), or ballot in which voters say yes or no to an issue. Each time, the French strongly supported him. To understand why, we must look at his policies.

## France Under Napoleon

During the consulate and empire, Napoleon consolidated power, strengthening the central government. Order, security, and efficiency replaced liberty, equality, and fraternity as the slogans of the new regime.

# CAUSE AND EFFECT

## Long-Term Causes

Corrupt, inconsistent, and insensitive leadership
Prosperous members of Third Estate resent privileges of First and Second estates
Spread of Enlightenment ideas

## Immediate Causes

Huge government debt
Poor harvests and rising price of bread
Failure of Louis XVI to accept financial reforms
Formation of National Assembly
Storming of Bastille

## THE FRENCH REVOLUTION

## Immediate Effects

France adopts its first written constitution
French feudalism ends
Declaration of the Rights of Man and the Citizen adopted
Monarchy abolished
Revolutionary France fights coalition of European powers
Reign of Terror

## Long-Term Effects

Napoleon gains power
Napoleonic Code established
French conquests spark nationalism
French public schools set up

## Connections Today

French people remain proud of Napoleon's glory days
French law reflects Napoleonic Code
Metric system, set up after revolution, in use worldwide
After centuries of power, French political and military influence declines in Europe

*Interpreting a Chart* Once it began, the French Revolution moved swiftly. Its long-term causes, however, had been building up for decades. ■ Why is the rise of Napoleon considered a long-term effect rather than an immediate effect?

**Reforms.** To restore prosperity, Napoleon modernized finance. He regulated the economy to control prices, encourage new industry, and build roads and canals. To ensure well-trained officials and military officers, he promoted a system of public schools under strict government control.

At the same time, Napoleon backed off from some social reforms of the revolution. He made peace with the Catholic Church in the Concordat of 1801. The Concordat kept the Church under state control but recognized religious freedom for Catholics. Revolutionaries who opposed the Church denounced the agreement, but Catholics welcomed it.

Napoleon won support across class lines. He encouraged émigrés to return, provided they took an oath of loyalty. Peasants were relieved when he recognized their right to lands they had bought from Church and nobles during the revolution. The middle class, who had benefited most from the revolution, approved Napoleon's economic reforms and the restoration of order after years of chaos. Napoleon also made all "careers open to talent," a popular policy among those who remembered the old aristocratic monopoly of power. Napoleon's chief opposition came from royalists on the right and republicans on the left.

**Napoleonic Code.** Among Napoleon's most lasting reforms was a new law code, popularly called the Napoleonic Code. It embodied Enlightenment principles such as the equality of all citizens before the law, religious toleration, and advancement based on merit.

But the Napoleonic Code undid some reforms of the French Revolution. Women, for example, lost most of their newly gained rights under the new code. The law considered women minors who could not exercise the rights of citizenship. Male heads of households regained complete authority over their wives and children. Again, Napoleon valued order and authority over individual rights.

## Subduing an Empire

From 1804 to 1814, Napoleon furthered his reputation on the battlefield. He successfully faced down the combined forces of the greatest European powers. Year after year, he marshaled the military might of France to field enormous armies. He took great risks and even suffered huge losses. "I grew up on the field of battle," he once said, "and a man such as I am cares little for the life of a million men." By 1810, his Grand Empire reached its greatest extent. "We are babes in the hands of a giant," sighed Czar Alexander I of Russia.

As a military leader, Napoleon valued rapid movements and made effective use of his large armies. He developed a new plan for each battle, so opposing generals could never anticipate what he would do next. His enemies paid tribute to his leadership. Napoleon's presence on the battlefield, said one, was "worth 40,000 troops." The map on the right highlights Napoleon's most celebrated strategic victory, the Battle of Austerlitz.

**The Grand Empire.** Napoleon redrew the map of Europe. He annexed, or added outright, some areas to France, including the Netherlands and Belgium as well as parts of Italy and Germany. He abolished the tottering Holy Roman Empire and created a 38-member Confederation of the Rhine under French protection. He cut Prussian territory in half, turning part of old Poland into the Grand Duchy of Warsaw. And he forced alliances on European powers from Madrid to Moscow. At various times, the rulers of Austria, Prussia, and Russia reluctantly signed treaties with the "Corsican upstart," as his enemies called him. (See the map on page 499.)

Napoleon put friends and family members on the thrones of Europe. He unseated the king of Spain and placed his own brother, Joseph Bonaparte, on the throne. Napoleon also divorced his wife, Josephine, to marry a Hapsburg princess, the niece of Marie Antoinette. He and his heirs could then claim kinship with the ancient ruling families of Europe.

**France versus Britain.** Britain alone remained outside Napoleon's European empire. With only a small army, Britain relied on its sea power to stop Napoleon's drive to rule the continent. In 1805, Napoleon prepared to invade England. But at the Battle of Trafalgar, fought off the southwest coast of Spain, British admiral Horatio Nelson smashed a French fleet. During the battle, Nelson was fatally shot by a French sniper but lived long enough to learn of the

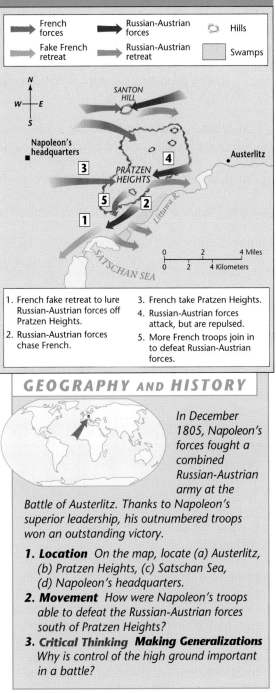

## Battle of Austerlitz, 1805

| → French forces | → Russian-Austrian forces | Hills |
| → Fake French retreat | → Russian-Austrian retreat | Swamps |

1. French fake retreat to lure Russian-Austrian forces off Pratzen Heights.
2. Russian-Austrian forces chase French.
3. French take Pratzen Heights.
4. Russian-Austrian forces attack, but are repulsed.
5. More French troops join in to defeat Russian-Austrian forces.

### GEOGRAPHY AND HISTORY

In December 1805, Napoleon's forces fought a combined Russian-Austrian army at the Battle of Austerlitz. Thanks to Napoleon's superior leadership, his outnumbered troops won an outstanding victory.

1. **Location** On the map, locate (a) Austerlitz, (b) Pratzen Heights, (c) Satschan Sea, (d) Napoleon's headquarters.
2. **Movement** How were Napoleon's troops able to defeat the Russian-Austrian forces south of Pratzen Heights?
3. **Critical Thinking** *Making Generalizations* Why is control of the high ground important in a battle?

British victory. His last words were, "Thank God, I have done my duty."

With an invasion ruled out, Napoleon tried to strike at Britain's lifeblood, its commerce. He waged economic warfare through the Continental System, which closed European ports to British goods. Britain responded with its own blockade of European ports. A blockade involves shutting off ports to keep people or supplies from moving in or out. During their long struggle, both Britain and France seized neutral ships suspected of trading with the other side. British attacks on American ships sparked anger in the United States and eventually triggered the War of 1812.

**Successes and failures.** In the end, Napoleon's Continental System failed to bring Britain to its knees. Although British exports declined, its powerful navy kept open vital trade routes to the Americas and India. Meanwhile, restrictions on trade hurt Europe, created a scarcity of goods, and sent prices soaring. Resentful European merchants ignored Napoleon's ban on British goods and engaged in widespread smuggling.

Still, for years the French celebrated unforgettable successes. Napoleon's triumphs boosted French nationalism. Great victory parades filled the streets of Paris with cheering crowds. To this day the glory and grandeur of the age of Napoleon are a source of pride to many French citizens.

## SECTION 4 REVIEW

1. **Identify** (a) Consulate, (b) Concordat of 1801, (c) Napoleonic Code, (d) Battle of Trafalgar, (e) Confederation of the Rhine, (f) Continental System.
2. **Define** (a) plebiscite, (b) annex, (c) blockade.
3. (a) Describe Napoleon Bonaparte's rise to power. (b) Why did many French support him?
4. How did Napoleon's policies both extend and turn back the reforms of the French Revolution? Give examples.
5. (a) How did Napoleon come to dominate most of Europe? (b) Why did his efforts to subdue Britain fail?
6. **Critical Thinking** **Drawing Conclusions** Why do you think both royalists and republicans opposed Napoleon?
7. *ACTIVITY* Draw a political cartoon commenting on the rivalry between Britain and Napoleonic France, from either a British or French point of view.

## 5 The End of an Era

### Guide for Reading

■ What events led to Napoleon's downfall?

■ What principles guided leaders at the Congress of Vienna?

■ How did the Congress of Vienna seek to impose a new order on Europe?

■ **Vocabulary** *guerrilla warfare, abdicate, legitimacy*

Napoleon watched the battle for the Russian city of Smolensk from a chair outside his tent. As fires lit up the walled city, he exclaimed;

"It's like Vesuvius erupting. Don't you think this is a beautiful sight?"

"Horrible, Sire," replied an aide.

"Bah!" snorted Napoleon. "Remember, gentlemen, what a Roman emperor said: 'The corpse of an enemy always smells sweet.'"

In 1812, Napoleon pursued his dream of empire by invading Russia. The campaign began a chain of events that eventually led to his downfall. Napoleon's final defeat brought an end to the era of the French Revolution.

### Challenges to Napoleon's Empire

Under Napoleon, French armies spread the ideas of the revolution across Europe. They backed liberal reforms in the lands they conquered. In some places, they helped install revolutionary governments that abolished titles of nobility, ended Church privileges, opened careers to men of talent, and ended serfdom and manorial dues. The Napoleonic Code, too, was carried across Europe. French occupation sometimes brought economic benefits as well, by reducing trade barriers and stimulating industry.

Yet Napoleon's successes contained the seeds of defeat. While nationalism spurred French armies to success, it worked against them, too. Many Europeans who welcomed the ideas of the French Revolution nevertheless saw Napoleon's armies as foreign oppressors. They

# Napoleon's Power in Europe, 1812

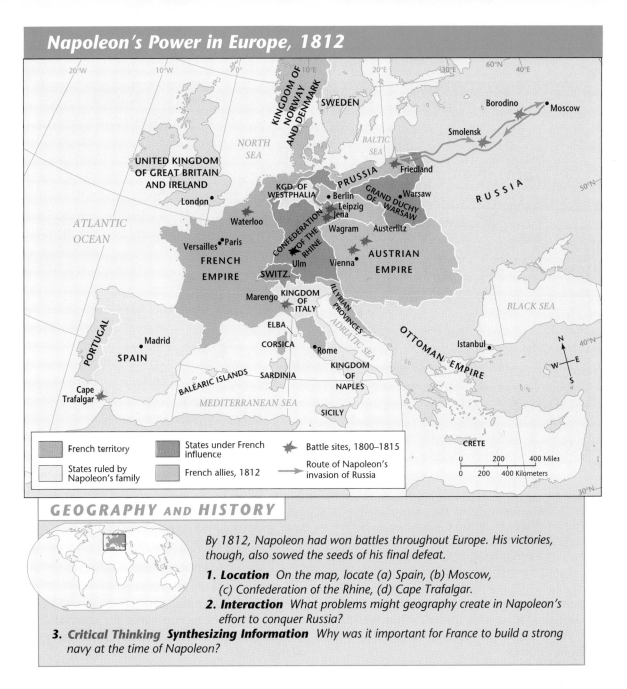

## GEOGRAPHY AND HISTORY

By 1812, Napoleon had won battles throughout Europe. His victories, though, also sowed the seeds of his final defeat.

1. **Location** On the map, locate (a) Spain, (b) Moscow, (c) Confederation of the Rhine, (d) Cape Trafalgar.
2. **Interaction** What problems might geography create in Napoleon's effort to conquer Russia?
3. **Critical Thinking** **Synthesizing Information** Why was it important for France to build a strong navy at the time of Napoleon?

---

resented the Continental System and Napoleon's effort to impose French culture.

From Rome to Madrid to the Netherlands, nationalism unleashed revolts against France. In the German states, leaders encouraged national loyalty among German-speaking people to counter French influence.

**Resistance in Spain.** Resistance to foreign rule bled French occupying forces in Spain. In 1808, Napoleon replaced the king of Spain with his own brother, Joseph Bonaparte. He also introduced liberal reforms that sought to undermine the Spanish Catholic Church. But many Spaniards remained loyal to their former king and devoted to the Church. When they resisted the invaders, well-armed French forces responded with brutal repression. Far from crushing resistance, the French reaction further inflamed Spanish nationalism.

Spanish patriots conducted a campaign of guerrilla warfare, or hit-and-run raids, against the French. (In Spanish, *guerrilla* means "little war.") Small bands ambushed French supply trains or troops before melting into the countryside. These attacks kept large numbers of French soldiers tied down in Spain, when

**The Third of May, 1808** *This painting by the Spanish artist Francisco Goya shows the execution of Spaniards by Napoleon's troops. The man about to be shot throws out his arms, a martyr for the cause of liberty. The faceless French soldiers embody the inhumanity of war. Artists like Goya shifted away from the heroic, classical style of Jacques Louis David toward more emotional scenes.* **Art and Literature** *Why do you think Goya painted the scene as taking place at night? What effect does the lantern create?*

Napoleon needed them elsewhere. Eventually, the British sent an army under Arthur Wellesley, later the Duke of Wellington, to help the Spanish fight France.

**Defeat in Russia.** Despite revolts in Spain and elsewhere, Napoleon continued to seek new conquests. In 1812, Alexander I of Russia resigned from the Continental System. Napoleon responded by assembling his Grand Army. About 600,000 soldiers from France and other countries invaded Russia.

To avoid battles with Napoleon, the Russians retreated eastward, burning crops and villages as they went. This "scorched earth" policy left the French hungry and cold as winter came. Napoleon entered Moscow in September. He realized, though, that he could not feed and supply his army through the long Russian winter. In October, he turned homeward.

The 1,000-mile retreat from Moscow turned into a desperate battle for survival. The French general Michel Ney described the grim scene:

66The army marches covered in great snowflakes. The stragglers fall to the lances of the Cossacks. As for me, I cover the retreat. Behind files the army with broken ranks. It is a mob without purpose, famished, feverish. . . . General Famine and General Winter, rather than the Russian bullets, have conquered the Grand Army.99

Only about 100,000 soldiers of the once-proud Grand Army survived. Many died. Others deserted. Napoleon himself rushed back to Paris to raise a new force to defend France. His reputation for success, however, was shattered.

## Downfall of Napoleon

The disaster in Russia brought a new alliance of Russia, Britain, Austria, and Prussia against a weakened France. In 1813, they defeated Napoleon in the Battle of the Nations at Leipzig. The next year, as his enemies closed in on France, Napoleon abdicated, or stepped down from power. The victors exiled him to Elba, an island in the Mediterranean. They then recognized Louis XVIII, brother of Louis XVI, as king of France.

**Napoleon returns.** The restoration of Louis XVIII did not go smoothly. The Bourbon king agreed to accept the Napoleonic Code and honor the land settlements made during the revolution. However, many émigrés rushed back to France bent on revenge. An economic depression and the fear of a return to the old regime helped rekindle loyalty to Napoleon.

As the victorious allies gathered for a general peace conference in Vienna, Napoleon escaped his island exile and returned to France. Soldiers flocked to his banner. As citizens cheered Napoleon's advance, Louis XVIII fled. In March 1815, the emperor of the French entered Paris in triumph.

**Waterloo.** Napoleon's triumph was short-lived. His star soared for only 100 days, while the allies reassembled their forces. On June 18, 1815, the opposing armies met near the town of Waterloo in Belgium. British forces under the Duke of Wellington and a Prussian army commanded by General Blücher crushed the French in an agonizing day-long battle. Once again, Napoleon was forced to abdicate and go into exile on St. Helena, a lonely island in the South Atlantic. This time, he would never return.

**Legacy of Napoleon.** Napoleon died in 1821, but his legend lived on in France and around the world. His contemporaries as well as historians have long debated his legacy. Was he "the revolution on horseback," as he claimed? Or was he a traitor to the revolution?

No one, though, questions Napoleon's impact on France and on Europe. The Napoleonic Code consolidated many changes of the revolution. The France of Napoleon was a centralized state with a constitution. Elections were held with expanded, though limited, suffrage. Many more citizens had rights to property and access

*Retreat From Moscow* This British cartoon depicts Napoleon's retreat from Moscow. Hundreds of thousands of French soldiers died during their long trek across Russia's frozen landscape. *Global Interaction* Why do you think this cartoonist made light of the suffering of Napoleon's army?

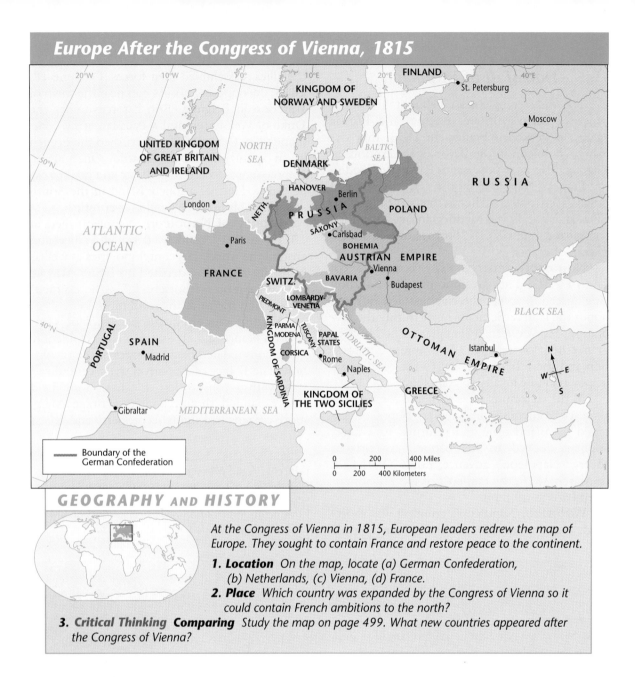

# Europe After the Congress of Vienna, 1815

Boundary of the German Confederation

0    200    400 Miles
0    200    400 Kilometers

## GEOGRAPHY AND HISTORY

At the Congress of Vienna in 1815, European leaders redrew the map of Europe. They sought to contain France and restore peace to the continent.

1. **Location** On the map, locate (a) German Confederation, (b) Netherlands, (c) Vienna, (d) France.
2. **Place** Which country was expanded by the Congress of Vienna so it could contain French ambitions to the north?
3. **Critical Thinking** **Comparing** Study the map on page 499. What new countries appeared after the Congress of Vienna?

to education than under the old regime. Still, French citizens lost many rights promised so fervently by republicans during the Convention.

On the world stage, Napoleon's conquests spread the ideas of the revolution. He failed to make Europe into a French empire. Instead, he sparked nationalist feeling across Europe. The abolition of the Holy Roman Empire would eventually help in creating a new Germany. Napoleon also had a dramatic impact across the Atlantic. In 1803, his decision to sell France's vast Louisiana Territory to the American government doubled the size of the United States and ushered in an age of American expansion.

## The Congress of Vienna

After Waterloo, diplomats and heads of state again sat down at the Congress of Vienna. They faced the monumental task of restoring stability and order in Europe after 25 years of war.

**Glittering spectacle.** The Congress met for 10 months, from September 1814 to June 1815. It was a brilliant gathering of European leaders. Diplomats, courtiers, and royalty dined and danced, attended concerts and ballets, and enjoyed hunting parties and picnics arranged by their host, Emperor Francis I of Austria. Beneath the glittering spectacle, paid spies slipped in and out of rented palaces, anxious to find out who was saying what to whom.

**Serious work.** While the entertainment kept thousands of smaller players busy, the real work fell to Prince Clemens von Metternich of Austria, Czar Alexander I of Russia, and Lord Robert Castlereagh (KAS uhl ray) of Britain. Defeated France was also invited to send a representative to Vienna, Prince Maurice Talleyrand.

The chief goal of the Vienna decision makers was to create a lasting peace by establishing a balance of power and protecting the system of monarchy. Each of the leaders also pursued his own goals. Metternich, the dominant figure at the Congress, wanted to restore the *status quo* (Latin for "the way things are") of 1792. Alexander I urged a "holy alliance" of Christian monarchs to suppress future revolutions. Lord Castlereagh was determined to prevent a revival of French military power. The aged diplomat Talleyrand shrewdly played the other leaders against one another to get defeated France accepted as an equal partner.

### *The Vienna Settlement*

Despite clashes and controversies, the diplomats at Vienna finally worked out a framework for peace. Their decisions set the stage for European politics for the next 100 years.

**Balance of power.** The peacemakers redrew the map of Europe. (See the map on page 502.) To contain French ambitions, they ringed France with strong countries. In the north, they added Belgium and Luxembourg to Holland to create the kingdom of the Netherlands. To prevent French expansion eastward, they gave Prussia lands along the Rhine River. They also allowed Austria to reassert control over northern Italy. This policy of containment proved fairly successful in maintaining the peace.

**Stability.** To turn back the clock to 1792, the architects of the peace promoted the principle of legitimacy, restoring hereditary monarchies that the French Revolution or Napoleon had unseated. Even before the Congress began, they had put Louis XVIII on the French throne. Later, they restored "legitimate" monarchs in Portugal, Spain, and the Italian states.

To protect the new order, Metternich pushed to create the Concert of Europe, a peacekeeping organization. It included all of the major European states. Leaders pledged to maintain the balance of power and to suppress any uprisings inspired by the ideas of the French Revolution.

**Problems of the peace.** The Vienna statesmen achieved their immediate goals. However, they failed to foresee how powerful new forces such as nationalism would shake the foundations of Europe. They redrew national boundaries without any concern for national cultures.

In Germany, they created a loosely organized German Confederation with Austria as its official head. But Germans who had battled Napoleon were already dreaming of a strong united German nation. Their dream would not come true for more than 50 years, but the story of German unification began in this period.

**Looking ahead.** Many people inspired by revolutionary ideals condemned the Vienna settlement. Still, the general peace lasted for a hundred years. Europe would not see war on a Napoleonic scale until 1914.

Yet the ideals of the French Revolution were not destroyed. In the next decades, its slogan and goals would inspire people in Europe and Latin America to seek equality and liberty. (See Chapter 21.) The spirit of nationalism ignited by Napoleon remained a powerful force.

## SECTION 5 REVIEW

1. **Identify** (a) Waterloo, (b) Clemens von Metternich, (c) Concert of Europe.
2. **Define** (a) guerrilla warfare, (b) abdicate, (c) legitimacy.
3. How did Napoleon's success contain the seeds of his defeat?
4. (a) What were the chief goals of the Congress of Vienna? (b) Describe three actions taken to achieve these goals.
5. *Critical Thinking* **Drawing Conclusions** Do you agree that Napoleon was "the revolution on horseback"? Why or why not?
6. *ACTIVITY* Imagine that it is 1816 and you are Napoleon, Metternich, or a former French revolutionary. Write a letter in which you evaluate the events of the last 30 years.

# Skills for Success

**Critical Thinking**  **Writing and Researching**  **Maps, Charts, and Graphs**  **Speaking and Listening**

## Identifying Relevant Facts

When researching a specific topic, students of history must wade through a large amount of information. Then, they must make decisions regarding which facts are relevant. Relevant information can be defined as information that has a clear and significant relationship to the subject under investigation. Information that provides examples, details, facts, and reasons about a topic or issue is relevant.

In gathering information about a topic or issue, historians begin to recognize key words, key people, key locations, and key dates. They make a mental or written list of key terms and skim through sources of information to see if any of these terms appears. In this way, they are able to locate relevant information quickly and efficiently.

Imagine that you are preparing a paper about the Reign of Terror. Look at the information on the right, and then answer the following questions.

**1** **Decide which information provides *examples* and *details* relevant to the topic under discussion.** (a) Which statement illustrates that the Committee of Public Safety ruled with almost dictatorial powers? (b) Is statement L relevant to the topic of the Reign of Terror? Explain. (c) Is statement B relevant to the topic? Explain.

**2** **Review information to see if it provides *background* and *reasons* relating to the topic.** (a) Which statements provide reasons why the Reign of Terror began and why it came to an end? (b) What facts does statement D contain? Is it relevant to the topic? Explain.

**3** **Draw conclusions about the relevance of the information.** (a) What are some key words, names, and dates that appear in the statements that are relevant to the Reign of Terror? (b) Which statements would be relevant to a discussion of the rise and fall of Napoleon? (c) Which statements would be relevant to a discussion of the effects of the revolution?

***Beyond the Classroom*** Make a list of your hobbies or extracurricular interests. Look through several newspapers and magazines for articles relevant to your interests. Circle any statements that contain examples, reasons, facts, and details about your hobbies or interests.

---

**TOPIC: *The Reign of Terror***

**A.** By 1794, supporters of the revolution began to question the need for constant executions. In July, Robespierre was arrested and executed.

**B.** The revolution transformed daily life in France. Society became more democratic and most feudal customs were abolished.

**C.** In the face of domestic and foreign threats, the National Convention took drastic action. It set aside the constitution and created a Committee of Public Safety with almost dictatorial powers.

**D.** Napoleon found that many people were dissatisfied with the Directory. With the help of troops loyal to him, Bonaparte and two directors overthrew the government in 1799.

**E.** By the 1770s, the economic situation in France began to deteriorate. Attempts to turn the economy around failed in part because of the resistance of the nobles and in part because King Louis XVI was a weak ruler.

**F.** The National Assembly abolished feudalism and introduced sweeping religious reforms.

**G.** The French Revolution began in 1789 when peasants and workers became frustrated by the government's inaction.

**H.** The campaign known as the Reign of Terror lasted from July 1793 to July 1794.

**I.** In 1814, Napoleon's enemies invaded France, forcing the emperor to abdicate.

**J.** Maximilien Robespierre led the Committee of Public Safety during the Reign of Terror.

**K.** To uncover traitors, the Committee of Public Safety sent agents across France. Traitors were tried and, if found guilty, sent to the guillotine.

**L.** Between 20,000 and 40,000 French people were executed.

# CHAPTER 19 REVIEW

## Building Vocabulary

Select *five* vocabulary words from the chapter. Write each word on a separate slip of paper. Then, write the definition for each word on other slips of paper. Scramble the slips and exchange them with another student. Match the words with their definitions, and then check each other's results.

## Reviewing Chapter Themes

1. **Political and Social Systems** (a) Why were many French dissatisfied with the ancien regime? (b) Describe one major political or social reform that emerged during *each* of the four phases of the French Revolution.
2. **Religions and Value Systems** (a) What role did Enlightenment values and ideas play in the French Revolution? (b) How did the leaders of the revolution try to encourage revolutionary values in everyday life?
3. **Impact of the Individual** Describe four ways that the career of Napoleon Bonaparte affected France and Europe.
4. **Continuity and Change** (a) How did the Congress of Vienna attempt to turn back the effects of the French Revolution? (b) In what ways did this attempt fail?

## Thinking Critically

1. **Analyzing Primary Sources** Looking back at the events leading to the revolution, a French noble wrote, "The most striking of the country's troubles was the chaos in its finances, the result of years of extravagance intensified by the expense of the American War of Independence. . . . No one could think of any remedy, except to search for fresh funds as the old ones were exhausted." (a) Does this statement accurately describe the situation in France in 1789? (b) How does the writer seem to feel about it? (c) Do you agree that the financial crisis was the main cause of the revolution? Explain. (★ See *Skills for Success*, page 154.)
2. **Defending a Position** The Declaration of the Rights of Man has been called the "death certificate" of the old regime. Do you agree? Why or why not?

3. **Analyzing Literature** Reread the two passages by William Wordsworth on pages 488 and 492. (a) What mood does Wordsworth express in the first passage? (b) What mood does he express in the second passage? (c) What accounts for the change in Wordsworth's attitude toward the French Revolution? (★ See *Skills for Success*, page 234.)
4. **Comparing** Review Chapter 17, pages 432–433. (a) In what ways were the English Civil War and the French Revolution similar? (b) In what ways were they different? (c) Which do you think was more radical? Why?
5. **Linking Past and Present** Most historians agree that the French Revolution was a great turning point in European history. What events and ideas that emerged during the French Revolution are still a part of our political and social views today?

### For Your Portfolio

Your class has been asked to produce a public television documentary series on the French Revolution. Your assignment is to work with a crew of four students to prepare one of the segments.

1. Choose from one of these topics: The Way It Was, The Outbreak of the Revolution, A Moderate Start, The Radicals Take Over, The Rise and Fall of Napoleon, or Peace Again.
2. Review the relevant pages in your textbook and consult library resources for additional research on your segment. You will also want to note documents, photographs, maps, and other visuals that can be used in the documentary.
3. Decide on the kinds of elements you might include. Some possibilities include interviews, commentary, reenactments, and quotations from people or publications of the time. If possible, view sample documentaries to see how they are assembled.
4. Work with your crew to write your segment. Indicate in the script which visuals are to be used at what points. (Your teacher may ask you to videotape a rough version of your segment.)
5. Present your segment to the class. Follow it up with a discussion of the content.

# The Industrial Revolution Begins

## (1750–1850)

### CHAPTER OUTLINE

1  **Dawn of the Industrial Age**
2  **Britain Leads the Way**
3  **Hardships of Early Industrial Life**
4  **New Ways of Thinking**

On September 15, 1830, an excited crowd gathered at the bustling seaport of Liverpool, England. They had come to celebrate the opening of the Liverpool & Manchester, the world's first public steam-operated railway.

The 600 specially invited guests climbed aboard the gaily decorated trains. The engineer signaled that all was ready. Slowly, the shiny locomotives moved out of the station.

About halfway along the route, the locomotives stopped to take on water. Several passengers climbed down to get a closer look at the engines. Among them was William Huskisson, president of Britain's Board of Trade.

Suddenly, another locomotive steamed up the track. Startled guests clambered to safety. "Huskisson! For God's sake, get to your place!" shouted someone. But in his hurry, Huskisson stumbled and fell. The approaching engine ran him over and crushed his leg.

Stunned passengers lifted the injured man onto another train. The rescue locomotive roared to the nearest town. But despite a doctor's efforts, Huskisson died of his wounds.

The tragedy took the joy out of the occasion. Still, people noted the amazing speed attained by the engine carrying the wounded Huskisson. An astonished observer reported:

> 66 The . . . engine conveyed the wounded
> body of the unfortunate gentleman
> a distance of about 15 miles in 25 minutes, or at the rate of 36 miles an hour.
> This incredible speed burst upon the
> world with the effect of a new and
> unlooked-for phenomenon. 99

Despite the sad events of opening day, investors flocked to the new railroad. Soon railroads were sprouting everywhere, creating fabulous fortunes for builders and speeding people and goods to distant destinations.

Steam-powered railroads were part of the enormous transformation known as the Industrial Revolution. The Industrial Revolution refers to the shift of production from simple hand tools to complex machines, and from human and animal power to steam power.

The Industrial Revolution was a crucial turning point in history. The changes that began in Western Europe 250 years ago have spread around the globe. In this chapter we will look at the early Industrial Revolution in its birthplace in Britain, from about 1750 to 1850.

**FOCUS ON** these questions as you read:

■ **Continuity and Change**
How did the Industrial Revolution transform traditional ways of life?

■ **Economics and Technology**
What role did capital and technology play in the Industrial Revolution?

■ **Impact of the Individual**
How did individual contributions shape the industrial age?

■ **Political and Social Systems**
Why did new social and political philosophies develop during the industrial age?

### TIME AND PLACE

**An Industrial Town** *Iron and coal were key ingredients of the Industrial Revolution. Coal powered the steam engines in Europe's new factories. Iron was used in railroads, bridges, and machines. Here, blast furnaces, used to purify iron ore, light up the sky of an early industrial town.* **Continuity and Change** *Based on this picture, how do you think the Industrial Revolution changed the European landscape? Explain.*

## HUMANITIES LINK

*Art History* Joseph Wright, *An Iron Forge* (page 511).
*Literature* In this chapter, you will encounter passages from the following works of literature: Alfred, Lord Tennyson, "Ode Sung at the Opening of the International Exhibition" (page 510); Charles Dickens, *Hard Times* (page 516).

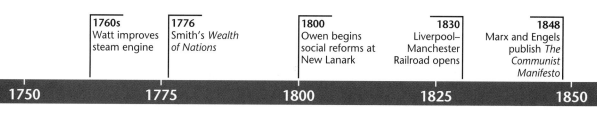

| **1760s** | **1776** | **1800** | **1830** | **1848** |
| Watt improves steam engine | Smith's *Wealth of Nations* | Owen begins social reforms at New Lanark | Liverpool–Manchester Railroad opens | Marx and Engels publish *The Communist Manifesto* |

1750     1775     1800     1825     1850

# 1 Dawn of the Industrial Age

## Guide for Reading

- What factors contributed to a second agricultural revolution?
- Why did populations soar in Europe?
- What energy sources powered the Industrial Revolution?
- **Vocabulary** *enclosure*

For thousands of years after the rise of civilization, most people lived and worked in small farming villages. A chain of events set in motion in the mid-1700s changed that way of life forever.

The Industrial Revolution started in Britain. Unlike most political revolutions, it was neither sudden nor swift. Instead, it was a long, slow, uneven process in which production shifted from simple hand tools to complex machines. New sources of power replaced human and animal power. In the 250 years since it began, the Industrial Revolution has spread from Britain to the rest of Europe and North America, and then around the globe.

## A Turning Point in History

In 1750, most people worked the land, using simple handmade tools. They lived in simple cottages lit by firelight and candles. They made their own clothes and grew their own food. In nearby towns, they might exchange goods at a weekly outdoor market.

Like their peasant ancestors, these people knew little of the world that existed beyond their village. The few who left home traveled only as far as their feet or a horse-drawn cart could take them. Those bold adventurers who dared to cross the seas were at the mercy of winds that filled billowing sails.

Then the Industrial Revolution began. For growing numbers of people, the rural way of life began to disappear. By the 1850s, many country villages had grown into industrial towns and cities. Their inhabitants bought food and clothing in stores that offered a large variety of machine-made goods. They worked indoors behind a counter, desk, or factory machine. Their homes were multistory tenements.

Industrial-age travelers moved rapidly by train or steamship. Urgent messages flew along telegraph wires. New inventions and scientific "firsts" poured out each year. Between 1845 and 1855, for example, an American dentist used an anesthetic for the first time, a French physicist measured the speed of light, and a German chemist developed the Bunsen burner. Elias Howe made the first sewing machine, and a Hungarian doctor introduced antiseptic methods to reduce the risk of women dying in childbirth.

Still more stunning changes occurred in the next century, creating our familiar world of skyscraper cities and carefully tended suburbs. Cars and televisions, air travel and antibiotics, and a mass of other goods and services made their appearance.

How and why did these great changes occur? Historians point to a series of interrelated causes that helped trigger the industrialization of the West.

## A New Agricultural Revolution

Oddly enough, the Industrial Revolution was made possible in part by a change in the farming fields of Western Europe. In Chapter 1, you read about an agricultural revolution some 11,000 years ago, when people learned to farm and domesticate animals. About 300 years ago, a second agricultural revolution took place. It greatly improved the quality and quantity of farm products.

**Improved methods of farming.** The Dutch led the way in the new agricultural revolution. In the 1600s, they built earthen walls known as dikes to reclaim land from the sea. They combined smaller fields into larger ones to

**ISSUES** *For* **TODAY**

The Industrial Revolution transformed the way people lived and worked. How does technology affect the way people live?

This four Wheel Drill Plow, with a Seed and a Manure Hopper, was first Invented in the Year 1745 and is now in Use with Wm Ellis at Little Gaddesden near Hempstead in Hertfordshire, where any person may View the same. It is so light that a Man may Draw it, but Generally drawn by a pony or little Horse —

**Improved Farm Machinery**
Jethro Tull's seed drill planted seeds in straight lines. Since crops planted this way grew in neat rows, they could be weeded with another new invention, the horse-drawn hoe, instead of by hand. **Continuity and Change** Does Tull's seed drill have anything in common with modern farm equipment? Explain.

make better use of the land and used fertilizer from livestock to renew the soil.

In the 1700s, British farmers expanded on Dutch experiments. Some farmers mixed different kinds of soils to get higher crop yields. Others tried out new methods of crop rotation. Lord Charles Townshend won the nickname "Turnip Townshend" for urging farmers to grow turnips, which restored exhausted soil. Jethro Tull invented a mechanical device, the seed drill, to aid farmers. It deposited seeds in rows rather than scattering them wastefully over the land. Another pioneer, Robert Bakewell, bred stronger horses for farmwork and fatter sheep and cattle for meat.

Educated farmers exchanged news of experiments through farm journals. King George III himself, nicknamed "Farmer George," wrote articles about his model farm near Windsor Castle.

**Enclosure movement.** Meanwhile, rich landowners pushed ahead with enclosure, the process of taking over and fencing off land formerly shared by peasant farmers. In the 1500s, they had enclosed land to gain pastures for sheep and increased wool output. By the 1700s, they wanted to replace the strip farms of medieval times with larger fields that could be cultivated more efficiently.

As millions of acres were enclosed, farm output rose. Profits also rose because large fields needed fewer people to work them. But such progress had a human cost. Many farm laborers were thrown out of work. Small farmers were forced off their land because they could not compete with large landholders. Villages shrank as cottagers left in search of work.

In time, jobless farmworkers migrated to towns and cities. There, they formed a growing labor force that would tend the machines of the Industrial Revolution.

## The Population Explosion

The agricultural revolution contributed to a rapid growth of population. This population explosion has continued, although today, the center of growth has shifted from the western world to developing nations outside Europe.

Precise population statistics for the 1700s are rare, but those that do exist are striking. Britain's population, for example, soared from about 5 million in 1700 to almost 9 million in 1800. The population of France rose from 18 million in 1715 to 26 million in 1789. The population of Europe as a whole shot up from roughly 120 million to about 190 million in the same period. Such growth was unlike any in earlier history. Yet in the 1800s, populations would climb still higher.

The population boom of the 1700s was due more to declining death rates than to rising birthrates. The agricultural revolution reduced the risk of famine. Because they ate better, women were healthier and had stronger babies. Some deadly diseases, such as bubonic plague, had faded away. In the 1800s, better hygiene and sanitation along with improved medical care further slowed deaths from disease.

## An Energy Revolution

A third factor that helped trigger the Industrial Revolution was an "energy revolution."

From the beginning of human history, the energy for work was provided mostly by the muscles of humans and animals. In time, water mills and windmills were added to muscle power.

In the 1700s, inventive minds found ways to use water power more efficiently. Giant water wheels powered machines in the first factories. People also harnessed new sources of energy. Among the most important was coal, used to develop the steam engine. In 1712, inventor Thomas Newcomen had developed a steam engine powered by coal to pump water out of mines. About 1769, James Watt improved on Newcomen's engine. Watt's steam engines would become the vital power source of the early Industrial Revolution.

Watt linked up with a shrewd partner, Matthew Boulton, who saw the potential of steam engines. He told the king of England:

66Your Majesty, I have at my disposal what the whole world demands: something which will uplift civilization more than ever by relieving man of all undignified drudgery. I have *steam power*.99

## SECTION 1 REVIEW

1. **Identify** (a) Charles Townshend, (b) Jethro Tull, (c) Robert Bakewell, (d) Thomas Newcomen, (e) James Watt.
2. **Define** enclosure.
3. How did each of the following affect agriculture in the 1700s and 1800s: (a) new farming methods, (b) mechanical inventions, (c) enclosure?
4. Identify three causes of the population explosion in Europe in the 1700s and 1800s.
5. (a) What role did the steam engine play in the Industrial Revolution? (b) What energy source powered the steam engine?
6. *Critical Thinking* **Recognizing Causes and Effects** What were the immediate and long-term effects of the agricultural revolution?
7. *ACTIVITY* Keep a log of your activities for one week. Next to each activity, indicate how it might have been different if you lived in the pre-industrial world.

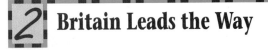

# 2 Britain Leads the Way

## Guide for Reading

■ Why was Britain the first nation to industrialize?

■ Why were coal and iron important to the industrial age?

■ How did industrialization change the textile industry?

■ **Vocabulary** *factory, turnpike*

Visitors crowded into London's Crystal Palace in 1851. The immense structure housed the Great Exhibition, a display of the "Works of Industry of all Nations." The palace itself was specially built for the occasion. A vast cavern of glass and iron, it symbolized the triumph of the industrial age.

This early world's fair, and a second one in 1862, offered an awesome array of machines, works of art, and other exhibits. Britain's leading poet, Alfred Tennyson, wrote:

66. . . lo! the giant aisles
    Rich in model and design;
    Harvest-tool and husbandry,
    Loom and wheel and enginery,
    Secrets of the sullen mine,
    Steel and gold, and coal and wine,
    Fabric rough or fairy-fine . . .
    And shapes and hues of Art divine!
    All of beauty, all of use
    That one fair planet can produce.99

In the century before the exhibitions, Britain had been the first nation to industrialize. Its success became the model for others, in Europe and around the world.

## *Why Britain?*

Why did the Industrial Revolution begin in Britain? Historians have identified a number of key factors that helped Britain take an early lead in industry.

**Natural resources.** Though a relatively small nation, Britain had large supplies of coal to power steam engines. It also had plentiful iron to build the new machines.

**Human resources.** A large number of workers were needed to mine the coal and iron, build the factories, and run the machines. The agricultural revolution of the 1600s and 1700s freed many men and women in Britain from farm labor. The population boom that resulted further swelled the available work force.

**New technology.** Britain had been a center of the Scientific Revolution, which had focused attention on the physical world and developed new devices for managing it. In the 1700s, Enlightenment thinkers promoted the idea of progress through technology. The *Encyclopedia* compiled by the French philosophe Diderot, for example, included articles on technology as well as on social and political reform. In the 1700s, Britain had plenty of skilled mechanics who were eager to meet the growing demand for new, practical inventions.

Technology was an important part of the Industrial Revolution, but it did not cause it. After all, other societies, such as the ancient Greeks or Chinese, had advanced technology for their time but did not move on to industrialization. Only when other necessary conditions existed, including demand and capital, did technology pave the way for industrialization.

**Economic conditions—capital and demand.** In the 1700s, trade from a growing overseas empire helped the British economy prosper. The business class accumulated capital, or wealth to invest in enterprises such as mines, railroads, and factories. (See page 467.) A large number of these entrepreneurs were ready to risk their capital in new ventures.

**An Iron Forge** In the late 1700s, most artists ignored the Industrial Revolution, which was changing the world around them. They thought that bleak factories and banging machinery were not proper subjects for art. But factory scenes fascinated English artist Joseph Wright, whose home town of Derby was a center of industry. In this painting, a giant hammer driven by a water wheel pounds a piece of white-hot iron. The red glow of the forge tints the faces of the master, his wife, and children. **Art and Literature** How are the children reacting to the sight of the forge?

At home, the population explosion boosted demand for goods. However, a growing population alone would not have resulted in increased production. General economic prosperity was also needed to enable not only the middle and upper classes but also artisans and farmers to afford the new consumer goods.

**Political and social conditions.** Britain had a stable government that supported economic growth. It built a strong navy to protect its empire and overseas trade. Although members of the upper class tended to look down on business and business people, they did not reject the great wealth produced by the new entrepreneurs.

# Technology of the British Industrial Revolution

| Invention | Description | Impact | Connections Today |
|---|---|---|---|
| **Improved steam engine** (James Watt) | Improved version of steam engine that used coal rather than water power. First used to pump water from mines and to forge iron. By the late 1780s, powered machines in cotton mills. | Steam engines provided power for early Industrial Revolution. They led to the factory system, early assembly lines, and rapidly growing production. | Steam engines are still used today to power giant ocean liners, pile drivers, and electric generators. |
| **Spinning mule** (Samuel Crompton) | Spinning device that combined the features of the spinning jenny, which made it possible to spin many threads at one time, and the water frame, which could produce strong cotton threads. | Produced stronger, finer thread; helped create demand for factories; supply of thread exceeded weavers' ability to use; this spurred invention of better weaving machines. | Today's spinning machines use computers to ensure strong and even threads. They can spin even the coarsest natural fibers, such as hemp and flax. |
| **Steam-powered locomotive** (George Stephenson) | Steam-powered vehicle used to pull a train. The "iron horse" moved faster and could haul heavier loads than a horse could. | Revolutionized transportation. Created demand for iron for rails and trains; created jobs building and running railroads; linked people far and wide. | Railroads, powered by electricity and diesel fuel, carry tons of freight and millions of passengers each year. High-speed passenger trains in Europe and Japan can reach 185 mph. |
| **Dynamo** (Michael Faraday) | Electric generator that worked by rotating a coil of wire between the poles of a magnet, which created electric current. | Development of electric power was critical to later industrial developments. By late 1800s, other inventors had found ways to use electric power to run machines and light up whole cities. | All electric generators and transformers work on the principle of Faraday's dynamo. In the 1990s, the U.S., Russia, and China together produced and used 42 percent of the world's total electric power. |

**Interpreting a Chart** *Beginning in the mid-1700s, inventors in Britain applied scientific principles to practical problems. The technological advances that they made helped trigger the Industrial Revolution.*
■ *Review the definition of the Industrial Revolution on page 506. How does each of the inventions on the chart fit that definition?*

Religious attitudes also played a role in the growth of British industry. Many entrepreneurs came from religious groups that encouraged thrift and hard work. At the same time, for many people, worldly problems had become more important than concern about life after death. Thus, inventors, bankers, and other risk-takers felt free to devote their energies to material achievements.

## The Age of Iron and Coal

New technologies in the iron industry were key to the Industrial Revolution. Iron was needed for machines and steam engines. Producing high-quality iron, however, required large quantities of fuel, which in the past had most often been wood. Over the centuries, Britain had cleared most of its trees. In the 1700s, the British turned to coal for fuel.

The Darby family of Coalbrookdale were leaders in developing Britain's iron industry. In 1709, Abraham Darby began to use coal instead of wood for smelting iron, that is, separating iron from its ore. When he discovered that coal gave off impurities that damaged the iron, Darby found a way to remove the impurities from coal.

Darby's experiments led him to produce better-quality and cheaper iron. His son and grandson improved on his methods. In 1779, his grandson, Abraham Darby III, made the world's first cast iron bridge. In the years that followed, high-quality iron found more and more uses, especially after the world turned to building railroads.

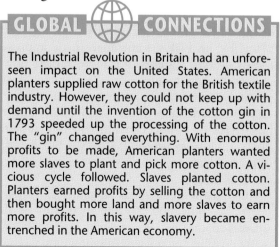

**GLOBAL CONNECTIONS**

The Industrial Revolution in Britain had an unforeseen impact on the United States. American planters supplied raw cotton for the British textile industry. However, they could not keep up with demand until the invention of the cotton gin in 1793 speeded up the processing of the cotton. The "gin" changed everything. With enormous profits to be made, American planters wanted more slaves to plant and pick more cotton. A vicious cycle followed. Slaves planted cotton. Planters earned profits by selling the cotton and then bought more land and more slaves to earn more profits. In this way, slavery became entrenched in the American economy.

## Revolutionary Changes in the Textile Industry

Important changes also took place in Britain's largest industry—textiles. Indeed, it was in this industry that the Industrial Revolution first took hold.

**The early industry.** In the 1600s, cotton cloth imported from India had become increasingly popular. British merchants tried to organize a cotton cloth industry at home. They developed the putting out system. (See page 413.) They distributed imported raw cotton to peasant families who spun it into thread and then wove the thread into cloth. Skilled artisans in the towns finished and dyed the cloth.

Under the putting out system, production was slow. As the demand for cloth grew, inventors came up with a string of remarkable devices that revolutionized the British textile industry. (See the chart on page 512.)

**Major inventions.** Among the inventions was John Kay's flying shuttle. Using Kay's device, weavers worked so fast that they soon outpaced spinners. James Hargreaves solved that problem by producing the spinning jenny in 1764, which spun many threads at the same time.

A few years later, Richard Arkwright invented the waterframe, using water power to speed up spinning still further. Arkwright, who had begun life as a barber, was typical of Britain's hard-working and highly disciplined entrepreneurs. An observer noted:

> 66[Arkwright] commonly labored in his [many] concerns from five o'clock in the morning till nine at night; and when considerably more than fifty years of age . . . he encroached upon his sleep, in order to gain an hour each day to learn English grammar.99

**The first factories.** The new machines doomed the old putting out system of manufacturing. They were too large and expensive to be operated at home. Instead, manufacturers built long sheds to house the machines. At first, they located the sheds near rapidly moving streams, which provided water power to run the machines. Later, machines were powered by steam engines.

Import routes
of raw cotton

Export routes
of cotton cloth

## GEOGRAPHY AND HISTORY

As the textile industry grew, Great Britain needed ever-increasing supplies of raw cotton for its mills. It also sought out new markets for finished cotton cloth.

1. **Location** On the map, locate (a) Great Britain, (b) United States, (c) British West Indies.
2. **Movement** (a) Name two overseas sources that supplied raw cotton to Britain. (b) Name two overseas markets to which Britain exported its cotton cloth.
3. **Critical Thinking** **Predicting Consequences** What might have happened to the British cotton industry if Britain had lost control of its colony in India?

Spinners and weavers came each day to work in these first factories—as these places that brought together workers and machines to produce large quantities of goods came to be called. Early observers were awed at the size and output of these establishments. As a writer of the 1800s commented:

66Those vast brick buildings, . . . towering to the height of 70 or 80 feet, . . . now perform labors which formerly employed whole villages. In the steam loom factories, the cotton is carded, roved, spun, and woven into cloth, and the same [amount] of labor is now performed in one of these structures which formerly occupied the industry of an entire district.99

## Revolution in Transportation

As factories sprang up and production increased, entrepreneurs needed faster and cheaper methods of moving goods from place to place. In the 1700s, individuals made improvements in local systems of transportation. Some capitalists invested in turnpikes, which were privately built roads that charged a fee to travelers who used them. Others had canals dug to link rivers or connect inland towns to coastal ports. Engineers also built stronger bridges and upgraded harbors to help the rapidly expanding overseas trade.

**On land.** The great revolution in transportation, however, was the invention of the steam locomotive. It was this invention that made possible the growth of railroads.

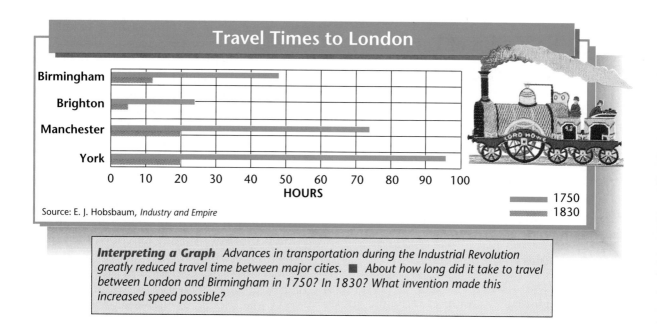

## Travel Times to London

HOURS

Birmingham
Brighton
Manchester
York

0 10 20 30 40 50 60 70 80 90 100

Source: E. J. Hobsbaum, *Industry and Empire*

— 1750
— 1830

**Interpreting a Graph** *Advances in transportation during the Industrial Revolution greatly reduced travel time between major cities.* ■ *About how long did it take to travel between London and Birmingham in 1750? In 1830? What invention made this increased speed possible?*

In the early 1800s, pioneers like George Stephenson developed steam-powered locomotives to pull carriages along rails. As we saw on page 506, the world's first major rail line, from Liverpool to Manchester in England, opened in 1830. In the following decades, railroads got faster and railroad building boomed. By 1870, rail lines crisscrossed Britain, Europe, and eastern North America.

**On sea.** Other inventors applied steam power to improve shipping. Scottish builders made the first paddle wheel steamboats to pull barges along canals. In 1807, an American, Robert Fulton, used Watt's steam engine to power the *Clermont* up the Hudson River. Fulton's steamboat traveled at a record-breaking speed of more than five miles an hour!

Designing steamships for ocean voyages was more difficult. The coal needed for the voyage took up much of the cargo space. But by the late 1800s, steam-powered freighters with iron hulls were carrying 10 to 20 times the cargo of older wooden ships.

### Looking Ahead

As the Industrial Revolution got under way, it triggered a chain reaction. In response to growing demand, inventors developed machines that could produce large quantities of goods more efficiently. As the supply of goods

increased, prices fell. Lower prices made goods more affordable and thus created more consumers who further fed the demand for goods.

The Industrial Revolution did more than change the way goods were made. It affected people's whole way of life. In the 1800s, a tidal wave of economic and social changes swept the industrializing nations of the world.

## SECTION 2 REVIEW

1. **Identify** (a) Abraham Darby, (b) John Kay, (c) James Hargreaves, (d) Richard Arkwright, (e) Robert Fulton.
2. **Define** (a) factory, (b) turnpike.
3. Describe five factors that contributed to the Industrial Revolution in Britain.
4. Explain how each of the following was key to industrialization: (a) coal, (b) iron, (c) better methods of transportation.
5. How did the Industrial Revolution transform the textile industry?
6. *Critical Thinking* **Analyzing Information** Explain how each of the following helped contribute to demand for consumer goods in Britain: (a) population explosion, (b) general economic prosperity.
7. *ACTIVITY* Create a concept map that shows the major causes of the Industrial Revolution and how they were related.

## 3 Hardships of Early Industrial Life

### Guide for Reading

- How did the factory system change workers' lives?

- What problems did the industrial working class face?

- What were the costs and benefits of the Industrial Revolution?

- **Vocabulary** *urbanization*

The Industrial Revolution brought great riches to most of the entrepreneurs who helped set it in motion. For the millions of workers who crowded into the new factories, however, the industrial age brought poverty and harsh living conditions. In *Hard Times,* the British novelist Charles Dickens describes a typical factory town and the people who live in it:

> 66It was a town of machinery and tall chimneys, out of which interminable serpents of smoke trailed themselves forever and ever. . . . It had a black canal in it, and a river that ran purple with ill-smelling dye. [It was] inhabited by people . . . who all went in and out at the same hours, . . . to do the same work, and to whom every day was the same as yesterday and tomorrow, and every year the counterpart of the last and the next.99

In time, reforms would curb many of the worst abuses of the early industrial age in Europe and the Americas, and people at all levels of society would benefit from industrialization. Until then, working people could look forward only to lives marked by dangerous working conditions; unsafe, unsanitary, and overcrowded housing; and unrelenting poverty.

### The New Industrial City

The Industrial Revolution brought rapid urbanization, or a movement of people to cities. Changes in farming, soaring population growth, and an ever-increasing demand for workers led masses of people to migrate from farms to cities. Almost overnight, small towns around coal or iron mines mushroomed into cities. Other cities grew up around the factories that entrepreneurs built in once-quiet market towns. In these new, overcrowded urban centers, misery festered.

The market town of Manchester numbered 17,000 people in the 1750s. Within a few years, it exploded into a center of the textile industry. Its population soared to 40,000 by 1780 and 70,000 by 1801. Visitors described the "cloud of coal vapor" that polluted the air, the pounding noise of steam engines, and the filthy stench of its river "filled with waste dye-stuffs."

In Manchester, as elsewhere, a gulf divided the urban population. The wealthy and the middle class lived in pleasant neighborhoods. Vast numbers of poor, however, struggled to survive in foul-smelling slums. They packed into tiny rooms in tenement buildings. No light filtered through the dark, narrow alleys. They had no running water, only community pumps. There was no sewage or sanitation system, and wastes and garbage rotted in the streets. Cholera and other diseases spread rapidly. In time, reformers pushed for laws to improve conditions in city slums. (See Chapter 24.)

### The Factory System

The heart of the new industrial city was the factory. There, the technology of the machine age imposed a harsh new way of life on workers.

**Rigid discipline.** The factory system differed greatly from farmwork. In rural villages, people worked hard, but their work varied according to the season. In factories, workers faced a rigid schedule set by the factory whistle. "While the engine runs," said an observer, "people must work—men, women, and children are yoked together with iron and steam."

Working hours were long. Shifts lasted from 12 to 16 hours. Weary workers suffered accidents from machines that had no safety devices. They might lose a finger, a limb, or even their lives. Workers were exposed to other dangers, as well. Coal dust destroyed the lungs of miners, while textile workers constantly breathed air filled with lint. If workers were sick or injured, they lost their jobs.

**Women workers.** Women made up much of the new industrial work force. Employers often preferred women workers to men. They thought women could adapt more easily to machines and were easier to manage than men. More important, they were able to pay women less than men, even for the same work.

Factory work created special problems for women. Their new jobs took them out of their homes for 12 hours or more a day. They then returned to crowded slum tenements to feed and clothe their families, clean, and cope with sickness and other problems. Family life had been hard for poor rural cottagers. In industrial towns, it was even grimmer.

**Child labor.** Factories and mines hired many boys and girls. Nimble-fingered and quick-moving children changed spools in textile mills. Others clambered through narrow mine shafts, pushing coal carts.

Since children had helped with farmwork, parents accepted the idea of child labor. And the wages the children earned were needed to help support the family. One mother told investigators of her 10-year-old child who worked in the mines from six in the morning until eight at night. "It would hurt us," she said, "if children were prevented from working till [they were] 11 or 12 years old, because we've not jobs enough to live now as it is."

Employers often hired orphans, making deals with local officials who were glad to have the children taken off their hands. Orphans worked long hours for a minimum of food. Overseers beat children accused of idling. A few enlightened factory owners did provide basic education and a decent life for child workers. More often, though, children, like their parents, were slaves to the machines.

## Patience Kershaw's Life Underground

The horrors of child labor were slowly exposed in the 1830s and 1840s, when British lawmakers looked into abuses in factories and mines. Government commissions heard about children as young as five years old working in factories. Some died. Others were stunted in growth or had twisted limbs. Most remained uneducated.

**A 12-hour workday.** From 17-year-old Patience Kershaw, members of the Ashley Mines Commission heard about life in the coal mines:

> **❝**My father has been dead about a year. My mother is living and has 10 children, 5 lads and 5 lasses. The oldest is about 30, the youngest is 4. Three lasses go to mill. All the lads are [coal miners].**❞**

Kershaw's sisters had started in the mines but switched to mill work. One changed jobs when her legs swelled from standing in the cold water that covered the mine floor.

Kershaw herself worked in the mines. Her job was "hurrying"—pushing carts of coal to the surface of the mine:

> **❝**I go to [the mine] at 5 o'clock in the morning and come out at 5 in the evening. . . . I hurry in the clothes I have now got on, trousers and ragged jacket. The bald place upon my head is made by [pushing] the corves [carts

**Working Underground** *Thousands of children worked in Britain's coal mines during the Industrial Revolution. In the cramped, narrow mine shafts, children crawled on all fours, pushing coal carts or dragging them behind. "Some places are scarcely fit for a dog to go in, not being more than from two feet and a half to a yard in height," one young miner said.* **Economics and Technology** *Why did many parents resist efforts to end child labor?*

full of coal]. . . . I hurry the corves a mile and more underground and back. . . . I wear a belt and chain . . . to get the corves out.**99**

Kershaw said that the men she worked with beat her if she did not work quickly enough. And "the boys sometimes pull me about. I am the only girl in the pit. There are about 20 boys and 15 men."

**Efforts at reform.** Like many other working poor, Kershaw had entered the mines as a small child. In a tangle of underground tunnels, men, women, and children mined coal to fuel the engines of the Industrial Revolution.

Kershaw probably never saw the Ashley Mines Commission report. Besides, since she had never attended school, she could not have read it in any case. But in 1842, her testimony shocked many people in Britain. Slowly, Parliament passed laws to regulate the employment of children in mines and factories. ▨

## The Working Class

In rural villages, farm families had ties to a community where they had lived for generations. When they moved to the new industrial cities, they felt lost and bewildered. In time, though, factory and mine workers developed their own sense of community.

**Protests.** As the Industrial Revolution began, weavers and other skilled artisans resisted the new "labor-saving" machines that were costing them their jobs. They smashed machines and burned factories. Such rioters in England were called Luddites after a mythical figure, Ned Ludd, who supposedly destroyed machines in the 1780s.

Protests met harsh repression. Luddites were hanged or sent to penal colonies in Australia. When workers held a rally in Manchester in 1819, soldiers charged the crowd, killing a dozen and injuring hundreds more. For years, workers were forbidden to form labor unions to bargain for better pay and working conditions. Strikes were outlawed.

**Spread of Methodism.** Many working-class people found comfort in a new religious movement. In the mid-1700s, John Wesley had been the leader of a religious revival and founded the Methodist Church. Wesley stressed the need for a personal sense of faith. He urged Christians to improve their lot by adopting sober, moral ways.

Methodist meetings featured hymns and sermons promising forgiveness of sin and a better life to come. Methodist preachers took this message of salvation into the slums. There, they sought to rekindle self-confidence and hope among the working poor. They set up Sunday schools where followers not only studied the Bible but also learned to read and write. Methodists helped channel workers' anger away from revolution and toward social reform.

**Worker Protests** *On a hot August day in 1819, workers in the industrial city of Manchester gathered to hear several reformers speak. Suddenly, soldiers attacked the crowd, killing a dozen people and wounding hundreds more.* **Art and Literature** *Do you think the artist who created this cartoon sympathized with the workers or the soldiers? Explain.*

# PARALLELS THROUGH TIME

## Frankenstein

In 1816, a teenager named Mary Shelley (below left) had a nightmare vision that "so possessed my mind that a thrill of fear ran through me." Shelley's nightmare inspired her to write *Frankenstein*, a novel about a scientist who tries to make a human being but creates a monster instead. The story reflected the fear of many Europeans during the Industrial Revolution that humans were using technology to tamper with nature.

**Linking Past and Present** Why did people during the Industrial Revolution worry that technology had gone too far? Are those concerns still valid today?

**PAST** In Shelley's novel, the monster is not a grunting brute. Instead, he is an intelligent but hideously ugly and evil creature who reads poetry and argues cleverly with Victor Frankenstein, his creator. "Why," he piteously asks, "did you form a monster so hideous that even you turned from me in disgust?"

**PRESENT** The story of Frankenstein and his monster has continued to capture the popular imagination. A silent movie based on the tale was made in 1910, and a film featuring Boris Karloff (above right) as the monster was one of the biggest hits of the 1930s. Mel Brooks made Young Frankenstein, a spoof on the original story, in the 1970s, and in 1994 still another version starring Robert De Niro was released.

---

## The New Middle Class

Those who benefited most from the Industrial Revolution were the entrepreneurs who set it in motion. This new middle class came from several groups. Some were merchants who invested their profits in factories. Others were inventors or skilled artisans who turned their technological know-how into a ticket to a better life. Some rose from "rags to riches," a pattern that the age greatly admired.

Middle-class families lived in solid, well-furnished homes. They dressed well and ate large meals. Middle-class men made their influence felt in Parliament, where they opposed any effort to regulate factories or legalize labor unions.

As a sign of their new standard of living, middle-class women were encouraged to become "ladies." They took up "ladylike" activities, such as drawing, embroidery, or playing the piano. A "lady" did not work outside the home. She was also discouraged from doing the physical labor of housework. The first thing a family's new wealth acquired was a maid servant. The family then set about educating their daughters to provide a happy, well-furnished home for their future husbands. Sons learned to become businessmen.

The new middle class valued hard work and the determination to "get ahead." They had confidence in themselves and often little sympathy for the poor. If they thought of the faceless millions in the factories and mines, they generally supposed the poor to be responsible for their own misery. Some believed the poor were so lazy or ignorant that they could not "work their way up" out of poverty.

*Chapter 20* **519**

## Benefits and Problems

Since the 1800s, people have debated whether the Industrial Revolution was a blessing or a curse. The hardships brought by the early industrial age were terrible. Said English writer Thomas Carlyle, "Something [ought] to be done."

In time, "something" would be done. Reformers pressed for laws to improve working conditions. (See Chapter 22.) Unions won the right to bargain with employers for better wages and hours. Eventually, working-class men gained the right to vote, which gave them political power. Some workers founded political parties and movements that sought swifter, more radical solutions.

Despite the social problems created by the Industrial Revolution—low pay, unemployment, dismal living conditions—the industrial age did bring material benefits. As demand for mass-produced goods grew, new factories opened, creating more jobs. Wages rose so that workers had enough left after paying rent and buying food to buy a newspaper or visit a music hall. As the cost of railroad travel fell, people could visit family in other towns. Horizons widened, opportunities increased.

Industrialization continues to spread around the world today. Often, it begins with great suffering. In the end, it produces more material things for more people.

## SECTION 3 REVIEW

1. **Identify** (a) Luddite, (b) John Wesley, (c) Methodism.
2. **Define** urbanization.
3. Describe working conditions in an early factory.
4. What special problems did factory work create for women?
5. How did the conditions of the early industrial age improve over time?
6. *Critical Thinking* **Comparing** Compare the life of a farmworker with that of a factory worker in the early industrial age.
7. *ACTIVITY* Write five questions for an interview with Patience Kershaw.

# 4 New Ways of Thinking

## Guide for Reading

- What economic ideas helped shape the industrial age?
- What reforms did individual thinkers urge?
- How was socialism linked to the Industrial Revolution?
- **Vocabulary** *utilitarianism, socialism, communism, proletariat*

Everywhere in his native England, Thomas Malthus saw the effects of the population explosion—crowded slums, hungry families, and widespread misery. After careful study, in 1798 he published an "Essay on the Principle of Population." Poverty and misery, he concluded, were unavoidable because the population was increasing faster than the food supply. Malthus wrote:

66The power of population is [far] greater than the power of the Earth to produce subsistence for man.99

Malthus was one of many thinkers who tried to understand the staggering changes taking place in the early industrial age. As heirs to the Enlightenment, these thinkers looked for natural laws that governed the world of business and economics. Their ideas would influence governments in the years ahead.

## Laissez-Faire Economics

During the Enlightenment, physiocrats argued that natural laws should be allowed to operate without interference. As part of this philosophy, they believed that government should not interfere in the free operation of the economy. In the early 1800s, middle-class business leaders embraced this laissez-faire, or "hands-off," approach.

**Legacy of Adam Smith.** The prophet of laissez-faire economics was Adam Smith. (See page 460.) Smith believed that a free market—

the unregulated exchange of goods and services—would eventually help everyone, not just the rich.

The free market, Smith said, would produce more goods at lower prices, making them affordable by everyone. A growing economy would also encourage capitalists to reinvest profits in new ventures. Supporters of this free enterprise capitalism pointed to the successes of the industrial age, in which government had played no part.

**Malthus on population.** Like Smith's *Wealth of Nations,* Thomas Malthus's writings on population shaped economic thinking for generations. As you have read on page 520, Malthus grimly predicted that population would outpace the food supply. The only checks on population growth, he said, were war, disease, and famine. As long as population kept increasing, he went on, the poor would suffer. He thus urged families to have fewer children.

In the early 1800s, many people accepted Malthus's bleak view. It was too pessimistic, however. Although the population boom continued, the food supply grew even faster. As the century progressed, living conditions for the western world also slowly improved. And then people did begin having fewer children. In the 1900s, population growth ceased to be a problem in western countries, though it still afflicted some nations elsewhere.

**Ricardo on wages.** Another influential British economist, David Ricardo, agreed with Malthus that the poor had too many children. In his "iron law of wages," Ricardo noted that when wages were high, families had more children. But more children increased the supply of labor, which led to lower wages and higher unemployment. Like Malthus, Ricardo held out no hope for the working class to escape poverty. Because of such gloomy predictions, economics became known as the "dismal science."

Neither Malthus nor Ricardo was a cruel man. Yet both opposed any government help for the poor. To these supporters of laissez-faire economics, the best cure for poverty was not government relief but the unrestricted "laws of the free market." Individuals, they felt, should be left to improve their lot through thrift, hard work, and limiting the size of their family.

## The Utilitarians

Others revised laissez-faire doctrines to justify some government intervention. By 1800, Jeremy Bentham was preaching utilitarianism, the idea that the goal of society should be "the greatest happiness for the greatest number" of its citizens. To Bentham, laws or actions should be judged by their "utility." Did they provide

*Overcrowding in a London Slum* Thomas Malthus warned that the population explosion was causing widespread misery throughout England. Here, French artist Gustave Doré captures the squalor and overcrowded conditions of a London slum. **Political and Social Systems** What did Malthus recommend as a solution to the problems of the early industrial age?

more pleasure (happiness) than pain? He strongly supported individual freedom, which he believed ensured happiness. At the same time, he saw the need for government to intervene under certain circumstances.

Bentham's chief follower, John Stuart Mill, also argued that actions are right if they promote happiness and wrong if they cause pain. He reexamined the idea that unrestricted competition in the free market was always good. Often, he said, it favored the strong over the weak.

Although he believed strongly in individual freedom, Mill wanted the government to step in to improve the hard lives of the working class. He further called for giving the vote to workers and women. These groups could then use their political power to win reforms. Mill and other utilitarians worked for reforms in many areas, from child labor to public health.

Most middle-class people rejected Mill's ideas. Only in the later 1800s were his views slowly accepted. Today's democratic governments, however, have absorbed many ideas from Mill and the utilitarians.

## Emergence of Socialism

While the champions of laissez-faire economics praised individual rights, other thinkers focused on the good of society in general. They condemned the evils of industrial capitalism, which they believed had created a gulf between rich and poor. To end poverty and injustice, they offered a radical solution—socialism. Under socialism, the people as a whole rather than private individuals would own and operate the "means of production"—the farms, factories, railways, and other large businesses that produced and distributed goods.

Socialism grew out of the Enlightenment faith in progress, its belief in the basic goodness of human nature, and its concern for social justice. The goal of socialists was a society that operated for the welfare of all the people. In a socialist society, one reformer predicted:

**"**There will be no war, no crime, no administration of justice, as it is called, no government. Besides there will be neither disease, anguish, melancholy,

nor resentment. Every man will seek . . . the good of all.**"**

**The Utopians.** Early socialists tried to build self-sufficient communities in which all work was shared and all property was owned in common. When there was no difference between rich and poor, they felt, fighting between people would disappear. These early socialists were called Utopians, after Thomas More's ideal community. (See page 351.) The name implied that they were impractical dreamers. However, the Utopian Robert Owen did set up a model community to put his ideas into practice.

**Robert Owen.** A poor Welsh boy, Owen became a successful mill owner. Unlike most self-made industrialists at the time, he refused to use child labor. He campaigned vigorously for child labor laws and encouraged labor unions.

Owen insisted that the conditions in which people lived shaped their character. To prove his point, he set up his factory in New Lanark, Scotland, as a model village. He built homes for workers, opened a school for children, and generally treated employees well. He showed that an employer could offer decent living and working conditions and still run a profitable business. By the 1820s, many people were visiting New Lanark to observe Owen's reforms.

## The "Scientific Socialism" of Karl Marx

In the 1840s, Karl Marx, a German philosopher, condemned the ideas of the Utopians as unrealistic idealism. He put forward a new theory, "scientific socialism," which he claimed was based on a scientific study of history.

As a young man in Germany, Marx agitated for reform. Forced to leave his homeland because of his radical ideas, he lived first in Paris and then settled in London. He teamed up with another German socialist, Friedrich Engels, whose father owned a textile factory in England.

In 1848, Marx and Engels published a pamphlet, *The Communist Manifesto*. "A spectre is haunting Europe," it began, "the spectre of communism." Communism is a form of socialism that sees class struggle between employers and employees as inevitable.

**Marxism.** In the *Manifesto,* Marx theorized that economics was the driving force in history. The entire course of history, he argued, was "the history of class struggles" between the "haves" and "have-nots." The "haves" have always owned the means of production and thus controlled society and all its wealth. In industrialized Europe, Marx said, the "haves" were the bourgeoisie, or middle class. The "have-nots" were the proletariat, or working class.

According to Marx, the modern class struggle pitted the bourgeoisie against the proletariat. In the end, he predicted, the proletariat would triumph. It would then take control of the means of production and set up a classless, communist society. In such a society, the struggles of the past would end because wealth and power would be equally shared.

Marx despised capitalism. He believed it created prosperity for a few and poverty for many. He called for an international struggle to bring about its downfall. "Working men of all countries," he urged, "unite!"

**Impact.** At first, Marxist ideas had little impact. In time, however, they would have worldwide effects. In Western Europe, socialist political parties emerged. Many of them absorbed Marxist ideas, including the goal of a classless society.

In the late 1800s, Russian socialists embraced Marxism, and the Russian Revolution of 1917 set up a communist-inspired government. (See Chapter 28.) Later, revolutionaries around the world would adapt Marxist ideas to their own ends.

**Weaknesses.** Marx claimed his ideas were based on scientific laws. However, many of the assumptions on which he based his theories were wrong. He predicted that the misery of the proletariat would touch off a world revolution. Instead, by 1900, the standard of living of the working class improved. As a result, Marxism lost much of its appeal in industrially developed western countries.

Marx also predicted that workers would unite across national borders to wage class warfare. Instead, nationalism won out over working-class loyalty. In general, people felt stronger ties to their own countries than to the international communist movement.

***Champion of the Working Class*** *Karl Marx was a social philosopher and revolutionary. He argued that history was a struggle between the classes that would end with the victory of the working class.*
***Global Interaction*** *Marx was born in Germany but lived for more than 30 years in London. How might living in London during the early industrial age have influenced Marx's ideas?*

## SECTION 4 REVIEW

1. **Identify** (a) Thomas Malthus, (b) "iron law of wages," (c) John Stuart Mill, (d) Utopians, (e) *The Communist Manifesto.*
2. **Define** (a) utilitarianism, (b) socialism, (c) communism, (d) proletariat.
3. (a) Which group of people supported the free-market ideas of Adam Smith? (b) Why?
4. How did Utopian socialists propose to end the miseries brought by the Industrial Revolution?
5. (a) Describe Karl Marx's view of history. (b) How have events challenged that view?
6. *Critical Thinking* **Linking Past and Present** Choose *one* economic or political theory discussed in this section. Then, analyze it in relation to life today.
7. *ACTIVITY* Make a chart outlining the main ideas of the individuals discussed in this section. Then, compare *two* of them.

# Skills for Success

## Recognizing Faulty Reasoning

Whenever you participate in a discussion or a debate, your goal is to convince the other side that your opinion is logical and correct. You begin your argument with a **premise**, a statement that is the basis for your argument. You then build on your premise by adding reasons and persuasions. You try to reach a **conclusion** that is so sound that the other side has no choice but to agree with you.

Whether or not you prevail in the discussion may depend on how well you reason from your basic premise to your conclusion. Many people employ **faulty reasoning** during discussions. Faulty reasoning happens when you make an error in thinking or argument. Three common types of faulty reasoning are (1) attacking your opponents rather than their arguments, (2) incorrectly stating cause-and-effect relationships, and (3) using circular arguments, that is, giving a conclusion that simply restates your premise.

In the dialogue below, several students are discussing the Industrial Revolution. Read the dialogue, and follow the steps to identify the faulty reasoning.

**1** **Identify personal attacks.** (a) Which student is focusing on the person arguing rather than on the argument itself? (b) What argument does this student use? (c) Why is this faulty reasoning?

**2** **Identify incorrect statements of cause-and-effect relationships.** (a) What position does Student B take on the issue of the Industrial Revolution? (b) What argument does Student B use to support this position? (c) Describe Student C's position and argument. (d) Compare the arguments of Student B and Student C. Which is an example of faulty reasoning? Explain.

**3** **Identify circular arguments.** (a) Which student uses circular reasoning to support his or her argument? (b) What arguments does this student use? (c) How is it an example of circular reasoning?

***Beyond the Classroom*** Editorials, political speeches, and advertisements often employ faulty reasoning. In a newspaper or news magazine, locate one example of each type of faulty reasoning described above.

---

**Student A:**
"I do not see how anyone can question the benefits of the Industrial Revolution. Without the Industrial Revolution, think of all the machines and scientific advances we wouldn't have today."

**Student B:**
"I don't agree that the Industrial Revolution was such a good thing. After all, it caused a lot of suffering and dislocation. In 1860, almost immediately after the Industrial Revolution, the Civil War broke out in the United States. And shortly after that, World War I began in Europe. In fact, I think hardly anything good came out of the Industrial Revolution at all."

**Student C:**
"That's not so! The Industrial Revolution also produced labor unions and the middle class and expanded political representation for the working class."

**Student D:**
"Your reasoning is all wrong! Those changes were produced by reformers who could see that industry was taking advantage of people. Just because a middle-class housewife has 20 machines to do her work does not make her life any better. She's still got to run the machines!"

**Student E:**
"I'd expect *you* to make a statement like that. After all, you still use a pencil and paper to do your homework. You just don't like machines!"

# CHAPTER 20 REVIEW

## Building Vocabulary

Review the vocabulary words in this chapter. Then, use *five* of these vocabulary words and their definitions to create a matching quiz. Exchange quizzes with another student. Check each other's answers when you are finished.

## Reviewing Chapter Themes

1. **Continuity and Change** Describe how the Industrial Revolution affected each of the following: (a) population, (b) cities, (c) working and living conditions, (d) women and children.
2. **Economics and Technology** Why did the Industrial Revolution begin in Britain?
3. **Impact of the Individual** How did inventors help to transform the British textile industry? Give two examples.
4. **Political and Social Systems** (a) What were the goals of early socialists? (b) What were the strengths and weaknesses of Karl Marx's political theories?

## Thinking Critically

1. **Recognizing Causes and Effects** Why were the agricultural revolution and the energy revolution necessary to the Industrial Revolution? ( ★ See *Skills for Success*, page 18.)
2. **Analyzing Literature** Compare Tennyson's lines about the Great Exposition on page 510 with Dickens's description of a factory town on page 516. (a) What is the mood of each? (b) What picture does each writer present of the Industrial Revolution? (c) How might you account for the difference? ( ★ See *Skills for Success*, page 234.)
3. **Analyzing Political Cartoons** Study the political cartoon on page 518. (a) What is the subject of the cartoon? (b) Who are the men on horseback? (c) Who are the people under attack? (d) What do you think was the artist's purpose in creating the cartoon? Explain. ( ★ See *Skills for Success*, page 580.)
4. **Defending a Position** Do you think that the Industrial Revolution was a blessing or a curse? Use material from the chapter to defend your position.

5. **Linking Past and Present** Thinkers in the 1800s disagreed about the role of government in helping the poor. David Ricardo believed that individuals should be left to improve their own lot through thrift, hard work, and limiting the size of their families. The utilitarians wanted government to help the working class. Give three examples to show that this debate about the role of government and the poor continues today.
6. **Synthesizing Information** Why do historians consider the Industrial Revolution to be a major turning point in history? ( ★ See *Skills for Success*, page 896.)

## For Your Portfolio

In this assignment, your class will form a debating society. You will work with classmates as part of a team to debate topics related to the chapter.

1. Begin by reviewing the rules for formal debates. ( ★ See *Skills for Success*, page 628.) Then, decide how much time you will allow for the arguments and rebuttals in each debate.
2. With the class, decide on five debate topics based on Chapter 20. Possible topics include: Could the Industrial Revolution Have Started as Successfully in a Country Other Than Britain? Were the Results of the Industrial Revolution a Blessing or Curse? You might also consider framing a debate around the ideas of thinkers such as Malthus, Smith, Ricardo, Bentham, Mill, or Marx. Assign two teams (affirmative and negative) to each topic that the class plans to debate.
3. Work with your team to prepare arguments for your side in the debate. Use library resources to research facts to support your position.
4. Rehearse your arguments and prepare your speech. Remember: A persuasive speech has an introduction, a presentation of major points and evidence, and a conclusion. Also, try to remember to anticipate the opposing arguments.
5. Take turns holding the debates while the rest of the class serves as an audience. Discuss the points made in each debate and note any important points that were not made.

# Revolutions in Europe and Latin America

## (1790–1848)

## CHAPTER OUTLINE

1  **An Age of Ideologies**
2  **To the Barricades!**
3  **Latin American Wars of Independence**

It started out as an ordinary evening at Brussels' Théâtre de la Monnaie. It was August 25, 1830, and the city's residents had turned out to see a popular new opera, *La Muette de Portici*. Slowly, the audience settled into their seats. They looked forward to an enjoyable but quiet evening. Surely, no one would have predicted that this evening's performance would spark a revolution!

The opera is set in Naples, Italy. The year is 1647, and Naples is under Spanish rule. The hero, a young fisherman named Masaniello, yearns to free his country. In the second act, he sings of his love for his land:

66Sacred love of country
    Restore to us our daring and
       our pride!
    My country gave me life
    And I shall give it liberty.99

The Belgian audience listened raptly to Masaniello's words. For 15 years, since the Congress of Vienna, Belgians had been forced to live under Dutch rule. As the tenor lingered over the last lines of the aria, the audience rose to their feet and joined their voices to his.

Crowds milling around outside the theater took up the song. Demonstrations soon evolved into riots and then full-scale revolt against Dutch rule. Within days, the Belgians had succeeded in ejecting the Dutch from their country. By year's end, they had won independence.

The Brussels revolt was part of a wave of violent uprisings that swept Western Europe in the first half of the 1800s. Across the continent, minor incidents flared into revolution. This "age of revolutions," as it is sometimes called, was fueled by the political ideas of the French Revolution and the economic problems caused by the Industrial Revolution.

In the aftermath of the Congress of Vienna, the great powers sought to silence liberal and nationalist demands. But simmering discontent erupted in three major revolutionary outbreaks—in the 1820s, 1830, and 1848. Rebels, divided by class interests, were soon crushed. Still, the uprisings sent a chilling message to rulers across Europe. The winds of liberalism and nationalism also swept across the Atlantic, igniting wars of independence in Latin America.

**FOCUS ON** these questions as you read:

■ **Political and Social Systems**
  How were revolutionaries seeking to change the European political and social system?

■ **Economics and Technology**
  How did economic changes contribute to revolutionary unrest in Europe?

■ **Continuity and Change**
  How were the revolutions of the early 1800s an outgrowth of the French Revolution?

■ **Global Interaction**
  How did events and ideas in Europe affect the people of Latin America?

## TIME AND PLACE

**The Spirit of Revolution** In 1830 and again in 1848, the streets of European cities seethed with rebellion. As in 1789, the revolts began in Paris and spread across the continent. In time, the revolutionary spark jumped the Atlantic and ignited uprisings in the Americas. Here, a French crowd storms the barricades. **Art and Literature** Do you think the painter supported the rebels? Explain.

## HUMANITIES LINK

**Art History** Honoré Daumier, *"You Have the Floor"* (page 532).
**Literature** In this chapter, you will encounter passages from the following works of literature: Daniel Auber, Eugène Scribe, Germaine Delavigne, *La Muette de Portici* (page 526); Stendhal, *The Charterhouse of Parma* (page 528).

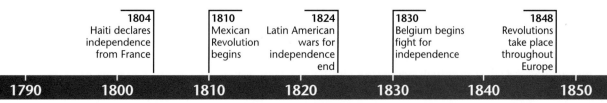

| | | | | |
|---|---|---|---|---|
| **1804** Haiti declares independence from France | **1810** Mexican Revolution begins | **1824** Latin American wars for independence end | **1830** Belgium begins fight for independence | **1848** Revolutions take place throughout Europe |

1790 — 1800 — 1810 — 1820 — 1830 — 1840 — 1850

# 7 An Age of Ideologies

## Guide for Reading

- How did the goals of conservatives and liberals differ?

- How did nationalism pose a challenge to the old order?

- Why was Europe plagued by constant unrest after 1815?

- **Vocabulary** *ideology, universal manhood suffrage, autonomy*

**The Conservative Order** European conservatives were determined to preserve the old order. At the heart of that order was the monarchy, symbolized by the Hapsburg coat of arms shown here. **Political and Social Systems** What other institutions were part of the old order?

A "revolutionary seed" had been planted in Europe, warned Prince Clemens von Metternich. The ideas spread by the French Revolution and Napoleon Bonaparte, he believed, not only threatened Europe's monarchs. They also undermined its basic social values:

> 66Kings have to calculate the chances of their very existence in the immediate future. Passions are let loose and [join] together to overthrow everything that society respects as the basis of its existence: religion, public morality, laws, customs, rights, and duties, all are attacked, confounded, overthrown, or called in question.99

At the Congress of Vienna, the European powers had sought to uproot that "revolutionary seed." Other voices, however, kept challenging the order imposed in 1815. The clash of people with opposing ideologies, or systems of thought and belief, plunged Europe into a period of turmoil that lasted more than 30 years.

## Preserving the Old Order

The Congress of Vienna was a clear victory for conservative forces. Who were these forces? And what did they want?

Conservatives included monarchs and members of their government, noble landowners, and church leaders. They supported the political and social order that had come under attack during the French Revolution. They had

benefited in many ways from the old order. Conservative ideas also appealed to peasants, who wanted to preserve traditional ways.

**Goals.** The conservatives in 1815 had very different goals from conservatives in the United States today. Conservatives of the early 1800s wanted to turn back the clock to the way things had been before 1789. They wanted to restore to power the royal families that had lost their thrones when Napoleon swept across Europe. They accepted the hierarchy of social classes. The lower classes, they felt, should respect and obey their social superiors. Conservatives also backed an established church—Catholic in Austria and the southern European countries, Orthodox in Eastern Europe, and Protestant in Britain, the Netherlands, Prussia, and the Scandinavian lands.

**Attitude toward change.** Conservatives believed that talk about natural rights and constitutional government could lead only to chaos, as it had in France in 1789. If change had to come, they argued, it must come slowly. A character in a novel by the French writer Stendhal expresses the conservative view:

> 66The words *liberty, justice,* and *happiness of the greatest number* are criminal. They give men's minds a habit of discussion. Man ends by distrusting . . . the authority of the princes set up by God.99

Conservatives equated their own interests with peace and stability for all people. Conservative leaders like Metternich opposed freedom of the press. They urged monarchs throughout Europe to suppress revolutionary ideas and crush protests in their own countries. Metternich also proposed that monarchs should step in to defeat successful revolutions in neighboring lands. ( ★ See *Skills for Success*, page 544.)

## *The Liberal Challenge*

Challenging the conservatives at every turn were the liberals. In the early 1800s, liberals embraced Enlightenment ideas spread by the French Revolution. They spoke out against divine-right monarchy, the old aristocracy, and established churches. They defended the natural rights of individuals to liberty, equality, and property.

Because liberals spoke mostly for the bourgeoisie, or middle class, their ideas are sometimes called "bourgeois liberalism." Liberals included business owners, bankers, and lawyers, as well as politicians, newspaper editors, writers, and others who helped to shape public opinion.

**Political ideas.** Liberals wanted governments to be based on written constitutions and separation of powers. They called for rulers elected by the people and responsible to them. Thus, most liberals favored a republican form of government over a monarchy, or at least wanted the monarch to be limited by a constitution.

The liberals of the early 1800s saw the role of government as limited to protecting basic rights such as freedom of thought, speech, and religion. They believed that only male property owners or others with a financial stake in society should have the right to vote. Only later in the century would liberals throw their support behind the principle of universal manhood suffrage, giving all adult men the right to vote, and social reforms. John Stuart Mill, an influential English liberal, was a notable exception, who urged equal rights for women.

**Economic views.** Liberals strongly supported the laissez-faire economics of Adam Smith and David Ricardo. (See page 460.) They saw the free market as an opportunity for capitalist entrepreneurs to succeed. As capitalists and often employers, liberals had different goals from those of workers laboring in factories, mines, and other enterprises of the early Industrial Revolution.

## *Nationalist Stirrings*

Another challenge to Metternich's conservative order came from nationalists. Like liberalism, nationalism was an outgrowth of the Enlightenment and the French Revolution. Also like liberalism, it ignited a number of revolts against established rule.

**Goals.** For centuries, European rulers had won or lost lands in war. They exchanged territories and the people who lived in them like pieces in a game. Regions also passed back and forth with various marriages between royal families. As a result of all this land swapping, by 1815 Europe had several empires that included many nationalities. The Austrian, Russian, and Ottoman empires, for example, each included diverse peoples.

Unifying and gaining independence for people with a common national heritage became a major goal of nationalists in the 1800s. Each national group, they believed, should have its own state.

While nationalism gave people with a common heritage a sense of identity and a goal—establishment of their own homeland—it also had negative effects. It often bred intolerance and led to persecution of national or ethnic minorities.

**Revolts in the Balkans.** The Balkans, in southeastern Europe, were home to many ethnic groups. In the early 1800s, several Balkan peoples rebelled against the Ottomans, who had ruled them for more than 300 years.

The first Balkan people to revolt were the Serbs. In two major rebellions between 1804 and 1817, the Serbs suffered terrible defeats. In the end, however, they achieved autonomy, or self-rule, within the Ottoman empire. The bitter

**ISSUES** *For* **TODAY** Conservatives in the 1800s tried to preserve the old social order by holding back the forces of change. How can the need for social and political change be balanced with the desire for a stable society?

struggle fostered a sense of Serbian identity. A revival of Slavic literature and culture added to the sense of nationhood.

**Independence for the Greeks.** In 1821, the Greeks, too, revolted, seeking to end centuries of Ottoman rule. At first, the Greeks were badly divided. But years of suffering in long, bloody wars of independence helped shape a national identity.

Leaders of the rebellion justified their struggle as "a national war, a holy war, a war the object of which is to reconquer the rights of individual liberty." They appealed for support to Western Europeans, who admired ancient Greek civilization.

The Greeks won sympathy in the West. In the late 1820s, Britain, France, and even conservative Russia forced the Ottomans to grant independence to some Greek provinces. By 1830, Greece was independent. The European powers, however, pressured the Greeks to accept a German king, a move meant to show that they did not support revolution. Still, liberals were enthusiastic, while nationalists everywhere saw reasons to hope for a country of their own.

## Challenges to the Old Order

Several other challenges to the Vienna settlement erupted in the 1820s. Revolts occurred along the southern fringe of Europe. In Spain, Portugal, and the Italian states, rebels demanded constitutional governments.

Metternich urged conservative rulers to crush the uprisings. A French army marched into Spain to suppress a revolt, while Austrian forces crossed the Alps to smash Italian rebels.

Troops dampened the fires of liberalism and nationalism in western and southern areas of Europe, but could not smother them. In the next decades, sparks would flare anew. Added to liberal and nationalist demands were the goals of the new industrial working class. By the mid-1800s, social reformers and agitators were urging workers to support socialism or some other way of reorganizing property ownership, further contributing to the unrest of this period.

*Greek Independence* Inspired by the nationalism that was sweeping Europe, the Greeks proclaimed independence. For a decade, they battled their Ottoman rulers. At last, after the British, French, and Russians intervened, the Turks granted Greece independence. Here, a victorious Greek soldier raises the national flag over a defeated enemy. **Art and Literature** Compare this painting with that on page 527. How does each represent the spirit of nationalism?

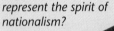

SECTION **1** REVIEW

1. **Identify** (a) conservatives, (b) liberals, (c) nationalists.
2. **Define** (a) ideology, (b) universal manhood suffrage, (c) autonomy.
3. (a) Which groups backed conservative ideas? Why? (b) How did the political goals of conservatives differ from those of liberals?
4. How did nationalists threaten the system set up by Metternich?
5. *Critical Thinking* **Applying Information** How did ideologies like liberalism and nationalism contribute to unrest?
6. *ACTIVITY* Create a series of political cartoons expressing the point of view of each of the following groups: (a) conservatives, (b) liberals, (c) nationalists.

# To the Barricades!

## Guide for Reading

- Why did revolts break out in France in 1830 and 1848?

- How did revolutions in France affect other parts of Europe?

- Why did the revolts of 1830 and 1848 generally fail to achieve their goals?

The quick suppression of liberal and nationalist uprisings in the 1820s did not end Europe's age of revolutions. "We are sleeping on a volcano," warned Alexis de Tocqueville, a liberal French leader who saw widespread discontent. "Do you not see that the Earth trembles anew? A wind of revolution blows, the storm is on the horizon."

In 1830 and 1848, Europeans saw street protests explode into full-scale revolts. As in 1789, the upheavals began in Paris and radiated out across the continent.

## France After the Restoration

When the Congress of Vienna restored Louis XVIII to the French throne, he prudently issued a constitution, the Charter of French Liberties. It created a two-house legislature and allowed limited freedom of the press. Still, while Louis was careful to shun absolutism, the king retained much power.

**Efforts at compromise.** Louis's efforts at compromise satisfied few people. Ultraroyalists, supporters on the far right, despised constitutional government and wanted to restore the old regime. The "ultras" included many high clergy and emigré nobles who had returned to France after the Revolution.

The ultras faced bitter opposition from other factions. Liberals wanted to extend suffrage and win a share of power for middle-class citizens like themselves. On the left, radicals yearned for a republic like that of the 1790s. And in working-class slums, men and women wanted what they had wanted in 1789—a decent day's pay and bread they could afford.

**The July revolution.** When Louis XVIII died in 1824, his brother, Charles X, inherited the throne. Charles, a strong believer in absolutism, rejected the very idea of the charter. In July 1830, he suspended the legislature, limited the right to vote, and restricted the press.

Liberals and radicals responded forcefully to the king's challenge. In Paris, angry citizens threw up barricades across the narrow streets. From behind them, they fired on the soldiers and pelted them with stones and roof tiles. Within days, rebels controlled Paris. The revolutionary tricolor flew from the towers of Notre Dame cathedral. A frightened Charles X abdicated and fled to England.

With the king gone, radicals wanted to set up a republic. Moderate liberals, however, insisted on a constitutional monarchy. The Chamber of Deputies, the lower house of the French legislature, chose Louis Philippe as king. He was a cousin of Charles X and in his youth, had supported the revolution of 1789.

**The "citizen king."** The French called Louis Philippe the "citizen king" because he owed his throne to the people. Louis got along well with the liberal bourgeoisie. Like them, he dressed in a frock coat and top hat. Sometimes, he strolled the streets, shaking hands with well-wishers. Liberal politicians and professionals filled his government.

Under Louis Philippe, the upper bourgeoisie prospered. Louis extended suffrage, but only to France's wealthiest citizens. The vast majority of the people still could not vote. Louis Philippe's other policies also favored the middle class at the expense of the workers.

## The French Revolution of 1848

In the 1840s, discontent grew. Radicals formed secret societies to work for a French republic. Utopian socialists called for an end of private ownership of property. (See Chapter 20.) Even liberals denounced Louis Philippe's government for corruption and called for expanded suffrage.

Toward the end of the decade, an economic slump shut down factories. Harvests were poor. People lost their jobs and bread prices soared. Scandals involving high officials filled the newspapers. As in 1789, Paris was ripe for revolution.

*"You have the floor; explain yourself!"*

**"You Have the Floor"** The political cartoons of French artist Honoré Daumier combine masterful line drawings with a sharp wit. His works were immensely influential in calling attention to the social injustices of the time. In this drawing, Daumier depicts a court scene. The defendant, mouth gagged and arms pinned down by his prosecutors, stands before the judge. The judge snarls, "You have the floor; explain yourself!" **Art and Literature** What do the judge's words mean? Based on the cartoon, what is Daumier's view of the French justice system?

**"February Days."** In February 1848, when the government took steps to silence critics and prevent public meetings, angry crowds took to the streets. During the "February Days," iron railings, overturned carts, paving stones, and toppled trees again blocked the streets of Paris. Church bells rang alarms, while women and men on the barricades sang the revolutionary "La Marseillaise." A number of demonstrators clashed with royal troops and were killed.

As the turmoil spread, Louis Philippe abdicated. A group of liberal, radical, and socialist leaders proclaimed the Second Republic. (The First Republic had lasted from 1792 until 1804, when Napoleon became emperor.)

From the start, deep differences divided the new government. Middle-class liberals were interested in political reforms such as constitutions. Socialists wanted far-reaching social and economic change that would help hungry workers. In the early days of the new republic, the socialists forced the government to set up national workshops to provide jobs for the unemployed.

**"June Days."** By June, however, upper- and middle-class interests had won control of the government. They saw the national workshops as a waste of money, and they shut them down.

Furious, workers took to the streets of Paris, rallying to the cry "Bread or Lead!" This time, however, bourgeois liberals turned violently against the protesters. Peasants, who feared that socialists might take their land, also attacked the rioting workers. At least 1,500 people were killed before the government crushed the rebellion.

The fighting of the "June Days" left a bitter legacy. The middle class both feared and distrusted the left, while the working class nursed a deep hatred for the bourgeoisie.

**Louis Napoleon.** Toward the end of the year, the National Assembly, dominated by forces who wanted to restore order, issued a constitution for the Second Republic. It created a strong president and a one-house legislature. But it also gave the vote to all adult men, the widest suffrage in the world at the time. Nine million Frenchmen now could vote, compared to only 200,000 who had that right before.

When elections for president were held, the overwhelming winner was Louis Napoleon, nephew of Napoleon Bonaparte. The "new" Napoleon attracted the working classes by presenting himself as a man who cared about social issues such as poverty. At the same time, his famous name, linked with order and authority as well as with France's past glories, helped him with conservatives.

Once in office, Louis Napoleon used his position as a steppingstone to greater power. By 1852, he had proclaimed himself emperor, taking the title Napoleon III. (He was the third Napoleon because the son of Napoleon I, Napoleon II, had died in his youth without ever ruling France.) Thus ended the short-lived Second Republic.

Like his celebrated uncle, Louis Napoleon used a plebiscite to win public approval for his seizure of power. A stunning 90 percent of voters supported his move to set up the Second Empire. Many saw a monarchy as more stable than a republic. Millions of French also recalled the glory days of Napoleon Bonaparte and hoped that his nephew would restore the magic. A few voters even thought he was the old Napoleon, miraculously still alive and returned from exile!

In fact, Napoleon III, like Louis Philippe, ruled at a time of rapid economic growth. For the bourgeoisie, the early days of the Second Empire brought prosperity and contentment. In time, however, Napoleon III would embark on foreign adventures that brought down his empire and ended France's long leadership in Europe.

## "Europe Catches Cold"

In both 1830 and 1848, the revolts in Paris inspired uprisings elsewhere in Europe. As Metternich said, "When France sneezes, Europe catches cold." Most uprisings were suppressed. But here and there, rebels did force changes on conservative governments. Even when they failed, they frightened rulers badly enough to encourage reform later in the century.

**Belgium.** The one notable success for Europe's revolutionaries in 1830 took place in Belgium. In 1815, the Congress of Vienna had united the Austrian Netherlands (present-day Belgium) and the Kingdom of Holland under the Dutch king. The Congress had wanted to create a strong barrier against French expansion.

The Belgians resented the new arrangement. The Belgians and Dutch had different languages, religions, and economic interests. The Belgians were Catholic, while the Dutch were Protestant. The Belgian economy was based on manufacturing; the Dutch, on trade.

In 1830, news of the Paris uprising that toppled Charles X ignited a revolutionary spark in Belgium. Students and workers threw up barri-

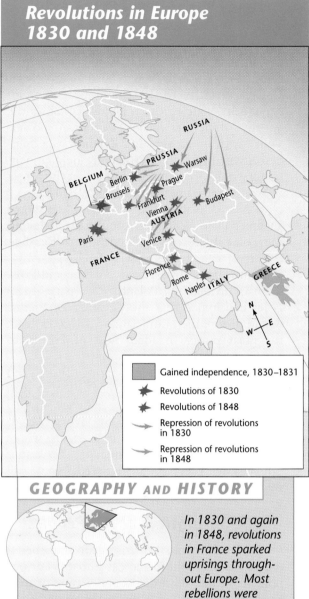

### Revolutions in Europe 1830 and 1848

Gained independence, 1830–1831

★ Revolutions of 1830

★ Revolutions of 1848

→ Repression of revolutions in 1830

→ Repression of revolutions in 1848

**GEOGRAPHY AND HISTORY**

In 1830 and again in 1848, revolutions in France sparked uprisings throughout Europe. Most rebellions were quickly crushed. Still, they were a warning to Europe's rulers that the old order was changing.

1. **Location** On the map, locate (a) Paris, (b) Warsaw, (c) Prague, (d) Italy.
2. **Place** (a) Which countries gained independence in 1830 and 1831? (b) Name two places where revolutions took place in 1830. In 1848.
3. **Critical Thinking** **Making Inferences** How can you tell from the map that the revolution in Budapest was unsuccessful?

cades in Brussels, the capital. The Dutch king turned to the other European powers for help. Britain and France, however, believing they would benefit from the separation of Belgium and Holland, supported Belgian demands for independence. The conservative powers—Austria, Prussia, and Russia—were too busy putting down revolts of their own to become involved.

As a result, in 1831, Belgium became an independent state with a liberal constitution. Shortly after, the major European powers signed a treaty recognizing Belgium as a "perpetually neutral state." Protecting Belgian neutrality would be an important issue at the outset of World War I, in 1914. (See page 700.)

**Poland.** Nationalists in Poland also staged an uprising in 1830. But, unlike the Belgians, the Poles failed to win independence for their country.

In the late 1700s, Russia, Austria, and Prussia had divided up Poland. (See page 443.) Poles had hoped that the Congress of Vienna would restore their homeland in 1815. Instead, the great powers handed most of Poland to Russia.

In 1830, Polish students, army officers, and landowners rose in revolt. They failed to gain widespread support, however, and were brutally crushed by Russian forces. Survivors fled to Western Europe and the United States, where they kept alive the dream of freedom. "Poland is not yet lost," they proudly declared, "while still we live."

## The Springtime of the Peoples

In 1848, revolts in Paris again unleashed a tidal wave of revolution across Europe. For opponents of the old order, it was a time of such hope that they called it the "springtime of the peoples." Michael Bakunin, a young Russian revolutionary, recalled the feeling of unlimited possibilities:

> **66**It seemed as if the entire world was turned upside down. The improbable became commonplace, the impossible possible. . . . If someone had said, 'God has been driven from heaven and a republic has been proclaimed there,' . . . no one would have been surprised.**99**

**Sources of discontent.** Revolution in France was the spark that touched off the revolts. But grievances had been piling up for years.

Unrest came from many sources. Middle-class liberals wanted a greater share of political power for themselves, as well as protections for the basic rights of all citizens. Workers demanded relief from the miseries of the spreading Industrial Revolution. And nationalists of all classes ached to throw off foreign rule. By 1848, discontent was so widespread that it was only a matter of time before it exploded into full-scale revolution.

**Metternich falls.** In the Austrian empire, revolt first broke out in Vienna, taking the government by surprise. Metternich, who had dominated Austrian politics for more than 30 years, tried to suppress the students who took to the streets. But when workers rose up to support the students, Metter-nich resigned and fled in disguise. The Austrian emperor promised reform.

▲ *Metternich flees in disguise*

Revolution quickly spread to other parts of the empire. In Budapest, Hungarian nationalists led by Louis Kossuth demanded an independent government. They also called for an end to serfdom and a written constitution to protect basic rights. In Prague, the Czechs made similar demands. Overwhelmed by events, the Austrian government agreed to the reforms.

Any gains were short-lived, however. The Austrian army soon regained control of Vienna and Prague. With Russian help, Austrian forces also smashed the rebels in Budapest. Many were imprisoned or executed or forced into exile.

**Revolution in Italy.** Uprisings also erupted in the Italian states. Nationalists wanted to end domination of Italy by the Austrian Hapsburgs. As elsewhere, nationalist goals were linked to demands for liberal reforms such as constitutional government. Workers suffering economic hardships demanded even more radical changes.

**Italy in Revolt** *Throughout Italy, nationalists rose up to end Austrian domination. Here, rebels in Venice hurl cobblestones at well-armed Austrian forces.* **Political and Social Systems** *What other goals did Italian nationalists pursue?*

From Venice in the north to Naples in the south, Italians set up independent republics. Revolutionaries even expelled the pope from Rome and installed a nationalist government. (See Chapter 23.)

Before long, however, the forces of reaction surged back here, too. Austrian troops ousted the new governments in northern Italy. A French army restored the pope to power in Rome. In Naples, local rulers betrayed their promises to the rebels, canceling the reforms they had reluctantly accepted.

**Turmoil in the German states.** In the German states, university students passionately demanded national unity and liberal reforms. Economic hard times and a potato famine brought peasants and workers into the struggle. Workers destroyed the machines that threatened their livelihood, while peasants burned the homes of wealthy landowners.

Women, too, plunged into the struggle. A German woman explained her reasons for fighting alongside her husband:

66You know it was not [enthusiasm for] war that called me, but love. Yet I must confess—hate, too, a burning hate generated in the struggle against tyrants and oppressors of sacred human rights.99

In Prussia, liberals forced King Frederick William IV to agree to a constitution written by an elected assembly. Within a year, though, he dissolved the assembly. Later, he issued his own constitution keeping power in his own hands or those of the upper classes.

**Frankfurt Assembly.** Throughout 1848, delegates from many German states met in the Frankfurt Assembly. "We are to create a consti-tution for Germany, for the whole land," declared one leader with boundless optimism.

Divisions soon emerged. Delegates debated endlessly on such topics as whether the new Germany should be a republic or a monarchy, and whether or not to include Austria in a united German state. Finally, the assembly offered Prussia's Frederick William IV the crown of a united Germany. To their dismay, the conservative king rejected the offer because it came not from the German princes but from the people— "from the gutter," as he described it. By early 1849, the assembly was dissolved, under threat from the Prussian military.

Outside the assembly, liberals clashed with workers whose demands were too radical for middle-class reformers to accept. Conservative forces rallied, dousing the last flames of revolt.

**GLOBAL CONNECTIONS**

The defeat of liberal forces in Europe in 1848 had a profound effect on the other side of the world. By the 1850s, Japan would begin to emerge from centuries of self-imposed isolation. Seeking to modernize, the new leaders of Japan looked to Europe for examples. The nation that they chose as a model was the conservative, militaristic Germany that had emerged after the defeat of the liberals in 1848. As a result, modern Japan, like Germany after 1848, was marked by political conservatism and emphasis on a strong military.

Hundreds were killed. Many more went to prison. And thousands of Germans left their homeland, most for the cities of the United States.

## Looking Ahead

By 1850, the flickering light of rebellion faded, ending the age of liberal revolution that had begun in 1789. Why did the uprisings fail? In general, revolutionaries did not have mass support. In Poland in 1830, for example, peasants did not take part in the uprising. In 1848, a growing gulf divided workers seeking radical economic change and liberals pursuing moderate political reform.

By mid-century, Metternich was gone from the European scene. Still, his conservative system remained in force. In the decades ahead, liberalism, nationalism, and socialism would win successes not through revolution but through political activity. Ambitious political leaders would unify Germany and Italy. Workers would campaign for reforms through unions and the ballot box, as they increasingly won the right to vote.

## SECTION 2 REVIEW

1. **Identify** (a) Charter of French Liberties, (b) Charles X, (c) Louis Philippe, (d) Louis Napoleon, (e) Louis Kossuth, (f) Frankfurt Assembly.
2. (a) What were the causes of the French revolution of 1830? (b) What were its effects?
3. How was the French revolution of 1848 really two revolutions?
4. Why did conservative leaders in Europe fear news of revolutions in France?
5. Why did most revolts in the 1830s and 1840s fail?
6. *Critical Thinking* **Identifying Alternatives** Do you think that European rulers could have prevented nationalist revolts by allowing reforms? Why or why not?
7. *ACTIVITY* Create a "docudrama" for television based on the "February Days" and "June Days" during the French revolution of 1848.

## 3 Latin American Wars of Independence

### Guide for Reading

■ What were the long-term causes of the revolutions in Latin America?

■ How did Haiti's struggle for freedom differ from independence fights in other parts of Latin America?

■ How did Mexico and the nations of South America win independence?

Like many wealthy Latin American* creoles, young Simón Bolívar (boh LEE vahr) was sent to Europe to complete his education. There, he became a strong admirer of the ideals of the French Revolution.

One afternoon, Bolívar and his Italian tutor sat talking about freedom and the rights of ordinary people. Bolívar's thoughts turned to his homeland, held as a colony by Spain. He fell on his knees and swore a solemn oath:

❝I swear before God and by my honor never to allow my hands to be idle nor my soul to rest until I have broken the chains that bind us to Spain.❞

In later years, Bolívar would fulfill his oath, leading the struggle to liberate northern South America from Spain. Elsewhere in Latin America, other leaders organized independence movements. By 1825, most of Latin America had been freed from colonial rule.

### Climate of Discontent

By the late 1700s, the revolutionary fever that gripped Western Europe had spread to Latin America. There, discontent was rooted in

---

*Latin America refers to the regions in Middle and South America colonized by Europeans, especially the Spanish, French, and Portuguese, whose languages are rooted in Latin. It includes Spanish-speaking countries from Mexico to Argentina, Portuguese-speaking Brazil, and French-speaking Haiti.

the social, racial, and political system that had emerged during 300 years of Spanish rule.

**Ethnic and social hierarchy.** Spanish-born peninsulares dominated Latin American political and social life. Only they could hold top jobs in government and the Church. Many creoles—the European-descended Latin Americans who owned the haciendas, ranches, and mines—bitterly resented their second-class status. Merchants fretted under mercantilist policies that tied the colonies to Spain. "Commerce ought to be as free as air," declared one colonial merchant.

Meanwhile, a growing population of mestizos and mulattoes were angry at being denied the status, wealth, and power that were available to whites. Native Americans suffered economic misery under the Spanish, who had conquered the lands of their ancestors. In the Caribbean region and parts of South America, masses of enslaved Africans who worked on plantations longed for freedom.

Beyond dissatisfaction with Spanish rule, the different classes had little in common. In fact, they distrusted and feared one another. At times, they worked together against the Spanish. But once independence was achieved, the creoles, who had led the revolts, dominated the governments.

**Enlightenment ideas.** In the 1700s, educated creoles read the works of Enlightenment thinkers such as Voltaire, Rousseau, and Montesquieu. They watched colonists in North America throw off British rule. Translations of the Declaration of Independence and the Constitution of the United States even circulated among the creole elite.

Women actively participated in the exchange of ideas. In some cities, women hosted and attended salons, called *tertulias,* where independence and revolution were discussed.

During the French Revolution, young creoles like Simón Bolívar traveled in Europe and were inspired by the ideals of "liberty, equality, and brotherhood." Still, while Enlightenment ideas and revolutions in other lands touched off debates, most creoles were reluctant to act.

**Napoleon.** The spark that finally ignited widespread revolt in Latin America was Napoleon's invasion of Spain in 1808. Napoleon ousted the Spanish king and placed his brother

*Social Classes in Latin America* These portraits, both by Edouard Pingret, paint contrasting pictures of life in colonial Latin America. The wealthy women at top are probably peninsulares, Spanish-born settlers who dominated political and social life. At the opposite end of the social scale was the Native American woman, at bottom. This inequality between classes fed discontent and in time resulted in uprising. **Diversity** What other classes made up the social hierarchy in Latin America?

Joseph on the Spanish throne. Latin American leaders saw Spain's weakness as an opportunity to reject foreign domination and demand independence from colonial rule.

## Haiti's Struggle

Even before Spanish colonists hoisted the flag of freedom, revolution had erupted elsewhere in Latin America, in a French-ruled colony on the island of Hispaniola. Haiti, as it is now called, was France's most valued possession in the 1700s.

In Haiti, French planters owned great sugar plantations worked by nearly a half million enslaved Africans. The sugar trade was hugely profitable, but conditions for enslaved workers were horrendous. Many were cruelly overworked and underfed. Haiti also had a population of both free and enslaved mulattoes. Free mulattoes, however, had few rights and were badly treated by the French.

In the 1790s, revolutionaries in France were debating ways to abolish slavery in the West Indies. However, debating the issue in Paris did not help enslaved Haitians gain their freedom. Embittered by suffering and inspired by talk of liberty and equality, they took action. In 1791, a slave revolt exploded in northern Haiti. Under the able leadership of Toussaint L'Ouverture (too SAN loo vuhr TYOOR), Haitians would fight for freedom and pave the way for throwing off French rule.

## Toussaint L'Ouverture

 Toussaint L'Ouverture was born into slavery in Haiti. But his father, the son of a noble West African family, had only recently been brought to the West Indian island. He taught the boy to take pride in his African heritage.

Toussaint learned to speak both French and the African language of his ancestors. Thanks to a kind master, he also learned to read. He pored over stories of slave revolts in ancient Rome and of military heroes like Julius Caesar.

In time, Toussaint read the works of the French philosophes. One passage, in particular, impressed him:

66Nations of Europe, your slaves need neither your generosity nor your advice to break the . . . yoke that oppresses them. All they need is a brave leader. Who will he be? There is no doubt that he will appear. He will come and raise the sacred standard of liberty.99

Toussaint determined to be that "brave leader" and bring his people to liberty.

**The uprising begins.** When a slave revolt broke out in 1791, Toussaint was nearly 50 years old. His intelligence and military skills soon earned him the position of leader.

The struggle was long and complex. Toussaint's army of former slaves faced many enemies. Mulattoes, promised high pay, joined French planters against the rebels. France,

*Toussaint L'Ouverture* A self-educated former slave, Toussaint L'Ouverture led Haitians in a revolt against French rule. Although Toussaint was captured and killed, his followers eventually won independence. In 1820, Haiti became a republic, the only nonslave nation in the Western Hemisphere. **Impact of the Individual** Compare this portrait with the portrait of Napoleon on page 495. What impression is each artist trying to create?

Spain, and Britain each sent armies to Haiti. The fighting took more lives than any other revolution in the Americas.

**An inspiring commander.** Although untrained, Toussaint was a brilliant general. He was also an inspiring commander. On the eve of one crucial battle, he issued this stirring call to his army:

66Do not disappoint me. Prove yourselves men who know how to value liberty and how to defend it. . . . We are fighting so that liberty—the most precious of all earthly possessions—may not perish. We are fighting to preserve it for ourselves, for our children, for our brothers, for our fellow citizens.99

**Rebuilding.** By 1798, Toussaint had achieved his goal—enslaved Haitians had been freed. And even though Haiti was still a French colony, Toussaint's forces controlled most of the island.

Toussaint set about rebuilding the country, which had been destroyed by long years of war. By offering generous terms, he won the support of French planters. He set out to improve agriculture, expand trade, and give Haiti a constitution. He even tried to heal rifts between classes by opening his government to whites and mulattoes as well as Africans.

**Renewed struggle.** In France, meantime, Napoleon Bonaparte rose to power. He determined to regain control over Haiti. In 1802, he sent a large army to the island.

Toussaint again took up arms, this time to fight for full independence. His guerrilla forces were aided by a deadly ally, yellow fever, which took a growing toll on the invaders. In April 1802, with soldiers dying at the rate of a hundred a day, the French agreed to a truce, or temporary peace.

**"The tree of black liberty."** Shortly after, a trusted French friend lured Toussaint to his house, where he betrayed him. Soldiers seized the Haitian leader and hustled him in chains onto a French warship. As the ship sailed, Toussaint told the captain:

66In overthrowing me, the French have only felled the tree of black liberty in

Haiti. It will shoot up again, for it is deeply rooted, and its roots are many.99

Ten months later, in a cold mountain prison in France, Toussaint died. But Haiti's struggle for freedom continued. In 1804, Haitian leaders declared independence. With yellow fever destroying his army, Napoleon abandoned Haiti. In the years ahead, rival Haitian leaders fought for power. Finally, in 1820, Haiti became a republic, the only nonslave nation in the Western Hemisphere. ▣

## A Call to Freedom in Mexico

The slave revolt in Haiti frightened creoles in Spanish America. While they wanted power themselves, most had no desire for economic or social changes that might threaten their way of life. In 1810, however, a creole priest in Mexico, Father Miguel Hidalgo (hih DAHL goh), raised a cry for freedom that would echo across the land.

**El Grito de Dolores.** Father Hidalgo presided over the poor rural parish of Dolores. On the morning of September 16, 1810, he rang the church bells summoning the people to prayer. When they gathered, he startled them with an urgent appeal. We do not know his exact words, but his message is remembered:

66My children, will you be free? Will you make the effort to recover the lands stolen from your forefathers by the hated Spaniards 300 years ago?99

Father Hidalgo's speech became known as "el Grito de Dolores"—the cry of Dolores. It called the people of Mexico to fight for "Independence and Liberty."

Poor Mexicans rallied to Father Hidalgo. A ragged army of poor mestizos and Native Americans marched to the outskirts of Mexico City. At first, some creoles supported the revolt. However, they soon rejected Hidalgo's call for an end to slavery and his plea for reforms to improve conditions for Native Americans. They felt that these policies would cost them power. They also believed that the Indians deserved their lot in life.

After some early successes, the rebels faced growing opposition. Less than a year after he

# PARALLELS THROUGH TIME

## National Flags

For most of history, flags were emblems of an army or a royal family. With the rise of nationalism, however, national flags began to emerge. Today, each nation has a flag whose design represents the ideals of its people.

**Linking Past and Present** Why do you think designing a flag is often one of the first things a new nation does?

**PAST** *Each new nation of Latin America adopted its own flag. The yellow-blue-red flag of Venezuela symbolized the gold of the Americas separated from Spain by the blue ocean. Argentina borrowed its blue-white-blue flag from fleets that attacked Spanish ports during the colonial era.*

**PRESENT** *These flags represent nations that gained independence since 1945. The Star of David on the Israeli flag symbolizes the quest for a Jewish homeland. The shield and crossed spears of Kenya's flag recall its proud struggle for independence.*

---

issued the "Grito," Hidalgo was captured and executed, and his followers scattered.

**José Morelos.** Another priest picked up the banner of revolution. Father José Morelos was a mestizo who called for wide-ranging reform. He wanted to improve conditions for the majority of Mexicans, abolish slavery, and give the vote to all men. For four years, Morelos led rebel forces before he, too, was captured and shot in 1815.

Spanish forces, backed by conservative creoles, hunted down the surviving guerrillas. They had almost succeeded in ending the rebel movement when events in Spain had unexpected effects on Mexico.

**Independence achieved.** In Spain in 1820, liberals forced the king to issue a constitution. This alarmed Agustín de Iturbide (ee toor BEE day), a conservative creole in Mexico. Iturbide feared that the new Spanish government might impose liberal reforms on the colonies as well.

Iturbide had spent years fighting Mexican revolutionaries. Suddenly in 1821, he reached out to them. Backed by creoles, mestizos, and Native Americans, he overthrew the Spanish viceroy. Mexico was independent at last.

Iturbide took the title Emperor Agustín I. Soon, however, liberal Mexicans toppled the would-be monarch and set up the Republic of Mexico.

Although Mexico was free of Spanish rule, the lives of most people changed little. Military leaders dominated the government and ruled by force of arms. The next 100 years would see new struggles to improve conditions for Mexicans. These struggles would be even more complicated by the intervention of foreign powers, including the United States.

## New Republics in Central America

Spanish-ruled lands in Central America declared independence in the early 1820s. Iturbide tried to add these areas to his Mexican empire. After his overthrow, local leaders set up a republic called the United Provinces of Central America.

The union was short-lived. It soon fragmented into the separate republics of Guatemala, Nicaragua, Honduras, El Salvador, and Costa Rica. Like Mexico, the new nations faced many social and economic problems.

## Revolutions in South America

In South America, Native Americans had rebelled against Spanish rule as early as the 1700s. These rebellions had limited results, however. It was not until the 1800s that discontent among the creoles sparked a widespread drive for independence.

**An early challenge.** The strongest challenge by Native Americans was led by Tupac Amaru, who claimed descent from the Incan royal family. He demanded that the government end the brutal system of forced Indian labor. Spanish officials rejected the demand for reform.

In 1780, Tupac Amaru organized a revolt. A large army crushed the rebels and captured and killed their leader. But the revolt did have effects. The Spanish king ordered officials to look into the system of forced labor and eventually abolished it.

**A long struggle.** In the early 1800s, widespread discontent began to surface among other South Americans. Educated creoles like Simón Bolívar, whom you read about at the beginning of the section, had applauded the French and American revolutions. They dreamed of winning their own independence.

In 1808, when Napoleon Bonaparte occupied Spain, Bolívar and his friends saw it as a signal to act. Bolívar by then had returned to South America. In 1810, he led an uprising that established a republic in his native Venezuela.

Bolívar's new republic was quickly toppled by conservative

▲ Simón Bolívar

# CAUSE AND EFFECT

### Long-Term Causes

European domination of Latin America
Spread of Enlightenment ideas
American and French revolutions
Growth of nationalism in Latin America

### Immediate Causes

Creoles, mestizos, and Indians resent colonial rule
Revolutionary leaders emerge
Napoleon invades Spain and ousts Spanish king

## INDEPENDENCE MOVEMENTS IN LATIN AMERICA

### Immediate Effects

Toussaint leads slave revolt in Haiti
Colonial rule ends in much of Latin America
Attempts made to rebuild economies

### Long-Term Effects

18 separate republics set up
Continuing efforts to achieve stable democratic governments and to gain economic independence

### Connections Today

Numerous independent nations in Latin America
Ongoing efforts to bring prosperity and democracy to people in Latin America

*Interpreting a Chart* By 1825, most of Latin America had become independent. Growth of nationalism and discontent with colonial rule played a role in bringing about the independence movements. ■ What was one immediate effect of Latin American independence movements? Which effect of independence movements in Latin America continues to this day?

# Independent Nations of Latin America About 1844

Independent nations with date of independence

*United Provinces of Central America had dissolved by 1841, Gran Colombia by 1830

OREGON COUNTRY

UNITED STATES

PACIFIC OCEAN

ATLANTIC OCEAN

MEXICO 1821

GULF OF MEXICO

Mexico City

BAHAMAS (Br.)

HAITI 1804

CUBA

DOMINICAN REPUBLIC 1844

PUERTO RICO

BRITISH HONDURAS

JAMAICA

CARIBBEAN SEA

GUATEMALA 1839
EL SALVADOR 1839
HONDURAS 1838
NICARAGUA 1838
COSTA RICA 1838

UNITED PROVINCES OF CENTRAL AMERICA*

Caracas

TRINIDAD

VENEZUELA 1830

BRITISH GUIANA
DUTCH GUIANA
FRENCH GUIANA

PANAMA (part of Colombia)

Bogotá

COLOMBIA 1819

GRAN COLOMBIA*

Equator

Quito

ECUADOR 1822

BRAZIL 1822

Lima

PERU 1824

BOLIVIA 1825

La Paz

N
W    E
S

PARAGUAY 1811

Rio de Janeiro

Asunción

CHILE 1818

ARGENTINA 1816

URUGUAY 1828

Santiago

Buenos Aires

Montevideo

PATAGONIA

0    750    1500 Miles
0    750    1500 Kilometers

FALKLAND ISLANDS (Argentine until 1833)

## Latin America About 1790

NEW SPAIN

UNITED STATES

Mexico City

BAHAMAS (Br.)

HISPANIOLA

CUBA

WEST INDIES

GUIANAS

Bogotá

NEW GRANADA

BRAZIL

Lima

PERU

LA PLATA

Rio de Janeiro

Buenos Aires

British
Dutch
French
Portuguese
Spanish

0    750    1500 Miles
0    750 1500 Kilometers

## GEOGRAPHY AND HISTORY

In the late 1700s, Europeans controlled most of Latin America. Wars of independence erupted across the region, however, and by the mid-1800s, a number of new nations had been born.

1. **Location** (a) On the main map, locate the following: Mexico, Gran Colombia, Haiti. (b) On the inset map, locate the following: La Plata, New Spain.

2. **Place** (a) Which countries had been carved out of New Granada by 1844? (b) Which independent countries had been part of New Spain?

3. **Critical Thinking** **Synthesizing Information** In a sentence, summarize the information shown on these two maps. Then, explain why the mapmaker needed to include an inset map.

forces. For years, civil war raged in Venezuela. The revolutionaries suffered many setbacks, and twice Bolívar was forced into exile on the island of Haiti.

Then, Bolívar conceived a daring plan. He would march his army across the Andes and attack the Spanish at Bogotá, the capital of the viceroyalty of New Granada (present-day Colombia). First, he cemented an alliance with the hard-riding *llaneros*, or Venezuelan cowboys. Then in a grueling campaign, he led an army through swampy lowlands and over the snow-capped mountains. Finally, in August 1819, he swooped down to take Bogotá from the surprised Spanish.

Other victories followed. By 1821, Bolívar had freed Caracas, Venezuela. "The Liberator," as he was now called, then moved south into Ecuador, Peru, and Bolivia. There, he joined forces with another great South American leader, José de San Martín.

**San Martín.** Like Bolívar, San Martín was a creole. He was born in Argentina but went to Europe for military training. In 1816, this gifted general helped Argentina win freedom from Spain. He then joined the independence struggle in other areas. He, too, led an army across the Andes, from Argentina into Chile. He defeated the Spanish in Chile before moving into Peru to strike further blows against colonial rule.

Bolívar and San Martín tried to work together, but their views were too different. In 1822, San Martín stepped aside, letting Bolívar's forces win the final victories against Spain.

**Dreams and disappointments.** The wars of independence had ended by 1824. Bolívar now worked tirelessly to unite the lands he had liberated into a single nation, called Gran Colombia. Bitter rivalries, however, made that impossible. Before long, Gran Colombia split into three countries: Venezuela, Colombia, and Ecuador.

Bolívar faced another disappointment as power struggles among rival leaders triggered violent civil wars. Spain's former South American colonies faced a long struggle to achieve stable governments—and an even longer one for democracy. (See Chapter 26.) Before his death in 1830, a discouraged Bolívar wrote, "We have achieved our independence at the expense of everything else." Contrary to his dreams, no social revolution took place. South America's common people had simply changed one set of masters for another.

## Independence for Brazil

No revolution or military campaigns were needed to win independence for Brazil. When Napoleon's armies conquered Portugal, the Portuguese royal family fled to Brazil. During his stay in Brazil, the Portuguese king introduced many reforms, including free trade.

When the king returned to Portugal, he left his son Dom Pedro to rule Brazil. "If Brazil demands independence," the king advised Pedro, "proclaim it yourself and put the crown on your own head."

In 1822, Pedro followed his father's advice. He became emperor of an independent Brazil. He accepted a constitution that provided for freedom of the press and religion as well as an elected legislature. Brazil remained a monarchy until 1889, when social and political turmoil led it to become a republic.

## SECTION 3 REVIEW

1. **Identify** (a) Toussaint L'Ouverture, (b) Miguel Hidalgo, (c) el Grito de Dolores, (d) José Morelos, (e) Agustín de Iturbide, (f) Tupac Amaru, (g) Simón Bolívar, (h) José de San Martín, (i) Dom Pedro.
2. How did the colonial class system contribute to discontent in Latin America?
3. (a) What was the first step on Haiti's road to independence? (b) What role did Toussaint L'Ouverture play in Haiti's struggle?
4. Why did creoles in Mexico refuse to support Hidalgo or Morelos?
5. (a) What was Bolívar's goal for South America? (b) Did he achieve his goal? Explain.
6. *Critical Thinking* **Comparing** Compare the ways Mexico and Brazil achieved independence.
7. *ACTIVITY* Imagine that you have been hired by the French government. Create a "wanted" poster for the capture of Toussaint L'Ouverture.

# Skills for Success

**Critical Thinking** | **Writing and Researching** | **Maps, Charts, and Graphs** | **Speaking and Listening**

## Identifying Ideologies

An ideology is a system of thought that seeks to define the proper nature of government and society. Liberalism, conservatism, communism, capitalism, and democracy are all examples of ideologies.

People do not always declare outright what ideologies they follow. However, you can identify their ideology by analyzing what they say.

The statements below reflect basic ideas of conservativism and liberalism, two opposing ideologies of the 1800s. Read the statements, and then follow the steps to identify the ideology each statement represents.

**1** **Identify the subject of the statement.** (a) What is the main subject of Prince Metternich's statement? Of Jeremy Bentham's statement? (b) How are the two subjects related?

**2** **List the major points of the statement.** (a) According to Metternich, how does a king fulfill his duties? (b) What rule does Metternich believe should guide change in government? (c) What does Metternich say should be the goal of rulers at a time of unrest? (d) According to Bentham, what should be the goal of government? (e) What does Bentham believe is the goal of governments ruled by kings? (f) Which form of government does he prefer? Why?

**3** **Identify the speaker's ideology.** (a) According to Metternich, from whom do kings get their power? (b) From what sources does the basic rule about governmental change come? (c) According to Bentham, from whom should a government get its power? (d) What does Bentham believe about human nature that will ensure good representative government? (e) What ideology does each speaker represent? Explain.

***Beyond the Classroom*** Conservative and liberal ideologies still exist today. However, they have changed since the 1800s. Use reference sources to find out what each "ism" stands for today. Then, watch two or more TV talk shows, and identify whether each is liberal or conservative. Be prepared to support your answer.

---

### *Prince Clemens von Metternich*

**❝**I am a true friend to order and public peace. As such . . . I am absolutely convinced that the governments ruled by kings must . . . stop the rioting and social unrest. By taking whatever steps are necessary, the kings will fulfill the duties which God . . . has given them the power to do. . . .

Centuries of experience and history have shown that one rule guides how governments and citizens should behave when it comes to change. This rule declares 'that no one should ever dream of changing or reforming society when emotions are out of control. If such is the case, the wisest thing to do is to maintain things the way they are.' So let the kings of all nations vigorously establish stability, let all their decrees and actions reflect it.**❞**

---

Adapted from Prince Metternich, *Secret Memorandum for Alexander 1*, December 15, 1820.

### *Jeremy Bentham*

**❝**In every society, a government should work for the greatest happiness of the greatest number of its citizens. . . . What we have now are governments by kings which work for the greatest happiness for themselves. . . . A king has no reason to see that his subjects are happy and content . . . since his subjects have no say in whether he will be ruler or not. . . . Under a representative democracy [in which men elect their government leaders], the goal is the greatest happiness of the greatest number. . . . Because every human being is most interested in gaining happiness for himself, every human being pursues that line of conduct which . . . will contribute the most to his happiness . . . [electing leaders that will help him gain happiness].**❞**

---

Adapted from Jeremy Bentham, *Constitutional Code for the Use of All Nations*, 1827, 1830.

# CHAPTER 21 REVIEW

## Building Vocabulary

Review the following vocabulary from this chapter: *ideology, universal manhood suffrage, autonomy, nationalism, peninsular, creole, mulatto, mestizo.* Write sentences using each of these terms, leaving blanks where the terms would go. Exchange your sentences with another student and fill in the blanks on each other's lists.

## Reviewing Chapter Themes

1. **Political and Social Systems** What were the goals and achievements of each of the following groups in Europe in the 1800s: (a) conservatives, (b) liberals, (c) nationalists, (d) socialists?
2. **Economics and Technology** What role did economics play in the French revolution of 1848?
3. **Continuity and Change** What ideas did the revolutionaries of the 1800s owe to the French Revolution of 1789?
4. **Global Interaction** (a) What European ideas influenced Latin Americans in their struggle for independence? (b) How did Napoleon's invasion of Spain encourage Latin Americans to rebel against colonial rule?

## Thinking Critically

1. **Recognizing Causes and Effects** How did ideologies like liberalism and nationalism contribute to unrest in Europe in the 1800s? ( ★ See *Skills for Success*, page 18.)
2. **Recognizing Points of View** In 1847, King Frederick William IV of Prussia rejected the idea of a constitution with the following words: "Neither now nor ever will I allow a scribbled sheet of paper to intervene like a second Providence between our God in Heaven and this land of ours." (a) What reason does Frederick William give for opposing a constitution? (b) How might a supporter of liberalism answer Frederick William's argument? ( ★ See *Skills for Success*, page 280.)
3. **Comparing** Compare the situation in Paris at the time of the French revolution of 1789 with that during the revolution of 1848. (a) How were they similar? (b) How were they different?
4. **Analyzing Information** You have read Metternich's comment "When France sneezes, Europe catches cold." What did he mean?
5. **Making Inferences** (a) Why do you think it was hard for Europeans in the 1800s to work together to achieve their revolutionary goals? (b) Why did conservative governments often survive the revolutions designed to overthrow them?
6. **Predicting Consequences** Do you think that the suppression of nationalist revolutions in the mid-1800s put an end to nationalism? Why or why not? ( ★ See *Skills for Success*, page 974.)
7. **Synthesizing Information** (a) Identify the major goal of each of the following leaders: Toussaint L'Ouverture, Miguel Hidalgo, Simón Bolívar. (b) Did each achieve his goal? Explain. ( ★ See *Skills for Success*, page 896.)

## For Your Portfolio

Imagine that you have been asked by a publisher to help retell events from history in comic book form. You will work with a group of classmates to produce a comic book about the age of revolution in Europe and Latin America.

1. Begin by selecting an event from this chapter as the subject of your comic book. For example, you might focus on the revolts in the Balkans or Greece, the French uprisings in 1830 or 1848, or the wars of independence in Latin America.
2. Divide up the responsibilities of the assignment among your group. Assign some members to do research, others to write dialogue and narrative. Still others can draw the pictures. Finally, another group can assemble the book.
3. With your group, outline the story you will tell. Decide how many pages your comic book will be and what you will feature in your illustrations.
4. After research is completed, have the writers set down the story for your comic book. Remember, most of a comic book story is told in dialogue. Writers may want to use comic book symbols for loud noises, exclamations, and so on.
5. Have artists illustrate the story. Writers and artists should consult as necessary.
6. Share your history comic with the class. Be prepared to answer questions about your story.

# *Unit-in-Brief*

## Enlightenment and Revolution

**Chapter 18** The Enlightenment and the American Revolution (1715–1800)

The Enlightenment was a movement in Western Europe and North America that sought to discover natural laws and apply them to social, political, and economic problems. Since the 1700s, Enlightenment ideas have spread around the world, creating upheaval and change as they have challenged established traditions.

- Enlightenment thinkers called philosophes applied the methods of science to their efforts to understand and improve society.
- The ideas of thinkers such as Locke, Montesquieu, and Rousseau would later justify revolutions and inspire principles of representative government.
- Physiocrats rejected mercantilism in favor of laissez-faire economics.
- Despite a growing middle class, most Europeans remained peasants who lived in small rural villages, untouched by Enlightenment ideas.
- England established a constitutional monarchy and built the most powerful commercial empire in the world.
- After years of growing dissent, Britain's North American colonies won independence in the American Revolution.
- Inspired by Enlightenment ideas, the United States adopted a constitution that would serve as a model for other democratic nations.

**Chapter 19** The French Revolution and Napoleon (1789–1815)

Between 1789 and 1815, the French Revolution destroyed an absolute monarchy and disrupted a social system that had existed for over a thousand years. These events ushered in the modern era in European politics.

- France was burdened by an outdated social class system, a severe financial crisis, and a monarchy too indecisive to enact reforms.
- In 1789, dissatisfied members of the middle class called for a constitution and other reforms. Meanwhile, hunger and social resentment sparked rioting among peasants and poor city dwellers.
- In the first phase of the French Revolution, moderates attempted to limit the power of the monarchy and guarantee basic rights.
- In 1793, as enemies outside France denounced the revolution, radicals executed the king and queen and began a Reign of Terror.
- From 1799 to 1815, Napoleon Bonaparte consolidated his power within France and subdued the combined forces of the greatest powers of Europe.
- Under Napoleon, French armies spread the ideas of revolution across Europe.
- In 1815, the Congress of Vienna sought to undo the effects of the French Revolution and the Napoleonic era.

## Chapter 20 The Industrial Revolution Begins (1750–1850)

During the 1700s, production began to shift from simple hand tools to complex machines and new sources of energy replaced human and animal power. Known as the Industrial Revolution, this transformation marked a crucial turning point in history and changed the lives of people all over the world.

- An agricultural revolution contributed to a population explosion that, in turn, fed the growing industrial labor force.
- Abundant resources and a favorable business climate allowed Britain to take an early lead in industrialization.
- New sources of energy, such as coal and steam, fueled factories and paved the way for faster means of transporting people and goods.
- A series of remarkable inventions revolutionized the British textile industry and led to the creation of the first factories.
- Rapid urbanization and the rise of the factory system at first created dismal living and working conditions.
- Laissez-faire economists, utilitarians, and socialists put forth their own ideas for solving the problems of industrial society.
- Karl Marx promoted communism, a radical form of socialism that would have a worldwide influence.

## Chapter 21 Revolutions in Europe and Latin America (1790–1848)

With the Congress of Vienna, the great powers sought to return to the political and social order that had existed prior to 1789. However, in the early 1800s, a wave of violent uprisings swept across Western Europe and Latin America, fueled by the political ideas of the French Revolution and the economic problems of the Industrial Revolution.

- Two opposing ideologies emerged in Europe. Liberals embraced Enlightenment ideas about democracy and individual rights, while conservatives sought to preserve the old political and social order.
- Nationalism inspired independence movements among peoples with a shared heritage but also bred intolerance and persecution of minorities.
- In 1830 and 1848, ideological tensions and social inequalities sparked uprisings in France and elsewhere in Europe. Although most of these democratic revolutions were suppressed, they served to hasten reform later in the century.
- In Latin America, discontent with foreign domination led to a series of independence movements that freed most of the region from colonial rule by 1825.

# A Global View

## How Did the New Ideas of the Enlightenment Lead to a Wave of Democratic Revolutions?

During the later 1700s and the early 1800s, new ideas brought revolutionary changes in western society and government. The Enlightenment, the American and French revolutions, and the Industrial Revolution all made this period a turning point in western history.

### Ideas and Machines

Voltaire, Rousseau, and other thinkers of the French Enlightenment urged radical changes in government. They proposed limitations on governmental power and favored enlightened rule dedicated to the welfare of the people. Their ideas were partly inspired by the example of France's powerful neighbor across the English Channel. British monarchs actually shared power with Parliament, which included elected representatives of at least some of the people.

The Industrial Revolution also made key contributions to social change. In the beginning, industrialization created a poverty-stricken new working class. The demands of this class for improved living conditions would lead to major political changes in later years. At the same time, however, increased productivity would bring great material wealth.

### Revolutions in Europe

In the late 1700s, France, Europe's greatest power, confronted many economic, social, and political problems. These problems finally exploded in the French Revolution of 1789.

During the tumultuous years that followed, revolutionaries who were inspired by the ideas of the Enlightenment overthrew the French monarchy. They stripped the Church of its power and the ruling aristocracy of its land. Leaders like Robespierre also launched a savage Reign of Terror, which claimed the lives of thousands of people.

Out of this revolutionary chaos, a new ruler rose to power. Napoleon Bonaparte greatly strengthened the French government and conquered most of Europe. An alliance of all the other great powers finally

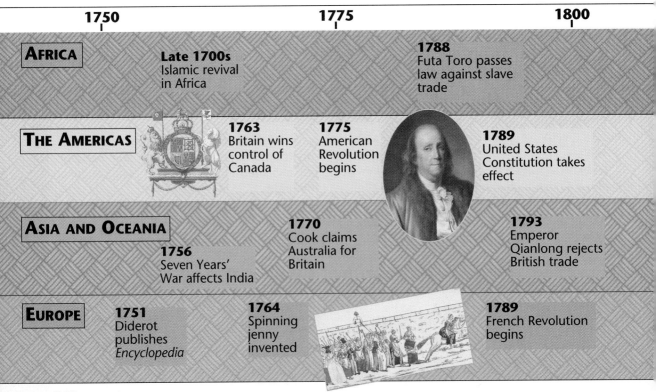

**1750**

**1775**

**1800**

**AFRICA**

**Late 1700s**
Islamic revival
in Africa

**1788**
Futa Toro passes
law against slave
trade

**THE AMERICAS**

**1763**
Britain wins
control of
Canada

**1775**
American
Revolution
begins

**1789**
United States
Constitution takes
effect

**ASIA AND OCEANIA**

**1756**
Seven Years'
War affects India

**1770**
Cook claims
Australia for
Britain

**1793**
Emperor
Qianlong rejects
British trade

**EUROPE**

**1751**
Diderot
publishes
*Encyclopedia*

**1764**
Spinning
jenny
invented

**1789**
French Revolution
begins

defeated him at Waterloo in 1815.

Though the French Revolution had failed, the problems that had caused it persisted. As a result, Europeans rose in revolt in many lands in 1830 and 1848. Though most of these revolutions also failed, they made the need for reform clear.

## Revolutions in the Americas

More successful revolutions blazed up in Europe's American colonies. In both North and South America, Enlightenment ideas and economic grievances drove the colonists to revolt. Once free of European control, the former colonists established republics with elected governments rather than hereditary monarchies.

The first American revolution began in 1775 in Britain's North American colonies. After a hard struggle, George Washington and his colleagues freed the 13 colonies. The United States Constitution gave the new nation a republican government which guaranteed the rights of the people.

The United States experiment in democracy helped inspire revolutions in Spain's Latin American colonies. By 1825, a string of independent Spanish-speaking republics stretched from Argentina to Mexico. During this period, Haiti gained independence from France, while Brazil broke away from Portugal.

In the Americas as in Europe, most people did not yet have the right to vote. Still, most of two continents had been freed from European rule.

## Looking Ahead

By the mid-1800s, most of the world was still ruled by autocratic monarchs, and Europe's remaining overseas colonies had no democratic rights. Still, the "age of democratic revolutions" left a legacy of accelerating change. Enlightenment political ideas would develop further over the next two centuries. Europe and the Americas would continue to build increasingly democratic governments, and democratic ideas would begin to spread beyond the West.

**ACTIVITY** Choose two events and two pictures from the time line below. For each, write a sentence explaining how it relates to the themes expressed in the Global View essay.

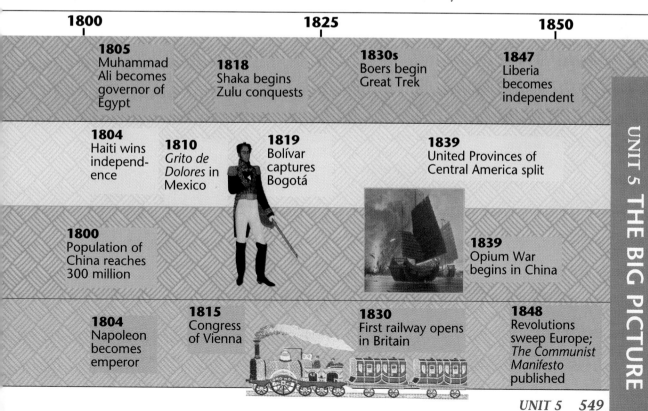

| 1800 | 1825 | 1850 |

**1805** Muhammad Ali becomes governor of Egypt

**1818** Shaka begins Zulu conquests

**1830s** Boers begin Great Trek

**1847** Liberia becomes independent

**1804** Haiti wins independence

**1810** Grito de Dolores in Mexico

**1819** Bolívar captures Bogotá

**1839** United Provinces of Central America split

**1800** Population of China reaches 300 million

**1839** Opium War begins in China

**1804** Napoleon becomes emperor

**1815** Congress of Vienna

**1830** First railway opens in Britain

**1848** Revolutions sweep Europe; The Communist Manifesto published

# You Decide

## Exploring Global Issues

### What Limits Should There Be on Freedom of Speech?

"I do not agree with a word that you say, but I will defend to the death your right to say it." Whether or not Voltaire said these exact words, he passionately believed in this idea. Since then, people everywhere have quoted these words to uphold the right to free speech.

But are there limits to freedom of speech? And, if so, what are they? To begin your investigation, examine these viewpoints.

**ENGLAND**
**1859**

In his influential work *On Liberty,* the philosopher John Stuart Mill stated his belief that democracy required the free exchange of ideas:

66If all mankind minus one were of one opinion, and only one person were of the contrary opinion, mankind would be no more justified in silencing that one person, than he, if he had the power, would be justified in silencing mankind.99

**UNITED STATES**
**1919**

Supreme Court justice Oliver Wendell Holmes gave a famous definition of the limits of free speech in the case of *Schenck* v. *United States:*

66The most stringent protection of free speech would not protect a man in falsely shouting fire in a theater and causing a panic.99

**FRANCE**
**1940**

During wartime, democratic governments have restricted free speech in the interests of security. "Silence," warns this poster from World War II. "The enemy hears your secrets." ▶

SILENCE

L'ENNEMI..
GUETTE VOS CONFIDENCES

**CHINA**
**1957**

Mao Zedong founded a government in China based on the ideas of the communist philosopher Karl Marx:

66What should our policy be towards non-Marxist ideas? As far as unmistakable counterrevolutionaries and saboteurs of the socialist cause are concerned, the matter is easy. We simply deprive them of their freedom of speech.99

**IRAN**

1979

The same year he was overthrown, Shah Muhammad Reza Pahlavi had denounced the dangers of uncontrolled free speech:

**66**Freedom of thought, freedom of thought! Democracy, democracy! With five-year-old children going on strike and parading through the streets? That's democracy? That's freedom of thought?**99**

**SOUTH AFRICA**

1980s

In the face of protests from the black majority, the minority government of South Africa took many measures to limit free speech, including censoring news reports like this one. ▶

dela!" echoed through the stadium as the wife of Nelson Mandela, the long-imprisoned black leader, arrived. ▮

▮ she told the workers. ▮

▮ Union leaders have asked miners to stay away from the pits this Wednesday as a gesture of protest and mourning.

**CANADA**

1985

The criminal code of Canada outlaws public remarks against religious, racial, or ethnic groups:

**66**Every one who, by communicating statements other than in private conversation, willfully promotes hatred against any identifiable group is guilty of . . . an indictable offense and is liable to imprisonment for a term not exceeding two years.**99**

## COMPARING VIEWPOINTS

1. Which of the viewpoints represented here seems to place the fewest restrictions on freedom of speech?
2. Mao Zedong and the shah of Iran were both authoritarian dictators. How are their viewpoints similar or different?
3. When should free speech in a democracy be restricted according to Holmes? According to the poster? According to the Canadian criminal code?

### YOUR INVESTIGATION

**ACTIVITY**

1. Find out more about other viewpoints related to this topic. You might investigate one or more of the following:

 ▪ The Alien and Sedition acts, enacted in the United States in 1798.
 ▪ Wartime censorship in Allied nations during World War I.
 ▪ Restrictions on free speech in Iran since the overthrow of the shah.
 ▪ The contrasting policies toward dissent of Soviet leaders Leonid Brezhnev and Mikhail Gorbachev.
 ▪ Recent debates in the United States about forms of "symbolic speech," such as flag burning.

2. Decide which viewpoint you agree with most closely and express it in your own way. You may do so in an essay, a cartoon, a poem, a drawing or painting, a song, a skit, a video, or some other way.

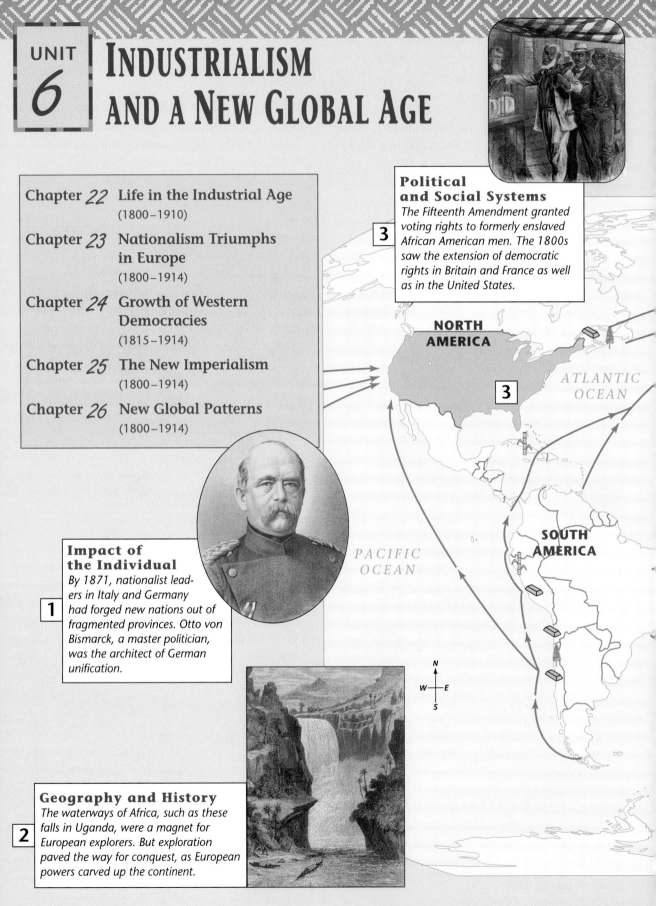

# UNIT *6*

# INDUSTRIALISM AND A NEW GLOBAL AGE

**Political and Social Systems**

**3** *The Fifteenth Amendment granted voting rights to formerly enslaved African American men. The 1800s saw the extension of democratic rights in Britain and France as well as in the United States.*

**NORTH AMERICA**

*ATLANTIC OCEAN*

**3**

*PACIFIC OCEAN*

**SOUTH AMERICA**

**Impact of the Individual**

**1** *By 1871, nationalist leaders in Italy and Germany had forged new nations out of fragmented provinces. Otto von Bismarck, a master politician, was the architect of German unification.*

**Geography and History**

**2** *The waterways of Africa, such as these falls in Uganda, were a magnet for European explorers. But exploration paved the way for conquest, as European powers carved up the continent.*

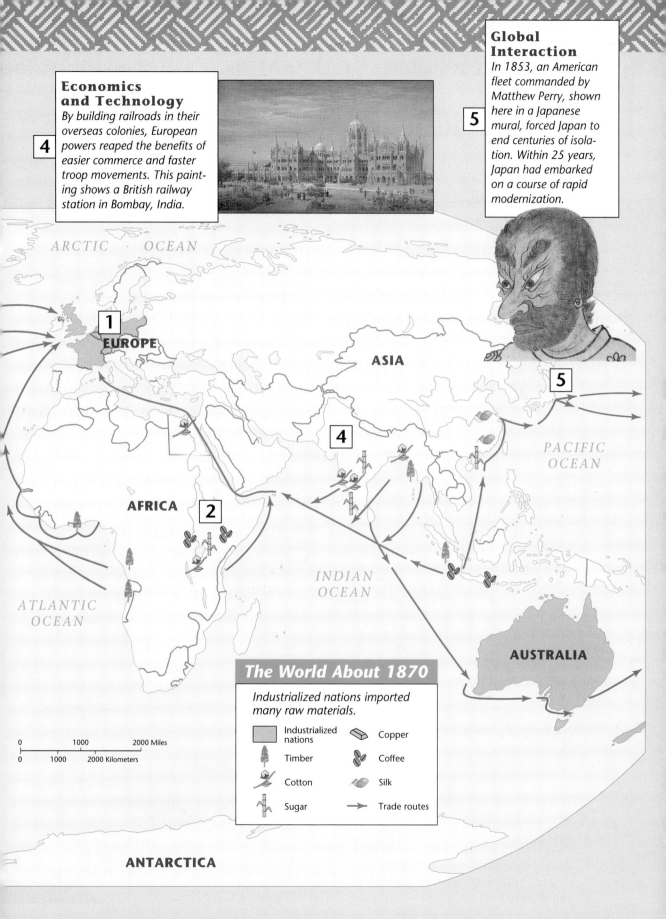

**Economics
and Technology**

4

By building railroads in their overseas colonies, European powers reaped the benefits of easier commerce and faster troop movements. This painting shows a British railway station in Bombay, India.

**Global
Interaction**

5

In 1853, an American fleet commanded by Matthew Perry, shown here in a Japanese mural, forced Japan to end centuries of isolation. Within 25 years, Japan had embarked on a course of rapid modernization.

ARCTIC OCEAN

1

EUROPE

ASIA

4

AFRICA

2

PACIFIC OCEAN

5

INDIAN OCEAN

ATLANTIC OCEAN

AUSTRALIA

**The World About 1870**

*Industrialized nations imported many raw materials.*

| | Industrialized nations | | Copper |
| | Timber | | Coffee |
| | Cotton | | Silk |
| | Sugar | → | Trade routes |

0    1000    2000 Miles
0    1000    2000 Kilometers

ANTARCTICA

# Life in the Industrial Age

## (1800–1910)

The great French scientist Louis Pasteur (pas TYOOR) was working in his laboratory on July 6, 1885. Suddenly, a woman rushed in, clutching her limping nine-year-old son. The mother explained that the boy had been savagely attacked by a dog two days before.

Though not a doctor, Pasteur agreed to examine the wounded child. He noted that the boy "had numerous bites . . . some of them very deep that made walking difficult." Still, the bites were not what worried Pasteur. The great danger was rabies, a deadly disease of the nervous system, which could be transmitted through the bite of a "mad dog." There was no known cure.

Pasteur had been studying rabies for five years. He had even saved the lives of some dogs. But he had never tried his treatment on humans. Still, two physicians agreed that, without treatment, the boy would die. Under Pasteur's direction, a doctor gave the boy a series of injections over 10 days. In great anxiety, Pasteur watched and waited. "All is going well," he wrote after five days. "If the lad keeps well during the following weeks, I think the experiment will be sure to succeed."

All summer, the boy continued to thrive. In October, Pasteur was able to report to the French Academy of Sciences:

> **66**After I might say innumerable experiments, I have arrived at a preventive method, practical and prompt, the success of which has been so convincing in dogs that I have confidence of its general application in all animals and even in man.**99**

In the 1800s, medicine and other sciences stretched the frontiers of knowledge. Some discoveries, like Pasteur's rabies vaccine, helped people live longer, healthier lives. Others, applied to the growing world of industry, led to the development of thousands of inventions.

From the mid-1800s, industrialism spread rapidly across Europe to North America and beyond. During this second Industrial Revolution, the western world acquired greater wealth and power than any other society in the past. Big businesses emerged that dwarfed those of other eras. Economic and social changes transformed daily life. By the early 1900s, the western world had acquired much of the structure and patterns of life that are familiar to us today.

**FOCUS ON** these questions as you read:

- **Economics and Technology**
  How did science and new ways of doing business promote industrial growth?

- **Religions and Value Systems**
  What social, economic, and intellectual developments reshaped western social values?

- **Art and Literature**
  How did literature, music, and visual arts reflect changing attitudes and values?

- **Impact of the Individual**
  What important contributions were made by individuals in science, business, and the arts?

**TIME AND PLACE**

**The New Cities** *The rapidly growing cities of the industrial world attracted people of all social classes. The well-to-do mother and daughter walking down this street lived a far different life from the flower seller or the men working on the pavement.* **Continuity and Change** *Compare this painting to the earlier engraving by Gustave Doré on page 521. How do they emphasize different aspects of city life?*

## HUMANITIES LINK

*Art History* Edvard Munch, *Spring Evening on Karl Johan Street, Oslo* (page 565).
*Literature* In this chapter, you will encounter passages from the following works of literature: Emile Zola, *Germinal* (page 561); Elizabeth Gaskell, *Cranford* (pages 567–568); William Wordsworth, "It is a beauteous evening, calm and free" (page 572); Charles Dickens, *Oliver Twist* (pages 575–576); Henrik Ibsen, *A Doll's House* (pages 578–579).

| 1807 | 1846 | 1859 | 1870s | 1903 |
|------|------|------|-------|------|
| Industrial Revolution spreads to Belgium | Anesthesia first used in surgery | *On the Origin of the Species* published | Impressionists develop new style of painting | Wright brothers invent airplane |

| 1800 | 1820 | 1840 | 1860 | 1880 | 1900 | 1920 |

# The Industrial Revolution Spreads

## Guide for Reading

- How did the industrialized world expand in the 1800s?

- How was technology linked to economic growth?

- Why did big business emerge in the late 1800s?

- **Vocabulary** *interchangeable parts, assembly line, corporation, cartel*

The first phase of industrialism had largely been forged from iron, powered by steam engines, and driven by the British textile industry. By the mid-1800s, the Industrial Revolution entered a new phase. New industrial powers emerged. New factories powered by new sources of energy used new processes to turn out new products. And new forms of business organization led to the rise of giant new companies. As a new century—our century—dawned, this "second" Industrial Revolution transformed the economies of the western world.

## New Industrial Powers

In the early Industrial Revolution, Britain stood alone as the world's industrial giant. To protect its head start, Britain tried to enforce strict rules against exporting inventions.

For a while, the rules worked. Then, in 1807, a British mechanic, William Cockerill, opened factories in Belgium for the manufacture of spinning and weaving machines. Belgium thus became the first European nation outside Britain to industrialize. By the mid-1800s, other nations had joined the race, and several newcomers were challenging Britain's industrial supremacy.

**The new pacesetters.** Why did other nations catch up so quickly to Britain? First, nations such as Germany, France, and the United States had more abundant supplies of coal, iron,

and other resources than did Britain. Also, they had the advantage of being able to follow Britain's lead. Like Belgium, latecomers often borrowed British experts or technology. The first American textile factory was built in Pawtucket, Rhode Island with plans smuggled out of Britain. American inventor Robert Fulton powered his steamboat with one of James Watt's steam engines.

Two countries in particular thrust their way to industrial leadership. Germany united into a powerful nation in 1871. (See Chapter 23.) Within a few decades, it became Europe's leading industrial power. Across the Atlantic, the United States advanced even more rapidly, especially after the Civil War. By 1900, American industry led the world in production.

**Uneven development.** Other nations industrialized more slowly, especially those in eastern and southern Europe. These nations often lacked natural resources or the capital to invest in industry. While Russia did have resources, social and political conditions slowed its economic development. Only in the late 1800s, more than 100 years after Britain, did Russia lumber toward industrialization.

In East Asia, however, Japan offered a remarkable success story. Although it lacked many basic resources, it industrialized rapidly after 1868. (See Chapter 26.) Canada, Australia, and New Zealand also built thriving industries.

**Impact.** Like Britain, the new industrial nations underwent social changes, such as rapid urbanization. Men, women, and children worked long hours in difficult and dangerous conditions. As you will read, by 1900, these conditions had begun to improve in many industrialized nations.

The factory system produced huge quantities of new goods at low-

*New industrial* ▶
*products—a sewing machine (top) and a coffeemaker (bottom)*

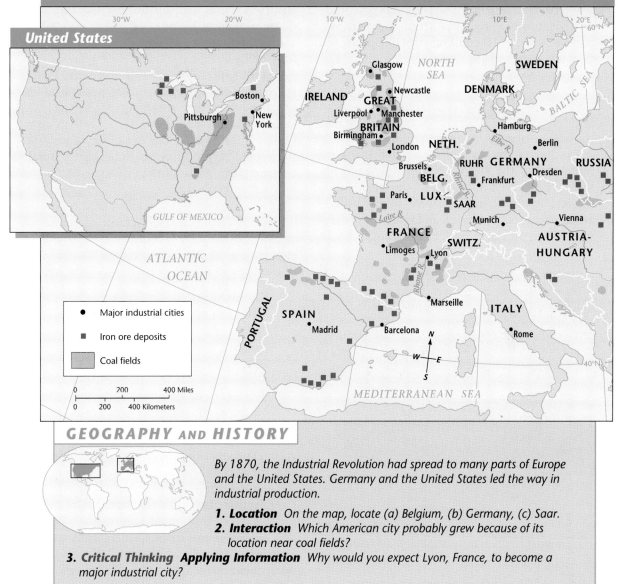

## Industrial Growth About 1870

**United States**

Boston
Pittsburgh • New York

GULF OF MEXICO

ATLANTIC OCEAN

Glasgow — NORTH SEA — SWEDEN
Newcastle — DENMARK
IRELAND — GREAT
Liverpool • Manchester — Hamburg
BRITAIN — Berlin
Birmingham — London — NETH.
Brussels — RUHR GERMANY — RUSSIA
BELG. — Frankfurt — Dresden
Paris — LUX. — SAAR
FRANCE — Munich — Vienna
SWITZ. — AUSTRIA-HUNGARY
Limoges — Lyon
Marseille — ITALY
PORTUGAL — SPAIN — Rome
Madrid — Barcelona
MEDITERRANEAN SEA

● Major industrial cities
■ Iron ore deposits
▨ Coal fields

0    200    400 Miles
0  200  400 Kilometers

### GEOGRAPHY AND HISTORY

By 1870, the Industrial Revolution had spread to many parts of Europe and the United States. Germany and the United States led the way in industrial production.

**1. Location** On the map, locate (a) Belgium, (b) Germany, (c) Saar.
**2. Interaction** Which American city probably grew because of its location near coal fields?
**3. Critical Thinking Applying Information** Why would you expect Lyon, France, to become a major industrial city?

er prices than ever before. In time, workers were buying goods that in earlier times only the wealthy could afford. The demand for goods created jobs, as did the building of cities, railroads, and factories. Politics changed, too, as leaders had to meet the demands of an industrial society.

Globally, industrial nations competed fiercely, altering patterns of world trade. Thanks to their technological and economic advantage, western powers came to dominate the world more than ever before. (See Chapters 25 and 26.)

## New Methods of Production

The basic characteristics of the factory system remained the same. Factories still used large numbers of workers and power-driven machines to mass-produce goods. To improve the efficiency of the system, manufacturers designed products with interchangeable parts, identical components that could be used in place of one another. Interchangeable parts simplified both assembly and repair.

Later, manufacturers introduced another new method of production, the assembly line.

Workers on an assembly line add parts to a product that moves along a belt from one work station to the next. Like interchangeable parts, the assembly line made production faster and cheaper, lowering the price of goods.

## Technology and Industry

The marriage of science and industry spurred economic growth. Early industrial inventions like the steam engine were generally the work of gifted tinkerers. By the later 1800s, though, many companies were hiring professional chemists, biologists, and engineers to develop new products and technologies. These creative experts sped up the breathtaking pace of technological change. ( ■ See *You Decide,* "Is Technology a Blessing or a Curse?" pages 688–689.)

**Steel.** In 1856, British engineer Henry Bessemer developed a process to purify iron ore and produce a new substance, steel. Steel was lighter, harder, and more durable than iron. Others improved on the Bessemer process, so steel could be produced very cheaply. It rapidly became the major material used in tools, bridges, and railroads.

Just as steam was a symbol of the first Industrial Revolution, steel became a symbol for the second. Observers commented on the awesome power of the huge steel mills where tons of molten metal were poured into giant mixers:

> **❝**At night the scene is indescribably wild and beautiful. The flashing fireworks, the terrific gusts of heat, the gaping, glowing mouth of the giant chest, the quivering light from the liquid iron, the roar of a nearby converter . . . combine to produce an effect on the mind that no words can translate.**❞**

As steel production soared, industrialized countries measured their success in steel output. (See the graph at left.)

**Chemicals.** Chemists created hundreds of new products, from medicines such as aspirin to new perfumes and soaps to margarine, the first artificially produced foodstuff. Newly developed chemical fertilizers played a key role in increasing food production.

The Swedish chemist Alfred Nobel invented dynamite, an explosive much safer than those used at the time. It became widely used in construction as well as in warfare—much to Nobel's dismay. Nobel earned a huge fortune from dynamite, which he willed to fund the Nobel prizes. (See page 694.)

**Electricity.** A new power source, electricity, was put to work in the late 1800s. Scientists like Benjamin Franklin had tinkered with electricity a century earlier. The Italian scientist Alessandro Volta developed the first battery about 1800. Later experimenters created the dynamo, which generated electricity. In the 1870s, the American inventor Thomas Edison

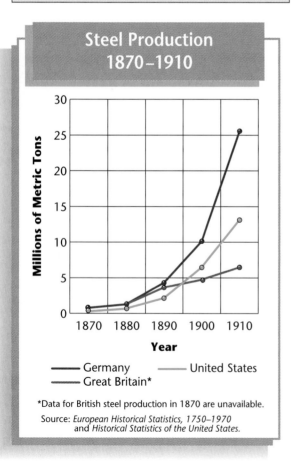

**Interpreting a Graph** *Before the introduction of the Bessemer process, industrialized nations produced only a few thousand tons of steel a year. By the end of the 1800s, steel production was measured in the millions.* ■ *Which nation led in steel production in 1890? In 1900? How much steel did Germany produce in 1900?*

### Steel Production 1870–1910

Millions of Metric Tons vs. Year

— Germany  — United States
— Great Britain*

*Data for British steel production in 1870 are unavailable.

Source: *European Historical Statistics, 1750–1970* and *Historical Statistics of the United States.*

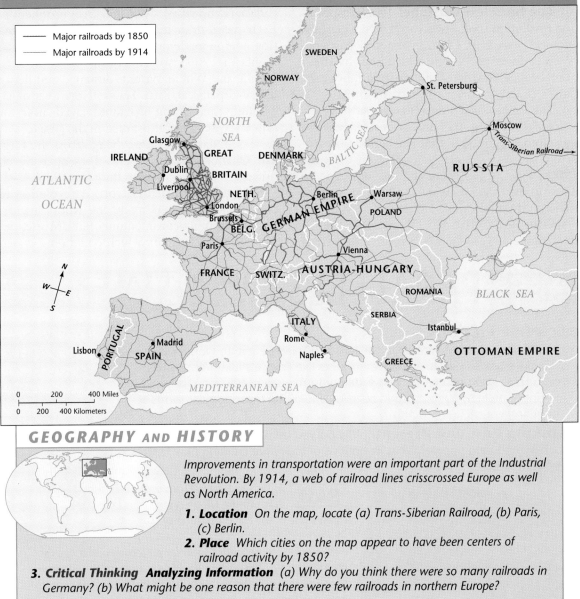

## Growth of Railroads, 1850–1914

Major railroads by 1850
Major railroads by 1914

NORTH SEA

SWEDEN

NORWAY

St. Petersburg

Moscow

Trans-Siberian Railroad →

RUSSIA

IRELAND

Glasgow

GREAT BRITAIN

DENMARK

BALTIC SEA

Dublin
Liverpool

NETH.

Berlin

Warsaw

ATLANTIC OCEAN

London

GERMAN EMPIRE

POLAND

Brussels

BELG.

Paris

FRANCE

SWITZ.

Vienna

AUSTRIA-HUNGARY

ROMANIA

BLACK SEA

SERBIA

Istanbul

PORTUGAL

Lisbon

Madrid

SPAIN

ITALY

Rome

Naples

GREECE

OTTOMAN EMPIRE

MEDITERRANEAN SEA

N W E S

0    200    400 Miles
0    200    400 Kilometers

### GEOGRAPHY AND HISTORY

Improvements in transportation were an important part of the Industrial Revolution. By 1914, a web of railroad lines crisscrossed Europe as well as North America.

1. **Location**  On the map, locate (a) Trans-Siberian Railroad, (b) Paris, (c) Berlin.
2. **Place**  Which cities on the map appear to have been centers of railroad activity by 1850?
3. **Critical Thinking  Analyzing Information**  (a) Why do you think there were so many railroads in Germany? (b) What might be one reason that there were few railroads in northern Europe?

made the first electric light bulb. Soon, Edison's "incandescent lamps" illuminated whole cities. The pace of city life quickened, and factories could remain productive after dark.

By the 1890s, cables carried electrical power from dynamos to factories. Electricity quickly replaced steam as the dominant source of industrial power.

### The Shrinking World

During the second Industrial Revolution, transportation and communications were trans-formed by technology. Steamships replaced sailing ships, and railroad building took off. In Europe and North America, rail lines connected inland cities and seaports, mining regions and industrial centers. In the United States, a transcontinental railroad provided rail service from the Atlantic to the Pacific. In the same way, Russians built the Trans-Siberian Railroad, linking Moscow in European Russia to Vladivostok on the Pacific. Railroad tunnels and bridges crossed the Alps in Europe and the Andes in South America. Passengers and goods rode on rails in India, China, Egypt, and South Africa.

**The horseless carriage.** The transportation revolution took a new turn when a German engineer, Nikolaus Otto, invented a gasoline-powered internal combustion engine. In 1887, his colleague Gottlieb Daimler (DĪM luhr) used Otto's engine to power the first automobile.

The French nosed out the Germans as early automakers. Then the American Henry Ford started making models that reached the breathtaking speed of 25 miles an hour. In the early 1900s, Ford began using the assembly line to mass-produce cars, making the United States a leader in the automobile industry.

**Conquest of the air.** The internal combustion engine powered more than cars. Motorized threshers and reapers boosted farm production. Even more dramatically, the internal combustion engine made possible the dream of human flight. In 1903, two American bicycle makers, Orville and Wilbur Wright, designed and flew a flimsy airplane at Kitty Hawk, North Carolina. Though their flying machine stayed aloft for only a few seconds, it ushered in the air age.

Soon, daredevils were flying across the English Channel and the Alps. Passenger travel, however, would not begin until the 1920s.

**Rapid communication.** A revolution in communications also made the world smaller. An American inventor, Samuel F. B. Morse, developed the telegraph, which could send coded

# PARALLELS THROUGH TIME

## Science Fiction

The dizzying rate of invention in the late 1800s led people to wonder what marvels might come next. Imaginative novelists like France's Jules Verne and England's H. G. Wells pioneered a new literary form—science fiction. Today, in print or on film, science fiction remains one of the most popular forms of entertainment.

**Linking Past and Present** Why do you think science fiction has had such an enduring appeal? What inventions of today are creating new fantasies about the future?

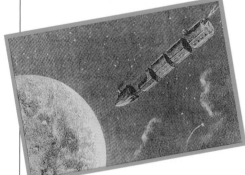

**PAST** *In his 1865 novel* From the Earth to the Moon, *Verne created one of the earliest pictures of space travel. Passengers on this rocket traveled in luxury, with padded walls for protection and a dog for companionship. The anchor would be tossed out the window to secure the vessel on the moon's surface. Verne also correctly predicted that space travelers would experience weightlessness.*

**PRESENT** *Beam us up! Inspired by modern advances in physics and computer technology, the creators of* Star Trek *made an enormous leap of imagination from the visions of Verne's day.*

messages over wires by means of electricity. His first telegraph line went into service between Baltimore and Washington, D.C., in 1844. By the 1860s, an undersea cable was relaying messages between Europe and North America.

Communication soon became even faster. In 1876, the Scottish-born American inventor Alexander Graham Bell patented the telephone. By the 1890s, the Italian pioneer Guglielmo Marconi had invented the radio. In 1901, Marconi transmitted a radio message from Britain to Canada, using Morse's dot-and-dash code. He later recalled:

> 66 Shortly before mid-day I placed the single earphone to my ear and started listening. . . . The answer came at 12:30 when I heard, faintly but distinctly, *pip-pip-pip*. . . . The electric waves sent out into space from Poldhu had traversed the Atlantic—the distance, enormous as it seemed then, of 1,700 miles. . . . I now felt for the first time absolutely certain that the day would come when mankind would be able to send messages without wires not only across the Atlantic, but between the farthermost ends of the earth. 99

As Marconi foresaw, radio would become part of today's global communications network that links every corner of the world.

## New Directions for Business

New technologies required the investment of large amounts of money. To get the needed capital, entrepreneurs developed new ways of organizing businesses. Owners sold stock, or shares in their companies, to investors. Each stockholder thus became owner of a tiny part of a company.

**Rise of big business.** By the late 1800s, what we call "big business" came to dominate industry. Large-scale companies such as steel foundries needed so much capital that they sold hundreds of thousands of shares. These businesses formed giant corporations, businesses that are owned by many investors who buy shares of stock. Stockholders risk only the amount they invest in the company and cannot

be held personally responsible for any debts of the corporation.

With large amounts of capital, corporations could expand into many areas. In the novel *Germinal* by the French writer Emile Zola, two investors discuss the growth of a large coal mining company:

> 66 'And is your company rich?' asked Etienne. . . .
>
> 'Ah! yes. Ah! yes. . . . Ten thousand workers, concessions reaching over sixty-seven towns, an output of five thousand tons a day, a railway joining all the pits, and workshops, and factories! Ah! yes! Ah, yes! There's money there!'"

**Move toward monopolies.** Powerful business leaders created monopolies and trusts, huge corporate structures that controlled entire industries or areas of the economy. In Germany, Alfred Krupp inherited a steelmaking business from his father. He bought up coal and iron mines as well as ore shipping lines that fed the steel business. Later, he and his son acquired plants that manufactured tools, railroad cars, and weapons. In the United States, John D. Rockefeller built Standard Oil Company of Ohio into an empire. By gaining control of oil wells, oil refineries, and oil pipelines, he dominated the American petroleum industry.

In their pursuit of profit, ruthless business leaders destroyed competing companies. Some lowered prices to force competitors out of business. Then, with the competition gone, they were free to raise prices to any level. Sometimes, a group of large corporations would form a cartel, an association to fix prices, set production quotas, or divide up markets. In Germany, a single cartel fixed prices for 170 coal mines. An international shipping cartel of British, German, French, Dutch, and Japanese shippers came close to setting freight rates on the sea lines of the world.

**Move toward regulation.** The rise of big business created a stormy debate. Some people saw the Krupps and Rockefellers as "captains of industry." Supporters praised their vision and skills. They pointed out that capitalists invested their great wealth in worldwide ventures, such

# CAUSE AND EFFECT

## Causes

Increased agricultural productivity

Growing population

New sources of energy, such as steam and coal

Growing demand for textiles and other mass-produced goods

Improved technology

Available natural resources, labor, and money

Strong, stable governments that promoted economic growth

## INDUSTRIAL REVOLUTION

## Immediate Effects

Rise of factories

Changes in transportation and communication

Urbanization

New methods of production using machines and steam power

Changes in workers' way of life and rise of urban working class

Growth of reform movements, including liberalism, socialism, and Marxism

## Long-Term Effects

Growth of labor unions

Increase in new, relatively inexpensive products

Spread of industrialization globally

Development of large corporations and other new ways of organizing businesses

Expansion of public education

Expansion of middle class

Fierce competition among industrialized nations for world trade

Progress in medical care and nutrition

Growth of women's movement

## Connections Today

Improvements in world health

Growth in population

Industrialization in developing nations

New sources of energy, including petroleum and nuclear power

Mass media and mass entertainment

Efforts to regulate world trade through international agreements

---

*Interpreting a Chart* Economics and technology sparked the Industrial Revolution. The long-term effects, however, touched nearly every aspect of life. ■ Identify two social and two economic effects of the Industrial Revolution.

---

as railroad building, that employed thousands of workers and added to general prosperity.

To others, the aggressive magnates were "robber barons." Any effort to destroy competition, critics argued, hurt the free-enterprise system. Reformers called for laws to prevent monopolies and regulate large corporations. By the early 1900s, some governments did move against monopolies. However, the political and economic power of business leaders often hindered efforts at regulation. ( ★ See *Skills for Success,* page 580.)

**Looking ahead.** By the late 1800s, European and American corporations were setting up operations around the world. Banks invested vast sums in undertakings such as building ports, railroads, and canals. As western capital flowed into Africa, Asia, and Latin America, western powers became increasingly involved in these regions, as you will read in Chapters 25 and 26.

## SECTION 1 REVIEW

1. **Identify**  (a) Bessemer process, (b) Thomas Edison, (c) Gottlieb Daimler, (d) Henry Ford, (e) Wilbur and Orville Wright, (f) Guglielmo Marconi, (g) Alfred Krupp.
2. **Define**  (a) interchangeable parts, (b) assembly line, (c) corporation, (d) cartel.
3. (a) How did the Industrial Revolution spread in the 1800s? (b) Why were other nations able to challenge Britain's leadership in industry?
4. How did science help industry expand? Give three examples.
5. How did the need for capital lead to new ways of organizing business?
6. *Critical Thinking* **Ranking** Which *three* technological advances in this section do you think were most important? Explain.
7. *ACTIVITY* Draw a political cartoon supporting or opposing laws against business monopolies in the late 1800s.

# 2 The World of Cities

## Guide for Reading

- What was the impact of medical advances in the late 1800s?

- How did cities expand and change?

- Why did conditions for workers improve?

In the 1870s, a citizen of Berlin, Germany, boasted of his city's remarkable growth. "We have already 800,000 inhabitants, next year we shall have 900,000, and the year after that a million." He predicted that Berlin's population would soon compete with those of Paris and even London.

Cities grew as rural people streamed into urban areas. By the end of the century, European and American cities had begun to take on many of the features of cities today.

## *Medicine and Population*

The population explosion that had begun in the 1700s continued. Between 1800 and 1900, the population of Europe more than doubled. This rapid growth was not due to larger families. In fact, families in most industrializing countries had fewer children. Instead, populations soared because the death rate fell. People ate better and enjoyed longer lives, thanks in part to improved methods of farming, food storage, and distribution. Medical advances and improvements in public sanitation also slowed death rates.

**The fight against disease.** Since the 1600s, scientists had known of microscopic organisms, or microbes. Some scientists speculated that microbes might cause certain diseases. Yet most doctors scoffed at this "germ theory." Not until 1870 did Louis Pasteur clearly show the link between germs and disease. As you read, Pasteur developed a vaccine for rabies as well as a process, called pasteurization, to kill disease-carrying microbes in milk.

In the 1880s, the German doctor Robert Koch identified the bacteria that caused tuberculosis, a respiratory disease that claimed about 30 million human lives in the 1800s. The search

CHOLERA PREVENTIVE COSTUME.

*Battling Disease?* *This German cartoon from the 1830s shows a man trying to protect himself from cholera by wearing a skin of rubber, yards of flannel, and a copper plate over his heart. He carries with him juniper berries, peppercorns, camphor, smelling salts, a cigar, and other "medicines" supposed to prevent infection.* **Economics and Technology** *What point do you think this cartoonist was making?*

for a tuberculosis cure, however, took half a century. By 1914, yellow fever and malaria had been traced to microbes carried by mosquitoes.

As people understood how germs caused disease, they bathed and changed their clothes more often. In western cities, better hygiene caused a marked drop in the rate of disease and death.

**In the hospital.** In 1846, a Boston dentist, William Morton, introduced anesthesia to relieve pain during surgery. The use of anesthetics allowed doctors to experiment with operations that had never before been possible.

Yet, throughout the century, hospitals could be dangerous places. Surgery was performed with dirty instruments in dank operating rooms. Often, a patient would survive an operation, only to die days later of infection. For the poor, being admitted to a hospital was often a death sentence. Wealthy or middle-class patients insisted on treatment in their own homes.

"The very first requirement in a hospital," said British nurse Florence Nightingale, "is that

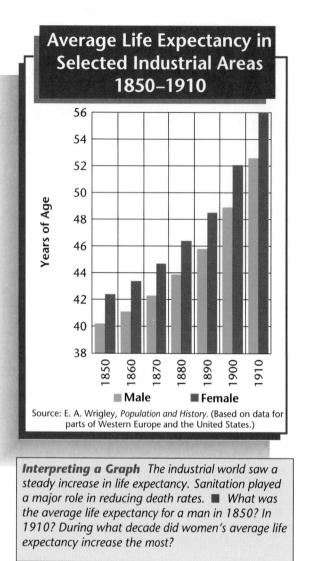

## Average Life Expectancy in Selected Industrial Areas 1850–1910

Years of Age

■ Male ■ Female

Source: E. A. Wrigley, *Population and History.* (Based on data for parts of Western Europe and the United States.)

*Interpreting a Graph* The industrial world saw a steady increase in life expectancy. Sanitation played a major role in reducing death rates. ■ What was the average life expectancy for a man in 1850? In 1910? During what decade did women's average life expectancy increase the most?

it should do the sick no harm." As an army nurse during the Crimean War, Nightingale insisted on better hygiene in field hospitals. Back home, she worked to introduce sanitary measures in British hospitals. She also founded the world's first school of nursing.

The English surgeon Joseph Lister discovered how antiseptics prevented infection. He insisted that surgeons wash their hands before operating and sterilize their instruments. Eventually, the use of antiseptics drastically reduced deaths from infection.

## The Life of the Cities

As industrialization progressed, cities came to dominate the West. City life, as old as civilization itself, underwent dramatic changes.

**The changing city landscape.** Growing wealth and industrialization altered the basic layout of European cities. City planners gouged out spacious new squares and boulevards. They lined these avenues with government buildings, offices, department stores, and theaters.

The most extensive urban renewal took place in Paris in the 1850s. Napoleon III's chief planner, Georges Haussmann, destroyed many tangled medieval streets full of tenement housing. In their place, he built wide boulevards and splendid public buildings. The project put many people to work, decreasing the threat of social unrest. The wide boulevards also made it harder for rebels to put up barricades and easier for troops to reach any part of the city.

As the century progressed, settlement patterns shifted. The rich developed pleasant residential neighborhoods on the outskirts of the city. The poor tended to crowd into slums near the city center, within reach of factories. Trolley lines made it possible to live in one part of the city and work in another.

**Sidewalks, sewers, and skyscrapers.** Paved streets made urban areas much more livable. First gas lamps, then electric street lights, increased safety at night. Cities organized police forces and expanded fire protection.

Beneath the streets and sidewalks, new sewage systems helped make cities healthier places to live. City reformers realized that clean water supplies were necessary to combat epidemics of cholera and tuberculosis. The massive new sewer systems of London and Paris were costly, but they cut death rates dramatically.

By the late 1800s, architects began using steel to construct soaring buildings. The metal Eiffel Tower became a symbol of Paris. In the United States, architects like Louis Sullivan pioneered a new structure, the skyscraper. In large cities, single-family middle-class homes gave way to multistory apartment buildings.

**Slums.** Despite urban improvements, city life remained harsh for the poor. Some working-class families could afford better clothing, newspapers, or tickets to a music hall. But they went home to small, cramped row houses or tenements in overcrowded neighborhoods.

In the worst tenements, whole families were often crammed into a single room. Unemployment or illness meant lost wages that could ruin

**Spring Evening on Karl Johan Street, Oslo** *This haunting street scene by the Norwegian painter Edvard Munch depicts the anonymous life of a big city. Munch was a pioneer in a style called expressionism. Expressionists used bold distortions and violent colors to explore complex, tortured emotional states.* **Art and Literature** *How does Munch express the idea of anonymity?*

a family. High rates of crime and alcoholism were a constant curse. Conditions had improved somewhat from the early Industrial Revolution, but slums remained a fact of city life.

**The lure of the city.** Despite their drawbacks, cities attracted millions of new residents. Many were drawn as much by the excitement as by the promise of work. Music halls, opera houses, and theaters provided entertainment for every taste. Museums and libraries offered educational opportunities. Sports, from tennis and horse racing to bare-knuckle boxing, drew citizens of all classes. Tree-lined parks offered a chance for fresh air, walks, and picnics.

The London *Times* described the hustle and bustle of holiday crowds in the late 1800s:

66Cyclists of both sexes covered the
    roads. River steamers and pleasure
boats carried their thousands to Kew and the upper reaches of the Thames. The London parks were crowded. The Botanic Gardens and Zoological Gardens . . . and the flowers of Batersea Park drew large crowds all day.99

Few of these enjoyments were available in country villages. For residents and tourists alike, cities were magnetic centers of action.

## Working-Class Struggles

Workers tried to improve the harsh conditions of industrial life. They protested low wages, long hours, unsafe conditions, and the constant threat of unemployment. At first, employers and governments tried to silence protesters. Strikes and unions were illegal. Worker demonstrations were crushed.

**The Rise of Trade Unions** *Trade unions did more than fight for higher wages and better conditions. They also gave workers a sense of dignity and pride. This was the emblem for a trade union whose members were engineers, machinists, and metalworkers.* **Economics and Technology** *How do the images in this emblem glorify labor?*

By mid-century, workers slowly began to make progress. They formed mutual-aid societies to help sick or injured workers. Women as well as men joined socialist parties or organized unions. The revolutions of 1830 and 1848 left vivid images of worker discontent, which governments could not ignore.

**Steps to reform.** By the late 1800s, most western countries had granted all men the vote. Workers also won the right to organize unions to bargain on their behalf. Germany legalized labor unions in 1869. Britain, Austria, and France followed. Unions grew rapidly. In France, union membership grew from 140,000 in 1890 to over a million in 1912.

Pushed by unions, reformers, and working-class voters, governments passed laws regulating conditions in factories and mines. Early laws forbade employers to hire children under the age of 10. Later laws outlawed child labor entirely and banned the employment of women in mines. Other laws limited work hours and improved safety conditions. By 1909, British coal miners had won an eight-hour day, setting a standard for workers in other countries.

First in Germany, then elsewhere, western governments set up programs for old-age pensions, as well as disability insurance for workers who were hurt or became ill. These programs protected workers from dying in poverty once they were no longer able to work.

**Rising standards of living.** Wages varied across the industrialized world. Unskilled laborers earned much less than skilled workers. Women factory workers received less than half the pay of men doing the same work. Farm laborers lagged seriously behind. They barely scraped by during the economic slump of the late 1800s. Periods of unemployment brought desperate hardships to industrial workers and helped boost union membership.

Overall, the standard of living for workers improved. Families ate more varied diets, lived in better homes, and dressed in inexpensive, mass-produced clothing. Advances in medicine ensured healthier lives. Some workers even moved to the suburbs, traveling to work on cheap subways and trams. Still, the gap between workers and the middle class widened.

## SECTION 2 REVIEW

1. **Identify** (a) Louis Pasteur, (b) Robert Koch, (c) Florence Nightingale, (d) Joseph Lister.
2. Why did Europe's population grow in the late 1800s?
3. Describe three ways that city life changed in the later Industrial Revolution.
4. What laws helped workers in the late 1800s?
5. *Critical Thinking* **Linking Past and Present** How was city life in the 1800s similar to or different from city life today?
6. *ACTIVITY* Imagine that you have moved from a rural village to London or Paris in the late 1800s. Write a letter home describing your feelings about city life.

## 3 Changing Attitudes and Values

### Guide for Reading

- What new social hierarchy emerged in industrialized nations?
- What ideals shaped the middle class?
- What changes did some women seek?
- How did science challenge traditional beliefs?
- **Vocabulary** *women's suffrage, racism, social gospel*

66 Once a woman has accepted an offer of marriage, all she has . . . becomes virtually the property of the man she has accepted as husband. 99

This advice appeared in *The What-Not, or Ladies' Handbook* in 1859. Not all women, though, accepted such restrictions. Anna Mozzoni, a crusader for women's rights in Italy, denounced the legal status of women:

66 For her, taxes but not an education; for her, sacrifices but not employment; for her, strict virtue but not honor; . . . for her, the capacity to be punished but not the right to be independent. 99

The debate about women's rights was one of several challenges to traditional views in the late 1800s. At the same time, middle-class ways came increasingly to dominate western society.

### A Shifting Social Order

The Industrial Revolution slowly changed the old social order in the western world. For centuries, the two main classes were nobles and peasants. Their roles were defined by their relationship to the land. While middle-class merchants, artisans, lawyers, and officials played important roles, they still occupied a secondary position in society. With the spread of industry, a more complex social structure emerged.

By the late 1800s, Western Europe's new upper class included superrich industrial and business families as well as the old nobility. Wealthy entrepreneurs married into aristocratic families, gaining the status of noble titles. Nobles needed the money brought by the industrial rich to support their lands and lifestyle. By tradition, the upper class held the top jobs in government and the military.

Below this tiny elite, a growing middle class was pushing its way up the social ladder. Its highest rungs were filled with midlevel business people and professionals such as doctors, scientists, and lawyers. With comfortable incomes, they enjoyed a wide range of material goods. Next came the lower middle class, which included teachers, office workers, shopowners, and clerks. On much smaller incomes, they struggled to keep up with their "betters."

At the base of the social ladder were workers and peasants. In highly industrialized Britain, workers made up more than 30 percent of the population in 1900. In Western Europe and the United States, the number of farmworkers fell, but many families still worked the land. The rural population was even higher in eastern and southern Europe.

### Middle-Class Values

By mid-century, the modern middle class had evolved its own way of life. The nuclear family lived in a large house, or perhaps in one of the new apartment houses. Rooms were crammed with large overstuffed furniture, and paintings and photographs lined the walls. Clothing reflected middle-class tastes for luxury and respectability.

A strict code of etiquette governed social behavior. Rules dictated how to dress for every occasion, when to write letters, and how long to mourn relatives who died. In Elizabeth Gaskell's novel *Cranford,* a young woman is instructed about how to pay a social call:

66 'It is the third day; I dare say your mamma has told you, my dear, never to let more than three days elapse between receiving a call and returning it; and also, that you are never to stay longer than a quarter of an hour.'

**Middle-Class Fashion** *While fashions changed through the 1800s, clothing for women and men reflected middle-class values of luxury and respectability. The gentlemen on the left sport the latest French styles. Below, servants use tongs to lower a woman's dress over her many layers of petticoats.* **Continuity and Change** *Compare these styles with clothing today. What details have remained the same? What has changed?*

'But am I to look at my watch? How am I to find out when a quarter of an hour has passed?'

'You must keep thinking about the time, my dear, and not allow yourself to forget it in conversation.'**"**

Parents strictly supervised their children, who were expected to be "seen but not heard." A child who misbehaved was considered to reflect badly on the entire family. Servants, too, were seen as a reflection of their employers. Even a small middle-class household was expected to have at least a cook and a housemaid.

**Courtship and marriage.** As in the past, middle-class families had a large say in choosing whom their children married. At the same time, young people had more freedom to choose a marriage partner. The notion of "falling in love" was more accepted than ever before.

Yet most women and men carefully considered the practical side of marriage. Mothers and daughters discussed the "likely prospects" of a possible husband. A young man was expected to court his bride-to-be with tender sentiments. But he also had to convince her father that he could support her in style. Until the late 1800s in most western countries, a husband controlled his wife's property, so marriage contracts were drawn up to protect a daughter's property rights.

**"Home, sweet home."** Within the family circle, the division of labor between wife and husband changed. In earlier times, middle-class women had often helped run family businesses out of the home. By the later 1800s, most middle-class husbands went to work in an office or shop. A successful husband was one whose income was enough to keep his wife at home. Women spent their working hours raising children, directing the servants, and perhaps doing religious or charitable service.

Books, magazines, and popular songs supported a "cult of domesticity" that idealized women and the home. Sayings like "home, sweet home" were stitched into needlework and hung on parlor walls. The ideal woman was seen as a tender, self-sacrificing caregiver who provided a nest for her children and a peaceful refuge for her husband.

This ideal rarely applied to the lower classes. Working-class women labored for low pay in garment factories or worked as domestic servants. Young women might leave domestic service after they married but often had to seek other employment. Despite long days working for wages, they were still expected to take full responsibility for child care and homemaking.

## Rights for Women

Some individual women and women's groups protested restrictions on women. Like earlier pioneers Olympe de Gouges (page 493) and Mary Wollstonecraft (page 460), they sought a broad range of rights. Across Europe and the United States, politically active women campaigned for fairness in marriage, divorce, and property laws. Women's temperance unions battled to combat the effects of alcoholism on family life.

These reformers faced many obstacles. In Europe and the United States, women could not vote. They were barred from most schools and had little, if any, protection under the law. A woman's husband or father controlled her property.

**Early voices.** Before 1850, some women had become leaders in the union movement. Others, mostly from the middle class, had campaigned for the abolition of slavery. In the process, they realized the severe restrictions on their own lives. In the United States, Elizabeth Cady Stanton and Susan B. Anthony crusaded against slavery before organizing a movement for women's rights.

Many women broke the barriers that kept them out of universities and professions. By the late 1800s, a few brave women overcame opposition to train as doctors or lawyers. Others became explorers, researchers, or inventors, often without recognition. For example, Julia Brainerd Hall worked with her brother to develop an aluminum-producing process. Their company became hugely successful, but Charles Hall received almost all of the credit.

**The suffrage struggle.** By the late 1800s, married women in some countries had won the right to control their own property. The struggle for political rights proved far more difficult. In the United States, the Seneca Falls Convention of 1848 demanded the right to vote for women. In Europe, groups dedicated to women's suffrage, or votes for women, emerged in the later 1800s.

Among men, some liberals and socialists supported women's suffrage. In general, though, suffragists faced intense opposition. Some critics claimed that women were too emotional to be allowed to vote. Others argued that women needed to be "protected" from grubby politics or that a woman's place was in the home, not in government. To such claims, Sojourner Truth, an African American campaigner for women's rights, replied:

> 66Nobody ever helps me into carriages, or over mudpuddles, or gives me any best place! And ain't I a woman? Look at me! Look at my arm! I have ploughed, and planted, and gathered into barns, and no man could head me! And ain't I a woman? I could work as much and eat as much as a man—when I could get it—and bear the lash as well! And ain't I a woman?99

On the edges of the western world, women made faster strides. In New Zealand, Australia, and some western territories of the United States, women won the vote before 1900. There, women who had "tamed the frontier" alongside men were not dismissed as weak and helpless. In Europe and most of the United States, however, the suffrage struggle succeeded only after World War I. You will read about the suffrage movement in various countries in Chapter 24.

## The Growth of Schools

By the late 1800s, reformers convinced governments to set up public schools and require basic education for all children. Teaching "the three Rs"—reading, writing, and 'rithmetic—was thought to produce better citizens. In addition, industrialized societies realized the need for a literate work force. Schools taught punctuality, obedience to authority, disciplined work habits, and patriotism. In European schools, children also received basic religious education.

**Public education.** At first, elementary schools were primitive. Many teachers had little schooling themselves. In rural areas, students attended class only when they were not needed on the farm or in their parents' shops.

By the late 1800s, more and more children were in school, and the quality of elementary education improved. Also, governments were expanding secondary schools, known as high schools in the United States. In secondary schools, students learned the "classical languages," Latin and Greek, along with history and mathematics.

In general, only middle-class families could afford to have their sons attend these schools, which trained students for more serious study or for government jobs. Middle-class girls were sent to school primarily in the hopes that they might marry well and become better wives and mothers.

**Higher education.** Universities expanded in this period, too. Most students were the sons of middle- or upper-class families. The university curriculum emphasized ancient history and languages, philosophy, religion, and law. By the late 1800s, universities added courses in the sciences, especially in chemistry and physics. At the same time, engineering schools trained students who would help build the new industrial society.

Some women sought greater educational opportunities. By the 1840s, a few small colleges for women opened, including Bedford College in England and Mount Holyoke in the United States. In 1863, the British reformer Emily Davies campaigned for female students to be allowed to take the entrance examinations for Cambridge University. She succeeded, but as late as 1897, male Cambridge students rioted against granting degrees to women. (See the picture on page 571.)

## The Challenge of Science

"Science moves, but slowly, slowly creeping on from point to point," wrote the British poet Alfred Tennyson. As you have seen, science in the service of industry brought great changes in

the later 1800s. At the same time, researchers advanced startling theories about the natural world. Their ideas challenged long-held ideas.

**Atomic theory.** A crucial breakthrough came in the early 1800s when the English Quaker schoolteacher John Dalton developed modern atomic theory. The ancient Greeks had speculated that all matter was made of tiny particles called atoms. Dalton showed how different kinds of atoms combine to make all chemical substances. In 1869, the Russian chemist Dmitri Mendeleyev (mehn duh LAY ehv) drew up a table that grouped elements according to their atomic weights. Mendeleyev's table became the basis for the periodic table of elements used by scientists today.

**The age of the Earth.** The new science of geology opened disturbing avenues of debate. In his *Principles of Geology* (1830–1833), Charles Lyell offered evidence to show that the Earth had formed over millions of years. His successors concluded that the Earth was at least two billion years old and that life had not appeared until long after Earth was formed. These ideas did not seem to agree with biblical accounts of creation.

Archaeology added other pieces to an emerging debate about the origins of life on Earth. In 1856, workers in the Neander valley of Germany accidentally uncovered the fossilized bones of prehistoric people, whom scientists called Neanderthal. Later scholars found fossils of other prehistoric humans and animals. These pioneering archaeologists had limited evidence and often drew mistaken conclusions. But as more discoveries were made around the world, scholars developed new ideas about early human life.

## The Darwin Furor

The most disturbing new idea came from the British naturalist Charles Darwin. In 1859, after years of research, he published *On the Origin of Species*. Darwin argued that all forms of life had evolved into their present state over millions of years. To explain the long, slow process of evolution, he put forward his theory of natural selection.

**Theory of natural selection.** Darwin adopted Malthus's idea that all plants and ani-

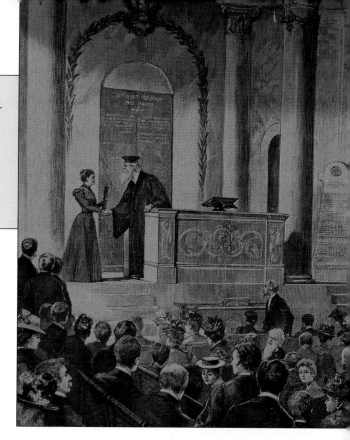

mals produced more offspring than the food supply could support. As a result, he said, members of each species constantly competed to survive. Natural forces "selected" those with physical traits best adapted to their environment. For example, short-necked giraffes, unable to reach the tender leaves at the top of trees, would starve. Longer-necked giraffes would survive and pass the trait on to their offspring. This process of natural selection later came to be called "survival of the fittest."

Over time, said Darwin, natural selection would give rise to entirely new species. He applied this theory to humans. "Man," he declared, "is descended from some less highly organized form." He claimed that humans, like all life forms, were still evolving.

**The uproar.** Like the ideas of Nicolaus Copernicus and Galileo Galilei in earlier times, Darwin's theory ignited a furious debate between scientists and theologians. To many Christians, the Bible contained the only true account of creation. It told how God created the world and all forms of life within seven days. Darwin's theory, they argued, reduced people to the level of animals and undermined belief in God and the soul.

While some Christians eventually came to accept the idea of evolution, others did not. Controversy over Darwin's theory has continued to the present day.

**Social Darwinism.** Darwin himself never promoted any social ideas. However, some thinkers used Darwin's theories to support their own beliefs about society. Their ideas became known as Social Darwinism, applying the idea of survival of the fittest to war and economic competition. Industrial tycoons, argued Social Darwinists, earned their success because they were more "fit" than those they put out of business. War brought progress by weeding out weak nations. Victory was seen as proof of superiority.

Social Darwinism encouraged racism, the belief that one racial group is superior to another. By the late 1800s, many Europeans and Americans claimed that the success of western civilization was due to the supremacy of the white race. Karl Pearson, a British mathematician, wrote:

> 66History shows me one way, and one way only, in which a high state of civilization has been produced, namely the struggle of race with race, and the survival of the physically and mentally fitter race.99

By the end of the century, such ideas would be used to justify the global expansion of European power. (See Chapter 25.)

## Christianity in the Industrial Age

Despite the challenge of new ideas, Christianity continued to be a major force in western society. Churches remained at the center of communities, and church leaders influenced political, social, and educational developments.

The grim realities of industrial life stimulated feelings of compassion and charity in many Christians. In Europe, Christian labor unions and political parties pushed for reforms. Individuals and church groups tried to help the working poor. Catholic priests and nuns set up schools and hospitals in urban slums.

In Europe and the United States, Protestant churches backed the social gospel, a movement that urged Christians to social service. They campaigned for reforms in housing, health care, and education. By 1878, William and Catherine Booth had set up the Salvation Army in London. It both spread Christian teachings and provided social services. Their daughter Evangeline Booth later helped bring the Salvation Army to the United States and Canada.

▲ *Evangeline Booth with two homeless children*

## SECTION 3 REVIEW

1. **Identify** (a) "cult of domesticity," (b) atomic theory, (c) Charles Lyell, (d) natural selection, (e) Salvation Army.
2. **Define** (a) women's suffrage, (b) racism, (c) social gospel.
3. Describe middle-class life in the late 1800s in terms of (a) social behavior, (b) marriage, (c) the home.
4. (a) What were the main goals of the women's movement? (b) Why did it face strong opposition?
5. Why did the ideas of Charles Darwin cause controversy?
6. *Critical Thinking* **Defending a Position** Why do you think reformers pushed for free public education?
7. *ACTIVITY* Create a diagram illustrating the new social hierarchy that emerged during the Industrial Revolution.

# 4 A New Culture

## Guide for Reading

■ What themes shaped romantic art, literature, and music?

■ How did realists respond to the industrial world?

■ How did the visual arts change?

■ **Vocabulary** *romanticism, realism, impressionism*

In the 1800s, many writers turned away from the harsh realities of industrial life to celebrate the natural world. The English poet William Wordsworth described the peace and beauty of sunset:

66It is a beauteous evening, calm and free,
The holy time is quiet as a Nun
Breathless with adoration; the broad sun
Is sinking down in its tranquillity;
The gentleness of heaven broods o'er the Sea.99

Other writers, however, took a different approach. They made the grim industrial world the subject of their work.

## *The Revolt Against Reason*

Wordsworth was part of a movement called romanticism. From about 1750 to 1850, romanticism shaped western literature and arts. Romantic writers, artists, and composers rebelled against the Enlightenment emphasis on reason. Using new verse forms, bold colors, or the swelling sounds of the orchestra, romantics sought to excite strong emotions.

**The romantic hero.** Romantic writers created a new kind of hero. He was a mysterious, melancholy figure who felt out of step with society. "My joys, my grief, my passions, and my powers,/Made me a stranger," wrote Britain's Lord Byron. Byron himself became a larger-than-life figure equal to those he created. After a rebellious, wandering life, he joined Greek forces battling for freedom. When he died of a fever in Greece, his legend bloomed. In fact, the moody, isolated romantic hero came to be described as "Byronic."

The romantic hero often hid a guilty secret and faced a grim destiny. Johann Wolfgang von Goethe (GEH tuh), Germany's greatest writer, recast an old legend into the dramatic poem *Faust*. The aging scholar Faust makes a pact with the devil, exchanging his soul for youth. After much agony, Faust wins salvation by accepting his duty to help others.

**Romance of the past.** Like Goethe, British and French writers combed history, legend, and folklore. Sir Walter Scott's novels and ballads evoked the turbulent history of Scottish clans or medieval knights. Alexandre Dumas (doo MAH) and Victor Hugo re-created France's past in novels like *The Three Musketeers* and *The Hunchback of Notre Dame*.

Architects, too, were inspired by old styles and forms. Churches and other buildings, including the British Houses of Parliament, were modeled on medieval Gothic styles. To people living in the 1800s, medieval towers and lacy stonework conjured up images of a glorious past.

**Romanticism in art.** Painters, too, broke free from the discipline and strict rules of the Enlightenment. Landscape painters like John Constable sought to capture the beauty and power of nature. Using bold brush strokes and colors, the brilliant landscape painter J.M.W. Turner showed tiny human figures struggling against sea and storm.

Romantics painted many subjects, from simple peasant life to medieval knights to current events. Bright colors conveyed violent energy and emotion. The French painter Eugène Delacroix (deh luh KRWAH) filled his canvases with dramatic action. In *Liberty Leading the People*,

**Romanticism in Art** *This 1823 landscape by John Constable shows a view of England's Salisbury Cathedral. The painting transports the viewer far from the noise, poverty, and gloom of industrial London.* **Art and Literature** *Reread the lines by William Wordsworth on page 572. How do the poem and the painting convey similar romantic themes?*

the Goddess of Liberty carries the revolutionary tricolor as French citizens rally to the cause.

**Music of the romantics.** Romantic composers also sought to inspire deep emotions. The piano music of the Hungarian Franz Liszt moved audiences to laugh or weep at the passion of his playing. Other composers wove traditional folk melodies into their works to glorify their nations' past. In his piano works, Frederic Chopin (SHOH pan) used Polish peasant dances to convey the sorrows and joys of people living under foreign occupation.

The orchestra as we know it today took shape in the early 1800s. The first composer to take full advantage of the broad range of instruments was a brooding genius who shared many traits of the romantic hero—Ludwig van Beethoven.

### A Tortured Musical Genius

It was Ferdinand Ries who brought the bad news to Beethoven. The brilliant composer had recently dedicated a new symphony to Napoleon Bonaparte. He had even inscribed the French general's name on the title page. Like many young Germans, Beethoven admired Napoleon as the heroic defender of "the rights of man."

But then, in 1804, Napoleon had declared himself emperor of France. Ries later recalled Beethoven's reaction:

> 66He broke into a rage and cried, 'So he is no more than a common mortal! And from now on he will trample on the rights of man and further only his own ambition. And from now on he will consider himself superior to everybody and become a tyrant!' Beethoven went to the table, snatched the title page of the manuscript, tore it in half and threw it on the floor.99

Despite his raging fury, Beethoven did not destroy his Bonaparte Symphony. Instead, he changed the title to *Eroica,* or "Heroic." To Beethoven, the music was far more important than the man.

**Ludwig van Beethoven** *Beethoven's wild hair and intense eyes have been immortalized in paintings and sculpture. You can almost sense the fury and inspiration that consumed him as he scribbled the lines, below right, from an 1808 composition.* **Impact of the Individual** *Why do you think Beethoven has been one of the most admired figures in world culture?*

**A fiery talent.** Beethoven's life spanned the revolutionary era, from 1770 to 1827. His symphonies combined classical forms with the stirring range of sound favored by the romantics. He wrote from the heart, conveying intense emotional struggle.

Beethoven was a proud, difficult, extravagant man. In fact, he felt he had much in common with Napoleon. They were almost the same age. Through talent, energy, and ambition, each had risen from a lowly station to carve out his own destiny. These were the qualities that inspired the *Eroica.*

**Eroica.** At first, the new symphony did not please listeners. An early critic complained that, in spite of "startling and beautiful passages," the symphony had "too much that is glaring and bizarre." Beethoven, who conducted the first performance, angered the audience by refusing to nod in response to applause.

Some listeners, though, recognized the genius of the *Eroica.* Critics have suggested that it mirrors the spirit of both Beethoven and his ex-hero Napoleon. The first movement expresses a sweeping determination to succeed. Later, a funeral march expresses the power of the hero to survive death and despair. The symphony rushes on to a triumphant conclusion—the victory of the creative spirit.

**Triumph and tragedy.** After the *Eroica,* Beethoven went from masterpiece to masterpiece. In all, he produced nine symphonies, an opera, and dozens of shorter pieces. In the famous opening four notes of his Fifth Symphony, Beethoven captured the feeling of "Fate knocking at the door." His Ninth Symphony features the stirring choral "Ode to Joy," a favorite in both concert halls and churches.

Yet Beethoven's career was haunted by perhaps the greatest tragedy a musician can face. About 1798, he began to lose his hearing. Advancing deafness sparked outbursts of rage and depression. He alienated friends, lived in a chaotic, messy house, and once looked so ragged that he was arrested as a tramp. Late in life, he became totally deaf. Still, he continued to compose and conduct—music that he himself would hear only in his mind.

More than 20,000 admirers marched at Beethoven's funeral in 1827. A speaker summed up his tortured life:

66He withdrew from men after he had given them everything and received nothing in return. He remained solitary. . . . But even unto his grave he preserved a human heart for all who are human. . . . Thus he lived, thus he died, and thus he shall live forever.99

The prediction came true. Today, audiences all over the world still buy recordings and flock to performances of Beethoven's works. ■

## *The Call to Realism*

By the mid-1800s, a new artistic movement, realism, took hold in the West. Realism was an attempt to represent the world as it was, without the sentiment associated with romanticism. Realists often looked at the harsher side of life in cities or villages. Many writers and artists were committed to improving the lot of the unfortunates whose lives they described.

**The novel.** The English novelist Charles Dickens vividly portrayed the lives of slum dwellers and factory workers, including children. In *Oliver Twist,* he told the story of a nine-year-old orphan raised in a grim poorhouse. One day, Oliver asks for extra food:

66Child as he was, he was desperate with hunger, and reckless with misery. He rose from the table, and advancing on the master, basin and spoon in hand, said, somewhat alarmed at his own [boldness]:

'Please, sir, I want some more.'

The master was a fat, healthy man, but he turned very pale. He gazed in

***The World of Dickens*** Dozens of beloved characters poured from the pen of Charles Dickens— from Oliver Twist and David Copperfield, to Ebenezer Scrooge and Tiny Tim in A Christmas Carol. Dickens's novels were often published in installments. Families eagerly gathered to hear the latest chapters read out loud and find out what happened next. **Continuity and Change** Dickens's novels often shed light on social problems. What kinds of people might Dickens write about today?

stupefied astonishment at the small rebel for some seconds. . . . 'What!' said the master at length, in a faint voice.

'Please, sir,' replied Oliver, 'I want some more.'

The master aimed a blow at Oliver's head with the ladle, pinioned him in his arms, and shrieked aloud.**"**

Later, Oliver runs away to London. There he is taken in by Fagin, a villain who trains homeless children to become pickpockets. *Oliver Twist* shocked middle-class readers with its picture of poverty and urban crime.

Victor Hugo moved from romantic to realistic novels. In *Les Miserables* (mih zehr AHB luh), he revealed how hunger drove a good man to crime and how the law hounded him ever after. Emile Zola's *Germinal* is a novel of class warfare in the mining industry. (See page 561.) To Zola's characters, neither the Enlightenment's faith in reason nor romantic feelings mattered at all.

**Drama.** The Norwegian dramatist Henrik Ibsen brought realism to the stage. His plays attacked the hypocrisy he saw around him. *A Doll's House* showed a woman caught in a straitjacket of social rules. In *An Enemy of the People,* a doctor discovers that the water in a local spa is polluted. Because the town's economy depends on its spa, the citizens denounce the doctor and suppress the truth. Ibsen's realistic dramas had a wide influence in Europe and the United States. (📖 See *World Literature,* "A Doll's House," pages 578–579.)

**Realism in art.** Painters also represented the realities of their time. Rejecting the romantic emphasis on imagination, they focused on ordinary subjects, especially working-class men and women. "I cannot paint an angel," said the French realist Gustave Courbet (koor BAY), "because I have never seen one." Instead, he painted works such as *The Stone Breakers,* which shows two rough laborers on a country road.

## Women Writers Win Recognition

By the mid-1800s, a growing number of women were getting their works into print. In northern England, the sisters Charlotte, Emily, and Anne Brontë lived quietly at home, the dutiful daughters of a country clergyman. But every day, they wrote. Using the names Currer, Ellis, and Acton Bell, they found a publisher for their poems and novels. Later, the publisher was shocked to discover his authors were women.

Charlotte Brontë's novel *Jane Eyre* follows the sufferings of an orphaned governess and her love for Mr. Rochester, a brooding, Byronic hero. In *Wuthering Heights,* Emily Brontë told a dramatic story of doomed love against the backdrop of the stormy Yorkshire moors.

In France, Aurore Dupin Dudevant (doo duh VAHN) published a highly successful novel, *Indiana,* under the name George Sand. Soon, critics were ranking her among the finest French writers. Sand defied convention by dressing like a man, complete with top hat and cigar.

In the United States, Harriet Beecher Stowe created a sensation with her first novel, *Uncle Tom's Cabin.* Its depiction of the lives of plantation slaves helped mold antislavery opinion. Kate Chopin's 1899 novel *The Awakening,* like Ibsen's *A Doll's House,* showed a wife rebelling against her restricted life. Yet Chopin's work was largely unappreciated until the 1960s.

## New Directions in the Visual Arts

By the 1840s, a new art form, photography, was emerging. Louis Daguerre (dah GAYR) in France and William Fox Talbot in England had improved on earlier technologies to produce successful photographs. At first, many photos were stiff-posed portraits of middle-class families or prominent people. Other photographs reflected the romantics' fascination with faraway places.

▲ *Camera, about 1845*

**ISSUES** *For* **TODAY** — Artists and writers responded in varying ways to the tremendous changes of the industrial era. How do you think literature and the arts reflect social and technological developments?

**Post-Impressionism** *Vincent van Gogh's unique brushwork lent a dreamlike quality to everyday subjects. His fields, flowers, and faces are some of the most recognized images in art today.* **Art and Literature** *Compare and contrast Van Gogh's cathedral to Constable's on page 573.*

In time, photographers used the camera to expose slum conditions and other social ills. Photographs provided shocking evidence to prod governments toward reform. Photographers also went to war. During the American Civil War, Mathew B. Brady preserved a vivid, realistic record of the corpse-strewn battlefields.

**The impressionists.** Photography posed a challenge to painters. Why try for realism, some artists asked, when a camera could do the same thing better? By the 1870s, a group of painters took art in a new direction, seeking to capture the first fleeting impression made by a scene or object on the viewer's eye. The new movement, known as impressionism, took root in Paris, capital of the western art world.

Since the Renaissance, painters had carefully finished their paintings so that not a brush stroke showed. But impressionists like Claude Monet (moh NAY) and Edgar Degas (day GAH) brushed strokes of color side by side without any blending. According to new scientific studies of optics, the human eye would mix these patches of color. (See the painting on page 579.)

By concentrating on visual impressions rather than realism, artists achieved a fresh view of familiar subjects. Monet, for example, painted the cathedral at Rouen (roo AHN), France, dozens of times from the same angle, capturing how it looked in different lights at different times of day.

**The post-impressionists.** Later painters, called post-impressionists, developed a variety of styles. Georges Seurat (suh RAH) arranged small dots of color to define the shapes of objects. The Dutch painter Vincent van Gogh experimented with sharp brush lines and bright color. Desperately poor, he sold few paintings in his short, unhappy life. Today, Van Gogh's masterpieces have sold for millions of dollars apiece.

Paul Gauguin (goh GAN) developed a bold, personal style. He rejected the materialism of Western life and went to live on the island of Tahiti. In his paintings, people look flat as in medieval stained-glass windows or "primitive" folk art. But his brooding colors and black outlining of shapes convey intense feelings and images.

## SECTION 4 REVIEW

1. **Identify** (a) Lord Byron, (b) Johann Wolfgang von Goethe, (c) Ludwig van Beethoven, (d) the Brontës, (e) George Sand, (f) Claude Monet, (g) post-impressionists.
2. **Define** (a) romanticism, (b) realism, (c) impressionism.
3. (a) How did romantics respond to industry? (b) Describe three subjects they favored.
4. How did each of the following explore realistic themes: (a) Charles Dickens, (b) Henrik Ibsen, (c) Gustave Courbet?
5. How did photography influence the development of painting in the late 1800s?
6. *Critical Thinking* **Linking Past and Present** Compare the ideal of a romantic hero of the 1800s to the ideal of a romantic hero today. How are they similar or different?
7. *ACTIVITY* Write a review of one of the paintings in this chapter. Consider such questions as: What style is used? What is the artist trying to do? What is your impression of the work?

# *World Literature*

## A Doll's House

### Henrik Ibsen

**Introduction** *By today's standards,* A Doll's House *is not a shocking play. In 1879, though, Henrik Ibsen's drama stunned audiences, first in Norway, then throughout Europe and the United States. Unlike the heroic or romantic dramas that were popular,* A Doll's House *presented a realistic picture of middle-class life. In addition, Ibsen challenged many accepted social ideas, especially about marriage.*

*At the start of the play, Torvald Helmer, a lawyer, and his wife, Nora, are happily married. But a crisis causes Nora to question her role. The following scene occurs near the end of the play.*

**HELMER.** *(Speaking to NORA, who is offstage)* How snug and nice our home is, Nora. You're safe here; I'll keep you like a hunted dove I've rescued out of a hawk's claws; I'll bring peace to your poor, shuddering heart. . . . For a man there's something indescribably sweet and satisfying in knowing he's forgiven his wife—and forgiven her out of a full and open heart. It's as if she belongs to him in two ways now: in a sense, he's given her fresh into the world again, and she's become his wife and his child as well. From now on that's what you'll be to me—you little, bewildered, helpless thing. Don't be afraid of anything, Nora; just open your heart to me, and I'll be conscience and will to you both— *(NORA enters in her regular clothes.)* What's this? Not in bed? You've changed your dress?

**NORA.** Yes, Torvald, I've changed my dress.

**HELMER.** But why now, so late? . . .

**NORA.** Sit down, Torvald; we have a lot to talk about.

**HELMER.** Nora—what is this? That hard expression—

**NORA.** Sit down. This'll take some time. I have a lot to say.

**HELMER.** You worry me, Nora. And I don't understand you.

**NORA.** No, that's exactly it. You don't understand me. And I've never understood you either—until tonight. No, don't interrupt. You can just listen to what I say. We're closing our accounts, Torvald.

**HELMER.** How do you mean that?

**NORA.** Doesn't anything strike you about our sitting here like this?

**HELMER.** What's that?

**NORA.** We've been married now eight years. Doesn't it occur to you that this is the first time we two, you and I, man and wife, have ever talked seriously together?

**HELMER.** What do you mean—seriously?

**NORA.** In eight whole years—longer even—right from our first acquaintance, we've never exchanged a serious word. . . .

**HELMER.** But dearest, what good would that ever do you?

**NORA.** That's the point right there: you've never understood me. I've been wronged greatly, Torvald—first by Papa, and then by you.

**HELMER.** What? By us—the two people who've loved you more than anyone else?

**NORA.** *(Shaking her head)* You never loved me. You've thought it fun to be in love with me, that's all.

**HELMER.** Nora, what a thing to say!

**NORA.** Yes, it's true now, Torvald. When I lived at home with Papa, he told me all his opinions, so I had the same ones too; or if they were different I hid them, since he wouldn't have cared for that. He used to call me his doll-child, and he played with me the way I played with my dolls. Then I came into your house—

**HELMER.** How can you speak of our marriage like that?

**NORA.** *(Unperturbed)* I mean, then I went from Papa's hands into yours. You arranged everything to your own taste, and so I got the same taste as you—or I pretended to; I can't remember. I guess a little of both, first one,

then the other. Now when I look back, it seems as if I'd lived here like a beggar—just from hand to mouth. I've lived by doing tricks for you, Torvald. But that's the way you wanted it. It's a great sin what you and Papa did to me. You're to blame that nothing's become of me.

HELMER. Nora, how unfair and ungrateful you are! Haven't you been happy here?

NORA. No, never. I thought so—but I never have.

HELMER. Not—not happy!

NORA. No, only lighthearted. And you've always been so kind to me. But our home's been nothing but a playpen. I've been your doll-wife here, just as at home I was Papa's doll-child. And in turn the children have been my dolls. I thought it was fun when you played with me, just as they thought it was fun when I played with them. That's been our marriage, Torvald.

HELMER. There's some truth in what you're saying—under all the raving exaggeration. But it'll all be different after this. Playtime's over; now for the schooling.

NORA. Whose schooling—mine or the children's?

HELMER. Both yours and the children's, dearest.

NORA. Oh, Torvald, you're not the man to teach me to be a good wife to you.

HELMER. And you can say that?

NORA. And I—how am I equipped to bring up children?

HELMER. Nora!

NORA. Didn't you say a moment ago that that was no job to trust me with?

HELMER. In a flare of temper! Why fasten on that?

NORA. Yes, but you were so very right. I'm not up to the job. There's another job I have to do first. I have to try to educate myself. You can't help me with that. I've got to do it alone. And that's why I'm leaving you now.

HELMER. *(Jumping up)* What's that?

NORA. I have to stand completely alone, if I'm ever going to discover myself and the world out there.

Source: Henrik Ibsen, *A Doll's House*, translated by Rolf Fjelde (New York: New American Library, 1965).

## Thinking About Literature

1. List five phrases or nicknames Torvald uses that reveal his attitude toward his wife.
2. (a) According to Nora, how was she "wronged" by her father and her husband? (b) What does she intend to do about it?
3. *Critical Thinking* **Synthesizing Information** Review the subsections Middle-Class Values on pages 567–568 and Rights for Women on page 569. (a) Does the Helmers' marriage fit the middle-class ideal of the time? Explain. (b) Nora expresses a need to educate herself. Why do you think many women in the late 1800s fought for the right to an education?

# Skills for Success

**Critical Thinking**

**Writing and Researching**

**Maps, Charts, and Graphs**

**Speaking and Listening**

## Analyzing Political Cartoons

Political cartoons express a person's point of view on a current event or issue. The purpose of the cartoon is to make a statement and to sway the opinions of others. To do this, the cartoonist often uses humor and exaggeration.

Many political cartoons rely on symbols to convey their message. The dove, for example, is a symbol of peace. In interpreting a cartoon, it is important to examine all of the images and words to determine the cartoonist's point of view.

The cartoon below appeared in the American magazine *The Verdict* in 1899. The title of the cartoon is "The Menace of the Hour." Examine the cartoon and then answer the following questions:

**1** **Identify the symbols in the cartoon.** (a) What does the octopus-like monster represent? (b) What do its tentacles represent? (c) What is the monster doing to the city?

**2** **Analyze the meaning of the cartoon.** (a) Identify three types of businesses that, according to this cartoon, are controlled by monopolies. (b) Why is one of the monster's tentacles labeled "Political Pull"? (c) Explain the title of the cartoon. (d) What statement is the cartoonist making about big business?

**3** **Draw conclusions about the cartoonist's point of view.** (a) What does the cartoonist think about monopolies? (b) Do you think this cartoonist would view business leaders as "captains of industry" or "robber barons"? (c) How do you think this cartoonist probably felt about government regulation of big business? Explain.

***Beyond the Classroom*** Locate a political cartoon in a newspaper or magazine. Identify the topic of the cartoon and any symbols the cartoonist has used. Then, analyze the cartoon and determine the cartoonist's point of view.

# CHAPTER 22 REVIEW

## Building Vocabulary

Review the vocabulary words in this chapter. Then, use *eight* of these words to create a crossword puzzle. Exchange puzzles with a classmate. Complete the puzzles and then check each other's answers.

## Reviewing Chapter Themes

1. **Economics and Technology**  Give examples of how *three* of the following developments affected western economies and societies in the 1800s: (a) new manufacturing processes and products, (b) developments in transportation and communication, (c) advances in medical science, (d) the rise of corporations, (e) the rise of labor unions.
2. **Religions and Value Systems**  (a) How did the middle class shape attitudes and values? (b) Describe two challenges to traditional ideas.
3. **Art and Literature**  (a) Compare romantic writers to realist writers in terms of goals and subject matter. (b) How did styles in the visual arts change between 1800 and 1900?
4. **Impact of the Individual**  Choose one inventor, one scientist, and one artist or writer discussed in this chapter. (a) Describe how each of them contributed to the development of industrial culture. (b) Many of these individuals have been called "builders of the modern world." Do you agree with this statement? Explain.

## Thinking Critically

1. **Linking Past and Present**  (a) How did the second phase of the Industrial Revolution differ from the first phase? (b) Some historians have suggested that we are now in the midst of the "third" Industrial Revolution. Do you agree or disagree? Explain.
2. **Recognizing Points of View**  Review the discussion of laissez-faire economics on page 460. (a) Which side do you think Adam Smith would have taken in the debate over regulating monopolies? Explain. (b) Do you think David Ricardo would have favored the organization of labor unions? Explain. ( ★ See *Skills for Success,* page 280.)

3. **Applying Information**  John Hollingshead, a British journalist describing London in 1862, wrote that "the spreading limbs of a great city may be healthy and vigorous, while its heart may gradually become more choked and decayed." Does this description agree with what you have read about cities in the later 1800s? Explain.
4. **Identifying Main Ideas**  Reread Sojourner Truth's words on page 569 and summarize her main point in your own words.
5. **Analyzing Literature**  Reread the selection from *Oliver Twist* on page 575–576. (a) What is Oliver's manner when he asks for more food? (b) Why does Dickens include the detail that "the master was a fat, healthy man"? (c) How does the master react to Oliver's request? What does this suggest about him? (d) What overall impression does Dickens give about the institutions that were meant to help the poor? ( ★ See *Skills for Success,* page 234.)

### For Your Portfolio

For this assignment you will work with a group of classmates to write a script for a dramatic presentation of some aspect of life in the Industrial Age.

1. Begin by reviewing the content of this chapter and deciding on an incident, invention, scene, story, or person to feature in your dramatic presentation.
2. Discuss with your group what characters to include in your dramatization. You should include at least one character for each group member to portray.
3. Use library resources to research additional information for your script.
4. Outline the story you will present. Plan to portray authentic values and attitudes in your story as well as the consequences of the events you cover. Then, write the script. Include directions for the sets, props, costumes, and staging if you like.
5. Rehearse the script with your group. Make any changes you need to improve the story. Then, present your drama for the class.

# CHAPTER

## 23

# Nationalism Triumphs in Europe

## (1800–1914)

## CHAPTER OUTLINE

1 **Building a German Nation**
2 **Strengthening Germany**
3 **Unifying Italy**
4 **Nationalism Threatens Old Empires**
5 **Russia: Reform and Reaction**

The Prussian legislators waited restlessly for Otto von Bismarck, the king's new chancellor, to speak. They knew he wanted them to vote more money to build up the Prussian army. Liberal members of the parliament, however, opposed the move.

At last, Bismarck rose. He was a tall man with a bristling mustache and hard, unyielding eyes. In harsh tones, he dismissed the concerns of the liberal opposition:

> 66Germany does not look to Prussia's liberalism, but to her power. . . . The great questions of the day are not to be decided by speeches and majority resolutions—that was the mistake of 1848 and 1849—but by blood and iron!99

Bismarck delivered his "blood and iron" speech in 1862. It set the tone for his policies in the years ahead. Bismarck had no respect for representative government. He was determined to build a strong, unified German nation, led by his state of Prussia. He meant to do so with or without the help of parliament.

A master of power politics at home and abroad, Bismarck dominated European affairs from 1862 to 1890. Once, when he was warned that Britain might oppose him on a certain issue, he replied:

> 66What is England to me? The importance of a state is measured by the number of soldiers it can put into the field of battle. . . . *It is the destiny of the weak to be devoured by the strong.*99

The last half of the 1800s can be called the age of nationalism. In this period, a new political order emerged in Europe. Bismarck welded the German states into a powerful empire. A divided Italy found political unity. And throughout the European continent, strong leaders harnessed national feeling to encourage industrialism and modernization.

In some countries, nationalism was a divisive rather than a unifying force. It strained Austria's multinational empire. It led Russian czars to suppress the cultures of national minorities within their land. To this day, nationalism has remained a powerful force that has both unified countries and sparked rivalries, conflicts, and great bloodshed.

**FOCUS ON** these questions as you read:

- **Political and Social Systems**
  What effect did nationalism and demands for reform have on European governments?

- **Impact of the Individual**
  How did tough-minded political leaders contribute to the unification of Germany and of Italy?

- **Diversity**
  How did nationalism affect ethnically diverse empires in central and Eastern Europe?

- **Religions and Value Systems**
  How were religion and nationalism linked in the Russian empire?

## TIME AND PLACE

**Triumph of Nationalism** *After stunning victories over Austria and France, German leaders met in the palace at Versailles in 1871 to proclaim William I emperor of a united Germany. Here, William (on steps) takes the oath of office. William's chancellor and the architect of German unification, Otto von Bismarck (at center, in white jacket), looks on.* **Global Interaction** *How does the scene mark a shift of European power and a triumph of nationalism?*

## HUMANITIES LINK
*Art History* Photographs of German workers (page 589).
*Literature* In this chapter, you will encounter passages from the following works of literature: Ernst Morris Arndt, "The German's Fatherland" (page 584); Alexander Pushkin, "Ode to Freedom" (page 598).

| 1814 | 1831 | 1862 | 1871 | 1905 | 1914 |
|------|------|------|------|------|------|
| Congress of Vienna begins | Giuseppe Mazzini founds Young Italy | Otto von Bismarck named Chancellor of Prussia | Germany is united under Second Reich | Russian Revolution of 1905 | World War I begins |

| 1800 | 1820 | 1840 | 1860 | 1880 | 1900 | 1920 |
|------|------|------|------|------|------|------|

# 1 Building a German Nation

## Guide for Reading

- How did early German nationalism pave the way for unity?

- What role did Bismarck play in the unification of Germany?

- What were the immediate cause and the immediate results of the Franco-Prussian War?

German nationalism developed gradually. In the early 1800s, romantic writers spoke of a unique "German national character" shaped by ancient traditions. Philosophers and poets promoted the idea of a German nation. In a widely admired poem, "The German's Fatherland," poet Ernst M. Arndt tapped into this patriotic feeling:

66Where is the German's Fatherland?
Name me its farthest bound!
'Wherever rings the German tongue,
Wherever its hymns to God are sung,
There shall it be!
There, brave German, make your
Germany!'99

The early calls to nationhood came mostly from students and intellectuals. Their efforts to unite Germans faltered in the face of Metternich's conservative ideas. In the mid-1800s, however, an aggressive leader named Otto von Bismarck imposed a Prussian brand of nationhood on all of Germany.

## First Steps

In the early 1800s, German-speaking people lived in a host of small and medium-sized states as well as in Prussia and the Austrian Hapsburg empire. (See the map on page 502.) Napoleon's invasions unleashed new forces in these territories.

**Impact of Napoleon.** Between 1807 and 1812, Napoleon made important territorial

changes in the German-speaking lands. He added lands along the Rhine River to France. He dissolved the Holy Roman Empire and organized a number of German states into a French-controlled Rhine Confederation.

At first, some Germans welcomed the French emperor as a hero with enlightened, modern policies. He encouraged freeing of the serfs, made trade easier, and abolished laws against Jews.

At the same time, Napoleon's conquests sparked German nationalism. People who had fought to free their lands from French rule began to demand a unified German state.

At the Congress of Vienna, Metternich opposed nationalist demands. He pointed out that a united Germany would require dismantling the governments of the many separate German states. Instead, the conservative peacemakers created the German Confederation, a weak body headed by Austria.

**Prussian leadership.** In the 1830s, Austria's great rival, Prussia, took the lead in creating an economic union called the Zollverein (TSAWL fuh rīn). It dismantled tariff barriers between many of the German states. Still, despite this step toward economic unity, Germany remained politically fragmented.

In 1848, liberals meeting in the Frankfurt Assembly once more took up the demand for German political unity. (See page 535.) They offered the throne of a united German state to King Frederick William IV of Prussia. The Prussian ruler rejected the notion of a throne offered by "the people." Again, Germany remained divided, but the stage was set for Prussian leadership.

## Bismarck: Architect of German Unity

Otto von Bismarck succeeded where others had failed. He came from Prussia's Junker (YUNG ker) class, which was made up of conservative landowning nobles. Bismarck served Prussia as a diplomat in Russia and France before King William I made him chancellor, or prime minister, in 1862. Within a decade, the new chancellor had used his policy of "blood and iron" to unite the German states under Prussian rule.

law. The state must survive at any price; it cannot go into the poorhouse, it cannot beg, it cannot commit suicide; in short, it must take wherever it can find the essentials of life. **99**

Oddly enough, Bismarck, the architect of German unity, was not really a German nationalist. His primary loyalty was to the Hohenzollerns, the ruling dynasty of Prussia. He regarded uniting Germany as a means to make the Hohenzollerns master of all the German states.

**Strengthening the army.** As chancellor, Bismarck moved first to build up the Prussian army. Despite his "blood and iron" speech (see page 582), the liberal legislature refused to vote funds for the military. Bismarck would not be thwarted. He simply used money that had been collected for other purposes to strengthen the army. With a powerful, well-equipped military, he was ready to pursue an aggressive foreign policy.

## Victory in Three Wars

In the next decade, Bismarck led Prussia into three wars. Each war increased Prussian prestige and power while paving the way for German unity.

**Schleswig and Holstein.** Bismarck's first maneuver was to form an alliance in 1864 with Austria. They then moved to seize the provinces of Schleswig and Holstein from Denmark. After a brief war, Prussia and Austria "liberated" the two provinces, which were largely inhabited by Germans, and divided up the spoils. Austria was to administer Holstein and Prussia was to administer Schleswig.

**War with Austria.** In 1866, Bismarck invented an excuse to attack Austria. The Austro-Prussian War lasted just seven weeks and ended in a decisive Prussian victory. Prussia then annexed, or added, not only Holstein but several other north German states.

Bismarck dissolved the Austrian-led German Confederation and created a new North German Confederation dominated by Prussia. But the master of Realpolitik did not enforce harsh terms of peace. Instead, he allowed Austria and four other southern German states to

**The Roots of German Nationalism** In 1812, Jacob and Wilhelm Grimm published the first of a series of folk tales they had collected from peasant villages throughout Germany. They hoped that their work would help unify the German people by giving them a sense of their common heritage. An illustration from one of the most popular tales, "Hansel and Gretel," is shown here. **Art and Literature** What stories do Americans share as part of their cultural heritage?

**Master of Realpolitik.** Bismarck's success was due in part to his strong will and his ability to manipulate others. He was a master of Realpolitik, or realistic politics based on a tough-minded evaluation of the needs of the state. In Bismarck's view, the ends justified the means. Power was more important than principles such as liberalism.

A contemporary of Bismarck reflected the ideas of Realpolitik when he explained why national leaders sometimes had to make ruthless decisions:

**66**For the state, in contrast to the individual, self-preservation is the supreme

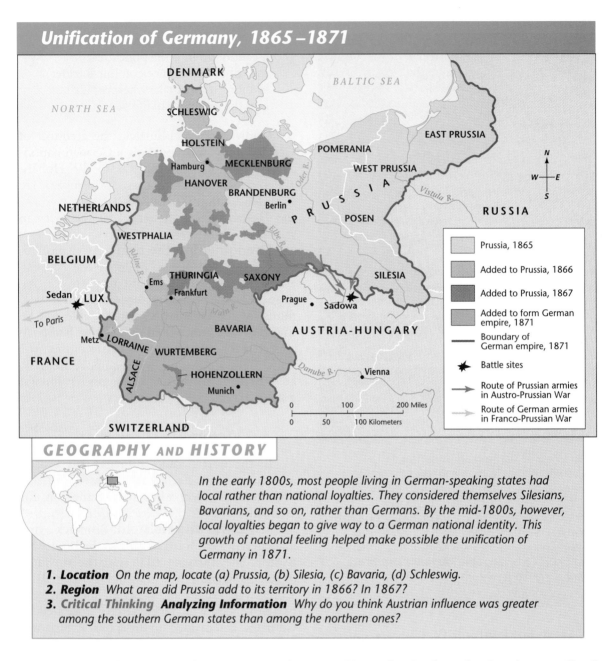

## Unification of Germany, 1865–1871

**Map legend:**
- Prussia, 1865
- Added to Prussia, 1866
- Added to Prussia, 1867
- Added to form German empire, 1871
- Boundary of German empire, 1871
- ★ Battle sites
- → Route of Prussian armies in Austro-Prussian War
- → Route of German armies in Franco-Prussian War

**Map labels:** DENMARK, BALTIC SEA, NORTH SEA, SCHLESWIG, HOLSTEIN, EAST PRUSSIA, POMERANIA, WEST PRUSSIA, Hamburg, MECKLENBURG, HANOVER, BRANDENBURG, PRUSSIA, Berlin, POSEN, RUSSIA, Vistula R., Oder R., NETHERLANDS, WESTPHALIA, Elbe R., BELGIUM, Rhine R., THURINGIA, SAXONY, SILESIA, Sedan, LUX., Ems, Frankfurt, Prague, Sadowa, To Paris, Metz, LORRAINE, WURTEMBERG, BAVARIA, AUSTRIA-HUNGARY, Main R., FRANCE, ALSACE, HOHENZOLLERN, Munich, Danube R., Vienna, SWITZERLAND

Scale: 0 100 200 Miles / 0 50 100 Kilometers

## GEOGRAPHY AND HISTORY

In the early 1800s, most people living in German-speaking states had local rather than national loyalties. They considered themselves Silesians, Bavarians, and so on, rather than Germans. By the mid-1800s, however, local loyalties began to give way to a German national identity. This growth of national feeling helped make possible the unification of Germany in 1871.

1. **Location** On the map, locate (a) Prussia, (b) Silesia, (c) Bavaria, (d) Schleswig.
2. **Region** What area did Prussia add to its territory in 1866? In 1867?
3. **Critical Thinking** *Analyzing Information* Why do you think Austrian influence was greater among the southern German states than among the northern ones?

remain independent. Bismarck's motives, as always, were strictly practical. "We had to avoid leaving behind any desire for revenge," he later wrote.

**The Franco-Prussian War.** The Prussian victory worried Napoleon III in France. A growing rivalry between the two nations led to the Franco-Prussian War of 1870. The immediate cause was a struggle over the vacant Spanish throne. When a relative of the Prussian king was offered the throne, France protested. It feared the spread of Prussian influence to its southern border.

Bismarck seized on the situation to rally all Germans—no matter where they lived—against Napoleon III. Germans recalled only too well the invasions of Napoleon I some 60 years earlier. Bismarck played up the image of the French menace to spur German nationalism. For his part, Napoleon III did little to avoid war, hoping to mask problems at home with military glory.

Bismarck helped the crisis along by rewriting and then releasing to the press a telegram that reported on a meeting between King William I and the French ambassador. Bismarck's editing of the "Ems dispatch" made it seem that William I had insulted the Frenchman. Furious, Napoleon III declared war on Prussia, as Bismarck hoped. Cries of "On to Berlin!" filled the streets of Paris. The fighting, however, quickly proved otherwise.

A superior Prussian force, helped by troops from other German states, smashed the badly organized, poorly supplied French soldiers. Napoleon III, old and ill, surrendered after a few weeks of fighting. France had to accept a humiliating peace. The French defeat led to the downfall of the Second Empire, as you will read in Chapter 24.

*"The Great German Ogre"* As part of his plan to unify Germany, Bismarck provoked the French into the disastrous Franco-Prussian War. This cartoon, titled *"The Great German Ogre,"* shows the French view of the German chancellor. **Political and Social Systems** How does the cartoonist show his dislike of Bismarck?

N° 11.

LE GRAND ÔGRE ALLEMAND.

Les grands et petits seigneurs hobereaux des voisins pays s'étant permis de lui tenir tête et d'agir contre son gré ; il chaussa incontinent ses tant fameuses bottes de sept lieues, s'élança contre eux et les écrasa comme un tas de mouches. Comme avait moult grand appétit volontiers les voulaient tous dévorer tout crus avec leurs sujets ; mais craignant une indigestion... &.ª ( Extrait d'une vieille légende )

## The German Empire

Delighted by the victory over France, princes from the southern German states and the North German Confederation persuaded William I of Prussia to take the title kaiser (KĪ zer), or emperor. In January 1871, German nationalists celebrated the birth of the Second Reich, or empire. They called it that because they considered it heir to the Holy Roman Empire founded by King Otto the Great in the 900s and abolished by Napoleon I in 1806.

Success, as Bismarck had predicted, came from a policy of "blood and iron." He had dealt shattering blows to two great powers, Austria and France. The newly united Germany soon vaulted into a leading role in Europe. What an odd twist of fate that a conservative Prussian noble had created a united German nation, the goal set by liberals and nationalists in the early 1800s!

A constitution drafted by Bismarck set up a two-house legislature for the Second Reich. The Bundesrat, or upper house, was appointed by the rulers of the German states. The Reichstag, or lower house, was elected by universal male suffrage. Still, the new German nation was far from democratic, since the Bundesrat could veto any decisions of the Reichstag. Real power remained in the hands of the emperor and his chancellor.

## SECTION 1 REVIEW

1. **Identify** (a) Zollverein, (b) Realpolitik, (c) Schleswig and Holstein, (d) Austro-Prussian War, (e) North German Confederation, (f) Franco-Prussian War, (g) William I, (h) Second Reich.
2. What steps were taken toward German unity before 1850?
3. Describe the goals and policies of Otto von Bismarck.
4. Prussia fought three wars to unite Germany. Explain how each helped achieve that goal.
5. *Critical Thinking* **Applying Information** Identify three examples of Bismarck's use of Realpolitik.
6. *ACTIVITY* Create an illustrated map and time line showing the unification of Germany.

# 2 Strengthening Germany

## Guide for Reading

- What forces spurred the growth of the German economy?
- What domestic policies did Bismarck pursue?
- What were the goals of William II?

In January 1871, German princes gathered in the glittering Hall of Mirrors at the French palace of Versailles. (See the painting on page 583.) They had just defeated Napoleon III in the Franco-Prussian War and had chosen Louis XIV's palace to proclaim the new German empire. The symbolism was clear. French domination of Europe, dating from the age of Louis XIV, had ended. Germany, headed by William I and his chancellor, Otto von Bismarck, was the new power in Europe.

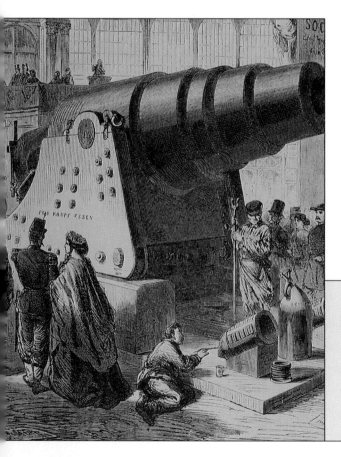

## The German Industrial Giant

In the aftermath of unification, the German empire emerged as the industrial giant of the European continent. By the late 1800s, German chemical and electrical industries set the standard worldwide. German shipping was second only to Britain's among the European powers.

**Economic progress.** Germany's spectacular growth was due in part to ample iron and coal resources, the basic ingredients for industrial development. A disciplined and educated work force also helped the economy, while a rapidly growing population—from 41 million in 1871 to 67 million by 1914—provided a huge home market and a highly skilled work force.

The new nation also benefited from earlier progress. During the 1850s and 1860s, Germans had founded large companies and built many railroads. The house of Krupp boomed after 1871, becoming an enormous industrial complex producing steel and weapons for a world market. (See page 561.) Between 1871 and 1914, the business tycoon August Thyssen built a small steel factory of 70 workers into a giant empire with 50,000 employees.

**Science, government, and industry.** German industrialists were the first to see the value of applied science in developing new products such as synthetic chemicals and dyes. They supported research and development in the universities and hired trained scientists to solve technological problems in their factories.

The German government promoted economic development. After 1871, it issued a single currency for Germany, reorganized the banking system, and coordinated railroads built by the various German states. When a worldwide depression hit in the late 1800s, it raised tariffs to protect home industries from foreign

*"Arsenal of the World"* Here, visitors to an international industrial exhibition admire a huge cannon produced by the Krupp works. By the time he died in 1887, Alfred Krupp had turned his family business into the "arsenal of the world." He had armed 46 different countries and was awarded military decorations by Russia, Belgium, Sweden, Spain, the Ottoman empire, Japan, and Brazil. ***Economics and Technology*** What advantages would a cannon like this one offer to an army?

competition. The new German empire was determined to maintain economic strength as well as military power.

## The Iron Chancellor

As chancellor, Bismarck pursued several foreign policy goals. He sought to keep France weak and isolated while building strong links with Austria and Russia. He respected British naval power but did not seek to compete in that arena. "Water rats," he said, "do not fight with land rats." Later, he took a more aggressive stand against Britain as the two nations competed for empire overseas. (See Chapter 25.)

On the domestic front, Bismarck applied the same ruthless methods he had used to achieve unification. The Iron Chancellor, as he was called, sought to erase local loyalties and crush all opposition to the imperial state. He targeted two groups, the Catholic Church and the socialists. In his view, both posed a threat to the new German state.

**Campaign against the Church.** After unification, Catholics made up about a third of the German population. The Lutheran Bismarck distrusted Catholics, especially the clergy, whose first loyalty, he believed, was to the pope.

In response to what he saw as the Catholic threat, Bismarck launched the Kulturkampf, or "battle for civilization." His goal was to make Catholics put loyalty to the state above allegiance to the Church. The chancellor had laws passed that gave the state the right to supervise Catholic education and approve the appointment of priests. Other laws closed some religious orders, expelled the Jesuits from Prussia, and made it compulsory for couples to be married by civil authority.

Bismarck's moves against the Catholic Church backfired. The faithful rallied behind the Church, and the Catholic Center party gained strength in the Reichstag. A realist, Bismarck saw his mistake and made peace with the Church.

**Campaign against the socialists.** Bismarck also saw a threat to the new Germany in the growing power of socialism. By the late 1870s, German Marxists had organized the Social Democratic party, which called for a true parliamentary democracy and laws to improve

***Photographs of German Workers*** *The invention of photography in the mid-1800s created a new art form. Photographers learned to use light and design to "paint" pictures. Soon, photos became a way to depict real life and to protest or comment about it. These photographic portraits are from a series depicting German workers at the beginning of the 1900s.* **Art and Literature** *What techniques did the photographer use to give the photographs an artistic quality? What do you think the photographer is trying to say about German workers?*

conditions for the working class. Bismarck feared that socialists would undermine the loyalty of German workers and turn them toward revolution. He had laws passed that dissolved socialist groups, shut down their newspapers, and banned their meetings. Once again, repression backfired, unifying workers in support of the socialist cause.

Bismarck then changed course. He set out to woo workers away from socialism by sponsoring laws to protect them. By the 1890s, Germans had health and accident insurance as well as old-age insurance to provide retirement benefits. Thus, under Bismarck, Germany was a pioneer in social reform. Its system of economic safeguards became the model for other European nations.

Bismarck was frank about the goals of his social reforms:

66Give the workingman the right to work as long as he is healthy, assure him care when he is sick, and maintenance when he is old . . . then the socialists will sing their siren songs in vain, and the workingmen will cease to throng to their banner.99

Bismarck's plan was only partly successful. Although workers benefited from his measures, they did not abandon socialism. In fact, the Social Democratic party continued to grow in strength. By 1912, it had the most seats in the Reichstag. Yet Bismarck's program showed that workers could improve their condition without the upheaval of a revolution. Later, Germany and other European nations would build on Bismarck's social policies, greatly increasing government's role in providing for the needs of its citizens. (See Chapter 33.)

## A Confident New Kaiser

In 1888, William II succeeded his grandfather as kaiser. The new emperor was supremely confident of his abilities and wished to put his own stamp on Germany. In 1890, he shocked Europe by asking the dominating Bismarck to resign. "There is only one master in the Reich, and that is I," he said.

William II seriously believed in his divine right to rule. As he put it:

66My grandfather considered that the office of king was a task that God had assigned to him. . . . That which he thought I also think. . . . Those who wish to aid me in that task . . . I welcome with all my heart; those who oppose me in this work I shall crush.99

Not surprisingly, William resisted efforts to introduce democratic reforms. At the same time, his government provided services, from social welfare benefits to cheap transportation and electricity. An excellent system of public schools, begun under Bismarck, taught students obedience to the emperor along with the "three R's."

Like his grandfather, William II lavished funds on the German military machine, already the most powerful in Europe. He also launched an ambitious campaign to expand the German navy and win an overseas empire to rival those of Britain and France. You will see in later chapters how William's nationalism and aggressive military stance helped increase tensions on the eve of World War I.

▲ *Kaiser William II*

## SECTION 2 REVIEW

1. **Identify** Kulturkampf.
2. Why did Germany become an industrial giant in the late 1800s?
3. (a) Describe the social reforms adopted under Bismarck. (b) Why did he favor these reforms?
4. (a) Why did William II dismiss Bismarck as chancellor? (b) What policies did William introduce?
5. *Critical Thinking* **Recognizing Causes and Effects** Why do you think supporters of democratic government had little hope of success in Germany in the late 1800s?
6. *ACTIVITY* Write an obituary for Bismarck that evaluates his strengths and weaknesses.

# 3 Unifying Italy

## Guide for Reading

- What forces hindered Italian unity?
- How did individual leaders help forge the Italian nation?
- What problems did Italy face after 1861?
- **Vocabulary** *anarchist*

Sixteen-year-old Giuseppe Mazzini (joo ZEHP pee mah TSEE nee) was walking with his mother in Genoa in 1821. A few weeks earlier, Austrian forces had crushed a revolt in northern Italy. Mazzini later recalled how he and his mother were stopped by a "tall, black-bearded man":

> ❝He held out a white handkerchief, merely saying, 'For the refugees of Italy.' My mother . . . dropped some money into the handkerchief. . . . That day was the first in which a confused idea presented itself to my mind . . . an idea that we Italians could and therefore ought to struggle for the liberty of our country.❞

In time, Mazzini would become a revolutionary devoted to the cause of Italian unity. But when an Italian nation finally emerged, it was not the work of revolutionaries. Just as German unity was spearheaded by Prussia and Bismarck, Italian unification was brought about by the efforts of a single, powerful state—the kingdom of Sardinia—and of a shrewd and ruthless politician—Count Camillo Cavour.

## The Italian Peninsula

For centuries, Italy had been a battleground for ambitious foreign and local princes. Frequent warfare and foreign rule had led people to identify with local regions. The people of Florence considered themselves Tuscans, those of Venice Venetians, the people of Naples Neapolitans, and so on. But as in Germany, the invasions of Napoleon had sparked dreams of national unity.

The Congress of Vienna, however, ignored the demands of nationalists. To Metternich, Italy was merely a "geographical expression," not a nation. Moreover, a divided Italy suited Austrian interests. At Vienna, Austria took control of much of northern Italy, while Hapsburg monarchs ruled various other Italian states. In the south, a French Bourbon ruler was put in charge of Naples and Sicily.

In response, nationalists organized secret patriotic societies and focused their efforts on expelling Austrian forces from northern Italy. Between 1820 and 1848, nationalist revolts exploded across the region. Each time, Austria sent troops to crush the rebels.

**Mazzini's Young Italy.** In the 1830s, the nationalist leader Giuseppe Mazzini founded Young Italy. The goal of this secret society was "to constitute Italy, one, free, independent, republican nation."

**Verdi, an Italian Nationalist** *Opera composer Giuseppi Verdi was an ardent Italian nationalist, and he used his music to rouse Italians to the nationalist cause. His opera* I Lombardi *told of Italian heroism during the Crusades. On opening night in 1843, its thinly disguised anti-Austrian themes whipped the audience into a riot.* **Continuity and Change** *Do people today use theater and music to promote a cause? Give examples to support your answer.*

# PARALLELS THROUGH TIME

## The Red Cross

The International Red Cross operates in nearly every country of the world. It was founded in 1863 to provide relief in wartime. Participating governments agreed to care for victims whether they were from enemy or friendly countries. In later years, the Red Cross expanded to include many peacetime activities, such as first aid training, blood banks, child care, and water safety.

**Linking Past and Present** Why do you think a "neutral" organization was needed to care for war victims? Do you think the Red Cross is still needed today? Explain.

**PAST** In 1859, a Swiss banker, Jean-Henri Dunant (left), witnessed a battle between Italian, French, and Austrian forces in Lombardy. Horrified at the suffering—nearly 40,000 casualties—Dunant helped to organize the International Red Cross to help victims of war. One of the first groups of Red Cross volunteers, during the Franco-Prussian War in 1870, is shown below.

**PRESENT** Today, the Red Cross operates in more than 100 countries. A sister organizaton, the Red Crescent, above, is active in Muslim nations.

---

In 1849, Mazzini helped set up a revolutionary republic in Rome, but French forces soon toppled it. Like many other nationalists, Mazzini spent much of his life in exile, plotting and dreaming of a united Italy.

**The tide of nationalism.** "Ideas grow quickly," Mazzini once said, "when watered by the blood of martyrs." Although revolution had failed, nationalist agitation had planted seeds for future harvests.

To nationalists like Mazzini, a united Italy made sense not only because of geography but because of a common language and shared tra-

ditions. They reminded Italians of the glories of ancient Rome and the medieval papacy. To others, unity made practical economic sense. It would end trade barriers between the various Italian states, encourage railroad building, and stimulate industry.

## The Struggle for Italy

After 1848, leadership of the Risorgimento (ree sor jee MEHN toh), or Italian nationalist movement, passed to the small kingdom of Sardinia. (See the map on page 594.) Its constitutional monarch, Victor Emmanuel II, hoped to join other states to his own.*

**Cavour.** In 1852, Victor Emmanuel appointed Count Camillo Cavour as his prime minister. The new prime minister came from a noble family but favored liberal goals. He was a flexible, practical, crafty politician, willing to use almost any means to achieve his goals. Like Bismarck in Prussia, Cavour believed in Realpolitik. Also like Bismarck, he was a monarchist devoted to the interests of his royal master.

Once in office, Cavour moved first to reform Sardinia's economy. He improved agriculture, had railroads built, and encouraged commerce by supporting free trade. Cavour's long-term goal, however, was to expel Austrian power from Italy and add Lombardy and Venetia to Sardinia.

**Intrigue with France.** In 1855, led by Cavour, Sardinia joined Britain and France in the Crimean War against Russia. Although the fighting brought no rewards of territory, it did give Sardinia a voice at the peace conference. It also made Napoleon III take notice of the little Italian kingdom.

In 1858, Cavour negotiated a secret deal with Napoleon, who promised to aid Sardinia in case it faced a war with Austria. A year later, the shrewd Cavour provoked that war. With French help, Sardinia defeated Austria and annexed Lombardy. Meanwhile, nationalist groups overthrew Austrian-backed rulers in several other northern Italian states. These states then voted to join with Sardinia.

**Garibaldi's Red Shirts.** Next, attention shifted to the kingdom of the Two Sicilies in southern Italy. There, Giuseppe Garibaldi, a longtime nationalist and an ally of Mazzini, was ready for action. Like Mazzini, Garibaldi wanted to create an Italian republic. He did not, however, hesitate to accept aid from the monarchist Cavour. By 1860, Garibaldi had recruited a force of 1,000 red-shirted volunteers. Cavour provided weapons and allowed two ships to take Garibaldi and his "Red Shirts" south to Sicily.

With surprising speed, Garibaldi's forces won control of Sicily, crossed to the mainland, and marched triumphantly north to Naples. Later, Garibaldi recalled the Red Shirts' glorious campaign:

> **❝**O noble Thousand! . . . I love to remember you! . . . 'Where any of our brothers are fighting for liberty, there all Italians must hasten!'—such was your motto, and you hastened to the spot without asking whether your foes were few or many.**❞**

**Unity at last.** Garibaldi's success alarmed Cavour, who feared the nationalist hero would set up a republic in the south. To prevent this,

---

*The kingdom of Sardinia included Piedmont, Nice, and Savoy, as well as the island of Sardinia.

*Giuseppe Garibaldi* "I offer neither pay, nor quarters, nor provisions," Garibaldi warned his troops. "I offer hunger, thirst, forced marches, battles, and death. Let him who loves his country in his heart, and not with his lips only, follow me." His loyal Red Shirts did follow their beloved leader to victory. Garibaldi had learned techniques of guerrilla warfare during a 12-year exile in South America, where he joined wars of liberation in Brazil and Uruguay. ***Impact of the Individual*** *What qualities might inspire people to follow a leader like Garibaldi?*

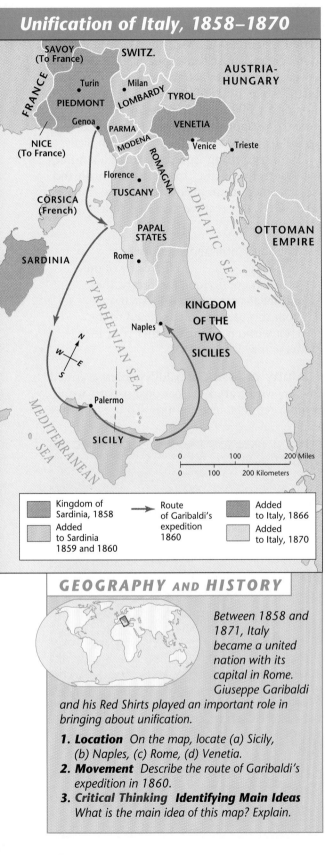

## Unification of Italy, 1858–1870

Kingdom of Sardinia, 1858

Added to Sardinia 1859 and 1860

Route of Garibaldi's expedition 1860

Added to Italy, 1866

Added to Italy, 1870

### GEOGRAPHY AND HISTORY

Between 1858 and 1871, Italy became a united nation with its capital in Rome. Giuseppe Garibaldi and his Red Shirts played an important role in bringing about unification.

1. **Location** On the map, locate (a) Sicily, (b) Naples, (c) Rome, (d) Venetia.
2. **Movement** Describe the route of Garibaldi's expedition in 1860.
3. **Critical Thinking  Identifying Main Ideas** What is the main idea of this map? Explain.

Cavour sent Sardinian troops to deal with Garibaldi. The Sardinians overran the Papal States and linked up with Garibaldi in Naples.

In a patriotic move, Garibaldi turned over Naples and Sicily to Victor Emmanuel. Shortly after, southern Italy voted to approve the move, and in 1861, Victor Emmanuel II was crowned king of Italy.

Two areas remained outside the new Italian nation: Rome and Venetia. Cavour died in 1861, but his successors completed his dream. In a deal negotiated with Bismarck, Italy acquired Venetia in the peace treaty that ended the Austro-Prussian War in 1866. During the Franco-Prussian War in 1870, France was forced to withdraw its troops from Rome. Italian troops entered the city, and Rome became the capital of the new nation. For the first time since the fall of the Roman empire, Italy was a united land.

## Trials of the New Nation

Young Italy faced a host of problems. Like the many states Bismarck cemented into the German empire, Italy had no tradition of unity. Most Italians felt stronger ties to local areas than to the new nation. Regional disputes left Italy unable to solve critical national issues.

**Divisions.** The greatest regional differences were between Italians in the north and those in the south. The north was richer and had more cities than the south. For centuries, northern Italian cities had flourished as centers of business and culture. The south was rural and poor. Its population was booming, but illiterate peasants wrung a meager existence from the exhausted farmland.

Hostility between the state and the Roman Catholic Church further divided Italy. Popes bitterly resented the seizure of the Papal States and of Rome. The government granted the papacy the small territory of the Vatican. Popes, however, saw themselves as "prisoners" and urged Italian Catholics—almost all Italians—not to cooperate with their new government.

**Turmoil.** Under Victor Emmanuel, Italy was a constitutional monarchy with a two-house legislature. The king appointed members to the upper house, which could veto bills passed by the lower house. Although the lower house had elected representatives, only a small number of men had the right to vote.

In the late 1800s, unrest increased as radicals on the left struggled against a conservative government. Socialists organized strikes while anarchists, people who want to abolish all government, turned to sabotage and violence. Slowly, the government extended suffrage to more men and passed laws to improve social conditions. Still, the turmoil continued. To distract attention from troubles at home, the government set out to win an overseas empire. (See page 639.)

**Progress.** Despite its problems, Italy did develop economically, especially after 1900. Although it lacked important natural resources such as coal, industries did sprout up in northern Italy. Industrialization, of course, brought urbanization as peasants flocked to the cities to work in factories. Reformers campaigned to improve education and working conditions.

The population explosion of this period created tensions, but an important safety valve was emigration. Many Italians left for the United States, Canada, and Latin American lands.

**Looking ahead.** By 1914, the country was significantly better off than it had been in 1861. But it was hardly prepared for the great war that broke out in that year and into which it would soon be drawn.

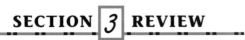

## SECTION 3 REVIEW

1. **Identify** (a) Giuseppe Mazzini, (b) Risorgimento, (c) Victor Emmanuel II, (d) Camillo Cavour, (e) Giuseppe Garibaldi.
2. **Define** anarchist.
3. (a) What obstacles to unity did Italian nationalists face? (b) What conditions favored unity?
4. What steps did Cavour take to promote Italian unity?
5. Describe the problems Italians faced after unification.
6. *Critical Thinking* **Comparing** Compare the goals and methods of Cavour in Italy and Bismarck in Germany. (a) How are they similar? (b) How are they different?
7. *ACTIVITY* Create a comic strip showing the events leading to Italian unification.

# 4 Nationalism Threatens Old Empires

## Guide for Reading

■ How was nationalism a divisive force in the Austrian empire?

■ Why was the Dual Monarchy formed?

■ Why did conflicts erupt in the Balkans?

While nationalism united people in Germany and Italy, it undermined old empires in Eastern Europe. The Austrian Hapsburgs and the Ottoman Turks ruled lands that included diverse ethnic groups. Nationalist feelings among these subject people contributed to tensions in Europe.

## A Fading Power

In 1800, the Hapsburgs were the oldest ruling house in Europe. Besides their homeland of Austria, they had acquired over the centuries Bohemia and Hungary, as well as parts of Romania, Poland, Ukraine, and northern Italy.

**Challenge of change.** Since the Congress of Vienna, the Austrian emperor Francis I and Metternich, his foreign minister, upheld conservative goals against liberal forces. "Rule and change nothing," the emperor told his son. Under Francis and Metternich, newspapers could not even use the word *constitution.* The government tried to limit industrial development, which would threaten traditional ways of life.

Austria, however, could not hold back the changes that were engulfing Europe. By the 1840s, factories were springing up, and the Hapsburgs were facing the familiar problems of industrial life—the growth of cities, worker discontent, and the stirrings of socialism.

**ISSUES** *For* **TODAY**

During the 1800s, nationalism helped to reshape the map of Europe. How is nationalism both a unifying and a divisive force?

**A patchwork of people.** Equally disturbing to the old order were the urgent demands of nationalists. The Hapsburgs presided over a multinational empire. Of its 50 million people at mid-century, less than a quarter were German-speaking Austrians. Almost half belonged to different Slavic groups, including Czechs, Slovaks, Poles, Ukrainians, Serbs, Croats, and Slovenes. Often, rival groups shared the same region. The empire also included large numbers of Hungarians and Italians. ( ★ See *Skills for Success*, page 604.)

The Hapsburgs ignored nationalist demands as long as they could. "Peoples?" Francis I once exclaimed. "What does that mean? I know only subjects." As you have read, when nationalist revolts broke out across the empire in 1848, the government crushed them.

**Early reforms.** Amid the turmoil, 18-year-old Francis Joseph inherited the throne. He would rule until 1916, presiding over the empire during its fading days into World War I.

An early challenge came when Austria suffered its humiliating defeat by France and Sardinia in 1859. (See page 593.) Francis Joseph realized he needed to strengthen the empire at home and made some reforms. He granted a new constitution that set up a legislature. This body, however, was dominated by German-speaking Austrians. The reforms thus satisfied none of the empire's other national groups. The Hungarians, especially, were determined to settle for nothing less than self-government.

## The Dual Monarchy

Austria's disastrous defeat in 1866 in the war with Prussia brought renewed pressure from the Hungarians. A year later, Francis Deák (deh AHK), a moderate Hungarian leader, helped work out a compromise that created the Dual Monarchy of Austria-Hungary.

Under the agreement, Austria and Hungary were separate states. Each had its own constitution and parliament. Francis Joseph ruled as emperor of Austria and king of Hungary. The two states shared ministries of finance, defense, and foreign affairs but were independent of each other in all other areas.

While Hungarians welcomed the compromise, other subject people resented it. Restlessness increased among various Slavic groups, especially the Czechs in Bohemia. Some leaders called on Slavs to unite, insisting that "only through liberty, equality, and fraternal solidarity" could Slavs fulfill their "great mission in the history of mankind." By the early 1900s, nationalist discontent often left the government paralyzed in the face of pressing problems.

## Balkan Nationalism

Like the Hapsburgs, the Ottomans ruled a multinational empire. It stretched from Eastern Europe and the Balkans to North Africa and the Middle East. There, as in Austria, nationalist demands tore at the fabric of the empire. (You will

**Hub of the Hapsburg Empire**
The Hapsburg empire boasted many fine cities, but none equaled Vienna at the turn of the century. With its great churches, Gothic palaces, fine museums, and stately tree-lined avenues, Vienna was a magnet that attracted many of the best minds and talents of Europe. Here, Vienna's leading citizens enjoy an evening of gaiety at an imperial ball.
**Political and Social Systems**
Based on this painting, make a generalization about the Hapsburg ruling class.

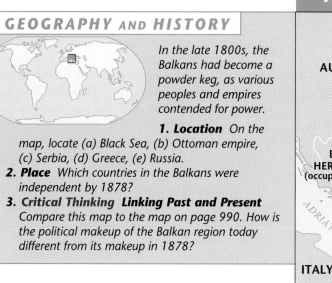

In the late 1800s, the Balkans had become a powder keg, as various peoples and empires contended for power.

**1. Location** On the map, locate (a) Black Sea, (b) Ottoman empire, (c) Serbia, (d) Greece, (e) Russia.

**2. Place** Which countries in the Balkans were independent by 1878?

**3. Critical Thinking** *Linking Past and Present* Compare this map to the map on page 990. How is the political makeup of the Balkan region today different from its makeup in 1878?

## The Balkans, 1878

read about Ottoman efforts to stem their decline in Chapter 25.)

In the Balkans, Serbia had won autonomy in 1817 and the southern part of Greece won independence in the 1830s. (See Chapter 21.) But many Serbs and Greeks still lived in the Balkans under Ottoman rule. The Ottoman empire was also home to other national groups, such as the Bulgarians and Romanians. During the 1800s, various subject people revolted against the Ottomans, hoping to set up their own independent states.

These nationalist stirrings became mixed up with the ambitions of the great European powers. In the mid-1800s, Europeans saw the Ottoman empire as a "dying man," and they scrambled eagerly to divide up its territories. Russia pushed southward toward Constantinople. Austria-Hungary eventually gained the provinces of Bosnia and Herzegovina, angering the Serbs who hoped for greater power there themselves. Meanwhile, Britain and France each set their sights on other Ottoman lands.

In the end, a complex web of competing interests contributed to a succession of crises and wars. Russia fought several wars against the Ottomans. France and Britain sometimes joined the Russians and sometimes the Ottomans. Germany supported Austrian authority over the national groups but encouraged the Ottomans, too, because of their strategic location at the eastern end of the Mediterranean. In between, the subject nationalities revolted and then fought among themselves. By the early 1900s, observers were referring to the region as the "Balkan powder keg." The explosion that came in 1914 helped set off World War I.

## SECTION 4 REVIEW

1. **Identify** Francis Joseph.
2. How did nationalism affect each of the following: (a) Austrian empire, (b) Ottoman empire?
3. (a) What was the Dual Monarchy? (b) Why did it fail to end nationalist demands?
4. Give two reasons why the Balkans were a trouble spot in the 1800s.
5. **Critical Thinking** *Solving Problems* Do you think that the Hapsburgs or Ottomans could have built a modern nation from their multinational empires? Explain.
6. *ACTIVITY* Create a concept map of nationalism as a positive and a negative force.

# Russia: Reform and Reaction

## Guide for Reading

- Why did attempts to reform Russia often fail?

- How did Russia try to modernize and industrialize?

- What were the causes and results of the revolution of 1905?

- **Vocabulary** *zemstvo, pogrom, refugee*

The ideas of the French Revolution inspired Russia's great poet Alexander Pushkin to write his "Ode to Freedom":

66I will sing the freedom of the world,
  And strike down the [evil] sitting on
    the throne,
  Tyrants of the world tremble!
  And you, fallen slaves, take heart
    and hear.
  Arise!99

In the early 1800s, romantics like Pushkin dreamed of freeing Russia from autocratic rule, economic backwardness, and social injustice. But efforts to modernize Russia had little success. Between 1801 and 1914, repression outweighed reform, as czars imprisoned critics or sent them into icy exile in Siberia.

## The Russian Colossus

By 1800, Russia was not only the largest, most populous nation in Europe but also a great world power. Since the 1600s, explorers had pushed the Russian frontier eastward across Siberia to the Pacific. (See the map on page 442.) Peter and Catherine had added lands on the Baltic and Black seas, and czars in the 1800s had expanded into Central Asia. Russia thus acquired a huge multinational empire, part European and part Asian.

Other European nations looked on the Russian colossus, or giant, with wonder and misgiving. It had immense natural resources. Its vast size gave it global interests and influence. But Western Europeans disliked its autocratic government and feared its expansionist aims.

**Obstacles to progress.** Despite efforts by Peter and Catherine to westernize Russia, it remained economically undeveloped. By the 1800s, czars saw the need to modernize but resisted reforms that would undermine absolute rule. While they wavered, Russia fell further behind Western Europe in economic and social developments.

A great obstacle to progress was the rigid social structure. Landowning nobles dominated society and rejected any change that would threaten their privileges. The middle class was too small to have much influence. The majority of Russians were serfs, laborers bound to the land. While serfdom had almost disappeared in Western Europe by the 1700s, it survived and spread in Russia.

**The shame of serfdom.** Masters exercised almost total power over their serfs. In his autobiography, Peter Kropotkin, a noble who

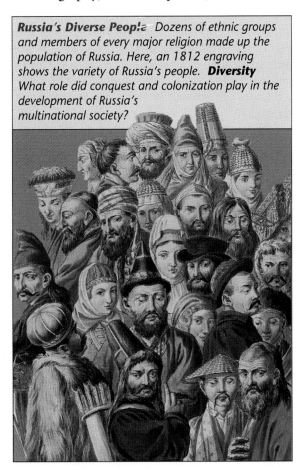

*Russia's Diverse People* Dozens of ethnic groups and members of every major religion made up the population of Russia. Here, an 1812 engraving shows the variety of Russia's people. **Diversity** What role did conquest and colonization play in the development of Russia's multinational society?

became a revolutionary, described the brutal treatment of serfs:

> **❝**I heard . . . stories of men and women torn from their families and their villages, and sold, or lost in gambling, or exchanged for a couple of hunting dogs, and then transported to some remote part of Russia to create a [master's] new estate; . . . of children taken from their parents and sold to cruel masters; . . . of flogging . . . that occurred daily with unheard-of cruelty.**❞**

The majority of serfs were peasants. Others might be servants, artisans, or soldiers forced into the czar's army. As industry expanded, masters sent serfs to work in factories but took much of their pay. Many enlightened Russians knew that serfdom was inefficient. As long as most people had to serve the whim of their masters, Russia's economy would remain backward. Landowning nobles had no incentive to improve agriculture and took little interest in industry.

▲ *Russian serf*

## Three Pillars of Russian Absolutism

For centuries, czars had ruled with absolute power, imposing their will on their subjects. The Enlightenment and French Revolution had almost no effect on Russian autocracy.

**Alexander I.** When Alexander I inherited the throne in 1801, he seemed open to liberal ideas. The new czar eased censorship and promoted education. He even talked about freeing the serfs.

By the time Napoleon invaded Russia in 1812, however, Alexander had drawn back from reform. Like earlier czars, he feared losing the support of nobles. At the Congress of Vienna, he joined the conservative powers in opposing liberal and nationalist impulses in Europe.

**Revolt and repression.** When Alexander I died in 1825, a group of army officers led an uprising, known as the Decembrist Revolt. They had picked up liberal ideas while fighting Napoleon in Western Europe and now demanded a constitution and other reforms. The new czar, Nicholas I, quickly suppressed the Decembrists and then cracked down on all dissent.

Nicholas used police spies to hunt out critics. He banned books from Western Europe that might spread liberal ideas. Only approved textbooks were allowed in schools and universities. Many Russians with liberal or revolutionary ideas were judged to be insane and shut up in mental hospitals. Up to 150,000 others were exiled to Siberia. The American humorist Mark Twain once quipped:

> **❝**In Russia, whenever they catch a man, woman, or child that has got any brains or education or character, they ship that person straight to Siberia. It is admirable. . . . It keeps the general level of Russian intellect and education down to that of the Czar.**❞**

**"Orthodoxy, autocracy, and nationalism."** To bolster his regime, Nicholas I embraced the pillars of Russian absolutism symbolized in the motto: "Orthodoxy, autocracy, and nationalism." Orthodoxy referred to the strong ties between the Russian Orthodox Church and the government. Autocracy was the absolute power of the state. Nationalism involved respect for Russian traditions and suppression of non-Russian groups within the empire.

Still, Nicholas realized that Russia needed to modernize. He issued a new law code and made some economic reforms. He even tried to limit the power of landowners over serfs. But he could see no way to change the system without angering Russian nobles. Before he died, he told his son: "I am handing you command of the country in a poor state."

## Reforms of Alexander II

Alexander II came to the throne in 1855 during the Crimean War. The war had broken

out after Russia tried to seize Ottoman lands along the Danube. Britain and France stepped in to help the Turks, invading the Crimean peninsula that juts into the Black Sea. The war, which ended in a Russian defeat, revealed the country's backwardness. It had only a few miles of railroads, and the military bureaucracy was hopelessly inefficient.

**Emancipation.** A widespread popular reaction followed. Liberals demanded changes and students demonstrated for reform. Pressed from all sides, Alexander II finally agreed to reforms. In 1861, he issued a royal decree emancipating, or freeing, the serfs.

Freedom brought problems. Former serfs had to buy the land they had worked for so long. Many were too poor to do so. Also, the lands allotted to peasants were often too small to farm efficiently or to support a family. As a result, peasants remained poor, and discontent festered.

Still, emancipation was a turning point. Many peasants moved to the cities, taking jobs in factories and building Russian industries. Equally important, freeing the serfs boosted the drive for further reform.

**Other reforms.** Along with emancipation, Alexander set up a system of local government. Elected assemblies, called zemstvos, were made responsible for matters such as road repair, schools, and agriculture. At the local level, at least, Russians gained some experience of open discussion and self-government.

The czar also introduced legal reforms based on ideas such as trial by jury. He eased censorship and tried to reform the military. A soldier's term of service was reduced from 25 years to 15, and brutal discipline was limited. Alexander also encouraged the growth of industry in Russia.

A movement to liberate women swept the urban centers of Russia. Since university education was denied them in Russia, hundreds of privileged young women left their homes and families to study abroad. Many became supporters of the goal of popular revolution.

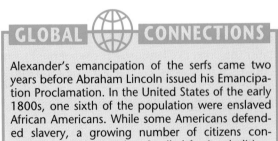

**GLOBAL CONNECTIONS**

Alexander's emancipation of the serfs came two years before Abraham Lincoln issued his Emancipation Proclamation. In the United States of the early 1800s, one sixth of the population were enslaved African Americans. While some Americans defended slavery, a growing number of citizens condemned it as immoral and called for its abolition. At last, in 1861, agitation over the issue involved the nation in a civil war. Not until after peace was restored in 1865 did slavery finally end.

## Return to Reaction

Alexander's reforms failed to satisfy many Russians. Peasants had freedom but not land. Liberals wanted a constitution and elected legislature. Radicals, influenced by socialist ideas from the West, demanded even more revolutionary changes. The czar, meantime, moved away from reform and toward repression.

**Revolutionary currents.** In the 1870s, some socialists carried the message of reform to the peasants. They went to live and work among the peasants, sometimes preaching rebellion. These educated young men and women had little success. The peasants scarcely understood them and sometimes turned them over to the police.

The failure of the "Go to the People" movement and renewed government repression sparked anger among radicals. Some turned to terrorism. A revolutionary group calling itself the People's Will assassinated officials and plotted to kill the czar. Their first attempts failed. Then, on a cold March day in 1881, terrorists hurled two bombs at Alexander's carriage. One struck down several guards. The second killed the "czar emancipator."

**Crackdown.** Alexander III responded to his father's assassination by reviving the harsh methods of Nicholas I. To wipe out liberals and revolutionaries, he increased the power of the secret police, restored strict censorship, and exiled critics to Siberia. He relied on his adviser and former tutor, Constantine Pobedonostsev (puh beh duh NAWS tsehv), who rejected all talk of democracy and constitutional government as "the lies of hollow and flabby people."

The czar also launched a program of Russification aimed at suppressing the cultures of non-Russian people within the empire. Alexander insisted on one language, Russian, and one church, the Russian Orthodox Church. Poles, Ukrainians, Finns, Armenians, and many others suffered persecution. The Russification campaign also targeted Jews and Muslim people throughout the empire.

**Persecution and pogroms.** Russia had acquired a large Jewish population when it carved up Poland and expanded into Ukraine. Under Alexander III, persecution of Russian Jews increased. He limited the number of Jews allowed to study in universities and practice professions such as law and medicine. He revived old laws that forced Jews to live in certain restricted areas.

Official persecution encouraged violent mob attacks on Jews, known as pogroms. Gangs beat and killed Jews and looted and burned their homes and stores. The police did nothing to stop the violence. Faced with savage persecution, many Jews escaped from Russia. They became refugees, or people who flee their homeland to seek safety elsewhere. Large numbers of Jews went to the United States. Though they often faced prejudice there, they were safe from pogroms and official persecution. Jewish immigrants sent joyful news back to Russia: "There is no czar in America!"

**A Jewish Village** The center of Russian Jewish life was the shtetl, or village. From day to day, Russia and the czar seemed far away from the village community. "The world was divided into two parts," recalled one Jewish woman, "Polotzk, the place where I lived, and a strange land called Russia." Yet, at any moment, a pogrom might shatter the peace of the shtetl. **Global Interaction** Why did many Jewish families flee to the United States?

## Building Russian Industry

Under Alexander III and his son, Nicholas II, Russia finally entered the industrial age. In the 1890s, Count Serge Witte, finance minister to Nicholas, made economic development a key goal. Witte encouraged railroad building to link iron and coal mines to factories and to transport goods across Russia. He secured foreign capital to invest in transportation and industry. Loans from France helped build the Trans-Siberian Railway. Begun in the 1890s, it stretched 5,000 miles (8,000 km) from European Russia to the Pacific Ocean.

The drive to industrialize increased political and social problems. Government officials and business leaders applauded and encouraged economic growth. Nobles and peasants opposed it, fearing the changes brought by the new ways.

Industrialization also created social ills as peasants flocked to cities to work in factories. There, they faced long hours and low pay in dangerous conditions. In the slums around the factories, poverty, disease, and discontent multiplied.

Radicals sought supporters among the new industrial workers. At factory gates, socialists handed out pamphlets that preached the revolutionary ideas of Karl Marx. Among the revolutionaries of the 1890s was young Vladimir Ulyanov, whose older brother had been executed for plotting to kill Alexander III. Like many revolutionaries, Ulyanov used an alias, or false name—Lenin. In 1917, Lenin would take power in a revolution that transformed Russia. (See Chapter 28.)

## The "Little Father" Betrays His People

War broke out between Russia and Japan in 1904. (See Chapter 26.) Nicholas II called on his people to fight for "the Faith, the Czar, and the Fatherland." But despite their efforts, the Russians suffered one humiliating defeat after another.

**A peaceful march.** News of the disasters unleashed pent-up discontent created by years of oppression. Protesters poured into the streets. Workers struck with demands for shorter hours and better wages. Liberals called for a constitution and reforms to overhaul an inefficient, corrupt government.

As the crisis deepened, a young Orthodox priest, Father George Gapon, organized a march for Sunday, January 22, 1905. He felt certain that the "Little Father," as Russians called the czar, would help his people if only he understood their sufferings.

The parade flowed through the icy streets of St. Petersburg toward the czar's Winter Palace. Chanting prayers and singing hymns, workers carried holy icons and pictures of the czar. They also brought a petition addressed to Nicholas:

> **“**We, the workers of St. Petersburg, with our wives, our children, and our aged and feeble parents, have come to you, Sire, in search of justice and protection. We have fallen into poverty, we are oppressed, we are . . . treated as slaves. . . . Do not refuse to protect your people. Raise us from the grave of arbitrary power, poverty, and ignorance. . . . Free us from the intolerable oppression of officials. Destroy the wall between yourself and your people—and let us govern the country with you.**”**

**Bloody Sunday.** Fearing the marchers, the czar had fled the palace and called in soldiers. As the people approached, they saw troops lined up across the square. Suddenly, a crack of gunfire rang out, followed by another and another. Men and women reeled and fell. Hundreds lay dead in the snow. One marcher cried out: "How dare they shoot at a religious procession, at the portraits of the czar?"

A woman stumbling away from the scene of the massacre moaned: "The czar has deserted us! They shot away the orthodox faith." Indeed, the slaughter marked a turning point for Russians. "Bloody Sunday" killed the people's faith and trust in the czar.

## The Revolution of 1905

In the months that followed Bloody Sunday, discontent exploded across Russia. Strikes multiplied. In some cities, workers took over lo-

**Bloody Sunday** *The Russian people's faith in the czar was badly shaken by the events of Bloody Sunday. This illustration shows peaceful marchers being gunned down near the czar's Winter Palace in St. Petersburg. In the center stands Father Gapon, pleading vainly for mercy.* **Political and Social Systems** *How did the events of Bloody Sunday help spark the Revolution of 1905?*

cal government. In the countryside, peasants revolted, demanding land. Minority nationalities called for autonomy. Terrorists targeted officials, and some assassins were cheered as heroes by discontented Russians.

At last, the clamor grew so great that Nicholas was forced to announce sweeping reforms. In the October Manifesto, he promised "freedom of person, conscience, speech, assembly, and union." He agreed to summon a Duma, or elected national legislature. No law, he declared, would go into effect without approval by the Duma.

**Results of the revolution.** The manifesto won over moderates, leaving socialists isolated. Divisions between these groups helped the czar, who had no intention of letting strikers, revolutionaries, and rebellious peasants challenge him.

In 1906, the first Duma met, but the czar quickly dissolved it when leaders criticized the government. Nicholas then appointed Peter

Stolypin (stuh LEE pihn), a conservative, as prime minister. Arrests, pogroms, and executions followed as Stolypin sought to restore order. Russians bitterly dubbed the hanging noose "Stolypin's necktie." A popular song mocked the czar's promises in the October Manifesto:

> **66**The czar became frightened,
> He issued a manifesto:
> That the dead be given liberty,
> The living be arrested.**99**

Stolypin realized that Russia needed reform, not just repression. To regain peasant support, he introduced moderate land reforms. He strengthened the zemstvos and improved education before he was assassinated in 1911. Several more Dumas met during this period, but new voting laws made sure they were conservative. By 1914, Russia was still an autocracy, simmering with peasant and worker unrest.

## SECTION 5 REVIEW

1. **Identify** (a) Decembrist Revolt, (b) Crimean War, (c) Alexander II, (d) People's Will, (e) Russification, (f) Serge Witte, (g) Bloody Sunday, (h) October Manifesto, (i) Peter Stolypin.
2. **Define** (a) zemstvo, (b) pogrom, (c) refugee.
3. (a) Why was Russia a relatively backward country in the 1800s? (b) What reforms did Russia undertake?
4. What steps did Russia take to industrialize in the late 1800s?
5. (a) What were the causes of the revolution of 1905? (b) How did Nicholas II respond to the widespread turmoil?
6. *Critical Thinking* **Analyzing Information** Alexander II declared that it is "better to abolish serfdom from above than to wait until it will be abolished by a movement from below." What did he mean by this?
7. *ACTIVITY* Make a set of playing cards picturing each of the czars discussed in the section. On each card, list the goals and achievements of the czar. Color code the cards according to whether the czar was a reformer or a reactionary.

# Skills for Success

Critical Thinking | Writing and Researching | **Maps, Charts, and Graphs** | Speaking and Listening

## Drawing Inferences From Maps

Maps present a great deal of information in a small space. Most of the information is furnished directly, through color and symbols. Other information may be obtained by *drawing inferences*. Drawing inferences from a map usually involves two processes: (1) identifying information that the map presents indirectly, and (2) recalling and applying knowledge that you already have.

Not everyone will draw the same inferences from one map. Every person has his or her own store of previous knowledge, and every person reasons differently. Thus, the inferences you draw from a map may be different from those that someone else draws from the same map.

**National Groups of Eastern Europe About 1870**

The map below and the map on page 597 show the Balkan region in about 1870 and 1878. Study the two maps. Then, follow the steps below to draw inferences about the Balkan region and its population.

**1** **Identify information on the maps.**
(a) What region of the world do both maps show? (b) What is the subject of the map below? (c) What is the subject of the map on page 597?

**2** **Decide what information is implied.** Compare the two maps to identify information that is implied but not directly stated. (a) Identify two multinational empires shown on the map. (b) List the national groups who lived in one of these empires about 1870. (c) Did the country in which some national groups lived change in 1878? How do you know?

**3** **Combine prior knowledge with information from the maps.** Recall information that you learned in the chapter about national groups to answer these questions: (a) How did national groups encourage the drive for German unity? For Italian unity? (b) How did national groups affect Austria-Hungary and the Ottoman empire?

**4** **Draw inferences about the 1878 border changes.** (a) How might national groups react to the border changes? To a change in rulers? (b) How might rulers react to the border changes? To a change in national groups under their rule? (c) What positive effects and consequences might take place? What negative effects? Compare and discuss your inferences and reasoning with others.

*Beyond the Classroom* With a partner, find a map or pair of maps in your local newspaper or in a national news magazine. Work together to identify the information presented on the map(s). Then, apply geographic or historical knowledge to draw inferences about the map's region or population.

## Building Vocabulary

Review the following vocabulary from this chapter: *nationalism, Realpolitik, anarchist, serf, absolutism, autocracy, emancipation, zemstvo, pogrom, refugee.* Write sentences using each of these words, leaving blanks where the words would go. Exchange your sentences with another student, and fill in the blanks on each other's lists.

## Reviewing Chapter Themes

1. **Political and Social Systems** How did nationalism spark the drive for unification of (a) Germany, (b) Italy?
2. **Impact of the Individual** (a) What role did Bismarck play in German unification? (b) What policies did he pursue after unification? (c) How did Cavour help to unify Italy?
3. **Diversity** (a) What problems did nationalism create in the Austrian empire? (b) What steps did the emperor take to resolve these problems? (c) How did nationalist demands hasten the decline of the Ottoman empire?
4. **Religions and Value Systems** (a) What obstacles to progress did Russia face in the early 1800s? (b) How did the czars try to strengthen the autocracy? (c) What reforms did they introduce?

## Thinking Critically

1. **Analyzing Fine Art** Study the painting on page 583. (a) What is the subject of the painting? (b) Where does the scene take place? What was the special symbolism of that location? (c) Who seems to be the central figure of the painting? (d) What conclusions can you draw from this about the power structure in Germany at the time? ( ★ See *Skills for Success*, page 368.)
2. **Comparing** How did the nationalism represented by Bismarck differ from the nationalism embraced by European liberals in the early 1800s?
3. **Applying Information** (a) Define Realpolitik. (b) Then, give *four* examples to show how Bismarck and Cavour were followers of this approach.
4. **Linking Past and Present** Is nationalism a force in the world today? Give examples to support your answer.
5. **Drawing Conclusions** Why do you think the Russian czars in the 1800s moved back and forth between reform and repression?
6. **Making Inferences** What do the events of Bloody Sunday tell you about the relationship between the czar and the Russian people?
7. **Predicting Consequences** Based on your reading of the chapter, predict the consequences of the following: (a) German humiliation of France in the Franco-Prussian War, (b) growth of German nationalism and militarism in the late 1800s, (c) failure to satisfy nationalist ambitions in Austria-Hungary, (d) weakening of the Ottoman empire. ( ★ See *Skills for Success*, page 974.)

## For Your Portfolio

Historical fiction is a form of literature that is based on people and events from history. For this assignment, you will write a short piece of historical fiction. Your story should relate to people and events that you studied in the chapter.

1. Begin by reviewing the chapter. Then, decide on the time and place in which you will set your story and the characters you will include in it. Jot down facts that you might use in the story. Record each fact on a separate index card. Include as many details as possible.
2. Brainstorm a story plot. Decide if your characters will be purely fictional or figures from history or both. You might also find it helpful to skim published works of historical fiction.
3. Use library resources to research the period, events, and historical figures you will include. For example, if you are writing about the unification of Italy, you might want to find out more about Garibaldi's Red Shirts.
4. Write a first draft. Ask a classmate to serve as an editor to help you review the story. Revise your story as necessary. Finally, give your story an interesting title.
5. Share your finished story with the class. Be prepared to discuss how it reflects the history on which it is based.

CHAPTER 24

# Growth of Western Democracies

(1815–1914)

## CHAPTER OUTLINE

1 **Britain Becomes More Democratic**
2 **A Century of Reform**
3 **Division and Democracy in France**
4 **Expansion of the United States**

Charles Egremont is proud to be British. The son of a privileged family, he had grown up at a time when his nation's prosperity and prestige were soaring to remarkable heights. One day he boasts to some strangers that Victoria, the queen of England, "reigns over the greatest nation that ever existed."

"Which nation?" asks one of the strangers, "for she reigns over two":

> "'Two nations: between whom there is no [communication] and no sympathy; who are as ignorant of each other's habits, thoughts, and feelings, as if they were dwellers in different zones or inhabitants of different planets; who are formed by a different breeding, are fed by a different food, are ordered by different manners, and are not governed by the same laws.'"

Surprised, Egremont wonders what these "two nations" are. The stranger replies, "THE RICH AND THE POOR."

Charles Egremont is the hero of Benjamin Disraeli's novel *Sybil.* Disraeli was familiar with Britain's "two nations." A leading political figure, he moved in the world of aristocratic luxury and elegance. In the 1840s, however, travels around Britain opened his eyes to the appalling poverty of factory towns and rural villages.

Disraeli did more than write about the gap between rich and poor. As prime minister and leader of the Conservative party, he worked to achieve many needed reforms.

The Industrial Revolution uprooted old ways of life. Prosperity offered unimagined opportunities. Left behind in this age of great material progress, however, masses of people were condemned to wretched poverty. In response to changing conditions, reformers demanded the vote and other rights. In Germany and Russia, repressive governments stemmed the tide of change. But Britain, France, and the United States slowly extended democratic rights.

In all three of these western democracies, many people struggled for social reform. Factory workers, farmers, women, and others slowly made gains. Their efforts paved the way for great improvements in the quality of life in our own century.

**FOCUS ON** these questions as you read:

- **Political and Social Systems**
  How did Britain, France, and the United States become more democratic?
- **Continuity and Change**
  How did western democracies adapt to the new demands of industrial society?
- **Religions and Value Systems**
  What role did nationalism play in the western democracies?
- **Diversity**
  How did women and members of religious and ethnic groups seek greater rights?

## TIME AND PLACE

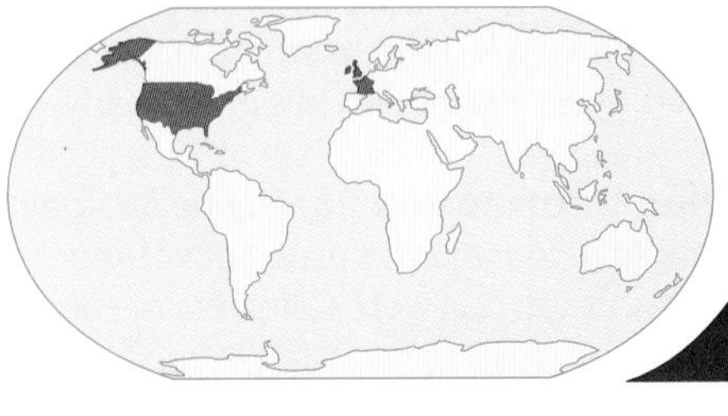

The Victorian Age  This 1887 plate honors Queen Victoria, the longest-ruling monarch in British history. She held little political power, but her strict code of behavior and morality set a standard for her time. For Britain, Victoria's reign was a time not only of power and prosperity but also of political reform.  **Political and Social Systems**  Review what you have learned about the British political system. Why did British monarchs hold little political power by the time of Victoria?

## HUMANITIES LINK

**Art History**  Hannah Stokes, *Trade and Commerce Quilt* (page 626).
**Literature**  In this chapter, you will encounter passages from the following works of literature: Benjamin Disraeli, *Sybil* (page 606); Emma Lazarus, "The New Colossus" (page 622).

| **1832** Reform Bill becomes law in Britain | **1845** "Great Hunger" in Ireland | **1865** United States Civil War ends | **1894** Dreyfus affair begins | **1909** French Union for Women's Suffrage founded |
|---|---|---|---|---|

| 1815 | 1835 | 1855 | 1875 | 1895 | 1915 |

# 1 Britain Becomes More Democratic

## Guide for Reading

- Why did reformers seek to alter Parliament in the 1800s?

- What role did political parties play in the Victorian era?

- How did Britain achieve universal male suffrage?

Earl Grey, Britain's prime minister, must have felt nervous as he stood up in the House of Lords. His goal was to win support for a new election reform bill. Many Lords feared that the bill was a first step toward giving too much power to the "rabble"—the uneducated masses of common people.

Still, Grey proceeded boldly. The present system of elections, he declared, was desperately in need of reform. No one supported it. It was condemned "by all authority, by all reason . . . and by the common law of the land." Grey continued:

66 The removal of this vicious and corrupt system, so far from tending to endanger the Constitution, in my opinion, will tend materially to improve and strengthen it. 99

In the end, Grey won his point. Later historians agreed that the Reform Bill of 1832 was a turning point in British politics.

The British parliamentary system would face other challenges over the next 80 years. Again and again, Britain would show the way to achieve greater democracy through reform rather than revolution.

## Reforming Parliament

In 1815, Britain was a constitutional monarchy with a parliament and two political parties. Still, it was far from democratic. Parliament, you will recall, was made up of the House of Lords and the House of Commons. The Lords were hereditary nobles and high-ranking clergy in the Church of England. They had the right to veto any bill passed by the House of Commons.

Members of the Commons were elected. Still, less than five percent of the people could vote. Wealthy country squires and landowning nobles dominated politics and heavily influenced voters. In certain towns, local landowners even had the right to name members of Parliament. In addition, old laws banned Catholics and non-Anglican Protestants from voting or serving in Parliament.

**Pressure for change.** In the 1820s, reformers pushed to end religious restrictions. After fierce debate, Parliament finally granted Catholics and non-Anglican Protestants equal political rights.

An even greater battle was brewing to make Parliament more representative. During the Industrial Revolution, centers of population shifted. Some old rural towns lost so many people that there were few or no voters. Yet these so-called "rotten boroughs" still sent members to Parliament, chosen by powerful local landowners. At the same time, populous new industrial cities like Manchester and Birmingham had no seats in Parliament at all.

**Reform Bill of 1832.** In 1830, as revolts flared on the continent, Whigs and Tories* battled over a reform bill. In the streets, supporters of reform chanted, "The Bill, the whole Bill, and nothing but the Bill!" Their shouts seemed to echo the cries of revolutionaries on the continent.

Parliament finally passed the Great Reform Act in 1832. It redistributed seats in the House of Commons, giving representation to large towns and eliminating rotten boroughs. It also enlarged the number of voters by granting suffrage to men with a certain amount of property.

The Reform Bill of 1832 did not bring full democracy, but it did give a greater political voice to men in the middle class. Landowning nobles, however, remained a powerful force in the government and economy.

---

*The Whig party had increasingly come to represent middle-class and business interests. The Tory party spoke for nobles, landowners, and others whose interests and income were rooted in agriculture. (See Chapter 18.)

**Chartism.** Many workers rejected the reform bill and called for more radical change. In the 1830s, protesters drew up the People's Charter, a petition that demanded universal male suffrage, a secret ballot, annual parliamentary elections, and salaries for members of Parliament. Their movement became known as Chartism. (Although Chartists did not call for women's rights, women in the Chartist movement organized the first British association to work for women's suffrage.)

Twice the Chartists presented petitions with over a million signatures to Parliament. Both petitions were ignored. In 1848, as revolutions swept Europe, the Chartists prepared a third petition and organized a march on Parliament. Fearing violence, the government moved to suppress the march. Soon after, the unsuccessful Chartist movement declined. In time, however, Parliament would pass most of the major reforms proposed by the Chartists.

## The Victorian Age

By the mid-1800s, the great symbol in British life was Queen Victoria. Her reign, from 1837 to 1901, was the longest in British history. Although she exercised little real political power, she set the tone for what is today called the Victorian age.

**Symbol of a nation's values.** As queen, Victoria came to embody the values of her age. These Victorian ideals included duty, thrift, honesty, hard work—and, above all, respectability. Today, we associate most of these qualities with the Victorian middle class. (See pages 567–568.) However, people at all levels of society shared these ideals, even if they could not al-

ways live up to them. Victoria herself embraced a strict code of morals and manners. As a young woman, she married a German prince, Albert, and they raised a large family. Although she outranked Albert, she treated him with the devotion a dutiful wife was expected to have for her husband. When he died in 1861, Victoria went into deep mourning and dressed in black for the rest of her reign. A fond grandmother to her 38 grandchildren, she worried that manners were becoming far too loose and informal. "Young people," she fretted, "are getting very American I fear in their lives and ways."

**Queen of a changing nation.** Under Victoria, the British middle class—and many members of the working class—felt great confidence in the future. That confidence grew as Britain expanded its already huge empire. (See Chapter 25.) Victoria, the empress of India and ruler of some 300 million subjects around the world, became a revered symbol of British might.

As she aged from teenaged queen to grieving widow to revered national symbol, Victoria witnessed tremendous political changes. She herself commented on the growing agitation for social reform:

❝The lower classes are becoming so well-informed, are so intelligent and earn their bread and riches so deservedly, that they cannot and ought not to be kept back.❞

As the Victorian era went on, reformers continued the push toward greater democracy.

## Politics Transformed

In the 1860s, a new era opened in British politics. The old political parties regrouped under new leadership. Benjamin Disraeli, whom you read about at the beginning of this chapter, forged the old Tory party into the modern

# PARALLELS THROUGH TIME

## The Art of Caricature

A caricature is a portrait that exaggerates the subject's face and other features. In the hands of a political cartoonist, caricature can be a powerful weapon. A good-natured caricature, however, can bring a smile even to the face of the victim.

**Linking Past and Present** Where would you be likely to find caricatures of famous people today?

**PAST** As the leading political figures of Victorian Britain, William Gladstone, right, and Benjamin Disraeli, below, were often the subject of caricatures.

**PRESENT** Political figures are not the only people who are caricatured. These modern caricatures depict pop stars Stevie Wonder (above) and Bruce Springsteen (below).

Conservative party. The Whigs, led by William Gladstone, evolved into the Liberal party. Between 1868 and 1880, as the majority in Parliament swung between the two parties, Gladstone and Disraeli alternated as prime minister. Both men fought for important reforms.

**Universal male suffrage.** In 1867, Disraeli's Conservative party pushed through a bill to give the vote to many working-class men. Conservatives backed the measure to win working-class support. The Reform Bill of 1867 almost doubled the size of the electorate.

In the 1880s, it was Gladstone and the Liberal party's turn to expand suffrage. Their reforms extended the vote to farmworkers and most other men. By century's end, almost-universal male suffrage, the secret ballot, and other Chartist ambitions had been achieved.

**Limiting the Lords.** In the early 1900s, Liberals in the House of Commons pressed ahead with social reforms. But many bills passed by the Commons met defeat in the House of Lords. In particular, the Lords used their veto power to block any attempt to increase taxes on the wealthy.

In 1911, a Liberal government passed measures to restrict the power of the Lords. For example, the new law would end their power to veto tax bills. Getting the Lords to approve the law was not easy. When the government threatened to have the king create enough new lords to approve the law, the Lords backed down.

People hailed the change as a victory for democracy. In time, the House of Lords, like the monarchy, became largely a ceremonial institution with little real power. The elected House of Commons would reign supreme.

## SECTION 1 REVIEW

1. **Identify** (a) rotten boroughs, (b) Chartism, (c) Victoria, (d) Benjamin Disraeli, (e) William Gladstone.
2. (a) In what ways was the British system of government not democratic in the early 1800s? (b) How did the Reform Bill of 1832 make Parliament more representative?
3. How did British political parties evolve in the 1800s?
4. (a) What groups gained the right to vote after 1860? (b) Why did reformers seek to limit the power of the House of Lords?
5. *Critical Thinking* **Drawing Conclusions** Why do you think the Chartists demanded (a) a secret ballot rather than public voting, (b) salaries for members of Parliament?
6. *ACTIVITY* Imagine that you are a land-owning aristocrat or a wealthy middle-class merchant. Write a letter to a friend of the same social class about the Reform Bill of 1832.

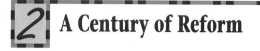

# A Century of Reform

## Guide for Reading

- What social and economic reforms did Britain pass in the 1800s?

- How did British women work to win the vote?

- What were the goals of Irish nationalists?

- **Vocabulary** *home rule*

Lying in a British prison hospital, Lady Constance Lytton refused to eat voluntarily. Her hunger strike, she vowed, would go on until the government gave the vote to women. Lytton later recalled:

> ❝I was visited again by the Senior Medical Officer, who asked me how long I had been without food. I said I had eaten a buttered scone and a banana sent in by friends to the police station on Friday at about midnight. He said, 'Oh, then, this is the fourth day; that is too long, I shall feed you, I must feed you at once.'❞

In the end, the doctor—with the help of five prison matrons—force-fed Lytton through a tube. Yet the painful ordeal failed to weaken her resolve. "No surrender," she whispered.

Lytton's 1910 hunger strike was part of the long struggle for women's suffrage in Britain. Suffragists were not the only people to fight for reform. Between 1815 and 1914, Parliament responded to widespread discontent with a series of important laws.

## Economic and Social Reforms

During the 1800s, Parliament gradually passed a series of social and economic reforms. Many laws were designed to help the men, women, and children whose labor supported the new industrial society.

**Free trade.** Britain, like other European nations, taxed foreign imports in order to protect local economies. (See page 414.) In the early 1800s, controversy erupted over the Corn Laws, which imposed high tariffs on imported grain. (In Britain, "corn" refers to all cereal grains, such as wheat and oats.) Farmers and wealthy landowners supported the Corn Laws because they kept the price of British grain high. Middle-class business leaders, however, fought to repeal the Corn Laws. Repeal, they argued, would make bread cheaper for city workers and would also open up trade in general.

Parliament finally repealed the Corn Laws in 1846. Liberals hailed the repeal as a victory for free trade and laissez-faire capitalism. However, economic hard times led Britain and other European countries to impose protective tariffs on many goods again by the early 1900s.

**Abolition of slavery.** Middle-class reformers also campaigned against slavery. Enlightenment thinkers had first turned the spotlight on the evils of the slave trade. The Congress of Vienna had condemned it but taken no action. In Britain, liberals preached the immorality of slavery. Finally, in 1834, slavery was outlawed in all British colonies. Still, British textile manufacturers continued to import cheap cotton produced by enslaved African Americans in the United States.

**Crime and punishment.** Other reforms were aimed at the criminal justice system. In the early 1800s, more than 200 crimes were punishable by death. Such capital offenses included, not only murder, but also shoplifting, sheep stealing, or impersonating an army veteran. In practice, some juries refused to convict criminals because the punishments were so harsh. Executions were public occasions, and the hanging of a well-known murderer might attract thousands of curious spectators.

Victorian reformers began to reduce the number of capital offenses. By 1850, the death penalty was reserved for murder, piracy, treason, and arson. Many petty criminals were instead transported to penal colonies in the new British territories of Australia and New Zealand. (See Chapter 26.) In 1868, Parliament ended public hangings. Additional reforms improved prison conditions and outlawed imprisonment for debt.

**Victories for workers.** In Chapter 20, you read about harsh conditions for early industrial workers. Gradually, Parliament passed laws to regulate conditions in factories and mines. In 1842, for example, mineowners were forbidden to employ women or children under age 10. An 1847 law limited women and children to a 10-hour day. Later in the 1800s, the government regulated many safety conditions in factories and mines—and sent inspectors to see that the laws were enforced. Other laws set minimum wages and maximum hours of work.

Early in the Industrial Revolution, labor unions were outlawed. Under pressure, government and business leaders slowly accepted worker organizations. Trade unions were made legal in 1825. At the same time, though, strikes remained illegal.

Despite restrictions, unions spread, and gradually they won additional rights. Between 1890 and 1914, union membership soared. Besides winning higher wages and shorter hours for workers, unions pressed for other laws to improve the lives of the working class.

**Other reforms.** During the late 1800s, both political parties enacted reforms. Disraeli sponsored laws to improve public health and housing for workers in cities. Under Gladstone, an Education Act called for free elementary education for all children. Gladstone also pushed to open up government jobs based on merit rather than birth or wealth.

Another force for reform was the Fabian Society, a socialist organization founded in 1883. The Fabians promoted gradual change through legal means rather than by violence. Though small in number, the Fabians had a strong influence on British politics.

In 1900, socialists and union members backed the formation of a new political party, which became the Labour party. ("Labour" is the British spelling of "labor.") The Labour party would grow in power and membership until, by the 1920s, it surpassed the Liberal party as one of Britain's two major parties.

In the early 1900s, Britain began to pass social welfare laws modeled on those Bismarck had introduced in Germany. They protected workers with accident, health, and unemployment insurance as well as old-age pensions. One result of such reforms was that Marxism gained only limited support among the British working classes. The middle class hailed reforms as proof that democracy was working.

# Nineteenth-Century Reforms in Great Britain

| Area of Reform | Laws Enacted | Connections Today |
|---|---|---|
| **Representative government**  | **1832:** Reform Act gave representation to new industrial towns and eliminated many rotten boroughs. **1858:** Law ended property qualifications for members of Parliament. **1911:** Law restricted powers of House of Lords; elected House of Commons became supreme. | Britain combines centuries-old monarchy with democratic government. Majority party in elected House of Commons chooses cabinet and prime minister. House of Commons open to all citizens regardless of ethnic origin, creed, or gender. |
| **Voting rights** | **1829:** Parliament gave Catholics the right to vote and hold most public offices. **1867:** Reform Act gave suffrage to many working-class men. **1884:** Law extended suffrage to most farmers and other men. **1918:** Women won the right to vote. | Today, all British citizens have the right to vote. |
| **Rights of workers**  | **1825:** Trade unions were legalized. **1840s to 1910s:** Parliament passed laws • limiting child labor • regulating work hours for women and children • regulating safety conditions in mines and factories • setting minimum wages • providing for accident and unemployment insurance • sending inspectors to enforce the laws | In 1900, trade unions founded and helped finance the Labour party, which has become one of the major political parties in Great Britain. Unions are still very influential in shaping the party's policies. |
| **Education** | **1870:** Education Act set up local elementary schools run by elected school boards. **1902:** Law created a system of state-aided secondary schools. Industrial cities such as London and Manchester set up public universities. | Education from kindergarten through high school is free and compulsory. All British students who pass a series of demanding tests may attend one of Britain's 46 state universities for a minimal fee. |

*Interpreting a Chart* In the 1800s and early 1900s, Parliament passed dozens of reform measures. In addition to the acts listed here, new laws overhauled criminal justice, promoted public health, and set standards for housing. ■ Based on this chart, how is the British educational system similar to that of the United States? How is it different?

## Votes for Women

In Britain, as elsewhere, women struggled for the right to vote against strong opposition. Just as Parliament had rejected the Chartist demand for universal male suffrage in 1848, so it resisted the demands of the women's suffrage movement. Women themselves were divided on the issue. Some women opposed suffrage altogether. Queen Victoria, for example, called the suffrage struggle "mad, wicked folly." Even women in favor of suffrage disagreed about how best to achieve it.

**Suffragists revolt.** By the early 1900s, Emmeline Pankhurst, a leading suffragist, had become convinced that only aggressive tactics would bring victory. Radical suffragists interrupted speakers in Parliament, shouting, "Votes for women!" They collected petitions and organized huge public demonstrations. Describing one mass rally in London's Hyde Park, a newspaper wrote that "so many people have never before stood in one square mass anywhere in England."

▲ *Emmeline Pankhurst*

When peaceful efforts brought no results, some women turned to violent protest. They smashed windows or burned buildings. Pankhurst declared:

66There is something that governments care far more for than human life, and that is the security of property, so it is through property that we shall strike the enemy.99

Pankhurst and other women, including her daughters Christabel and Sylvia, were arrested and jailed. As you read, some went on hunger strikes and were force-fed through tubes.

**A belated victory.** Many middle-class women disagreed with such radical actions. Yet they, too, spoke up in support of votes for women and equality under the law. Not until 1918, however, did Parliament finally grant suffrage to women over age 30. Younger women did not win the right to vote for another decade.

## "Ireland for the Irish"

Throughout the 1800s, Britain faced the ever-present "Irish question." The English had begun conquering Ireland in the 1100s. In the 1600s, English and Scottish settlers colonized Ireland, taking possession of much of the best farmland. (See pages 466–467.)

The Irish never accepted rule by the English. The Irish bitterly resented settlers, especially absentee landlords who held large tracts of land. Many Irish peasants lived in desperate poverty, while paying high rents to English landlords. In addition, the Irish, most of whom were Catholic, had to pay tithes to support the state Anglican church. Under these conditions, resistance and rebellion were common.

**Irish nationalism.** Like the national minorities in the Austrian empire, Irish nationalists campaigned vigorously for freedom in the 1800s. "My first object," said nationalist leader Daniel O'Connell, "is to get Ireland for the Irish."

Under pressure from O'Connell and other Irish nationalists, Britain slowly moved to improve conditions in Ireland. In 1829, Parliament passed the Catholic Emancipation Act, which allowed Irish Catholics to vote and hold political office. Yet many injustices remained. Absentee landlords could evict tenants almost at will. Other British laws forbade the teaching and speaking of the Irish language.

**The Great Hunger.** Under British rule, three quarters of Irish farmland was used to grow crops that were imported to England. The potato, introduced from the Americas, became the main source of food for most of the Irish people themselves. Still, potatoes were abundant and nutritious enough to support a growing population.

Then, in 1845, disaster struck. A blight, or disease, destroyed the potato crop. Other crops, such as wheat and oats, were not affected. Yet British landowners continued to ship these crops outside Ireland, leaving little for the Irish except the blighted potatoes. The result was a terrible famine that the Irish called the "Great Hunger."

Visitors to Ireland described many "scenes of frightful hunger." One man told of entering what he thought was a deserted village:

> **&&**In the first [home], six famished and ghastly skeletons, to all appearances dead, were huddled in a corner on some filthy straw, their sole covering what seemed a ragged horsecloth. . . . I approached with horror, and found by a low moaning they were alive—they were in a fever, four children, a woman and what had once been a man. . . . In a few minutes I was surrounded by at least 200 such phantoms, such frightful spectres as no words can describe, either from famine or from fever.**&&**

In four years, at least one million Irish died of starvation or disease. Millions more emigrated to the United States and Canada. The Great Hunger left a legacy of Irish bitterness toward the English that still exists today.

**Struggle for home rule.** Throughout the century, Irish demands for self-rule intensified. The turmoil also disrupted English politics. At times, political parties were so deeply split over the Irish question that they could not take care of other business.

As prime minister, Gladstone pushed for reforms in Ireland. He ended the use of Irish tithe money to support the Anglican church and tried to ease the hardships of Irish tenant farmers. New laws prevented landlords from charging unfair rents and protected the rights of tenants to the land they worked.

In the 1870s, Irish nationalists found a rousing leader in Charles Stewart Parnell. He rallied Irish members of Parliament to press for home rule, or local self-government. The debate dragged on for decades. Finally, in 1914, Parliament passed a home rule bill. But it de-

**Erin Go Bragh** *Portraits of leading Irish nationalists ring this patriotic banner. The banner includes many symbols of Irish pride, including the shamrock and the traditional Irish harp. The phrase* Erin Go Bragh *can be translated as "Ireland Forever!"* **Art and Literature** *What do you think the figures in the center of the wreath represent?*

layed putting the new law into effect when World War I broke out that year. As you will read in Chapter 30, the southern counties of Ireland finally became independent in 1921.

## SECTION 2 REVIEW

1. **Identify** (a) Corn Laws, (b) Fabian Society, (c) Emmeline Pankhurst, (d) Catholic Emancipation Act, (e) Great Hunger, (f) Charles Stewart Parnell.
2. **Define** home rule.
3. Describe three social reforms that helped the British working class.
4. What actions did women suffragists take to achieve their goals?
5. (a) Why did Irish nationalists oppose British rule? (b) Describe two reforms that improved conditions in Ireland.
6. *Critical Thinking* **Defending a Position** Do you agree that the tactics used by suffragists like Emmeline Pankhurst were necessary? Why or why not?
7. *ACTIVITY* Design a poster that an Irish nationalist of the 1800s might have used to win support for home rule.

**GLOBAL CONNECTIONS**

Americans rushed to the aid of the starving Irish. Quakers were the first to organize relief efforts. Catholic churches, Jewish synagogues, and women's groups worked to raise funds. The Choctaw Indians, still recovering from their own food shortages, contributed over $700—a large sum in the 1840s. The American government encouraged food shipments by announcing that no road or canal tolls would be charged on any supplies headed for Ireland.

## 3 Division and Democracy in France

### Guide for Reading

- What domestic and foreign policies did Napoleon III pursue?
- What steps toward democracy did the Third Republic take?
- What were the results of the Dreyfus affair?
- **Vocabulary** *coalition*

The news sent shock waves through Paris. An entire French army under the emperor Napoleon III had surrendered to the Prussians at the city of Sedan. Still worse, Prussian forces were about to advance on Paris. Could the city survive?

Georges Clemenceau (KLEHM uhn soh), a young doctor turned politician, passionately urged Parisians to resist the Prussian onslaught:

66 Citizens, must France destroy herself and disappear, or shall she resume her old place in the vanguard of nations? . . . Each of us knows his duty. We are children of the Revolution. Let us seek inspiration in the example of our forefathers in 1792, and like them we shall conquer. Long live France! 99

For four months, Paris did resist the German siege. Surrounded by Prussian troops, starving Parisians were reduced to catching rats and slaughtering circus animals for food. The siege did not end until January 1871, when the French government at Versailles accepted Prussia's terms.

The Franco-Prussian War ended the long period of unquestioned French domination of Europe that had begun under Louis XIV. Yet the nation survived its crushing defeat. The Third Republic rose on the ruins of Napoleon III's Second Empire. Economic growth, democratic reforms, and the fierce nationalism expressed by Clemenceau all played a part in shaping modern France.

### France Under Napoleon III

As you read in Chapter 21, Napoleon III rose to power after the revolution of 1848. His appeal cut across lines of class and ideology. The bourgeoisie saw him as a strong leader who would restore order. At the same time, his promise to end poverty gave hope to the lower classes. People of all classes were attracted by his magical name, a reminder of the days when France had towered over Europe. Unlike his famous uncle, however, Napoleon III would bring France neither glory nor an empire.

**Limits on liberty.** On the surface, the Second Empire looked like a constitutional monarchy. In fact, Napoleon III ruled almost like a dictator. He held the power to appoint his cabinet, the upper house of the legislature, and many officials. Although the assembly was elected by universal male suffrage, appointed officials "managed" elections so that supporters of the emperor would win. Debate was limited, and newspapers faced strict censorship.

In the 1860s, the emperor began to ease these controls. He lifted some censorship and gave the legislature more power. On the eve of his disastrous war with Prussia, he even issued a new constitution that extended democratic rights.

**Economic growth.** Like much of Europe, France prospered at mid-century. Napoleon promoted investment in industry and large-scale ventures such as railroad building. During this period, a French entrepreneur, Ferdinand de Lesseps (duh LEHS uhps), organized the building of the Suez Canal to link the Mediterranean with the Red Sea and thus the Indian Ocean.

Napoleon III sponsored huge public works programs, such as the rebuilding of Paris, that employed vast numbers of workers. (See page 564.) He also legalized labor unions, extended public education to girls, and created a small public health program. Apparently, the emperor was genuinely concerned over the hard lives of the poor. Yet in France, as in other industrializing nations, many people lived in shocking poverty.

**Foreign affairs.** Napoleon III's worst failures were in warfare and diplomacy. In the 1860s, he attempted to place Maximilian, an

Austrian Hapsburg prince, on the throne of Mexico. Through Maximilian, Napoleon hoped to turn Mexico into a French satellite. But after a large commitment of troops and money, the adventure failed. Mexican patriots resisted fiercely and the United States protested. After four years, France withdrew its army. Maximilian was overthrown and shot by Mexican patriots. (See page 674.)

Napoleon did enjoy some military successes. Yet they were almost as costly as his failures. He helped Italian nationalists defeat Austria, gaining Nice (NEES) and Savoy for France. This victory backfired when a united Italy emerged as a strong rival on the border of France. And, though France and Britain won the Crimean War against Russia, France had little to show for its terrible losses except a small foothold in the Middle East.

**A humiliating defeat.** At this time, France grew increasingly concerned about the rise of a great European rival, Prussia. The Prussian leader Otto von Bismarck shrewdly manipulated French worries to lure Napoleon into war in 1870.

As you read, the Franco-Prussian War was a disaster for France. After his humiliating surrender at Sedan, Napoleon III was overthrown. In 1871, the newly elected French National Assembly accepted a harsh peace with Germany. France had to surrender the provinces of Alsace and Lorraine and pay a huge sum to Germany. The bitter sting of defeat left the French burning to avenge their loss.

## The Paris Commune

The war brought another catastrophe. In 1871, while Prussians still occupied eastern France, an uprising broke out in the French capital. The rebels set up the Paris Commune. Like the radical government during the French Revolution, its goal was to save the Republic from royalist control.

Communards, as the rebels were called, included workers and socialists as well as bourgeois republicans. As patriots, they rejected the peace with Germany that the National Assembly had signed. Radicals dreamed of a new socialist order and hoped to rebuild France into a loose federation of communes.

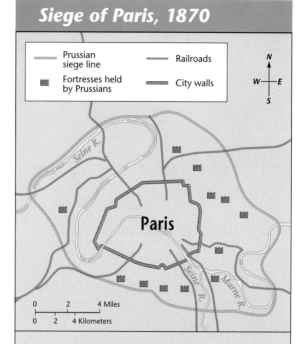

### Siege of Paris, 1870

Prussian siege line
Fortresses held by Prussians
Railroads
City walls

Seine R.

Paris

Seine R.

Marne R.

0    2    4 Miles
0    2    4 Kilometers

*A Message to the Outside World* In the 1870 painting below, a Parisian woman, rifle in hand, salutes a balloon as it rises and drifts beyond the horizon. During the four-month siege, Prussian troops cut Paris off from the outside world. (See the map above.) Balloons were the only means of communication between Paris and the rest of Europe. **Art and Literature** How does the painting convey both pride and despair?

**History in Flames** *Like much of Paris, the Tuileries Palace was burned during the Paris Commune of 1871. Built in 1564, the palace was later expanded by some of France's greatest architects. During the early years of the French Revolution, it was the residence of the king and queen. (See page 487.)*
**Continuity and Change** *Why do you think rebels tried to destroy a place of such cultural value to France?*

The National Assembly ordered the Commune to disband. When it refused, the government sent troops to besiege Paris. For weeks, civil war raged. An English visitor described the scene:

66 'Paris the beautiful' is Paris the ghastly, Paris the battered, Paris the burning, Paris the blood-spattered now. And this is the nineteenth century, and Europe professes civilization, and France boasts of culture, and Frenchmen are braining one another with the butt end of muskets, and Paris is burning.99

As government troops advanced, the rebels toppled great Paris monuments and slaughtered hostages. In the final blood bath, government forces butchered some 20,000 Communards. The suppression of the Paris Commune left bitter memories that deepened social divisions within France.

## The Third Republic

Born out of defeat and political chaos in 1871, the Third Republic remained in place for 70 years. The new Republic had a two-house legislature. The lower house, or Chamber of Deputies, was elected by universal male suffrage and had great influence. Together with the Senate, it elected the president of the Republic. He had little power and served mostly as a figurehead. The real political power was in the hands of the premier (prih MIR), or prime minister.

**Coalition governments.** Unlike Britain, with its two parties, France had many parties reflecting the wide splits within the country. Among them were divine-right royalists, constitutional monarchists, ultranationalists, moderate republicans, and radicals.

With so many parties, no single party could win a majority in the legislature. In order to govern, politicians had to form coalitions, or alliances of various parties. Once a coalition controlled enough votes, it could then name a premier and form a cabinet.

Multiparty systems and coalition governments are common in continental Europe. This system allows citizens to vote for a party that most nearly matches their own beliefs. Coalition governments, however, are often unstable. If one party deserts a coalition, the government might lose its majority in the legislature. The government then falls, and new elections must be held. In the first 10 years of the Third Republic, 50 different coalition governments were formed and fell.

**Scandals.** Despite frequent changes of governments, France made economic progress. It paid Germany the huge sum required by the peace treaty and expanded its overseas empire, as you will read in Chapter 25. But in the 1880s and 1890s, a series of political scandals shook public trust in the government.

One crisis erupted when a popular minister of war, General Georges Boulanger (boo lahn ZHAY), rallied royalists and ultranationalists eager for revenge on Germany. Accused of plotting to overthrow the Republic, Boulanger fled to Belgium and later committed suicide. In another scandal, members of the government were charged with bribery and corruption in connection with an attempt to build a canal across Panama. A nephew of the president was even caught selling nominations for the Legion of Honor, France's highest award. The president was forced to resign.

The most disturbing scandal began in 1894, when an army officer, Alfred Dreyfus, was unjustly convicted of spying. The Dreyfus affair scarred French politics and society for decades.

### The Dreyfus Affair

Under a leaden January sky, Captain Alfred Dreyfus stood at attention. "Alfred Dreyfus," declared his commanding general, "you are unworthy of your uniform. In the name of the French people, we degrade you."

The condemned man cried out, "I am innocent. I swear I am innocent. Long live France!" Ignoring the cry, a soldier approached. He ripped the gold braid from the captain's uniform, tore the buttons off his tunic, and broke his sword. The humiliating punishment was just one more horror in a tragic nightmare for Alfred Dreyfus.

**Charge of treason.** A few months earlier, in October 1894, Dreyfus had been arrested on charges of spying for Germany. A high-ranking member of the French army, Dreyfus had access to many military secrets. The military court that convicted Dreyfus claimed that there was plenty of written evidence against him. Yet the War Department kept that evidence in a "secret file." Even Dreyfus's own lawyers had not been al-

lowed to see the evidence against their client. The army claimed that secrecy was necessary to protect France.

There were more sinister reasons behind the army's eagerness to convict Dreyfus. Most of the military elite detested Dreyfus because he was the first Jew to reach a high position in the French army. He made a convenient scapegoat, or person chosen to take the blame, for the security leak in the high command.

After his conviction, Dreyfus was condemned to lifetime confinement on Devil's Island, a tiny tropical isle off the coast of South America. He left France still proclaiming his innocence.

**"I accuse."** The case might have faded from the headlines, but another man, Major Ferdinand Esterhazy, was soon charged as a spy. Dreyfusards, or supporters of Dreyfus, claimed that Esterhazy was guilty of the crime for which Dreyfus had been convicted. Esterhazy was a spendthrift and gambler. But he was also a member of the French nobility. Despite strong evidence, a secret military court cleared him of all charges. Esterhazy then fled the country.

Eventually, the case caught the attention of the novelist Emile Zola. (See page 576.) He began to untangle the web of official lies. Early in 1898, he put his pen into action.

"J'Accuse!" blazed the newspaper headline. "I Accuse!" In a blistering article, Zola charged the army and government officials with suppressing the truth and falsifying evidence. To protect "the honor of the army," said Zola, they had knowingly condemned an innocent man.

Zola knew he could be charged with libel. Indeed, he welcomed a trial:

> **66** I have but one passion—that of light. . . . Let them dare to bring me before the court of appeals and let an inquiry be made in broad daylight. I wait. **99**

**A long struggle.** As the Dreyfus affair dragged on, it tore France apart. Ultranationalists, royalists, and Church officials charged the Dreyfusards with undermining France. Paris echoed with cries of "Long live the Republic!" "Long live the army!" "Death to traitors!" and "Down with the Jews!"

Dreyfusards were mostly liberals and republicans who upheld ideals of justice and equality. Few in number, they faced the wrath of an enraged public. Zola himself was convicted of libel and fled into exile.

Gradually, though, the Dreyfusards made progress. Under pressure, the army released evidence against Dreyfus. Much of it turned out to have been forged. In 1899, Esterhazy confessed to being both the forger and the spy.

**The fate of Dreyfus.** After almost five years in a hellish prison, Dreyfus was brought back to France for a new trial. The tropical climate, fevers, chains, and brutal treatment by guards had destroyed his health. Yet he still professed his faith in the army.

At his trial, the army again protected its honor by convicting Dreyfus. But this time, the president of France, convinced of the officer's innocence, pardoned Dreyfus.

For Dreyfus and his supporters, a pardon was not enough. It still implied that Dreyfus was guilty. Finally, in 1906, his conviction was overturned. Alfred Dreyfus was reinstated in the army and awarded the Legion of Honor. Emile Zola, though, did not witness this final triumph.

He had died four years earlier without ever having met Dreyfus.

The reinstatement of Dreyfus was, in the end, a victory for French justice and democracy. The political scars of the Dreyfus affair, however, took years to heal. ▨

## Calls for a Jewish State

The Dreyfus case reflected the rise of anti-Semitism in Europe. The Enlightenment and French Revolution had spread ideas about religious toleration. In Western Europe, some Jews—especially those who had converted to Christianity—had gained jobs in government, universities, and other areas of life. A few were successful in banking and business, though most struggled to survive in the ghettos of Eastern Europe or slums of Western Europe.

By the late 1800s, however, anti-Semitism was again on the rise. Anti-Semites were often members of the lower middle class who felt insecure in their social and economic position. Steeped in the new nationalist fervor, they adopted an aggressive intolerance for outsiders and a violent hatred of Jews.

*"J'Accuse!"* Before the Dreyfus affair, Emile Zola (right) was already known as a passionate defender of the underdog. On January 13, 1898, the newspaper Aurore *printed Zola's stinging defense of Alfred Dreyfus (left). It sold 200,000 copies in one day.* **Global Interaction** *How did the world outside France react to the Dreyfus affair?*

**A Home for Jews** Zionists met on this desert landscape in 1909 to make plans for the Jewish city of Tel Aviv. The city was finally founded in 1949, just after the creation of the nation of Israel. Today, nearly a quarter of Israel's population live in Tel Aviv and its surrounding metropolis. **Geography and History** Why did Jews want to make their home in a place that appeared so empty and forbidding?

The Dreyfus case and the pogroms in Russia (see Chapter 23) stirred Jewish leaders to action. In 1896, Theodor Herzl (HEHRT suhl), a Hungarian Jewish journalist living in France, published *The Jewish State*. In it, he called for Jews to form their own separate state, where they would have the rights and freedoms denied to them in European countries. Herzl helped launch the modern form of Zionism, the movement devoted to rebuilding a Jewish state in Palestine. Since the Romans had destroyed Jerusalem in A.D. 70, many Jews had kept alive this dream.

In 1897, Herzl organized the first world congress of Zionists in Basel, Switzerland. Afterward, he wrote in his diary:

> 66 At Basel, I founded the Jewish state. If I were to say this today, I would be greeted by universal laughter. In five years, perhaps, and certainly in 50, everyone will see it. 99

Just over 50 years later, Zionists in Palestine founded the modern nation of Israel.

## Reforms in France

Though shaken by the Dreyfus affair, the French government accomplished some serious reforms in the early 1900s. Like Britain, France adopted laws regulating wages, hours, and safety conditions for workers. It set up a system of free public elementary schools to provide basic education for all. Creating public schools was also a way to end the monopoly on education of the Roman Catholic Church.

**Separating church and state.** Like Bismarck in Germany, France tried to limit the power of the Church and end its involvement in government. Supporters of the French republic viewed the Church as a conservative force that opposed progressive policies. In the Dreyfus affair, it had backed the interests of the army and the ultranationalists.

The government therefore closed Church schools along with many monasteries and convents. In 1905, it passed a law to separate church and state and stopped paying the salaries for the clergy. Catholics, Protestants, and Jews enjoyed freedom of worship, but none had any special treatment from the government.

**Women's rights.** Under the Napoleonic Code, French women had few rights. Women could not even control their own property. By the 1890s, a growing women's rights movement sought legal reforms. Some gains were made, such as an 1896 law that gave married women the right to their own earnings.

In 1909, Jeanne-Elizabeth Schmahl founded the French Union for Women's Suffrage. She

**ISSUES** *For* **TODAY**

In the western democracies, reformers campaigned for wider suffrage and other rights. What rights should a democracy guarantee to its citizens?

argued that women should be allowed to vote because they had become better educated and more independent. Rejecting the radical tactics used in Britain, Schmahl and other women sought the vote through legal means. Yet even liberal men were reluctant to grant women suffrage. They feared that women would vote for Church and conservative causes. In the end, French women would not gain the right to vote until 1944.

**Looking ahead.** By 1914, France was the largest democratic country on the European continent, with a constitution that protected basic rights. A wide range of parties put up candidates for office. France's economy was generally prosperous, and its overseas empire was second only to that of Britain.

Yet the outlook was not all smooth. Coalition governments rose and fell at the slightest pressure. To the east across the Rhine River loomed the industrial might of Germany. Many French citizens were itching for a chance to revenge the defeat in the Franco-Prussian War and liberate the "lost provinces" of Alsace and Lorraine. That chance came in 1914, when all of Europe exploded into World War I. (See Chapter 27.)

## SECTION 3 REVIEW

1. **Identify** (a) Paris Commune, (b) Georges Boulanger, (c) Alfred Dreyfus, (d) Theodor Herzl, (e) Jeanne-Elizabeth Schmahl.
2. **Define** coalition.
3. (a) Describe the government of France during the Second Empire. (b) How did France become more democratic during the Third Republic?
4. Describe how each of the following heightened divisions within France: (a) the suppression of the Paris Commune, (b) the Dreyfus affair.
5. *Critical Thinking* **Solving Problems** (a) What solution did Zionists propose for the problem of widespread anti-Semitism? (b) Why do you think they felt it was the best solution?
6. *ACTIVITY* Draw a political cartoon about one of the domestic or foreign policies of Napoleon III.

## 4 Expansion of the United States

### Guide for Reading

- How did the United States expand in the 1800s?
- What changes made the United States more democratic?
- What were the causes and effects of the Civil War?
- **Vocabulary** *segregation, isolationism*

For many Irish families fleeing the Great Hunger, Russian Jews escaping pogroms, or poor Italian farmers seeking economic opportunity, the answer was the same—America! In "The New Colossus," Emma Lazarus expressed the hopes of millions of immigrants:

“Give me your tired, your poor,
  Your huddled masses yearning to
    breathe free,
  The wretched refuse of your teeming
    shore.
  Send these, the homeless, tempest-
    tossed to me.
  I lift my lamp beside the golden
    door. ”

Lazarus's poem was later inscribed on the base of the Statue of Liberty.

In the 1800s, the United States was a beacon of hope for many people. At the same time, the nation grew rapidly in economic strength. Not everyone shared in the prosperity or the ideals of democracy. Still, by the turn of the century, Americans were increasingly proud of their status as an emerging world power.

### From Sea to Sea

In 1800, the United States extended from the Atlantic coast to the Mississippi River. A hundred years later, it had grown tremendously, reaching across the continent and beyond.

In 1803, President Thomas Jefferson bought the Louisiana territory from France. In

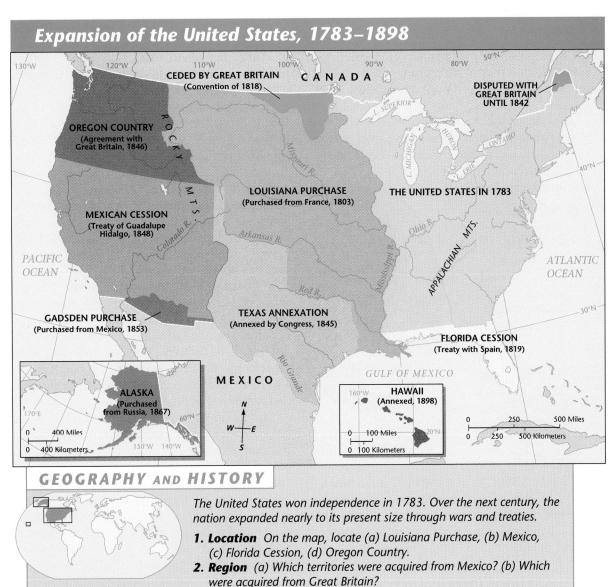

# Expansion of the United States, 1783–1898

CEDED BY GREAT BRITAIN
(Convention of 1818)

CANADA

DISPUTED WITH
GREAT BRITAIN
UNTIL 1842

OREGON COUNTRY
(Agreement with
Great Britain, 1846)

LOUISIANA PURCHASE
(Purchased from France, 1803)

THE UNITED STATES IN 1783

MEXICAN CESSION
(Treaty of Guadalupe
Hidalgo, 1848)

PACIFIC
OCEAN

ATLANTIC
OCEAN

GADSDEN PURCHASE
(Purchased from Mexico, 1853)

TEXAS ANNEXATION
(Annexed by Congress, 1845)

FLORIDA CESSION
(Treaty with Spain, 1819)

MEXICO

GULF OF MEXICO

ALASKA
(Purchased
from Russia, 1867)

HAWAII
(Annexed, 1898)

## GEOGRAPHY AND HISTORY

The United States won independence in 1783. Over the next century, the nation expanded nearly to its present size through wars and treaties.

1. **Location** On the map, locate (a) Louisiana Purchase, (b) Mexico, (c) Florida Cession, (d) Oregon Country.
2. **Region** (a) Which territories were acquired from Mexico? (b) Which were acquired from Great Britain?
3. **Critical Thinking Analyzing Information** Notice the scales of miles and kilometers on the main map and two inset maps. Why are the scales different on each map?

one stroke, the Louisiana Purchase virtually doubled the size of the nation. By 1850, the United States included other territories, such as Florida, Oregon, and the Lone Star Republic of Texas. The Mexican War of 1846 added California and the southwestern territories.

**Manifest destiny.** With growing pride and confidence, Americans talked of their "manifest destiny." The United States, they said, had a clear right to spread across the continent. Some people even urged expansion "from Panama to Hudson's Bay"—to include Canada and Mexico. In fact, the United States did go far afield. In 1867, it bought Alaska from Russia and in 1898 annexed the Hawaiian Islands.

During the 1800s, settlers flocked to newly acquired western lands. The discovery of gold in California drew floods of easterners. Other people, like the Mormons, sought a place to practice their religion freely. Still others headed west in the spirit of adventure.

**Native Americans.** The waves of settlers brought tragedy to Native Americans. The pattern begun in colonial days continued throughout the 1800s. Newcomers pushed the Indians off their lands, sometimes by treaty, but more often by force. In the 1830s, the Cherokees and other Indian nations were forced to leave their homes in the southeastern United States and move west of the Mississippi.

Some Native American nations resisted the invaders, but they were outgunned and outnumbered. As settlers moved westward, they destroyed the buffalo herds on which the Plains Indians depended. Survivors suffered spiritual as well as physical defeat. After a long, courageous resistance, Chief Joseph of the Nez Percé nation wearily surrendered to forces of the federal government in 1877:

▲ *Chief Joseph of the Nez Percé*

66 Our chiefs are killed. . . . He who led the young men is dead. It is cold, and we have no blankets; the little children are freezing to death. . . . I am tired of fighting. My heart is sick and sad. From where the sun now stands I will fight no more forever. 99

By the 1890s, most surviving Native Americans had been driven onto reservations, usually the least desirable parts of a territory. There, the first inhabitants of the continent suffered poverty and the further loss of their traditions.

## Expanding Democracy

In 1800, the United States had the most liberal suffrage in the world, but still only white men who owned property could vote. States slowly chipped away at requirements. By the 1830s, most white men had the right to vote. Democracy was far from complete, however. Women, Native Americans, and free blacks had no vote. Enslaved African Americans had no rights at all.

By mid-century, reformers were campaigning for many changes. Some demanded a ban on the sale of alcoholic beverages. Others called for better treatment of the mentally ill or pushed for free elementary schools. Two crusades, especially, highlighted the limits of American democracy—the abolition movement and the women's rights movement.

**Calls for abolition.** In the early 1800s, a few Americans denounced slavery and demanded its abolition. Frederick Douglass, who had himself escaped slavery, spoke eloquently in the North about the evils of slavery. William Lloyd Garrison pressed the antislavery cause through his newspaper, the *Liberator.*

By the 1850s, the battle over slavery intensified. As new states entered the union, pro- and antislavery forces met in violent confrontations to decide whether slavery would be legal in the new state. Harriet Beecher Stowe's novel, *Uncle Tom's Cabin,* helped convince many northerners that slavery was a great social evil.

**Women's rights movement.** Women worked hard in the antislavery movement. Lucretia Mott and Elizabeth Cady Stanton, for example, traveled to London for the World Antislavery Convention—only to find they were unwelcome because they were women. Gradually, American women began to protest the laws and customs that limited their lives.

In 1848, Mott and Stanton organized the Seneca Falls Convention in New York to discuss the problems faced by women. The convention passed a resolution, based on the Declaration of Independence. "We hold these truths to be self evident: that all men and women are created equal." The women's rights movement set as its goal equality before the law, in the workplace, and in education. Like women in Europe, American women also demanded the vote.

## Civil War and After

Economic differences, as well as the slavery issue, drove the North and South apart. The division reached a crisis in 1860 when Abraham Lincoln was elected president. Lincoln opposed extending slavery into new territories. Southerners feared that he would eventually abolish slavery altogether and that the federal government would infringe on their states' rights.

**The Civil War.** Soon after Lincoln's election, most southern states seceded from the Union and formed the Confederate States of America. This action sparked the Civil War. From 1861 to 1865, the agonizing ordeal divided families as well as a nation.

The South had fewer resources, people, and industry than the North. Still, southerners fought fiercely to defend their cause. They won many early victories. At one point, Confederate armies under General Robert E. Lee drove northward as far as Gettysburg, Pennsylvania. In a bloody three-day battle, the Union army turned back the southern advance for good.

In the last years of the war, Lincoln's most successful general, Ulysses S. Grant, used the massive resources of the North to launch a full-scale offensive against the South. After devastating losses on both sides, the Confederacy finally surrendered in 1865. The struggle cost more than 600,000 lives—the largest casualty figures of any American war. Although the war left a bitter legacy, it did guarantee that the nation would remain united.

**Challenges for African Americans.** During the war, Lincoln emancipated enslaved African Americans in the South. After the war, three amendments to the Constitution banned slavery throughout the country and granted political rights to African Americans. Under the Fifteenth Amendment, for example, African American men won the right to vote.

Despite these amendments, African Americans faced many restrictions. In the South, "Jim Crow" laws imposed segregation, or legal separation of the races, in hotels, hospitals, schools, and other public places. Other laws bypassed the Fifteenth Amendment to prevent African Americans from voting. Thus, in the United States, as in Europe, democracy remained a goal rather than a reality for many citizens.

African Americans also faced economic hardships. Freed from slavery but without land, many ended up working as tenant farmers. To escape the bleak poverty of the postwar South, some headed west. There, they became cowhands or farmed their own lands. Others migrated to the northern cities, seeking jobs in the factories that were springing to life.

## Economic Successes

Like Western Europe, the United States plunged into the Industrial Revolution. With seemingly unlimited natural resources and the help of European capital, the economy boomed. By 1900, the nation led the world in industrial and agricultural production.

Farm output soared as settlers flooded into the fertile farmlands of the Midwest. Inventions

**Fighting for Freedom** About 178,000 African Americans volunteered to serve in the Union Army during the Civil War. Of these, 21 were awarded the Medal of Honor. The secretary of war noted that the African American regiments "have proved themselves among the bravest of the brave, performing deeds of daring and shedding their blood with . . . heroism." **Diversity** Why do you think many African Americans were eager to fight for the Union cause?

**Trade and Commerce Quilt** *This quilt, made around 1830 by Hannah S. Stokes, celebrates the bustling sea trade of that period. Its design includes rowboats, sailing ships, and the newly invented steamship. Quilting provided a creative outlet for women living in lonely stretches of rural America. A quilt like this one might take more than a year to complete.* **Art and Literature** *Art historians classify quilts as "folk art." What do you think this phrase means?*

**Transportation.** A growing network of transportation and communication aided economic growth. In the early 1800s, canals and turnpikes helped farmers and entrepreneurs in the young nation. Later, railroads crisscrossed the country. The first transcontinental railroad was completed in 1869, opening up new opportunities for settlement and growth.

In the early 1900s, Americans took to the automobile faster than Europeans. Henry Ford's "Model T" became the symbol of the new automobile era. "When I'm through," Ford boasted, "everybody will be able to afford one, and about everybody will have one."

## Seeking Reform

In the United States, as in Europe, the growing prosperity was not shared by all. The Industrial Revolution brought urbanization as millions of people left the farms for jobs in the cities. In city slums, disease, poverty, and unemployment were daily threats. In factories, wages were low and conditions were often brutal.

**Labor unions.** By the late 1800s, American workers were organizing labor unions to defend their interests. Through unions such as the American Federation of Labor, they sought better wages, hours, and working conditions. Struggles with management sometimes erupted into violent confrontations. Slowly, however, workers made gains.

In the economic hard times of the late 1800s, farmers, too, organized to defend their interests. In the 1890s, they joined city workers to support the new Populist party. The Populists never became a major party, but their platform of reforms, such as an eight-hour workday, eventually became law.

**Immigrants.** The nation's population soared as millions of immigrants arrived in the 1800s and early 1900s. They represented nearly every nationality and ethnic group, including Irish, German, Chinese, Italian, Japanese, Eastern European Jews, and many others.

Typically, European immigrants settled first in cities on the Atlantic coast, while Asian immigrants filled cities on the Pacific coast. In time, newcomers spread out across the country. They worked in mines and factories, built canals and railroads, and opened up farmlands in the West.

like Cyrus McCormick's mechanical reaper increased production. Later, mechanical plows and threshers further revolutionized farming.

**Industrial output.** Industry grew even more rapidly. As in Europe, early progress came in the textile industry. Cotton mills used machines and cheap labor to turn out great quantities of mass-produced goods. Rich coal and iron resources fed other industries. A huge work force, swelled by waves of immigrants, labored in mines and factories.

After the Civil War, production and profits in many industries shot up. As in Europe, giant monopolies controlled whole industries. (See page 561.) Scottish-born Andrew Carnegie built the nation's largest steel company, while John D. Rockefeller's Standard Oil Company dominated the world's petroleum industry.

**Coming to America** *Immigrants often settled near relatives and friends who had come before them. This Italian family might have ended up in a "Little Italy" in New York or another major city.* **Diversity** *Pick a member of the family in this photograph and describe how he or she probably felt upon landing in America.*

The newcomers made the United States "a nation of nations," with roots around the world.

Immigrants faced harsh conditions in crowded slum tenements. Often, newcomers suffered from prejudice and even violence from native-born Americans. In the West, whites hostile to Chinese workers pushed for laws to end immigration from China. For the first time, the United States began to close its "golden" door.

**Progressive movement.** By 1900, reformers known as Progressives again pressed for change. They sought laws to ban child labor, limit working hours, regulate monopolies, and give voters more power. Another major goal of the Progressives was votes for women. Copying the tactics used in Britain, American suffragists finally won the vote in 1920, when the Nineteenth Amendment went into effect.

## Becoming a World Power

By 1900, the United States was the world's leading industrial giant. It was also acquiring a new role—that of a global power. Its ships had opened up Japan to western trade. (See Chapter 26.) In the Spanish American War of 1898, the United States acquired overseas territories, including the Philippines, Guam, and Puerto Rico.

Many Americans wanted to maintain their tradition of isolationism, or limited involvement in world affairs. Expansionists, however, urged the nation to pursue global economic and military interests. "Whether they will or no, Americans must now begin to look outward," wrote influential expansionist Alfred T. Mahan in 1890. "The growing production of the country demands it."

In 1914, rivalries among European nations exploded into global war. Although the United States was already a world power, it tried to stay out of the conflict. As you will read, World War I eventually forced the United States to take an even greater role on the world stage.

## SECTION 4 REVIEW

1. **Identify** (a) Louisiana Purchase, (b) manifest destiny, (c) Frederick Douglass, (d) Seneca Falls Convention, (e) Abraham Lincoln, (f) Fifteenth Amendment, (g) Progressives.
2. **Define** (a) segregation, (b) isolationism.
3. Give one example of how the United States grew in each of these areas in the 1800s: (a) territory, (b) population, (c) economy.
4. Describe two ways that reformers tried to make the United States more democratic.
5. (a) What issues divided the North and South? (b) Describe two results of the Civil War.
6. *Critical Thinking* **Recognizing Causes and Effects** Why do you think economic growth helped make the United States a world power?
7. *ACTIVITY* Write two four-line poems about the United States in the 1800s. Each poem should express the viewpoint of one of the following: a settler in the western United States, a Native American, a supporter of women's rights, a formerly enslaved African American, a business leader, an immigrant.

# Skills for Success

## Holding a Debate

There are two kinds of debates: formal and informal. Informal debates may be any reasoned discussion of opposing viewpoints. Formal debates, like those held in schools across the country, follow a set format.

In the most widely used debate format, each side has two team members. The issue to be discussed is stated as a proposition, or a statement that can be answered yes or no. One side takes the affirmative position, that is, argues in favor of the proposition. The other side takes the negative position, that is, argues against the proposition.

The debate is divided into two parts. During the constructive speeches, a debater on each side presents prepared arguments in favor of his or her position. During rebuttal, debaters try to refute the arguments given by the opposing side. Debate is subject to time limitations so that both sides have equal time for presenting and rebutting arguments.

Imagine that you are going to debate the affirmative side of the following proposition:

*RESOLVED, that a two-party political system is preferable to a multiparty system.*

Read the following directions and answer the questions.

**1 Prepare a brief in favor of your position.** A brief is a written outline of each of the arguments on one side of the debate. (a) What would the affirmative side in the debate need to prove? (b) From your reading of the chapter, list two points that might support the affirmative position.

**2 Locate factual information to support each of your arguments.** The strength of an argument is based on the facts that are presented to support it. (a) What kinds of factual information would support your arguments? (b) Where might you look to find these facts?

**3 Prepare your speech.** A persuasive constructive speech has three parts: an introduction; a discussion of contentions, or points, and supporting evidence; and a conclusion. You might use the outline given here as a model.

(a) Which part of the speech do you think should take the most time? Why? (b) Write a concluding statement summarizing your side of the debate. (c) Why do you think it is important to practice and time your constructive speech before the debate?

**4 Anticipate the arguments of the opposing side.** (a) Identify what the negative side needs to prove. (b) List two contentions the negative side would be likely to present. (c) What arguments could you use to rebut these arguments?

*Beyond the Classroom* On some television news programs, participants informally debate the pros and cons of newsworthy issues. Watch one of these programs and take notes. Write down what the debate issue was and what arguments each side presented to support its position. Report on the debate to your class.

---

**Outline of an Affirmative Brief**

*Introduction*

I. The cause for discussion is as follows:
   A.
   B.

II. The issues are as follows:
   A.
   B.

III. The affirmative will establish the following points:
   A.
   B.

*Discussion*

I. First contention states
   A. First supporting fact
   B. Second supporting fact

II. Second contention states
   A. First supporting fact
   B. Second supporting fact

*Conclusion*

I. Since...; (relate to contention I)

II. Since...; (relate to contention I)

Therefore,...(state proposition)

# CHAPTER 24 REVIEW

## Building Vocabulary

Review the following vocabulary from this chapter: *democracy, suffrage, free market, home rule, bourgeoisie, socialism, coalition, segregation, isolationism.* Write sentences using *six* of these terms, leaving blanks where the terms would go. Exchange your sentences with another student and fill in the blanks on each other's lists.

## Reviewing Chapter Themes

1. **Political and Social Systems** (a) How did British parliamentary traditions evolve during the 1800s? (b) Describe how the French political system under the Third Republic differed from that of Britain and the United States.
2. **Continuity and Change** (a) How did lawmakers in the industrial world respond to the growing importance of city dwellers and factory workers? Give three examples from Britain, France, or the United States. (b) What changes in women's rights did reformers support?
3. **Religions and Value Systems** Describe how *three* of the following were related to nationalism: (a) the prestige of Queen Victoria, (b) the demands for Irish home rule, (c) the revolt of the Paris Commune, (d) the rise of Zionism, (e) the idea of manifest destiny.
4. **Diversity** (a) What challenges did African Americans face after the Civil War? (b) How did the United States become a "nation of nations"?

## Thinking Critically

1. **Analyzing Literature** Reread the excerpt from *Sybil* on page 606. (a) Restate the young stranger's main idea in your own words. (b) Why is Egremont surprised by this view of Britain? (c) Based on what you have read, would you consider this novel a reliable source of information about Britain in the early 1800s? Why or why not? (★ See *Skills for Success*, page 234.)
2. **Recognizing Causes and Effects** (a) List two long-term and two immediate causes of the Great Hunger. (b) List two immediate effects. (c) Why do you think the famine sparked lasting feelings of bitterness against Britain? (★ See *Skills for Success*, page 18.)

3. **Drawing Conclusions** Britain and France faced many similar political and social problems in the 1800s. Why do you think Britain was able to avoid the revolutions and instability that plagued France?
4. **Applying Information** A historian wrote, "'J'Accuse!' was an act of courage and it was also an act of faith." Based on what you have read about the Dreyfus case, what do you think she meant by this?
5. **Identifying Main Ideas** Reread the subsection Expanding Democracy on page 624. Then, write a sentence summarizing the main idea of this subsection.
6. **Linking Past and Present** The United States still continues to attract large numbers of immigrants from around the world. Do people come to the United States today for the same reasons that immigrants came in the late 1800s and early 1900s? Explain.

## For Your Portfolio

For this assignment you and a group of classmates will work together to publish a newspaper of events in the 1890s.

1. Decide who will fill each of the following roles: reporters, editors, feature writers, editorial writers, political cartoonists, reviewers, layout and production editors.
2. Hold a news conference to decide on and assign articles for the paper. News articles might include Expanded Suffrage in Britain, Social and Economic Reforms in Britain, The Dreyfus Affair in France, Zionist Movement, Rise of Labor Unions in America. Feature articles might include The Victorian Age in England, A History of the Reform Movement in England, Emmeline Pankhurst's Fight for Women's Suffrage, Charles Stewart Parnell of Ireland, Immigration in the United States. Reviews might focus on books by Emile Zola and other writers of the time. Editorials and cartoons should reflect a point of view on an issue of the period.
3. Set aside time to research, write, and edit the stories.
4. If available, use a computer to design and produce your newspaper pages. Pass out copies of the newspaper to other world history classes.

*Chapter 24* **629**

# The New Imperialism

## (1800–1914)

## CHAPTER OUTLINE

In the late 1800s, Europeans seized almost the entire continent of Africa. A few critics opposed the expansion. But most Europeans applauded the move. As French statesman and historian Gabriel Hanotaux wrote of his nation's colonizing activities:

> 66 I can think of nothing more heartening than the spectacle of the struggle waged for a century by the sons of civilized Europe against the sphinx that guards the mystery of Africa. 99

Hanotaux's attitude was typical among westerners. The West, they believed, was modern and enlightened. It had to bring "civilization" to the "backward" people of Africa and Asia.

Europeans had other motives, as well, for expanding around the globe. In the words of British empire builder Frederick Lugard:

> 66 There are some who say we have no *right* to Africa at all, that 'it belongs to the natives.' I hold that our right is the necessity that is upon us to provide for our ever-growing population—either by opening new fields for emigration, or by providing work and employment . . . and to stimulate trade by finding new markets. 99

At the beginning of the 1800s, westerners had relatively little influence outside their own lands. With the Industrial Revolution, however, western nations gained extraordinary power. By the end of the century, they had carved out empires around the globe. During the "age of imperialism," from 1870 to 1914, they dominated other peoples and brought distant lands under their control.

In this chapter and the next one, we will look at how and why western industrial powers won global empires. We will also learn how people in the lands targeted for takeover fought to preserve their own cultures and traditions. When foreign powers pushed at their doors, they resisted, often in fierce but ultimately unsuccessful wars.

**FOCUS ON** these questions as you read:

- **Economics and Technology**
  How was the Industrial Revolution linked to imperialism?

- **Global Interaction**
  How did western powers gain global empires?

- **Political and Social Systems**
  What conditions in Africa and Asia helped western powers make inroads there?

- **Continuity and Change**
  How did people in Africa and Asia respond to western imperialism?

## TIME AND PLACE

**Growing European Empires** *Europeans took control of much of Africa, Asia, and the Middle East in the 1800s. Early contacts between Europeans and local leaders were often polite, as in this meeting between a British naval officer and the king of Ambriz in Africa. Both sides knew, however, that behind the friendly gestures stood gunboats, cannons, and rifles that the Europeans would use to expand their imperialist rule.* **Continuity and Change** *Do foreign diplomats today conceal their nations' real motives and goals? Explain.*

## HUMANITIES LINK

*Art History* Indian miniature painting (page 648).
*Literature* In this chapter, you will encounter a passage from the following work of literature: Rudyard Kipling, "White Man's Burden" (page 633).

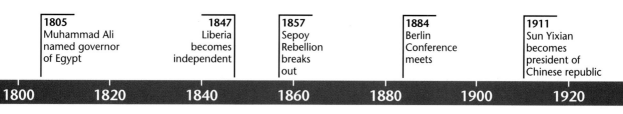

| 1805 | 1847 | 1857 | 1884 | 1911 |
|---|---|---|---|---|
| Muhammad Ali named governor of Egypt | Liberia becomes independent | Sepoy Rebellion breaks out | Berlin Conference meets | Sun Yixian becomes president of Chinese republic |

| 1800 | 1820 | 1840 | 1860 | 1880 | 1900 | 1920 |

# 1  A Western-Dominated World

## Guide for Reading

- Why did European imperialism grow in the late 1800s?

- What groups supported the new imperialism?

- How did Europeans rule their overseas empires?

- **Vocabulary** *imperialism, protectorate, sphere of influence*

When Edward VII inherited the British throne in 1901, his empire extended far beyond Britain. One writer boasted, "The sun never sets" on the British empire. In other words, since the empire circled the globe, the sun always shone on some part of it. Another writer noted:

> 66His Majesty rules over one continent, a hundred peninsulas, five hundred promontories, a thousand lakes, two thousand rivers, and ten thousand islands. . . . The empire to which [Queen] Victoria acceded in 1837 covered a sixth of the land of the world; that of King Edward covers nearly a quarter. The [British flag] has unfolded itself . . . over two acres of new territory every time the clock has ticked since 1800.99

Like Britain, other western powers built overseas empires in the late 1800s. The Industrial Revolution and the growth of science and technology had transformed the West. Armed with new economic and political power, western nations set out to dominate the world.

## The New Imperialism

European imperialism did not begin in the 1800s. Imperialism is the domination by one country of the political, economic, or cultural life of another country or region. As you have read, European nations won empires in the Americas after 1492, established colonies in India and Southeast Asia, and gained toeholds on the coasts of Africa and China. (See Chapters 15 and 16.) Despite these gains, between 1500 and 1800, Europe had little influence on the lives of the peoples of China, India, or Africa.

By the 1800s, Europe had developed politically and economically. Strong, centrally governed nation-states had emerged. The Industrial Revolution greatly strengthened European economies, and westerners had a new sense of confidence in themselves. Inspired by these changes, Europeans embarked on that path of aggressive expansion that today's historians call the "new imperialism." In just a few decades, from about 1870 to 1914, they brought much of the world under their control.

## Motives of the New Imperialists

Like other key developments in world history, the new imperialism exploded out of a combination of causes. They can be grouped into four main categories.

**Economic interests.** The Industrial Revolution created needs that spurred overseas expansion. Manufacturers wanted access to natural resources such as rubber, petroleum, manganese for steel, and palm oil for machinery. They also looked to expand their markets around the globe. Bankers sought ventures in far-flung parts of the world in which to invest their profits. Colonies also offered a valuable outlet for Europe's rapidly expanding population.

**Political and military interests.** Closely linked to economic motives were political and military issues. Steam-powered merchant ships and naval vessels needed bases around the world to take on coal and supplies. Industrial powers seized islands or harbors to satisfy these needs.

Nationalism played an important role, too. When France, for example, moved into West

**ISSUES For TODAY**

Advanced technology and a strong military enabled western nations to exert their will around the globe. What are the responsibilities of powerful nations toward those that are less powerful?

**Exploiting Natural Resources**
Tropical colonies supplied Europe with many valuable products. These workers in Ceylon (modern-day Sri Lanka) load crates of tea for shipment abroad. **Global Interaction** For what other purposes did European nations seek colonies?

Africa, rival nations like Britain and Germany seized lands nearby to halt further French expansion. Western leaders also claimed colonies were needed for national security. Sometimes, they were acquired for the prestige of ruling a global empire.

**Humanitarian and religious goals.** Many westerners felt a genuine concern for their "little brothers" beyond the seas. Missionaries, doctors, and colonial officials believed they had a duty to spread what they saw as the blessings of western civilization, including its medicine, law, and Christian religion. In his poem "White Man's Burden," Rudyard Kipling expressed this mission:

    66Take up the White Man's Burden—
      Send forth the best ye breed—
      Go bind your sons to exile
      To serve your captives' need;
      To wait in heavy harness
      On fluttered folk and wild—
      Your new-caught, sullen peoples
      Half-devil and half-child.99

**Social Darwinism.** Behind the idea of a civilizing mission was a growing sense in the West of racial superiority. Many westerners had embraced the scientific-sounding ideas of Social Darwinism. They applied Darwin's ideas about natural selection and survival of the fittest to hu-

man societies and nations. European races, they argued, were superior to all others, and imperial conquest and destruction of weaker races were simply nature's way of improving the human species! As a result, millions of nonwesterners were robbed of their cultural heritage.

**Empire builders and critics.** Many people were involved in the new imperialism. Leading the way were soldiers, merchants, settlers, missionaries, and explorers. In Europe, imperial expansion found favor with all classes, from bankers and manufacturers to workers.

Yet critics did speak out. Some opponents argued that colonialism was a tool of the rich. Others said it was immoral. Westerners, they pointed out, were moving toward greater democracy at home but were imposing undemocratic rule on other people.

## Down the Barrel of a Gun

Western imperialism succeeded for a number of reasons. While European nations had grown stronger in the 1800s, several older civilizations were in decline, especially the Ottoman Middle East, Mughal India, and Qing China. In West Africa, wars among African peoples and the draining effect of the slave trade had undermined established empires, kingdoms, and city-states. Newer African states were not strong enough to resist the western onslaught.

**Western advantages.** Europeans had the advantages of strong economies, well-organized governments, and powerful armies and navies.

▼ *Maxim machine gun*

Superior technology and improved medical knowledge also played a role. Quinine and other new medicines helped Europeans survive deadly tropical diseases. And, of course, advances such as Maxim machine guns, repeating rifles, and steam-driven warships were very strong arguments in persuading Africans and Asians to accept western control. As an English writer sarcastically noted:

66Whatever happens, we have got
 The Maxim gun, and they have not.99

**Resistance.** Africans and Asians strongly resisted western expansion. Some people fought the invaders, even though they had no weapons to equal the Maxim gun. As you will read, ruling groups in certain areas tried to strengthen their societies against outsiders by reforming their own Muslim, Hindu, or Confucian traditions. Finally, western-educated Africans and Asians organized nationalist movements to expel the imperialists from their lands.

## Forms of Imperial Control

The new imperialism took several forms. Among them were colonies, protectorates, and spheres of influence.

**Colonies.** In some areas, imperial powers established colonies. They sent out governors, officials, and soldiers to control the people and set up a colonial bureaucracy. Often, a handful of colonial officials ruled the local people and sought to transform their society.

France and Britain, the leading imperial powers, developed different kinds of colonial rule. The French practiced direct rule, sending officials from France to administer their colonies. Their goal was to impose French culture on their colonies and turn them into French provinces.

The British, by contrast, relied on a system of indirect rule. They used sultans, chiefs, or other local rulers as their agents in governing their colonies. They then encouraged the children of the local ruling class to get an education in Britain. In that way, a new generation was groomed to become agents of indirect rule—and of western civilization.

**Protectorates.** Sometimes, a western power established a protectorate. In a protectorate, local rulers were left in place. The ruler was, however, expected to accept the advice of European advisers on issues such as trade or missionary activity. A protectorate had certain advantages over a colony. It cost less to run than a colony did, and it did not require a large commitment of military or naval support unless a crisis occurred.

**Spheres of influence.** A third form of western control was the sphere of influence, an area in which an outside power claimed exclusive investment or trading privileges. Europeans carved out these spheres in China and elsewhere to prevent conflicts among themselves. The United States claimed Latin America as its sphere of influence.

## SECTION 1 REVIEW

1. **Identify** (a) new imperialism, (b) direct rule, (c) indirect rule.
2. **Define** (a) imperialism, (b) protectorate, (c) sphere of influence.
3. Describe three causes for the new imperialism.
4. What advantages did a protectorate have over a colony?
5. *Critical Thinking* **Analyzing Information** Review the poem on page 633. What is Kipling referring to when he uses the term "White Man's Burden"? Explain.
6. *ACTIVITY* Write a sentence offering a defense of the new imperialism that might have been offered by each of the following Europeans: (a) missionary, (b) merchant, (c) steel manufacturer, (d) banker.

# The Partition of Africa

## Guide for Reading

- What forces were shaping Africa before 1880?

- Which European countries carved up Africa?

- How did Africans resist European imperialism?

In 1890, Chief Machemba of the Yao people in East Africa wrote in Swahili to a German officer:

> I have listened to your words but can find no reason why I should obey you—I would rather die first. . . . If you desire friendship, then I am ready for it, today and always. But I cannot be your subject. If you desire war, then I am ready.

In the late 1800s, Germany and other European powers swept into Africa. Within about 20 years, they had carved up the continent and dominated its millions of people. Many, like the Yao, resisted. But despite their efforts, they could not hold back the tide of European conquest.

## On the Eve of the Scramble

In the early 1800s, westerners knew little about Africa. They called it the "dark continent," meaning the unknown land. Although they had built trading posts on the coasts, their maps of the interior were blank, or filled with imaginary features.

In the later 1800s, however, European nations sent explorers to Africa and later became involved in a "scramble" for African colonies. To understand the impact of European domination, we need to look at Africa in the early 1800s, before the scramble began.

**A diverse land.** Africa is a huge continent, four times the size of Europe. Across its many regions—the blank areas on European maps—people had evolved diverse cultures. They spoke hundreds of languages and had developed varied governments. Some people lived in large centralized states, others in village communities, still others in herding or food-gathering societies.

**North Africa.** North Africa includes the fertile land along the Mediterranean and the enormous Sahara. Since before 1800, the region has had close ties to the Muslim world. From the 1400s, much of North Africa, including Egypt, was ruled by the Ottoman empire. But by the 1800s, Ottoman control was weakening. You will read about Egypt and the Ottoman empire later in this chapter.

**West Africa.** On the grassy plains of West Africa, an Islamic reform movement had unleashed forces for change. (See page 409.) Leaders like Usman dan Fodio preached jihad, a holy struggle, to revive and purify Islam. Under these leaders, several new Muslim states arose, built on trade, farming, and herding.

In the forest regions, strong states like the Asante kingdom had grown up. (See page 409.) The Asante traded with both Europeans and Muslims. Asante power was limited, however. They controlled many smaller states that felt no loyalty to the central government. These tributary states were ready to turn to other protectors who might help them defeat their overlords. The European imperialists would exploit that lack of unity.

**East Africa.** Islam had long influenced the region from the Red Sea down the coast of East Africa. Port cities like Mombasa and Kilwa had suffered setbacks when the Portuguese arrived in the early 1500s. Yet East Africans still sent trading ships to the Red Sea or Persian Gulf. Their cargoes were human captives marched from the interior to the coast to be shipped as slaves to the Middle East. Ivory and copper from Central Africa were also brought to the coast, where they were exchanged for Indian cloth and firearms.

**Southern Africa.** In the early 1800s, southern Africa was in turmoil. Shaka, you will recall, united the Zulu nation. His conquests, however, set off mass migrations and wars, creating chaos across much of the region. By the 1830s, the Zulus were also battling the Boers, who were migrating north from the Cape Colony.

## European Contacts Increase

In the 1500s and 1600s, Europeans traded along the coasts of Africa. Difficult geography and deadly diseases like malaria and sleeping sickness kept them from reaching the interior. Medical breakthroughs and river steamships changed all that in the 1800s.

**Impact of the slave trade.** For centuries, Europeans had taken enslaved Africans to work the plantations and mines of the Americas. Arabs and Africans had also traded in slaves.

Beginning in the early 1800s, European nations slowly outlawed the slave trade. In Britain and the United States, abolitionists promoted the idea of returning freed slaves to Africa. In 1787, the British organized Sierra Leone in West Africa as a colony for freed slaves. Later, some free blacks from the United States settled nearby Liberia. By 1847, after much hardship, Liberia became an independent republic.

Slavery still existed, however. Arab and African slave traders continued to send human beings from Central and East Africa to work as slaves in the Middle East and Asia well into the late 1800s. Thus, the demand for slaves remained, and the slave trade in Africa continued.

**Explorers.** In the early 1800s, European explorers began pushing into the interior of Africa. Daring adventurers like Mungo Park and Richard Burton set out to map the course and sources of the great African rivers such as the Niger, Nile, and Congo. Some explorers were self-promoters who wrote glowing accounts of their bold deeds. While they were fascinated by African geography, they had little understanding of the peoples they met. All, however, endured great hardships in pursuit of their dreams.

**Missionaries.** Catholic and Protestant missionaries followed the explorers. All across Africa, they sought to win souls to Christianity.

The missionaries were sincere in their desire to help Africans. They built schools and medical clinics alongside churches. They also focused attention on the evils of the slave trade.

Still, missionaries, like most westerners, took a paternalistic view of Africans. They saw them as children in need of guidance. To them, African cultures and religions were "degraded." They urged Africans to reject their own traditions in favor of western civilization.

**Livingstone.** The best known explorer-missionary was Dr. David Livingstone. For 30 years, he crisscrossed the African continent. He wrote about the many peoples he met with more sympathy and less bias than did most Europeans. He relentlessly opposed the slave trade, which remained a profitable business for some African rulers. The only way to end this cruel traffic, he believed, was to open up the interior of Africa to Christianity and trade.

Livingstone blazed a trail that others soon followed. In 1869, the journalist Henry Stanley trekked into Central Africa to find Livingstone, who had not been heard from for years. He finally tracked him down in 1871 in what is today Tanzania, greeting him with the now-legendary phrase "Dr. Livingstone, I presume?"

*King Njoya's Throne* King Njoya of Bamum, in modern-day Cameroon, impressed German colonizers with his orderly government and disciplined army. Njoya sent this ornate wooden throne as a gift to the German kaiser William II in 1908. ***Political and Social Systems*** How did Njoya's gift to Kaiser William suggest equality between the two rulers?

## The Great Scramble Begins

Shortly afterward, Stanley took a new assignment. King Leopold II of Belgium hired him to explore the Congo River basin and arrange trade treaties with African leaders. Publicly, Leopold spoke of a civilizing mission to carry the light "that for millions of men still plunged in barbarism will be the dawn of a better era." Privately, he dreamed of conquest and profit.

Leopold's activities in the Congo (present-day Zaire) set off a scramble by other European nations. Before long, Britain, France, and Germany were pressing rival claims to the region.

**Berlin Conference.** To avoid bloodshed, European powers met at an international conference in 1884. It took place not in Africa but in Berlin, Germany. No Africans were invited.

At the Berlin Conference, European powers recognized Leopold's private claims to the Congo Free State but called for free trade on the Congo and Niger rivers. They further agreed that a European power could not claim any part of Africa unless it had set up a government office there. This principle led Europeans to send officials who would exert their power over local rulers.

The rush to colonize Africa was on. With little understanding of or regard for traditional African patterns of settlement or ethnic boundaries, Europeans drew borders and set up frontiers as they carved out their claims. A British politician observed:

> 66We have been engaged in drawing lines upon maps where no white man's foot has ever trod. We have been giving away mountains and rivers and lakes to each other, only hindered by the small impediment that we never knew exactly where the mountains and rivers and lakes were.99

In the 20 years after the Berlin Conference, the European powers partitioned almost the entire continent. Only Ethiopia and Liberia remained independent. (See the map on page 638.)

**Horrors in the Congo.** Leopold and other wealthy Belgians, meantime, exploited the riches of the Congo, including its copper, rubber, and ivory. Soon, horrifying stories filtered out of the region. They told of Belgian overseers torturing and brutalizing villagers. Forced to work for almost nothing, unwilling laborers were savagely beaten or had hands and ears amputated. The population of some areas declined drastically.

Eventually, international outrage forced Leopold to turn over his colony to the Belgian government. It became the Belgian Congo in 1908. Under Belgian rule, the worst abuses of the state were ended. Still, the Belgians regarded the Congo as a possession to be exploited for their own enrichment, and African inhabitants were given little or no role in either the government or economy of the colony.

## Carving Up a Continent

In the 1800s, France took a giant share of Africa. In 1830, it had invaded and conquered Algeria in North Africa. The victory cost tens of thousands of French lives and killed many times more Algerians. Later, France extended its influence along the Mediterranean into Tunisia and won colonies in West and Central Africa. At their height, French holdings in Africa were as large as the continental United States.

Britain's share of Africa was smaller and more scattered than that of France. However, it included more heavily populated regions with many rich resources. Britain took chunks of West and East Africa. It gained control of Egypt, as you will read, and pushed south into the Sudan. It also ruled much of southern Africa.

**The Boer War.** Britain had acquired the Cape Colony in southern Africa from the Dutch in 1806. The Boers—Dutch farmers—resented British rule and had migrated north to found their own republics.

In the late 1800s, the discovery of gold and diamonds in the Boer republics set off the Boer War. The war, which lasted from 1899 to 1902, involved bitter guerrilla fighting. The British won, but at great cost.

In 1910, the British united the Cape Colony and the former Boer republics into the Union of South Africa. The new constitution set up a government run by whites and laid the foundation for a system of complete racial segregation that would remain in force until 1993. (See page 742.)

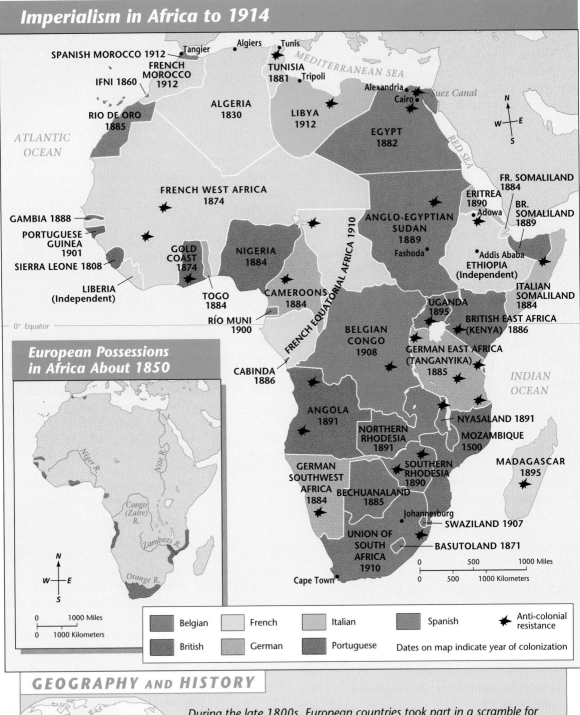

## Imperialism in Africa to 1914

SPANISH MOROCCO 1912
FRENCH MOROCCO 1912
IFNI 1860
RIO DE ORO 1885
Tangier
Algiers
Tunis
TUNISIA 1881
Tripoli
MEDITERRANEAN SEA
Alexandria
Cairo
Suez Canal

ALGERIA 1830
LIBYA 1912
EGYPT 1882
RED SEA

ATLANTIC OCEAN

FRENCH WEST AFRICA 1874

FR. SOMALILAND 1884
ERITREA 1890
Adowa
BR. SOMALILAND 1889

GAMBIA 1888
PORTUGUESE GUINEA 1901
SIERRA LEONE 1808
LIBERIA (Independent)

GOLD COAST 1874
NIGERIA 1884
TOGO 1884
CAMEROONS 1884
RÍO MUNI 1900

ANGLO-EGYPTIAN SUDAN 1889
Fashoda
Addis Ababa
ETHIOPIA (Independent)
ITALIAN SOMALILAND 1884

0° Equator

FRENCH EQUATORIAL AFRICA 1910
BELGIAN CONGO 1908
UGANDA 1895
BRITISH EAST AFRICA (KENYA) 1886
GERMAN EAST AFRICA (TANGANYIKA) 1885
INDIAN OCEAN

CABINDA 1886

ANGOLA 1891
NORTHERN RHODESIA 1891
NYASALAND 1891
MOZAMBIQUE 1500
MADAGASCAR 1895

European Possessions in Africa About 1850

Niger R.
Nile R.
Congo (Zaire) R.
Zambezi R.
Orange R.

GERMAN SOUTHWEST AFRICA 1884
BECHUANALAND 1885
SOUTHERN RHODESIA 1890
Johannesburg
SWAZILAND 1907
BASUTOLAND 1871
UNION OF SOUTH AFRICA 1910
Cape Town

0    500    1000 Miles
0    500    1000 Kilometers

0    1000 Miles
0    1000 Kilometers

| Belgian | French | Italian | Spanish | ★ Anti-colonial resistance |
| British | German | Portuguese | Dates on map indicate year of colonization |

## GEOGRAPHY AND HISTORY

During the late 1800s, European countries took part in a scramble for Africa. They claimed control of nearly the whole continent by 1914. Only Ethiopia and Liberia remained independent.

1. **Location** On the main map, locate (a) Algeria, (b) Nigeria, (c) Angola, (d) Eritrea, (e) Cameroons, (f) Southern Rhodesia.
2. **Region** In which part of Africa were most of France's possessions located by 1914?
3. **Critical Thinking Making Inferences** How can you tell from the map that Africans did not willingly accept European domination?

"Our place in the sun." Other European powers joined the scramble, in part to bolster their national image, in part to further their economic growth and influence. The Portuguese carved out large colonies in Angola and Mozambique. Italy reached across the Mediterranean to occupy Libya and then pushed into the "horn" of Africa, at the southern end of the Red Sea. Italian efforts to conquer Ethiopia, however, ended in a stinging defeat.

The newly united German empire took lands in eastern and southwestern Africa. A German politician, trying to ease the worries of European rivals, explained, "We do not want to put anyone in the shade, but we also demand our place in the sun."

## Africans Fight Back

Europeans met armed resistance across the continent. The Algerians battled the French for years. Samori Touré fought French forces in West Africa, where he was building his own empire. The British battled the Zulus in southern Africa and the Asante in West Africa. When all seemed lost and their king exiled, the Asante put themselves under the command of their queen, Yaa Asantewaa. She led the fight against the British in the last Asante war.

Another woman who became a military leader was Nehanda, of the Shona in Zimbabwe. Although a clever tactician, Nehanda was captured and executed. However, her memory inspired later generations to fight for freedom.

In East Africa, the Germans fought wars against people like the Yao and Herero. Among some groups, resistance was weakened by an 1897 epidemic of rinderpest, a cattle disease that destroyed their herds. Still, they fought fiercely, especially in the Maji-Maji Rebellion of 1905. Only by using a scorched-earth policy that left thousands of local people to starve to death did the Germans triumph in the end.

**Ethiopia survives.** Successful resistance was mounted by Ethiopia. This ancient Christian kingdom had survived in the highlands of East Africa. But, like feudal Europe, it had been divided up among a number of rival princes who ruled their own domains.

In the late 1800s, a reforming ruler, Menelik II, began to modernize his country. He hired European experts to plan modern roads and bridges and set up a western school system. He imported the latest weapons and European officers to help train his army. Thus, when Italy invaded Ethiopia in 1896, Menelik was prepared. At the battle of Adowa (ah DUH wah), the Ethiopians smashed the Italian invaders. Ethiopia was the only African nation, aside from Liberia, to preserve its independence.

▲ Emperor Menelik II

**Impact.** During the age of imperialism, a western-educated African elite emerged. Some middle-class Africans admired western ways and rejected their own culture. Others valued their African traditions and condemned western societies that upheld liberty and equality for whites only. By the early 1900s, African leaders were forging nationalist movements to pursue self-determination and independence.

## SECTION 2 REVIEW

1. **Identify** (a) Sierra Leone, (b) Liberia, (c) David Livingstone, (d) Berlin Conference, (e) Congo Free State, (f) Boer War, (g) Nehanda, (h) Menelik II, (i) Adowa.
2. Describe one development in each region of Africa in the early 1800s.
3. How did Ethiopia maintain its independence?
4. Describe three examples of African resistance to European colonization.
5. *Critical Thinking* **Making Inferences** (a) Why do you think the Europeans held the Berlin Conference without inviting any Africans? (b) What might be the effect of this exclusion upon later African leaders?
6. *ACTIVITY* Imagine that you live in one of the African lands discussed in Section 2. Write a poem about the European colonization of your land.

# 3 European Challenges to the Muslim World

## Guide for Reading

- What problems did the Ottoman empire face?
- How did Egypt seek to modernize?
- Why did Iran become a focus of European interest?
- **Vocabulary** *genocide*

"Europe is a molehill," said Napoleon Bonaparte in 1797. He felt it offered too few chances for glory. "We must go to the East," he declared. "All great glory has been acquired there." Following through, in 1798 Napoleon invaded Egypt.

Napoleon's attack on Egypt opened a new era in European contacts with the Muslim world. It focused attention on the fading power of the Ottoman empire. By the early 1800s, European countries were nibbling at the fringes of the Muslim world. Before long, they would strike at its heartlands.

## Ferment in the Muslim World

The Muslim world extended from western Africa to Southeast Asia. (See the map on page 261.) In the 1500s, three giant Muslim empires ruled much of this world—the Mughals in India, the Ottomans in the Middle East, and the Safavids in Iran. By the 1700s, all three were in decline.

The decay had many causes. Central governments had lost control over powerful groups such as landowning nobles, military elites, and urban craft guilds. Corruption was widespread. In some places, Muslim scholars and religious leaders were allied with the state. In other areas, they helped to foment discontent against the government.

**Islamic reform movements.** In the 1700s and early 1800s, reform movements sprang up across the Muslim world. Most stressed religious piety and obedience to strict rules of behavior. The Wahhabi movement in Arabia, for example, rejected the schools of theology and law that had emerged in the Ottoman empire. In their place, they wanted to recapture the purity and simplicity of Muhammad's original teachings. An Arab prince led the Wahhabis against Ottoman rule. Although the revolt was crushed, the Wahhabi movement survived. Its teachings are influential in the kingdom of Saudi Arabia today.

Islamic revivals rose in Africa, too. As you have read, Usman dan Fodio led the struggle to reform Muslim practices. (See page 409.) In the Sudan, south of Egypt, Muhammad Ahmad announced that he was the Mahdi, the long-awaited savior of the faith. In the 1880s, the Mahdi and his followers fiercely resisted British expansion into the region. In modern Sudan, followers of the Mahdi still have great influence.

**European pressure.** Added to internal ferment and decay, the old Muslim empires faced western imperialism. Through a mix of diplomacy and military threat, European powers won treaties giving them favorable trading terms. They then demanded special rights for their citizens in the region and used excuses such as the need to protect those rights to intervene in local affairs. Sometimes, they took over an entire region.

## Challenges to the Ottoman Empire

At its height, the Ottoman empire had extended across the Middle East, North Africa, and parts of Eastern Europe. By 1800, however, it was facing serious challenges. Ambitious pashas, or provincial rulers, had increased their power. Economic problems and corruption also contributed to Ottoman decay.

**Nationalist revolts.** As ideas of nationalism spread from Western Europe, internal revolts posed constant challenges within the multi-ethnic Ottoman empire. Subject peoples in Eastern Europe, the Middle East, and North Africa threatened to break away. In the Balkans, Greeks, Serbs, Bulgarians, and Romanians gained their independence. (See pages 529–530.) Revolts against Ottoman rule also erupted in Arabia, Lebanon, and Armenia. The Ottomans suppressed these uprisings, but another valuable territory, Egypt, slipped out of their control.

**European involvement.** Britain, France, and Russia each sought to benefit from the slow crumbling of the Ottoman-held empire. France, which had seized Algeria in the 1830s, cast its eyes on other Ottoman-held territory. Russia schemed to gain control of the Turkish Straits—the Bosporus and Dardanelles—which would give it access to the Mediterranean Sea. Britain tried to thwart Russia's ambitions, which it saw as a threat to its own power in the Mediterranean and beyond it to India. And in 1898, the new German empire jumped onto the bandwagon, hoping to increase its influence in the region by building a Berlin-to-Baghdad railway.

During the Crimean War, which you read about in Chapter 23, the British and French had helped the Ottomans resist Russian expansion. By the late 1800s, however, France and Britain had extended their own influence over Ottoman lands.

## Efforts at Reform

Since the late 1700s, Ottoman rulers had seen the need for reform. Several sultans looked to the West for ideas. They reorganized the bureaucracy and system of tax collection. They built railroads, improved education, and hired European officers to train a modern military. Young men were sent to the West to study the new sciences and technology. Many returned home with western ideas about democracy and equality.

**Successes and failures.** The reforms brought better medical care and revitalized farming. These improvements, however, were a mixed blessing. Better living conditions resulted in a population explosion. The growing population increased pressure on the land, which led to unrest.

*A Crossroads of the World* Constantinople, at the crossroads of Europe and Asia, was the capital of the vast Ottoman empire. People from all over the world met and traded in the city. Here, Europeans mingle with Ottoman subjects from different parts of the empire on the banks of the Bosporus. In the background is Hagia Sophia, a giant Islamic mosque built originally as a Christian cathedral. (See the picture on page 237.) **Diversity** How does the artist portray the diversity of the gathering?

The adoption of western ideas about government also increased tension. Many officials objected to changes that were inspired by a foreign culture. For their part, repressive sultans rejected reform and tried to rebuild the autocratic power enjoyed by earlier rulers.

**Young Turks.** In the 1890s, a group of liberals formed a movement called the Young Turks. They insisted that reform was the only way to save the empire. In 1908, the Young Turks overthrew the sultan. Before they could achieve their planned reforms, however, the Ottoman empire was plunged into the world war that erupted in 1914.

**Massacre of Armenians.** Meanwhile, Turkish nationalism had grown rapidly. In the 1890s, it took an ugly, intolerant course.

Traditionally, the Ottomans had let minority nationalities live in their own communities and practice their own religions. By the 1890s, however, nationalism was igniting new tensions, especially between Turks and minority peoples who sought their own states. These tensions triggered a brutal genocide of the Armenians, a Christian people concentrated in the mountainous eastern region of the empire. Genocide is a deliberate attempt to destroy an entire religious or ethnic group.

The Muslim Turks distrusted the Christian Armenians and accused them of supporting Russian plans against the Ottoman empire. When Armenians protested repressive Ottoman policies, the sultan had tens of thousands of them slaughtered. Survivors fled, many of them to the United States. Still, over the next 25 years, a million or more Armenians in the Ottoman empire were killed.

## Egypt Seeks to Modernize

Egypt in 1800 was a semi-independent Ottoman province. In the early 1800s, it made great strides toward reform. Its success was due to Muhammad Ali, an Albanian Muslim soldier who was appointed governor of Egypt in 1805.

**Muhammad Ali.** Muhammad Ali is sometimes called the "father of modern Egypt." He was an ambitious soldier who led an unsuccessful attempt to drive Napoleon from Egypt in 1799 and later conquered the neighboring lands of Arabia, Syria, and Sudan. To strengthen Egypt, he introduced a number of political and economic reforms.

Muhammad Ali improved tax collection, reorganized the landholding system, and backed large irrigation projects to increase farm output. By expanding cotton production and encouraging industry, he involved Egypt in world trade. Muhammad Ali also brought in western military experts to help him build a well-trained, modern army. Before he died in 1849, he had set Egypt on the road to becoming a complex industrialized society and made it a major Middle Eastern power.

**The Suez Canal.** Muhammad Ali's successors lacked his skills, and Egypt came increasingly under foreign control. In 1859, a French entrepreneur, Ferdinand de Lesseps, organized a company to build the Suez Canal. This 100-mile waterway links the Mediterranean and Red seas. (See the map on the next page.) Europeans hailed its opening in 1869 because it greatly shortened the sea route from Europe to South and East Asia. To Britain, especially, the canal was a "lifeline" to India.

In 1875, the ruler of Egypt found himself unable to repay loans he had contracted for the canal and other modernization projects. To pay his debts, he was forced to sell his shares in the canal. British prime minister Disraeli quickly bought them, giving Britain a controlling interest in the canal.

**A British protectorate.** Britain quickly expanded its influence over Egypt. When a nationalist revolt erupted in 1882, Britain made Egypt a protectorate. In theory, the governor of Egypt was an official of the Ottoman government. In fact, he followed policies dictated by Britain.

Under British influence, Egypt continued to modernize. At the same time, however, nationalist discontent simmered and flared into protests and riots well into the next century.

## Iran and the Western Powers

Like the Ottoman empire, Iran faced major challenges in the 1800s. The Qajar (kah JAHR) shahs, who ruled Iran from 1794 to 1925, exercised absolute power like the Safavids before them. Still, they did take steps to introduce reforms. The government improved finances and

# PARALLELS THROUGH TIME

## Shortcuts

Throughout history, people have taken advantage of new technology to create better and shorter ways of "getting there." The resulting works of engineering altered the face of the Earth, connecting oceans and continents and bringing people closer together.

**Linking Past and Present** Identify a structure that permits you to move easily from one place to another. How would your life be different without that structure?

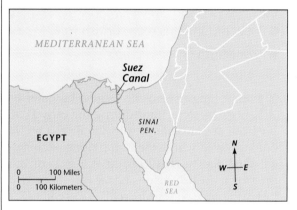

**PAST** The Suez Canal, which connects the Mediterranean and Red seas, opened in 1869. A French company headed by Ferdinand de Lesseps built the canal, but money and labor for the project came mainly from Egypt. The canal cut the distance between Europe and the East by thousands of miles and placed Egypt at the center of world trade routes. (See the map, left, and picture, below.)

**PRESENT** The first plan to dig a tunnel under the English Channel was submitted to Napoleon Bonaparte in 1802. Almost 200 years later, work on the project finally began. The 31-mile tube, through which both trains and cars can travel, opened in 1994. (See the picture and map below.)

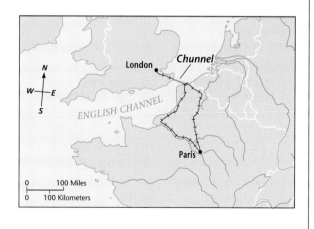

sponsored the building of telegraph lines and railroads. It even experimented with a liberal constitution.

Reform, however, did not save Iran from western imperialism. Both Russia and Britain battled for influence in the area. Russia wanted to protect its southern frontier and expand into Central Asia. Britain was concerned about protecting its interests in India.

For a time, each nation set up its own sphere of influence in Iran. Russia operated in the north and Britain in the south. The discovery of oil in the early 1900s upset the balance. Russia and Britain intrigued for control of Iranian oil fields. By 1914, Russia had sent troops into the region, giving it a dominant position.

Concessions, or economic rights granted to foreign powers, outraged Iranian nationalists. Nationalists included two very different groups. Some Iranians, especially the urban middle class, wanted to move swiftly to adopt western ways. Others, led by Muslim religious leaders, condemned the government and western influences. The religious leaders often spoke for the masses of the people who lived in rural poverty and resented government interference.

## SECTION 3 REVIEW

1. **Identify** (a) Mahdi, (b) Young Turks, (c) Muhammad Ali, (d) Suez Canal.
2. **Define** genocide.
3. Identify three causes of Ottoman decline.
4. (a) What reforms did Muhammad Ali introduce in Egypt? (b) How did Egypt come under British control?
5. Why did Iran become a center of imperialist interest?
6. *Critical Thinking* **Linking Past and Present** How might nationalism sometimes lead to intolerance? Give a present-day example .
7. *ACTIVITY* On an outline map of the world, draw the route of a ship traveling from Europe to Asia before and after the Suez Canal. Use your completed map to calculate the distance of each route. Then, write a sentence explaining why Europeans welcomed the canal.

# 4 The British Take Over India

## Guide for Reading

- What were the causes and results of the Sepoy Rebellion?
- What effects did British rule have on India?
- How did Indians resist British rule?
- **Vocabulary** *cash crop*

Ranjit Singh ruled the large Sikh empire in northwestern India during the early 1800s. He had cordial dealings with the British but saw only too well where their ambitions were headed. One day, he was looking at a map of India on which British-held lands were shaded red. "All will one day become red!" he predicted.

Not long after Ranjit Singh's death in 1839, the British conquered the Sikh empire. They added its 100,000 square miles to their steadily growing lands. As Singh had forecast, India was falling under British control, and the map of the subcontinent was almost entirely red.

## The East India Company

In the early 1600s, the British East India Company obtained trading rights on the fringe of the Mughal empire. (See Chapter 15.) As Mughal power declined, the company expanded its influence. By the mid-1800s, it controlled three fifths of India.

**A divided land.** How were the British able to conquer such a vast territory? The answer lies in the land's diversity. Even when Mughal power was at its height, India was home to many people and cultures. As Mughal power crumbled, India fragmented. Indians speaking dozens of different languages and with different traditions were not able to unite against the newcomers.

The British took advantage of this ferment by playing off rival princes against each other. Where diplomacy or intrigue did not work, their superior weapons overpowered local rulers.

**British policies.** The East India Company's main goal in India was to make money, and leading officials often got very rich. At the same time, the company did work to improve roads, preserve peace, and reduce banditry.

By the early 1800s, British officials introduced western education and legal procedures. Missionaries tried to convert Indians to Christianity, which they felt was far superior to Indian religions. The British also pressed for social change. They worked to end slavery and the caste system and to improve the position of women within the family. One law outlawed sati, a Hindu custom practiced mainly by the upper classes. It called for a widow to join her husband in death by throwing herself on his funeral fire.

## The Sepoy Rebellion

Indians from all social classes resented British interference and domination. Well-educated Indians were shut out of high posts. In line with mercantilist policy, the British kept Indians from engaging in large-scale manufacturing, which hurt the business class. Peasants felt the impact of the British-imposed economic policies and were angry at laws that violated ancient customs and traditions.

**Unpopular moves.** In the 1850s, the East India Company took several unpopular steps. First, it required sepoys—Indian troops—to serve anywhere, either in India or overseas. For high-caste Hindus, however, overseas travel was an offense against their religion. The second cause of discontent was a new law that allowed Hindu widows to remarry. Hindus viewed both moves as a Christian conspiracy to undermine their beliefs.

The final insult came in 1857, when the British issued new rifles to the sepoys. Troops were told to bite off the tips of cartridges before loading them into the rifles. The cartridges, however, were greased with animal fat—either from cows, which Hindus considered sacred, or from pigs, which were forbidden to Muslims. When the troops refused the order to "load rifles," they were dismissed without pay and sent home in disgrace.

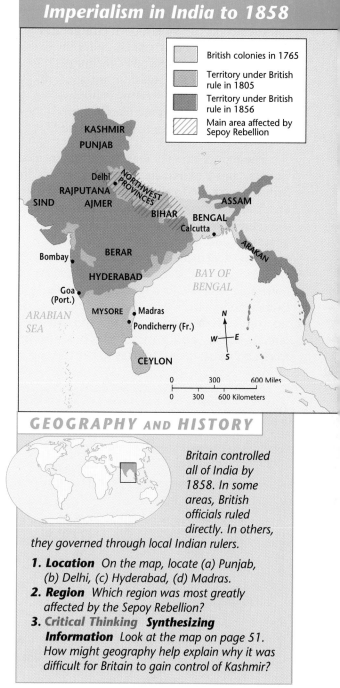

### Imperialism in India to 1858

British colonies in 1765

Territory under British rule in 1805

Territory under British rule in 1856

Main area affected by Sepoy Rebellion

KASHMIR
PUNJAB
Delhi
NORTHWEST PROVINCES
RAJPUTANA
SIND
AJMER
BIHAR
ASSAM
BENGAL
Calcutta
ARAKAN
Bombay
BERAR
HYDERABAD
BAY OF BENGAL
Goa (Port.)
ARABIAN SEA
MYSORE
Madras
Pondicherry (Fr.)
CEYLON

0    300    600 Miles
0    300    600 Kilometers

## GEOGRAPHY *AND* HISTORY

Britain controlled all of India by 1858. In some areas, British officials ruled directly. In others, they governed through local Indian rulers.

1. **Location** On the map, locate (a) Punjab, (b) Delhi, (c) Hyderabad, (d) Madras.
2. **Region** Which region was most greatly affected by the Sepoy Rebellion?
3. *Critical Thinking* **Synthesizing Information** Look at the map on page 51. How might geography help explain why it was difficult for Britain to gain control of Kashmir?

**On to Delhi.** Angry sepoys rose up against their British officers. The Sepoy Rebellion swept across northern and central India. Several sepoy regiments marched off to Delhi, the old Mughal capital. There, they hailed the last Mughal ruler as their leader. Other sepoys issued a document calling on both Hindus and Muslims for their support:

66It is well known to all, that in this age the people of [India], both Hindus and Muslims, are being ruined under the tyranny and oppression of the infidel and treacherous English. It is therefore the duty of all the wealthy people of India . . . to stake their lives and property for the well being of the public.99

The sepoys brutally massacred British men, women, and children in some places. But the British soon rallied and crushed the revolt. They then took terrible revenge for their earlier losses, torching villages and slaughtering thousands of unarmed Indians.

**The aftermath.** The Sepoy Rebellion left a bitter legacy of fear, hatred, and mistrust on both sides. It also brought major changes in British policy. In 1858, Parliament ended the rule of the East India Company and put India directly under the British crown. It sent more troops to India, taxing Indians to pay the cost of these occupying forces. While it slowed the "reforms" that had angered Hindus and Muslims, it continued to develop India for its own economic benefit. ■

## The "Brightest Jewel"

After 1858, Parliament set up a system of colonial rule in India. A British viceroy in India governed in the name of the queen, and British officials held the top positions in the civil service and army. Indians filled most other jobs. With their cooperation, the British made India the "brightest jewel" in the crown of their empire.

British policies were designed to fit India into the overall British economy. At the same time, British officials felt they were helping India to modernize. In their terms, modernizing meant adopting not only western technology but also western culture.

**An unequal partnership.** Britain saw India both as a market and as a source of raw ma-

*The Sepoy Rebellion* Resentment of foreign rule exploded in the Sepoy Rebellion. The uprising revealed deep-seated hostility toward British exploitation as well as anger at western attempts to change Indian society. Horrifying atrocities occurred on both sides before the uprising was suppressed. **Diversity** How was the Sepoy Rebellion a clash of cultures?

terials. To this end, the British built roads and an impressive railroad network. Improved transportation let the British sell their factory-made goods across the subcontinent and carry Indian cotton, jute, wheat, and coal to coastal ports for transport to factories in England. New methods of communication, such as the telegraph, also gave Britain better control of India.

After the Suez Canal opened in 1869, British trade with India soared. But it remained an unequal partnership, favoring the British. The British flooded India with inexpensive, machine-made textiles, ruining India's once-prosperous hand-weaving industry.

Britain also transformed Indian agriculture. It encouraged nomadic herders to settle into farming and pushed farmers to grow **cash crops,** such as cotton and jute, that could be sold on the world market. Clearing new farmlands led to massive deforestation, or cutting of trees, and other environmental destruction.

**Population and famine.** The British introduced medical improvements. At the same time, new farming methods increased food production. The result was rapid population growth. The rising numbers, however, put a strain on the food supply, especially as farmland was turned over to growing cash crops instead of food. In the late 1800s, terrible famines swept India. Railroads could carry food to the stricken areas, but overall, millions of Indian peasants sank deeply into poverty.

**Benefits of British rule.** On the positive side, British rule brought peace and order to the countryside. The British revised the legal system to promote justice for Indians regardless of class.

The upper classes benefited from some British policies. They sent their sons to British schools, where they were trained for posts in the civil service and military. Indian landowners and princes, who still ruled their own territories, grew rich from exporting cash crops. Railroads helped Indians move around the country, while the telegraph and postal system let them communicate more easily than ever before. Greater contact helped bridge regional differences and opened the way for Indians to develop a sense of national unity.

## Indians and British: Viewing Two Cultures

During the age of imperialism, Indians and British developed different views of each other's culture. Educated Indians were divided in their opinion of the British. Some were impressed by British power and technology and urged India to follow a western model of progress. These mostly upper class Indians learned English and adopted western ways. Other Indians felt that the answer to change lay with their own Hindu or Muslim cultures.

**Ram Mohun Roy.** In the early 1800s, Ram Mohun Roy combined both views. A great scholar, he knew Sanskrit, Persian, and Arabic classics, as well as English, Greek, and Latin works. Roy felt that India could learn from the West. At the same time, he wanted to revitalize and reform traditional Indian culture.

Roy condemned some traditions, such as rigid caste distinctions, child marriage, sati, and purdah, the isolation of women in separate quarters. But he also set up learned societies that helped revive pride in Indian culture. Because of his influence on later leaders, he is often hailed today as the founder of Indian nationalism.

**Western attitudes.** The British disagreed among themselves about India. A few admired Indian theology and philosophy. As western scholars translated Indian classics, they acquired respect for India's ancient heritage. Western writers and philosophers borrowed ideas from Hinduism and Buddhism.

On the other hand, most British people knew little about Indian achievements and dismissed Indian culture with contempt. In an essay on whether Indians should be taught in English or their own languages, the English historian Thomas Macaulay wrote that "a single

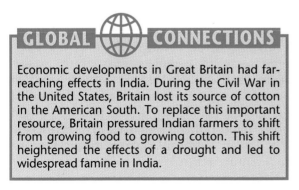

**GLOBAL CONNECTIONS**

Economic developments in Great Britain had far-reaching effects in India. During the Civil War in the United States, Britain lost its source of cotton in the American South. To replace this important resource, Britain pressured Indian farmers to shift from growing food to growing cotton. This shift heightened the effects of a drought and led to widespread famine in India.

**Indian Miniature Painting** *Like India itself, Indian art blends the traditions of different cultures. The art of miniature painting was carried to Mughal India from Persia in the 1500s, part of the flow of ideas and customs within the Muslim world. The art form evolved in India, where painters often used the small paintings to tell a story. After the arrival of Europeans, Indian artists began to adopt western styles of perspective as well. This miniature painting, from about 1880, shows British colonel James Todd riding an elephant.* **Art and Literature** *Based on the painting, what was Colonel Todd's position in society? Explain.*

shelf of a good European library is worth the whole native literature of India and Arabia."

## Growing Nationalism

During the years of British rule, a class of western-educated Indians emerged. In the view of Macauley and others, this elite class would bolster British power:

❝We must at present do our best to form a class who may be interpreters between us and the millions whom we govern; a class of persons, Indian in blood and color, but English in taste, in opinions, in morals, and in intellect.❞

As it turned out, exposure to European ideas had the opposite effect. By the late 1800s, western-educated Indians were spearheading a nationalist movement. Schooled in western ideals such as democracy and equality, they dreamed of ending imperial rule.

**Indian National Congress.** In 1885, nationalist leaders organized the Indian National Congress, which became known as the Congress party. Its members were mostly professionals and business leaders who believed in peaceful protest to gain their ends. They called for greater democracy, which they felt would bring more power to Indians like themselves. The Indian National Congress looked forward to eventual self-rule but supported western-style modernization.

Other Indian nationalists, however, took a more radical, anti-British stand. They wanted to restore Indian languages and Hindu and Muslim cultures.

**Muslim League.** At first, Muslims and Hindus worked together for self-rule. In time, however, Muslims grew to resent Hindu domination of the Congress party. They also worried that a Hindu-run government would oppress Muslims. In 1906, Muslims formed the Muslim League to pursue their own goals. Soon, they were talking of a separate Muslim state.

**Looking ahead.** By the early 1900s, protests and resistance to British rule increased. More and more Indians demanded not simply self-rule but complete independence. Their goal finally would be achieved in 1947, but only after a long struggle against the British and a nightmare of bloody conflict between Hindus and Muslims.

## SECTION 4 REVIEW

1. **Identify** (a) East India Company, (b) Sepoy Rebellion, (c) Ram Mohun Roy, (d) Indian National Congress, (e) Muslim League.
2. **Define** cash crop.
3. (a) What were the immediate causes of the Sepoy Rebellion? (b) What were the long-term causes?
4. (a) What were the goals of the East India Company in India? (b) What policies did the British government pursue in India after 1858?
5. How did British rule lead to growing Indian nationalism?
6. *Critical Thinking* **Applying Information** Review the definition of *racism* on page 571. Then, explain how the following statement by a British general serving in India in the mid-1800s reflects racism: "However well-educated and clever a native may be, and however brave he may prove himself, I believe that no rank we can bestow on him would cause him to be considered an equal of the British officer."
7. *ACTIVITY* Use the information in this chapter and in Chapter 15 to create an illustrated time line of British rule in India.

---

## 5 China and the New Imperialism

### Guide for Reading

■ What rights did westerners seek in China?

■ How did internal problems weaken China?

■ What were the goals of Chinese reformers?

■ **Vocabulary** *balance of trade, trade deficit, indemnity, extraterritoriality*

By the 1830s, British merchant ships were arriving in China, loaded with opium to sell to the Chinese. Lin Zexu (LIHN DZEH SHOO), a Chinese official, complained bitterly to Britain's Queen Victoria. "I have heard that smoking opium is strictly forbidden in your country," he wrote. "Why do you let this evil drug be sent to harm people in other countries?"

For centuries, the Chinese had strictly controlled foreign trade, ensuring that it was in China's favor. By the 1800s, however, western nations were using their growing power to weave a web of influence over East Asia just as they were doing in the rest of the world.

### The Trade Issue

As you read in Chapter 15, Chinese rulers placed strict limits on foreign traders. European merchants were restricted to a small area around Guangzhou in southern China. China sold them silk, porcelain, and tea in exchange for gold and silver. Under this arrangement, China enjoyed a favorable balance of trade, exporting more than it imported. Westerners, on the other hand, had a trade deficit with China, buying more from the Chinese than they sold them. In 1793, the British requested increased trading rights. The emperor Qianlong refused, saying that there was nothing in the West that China needed. (See page 388.)

By the late 1700s, two developments were underway that would transform China's relations with the western world. First, China

**A Shameful War** *The Opium War began when Chinese officials tried to keep British ships from bringing the addictive drug into China. Here, a British warship sinks Chinese junks during the war.*
**Economics and Technology** *How does the picture convey Britain's superior technology in warfare?*

entered a period of decline. Second, the Industrial Revolution created a need for expanded markets for European goods. At the same time, it gave the West the military power to back its demands for such markets.

**The Opium War.** During the late 1700s, British merchants discovered that they could make huge profits by trading opium grown in India for Chinese tea, which was popular in Britain. Soon, many Chinese had become addicted to the drug. Silver flowed out of China in payment for the drug, disrupting the economy.

The Chinese government outlawed opium and executed Chinese drug dealers. They called on Britain to stop the trade. The British refused, insisting on the right of free trade.

In 1839, Chinese warships clashed with British merchants. The incident triggered what became known as the Opium War. During the war, Britain flexed its new industrial might. Its gunboats, equipped with the latest in firepower, bombarded Chinese coastal and river ports. With outdated weapons and fighting methods, the Chinese were easily defeated.

**Unequal treaties.** In 1842, Britain made China accept the Treaty of Nanjing. It was the first of a series of "unequal treaties" that forced China to give up rights to western powers. France and the United States soon signed similar treaties with China.

The treaty gave Britain a huge indemnity, or payment for losses in the war. The British also gained the island of Hong Kong, near Guangzhou. (See the map on page 652.) China had to open five ports to foreign trade and grant British citizens in China extraterritoriality, the right to live under their own laws and be tried in their own courts. Finally, the treaty included a "most favored nation clause." It said that if the Chinese granted rights to another nation, Britain would automatically receive the same rights.

The Opium War set a pattern for later encounters between China and the West. During the mid-1800s, western powers squeezed China to win additional rights, such as opening more ports to trade and letting Christian missionaries preach in China.

## Internal Pressures

By the 1800s, the Qing dynasty was in decline. Irrigation systems and canals were poorly maintained, leading to massive flooding of the Huang He Valley and its rich farmlands. The population explosion that had begun a century earlier created a terrible hardship for China's peasants. An extravagant court, widespread official corruption, and tax evasion by the rich added to the peasants' burden. Even the honored civil service system was rocked by bribery and cheating scandals.

**The Taiping Rebellion.** As poverty and misery increased, peasants rebelled. The Taiping Rebellion, which lasted from 1850 to 1864, was probably the most devastating peasant revolt in history. The leader, Hong Xiuquan (howng shyoo CHWAHN), was a village schoolteacher who had failed the civil service exams four times. Inspired by religious visions, he set himself up as a revolutionary prophet. He wanted to establish a "Heavenly Kingdom of Great Peace"—the Taiping (tī PIHNG).

Hong was influenced by the teachings of Christian missionaries, and he was disappointed when westerners refused to help his cause. Hong endorsed radical social ideas, including land reform, community ownership of property, equality of women and men, and strict morality. Above all, he called for an end to the hated Qing dynasty.

The Taiping rebels won control of large parts of China. They held out for 14 years. In the end, the government relied on regional governors and generals to crush the rebellion.

**Effects.** The Taiping Rebellion almost toppled the Qing dynasty. It is estimated to have caused the deaths of between 20 million and 30 million Chinese. The lower Yangzi basin, the heartland of the revolt, was largely destroyed. The Qing government survived, but it had to share power with regional commanders who rebuilt the region and their power base.

During the rebellion, Europeans kept up pressure on China. Russia seized lands along the Amur River in northern China. It then built the great port of Vladivostok on the Pacific coast.

## Reform Efforts

By the mid-1800s, educated Chinese were divided over the need to adopt western ways. Most scholar-officials saw no reason to foster new industries, since China's wealth—and taxes—came from land. Although Chinese merchants were allowed to do business, they were not seen as a source of economic prosperity.

Scholar-officials also disapproved of the ideas of western missionaries, whose emphasis on individual choice challenged the Confucian order. They saw western technology as dangerous, too, because it threatened Confucian ways that had served China successfully for so long.

The imperial court was a center of conservative opposition. By the late 1800s, the empress Ci Xi (tsee SHYEE) had gained power. A strong-willed ruler, she surrounded herself with advisers who were deeply committed to Confucian traditions.

**Self-strengthening movement.** Some Chinese wanted to adapt western ideas. But others worried that technology such as railroads and steamships would bring unwelcome changes. "One thing will lead to another," they said, "and we will not be able to refuse them." ( ★ See *Skills for Success*, page 654.)

In the 1860s, reformers launched what became known as the "self-strengthening movement." They imported western technology, setting up factories to make modern weapons. They developed shipyards, railroads, mining, and light industry. The Chinese translated not

**Empress Ci Xi** *The Empress Ci Xi ruled China from 1862 until her death in 1908. Through most of her reign, she blocked efforts to modernize the nation, accusing reformers of being traitors and having them jailed, exiled, or even executed.* **Political and Social Systems** *Why did conservative Chinese reject reform?*

only western works of science but also works by Europeans on government and the economy. The movement made limited progress, however, because the government did not rally behind it. Also, while China was undertaking a few selected reforms, the western powers—and nearby Japan—were moving ahead rapidly.

**War with Japan.** The island nation of Japan modernized rapidly after 1868. (See Chapter 26.) It then joined the western imperialists in the competition for global empire.

In 1894, Japanese pressure on China led to war. It ended in disaster for China, with Japan gaining Korea, the Liaotung Peninsula, and Taiwan. (See the map on page 652.) When the two powers met at the peace table, there was a telling difference. Japanese officials were dressed in western clothes, the Chinese in traditional robes.

**Spheres of influence.** The crushing defeat revealed China's weakness. Western powers moved swiftly to carve out spheres of influence along the Chinese coast. The British took the Yangzi Valley. The French acquired the territory near Indochina. Germany got the Shandong

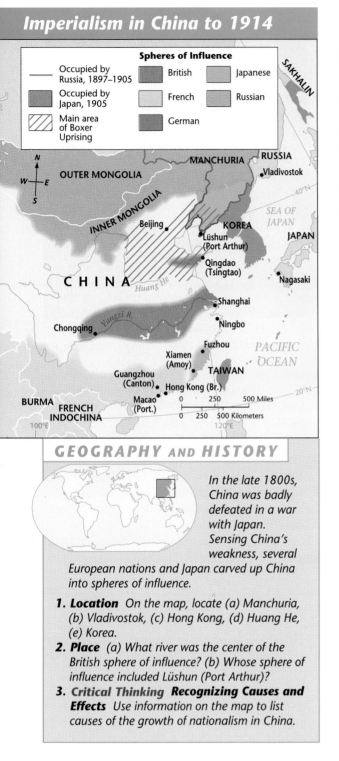

## Imperialism in China to 1914

**Spheres of Influence**

— Occupied by Russia, 1897–1905
▨ Occupied by Japan, 1905
▨ Main area of Boxer Uprising
■ British
☐ French
■ German
■ Japanese
■ Russian

### GEOGRAPHY AND HISTORY

In the late 1800s, China was badly defeated in a war with Japan. Sensing China's weakness, several European nations and Japan carved up China into spheres of influence.

1. **Location** On the map, locate (a) Manchuria, (b) Vladivostok, (c) Hong Kong, (d) Huang He, (e) Korea.
2. **Place** (a) What river was the center of the British sphere of influence? (b) Whose sphere of influence included Lüshun (Port Arthur)?
3. **Critical Thinking** *Recognizing Causes and Effects* Use information on the map to list causes of the growth of nationalism in China.

Peninsula in northern China. Russia received the Liaotung Peninsula (which the European powers had forced Japan to return to China), also in northern China.

The United States, a longtime trader with the Chinese, did not take part in the carving up of China. It feared that European powers might shut out American merchants. A few years later, in 1899, it called for a policy that would keep Chinese trade open to everyone on an equal basis. The imperial powers more or less accepted the idea of an Open Door Policy, as it came to be called. No one, however, consulted the Chinese about the policy.

**Hundred Days of Reform.** Defeated by Japan and humiliated by westerners, the Chinese looked for a scapegoat. Reformers blamed conservative officials for being "soundly asleep atop a pile of kindling." They argued that Confucius himself was a reformer and that China could not look to a golden age in the past but must modernize as Japan had.

In 1898, a young emperor, Guang Xu (gwawng SHYOO), launched the Hundred Days of Reform. New laws set out to modernize the civil service exams, streamline government, and encourage new industries. Reforms affected schools, the military, and the bureaucracy. Conservatives at court soon rallied. The emperor was imprisoned, and the aging empress Ci Xi reasserted control. Reformers fled for their lives.

## The Empire Crumbles

As the century ended, China was in turmoil. Anger against foreigners was growing. While the Chinese welcomed some western ideas, they resented Christian missionaries who belittled Chinese thinkers like Confucius. The presence of foreign troops was another source of discontent. Protected by extraterritoriality, foreigners could ignore Chinese laws and live in their own protected communities. In their parks, signs announced "Dogs and Chinese Not Allowed."

**Boxer Uprising.** Antiforeign feeling finally exploded in the Boxer Uprising. In 1899, a group of Chinese had formed a secret society, the Righteous Harmonious Fists. Westerners watching them train in the martial arts dubbed them Boxers. Their goal was to drive out the "foreign devils" who were polluting the land with their un-Chinese ways, strange buildings, machines, and telegraph lines. One group, called the Red Lantern, was made up primarily of young women. They carried red handkerchiefs and lanterns and were believed to have supernatural powers to stop foreign bullets.

**Father of Modern China** *Sun Yixian combined the ideas of Confucius with western ideas about religion, democracy, and socialism. His Three Principles of the People—nationalism, democracy, and economic security—became the guiding ideas of the Chinese republic.* **Global Interaction** *How did the thinking of Sun Yixian represent a global exchange of ideas?*

In 1900, the Boxers attacked foreign communities across China. In response, the western powers and Japan organized a multinational force. It crushed the Boxers and rescued foreigners besieged in Beijing. The empress Ci Xi had at first supported the Boxers but reversed her policy as they retreated.

**Aftermath.** China once again had to make concessions to foreigners. The defeat, however, forced even Chinese conservatives to support westernization. In a rush of reforms, China admitted women to schools and stressed science and mathematics in place of Confucian thought. More students were sent abroad to study.

China expanded economically, as well. Mining, shipping, railroads, banking, and exports of silk, tobacco, soybeans, and other commodities grew. With foreign capital, small-scale Chinese industry developed. A Chinese business class emerged, and a new urban working class began to press for rights as western workers had done.

**Three Principles of the People.** Although the Boxer Uprising failed, the flames of Chinese nationalism spread. Reformers wanted to strengthen China's government. By the early 1900s, they had introduced a constitutional monarchy. Some reformers called for a republic.

A passionate spokesman for a Chinese republic was Sun Yixian* (soon yee SHYAHN). Sun had studied and traveled in the West. In the early 1900s, he organized the Revolutionary Alliance. His goal was to rebuild China on "Three Principles of the People." The first principle was

nationalism, freeing China from foreign domination. The second was democracy, or representative government. The third was "livelihood," or economic security for all Chinese.

**Birth of a republic.** When Ci Xi died in 1908 and a two-year-old boy inherited the throne, China slipped into chaos. In 1911, uprisings in the provinces swiftly spread. Peasants, workers, students, local warlords, and even court politicians helped topple the dynasty and end China's 2,000-year-old monarchy.

Sun Yixian hurried home from a trip to the United States. In December 1911, he was named president of the new Chinese Republic. From the outset, the republic faced overwhelming problems. For the next 37 years, China was almost constantly at war with itself or fighting off foreign invasion.

## SECTION 5 REVIEW

1. **Identify** (a) Opium War, (b) Treaty of Nanjing, (c) Taiping Rebellion, (d) Ci Xi, (e) Open Door Policy, (f) Hundred Days of Reform, (g) Boxer Uprising, (h) Sun Yixian.
2. **Define** (a) balance of trade, (b) trade deficit, (c) indemnity, (d) extraterritoriality.
3. How did western powers gain rights in China?
4. What internal problems did the Qing dynasty face?
5. (a) What were the goals of Chinese reformers? (b) Why did they have a hard time putting their reforms into action?
6. *Critical Thinking* **Making Inferences** How was Britain's push into China linked to British imperialism in India?
7. *ACTIVITY* Organize a debate between a British merchant and a Chinese government official about the opium trade in China.

---

*In earlier history books, this name appears as Sun Yat-sen.

# Skills for Success

## Identifying Alternatives

Throughout history, nations have made choices about the future. To do so, they had to identify the alternatives and project the consequences.

In the mid-1800s, the Chinese were divided over whether or not to accept a proposal to invite westerners to teach mathematics and astronomy. The excerpts below present alternative responses. The first excerpt presents the views of Woren, tutor to the emperor. The second excerpt is by the Zongli Yamen, a government board that handled relations with the West. Read the excerpts and follow the steps to identify the alternatives and analyze their consequences.

**1 Identify the problem.** Before you can identify alternatives, you must identify the problem. (a) What is the issue that both excerpts address? (b) Who is presenting the alternative solutions?

**2 Identify alternative solutions.** (a) What solution does Woren propose? (b) What argument does he use to support his position? (c) What solution does the Zongli Yamen offer? (d) What should the Chinese do to strengthen themselves to meet the western challenge, according to the Zongli Yamen?

**3 Evaluate the arguments.** Examine the arguments used in presenting an alternative for "loaded" language or bias. (a) What phrase does Woren use to describe westerners? What does this phrase tell about his attitude toward westerners? (b) What impression does the Zongli Yamen hope to convey by characterizing their plan as "long-term policy"? (c) Why is it important that the decision maker be aware of hidden distortion or other bias?

**4 Project the consequences.** Every alternative will, if put into action, produce consequences—negative, positive, or both. (a) According to Woren, what will be the effect of western mathematics on China? (b) What does Woren believe is the only way to build a great nation? (c) What does the Zongli Yamen believe will result from adopting western technology and learning? (d) What does it think would be the consequence of Woren's proposed alternative of using propriety and righteousness to curb western influence in China?

## Beyond the Classroom

Select an issue in today's news. Identify at least two alternatives for dealing with the issue, and project their consequences. Write a paragraph supporting one alternative.

---

*Woren*

"Mathematics . . . should indeed be learned by scholars, . . . but astronomy and mathematics are of very little use. If these subjects are going to be taught by westerners as regular studies, the damage will be great. . . . [I have] learned that the way to establish a nation is to lay emphasis on propriety and righteousness. . . . If we seek trifling arts and respect barbarians as teachers, . . . all that can be accomplished is the training of mathematicians. From ancient to modern times, [I have] never heard of anyone who could use mathematics to raise the nation from a state of decline or to strengthen it in time of weakness."

*The Zongli Yamen*

"While merely to get along with [westerners] for the time being is all right, it is not possible in this way to protect ourselves for . . . decades to come. Therefore [we] have pondered a long-term policy. . . . Proposals to learn the written and spoken languages of foreign countries, the various methods of making machines, . . . the investigations of [foreign] customs and social conditions, . . . all these . . . represent nothing other than a struggle for self-strengthening.

Woren considers our action a hindrance. . . . If he has no other plan than to use . . . propriety and righteousness as a shield, and . . . if he says [this] could accomplish diplomatic negotiations and be sufficient to control the life of our enemies, your ministers do not . . . believe it."

---

Source: Ssu-yü Teng and John K. Fairbank, *China's Response to the West* (Cambridge, MA: Harvard University Press, 1954).

## Building Vocabulary

Review the vocabulary words in this chapter. Then, use *six* of these words to create a crossword puzzle. Exchange puzzles with a classmate. Complete the puzzles and then check each other's answers.

## Reviewing Chapter Themes

1. **Economics and Technology** Describe the relationship between the Industrial Revolution and the new imperialism.
2. **Global Interaction** (a) Describe how European nations extended their influence in *one* of the following regions of the world: Africa, the Middle East, China. (b) Why were Europeans able to extend their influence in this region?
3. **Political and Social Systems** (a) What forces were affecting the Muslim world in the 1800s? (b) How did Islamic reform movements seek to deal with the problems of the day? (c) Identify two effects of these reform efforts.
4. **Continuity and Change** (a) Identify one positive and one negative effect of British rule on the people of India. (b) How did the Indians turn western ideas against their western rulers?

## Thinking Critically

1. **Making Inferences** Why do you think people from all social classes in the West supported the new imperialism?
2. **Recognizing Bias** Western imperialists viewed European culture as "modern" and the culture of the rest of the world as "backward." How do you think nonwesterners might have responded to that view? ( ★ See *Skills for Success*, page 390.)
3. **Predicting Consequences** How do you think modernization might have occurred in Asia and Africa without interference by the imperialist powers? ( ★ See *Skills for Success*, page 974.)
4. **Linking Past and Present** The opening of the Suez Canal in 1869 transformed world trade. Why do you think  the canal might be less important today?
5. **Defending a Position** Do you think that the British were right to try to outlaw traditions such as the caste system and sati, which were an important part of Indians' religious beliefs? Defend your position.
6. **Analyzing Information** Western industrial nations colonized Africa and India in the 1800s. Why do you think they did not choose to colonize China?
7. **Synthesizing Information** Review the chart of the Chinese dynastic cycle on page 62. How did China in the 1800s reflect a downswing in the dynastic cycle? ( ★ See *Skills for Success*, page 896.)
8. **Comparing** Several nonwestern nations embarked on programs of western-style reform and modernization in the late 1800s. (a) Describe the reform efforts of *three* of the following: Ethiopia, Egypt, the Ottoman empire, China. (b) Compare the results of these efforts. Which succeeded and which failed? Why?

### *For Your Portfolio*

Imagine that your class has been asked to create a historical atlas for other world history students. Your atlas will be based on information in this chapter and will cover the years 1800 to 1914.

1. Meet with classmates to decide what maps to include in your atlas. Some possible map subjects: the Ottoman empire; the Central and East African slave trade; explorations of Mungo Park, Richard Burton, and David Livingstone; European colonies in Africa; Islamic revivals in Africa; newly independent nations in Eastern Europe; the Suez Canal; British rule in India; and European influence in China.
2. Use your textbook, atlases, encyclopedias, and other resources to prepare the maps. You might work in small groups to create each map. Remember to label all important places and to include standard map devices such as a scale of miles/kilometers, a directional arrow or compass rose, and any necessary legends.
3. Write a caption or short paragraph explaining the historical significance of each map. Be sure each map is dated and given a title.
4. Compile the finished maps into a historical atlas. Place the atlas in a resource center where other students can use it.

# New Global Patterns

## (1800–1914)

**CHAPTER OUTLINE**

1 Japan Modernizes
2 Southeast Asia and the Pacific
3 Self-Rule for Canada, Australia, and New Zealand
4 Economic Imperialism in Latin America
5 Impact of Imperialism

Siam—the land we now call Thailand—faced danger on all sides in the mid-1800s. Western powers were encircling the ancient kingdom, vying with one another for its control.

The burden of meeting this challenge fell to King Mongkut. Before inheriting the throne, he had been a Buddhist monk. During that time, he had studied foreign languages and read widely on modern science and mathematics. As king, he thus had a greater understanding of the West than many other Asian rulers. In a long letter to the Siamese ambassador in Paris, he mused on the problems facing their land:

66Being, as we now are, surrounded on two or three sides by powerful nations, what can a small nation like us do? Supposing we were to discover a gold mine in our country, from which we could obtain [much] gold, enough to buy a hundred warships. Even with this, we would still be unable to fight them, because we would have to buy those very same warships and all the armaments from them.99

Besides, Mongkut added, western powers could refuse to sell arms to Siam, and the Siamese could not yet make the weapons themselves.

Mongkut's solution was to modernize his country. From 1851 to 1868, he cautiously introduced political, economic, and social reforms. Later, his son, Chulalongkorn, picked up

the pace. While both had to grant some rights to western powers, Siam remained an independent kingdom during the Age of Imperialism.

In Chapter 25, you saw how Europeans competed for empire in Africa and parts of Asia. This chapter focuses on two related themes. First, how did people in different parts of the globe respond to western imperialism? Second, how did imperialism affect the cultures of these people?

**FOCUS ON** these themes as you read:

■ **Continuity and Change**
How did western domination threaten traditional cultures around the world?

■ **Economics and Technology**
How did imperialism create a new western-dominated world economy?

■ **Political and Social Systems**
Why did Latin American nations have a hard time achieving political stability?

■ **Diversity**
How did responses to imperialism differ in various parts of the world?

■ **Geography and History**
How did the migration of English-speaking people to Canada, Australia, and New Zealand shape their emergence as independent countries?

**TIME AND PLACE**

***Influence of the West*** *Japan was one of the few nations to escape western domination. It did so by copying the West, transforming itself into a modern industrial power set on its own imperialist path. This painting shows the gaslights at Japan's first industrial fair, in 1877.*
***Global Interaction*** *What evidence of western influence can you find in the painting?*

## HUMANITIES LINK

***Art History*** Maori wood carving (page 671).
***Literature*** In this chapter, you will encounter passages from the following works of literature: Fukuzawa Yukichi, *Autobiography* (pages 660 and 661); Rudyard Kipling, "The Ballad of East and West" (page 678).

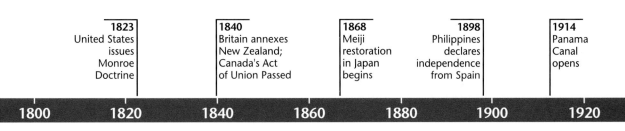

| | | | | |
|---|---|---|---|---|
| **1823**<br>United States<br>issues<br>Monroe<br>Doctrine | **1840**<br>Britain annexes<br>New Zealand;<br>Canada's Act<br>of Union Passed | **1868**<br>Meiji<br>restoration<br>in Japan<br>begins | **1898**<br>Philippines<br>declares<br>independence<br>from Spain | **1914**<br>Panama<br>Canal<br>opens |

| 1800 | 1820 | 1840 | 1860 | 1880 | 1900 | 1920 |
|---|---|---|---|---|---|---|

# 1 Japan Modernizes

## Guide for Reading

■ Why did Japan open its doors to western influences?

■ Why was Japan able to modernize rapidly?

■ How did Japan become an imperialist power?

■ **Vocabulary** *zaibatsu, homogeneous society*

In 1853, the United States displayed its new military might, sending a naval force to make Japan open its ports to trade. Japanese leaders debated how to respond. Some resisted giving up their 215-year-old policy of seclusion. "We should . . . observe the ways of our ancestors, which is the safest and most dignified policy for the country," they said.

Other Japanese disagreed. Lord Ii, for example, pointed out:

66[Foreign states] have invented the steamship . . . and introduced radical changes in the art of navigation. They have also built up their armies . . . and are possessed of weapons of great power and precision. . . . If we cling to our [outdated] systems, heaven only knows what disaster may befall our Empire.99

In the end, Japan chose to abandon its centuries of isolation. As a defense against western imperialism, it decided to learn from the West. It swiftly transformed itself into a modern industrial power and then set out on its own imperialist path.

## Strains in Tokugawa Japan

The Tokugawa shoguns, who had gained power in 1600, reimposed centralized feudalism, closed Japan to foreigners, and forbade Japanese to travel overseas. (See Chapter 15.) Their only window on the world was through Nagasaki, where the Dutch were allowed very limited trade.

For 215 years, Japan developed in near isolation. During that time, the economy expanded, especially internal commerce. But economic growth brought changes that put severe strains on the country.

Like China, Japan drifted into decline in the 1800s. Shoguns were no longer strong leaders, and corruption was common. Discontent simmered throughout Japanese society.

Daimyo suffered financial hardship because their wealth was in land. In a commercial economy, money was needed. Daimyo also had the heavy expense of maintaining households in both Edo and their own domains. Every other year, they traveled with their servants from one site to the other, a costly undertaking.

Lesser samurai were unhappy because they were no longer fighters. Many were government bureaucrats. Even though they were noble, they lacked the money to live as well as urban merchants.

For their part, merchants resented their place at the bottom of the social ladder. No matter how rich they were, they had no political power. Prestigious positions went only to nobles. Peasants, meanwhile, suffered under heavy taxes. Some fled to the cities. Others rose in rebellion.

The government responded by trying to revive old ways, emphasizing farming over commerce and extolling the virtues of simple moral values. Efforts at reform had scant success, which left many groups with little loyalty to the old system.

## Opening Up Japan

While the shogun faced troubles at home, disturbing news reached him from abroad. With alarm, he listened to reports of how the British had defeated China in the Opium War and how the imperialists had forced China to sign the unequal treaties. Surely, it would not be long before western powers began seeking trading rights in Japan.

**Foreign pressure.** Then, in July 1853, a fleet of well-armed American ships commanded by Commodore Matthew Perry sailed into Tokyo Bay. Perry had a letter from the President of the United States. It demanded that Japan open its ports to trade.

**Traditional Japan** *Before the 1850s, Japanese society developed largely in isolation from the western world. In this traditional Japanese painting, a woman inspects a piece of fine cloth.* **Global Interaction** *How do you think isolation might have affected Japanese attitudes toward foreigners?*

The shogun's advisers debated what to do. As Lord Ii noted, Japan did not have the ability to defend itself against the powerful United States Navy. In the Treaty of Kanagawa in 1854, the shogun agreed to open two Japanese ports to American ships, though not for trade.

The United States soon won trading and other rights, including the right of extraterritoriality and a "most favored nation" clause. (See page 650.) Britain, France, and Russia demanded and won similar rights. Like the Chinese, the Japanese deeply resented the humiliating terms of the unequal treaties. Some bitterly criticized the shogun for not taking a strong stand against the foreigners.

**Crisis and revolt.** Foreign pressure deepened the social and economic unrest. As the crisis worsened, many young, reform-minded samurai rallied around the emperor, long regarded as a figurehead. "Honor the emperor," "Expel the barbarian," were their cries.

In 1867, discontented daimyo and samurai led a revolt that unseated the shogun and "restored" the emperor to power. He moved from Kyoto, the old imperial capital, to the shogun's palace in Edo, which was renamed Tokyo, or "eastern capital."

**Meiji restoration.** The young emperor, just 15 years old, began a long reign. This period from 1868 to 1912, known as the Meiji (MAY jee) restoration, was a turning point in Japanese history.

Meiji means "enlightened rule." The Meiji reformers, who ruled in the emperor's name, were determined to strengthen Japan against the West. Their goal was summarized in their motto, "A rich country, a strong military."

The new leaders set out to study western ways, adapt them to Japanese needs, and eventually beat westerners at their own game. In 1871, members of the Meiji government traveled abroad to learn about western governments, economies, technology, and customs. The government brought western experts to Japan and sent young samurai to study in Europe and the United States.

## Fukuzawa Yukichi Travels Abroad

An early Japanese visitor to the West was Fukuzawa Yukichi. As a student, he had learned first Dutch and then English. In 1860, even before the Meiji restoration, he sailed on the first Japanese ship to cross the Pacific and visit California. Later, he traveled in Europe. In his *Autobiography,* he set out to explain western culture to the Japanese and Japanese culture to the West.

**Pride in Japan.** As the *Kanrin-Maru* set sail for the United States, Fukuzawa was filled with pride. The Japanese had seen their first steamship in 1853 when Commodore Perry arrived. Two years later, they began studying modern navigation. And in 1860, a Japanese steamship was crossing the Pacific. Fukuzawa marveled:

66This means that about seven years after the first sight of a steamship, after only about five years of practice, the Japanese made a trans-Pacific crossing without help from foreign experts. I think we can without undue pride boast before the world of this courage and skill. . . . Even Peter the Great of Russia, who went to Holland to study navigation . . . could not have equalled this feat of the Japanese.99

**Exploring a new world.** After 37 stormy days at sea, the *Kanrin-Maru* reached San Francisco. There, the Japanese visitors saw many unfamiliar sights. They were stunned to find the hotel floor covered with "valuable carpets that in Japan only the more wealthy could buy . . . at so much a square inch to make purses." Even more shocking, "Upon this costly fabric walked our hosts wearing shoes with which they had come in from the streets!" (At home, the Japanese, who highly value cleanliness, remove their shoes before entering a house.)

Among Fukuzawa's more confusing experiences were drinks served with "strange fragments floating in them." He told how "Some of the party swallowed these floating particles; others expelled them suddenly; others bravely chewed them." Upon closer inspection they

***A Japanese Student of Western Ways*** *Fukuzawa Yukichi was an early student of western ways. Among other things, he became a strong supporter of equality for women. "Society should give women the same rank as men," he wrote. Here, Fukuzawa poses with an American girl during his visit to the United States.* **Global Interaction** *Why did the Meiji government send people abroad to study western ways?*

learned that the particles were ice. "Hardly did we expect to find *ice* in the warm spring weather," they said.

Among many bewildering American customs was a dancing party. "To our dismay, we could not make out what they were doing. The ladies and gentlemen seemed to be hopping about the room together. As funny as it was, we knew it would be rude to laugh, and we controlled our expressions with difficulty as the dancing went on."

**Modern ways.** The Japanese examined telegraphs and visited a sugar refinery. Fukuzawa, however, was more interested in American life than in industry, which he had read about in books. He was stunned at the "enormous waste of iron everywhere":

> 66In garbage piles, on the seashores—everywhere—I found lying old oil tins, empty cans, and broken tools. This was remarkable to us, for in [Tokyo] after a fire, there would appear a swarm of people looking for nails in the ashes.99

Later, on a visit to Europe, Fukuzawa had his first view of democratic politics. In London, he tried to figure out how Parliament worked. He had read about "bands of men called political parties . . . who were always fighting against each other in the government." But he found it hard to understand how they could be "fighting in peacetime" and how "enemies in the House" could share a table and friendly talk in a restaurant. "It took me a long time, and some tedious thinking, before I could gather a general notion of these separate mysterious facts."

Individuals like Fukuzawa introduced the Japanese to the West and westerners to Japan. In a few generations, their efforts would help Japan become a global power.

## *Reforms Under the Meiji*

The Meiji reformers faced an enormous task. They were committed to replacing the rigid old feudal order with a new political and social system and to building a modern economy. Change did not come easily. It involved setbacks and confusion. In the end, however, Japan adapted foreign ideas with amazing success.

**Government.** The reformers wanted to create a strong central government, equal to those of western powers. After studying various European governments, they adapted the German model. In 1889, the emperor issued the Meiji constitution. It set forth the principle that all citizens were equal before the law. Like the German system, however, it gave the emperor autocratic power. A legislature, or Diet, was formed, made up of one elected house and one house appointed by the emperor. But its powers were strictly limited. Suffrage, too, was limited.

Japan then established a western-style bureaucracy with separate departments to supervise finance, the army, the navy, and education. To strengthen the military, it turned to western technology and ended the special privilege of samurai. In the past, samurai alone were warriors. In modern Japan, as in the modern West, all men were subject to military service.

**The economy.** Meiji leaders made the economy a major priority. They encouraged Japan's business class to adopt western methods. The government set up a banking system, built railroads, improved ports, and organized a telegraph and postal system.

> *A Textile Workshop* Japanese manufacturing grew rapidly in the late 1800s. As in Europe and the United States, women played a key role in Japan's industrial revolution. In this 1897 print, women make clothing in a Japanese workshop. ***Economics and Technology*** Which steps in the process seem to have been influenced by western technology?

To get industries started, the government typically built factories and then sold them to wealthy business families who developed them further. With such support, business dynasties like the Kawasaki family soon ruled over industrial empires that rivaled those of the Rockefellers in the United States or the Krupps in Germany. These powerful banking and industrial families were known as zaibatsu (ZĪ BAHT SOO).

By the 1890s, industry was booming. With modern machines, silk manufacturing soared. Shipyards, copper and coal mining, and steelmaking also helped make Japan an industrial powerhouse. As in other industrial countries, the population grew rapidly, and many peasants flocked to the growing cities for work.

**Social change.** The constitution, as you have seen, ended legal distinctions between classes, thus freeing people to build the nation. The government set up schools and a university. It hired westerners to teach the new generation modern technology.

Despite the reforms, class distinctions survived in Japan as they did in the West. Also, although literacy increased and some women gained an education, women in general were still assigned a secondary role in society.

The reform of the Japanese family system, and women's position in it, became the topic of major debates in the 1870s. Reformers wanted women to become full partners in the process of nation building and to learn skills that would allow them to live on their own. While the government agreed to some increases in education for women, it dealt harshly with other attempts at change. It passed laws reestablishing the most oppressive model of the family. It took away earlier political and legal rights that women had won. After 1898, Japanese women were forbidden any political participation and legally were lumped together with minors.

**Amazing success.** During the Meiji period, Japan modernized with amazing speed. Its success was due to a number of causes. It was a homogeneous society—that is, it had a common culture and language that gave it a strong sense of identity. Economic growth during Tokugawa times had set Japan on the road to development. Also, the Japanese had experience in learning from foreigners. Centuries before, they had selectively borrowed and adapted ideas from China.

Then, too, like other people faced with western imperialism, the Japanese were determined to resist foreign rule. In fact, in the 1890s, Japan was strong enough to force western powers to revise the unequal treaties. By then, it was already competing with the West and acquiring its own overseas empire.

## Competition for Empire

As with western industrial powers, Japan's economic needs fed its imperialist desires. A small island nation, Japan lacked many basic resources, including coal, essential for its industrial growth. Yet, spurred by nationalism and a strong ambition to equal the West, Japan built an empire. With its modern army and navy, it maneuvered for power in East Asia.

In 1894, rivalry between Japan and China over Korea led to war. Although China had far greater resources, Japan had benefited from modernization. To the surprise of China and the West, Japan won easily. It used its victory to gain treaty ports in China and rights to rule the island of Taiwan.

Ten years later, Japan successfully challenged Russia, its rival for power in Korea and Manchuria. (See the map on page 652.) During the Russo-Japanese War, Japan's armies defeated Russian troops in Manchuria, and its navy destroyed almost the entire Russian fleet. For the first time in modern history, an Asian power humbled a European nation. In the 1905 Treaty of Portsmouth, Japan gained control of Korea as well as rights in parts of Manchuria. This foothold on the mainland would fuel its ambitions in East Asia.

## Korea: A Focus of Competition

Imperialist rivalries put the spotlight on Korea. Located at a crossroads of East Asia, it was a focus of competition among Russia, China, and Japan. (See the map on page 321.)

**"A shrimp among whales."** Although Korea had long been influenced by its powerful Chinese neighbor, it had its own traditions and government. Like China and Japan, it had shut its doors to foreigners in early modern times. It

**Expanding in Asia** *Japan tested its new strength in wars against China and Russia. Here, Japanese troops occupy Seoul, Korea, during the Russo-Japanese War.* **Geography and History** *Why was Korea a focus of competition?*

ever before, but most of it went to feed the Japanese.

The Japanese were as unpopular in Korea as western imperialists were elsewhere. They imposed harsh rule on their colony and deliberately set out to erase the Korean language and identity. Repression bred resentment. And resentment, in turn, nourished a Korean nationalist movement.

Nine years after annexation, a nonviolent protest against the Japanese began on March 1, 1919, and soon spread throughout Korea. The Japanese crushed the uprising and massacred many Koreans. The March First Movement became a rallying symbol for Korean nationalists.

**Looking ahead.** The Koreans would have to wait many years for freedom. By the early 1900s, Japan was the strongest power in Asia. In competition with western nations, it continued to expand in East Asia during the years ahead. In time, Japanese ambitions to control a sphere of influence in the Pacific would put it on a collision course with several western powers, especially Britain and the United States.

did, however, maintain relations with China and sometimes with Japan.

By the 1800s, Korea faced growing pressure from outsiders. As Chinese power declined, Russia expanded into East Asia. Then, as Japan industrialized, it too eyed Korea. Once again, Korea saw itself as "a shrimp among whales."

In 1876, Japan used its superior power to force Korea to open its ports to Japanese trade. Faced with similar demands from western powers, the Hermit Kingdom had to accept humiliating unequal treaties.

As Japan extended its influence in Korea, it came into conflict with China, which still saw Korea as a tributary state. After defeating China and then Russia, Japan made Korea a protectorate. In 1910, it annexed Korea outright, ending Korean independence and absorbing the kingdom into the Japanese empire.

**Japanese rule.** Japan ruled Korea for 35 years. Like western imperialists, the Japanese set out to modernize their possession. They built factories, railroads, and communications systems in Korea. Development, however, generally benefited the colonial power, Japan. Under Japanese rule, Koreans produced more rice than

## SECTION 1 REVIEW

1. **Identify** (a) Matthew Perry, (b) Treaty of Kanagawa, (c) Meiji restoration, (d) Russo-Japanese War.
2. **Define** (a) zaibatsu, (b) homogeneous society.
3. (a) What problems did Tokugawa Japan face in the early 1800s? (b) Why did Japan end 200 years of seclusion?
4. (a) List three ways in which Japan modernized. (b) Explain how each helped strengthen Japan so that it could resist western pressure.
5. Why did Japan want to build an overseas empire?
6. *Critical Thinking* **Predicting Consequences** What do you think might have happened if Japan had not rushed to modernize in the late 1800s? Give reasons for your answer.
7. *ACTIVITY* Write a dialogue between two advisers to the shogun giving arguments for and against opening up Japan to the West in the mid-1800s.

# Southeast Asia and the Pacific

## Guide for Reading

- ■ What effect did imperialist rivalries have on Southeast Asia?

- ■ Why was Thailand able to remain independent?

- ■ How did the United States expand in the Pacific?

A Vietnamese official, Phan Thanh Gian, faced a dilemma in 1867. The French were threatening to invade. As a patriot, Phan Thanh Gian wanted to resist. But as a devoted follower of Confucius, he was obliged "to live in obedience to reason." And based on the facts, he concluded that the only reasonable course was to surrender:

66 The French have immense warships,
filled with soldiers and armed with
huge cannons. No one can resist them.
They go where they want, the
strongest [walls] fall before them. 99

Phan Thanh Gian made his choice with a heavy heart. By avoiding a useless war that would hurt his people, he became a traitor to his king. For that decision, he wrote, "I deserve death."

Leaders throughout Southeast Asia faced the same dilemma during the Age of Imperialism. As they had in Africa, western industrial powers gobbled up the region in their relentless race for raw materials, new markets, and Christian converts.

## Colonizing Southeast Asia

Southeast Asia commanded the sea lanes between India and China and had long been influenced by both civilizations. In the 1500s and 1600s, European merchants gained footholds in the region, but most of the Southeast Asian peoples remained independent. When the Industrial Revolution set off the Age of Imperial-

ism in the 1800s, the situation changed. Westerners played off local rivalries and used their modern armies and technology to colonize much of Southeast Asia.

**Dutch colonies.** In the 1600s, the Dutch East India Company gained control of the fabled riches of the Moluccas, or Spice Islands. (See the map on page 384.) They then reached out to dominate the rest of Indonesia. The Dutch expected their Southeast Asian colonies to produce profitable crops of coffee and indigo as well as spices.

**British inroads.** In the early 1800s, rulers of Burma (present-day Myanmar) clashed with the British, who were expanding eastward from India. At first, the Burmese misjudged British strength. In several wars, they suffered disastrous defeats. By the 1880s, Britain had annexed Burma as part of its Indian empire. The Burmese, however, constantly resisted British rule.

The British also pushed south through the Malay Peninsula. The bustling port of Singapore, on the sea route between the Indian Ocean and the China Sea, grew up at the southern tip of Malaya. Soon, rubber and tin from Malaya along with profits from Asian trade were flowing through Singapore to enrich Britain.

**French Indochina.** The French meanwhile were building an empire on the Southeast Asian mainland. In the early 1800s, French missionaries began winning converts in what is today Vietnam. The region had long been influenced by Confucian traditions. Vietnamese officials tried to suppress Christianity by killing converts and missionary priests.

As with Burma and the British, the Vietnamese misjudged European power. In the 1860s, the French invaded and seized a chunk of Vietnam. Over the next decades, they added more lands, eventually seizing all of Vietnam, Laos, and Cambodia. The French and other westerners referred to these holdings as French Indochina.

**European rule.** By the 1890s, Europeans controlled most of Southeast Asia. They introduced modern technology and expanded commerce and industry. They set up new enterprises to mine tin and harvest rubber, brought in new crops of corn and cassava, and built harbors and railroads. But as you will read later in this chap-

**The French in Indochina** By the 1890s, France controlled most of modern-day Vietnam, Cambodia, and Laos. The French allowed local rulers to keep their titles but forced them to give key powers to colonial officials. At left, a French colonial governor meets with the king of Laos. The king is dressed in traditional clothes but wears a pair of western-style shoes. Below, a Laotian man pulls a French woman in a rickshaw. The rickshaw was based on a French vehicle. It was introduced to Japan by missionaries in the late 1800s and spread to other parts of East and Southeast Asia. **Political and Social Systems** Why do you think the French allowed rulers to keep their titles?

ter, these changes benefited Europeans far more than the people of Southeast Asia.

Many Chinese migrated to Southeast Asia to escape hardship and turmoil at home and to benefit from growing economic opportunities. Despite local resentment, these communities of "overseas" Chinese formed vital networks in trade, banking, and other economic activities.

## Thailand Survives

Sandwiched between British-ruled Burma and French Indochina lay the kingdom of Siam. As you have read at the beginning of this chapter, Siam escaped becoming a European colony partly because its rulers did not underestimate western power and avoided incidents that might provoke invasion.

Although King Mongkut had to accept some unequal treaties, he set Siam on the road to modernization. He and his son, Chulalongkorn, who ruled from 1868 to 1910, reformed government, modernized the army, and hired western experts to train Thais in the new technology. They abolished slavery and gave

women some choice in marriage. Thai students traveled abroad and spread western ways when they returned home. As Siam modernized, Chulalongkorn bargained to remove the unequal treaties.

In the end, both Britain and France saw the advantage of making Thailand a buffer, or neutral zone, between them. In the early 1900s, they guaranteed its independence. But then, to stop other imperialist powers from pushing into Siam, each set up its own sphere of influence there.

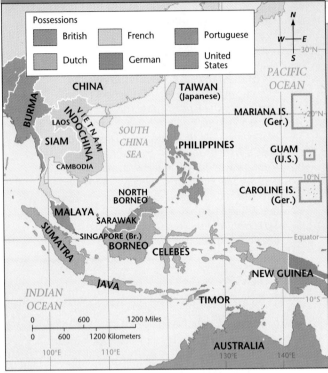

## Imperialism in Southeast Asia and the Pacific

**Possessions**

- British
- Dutch
- French
- German
- Portuguese
- United States

### GEOGRAPHY AND HISTORY

The lure of spices first brought Europeans to Southeast Asia. Then the Industrial Revolution spurred European traders to search for raw materials to fuel the new industries. In Southeast Asia, they found such products as tin and rubber.

1. **Location** On the map, locate (a) New Guinea, (b) Siam, (c) Singapore, (d) Philippines (e) Indochina.
2. **Region** Which European countries claimed territory on the mainland?
3. **Critical Thinking** **Synthesizing information** Review the discussion of earlier encounters between Europeans and the peoples of Southeast Asia, on pages 382–384. Based on that information, why do you think the Dutch controlled the largest area in Southeast Asia around 1914?

## Imperialism and Nationalism in the Philippines

In the 1500s, Spain had seized the Philippines and extended its rule over the islands. Catholic missionaries spread Christianity among the Filipinos, and the Catholic Church gained enormous power and wealth. Many Filipinos accused the Church of abusing its position. By the late 1800s, their anger had fueled strong resistance to Spanish rule.

The United States became involved in the fate of the Philippines almost by accident. In 1898, war broke out between Spain and the United States over Cuba's independence from Spain. (See page 677.) During the Spanish-American War, American battleships destroyed the Spanish fleet which was stationed in the Philippines. Seizing the moment, Filipino leaders declared their independence from Spain. Rebel soldiers threw their support into the fight against Spanish troops.

In return for their help, the Filipino rebels had expected the Americans to recognize their independence. The peace settlement with Spain, however, placed the Philippines under American control.

Bitterly disappointed, Filipino nationalists renewed their struggle. From 1899 to 1901, Filipinos led by Emilio Aguinaldo (ah gee NAHL doh) battled American forces. Thousands of Americans and hundreds of thousands of Filipinos died. In the end, the Americans crushed the rebellion. The United States set out to modernize the Philippines, promising Filipinos self-rule some time in the future.

## Western Powers in the Pacific

In the 1800s, the industrial powers began to take an interest in the islands of the Pacific.* At first, American, French, and British whaling and sealing ships looked for bases to take on supplies. Missionaries, too, moved into the Pacific region. As in Africa, they opened the way for political involvement.

**Samoa.** In 1878, the United States secured an "unequal treaty" from Samoa, gaining rights such as extraterritoriality and a naval sta-

---

*The thousands of islands splashed across the Pacific are known as Oceania. Besides Australia and New Zealand, Oceania includes three regions: Melanesia, Micronesia, and Polynesia. (See the map on page 994.)

tion. Other nations gained similar agreements. As their rivalry increased, the United States, Germany, and Britain agreed to a triple protectorate over Samoa.

**Hawaii.** From the mid-1800s, American sugar growers pressed for power in Hawaii. When the Hawaiian queen Liliuokalani (lee lee oo oh kah LAH nee) tried to reduce foreign influence, American planters overthrew her in 1893. They then asked the United States to annex Hawaii, which it did in 1898. Supporters of annexation argued that if the United States did not take Hawaii, Britain or Japan might do so.

**Looking ahead.** By 1900, the United States, Britain, France, and Germany had claimed nearly every island in the Pacific. Japan, too, wanted a share of the region. Eventually, it would gain German possessions in the Pacific, setting the stage for a growing rivalry with the United States.

▲ *Queen Liliuokalani*

## SECTION 2 REVIEW

**1. Identify** (a) French Indochina, (b) Chulalongkorn, (c) Emilio Aguinaldo, (d) Queen Liliuokalani.

**2.** (a) Which European nations set up colonies in Southeast Asia? (b) What products did they take from these colonies?

**3.** What steps did Thailand take to preserve its independence?

**4.** How did the United States acquire each of the following: (a) Philippines, (b) Samoa, (c) Hawaii?

**5. Critical Thinking Comparing** Compare the partition of Southeast Asia to the partition of Africa during the Age of Imperialism. (a) How was it similar? (b) How was it different?

**6. ACTIVITY** Create a map and time line showing colonization of Southeast Asia and the Pacific during the Age of Imperialism.

## 3 Self-Rule for Canada, Australia, and New Zealand

### Guide for Reading

- How did Canada achieve self-rule?
- How did Australia and New Zealand emerge as independent nations?
- What effects did colonization have on the Aborigines and Maoris?

■ **Vocabulary** *indigenous, penal colony*

The pattern of imperialism in the British colonies of Australia and New Zealand differed from that in other parts of the world. The indigenous (ihn DIHJ uh nuhs), or original, inhabitants of these regions were relatively few in number, and white settlers quickly subdued and replaced them. Still, the process of "replacement" was as deadly as it had been when Europeans settled the Americas some 200 years earlier.

These two English-speaking colonies, as well as Canada, won independence faster and with greater ease than England's territories in Africa or Asia. One reason was that nonwestern peoples had no cultural roots in western-style government. However, western racial attitudes also played a part. Imperialist nations like Britain felt that whites could govern themselves. Nonwhites in places like India were thought to be incapable of shouldering such responsibility.

### The Canadian Pattern

Canada's first European rulers, you will recall, were the French. (See page 401.) When France lost Canada to Britain in 1763, thousands of French-speaking settlers remained there. After the American Revolution, an estimated 30,000 or more colonists who had remained loyal to Britain fled to Canada. Unlike the French-speaking Catholics, the newcomers were English-speaking and Protestant. Rivalries between the two groups have been an ongoing theme in Canada's history ever since.

**A Blending of Cultures** *Canadian culture blends English, French, and Native American traditions. This is the symbol of the "Mounties," the Canadian mounted police, formed in 1873. The crown stands for the British monarchy, while the buffalo and maple leaves represent the Americas.* **Diversity** *How does the Mounties' symbol reflect Canada's French heritage?*

Native Americans formed another strand of the Canadian heritage. In the 1790s, various Native American people still lived in eastern Canada. Others remained largely undisturbed by white settlers in the west and north.

**The two Canadas.** To ease ethnic tensions, Britain passed the Canada Act in 1791. It created two provinces: English-speaking Upper Canada (now Ontario) and French-speaking Lower Canada (now Quebec). Each had its own laws, legislature, and royal governor. French traditions and the Catholic Church were protected in Lower Canada, while English traditions and laws guided Upper Canada.

During the early 1800s, unrest grew in both colonies. The people of Upper Canada resented the power held by a small British elite. In Lower Canada, too, people felt that British officials ignored their needs. In 1837, discontent flared into rebellion in both Upper and Lower Canada. "Put down the villains who oppress and enslave our country," cried William Lyon Mackenzie, a leader of the Upper Canada revolt.

**The Durham Report.** The British had learned a lesson from the American Revolution. While they hurried to put down the disorder, they sent an able politician, Lord Durham, to study the causes of the unrest. In 1839, the Durham Report called for the two Canadas to be reunited and given control over their own affairs.

In 1840, Parliament passed the Act of Union, a major step toward self-government. It gave Canada an elected legislature to determine domestic policies. Britain kept control of foreign policy and trade.

**Dominion of Canada.** Like the United States, Canada expanded westward in the 1800s. Two Canadians, John Macdonald and George Etienne Cartier, urged confederation, or unification, of all Canada's provinces. Like many Canadians, Macdonald and Cartier feared that the United States might try to dominate Canada. A strong union, they felt, would strengthen Canada against American ambitions and help it develop economically.

Britain finally agreed. In 1867, it passed the British North America Act of 1867, creating the Dominion of Canada. It united four provinces in a self-governing nation. Six additional provinces joined the union in later years.

As a dominion, Canada had its own parliament, modeled on Britain's. By 1900 it had some control over its own foreign policy. Still, although self-governing, Canada maintained close ties with the British monarchy.

**Expansion.** John Macdonald, Canada's first prime minister, encouraged expansion across the continent. To unite the far-flung regions of Canada, he called for a transcontinental railroad. In 1885, the Canadian Pacific Railway opened, linking eastern and western Canada. Wherever the railroad went, settlers followed. It moved people and products, such as timber and manufactured goods, across the country.

As in the United States, westward expansion destroyed the way of life of Native Americans in Canada. Most were forced to sign treaties giving up their lands. Some resisted. Louis Riel led a revolt of the Métis, people of mixed Native American and European descent. Many were French-speaking Catholics who accused the government of stealing their land and trying to destroy their language and religion. Govern-

# Geography of Australia and New Zealand

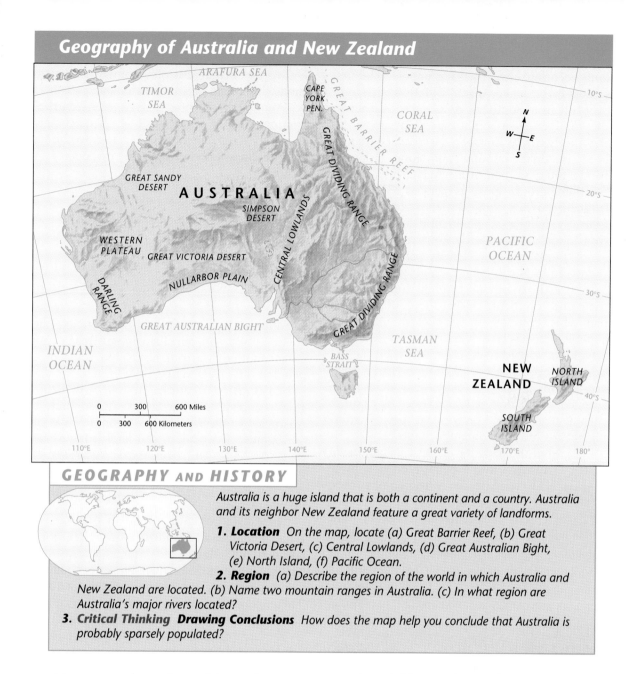

## GEOGRAPHY AND HISTORY

Australia is a huge island that is both a continent and a country. Australia and its neighbor New Zealand feature a great variety of landforms.

1. **Location** On the map, locate (a) Great Barrier Reef, (b) Great Victoria Desert, (c) Central Lowlands, (d) Great Australian Bight, (e) North Island, (f) Pacific Ocean.
2. **Region** (a) Describe the region of the world in which Australia and New Zealand are located. (b) Name two mountain ranges in Australia. (c) In what region are Australia's major rivers located?
3. **Critical Thinking** **Drawing Conclusions** How does the map help you conclude that Australia is probably sparsely populated?

ment troops put down the uprising and executed Riel.

**Immigration.** In the late 1800s and early 1900s, immigrants flooded into Canada from Europe and Asia. Newcomers from Germany, Italy, Poland, Russia, Ukraine, China, and Japan enriched Canada economically and culturally.

By 1914, Canada was a flourishing nation. Still, two issues plagued Canada. First, French-speaking Canadians desperately tried to preserve their separate heritage, making it hard for Canadians to create a single national identity. Second, the United States exerted a powerful economic and cultural influence that threatened to domi-nate its neighbor to the north. Both issues have continued to affect Canada to the present day. (See Chapter 33.)

## Europeans in Australia

The Dutch in the 1600s were the first Europeans to reach Australia—the world's smallest continent. In 1770, Captain James Cook claimed Australia for Britain. For a time, however, it remained too distant to attract European settlers.

**The first settlers.** Like most regions claimed by imperialist powers, Australia had long been inhabited by other people. The first settlers had reached Australia 50,000 years ago, probably from Southeast Asia, and spread across the continent. Cut off from the larger world, the Aborigines, as Europeans later called them,* lived in small hunting and food-gathering bands, much as their Stone Age ancestors had. Aborigine groups spoke as many as 250 distinct languages. When white settlers arrived in Australia, the indigenous population suffered disastrously, just as it had in the Americas.

**A penal colony.** Events halfway around the world in North America and Britain ended Australia's isolation and brought Europeans to the island continent. During the 1700s, Britain had sent convicts to its North American colonies, especially to Georgia. The American Revolution closed that outlet just when the Industrial Revolution was disrupting British society. Prisons in London and other cities were jammed with poor people arrested for crimes such as stealing food or goods to pawn, agitating against the government, or murder.

To fulfill the need for prisons, Britain made Australia into a penal colony, a place to send people convicted of crimes. The first ships, carrying about 700 convicts, arrived in Botany Bay, Australia, in 1788. The men,

▼ Convicts arriving at an Australian penal colony

women, and children who survived the grueling eight-month voyage faced more hardships on shore. Many were city dwellers with no farming skills.

---

*Aborigine* was a word used by Europeans to denote the earliest people to live in a place. Today, many Australian Aborigines call themselves Kooris.

Under the brutal discipline of soldiers, work gangs cleared land for the settlement.

Among these first arrivals was Matthew Everingham, who at the age of 14 had been given a seven-year sentence for stealing two books. Despite illness and beatings, he dreamed of the future:

❝I have now two years and seven months to remain a convict and then I am at liberty to act as a free-born Englishman ought to. . . . I am yet but young, only 19. If my health is spared I shall not be one jot the worse for being transported.❞

Everingham later married another convict, Elizabeth Rimes, and remained in Australia. Their descendants carved out farms and some prospered in their rugged new homeland.

**Into the Outback.** In the early 1800s, Britain encouraged free citizens to emigrate to Australia by offering them land and tools. As the newcomers occupied coastal lands, they thrust aside or killed the Aborigines. After settlers found that sheep herding was suited to the land and climate, a prosperous wool industry grew up in Australia.

In 1851, gold was found in eastern Australia. The resulting gold rush brought a population boom. Many gold hunters stayed on to become ranchers and farmers. They pushed into the rugged interior known as the Outback. There, too, they displaced the Aborigines and carved out huge sheep ranches and wheat farms. By the late 1800s, Australia had won a place in a growing world economy.

**Achieving self-government.** Like Canada, Australia was made up of separate colonies scattered around the continent. During the Age of Imperialism, Britain worried about interfer-

**GLOBAL CONNECTIONS**

European nations often punished people convicted of crimes by sending them to far-off places. Russia sent convicts to Siberia. France created a penal colony on Devil's Island, off the coast of South America. Before they hit upon Australia, the British tried to make West Africa a dumping ground for "undesirable" citizens.

ence from other powers. To counter this threat and to boost development, it responded to Australian demands for self-rule. In 1901, Britain helped the colonies unite into the independent Commonwealth of Australia. The new country kept its ties to Britain by recognizing the British monarch as its head of state.

The Australian constitution drew on both British and American models. Like the United States Constitution, it set up a federal system that limited the power of the central government. Its Parliament has a Senate and House of Representatives, but its executive is a prime minister chosen by the majority party in Parliament. Unlike Britain and the United States, Australia quickly granted women the right to vote. It also was the first nation to introduce the secret ballot.

## New Zealand

Far to the southeast of Australia lies New Zealand. In 1769, Captain Cook claimed its islands for Britain. Missionaries landed there in 1814 to convert the local people, the Maoris, to Christianity.

**Maori struggles.** Unlike Australia, where the Aborigines were spread thinly across a large continent, the Maoris were concentrated in a smaller area. They were descended from seafaring people who had reached New Zealand from Polynesia in the 1200s. Unlike the nomadic Aborigines, the Maoris were settled farmers. They were also a warlike people, determined to defend their land.

Missionaries were followed by white settlers, attracted by the mild climate and good soil. They introduced sheep and cattle and were soon exporting wool, mutton, and beef. In 1840,

**Maori Wood Carving** *Wood carving was a highly respected art among the Maoris. Carved figures served a religious function, affirming a community's ties to its gods and ancestors. The head was given special prominence because the Maoris believed that the soul resided in the head. The intricate curving surface designs imitate the tattoos worn by Maori people. This figure stood outside a Maori meeting house.* **Art and Literature** *Review the Art History lesson on page 243. How did Maori wood carvings and Byzantine icons serve a similar function?*

Britain annexed New Zealand. The move was designed in part to keep out other imperialist powers.

As colonists poured in, they took over more and more of the land, leading to fierce wars with the Maoris. Many Maoris died in the struggle. Still more perished from disease, alcoholism, and other misfortunes that came with European colonization.

By the 1870s, resistance crumbled. The Maori population had fallen drastically, from 250,000 to less than 50,000. Only in recent years has the Maori population started to grow once more.

**Self-government.** Like settlers in Australia and Canada, white New Zealanders sought self-rule. In 1907, they won independence, with their own parliament, prime minister, and elected legislature. They, too, preserved close ties to the British empire.

New Zealand pioneered in several areas of democratic government. In 1893, it became the first nation to give suffrage to women. Later, it was in the forefront of other social reforms, passing laws to guarantee old-age pensions and a minimum wage for all workers.

## SECTION 3 REVIEW

1. **Identify** (a) Upper Canada, (b) Lower Canada, (c) John Macdonald, (d) British North America Act, (e) Aborigines, (f) Maoris.
2. **Define** (a) indigenous, (b) penal colony.
3. (a) How did ethnic tensions affect Canada? (b) What steps led to Canadian self-rule?
4. (a) Who were the first white settlers in Australia? (b) What traditions influenced Australian government?
5. (a) Why did Maoris fight colonists in New Zealand? (b) What democratic advances were made by New Zealand?
6. *Critical Thinking* **Analyzing Information** Why might young nations like Australia and New Zealand have been willing to grant women the right to vote before European nations did so?
7. *ACTIVITY* Imagine you are a teenage prisoner who was transported to Australia. Write a short story about your experiences.

# 4 Economic Imperialism in Latin America

## Guide for Reading

- What problems did Latin American nations face in the 1800s?
- How were Latin American nations linked to the world economy?
- How did the United States gain influence in Latin America?
- **Vocabulary** *regionalism, caudillo, economic dependence, peonage*

During the Age of Imperialism, Latin American nations found their economies increasingly dependent on those of more developed countries. Britain, and later the United States, invested heavily in Latin America. Both then intervened to protect their interests there.

## Problems Facing the New Nations

Simón Bolívar had hoped to create strong ties among the nations of Latin America. After all, most people shared a common language, religion, and cultural heritage. But feuds among leaders, geographic barriers, and local nationalism shattered that dream. In the end, 20 separate nations emerged. (See the map on page 542.)

These new nations wrote constitutions modeled on that of the United States. They set up republics with elected legislatures. During the 1800s, however, most Latin American nations were plagued by revolts, civil war, and dictatorships.

**Colonial legacy.** Many problems had their origins in colonial rule. Spain and Portugal had kept tight control on their colonies, giving them little experience with self-government. The wars of independence barely changed the colonial hierarchy. Creoles simply replaced peninsulares as the new ruling class. The Roman Catholic Church kept its privileged position and still controlled huge amounts of land.

For most people—mestizos, mulattoes, blacks, and Indians—life did not improve after independence. The new constitutions guaranteed equality before the law, but deep-rooted inequalities remained. Voting rights were limited. Racial prejudice was widespread, and land remained in the hands of a few. Owners of haciendas ruled their great estates, and the peasants who worked them, like medieval European lords.

**Instability.** With few roads and no tradition of unity, the new nations were weakened by regionalism, loyalty to a local area. Local strongmen, called caudillos, assembled private armies to resist the central government. At times, popular caudillos gained national power. They looted the treasury and ignored the constitution. Supported by the military, they ruled as dictators.

Power struggles led to frequent revolts that changed little except the name of the leader. In the long run, power remained in the hands of a privileged few who had no desire to share it.

As in Europe, the ruling elite in Latin America was divided between conservatives and liberals. (See pages 536–537.) Conservatives defended the old social order, favored press censorship, and strongly supported the Catholic Church. Liberals backed laissez-faire economics, religious toleration, and freedom of the press. They wanted to weaken the Catholic Church by breaking up its landholdings and ending its

**The Caudillo**
In many Latin American countries, caudillos won power by appealing to the masses. "I am one of you, poor and humble," one caudillo declared. Once in power, however, caudillos usually followed policies that helped the rich. **Political and Social Systems** What factors hindered growth of democratic self-government in Latin America?

monopoly on education. Liberals saw themselves as enlightened supporters of progress but often showed little concern for the needs of the majority of the people.

## The Economics of Dependence

Under colonial rule, mercantilist policies made Latin America economically dependent on Spain and Portugal. Colonies sent raw materials such as sugar, cotton, or precious metals to the parent country and had to buy manufactured goods from them. Strict laws kept colonists from trading with other countries or building local industries that might compete with the parent country.

After independence, this pattern changed very little. The new republics did adopt free trade, welcoming all comers. Britain and the United States rushed into the new markets, replacing Spain as the chief trading partner in Latin America. But Latin America remained as economically dependent as before.

Economic dependence occurs when less developed nations export raw materials and commodities to industrial nations and import manufactured goods, capital, and technological know-how. The relationship is unequal because the more developed nation controls prices and the terms of trade.

**Foreign influence.** In the 1800s, foreign goods flooded into Latin America, creating large profits for foreigners and for a handful of local business people. At mid-century, an American diplomat described how British capital and goods were everywhere in Brazil. "British pottery, British articles of glass, iron or wood," he wrote, "are as common as woolens and cotton cloth." He then continued:

66Great Britain supplies Brazil with its steam and sailing ships, and paves and repairs its streets, lights its cities with gas, builds its railways, exploits its mines, is its banker, puts up its telegraph wires, carries its mail, builds its furniture, motors, and wagons.99

Foreign investment, which could yield enormous profits, was often accompanied by interference. British, American, or other investors might pressure their own governments to take action if political events or reform movements in a Latin American country seemed to threaten their interests.

**Economic growth.** After 1850, some Latin American economies did grow. With foreign capital, they developed mining and agriculture. Chile exported copper and nitrates, while Argentina expanded livestock and wheat growing. Brazil added coffee and rubber to its traditional export crop of sugar. By the early 1900s, Venezuela and Mexico were developing important oil industries.

Throughout the region, foreigners invested in modern ports and railroads to carry goods from the interior to coastal cities. As in the United States, European immigrants flooded into Latin America. The newcomers helped to promote economic activity, and a small middle class emerged.

Thanks to trade, investment, technology, and migration, Latin American nations moved into the world economy. Yet development was limited. Local industries grew slowly, in part because of the social structure. The tiny elite at the top benefited from the economic upturn. Their wealth grew, but very little trickled down to the masses of people at the bottom. The poor earned too little to buy consumer goods. Without a strong demand, many industries failed to develop.

## Mexico's Struggle for Stability

During the 1800s, each Latin American country followed its own course. In this section, we will explore the experiences of Mexico as an example of the challenges facing Latin American nations.

Large landowners, army leaders, and the Catholic Church dominated Mexican politics. However, bitter battles between conservatives and liberals led to revolts and the rise of dictators. Deep social divisions separated wealthy creoles from mestizos and Indians who lived in desperate poverty.

**Santa Anna.** Between 1833 and 1855, an ambitious and cunning caudillo, Antonio López de Santa Anna, gained and lost power many times. At first, he posed as a liberal reformer. Soon, however, he reversed his stand and crushed efforts at reform.

In Mexico's northern territory of Texas, discontent against Santa Anna grew. Settlers from the United States began an independence movement. In 1835, American settlers and some Mexicans in Texas revolted and the next year set up an independent republic. In 1845, the United States annexed Texas. Mexicans were outraged by this act, which they saw as a declaration of war. In the fighting that followed, the United States invaded Mexico. In Mexico City, young military cadets fought to the death rather than surrender.

Despite the bravery of these "boy heroes," Mexico lost the Mexican War. And in the treaty ending the war, it lost almost half its territory. This defeat shook the creole ruling class and triggered new violence between conservatives and liberals.

**La Reforma.** In 1855, Benito Juárez (WAHR ehz) and other liberals seized power, opening La Reforma, an era of reform. Juárez, a Zapotec Indian, offered hope to the oppressed people of Mexico. He and his fellow reformers revised the Mexican constitution to strip the military of power and end the special privileges of the Church. They ordered the Church to sell unused lands to peasants.

Conservatives resisted La Reforma, unleashing a civil war. In 1861, Juárez was elected president. He used his new office to expand reforms. His wealthy opponents turned to Europe for help. In 1863, Napoleon III sent troops to Mexico and set up Austrian archduke Maximilian as Mexican emperor. (See page 617.)

For four years, Juárez led Mexicans in battle against conservative and French forces. When France withdrew its troops, Maximilian was captured and shot. In 1867, Juárez was returned to power. Although he tried to renew reform, opponents resisted. Juárez, who died in office in 1872, never achieved all the reforms he envisioned. He did, however, help unite Mexico, bring mestizos into political life, and separate church and state.

**"Order and Progress."** After Juárez died, General Porfirio Díaz, a hero of the war against the French, gained power. From 1876 to 1880 and 1884 to 1911, he ruled as a dictator. In the name of "Order and Progress," he strengthened the army, local police, and central government. Any opposition was brutally crushed.

## Cowboys

In South America as in the western United States, cowboys became folk heroes. From Argentina to Mexico, *gauchos* and *vaqueros* herded cattle on the rugged frontier. The heyday of the cowboy was brief, but the cowboy lives on in songs, novels, films, and television shows.

**Linking Past and Present**  Cowboy legends became popular at a time when the open frontier was disappearing in both South and North America. Why did cowboys become heroes at such a time? Why are they still popular?

**PAST**  The story of *Martín Fierro* fascinated the people of Argentina in the 1870s. The hero, a gaucho, told of his adventures on the vast plains of central Argentina.

**PRESENT**  In the United States, "westerns" once dominated both movies and television. *The Virginian* was a best-selling novel at the turn of the century, a hit movie in 1929, and a popular television show in the 1960s. Westerns have made a comeback in recent years with the success of *Wyatt Earp,* below, and other movies.

---

Under his harsh rule, Mexico made impressive economic advances. It built railroads, increased foreign trade, developed some industry, and expanded mining. Growth, however, had a high cost. Capital for development came from foreign investors, to whom Díaz granted special rights. He also let wealthy landowners buy up Indian lands.

The rich prospered, but most Mexicans continued in grinding poverty. Many Indians and mestizos fell into peonage to their employers. In the peonage system, hacienda owners would give workers advances on their wages and require them to stay on the hacienda until they had paid back what they owed. Wages remained low, and workers were rarely able to repay the hacienda owner. Many children died in infancy. Others worked 12-hour days and never learned to read or write.

In the early 1900s, pressure mounted for real change. Middle-class Mexicans demanded democracy. Urban and rural workers joined protests and strikes. In 1910, Mexico plunged into revolution. It was one of the world's major

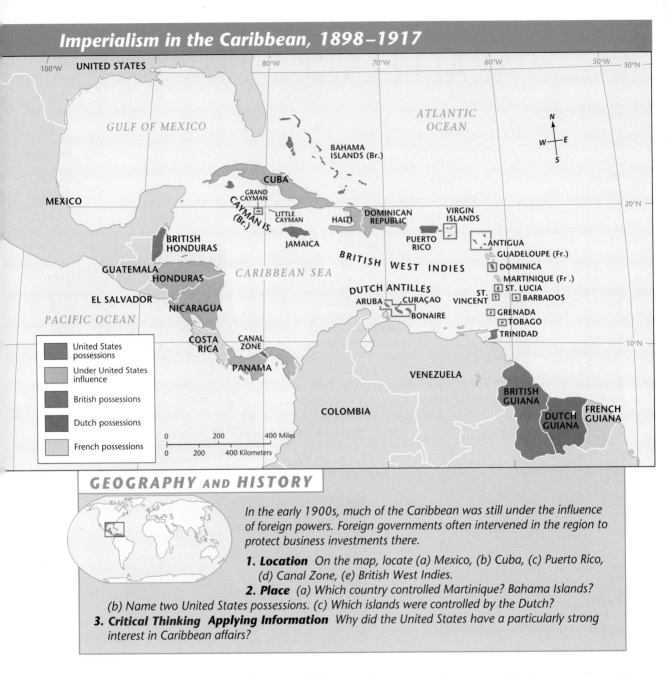

## Imperialism in the Caribbean, 1898–1917

UNITED STATES

GULF OF MEXICO

ATLANTIC OCEAN

MEXICO

CUBA

GRAND CAYMAN
CAYMAN IS. (Br.)
LITTLE CAYMAN

BAHAMA ISLANDS (Br.)

HAITI
DOMINICAN REPUBLIC

VIRGIN ISLANDS

PUERTO RICO

ANTIGUA
GUADELOUPE (Fr.)
DOMINICA
MARTINIQUE (Fr.)
ST. LUCIA
BARBADOS

BRITISH HONDURAS

JAMAICA

BRITISH WEST INDIES

GUATEMALA
HONDURAS

CARIBBEAN SEA

DUTCH ANTILLES
ARUBA   CURAÇAO
BONAIRE

ST. VINCENT

GRENADA
TOBAGO
TRINIDAD

EL SALVADOR
NICARAGUA

PACIFIC OCEAN

COSTA RICA
CANAL ZONE
PANAMA

VENEZUELA

COLOMBIA

BRITISH GUIANA
DUTCH GUIANA
FRENCH GUIANA

**Legend:**
- United States possessions
- Under United States influence
- British possessions
- Dutch possessions
- French possessions

0    200    400 Miles
0  200  400 Kilometers

### GEOGRAPHY AND HISTORY

In the early 1900s, much of the Caribbean was still under the influence of foreign powers. Foreign governments often intervened in the region to protect business investments there.

**1. Location** On the map, locate (a) Mexico, (b) Cuba, (c) Puerto Rico, (d) Canal Zone, (e) British West Indies.

**2. Place** (a) Which country controlled Martinique? Bahama Islands? (b) Name two United States possessions. (c) Which islands were controlled by the Dutch?

**3. Critical Thinking Applying Information** Why did the United States have a particularly strong interest in Caribbean affairs?

---

upheavals and the first true social revolution in Latin America. (See Chapter 29.)

## Colossus of the North

As nations like Mexico tried to build stable governments, a neighboring republic, the United States, was expanding across North America. At first, the young republics in the western hemisphere looked favorably on each other. Bolívar praised the United States as a "model of political virtues and moral enlightenment." In time, however, Latin American nations felt threatened by the "Colossus of the North," the

giant power that cast its shadow over the entire hemisphere.

**The Monroe Doctrine.** In the 1820s, Spain plotted to recover its American colonies. Britain opposed any move that might close the door to trade with Latin America. It asked the United States to join it in a statement opposing any new colonization of the Americas.

President James Monroe, however, wanted to avoid any "entangling alliance" with Britain. Acting alone, in 1823 he issued the Monroe Doctrine. "The American continents," it declared, "are henceforth not to be considered as subjects for future colonization by any European powers." The United States lacked the military power to enforce the doctrine. But knowledge that Britain was willing to use its strong navy to support the doctrine discouraged European interference. For more than a century, the Monroe Doctrine would be the key to United States policy in the Americas.

**Expansion.** As a result of the war with Mexico, in 1848 the United States acquired the thinly populated regions of northern Mexico, including the Colorado River valley and California. The victory fed dreams of future expansion. Boasted one journalist:

> 66The North Americans will spread out far beyond their present bounds. New territories will be planted, declare their independence, and be annexed. We have New Mexico and California! We will have Old Mexico and Cuba!99

For decades, Cuban patriots had battled to free their island from Spanish rule. As they began to make headway, the United States joined their cause, declaring war on Spain in 1898. The brief Spanish-American War ended in a crushing defeat for Spain.

In the peace treaty ending the war, the United States acquired Puerto Rico in the Caribbean and the Philippines and Guam in the Pacific. Cuba was granted independence, but in 1901 the United States forced Cubans to add the Platt Amendment to their constitution. It gave the United States naval bases in Cuba and the right to intervene in Cuban affairs.

**Intervention.** American investments in Latin America soared in the early 1900s. Citing the need to protect those investments, in 1904 the United States issued the Roosevelt Corollary to the Monroe Doctrine. Under this policy, the United States claimed "international police power" in the Western Hemisphere. When the Dominican Republic failed to pay its foreign debts, the United States sent in troops. It collected customs duties, paid off the debts, and remained there for years.

In the next decades, the United States sent troops to Cuba, Haiti, Mexico, Honduras, Nicaragua, and other countries. Like European powers in Africa and Asia, the United States intervened in the Caribbean to protect American lives and investments.

**Panama Canal.** From the late 1800s, the United States had wanted to build a canal across Central America. A canal would let the American fleet move swiftly between the Atlantic and Pacific oceans and protect its coastlines on either side of the continent. It would also greatly reduce the cost of trade between the two oceans.

Panama, however, belonged to Colombia, which refused to sell the United States land for the canal. In 1903, the United States backed a revolt by Panamanians against Colombia. The Panamanians quickly won independence and gave the United States land to build the canal.

The Panama Canal opened in 1914. It was an engineering marvel that boosted American trade and shipping worldwide. To people in Latin America, however, the canal was another example of "Yankee imperialism." In those years, nationalist feeling in the hemisphere was often expressed as anti-Americanism. (In 1978, the United States agreed to a series of treaties that would grant Panama control over the Canal Zone by the year 2000.)

## SECTION 4 REVIEW

1. **Identify** (a) Antonio López de Santa Anna, (b) Benito Juárez, (c) Porfirio Díaz, (d) Colossus of the North, (e) Monroe Doctrine, (f) Spanish-American War, (g) Roosevelt Corollary, (h) Panama Canal.
2. **Define** (a) regionalism, (b) caudillo, (c) economic dependence, (d) peonage.
3. (a) Why did Latin American nations have trouble building stable governments? (b) How did Mexico's experience in the 1800s reflect the problems facing Latin American nations?
4. (a) How did Latin America become part of the global economy? (b) Why was the region's economic growth limited?
5. Why did Latin American nations feel threatened by the United States?
6. *Critical Thinking* **Defending a Position** (a) Why do poor nations encourage foreign investment? (b) Do you think foreign investors should have the right to intervene to protect their investments? Why or why not?
7. *ACTIVITY* Imagine you are a Latin American in the late 1800s. Draw a political cartoon depicting the "Colossus of the North."

# Impact of Imperialism

## Guide for Reading

- What were the main features of the new world economy?

- How did imperialism affect both western cultures and traditional cultures around the world?

- How did imperialism fuel tensions among industrial powers?

In 1900, Rudyard Kipling was among the most popular writers in the English-speaking world. Kipling was born in British-ruled India and, after being educated in England, returned to India as a journalist for a number of years. His stories and poems, such as "White Man's Burden," often glorified imperialism or presented it as a romantic adventure. (See page 633.)

Like most westerners, Kipling emphasized differences between what he saw as "exotic" India and his own English culture. In a famous poem, "The Ballad of East and West," however, he recounted a dramatic clash between equals: a gallant Afghan chief and a heroic British officer. Though enemies, the two men respect each other and act with nobility and courage. The poem begins and ends with these lines:

> 66Oh, East is East, and West is West;
> and never the twain shall meet,
> Till Earth and Sky stand presently at
> God's great Judgment Seat;
> But there is neither East nor West,
> Border, nor Breed, nor Birth,
> When two strong men stand face to
> face, though they come from the
> ends of the Earth!99

The Age of Imperialism brought confrontations between differing cultures "from the ends of the Earth." By 1900, western nations had unfurled their flags over much of the globe. That expansion set off radical changes that reshaped the lives of subject people from Africa to Southeast Asia and the Pacific. For their western rulers, too, imperialism would bring dramatic economic, political, and cultural changes.

## New Economic Patterns

During the Age of Imperialism, a truly global economy emerged. It was dominated by the industrialized nations of the West, especially the United States, Britain, France, and Germany. From these nations, machine-made goods, investment capital, and technology flowed to the rest of the world. In return, the people of Africa, Asia, and Latin America provided agricultural goods, natural resources, and cheap labor. Most profits from this global exchange went to the industrialized nations.

The demands of the new world economy disrupted traditional local economies in Africa and Asia. As in Europe before the Industrial Revolution, most people on these continents grew and produced goods by hand for local use. Under colonial rule, they were forced to supply products such as rubber, copper, and coffee needed by the industrial world.

**Money economy.** Western capitalists developed plantations and mines but relied on a steady supply of local labor to work them. At the same time, colonial rulers introduced a money economy that replaced the old barter system. To

▲ Colonial money

cover the expense of governing their colonies, colonial authorities imposed heavy taxes on their subjects. The only way that people could earn money to pay the taxes was by working on plantations, in mines, or on projects such as railroad building.

Families were disrupted as men left their homes and villages to work in distant mines or cities. In southern and eastern Africa, especially, many men became migrant workers. Their departure shattered families and undermined village life as women were left alone to grow food and support their children. In other parts of the world, such as Japan and Latin America, sons were kept at home to farm while daughters were sent to cities to find work as domestics or in the growing textile industry.

**Dependency.** Mass-produced goods from the industrialized world further disrupted traditional economies. India, for example, was seen by Britain as a great market for its goods. It flooded the subcontinent with cheap, factory-made cloth. The British textile industry flourished. Indian weavers who produced cloth by hand, however, could not compete and were ruined. Elsewhere, too, artisans and handcraft industries were destroyed.

Local economies that had once been self-sufficient became dependent on the industrial powers, which bought their raw materials and supplied them with manufactured goods. When the demand and prices for crops or minerals were high, colonies prospered. When demand and prices fell, people suffered. In addition, because many workers were producing export crops rather than food for local consumption, famines occurred in lands that had once fed themselves.

**Modernization.** Colonial rule did bring some economic benefits. Westerners laid the groundwork for modern banking systems. They introduced new technology and built modern communication and transportation networks. Capitalists invested huge sums in railroad building to boost the export economy. Railroads linked plantations and mines to ports, which developers also modernized.

From China to Chile, some local leaders and business people benefited from the new economic system. Countries like Argentina, Brazil, and Chile, for example, used export profits to develop industry, buy modern farm equipment, and promote growth.

## Cultural Impact

During the Age of Imperialism, Europeans were convinced of their own superiority and believed they had a mission to "civilize" the world.

# CAUSE AND EFFECT

### Causes

Industrial Revolution strengthens the West
Newly industrialized nations seek new markets and raw materials
European nations compete for power and prestige
Europeans feel duty to spread western culture

## *NEW IMPERIALISM*

### Immediate Effects

Europeans claim and conquer large empires in Africa and Asia
Ottoman and Qing empires attempt reforms to meet imperialist challenge
Local people resist European domination
Japan modernizes along western lines
Europeans pursue economic imperialism in Latin America
United States acquires territories in Caribbean and Pacific

### Long-Term Effects

New global economy emerges
Traditional cultures and economies disrupted around the world
Western culture spreads around the globe
Resistance to imperial rule evolves into nationalist movements
European competition for empire contributes to outbreak of two world wars

### Connections Today

Civil wars disrupt nations of Africa and Asia
Latin American nations struggle to build stable democracies

*Interpreting a Chart* At the beginning of the 1800s, westerners had little influence outside their own lands. But with the Industrial Revolution, they gained the power to carve out empires around the globe. ■ Identify two other causes for the "new imperialism." How are the effects of the new imperialism still felt in Africa and Asia today?

(See page 633.) Cecil Rhodes, a leading promoter of British imperialism, declared:

> 66The more of the world we inhabit the better it is for the human race. . . . If there be a God, I think what he would like me to do is to paint as much of the map of Africa British red as possible.99

**Westernization.** As westerners conquered other lands, they pressed subject people to accept "modern" ways. By this, they meant western ideas, government, technology, and culture. Thus, during the Age of Imperialism, modernization and westernization came to be seen as one and the same.*

Many nonwesterners, especially in conquered lands, came to accept a belief in western superiority. The successes of the western imperialist nations sapped their confidence in their own cultures. To share in the material advantages of western society, business and professional people and others who had contact with westerners learned western languages, wore western clothing, and embraced many western ways.

Other nonwesterners, however, had great misgivings about abandoning their own age-old traditions. They greatly resented—and often strongly resisted—western efforts to force new ways on them.

The new imperialism spread western culture around the world. Still, many regions were able to escape its influence. In Africa, the Middle East, and Asia, many farming villagers and nomadic herders had virtually no contact with westerners. As a result, their lives continued largely unchanged.

**Schools and hospitals.** Western culture was often spread by missionaries who built schools and hospitals. They taught children basic literacy and trained young men for jobs in colonial governments.

Western medicine brought benefits. Missionaries introduced medical breakthroughs such as vaccines and modern methods of hygiene that saved lives. At the same time, however, modern medicine undermined traditional herbalists and local healers.

**Religion.** Missionaries spread their Christian faith across the globe. They had great success in some areas. In southern Africa, for example, Christianity became widespread, although Africans adapted its teachings and beliefs to their own traditions. In regions where other world religions or belief systems such as Islam, Hinduism, Buddhism, and Confucianism were deeply rooted, Christian missionaries won fewer converts.

**Old and new ways.** The pressure to westernize forced people to reevaluate their traditions. In Asia, people were proud of their ancient civilizations. On the other hand, they did work to discourage some customs, such as sati in India or footbinding in China. In the end, many nonwestern cultures created a complex blend of old and new ways.

As people moved into cities that had become westernized, many still felt the pull of the past. "People come to the city because they want to live like Europeans," admitted one Nigerian, "but we still feel close to our village and always go back to visit it."

**Impact on western culture.** Western cultures changed, too, during the Age of Imperialism. The Columbian Exchange that had begun in 1492 picked up speed in the 1800s. (See page 410.) Westerners drank coffee from Brazil and tea from Sri Lanka. They ate bananas from Honduras and pineapples from Hawaii. Their factories turned out products made from rubber harvested on plantations in Southeast Asia or South America.

Archaeologists and historians slowly unearthed evidence about ancient civilizations previously unknown to the West. Westerners who studied Hindu and Buddhist texts, Chinese histories, or Japanese poetry realized they had much to learn from other civilizations. The arts of Japan, Persia, Africa, and Southeast Asia influenced western sculptors and painters. West-

---

*The process of modernization along western lines has continued to the present. In today's world, however, modernization and westernization are often seen as separate and different courses. (See page 839.)

**ISSUES For TODAY** Western imperialist nations pressured their overseas colonies to adopt "modern" ways. How does modernization affect traditional cultures?

ern manufacturers also copied designs from other lands, launching fashions for Egyptian furniture, Japanese kimonos, and Chinese embroidery screens.

## New Political Tensions

Imperialism had global political consequences, as you have seen. Europeans claimed and conquered large empires in Africa and Asia. They disrupted traditional political units such as tribes and small kingdoms. Often, they united rival people under a single government, imposing stability and order where local conflicts had raged for centuries.

By the early 1900s, however, resistance to imperialism was taking a new course. In Africa and Asia, western-educated elites were organizing nationalist movements to end colonial rule.

At the same time, the competition for empire was fueling tensions among western powers. In the Sudan in 1898, British forces expanding south from Egypt and French forces

pushing east from West Africa met at Fashoda. An armed clash was barely avoided. Elsewhere, the British and Russians played a cat-and-mouse game in Central Asia. The Great Powers—Germany, Britain, France, and Russia—tried to thwart one another's ambitions in Ottoman lands. More than once, Germany and France teetered on the brink of war over Morocco in North Africa. In 1914 and again in 1939, imperialist ambitions would contribute to the outbreak of two shattering world wars.

## SECTION 5 REVIEW

1. (a) What did nonwestern lands contribute to the new global economy? (b) What did western nations contribute?
2. (a) What did westerners mean by modernization? (b) What are two ways that imperialism affected the cultures of subject people?
3. Why did imperialism lead to increased tensions among industrial powers?
4. *Critical Thinking* **Analyzing Information** List the benefits and disadvantages brought by colonial rule. Do you think subject people were better or worse off as a result of the Age of Imperialism? Explain.
5. *ACTIVITY* Create a flowchart showing the movement of goods and money in the global economy that emerged in the late 1800s. Be sure to include the effects that the new world economy had on the traditional economies of the unindustrialized nations. Use original drawings or pictures from magazines to illustrate your completed flowchart.

# Skills for Success

**Critical Thinking**

**Writing and Researching**

**Maps, Charts, and Graphs**

**Speaking and Listening**

## Using CD-ROM

Many computers allow you to access CD-ROMs. A CD-ROM—compact disc/read-only memory—may contain an encyclopedia, dictionary, atlas, or other reference works.

The screens below are examples of what you will see when you use a CD-ROM for research. Study the screens and follow the steps to research the Australian Aborigines.

**1 Start your research.** Study Screen 1. (a) Which source would you select to find the correct spelling of *Aborigine*? (b) Which source(s) would you select to write a report on the Aborigines?

**2 Narrow your search.** (a) What does Screen 2 show? (b) Which subject would you choose to find out about the Aborigines' religion?

(c) Which subject would you select to learn how the Aborigines arrived in Australia?

**3 Research your topic.** (a) What topic is being researched on Screen 3? (b) Who are the Aborigines? (c) Where do most Aborigines live?

**4 Search for additional information.** A list of Associated Topics often appears at the end of an article, as on Screen 4. (a) Which Associated Topic would you select to find out the number of Aborigines in Australia? (b) Which topic would you search to find out where the earliest Aborigines settled?

*Beyond the Classroom* Select a topic from the chapter. Then, use the CD-ROM encyclopedia at your local library to research your topic. List at least two new facts that you learn from the CD-ROM.

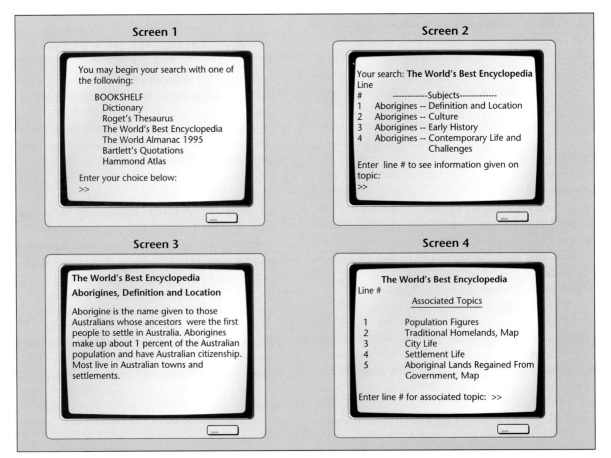

**Screen 1**

You may begin your search with one of the following:

BOOKSHELF
Dictionary
Roget's Thesaurus
The World's Best Encyclopedia
The World Almanac 1995
Bartlett's Quotations
Hammond Atlas

Enter your choice below:
>>

**Screen 2**

Your search: **The World's Best Encyclopedia**
Line
\#           ------------Subjects-------------
1     Aborigines -- Definition and Location
2     Aborigines -- Culture
3     Aborigines -- Early History
4     Aborigines -- Contemporary Life and
                     Challenges

Enter line \# to see information given on topic:
>>

**Screen 3**

The World's Best Encyclopedia
**Aborigines, Definition and Location**

Aborigine is the name given to those Australians whose ancestors were the first people to settle in Australia. Aborigines make up about 1 percent of the Australian population and have Australian citizenship. Most live in Australian towns and settlements.

**Screen 4**

The World's Best Encyclopedia
Line \#
        Associated Topics

1     Population Figures
2     Traditional Homelands, Map
3     City Life
4     Settlement Life
5     Aboriginal Lands Regained From
       Government, Map

Enter line \# for associated topic: >>

## Building Vocabulary

Review the vocabulary words in this chapter. Then, use *five* of these vocabulary words and their definitions to create a matching quiz. Exchange your quiz with another student. Check each other's answers when you are finished.

## Reviewing Chapter Themes

1. **Continuity and Change** (a) Describe three economic changes brought by western imperialism. (b) Describe three cultural changes. (c) Do you think these changes were positive or negative? Explain.
2. **Economics and Technology** (a) Describe the new global economy that emerged during the Age of Imperialism. (b) How did the new world economy affect local economies in Africa and Asia? (c) How did it affect the economies of Latin American nations?
3. **Political and Social Systems** (a) What challenges did Mexico face in its efforts to establish political stability? (b) How did Mexico's problems reflect the experience of most Latin American nations in the Age of Imperialism?
4. **Diversity** How did each of the following respond to western imperialism: (a) Japan, (b) Thailand, (c) French Indochina?
5. **Geography and History** (a) How did Australia achieve self-rule? (b) How did this reflect its settlement by English-speaking people?

## Thinking Critically

1. **Synthesizing Information** How was imperialism the "child" of the Industrial Revolution? (★ See *Skills for Success*, page 896.)
2. **Comparing** Compare Japan's response to western imperialism with that of China. (a) How were they similar? (b) How were they different?
3. **Linking Past and Present** (a) List the reasons that Japan responded successfully to the challenge of western imperialism. (b) Do you think that the United States today has a similar ability to adapt to new situations? Explain.
4. **Comparing** Compare the partition of Southeast Asia to the partition of Africa. (a) How were they similar? (b) How were they different?

5. **Solving Problems** If you were a ruler in Southeast Asia during the Age of Imperialism, what steps would you have taken to prevent your country from being colonized?
6. **Analyzing Information** (a) Compare the way that Canada and the United States achieved independence from Britain. (b) How might Britain's experience in the American Revolution have affected its response to demands for self-rule by other English-speaking colonies?
7. **Applying Information** (a) What principle did the United States put forth in the Monroe Doctrine? (b) How did the United States use the Monroe Doctrine to support its intervention in Latin America?
8. **Defending a Position** Mexican president Porfirio Díaz defended his regime: "We were harsh. Sometimes we were harsh to the point of cruelty. But it was necessary then to the life and progress of the nation." Do you agree or disagree with Díaz's view that the end justifies the means? Defend your position.

## For Your Portfolio

   Imagine that you are a world traveler during the 1800s. You will write journal entries for visits that you make to a place at two different times.

1. Begin by choosing one of the following destinations: Japan, Korea, Indonesia, Indochina, Burma, Siam, the Philippines, Canada, Australia, New Zealand, Mexico, Panama.
2. Select two time periods for your visits. These should be far enough apart for you to observe major changes that have occurred between them. These changes might be the result of specific events or of forces such as imperialism or modernization. For example, if you choose Japan, your journal might describe visits before and after Commodore Perry's arrival.
3. Consult library resources for additional information about the place you will visit at the times you have chosen.
4. Write your journal entries. Make sure that your observations reflect changes that occurred in the country between your two visits.
5. Take turns reading your journals aloud with classmates. Be ready to answer questions.

# Unit-in-Brief

## UNIT 6

# Industrialism and a New Global Age

### Chapter 22 Life in the Industrial Age
#### (1800–1910)

From the mid-1800s, industrialism spread rapidly across Europe to North America and beyond. This second Industrial Revolution transformed the economies of the world and solidified patterns of life familiar to us today.

- By the mid-1800s, other western nations, particularly Germany and the United States, were challenging Britain's position as the world's industrial giant.
- Steel, electricity, and advances in communications and transportation marked the second Industrial Revolution.
- By the late 1800s, "big business" came increasingly to dominate the industrial world.
- With the spread of industry, a more complex social structure, dominated by middle-class values, evolved. Although the poor continued to endure harsh conditions, the overall standard of living for workers improved.
- Artistic movements such as romanticism, realism, and expressionism reflected various responses to social and technological changes.

### Chapter 23 Nationalism Triumphs in Europe
#### (1800–1914)

The 1800s saw an upsurge of nationalism in Europe. Nationalism unified some countries and sparked divisiveness and conflict in others.

- Between 1862 and 1890, Otto von Bismarck molded the German states into a powerful empire. To strengthen the German state, Bismarck promoted economic development, aggressive foreign policy goals, and domestic reforms.
- Although nationalist forces unified Italy in 1870, a long history of fragmentation created a host of problems for the new state.
- Nationalist feelings among diverse ethnic groups in Eastern Europe created widespread unrest and helped hasten the decline of the Ottoman and Hapsburg empires.
- Reluctant to surrender absolute power, Russian czars of the 1800s swung between reform and repression.

### Chapter 24 Growth of Western Democracies
#### (1815–1914)

In Britain, France, and the United States, reformers struggled for an extension of democratic rights and social change. Although many inequalities persisted, these efforts paved the way for great improvements in the quality of life.

- The British Parliament passed a series of reforms designed to help those whose labor supported the new industrial society. Suffrage was extended to all male citizens, prompting women to seek the vote as well.

- Following its defeat in the Franco-Prussian War and a fierce internal revolt, France established the Third Republic, which instituted a series of important reforms.
- By 1900, the United States had become the world's leading industrial giant, a global power, and a magnet for immigrants seeking freedom and opportunity.

## Chapter 25  The New Imperialism
### (1800–1914)

During the 1800s, European powers embarked on a period of aggressive expansion known as the Age of Imperialism. Despite fierce resistance, these powers brought much of the world under their control between 1870 and 1914.

- The Industrial Revolution gave western powers both the means and the motives to seek global domination.
- With little regard for traditional patterns of settlement, European powers partitioned almost the entire African continent.
- Taking advantage of the slowly crumbling Ottoman empire, Britain, France, and Russia competed to extend their influence over Algeria, Egypt, and other Ottoman lands.
- Britain set up a profitable system of colonial rule, controlling over 60 percent of India.
- Western powers carved out spheres of influence along the Chinese coast. China unsuccessfully tried to resist foreign influence with belated efforts at modernization and reform.

- By the early 1900s, leaders in many colonized regions were forging their own nationalist movements.

## Chapter 26  New Global Patterns
### (1800–1914)

Imperialism resulted in a global exchange that profited industrial nations but disrupted local economies in Africa, Asia, and Latin America. Radical changes reshaped the lives of both subject peoples and westerners.

- As a defense against western imperialism, Japan transformed itself into a modern industrial power and set out on its own imperialist path.
- By 1900, western powers had claimed most islands in the Pacific and divided up most of Southeast Asia.
- The British colonies of Canada, Australia, and New Zealand won independence relatively quickly.
- Although Latin American nations struggled to set up stable governments and economies, a pattern of military rule and economic dependency emerged.
- The United States created its own sphere of influence in the Western Hemisphere.
- Europeans forced subject peoples to accept western ideas about government, technology, and culture.

# A Global View

## How Did Industrialization, Nationalism, and the Growth of Democracy Reshape the World?

As we saw in Unit 3, the first global age began with European expansion in the late 1400s. In the 1800s, a second wave of expansion extended western power to almost all parts of the world. Forces that were reshaping the West itself thus took on a new global importance.

### The Age of Steam

During the early 1800s, the Industrial Revolution spread from Britain to Europe and the Americas. Modern industrial cities emerged, built around the new factories. In the cities, the middle classes lived in elegant neighborhoods, while most workers survived in slum tenements.

The citizens of this new industrial society began to develop new views and values. Many admired the middle-class virtues that made the system work. Others challenged established institutions.

### New Nations

Kindled by the Napoleonic wars, nationalism reshaped Europe. All peoples, nationalists insisted, had a right to their own countries. This call to nationhood was echoed by Irish nationalists seeking freedom from British rule and, later, by Zionists who sought a Jewish state.

Inspired in part by nationalism, two new European states emerged in the late 1800s. Led by the dynamic kingdom of Sardinia, most of the separate states of Italy were united by 1861. A decade later, Bismarck's Prussia, already one of Europe's great powers, forged a united German empire.

Elsewhere, nationalism was a threat to unity. Both Austria and the Ottoman empire faced disintegration as their multinational populations called for "national self-determination." Czarist Russia confronted this problem along with demands for economic, political, and social reforms.

### Spread of Democracy

In Western Europe and North America, democratic ideas were the main force for

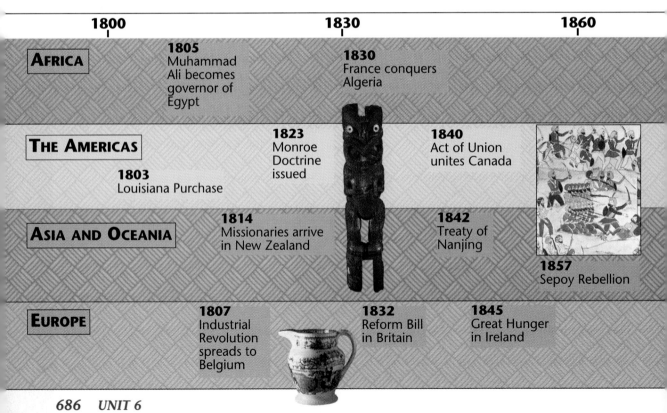

| | 1800 | 1830 | 1860 |
|---|---|---|---|
| **AFRICA** | **1805** Muhammad Ali becomes governor of Egypt | **1830** France conquers Algeria | |
| **THE AMERICAS** | **1803** Louisiana Purchase | **1823** Monroe Doctrine issued | **1840** Act of Union unites Canada |
| **ASIA AND OCEANIA** | **1814** Missionaries arrive in New Zealand | | **1842** Treaty of Nanjing · **1857** Sepoy Rebellion |
| **EUROPE** | **1807** Industrial Revolution spreads to Belgium | **1832** Reform Bill in Britain | **1845** Great Hunger in Ireland |

political change. In Britain, where Parliament had come to share royal power, genuine democracy began to emerge, as a series of reform bills gave the vote to most male citizens. People also demanded—and got—more social reforms, from child labor laws to public education.

Democratic reforms also came to France and the United States. The French Third Republic built on the foundation laid by the French Revolution of 1789. Despite such setbacks as the Dreyfus affair, France increasingly lived up to its democratic principles of liberty and equality.

Still, the United States was perhaps the world's most successful democracy. After the abolition of slavery, male suffrage was widespread. The economic boom of the "gilded age" of the late 1800s also made America the most productive of all industrial states.

## Expanding Empire

Democratic and nationalistic ideals, however, did not stop western powers from imposing their will on other peoples. Driven by a variety of motives, imperialists were now equipped with new weapons produced by the Industrial Revolution.

The New Imperialism seemed unstoppable. Its leaders included old colonial powers like Britain and France, as well as Germany, Belgium, and Japan. By 1900, imperialist powers had divided up almost all of Africa and dominated most of Asia. While Latin American nations retained their independence, they were subject to economic domination and, occasionally, military intervention.

## Looking Ahead

The forces that shaped the 1800s would continue into the next century. Industrial development would reach new heights. Nationalism would kindle wars, fragment empires, and forge new states. Democracy would survive challenges to spread to many new lands. And the effects of imperialism would last long after most colonies won independence.

**ACTIVITY** Choose two events and two pictures from the time line below. For each, write a sentence explaining how it relates to the themes expressed in the Global View essay.

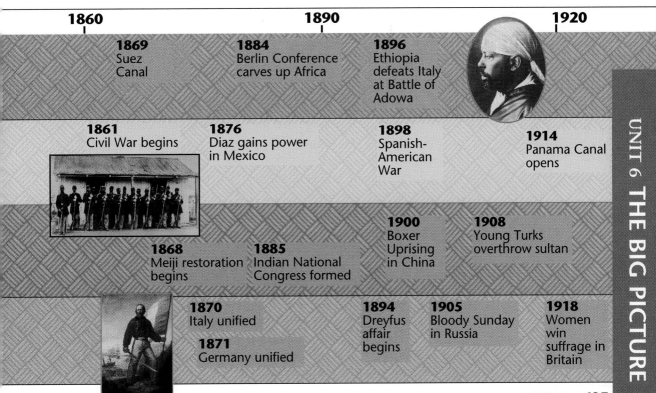

1860

1890

1920

**1869**
Suez Canal

**1884**
Berlin Conference carves up Africa

**1896**
Ethiopia defeats Italy at Battle of Adowa

**1861**
Civil War begins

**1876**
Diaz gains power in Mexico

**1898**
Spanish-American War

**1914**
Panama Canal opens

**1900**
Boxer Uprising in China

**1908**
Young Turks overthrow sultan

**1868**
Meiji restoration begins

**1885**
Indian National Congress formed

**1870**
Italy unified

**1871**
Germany unified

**1894**
Dreyfus affair begins

**1905**
Bloody Sunday in Russia

**1918**
Women win suffrage in Britain

UNIT 6 THE BIG PICTURE

# You Decide

## Exploring Global Issues

### Is Technology a Blessing or a Curse?

To Mary Shelley, the Industrial Revolution sparked the nightmare of the Frankenstein monster. To Jules Verne, it inspired dreams of traveling to the moon or far beneath the sea. Today, these two visions still reflect people's hopes and fears about technology. Should we welcome all technological advances as signs of progress? Or do the dangers of technology far outweigh the benefits? To begin your investigation, examine these viewpoints:

**UNITED STATES**

**1867**

Industrial nations of the 1800s sponsored huge industrial expositions to show off the products of their technology. Here, visitors admire a gear-cutting machine at an exhibition in Philadelphia. ▶

**IRELAND**

**1895**

Writer and wit Oscar Wilde saw technology as a tool for cultural progress:

❝The fact is, that civilization requires slaves. . . . Unless there are slaves to do the ugly, horrible, uninteresting work, culture and contemplation become almost impossible. Human slavery is wrong, insecure, and demoralizing. On mechanical slavery, on the slavery of the machine, the future of the world depends.❞

**INDIA**

**1955**

As nations such as India gained independence, Prime Minister Jawaharlal Nehru commented on their need for technological development:

❝There can be no real well-being or advance in material standards in India without the big factory. I shall venture to say that we cannot even maintain our freedom and independence as a nation without the big factory and all that it represents.❞

**FRANCE**

**1964**

Writer Jacques Ellul commented on the effects of technology in his book *The Technological Society*:

❝The machine tends not only to create a new human environment, but also to modify man's very essence. . . . He must adapt himself, as though the world were new, to a universe for which he was not created. He was made to go six kilometers an hour, and he goes a thousand. He was made to eat when he was hungry and to sleep when he was sleepy; instead, he obeys a clock. He was made to have contact with living things, and he lives in a world of stone.❞

## IRAN

**1964**

Ruhollah Khomeini, a Muslim reformer, belittled the technological progress of the western powers who dominated his country:

> Let them go all the way to Mars or beyond the Milky Way; they will still be deprived of true happiness. . . . For the solution of social problems and the relief of human misery require foundations in faith and morals; merely acquiring material power and wealth, conquering nature and space, have no effect in this regard.

## JAPAN

**1984**

Ikeda Daisaku spoke of the effects of technology from the viewpoint of a Buddhist philosopher:

> The man who rides in a car all of the time loses the ability to walk long distances vigorously. Even when we employ mechanical devices, we must realize that it is we human beings who are at the controls and that whether the machine is a blessing or curse depends on what is inside us.

## SOUTH AFRICA

**1986**

This cartoon uses imagery borrowed from the pyramid builders of ancient Egypt to comment on modern technology. ▶

---

### COMPARING VIEWPOINTS

**1.** Which views represented here seem least critical of modern technology?

**2.** Both India and Iran sought to free themselves from western domination. How does Nehru's view of western technology differ from Khomeini's?

**3.** How is Ellul's view of technology similar to Ikeda's?

**4.** How do Wilde and the cartoonist use the same image to express different viewpoints?

### YOUR INVESTIGATION

**ACTIVITY**

**1.** Find out more about other viewpoints related to this topic. You might investigate one or more of the following:

- The Luddite movement in early industrial Britain.

- The view of technology depicted in a work of science fiction, such as the novel *The Shape of Things to Come* by H. G. Wells, the play *R.U.R.* by Karel Capek, or the American movie *War Games.*

- Debates over the "rationing" of modern medical technology, such as kidney dialysis or organ transplants.

- The history and effects of robotics in Japan.

- Commentary on an industrial disaster, such as the chemical leakage at Bhopal, India, or the nuclear accident at Chernobyl, Ukraine.

**2.** Decide which viewpoint you agree with most closely and express it in your own way. You may do so in an essay, a cartoon, a poem, a drawing or painting, a song, a skit, a video, or in some other way.

# WORLD WARS AND REVOLUTIONS

**Impact of the Individual**

*Mohandas Gandhi led India's drive for independence from British rule. He urged Indians to use methods of non-violent protest, such as using home-spun rather than British cotton.*

**2**

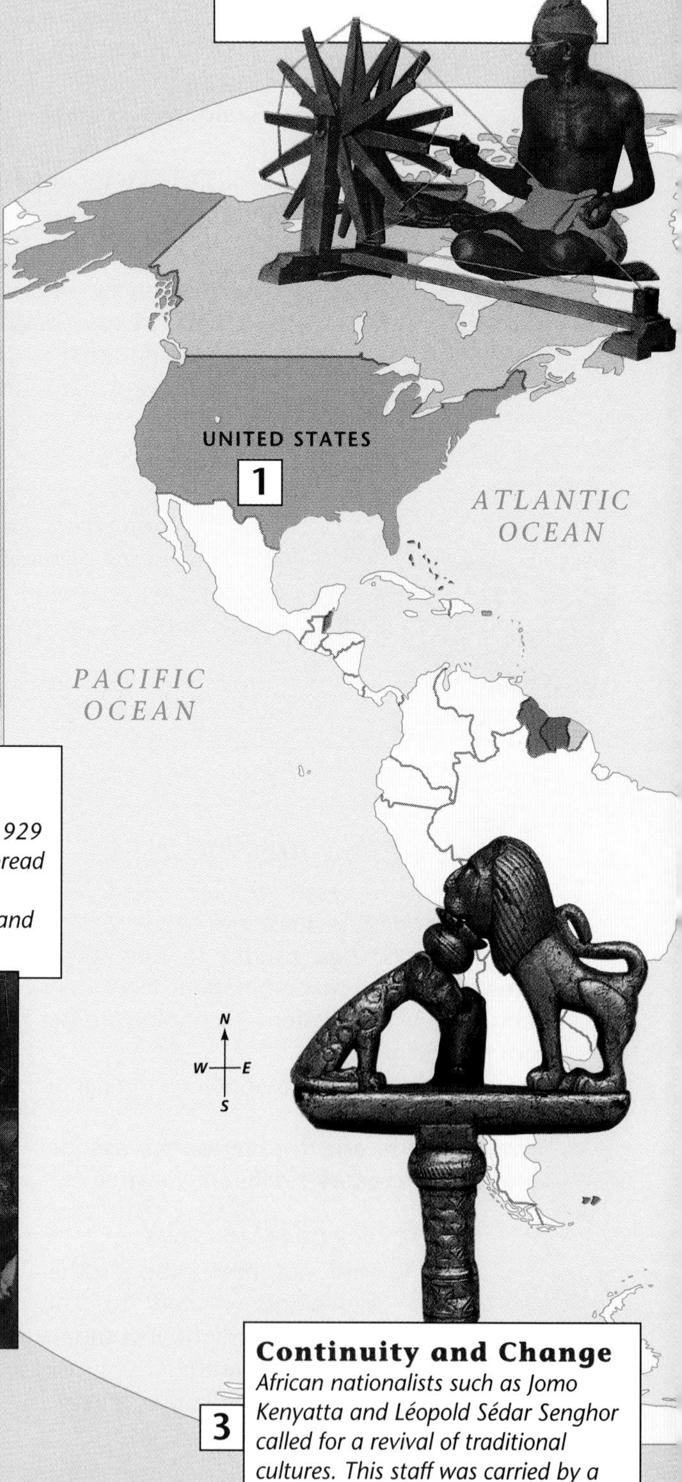

UNITED STATES

**1**

*ATLANTIC OCEAN*

*PACIFIC OCEAN*

**Economics and Technology**

**1** *The Great Depression began in 1929 in the United States. It quickly spread to the rest of the world, bringing hardship both to urban workers and to rural families, like this one.*

N
W—E
S

**Continuity and Change**

**3** *African nationalists such as Jomo Kenyatta and Léopold Sédar Senghor called for a revival of traditional cultures. This staff was carried by a student of African languages.*

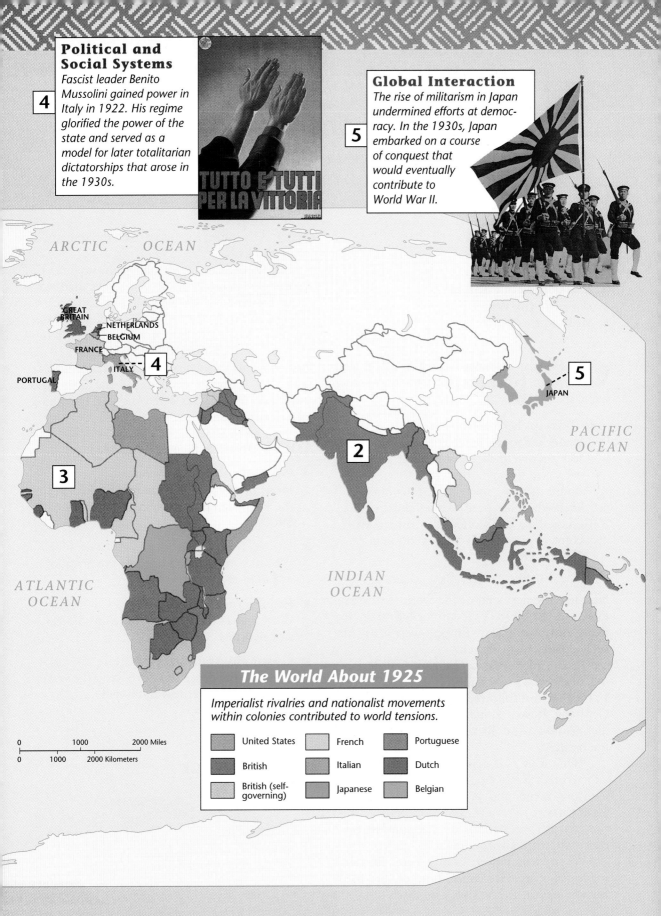

## Political and Social Systems

**4**

*Fascist leader Benito Mussolini gained power in Italy in 1922. His regime glorified the power of the state and served as a model for later totalitarian dictatorships that arose in the 1930s.*

TUTTO E TUTTI
PER LA VITTORIA

## Global Interaction

**5**

*The rise of militarism in Japan undermined efforts at democracy. In the 1930s, Japan embarked on a course of conquest that would eventually contribute to World War II.*

ARCTIC OCEAN

GREAT BRITAIN
NETHERLANDS
BELGIUM
FRANCE
ITALY **4**
PORTUGAL

**5**
JAPAN

PACIFIC OCEAN

**2**

ATLANTIC OCEAN

**3**

INDIAN OCEAN

AUSTRALIA

### The World About 1925

*Imperialist rivalries and nationalist movements within colonies contributed to world tensions.*

0   1000   2000 Miles
0   1000   2000 Kilometers

- United States
- British
- British (self-governing)
- French
- Italian
- Japanese
- Portuguese
- Dutch
- Belgian

# World War I and Its Aftermath

## (1914–1919)

On Monday evening, August 3, 1914, Vera Brittain, a young English woman, wrote in her diary:

> 66Today has been far too exciting to enable me to feel at all like sleep—in fact it is one of the most thrilling I have ever lived through, though without doubt there are many more to come. That which has been so long anticipated by some and scoffed at by others has come to pass at last—Armageddon in Europe!99

"Armageddon" is a decisive, catastrophic conflict, like the fiery end-of-the-world battle predicted in the Bible. That summer, Brittain and many other people in Europe were sure that such a conflict had arrived.

In late July, Austria-Hungary had declared war on Serbia, a tiny nation in Eastern Europe. In the days that followed, other major powers—Germany, Russia, France—had joined the conflict. Would Great Britain, too, be drawn into the battle?

"One feels as if one were dreaming," Brittain wrote. "Every hour brings fresh and momentous events and one must stand still and await catastrophes each even more terrible than the last. All the nations of this continent are ready with their swords drawn."

When war finally came, Vera Brittain's world fell apart. Her fiancé, brother, and many friends died in the terrible slaughter of World War I. As a nurse, she herself saw the tragedy of shattered lives.

By 1914, Europeans had enjoyed almost a century without a major war. They had witnessed incredible changes. Rapid advances in science and industry had fed a belief in unlimited progress, peace, and prosperity. That confidence came crashing down in August 1914, buried in an avalanche of death and destruction. For Vera Brittain's generation—the ones who survived—World War I marked the beginning of a disturbing new age.

**FOCUS ON** these themes as you read:

- **Political and Social Systems**
  How did political and military rivalries push the European powers toward war in the early 1900s?

- **Global Interaction**
  Why did World War I become the first global war in history?

- **Economics and Technology**
  What impact did total war have on soldiers and civilians?

- **Continuity and Change**
  How did the peace treaties ending the war lead to both bitterness and hope?

## TIME AND PLACE

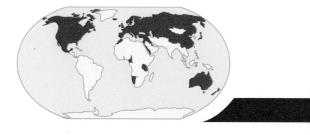

*A Vision of Destruction*  German artist Ludwig Meidner painted this nightmarish landscape in 1913. The following year, Europe was embroiled in World War I. It would become the most destructive conflict in world history up to that time. **Art and Literature** Compare this painting with the excerpts from Vera Brittain's diary on page 692. What do the two sources tell you about the mood in Europe on the eve of World War I?

## HUMANITIES LINK

*Art History*  C.R.W. Nevinson, *Return to the Trenches* (page 706).
*Literature*  In this chapter you will encounter passages from the following works of literature: Vera Brittain, *Chronicle of Youth* (page 692); Siegfried Sassoon, "Suicide in the Trenches" (page 705).

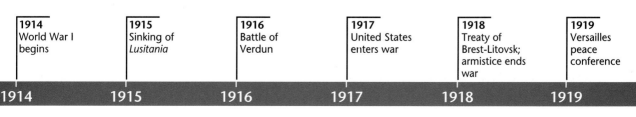

| 1914 World War I begins | 1915 Sinking of *Lusitania* | 1916 Battle of Verdun | 1917 United States enters war | 1918 Treaty of Brest-Litovsk; armistice ends war | 1919 Versailles peace conference |
|---|---|---|---|---|---|
| 1914 | 1915 | 1916 | 1917 | 1918 | 1919 |

# 1 The Stage Is Set

## Guide for Reading

- Why did many people in the early 1900s believe that war was unlikely?
- What forces pushed Europe toward war?
- What were the causes and effects of European alliances?
- **Vocabulary** *militarism*

To many, war seemed far away in the decades before 1914. After a century of relative peace, idealists hoped for a permanent end to war. "The future belongs to peace," said French economist Frédéric Passy.

Others were far less hopeful. "I shall not live to see the Great War," warned German chancellor Otto von Bismarck, "but you will see it, and it will start in the east." It was Bismarck's prediction, rather than Passy's, that came true.

### Pressure for Peace

The late 1800s and early 1900s saw serious efforts to end the scourge of war. Alfred Nobel, the Swedish inventor of dynamite, came to regret the military uses of his invention. In his will, he set up the Nobel Peace Prize to reward each year the individual whose work advanced the cause of peace.

The struggle for women's suffrage throughout Europe supported the peace movement. Aletta Jacobs, the first woman doctor in the Netherlands, argued that if women won the vote, they would be able to prevent wars:

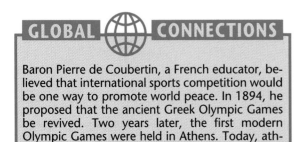

**GLOBAL CONNECTIONS**

Baron Pierre de Coubertin, a French educator, believed that international sports competition would be one way to promote world peace. In 1894, he proposed that the ancient Greek Olympic Games be revived. Two years later, the first modern Olympic Games were held in Athens. Today, athletes from around the world still compete every four years in the summer and winter Olympics.

**66**Yes, the women will do it. They don't feel as men do about war. They are the mothers of the race. Men think of the economic results, women think of the grief and pain.**99**

Organizations such as the Women's International League for Peace and Freedom gave women a way to voice their concerns.

Governments, too, backed peace efforts. In 1899, the First Universal Peace Conference brought together leaders of many nations in The Hague in the Netherlands. There, they set up a world court to settle disputes between nations. The Hague Tribunal, as the court was called, could not force nations to submit their disputes, nor could it enforce its rulings. Still, it was a step toward keeping the peace.

At the same time, other powerful forces were pushing Europe to the brink of war. They included aggressive nationalism, economic competition, imperialism, an arms race, and rival alliance systems.

### Aggressive Nationalism

Nationalism can be a positive force, binding together a nation's people. People enjoy such patriotic celebrations as St. Patrick's Day in Ireland or Cinco de Mayo in Mexico. At the same time, national pride can fuel bitter conflicts. In the early 1900s, aggressive nationalism was a leading cause of international tension.

**Alsace and Lorraine.** Nationalism was strong in both Germany and France. Germans were proud of their new empire's military power and industrial leadership. France longed to regain its position as Europe's leading power.

The French were still bitter about their defeat in the Franco-Prussian War. (See page 617.) They especially resented German occupation of the border provinces Alsace and Lorraine. Patriotic French citizens longed for revenge against Germany and recovery of the "lost provinces."

**Pan-Slavism.** In Eastern Europe, Russia sponsored a powerful form of nationalism called Pan-Slavism. According to Pan-Slavism, all Slavic peoples shared a common nationality. As the largest Slavic country, Russia felt that it had a duty to lead and defend all Slavs. By 1914, it stood ready to support Serbia, an ambitious young Slavic nation, against any threat.

**Crises in the Balkans.** Two old multinational empires particularly feared rising nationalism in Eastern Europe. Austria-Hungary was worried that nationalism might foster rebellion among the many minority populations within its empire. Ottoman Turkey felt threatened by new nations on its borders, such as Serbia and Greece. Serbia was especially aggressive. It dreamed of creating and ruling a South Slav state.

In 1912, several Balkan states attacked Turkey. The next year, they fought among themselves over the spoils of war. These brief but bloody Balkan wars raised tensions to a fever pitch. By 1914, the Balkans were the "powder keg of Europe." A tiny spark might lead to an explosion.

## Economic and Imperial Rivalries

Economic rivalries further poisoned the international atmosphere. The British felt threatened by Germany's rapid economic growth. By 1900, Germany's new, modern factories increasingly outproduced Britain's older ones. Britain therefore had strong economic reasons to oppose Germany in any conflict. Germany, in turn, thought the other great powers did not give them enough respect.

Imperialism also divided European nations. In 1905 and again in 1911, competition for colonies brought France and Germany to the brink of war. Germany wanted to keep France from imposing a protectorate on the Muslim kingdom of Morocco. Although diplomats kept the peace, Germany gained some territory in central Africa. As a result of the two Moroccan crises, Britain and France began to form closer ties against Germany.

## Militarism and the Arms Race

The late 1800s saw a rise in militarism, the glorification of the military. Under militarism, the armed forces and readiness for war came to dominate national policy. Militarists painted war in romantic colors. Young men dreamed of blaring trumpets and heroic cavalry charges—not at all the sort of conflict they would soon face.

The rise in militarism grew partly out of the ideas of Social Darwinism. (See page 571.) Echoing the idea of "survival of the fittest," the German militarist Friedrich von Bernhardi claimed that war was "a biological necessity of the first importance."

**The arms race.** As international tensions grew, the great powers expanded their armies and navies. The result was an arms race that further increased suspicions and made war more likely.

The fiercest competition was the naval rivalry between Britain and Germany. To protect its vast overseas empire, Britain had built the world's most respected navy. When Germany began to acquire colonies, it began to build up its own navy. Kaiser William II boasted:

> **❝**All the long years of my reign, my colleagues, the monarchs of Europe, have paid no attention to what I have to say. Soon, with my great navy to endorse my words, they will be more respectful.**❞**

Suspicious of Germany's motives, Britain increased its naval spending. In a British cartoon of the time, one man warns another, "We must build a bigger navy than the enemy will build

## Toy Soldiers

Miniature soldiers have been found in the tombs of ancient Egypt. During the Middle Ages, noble children staged mock jousts with wooden knights. Later, young rulers like Louis XIV and Peter the Great learned military strategy by playing with toy armies. Not until the 1700s, though, were mass-produced toy soldiers widely available to ordinary children.

**Linking Past and Present** Some parents today object to "war toys." Do you agree or disagree? Explain.

**PAST** *In the early 1900s, as world powers built up their armies, toymakers did the same. The British regiment at right came in a box that boasted of their worldwide exploits. Below, an Austro-Hungarian cavalry struts proudly. American marines, Japanese infantrymen, Zulu warriors, and Indian troops mounted on elephants—all were reproduced in miniature.*

**PRESENT** *Plastic soldiers and posable "action figures," such as G.I. Joe™ (right), have largely replaced the tin or lead figurines of earlier times.*

---

when he hears we're building a bigger navy than he's building."

**Military leaders.** Fear of war gave military leaders more influence. On matters of peace and war, governments turned to military leaders for advice. German generals and British admirals enjoyed great respect and got more funds to build up their forces. As militarism and the arms race fed each other, tensions grew.

### A Tangle of Alliances

Fear and distrust led the great powers to protect themselves through alliances. Nations signed treaties pledging to defend each other. These alliances were intended to create powerful combinations that no one would dare attack. Gradually, two huge alliances emerged.

**The Central Powers.** The first alliances had their origins in Bismarck's day. He was aware that France longed to avenge its humiliating defeat in the Franco-Prussian War. Knowing that France would not attack Germany without help, Bismarck signed treaties with the other great powers. In 1881, Germany joined an alliance with Austria-Hungary and Russia. The next year, Germany formed the Triple Alliance with Austria-Hungary and Italy.

After Bismarck resigned, Kaiser William II pursued his own policies. He preserved the Triple Alliance but allowed Germany's treaty with Russia to lapse. Thus, Russia was free to seek new allies.

In 1914, when war did erupt, Germany and Austria-Hungary fought on the same side. They became known as the Central Powers.

**The Allies.** A rival bloc took shape in 1894, when France and Russia signed an alliance. In 1904, France and Britain signed an *entente cordiale* (ahn TAHNT kawr DYAHL), or "friendly understanding." Though not as binding as a treaty, the entente led to close military and diplomatic ties. Three years later, Britain signed a similar agreement with Russia. When war began, these powers became known as the Allies.

**Consequences.** Other states were drawn into alliances. Germany signed a treaty with the Ottoman empire, while Britain drew close to Japan. Rather than easing tensions, the growth of rival alliance systems made governments increasingly nervous. A local conflict could easily mushroom into a general war. In 1914, that threat became a horrifying reality.

## SECTION 1 REVIEW

1. **Identify** (a) Alfred Nobel, (b) Pan-Slavism, (c) Central Powers, (d) Allies.
2. **Define** militarism.
3. (a) What was the purpose of the Hague Tribunal? (b) How was its power limited?
4. Describe how each of the following inflamed tensions in Europe: (a) nationalism, (b) imperialism, (c) militarism.
5. (a) Why did European nations form alliances? (b) How did the alliance systems increase fears of war?
6. *Critical Thinking* **Past and Present** Do you think the idea of going to war excites young people today in the same way it did in the early 1900s? Why or why not?
7. *ACTIVITY* Choose someone living today that you would nominate for the Nobel Peace Prize. Write a brief paragraph explaining why you think he or she deserves the honor.

## 2 The Guns of August

### Guide for Reading

■ How did ethnic tensions in the Balkans spark a political assassination?

■ How did conflict between Austria-Hungary and Serbia widen?

■ Whom do historians blame for the outbreak of World War I?

■ **Vocabulary** *ultimatum, mobilize, neutrality*

In April of 1913, Bertha von Suttner wrote a grim prediction in her diary:

66All in all, it seems to me that the great European disaster is well on its way. If so many seeds have been sown, surely the weeds will sprout up soon and surely so much stockpiled gunpowder will explode.99

"Peace Bertha" died on June 20, 1914. Eight days later, an assassin's bullet set off the "gunpowder" and ignited a war that engulfed much of the world for four bloody years.

### A Murder With Millions of Victims

On a spring night in 1914, a small group of young revolutionaries huddled around a cafe table in Belgrade, Serbia. By the light of a flickering gas lamp, they read a news article. It announced that Archduke Francis Ferdinand of Austria-Hungary would visit Sarajevo (sar uh YAY voh), the capital of neighboring Bosnia, on June 28.

The Serbians were outraged. June 28 was the date on which Serbia had been conquered by the Ottoman empire in 1389. (See page 251.) On the very same date in 1912, Serbia had at last freed itself from Turkish rule. But Bosnia, home to many Serbs, was still ruled by Austria-Hungary. Now Francis Ferdinand, heir to the Austrian throne, had chosen June 28 to come to Bosnia! "Our decision was taken almost immediately," recalled one of the group. "Death to the tyrant!"

**The killer.** Among the group was a youth of 19 named Gavrilo Princip (GAHV ree loh PREEN tseep). Princip's family were Serb farmers who made a meager living in Bosnia. Having grown up under Austrian rule, he felt that he must take action against the oppressors.

Princip joined Unity or Death, a terrorist group commonly known as the Black Hand. Organized by Bosnian Serbs, its goal was to organize all South Slav peoples into a single nation. On June 28, Princip would be waiting on the streets of Sarajevo.

**The victims.** June 28 was a special date for Francis Ferdinand as well. Exactly 14 years earlier, he had married Countess Sophie Chotek. The love match brought both joy and bitterness. The Hapsburg royal family snubbed Sophie, because of her lower social rank. Still, Francis Ferdinand sought ways to make sure she was acknowledged. When his duties took him to Sarajevo on their anniversary, he decided to bring his wife along.

Politically, Francis Ferdinand was not a supporter of democracy. Yet he recognized how nationalism was threatening the Hapsburg empire. He even anticipated making some concessions to the Slavs. This view made him unpopular with hard-liners on both sides. Conservative Austrians saw him as too soft. Serbian radicals feared concessions might weaken their movement.

The archduke ignored warnings of anti-Austrian unrest in Sarajevo. On the morning of June 28, he dictated a telegram for his daughter:

66Mama and I are very well . . . We gave a large dinner party yesterday and this morning there is a big reception in Sarajevo. Another large dinner party after that and then we are leaving. . . . Dearest love to you all. Papa.99

**Murder in Sarajevo.** A few hours later, the royal motorcade drove through Sarajevo. Stationed along the route were seven members of the Black Hand. Several carried crude hand bombs and pistols. The first two conspirators lost their nerve as the cars passed. The third hurled his bomb. It missed the archduke's car but injured an officer in another car. After stopping to see what happened, the royal couple continued with the day's program.

Meanwhile, despite the failure of his co-conspirators, Gavrilo Princip held firm to his plan. He stayed near the route the motorcade would follow later in the day.

Leaving the town hall, the archduke asked to visit the officer who had been wounded in the bombing. But no one told the chauffeur to drive to the hospital. Instead, he followed the old route. When told to change directions, he stopped to put the car in reverse—right at the spot where Princip stood. Seizing his opportunity, he sprang toward the car and fired twice into the back seat.

Horrified guards hurled themselves upon the killer. It was too late—the royal couple had been struck. According to one witness, the archduke gasped, "Sophie, Sophie, don't die. Stay alive for the children!" Within minutes, both were dead.

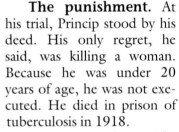

▲ New York Times *headline of June 29, 1914*

**The punishment.** At his trial, Princip stood by his deed. His only regret, he said, was killing a woman. Because he was under 20 years of age, he was not executed. He died in prison of tuberculosis in 1918.

For Europe, the punishment was more severe. The archduke and his wife were the first victims of a war that killed millions. ■

### Peace Unravels

News of his nephew's assassination shocked the aging Austrian emperor, Francis Joseph. He and his government in Vienna blamed Serbia. Serbia would stop at nothing, they believed, to achieve its goal of a South Slav empire. The Austrians

**"Who Did It?"** One by one, the major powers of Europe were drawn into the dispute between Serbia and Austria-Hungary. This cartoon appeared in an American newspaper in 1914, just after war broke out. **Global Interaction** What point is this cartoon making about the events leading up to the war?

decided that their only course was to punish Serbia.

**A harsh ultimatum.** Austria sent Serbia a sweeping ultimatum, or final set of demands. To avoid war, said the ultimatum, Serbia must end all anti-Austrian agitation and punish any Serbian official involved in the murder plot. It must even let Austria join in the investigation.

Serbia agreed to most, but not all, of the terms. This partial refusal gave Austria the opportunity to take decisive action. On July 28, Austria declared war on Serbia.

**Capital to capital.** A war between a major power and a small Balkan state might have been another "summer war," like most European wars of the past century. But as diplomats sent notes from capital to capital, larger forces drew the great powers deeper into conflict.

Austria might not have pushed Serbia into war without the backing of its longtime ally, Germany. In Berlin, Kaiser William II was horrified at the assassination of a royal heir. He advised Francis Joseph to take a firm stand toward Serbia and assured him of German support. Thus, instead of urging restraint, the kaiser gave Austria a "blank check."

Serbia meanwhile sought help from Russia, the champion of Slavic nations. From St. Petersburg, Nicholas II telegraphed William II. The czar asked the kaiser to urge Austria to soften its demands. When this plea failed, Russia began to mobilize, or prepare its military forces for war. Germany responded by declaring war on Russia.

Russia, in turn, appealed to its ally France. In Paris, nationalists saw a chance to avenge France's defeat in the Franco-Prussian War. Though French leaders had some doubts, they gave Russia the same kind of backing Germany offered Austria. When Germany demanded that France remain neutral, France refused. Germany then declared war on France. By early August, the battle lines were hardening.

**The Schlieffen Plan.** Italy and Britain remained uncommitted. Italy decided to remain neutral for the time being. Neutrality is a policy of supporting neither side in a war. Britain had to decide quickly whether or not to support its ally France. Then Germany's war plans suddenly made the decision for Britain.

Germany's worst fear was a war on two fronts, with France attacking from the west and Russia from the east. Years earlier, General Alfred Schlieffen (SHLEE fuhn) had developed a strategy to avoid a two-front war. Schlieffen reasoned that Russia's lumbering military would be slow to mobilize. Under the Schlieffen Plan, Germany first had to defeat France quickly. Then it would fight Russia.

**ISSUES** *For* **TODAY** The Balkan "powder keg" and the complex web of alliances were key ingredients in the outbreak of World War I. What conditions can increase the possibility of war?

## Europe, 1914

NORWAY
SWEDEN
NORTH SEA
DENMARK
IRELAND
GREAT BRITAIN
NETH.
RUSSIA
ATLANTIC OCEAN
BELGIUM
LUX.
GERMANY
FRANCE
SWITZ.
AUSTRIA-HUNGARY
ROMANIA
ITALY
SERBIA
MONTENEGRO
BULGARIA
BLACK SEA
PORTUGAL
SPAIN
ALBANIA
OTTOMAN EMPIRE
GREECE
MEDITERRANEAN SEA

0   250   500 Miles
0   250   500 Kilometers

Central Powers
Allies
Neutral nations
Neutral nations that later joined the Central Powers
Neutral nations that later joined the Allies

### GEOGRAPHY AND HISTORY

By 1914, the major European powers formed rival alliances. Some neutral nations later joined one side or the other.

1. **Location** On the map, locate (a) Germany, (b) Austria-Hungary, (c) France, (d) Serbia.
2. **Place** (a) Which countries remained neutral throughout the war? (b) Which neutral nations eventually joined the Central Powers?
3. **Critical Thinking** **Predicting Consequences** What disadvantage did Germany face because of its location?

To ensure a quick victory in the west, the Schlieffen Plan required German armies to march through Belgium, then swing south behind French lines. On August 3, Germany invaded Belgium. However, Britain and other European powers had signed a treaty guaranteeing Belgian neutrality. Outraged by the invasion of Belgium, Britain declared war on Germany.

## Whose Fault?

How could an assassination lead to all-out war in just a few weeks? During the war, each side blamed the other. Afterward, the victorious Allies put the blame on Germany. Today, most historians agree that all parties must share blame for a catastrophe nobody wanted.

Each great power believed its cause was just. Austria wanted to punish Serbia for encouraging terrorism. Germany felt that it must stand by its one dependable ally, Austria. Russia saw the Austrian ultimatum to Serbia as an effort to oppress Slavic peoples. France feared that if it did not support Russia, it would have to face Germany alone later. Britain felt committed to protect Belgium but also feared the powerful German force just across the English Channel. (☑ See *You Decide,* "Is War Ever Justified?" pages 820–821.)

**"The lamps are going out."** Although leaders made the decisions, most people on both sides were equally committed to military action. Young men rushed to enlist, cheered on by women and their elders. Now that war had come at last, it seemed an exciting adventure.

British diplomat Edward Grey was less optimistic. As armies began to move, he predicted, "The lamps are going out all over Europe. We shall not see them lit again in our lifetime."

### SECTION 2 REVIEW

1. **Identify** (a) Francis Ferdinand, (b) Gavrilo Princip, (c) Black Hand, (d) Schlieffen Plan.
2. **Define** (a) ultimatum, (b) mobilize, (c) neutrality.
3. (a) Why did Serbian nationalists plot the assassination of Francis Ferdinand? (b) How did Austria react to the assassination?
4. Describe how each of the following nations got involved in the conflict: (a) Germany, (b) Russia, (c) France, (d) Britain.
5. **Critical Thinking** **Drawing Conclusions** Do you think that war could have been avoided in 1914? Why or why not?
6. *ACTIVITY* Choose one of the European powers involved in the outbreak of World War I. From that nation's point of view, draw a cartoon assigning blame for the war.

# 3 A New Kind of Conflict

## Guide for Reading

- Why did a stalemate develop on the western front?

- What forces made World War I different from earlier wars?

- How did the war become a global conflict?

"The Great War," as newspapers soon called it, was the largest war in history up to that time. The French mobilized almost 8.5 million men, the British 9 million, the Russians 12 million, and the Germans 11 million.

For those who fought, the statistics were more personal. "At least one in three of my generation in school died," recalled one survivor. Another young man wrote:

66One out of every four men who went out to the World War did not come back again, and of those who came back, many are maimed and blind and some are mad.99

The early enthusiasm for the war soon faded. There were no stirring cavalry charges, no quick and glorious victories. This was a new kind of war, far deadlier than any before.

## The Western Front

As the war began, German forces swept through Belgium toward Paris. German generals, however, soon violated the Schlieffen Plan. Russia mobilized more quickly than expected. After Russian forces won a few small victories in eastern Prussia, Germany hastily shifted some troops to the east. That move weakened German forces in the west. When British troops reached France, the German offensive stalled.

Both sides then dug in for the winter. They did not know that the battle lines would remain almost unchanged for four years. Every year, each side tried to advance—and failed.

**Trench warfare.** On the Western Front, the warring armies burrowed into a vast system of trenches, stretching from the Swiss frontier to the English Channel. A war correspondent described the scene:

66To say where the trenches began and where they ended is difficult. . . . There were vast stretches of mud, of fields once cultivated, but now scarred with pits, trenches, rusty barbed wires. The roads were rivers of clay. They were lined with dugouts, cellars, and caves.99

An underground network linked bunkers, communications trenches, and gun emplacements. There, millions of soldiers roasted under the broiling summer sun or froze through the

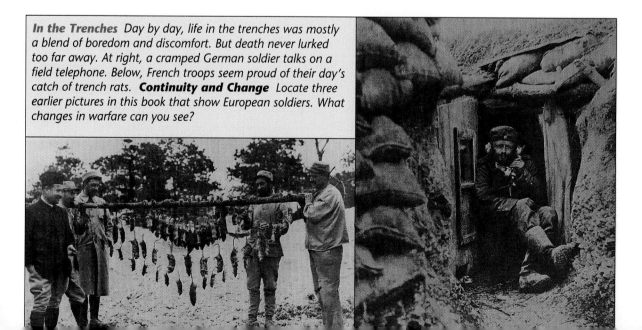

*In the Trenches* Day by day, life in the trenches was mostly a blend of boredom and discomfort. But death never lurked too far away. At right, a cramped German soldier talks on a field telephone. Below, French troops seem proud of their day's catch of trench rats. **Continuity and Change** Locate three earlier pictures in this book that show European soldiers. What changes in warfare can you see?

long winters. They shared their food with rats and their beds with lice.

Between the opposing trench lines lay "no man's land." In this empty tract, pocked with shell holes, every house and tree had long since been destroyed. Through coils of barbed wire, soldiers peered over the edge of their trenches, watching for the next attack. They themselves would have to charge into this man-made desert when officers gave the order.

Sooner or later, soldiers would obey the order to go "over the top." With no protection but their rifles and helmets, they charged across no man's land toward the enemy lines. With luck, they might overrun a few trenches. In time, the enemy would launch a counterattack, with similar results. Each side then rushed in reinforcements to replace the dead and wounded. The struggle continued, back and forth, over a few hundred yards of territory.

**Costly battles.** In 1916, both the Allies and Central Powers launched massive offensives to break the stalemate. German forces tried to overwhelm the French at Verdun (vuhr DUHN). The French sent up the battle cry "They shall not pass." The French defenders held firm, but the struggle cost more than a half-million casualties on both sides.

An Allied offensive at the Somme (SAHM) River was even more costly. In a single grisly day, 60,000 British soldiers were killed or wounded. In the five-month battle, over one million soldiers were killed, without either side winning an advantage.

**A war of machines.** Modern weapons added greatly to the destructiveness of the war. In 1914, German artillery could shell enemy lines from a distance of 15 miles away. By 1918, they were shelling Paris from battle lines 70 miles away.

World War I was truly the first mechanized war. The Quick Study Chart on page 703 details some of the technology that helped turn the war into a seemingly endless ordeal.

## Other European Fronts

On the Eastern Front, battle lines swayed back and forth, sometimes over large areas. Casualties rose even higher than in the west, but the results were just as indecisive.

**Disasters for Russia.** In August 1914, Russian armies pushed into eastern Germany. Then, at the battle of Tannenberg, they suffered one of the worst defeats of the war. Reeling, the Russians retreated. After Tannenberg, armies in the east fought on Russian soil.

As the least industrialized of the great powers, Russia was poorly equipped to fight a modern war. Troops sometimes lacked even rifles. Still, Russian commanders continued to fling masses of peasant soldiers into combat.

**War in the south.** Southeastern Europe was another battleground. In 1915, Bulgaria joined the Central Powers and helped crush its old rival Serbia. Italy, meanwhile, joined the Allies to gain Austrian-ruled lands inhabited by Italians. Caporetto, the major battle on the Italian front, was as disastrous for Italy as Tannenberg had been for Russia.

## The War Beyond Europe

Though most of the fighting took place in Europe, World War I was a global conflict. At sea, Britain blockaded Germany, while German U-boats sank ships crossing the Atlantic toward Allied ports. Such unrestricted submarine warfare outraged neutral countries, especially the United States.

**War and the colonies.** European colonies were drawn into the struggle. The Allies overran scattered German colonies in Africa and Asia. They also turned to their own colonies and dominions for troops, laborers, and supplies. Canada, Australia, and New Zealand sent troops to Britain's aid. Colonial recruits from British India and French West Africa fought on European battlefields.

People in the colonies had mixed feelings about serving. Many volunteered eagerly, expecting that their service would be a step toward citizenship or independence. Others were reluctant to serve the imperial powers. A South African man remarked:

❝When we speak of joining . . . our women curse and spit at us, asking us whether the Government, for whom we propose to risk our lives, is not the one which sends the police to our houses at night.❞

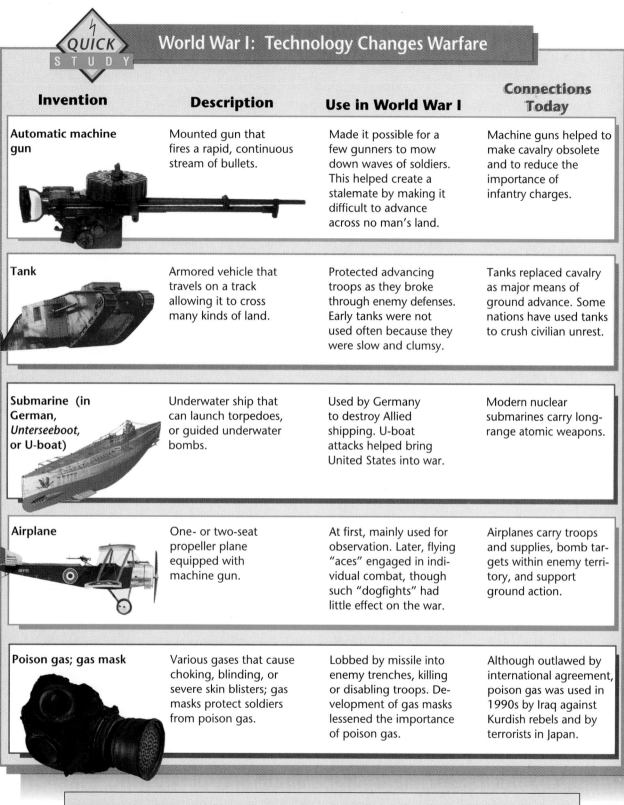

## QUICK STUDY

# World War I: Technology Changes Warfare

| Invention | Description | Use in World War I | Connections Today |
|---|---|---|---|
| **Automatic machine gun** | Mounted gun that fires a rapid, continuous stream of bullets. | Made it possible for a few gunners to mow down waves of soldiers. This helped create a stalemate by making it difficult to advance across no man's land. | Machine guns helped to make cavalry obsolete and to reduce the importance of infantry charges. |
| **Tank** | Armored vehicle that travels on a track allowing it to cross many kinds of land. | Protected advancing troops as they broke through enemy defenses. Early tanks were not used often because they were slow and clumsy. | Tanks replaced cavalry as major means of ground advance. Some nations have used tanks to crush civilian unrest. |
| **Submarine (in German, *Unterseeboot*, or U-boat)** | Underwater ship that can launch torpedoes, or guided underwater bombs. | Used by Germany to destroy Allied shipping. U-boat attacks helped bring United States into war. | Modern nuclear submarines carry long-range atomic weapons. |
| **Airplane** | One- or two-seat propeller plane equipped with machine gun. | At first, mainly used for observation. Later, flying "aces" engaged in individual combat, though such "dogfights" had little effect on the war. | Airplanes carry troops and supplies, bomb targets within enemy territory, and support ground action. |
| **Poison gas; gas mask** | Various gases that cause choking, blinding, or severe skin blisters; gas masks protect soldiers from poison gas. | Lobbed by missile into enemy trenches, killing or disabling troops. Development of gas masks lessened the importance of poison gas. | Although outlawed by international agreement, poison gas was used in 1990s by Iraq against Kurdish rebels and by terrorists in Japan. |

**Interpreting a Chart** *World War I was the first modern, fully industrialized war. Some weapons, such as machine guns, altered the nature of the fighting. Other new technology, such as tanks and airplanes, did not have their greatest impact until years later.* ■ *Which invention on this chart do you think has done the most to change how wars are fought? Explain.*

# Europe at War, 1914–1918

NORWAY
SWEDEN
Petrograd
Moscow
Jutland
DENMARK
NORTH SEA
BALTIC SEA
RUSSIA
IRELAND
GREAT BRITAIN
Tannenberg
NETH.
Brest-Litovsk
London
Berlin
Warsaw
UKRAINE
Ypres
GERMANY
Oder R.
Somme R.
BELG.
LUX.
Rhine R.
GALICIA
Paris
Prague
ATLANTIC OCEAN
Verdun
Vienna
Budapest
FRANCE
SWITZ.
AUSTRIA-HUNGARY
BLACK SEA
Caporetto
Venice
Danube R.
ROMANIA
ITALY
BOSNIA
Sarajevo
SERBIA
BULGARIA
MONTENEGRO
Istanbul
PORTUGAL
SPAIN
CORSICA (Fr.)
Rome
Gallipoli
OTTOMAN EMPIRE
SARDINIA (It.)
ALBANIA
GREECE
Dardanelles
CYPRUS (Br.)
Jerusalem
MEDITERRANEAN SEA
AFRICA

**Legend:**
- Allies, 1918
- Central Powers 1918
- Neutral nations
- Farthest advance by Central Powers
- ★ Battle sites

0    250    500 Miles
0    250    500 Kilometers

## GEOGRAPHY AND HISTORY

World War I was fought on many fronts, with massive losses of life and property.

1. **Location** On the map, locate (a) Sarajevo, (b) Verdun, (c) Somme River, (d) Tannenberg, (e) Caporetto, (f) the Dardanelles.
2. **Movement** How far into France did the Central Powers advance?
3. **Critical Thinking** **Comparing** Compare this map with the Time and Place map on page 692. Why do the two maps show different areas?

**Non-European powers.** The Ottoman empire joined the Central Powers in 1914. The Turks then closed off Allied ships from the Dardanelles, a strategic link to the Black Sea and Russia. (See the map above.) The Allies sent a massive force of British, Indian, Australian, and New Zealand troops to open up the strait. At the battle of Gallipoli (guh LIHP uh lee), Turkish troops tied down the trapped Allies on the beaches. A British soldier described the futility of the struggle that followed:

66On June 4th we went over the top. We took the Turks' trench and held it. It was called Hill 13. The next day we were relieved and told to rest for three hours, but it wasn't more than half an hour before the relieving regiment came running back. The Turks had returned and recaptured their trench. On June 6th my favorite officer was killed and no end of us butchered, but we managed to get hold of Hill 13 again. We found a great muddle, carnage and men without rifles shouting, 'Allah! Allah!,' which is God's name in the Turkish language. Of the 60 men I had started out to war from Harwich with, there were only three left.**99**

In January 1916, after 10 months and more than 200,000 casualties, the Allies finally withdrew from the Dardanelles. In turn, the Ottoman empire was hard hit in the Middle East. Arab nationalists, supported by the British, attacked Turkish outposts in their own struggle for freedom.

Japan, allied to Britain, used the war as an excuse to seize German outposts in China and islands in the Pacific. It also tried to impose a protectorate on China. The world's other great industrial power, the United States, tried to remain neutral. However, as you will read, it was eventually drawn into the war as well.

## SECTION 3 REVIEW

1. **Identify** (a) Western Front, (b) no man's land.
2. (a) Why did the war turn into a stalemate? (b) How was trench warfare conducted?
3. Describe how three new weapons affected the course of the war.
4. What role did Europe's overseas colonies play in World War I?
5. *Critical Thinking* **Predicting Consequences** Governments on both sides tried to keep full casualty figures and other bad news from reaching the public. What effect do you think disastrous defeats such as Tannenberg, Caporetto, or Gallipoli would have had on the attitude of people back home?
6. *ACTIVITY* With a partner, prepare an interview between a war correspondent and a soldier fighting on the Western Front during World War I.

# 4 Winning the War

## Guide for Reading

- How did World War I become a total war?
- What role did women play in the war effort?
- What impact did events in Russia and the United States have on the course of World War I?
- **Vocabulary** *total war, propaganda, atrocity, armistice*

By 1917, European societies were cracking under the strain of war. Instead of praising the glorious deeds of heroes, war poets began denouncing the leaders whose errors wasted so many lives. In "Suicide in the Trenches," the British poet and soldier Siegfried Sassoon captured the bitter mood:

**66**You smug-faced crowds with
    kindling eye
Who cheer when soldier lads march by,
Sneak home and pray you'll
    never know
The hell where youth and
    laughter go.**99**

Three years into the war, a revolution in Russia and the entry of the United States into the war would upset the balance of forces and finally end the long stalemate.

## Effects of the Stalemate

As the struggle wore on, nations realized that a modern, mechanized war required the total commitment of their whole society. The result was what we today call total war, the channeling of a nation's entire resources into a war effort.

**Economic impact.** Early on, both sides set up systems to recruit, arm, transport, and supply armies that numbered in the millions. All of the warring nations except Britain imposed universal military conscription, or "the draft,"

**Returning to the Trenches** British artist C.R.W. Nevinson painted in a new style called Futurism. The aim of Futurist art was to express a sense of motion and an increasingly mechanized world. In this painting, individual soldiers interlock like parts of a giant, impersonal machine. Nevinson saw trench warfare firsthand as a member of the British medical corps. **Art and Literature** Why was Futurism a fitting style for a painting about World War I?

which required all young men to be ready for military or other service.

Governments raised taxes and borrowed huge amounts of money to pay the costs of war. They rationed food and other products, from boots to gasoline. In addition, they introduced other economic controls, such as setting prices and forbidding strikes.

**Propaganda war.** Total war meant controlling public opinion. Even in democratic countries, special boards censored the press. Their aim was to keep complete casualty figures and other discouraging news from reaching the people. Government censors also restricted popular literature, historical writings, motion pictures, and the arts.

Both sides waged a propaganda war. Propaganda is the spreading of ideas to promote a cause or damage an opposing cause. In Germany, people learned to sing a "Hymn of Hate" against the British:

> 66Hate by water and hate by land;
> Hate of the head and hate of the hand;
> We love as one, we hate as one;
> We have *one* foe and one alone—
> ENGLAND!99

Allied propaganda often played up Germany's invasion of Belgium as a barbarous act. The British and French press circulated tales of atrocities, horrible acts against innocent people. Often, these stories were greatly exaggerated versions of misreported incidents. Many were completely made up. ( ★ See *Skills for Success*, page 714.)

## Women at War

Women played a major part in total war. As millions of men left to fight, women took over their jobs and kept national economies going. Many women worked in war industries, manufacturing weapons and supplies. Others joined women's branches of the armed forces. When food shortages threatened Britain, volunteers in the Women's Land Army went to the fields to grow their nation's food.

**At the front.** Military nurses shared the dangers of the men whose wounds they tended. At aid stations close to the front lines, they worked around the clock, especially after a big "push" brought a flood of casualties. In her diary, Vera Brittain describes sweating through 90-degree days in France, "stopping hemorrhages, replacing intestines, and draining and reinserting innumerable rubber tubes" with "gruesome human remains heaped on the floor" around her feet.

Some women became national heroes. Edith Cavell, a British nurse, ran a Red Cross hospital in Belgium even after the German invasion. When the Germans discovered that she was helping Allied prisoners escape, they shot her as a spy. Allied propaganda made Cavell a symbol of German brutality, although women on both sides were executed as spies.

**Looking ahead.** War work gave women a new sense of pride and confidence. After the war, most women had to give up their jobs to men returning home. Still, they had challenged the idea that women were too "delicate" for demanding and dangerous jobs. In many countries, including Britain and the United States, women's support for the war effort helped them finally win the right to vote, after decades of struggle.

## Collapsing Morale

By 1917, the morale of both troops and civilians had plunged. Germany was sending 15-year-old recruits to the front. Britain was on the brink of bankruptcy. Long casualty lists, food shortages, and the failure of generals to win promised victories led to calls for peace.

As morale collapsed, troops mutinied in some French units. In Italy, many soldiers de-

**Serving Her Country** Posters like this one recruited thousands of women to serve in the Royal Air Force. Their work on the ground supported the exploits of daredevil flying aces in the air. **Continuity and Change** How does this poster both reinforce and challenge traditional notions of "women's work"?

serted after the defeat at Caporetto. In Russia, soldiers left the front to join in a full-scale revolution back home.

**Revolution in Russia.** Three years of war had hit Russia especially hard. Stories of incompetent generals and corruption destroyed public confidence. In March 1917, bread riots in St. Petersburg mushroomed into a revolution that brought down the Russian monarchy. (You will read more about the causes and effects of the Russian Revolution in Chapter 28.)

At first, the Allies welcomed the overthrow of the czar. They hoped Russia would institute a democratic government and become a stronger ally. But later that year, when V. I. Lenin came to power, he promised to pull Russian troops out of the war. Early in 1918, Lenin signed the Treaty of Brest-Litovsk (brehst lih TAWFSK) with Germany. The treaty ended Russian participation in World War I.

**Impact on the war.** Russia's withdrawal had an immediate impact on the war. With Russia out of the struggle, Germany could concentrate its forces on the Western Front. In the spring of 1918, the Central Powers stood ready to achieve the great breakthrough they had sought so long.

## The United States Declares War

Soon after the Russian Revolution began, however, another event altered the balance of forces. The United States, which so far had stayed out of the fighting, declared war on Germany. Why did the United States exchange neutrality for war in 1917?

**Unrestricted submarine warfare.** One major reason was German submarine attacks on merchant and passenger ships carrying American citizens. Many of these ships were carrying supplies to the Allies. But President Woodrow Wilson insisted that Americans, as citizens of a neutral country, had a right to safe travel on the seas.

In May 1915, a German submarine torpedoed the British liner *Lusitania*. Almost 1,200 passengers were killed, including 128 Americans. Germany justified the attack, arguing that the *Lusitania* was carrying weapons. When Wilson threatened to cut off relations with Germany, though, Germany agreed to restrict its submarine campaign. Before attacking any ship, U-boats would surface and give warning, allowing neutral passengers to escape to the lifeboats. In January 1917, however, Germany angered Wilson by resuming unrestricted submarine warfare.

**Cultural ties.** The United States had other reasons to support the Allies. Many Americans felt ties of culture and language to Britain. Americans were also sympathetic to France as another democracy. Still, some German Americans favored the Central Powers. So did many Irish Americans, who resented Britain's domination of Ireland, and Russian Jewish immigrants, who did not want to be allied with the czar.

**Zimmermann note.** In early 1917, the British intercepted a message from the German foreign minister, Arthur Zimmermann, to his ambassador in Mexico. Zimmermann promised that, in return for Mexican support, Germany would help Mexico "to reconquer the lost territory in New Mexico, Texas, and Arizona." Britain revealed the Zimmermann note to the American government. When the note became public, anti-German feeling intensified in the United States.

**"The Yanks are coming!"** In April 1917, Wilson asked Congress to declare war on Germany. "We have no selfish ends to serve," he stated. Instead, he painted the conflict idealistically as a war "to make the world safe for democracy" and as a "war to end war."

First, the United States needed months to recruit, train, supply, and transport a modern army across the Atlantic. By 1918, about two million of these fresh American soldiers had joined the war-weary Allied troops fighting on the Western Front. The confidence of these Americans was captured in "Over There," a popular song by George M. Cohan. "The Yanks are coming!" it promised. "And we won't come back/ Till it's over, over there!"

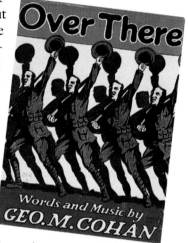

▲ *Sheet music for "Over There"*

Although relatively few American troops got into combat, they proved to be good fighters. Their arrival gave Allied troops a much-needed morale boost. Just as important to the debt-ridden Allies was the financial aid provided by the United States.

**The Fourteen Points.** Though he had failed to maintain American neutrality, Wilson still hoped to be a peacemaker. In January 1918, he issued the Fourteen Points, a list of his terms for resolving this and future wars. He called for an end to secret treaties, freedom of the seas, free trade, and large-scale reductions of arms. Wilson also favored self-determination, by which the peoples of Eastern Europe would choose their own form of government. All those issues, he felt, had helped cause the war. Finally, he urged the creation of a "general association of nations" to keep the peace in the future.

## Campaign to Victory

A final showdown got underway in early 1918. In March, the Germans launched a huge offensive that pushed the Allies back 40 miles by July. But the effort exhausted the Germans. The Allies then launched a counterattack, slowly driving German forces back across France and Belgium. In September, German generals told the kaiser that the war could not be won.

The German people showed their monarch their frustration as uprisings exploded among hungry city dwellers. German commanders advised the kaiser to step down, as the czar had done. William II did so in early November, fleeing into exile in the Netherlands.

By autumn, Austria-Hungary was also reeling toward collapse. As the government in Vienna tottered, the subject nationalities revolted, splintering the empire of the Hapsburgs.

The new German government sought an armistice, or agreement to end fighting, with the Allies. At 11 A.M. on November 11, 1918, the Great War at last came to an end.

---

## SECTION 4 REVIEW

1. **Identify** (a) Women's Land Army, (b) Edith Cavell, (c) Treaty of Brest-Litovsk, (d) Woodrow Wilson, (e) Fourteen Points.
2. **Define** (a) total war, (b) propaganda, (c) atrocity, (d) armistice.
3. How did wartime governments attempt to control (a) national economies, (b) public opinion?
4. Describe two ways that World War I affected women.
5. (a) Why did Russia withdraw from the Allies? (b) Why did the United States declare war on Germany?
6. *Critical Thinking* **Analyzing Information** Why is 1917 considered to be a turning point in the war?
7. *ACTIVITY* Imagine that you are a soldier fighting for the Allies or for the Central Powers. Write a letter home describing your feelings about the armistice.

---

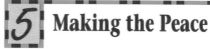

# 5 Making the Peace

### Guide for Reading

■ What problems did Europeans face in 1918?

■ How did the Big Three disagree over the peace?

■ What were the results of the Paris Peace Conference?

■ **Vocabulary** *reparations, mandate*

Just weeks after the war ended, President Wilson boarded the steamship *George Washington*, bound for France. He had decided to go in person to Paris, where Allied leaders would make the peace. Wilson was certain that he could solve the problems of old Europe. "Tell me what is right," Wilson urged his advisers, "and I'll fight for it."

Sadly, it would not be that easy. Europe was a shattered continent. Its problems, and those of the world, would not be solved at Paris, or for many years afterward.

## The Costs of War

The human and material costs of the war were staggering. More than 8.5 million people were dead. Double that number had been wounded, many handicapped for life. Famine threatened many regions. The devastation was made even worse in 1918 by a deadly epidemic

▲ *French war orphans*

## Casualties of World War I

| Allies | Deaths in Battle | Wounded in Battle |
|---|---|---|
| France | 1,357,800 | 4,266,000 |
| British empire | 908,371 | 2,090,212 |
| Russia | 1,700,000 | 4,950,000 |
| Italy | 462,391 | 953,886 |
| United States | 50,585 | 205,690 |
| Other | 502,421 | 342,585 |
| **Central Powers** | | |
| Germany | 1,808,546 | 4,247,143 |
| Austria-Hungary | 922,500 | 3,620,000 |
| Ottoman empire | 325,000 | 400,000 |

Source: R. E. Dupuy and T. N. Dupuy,
*The Encyclopedia of Military History*

*Interpreting a Chart* World War I resulted in far more casualties than any previous war. In countries such as Britain, France, and Germany, hardly a family emerged untouched. ■ Which nation suffered the most military deaths among the Allies? Among the Central Powers? Why did the United States suffer relatively few casualties?

of influenza. In just a few months, the flu swept around the world, killing more than 20 million people—twice as many as the war itself.

**Financial burdens.** In battle zones from France to Russia, homes, farms, factories, roads, and churches had been shelled into rubble. Rebuilding and paying huge national war debts would burden an already battered world.

Shaken and disillusioned, people everywhere felt bitter about the war. The Allies blamed the conflict on their defeated foes and insisted that the losers make reparations, or payments for war damage. The stunned Central Powers, who had viewed the armistice as a cease-fire rather than a surrender, looked for scapegoats on whom to blame their defeat.

**Political turmoil.** Under the stress of war, governments had collapsed in Russia, Germany, Austria-Hungary, and the Ottoman empire. Political radicals dreamed of building a new social

order from the chaos, as revolutionaries in Russia seemed to be doing. Conservatives warned against the spread of bolshevism, or communism, as it came to be called.

Unrest also swept through Europe's colonial empires. African and Asian soldiers had discovered that the imperial powers were not as invincible as they seemed. Colonial troops returned home with a more cynical view of Europeans and renewed hopes for independence.

### The Paris Peace Conference

To a weary and angry world, Woodrow Wilson seemed a symbol of hope. His talk of democracy and self-determination raised expectations for a just and lasting peace, even in defeated Germany. As he rode along the broad Paris boulevards, crowds cheered wildly. Overhead, a giant banner proclaimed, "Honor to Wilson the Just."

**The Big Three.** Wilson was one of three strong personalities who dominated the Paris Peace Conference. A dedicated reformer, Wilson was so sure of his rightness that he could be hard to work with. Urging "peace without victory," he wanted the Fourteen Points to be the basis of the peace.

The other Allies had different aims. The British prime minister, David Lloyd George, knew that the British people demanded harsh treatment for Germany. He promised that he would build a postwar Britain "fit for heroes"— a goal that would cost money. The French leader, Georges Clemenceau, bore the nickname "the Tiger" for his fierce war policy. His chief goal was to weaken Germany so that it could never again threaten France. "Mr. Wilson bores me with his Fourteen Points," complained Clemenceau. "Why, God Almighty has only ten!"

**Difficult issues.** Crowds of other representatives circled around the "Big Three" with their own demands and interests. Among the most difficult issues were the secret agreements made by the Allies during the war. Italy had signed one such treaty. Its prime minister, Vittorio Orlando, insisted on gaining for Italy lands that were once ruled by Austria-Hungary. Such secret agreements violated Wilson's principle of self-determination.

Self-determination posed other problems. Many people who had been ruled by Russia, Austria-Hungary, or the Ottoman empire now demanded national states of their own. The territories claimed by these peoples often overlapped, so it was impossible to satisfy them all.

Faced with conflicting demands, Wilson had to compromise on his Fourteen Points. On one point, though, he stood firm. His dream was to create an international League of Nations to guarantee peace for the future. With the league in place, he felt sure that any mistakes made in Paris could be corrected in time.

## The Treaty of Versailles

In June 1919, the peacemakers summoned representatives of the new German Republic to the palace of Versailles outside Paris. The Germans were ordered to sign the treaty drawn up by the Allies.

The German delegates read the document with growing horror. It forced Germany to assume full blame for causing the war:

> **66** The Allied and Associated Governments affirm, and Germany accepts, the responsibility of Germany and her allies for causing all the loss and damage to which the Allied and Associated Governments and their nationals have been subjected as a consequence of the war imposed on them by the aggression of Germany and her allies. **99**

The treaty also imposed huge reparations that would put an already damaged German economy under a staggering burden. The reparations covered not only the destruction caused by the war, but also pensions for millions of Allied soldiers or their widows and families. The total cost of German reparations would come to over $30 billion.

Other clauses were aimed at weakening Germany. The treaty severely limited the size of the once-feared German military machine. It returned Alsace and Lorraine to France, removed hundreds of square miles of territory from western and eastern Germany, and stripped Germany of its overseas colonies.

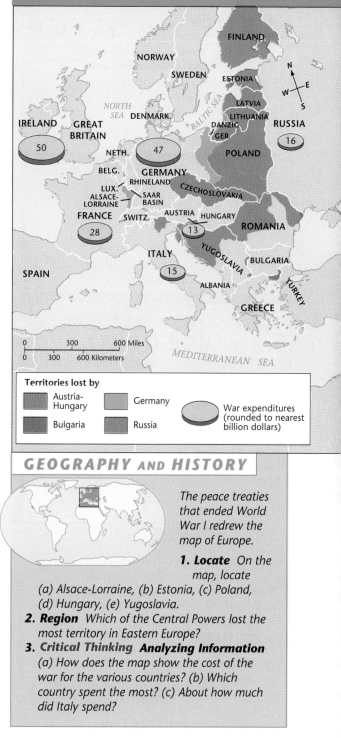

### Europe After World War I

**Territories lost by**

- Austria-Hungary
- Bulgaria
- Germany
- Russia
- War expenditures (rounded to nearest billion dollars)

### GEOGRAPHY AND HISTORY

The peace treaties that ended World War I redrew the map of Europe.

1. **Locate** On the map, locate (a) Alsace-Lorraine, (b) Estonia, (c) Poland, (d) Hungary, (e) Yugoslavia.
2. **Region** Which of the Central Powers lost the most territory in Eastern Europe?
3. **Critical Thinking** Analyzing Information (a) How does the map show the cost of the war for the various countries? (b) Which country spent the most? (c) About how much did Italy spend?

The Germans signed because they had no choice. But German resentment of the Treaty of Versailles would poison the international climate for 20 years—and help spark an even more deadly world war. (See Chapter 31.)

# CAUSE AND EFFECT

## Long-Term Causes

Imperialist and economic rivalries among European powers
European alliance system
Militarism and arms race
Nationalist tensions in Balkans

## Immediate Causes

Austria-Hungary annexation of Bosnia and Herzegovina
Fighting in the Balkans
Assassination of Archduke Francis Ferdinand
German invasion of Belgium

## WORLD WAR I

## Immediate Effects

Enormous cost in lives and money
Russian Revolution
Creation of new nations in Eastern Europe
Requirement that Germany pay reparations
German loss of its overseas colonies
Balfour Declaration
League of Nations

## Long-Term Effects

Economic impact of war debts on Europe
Emergence of United States and Japan as important powers
Growth of nationalism in colonies
Rise of fascism
World War II

## Connections Today

Ethnic tensions in Balkans
International agreement banning poison gas
Use of airplanes and submarines for military purposes
Arab-Israeli conflict

## Other Settlements

The Allies drew up separate treaties with the other Central Powers. These treaties redrew the map of Eastern Europe.

**Self-determination in action.** A band of new nations emerged where the German, Austrian, and Russian empires had once ruled. These nations included the Baltic states of Lithuania, Latvia, and Estonia. (See the map on page 711.) Poland regained independence after more than 100 years of foreign rule.

Three new republics—Czechoslovakia, Austria, and Hungary—rose in the old Hapsburg heartland. In the Balkans, the peacemakers created a new South Slav state, Yugoslavia, dominated by Serbia. Eastern Europe, however, remained a center of conflict, as you will read.

**Mandate system.** European colonies in Africa, Asia, and the Pacific had looked to the Paris Peace Conference with high hopes. Many people from these lands had fought alongside Europeans. Colonial leaders expected that the peace would bring new respect and an end to imperial rule. They took up Wilson's call for self-determination.

However, the leaders at Paris applied the principle of self-determination only to parts of Europe. Outside Europe, the victorious Allies added to their existing overseas empires. The treaties created a system of mandates, or territories that were administered by western powers. Britain and France gained mandates over German colonies in Africa and Ottoman lands in the Middle East. In theory, mandates were to be held and modernized until they were able to "stand alone." In practice, they practically became European colonies. From Africa to the Middle East and across Asia, colonized peoples felt betrayed by the peacemakers.

**Unfulfilled goals.** Germany was not the only power dissatisfied by the peace. Italy was angry because it did not get all the lands promised in its secret treaty with the Allies.

*Interpreting a Chart* World War I grew out of rivalries among the nations of Europe. But its effects are still being felt around the world today. ■ What single event sparked the outbreak of World War I? Which long-term effect of World War I do you think is most important today? Why?

sioned with war and its consequences, the United States chose to play a lone hand in world affairs.

As time soon revealed, the league was powerless to prevent aggression or war. Still, it was a first step toward something genuinely new—an international organization dedicated to maintaining peace and advancing the interests of all peoples.

Japan protested the refusal of western nations to recognize its claims in China. At the same time, China was forced to accept Japanese control over some former German holdings. (See page 752.) Russia, excluded from the peace talks, resented the reestablishment of a Polish nation and three independent Baltic states on lands that had been part of the Russian empire.

All of these discontented nations bided their time. They waited for a chance to revise the peace settlements in their favor.

## Hopes for Global Peace

The Paris Peace Conference offered one beacon of hope in the League of Nations. In the aftermath of the war, millions of people looked to the league to ensure the peace. More than 40 nations joined the league. They agreed to negotiate disputes rather than resort to war. Members of the league promised to take common action, economic or even military, against any aggressor state.

Wilson's dream had become a reality. Yet his own Senate refused to ratify the treaty and the United States never joined the league. Disillu-

## SECTION 5 REVIEW

1. **Identify** (a) David Lloyd George, (b) Georges Clemenceau, (c) Treaty of Versailles, (d) League of Nations.
2. **Define** (a) reparations, (b) mandate.
3. Describe conditions in Europe after World War I.
4. (a) Explain three issues to be settled at the Paris Peace Conference. (b) How did Wilson's goals for the peace differ from those of other Allied leaders?
5. How did the treaties both follow and violate Woodrow Wilson's principle of self-determination?
6. *Critical Thinking* **Making Inferences** Wilson's closest adviser wrote, "Looking at the conference in retrospect, there is much to approve and much to regret." What do you think he might have approved? What might he have regretted?
7. *ACTIVITY* Write an editorial or draw a cartoon about the Treaty of Versailles that might have appeared in a German newspaper in 1919.

# Skills for Success

## Recognizing Propaganda

Propaganda consists of ideas, information, or rumors that are spread deliberately for the purpose of influencing people's thoughts or actions. The goal of propagandists, or those who create and spread propaganda, is to further their own cause or damage an opposing cause. The information given may be true. However, it is usually only one side of an issue or may be presented in a distorted manner.

Propagandists use several techniques to shape the way people perceive an issue. One technique is to present half-truths. This involves supplying only those facts that support a cause or point of view. A second technique is to engage in name-calling. Describing one's opponents or enemies as "barbar-

ians" is an example of name-calling. A third propaganda technique is to identify a cause with a famous person or noble idea. A fourth technique is to use symbols or images that show the other side in the worst possible light.

Propaganda has been used throughout history. During World War I, both the Allies and the Central Powers used propaganda to win and maintain public support for the war effort. One of the most frequently used means of spreading propaganda was posters. The poster below was printed in Britain in 1915. Examine the poster, then answer the following questions:

**1** **Identify the use of propaganda techniques.** (a) Does the British poster contain any half-truths? Explain. (b) Does the poster make use of name-calling? Explain. (c) What details of the attack are included? (d) What symbols or images are used to present the Central Powers in the worst possible light?

**2** **Analyze the emotional appeal of the propaganda.** (a) Why does this poster concentrate on a single household? (b) What emotions might this poster have stirred up in the people of Great Britain? Why? (c) How is the emotional appeal of the poster at left similar to and different from that of the poster on page 707?

**3** **Draw conclusions.** (a) Who do you think paid for and distributed this poster? (b) Who was the intended audience? (c) What was the main goal? (d) How do you think propaganda affected the course of the war?

***Beyond the Classroom*** Recognizing propaganda is an important skill as you evaluate information. If you are aware of how others are trying to influence your opinion, you can make better judgments. Look for examples of propaganda on television and in newspapers. These may include campaign advertisements, commercials, public service messages, and political cartoons. Report to the class on what the message was and what propaganda techniques were used.

MEN OF BRITAIN !
WILL YOU STAND THIS ?

Nº 2 Wykeham Street, SCARBOROUGH, after the German bombardment on Dec! 16ᵗʰ. It was the Home of a Working Man. Four People were killed in this House including the Wife aged 58, and Two Children the youngest aged 5.

78 Women & Children were killed and 228 Women & Children were wounded by the German Raiders
ENLIST NOW

## Building Vocabulary

Write sentences using *five* of the vocabulary words from this chapter, leaving blanks where the vocabulary words would go. Exchange your sentences with another student and fill in the blanks on each other's lists.

## Reviewing Chapter Themes

1. **Political and Social Systems** (a) Why did the great powers seek alliances in the late 1800s and early 1900s? (b) What effect did these alliances have on the international atmosphere? (c) Describe how the alliance system operated in the summer of 1914.
2. **Global Interaction** Describe how each of the following became involved in a war that broke out in Europe: (a) colonized lands in Africa and Asia, (b) Japan, (c) the Ottoman empire, (d) the United States.
3. **Economics and Technology** (a) Why was World War I more destructive than earlier wars? (b) How did the war affect the economies of European nations?
4. **Continuity and Change** (a) How did the Paris Peace Conference try to deal with the issues that caused the war? (b) Why were many nations dissatisfied with the peace settlement?

## Thinking Critically

1. **Linking Past and Present** (a) What efforts were made to promote world peace before and after World War I? (b) How do individuals and governments work for peace today?
2. **Analyzing Political Cartoons** Study the cartoon on page 699. (a) What attitude does the cartoonist seem to have toward the major powers of Europe? (b) How does the cartoon reflect the position of the United States at the beginning of the war? (c) Based on your reading, does this cartoon accurately depict the crisis leading up to World War I? (★ See *Skills for Success,* page 580.)
3. **Recognizing Causes and Effects** How did the Industrial Revolution affect the course of World War I? (★ See *Skills for Success,* page 18.)

4. **Analyzing Literature** Reread the lines by Siegfried Sassoon on page 705. (a) To whom is Sassoon speaking? (b) What attitude does he express? (c) What do these lines suggest about the experience of fighting in the trenches? (★ See *Skills for Success,* page 234.)
5. **Defending a Position** Some women suffragists opposed World War I, arguing that they could not support a government that would not let them vote. Other suffragists urged women to support the war effort as a way of winning the vote. If you had been a suffragist, which of these two positions would you have supported? Explain. (Remember, you would not know the outcome of the war in advance.)
6. **Analyzing Information** (a) What do you think Woodrow Wilson meant by "peace without victory"? (b) Why do you think the European Allies were unwilling to accept this idea?

## For Your Portfolio

Imagine that you and two classmates are members of a British propaganda team early in 1917. Your assignment is to produce propaganda that will convince Americans to support the Allies.

1. Begin by reviewing with your partners the Skill Lesson on the opposite page and the discussion of propaganda on page 706.
2. Make a list of reasons for the United States to support the Allies or oppose the Central Powers. Use this list to decide on a focus for your propaganda campaign. (You might do further research on certain topics, such as the invasion of Belgium or the sinking of the *Lusitania.*)
3. Decide what form your propaganda will take. You might write a speech, create a poster, write a song, or prepare a skit. (The Allies and Central Powers also made propaganda films. If you decide to present a scene from a movie, remember that movies during this period were silent.)
4. Prepare your propaganda and present it to the class. Afterward, discuss the following questions: (a) Which propaganda was most effective? Why? (b) Which propaganda seemed to exaggerate the most? The least? (c) Why is it important for people to be aware of how propaganda works?

# Revolution in Russia

## (1917–1939)

## CHAPTER OUTLINE

As he watched the Bolsheviks celebrate their victory in November 1917, N. N. Sukhanov (soo KAHN awf) was both excited and nervous. In just a few months, these radical revolutionaries had seized power in Russia. Their leader, Lenin, and his comrades rose before a cheering crowd, savoring their triumph. Everyone sang the "Internationale," the anthem for supporters of worldwide socialism. "The mass of delegates," recalled Sukhanov, "were permeated by the faith that all would go well in the future too."

Sukhanov was not so sure. Like many Russians, he had long dreamed of the moment when the czar would be gone and the government would undertake much-needed changes. Like the Bolsheviks, he, too, was a socialist. But he feared these determined revolutionaries:

> 66Applause, hurrahs, caps flung up in the air . . . But I didn't believe in the success, in the rightness, or in the historic mission of a Bolshevik regime. Sitting in the back seats, I watched this celebration with a heavy heart. How I longed to join in and merge with this mass and with its leaders in a single feeling! But I couldn't.99

Time would later justify Sukhanov's worst fears. In 1931, he himself would be arrested by the new government's secret police, to vanish like millions of others into a brutal forced-labor camp. The revolution that many Russians had welcomed in 1917 would have costs that they never anticipated.

Like the American and French revolutions, the Russian Revolution began with a small incident—bread riots in the capital. But it soon mushroomed into one of the most important events of the century. Leaders like Lenin were determined to create a new society based on the ideas of Karl Marx. Certain that capitalism was destined to fall, they harbored ambitions to spread communist revolution around the world.

The worldwide revolution that Marx had predicted never took place. But Lenin and his successors would transform czarist Russia into the communist Soviet Union. For almost 75 years, Soviet experiments in one-party politics and a state-run economy would serve as a model for revolutionaries from China to Cuba.

**FOCUS ON** these themes as you read:

■ **Continuity and Change**
How did political, social, and economic conditions in czarist Russia spark a revolution?

■ **Impact of the Individual**
What roles did Lenin and Stalin play in the emergence of the Soviet Union?

■ **Economics and Technology**
How did the Soviet economy develop?

■ **Political and Social Systems**
How did the Soviet Union become a totalitarian state?

## TIME AND PLACE

*A New Russia*  The year 1917 saw two revolutions in Russia. The first overthrew the czar. The second led to the creation of the world's first communist nation, the Soviet Union. Here, the Soviet Red Army parades in Moscow past a statue of Lenin, leader of the communist takeover. The city is decorated in red, the color of the revolution. **Art and Literature**  Do you think this painter admired the revolution? How can you tell?

## HUMANITIES LINK

*Art History*  Sergei Eisenstein, *Battleship Potemkin* (page 728).
*Literature*  In this chapter, you will encounter passages from the following works of literature: Mikhail Sholokhov, *And Quiet Flows the Don* (page 723); Vladimir Mayakovsky, "Vladimir Ilyich Lenin" (page 732); Anna Akhmatova, "Requiem" (page 732).

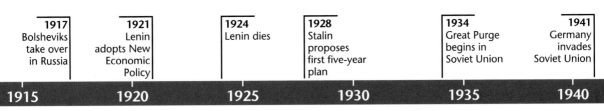

| 1917 Bolsheviks take over in Russia | 1921 Lenin adopts New Economic Policy | 1924 Lenin dies | 1928 Stalin proposes first five-year plan | 1934 Great Purge begins in Soviet Union | 1941 Germany invades Soviet Union |

1915    1920    1925    1930    1935    1940

# 1  Two Revolutions in Russia

## Guide for Reading

- Why did revolution break out in Russia in 1917?
- What were the goals of Lenin and the Bolsheviks?
- What problems did the Bolsheviks face?

- **Vocabulary** *soviet*

On Easter 1913, Czar Nicholas II gave his wife, Alexandra, a fabulous jeweled egg, made by the world-famous jewelry firm of Fabergé (fab uhr ZHAY). The egg's enamel shell held tiny portraits of all the Romanovs who had reigned since Michael Romanov was elected to rule Russia in 1613. Balls, parades, and other ceremonies marked the 300th anniversary of the Romanov dynasty. Everywhere, Russians cheered wildly for the czar and his family.

Years later, an exiled Russian noblewoman recalled the anniversary celebrations:

66 Nobody seeing those
enthusiastic crowds
could have imagined that
in less than four years,
Nicky's very name would
be splattered with mud
and hatred.99

▲ *Fabergé egg given by Nicholas II to his wife*

After the Revolution of 1905, Nicholas had failed to solve Russia's basic problems. Discontent sparked new eruptions. In March 1917, the first of two revolutions would topple the Romanov dynasty and pave the way for even more radical changes.

## Revolutionary Rumblings

In 1914, the huge Russian empire stretched from Eastern Europe to the Pacific. Compared to industrialized Western Europe, it was a backward land dominated by landowning nobles, priests, and an autocratic czar. Much of its majority peasant population endured in stark poverty. A small middle class and an urban working class were emerging as Russia began to industrialize.

**Unrest.** Under pressure, czars had made some reforms, but too few to ease the nation's crisis. (See page 603.) The elected Duma set up after the Revolution of 1905 had no real power. Moderates pressed for a constitution and social change. But Nicholas II, a weak and ineffectual man, blocked attempts to limit his authority. Like past czars, he relied on his secret police and other enforcers to impose his will. Adding to the problems of the government were a corrupt bureaucracy and an overburdened court system.

Outside the government, revolutionaries hatched radical plots. Some hoped to lead discontented peasants to overthrow the czarist regime. Marxists tried to ignite revolution among the proletariat—the growing class of factory and railroad workers, miners, and urban wage earners. To outwit government spies and informers, revolutionaries worked in secrecy under rigid discipline. A revolution, they believed, would occur, but the time was not yet ripe.

**World War I.** The outbreak of war in 1914 fired national pride and united Russians. Armies dashed to battle with enthusiasm. But like the Crimean and Russo-Japanese wars, World War I quickly strained Russian resources. Factories could not turn out enough supplies. The transportation system broke down, delivering only a trickle of needed materials to the front. By 1915, soldiers had no rifles, no ammunition, and no medical care. Badly equipped and poorly led, they died in staggering numbers. In 1915 alone, Russian casualties reached two million.

In a patriotic gesture, Nicholas II went to the front to take personal charge. The decision proved a disastrous blunder. The czar was no more competent than many of his generals. Worse, he left domestic affairs to the czarina, Alexandra. Many Russians already distrusted Alexandra because she was German born. She also knew little about government. As corruption and intrigue flourished, Alexandra came to rely more and more on the advice of a notorious "holy man" named Gregory Rasputin.

## Death of the Mad Monk

An illiterate Siberian peasant, Rasputin was not actually a monk in the Russian Orthodox Church. In fact, he was amazingly corrupt and fond of worldly pleasures. But his powerful personality helped him gain a widespread reputation as a healer.

No one believed in his "miraculous" powers more than the czarina. Time and again, he eased the suffering of her only son, Alexis. The boy suffered from hemophilia, an inherited disorder in which any injury can lead to uncontrollable bleeding. When doctors were not able to help, Rasputin stopped the prince's bleeding, apparently through hypnosis.

**A threat to Russia?** By 1916, Rasputin's influence over Alexandra reached new heights. At his say-so, officials could be appointed or dismissed. Those who flattered him won top jobs for which they were wholly unqualified. Yet Alexandra chose to ignore all warnings about Rasputin's evil nature. She insisted that he had been sent by God to save Russia and the Romanov dynasty. At a time when wise leadership was desperately needed, Russia was in the hands of a shady character known to his enemies as the "mad monk."

Members of the Duma, nobles, and the czar's relatives saw the danger. To save the

**The Mad Monk** *Both nobles and ordinary Russians hated Rasputin for his influence over the czarina. "He is hated," complained Alexandra, "because we love him." Rasputin once boasted that "the czar and czarina bow down to me, kneel to me, kiss my hands."* **Impact of the Individual** *How might Rasputin's appearance have added to his reputation as a "holy man" and a magical healer?*

monarchy, a group of five men hatched a plot to destroy Rasputin.

**A hard man to kill.** On December 29, 1916, Prince Felix Yussoupov (yoo SOO pawf), a nephew of the czar, lured Rasputin to his palace. The prince fed the "mad monk" cakes and wine laced with poison. Rasputin polished them off and talked on—for hours.

Yussoupov hurried upstairs to consult his nervous co-conspirators. He returned with a revolver and shot Rasputin. As the plotters examined the body, Rasputin suddenly leaped up and grabbed the prince, who fled in terror. One of the plotters described what happened next:

66What I saw would have been a dream if it hadn't been a terrible reality. Rasputin, who half an hour before lay dying in the cellar, was running quickly across the snow-covered courtyard toward the iron gate which led to the street.99

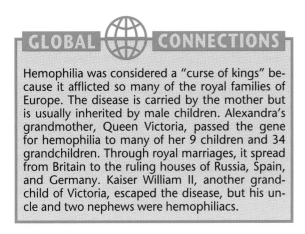

**GLOBAL CONNECTIONS**

Hemophilia was considered a "curse of kings" because it afflicted so many of the royal families of Europe. The disease is carried by the mother but is usually inherited by male children. Alexandra's grandmother, Queen Victoria, passed the gene for hemophilia to many of her 9 children and 34 grandchildren. Through royal marriages, it spread from Britain to the ruling houses of Russia, Spain, and Germany. Kaiser William II, another grandchild of Victoria, escaped the disease, but his uncle and two nephews were hemophiliacs.

Another shot felled Rasputin, who was then clubbed into stillness. The conspirators dropped the body into the icy Neva River. Later when it was found, doctors discovered that neither poison nor bullets had killed Rasputin. He had died by drowning.

**Rasputin's final warning.** News of Rasputin's death caused rejoicing in the capital. Alexandra, though, was desolate. Just weeks before, Rasputin had written her a letter predicting his murder. If he were killed by nobles, he warned, "None of your children or relations will remain alive for more than two years. They will be killed by the Russian people."

Rasputin's prophecy would enhance his legend. In 1917, the Romanov dynasty indeed came to an end. Its downfall, though, was not due to Rasputin's murder, but to long unsolved problems and the strains of war.

## The March Revolution

By March 1917,* disasters on the battlefield, combined with food and fuel shortages on the home front, brought the monarchy to collapse. In St. Petersburg (renamed Petrograd during the war), workers were going on strike. Marchers, mostly women, surged through the streets, shouting, "Bread! Bread!" Troops refused to fire on the demonstrators, leaving the government helpless. Finally, on the advice of military and political leaders, the czar abdicated.

Duma politicians then set up a provisional, or temporary, government. Middle-class liberals in the government began preparing a constitution for a new Russian republic. At the same time, they continued the war against Germany. That decision proved fatal. Most Russians were fed up with the war. Troops at the front were deserting and returning home in droves. Peasants wanted land. City workers demanded food and an end to the desperate shortages.

Outside the provisional government, revolutionary socialists plotted their own course. In Petrograd and other cities, they set up soviets,

---

*The revolutions of March and November 1917 are known to Russians as the February and October revolutions. In 1917, Russia still used an old calendar, which was 13 days behind the one used in Western Europe. Not until 1918 did Russia adopt the western calendar.

or councils of workers and soldiers. At first, the soviets worked democratically within the government. Before long, though, the Bolsheviks, a radical socialist group, took charge. The leader of the Bolsheviks was a determined revolutionary, V. I. Lenin.

## Lenin and the Bolsheviks

Lenin's real name was Vladimir Ilyich Ulyanov (ool YAHN awf). He was born in 1870 to a middle-class family. When he was 17, his older brother was arrested and hanged for plotting to kill Alexander III. The execution branded the entire family and instilled in young Vladimir a lifetime hatred for the czarist government. Still, he managed to finish his studies.

As a young man, he read the works of Karl Marx and participated in student demonstrations. He spread Marxist ideas among factory workers along with other socialists, including Nadezhda Krupskaya (nah DYEZH duh kroop SKĪ uh), the daughter of a poor noble family.

In 1895, Lenin and Krupskaya were arrested and sent to Siberia. During their imprisonment, they were married. After their release, they went into exile in Switzerland. There, they worked tirelessly to spread revolutionary ideas. A rival once described Lenin's total commitment to the cause:

> **66**There is no other man who is absorbed by the revolution 24 hours a day, who has no other thoughts but the thought of revolution, and who, even when he sleeps, dreams of nothing but the revolution.**99**

**A new view of Marx.** Lenin adapted Marxist ideas to Russian conditions. Marx had predicted that the industrial working class would rise spontaneously to overthrow capitalism. But Russia did not have a large urban proletariat. Instead, Lenin called for an elite group to lead the revolution and set up a "dictatorship of the proletariat." Though this revolutionary party represented a small percentage of socialists, Lenin gave them the name Bolsheviks, meaning "majority."

In Western Europe, many socialists had come to think that socialism could be achieved through gradual reforms such as higher wages, increased suffrage, and social welfare programs. The Bolsheviks rejected this approach. To Lenin, reforms were merely capitalist tricks to repress the masses. Only revolution, he said, could bring about needed changes.

**An exile returns.** In March 1917, Lenin was still in exile. As Russia stumbled into revolution, Germany saw a chance to weaken its enemy by helping Lenin return home. In a sealed train, it rushed the Bolshevik leader across Germany to the Russian frontier.

On April 16, 1917, Lenin stepped off the train in Petrograd. A crowd of fellow exiles and activists recently released from the czar's prisons met him at the station. Lenin triumphantly addressed the crowd:

> 66 Dear comrades, soldiers, sailors and workers, I am happy to greet in you the victorious Russian revolution, to greet you as the advance guard of the international proletarian army. . . . Any day may see the general collapse of European capitalism. The Russian revolution you have accomplished has dealt it the first blow and has opened a new epoch. . . . Long live the International Socialist Revolution! 99

## The November Revolution

Lenin threw himself into the work of furthering the revolution, assisted by another committed Marxist revolutionary, Leon Trotsky. To the hungry, war-weary Russian people, Lenin and the Bolsheviks promised "Peace, Land, and Bread."

That summer, the provisional government launched yet another disastrous new offensive against Germany. As troops mutinied and another grim winter closed in, the Bolsheviks made their move.

**The Bolshevik takeover.** In November 1917, squads of Red Guards—armed factory workers—joined mutinous sailors from the Russian fleet in attacking the provisional government. In a matter of days, Lenin's forces overthrew a government that no longer had any support.

In Petrograd, members of the government were meeting in an inner room at the Winter Palace. Suddenly, a young cadet entered the room to announce that Bolsheviks were storming the palace. "What are the provisional government's orders?" he asked.

"It's no use," one politician announced. "We give up. No bloodshed!"

*The Death of Old Russia* In the March Revolution, angry workers confronted the czar's troops in Petrograd. Instead of firing, the soldiers turned against their officers and joined the rebellion. "Cars full of soldiers with rifles and red flags are driving through the streets," one woman reported. "The crowd rushes toward them and shouts 'Hurray!'" **Political and Social Systems** Why do you think soldiers turned against their officers and the czar?

**Revolutionary Genius** *An iron will and brilliant mind made Lenin the natural leader of the Bolsheviks. Once in power, however, Lenin found his revolution threatened by enemies inside and outside the country. "The capitalists of England, America, and France are leading a war against Russia," he railed in one speech. Lenin told soldiers that the Red Army was invincible "because it combines millions of active peasants and workers who have now learned how to fight."* **Impact of the Individual** *How does this painting convey the impression that Lenin was an energetic, commanding leader?*

A moment later, armed men flooded into the room. The provisional government had fallen without a struggle.

**Bolsheviks in charge.** The Bolsheviks quickly seized power in other cities. In Moscow, it took a week of fighting to blast the local government out of the walled Kremlin. Moscow became the Bolsheviks' capital, and the Kremlin their headquarters.

"We shall now occupy ourselves in Russia in building up a proletarian socialist state," declared Lenin. The Bolsheviks ended private ownership of land and distributed land to peasants. Workers were given control of the factories and mines. A new red flag with an entwined hammer and sickle symbolized union between peasants and workers.

Millions of Russians thought they had at last won control of their lives. In fact, the Bolsheviks—renamed Communists—would soon become their new masters.

## Under Siege

After the Bolshevik Revolution, Lenin quickly sought peace with Germany. Despite its high cost, Russia signed the Treaty of Brest-Litovsk in March 1918, giving up a huge chunk of its territory and its population. (See page 707.) But the Communists needed all their energy to defeat a battery of enemies at home.

For three years, civil war raged. The newly formed Red Army battled the Whites, counter-revolutionaries who remained loyal to the czar. National groups that the czars had conquered also took up arms against the Red Army. Poland, Estonia, Latvia, and Lithuania broke free, but nationalists in Ukraine, the Caucasus, and Central Asia were eventually subdued.

**Allied invasion.** Foreign powers intervened, too. Japan seized land in East Asia that czarist Russia had once claimed. The Allies—Britain, France, and the United States—sent forces to help the Whites, who wanted to continue the war against Germany. Although the Allied forces failed, their presence roused Russian nationalism. In the long run, the invasion fed Communist distrust of the West.

**A costly triumph.** Both sides took brutal measures to win the civil war. Counterrevolutionary forces slaughtered captured Communists and tried to assassinate Lenin. To crush their enemies, the Communists unleashed a reign of terror. They organized their own secret police, the Cheka. Ordinary citizens were executed if they were suspected of counterrevolutionary activities. The former czar and czarina and their five children were shot to keep them from becoming a rallying symbol for counterrevolutionary forces.

The Communists adopted a policy known as "war communism." They took over banks, mines, factories, and railroads. Peasants were forced to deliver "surplus" food to hungry people in the cities. Peasant laborers were drafted into the military or into factory work.

Meanwhile, Trotsky turned the Red Army into an effective fighting force, under the close watch of Communist officials. Trotsky's passionate speeches roused soldiers to fight. So did the order to shoot every tenth man if a unit performed poorly—a tactic borrowed from the armies of ancient Rome. (See page 132.)

The great Russian writer Mikhail Sholokhov (SHAW luh kawf) described the civil war in his novel *And Quiet Flows the Don*. Here, a Red Army officer tells how he feels about executing Cossacks, peasants in the czar's cavalry:

66In real life there isn't a man who is without fear in battle, and not a man who can kill people without carrying— without getting morally scratched. I don't feel any regret for the officers. . . . But yesterday I had to shoot three Cossacks among the rest—three toilers. I began to bind one. . . . I happened to touch his hand, and it was as hard as sole-leather, covered with calluses. A black palm, all cuts and lumps.99

By 1921, the Communists had defeated their scattered foes. Although Lenin had triumphed, Russia was in chaos. Millions had died since the beginning of World War I. Famine stalked the land, killing millions. Lenin faced an immense job of rebuilding a nation and an economy in ruins.

## SECTION 1 REVIEW

1. **Identify** (a) Nicholas and Alexandra, (b) Gregory Rasputin, (c) Nadezhda Krupskaya, (d) Leon Trotsky, (e) Red Guard, (f) Whites, (g) Cheka, (h) Mikhail Sholokhov.
2. **Define** soviet.
3. (a) What was the immediate cause of the March Revolution? (b) What were the long-term causes?
4. (a) How did Lenin adapt Marxism to conditions in Russia? (b) Why were the Bolsheviks able to seize power in November 1917?
5. What problems did the Bolsheviks face after taking over the government?
6. *Critical Thinking* **Understanding Sequence** Make a list of entries for a time chart of key events in Russia in 1917. Your chart should clearly indicate how one event led to or influenced another.
7. *ACTIVITY* Write a letter that the czar might have written to the czarina, or the czarina to the czar, while he was away at the front during World War I.

 # From Lenin to Stalin

## Guide for Reading

- What policies did Russia pursue under Lenin?
- How did Stalin gain power?
- What were Stalin's economic goals?
- **Vocabulary** *command economy, collective, kulak*

In January 1924, tens of thousands of people lined up in Moscow's Red Square. They had come to view the body of Lenin, who had died a few days earlier.

Meanwhile, Lenin's party colleagues debated what to do with his corpse. His widow, Krupskaya, wanted him buried simply, next to his mother's grave in Petrograd. Communist party officials—including Joseph Stalin—had other ideas. They wanted Lenin preserved and put on permanent display. In the end, the party had its way. Lenin's body would remain on display in Red Square for more than 65 years.

By having Lenin preserved, Stalin wanted to show that he would carry on the goals of the revolution. In the years that followed, he used ruthless measures to win dictatorial power and impose a new order on Russia.

### Lenin Builds a Communist State

Lenin's first years as leader of Russia had been occupied in putting down civil war. Once his power was secure, he turned to his chief goal—building a classless society in which the means of production were in the hands of the people. As you will see, Lenin was never fully able to meet this Marxist goal.

**Government.** In 1922, the Communists produced a constitution that sounded both democratic and socialist. It set up an elected legislature, later called the Supreme Soviet, and gave all citizens over 18 the right to vote. All political power, resources, and means of production would belong to workers and peasants.

In practice, however, the Communist party, not the people, reigned supreme. Like the czars before them, the party used the army and secret police to enforce its will. The new government brought much of the old Russian empire under its rule. (See the map on page 725.) It then created the Union of Soviet Socialist Republics (USSR). Like the old Russian empire, the Soviet Union was a multinational state made up of diverse European and Asian peoples. In theory, each republic had certain rights. In reality, Russia, the largest republic, dominated the others.

**The NEP.** On the economic front, Lenin retreated from his policy of "war communism," which had brought the economy to near collapse. Under party control, factory and mine output had fallen. Peasants stopped producing grain, knowing it would only be seized by the government.

In 1921, Lenin adopted the New Economic Policy, or NEP. It allowed some capitalist ventures. While the state kept control of banks, foreign trade, and large industries, small businesses were allowed to reopen for private profit. The government also stopped squeezing peasants for grain. Under the NEP, they held on to small plots of land and freely sold their surplus crops.

Lenin's compromise with capitalism helped the Soviet economy recover and ended armed resistance to the new government. By 1928, food and industrial production had climbed back to prewar levels. The standard of living improved, too. But Lenin had always seen the NEP as a temporary retreat from communism. His successor would soon put the Soviet Union back on the road to "pure" communism.

## Stalin Gains Power

Lenin's sudden death in 1924 set off a power struggle among Communist leaders. The chief contenders were Trotsky and Joseph Stalin. Trotsky was a brilliant Marxist thinker, a skillful speaker, and an architect of the Bolshevik Revolution. Stalin, by contrast, was neither a scholar nor an orator. He was, however, a shrewd political operator and behind-the-scenes organizer.

**"Man of steel."** Stalin was born Joseph Djugashvili (joo guhsh VEE lee) to a poor family in Georgia, a region in the Caucasus Mountains. As a boy, he studied for the priesthood. But his growing interest in revolution brought him under the seminary's harsh discipline. Once, he was confined to a punishment cell for reading a novel about the French Revolution.

By 1900, Djugashvili had joined the Bolshevik underground and had taken the name Stalin, meaning "man of steel." He organized robberies to get money for the party and spent time in prison and in Siberian exile. He played a far less important role in the revolution and civil war than Trotsky. But in the 1920s, he became general secretary of the party. He used that position to build a loyal following who owed their jobs to him.

**Stalin versus Trotsky.** As early as 1922, Lenin had expressed grave doubts about Stalin's ambitious nature:

> 66Comrade Stalin, having become general secretary, has concentrated an enormous power in his hands; and I am not sure that he always knows how to use that power with sufficient caution.99

To Lenin, Stalin was "too rude." He urged the party to choose a successor "more tolerant, more loyal, more polite, and more considerate to comrades."

At Lenin's death, Trotsky and Stalin jockeyed for position. They differed on most issues, including the future of communism. Trotsky, a firm Marxist, urged support for a worldwide revolution against capitalism. Stalin took a more cautious view. Efforts to foster Marxist revolutions in Europe after World War I had failed. Instead, he wanted to concentrate on building socialism at home first.

With political cunning, Stalin put his own supporters into top jobs and isolated Trotsky within the party. Stripped of party membership, Trotsky fled into exile in 1929. Later, he was murdered in Mexico by a Stalinist agent.

## The Five-Year Plans

Once in power, Stalin set out to make the Soviet Union into a modern industrial power. In the past, said Stalin, Russia had suffered defeats because of its economic backwardness. In 1928, therefore, he proposed the first of several "five-year plans" aimed at building heavy industry, improving transportation, and increasing farm output.

# Soviet Union, 1917–1938

**EUROPE**
LITHUANIA
LATVIA
POLAND
FINLAND
ESTONIA
BELORUSSIAN SSR
•Leningrad
•Archangel
UKRAINIAN SSR
•Moscow
TURKEY
Stalingrad•
GEORGIAN SSR
ARMENIAN SSR
AZERBAIJAN SSR
RUSSIAN SOVIET FEDERATED SOCIALIST REPUBLIC
*Ob R.*
*Lena R.*
*Yenisei R.*
*Amur R.*
ARCTIC OCEAN
PACIFIC OCEAN
SEA OF OKHOTSK
SAKHALIN
*Volga R.*
BLACK SEA
CASPIAN SEA
ARAL SEA
KAZAKH SSR
L. BALKHASH
L. BAIKAL
IRAN
TURKMEN SSR
UZBEK SSR
KIRGHIZ SSR
AFGHANISTAN
TADZHIK SSR
CHINA
MONGOLIA
MANCHURIA
Vladivostok•
JAPAN
KOREA
INDIA

N W E S

| | |
|---|---|
| 0    500    1000 Miles | |
| 0   500  1000 Kilometers | |

Russian empire, 1914
Area controlled by Bolsheviks, 1919
Union of Soviet Socialist Republics 1938

## GEOGRAPHY AND HISTORY

*In the years following the Bolshevik Revolution, the Soviet Union extended control over many areas of the former Russian empire. It became the largest country in the world*

**1. Location** On the map, locate (a) Lithuania, (b) Georgian SSR, (c) Moscow, (d) Leningrad, (e) China.

**2. Region** Name three countries that had been part of the Russian empire in 1914 that were not part of the Soviet Union in 1938.

**3. Critical Thinking Applying Information** How does the map help explain why Russia became the most influential republic in the Soviet Union?

To achieve this economic growth, he brought all economic activity under government control. The Soviet Union developed a command economy, in which government officials made all basic economic decisions. Under Stalin, the government owned all businesses and allocated financial and other resources. By contrast, in a capitalist economy, the free market controls most economic decisions. Businesses are privately owned and operated by individuals for profit.

**Industrial growth.** Stalin's five-year plans set high production goals, especially for heavy industry and transportation. The government pushed workers and managers to meet these goals by giving bonuses to those who succeed-

ed—and by punishing those who did not. Between 1928 and 1939, large factories, hydroelectric power stations, and huge industrial complexes rose across the Soviet Union. Oil, coal, and steel production grew. Mining expanded, and new railroads were built.

**Mixed results.** Despite the impressive progress in some areas, Soviet workers had little to show for their sacrifices. Some former peasants did improve their lives, becoming skilled factory workers or managers. Overall, though, standards of living remained poor. Wages were low and consumer goods were scarce. Also, central economic planning was often inefficient, causing shortages in some areas and surpluses in others. Many managers, concerned only with meeting production quotas, turned out large quantities of low-quality goods.

During and after the Stalin era, the Soviet Union continued to produce well in heavy industry, such as the manufacture of farm machinery. But its planned economy failed to match the capitalist world in making consumer goods such as clothing, cars, and refrigerators.

## Revolution in Agriculture

Stalin also brought agriculture under government control. Under the NEP, peasants had held on to small plots of land. But Stalin saw that system as inefficient, as well as being a threat to state power. He forced peasants to give up their private plots and live on either state-owned farms or on collectives, large farms owned and operated by peasants as a group. Peasants were allowed to keep their houses and personal belongings, but all farm animals and implements were to be turned over to the collective. The state set all prices and controlled access to farm supplies.

On collectives, the government planned to provide tractors, fertilizers, and better seed, and to teach peasants modern farm methods. The government needed increased grain output to feed workers in the cities. Surplus grain would also be sold abroad to earn money to invest in industrial growth.

**A ruthless policy.** Peasants resisted collectivization by killing farm animals, destroying tools, and burning crops. The government responded with brutal force. An army officer described his horror at the orders he received:

&#10;&#10;I am an Old Bolshevik. . . . I worked in the underground against the czar and I fought in the civil war. Did I do all that in order that I should now surround villages with machine guns and order my men to fire indiscriminately into crowds of peasants? Oh, no, no!&#10;&#10;

**Lunch Break** During the revolution, the Communists had promised to give land to peasants. But under Stalin, the Soviet government forced peasants to give up their land and work on large, state-run farms. Workers on the collective farm shown here eat lunch together in the fields. **Economics and Technology** What does this photograph suggest about discipline on a collective farm?

Stalin targeted kulaks, or wealthy peasants, for special treatment. "We must smash the kulaks, eliminate them as a class," he stormed. The government confiscated kulaks' land and sent them to labor camps, where many thousands were executed or died from overwork.

**Effects.** Collectivization took a horrendous toll. Angry peasants often grew just enough to feed themselves. In response, the government seized all the grain, leaving the peasants to starve. This ruthless policy, combined with poor harvests, led to a terrible famine. Between five and eight million people died in Ukraine alone. Millions more died in other parts of the Soviet Union.

Although collectivization increased Stalin's control, it did not improve farm output. During the 1930s, grain production inched upward, but meat, vegetables, and fruits remained in short supply. Feeding the population would remain a major problem in the Soviet Union throughout its existence.

## The Great Purge

Even though Stalin's power was absolute, he harbored obsessive fears that rival party leaders were plotting against him. In 1934, he launched the Great Purge. In this reign of terror, Stalin and his secret police cracked down especially on Old Bolsheviks, party activists from the early days. His net soon widened to target army heroes, industrial managers, writers, and ordinary citizens. They were charged with a wide range of crimes, from counterrevolutionary plots to failure to meet production quotas.

Between 1936 and 1938, Stalin staged a series of spectacular public trials in Moscow. During these "show trials," former Communist leaders confessed to all kinds of crimes against the government. Confessions were made after prolonged torture or to save family or friends. Many purged party members were never tried but were sent to forced-labor camps in Siberia and elsewhere. Others were executed. Studies of secret police files have revealed that at least four million people were purged during the Stalin years. Of those, almost 800,000 were executed.

The purges destroyed the older generation of revolutionaries, replacing them with young party members who owed absolute loyalty to

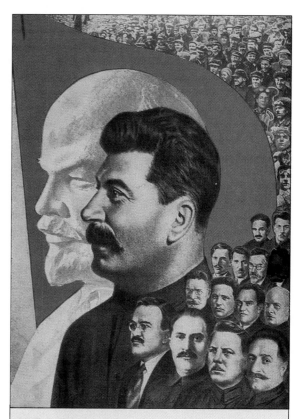

**Stalin's Dictatorship** *This 1933 propaganda poster presents Stalin as Lenin's heir. "Under Lenin's banner we won the October Revolution," the poster declares, "and under that banner we will achieve a world proletarian revolution." Many of the other Communist leaders shown on the poster would later become victims of Stalin's Great Purge.* **Political and Social Systems** *How did glorification of Lenin and Stalin contradict the original goals of the Russian Revolution?*

Stalin. The program of terror thus increased Stalin's power while impressing upon the Soviet people the dangers of disloyalty.

Among the victims of the purges were as many as 90 percent of the nation's military officers. This vacuum in military leadership would come back to haunt Stalin in 1941, when Nazi Germany invaded the Soviet Union. (See Chapter 31.)

## Foreign Policy

Between 1917 and 1939, the Soviet Union pursued divided foreign policy goals. As communists, both Lenin and Stalin wanted to bring

**Battleship Potemkin** *Motion pictures were the most original new art form of the twentieth century. Soviet director Sergei Eisenstein pioneered a technique called montage, cutting back and forth between clashing images. Eisenstein's 1925 silent film* Battleship Potemkin *dramatized the 1905 revolution. (See page 602.) This sequence shows a protest on a wide outdoor staircase in Odessa. In rapid succession, we see imperial troops firing on the crowd, a mother carrying her wounded son, and a baby carriage bouncing wildly down the steps. Although Eisenstein passionately supported the revolution, Stalin had many of his later films edited or banned.* **Art and Literature** *How did Eisenstein choose images that would shock and anger audiences? Give two examples.*

about the worldwide revolution that Marx had predicted. But as Russians, they wanted to guarantee their nation's security by winning the support of other countries. The result was a contradictory and generally unsuccessful foreign policy.

Soon after the revolution, Lenin organized the Communist International, or Comintern. It aided revolutionary groups around the world and encouraged colonial peoples to rise up against imperialist powers. At the same time, the Soviet Union sought to join the League of Nations and to improve diplomatic and trade relations with many western governments.

The Comintern's loud propaganda against capitalism made western powers highly suspicious of the Soviet Union. In the United States, fear of Bolshevik plots led to the Red Scare in the early 1920s. (See page 769.) Britain broke off relations with the Soviet Union when evidence revealed Soviet schemes to turn a 1926 strike into a revolution.

During the 1920s, the Soviet Union slowly won recognition from western powers and increased trade with capitalist countries. Eventually, it joined the League of Nations. Still, mistrust continued to poison relations, especially after the Great Purge. In the 1930s, Stalin urged Britain and France to join in an alliance against a new threat from Germany. But western suspicions of Soviet intentions made this impossible.

## SECTION 2 REVIEW

1. **Identify** (a) USSR, (b) NEP, (c) Great Purge, (d) Comintern.
2. **Define** (a) command economy, (b) collective, (c) kulak.
3. How did Lenin's economic policies change?
4. (a) How did Stalin differ from Trotsky? (b) Why was he able to gain power?
5. What were the goals and results of Stalin's five-year plans?
6. *Critical Thinking* **Defending a Position** Do you think western nations were justified in being suspicious of the Soviet Union in the 1920s and 1930s? Explain.
7. *ACTIVITY* Draw a political cartoon about the Great Purge from the viewpoint of one of the Old Bolsheviks.

# 3 Life in a Totalitarian State

## Guide for Reading

- How did the Communists promote their ideas?
- How did communism shape Soviet society?
- What policy did Stalin impose on the arts?

- **Vocabulary** *totalitarian state, socialist realism*

Stalin's propaganda mills created a fatherly image of the Soviet leader. Poets wrote hymns of praise to "the new Lenin" or "dear Comrade Stalin." Wrote one poet:

> ❝We receive our sun from Stalin,
> We receive our prosperous life
>   from Stalin. . . .
> Even the good life in the tundras filled
>   with snowstorms
> We made together with him,
> With the Son of Lenin,
> With Stalin the Wise.❞

From the 1930s until his death in 1953, Stalin tried to boost morale and faith in the communist system by making himself into a godlike figure. This "cult of personality" was one more pillar to support his absolute power.

## An "Iron Age" of Totalitarian Control

Marx had predicted that under communism the state would wither away. The opposite occurred under Stalin. He turned the Soviet Union into a totalitarian state. In this form of government, a one-party dictatorship attempts to regulate every aspect of the lives of its citizens. You have already seen how Stalin purged political rivals and imposed central government control over industry and agriculture.

To ensure obedience, Stalin's Communist party used secret police, censorship, and terror.

Police spies did not hesitate to open private letters or plant listening devices. Nothing appeared in print without official approval. Grumblers or critics were rounded up and sent to brutal labor camps, where many died.

**Propaganda.** Using modern technology, the party bombarded the public with relentless propaganda. Radios and loudspeakers blared into factories and villages. In movies, theaters, and schools, citizens heard about communist successes and the evils of capitalism. Newsreels and newspapers showed bumper harvests and new hydroelectric dams opening up, or proclaimed the misery of workers in the capitalist West. Billboards and posters urged workers to meet or exceed production quotas.

Stalinist propaganda also revived extreme nationalism. Headlines in the Communist party newspaper, *Pravda,* or "Truth," linked enemies at home to foreign agents:

> **"SPIES SOUGHT TO BREAK UP OUR COUNTRY AND RE-ESTABLISH POWER OF LAND-OWNERS AND CAPITALISTS IN U.S.S.R.—SHOOT THEM!"**

Those who supported Stalin's aims were often glorified as heroes. For example, the government put up statues honoring a 14-year-old boy who turned his own father over to the secret police for associating with kulaks.

**War on religion.** In accordance with the ideas of Marx, atheism became the official policy of the state. Early on, the Communists targeted the Russian Orthodox Church, which had strongly supported the czars. The party seized most religious property, converting many churches into offices and museums. Many priests and other religious leaders were killed or died in prison camps. Government-run museums set up exhibits discrediting miracles and other religious teachings.

Other religions were persecuted as well. At one show trial, 15 Roman Catholic priests were charged with "counterrevolutionary activities," such as teaching religion to the young. The state seized Jewish synagogues and banned the use of Hebrew. Stalin used anti-Semitic propaganda in his campaign against the Old Bolsheviks, many of whom were Jewish.

Islam was also officially discouraged. However, Muslims living in the Soviet Union generally faced fewer restrictions, partly because the Communists hoped to win support among colonized peoples in the Middle East.

**Communist ideology.** The Communists replaced religion with their own ideology. Like a religion, communist ideology had its own "sacred" texts—the writings of Marx and Lenin—and its own shrines, such as the tomb of Lenin. Portraits of Stalin replaced religious icons in Russian homes.

## *Changes in Soviet Society*

The Communists transformed Russian life. They destroyed the old social order of landowning nobles at the top and serfs at the bottom. But instead of creating a society of equals, as they promised, they created a society where a few elite groups emerged as a new ruling class.

**The new elite.** At the head of society were members of the Communist party. Only a small fraction of Soviet citizens were allowed to join the party. Many who did so were motivated by a desire to get ahead, rather than a belief in communist ideology.

The Soviet elite also included industrial managers, military leaders, scientists, and some artists and writers. The elite enjoyed benefits denied to most people. They had the best apartments in the cities and vacation homes in the country. They could shop at special stores for scarce consumer goods. Good shoes, noted one western visitor, distinguished the elite from the common citizen.

**Social benefits and drawbacks.** Although excluded from party membership, most people did enjoy benefits unknown before the revolution. Free education was offered to all. The state also provided free medical care, day care for children, inexpensive housing, and public transportation and recreation.

**ISSUES** *for* **TODAY** The Russian Revolution began with the overthrow of a monarchy but resulted in a totalitarian dictatorship. Why is it often difficult to establish democracy in a country without a tradition of democratic government?

While these benefits were real, the standard of living remained low. As elsewhere, industrial growth·led millions of people to migrate to cities. Although the state built massive apartment complexes, housing was scarce. Entire families might be packed into a single room. Bread was plentiful, but meat, fresh fruit, and other foods were in short supply.

**Education.** After the Russian Revolution, the Communists built schools everywhere and required all children to attend. Other schools taught adults to read and write, an opportunity few had enjoyed in czarist Russia. The state supported technical schools and universities as well.

Schools served important goals. Educated workers were needed to build a modern industrial state. In addition to basic skills, schools taught communist values, such as atheism, the glory of collective farming, and love of Stalin.

The Communist party also set up programs for students outside school. The youth organization Komsomol provided sports programs, cultural activities, and political classes to train teenagers for party membership. Sometimes, these young Communists would be sent to help harvest crops or participate in huge parades.

**Women.** Long before 1917, women such as Lenin's wife, Krupskaya, worked for the

# PARALLELS THROUGH TIME

## Fighting Illiteracy

Most ordinary people throughout history did not learn to read or write. Widespread literacy became a goal of industrialized nations only in the 1800s. Today, it is a major goal of developing nations. Illiteracy keeps individuals from reaching their full potential and also hinders economic growth.

**Linking Past and Present** Why do you think the Soviet government wanted people to learn to read? Why do democratic governments today want citizens to be educated?

### PAST

Before the revolution, few Russian peasants could read. The Soviet government built schools and launched campaigns to increase adult literacy. The Soviet poster at left proclaims, "Knowledge Will Break the Chains of Serfdom." Above, women in the Soviet republic of Turkmenistan attend classes.

ЗНАНИЕ
РАЗОРВЕТ ЦЕПИ РАБСТВА·

### PRESENT

Today, about 20 million adult Americans are functionally illiterate, unable to read well enough to carry out basic, day-to-day tasks. The poster at right encourages adults to join a government-sponsored literacy program. Below, an insurance company provides literacy training for workers.

You too can learn to read
Tu también puedes aprender

revolution, spreading radical ideas among peasants and workers. Some urged fellow Socialists to pay attention to women's needs. In 1905, Alexandra Kollontai (kawl uhn TĪ) noted "how little our party concerned itself with the fate of women of the working class and how meager was its interest in women's liberation." After the revolution, Kollontai became the only high-ranking woman to serve in Lenin's government. She vigorously campaigned for women's rights.

▲ *Soviet women working in a laboratory*

Under the Communists, women won equality under the law. They gained access to education and a wide range of jobs. By the 1930s, many Soviet women were working in medicine, engineering, or the sciences. By their labor, women contributed to Soviet economic growth. They worked in factories, in construction, and on collectives. Within the family, their wages were needed because men earned low salaries. The government provided day nurseries for children.

Despite new opportunities, women were expected to shoulder a double load. They spent a full day on the job, followed by a second shift caring for children and doing housework.

## The Arts and the State

The Bolshevik Revolution at first meant greater freedom for Russian artists and writers. They welcomed the chance to experiment with ideas and forms. The poet Vladimir Mayakovsky (mah yuh KAWF skee) exalted in the new society and praised revolutionary heroes:

**❝**Revolutions
   are the business of peoples;
  for individuals
    they're too heavy to wield,

yet Lenin
  ranked foremost
    among his equals
by his mind's momentum,
  his will's firm steel.**❞**

**Socialist realism.** "Art must serve politics," Lenin had insisted, but he generally did not interfere in artistic freedom. Under Stalin, however, the heavy hand of state control gripped the arts. Stalin forced artists and writers to conform to a style called **socialist realism.** Its goal was to boost socialism by showing Soviet life in a positive light. Artists and writers could criticize the bourgeois past or even, to a limited degree, point out mistakes under communism. Their overall message, though, had to promote hope in the socialist future. Popular themes for socialist-realist artists were peasants, workers, heroes of the revolution—and, of course, Stalin.

**Censorship.** Government controlled what books were published, what music was heard, and which works of art were put on display. Artists who ignored socialist-realist guidelines could not get materials, work space, or jobs.

Under Stalin, writers, artists, and composers faced persecution. The Jewish poet Osip Mandelstam was imprisoned, tortured, and exiled for composing a satirical verse about Stalin. Out of fear for his wife's safety, Mandelstam gave in and wrote an "Ode to Stalin."

Anna Akhmatova (ahk MAH taw vuh), one of Russia's greatest poets, fell out of favor because her poetry did not stress communist ideas. She went on writing poetry in secret. In "Requiem," she described the daily ordeal of trying to visit her 20-year-old son, imprisoned during the Stalinist terrors:

**❝**For seventeen long months my pleas,
  My cries have called you home.
  I've begged the hangman on my knees,
  My son, my dread, my own.
  My mind's mixed up for good, and I'm
  No longer even clear
  Who's man, who's beast, nor how
    much time
  Before the end draws near.**❞**

Although Akhmatova could not publish her works, friends memorized them to preserve her genius for future generations.

**Socialist Realism** Bold, heroic images were the trademark of socialist realism. Here, workers and farmers hold aloft the hammer and sickle, symbol of the Soviet Union. Bright sunbeams suggest a glorious future just ahead. (The letters CCCP stand for USSR in the Cyrillic alphabet.) **Religions and Value Systems** What Soviet values does this painting uphold?

Despite restrictions, some Soviet writers produced magnificent works. *And Quiet Flows the Don,* by Mikhail Sholokhov, passed the censor. (See page 723.) The novel tells the story of a man who spends years fighting in World War I, the Russian Revolution, and the civil war. Sholokhov later became one of the few Soviet writers to win the Nobel Prize for literature.

## Looking Ahead

Strict censorship, massive propaganda, and terror were instruments used by Stalin to ensure personal power and to push the Soviet Union toward modernization. By the time he died in 1953, the Soviet Union was a world leader in heavy industry, steel, and oil production. Along with the United States, it was one of the world's two military superpowers. Yet Stalin's efforts exacted a brutal toll.

The Soviet Union was not the only totalitarian state to emerge in the decades after World War I. In Western Europe, the 1920s and 1930s brought turmoil and economic hardship. As you will read in Chapter 30, dictators in Italy and Germany imposed their own ideologies that differed from Soviet communism. They, too, created one-party states and cults of personality to impose dictatorial rule on their people.

## SECTION 3 REVIEW

1. **Identify** (a) Komsomol, (b) Alexandra Kollontai, (c) Vladimir Mayakovsky, (d) Osip Mandelstam, (e) Anna Akhmatova.
2. **Define** (a) totalitarian state, (b) socialist realism.
3. How did Stalin make propaganda into a powerful weapon?
4. (a) How did the Communists attack religion? (b) What alternative did they offer to faith?
5. Describe three ways in which life under communism differed from life under the czars.
6. *Critical Thinking* **Applying Information** One historian has said that Soviet arts policy was "communism with a smiling face." What do you think he meant?
7. *ACTIVITY* Write a dialogue between a Russian peasant woman and her daughter who has become a factory worker. The two women might discuss religion, work, or the changing lives of women since the Russian Revolution.

# Skills for Success

## Documenting Your Sources

Most research reports and term papers require you to look at several sources in gathering the information you need. Every research report must contain a **bibliography,** a list of the sources you consulted. It is placed at the end of your paper.

A bibliography shows readers where your information came from. In this way, readers can determine whether the information in your report is accurate, current, and reliable. A bibliography also provides readers who want to learn more about the subject with additional references.

Bibliographies are written in a standard form. Each entry should contain all the information a reader needs to locate the source.

*For a book, include* author's name (last name first), title of the work (underlined or italic), place of publication, name of the publisher, and date of publication.

*For a magazine or journal article, include* author's name, title of the article (in quotation marks), name of the publication (underlined or italic), date of the publication, and page numbers.

*For a newspaper, include* headline of the article (in quotation marks), author (if given), name of newspaper (underlined or italic), date, edition, section, and page numbers.

*For an encyclopedia entry, include* title of the article, name of the encyclopedia, volume number, edition, the year of publication, and page numbers.

Imagine that you are writing a paper about Lenin. Look at the list of sources at right. Then, answer the following questions:

**1** **Make bibliography cards or a computer listing for each source.** (a) What would a bibliography card for Source C look like? (b) What would you list first in a bibliography card for Source A? (c) What would you list first in a bibliography card for Source D?

**2** **Arrange the bibliography cards or computer list in alphabetical order.** Sources are listed in alphabetical order by the authors' last names. Unsigned articles are alphabetized according to the first word of the article title (excluding *a, an,* or *the*). (a) Which of the sources below should appear first in the bibliography? Why? (b) Which should appear last? Why? (c) Where would you place Source B?

**3** **Review the entries for correct style and punctuation.** Use periods between the units (Author's name. Title. Publication data.) of the listing. Make sure book and publication titles are underlined or italic and article titles are in quotation marks. (a) Write a bibliography entry for Source D. (b) Write a bibliography entry for Source E.

***Beyond the Classroom*** Newspaper articles do not generally have written bibliographies. However, reporters must document the sources they used in writing their stories. Imagine that you are writing an article for a school newspaper on a topic of current interest. Make a list of sources you could use to write the story. Then, organize your list following the steps given above.

---

### Sources

**A.** An unsigned magazine article entitled "Lenin's Curse" that appeared in the magazine *The Economist* on April 27, 1991, on pages 11 and 12.

**B.** A book by Robert Service entitled *Lenin, a Political Life,* published in 1985 by Indiana University Press in Bloomington, Indiana.

**C.** A newspaper article written by the Associated Press entitled "Thousands Pay Respects to Lenin" that appeared in the first edition of the newspaper *The Oregonian* in Section A, page 8, on April 24, 1994.

**D.** An article entitled "Lenin, Vladimir Ilyich" on pages 335–336 in Volume 17 of the *Encyclopedia Americana,* published in 1994 by Grolier Inc. in Danbury, Connecticut.

**E.** A book by Robert Payne entitled *The Life and Death of Lenin,* published in 1964 by Simon and Schuster in New York.

## Building Vocabulary

Review the vocabulary words in this chapter. Then, use *five* of these vocabulary words and their definitions to create a matching quiz. Exchange your quiz with another student. Check each other's answers when you are finished.

## Reviewing Chapter Themes

1. **Continuity and Change** Describe how each of the following contributed to the March Revolution of 1917: (a) the rule of the czar, (b) World War I, (c) the economic situation in Russia.
2. **Impact of the Individual** (a) How did Lenin direct the Bolshevik takeover of Russia? (b) What methods did Stalin use to get and keep power? (c) Describe two ways that Stalin charted a new course for the Soviet Union.
3. **Economics and Technology** (a) Describe the goals of Lenin's New Economic Policy. (b) How did the Soviet command economy under Stalin differ from a capitalist economy?
4. **Political and Social Systems** Describe the Soviet totalitarian state in terms of (a) the role of the Communist party, (b) the "cult of personality," (c) the use of propaganda, (d) education.

## Thinking Critically

1. **Comparing** Review Chapter 19. Compare the Russian Revolution to the French Revolution in terms of (a) long-term causes, (b) immediate causes, (c) stages of the revolution, (d) world reaction.
2. **Applying Information** British statesman Winston Churchill commented that, in 1917, the Germans "turned upon Russia the most grisly of all weapons. They transported Lenin . . . like a plague bacillus from Switzerland into Russia." (a) What do you think Churchill meant? (b) Do you think his statement was accurate? Why or why not?
3. **Analyzing Literature** Reread the passage from *And Quiet Flows the Don* on page 723. (a) Why do you think the speaker feels no regret about shooting officers? (b) Why does he react differently to the Cossacks? (c) How does this passage reflect the mixed emotions of people

involved in wars and revolutions? ( ★ See *Skills for Success,* page 234.)
4. **Synthesizing Information** Review what you have read about Karl Marx and his theories in Chapter 20. (a) In what ways do you think Marx would have approved of the economic and social system set up by the Communists in the Soviet Union? (b) What might Marx have disapproved of in the Soviet system? ( ★ See *Skills for Success,* page 896.)
5. **Linking Past and Present** In the 1990s, the breakup of the Soviet Union led to a revival of open religious practices. Why do you think the Soviets were unsuccessful in their attempt to destroy religion?
6. **Analyzing Information** (a) Describe the Soviet policy toward the arts and literature. (b) How did writers like Anna Akhmatova and Osip Mandelstam risk danger in order to express themselves? (c) Why do you think creative freedom is important to writers and artists? Explain.

### *For Your Portfolio*

You have been given the opportunity to interview a figure from Russian or Soviet history. However, you must first submit your questions in writing. In this assignment you will prepare the questions for your interview.

1. Start by deciding whom you would like to interview. Choose from these people: Czar Nicholas II, Czarina Alexandra, Rasputin, V. I. Lenin, Leon Trotsky, an Old Bolshevik, Joseph Stalin, a member of the Communist party elite, Sergei Eisenstein, an Orthodox priest, Alexandra Kollontai, Anna Akhmatova, Osip Mandelstam.
2. Review the role played by this person in Russian or Soviet history. In addition to your textbook, consult library resources such as encyclopedias, biographies, and history books.
3. Prepare a list of interview questions. Be sure that these questions cannot be answered with just yes or no. ( ★ See *Skills for Success,* page 444.)
4. Submit your questions to the class without identifying the person they are addressed to. Can your classmates figure out who it is? Do your classmates think these questions will provoke thoughtful answers?

# CHAPTER 29

## Nationalism and Revolution Around the World

### (1914–1939)

## CHAPTER OUTLINE

1 Struggle for Change in Latin America
2 Nationalist Movements in Africa and the Middle East
3 India Seeks Self-Rule
4 Upheavals in China
5 Empire of the Rising Sun

In his gold-embroidered coat and elegant headdress, Emir Faisal cut a splendid figure at the Paris Peace Conference. The Arab leader went to Paris in 1919 to persuade the victorious Allies to stand by agreements they had made during World War I. Britain, he said, had promised to recognize Arab independence if the Arabs helped fight the Turks. In the meanwhile, however, Britain and France had secretly agreed to divide up Arab lands between themselves, canceling the promises "that were made to us before all the world." Angrily, Faisal continued:

66We have paid a heavy price for our liberty, but we are not exhausted. We are ready to fight on, and I cannot believe that the great rulers here assembled will treat us as did our former oppressors [the Ottoman Turks]. I think they will act from higher, nobler motives, but—if not—they should remember how badly it has turned out for our former oppressors.99

Faisal spoke to the Allies of Arab nationalism and of the Arabs' desire for unity. He pointed to Woodrow Wilson's principle of self-determination, to the splendors of Arab civilization, and to Arab contributions during the war. But even as Faisal spoke, British and French diplomats were working behind the scenes to create mandates over the Arab provinces of the shattered Ottoman empire.

Angry and frustrated, Faisal returned home empty-handed. He was not alone. Outside the Arab world, nationalists in Africa and Asia were also disappointed by the terms of the peace.

The postwar years from 1919 to 1939 saw a surge of hope around the world. They also brought great turmoil. Desire for democracy and self-determination contributed to explosive struggles in many regions. In Mexico and China, revolutions toppled governments and triggered civil wars. In Latin America, Africa, and Asia, continued western imperialism fueled the forces of nationalism. Everywhere, new leaders were slowly forging liberation movements that would change the face of the world.

FOCUS ON these questions as you read:

■ **Political and Social Systems**
How did nationalism and a desire for modernization affect countries around the world?

■ **Impact of the Individual**
How did nationalist leaders bring people together to change their countries?

■ **Economics and Technology**
How did the Great Depression affect world economies?

■ **Global Interaction**
What forces did anti-imperialism movements awaken?

## TIME AND PLACE

**A Wave of Nationalism** *The years after World War I saw dramatic changes in many parts of the world. The war had loosened the grip of European nations on their colonies. In Asia, Africa, and the Middle East, nationalists fought for independence. Nationalists in China faced internal divisions as well as foreign invaders. This poster celebrates the victory of the nationalist Guomindang over local Chinese warlords in the 1920s.* **Global Interaction** *Why do you think World War I encouraged nationalist movements in the developing world?*

## HUMANITIES LINK

***Art History*** Diego Rivera, *The History of Mexico* (page 740).
***Literature*** In this chapter, you will encounter passages from the following works of literature: Léopold Senghor, "Black Woman" (page 744); Rabindranath Tagore, "We Crown Thee King" (page 758).

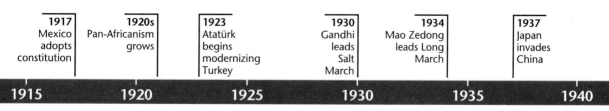

**1917**
Mexico adopts constitution

**1920s**
Pan-Africanism grows

**1923**
Atatürk begins modernizing Turkey

**1930**
Gandhi leads Salt March

**1934**
Mao Zedong leads Long March

**1937**
Japan invades China

1915    1920    1925    1930    1935    1940

# Struggle for Change in Latin America

## Guide for Reading

- Why did revolution erupt in Mexico in 1910?

- What were the effects of the Mexican Revolution?

- How did nationalism grow in Latin American countries?

- **Vocabulary** *nationalization*

The winds of revolution swept through Mexico between 1910 and 1920. "It is like a hurricane," says a peasant fighter in Mariano Azuela's novel *The Underdogs*. "If you're in it, . . . you're a leaf . . . blown by the wind." Azuela, a doctor, had fought with the rebel army of Pancho Villa. His novel captures the turmoil of the Mexican Revolution and details its effects on millions of Mexican men and women.

The Mexican Revolution unleashed radical forces. As the revolution spread, Indian peasants battled to end centuries of oppression and to win land. A century after Miguel Hidalgo raised the "cry of Dolores" (see page 539), the Mexican Revolution finally opened the door to social and economic reform.

## The Mexican Revolution

By 1910, the dictator Porfirio Díaz had ruled Mexico for almost 35 years, winning reelection as president again and again. On the surface, Mexico enjoyed peace and economic growth. Díaz welcomed foreign investors who developed mines, built railroads, and drilled for oil. (See pages 674–675.)

**Sources of discontent.** Prosperity benefited wealthy landowners, business people, and foreign investors. But most Mexicans were peasants who lived in desperate poverty. Without land or education, they had no hope for improvement. Their demands for land were ruthlessly crushed by the police or military.

Discontent rippled through Mexico in the early 1900s. Peasant land hunger could not be stifled forever. Factory workers and miners earning meager wages were restless and angry. And middle-class liberals, who embraced the ideals of democracy, opposed the Díaz dictatorship.

**The battle begins.** The unrest boiled over when Francisco Madero, a liberal reformer, demanded free elections in 1910. After being imprisoned by Díaz, he hoisted the flag of revolt. Soon, revolutionaries all across Mexico joined Madero's cause.

Faced with rebellion in several parts of the country, Díaz resigned in 1911. "Madero has unleashed a tiger, now let us see if he can control it," declared the dictator as he left Mexico. Díaz's taunt proved well founded. Madero became president of Mexico but within two years was murdered, probably on the orders of one of his generals, Victoriano Huerta. Huerta, himself, was soon forced to flee Mexico.

**A complex upheaval.** During the power struggle that followed, several radical leaders emerged. Among them was Francisco "Pancho" Villa, a hard-riding rebel from the north. He fought mostly for personal power but won the intense loyalty of his peasant followers.

In southern Mexico, Emiliano Zapata led a peasant revolt. Zapata, himself an Indian tenant farmer, understood the misery of peasant villagers who "own only the ground on which they stand. They suffer the horrors of poverty," he declared, because "the lands, woods, and water are monopolized by a few." The battle cry of the Zapatistas, as the rebels who followed Zapata were called, was *"Tierra y Libertad!"*—Land and Liberty!

◀ *A soldadera, or female soldier*

Fighting flared across Mexico for a decade, killing as many as a million Mexicans. Peasants, small farmers, ranchers, and urban workers were drawn into the violent struggle. *Soldaderas*, women soldiers, cooked, tended the wounded, and even fought alongside the men. Women marched with regular army units or joined hit-and-run guerrilla bands.

## Reforms

In 1917, Venustiano Carranza, a conservative, was elected president of Mexico. That year, he reluctantly approved a new constitution. With amendments, it is still in force today.

**A new constitution.** The Constitution of 1917 addressed three major issues: land, religion, and labor. It permitted the breakup of large estates, placed restrictions on foreigners owning land, and allowed nationalization, or government takeover, of natural resources. Church land was made "the property of the nation." The constitution set a minimum wage for workers and protected their right to strike.

Although the constitution gave suffrage only to men, it did give women some protection. Women doing the same job as men were entitled to the same pay. In response to pressures from women activists, Carranza also passed laws allowing married women to draw up contracts, to take part in legal suits, and to have equal authority with men in spending family funds.

**Social change.** At first, the constitution was just a set of goals to be achieved sometime in the future. But in the 1920s, as the government finally restored order after years of civil war, it began to carry out reforms.

The government helped some Indian communities regain lands that had been taken from them illegally in the past. It supported labor unions and launched a massive effort to combat illiteracy. Schools and libraries were set up. For the first time, Mexicans in rural areas who grew up speaking various Indian languages learned Spanish.

Dedicated teachers, often young women, worked for low pay. While they taught basic skills, they spread ideas of nationalism that began to bridge the gulf between the regions and the central government. As the revolutionary era ended, Mexico became the first Latin American nation to pursue real social and economic reforms for the majority of its people.

**The PRI.** In 1929, government leaders organized what later became the Institutional Revolutionary party (PRI). It has dominated Mexican politics ever since. The PRI managed to accommodate all groups in Mexican society, including business and military leaders, peasants, and workers. Its leaders backed social reform but suppressed political opposition. It also boosted industry. In 1938, the government nationalized foreign oil holdings, part of a program to reduce foreign influence.

## Rising Tide of Nationalism

Mexico's move to reclaim its oil fields from foreign investors reflected a growing spirit of nationalism in Latin America. It was directed largely at ending economic dependence on the industrial powers, especially the United States. (See page 673.)

**Economic nationalism.** During the 1920s and 1930s, world events affected Latin American economies. After World War I, trade fell off with Europe. New products such as synthetic textiles and nitrates competed with Latin American exports. The Great Depression that struck the United States in 1929 spread around the world in the 1930s. Prices for Latin American exports plunged as demand dried up. At the same time, the cost of imported consumer goods rose.

A tide of economic nationalism swept Latin American countries. They were determined to develop their own economies and end foreign economic control. Since consumers could no longer afford costly imports, local entrepreneurs set up factories to produce goods. They urged their governments to raise tariffs to protect the new industries. And, following Mexico's lead, some nations also nationalized resources or took over foreign-owned industries.

**ISSUES** *For* **TODAY**

In the 1920s, feelings of nationalism surged in the nations of Latin America. What conditions fuel the forces of nationalism?

**The History of Mexico** *As a young man, Diego Rivera studied painting in Europe. But after a while, his imitations of European art seemed "like a collection of masks and disguises." On his return to Mexico, Rivera began to paint in a bold, new style that drew on Mexican folk art. "It was as if I were being born anew," he wrote. "In everything I saw a potential masterpiece—the crowds, the markets, the festivals." In this mural, Rivera uses bright colors and bold forms to tell the story of Mexico. The mural moves from the Spanish conquest at the base to the victory of the Mexican Revolution at the top.* **Art and Literature** *How does Rivera's mural communicate a political message?*

The drive to create domestic industries had limited success. In Mexico, Argentina, Brazil, and a few other countries, some areas of manufacturing grew. Mexico and Venezuela also benefited from a growing demand for oil. But most Latin American nations did not have oil and lacked the resources to build large industries. As in the past, the unequal distribution of wealth hampered economic development.

**Cultural nationalism.** By the 1920s, an upsurge of national feeling led Latin American writers, artists, and thinkers to reject European influences. Instead, they took pride in their own unique culture, which blended western and Indian traditions. A Brazilian urged:

&& Let us forget the marble of the Acropolis and the towers of the Gothic cathedrals. We are the sons of the hills and the forests. Stop thinking of Europe. Think of America! &&

In Mexico, cultural nationalism was reflected in the revival of mural painting, a major art form of the Aztecs. In the 1920s and 1930s, Diego Rivera, José Clemente Orozco (oh RAHS koh), David Alfaro Siqueiros (sih KAY rohs), and other muralists created magnificent works that won worldwide acclaim. On the walls of public buildings, they portrayed the struggles of the Mexican people for liberty. They captured the desire of Indian peasants to regain land taken from them first by Spanish conquerors and later by foreigners during the Díaz era. The murals have been a great source of national pride ever since.

## The "Good Neighbor" Policy

During and after World War I, investments by the United States in the nations of Latin America soared, especially as British influence declined. The United States continued to play the role of "international policeman," intervening to restore order when it felt its interests were threatened.

During the Mexican Revolution, the United States supported leaders who it thought would protect American interests. In 1914, it bombarded the port of Vera Cruz to punish Mexico for imprisoning several American sailors. In 1916, it invaded Mexico after Pancho

Villa killed 17 Americans in New Mexico. Although the United States felt justified in these actions, they stirred up violent anti-Yankee sentiment in Mexico.

During the 1920s, anti-American feeling grew. In Nicaragua, Augusto César Sandino led a guerrilla movement against United States forces occupying his country. Many people throughout Latin America saw Sandino as a hero.

In the 1930s, President Franklin Roosevelt took a new approach to Latin America. He abandoned the Roosevelt Corollary, which had been used to justify military intervention. In its place, he pledged to follow "the policy of the good neighbor."

Under the Good Neighbor Policy, the United States withdrew troops it had stationed in Haiti and Nicaragua. It also lifted the Platt Amendment, which had limited Cuban independence. When Mexico nationalized foreign oil holdings, Roosevelt resisted demands by some Americans to intervene. The Good Neighbor Policy survived until 1945, when global tensions led the United States to intervene once again in the region.

## SECTION 1 REVIEW

1. **Identify** (a) Porfirio Díaz, (b) Zapatistas, (c) Diego Rivera, (d) Good Neighbor Policy.
2. **Define** nationalization.
3. Describe three causes of the Mexican Revolution.
4. Explain how the Constitution of 1917 addressed each of these issues: (a) land, (b) religion, (c) labor.
5. Give two examples of how nationalism helped shape Latin American republics in the 1920s and 1930s.
6. *Critical Thinking* **Analyzing Information** (a) How did world events affect the economy of Latin American nations during the 1920s and 1930s? (b) Do you think that a nation can avoid the effects of global events? Explain.
7. *ACTIVITY* Study the mural on page 740. Then, create a mural that illustrates an event in the Mexican Revolution.

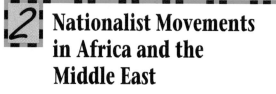

# 2 Nationalist Movements in Africa and the Middle East

## Guide for Reading

- How did African nationalism grow after World War I?

- How did nationalism help Turkey and Iran modernize?

- What were the goals of Arab nationalists?

- **Vocabulary** *apartheid*

The Kikuyu people of Kenya were outraged. Not only had the British taken their land, but they also treated the Kikuyu like second-class citizens. Jomo Kenyatta, a young Kikuyu leader, explained their anger in this way:

    66 If you woke up one morning and found that somebody had come to your house, and had declared that house belonged to him, you would naturally be surprised, and you would like to know by what arrangement. Many Africans found that, on land that had been in the possession of their ancestors from time immemorial, they were now working as squatters or as laborers. 99

The Kikuyu were among many African people who resented colonial rule. During the 1920s and 1930s, a new generation of leaders like Kenyatta, proud of their unique heritage, struggled to stem the tide of imperialism and restore Africa for Africans.

### Movements for Change in Africa

During the early 1900s, more and more Africans felt the impact of colonial rule. In Kenya and Rhodesia, for example, white settlers forced Africans off the best land. Those who were lucky enough to keep their land were forbidden to grow the most profitable crops—only Europeans could grow these. In Kenya, too, the

British made all Africans carry identification cards and restricted where they could live or travel.

Everywhere, Africans were forced to work on European-run plantations or in mines to earn money to pay taxes. Farmers who had kept their land had to grow cash crops. Increasingly, they lost their self-sufficiency and became dependent on European-made goods. Also, land converted to cash crops no longer produced food, which led to famines in some regions.

**Resistance.** Opposition to imperialism grew among Africans. Resistance took many forms. Those who had lost their lands to Europeans sometimes squatted, or settled illegally, on white-owned plantations. In cities, workers began to form unions, even though such activity was illegal.

Many western-educated Africans criticized the injustice of imperial rule. Although they had trained for professional careers, the best jobs went to Europeans. Inspired by President Woodrow Wilson's call for self-determination, they condemned the system that excluded Africans from the political life of their own lands. Some eagerly read Lenin's writings that claimed imperialism was the final stage of a corrupt and dying capitalist society. In Africa, as elsewhere around the world, socialism had a growing appeal.

**Protests.** While large-scale revolts were rare, protests were common. In Kenya, the Kikuyu protested the loss of their land, forced labor, heavy taxes, and the hated identification cards. The British jailed the Kikuyu leaders, but protests continued.

In West Africa, women had traditionally controlled the marketplaces and the farmland. In the 1920s, Ibo women in Nigeria denounced British policies that threatened their rights. They demanded a voice in decisions that affected them. The "Women's War," as it was called, became a full-fledged revolt. Women armed with machetes and sticks mocked British troops and shouted down officials who ordered them to disperse. In the end, the British silenced demonstrators with gunfire.

**South Africa.** Between 1910 and 1940, whites strengthened their grip on South Africa. They imposed a system of racial segregation that became known as **apartheid** (uh PAHRT hīt). Their goal was to ensure white economic power. New laws, for example, restricted better-paying jobs in mines to whites only. Blacks were pushed into low-paid, less-skilled work. As in Kenya, South African blacks had to carry passes at all times. They were evicted from the best land, which was set aside for whites, and forced to live on crowded "reserves," which were located in dry, infertile areas.

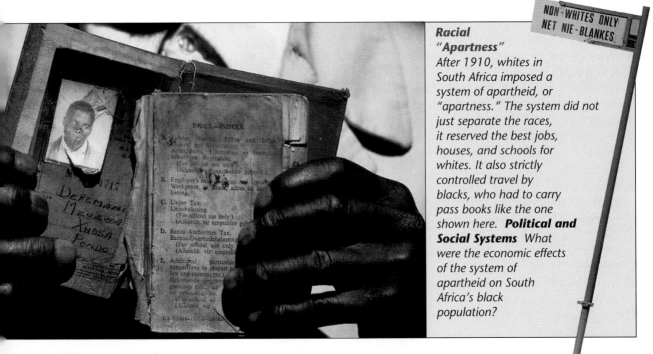

NON-WHITES ONLY
NET NIE-BLANKES

**Racial "Apartness"**
After 1910, whites in South Africa imposed a system of apartheid, or "apartness." The system did not just separate the races, it reserved the best jobs, houses, and schools for whites. It also strictly controlled travel by blacks, who had to carry pass books like the one shown here. **Political and Social Systems** What were the economic effects of the system of apartheid on South Africa's black population?

# PARALLELS THROUGH TIME

## Pride in Heritage

People all over the world share the desire to preserve their language, customs, religion, and culture. Often, they have to resist pressure to give up their heritage and assimilate. Immigrants to the United States, for example, become American citizens but still keep up ties to Mexico, China, Cuba, or Italy.

**Linking Past and Present** Why do you think people want to preserve their heritage? Do you think Americans today are more aware of ethnic pride? Explain.

**PAST** *After World War I, Pan-Africanism and négritude asserted the value of African culture. In the United States, artists and writers of the Harlem Renaissance rediscovered African traditions, as shown by Nancy Elizabeth Prophet's sculpture of a male head, at left. In Africa, nationalists like Jomo Kenyatta used cultural pride as a weapon against imperialism. Kenyatta's book* Facing Mount Kenya *expresses that pride.*

FACING
MOUNT KENYA
The Tribal Life of the Gikuyu

by
JOMO KENYATTA

with an Introduction by
B. MALINOWSKI
Ph.D. (Cracow); D.Sc. (London); Hon. D.Sc. (Harvard)
Professor of Anthropology in the University of London

**PRESENT**
*Today, people continue to celebrate their heritage throughout the world. Above, artist John Lightfoot uses traditional Native American colors and designs in his modern paintings. At left, a young Canadian of Scottish origin performs a traditional dance from the highlands of Scotland.*

---

Other laws further chipped away at the rights of blacks. In one South African province, educated blacks who owned property had been allowed to vote in local elections. In 1936, the government abolished that right. The system of segregation set up at this time would become even more restrictive after 1948. (See page 939.)

Yet South Africa was also home to a vital nationalist movement. African Christian churches and African-run newspapers demanded rights for black South Africans. In 1912, educated Africans organized a political party, later known as the African National Congress (ANC). Its members worked through legal means, protesting laws that restricted the freedom of black Africans. Their efforts, however, had no effect on the white government of South Africa. Still, the ANC did build a framework for later political action.

### Growing Self-Confidence

During the 1920s, a movement known as Pan-Africanism began to nourish the nationalist spirit. Pan-Africanism emphasized the unity of Africans and people of African descent around the world. Among its most inspiring leaders was

Jamaican-born Marcus Garvey. He preached a forceful message of "Africa for Africans" and demanded an end to colonial rule. Although he never visited Africa, his ideas influenced a new generation of African leaders.

**Pan-African Congress.** Led by the African American W.E.B. DuBois (doo BOIS), Pan-Africanists tried to forge a united front. DuBois organized the first Pan-African Congress in 1919. It met in Paris, where the victorious Allies were holding their peace conference. Delegates from African colonies, the West Indies, and the United States called on the Paris peacemakers to approve a charter of rights for Africans. Although the western powers ignored their demands, the Pan-African Congress established a tradition of cooperation among African leaders.

**Négritude.** French-speaking writers in West Africa and the Caribbean further awakened self-confidence among Africans. They expressed pride in their African roots through the *négritude* movement. Best known among them was the Senegalese poet Léopold Senghor, who celebrated Africa's rich cultural heritage. He fostered African pride by rejecting the negative views of Africa spread by colonial rulers. In his poem "Black Woman," he uses the image of an African woman to reflect on the beauty of Africa:

> **66**Black woman,
> Clothed in your color which is life,
> your form which is beauty!
> I grew up in your shadow, the
> sweetness of your hands bandaged
> my eyes,
> And here in the heart of summer and
> of noon, I discover you, promised
> land from the height of a burnt
> mountain,
> And your beauty strikes my heart,
> like the lightning of an eagle. **99**

Later, Senghor would take an active role in Senegal's drive to independence and would serve as its first president.

**Egypt.** African nationalism brought little political change, except to Egypt. During World War I, Egyptians had been forced to provide food and workers to help Britain. Simmering resistance to British rule flared as the war ended.

Western-educated officials, peasants, landowners, Christians, and Muslims united behind the Wafd (WAHFT) party, which launched strikes and riots.

In 1922, the British finally agreed to declare Egypt independent. In fact, however, British troops stayed in Egypt to guard the Suez Canal, and Britain remained the real power behind Egypt's King Faud.

In the 1930s, young Egyptians were attracted to the Muslim Brotherhood. This group fostered a broad Islamic nationalism that rejected western culture and denounced widespread corruption in the Egyptian government.

## Modernization in Turkey and Iran

Nationalism brought immense changes to the Middle East in the aftermath of World War I. The defeated Ottoman empire collapsed in 1918. Its Arab lands, as you read at the beginning of the chapter, were divided up between Britain and France. In Asia Minor, however, Turks resisted western control and fought to build a modern nation.

**Atatürk.** Led by the determined and energetic Mustafa Kemal, Turkish nationalists overthrew the sultan, defeated western occupation forces, and declared Turkey a republic. Kemal later took the name Atatürk, meaning "father of the Turks." Between 1923 and his death in 1938, Atatürk forced through an ambitious program of radical reforms. His goals were to modernize Turkey along western lines and create a secular state that separated religion from government.

**Westernization.** In a move that swept away centuries-old traditions, Atatürk replaced Islamic law with a new law code based on European models. He discarded the Muslim calendar in favor of the western (Christian) calendar and moved the day of rest from Friday, traditional with Muslims, to Sunday, in line with Christian practice.

Like Peter the Great in Russia, Atatürk forced his people to wear western dress. He replaced Arabic script with the western (Latin) alphabet, stating it was easier to learn. He closed religious schools but opened thousands of state schools to prepare young Turks for the challenges of modern society.

**A New Turkey** *Mustafa Kemal, known as Atatürk, pushed radical reforms to make Turkey a modern nation. "Surviving in the world of modern civilization depends upon changing ourselves," he declared. One change that he introduced was the replacement of Arabic with western script. Here, Atatürk reveals the new Turkish alphabet to a crowd in an Istanbul park.* **Impact of the Individual** *Why do you think Atatürk introduced the new alphabet himself in a public ceremony?*

Other reforms transformed the lives of women. They no longer had to veil their faces and were allowed to vote. Polygamy—the custom allowing men to have more than one wife—was banned. Given freedom to work outside the home, women became teachers, doctors, lawyers, and even politicians.

Under Atatürk, the government helped industry expand. It built roads and railroads, set up factories, and hired westerners to advise on how to make Turkey economically independent.

To achieve his reforms, Atatürk ruled with an iron hand. To many Turks, he was a hero who was transforming Turkey into a strong, modern power. Some Turkish Muslims, however, rejected his secular government. To them, the Quran and Islamic customs provided all needed guidance, from prayer and behavior to government, commerce, and education. (See Chapter 11.)

**Nationalism and reform in Iran.** Atatürk's reforms inspired nationalists in neighboring Iran. They greatly resented the British and Russians, who had won spheres of influence in their land. In 1925, an ambitious army officer, Reza Khan, overthrew the shah. He set up his own Pahlavi dynasty, with himself as shah.

Like Atatürk, Reza Khan rushed to modernize Iran and make it fully independent. He built factories, roads, and railroads and strengthened the army. He, too, adopted the western alphabet, forced Iranians to wear western clothing, and set up modern, secular schools. In addition, he moved to replace Islamic law with secular law and encouraged women to take part in public life. While the shah had the support of wealthy urban Iranians, Muslim religious leaders fiercely condemned his efforts to introduce western ways.

As Iran modernized, it won better terms from the British company that controlled its oil industry. It persuaded the British to give it a larger share of the profits and insisted that Iranian workers be hired at all levels. In the decades ahead, oil would become a major factor in Iranian economic and foreign affairs.

## Arab Nationalism and European Mandates

Arab nationalism blossomed after World War I and gave rise to Pan-Arabism. This nationalist movement built on the shared heritage of Arabs who lived in lands from the Arabian Peninsula through North Africa.* It emphasized their common history and language and recalled the golden age of Arab civilization. (See Chapter 11.) Pan-Arabism sought to free Arabs from foreign domination and unite them in

---

*The Arab Middle East included lands from the Arabian Peninsula through North Africa. Today, this area includes nations such as Syria, Jordan, Iraq, Egypt, Algeria, and Morocco.

## The Middle East, 1920s

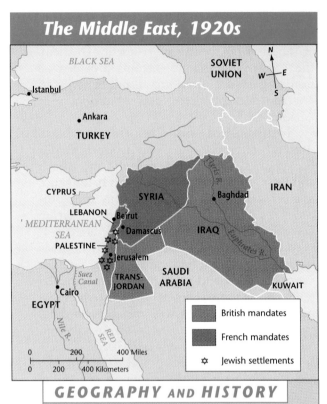

BLACK SEA

SOVIET UNION

Istanbul

Ankara

TURKEY

CYPRUS

SYRIA

Baghdad

IRAN

LEBANON
Beirut

Damascus

IRAQ

MEDITERRANEAN SEA

PALESTINE

Jerusalem

TRANS-JORDAN

SAUDI ARABIA

KUWAIT

Suez Canal

Cairo

EGYPT

Nile R.

RED SEA

Tigris R.

Euphrates R.

0    200    400 Miles
0    200    400 Kilometers

British mandates
French mandates
✡ Jewish settlements

## GEOGRAPHY AND HISTORY

After World War I, European nations sought to increase their influence in the Middle East. The League of Nations awarded Great Britain and France mandates in parts of the former Ottoman empire. In theory, a mandated territory was to be held until it was able to "stand alone." In practice, however, mandates became indistinguishable from European colonies.

1. **Location** On the map, locate (a) Syria, (b) Palestine, (c) Trans-Jordan, (d) Saudi Arabia, (e) Egypt, (f) Jerusalem, (g) Damascus, (h) Lebanon, (i) Suez Canal, (j) Mediterranean Sea.
2. **Place** (a) Which Middle Eastern countries became French mandates after World War I? (b) Which Middle Eastern countries became British mandates? (c) What was the status of Iran in the 1920s?
3. **Critical Thinking** **Applying Information** (a) Is this map a useful source of information about the European mandates in the Middle East? Why or why not? (b) Is it a useful source of information about the origins of the Arab-Jewish conflict in the Middle East? Explain your answer.

their own state. An Arab student spoke of this mission:

> 66 I am an Arab, and I believe that the Arabs constitute one nation. The sacred right of this nation is to be sovereign in her own affairs . . . to liberate the Arab homeland, to unite all its parts and to found [distinctively Arab] political, economic, and social institutions. 99

**Betrayal at the peace conference.** The mandates—territories administered by European nations—set up by the Paris Peace Conference outraged Arabs. During World War I, they had helped the Allies against the Central Powers, especially the Ottomans. In return, they had been promised independence. Instead, the Allies carved up the Ottoman lands, giving France mandates in Syria and Lebanon and Britain mandates in Palestine and Iraq. Later, Trans-Jordan was added to the British mandate.

Arabs felt betrayed by the West—a feeling that has endured to this day. During the 1920s and 1930s, their anger erupted in frequent protests and revolts against western imperialism. A major center of turmoil was the British mandate of Palestine. There, Arab nationalists faced European Zionists, or Jewish nationalists, with their own dreams of creating a Palestinian homeland.

**Promises in Palestine.** Since Roman times, Jews had dreamed of returning to Palestine. (See page 144.) In 1897, Theodor Herzl (HER tsuhl) responded to growing anti-Semitism in Europe by founding the modern Zionist movement. His goal was to rebuild a Jewish state in Palestine, "our ever-memorable historical home." Soon, a few Eastern European Jews migrated to Palestine, joining the small Jewish community that had survived there since biblical times.

During World War I, the Allies made two vague sets of promises. First, they promised Arabs their own kingdoms in former Ottoman lands, including Palestine. Then, in 1917, the British issued the Balfour Declaration to win support of European Jews. In it, Britain supported the idea of setting up "a national home for the Jewish people" in Palestine. The declaration noted, however, that "nothing shall be done which may prejudice the civil and religious rights of existing non-Jewish communities in Palestine." Those communities were Arab. The stage was thus set for conflict between Arab and Jewish nationalists.

**A bitter struggle.** In the 1930s, anti-Semitism in Germany and Eastern Europe forced many Jews to seek safety in Palestine. Despite great hardships, they set up factories, built new towns, and turned arid desert into irrigated farmland.

At first, some Arabs welcomed the money and modern technical skills that the newcomers brought with them. But as Jews poured into the land of Palestine, tensions between the two groups developed. Sometimes, Jewish settlers bought land from Arab landowners and then forced Arab tenants off the land. In the cities, Jewish factory owners often refused to hire Arabs. Angry Arabs attacked Jewish settlements, hoping to oust the Jews. For the rest of the century, Arab nationalists battled Zionists over a land that Arabs called Palestine and Jews called Israel. (See page 907.)

## SECTION 2 REVIEW

1. **Identify** (a) "Women's War," (b) négritude, (c) Léopold Senghor, (d) Atatürk, (e) Reza Khan, (f) Pan-Arabism, (g) Balfour Declaration.
2. **Define** apartheid.
3. (a) Why did Africans resent colonial rule? (b) How was Pan-Africanism an expression of African nationalism?
4. (a) How did Turkey and Iran seek to modernize? (b) How was modernization linked to nationalism?
5. (a) Why did Arabs resent the mandate system? (b) Why did Palestine become a center of conflict?
6. *Critical Thinking* **Analyzing Information** Why do you think leaders in Turkey and Iran tried to modernize their countries using western models?
7. *ACTIVITY* Imagine you are a member of the Pan-African movement in the 1920s. Use what you have learned about African culture in this and earlier chapters to write a speech extolling your unique heritage.

# 3 India Seeks Self-Rule

## Guide for Reading

- How did World War I strengthen Indian nationalism?
- How did Gandhi become a national hero?
- What goals did Muslims in India pursue?
- **Vocabulary** *civil disobedience*

Tensions were running high in Amritsar, a city in northern India. Protests against British rule had sparked riots and attacks on British residents. On April 13, 1919, a large but peaceful crowd jammed into a walled field in the heart of the city. The British commander, General Reginald Dyer, had banned public meetings, but Indians either ignored or had not heard the order.

As Indian leaders addressed the crowd, Dyer arrived with 50 soldiers. To clear the field, they opened fire on the unarmed men, women, and children. For 10 minutes, they rained death on the people trapped in the field, killing 379 and wounding more than 1,100. Dyer later claimed he had acted "to make a wide impression" and produce "a sufficient moral effect" on Indian protesters.

The Amritsar massacre was a turning point for many Indians. It convinced them of the evils of British rule. For Jawaharlal Nehru, a leading Indian nationalist, the incident made him realize "more vividly than I had ever done before, how brutal and immoral imperialism was and how it had eaten into the souls of the British upper classes." ( See *World Literature*, "We Crown Thee King," page 758.)

## *Moves Toward Independence*

The tragedy at Amritsar was linked to Indian frustrations after World War I. During the war, more than a million Indians had served overseas, suffering heavy casualties. As thousands died on distant battlefields, Indian nationalists grew increasingly angry that they had no freedom at home.

To quiet nationalist demands, the British promised India greater self-government after the war. But when the fighting ended, Britain proposed only a few minor reforms. Meanwhile, Britain's crackdown on protesters triggered riots and the brutal slaughter in Amritsar.

Since 1885, the Congress party had pressed for self-rule within the British empire. (See page 648.) After Amritsar, it began to call for full independence. But party members were mostly a middle-class, western-educated elite who had little in common with the masses of Indian peasants. In the 1920s, a new leader emerged, Mohandas Gandhi. He united all Indians behind the drive for independence. Adoring Indians dubbed him Mahatma, or "Great Soul."

## Mohandas Gandhi

Mohandas Gandhi came from a middle-class Hindu family. At age 19, he went to England to study law. After returning to India, he tried to set up his own law practice but soon joined an Indian law firm in South Africa. Thousands of Indians had gone to South Africa as indentured servants and then settled there. Some had prospered, but many were poor. All faced racial prejudice under South Africa's white rulers.

For 20 years, Gandhi fought laws that discriminated against Indians in South Africa. In his struggle against injustice, he adopted the weapon of nonviolent (passive) resistance. He called it *satyagraha,* or "soul-force." In 1914, Gandhi returned to India and joined the Congress party. His ideas inspired Indians of all religions and ethnic backgrounds and encouraged them to resist British rule.

**Nonviolence.** While leaders like Atatürk adopted western solutions to national problems, Gandhi embraced Hindu traditions. Above all, he preached the ancient doctrine of ahimsa, or nonviolence and reverence for all life. (See page 79.) He applied this idea to the fight against British rule. By using the power of love, he believed, people could convert even the worst wrongdoer to the right course of action. As Gandhi explained, passive resistance involved sacrifice and suffering:

> 66Passive [nonviolent] resistance is a method of securing rights by personal suffering. It is the reverse of resistance by arms. . . . If I do not obey [an unjust] law and accept the penalty for its breach, I use soul-force.99

**Western influence.** Gandhi's philosophy reflected western as well as Indian influences. He admired Christian teachings about love and had read the works of Henry David Thoreau, an American philosopher of the 1800s who believed in civil disobedience, the refusal to obey unjust laws.

Gandhi also embraced western ideas of democracy and nationalism. He rejected the inequalities of the caste system and fought hard to end the harsh treatment of untouchables. (See pages 87–88.) He urged equal rights for all Indians, women as well as men.

**Gandhi sets an example.** Abandoning western-style clothing, Gandhi dressed in the *dhoti,* the simple white garment traditionally worn by village Indians. During the 1920s and 1930s, he launched a series of nonviolent actions against British rule. He called for boycotts of British goods, especially textiles, and urged Indians to wear only cotton grown and woven in India. He worked to restore pride in India's traditional spinning and weaving industries, making the spinning wheel a symbol of the nationalist

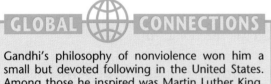

*Woman spinning* ▶

movement. Women joined the self-sufficiency movement in large numbers, learning to spin and weave their own clothes and producing as much as they could in their homes.

Through his own example, Gandhi inspired Indians to "get rid of our helplessness." His campaigns of civil disobedience attracted wide support. But when protests led to violent riots, Gandhi was deeply upset. He would fast, pray, and call on patriots to practice self-control.

## *The Salt March*

To mobilize mass support, Gandhi offered a daring challenge to Britain in 1930. He set out to end the British salt monopoly. Like earlier rulers in India, the British claimed the sole right to produce and sell salt. By taxing those sales, they collected money to maintain their government in India.

**The challenge.** To Gandhi, the government salt monopoly was an evil burden on the poor and a symbol of British oppression. Every-

**A Protest March** *The Salt March focused the attention of all India on Gandhi's challenge to the British. As Gandhi and his supporters walked from village to village, his message of opposition to British rule spread like wildfire. "If the awakening of the people in the country is true and real," Gandhi said, "the salt law is as good as abolished." When the marchers arrived at the sea, Gandhi lifted a lump of salt over his head and declared, "With this, I am shaking the foundations of the British empire."* **Impact of the Individual** *In what ways do you think Gandhi's personal example was important to the Indian independence movement?*

one needed salt to survive. But while natural salt was available in the sea, Indians were forbidden to touch it. They could only buy salt sold by the government.

Early in 1930, Gandhi wrote to the British viceroy in India, explaining his motives and goals. He stated his intention to break the law and condemned British rule as "a curse":

**66**[British rule] has impoverished the dumb millions by a system of progressive exploitation. . . . It has reduced us politically to serfdom. It has sapped the foundations of our culture . . . and degraded us spiritually.**99**

**While the world watched.** On March 12, Gandhi made good on his challenge. With 78 followers, he set out on a 240-mile march to the sea. As the tiny band passed through villages, crowds listened eagerly to Gandhi's message. They prayed for the protest's success, and some even joined the procession. By the time they reached the sea, the marchers numbered in the thousands.

Each day, reporters wired news of Gandhi's "salt march" to newspapers in India and around the globe. The world wondered what would happen when the small man in his simple white loin cloth broke the law. On April 6, Gandhi waded into the surf and picked up a lump of sea salt. A young woman marcher and poet, Sarojini Naidu, cried out: "Hail, law breaker!"

Gandhi urged Indians to follow his lead. Even though he was soon arrested and jailed, coastal villagers started collecting salt. Congress party leaders sold salt on city streets, displayed it to huge rallies—and went to jail. As Gandhi's campaign gained force, tens of thousands of Indians were dragged off to prison.

**An effective tool.** All around the world, newspapers thundered against Britain. Stories revealed how police brutally clubbed peaceful marchers who tried to occupy a government saltworks. "Not one of the marchers even raised an arm to fend off the blows," wrote an outraged American reporter.

The Salt March embarrassed Britain, which took pride in its democratic traditions. But in India, its officials were jailing thousands who asked only for basic freedoms that the British enjoyed in their own country.

**Toward freedom.** Gandhi's campaign of nonviolence and the self-sacrifice of his followers slowly forced Britain to agree to hand over some power to Indians and to meet other demands of the Congress party. Complete independence, however, would not be achieved until 1947, one year before the Mahatma's death. (See page 900.) ◼

## Looking Ahead

As India came closer to independence, Muslim fears of the Hindu majority increased. While millions of Muslims responded to Gandhi's campaigns, tensions between Hindus and Muslims often erupted into violence.

**A separate Muslim state.** During the 1930s, the Muslim League gained an able leader in Muhammad Ali Jinnah. Like Gandhi, Jinnah came from a middle-class background and had studied law in England. At first, he represented Muslim interests within the Congress party. Later, he threw his support behind the idea of a separate state for Muslims. It would be called Pakistan, meaning "land of the [ritually] pure."

**World War II.** India was moving toward independence when a new world war exploded in 1939. Britain outraged Indian leaders by postponing further action on independence and then bringing India into the war without consulting them. Angry nationalists launched a campaign of noncooperation and were jailed by the British. Millions of Indians, however, did help Britain during the war.

When the war ended in 1945, independence could no longer be delayed. But a new tragedy unfolded as Hindu-Muslim violence raged on the Indian subcontinent. (See Chapter 35.)

## SECTION 3 REVIEW

1. **Identify** (a) Amritsar, (b) Salt March, (c) Muhammad Ali Jinnah.
2. **Define** civil disobedience.
3. (a) How did World War I strengthen Indian resentment of British rule? (b) How did the Amritsar massacre change Indian goals?
4. (a) How did Gandhi revive Indian pride? (b) Describe Gandhi's method for resisting British rule.
5. How did the goal of Muslims in India change during the 1930s?
6. *Critical Thinking* **Analyzing Information** Why do you think civil disobedience is an effective weapon?
7. *ACTIVITY* Review the discussion of the Amritsar massacre on page 747. Then, write a headline about the event for (a) an Indian newspaper, (b) a British newspaper.

# 4 Upheavals in China

## Guide for Reading

- What problems did the new republic of China face?

- What were the goals of the May Fourth Movement?

- Why did civil war erupt between the Guomindang and the Communists?

Sun Yixian, "father" of the Chinese revolution, painted a grim picture of China after the overthrow of the Qing dynasty. "In comparison with other nations," he wrote, "we have the greatest population and the oldest culture, of 4,000 years' duration." Yet China, he noted, was "the poorest and weakest state in the world." Other countries were "the carving knife and the serving dish," and China was "the fish and the meat."

As the new Chinese republic took shape, nationalists like Sun Yixian set the goal of "catch-ing up and surpassing the powers, east and west." But that goal would remain a distant dream as China suffered the turmoil of civil war and foreign invasion.

## The Chinese Republic

In China, as you recall, the Qing dynasty collapsed in 1911. Sun Yixian hoped to rebuild China on the Three Principles of the People. (See page 653.) But he made little progress. China quickly fell into chaos.

**Internal problems.** In 1912, Sun Yixian stepped down as president in favor of a powerful general, Yuan Shikai. Sun hoped that Yuan would restore order and create a strong central government. But the ambitious general had other ideas. He tried to set up a new ruling

---

**A Chinese City** *China in the early 1900s was on the edge of major change. This picture shows the business district of Hangzhou, a major Chinese trading city for over 800 years. Hangzhou was opened to foreign trade in 1896. By the 1930s, it was a major railway hub and the site of China's first modern roads.* **Political and Social Systems** *What problems did China face in the early 1900s?*

dynasty, with himself as emperor. When Yuan died in 1916, China plunged into still greater disorder.

In the provinces, local warlords seized power. As rival armies battled for control, the economy collapsed and millions of peasants suffered terrible hardships. Warlords forced them to pay taxes to support their armies. The constant fighting ravaged the land. Bandits and famine added to their misery. A foreign observer compared the plight of China's peasants to "that of a man standing permanently up to his neck in water, so that even a ripple is enough to kill him."

**Foreign imperialism.** During this period of upheaval, foreign powers increased their influence over Chinese affairs. Foreign merchants, missionaries, and soldiers dominated the ports China had opened to trade. They also exerted influence inland.

In 1915, Japan put new pressure on its once-powerful neighbor. While western powers were distracted by World War I, Japan presented Yuan Shikai with Twenty-one Demands, which sought to make China a Japanese protectorate. Too weak to resist, Yuan gave in to some of the demands.

Then, in 1919, at the Paris Peace Conference, the victorious Allies gave Japan control over German possessions in China. That news infuriated Chinese nationalists, who blamed their leaders for "selling out" at Versailles.

**May Fourth Movement.** On May 4, 1919, student protests erupted in Beijing and later spread to cities across China—a startling event in those days. "China's territory may be conquered," they declared, "but it cannot be given away! The Chinese people may be massacred, but they will not surrender." Students organized boycotts of Japanese goods.

Student protests set off a cultural and intellectual ferment known as the May Fourth Movement. Like earlier reform movements, its goal was to strengthen China. Western-educated leaders blamed the imperialists' successes on China's own weakness. As in Meiji Japan, Chinese reformers wanted to learn from the West and use that knowledge to end foreign domination. Most reformers rejected Confucian traditions and many turned to western science and ideas such as democracy and nationalism to solve China's problems.

Women played a key role in the May Fourth Movement, as they had in earlier uprisings. They joined marches and campaigned to end arranged marriages, footbinding, and the seclusion of women within the home. Their work helped open doors for women in education and the economy.

**The appeal of Marxism.** Some Chinese turned to the revolutionary ideas of Marx and Lenin. The Russian Revolution seemed to offer a model of how a strong, well-organized party could transform a nation. And Soviet Russia was more than willing to train Chinese students and military officers to become the vanguard—or elite leaders—of a communist revolution. By the 1920s, a small group of Chinese communists had formed their own party.

## Leaders for a New China

In 1921, Sun Yixian and his Guomindang (gwoh meen DAWNG), or Nationalist, party established a government in south China. Sun planned to raise an army, defeat the warlords, and spread his government's rule over all of China. When western powers ignored pleas for help in building a democratic China, Sun decided "that the one real and genuine friend of the Chinese Revolution is Soviet Russia." Russian experts helped the Nationalists plan and carry out their campaign against the warlords.

**Jiang Jieshi.** After Sun's death in 1925, an energetic young army officer, Jiang Jieshi* (jyawng jeh SHEE), took over the Guomindang. He had received military training in Japan. While he was determined to reunite China, Jiang had little interest in either democracy or communism.

In 1926, Jiang Jieshi began a march into northern China, crushing local warlords as he advanced and capturing Beijing. In mid-campaign, he stopped to strike at the Chinese Communist party, which he saw as a threat to his power. While Jiang had the support of landlords and business leaders, the Communists were winning converts among the small proletariat in cities like Shanghai.

Early in 1927, on orders from Jiang, Guomindang troops slaughtered Communist party

*In earlier textbooks, this name is spelled Chiang Kai-shek.

members and the workers who supported them. In Shanghai and elsewhere, thousands of people were killed. Anger over the massacre would fuel a bitter civil war for the next 22 years.

**Mao Zedong.** Among the Communists who escaped Jiang's attack was a young revolutionary of peasant origins, Mao Zedong. Unlike earlier Chinese Communists, Mao believed the Communists should seek support not among the small urban working class but among the large peasant masses.

Although the Communists were pursued at every turn by Guomindang forces, Mao was optimistic of eventual success. "A single spark can start a prairie fire," he once observed. For a time, Mao and the Communists organized the peasants in southeastern China. They redistributed land to peasants and offered them schooling and health care.

**The Long March.** Jiang Jieshi, however, was determined to destroy the "Red bandits," as he called the Communists. He led the Guomindang in a series of "extermination campaigns" against them.

In 1934, in an epic retreat known as the Long March, Mao and about 100,000 of his followers fled the Guomindang. During the next year, they trekked more than 6,000 miles, facing daily attacks as they crossed rugged mountains, deep gorges, and mighty rivers. Only about 20,000 people survived the ordeal. For decades, the Long March stood as a symbol of Communist heroism to Chinese opposed to the Guomindang.

During the Long March, the Communists enforced strict discipline. Soldiers had to follow three main rules: Obey orders, "do not take a single needle or a piece of thread from the people," and turn in everything you capture. Further, they were to treat peasants politely, pay for goods they wanted, and avoid damaging crops. Such behavior made Mao's forces welcome among peasants who had suffered at the hands of the Guomindang.

At the end of the Long March, the Communists set up a new base in remote northern China. There, Mao rebuilt his forces and plotted new strategies. He claimed the great retreat as a victory. As he observed:

66The Long March is also a seeding-machine. It has sown many seeds in eleven provinces, which will sprout, grow leaves, blossom into flowers, bear fruit, and yield a crop in future.99

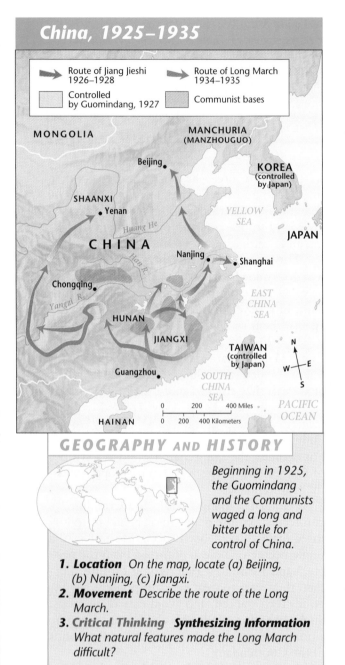

## China, 1925–1935

**Legend:**
- Route of Jiang Jieshi 1926–1928
- Route of Long March 1934–1935
- Controlled by Guomindang, 1927
- Communist bases

MONGOLIA

MANCHURIA (MANZHOUGUO)

Beijing

KOREA (controlled by Japan)

SHAANXI

Yenan

*Huang He*

*YELLOW SEA*

CHINA

JAPAN

*Han R.*

Nanjing

Shanghai

Chongqing

*Yangzi R.*

*EAST CHINA SEA*

HUNAN

JIANGXI

TAIWAN (controlled by Japan)

Guangzhou

*SOUTH CHINA SEA*

*PACIFIC OCEAN*

HAINAN

0    200    400 Miles
0    200    400 Kilometers

### GEOGRAPHY AND HISTORY

Beginning in 1925, the Guomindang and the Communists waged a long and bitter battle for control of China.

1. **Location** On the map, locate (a) Beijing, (b) Nanjing, (c) Jiangxi.
2. **Movement** Describe the route of the Long March.
3. **Critical Thinking** **Synthesizing Information** What natural features made the Long March difficult?

## Japanese Invasion

While Jiang was pursuing the Communists across China, the country faced another danger. In 1931, Japan invaded Manchuria in northeastern China, adding it to the growing Japanese empire. (See the map on page 756.) As Japanese aggression increased, some of Jiang's own generals began to doubt him. Why, they demanded, did he waste valuable resources fighting other Chinese instead of mobilizing against the foreign invaders? In the end, Jiang was forced to form a united front with the Communists against Japan.

In 1937, the Japanese struck again. This time, they attacked China proper. As airplanes bombed Chinese cities, highly disciplined and well-equipped Japanese troops overran eastern China, including Beijing and Guangzhou. Jiang Jieshi retreated to the interior and set up his capital at Chongqing (chawng CHIHNG). The Japanese set up their puppet government in Nanjing, the former Nationalist capital. The killing and brutality that accompanied their entry into the city became known as the "rape of Nanjing."

**Looking ahead.** From 1937 to 1945, the Guomindang, the Communists, and the Japanese were locked in a three-sided struggle. The bombing of Pearl Harbor in 1941 brought the United States not only into the war against Japan but into an alliance with the Chinese, as well. After Japan's defeat, the United States tried to prevent renewed civil war in China, but with no success. Within a few years, the Communists would triumph, and Mao would move to impose revolutionary change on China.

## SECTION 4 REVIEW

1. **Identify** (a) Yuan Shikai, (b) Twenty-one Demands, (c) May Fourth Movement, (d) Guomindang, (e) Jiang Jieshi, (f) Mao Zedong, (g) Long March, (h) rape of Nanjing.
2. Why did the new republic of China fall into chaos after 1912?
3. (a) What western ideas appealed to Chinese reformers? (b) How did these reformers plan to end the growth of foreign influence in China?
4. Describe the goals of each of the following: (a) Sun Yixian, (b) Jiang Jieshi, (c) Mao Zedong.
5. **Critical Thinking** **Recognizing Causes and Effects** How did the actions of foreign imperialist powers help to strengthen nationalism in China?
6. **ACTIVITY** Review Mao's statement about the Long March as a "seeding-machine." Draw a cartoon illustrating this statement.

# Empire of the Rising Sun

## Guide for Reading

- How did Japanese democracy grow during the 1920s?

- Why did the Great Depression undermine Japanese democracy?

- What policies did Japanese militarists pursue?

Solemn ceremonies marked the start of Emperor Hirohito's reign. A few honored participants gathered in the Secret Purple Hall. Other high-ranking guests sat in an outer chamber, able to hear but not to see the emperor.

In the hall, the new emperor sat stiffly on the ancient throne of Japan. Beside him sat his wife, the empress Nagako. With great care, he performed sacred purification rituals going back thousands of years. Calling on the spirits of his ancestors, he pledged "to preserve world peace and benefit the welfare of the human race."

The prime minister then made his own brief speech, ending with a ringing cry: "May the Lord Emperor live 10,000 years!" Instantly, the words echoed across Japan. "May the Lord Emperor live 10,000 years!" shouted millions of voices, invoking the traditional wish for a long and successful reign.

In fact, Hirohito reigned from 1926 to 1989—an astonishing 63 years. During those decades, Japan experienced remarkable successes and appalling tragedies. In this section, we will focus on the 1920s and 1930s, when the pressures of extreme nationalism and economic upheaval set Japan on a militaristic and expansionist path that would eventually engulf all of Asia.

### Liberal Changes of the 1920s

In the 1920s, Japan moved toward greater democracy. Political parties grew stronger, and elected members of the Diet—the Japanese parliament—exerted their power. By 1925, all adult men had won the right to vote. Western ideas about women's rights had brought a few changes. Overall, however, Japanese women remained subordinate to men, and they would not win suffrage until 1947.

**Economic growth.** During World War I, the Japanese economy enjoyed phenomenal growth. Its exports to the Allies soared. Also, while western powers battled in Europe, Japan expanded its influence in East Asia. As you have seen, it sought additional rights in China with the Twenty-one Demands.

By the 1920s, the powerful business leaders known as the zaibatsu strongly influenced politics through donations to political parties. They pushed for policies to favor international trade and their own interests. At the same time, in the spirit of world peace, Japan signed an agreement with the United States and Britain to limit the size of its navy. The government reduced military spending, signaling support for commercial over military expansion.

**Serious problems.** Behind this seeming well-being, Japan faced some grave problems. The economy grew more slowly in the 1920s than at any time since Japan had modernized. Rural peasants enjoyed none of the prosperity of city-dwellers. In the cities, factory workers earning low wages were attracted to the socialist ideas of Marx and Lenin. As they won the right to vote, socialists were elected to the Diet.

In the cities, too, the younger generation was in revolt against tradition. They adopted western fads and fashions and rejected family authority for the western notion of individual freedom.

During the 1920s, tensions between the government and the military simmered not far below the surface. Conservatives, especially military officers, blasted government corruption, including payoffs by powerful zaibatsu. They also condemned western influences for undermining basic Japanese values of obedience and respect for authority.

### The Nationalist Reaction

In 1929, the Great Depression rippled across the Pacific, striking Japan with devastating force. Trade, Japan's economic lifeline, suffered as foreign buyers could no longer afford Japanese silks and other exports. Prices for all exports plummeted. Unemployment in the

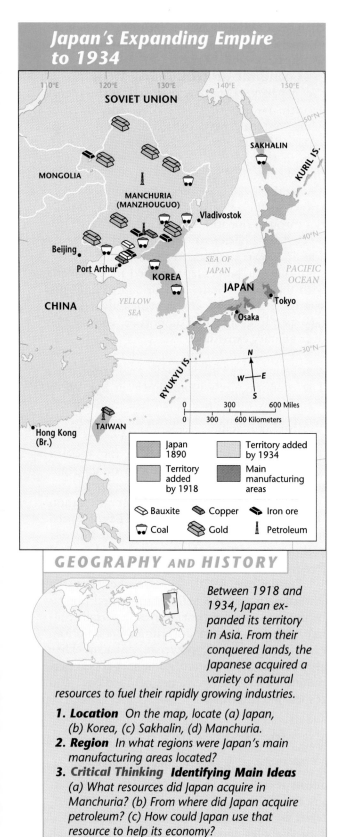

## Japan's Expanding Empire to 1934

Legend:
- Japan 1890
- Territory added by 1918
- Territory added by 1934
- Main manufacturing areas

Resources:
- Bauxite
- Coal
- Copper
- Gold
- Iron ore
- Petroleum

### GEOGRAPHY AND HISTORY

Between 1918 and 1934, Japan expanded its territory in Asia. From their conquered lands, the Japanese acquired a variety of natural resources to fuel their rapidly growing industries.

1. **Location** On the map, locate (a) Japan, (b) Korea, (c) Sakhalin, (d) Manchuria.
2. **Region** In what regions were Japan's main manufacturing areas located?
3. **Critical Thinking** *Identifying Main Ideas* (a) What resources did Japan acquire in Manchuria? (b) From where did Japan acquire petroleum? (c) How could Japan use that resource to help its economy?

cities soared, while in the countryside peasants were only a mouthful from starvation.

**A worsening crisis.** Economic disaster fed the discontent of the military and extreme nationalists, or ultranationalists. They condemned politicians for agreeing to western demands to stop overseas expansion. Western industrial powers, they pointed out, had long ago grabbed huge empires. By comparison, Japan's empire was tiny.

Japanese nationalists were further outraged by racial policies in the United States, Canada, and Australia that shut out Japanese immigrants. The Japanese took great pride in their achievements as a modern industrial power and bitterly resented being treated as second-class citizens of the world.

As the crisis worsened, nationalists demanded renewed expansion. An empire in Asia, they argued, would provide much-needed materials and an outlet for Japan's rapidly growing population. They set their sights on the Chinese province of Manchuria. (See the map at left.) It was rich in natural resources, and Japanese businesses had already invested heavily there.

**The Manchurian incident.** In 1931, a group of Japanese army officers provoked an incident that would provide an excuse to seize Manchuria. They blew up tracks on a Japanese-owned railroad line and claimed the Chinese had done it. In "self-defense," they then attacked Chinese forces. Without consulting their own government, the Japanese army conquered all of Manchuria and set up a puppet state there that they called Manzhouguo (mahn joh GWOH).

When the League of Nations condemned Japanese aggression, Japan simply withdrew from the league. When politicians in Tokyo objected to the army's high-handed actions, public opinion sided with the military. In the years ahead, the military would increase its power at home and expand Japan's empire abroad.

### Militarists in Power

By the early 1930s, ultranationalists were winning popular support for foreign conquests and a tough stand against the western powers. Members of "patriotic" societies assassinated a number of politicians and business leaders who opposed military expansion. Military leaders

**Militarists Rule Japan** *Japan's military steadily increased their power over the government during the 1930s. The army used propaganda, like this poster, to win public support.* **Art and Literature** *How did this poster appeal to Japanese patriotism?*

plotted to overthrow the government and, in 1936, briefly occupied the center of Tokyo.

**Traditional values revived.** Civilian government survived, but by 1937 it had been forced to accept military domination. To please the ultranationalists, it cracked down on socialists and ended most democratic freedoms. It revived ancient warrior values and built a cult around the emperor, who was believed to be descended from the sun goddess.

To spread its nationalistic message, the government focused on the schools. Students had to study *The Way of the Emperor's Subjects*. This government pamphlet deplored the Japanese adoption of western ideas:

66With the influx of European and American culture into this country, . . . individualism, liberalism, utilitarianism, and materialism began to assert them-

selves, with the result that the traditional character of the country was much impaired and the virtuous habits and customs bequeathed by our ancestors were affected unfavorably.99

To practice "the way of the emperor's subjects," students were taught absolute obedience to the emperor and service to the state.

**Renewed expansion.** During the 1930s, Japan took advantage of China's civil war to increase its influence there. In 1937, as you have read, its armies invaded the Chinese mainland. They committed terrible atrocities as they overran eastern China.

Japan expected to complete its conquest of China within a few years. But in 1939, while the two nations were locked in deadly combat, World War II broke out in Europe. That conflict swiftly spread to Asia, where France and Britain had large empires.

By 1939, Japan had joined with two aggressive European powers, Germany and Italy. That alliance, combined with renewed Japanese conquests, would turn World War II into a brutal, wide-ranging conflict waged not only across the continent of Europe but across Asia and the Pacific, as well.

## SECTION 5 REVIEW

1. **Identify** (a) Hirohito, (b) Manzhouguo.
2. How did Japan become more democratic in the 1920s?
3. (a) How did the Great Depression affect Japan's economy? (b) What political effects did it have on Japan?
4. (a) What goals did Japanese militarists pursue at home? (b) What goals did they pursue overseas?
5. *Critical Thinking* **Recognizing Causes and Effects** Why do you think a nation might turn to military leaders and extreme nationalists during a time of crisis?
6. *ACTIVITY* Review the discussion of the Manchurian incident on page 756. Then, write two telegrams reporting the incident, one by a Japanese soldier and the other by a Chinese soldier.

# World Literature

## "We Crown Thee King"

### Rabindranath Tagore

**Introduction** *Rabindranath Tagore was probably the most important Indian writer of this century. He produced numerous poems, short stories, plays, novels, essays, and travel books. One of his poems became India's national anthem. In 1913, Tagore became the first writer outside Europe to win the Nobel Prize for literature.*

*Like many educated Indians of his time, Tagore had an uneasy association with the Anglo-Indians, or the British living in India. In 1915, he accepted a knighthood from the British government. After the Amritsar massacre of 1919, however, he renounced his knighthood in protest. Tagore's 1916 short story "'We Crown Thee King'" explores the relationship between the British* sahibs, *or ruling class, and the Indian elite.*

Pramathanath was a Bachelor of Arts, and in addition was gifted with common sense. But he held no high official position; he had no handsome salary; nor did he exert any influence with his pen. There was no one in power to lend him a helping hand, because he desired to keep away from the Englishmen, as much as they desired to keep away from him. So it happened that he shone only within the sphere of his family and friends, and excited no admiration beyond it.

Yet this Pramathanath had once sojourned in England for some three years. The kindly treatment he received during his stay there overpowered him so much that he forgot the sorrow and humiliation of his own country, and came back dressed in European clothes. This rather grieved his brothers and his sisters at first, but after a few days they began to think that European clothes suited nobody better, and gradually they came to share his pride and dignity.

On his return from England, Pramathanath resolved that he would show the world how to associate with Anglo-Indians on terms of equality. Those of our countrymen who think that no such association is possible, unless we bend our knees to them, showed their utter lack of self-respect, and were also unjust to the English—so thought Pramathanath.

He brought with him letters of introduction from many distinguished Englishmen at home, and these gave him some recognition in Anglo-Indian society. He and his wife occasionally enjoyed English hospitality at tea, dinner, sports and other entertainments. Such good luck intoxicated him, and began to produce a tingling sensation in every vein of his body.

About this time, at the opening of a new railway line, many of the town, proud recipients of official favor, were invited by the Lieutenant-Governor to take the first trip. Pramathanath was among them. On the return journey, a European Sergeant of the Police expelled some Indian gentlemen from a railway-carriage with great insolence. Pramathanath, dressed in his European clothes, was there. He, too, was getting out, when the Sergeant said: "You needn't move, sir. Keep your seat, please."

At first Pramathanath felt flattered at the special respect shown to him. When, however, the train went on, the dull rays of the setting sun, at the west of the fields, now ploughed up and stripped of green, seemed in his eyes to spread a glow of shame over the whole country. Sitting near the window of his lonely compartment, he seemed to catch a glimpse of the downcast eyes of his Motherland, hidden behind the trees. As Pramathanath sat there, lost in reverie, burning tears flowed down his cheeks, and his heart burst with indignation.

He now remembered the story of a donkey who was drawing the chariot of an idol along the street. The wayfarers bowed down to the idol, and touched the dusty ground with their foreheads. The foolish donkey imagined that all this reverence was being shown to him. "The only difference," said Pramathanath to himself,

**British or Indian?** Like Rabindranath Tagore, many middle-class Indians were torn between British and Indian culture. Even Indian art mirrored the conflict. Some artists adopted European styles, while others blended Indian and European styles. This painting of an Indian woman by Ravi Varna is modeled closely on European portraits. **Art and Literature** Compare this painting with the one on page 648. How do they differ in style?

"between the donkey and myself is this: I understand today that the respect I receive is not given to me but to the burden on my back."

Arriving home, Pramathanath called together all the children of the household, and lighting a big bonfire, threw all his European clothes into it one by one. The children danced round and round it, and the higher the flames shot up, the greater was their merriment. After that, Pramathanath gave up his sip of tea and bits of toast in Anglo-Indian houses, and once again sat inaccessible within the castle of his house, while his insulted friends went about from the door of one Englishman to that of another, bending their turbaned heads as before.

[*A few years later, Nabendu Sekhar, a young Indian with political ambitions, marries one of Pramathanath's daughters. Nabendu tries to impress his new in-laws by showing off his connections with the British.*]

As if by mistake, he would often hand to his sisters-in-law sundry letters that his late father had received from Europeans. And when the cherry lips of those young ladies smiled sarcastically, and the point of a shining dagger peeped out of its sheath of red velvet, the unfortunate man saw his folly, and regretted it.

Labanyalekha, the eldest sister, surpassed the rest in beauty and cleverness. Finding an auspicious day, she put on the mantel-shelf of Nabendu's bedroom two pairs of English boots, daubed with vermilion, and arranged flowers, . . . incense, and a couple of burning candles before them in true ceremonial fashion. When Nabendu came in, [she] said with mock solemnity: "Bow down to your gods, and may you prosper through their blessings."

The third sister Kiranlekha spent many days in embroidering with red silk one hundred common English names such as Jones, Smith, Brown, Thomson, etc., on a cloth. When it was ready, she presented this [cloth] to Nabendu Sekhar with great ceremony.

The fourth, Sasankalekha, of tender age and therefore of no account, said: "I will make you a string of rosary beads, brother, with which to tell the names of your gods—the sahibs." Her sisters reproved her, saying: "Run away, you saucy girl."

Source: Rabindranath Tagore, *The Hungry Stones and Other Stories* (New York: The Macmillan Company, 1916).

## Thinking About Literature

1. **Vocabulary** Use the dictionary to find the meanings of the following words: sojourned, intoxicated, recipients, insolence, inaccessible, sundry, auspicious, vermilion, saucy.
2. How does the fable of the donkey and the idol remind Pramathanath of his own situation?
3. (a) Why do Pramathanath's daughters tease Nabendu Sekhar? (b) What point are they making?
4. *Critical Thinking* **Drawing Conclusions** (a) How does this story illustrate a cultural conflict within Indian society? (b) Judging by the story, how do you think Tagore felt about British rule in India?

# Skills for Success

## Interpreting Graphs

A graph is a mathematical drawing that shows numerical facts in picture form. A common kind of graph is a bar graph. Bar graphs are useful for showing changes in one or more sets of numbers over a period of time.

Study the bar graph below. Then follow the steps to draw some conclusions about Japan's foreign trade between World War I and World War II.

**1** **Identify the subject of the graph.** The title, labels, and key give you a general idea of the information presented. (a) What is the title of the graph? (b) What do the numbers on the vertical axis show? The horizontal axis? (c) What do the green and orange bars represent?

**2** **Read the data on the graph.** (a) What was the value of Japan's imports in 1920? In 1940? (b) What was the value of Japan's exports in 1920? In 1940? (c) A trade surplus occurs when exports exceed imports. A trade deficit occurs when imports are greater than exports. During which years did Japan have a trade deficit?

**3** **Interpret the graph.** (a) What was the general trend in the total amount of Japan's foreign trade between 1920 and 1940? (b) What happened to Japan's total foreign trade in 1930? What economic event that happened worldwide in 1930 might explain that change?

*Beyond the Classroom* Graphs are used extensively by economists to show current trends as well as to make predictions. In the business section of the newspaper, locate and study two graphs and the articles that accompany them. Present a short explanation of the graphs to the class.

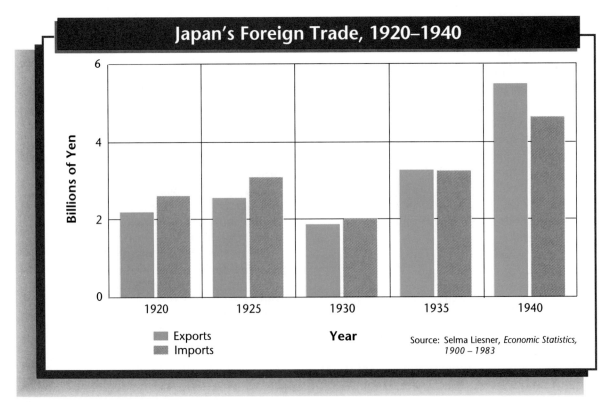

Japan's Foreign Trade, 1920–1940

Billions of Yen

■ Exports
■ Imports

Year

Source: Selma Liesner, *Economic Statistics, 1900 – 1983*

## Building Vocabulary

Review the following vocabulary from this chapter: *nationalization, nationalism, imperialism, apartheid, mandate, ahimsa, civil disobedience, warlord, zaibatsu, ultranationalist.* Write sentences using each of these terms, leaving blanks where the terms would go. Exchange your sentences with another student and fill in the blanks on each other's lists.

## Reviewing Chapter Themes

1. **Political and Social Systems** How did nationalism and the desire to modernize influence each of the following regions: (a) Latin America, (b) Africa?
2. **Impact of the Individual** (a) Compare the goals and methods of Mohandas Gandhi and Atatürk in reshaping their countries. (b) How did Jiang Jieshi and Mao Zedong differ in their goals for China?
3. **Economics and Technology** (a) Describe the economic effects of the Great Depression on Latin America. (b) What did Latin Americans do to combat the effects of the depression?
4. **Global Interaction** (a) Why did some Japanese resent the West? (b) How did Japanese militarists and ultranationalists exploit antiwestern feeling to strengthen their cause?

## Thinking Critically

1. **Making Inferences** (a) What were the three main issues addressed by the Mexican Constitution of 1917? (b) What groups do you think welcomed the constitution? (c) What groups might try to prevent the government from enforcing the constitution? Explain.
2. **Identifying Alternatives** (a) Based on your reading in this and earlier chapters, what different policies has the United States pursued toward the nations of Latin America in the past 150 years? (b) Identify at least one alternative approach that the United States might take toward these neighboring nations. Explain why you favor this alternative. (★ See *Skills for Success,* page 654.)
3. **Predicting Consequences** A British adviser at the Paris Peace Conference in 1919 made the following statement: "The Peace Conference has laid two eggs—Jewish nationalism and Arab nationalism: These are going to grow up into troublesome chickens." (a) What did he mean by this statement? (b) Based on what you have read about Arabs and Jews in Palestine, do you agree with his prediction? Explain. (★ See *Skills for Success,* page 974.)
4. **Linking Past and Present** (a) Describe Gandhi's methods of nonviolence and civil disobedience. (b) How were the methods used by the Reverend Martin Luther King, Jr., and other civil rights protesters in the United States in the 1960s similar to Gandhi's?
5. **Defending a Position** Some 80,000 Chinese Communists died during the Long March. Yet Communist leader Mao Zedong claimed the Long March as a victory. Do you agree or disagree with his assessment? Defend your position.
6. **Drawing Conclusions** Do you think the rise of the militarists in Japan could have been avoided? Why or why not?

## For Your Portfolio

A publisher of children's books has asked you to write a biography of a foreign leader. Your audience will be students in sixth grade.

1. Begin by reviewing the material on leaders discussed in this chapter. After reviewing the material, choose a leader for your biography.
2. Use the chapter text and library resources to research your biography. Find out facts on the person's childhood, rise to power, major influences, character, experience, ambitions, and philosophy of government. Try to locate several high-interest anecdotes to make the story come alive. If possible, locate photographs and other visual material that you can include.
3. Outline your biography. Then, write a draft using your outline.
4. Ask a classmate or your teacher to read your draft and make suggestions. Then, revise your biography. Make a final copy and add a title and cover.
5. Present your biography to students in a sixth-grade class.

# Crisis of Democracy in the West

## (1919–1939)

## CHAPTER OUTLINE

World War I ended in November 1918. Battlefields littered with debris were gradually cleared. Farms sprouted anew where tens of thousands had died. Restless heroes, who had survived the slaughter, tried to return to civilian life. For them, war had no romance. Erich Maria Remarque (ray  MAHRK), a German survivor of the trenches, captured their disillusionment in his 1929 novel *All Quiet on the Western Front*.

In the novel's last chapter, Paul Bäumer, a young German soldier, sits alone in a garden, recovering from a poison gas attack. At the age of 21, he is already a veteran of three years of combat. His friends are gone, killed by bullets, shrapnel, artillery explosions, or poison gas.

Now, in the autumn of 1918, he knows that the war is almost over. "The armistice is coming soon, I believe it now too. Then we will go home." But Bäumer cannot even imagine peace. He wonders how he can return to civilian life feeling used up, dead inside:

> 66Had we returned home in 1916, out of the suffering and the strength of our experience we might have unleashed a storm. Now if we go back we will be weary, broken, burnt out, rootless, and without hope. We will not be able to find our way any more.99

In fact, he never lives to see peace. He is killed in the last month of the war.

*All Quiet on the Western Front* captured the bitterness of survivors on both sides. Remarque dedicated the novel to "a generation of men who, even though they may have escaped its shells, were destroyed by the war."

After World War I ended, western nations worked to restore prosperity and ensure peace. But in the 1920s and 1930s, political and economic turmoil challenged democratic traditions. In Italy and Germany, people turned to dictators, whose seemingly simple solutions offered an escape from despair. Extremists pushed their own brand of ultranationalism and created scapegoats to blame for all their ills.

Today, we can see the mistakes and failures made between 1919 and 1939. As you read this chapter and the next one, though, think about why people responded as they did to each new crisis. Above all, why did the "war to end all wars" and Wilson's goal to create a "just and lasting peace" result in only a 20-year truce?

**FOCUS ON** these questions as you read:

- **Economics and Technology**
  What were the causes and effects of the Great Depression?

- **Art and Literature**
  How did writers and artists reflect the mood of postwar Europe and the United States?

- **Political and Social Systems**
  Why did some countries turn to authoritarian governments in the postwar era?

- **Religions and Value Systems**
  What values did fascism uphold?

## TIME AND PLACE

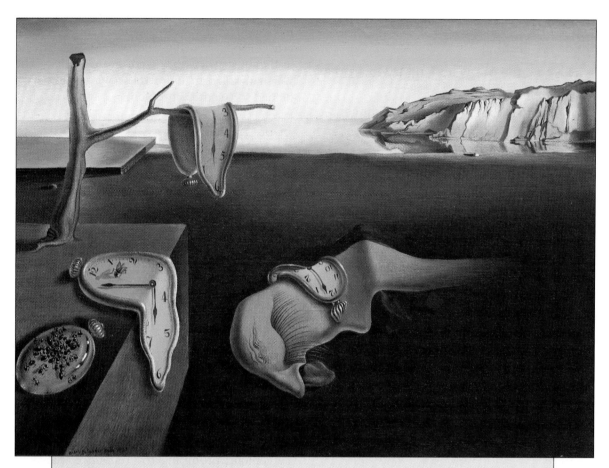

*An Uncertain World* The horrors of World War I shook many people's faith in human reason. Some artists turned instead to exploring the irrational world of dreams. This 1931 painting, The Persistence of Memory, *by the Spanish artist Salvador Dali seems to suggest a dream world where nothing is solid, even time. In the face of postwar confusion, others looked to powerful dictators for security.* **Art and Literature** *Can you think of ways that melting watches make sense as symbols of the postwar world?*

## HUMANITIES LINK

*Art History* Käthe Kollwitz, *War* (page 765).
*Literature* In this chapter, you will encounter passages from the following works of literature: Erich Maria Remarque, *All Quiet on the Western Front* (page 762); William Butler Yeats, "The Second Coming" (page 770); Thomas Hardy, "Drinking Song" (page 770).

| 1916 | 1922 | 1925 | 1929 | 1933 | 1938 |
|------|------|------|------|------|------|
| Easter Rising in Ireland | Mussolini takes power in Italy | Locarno treaties signed | Great Depression begins | Hitler becomes chancellor of Germany | Kristallnacht |

| 1915 | 1920 | 1925 | 1930 | 1935 | 1940 |

# 1 The Western Democracies

## Guide for Reading

- How did the postwar world try to ensure the peace?

- What challenges faced Britain, France, and the United States?

- How did the Great Depression affect western nations?

- **Vocabulary** *general strike*

"The belief in Progress," remarked a British clergyman in the early 1900s, "has been the working faith of the West for about a hundred and fifty years." Enlightenment thinkers had encouraged the belief that problems could be solved through reason. The Industrial Revolution bolstered confidence in technological and economic progress.

The catastrophe of World War I shattered this sense of optimism. People added up the staggering costs—10 million dead, more than 20 million wounded, unimaginable property losses. Economic and political crises would only add to the growing pessimism of the 1920s and 1930s.

## Postwar Problems

In 1919, three western democracies—Britain, France, and the United States—appeared powerful. They had ruled the Paris Peace Conference and boosted hopes for the spread of democracy to the new nations of Eastern Europe. Beneath the surface, however, postwar Europe faced grave problems.

At first, the most pressing issues were finding jobs for returning veterans and rebuilding war-ravaged lands. Many nations also owed huge debts because they had borrowed heavily to pay for the war. In the early postwar years, economic problems fed social unrest and made radical ideas more popular. The Russian Revolution unleashed fears of the spread of communism. (See Chapter 28.) Some people saw socialism as the answer to hardships. Others embraced nationalistic political movements.

Other troubles clouded the international scene. As you have read, the peace settlements dissatisfied many Europeans, especially in Germany and among various ethnic groups in Eastern Europe. Finally, Europe lacked strong leaders just when they were most needed. The war had killed many of those who might have helped solve critical problems.

## Pursuing Peace

During the 1920s, diplomats worked hard for peace. Many shared the fears of British prime minister Stanley Baldwin. "One more war in the West," he warned, "and the civilization of the ages will fall with as great a shock as that of Rome."

**The "spirit of Locarno."** Hopes soared in 1925 when representatives from seven European nations signed a series of treaties at Locarno, Switzerland. The treaties settled Germany's borders with France, Belgium, Czechoslovakia, and Poland. The Locarno treaties became the symbol of a new era. "France and Germany Ban War Forever," trumpeted a *New York Times* headline.

The "spirit of Locarno" was echoed in the Kellogg-Briand Pact of 1928. Almost every independent nation in the world signed onto this agreement, promising to "renounce war as an instrument of national policy." In this hopeful spirit, the great powers pursued disarmament. The United States, Britain, France, Japan, and other nations signed treaties to reduce the size of their navies. However, they failed to agree on limiting the size of their armies.

Despite grumblings about the Versailles treaty, people around the world put their hope in the League of Nations. From its headquarters in Geneva, Switzerland, the league encouraged cooperation and tried to get members to make a commitment to stop aggression. In 1926, after signing the Locarno agreements, Germany joined the league. Later, the Soviet Union was also admitted.

**Disturbances to the peace.** Although the Kellogg-Briand Pact outlawed war, there was no way of enforcing the ban. The League of Nations, too, was powerless to stop aggressors. It had also been damaged by the American refusal to join. In 1931, for example, the league

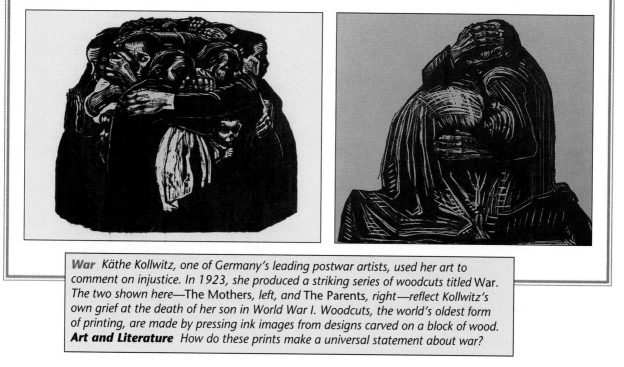

**War** Käthe Kollwitz, one of Germany's leading postwar artists, used her art to comment on injustice. In 1923, she produced a striking series of woodcuts titled War. The two shown here—The Mothers, *left, and* The Parents, *right*—reflect Kollwitz's own grief at the death of her son in World War I. Woodcuts, the world's oldest form of printing, are made by pressing ink images from designs carved on a block of wood. **Art and Literature** How do these prints make a universal statement about war?

vigorously condemned the Japanese invasion of Manchuria, but to no effect. (See page 756.) Other ambitious powers noted the league's weakness. In Chapter 31, you will see how ambitious dictators rearmed their military forces and pursued aggressive foreign policies.

## Recovery and Collapse

During the 1920s, Europe made a shaky recovery. Economies returned to peacetime manufacturing and trade. Veterans gradually found jobs. Middle-class families generally enjoyed a rising standard of living, with money to buy new products such as cars, refrigerators, and radios.

The United States emerged from the war as the world's leading economic power. American banks and businesses controlled a global network of trade and finance. American loans and investments backed the recovery in Europe. As long as the American economy was healthy, the global economy remained relatively prosperous.

**A dangerous imbalance.** Both the American and the world economy had weak spots, however. Oddly enough, a major problem was overproduction. The war had increased demand for raw materials from Africa, Asia, and Latin America. Improved technology and farm-

ing methods also contributed to higher output. When demand dwindled after the war, prices fell. Consumers benefited from the lower prices. But farmers, miners, herders, and other suppliers of raw materials suffered severe hardships.

At the same time, industrial workers won higher wages, which raised the price of manufactured goods. An imbalance emerged. Because farmers' earnings had fallen, they could afford fewer manufactured goods. Despite the slowing demand, factories kept pouring out goods. This imbalance, combined with other problems, undermined industrial economies. By the late 1920s, conditions were ripe for disaster.

**The crash.** Few people saw the looming danger. In the United States, prices on the New York Stock Exchange soared. Eager investors acquired stocks on margin, that is, they paid only part of the cost and borrowed the rest from brokers. In the autumn of 1929, jitters about the economy caused brokers to call in these loans. When investors were unable to repay, financial panic set in. Stock prices crashed, wiping out the fortunes of many investors.

**Spiraling disaster.** The stock market crash triggered the Great Depression of the 1930s, a painful time of global economic collapse. The crash created financial turmoil in the industrial world as American banks stopped making loans abroad and demanded repayment of foreign loans.

In the United States and elsewhere, banks failed and businesses closed, throwing millions out of work. The cycle spiraled steadily downward. The jobless could not afford to buy goods, so more factories had to close, which in turn increased the numbers of unemployed.

In once-prosperous western cities, people slept on park benches and lined up to eat in charity soup kitchens. Former business leaders sold apples in the street. In one of Britain's richest coal-mining regions, writer George Orwell observed poor families scrambling through the slag heaps:

66 The dumpy, shawled women, with their sacking aprons and their heavy black clogs, [were] kneeling in the cindery mud and the bitter wind searching for tiny chips of coal. . . . In winter they are almost desperate for fuel. It is more important almost than food. 99

**Global impact.** In desperation, governments tried to protect their economies from foreign competition. The United States imposed the highest tariffs in its history. The policy backfired because other nations retaliated by raising their tariffs. In the end, all countries lost access to the larger global market. As you read in Chapter 29, the Great Depression spread misery outside the industrial world.

As the depression dragged on, many people lost faith in the ability of democratic governments to solve the problems. Misery and hopelessness created fertile ground for extremists who promised radical solutions. Communists gloated over the failure of capitalism. Rightwing extremists played on themes of intense nationalism, the failure of democracy, the virtues of authoritarian rule, and the need to rearm.

## Britain in the Postwar Era

Even before the depression, Britain faced economic problems. Although it emerged victorious from the war, much of its overseas trade was lost. German U-boats had wreaked havoc on British shipping. The nation was deeply in debt, and its factories were out of date.

During the 1920s, unemployment was severe. Wages remained low, leading to worker unrest and frequent strikes. In 1926, a general strike, or strike by workers in many different industries at the same time, lasted nine days and involved some three million workers.

**Economics and politics.** During the 1920s, the Labour party surpassed the Liberal party in strength. (See page 612.) Labour leaders gained support among workers by promoting a gradual move toward socialism. The middle class, however, firmly backed the Con-

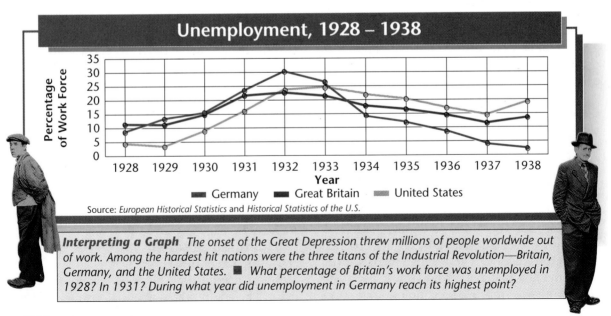

**Interpreting a Graph** The onset of the Great Depression threw millions of people worldwide out of work. Among the hardest hit nations were the three titans of the Industrial Revolution—Britain, Germany, and the United States. ■ What percentage of Britain's work force was unemployed in 1928? In 1931? During what year did unemployment in Germany reach its highest point?

servative party, which held power during much of this period. Widespread fear of communism contributed to a drift toward the right. After the general strike, Conservatives passed legislation limiting the power of workers to strike.

The Great Depression intensified the nation's economic woes. As the crisis worsened, Britain set up a coalition government with leaders from all three major parties. The government provided some unemployment benefits to ease the worst problems, but millions of people suffered great hardships.

**Irish independence.** At the war's end, Britain still faced the "Irish question." In 1914, you will recall, Parliament passed a home rule bill that was shelved when the war began. (See page 615.) Militant Irish nationalists, however, were unwilling to wait. On Easter 1916, a small group launched a revolt against British rule. Although the Easter Rising was quickly suppressed, the execution of 15 rebel leaders stirred wider support for their cause.

When Britain again failed to grant home rule in 1919, civil war erupted in Ireland. Members of the Irish Republican Army (IRA) carried on a guerrilla war against British forces and their supporters. Civilians were often caught in the middle of the violence.

In 1922, moderate leaders in Ireland and England finally reached an agreement. Most of Ireland became the independent Irish Free State, later called Eire. The largely Protestant northern counties (Ulster) remained under British rule. That settlement ended the worst violence. However, the IRA and many other nationalists never accepted the division of Ireland. In years to come, too, Catholics in the north faced discrimination. The status of Northern Ireland remained a thorny issue. (See page 855.)

**Commonwealth and empire.** Abroad, Britain took steps to satisfy the demands of Canada, Australia, New Zealand, and South Africa. In 1931, all four former colonies became fully self-governing dominions within the newly formed British Commonwealth of Nations. Although linked by economic and cultural ties, each member of the Commonwealth pursued its own course.

Despite challenges from nationalist groups, Britain's colonial empire still stretched around the globe. To the British, their empire remained

**A Change of Government** *After years of struggle, the Irish Free State finally won independence in 1922. Here, a statue of Queen Victoria is lowered from the roof of the building where Ireland's new parliament met.* **Continuity and Change** *How does this picture capture a symbolic moment?*

a source of wealth and pride. At the same time, Britain worked to improve agriculture, education, and medical care in its colonies while planning for gradual independence at some uncertain date.

**Foreign policy.** Britain's postwar foreign policy created tensions with its ally France. Almost from the signing of the Treaty of Versailles, British leaders wanted to relax the treaty's harsh treatment of Germany. They feared that if Germany became too weak, the Soviet Union would be able to expand and France might gain too much control on the continent. Britain's leniency toward Germany helped push France in the opposite direction.

## France Pursues Security

Like Britain, France emerged from World War I both a victor and a loser. Fighting on the Western Front had devastated northern France. The French had suffered enormous casualties. Survivors felt battered and insecure.

# CAUSE AND EFFECT

### Long-Term Causes

Worldwide interrelationship of governments, financial institutions, and industries

Huge debts resulting from costs of World War I

European dependence on American loans

Widespread use of credit

Overproduction of goods while demand was falling

Rising wages for industrial workers while farmers' earnings were falling

### Immediate Causes

New York stock market crash ruins investors who have borrowed and speculated on credit

Farmers who have purchased large machinery on credit are unable to make payments

Banks demand repayment of loans

American loans to other countries dry up

Without capital, businesses and factories fail

## WORLDWIDE ECONOMIC DEPRESSION

### Immediate Effects

Vast unemployment and misery

Growth of economic nationalism, with tariffs imposed to protect industries

Loss of faith in capitalism and democracy

Authoritarian leaders gain support

### Long-Term Effects

Nazis take control in Germany

Fascist leaders win support in Eastern Europe

Governments experiment with social programs

People blame scapegoats for economic woes

World War II begins

### Connections Today

Government monitoring of or control of national economies

Stricter controls on banks, credit, stock market

Continuation of social programs set up during depression

Monitoring of worldwide economic developments by international agencies

---

The French economy recovered fairly rapidly, thanks in part to German reparations and to territories gained from Germany, including Alsace and Lorraine. Later, the Great Depression did not hurt France as much as it did some countries. French industry was not as centralized in the hands of big business. Small workshops served local regions and were less affected by global trends.

**Coalition governments.** Still, economic swings did occur, adding to an unstable political scene. Political divisions and financial scandals continued to plague the Third Republic. (See Chapter 24.) Many parties—from conservatives to communists—competed for power. During the postwar years, France was again ruled by a series of coalition governments.

In 1936, several parties on the left united behind the socialist leader Leon Blum. His Popular Front government tried to solve labor problems and passed some social legislation. But it could not satisfy more radical leftists whose strikes soon brought down Blum's government. Thus, France, like Britain, muddled through a series of crises. Democracy survived, but the country lacked strong leadership that could respond to the clamor for change.

**The Maginot Line.** The chief French concern after the war was securing its borders against Germany. France deeply distrusted its neighbor across the Rhine, which had invaded in 1870 and 1914. To prevent a third invasion, it built massive fortifications along the border. The Maginot (MA zhee noh) Line, as this defensive "wall" was called, offered a sense of security—a false one. The line would be of little use when Germany again invaded in 1940.

In its quest for security, France strengthened its military and sought alliances with other countries, including the Soviet Union. It insisted on strict enforcement of the Versailles treaty and complete payment of reparations, hoping to keep the German economy weak.

*Interpreting a Chart* Today, economists still debate the causes and effects of the Great Depression. For most people at the time, however, the effects seemed simple—unemployment and misery. ■ What measures do governments today take to deal with the conditions that caused the Great Depression?

## Prosperity and Depression in the United States

The United States emerged from World War I in excellent shape. A late entrant into the war, it had suffered relatively few casualties and little loss of property. It led the world in industrial and agricultural output and helped finance the European recovery.

**Avoiding foreign entanglements.** As you have read, the United States stayed out of the League of Nations. Many Americans feared that joining the league might lead to involvement in future foreign wars. They insisted that the nation maintain its free hand in foreign affairs. Still, during the 1920s, the United States took a leading role in international diplomacy. It sponsored the Kellogg-Briand Pact, pressed for disarmament, and worked to reduce German reparations.

**Closing the door.** At the same time, the government moved to limit immigration from overseas. Millions of immigrants had poured into the United States between 1890 and 1914. (See page 627.) Some native-born Americans sought to exclude these newcomers, whose cultures differed from those of earlier settlers from northern Europe. In response, Congress passed laws limiting immigration from Europe. Earlier laws had already excluded Chinese immigrants and strictly limited Japanese immigration.

Fear of bomb-throwing radicals and the Bolshevik Revolution in Russia set off a "Red Scare" in 1919 and 1920. Police rounded up suspected foreign-born radicals, and a number were expelled from the United States.

**Boom and bust.** Communism had little appeal in the boom years of the 1920s. Middle-class Americans were enjoying the benefits of capitalism, stocking their homes with radios, refrigerators, and automobiles. Most Americans agreed with President Calvin Coolidge's slogan that "the business of America is business."

The 1929 stock market crash burst this bubble of prosperity. Banks failed, thousands of businesses closed, and unemployment spread misery everywhere. President Herbert Hoover firmly believed that the government should not intervene in private business matters. However, an angry public prompted him to try a variety of limited measures to solve the crisis.

**The New Deal.** In 1932, Americans elected a new President, Franklin D. Roosevelt, who projected an air of energy and optimism. "FDR" argued that government had to take an active role in combating the Great Depression. He introduced the New Deal, a massive package of economic and social programs.

Under the New Deal, the federal government became more directly involved in people's everyday lives than ever before. New laws regulated the stock market and protected bank depositors' savings. Government programs created jobs for the unemployed or gave aid to poverty-stricken farmers. The United States also set up a social security system. It provided old-age pensions and other benefits that major European countries had introduced years earlier.

The New Deal did not end the Great Depression, but it did ease the suffering for many. Still, some critics fiercely condemned the New Deal because it expanded the role of government so sharply. As a result of Roosevelt's policies, many Americans came to expect the government to intervene directly to promote their economic well-being. As you will read in Chapter 33, the debate about the role of government continues to influence American politics.

## SECTION 1 REVIEW

1. **Identify** (a) Locarno agreements, (b) Kellogg-Briand Pact, (c) IRA, (d) Commonwealth of Nations, (e) Leon Blum, (f) Maginot Line, (g) New Deal.
2. **Define** general strike.
3. (a) What steps did the major powers take to protect the peace? (b) Why did these moves have limited effects?
4. Explain how each of the following contributed to the Great Depression: (a) overproduction, (b) margin buying.
5. How did the Great Depression affect political developments in the United States?
6. *Critical Thinking* **Applying Information** How did Britain and France emerge from World War I as both victors and losers?
7. *ACTIVITY* Draw a political cartoon showing how the Great Depression undermined confidence in democracy.

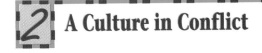

# A Culture in Conflict

## Guide for Reading

- What new ideas revolutionized science and thought?
- What artistic and literary trends emerged in the 1920s?
- How did women's lives change after World War I?
- **Vocabulary** *stream of consciousness, flapper*

In his poem "The Second Coming," the Irish poet William Butler Yeats summed up the feelings of many postwar writers and artists:

66Things fall apart; the centre cannot hold;
   Mere anarchy is loosed upon the world,
   The blood-dimmed tide is loosed, and
      everywhere
   The ceremony of innocence is
      drowned.99

It was not only the war and the Great Depression that fostered a sense of uncertainty. New ideas and scientific discoveries were challenging long-held ideas about the nature of the world.

### New Views of the Universe

The ancient Greeks were the first to propose that all matter is composed of tiny, indivisible atoms. Over the centuries, most scientists came to accept this idea. But discoveries made in the late 1800s and early 1900s showed that the atom was more complex than anyone suspected.

**Radioactivity.** By the early 1900s, the Polish-born French scientist Marie Curie and other scientists were experimenting with a process called radioactivity. They discovered that the atoms of certain elements, such as radium and uranium, spontaneously release charged particles. As scientists investigated radioactivity further, they discovered that it could change atoms of one element into atoms of another element. Such findings proved that atoms were not solid and indivisible.

**Relativity.** By 1905, the German-born physicist Albert Einstein advanced his theories of relativity. Einstein argued that space and time measurements are not absolute but are determined by many factors, some of them unknown. This idea raised questions about Newtonian science, which compared the universe to a machine that operated according to absolute laws.

In the postwar years, many scientists came to accept the theory of relativity. To much of the general public, however, Einstein's ideas seemed impossible to understand. And what they did understand disturbed them. Many feared that all the old certainties were crumbling. British writer Thomas Hardy echoed this mood of uncertainty:

66And now comes Einstein with a
      notion—
      Not yet quite clear
      To many here—
   That's there's no time, no space,
      no motion, . . .
   But just a sort of bending ocean.99

*A Fatal Discovery* Along with her husband, Pierre, Marie Curie won a Nobel prize for her groundbreaking research on radioactivity. But she paid a high price for knowledge. Curie's fingertips were often burned from handling deadly radioactive material. Although she shrugged off the danger to her health, she died in 1934 from radiation poisoning. Curie is shown here with her daughter Irene, who also went on to win a Nobel prize for her work with radioactive materials. *Impact of the Individual* Why do you think Curie ignored the health risks of her experiments?

Modern science seemed to reinforce the unsettling sense of a universe whirling beyond the understanding of human reason.

**Probing the mind.** The Austrian physician Sigmund Freud (FROID) also challenged faith in reason. He suggested that the unconscious mind drives much human behavior. Freud said that, in civilized society, learned values such as morality and reason help people repress, or check, powerful urges. But an individual feels constant tension between repressed drives and social training. This tension, argued Freud, may cause psychological illness or physical symptoms, such as paralysis or blindness.

Freud pioneered psychoanalysis, the study and treatment of the human mind. He analyzed dreams for clues to subconscious desires and developed ways to treat mental illnesses. His ideas had an impact far beyond medicine. Freud's work led writers and artists to explore the subconscious mind.

## The New Literature

In the 1920s, war novels, poetry, plays, and memoirs flowed off the presses. Works like Remarque's *All Quiet on the Western Front* exposed the grim horrors of modern warfare. Other writers heaped scorn on blundering military and political leaders. Their works reflected a powerful disgust with war that would color the European scene for decades.

**A loss of faith.** To many postwar writers, the war symbolized the moral breakdown of western civilization. In 1922, the American-born English poet T. S. Eliot published *The Waste Land*. This long poem portrays the modern world as spiritually empty and barren. In *The Sun Also Rises*, American novelist Ernest Hemingway shows the rootless wanderings of young people who lacked deep convictions. "I did not care what it was all about," says the narrator. "All I wanted to know was how to live in it."

**Literature of the inner mind.** As Freud's ideas became popular, some writers experimented with stream of consciousness. In this technique, a writer probes a character's random thoughts and feelings without imposing any logic or order. In novels like *To the Lighthouse* and *Mrs. Dalloway*, British novelist Virginia Woolf used stream of consciousness to explore the hidden thoughts of people as they go through the ordinary actions of their everyday lives.

The Irish novelist James Joyce went even further. In *Finnegan's Wake*, he explores the mind of a hero who remains sound asleep throughout the novel. To convey the freedom and playfulness of the unconscious mind, Joyce invented many words—including some, like bababadalgharaghtakamminarronnkonnbronnt- onnerronntuonnthunntrovarrhounawnskawnto- ohoohoordenenthurnuk, 100 letters long!

## Modern Art and Architecture

In the early 1900s, many western artists rejected earlier styles. Instead of trying to reproduce the real world, they explored other dimensions of color, line, and shape. Painters like Henri Matisse (mah TEES) outraged the public with their bold use of color and odd distortions. He and fellow artists were dubbed Fauves (FOHVZ), or Wild Beasts.

**Cubism.** Before the war, the Spanish artist Pablo Picasso and his friend Georges Braque (BRAHK) created a revolutionary new style, called Cubism. They broke three-dimensional objects into fragments and composed them into complex patterns of angles and planes. By redefining objects into separate shapes, they offered a new view of reality. (See page 681.)

Later artists, like the German Paul Klee (KLAY) and the Russian Vasily Kandinsky, moved even further from representing reality. They created abstract works—compositions of line, color, and shape with no recognizable subject matter at all.

**Dada and surrealism.** During and after the war, Dada burst onto the Paris art world. Dada was a revolt against civilization. Its goal was to "give the bourgeois a whiff of chaos." One Dadaist declared, "Dada is life without discipline or morality and we spit on humanity." Paintings by artists like Hans Arp and Max Ernst shocked, haunted, and disturbed viewers.

Cubism and Dada helped inspire surrealists like Salvador Dali. His dreamlike landscapes suggested Freud's notion of the chaotic unconscious mind. (See the painting on page 763.)

**Architecture.** Architects, too, rejected classical traditions and invented new styles to match an industrial, urban world. The famous Bauhaus school in Germany influenced architec-

# PARALLELS THROUGH TIME

## Stars and Their Fans

Since ancient times, crowds have cheered winning athletes, great actors, and other popular heroes. The relationship between stars and their fans got a big boost from technology in the 1920s. Radio and film brought people closer to their heroes than ever before.

**Linking Past and Present**  What might be some negative effects of admiring stars?

**PAST**  For movie fans of the 1930s, Hollywood stars like Swedish-born actress Greta Garbo, right, were symbols of beauty and style. At left, American track star Jesse Owens is welcomed home with a ticker-tape parade after winning four gold medals at the 1936 Olympics.

**PRESENT**  Fans of Elvis Presley, who died in 1977, still show their devotion to "the King" by flocking to his Tennessee home, Graceland. At the far right, fans of the Dallas Cowboys crowd to get an autograph.

ture by blending science and technology with design. Bauhaus designers used glass, steel, and concrete but little ornamentation.

The American architect Frank Lloyd Wright reflected the Bauhaus belief that the function of a building should determine its form. In designing houses, he used materials and forms that fit their environment.

## Popular Culture

New technologies helped create a mass culture shared by millions in the world's developed countries. Affordable cars gave middle-class people greater mobility. Movie stars made famous by Hollywood, such as Charlie Chaplin, had fans on every continent. Radios brought news, music, and sports into homes throughout the western world.

Many radios were tuned to the sounds of jazz. Jazz was pioneered by African American musicians who combined western harmonies with African rhythms. Jazz musicians, like trumpeter Louis Armstrong, took simple melodies and improvised endless subtle variations in beat and rhythm. They produced music that was both original and popular.

Europeans embraced American popular culture, with its greater freedom and willingness to experiment. The nightclub and the sound of jazz were symbols of that freedom. In fact, the 1920s are often referred to as the Jazz Age.

## A Changing Society

In the aftermath of World War I, many people yearned to return to "normalcy"—to life as it had been before 1914. But rebellious young people rejected the moral values and rules of the Victorian Age and chased after excitement. Gertrude Stein, an American writer living in Paris, called them the "lost generation." Others saw them as immoral pleasure-seekers.

**The flapper.** The reigning queen of the Jazz Age was the liberated young woman called the flapper. The first flappers were American, but their European sisters soon adopted the fashion. Flappers rejected old ways. Shocking their elders, they bobbed their hair and wore skirts far shorter than prewar fashions. They went out on dates unchaperoned, enjoyed wild

**Flappers and Homemakers** These two advertisements reflect contrasting images of women in the 1920s. Above, young flappers shop for the latest clothing styles. At right, a homemaker takes advantage of a new labor-saving device. **Continuity and Change** How do these ads reflect actual social changes?

new dance fads such as the Charleston, smoked, and drank in nightclubs.

**Women's lives.** For most women, the postwar period brought limited progress. During the war, women had held a wide range of jobs. While most returned to the home when the war ended, women's war work helped them win the vote in many western countries. A few women were elected to public office, such as Texas governor Miriam Ferguson or Lady Nancy Astor, the first woman to serve in the British Parliament.

Women continued to push open the doors to higher education. A few succeeded in what were considered "men's" fields. Even before the war, Marie Curie had won two Nobel prizes for her work in chemistry and physics. Still, like many other women, Curie had to balance her work with home duties. "I have a great deal of work," she lamented, "what with the house-keeping, the children, the teaching, and the laboratory, and I don't know how I shall manage it all."

By the 1920s, labor-saving devices were common in middle-class homes. Washing machines, vacuum cleaners, and canned foods freed women from many time-consuming household chores. Some women found paid work outside the home. Others took volunteer jobs, providing social services or raising funds for charities.

In the new atmosphere of emancipation, women pursued careers in many arenas—from sports to the arts. Women golfers, tennis players, swimmers, and pilots set new records. Women worked as newspaper reporters, published best-selling novels, and won recognition for their artwork. Most professions, though, were still dominated by men. Women doing the same work as men earned much less.

## SECTION 2 REVIEW

1. **Identify** (a) Marie Curie, (b) T. S. Eliot, (c) Virginia Woolf, (d) James Joyce, (e) Cubism, (f) Dada, (g) Bauhaus, (h) Jazz Age.
2. **Define** (a) stream of consciousness, (b) flapper.
3. Describe how the ideas of each of the following contributed to a sense of uncertainty in the postwar world: (a) Albert Einstein, (b) Sigmund Freud.
4. (a) What themes did postwar writers stress? (b) How did artists challenge older western traditions?
5. Describe three ways that women's lives changed in the postwar period.
6. *Critical Thinking* **Linking Past and Present** (a) How did technology shape popular culture in the 1920s? (b) What technologies are shaping popular culture today?
7. *ACTIVITY* Create flashcards for *six* individuals discussed in this section. On one side of each card, write the name of the person. On the other side, write a sentence describing his or her impact on postwar culture.

## 3 Fascism in Italy

### Guide for Reading

■ How did conditions in Italy favor Mussolini's rise to power?

■ How did Mussolini reshape Italy?

■ What were the values and goals of fascism?

Italo Balbo was disgusted with life back home in Italy. He had gone off to war in a spirit of patriotism. He returned to a land of economic chaos and political corruption:

❝I hated politics and politicians, who, in my opinion, had betrayed the hopes of soldiers, reducing Italy to a shameful peace. . . . Better to deny everything, destroy everything, in order to renew everything from the foundations.❞

Embittered and angry, Balbo joined a new movement, called fascism. Italy's Fascist party was led by a fierce nationalist, Benito Mussolini, who in the 1920s made himself dictator. His rise to power served as a model for ambitious strongmen elsewhere in Europe.

### *Rise of Mussolini*

In 1919, Italian nationalists were outraged by the Paris peace treaties. As one of the victorious Allies, Italy had expected to gain territory on the Adriatic. Instead, these lands became part of the newly created Yugoslavia. At the same time, disorders multiplied at home. Inspired in part by the Russian Revolution, peasants seized land and workers went on strike or took over factories. Their actions frightened the landowners and industrialists who had traditionally held power.

Amid the chaos, returning veterans faced unemployment. Trade declined and taxes rose. The government, split into feuding factions, seemed powerless to end the crisis.

**A fiery speaker.** Into this seething conflict stepped Benito Mussolini. The son of a socialist blacksmith and a devoutly religious schoolteacher, Mussolini had been a socialist in his youth. During the war, however, he switched loyalties, exchanging belief in class struggle for intense nationalism.

In 1919, he organized veterans and other discontented Italians into the Fascist party. They took their name from the Latin *fasces,* a bundle of sticks wrapped around an ax—a symbol of authority in ancient Rome. In fiery speeches, Mussolini spoke of reviving Roman greatness. He promised to end corruption and replace turmoil with order. With his jutting jaw and slashing phrases, Mussolini commanded attention.

**Seizing power.** Mussolini organized his supporters into "combat squads." These gangs, uniformed in black shirts, rejected the democratic process in favor of violent action. They broke up socialist rallies, smashed leftist presses, and attacked farmers' unions and cooperatives. Through terror and intimidation, "Black Shirts" ousted elected officials in northern Italy. Many Italians accepted these moves because they, too, had lost all faith in constitutional government.

In 1922, the Fascists made a bid for power. At a rally in Naples, they announced a "march on Rome" to demand that the government make changes. "On to Rome," chanted tens of thousands of Fascists who swarmed into the capital. Fearing civil war, King Victor Emmanuel III bowed to pressure. He asked Mussolini to form a government as prime minister. Without firing a shot, Mussolini thus obtained a legal appointment from the king.

## Mussolini's Italy

At first, Fascists held only a few cabinet posts. By 1925, though, Mussolini had assumed more power and taken the title *Il Duce* (EEL DOO chay), "The Leader." He suppressed rival parties, muzzled the press, limited the number of voters, and rigged elections. In provinces and towns, he replaced elected officials with Fascist supporters.

In theory, Italy remained a parliamentary monarchy. In fact, it was a dictatorship upheld by Fascist violence and terror. Critics were thrown into prison, forced into exile, or murdered outright. Secret police and propaganda bolstered the regime.

**Economic policy.** To encourage economic growth and end conflicts between owners and workers, Mussolini brought the economy under state control. Unlike socialists, though, he preserved capitalism. Under Mussolini's "corporate state," representatives of business, labor, government and the Fascist party controlled industry, agriculture, and trade. This policy did help business, and production increased. This success came, though, at the expense of workers, who were forbidden to strike and whose wages lagged.

*Fascist Propaganda* Mussolini prided himself on making the state more efficient. When he came to power, he fired thousands of bureaucrats who did little but collect their paychecks. He also strove to make Italy's notoriously slow trains run on time. This poster celebrates the introduction of new railroad cars for passengers. **Political and Social Systems** How does the image stress the fascist ideal of the "great man"?

FERROVIE DELLO STATO

LE PIU' RECENTI CARROZZE DI 3ª CLASSE

**Social policies.** To Fascists, the individual was unimportant except as a member of the state. Men, women, and children were bombarded with slogans glorifying the state and Mussolini. "Believe! Obey! Fight!" loudspeakers blared and posters proclaimed. Men were urged to be ruthless, selfless warriors for the glory of Italy. "A minute on the battlefield," they were told, "is worth a lifetime of peace."

Women were called on to "win the battle of motherhood." Those who bore more than 14 children were given a medal by Il Duce himself. Women were valued as wives and mothers but not as workers. "Machines and women," declared Mussolini, "are the two major causes of unemployment." Under the Fascists, women were pushed out of paid jobs or earned much less than men for the same work.

Still, Mussolini expected women to make sacrifices for the nation. He once asked them to donate their gold wedding bands to the treasury, handing out iron ones in exchange. The iron symbolized their contribution to a stronger nation.

**Fascist youth.** Shaping the young was a major Fascist goal. Fascist youth groups toughened children and taught them to obey strict military discipline. Boys and girls learned about the glories of ancient Rome. Young Fascists marched in torchlight parades, singing patriotic hymns and chanting "Mussolini is always right." By the 1930s, a generation of young soldiers stood ready to back Il Duce's drive to expand Italian power.

## What Is Fascism?

Historians still debate the real nature of fascist ideology. Mussolini coined the term, but fascists had no single unifying set of beliefs, as Marxists did. Today, we generally use the term to describe any authoritarian government that is not communist. In the 1920s and 1930s, though, fascism meant different things in different countries.

All forms of fascism, however, shared some basic features. It was rooted in extreme nationalism. Fascists glorified action, violence, discipline, and, above all, blind loyalty to the state. According to Mussolini:

> **"**Fascism conceives of the State as an absolute, in comparison with which all individuals or groups are relative, only to be conceived of in their relation to the State.**"**

▲ *Benito Mussolini*

Fascists were antidemocratic. They rejected the Enlightenment emphasis on reason and the concepts of equality and liberty spread by the French Revolution. To them, democracy led to greed, corruption, and weakness. They claimed it put individual or class interests above national goals and destroyed feelings of community. Instead, fascists emphasized emotion and the need for the citizen to serve the state.

Fascists also pursued aggressive foreign expansion. Their ideas were linked to Social Darwinism, with its notion of "survival of the fittest." (See page 571.) Fascist leaders glorified warfare as a necessary and noble struggle for survival. "War alone," said Mussolini, "brings up to its highest tension all human energy and puts the stamp of nobility upon peoples who have the courage to face it."

**Compared to communism.** Fascists were the sworn enemy of socialists and communists. While communists called for world revolution of the proletariat, fascists pursued nationalist goals. Fascists found allies among business leaders and wealthy landowners, as well as the lower middle class. Communists won support among the urban working class.

Despite these basic differences, there are significant similarities between these two ideolo-

**ISSUES** *For* **TODAY**

In Italy, supporters of fascism turned from democracy to one-party dictatorship. Under what circumstances might people be willing to sacrifice democratic rights and ideals?

## Features of Totalitarian States

1. **Single-party dictatorship**

2. **State control of economy**

3. **Police spies and state terrorism**

4. **Strict censorship and government control of media**

5. **Use of schools and media to indoctrinate and mobilize citizens**

6. **Unquestioning obedience to single ruler**

*Interpreting a Chart* Stalin's Soviet Union was on the opposite end of the political scale from Mussolini's Italy and Hitler's Germany. Yet all three totalitarian governments had important characteristics in common. ■ *Why is control of the media important in a totalitarian state? How did Mussolini use schools to indoctrinate young Fascists?*

gies. Both flourished during economic hard times by promoting extreme programs of social change. In both communist Russia and fascist Italy, dictators imposed totalitarian governments in order to bring about their social revolutions. In both, the party elite claimed to rule in the name of the national interest.

**Totalitarian rule.** Mussolini built the first totalitarian state, which served as a model for others. Fascist rule in Italy was never as absolute as Stalin's in the Soviet Union or the government Adolf Hitler would impose on Germany. All three governments, however, had some basic features in common. (See the chart above.)

**Appeal.** Given its restrictions on individual freedom, why did fascism appeal to many Italians? First, it promised a strong, stable government and an end to the political feuding that

had paralyzed democracy. Mussolini's intense nationalism also struck a chord among ordinary Italians. He revived national pride, pledging to make the Mediterranean Sea a "Roman lake" once more. Finally, Mussolini projected a sense of power and confidence at a time of disorder and despair.

At first, Il Duce received good press outside Italy, too. Newspapers in Britain, France, and North America applauded Mussolini. "He made the trains run on time," they said, giving an approving nod to the discipline and order of the new government. Only later, when Mussolini embarked on a course of foreign conquest, did western democracies protest his actions.

**Looking ahead.** Three systems of government competed for influence in postwar Europe. Democracy endured in Britain and France but faced an uphill struggle in economic hard times. Communism emerged in Russia and won support elsewhere, but many people saw it as a dangerous threat. In Italy, fascism offered a different formula. Its chest-thumping calls for action, national unity, and dedication to the state ignited patriotic feeling. As the Great Depression spread, other nations looked to leaders who preached fascist ideology.

## SECTION 3 REVIEW

1. **Identify** (a) Black Shirts, (b) Il Duce.
2. (a) What problems did Italy face after World War I? (b) How did these problems help Mussolini win power?
3. Describe two economic or social goals of Mussolini, and explain the actions he took to achieve each goal.
4. (a) What values did fascism promote? (b) List two similarities and two differences between fascism and communism.
5. *Critical Thinking* **Analyzing Information** Why do you think the fascists blamed democracy for problems in Italy?
6. *ACTIVITY* Many people today use the word *fascist* in discussing politics. Take a poll of several voters and ask what they think the word means. Then, write a paragraph or make a chart comparing these definitions to what fascism meant under Mussolini.

# 4  Hitler and the Rise of Nazi Germany

## Guide for Reading

- Why did the Weimar government fail?
- How did Hitler turn Germany into a totalitarian state?
- How did fascist leaders gain power in Eastern Europe?
- **Vocabulary** *concentration camp*

In November 1923, a German army veteran and leader of an extremist party, Adolf Hitler, tried to take a page from Mussolini's book. His brown-shirted thugs burst into a beer hall in Munich, Germany, where a political meeting was set to start. Hitler climbed onto a table and fired his pistol. "The National Socialist revolution has begun!" he shouted.

The coup failed, and Hitler was soon behind bars. But Hitler was a force that could not be ignored forever. Within a decade, he made a new bid for power. This time, he succeeded by legal means.

Hitler's rise to power is one of the most significant events of our century. His success raised disturbing questions that we still debate today. How did Germany, which had a liberal democratic government in the 1920s, become a totalitarian dictatorship in the 1930s? Why did Hitler gain the enthusiastic support of many Germans?

## Struggles of the Weimar Republic

In November 1918, as World War I was drawing to a close, Germany tottered on the brink of chaos. Under the threat of a socialist revolution, Kaiser William II abdicated. Moderate leaders signed the armistice and later, under protest, the Versailles treaty.

In 1919, the new German Republic drafted a constitution in the city of Weimar (vī mahr). It created a democratic government known as the Weimar Republic. The constitution set up a parliamentary form of government led by a prime minister, or chancellor. It gave both women and men the vote, and included a bill of rights.

**Unrest.** The Weimar government faced severe problems from the start. Politically, it was weak because Germany had many small parties. Like the French premier, the German chancellor had to form coalitions that easily fell apart.

The government came under constant fire from both the left and right. Communists demanded revolutionary changes like those Lenin had brought to Russia. Conservatives—including the old Junker nobility, military officers, and wealthy bourgeois—attacked the government as too liberal. To many conservatives, democracy meant weakness. They longed for another strong leader like Bismarck or the kaiser.

Germans of all classes blamed the government for the hated Versailles treaty, with its war-guilt clause and heavy reparations. (See Chapter 27.) In their bitterness, they looked for scapegoats. Many accused Marxists and Jews of an imaginary conspiracy to betray Germany.

**Inflation.** Economic disaster fed unrest. In 1923, when Germany fell behind in reparations payments, France occupied the coal-rich Ruhr Valley. Ruhr Germans turned to passive resistance, refusing to work. To support them, the government printed huge quantities of paper money. This move set off terrible inflation that spiraled out of control. The German mark became almost worthless. An item that cost 100 marks in July 1922 cost 944,000 marks by August 1923. A newspaper or loaf of bread cost tens of thousands of marks.

Inflation spread misery and despair. Salaries rose by billions of marks, but they still could not keep up with skyrocketing prices. Many middle-class families saw their savings wiped out.

**Recovery.** With help from the western powers, the government did bring inflation under control. In 1924, the United States won British and French approval for a plan to reduce German reparations payments. Under the Dawes Plan, France withdrew its forces from the Ruhr and American loans helped the German economy recover.

Germany began to prosper, but memories of the miseries of 1923 revived when the Great Depression hit. Germans turned to an energetic leader, Adolf Hitler, who promised to solve the economic crisis and restore German greatness.

## Adolf Hitler

Hitler was born in Austria in 1889. When he was 18, he went to Vienna, hoping to enter art school, but he was turned down. At this time, Vienna was the capital of the multinational Hapsburg empire. Austrian Germans were a minority, but they felt superior to Jews, Serbs, Poles, and other ethnic or religious groups. During his stay in Vienna, Hitler developed the fanatical anti-Semitism that would later play a major role in his rise to power.

Hitler later moved to Germany and fought in the German army during World War I. Like many ex-soldiers, he despised the Weimar government. In 1919, he joined a small group of right-wing extremists. Within a year, he was the unquestioned leader of the National Socialist German Workers, or Nazi, party. Like Mussolini, Hitler organized his supporters into fighting squads. Nazi "Storm Troopers" battled in the streets against communists and others they saw as enemies.

**Mein Kampf.** In 1923, as you have read, Hitler made a failed attempt to seize power in Munich. While in prison, he wrote *Mein Kampf* (My Struggle), the "holy book" of Nazi goals and ideology. *Mein Kampf* reflected Hitler's obsessions—extreme nationalism, racism, and anti-Semitism. Germans, he said, belonged to a superior "master race" of Aryans, or light-skinned Europeans, whose greatest enemy were the Jews. Hitler viewed Jews not as members of a religion but as a separate race. Echoing a familiar theme, he claimed that Germany had not lost the war but had been betrayed by Marxists, Jews, corrupt politicians, and business leaders.

In his recipe for revival, Hitler urged Germans wherever they lived to unite into one great nation. Germany must expand, he said, to gain *Lebensraum,* or living space, for its people. Slavs and other inferior races must bow to Aryan needs. To achieve its greatness, Germany needed a strong leader, or *Führer* (FYOO ruhr). Adolf Hitler was determined to become that leader.

**The road to power.** After leaving prison, Hitler renewed his table-thumping speeches. He found enthusiastic followers among veterans and lower-middle-class people who felt frustrated about the future. The Great Depression played into Hitler's hands. As unemployment

*"Yes! Leader, We Follow You!"* Nazi propaganda used simple slogans and images. The intelligence of ordinary people is small, Hitler said. Therefore, "all effective propaganda must be limited to a very few points and must harp on these in slogans until the last member of the public understands what you want him to understand." The pin above shows the swastika, symbol of the Nazi party. **Religions and Value Systems** Compare this poster to the one on page 775. How do they promote similar values?

rose, Nazi membership grew to almost a million. Hitler's program appealed to workers and business people alike. He promised to end reparations, create jobs, and rearm Germany.

With the government paralyzed by divisions, both Nazis and Communists won more seats in the Reichstag, or lower house of the legislature. Finally, in 1933, other conservative politicians decided Hitler must become chancellor. They despised him as a vulgar rabble-rouser but planned to use him for their own ends. Thus, like Mussolini in Italy, Hitler became head of state through legal means.

Within a year, Hitler was master of Germany. He suspended civil rights, destroyed the Communists, and disbanded other political parties. Germany became a one-party state. Nazi flags, with their black swastikas, waved across the country. Like Stalin in Russia, Hitler purged his own party, brutally executing Nazis he felt were disloyal. Nazis learned that the Führer demanded unquestioning obedience.

## Hitler's Third Reich

Once in power, Hitler moved to build a new Germany. Like Mussolini, Hitler appealed to nationalism by recalling past glories. Germany's First Reich, or empire, was the medieval Holy Roman Empire. The Second Reich was the empire forged by Bismarck in 1871. Under Hitler's new Third Reich, he boasted, the German master race would dominate Europe for 1,000 years.

Hitler soon repudiated the hated Versailles treaty. He began scheming to unite Germany and Austria. "Today Germany belongs to us," sang young Nazis. "Tomorrow, the world."

**A totalitarian state.** To achieve his goals, Hitler organized a brutal system of terror, repression, and totalitarian rule. Nazis controlled all areas of German life—from government to religion to schools. Elite, black-uniformed SS troops enforced the Führer's will. His secret police, the Gestapo, rooted out opposition.

Few Germans saw or worried about this terror apparatus taking shape. Instead, they cheered Hitler's accomplishments in ending unemployment and reviving German power.

**Economic policy.** To combat the Great Depression, Hitler launched large public works programs (as did Britain and the United States). Tens of thousands of people were put to work building highways and housing or replanting forests. Hitler also began a crash program to rearm Germany, in violation of the Versailles treaty. Demand for military hardware stimulated business and helped eliminate unemployment.

Like Mussolini, Hitler preserved capitalism but brought big business and labor under government control. Few objected to this loss of freedom because their standard of living rose. Nazi propaganda highlighted the improvements. Workers joined "Strength Through Joy" programs, which offered vigorous outdoor vacations that also made them physically fit for military service.

**Social policy.** Like Italian Fascists and Russian Communists, the Nazis indoctrinated young people with their racist ideology. In passionate speeches, the Führer urged young Ger-

▲ *Marchers at a Nazi rally*

mans to destroy their so-called "enemies" without mercy:

> 66Extremes must be fought by extremes. Against the infection of [Marxism], against the Jewish pestilence, we must hold aloft a flaming ideal. And if others speak of the World and Humanity, we must say the Fatherland—and only the Fatherland!99

On hikes and in camps, the "Hitler Youth" pledged absolute loyalty to Germany and undertook physical fitness programs to prepare for war. ( ★ See *Skills for Success,* page 784.)

Like Fascists in Italy, Nazis sought to limit women's roles. Women were dismissed from upper-level jobs and turned away from universities. "National Socialism will restore her to her true profession—motherhood." To raise the birthrate, Nazis offered "pure-blooded Aryan" women rewards for having more children. Hitler's goal to keep women in the home applied mainly to the privileged. As German industry expanded, women workers were needed.

## Purging German Culture

Nazis used the arts and education as propaganda tools. They denounced modern art and music, saying it was corrupted by Jewish influences. Instead, they sought to purge, or purify, German culture. The Nazis glorified old German myths such as those re-created in the operas of Richard Wagner.

School courses and textbooks were rewritten to reflect Nazi racial views. "We teach and learn history," said one Nazi educator, "not to say how things actually happened but to instruct the German people from the past." At huge public bonfires, Nazis burned books of which

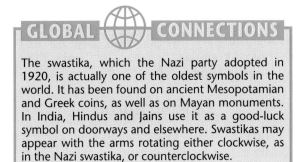

GLOBAL CONNECTIONS

The swastika, which the Nazi party adopted in 1920, is actually one of the oldest symbols in the world. It has been found on ancient Mesopotamian and Greek coins, as well as on Mayan monuments. In India, Hindus and Jains use it as a good-luck symbol on doorways and elsewhere. Swastikas may appear with the arms rotating either clockwise, as in the Nazi swastika, or counterclockwise.

they disapproved. *All Quiet on the Western Front* was one of many works that went up in flames. The Nazis viewed Remarque's novel as an insult to the German military.

**Nazism and the churches.** Hitler despised Christianity as "weak" and "flabby." He sought to replace religion with his racial creed. In an attempt to control the churches, the Nazis combined all Protestant sects into a single state church. They closed Catholic schools and muzzled the Catholic clergy.

Martin Niemoller, a German Protestant minister, was jailed for trying to help Jews. He later commented on the results of not speaking out against Nazism:

> 66The Nazis came first for the Communists. But I wasn't a Communist, so I didn't speak up. Then they came for the Jews, but I wasn't a Jew so I didn't speak up. Then they came for the trade unionists, but I wasn't a trade unionist so I didn't speak up. Then they came for the Catholics, but I was a Protestant so I didn't speak up.
>
> Then they came for me. By that time, there was no one left to speak up.99

**Campaign against the Jews.** In his fanatical anti-Semitism, Hitler set out to drive Jews from Germany. In 1935, the Nuremberg Laws placed severe restrictions on Jews. They were prohibited from marrying non-Jews, attending or teaching at German schools or universities, holding government jobs, practicing law or medicine, or publishing books. Nazis beat and robbed Jews and roused mobs to do the same. Many Jews, including Albert Einstein, fled the growing menace.

In November 1938, a German diplomat in Paris was shot by a young Jew whose parents had been mistreated in Germany. Hitler used the incident as an excuse to attack all Jews.

## Night of the Broken Glass

"Dead silence—not a sound to be heard in the town. The lamps in the street, the lights in the shops and in the houses are out. It is 3:30 A.M." In the German town of Emden, a small

A Vicious Campaign "We are going to destroy the Jews," Hitler said privately two months after Kristallnacht. In the picture above, Jewish-owned stores are marked with the word Jude, or Jew—a warning to "Aryans" not to shop there. Later, every Jew was required to wear a yellow Star of David in public. Yet the worst was still to come. **Diversity** Why do you think Hitler's campaign required that Jews be publicly identified?

Jewish boy was sleeping peacefully in his bed. Then, he recalled, the peace was shattered:

66Of a sudden noises in the street break into my sleep, a wild medley of shouts and shrieks. I listen, frightened and alarmed, until I distinguish words: 'Get out, Jews! Death to the Jews!'99

For this boy and for other Jews all over Germany, it was the beginning of a nightmare. This was *Kristallnacht* (krihs TAHL nahkt), or "Night of the Broken Glass."

**Two nights of terror.** The Kristallnacht riots took place on the nights of November 9 and 10, 1938. Nazi-led mobs attacked Jewish communities all over Germany. They smashed windows, looted shops, and burned synagogues. The boy in Emden recalled:

66Fists are hammering at the door. The shutters are broken open. We can hear the heavy cupboards crashing to the floor. Two Storm Troopers run upstairs, shouting at the top of their voices: 'Out with the Jews!'99

As the family stumbled downstairs, a gun was fired. "I am hit!" cried the boy's father. Still, the Storm Troopers forced the injured man and his family into the street. There, they watched in terror as other homes were plundered and Jews were beaten.

In Dusseldorf, a rabbi answered his phone at midnight. A terrified voice cried, "Rabbi, they're breaking up the synagogue hall and smashing everything to bits, they're beating the men, we can hear it from here." Before the rabbi could reply, fists pounded at his own door. Voices shouted, "Revenge for Paris! Down with the Jews!" Glass shattered, wood splintered, and footsteps thundered upstairs. The rabbi was dragged into the street. His books and typewriter were thrown out the windows onto the cobblestones below.

**Aftermath.** Kristallnacht brought such bad publicity to Hitler's Germany that it was not repeated. Yet Hitler made the Jewish victims pay for the damage. Tens of thousands of Jews were later sent to concentration camps, detention centers for civilians considered enemies of a state. Before long, Hitler and his henchmen were making even more sinister plans for what they would call the "final solution"—the extermination of all Jews. ◼

### Looking Ahead

In the 1930s, Germany became Europe's second fascist state. Germans of all classes responded to Hitler's hypnotic speeches and programs, which restored their national pride. Despite the warnings of some courageous Germans who realized what was happening, most individuals ignored the ugly side of Nazi rule. Those who opposed Nazism were not united and were soon silenced or sent to concentration camps.

While Hitler won absolute power at home, he moved boldly to expand Germany's power in Europe. As you will read in Chapter 31, Nazi aggression set the stage for the largest war the world has yet seen.

## Authoritarian Rule in Eastern Europe

Like Germany, most new nations in Eastern Europe slid from democratic to authoritarian rule in the postwar era. In 1919, a dozen countries were carved out of the old Russian, Hapsburg, Ottoman, and German empires. (See the map on page 711.) Though they differed from one another in important ways, they faced some common problems. They were small countries whose rural agricultural economies lacked capital to develop industry. Social and economic inequalities separated poor peasants from wealthy, semifeudal landlords. None had much experience in democracy.

**Ethnic nationalism.** Old rivalries between ethnic and religious groups created severe tensions. In Czechoslovakia, for example, Czechs and Slovaks were unwilling partners, while some Germans living in Czechoslovakia itched to become part of Germany itself. Serbs dominated the new state of Yugoslavia, but restless Slovenes and Croats living there pressed for autonomy or independence. In Poland, Hungary, and Romania, conflict flared among various ethnic minorities.

**Democracy retreats.** Economic problems and ethnic tensions contributed to instability, which in turn helped fascist rulers gain power. In Hungary, military strongman Nicholas Horthy (HOHR tee) overthrew a communist-led government in 1919. By 1926, Joseph Pilsudski (peel SOOT skee) had become dictator of Poland. Eventually, right-wing dictators emerged in every Eastern European country except Czechoslovakia and Finland. Like Hitler, they promised order and won the backing of the military and wealthy. They also turned to anti-

Semitism, using Jews as scapegoats for many national problems.

In the 1930s, Franklin Roosevelt tried to explain why so many nations had rejected democracy:

66Democracy has disappeared in several great nations, not because the people of those nations dislike democracy, but because they have grown tired of unemployment and insecurity, of seeing their children hungry while they sat helpless in the face of government confusion and government weakness. . . . Finally, in desperation, they chose to sacrifice liberty in the hope of getting something to eat.99

**Looking ahead.** While dictators in Eastern Europe could impose harsh regimes on their own lands, they could not change the region's political geography. As in earlier centuries, strong, aggressive neighbors eyed these small, weak states as tempting targets. Before long, Eastern Europe would fall into the orbit first of Hitler's Germany and then of Stalin's Soviet Union.

## SECTION 4 REVIEW

1. **Identify** (a) Ruhr Valley, (b) Dawes Plan, (c) *Mein Kampf*, (d) Third Reich, (e) Gestapo, (f) Nuremberg Laws, (g) Kristallnacht, (h) Nicholas Horthy, (i) Joseph Pilsudski.
2. **Define** concentration camp.
3. How did the failures of the Weimar Republic pave the way for the rise of Hitler?
4. (a) How did Hitler create a one-party dictatorship? (b) What racial and nationalistic ideas did Nazis promote?
5. Why did dictators gain power in much of Eastern Europe?
6. *Critical Thinking* **Defending a Position** Do you think that there are any circumstances when a government would be justified in banning books or censoring ideas? Explain.
7. *ACTIVITY* Draw a poster, write a poem, or compose a song about Kristallnacht from the point of view of a teenaged Jewish victim.

# Skills for Success

**Critical Thinking**

**Writing and Researching**

**Maps, Charts, and Graphs**

**Speaking and Listening**

## Analyzing Photographs

Photographs are a relatively new form of historical evidence. Since the mid-1800s, they have provided valuable information about the recent past.

Although a photograph shows real people in real settings, however, you must analyze it carefully. Some scenes may be candid, while others may have been staged for the camera. Photographers make many choices—such as subject, lighting, and camera angle—that influence how you perceive what is pictured in a photo. They may want you to appreciate the beauty of a scene or be shocked or moved by their photographs.

The photographs below were taken in Germany in 1938. Study the photographs and answer the following questions.

**1** **Identify the subject matter of the photographs.** (a) How old do the boys in each picture seem to be? (b) How can you tell that the boys in the photograph on the left belong to an official organization? (c) Based on your reading, what kind of organization is it? How can you tell? (d) What are the boys on the right doing? (e) How do you think they feel about their actions? How can you tell?

**2** **Analyze the reliability of the photographs as a source.** (a) How do these photographs support the information given on page 781? (b) Would you consider these photographs reliable sources of information? Why or why not? (c) What additional information might help you judge their reliability?

**3** **Use the photographs to draw conclusions about the historical period.** (a) What impression do the two pictures give you about the lives of youth in Nazi Germany? (b) What effects might this upbringing have on young people? (c) Why do you think Hitler and the Nazis encouraged activities like the ones shown here?

*Beyond the Classroom* Look through a newspaper and choose the two photographs that make the greatest impact on you. Analyze each photograph carefully, jotting down details such as facial expressions, body positions, hand gestures, and so on. Then read the story that accompanies the photograph and determine the photographer's motive for the picture. Does the photo clarify the news story or does it make an editorial statement?

## Building Vocabulary

Review the following vocabulary from this chapter: *general strike, stream of consciousness, flapper, ideology, dictator, nationalism, inflation, racism, anti-Semitism, concentration camp.* Write sentences using each of these words, leaving blanks where the words would go. Exchange your sentences with another student and fill in the blanks on each other's lists.

## Reviewing Chapter Themes

1. **Economics and Technology** (a) Describe one long-term and one immediate cause of the Great Depression. (b) How did the depression become worldwide? (c) How did the depression influence political developments in Europe?
2. **Art and Literature** Choose one postwar writer and one postwar artist. Explain how the work of each reflected a new view of the world.
3. **Political and Social Systems** Choose either Mussolini in Italy or Hitler in Germany. (a) What postwar conditions in that country favored the emergence of a strong dictator? (b) How did he gain power? (c) Describe three policies he used to build a strong totalitarian state.
4. **Religions and Value Systems** (a) What role did extreme nationalism and glorification of the state play in fascist ideology? (b) How did fascist values differ from democratic principles and goals?

## Thinking Critically

1. **Recognizing Points of View** "England can only be saved by direct action. When it's saved, we can begin to think about Parliament again." Based on what you have read, which of the three competing postwar ideologies does this statement express—democracy, fascism, or communism? Explain. ( ★ See *Skills for Success,* page 280.)
2. **Synthesizing Information** Review what you read about Adam Smith in Chapter 18 and about the liberal philosophy of the 1800s in Chapter 21. How did the New Deal challenge traditional free-market capitalism? ( ★ See *Skills for Success,* page 896.)

3. **Linking Past and Present** The manners and culture of the 1920s created a "generation gap" between young people and their elders. Do present-day manners and culture create a similar "generation gap"? Explain.
4. **Analyzing Primary Sources** Reread the words by Italo Balbo on page 774. (a) Why did Balbo and other ex-soldiers feel "betrayed" by politicians? (b) Describe his attitude toward Italy's postwar problems. (c) Why do you think fascism appealed to Balbo and many other Italians? ( ★ See *Skills for Success,* page 154.)
5. **Drawing Conclusions** Both Stalin in the Soviet Union and Hitler in Germany instituted ruthless campaigns against supposed enemies of the state. Why do you think dictators need to find scapegoats for their nation's ills?
6. **Identifying Main Ideas** Reread Martin Niemoller's words on page 781. Then, restate Niemoller's main point in your own words.

## *For Your Portfolio*

Your class has been asked to work on a museum exhibit representing the years between World War I and World War II. Your assignment is to prepare the annotated catalog for the exhibit.

1. Begin by reviewing information in the chapter. Then, work with classmates to make a list of what you'll include in the catalog. Make two headings: A (Event, Development, or Person) and B (How to Represent It). For example, if you list Postwar Disillusion in Germany under A, you might include *All Quiet on the Western Front* or Käthe Kollwitz's prints under B. Do further library research to come up with between 10 and 20 items.
2. Divide into teams to write the descriptions of the catalog entries.
3. Write the descriptions. Tell what the item is and how it represents an important event, trend, idea, or person during this period.
4. With the class, review the catalog entries and make any changes that are needed. If possible, find or make an illustration for each item.
5. Compile the entries into a catalog. Label it 1919–1939. Use your catalog as a class resource for your study of this period.

# World War II and Its Aftermath

## (1931–1949)

## CHAPTER OUTLINE

Here and there along the quiet Normandy beach, German officers peered through binoculars into the English Channel. Behind them, the French coast bristled with barbed wire. Metal tank traps spiked out of the sand. From dunes and cliffs, machine-gun nests and artillery pointed toward the sea.

Suddenly, through the thinning morning mist, a warship appeared. Soon, a dozen such silhouettes loomed into view, then a hundred, then more. It was dawn on June 6, 1944, and the largest naval invasion in history had just begun. As German guns roared into action, thousands of ships, carrying 176,000 American, British, Canadian, and French troops, began the assault on Nazi-controlled Europe. Cornelius Ryan, a war correspondent, later recalled the landing:

> 66The noise was deafening as the boats . . .
> churned steadily for shore. In the slop-
> ping, bouncing [landing] craft, the
> men had to shout to be heard over the
> diesels. . . . There were no heroes in
> these boats, just cold, miserable, anx-
> ious men.99

Despite heavy German resistance, the operation was a success. Allied troops were soon marching inland, through France to Germany. The "D-Day" invasion, as it is known, marked the beginning of the end of World War II.

World War II was the most costly conflict in history. It also had enormous impact on world politics, shifting the balance of power away from Western Europe into the hands of the United States and the Soviet Union. Finally, like all wars, World War II had a purely human dimension. For millions of people, it was not a page in history, but a daily struggle between life and death.

**FOCUS ON** these questions as you read:

- **Continuity and Change**
  Why was the world plunged into a second global conflict just two decades after World War I?

- **Economics and Technology**
  How did technology affect the nature of the fighting and the extent of destruction in World War II?

- **Political and Social Systems**
  How did totalitarian regimes carry out their goals during the war?

- **Global Interaction**
  How did World War II change the balance of world power?

- **Geography and History**
  How did geography influence the war in Eastern Europe and Russia?

## TIME AND PLACE

**World War II** *After only 20 years of peace, war engulfed Europe and the world once more in 1939. World War II was very different from World War I. Instead of a static war of trenches, it was mobile, high speed, and deadly. Airplanes, tanks, and warships moved troops quickly to the front. Battle lines shifted from tiny Pacific islands to the deserts of North Africa, from the steppes of Russia to the skies above London. The conflict killed tens of millions of men, women, and children. From its ashes arose a new world dominated by two superpowers, the United States and the Soviet Union. Here, Allied paratroopers land on a French beach on D-Day, June 6, 1944.*
**Economics and Technology** *What does this painting suggest about fighting during World War II?*

## HUMANITIES LINK

*Art History* Pablo Picasso, *Guernica* (page 790).
*Literature* In this chapter, you will encounter passages from the following works of literature: Cornelius Ryan, *The Longest Day* (page 786); W. H. Auden, "In Memory of W. B. Yeats" (page 792).

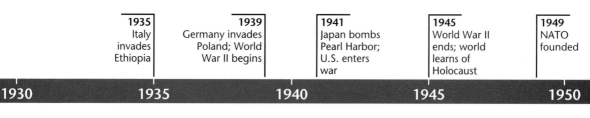

| 1935 | 1939 | 1941 | 1945 | 1949 |
|---|---|---|---|---|
| Italy invades Ethiopia | Germany invades Poland; World War II begins | Japan bombs Pearl Harbor; U.S. enters war | World War II ends; world learns of Holocaust | NATO founded |

1930      1935      1940      1945      1950

# 1 Aggression, Appeasement, and War

## Guide for Reading

- How did dictators undermine the peace in the 1930s?

- How was the Spanish Civil War a dress rehearsal for World War II?

- Why were the western democracies unable to stop aggressive dictators?

- **Vocabulary** *sanction, appeasement, pacifism*

In the last chapter, you saw how the western democracies tried to strengthen the framework for peace during the 1920s. In the 1930s, that structure crumbled. Dictators in Italy and Germany along with militarists in Japan pursued ambitious goals for empire. They scorned peace and glorified war. "In constant struggle," said Germany's Adolf Hitler, "mankind has become great—in eternal peace it must perish."

Unlike these dictators, leaders of the western democracies were haunted by memories of the Great War. Spurred by voters who demanded "no more war," the leaders of Britain, France, and the United States tried to avoid conflict through diplomacy. During the 1930s, the two sides tested each other's commitment and will.

## Early Challenges to World Peace

Challenges to peace followed a pattern throughout the 1930s. Dictators took aggressive action but met only verbal protests and pleas for peace from the democracies. Mussolini and Hitler viewed that desire for peace as weakness and responded with new acts of aggression. With hindsight, we can see the shortcomings of the democracies' policies. We must remember, however, that these policies were the product of long and careful deliberation. People at the time strongly believed that they would work.

**Japan on the move.** One of the earliest tests was posed by Japan. Japanese military lead-ers and ultranationalists felt that Japan should have an empire equal to those of the western powers. In pursuit of this goal, Japan seized Manchuria in 1931. (See page 756.) When the League of Nations condemned the aggression, Japan withdrew from the organization.

Japan's easy success strengthened the militarists. In 1937, Japanese armies overran much of eastern China. (See page 757.) Once again, western protests had no effect.

**Italy invades Ethiopia.** In Italy, Mussolini used his new, modern military to pursue his own imperialist ambitions. He looked first to Ethiopia, in northeastern Africa. Italy's defeat by the Ethiopians at the battle of Adowa in 1896 still rankled. (See page 639.)

In 1935, Italy invaded Ethiopia. Although the Ethiopians resisted bravely, their outdated weapons were no match for Mussolini's tanks, machine guns, poison gas, and airplanes. The Ethiopian king Haile Selassie (HI lee suh LAS ee) appealed to the League of Nations for help. The league voted sanctions, or penalties, against Italy for having violated international law. League members agreed to stop selling weapons or other war materials to Italy. But the sanctions did not extend to petroleum, which fueled modern warfare. Besides, the sanctions were not enforced. By early 1936, Italy had conquered Ethiopia.

**Hitler's challenge.** By then, Hitler, too, had tested the will of the western democracies and found it weak. First, he built up the German military in defiance of the Versailles treaty. Then, in 1936, he sent troops into the Rhineland—another treaty violation. The area belonged to Germany, but it lay on the frontier with France. (See the map on page 791.) In 1919, France had insisted that the Rhineland be a "demilitarized" zone, off-limits to German troops.

Hitler's successful challenge of the hated Versailles treaty increased his popularity in Germany. Western democracies denounced his moves but took no real action. Instead, they adopted a policy of appeasement, giving in to the demands of an aggressor in order to keep the peace.

**Why appeasement?** The policy of appeasement evolved for various reasons. France was demoralized, suffering from political divisions at home. It needed British support for any move against Hitler.

The British, however, had no desire to confront the German dictator. Some Britons thought that Hitler's actions were a justified response to the Versailles treaty, which they believed had been too harsh.

In both Britain and France, many saw Hitler as a defense against a worse evil—the spread of Soviet communism. Also, the Great Depression sapped the energies of the western democracies. Finally, widespread pacifism, or opposition to all war, and disgust with the last war pushed governments to seek peace at any price.

**Reaction in the United States.** As war clouds gathered in Europe in the mid-1930s, the United States Congress passed a series of Neutrality Acts. One law forbade the sale of arms to any nation at war. Others outlawed loans to warring nations and prohibited Americans from traveling on ships of warring powers. The fundamental goal of American policy, however, was to avoid involvement in a European war, not to prevent such a conflict.

**Rome-Berlin-Tokyo Axis.** In the face of the democracies' apparent weakness, Germany, Italy, and Japan formed what became known as the Rome-Berlin-Tokyo Axis. The three nations agreed to fight Soviet communism. They also agreed not to interfere with one another's plans for expansion. The agreement cleared the way for these anti-democratic, aggressor powers to take even bolder steps to bring other nations under their sway.

## The Spanish Civil War

In 1936, Spain plunged into civil war. Although the Spanish Civil War was a local struggle, it soon drew other European powers into the fighting.

**From monarchy to republic.** In the 1920s, Spain was a monarchy dominated by a landowning upper class, the Catholic Church, and the military. Most Spaniards were poor peasants or urban workers. In 1931, popular unrest against the old order forced the king to leave Spain. A republic was set up with a new, more liberal constitution.

The republican government passed a series of controversial reforms. It took over some

**No Help for Ethiopia** *Ethiopian king Haile Selassie, shown here, asked the League of Nations for help after Italy invaded his country in 1935. The league's weak response encouraged Mussolini to pursue the war in Ethiopia and gave a green light to the expansionist plans of other dictators.* **Impact of the Individual** *Do you think Haile Selassie was right to ask for help from the League of Nations? Explain.*

Church lands and ended Church control of education. It redistributed some land to peasants, gave women the vote, and ended some privileges of the old ruling class. These moves split the people of Spain. Communists and other leftists demanded more radical reforms. On the right, conservatives backed by the military rejected change. Clashes between leftists and rightists created chaos. Any moderate voices were drowned out.

**Nationalists versus Loyalists.** In 1936, a right-wing general, Francisco Franco, led a revolt that touched off a bloody civil war. Franco's forces, called Nationalists, rallied conservatives to their banner. Supporters of the republic, known as Loyalists, included communists, socialists, supporters of democracy, and others.

Several European powers quickly took sides. Hitler and Mussolini sent forces to help Franco. Like them, he was a nationalist and a foe of democracy and socialism. The Soviet Union and a handful of volunteers from the western democracies gave some support to the Loyalists. Britain, France, and the United States, however, remained neutral.

**A dress rehearsal.** Both sides committed unbelievable atrocities. The ruinous struggle took almost one million lives. Among the worst

**Guernica** *The bombing and strafing of the Spanish town of Guernica inspired one of Pablo Picasso's greatest works of art. The huge canvas, completed in 1937, is over 11 feet tall and 25 feet wide. By the 1930s, Picasso had moved beyond Cubism in his style of painting. (See page 772.) The distorted human and animal figures that in Cubist works were just images here symbolize the violent effects of war.* **Art and Literature** *Why do you think Picasso included horses and other animals in* Guernica? *What might be the symbolism of the oil lamp and the electric light?*

horrors was a German air raid on Guernica, a small Spanish market town of no military value. One April morning in 1937, German bombers streaked over the market square. They dropped their load of bombs and then swooped low to machine-gun people in the streets. An estimated 1,600 people were killed.

To Nazi leaders, the attack on Guernica was an "experiment" to see what their new planes could do. To the world, it was a grim warning of the destructive power of modern warfare, as well as a "dress rehearsal" for what was to come. Later, the Spanish artist Pablo Picasso created a massive painting, *Guernica,* shown above, that captured the brutality and terror of that day.

By 1939, Franco had triumphed. Once in power, he created a fascist dictatorship like those of Hitler and Mussolini. He rolled back earlier reforms, killed or jailed enemies, and used terror to promote order.

### German Aggression Continues

In the meantime, Hitler pursued his goal of bringing all German-speaking people into the Third Reich. He also took steps to gain "living space" for Germans in Eastern Europe. (See page 779.) Hitler, who believed in the superiority of the German, or Aryan, "race," thought that Germany had a right to conquer the inferior Slavs to the east. "Nature is cruel," he claimed, "so we may be cruel, too. . . . I have a right to remove millions of an inferior race that breeds like vermin."

**Austria annexed.** From the outset, Nazi propaganda had found fertile ground in Austria. By 1938, Hitler was ready to engineer the Anschluss, or union of Austria and Germany. Early that year, he forced the Austrian chancellor to appoint Nazis to key cabinet posts. When the Austrian leader balked at other demands, Hitler sent in the German army "to preserve order."

The Anschluss violated the Versailles treaty and created a brief war scare. But Hitler quickly silenced any Austrians who opposed the German takeover. And since the western democracies took no action, Hitler easily had his way.

**The Czech crisis.** Hitler's next victim was Czechoslovakia. At first, he insisted that the three million Germans in the Sudetenland in

## Aggression in Europe to 1939

### GEOGRAPHY AND HISTORY

Between 1936 and 1939, Germany and Italy repeatedly threatened the peace in Europe.

1. **Location** On the map, locate (a) Germany, (b) Italy, (c) Sudetenland, (d) Rhineland, (e) Albania, (f) Dachau.
2. **Region** Locate the region called the Polish Corridor. Why is that an appropriate name for the region?
3. **Critical Thinking** **Applying Information** (a) What example of Italian aggression in the 1930s is not shown on the map? (b) What changes on the map would be required in order to show that aggression?

western Czechoslovakia be given autonomy. The demand set off new alarms among the democracies.

Czechoslovakia was one of two remaining democracies in Eastern Europe (Finland was the other). Still, Britain and France were not willing to go to war to save it. As British and French leaders searched for a peaceful solution, Hitler increased his price. The Sudetenland, he said, must be annexed to Germany.

At the Munich Conference in September 1938, British and French leaders again chose appeasement. They caved in to Hitler's demands and then persuaded the Czechs to surrender the Sudetenland without a fight. In exchange, Hitler assured Britain and France that he had no further plans for expansion.

**"Peace for our time."** Returning from Munich, the British prime minister Neville Chamberlain told cheering crowds that he had achieved "peace for our time." In the House of Commons, he declared that the Munich Pact had "saved Czechoslovakia from destruction and Europe from Armageddon." The French

WONDER HOW LONG THE HONEYMOON WILL LAST?

**Nazi-Soviet Pact** *In 1939, a shocked world learned that Nazi Germany and the Soviet Union had signed a nonaggression treaty. As this cartoon suggests, the honeymoon between Hitler and Stalin would be short-lived. Less than two years later, Hitler launched a surprise attack on the Soviet Union.* **Political and Social Systems** *Why did two sworn enemies, Hitler and Stalin, join together in a pact?*

leader Edouard Daladier had a different reaction to the joyous crowds that greeted him in Paris. "The fools, why are they cheering?" he asked.

The Czech crisis revealed the Nazi menace. British politician Winston Churchill, who had long warned of the Nazi threat, judged the diplomats harshly: "They had to choose between war and dishonor. They chose dishonor; they will have war."

### The Plunge Toward War

As Churchill predicted, Munich did not bring peace. Instead, Europe plunged rapidly toward war. In March 1939, Hitler gobbled up the rest of Czechoslovakia. The democracies finally accepted the fact that appeasement had failed. At last thoroughly alarmed, they promised to protect Poland, most likely the next target of Hitler's expansion.

**Nazi-Soviet Pact.** In August 1939, Hitler stunned the world by announcing a nonaggres-

sion pact with his great enemy—Joseph Stalin, head of the Soviet Union. Publicly, the Nazi-Soviet Pact bound Hitler and Stalin to peaceful relations. Secretly, the two agreed (1) not to fight if the other went to war and (2) to divide up Poland and other parts of Eastern Europe between them.

The pact was based not on friendship or respect but on mutual need. The Nazis feared communism as Stalin feared fascism. But Hitler wanted a free hand in Poland. Also, he did not want to fight a war with the western democracies and the Soviet Union at the same time.

For his part, Stalin had sought allies among the western democracies against the Nazi menace. Mutual suspicions, however, kept them apart. By joining with Hitler, Stalin bought time to build up Soviet defenses. He also saw a chance for important territorial gains.

**Invasion of Poland.** On September 1, 1939, a week after the Nazi-Soviet Pact, German forces stormed into Poland. Two days later, Britain and France honored their commitment to Poland and declared war on Germany. World War II had begun. There was no joy at the news of war as there had been in 1914. The British poet W. H. Auden caught the mood of gloom in these lines:

&#10077;In the nightmare of the dark
All the dogs of Europe bark
And the living nations wait
Each sequestered in its hate.&#10078;

### Why War Came

Many factors contributed to World War II. You have learned some of the reasons behind Axis aggression. You have also seen why western democracies adopted a policy of appeasement. Today, historians often see the war as an effort to revise the 1919 peace settlement. The Versailles treaty had divided Europe into two camps—those who were satisfied with its terms and those who were not. Germany, Italy, Japan,

**ISSUES** *For* **TODAY**   Aggression by the Axis powers resulted in World War II. How can countries stop aggression by other nations?

and the Soviet Union all felt betrayed or excluded by the settlement and wanted to change it.

Since 1939, people have debated issues such as why the western democracies failed to respond forcefully to the Nazi threat and whether they could have stopped Hitler if they had responded. Dreading war, the democracies hoped that diplomacy and compromise would right old wrongs and prevent further aggression. They were distracted by political and economic problems and misread Hitler's intentions. A few people warned of the danger, but most disregarded even Hitler's declared goals in *Mein Kampf.* (See page 779.)

Many historians today think that Hitler might have been stopped in 1936, before Germany was fully rearmed. If Britain and France had taken military action then, they argue, Hitler would have had to retreat. But the French and British were unwilling to risk war. The experience of World War I and awareness of the destructive power of modern technology made the idea of renewed fighting unbearable. Unfortunately, when war came, it proved to be even more horrendous than anyone had imagined.

## SECTION 1 REVIEW

**1. Identify** (a) Haile Selassie, (b) Rome-Berlin-Tokyo Axis, (c) Guernica, (d) Anschluss, (e) Munich Conference, (f) Neville Chamberlain, (g) Nazi-Soviet Pact.
**2. Define** (a) sanction, (b) appeasement, (c) pacifism.
**3.** (a) List three acts of aggression by Italy, Germany, and Japan during the 1930s. (b) How did the western democracies respond to each?
**4.** How did the Spanish Civil War become a battleground for the competing political forces in the western world?
**5.** (a) Why did the western democracies follow a policy of appeasement? (b) How did the aggressor nations respond to appeasement?
**6.** *Critical Thinking* **Recognizing Causes and Effects** How was the Munich Conference a turning point in the road toward war?
**7.** *ACTIVITY* Make an illustrated time line titled "The Road to World War II."

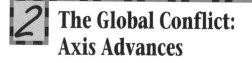

# 2 The Global Conflict: Axis Advances

## Guide for Reading

- How did new technologies affect the fighting in World War II?
- What goals did the Axis powers pursue in Europe and Asia?
- Why did Japan attack the United States?
- **Vocabulary** *blitzkrieg*

"Hitler will collapse the day we declare war on Germany," predicted a confident French general on the eve of World War II. He could not have been more wrong. World War II, the costliest war in history, lasted six years—from 1939 to 1945. It pitted the Axis powers, chiefly Germany, Italy, and Japan, against the Allied powers, which eventually included Britain, France, the Soviet Union, China, the United States, and 45 other nations.

Unlike World War I, with its dug-in defensive trenches, the new global conflict was a war of aggressive movement. In the early years, things went badly for the Allies as Axis forces swept across Europe, North Africa, and Asia, piling up victories.

### The First Onslaught

In September 1939, Nazi forces stormed into Poland, revealing the enormous power of Hitler's blitzkrieg, or "lightning war." First, German planes bombed airfields, factories, towns, and cities, and screaming dive bombers fired on troops and civilians. Then fast-moving tanks and troop transports roared into the country. The Polish army fought back but could not stop the motorized onslaught.

While Germany attacked from the west, Stalin's forces invaded from the east, grabbing areas promised under the Nazi-Soviet Pact. Within a month, Poland ceased to exist.

With Poland crushed, Hitler passed the winter without much further action. Stalin's armies, however, pushed on into the Baltic states of

Estonia, Latvia, and Lithuania. They also seized part of Finland, which put up stiff but unsuccessful resistance.

**Early Axis triumphs.** During that first winter, the French hunkered down behind the Maginot Line. (See page 768.) Britain sent troops to wait with them. Some reporters dubbed this quiet time the "phony war."

Then, in April 1940, the war exploded into action. Hitler launched a blitzkrieg against Norway and Denmark, both of which soon fell. Next, his forces slammed into the Netherlands and Belgium. Within weeks, Germany had overrun them, too.

**Miracle of Dunkirk.** By May, German forces were pouring into France. Retreating Allied forces were soon trapped between the advancing Nazis and the English Channel. In a desperate gamble, the British sent every available naval vessel, merchant ship, and even every pleasure boat across the choppy channel to pluck stranded troops off the beaches of Dunkirk and Ostend.

Despite German air attacks, the improvised armada ferried more than 300,000 troops to safety. This heroic rescue, dubbed the "miracle of Dunkirk," greatly raised British morale.

**France falls.** Meanwhile, German forces headed south toward Paris. Sensing an easy victory, Italy declared war on France and attacked from the south. Overwhelmed and demoralized, France surrendered.

On June 22, 1940, in a forest clearing in northeastern France, Hitler avenged the German defeat of 1918. He forced the French to sign the surrender documents in the same railroad car in which Germany had signed the armistice ending World War I. A young American reporter described the scene:

❝I observed [Hitler's] face. It was grave, solemn, yet brimming with revenge. There was also in it . . . a note of the triumphant conqueror, the defier of the world. There was something else, difficult to describe, in his expression; a sort of scornful, inner joy at being present at this great reversal of fate—a reversal he himself had wrought.❞

Following the surrender, Germany occupied northern France. In the south, the Germans set up a "puppet state," with its capital at Vichy (VIHSH ee). Some French officers escaped to England, where they set up a government-in-exile. Led by Charles de Gaulle, these "free French" worked to liberate their homeland. Inside France itself, resistance fighters turned to guerrilla tactics to harass the occupying German forces.

**The technology of modern warfare.** The whirlwind Nazi advance revealed the awesome power of modern warfare. Air power took a prominent role. After its tryout in Spain, the Luftwaffe, or German air force, perfected methods of bombing civilian as well as military targets. Hitler also used fast-moving armored tanks and troop carriers along with parachute troops to storm through Europe.

Technology created a war machine with even greater destructive power. Scientists and engineers working for the Axis and Allied governments improved the design and effectiveness of airplanes and submarines. They produced ever more deadly bombs and invented hundreds of new devices, such as radar to detect airplanes and sonar to detect submarines. At the same time, research also led to medical advances to treat the wounded and new synthetic products to replace scarce strategic goods.

## The Battle of Britain

With the fall of France, Britain stood alone. Hitler was sure that the British would sue for peace. But Winston Churchill, who had replaced Neville Chamberlain as prime minister, had other plans. For many years, Churchill had been a lone voice against the Nazi threat. In 1940, he rallied the British to fight on:

❝We shall defend our island, whatever the cost may be. We shall fight on the beaches, we shall fight on the landing grounds, we shall fight in the fields and in the streets, we shall fight in the hills; we shall never surrender.❞

Faced with this defiance, Hitler ordered preparation of Operation Sea Lion—the invasion of Britain. First, however, he set out to weaken Britain's air power and break the British will to resist. To achieve this goal, he launched massive air strikes against the island nation.

**The battle begins.** On August 12, 1940, the first wave of German bombers appeared over England's southern coast. The Battle of Britain had begun.

Racing to their planes, British Royal Air Force (RAF) fighter pilots rose into the air. They scrambled after the Germans until their fuel ran low. Landing, they snatched a few hours' sleep, refueled, and took off to fight again. A local resident commented on their bravery:

> **❝**I'd seen our RAF boys spiraling down. I'd also seen them do a victory roll when they shot a German airplane down. These boys went up day and night, in these Spitfires, almost stuck together with chewing gum.**❞**

For a month, the RAF valiantly battled the German Luftwaffe. Then the Germans changed their tactics, turning their attention from military targets to the bombing, or blitz, of London and other cities.

**The London blitz.** Late on the afternoon of September 7, German bombers appeared over London. All through the night, until dawn the next day, relays of aircraft showered high explosives and firebombs on the sprawling capital. For the next 57 nights, the bombing went on. German Stukas and Messerschmidts pounded docks and railways, buildings and homes. Much of the city was destroyed, and some 15,000 people lost their lives.

For Londoners, the blitz became a fact of life. Each night, they waited for the howl of air raid sirens that warned of the latest Luftwaffe assault. As searchlights swept the sky in search of the enemy, people took refuge wherever they could. Some hid in cellars under their homes, others in special shelters built in backyards. Thousands took shelter in cold subways, deep underground.

The city did not break under the blitz. Parliament continued to sit in defiance of the enemy. Citizens carried on their daily lives, seeking protection in shelters and then emerging when the all-clear sounded to resume their routine. One mother marveled at her own response to the nightly raids:

**London in Flames**
The Nazi blitz of London raged for two months in 1940. Each night, German bombers dropped tons of bombs, igniting fires that burned out of control. Each morning, Londoners picked through the rubble and counted the dead. The blitz destroyed some of the city's most precious buildings, but it failed to break the will of the English people. At right, a woman surveys the results of a raid. At far right, Londoners escape the bombs by bedding down in a subway station. **Religions and Value Systems** Why do you think the blitz failed to destroy British morale?

**❝**I never thought I could sit and read to children, say about Cinderella, while you could hear the German planes coming. Sometimes a thousand a night came over, in waves. We had a saying, 'I'm gonna getcha, I'm gonna getcha.' That's how the planes sounded. You'd hear the bomb drop so many hundred yards that way. And you'd think, Oh, that missed us. You'd think, My God, the next one's going to be a direct hit. . . . But you bore up. And I wasn't the bravest of people, believe me.**❞**

The Germans continued to bomb London and other cities off and on until June 1941. But contrary to Hitler's hopes, British morale was not destroyed. In fact, the bombing brought the British closer together in their determination to turn back the enemy.

**A German defeat.** The Battle of Britain showed that terror bombing could not defeat a determined people. By June 1941, Hitler had abandoned Operation Sea Lion in favor of a new campaign. This time, he targeted the Soviet Union. The decision to invade Russia helped save Britain. It also proved to be one of Hitler's most costly mistakes. ■

## Charging Ahead

While the Luftwaffe was blasting Britain, Axis armies were pushing into North Africa and the Balkans. In September 1940, Mussolini sent forces from Italy's North African colony of Libya into Egypt. When the British repulsed the invaders, Hitler sent a brilliant commander, General Erwin Rommel, to North Africa. The "Desert Fox," as he was nicknamed, chalked up a string of successes in 1941 and 1942. He pushed the British back across the desert toward Cairo, in Egypt. The British worried that he would seize the Suez Canal, thus severing their lifeline to India.

In 1940, Italian forces invaded Greece. When they met stiff resistance, German troops once again came to the rescue, and both Greece and Yugoslavia were added to the Axis empire. Even after the Axis triumph, however, Greek and Yugoslav guerrillas plagued the occupying forces.

Meanwhile, both Bulgaria and Hungary had joined the Axis alliance. By 1941, the Axis powers or their allies controlled most of Western Europe. (See the map on page 802.)

## Operation Barbarossa

In June 1941, Hitler embarked on Operation Barbarossa—the conquest of the Soviet Union.* Hitler's motives were clear. He wanted to gain "living space" for Germans and to win control of regions rich in resources. "If I had the Ural Mountains with their incalculable store of treasures in raw materials," he declared, "Siberia with its vast forests, and the Ukraine with its tremendous wheat fields, Germany under National Socialist leadership would swim in plenty." He also wanted to crush communism and defeat his powerful rival Joseph Stalin.

**The German advance.** In Operation Barbarossa, Hitler unleashed a new blitzkrieg. About three million Germans poured into Russia. They caught Stalin unprepared, his army still suffering from the purges that had wiped out many of its top officers. (See page 727.)

The Russians lost two and a half million soldiers trying to fend off the invaders. As they were forced back, they destroyed factories and farm equipment and burned crops to keep them out of enemy hands. But they could not stop the German war machine. By autumn, the Nazis had smashed deep into Russia and were poised to take Moscow and Leningrad. "The war is over," declared Hitler's propaganda minister Joseph Goebbels.

There, however, the German drive stalled. Like Napoleon's Grand Army in 1812, Hitler's forces were not prepared for the fury of Russia's "General Winter." By early December, temperatures plunged to –20 degrees. Thousands of German soldiers froze to death.

**Siege of Leningrad.** The Russians, meanwhile, suffered appalling hardships. In September 1941, the two-and-a-half-year siege of Leningrad began. Food was soon rationed to two pieces of bread a day. Desperate Leningraders ate almost anything. They chewed paper or boiled wallpaper scraped off walls because its paste was said

---

*The plan took its name from the Holy Roman emperor Frederick Barbarossa, who had won great victories in the East.

**War on Many Fronts** In sharply contrasting conditions, the German army made rapid advances during the early years of the war. At left, a tank division advances through the Russian snow during Operation Barbarossa. At right, German troops ride over the desert sands of North Africa. **Geography and History** What problems would an army face trying to maneuver in the desert? How did Russia's geography make it difficult to conquer?

to contain potato flour. Owners of leather briefcases boiled and ate them—"jellied meat," they called it.

More than a million Leningraders died during the German siege. The survivors, meanwhile, struggled to defend their city. Hoping to gain some relief for the exhausted Russians, Stalin urged Britain to open a second front in Western Europe. Although Churchill could not offer much real help, the two powers did agree to work together.

## Growing American Involvement

When the war began in 1939, the United States declared its neutrality. Although isolationist feeling remained strong, many Americans sympathized with the Poles, French, British, and others who battled the Axis powers. Later, President Roosevelt found ways around the Neutrality Acts to provide aid, including warships, to Britain as it stood alone against Hitler.

**The arsenal of democracy.** In early 1941, FDR convinced Congress to pass the Lend-Lease Act. It allowed him to sell or lend war materials to "any country whose defense the President deems vital to the defense of the United States." The United States, said Roosevelt, would not be drawn into the war, but it would become "the arsenal of democracy," supplying arms to those who were fighting for freedom.

**Atlantic Charter.** In August 1941, Roosevelt and Churchill met secretly on a warship in the Atlantic. The two leaders issued the Atlantic Charter, which set goals for the war—"the final destruction of the Nazi tyranny"—and for the postwar world. They pledged to support "the right of all peoples to choose the form of government under which they will live" and called for a "permanent system of general security."

## Japan Attacks

In December 1941, the Allies gained a vital boost when a surprise action by Japan suddenly pitched the United States into the war. From the late 1930s, Japan had been trying to conquer China. (See pages 756 and 757.) Although Japan occupied much of eastern China, the Chinese would not surrender. When war broke out in Europe in 1939, the Japanese saw a chance to grab European possessions in Southeast Asia. The rich resources of the region, including oil, rubber, and tin, would be of immense value in fighting the Chinese war.

**Growing tensions.** In 1940, Japan advanced into French Indochina and the Dutch East Indies (present-day Indonesia). To stop Japanese aggression, the United States banned

**Pearl Harbor** *By November 1941, American officials knew that Japan was planning an attack somewhere in the Pacific. Still, they were stunned by the bombing of the naval base at Pearl Harbor. Said one navy commander, "I didn't believe it when I saw the planes, and I didn't believe it when I saw the bombs fall." Here, an American battleship burns in Pearl Harbor.* **Political and Social Systems** *Why was the bombing of Pearl Harbor a turning point in World War II?*

the sale to Japan of war materials, such as iron, steel, and oil for airplanes. This move angered the Japanese.

Japan and the United States held talks to ease the growing tension. But extreme militarists such as General Tojo Hideki were gaining power in Japan. They did not want peace. Instead, they hoped to seize lands in Asia and the Pacific. The United States was interfering with their plans.

**Attack on Pearl Harbor.** With talks at a standstill, General Tojo ordered a surprise attack on the American fleet at Pearl Harbor, Hawaii. Early on December 7, 1941, Japanese airplanes struck. They damaged or destroyed 19 ships, smashed American planes on the ground, and killed more than 2,400 people.

The next day, a grim-faced President Roosevelt told the nation that December 7 was "a date which will live in infamy." He asked Congress to declare war on Japan. Three days later, Germany and Italy, as Japan's allies, declared war on the United States.

**Japanese victories.** In the long run, the Japanese attack on Pearl Harbor would be as serious a mistake as Hitler's invasion of Russia. But the months after Pearl Harbor gave no such hint. Instead, European and American possessions in the Pacific and in Southeast Asia fell one by one to the Japanese. They drove the Americans out of the Philippines and seized other American islands across the Pacific. They over-

ran the British colonies of Hong Kong, Burma, and Malaya, pushed deeper into the Dutch East Indies, and completed the takeover of French Indochina.

By the beginning of 1942, the Japanese empire stretched from Southeast Asia to the western Pacific Ocean. (See the map on page 805.) The Axis powers had reached the high point of their successes.

## SECTION 2 REVIEW

1. **Identify** (a) "phony war," (b) Dunkirk, (c) Winston Churchill, (d) Battle of Britain, (e) Operation Barbarossa, (f) Lend-Lease Act, (g) Atlantic Charter, (h) Pearl Harbor.
2. **Define** blitzkrieg.
3. How did new technologies make World War II a war of rapid movement?
4. What successes did the Axis have in Europe?
5. (a) What goals did Japan pursue in Asia? (b) Why did General Tojo order an attack on the United States?
6. *Critical Thinking* **Identifying Alternatives** Do you think that the United States could have stayed out of the war? Why or why not?
7. *ACTIVITY* Imagine that you are a teenager during the London blitz. Write a series of diary entries describing your experiences.

# 3 The Global Conflict: Allied Successes

## Guide for Reading

- How did the Axis powers treat the people they conquered?
- How did nations mobilize for total war?
- What battles were turning points in the war?

- **Vocabulary** *collaborator*

World War II was fought on a larger scale and in more places than any other war in history. It was also more costly in human life than any earlier conflict. Civilians were targets as much as soldiers. In 1941, a reporter visited a Russian town that had 10,000 people before the German invasion. The reporter found a lone survivor:

66[She was] a blind old woman who had gone insane. She was there when the village was shelled and had gone mad. I saw her wandering barefooted around the village, carrying a few dirty rags, a rusty pail, and a tattered sheepskin.99

From 1939 until mid-1942, the Axis ran up a string of successes. During those years, the conquerors blasted villages and towns and divided up the spoils. Then the Allies won some key victories. Slowly, the tide began to turn.

## Occupied Lands

While the Germans rampaged across Europe, the Japanese conquered an empire in Asia and the Pacific. Each set out to build a "new order" in the occupied lands.

**Nazi Europe.** Hitler's new order grew out of his racial obsessions. He set up puppet governments in Western European countries that were peopled by "Aryans" or related races. The Slavs of Eastern Europe were viewed as an inferior race. They were shoved aside to provide "living space" for Germans.

To the Nazis, occupied lands were an economic resource to be plundered and looted. One of Hitler's high officials bluntly stated his view:

66Whether nations live in prosperity or starve to death interests me only insofar as we need them as slaves for our culture.99

The Nazis systematically stripped countries of works of art, factories, and other resources. They sent thousands of Slavs and others to work as slave laborers in German war industries. As resistance movements emerged to fight German tyranny, the Nazis took savage revenge, shooting hostages and torturing prisoners.

**Nazi genocide.** The most savage of all policies was Hitler's program to kill Jews and others he judged "racially inferior," such as Slavs, Gypsies, and the mentally ill. At first, the Nazis forced Jews in Poland and elsewhere to live in ghettos. By 1941, however, Hitler and his supporters had devised plans for the "final solution of the Jewish problem"—the genocide, or deliberate destruction, of all European Jews.

To accomplish this goal, Hitler had "death camps" built in Poland and Germany, at places like Auschwitz and Bergen Belsen. The Nazis shipped Jews from all over occupied Europe to the camps. There, Nazi engineers designed the most efficient means of killing millions of men, women, and children.

As Jews reached the camps, they were stripped of their clothes and valuables. Their heads were shaved. Guards separated men from women and children from their parents. The young, old, and sick were targeted for immediate killing. Within a few days, they were herded into "shower rooms" and gassed. The Nazis worked others to death or used them for perverse "medical" experiments. By 1945, the Nazis had massacred more than six million Jews in what became known as the Holocaust. Almost as many other "undesirable" people were killed as well.

Jews resisted the Nazis even though they knew their efforts could not succeed. In October 1944, for example, a group of Jews in the Auschwitz death camp destroyed one of the gas chambers. The rebels were all killed. One woman, Rosa Robota, was tortured for days before

**The Holocaust** As German armies conquered new areas, the Nazis implemented their program to exterminate the Jewish people. Storm troopers rounded up Jewish men, women, and children, who were sent in cattle cars to death camps in Germany and Poland. More than six million Jews died in the Nazi Holocaust. **Continuity and Change** Do you think that the Holocaust could happen again today? Explain.

she was hanged. "Be strong and have courage," she called out to the camp inmates who were forced by the Nazis to watch her execution.

In some cases, friends, neighbors, or others concealed or protected Jews from the Holocaust. Italian peasants, for example, hid Jews in their villages, and Denmark as a nation saved almost all its Jewish population. Most often, however, people pretended not to see what was happening. Some were collaborators, helping the Nazis hunt down the Jews or, like the Vichy government in France, shipping tens of thousands of Jews to their death.

The scale and savagery of the Holocaust have been unequaled in history. The Nazis deliberately set out to destroy the Jews for no other reason than their religious and ethnic heritage. Today, the record of that slaughter is a vivid reminder of the monstrous results of racism and intolerance.

**The Co-Prosperity Sphere.** On the other side of the world, Japan wrapped itself in the mantle of anti-imperialism. Under the slogan "Asia for Asians," it created the Greater East Asia Co-Prosperity Sphere. Its self-proclaimed mission was to help Asians escape western colonial rule. In fact, its goal was a Japanese empire in Asia.

The Japanese treated the Chinese and other conquered people with great brutality, killing and torturing civilians everywhere. They seized food crops and made local people into slave laborers. Whatever welcome the Japanese had at first met as "liberators" was soon turned to hatred. In the Philippines, Indochina, and elsewhere, nationalist groups waged guerrilla warfare against the Japanese conquerors.

## The Allied War Effort

After the United States entered the war, the Allied leaders met periodically to hammer out their strategy. In 1942, the Big Three—Roosevelt, Churchill, and Stalin—agreed to finish the war in Europe first before turning their attention to the Japanese in Asia.

From the outset, the Allies distrusted one another. Churchill thought Stalin wanted to dominate Europe. Roosevelt felt that Churchill had ambitions to expand British imperial power. Stalin believed that the western powers wanted to destroy communism. At meetings and in writing, Stalin urged Roosevelt and Churchill to relieve the pressure on Russia by opening a second front in Western Europe. Not until 1944, however, did Britain and the United States make such a move. The British and Americans argued that they did not have the resources before then. Stalin saw the delay as a deliberate policy to weaken the Soviet Union.

**Total war.** Like the Axis powers, the Allies were committed to total war. Democratic governments in the United States and Britain increased their political power. They directed economic resources into the war effort, ordering factories to stop making cars or refrigerators and to turn out airplanes or tanks instead. Governments rationed consumer goods, from shoes to sugar, and regulated prices and wages. On the positive side, while the war brought shortages and hardships, it ended the unemployment of the depression era.

Under pressure of war, even democratic governments limited the rights of citizens. They censored the press and used slick propaganda to win public support for the war. In the United States and Canada, many citizens of Japanese descent lost their civil rights. On the West Coast, Japanese Americans even lost their freedom, as they were forced into internment camps after the government decided they were a security risk. The British took similar action against German refugees. Some 40 years later, the United States government would apologize to Japanese Americans for its wartime policy.

**Women help win the war.** As men joined the military and war industries expanded, millions of women replaced them in essential jobs. Women built ships and planes, produced munitions, and staffed offices. A popular British song recognized women's contributions:

> **❝**She's the girl that makes the thing that
>    drills the hole that holds the spring
> That drives the rod that turns the knob
>    that works the thingumebob. . . .
> And it's the girl that makes the thing
>    that holds the oil that oils the ring
> That works the thingumebob THAT'S
>    GOING TO WIN THE WAR!**❞**

British and American women served in the armed forces in auxiliary roles—driving trucks and ambulances, delivering airplanes, decoding

# PARALLELS THROUGH TIME

## Women in Wartime

As they have since ancient times, women in this century played key roles in times of war. On farms and in factories, women workers produced the food, weapons, and other supplies needed for the war effort. Other women served as translators, spies, nurses, and bomb experts.

**Linking Past and Present**  What opportunities did wartime service offer women during World War II? What opportunities do the armed forces offer women today?

**PAST**  Although the British and American armies did not allow women to serve in combat positions in World War II, women did serve in uniform as auxiliaries. In England, volunteers in the Women's Auxiliary Air Force (WAAF) worked alongside Royal Air Force pilots. Women also did dangerous work in the anti-Nazi resistance in occupied Europe. The Dutch woman below risked her life to distribute an anti-Nazi newspaper in Amsterdam.

**PRESENT**
Today, women play even more active roles in the armed forces. At right, women serve as soldiers in Operation Desert Storm. The Vietnam Women's Memorial, below, honors the women who lost their lives working in war zones as nurses and in other support positions.

# World War II in Europe and North Africa

NORWAY
FINLAND
SWEDEN
• Leningrad
ESTONIA
• Moscow
NORTH SEA
DENMARK
LATVIA
BALTIC SEA
LITHUANIA
SOVIET UNION
IRELAND
GREAT BRITAIN
Danzig • 1945 1944
1943
• London
POLAND
ATLANTIC OCEAN
1944
NETH.
1945 Berlin
1944
• Stalingrad
Dunkirk BELG.
Warsaw
1943
NORMANDY
• Paris
1945
1945
GERMANY
LUX. 1945
CZECHOSLOVAKIA
FRANCE
1944
• Vichy
SWITZ.
AUSTRIA
1945
VICHY FRANCE 1944
HUNGARY
1944
• Yalta
ITALY
ROMANIA
BLACK SEA
PORTUGAL
YUGOSLAVIA
BULGARIA
SPAIN
• Rome
Anzio
ALBANIA
TURKEY
• Salerno
1942
Palermo
GREECE
1942
Algiers
1944
1943
SP. MOROCCO
SYRIA
Casablanca
• Oran 1942
SICILY
1943
LEBANON
IRAQ
MOROCCO
Tunis
MEDITERRANEAN SEA
ALGERIA
TUNISIA
PALESTINE
TRANS-JORDAN
• Tripoli
1943
1942
El Alamein
Cairo •
SAUDI ARABIA
LIBYA
EGYPT
RED SEA

| | | |
|---|---|---|
| European Axis Powers, 1942 | | Allied territory, 1942 |
| Maximum extent of Axis control, 1942 | → | Allied advances |
| Neutral nations 1942 | ▪ | Concentration camps 1939–1945 |

0   250   500 Miles
0   250   500 Kilometers

## GEOGRAPHY AND HISTORY

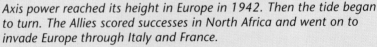

Axis power reached its height in Europe in 1942. Then the tide began to turn. The Allies scored successes in North Africa and went on to invade Europe through Italy and France.

**1. Location** On the map, locate (a) Vichy France, (b) Soviet Union, (c) El Alamein, (d) Berlin, (e) Normandy, (f) Palermo.

**2. Movement** (a) Describe the extent of the Axis advance to the east by 1942. (b) In what year did the Allies advance into Italy? (c) When did they advance through Romania?

**3. Critical Thinking Linking Past and Present** If you lived in Germany today, what do you think would be an appropriate way to commemorate the end of World War II?

messages, assisting at anti-aircraft sites. In occupied Europe, women fought in the resistance. Marie Fourcade, a French woman, directed 3,000 people in the underground and helped downed Allied pilots escape to safety.

Many Soviet women saw combat. Soviet pilot Lily Litvak, for example, shot down 12 German planes before she herself was killed.

## Turning Points

During 1942 and 1943, the Allies won several victories that would turn the tide of battle. The first turning points came in North Africa and Italy.

**El Alamein.** In Egypt, the British under General Bernard Montgomery finally stopped Rommel's advance during the long, fierce Battle of El Alamein. They then turned the tables on the Desert Fox, driving the Axis forces back across Libya into Tunisia.

Later in 1942, American general Dwight Eisenhower took command of a joint Anglo-American force in Morocco and Algeria. Advancing from the west, he combined with the British forces to trap Rommel's army, which surrendered in May 1943.

**Invasion of Italy.** Victory in North Africa let the Allies leap across the Mediterranean into Italy. In July 1943, a combined British and American army landed first in Sicily and then in southern Italy. They defeated the Italian forces there in about a month.

Italians, fed up with Mussolini, overthrew the Duce. The new Italian government signed an armistice, but the fighting did not end. Hitler sent German troops to rescue Mussolini and stiffen the will of Italians fighting in the north. For the next 18 months, the Allies pushed slowly up the Italian peninsula, suffering heavy losses against stiff German resistance. Still, the Italian invasion was a decisive event for the Allies because it weakened Hitler by forcing him to fight on another front.

## The Red Army Resists

Another major turning point in the war occurred in the Soviet Union. After their triumphant advance in 1941, the Germans were stalled outside Moscow and Leningrad. In 1942, Hitler launched a new offensive. This time, he aimed for the rich oil fields of the south. His troops, however, got only as far as the city of Stalingrad.

**Stalingrad.** The Battle of Stalingrad was one of the costliest of the war. Hitler was determined to capture Stalin's namesake city. Stalin was equally determined to defend it.

The battle began when the Germans surrounded the city. The Russians then encircled their attackers. As winter closed in, a bitter street-by-street, house-by-house struggle raged. Soldiers fought for two weeks for a single building, wrote a German officer. Corpses "are strewn in the cellars, on the landings and the staircases," he said.

Trapped, without food or ammunition and with no hope of rescue, the German commander finally surrendered in early 1943. The battle cost the Germans approximately 300,000 killed, wounded, or captured soldiers.

**Counterattack.** After the Battle of Stalingrad, the Red Army took the offensive. They lifted the siege of Leningrad and drove the invaders out of the Soviet Union. Hitler's forces suffered irreplaceable losses of troops and equipment. By early 1944, Soviet troops were advancing into Eastern Europe.

## Invasion of France

By 1944, the Allies were at last ready to open the long-awaited second front in Europe—the invasion of France. General Dwight Eisenhower was made the supreme Allied commander. He and other Allied leaders faced the enormous task of planning the operation and assembling troops and supplies. To prepare the way for the invasion, Allied bombers flew constant missions over Germany. They targeted factories and destroyed aircraft that might be used against the invasion force. They also destroyed many German cities.

The Allies chose June 6, 1944—D-Day, they called it—for the invasion of France. (★ See *Skills for Success*, page 814.) About 176,000 Allied troops were ferried across the English Channel. From landing craft, they fought their way to shore amid underwater mines and raking machine-gun fire. They clawed their way inland through the tangled hedges of Normandy. Finally, they broke through German defenses and advanced toward Paris. Meanwhile, other Allied forces sailed from Italy to land in southern France.

In Paris, French resistance forces rose up against the occupying Germans. Under pressure from all sides, the Germans retreated. On August 25, the Allies entered Paris. Joyous crowds in the "city of light" welcomed the liberators. Within a month, all of France was free. The next goal was Germany itself.

## SECTION 3 REVIEW

1. **Identify** (a) Holocaust, (b) Auschwitz, (c) Greater East Asia Co-Prosperity Sphere, (d) Battle of El Alamein, (e) Dwight Eisenhower, (f) Battle of Stalingrad, (g) D-Day.
2. **Define** collaborator.
3. (a) What was Hitler's "new order" in Europe? (b) How did the Japanese treat the people they conquered?
4. (a) How did democratic governments mobilize their economies for war? (b) How did they limit the rights of citizens?
5. How was each of the following battles a turning point in the war: (a) El Alamein, (b) Stalingrad?
6. *Critical Thinking* **Defending a Position** Do you think that democratic governments should be allowed to limit their citizens' freedoms during wartime? Defend your position.
7. *ACTIVITY* Write a poem or design a memorial commemorating the millions who died in the Holocaust.

## Toward Victory

### Guide for Reading

- What battles were turning points in the Pacific war?
- How did the Allied forces defeat Germany?
- Why did the United States use the atomic bomb on Japan?
- **Vocabulary** *kamikaze*

While the Allies battled to liberate Europe, fighting against the Japanese in Asia raged on. The war in Southeast Asia and the Pacific was very different from that in Europe. Most battles were fought at sea, on tiny islands, or in deep jungles. At first, the Japanese won an uninterrupted series of victories. By mid-1942, however, the tide began to turn.

### War in the Pacific

A major turning point in the Pacific war occurred just six months after the bombing of Pearl Harbor. In May and June 1942, American warships and airplanes severely damaged two Japanese fleets during the battles of the Coral Sea and Midway Island. These victories greatly weakened Japanese naval power and stopped the Japanese advance.

After the Battle of Midway, the United States took the offensive. That summer, under the command of General Douglas MacArthur, United States Marines landed at Guadalcanal in the Solomon Islands, the first step in an "island-hopping" campaign. The goal of the campaign was to recapture some Japanese-held islands while bypassing others. The captured islands served as stepping stones to the next objective. In this way, American forces gradually moved north from the Solomon Islands toward Japan itself. (See the map on page 805.)

On the captured islands, the Americans built air bases to enable them to carry the war closer to Japan. By 1944, American ships were blockading Japan, while American bombers pounded Japanese cities and industries.

# World War II in the Pacific

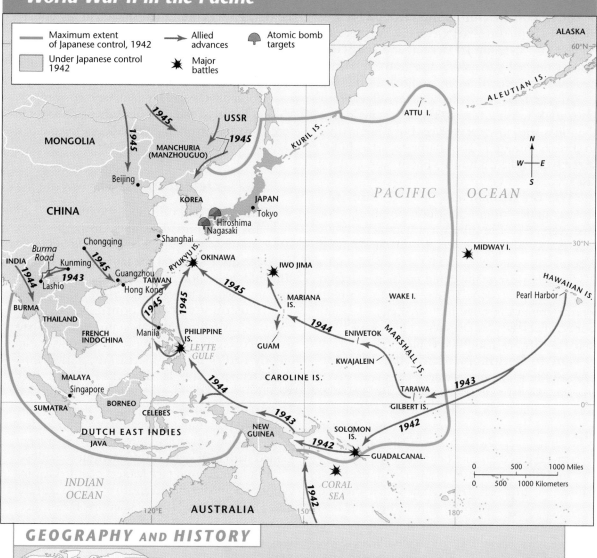

## GEOGRAPHY AND HISTORY

For six months after the bombing of Pearl Harbor, the Japanese won a series of uninterrupted victories. After the Battle of Midway, however, the Allies took the offensive in the Pacific. Their goal was to recapture the Philippines and invade Japan.

**1. Location** On the map, locate (a) Japan, (b) Midway Island, (c) Pearl Harbor, (d) Iwo Jima, (e) Hiroshima, (f) Burma Road, (g) Manchuria.

**2. Movement** (a) Did Japan ever gain control of New Guinea? Explain. (b) When did the Allies advance into Manchuria? (c) When did they reach the Philippines?

**3. Critical Thinking Making Inferences** How did geography make it difficult for Japan to keep control of its empire?

In October 1944, MacArthur began to retake the Philippines. The British meanwhile were pushing the Japanese back in the jungles of Burma and Malaya. Despite such setbacks, the militarists who dominated the Japanese government rejected any suggestions of surrender.

## The Nazis Defeated

Hitler, too, scorned talk of surrender. "If the war is to be lost," he declared, "the nation also will perish." To win the assault on "Fortress Europe," the Allies had to use devastating force.

**Battle of the Bulge.** After freeing France, the Allies battled toward Germany. As they advanced into Belgium in December 1944, Germany launched a massive counterattack. Hitler was throwing everything into a final effort.

At the bloody Battle of the Bulge, both sides took terrible losses. The Germans drove the Allies back in several places but were unable to break through. The Battle of the Bulge slowed the Allied advance, but it was Hitler's last success.

**The air war.** By this time, Germany was reeling under round-the-clock bombing. For two years, Allied bombers had hammered military bases, factories, railroads, oil depots, and cities.

By 1945, Germany could no longer defend itself in the air. In one 10-day period, bombing almost erased the huge industrial city of Hamburg. Allied raids on Dresden in February 1945 killed as many as 135,000 people.

**On to Berlin.** By March, the Allies had crossed the Rhine into western Germany. From the east, Soviet troops closed in on Berlin. Victory was only months away, but savage fighting continued. In late April, American and Russian soldiers met and shook hands at the Elbe River. Everywhere, Axis armies began to surrender.

In Italy, guerrillas captured and executed Mussolini. In Berlin, Hitler knew that the end was near. As Soviet troops fought their way into the city, Hitler committed suicide in his underground bunker. After just 12 years, Hitler's "thousand-year Reich" was a smoldering ruin.

On May 7, Germany surrendered. Officially, the war in Europe ended the next day, which was proclaimed V-E Day (Victory in Europe). Millions cheered the news, but the joy was tempered by the horrors and tragedies of the past six years.

## Defeat of Japan

With war won in Europe, the Allies poured their resources into defeating Japan. By mid-1945, most of the Japanese navy and air force had been destroyed. Yet the Japanese still had an army of two million men. The road to victory, it appeared, would be long and costly.

**Invasion versus the bomb.** Some American officials estimated that an invasion of Japan would cost a million or more casualties. At the bloody battles to take the islands of Iwo Jima and Okinawa, the Japanese had shown they would fight to the death rather than surrender. To save their homeland, young Japanese became *kamikaze* (kah mih KAH zee) pilots, who undertook suicide missions, crashing their planes loaded with explosives into American warships.

While Allied military leaders planned for invasion, scientists offered another way to end the war. Since the early 1900s, scientists had under-

*Meeting of the "Big Three"* The three main Allied leaders—(left to right) Churchill, Roosevelt, and Stalin—met several times during the war. Their last meeting, shown here, took place at the Soviet city of Yalta in February 1945. There, they planned "the whole shape and structure of post-war Europe." Roosevelt and Churchill agreed that Stalin had the right to control the governments of Eastern Europe after the war. This concession would become a key factor in the Cold War that began after 1945. **Global Interaction** Why do you think the Big Three went to the trouble to meet in person?

stood that matter, made up of atoms, could be converted into pure energy. (See page 770.) In military terms, this meant that, by splitting the atom, scientists could create an explosion far more powerful than any yet known. During the war, Allied scientists, some of them refugees from Hitler's Germany, raced to harness the atom. In July 1945, at Alamogordo, New Mexico, they successfully tested the first atomic bomb.

stood that matter, made up of atoms, could be converted into pure energy. (See page 770.) In military terms, this meant that, by splitting the atom, scientists could create an explosion far more powerful than any yet known. During the war, Allied scientists, some of them refugees from Hitler's Germany, raced to harness the atom. In July 1945, at Alamogordo, New Mexico, they successfully tested the first atomic bomb.

News of the test was brought to the new American President, Harry Truman. Truman had taken office after FDR died unexpectedly on April 12. Truman knew that the atomic bomb was a terrible new force for destruction. Still, after consulting with his advisers, he decided to use the new weapon.

At the time, Truman was meeting with Allied leaders in the city of Potsdam, Germany. They issued a warning to Japan to surrender or face "utter and complete destruction." When the Japanese ignored the deadline, the United States took action.

**GLOBAL CONNECTIONS**

After learning that American scientists had developed an atomic bomb, President Truman had jotted in his diary, "It's a good thing that Hitler's crowd or Stalin's did not discover this atomic bomb." Four years later, the Soviets had the bomb, too. Other nations soon joined the nuclear club. Britain conducted its first nuclear test in Australia in 1952. France followed suit in 1960. China was next. By the 1990s, Argentina, Brazil, India, Pakistan, and South Africa were all close to possessing a workable nuclear bomb.

**The Atomic Bomb** *In August 1945, the world entered the atomic age. On August 6 and August 9, American airplanes dropped single atomic bombs on the Japanese cities of Hiroshima and Nagasaki. The force of the explosions vaporized glass, metal, concrete, and human flesh. The center of Hiroshima, shown here, became a barren wasteland. Japan surrendered a few days after the second bombing.* **Religions and Value Systems** *What were some of the arguments for and against dropping the atomic bomb on Japan?*

**Hiroshima.** On August 6, 1945, an American plane dropped an atomic bomb on the mid-sized city of Hiroshima. Residents saw "a strong flash of light"—and then, total destruction. The bomb flattened four square miles and instantly killed more than 70,000 people. In the months that followed, many more would die from radiation sickness, a deadly after-effect from exposure to radioactive materials.

Truman warned the Japanese that if they did not surrender, they could expect "a rain of ruin from the air the like of which has never been seen on this Earth." And on August 8, the Soviet Union declared war on Japan and invaded Manchuria. Still, Japanese leaders did not respond. The next day, the United States dropped a second atomic bomb, on Nagasaki, killing more than 40,000 people.

Some members of the Japanese cabinet wanted to fight on. Other leaders disagreed. Finally, on August 10, Emperor Hirohito intervened—an action unheard of for a Japanese emperor—forcing the government to surrender. On September 2, 1945, the formal peace treaty was signed on board the American battleship

*Missouri*, which was anchored in Tokyo Bay. The war had ended.

**An ongoing controversy.** Dropping the atomic bomb on Japan brought a quick end to World War II. It also unleashed terrifying destruction. Ever since, people have debated whether or not the United States should have used the bomb.

Why did Truman use the bomb? First, he was convinced that Japan would not surrender without an invasion that would cost an enormous loss of both American and Japanese lives. Growing differences between the United States and the Soviet Union may also have influenced his decision. Truman may have hoped the bomb would impress the Soviets with American power. At any rate, the Japanese surrendered shortly after the bombs were dropped, and World War II was ended.

## Looking Ahead

After the surrender, American forces occupied the smoldering ruins of Japan. In Germany, meanwhile, the Allies had divided Hitler's fallen empire into four zones of occupation—French, British, American, and Russian. In both countries, the Allies faced difficult decisions about the future. How could they avoid the mistakes of 1919 and build the foundations for a stable world peace?

## SECTION 4 REVIEW

1. **Identify** (a) Battle of the Coral Sea, (b) Battle of the Bulge, (c) V-E Day, (d) Harry Truman.
2. **Define** kamikaze.
3. How did the United States bring the war closer to Japan?
4. (a) How did the Allies weaken Germany? (b) Why was the Battle of the Bulge significant?
5. *Critical Thinking* **Making Decisions** Imagine that you are President Truman. What information would you want before making the decision to drop an atomic bomb on Japan?
6. *ACTIVITY* Write a series of newspaper headlines reporting the final months of the war in Europe.

# 5 From World War to Cold War

## Guide for Reading

- What were the human and material costs of World War II?
- How did World War II change the global balance of power?
- What were the origins of the Cold War?
- **Vocabulary** *containment*

"Give me ten years and you will not be able to recognize Germany," said Hitler in 1933. His prophecy was correct—although not in the way he intended. In 1945, Germany was an unrecognizable ruin. Poland, Russia, Ukraine, Japan, and many other lands also lay in ruins. Total war had gutted cities, factories, harbors, bridges, railroads, farms, homes—and lives. Millions of refugees, displaced by war or liberated from prison camps, wandered the land. Amid the devastation, hunger and disease took large tolls for years after the fighting ended.

## Aftermath of War

While the Allies celebrated victory, the appalling costs of the war began to emerge. The global conflict had raged in Asia since Japan invaded China in 1937 and in Europe since 1939. It had killed as many as 75 million people worldwide. In Europe, about 38 million people lost their lives, many of them civilians. The Soviet Union suffered the worst casualties—more than 22 million dead.

Numbers alone did not tell the story of the Nazi nightmare in Europe or the Japanese brutality in Asia. In the aftermath of war, new atrocities came to light.

**Horrors of the Holocaust.** During the war, the Allies knew about the existence of Nazi concentration camps. But only at war's end did they learn the full extent of the Holocaust and the tortures and misery inflicted on Jews and others in the Nazi camps. General Dwight Eisenhower, who visited the camps, was stunned

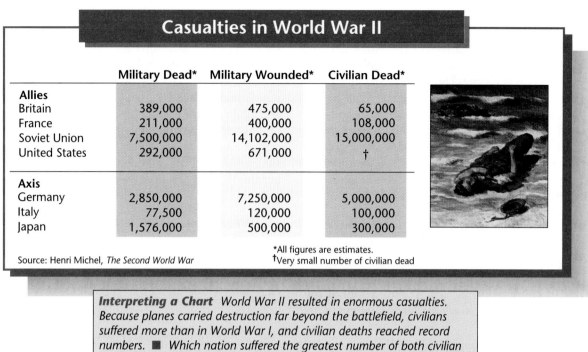

## Casualties in World War II

|  | Military Dead* | Military Wounded* | Civilian Dead* |
|---|---|---|---|
| **Allies** | | | |
| Britain | 389,000 | 475,000 | 65,000 |
| France | 211,000 | 400,000 | 108,000 |
| Soviet Union | 7,500,000 | 14,102,000 | 15,000,000 |
| United States | 292,000 | 671,000 | † |
| **Axis** | | | |
| Germany | 2,850,000 | 7,250,000 | 5,000,000 |
| Italy | 77,500 | 120,000 | 100,000 |
| Japan | 1,576,000 | 500,000 | 300,000 |

Source: Henri Michel, *The Second World War*

*All figures are estimates.
†Very small number of civilian dead

**Interpreting a Chart** *World War II resulted in enormous casualties. Because planes carried destruction far beyond the battlefield, civilians suffered more than in World War I, and civilian deaths reached record numbers.* ■ *Which nation suffered the greatest number of both civilian and military casualties?*

to come "face to face with indisputable evidence of Nazi brutality and ruthless disregard of every sense of decency."

Walking skeletons stumbled out of the death camps with tales of mass murder. The Nazi Rudolf Hoess, commander at Auschwitz, would admit that he had supervised the killing of two and a half million people, not counting those who died of disease or starvation.

**War crimes trials.** At wartime meetings, the Allies had agreed that Axis leaders should be tried for "crimes against humanity." In Germany, the Allies held war crimes trials in Nuremberg, where Hitler had staged mass rallies in the 1930s. A handful of top Nazis received death sentences. Others were imprisoned. Similar war crimes trials were held in Japan and Italy. The trials showed that political and military leaders could be held accountable for actions in wartime.

**Allied occupation.** The war crimes trials served another purpose. By exposing the savagery of the Axis regimes, they further discredited the Nazi, fascist, and militarist ideologies that had led to the war.

Yet disturbing questions haunted people then, as now. How had the Nazi horrors hap-

pened? Why had ordinary people in Germany, Poland, France, and elsewhere accepted and even collaborated in Hitler's "final solution"? How could the world prevent dictators from again terrorizing Europe or Asia?

The Allies tried to address those issues when they occupied Germany and Japan. The United States felt that strengthening democracy would ensure tolerance and peace. The western Allies built new governments with democratic constitutions to protect the rights of all citizens. In German schools, for example, Nazi textbooks and courses were replaced with a new curriculum that taught democratic principles.

### The United Nations

As in 1919, the World War II Allies set up an international organization to secure the peace. In April 1945, delegates from 51 nations met in San Francisco to draft a charter for the United Nations. The UN would last longer and play a much greater role in world affairs than its predecessor, the League of Nations.

Under the UN Charter, each member nation had one vote in the General Assembly, where members could debate issues. The much smaller Security Council was given greater power. Its five permanent members—the United States, the Soviet Union (today Russia), Britain, France, and China—all have the right to veto any council decision. The goal was to give these great powers the authority to ensure the peace. Often, however, differences among these powerful nations kept the UN from taking action on controversial issues.

The UN's work would go far beyond peacekeeping. The organization would take on many world problems—from preventing disease and improving education to protecting refugees and aiding nations to develop economically. UN agencies, like the World Health Organization and the Food and Agricultural Organization, have provided help for millions of people around the world. You will read more about the activities of the United Nations in later chapters.

## The Crumbling Alliance

Amid the rubble of war, a new power structure emerged that would shape events in the postwar world. In Europe, Germany was defeated. France and Britain were drained and exhausted. Two other powers, the United States and the Soviet Union, had brought about the final victory. Before long, these two nations would become superpowers with the economic resources and military might to dominate the globe. They would also become tense rivals in an increasingly divided world.

**Growing differences.** During the war, the Soviet Union and the nations of the West had cooperated to defeat Nazi Germany. By 1945, however, the wartime alliance was crumbling. Conflicting ideologies and mutual distrust divided the former Allies and soon led to the conflict known as the Cold War. The Cold War was a state of tension and hostility among nations without armed conflict between the major rivals. At first, the focus of the Cold War was Eastern Europe, where Stalin and the western powers had very different goals.*

---

*Stalin was deeply suspicious of other powers. Russia had been invaded by Napoleon's armies and by Germans in World Wars I and II. Also, the United States and Britain had both sent troops into Russia during World War I. (See page 722)

**Origins of the Cold War.** Stalin had two goals in Eastern Europe. First, he wanted to spread communism into the area. And second, he wanted to create a buffer zone of friendly governments as a defense against Germany, which had invaded Russia during World War I and again in 1941.

As the Red Army had pushed German forces out of Eastern Europe, it left behind occupying forces. At wartime conferences, Stalin tried to get the West to accept Soviet influence in the region. He bluntly claimed:

66Whoever occupies a territory also imposes his own social system. Everyone imposes his own system as far as his armies can reach. It cannot be otherwise.99

The Soviet dictator pointed out that the United States was not consulting the Soviet Union about peace terms for Italy or Japan, defeated and occupied by American and British troops. In the same way, Russia would determine the fate of the Eastern European lands overrun by the Red Army on its way to Berlin.

Roosevelt and Churchill rejected Stalin's view, making him promise "free elections" in Eastern Europe. Stalin ignored that pledge. Backed by the Red Army, local communists in Poland, Czechoslovakia, and elsewhere destroyed rival political parties and even assassinated democratic leaders. By 1946, Stalin had installed pro-Soviet communist governments throughout Eastern Europe.

**"An iron curtain."** Churchill had long distrusted Stalin. Early in 1946, on a visit to the United States, he warned of the new danger facing the war-weary world:

66A shadow has fallen upon the scenes so lately lighted by the Allied victories. . . . From Stettin in the Baltic to Trieste in the Adriatic, an iron curtain has descended across the Continent. Warsaw, Berlin, Prague, Vienna, Budapest, Belgrade, Bucharest, and Sofia, all these famous cities and populations around them lie in what I must call the Soviet sphere and all are subject to a very high and, in many cases, increasing measure of control from Moscow.99

## Divided Germany, 1945

BRITISH ZONE

Berlin

RUSSIAN ZONE

AMERICAN ZONE

FRENCH ZONE

0    75    150 Miles

0    75    150 Kilometers

NATO nations 1955

Warsaw Pact nations 1955

Other communist countries

Territory added to Soviet Union

0    250    500 Miles

0    250    500 Kilometers

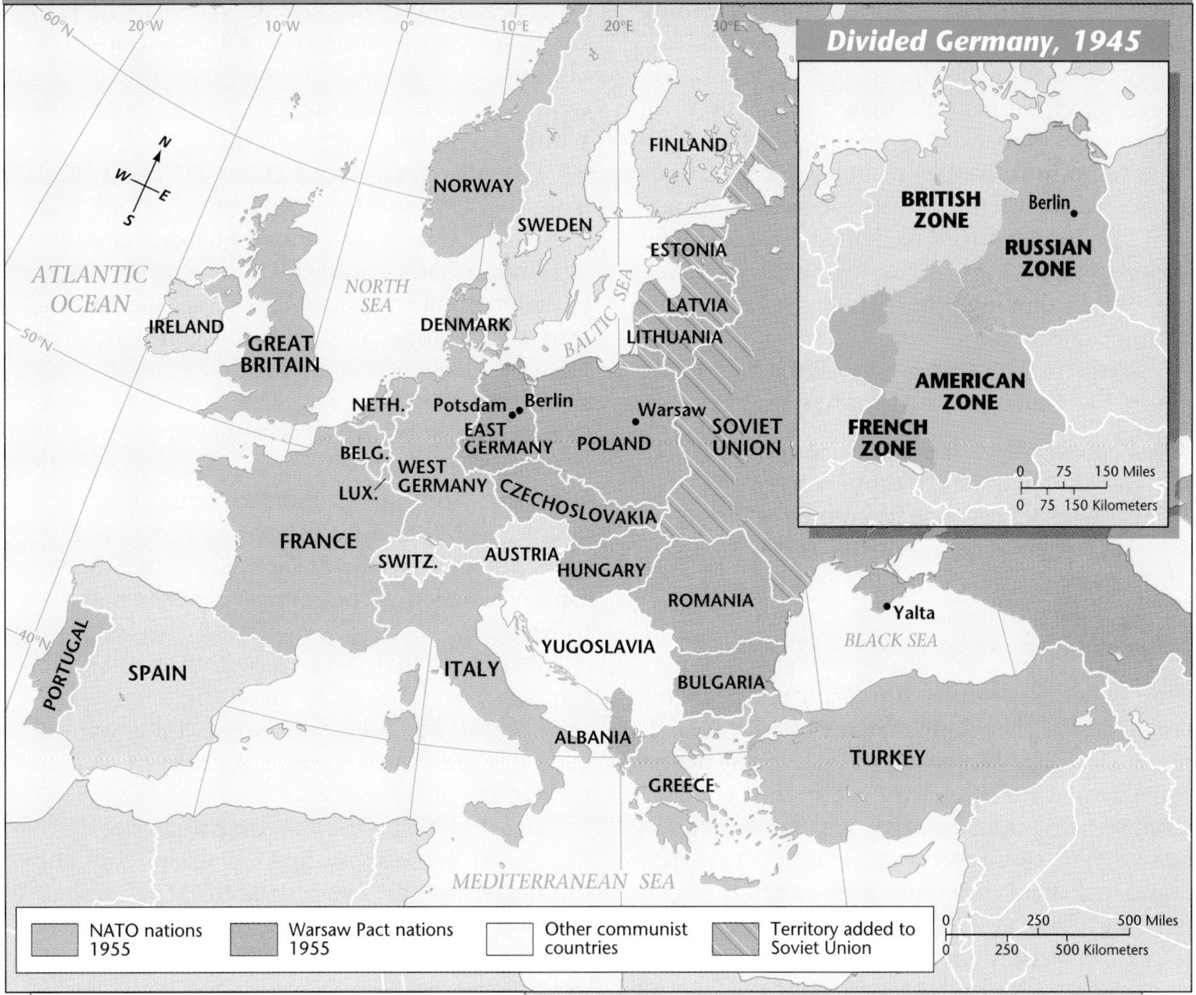

## GEOGRAPHY AND HISTORY

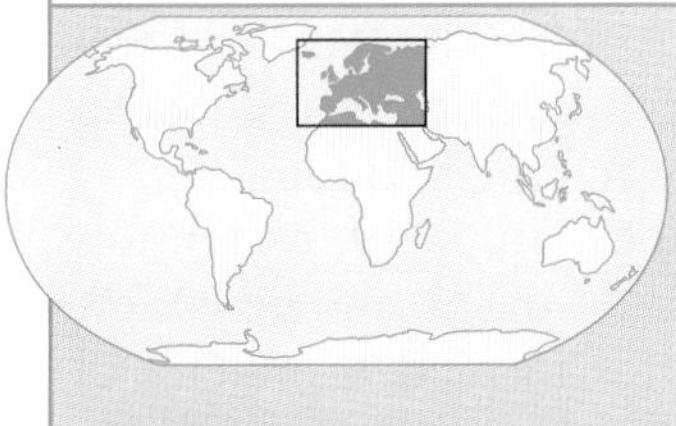

*By 1955, the Cold War was well underway in Europe. Western nations had joined to form NATO. In response, the Soviet Union formed the Warsaw Pact. Meanwhile, Germany, as well as the city of Berlin, was divided into communist and non-communist zones of occupation.*

1. **Location** On the main map, locate (a) West Germany, (b) East Germany, (c) Lithuania, (d) Warsaw Pact nations.
2. **Region** Use the inset map to identify the occupation zone in which Berlin was located.
3. **Critical Thinking** **Synthesizing Information** Why would Turkey be a likely locale for a Cold War conflict?

In the West, Churchill's "iron curtain" became a symbol of the Cold War. It expressed the growing fear of communism. More important, it described the division of Europe into an "eastern" and "western" bloc. In the East were the Soviet-dominated, communist countries of Eastern Europe. In the West were the western democracies, led by the United States.

## Containing Communism

Like Churchill, President Truman saw communism as an evil force creeping across Europe and threatening countries around the world, including China. To deal with that threat, the United States abandoned its traditional isolationism. Unlike after World War I, when it withdrew from global affairs, it took a leading role on the world stage after World War II.

When Stalin began to put pressure on Greece and Turkey, Truman took action. In Greece, Stalin backed communist rebels who were fighting to topple a right-wing monarchy supported by Britain. By 1947, however, Britain could no longer afford to defend Greece. Stalin was also menacing Turkey in the Dardanelles, the straits linking the Black Sea and the Mediterranean.

**Truman Doctrine.** On March 12, 1947, Truman outlined a new policy to Congress:

> **❝**I believe that it must be the policy of the United States to support free people who are resisting attempted subjugation by armed minorities or by outside pressures. . . . The free peoples of the world look to us for support in maintaining their freedoms.**❞**

This policy, known as the Truman Doctrine, would guide the United States for decades. It made clear that Americans would resist Soviet expansion in Europe or elsewhere in the world. Truman soon sent military and economic aid and advisers to Greece and Turkey so that they could withstand the communist threat.

The Truman Doctrine was rooted in the idea of containment, limiting communism to the areas already under Soviet control. George Kennan, the American statesman who first proposed this approach, believed that communism would eventually destroy itself. With "patient but firm and vigilant containment," he said, the United States could stop Soviet expansion. Stalin, however, saw containment as "encirclement" by the capitalist world that wanted to isolate the Soviet Union.

**The Marshall Plan.** Postwar hunger and poverty made Western European lands fertile ground for communist ideas. To strengthen democratic governments, the United States offered a massive aid package, called the Marshall Plan. Under it, the United States funneled food and economic assistance to Europe to help countries rebuild. Billions in American aid helped war-shattered Europe recover rapidly and reduced communist influence there.

President Truman also offered aid to the Soviet Union and its satellites in Eastern Europe. Stalin, however, saw the plan as a trick to knock Eastern Europe out of the Soviet orbit. He forbade Eastern European countries to accept American aid, promising that the Soviet Union would help them instead.

**Divisions in Germany.** Defeated Germany became another focus of the Cold War. The Soviet Union dismantled factories and other resources in its occupation zone, using them to help rebuild Russia. Above all, the Soviets feared the danger of a restored Germany. The western Allies, however, decided to unite their zones of occupation and encouraged Germans to rebuild industries.

Germany thus became a divided nation. In West Germany, the democratic nations let the people write a constitution and regain self-government. In East Germany, the Soviet Union installed a communist government tied to Moscow.

**Berlin airlift.** Stalin's resentment at western moves to rebuild Germany triggered a crisis over Berlin. The former German capital was occupied by all four victorious Allies even though it lay in the Soviet zone.

In 1948, Stalin tried to force the western Allies out of Berlin by sealing off all railroads and highways into the western sectors of the city. The western powers responded to the blockade by mounting a round-the-clock airlift. For almost a year, cargo planes supplied West Berliners with food and fuel. Their success forced the Soviets to end the blockade. The West had won a victory in the Cold War, but the crisis deepened the hostility between the two camps.

**Military alliances.** In 1949, as tensions grew, the United States, Canada, and nine Western European countries formed a military alliance. It was called the North Atlantic Treaty Organization (NATO). Members of NATO pledged to help one another if any one of them was attacked.

In 1955, the Soviet Union responded by forming its own military alliance, the Warsaw Pact. It included the USSR and seven satellite states in Eastern Europe. Unlike NATO, however, the Warsaw Pact was a weapon used by the Soviets to keep its satellites in order.

**The arms race.** Each side in the Cold War armed itself to withstand an attack by the other. At first, the United States, which had the atomic

Dec. 9 1961  THE NEW YORKER  Price 25 cents

Cover drawing by Korvarsky

**The Arms Race** *World War II and the Cold War changed American society. Before the war, the United States had spent less on the military than many European countries. After the war, military spending remained high, and the military became increasingly important to the economy. This postwar cartoon shows a toy store filled with missiles and other weapons.* **Art and Literature** *What point is the cartoonist making about postwar American society?*

The Cold War would last for more than 40 years. Rivalry between the hostile camps would not only divide Europe but would also fuel crises around the world. It would drain the resources of the United States and exhaust those of the Soviet Union. Though it would not erupt into large-scale fighting between the two superpowers, many small wars broke out, with the superpowers championing opposite sides. Meanwhile, the spread of ominous new weapons would more than once raise the specter of global destruction.

bomb, held an advantage. But Stalin's top scientists were under orders to develop an atomic bomb. When they succeeded in 1949, the arms race was on.

For four decades, the superpowers spent fantastic sums to develop new, more deadly nuclear and conventional weapons. They invested still more to improve "delivery systems"—the bombers, missiles, and submarines to launch these terrifying weapons of mass destruction. Soon, the global balance of power became, in Churchill's phrase, a "balance of terror."

**The propaganda war.** Both sides campaigned in a propaganda war. The United States spoke of defending capitalism and democracy against communism and totalitarianism. The Soviet Union claimed the moral high ground in the struggle against western imperialism. Yet linked to those stands, both sides sought world power.

**Looking ahead.** In 1945, the world hoped for an end to decades of economic crisis, bloody dictators, and savage war. Instead, it faced new tensions.

## SECTION 5 REVIEW

1. **Identify** (a) UN, (b) "iron curtain," (c) Truman Doctrine, (d) Berlin airlift, (e) NATO, (f) Warsaw Pact.
2. **Define** containment.
3. (a) Describe conditions that total war had created in Europe and Asia following World War II. (b) How did the Allies try to hold the Axis leaders responsible for the suffering they caused during the war?
4. (a) Who were the superpowers that emerged after World War II? (b) What were the main differences between them?
5. State two causes of the Cold War.
6. *Critical Thinking* **Recognizing Causes and Effects** Some historians argue that the Cold War began in 1918 when the World War I Allies, including the United States, sent forces to Russia to topple the Bolsheviks there. How might they support this position?
7. *ACTIVITY* Use Churchill's "iron curtain" image to create a political cartoon about the Cold War.

# Skills for Success

## Making Decisions

Decisions involve choices between alternatives. You have already learned how to identify alternatives and project their consequences. (See page 654.) In this lesson, you will build on that skill in order to learn how to make decisions.

During World War II, General Dwight Eisenhower had the task of preparing the invasion of France. The excerpt below is from his memoir, *Crusade in Europe*. Read the excerpt and follow the steps to analyze how and why Eisenhower chose June 6, 1944, for D-Day.

**1** **Identify the alternatives.** (a) What date had been set for the Normandy landing? (b) What other date did Eisenhower consider? Why?

**2** **Project the consequences for each alternative.** (a) What were possible consequences of a landing on June 5? (b) Of a landing on June 6? (c) What were possible consequences of postponing a landing past June 6?

**3** **Evaluate the consequences.** (a) What was Eisenhower's evaluation of a landing on June 5? (b) His evaluation of the forecast for June 6?

**4** **Make the decision.** After identifying alternatives and projecting and evaluating their consequences, decide which alternative has the greatest likelihood of success. (a) What did Eisenhower decide? (b) Why?

***Beyond the Classroom*** Use a newspaper to identify a current issue that affects your life. Identify the alternative solutions, project their consequences, and then evaluate the information to determine which solution would be best for you. Be prepared to defend your decision.

---

### Dwight D. Eisenhower

66 The government had established a deadline. . . . We met with the Meteorologic Committee twice daily. . . . At these meetings every bit of evidence was carefully presented, carefully analyzed, and carefully studied. . . . With the approach of the critical period the tension continued to mount as prospects for decent weather became worse and worse.

The final conference for determining the feasibility of attacking on the selected day, June 5, was scheduled for 4:00 A.M. on June 4. However, some of the attacking [groups] had already been ordered to sea, because if the entire force was to land on June 5, then some of the important elements stationed in northern parts of the United Kingdom could not wait.

When the commanders assembled on June 4 . . . the report we received was discouraging. Low clouds, high winds, and formidable wave action were predicted to make landing a most hazardous affair. The meteorologists said that air support would be impossible, naval gunfire would be ineffi-cient, and even the handling of small boats would be rendered difficult. . . . Weighing all factors, I decided that the attack would have to be postponed. . . .

[The next morning] . . . the first report was that the bad conditions predicted the day before . . . were actually prevailing and that if we had persisted in the attempt to land on June 5 a major disaster would almost surely have resulted. [They told us] that by the following morning a period of relatively good weather, heretofore completely unexpected, would ensue, lasting probably 36 hours. The long-term prediction was not good but they did give us assurance that this short period of calm weather would [occur].

The prospect was not bright because of the possibility that we might land the first several waves successfully and then find later build-up impractica-ble, and so have to leave the isolated original attack-ing forces easy prey to German counteraction. How-ever, the consequences of the delay justified great risk and I quickly announced the decision to go ahead with the attack on June 6. 99

## Building Vocabulary

(a) Classify each of the vocabulary words introduced in this chapter under one of the following themes: Economics and Technology, Political and Social Systems, Global Interaction. (b) Choose *one* word in each category and write a sentence explaining how that word relates to the theme.

## Reviewing Chapter Themes

1. **Continuity and Change** (a) Describe three acts of Axis aggression that contributed to the outbreak of World War II. (b) Describe three examples of Allied appeasement of the Axis powers. (c) How did the desire of the western democracies to avoid a repetition of World War I contribute to the outbreak of World War II?
2. **Economics and Technology** (a) Describe three new weapons or other military technology used during World War II. (b) How did this new technology make war more destructive? (c) Why did World War II have more civilian casualties than World War I?
3. **Political and Social Systems** (a) What policies did Germany follow in the lands that it occupied? (b) Why did Asians at first welcome the Japanese invaders? (c) Why did they later turn against Japan?
4. **Global Interaction** What differences developed between the western Allies and the Soviet Union?
5. **Geography and History** (a) Why did Hitler attack the Soviet Union? (b) Why was the attack an enormous mistake?

## Thinking Critically

1. **Analyzing Information** Why do you think some historians call the period from 1919 to 1939 the 20-year armistice?
2. **Defending a Position** Agree or disagree with the following statement: The western democracies could have prevented the outbreak of World War II. Defend your position.
3. **Applying Information** Hitler translated his hatred of Jews, Gypsies, Slavs, and others into a systematic program of genocide. How do ethnic, racial, and religious hatreds weaken society?

4. **Linking Past and Present** What lessons does the Holocaust have for us today?
5. **Recognizing Faulty Reasoning** (a) Why were the German invasion of the Soviet Union and the Japanese bombing of Pearl Harbor mistaken decisions of the Axis leaders? (b) Why do you think the Axis leaders made those decisions? ( ★ See *Skills for Success,* page 524.)
6. **Synthesizing Information** (a) How did the United States help the Allies during World War II? (b) Do you think participation by the United States was crucial to winning the war? Explain. ( ★ See *Skills for Success,* page 896.)
7. **Analyzing Information** Explain the following statement: World War II brought down several dictatorships but at the same time increased the power of the world's largest totalitarian state.
8. **Recognizing Causes and Effects** List two causes and two effects of the Cold War. ( ★ See *Skills for Success,* page 18.)

### For Your Portfolio

In Chapter 31, you have read about the major events of World War II. In this assignment, you will gain a closer view of the period by interviewing someone who lived during the war.

1. Review the information in the chapter.
2. Locate an adult—a family member, friend, neighbor, or teacher—who was born before World War II. Explain your assignment and request permission to tape an oral history.
3. Prepare a list of events that you would like the interviewee to comment on. For example, you might ask for recollections about Hitler's invasion of Poland or Japan's bombing of Pearl Harbor. You might also prepare questions about life on the home front. If you are interviewing someone who served in the war, you will want to ask about those experiences.
4. Hold a preliminary meeting with the person you will interview. Share the topics and questions you plan to cover. Offer the interviewee the chance to refresh his or her memory of the selected events. Finally, set the date and time for the interview.
5. Tape record the interview. Be sure to identify yourself and the other speaker on the tape.
6. Share the taped oral history with your class.

# *Unit-in-Brief*

## World Wars and Revolutions

### Chapter 27 World War I and Its Aftermath (1914–1919)

Many forces—including nationalism, militarism, and imperialist rivalries—propelled Europe into World War I. This massive conflict engulfed much of the world for four years and ushered in a new age of modern warfare.

- Two huge alliances emerged in Europe: the Central Powers, dominated by Germany and Austria-Hungary, and the Allies, led by France, Britain, and Russia.
- Although the assassination of Archduke Francis Ferdinand in 1914 ignited World War I, historians agree that all the major powers share blame for the conflict.
- Trench warfare and new weapons contributed to a stalemate on the Western Front.
- In 1917, the United States entered the war, allowing the Allies to achieve victory.
- The Paris peace conference imposed heavy penalties on Germany and redrew the map of Eastern Europe.

### Chapter 28 Revolution in Russia (1917–1939)

V. I. Lenin and his successors transformed czarist Russia into the communist Soviet Union. This experiment in single-party politics and a state-run economy would exert a powerful influence over the modern world for almost 75 years.

- In March 1917, political, social, and economic conditions in Russia sparked a revolution that overthrew the czar and paved the way for more radical changes.
- After leading the Bolsheviks to power in October 1917, Lenin hoped to build the classless, communist state envisioned by Karl Marx.
- Lenin's successor, Stalin, imposed "five-year plans" to build industry and farm output.
- Stalin created a totalitarian state, employing censorship, propaganda, and terror to ensure personal power and push the Soviet Union toward modernization.

### Chapter 29 Nationalism and Revolution Around the World (1914–1939)

Between 1919 and 1939, the desire for democracy and self-determination contributed to explosive struggles in many regions. New leaders in Africa, Latin America, and Asia built liberation movements that would change the world.

- The Mexican Revolution opened the door to social and economic reforms.
- Latin American leaders promoted economic nationalism, seeking to end dependence on the industrial powers.

- In Africa, a new generation of leaders called for an end to imperialism and reaffirmed traditional cultures.
- Arab nationalism gave rise to Pan-Arabism, a movement which sought to end foreign domination and unite Arabs in their own state.
- In India, Gandhi led a campaign of nonviolent resistance to British rule.
- In China, foreigners extended their spheres of influence. Later, communists and nationalists engaged in civil war.
- During the 1920s and 1930s, extreme nationalism and economic upheaval set Japan on a militaristic and expansionist path.

**Chapter 30** Crisis of Democracy
in the West
(1919–1939)

After World War I, western nations worked to restore prosperity and ensure peace. At the same time, political and economic turmoil in the 1920s and 1930s challenged democratic traditions and led to the rise of powerful dictators.

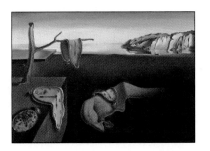

- The Great Depression of the 1930s created financial turmoil and widespread suffering throughout the industrialized world.
- Scientific discoveries, new trends in literature and the arts, and social changes all contributed to a sense of uncertainty.
- Three systems of government—democracy, communism, and fascism—competed for influence in postwar Europe.
- In Italy, Mussolini and his Fascist party took advantage of economic and political unrest to win power in the 1920s.

- In Germany, Hitler rose to power by appealing to extreme nationalism, anti-Semitism, anti-communism, and resentment of the Treaty of Versailles. In the 1930s, he turned Germany into a totalitarian Nazi dictatorship.

**Chapter 31** World War II
and Its Aftermath
(1931–1949)

Between 1939 and 1945, nations all over the globe fought World War II, the largest and most costly conflict in history. The war shifted the balance of world power from Western Europe to the United States and the Soviet Union.

- The Axis powers—Germany, Italy, and Japan—embarked on a course of aggression in the late 1930s. At first, France and Britain adopted a policy of appeasement but finally declared war when Hitler invaded Poland.
- The Axis at first enjoyed an unbroken string of victories in Europe.
- During the Holocaust, the Nazis systematically killed more than six million Jews, as well as millions of other people the Nazis considered undesirable.
- The Soviet Union and the United States joined the war on the Allied side. Allied victories in North Africa and Europe eventually led to the defeat of Germany.
- To force a Japanese surrender, the United States employed a powerful new weapon, the atomic bomb.
- World War II was followed by the Cold War, which pitted the western democracies, led by the United States, against the communist bloc, dominated by the Soviet Union.

# A Global View

## How Did World Events Reflect Growing Interaction?

Future historians may view the first half of the twentieth century as a giant step backward in human history. The events that swept the globe between 1900 and 1945 pitted many peoples around the world against one another or against their own governments.

The two world wars revealed a world that was violently divided. Revolutions tore through some of the world's largest nations. Cruel dictatorships arose in others. We might conclude that, at this point in history, people simply could not live together in harmony.

### A World Drawn Together

Amid such division, it is hard to see evidence of a world moving together. Yet these terrible events were also signs of a movement toward the globalization of history. The major events, trends, and even disasters of the period were, after all, increasingly global in scope.

World War I was fought mostly in Europe between European armies. But, as we have seen, non-Europeans also fought in that war, and there were battles beyond the continent. Certainly, the causes and consequences of World War I were global in scale.

The world economy in the early part of the century was still dominated by the West—German factories, American farms, stock exchanges in New York and London. But Japan was quickly joining the ranks of leading economic powers. In addition, ties of trade or empire linked Asia, Africa, and Latin America to the dominant economies.

Such economic connections meant that all regions were affected by the prosperity of the 1920s. But, by the same token, the Great Depression of the 1930s, which began in the United States, quickly escalated into a global disaster.

### Political Upheavals

The early 1900s also saw the longest and bloodiest revolutions in a century. Unlike the democratic revolutions that took place in Europe and Latin

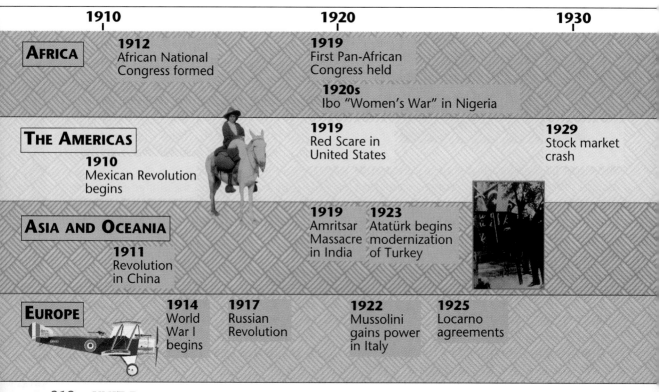

| 1910 | 1920 | 1930 |
|---|---|---|

**AFRICA**
1912 African National Congress formed
1919 First Pan-African Congress held
1920s Ibo "Women's War" in Nigeria

**THE AMERICAS**
1910 Mexican Revolution begins
1919 Red Scare in United States
1929 Stock market crash

**ASIA AND OCEANIA**
1911 Revolution in China
1919 Amritsar Massacre in India
1923 Atatürk begins modernization of Turkey

**EUROPE**
1914 World War I begins
1917 Russian Revolution
1922 Mussolini gains power in Italy
1925 Locarno agreements

America in the early 1800s, the revolutions of the twentieth century were global in scope.

The Russian Revolution under Lenin, the Chinese Revolution that climaxed with Mao's victory, and the long Mexican Revolution all served as inspirations or warnings to the rest of the world. At least in part because of these revolutions, rebellion against imperialism would soon boil up around the globe.

The brutal decade of the 1930s was an age of tyranny and aggression in Europe. This was the age of Hitler and Stalin and the beginning of the Nazi campaign against Jews that led to the Holocaust. But it was also the decade of Japanese militarism and aggression in East Asia, of Mussolini's invasion of Ethiopia, and of military regimes in Latin America. The brutality of the 1930s was not confined to the West.

Finally, World War II was beyond doubt a global conflict. Its major combatants included great powers of all continents except South America. Its theaters of war included Europe, Asia, Africa, and large sections of the Atlantic and Pacific oceans. Literally, no part of the globe escaped unscathed. The ruins that littered half the world in 1945 were grim evidence of the continuing globalization of history.

## Looking Ahead

More global confrontations waited in the second half of the century. During the decades after 1945, the old European empires collapsed and the Cold War divided the world between two global alliances. During the second half of the century also, the globe was drawn more closely together by closer economic ties, social contacts, and bonds of communications and culture. Today, no nation is farther from any other than the nearest television set—and Macdonald's, not even a dream in 1945, spans the globe.

All of these developments lay ahead as the world dug out of the ruins of World War II. The year 1945 thus marked the beginning of a new wave of global interdependence.

**ACTIVITY** Choose two events and two pictures from the time line below. For each, write a sentence explaining how it relates to the themes expressed in the Global View essay.

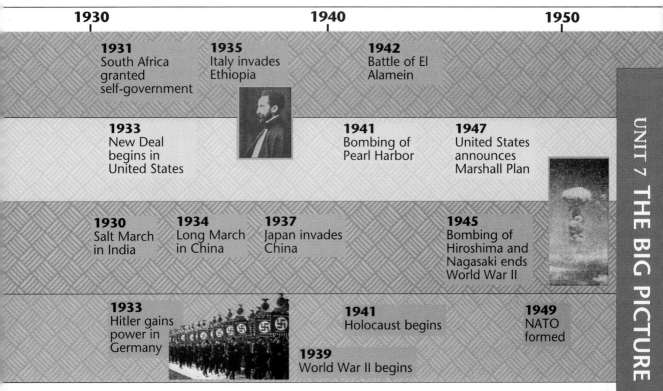

1930    1940    1950

**1931** South Africa granted self-government

**1935** Italy invades Ethiopia

**1942** Battle of El Alamein

**1933** New Deal begins in United States

**1941** Bombing of Pearl Harbor

**1947** United States announces Marshall Plan

**1930** Salt March in India

**1934** Long March in China

**1937** Japan invades China

**1945** Bombing of Hiroshima and Nagasaki ends World War II

**1933** Hitler gains power in Germany

**1941** Holocaust begins

**1949** NATO formed

**1939** World War II begins

# You Decide

## Exploring Global Issues

### *Is War Ever Justified?*

"Everlasting peace is a dream," declared the German military leader Helmuth von Moltke, "and war is a necessary part of God's arrangement of the world." Moltke spoke for militarists of all nationalities in the decades before World War I.

At the other extreme were the pacifists, who denounced war utterly. "A Christian cannot consistently uphold, and actively support, a government based on the sword," argued American pacifist Lucretia Mott.

Today, the debate continues. Should the risk of war be avoided at all costs? Or are there times when it may even be morally wrong to keep out of a conflict? To begin your investigation, examine these viewpoints:

**CHINA**

**300s B.C.**

The warrior-philosopher Sun Tzu wrote *The Art of War*, an influential handbook of military strategy:

66A government should not mobilize an army out of anger, military leaders should not provoke a war out of wrath. Act when it is beneficial, desist when it is not. Anger can revert to joy, wrath can revert to delight, but a nation destroyed cannot be restored to existence, and the dead cannot be restored to life.99

**AZTEC EMPIRE**

**1400s**

Like other world empires, the Aztecs glorified military might. This statue shows an elite Eagle Warrior, whose conquests kept the empire supplied with tribute money and sacrificial victims. ▷

**RUSSIA**

**1700s**

The empress Catherine the Great, whose conquests greatly increased Russian territory, wrote of the value of war:

66The only way to save our empires from the encroaching of the people is to engage in war, and thus substitute national passions for social aspirations.99

**CUBA**

**late 1800s**

Poet and revolutionary José Martí was a leader of his nation's fight against Spanish rule:

66Anyone is a criminal who promotes an avoidable war. And so is he who does not promote an inevitable civil war.99

**INDIA**

**1948**

Mohandas Gandhi, who led a nonviolent campaign to free India from British rule, denounced all forms of warfare and violence:

❝What difference does it make to the dead, the orphans and the homeless, whether the mad destruction is wrought under the name of totalitarianism or the holy name of democracy and liberty?❞

**UNITED STATES**

**1970s**

The women's group Another Mother Against War created this poster and slogan, which became popular on T-shirts, bumper stickers, and pins. ▷

**ZIMBABWE**

**1978**

Bishop Abel Muzorewa joined the struggle for majority rule in his nation and later served as prime minister:

❝I question whether God himself would wish me to hide behind the principles of nonviolence while innocent persons were being slaughtered.❞

---

### COMPARING VIEWPOINTS

1. Which statements or pictures do you think represent the most militaristic point of view? Which represent a pacifist viewpoint?
2. How is Sun Tzu's viewpoint similar to that of Martí?
3. Martí, Gandhi, and Muzorewa were all involved in movements to free their nations from colonial rule. Compare their views on the need for military action.

### YOUR INVESTIGATION

**ACTIVITY**

1. Find out more about other viewpoints related to this topic. You might investigate one or more of the following:
- The feudal military ideals of chivalry (Europe) and bushido (Japan).
- The history and philosophy of Quakerism.
- President Woodrow Wilson's war message to Congress in 1917.
- The life and work of a Nobel Peace Prize winner, such as Jane Addams of the United States, Albert Luthuli of South Africa, Mairead Corrigan and Betty Williams of Northern Ireland, or Oscar Arias Sanchez of Costa Rica.
- Contrasting positions on the appeasement of Hitler in the 1930s.
- Debates in the 1990s about the use of UN or American troops in the Persian Gulf, Haiti, Bosnia, or another trouble spot.

2. Decide which viewpoint you agree with most closely and express it in your own way. You may do so in an essay, a cartoon, a poem, a drawing or painting, a song, a skit, a video, or in some other way.

# THE WORLD TODAY

## Global Interaction

2

Today, millions of refugees live in various countries around the world. Here, at a camp in Zaire, the International Red Cross gives aid to refugees from a civil war in Rwanda.

1

## Political and Social Systems

1

*Chile was one of several nations that experienced a period of harsh military rule. After 16 years, civilian government was finally restored in 1989.*

## Impact of the Individual

**3** Soviet leader Mikhail Gorbachev was a key builder of today's world. His reforms paved the way for the independence of Eastern Europe, the breakup of the Soviet Union, and the end of the Cold War.

**3**

## Continuity and Change

**5** Today, ancient cultural traditions exist side by side with technological and social changes. In Thailand, this Buddhist monk lines up a shot with his state-of-the-art camera.

**4**

**5**

**2**

## The World Today

This photograph was created by combining hundreds of pictures taken by an orbiting weather satellite. It shows how the Earth would look from space, unobstructed by clouds.

## Economics and Technology

**4** Oil reserves have increased the strategic importance of the Middle East and the political clout of several Arab nations. These executives are inspecting a refinery in Saudi Arabia.

# The World Since 1945: An Overview

## (1945–Present)

## CHAPTER OUTLINE

1 The Changing Political Climate
2 Global Economic Trends
3 Changing Patterns of Life

In her short story "The Lake of Nothingness," Saudi writer Fawziyya al-Bakr describes the life of an unnamed business executive. He has carved out a successful career making deals with foreign companies. The rewards include a "luxurious American car. . . . First-class hotels. Luxurious seats in the planes, flying in and out of the capitals of money and business." Yet he is filled with a strange emptiness. He compares his new life to the world of his childhood:

> **❝**He remembered, tenderly, the mud hut he'd lived in when he was a boy. He'd gone barefoot and things had seemed friendlier then, even the insects and the dirt. And the neighbors, those good people, used to exchange smiles and food with them.**❞**

This fictional executive happens to be an Arab. But his story might have struck a familiar note in Singapore, Nigeria, or Bolivia. In the developing world, millions of people have flocked from small villages to growing cities. Some, like the man in the story, have prospered materially. Many more live poverty-stricken existences in crowded shantytowns. All, however, have had to adjust to a rapidly changing world.

In this unit, we are no longer looking at events that occurred centuries ago but at recent developments. Since 1945, the world has changed rapidly. More than 100 nations won independence as a result of the breakup of western colonial empires and, later, the collapse of the Soviet Union. Populations boomed, and technology revolutionized people's lives.

The recent past presents special problems for students of history. While we can see the immediate results of recent events, we cannot know their long-term impact. We lack the perspective of historians studying the distant past.

This chapter explores political, economic, and social trends and issues that have shaped the world since World War II. Some of those patterns will still be important 20, 50, or 100 years from now. Others may be less crucial. In the chapters that follow, we will look at how postwar trends affected individual regions.

FOCUS ON these questions as you read:

■ **Political and Social Systems**
What postwar developments have helped or hindered the spread of democracy?

■ **Global Interaction**
How has global interdependence increased in recent decades?

■ **Economics and Technology**
How does the gap between rich and poor nations affect the world?

■ **Geography and History**
Why have environmental issues attracted global attention?

■ **Continuity and Change**
How have modernization and westernization brought rapid social and cultural change?

## TIME AND PLACE

***An Urban Township*** *In the 1960s and 1970s, painter Jo Maseko depicted life in the black townships around Johannesburg, South Africa. The effects of urban poverty were heightened by the government's policy of apartheid. But the tin-roofed shacks and bustling streets of this township mirrored slums in other developing nations. Rapid urbanization has been a major feature of the world since 1945.* **Continuity and Change** *Review Chapter 20. What were the effects of rapid urbanization in Europe during the Industrial Revolution?*

## HUMANITIES LINK

***Art History*** Jean Tinguely, *M.K. III* (page 843).
***Literature*** In this chapter, you will encounter passages from the following works of literature: Fawziyya al-Bakr, "The Lake of Nothingness" (page 824); Nguyen Sa, "No Time" (page 837).

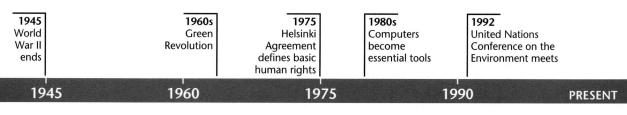

| 1945 World War II ends | 1960s Green Revolution | 1975 Helsinki Agreement defines basic human rights | 1980s Computers become essential tools | 1992 United Nations Conference on the Environment meets |
|---|---|---|---|---|
| 1945 | 1960 | 1975 | 1990 | PRESENT |

# 1 The Changing Political Climate

## Guide for Reading

■ Why did European overseas empires crumble after World War II?

■ How did the Cold War affect all regions of the world?

■ Why did new nations have problems building stable governments?

■ Why have ties among nations increased?

■ **Vocabulary** *nonaligned, interdependence, terrorism*

In 1972, President Julius Nyerere (nyuh RAIR ay) of Tanzania in East Africa spoke of the goals of struggling new nations:

66There is a world movement now against being pushed around. . . . This movement will succeed. Eventually, imperialism and racialism will become merely a chapter in the history of man—we shall hear about it in museums.99

The balance of world power changed dramatically after 1945. European influence declined while the United States and the Soviet Union emerged as superpowers locked in a tense Cold War. Perhaps the greatest change, however, was the collapse of western overseas empires and the emergence of dozens of new countries.

## The Great Liberation

The postwar decades brought a major turning point in world history when the colonial empires built by western powers during the Age of Imperialism crumbled. In Asia and Africa, people demanded and won freedom.

**Nationalism and independence.** Resistance to colonial rule had begun long before. By the 1930s, nationalist movements had taken root in Africa, Asia, and the Middle East. (See Chapter 29.) After World War II, nationalist

▲ *Postage stamps of former European colonies*

leaders like Gandhi in India insisted on independence.

At first, Britain, France, and other powers tried to hold on to their empires. But the war had exhausted their military and financial resources. With subject peoples ready to fight for freedom, many war-weary Europeans had no desire for further conflict.

The Cold War, too, undermined imperialism. The United States backed the right of people everywhere to self-determination. Its rival, the Soviet Union, also had long condemned western imperialism. Soon, both superpowers were seeking allies among emerging nations.

**Global impact.** Altogether, nearly 100 new countries emerged during this "great liberation." Some, such as India and Nigeria, were large in area or population. Many others, such as Nepal, Kuwait, or Lesotho, were small.

The new nations of Africa and Asia, as well as the countries of Latin America, became known as the developing world.* Although these nations differed greatly from one another, they shared common goals. All were determined to pursue modernization, which meant building stable governments and developing their countries economically. They followed different paths toward modernization, but many experienced similar challenges.

The needs and goals of developing nations transformed the postwar world. Most joined the United Nations, where they have become an important voice by uniting their interests and often voting as a bloc. Individually and in regional groups, a number of them have played significant roles in global political and economic affairs.

---

*During the Cold War, the term *Third World* was used to refer to these nations with less-advanced technology than the First World (the western industrial powers and Japan) or the Second World (the communist bloc nations).

## The Cold War Goes Global

The new nations emerged into a world dominated and divided by the Cold War. The United States and the Soviet Union competed for influence by offering economic and military aid to developing nations. Each superpower wanted new countries to adopt its ideology—either capitalism or socialism. Many new nations favored socialism, in part because their old colonial rulers had been capitalist. Other nations were attracted by the greater prosperity of the West.

**Nonaligned nations.** To avoid superpower rivalry, many new nations chose to remain nonaligned, that is, not allied to either side in the Cold War. The goal of the nonaligned movement was to reduce world tensions and promote economic policies that would benefit developing nations. India, which blended a democratic government with a socialist economy, was a leader in the nonaligned movement.

**Hot spots.** In Africa, Latin America, and Asia, local conflicts took on a Cold War dimension. Often, the United States and the Soviet Union supported opposite sides. Through such struggles, the superpowers confronted each other indirectly rather than head to head.

On occasion, the Cold War did erupt into "shooting wars," especially in Asia. Both Korea and Vietnam were torn by brutal conflicts in which the United States and the Soviet Union played crucial roles. (You will read about these wars in more detail in Chapter 34.)

**The Cold War ends.** The Cold War ended suddenly in 1991 when the Soviet Union collapsed. (See Chapter 33.) With this dramatic change, tensions eased and some long-standing conflicts were resolved. Many people hoped for a more peaceful world. But troubling local, regional, and global problems remained.

Within many nations—from Russia to Indonesia to Rwanda—ethnic groups pushed for autonomy, or independence. They wanted their own states to protect their identity. Other clashes occurred between rival religious groups or different clans. Often, however, economic or political struggles were at the root of ethnic clashes.

## New Nations Seek Stability

While new nations had high hopes for the future, they faced immense problems. In Africa, especially, nations inherited random colonial borders that mixed together people with different languages, religions, and ethnic identities. Colonial rulers, using a "divide and conquer" strategy, had often exploited ethnic rivalries. At independence, people in nations like Nigeria had few ties to unite them. (See page 934.)

The new nations wrote constitutions modeled on those of western democracies. Only a few, however, like India, were able to sustain democratic rule. In general, colonial rulers had done little to prepare the people for self-government in a postwar world. Many new nations were shaken by revolution or civil war. Often, a wealthy, western-educated elite controlled the government and economy. The great majority of people remained poor.

As problems multiplied, the military or authoritarian leaders often took over. Many times, these were the same people who had led the fight for liberation. They imposed order by

**The Nonaligned Ark** *This cartoon from a Bombay newspaper shows Indira Gandhi, longtime prime minister of India, sending out a dove of peace. India had assumed leadership of the nonaligned movement under Gandhi's father, Jawaharlal Nehru.* **Political and Social Systems** *According to this cartoon, what dangers did emerging nations face in the Cold War world? What was their goal?*

building one-party dictatorships. They banned other political parties, claiming that a multiparty system threatened stability. Leaders waved the banner of nationalism, hoping to overcome ethnic, religious, or regional divisions.

Despite setbacks, democracy did make some progress in the late 1980s and early 1990s. In Africa, Asia, and Latin America, nations that had been ruled by dictators or by a single party held multiparty elections. The outcome of these experiments in democracy remains uncertain given the problems that face developing nations and their lack of experience with forms of representative government.

## The Shrinking Globe

Since 1945, transportation and communications systems have made the world increasingly interdependent. Interdependence is the dependence of countries on goods, resources, and knowledge from other parts of the world. Political, economic, cultural, and other links have created both problems and opportunities. A number of international organizations deal with issues of global concern.

**The UN.** The United Nations was set up as a forum for settling disputes. (See page 809.) Its responsibilities, like its membership, have expanded greatly since 1945. The UN played a vital role in decolonization. Since then, it has tried to act as peacekeeper from Cambodia and the Middle East to Africa and the Balkans. Some UN interventions have been successful. Others have failed, often from an inability of members to agree on goals and methods.

UN agencies provide services for millions of people worldwide. The World Health Organization (WHO), for example, helped wipe out smallpox through its program of vaccinations. Today, WHO works with other groups to seek a solution to the AIDS crisis. Other UN programs spearhead campaigns to reduce malnutrition or ensure access to safe drinking water. The UN

has also sponsored global summits on issues such as the environment and population.

**Other organizations.** Many nations formed regional groups to promote trade or meet other common needs. Powerful regional trading blocs have emerged. In later chapters, you will see how such groups as the European Community, the North American Free Trade Association, and the Association of Southeast Asian Nations have worked to lower trade barriers and promote the free exchange of goods and services.

The importance of global trade was recognized by a series of international agreements known as the General Agreement on Tariffs and Trade (GATT). It tried to establish fair trade policies for all nations. At the highest levels, the Group of Seven, which represents the seven most productive economies—the United States, Canada, Japan, Germany, France, Britain, and Italy—has met annually to discuss common economic problems.

The World Bank and the International Monetary Fund (IMF) make loans to developing nations. Many other types of nongovernmental organizations have forged valuable global networks, including the International Olympic Committee and the International Red Cross.

## Enduring Issues

Many issues pose a challenge to world peace. Since the United States first exploded an atomic bomb in 1945, nations have poured resources into building nuclear weapons. The number of nuclear weapons grew from 3 in 1945 to over 50,000 in the 1980s.

**Nuclear weapons.** During the Cold War, efforts to curb the arms race had only limited success. In 1968, a number of nations signed the Nuclear Non-Proliferation Treaty (NPT), agreeing to halt the spread of nuclear weapons. As the treaty came up for renewal in the 1990s, though, some nations were unwilling to sign. They asked why a few countries like the United States and Russia could keep nuclear weapons and they could not. Still, in 1995, the NPT was renewed indefinitely.

**Arms trade.** Despite the end of the Cold War, military spending in many countries has

ISSUES For TODAY

Interdependence has created strong ties among rich and poor nations around the world. Do the benefits of increasing political and economic ties with other nations outweigh the dangers?

**Games for a Changing World** *In 1896, the first modern Olympic Games featured 311 male athletes from 13 nations. In 1992, the Olympic Games in Barcelona featured more than 10,000 male and female athletes from 172 nations. The 1992 games reflected other world changes. South Africa, after ending its system of apartheid, was allowed to send a team for the first time in 32 years. And, for the last time, athletes from the former Soviet Union competed as a unified team.* **Global Interaction** *Why are the Olympic Games a symbol of interdependence?*

continued to grow. In nations split by ethnic or other conflicts, arms dealers traffic in deadly weapons. Some people have condemned the international arms trade. Others defend the economic right of arms makers to produce and sell their goods on the free market.

**Terrorism.** Since the 1960s, the world has seen a rise in terrorist activity. Terrorism is the deliberate use of random violence, especially against civilians, to exact revenge or achieve political goals. Through bombings, kidnappings, airplane hijackings, and shootings, terrorists focused attention on their causes and tried to force governments to give in to their demands.

Militants on both sides of the conflict in Northern Ireland murdered civilians. In 1972, a radical group killed Israeli athletes at the Olympic Games to push its demands for a Palestinian state. In the 1990s, separate terrorist groups bombed the World Trade Center in New York City and released deadly nerve gas on a subway train in Tokyo. The random and secret nature of terrorist activities makes them difficult to prevent. To combat terrorism, some governments have passed tough laws and stepped up vigilance.

Some governments have been suspected of "state-sponsored terrorism," training and arm-ing extremists to carry out attacks abroad. Human rights groups and others also claim that governments engaged in terrorism when they used torture, murder, and illegal arrests against their own citizens.

**Human rights.** In 1948, UN members approved the Universal Declaration of Human Rights. The first article states:

> **❝**All human beings are born free and equal in dignity and rights. They are endowed with reason and conscience and should act towards one another in a spirit of brotherhood.**❞**

The document goes on to state that all people are entitled to basic rights and freedoms "without distinction of any kind, such as race, color, sex, language, property, birth or other status." These human rights include "the right to life, liberty, and security of person."

In 1975, 35 nations signed the Helsinki Agreement. It stated that freedom of speech, religion, and the press, and the right to a fair trial are basic human rights. The rights to earn a living and live in safety were also guaranteed.

Despite such agreements, human rights abuses such as torture and arbitrary arrest occurred around the world. At times, the world community pressed countries to stop those abuses. World pressure and economic sanctions, for example, helped push South Africa to end its system of apartheid. (See Chapter 36.)

Still, some leaders accused the West of trying to impose its own ideas about individual freedom. Some claim that their cultures value the community over the individual. Chinese leaders, for example, argued that national economic goals, such as improving the standard of living for its people, were more important than individual political freedoms.

**The question of intervention.** The human rights debate raises tough issues. Does the world community have a responsibility to intervene to end abuses? For example, the UN Charter forbids any action that violates the independence of a member nation. Yet in the 1990s, the UN sent peacekeepers to northern Iraq to protect the Kurds, an ethnic minority that was being persecuted by the government.

In the 1990s, Serbs in Bosnia killed or drove Muslims from their homes. (You will read about this conflict in Chapter 33.) World opinion was outraged, but for complex political reasons, the UN and western powers were reluctant to take military action against the Serbs. As ethnic conflict rose around the world, intervention continued to stir debate.

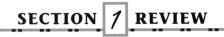

## SECTION 1 REVIEW

1. **Identify** (a) GATT, (b) NPT, (c) International Monetary Fund, (d) Universal Declaration of Human Rights, (e) Helsinki Agreement.
2. **Define** (a) nonaligned, (b) interdependence, (c) terrorism.
3. (a) Why did European nations lose their colonial empires after World War II? (b) What was one effect of the great liberation?
4. How did the Cold War become global?
5. Why did political instability plague many Third World nations?
6. *Critical Thinking* **Predicting Consequences** Is interdependence likely to make the world more peaceful ? Why or why not?
7. *ACTIVITY* Design an invitation to an international conference on nuclear arms, terrorism, or human rights.

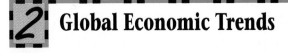

# 2 Global Economic Trends

## Guide for Reading

■ How is today's world divided along economic lines?

■ Why have developing nations made limited economic progress?

■ How are environmental and economic issues linked?

■ **Vocabulary** *multinational corporation, privatization, acid rain*

In 1969, Pope Paul VI expressed what he saw as a troubling mix of successes and failures in the modern age:

&&Ours is a time of problems, of gigantic problems. Everything is being transformed under the magic influence of science and technology. And every day, if we want to live with open eyes, we have a problem to study, to resolve.&&

As new nations won independence, they aspired to the high standard of living in the industrial world. Since the 1950s, however, a growing gulf has divided the world into rich and poor nations. A few developing nations have done well. Many others have not. In today's interdependent world, the stories of rich and poor nations are closely linked.

## *The Global North and South: Two Worlds of Development*

The Cold War created an ideological split between the communist East and the capitalist West. Today, an economic gulf divides the world into two spheres—the relatively rich nations of the global North and the relatively poor nations of the global South.

**Rich nations.** The global North includes the industrial nations of Western Europe and North America, as well as Japan and Australia. Most are located in the temperate zone north of the Equator. They control most of the world's wealth. Although pockets of poverty exist, the

# World Economy, 1990s

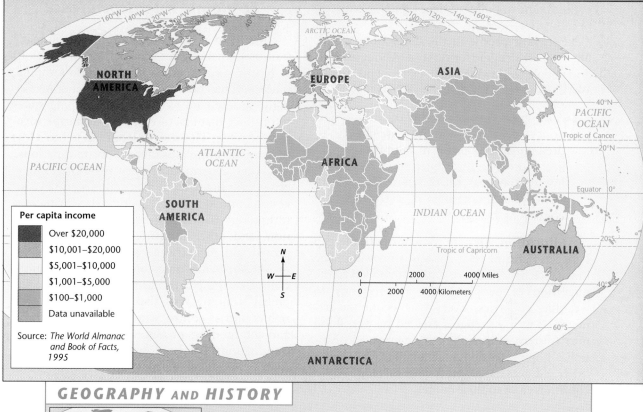

**Per capita income**
- Over $20,000
- $10,001–$20,000
- $5,001–$10,000
- $1,001–$5,000
- $100–$1,000
- Data unavailable

Source: *The World Almanac and Book of Facts, 1995*

## GEOGRAPHY AND HISTORY

*Per capita income is one measure of a country's wealth. By comparing the per capita income of different countries, you can make inferences about the well-being of people in those countries.*

**1. Location** On the map, locate (a) South America, (b) Europe, (c) Asia, (d) Africa, (e) North America.

**2. Region** (a) In which region do you find most of the countries with per capita income under $1,000? (b) In which region do you find most of the countries with per capita income over $10,000?

**3. Critical Thinking  Applying Information** How does this map illustrate the idea of the global North and global South?

standard of living in the North is generally high. Most people are literate, earn adequate wages, and have basic health services. Rich nations have a lower birthrate and higher life expectancy than do the nations of the global South. (★ See *Skills for Success,* page 844.)

With a few exceptions, such as socialist Sweden, most rich nations have basically capitalist economies. Economic decisions about what to produce and for whom are generally regulated by the free market, not by the government. Still, their governments support economic growth through transportation and communication systems, public education, and social services.

**Poor nations.** The global South refers to the developing world. Most of these nations lie in Asia, Africa, and Latin America in the zone between the tropics of Cancer and Capricorn. (See the map above.) The South has three quarters of the world's population and much of its natural resources. Some nations have enjoyed strong growth, especially the Asian "tigers"— Taiwan, Hong Kong, Singapore, and South Korea—and the oil-exporting nations of the Middle East. Overall, though, the global South remains generally poor and underdeveloped. Unlike the nations that industrialized in the 1700s and 1800s, newer nations have not had enough time to build up their capital, resources, or industries.

For most people in the developing world, life is a daily struggle for survival. About one billion people worldwide live in extreme poverty. A World Bank report noted:

> 66 A disproportionate number of [the poor]—perhaps two in five—are children under ten, mainly in large families. More than three quarters of them live in rural areas, the rest in urban slums—but almost all in very crowded conditions. 99

**Migration.** Despite some growth, the gap between rich and poor nations is growing. The imbalance has created resentment and led to the migration of people from poor regions to wealthier countries. Every year, economic refugees, as well as refugees created by war, flood into Western Europe, North America, and Australia, hoping to find a better life. Millions of other refugees, however, remain in Third World countries close to their homes.

*Looking for a Home* By the 1990s, there were more than 18 million refugees around the world. Here, a Vietnamese child peers out from behind the barbed wire at a crowded refugee camp in Hong Kong. **Global Interaction** What conditions cause people to flee their homelands?

## Economic Interdependence

Rich and poor nations are linked by many trade and financial ties. The nations of the global North control much of the world's capital, trade, and technology. But they depend increasingly on low-paid workers in developing states to produce manufactured goods as inexpensively as possible. This shift in labor has led to a loss of manufacturing jobs in many western nations.

Huge multinational corporations, enterprises with branches in many countries, have invested in the developing world. They bring new technology to mining, agriculture, transportation, and other industries. Rich nations also provide aid, technical advisers, and loans.

At the same time, however, poor nations claim that the North has a stranglehold on the global economy. With their great buying power, rich countries control the prices of most goods and commodities produced by the South. Also, multinational corporations remove many profits from developing countries and often limit workers' attempts to seek higher wages. As a result, some emerging nations see interdependence as a new form of imperialism.

**The oil crisis.** In an interdependent world, events in one country or region can affect people everywhere. A drastic example of this was the oil crisis of the early 1970s. All nations use oil for transportation and for products ranging from plastics to fertilizers. This demand has allowed nations with oil resources—from Venezuela to Britain—to seek the most favorable prices on the world market.

Much of the world's oil comes from the Middle East. In 1973, a political crisis in the Middle East led the Organization of Petroleum Exporting Countries (OPEC) to halt oil exports and then raise oil prices. (You will read more about the roots of this crisis in Chapter 35.) Oil shortages and soaring oil prices set off economic shock waves in industrialized nations. Suddenly, people in the United States and other nations realized how much they depended on imported oil. While some efforts were made to find other fuels or to conserve energy use, the energy crisis showed what impact a single vital product could have on the world economy.

**The debt crisis.** The oil crisis fed into another global economic development. Higher oil

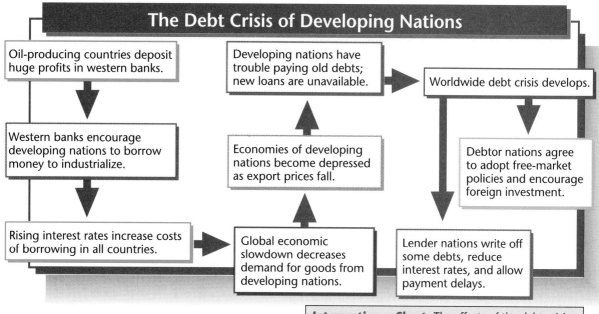

## The Debt Crisis of Developing Nations

Oil-producing countries deposit huge profits in western banks.

↓

Western banks encourage developing nations to borrow money to industrialize.

↓

Rising interest rates increase costs of borrowing in all countries.

→

Global economic slowdown decreases demand for goods from developing nations.

↑

Economies of developing nations become depressed as export prices fall.

↑

Developing nations have trouble paying old debts; new loans are unavailable.

→

Worldwide debt crisis develops.

↓

Debtor nations agree to adopt free-market policies and encourage foreign investment.

Lender nations write off some debts, reduce interest rates, and allow payment delays.

*Interpreting a Chart* The effects of the debt crisis varied from country to country. In general, though, the pressure of falling prices and high interest rates had a devastating effect on developing economies.
■ According to the flowchart, why did debtor nations have trouble repaying their loans?

prices brought riches to OPEC members. They deposited their oil earnings in western banks, which in turn invested the money to earn high interest.

Poor nations, needing capital to modernize, took loans offered by western banks. In the 1980s, however, bank interest rates rose, while the world economy slowed down. As demand for many of their goods fell, poor nations were unable to repay their debts or even the interest on their loans. Their economies stalled as they spent all their income from exports on payments to their foreign creditors.

The debt crisis hurt rich nations, too, as banks were stuck with billions of dollars of bad debts. The losses threatened the whole world financial system. To ease the crisis, the International Monetary Fund, the World Bank, and private banks worked out agreements with debtor nations. Lenders lowered interest rates or gave some nations more time to repay the loans. In some cases, debts were even canceled altogether.

In return, debtor nations had to agree to adopt free-market policies. Many turned from socialism to privatization, selling off state-owned industries to private investors. Nations hoped that more efficient private enterprises would produce higher-quality goods in the long run. Still, the immediate effects of privatization often hurt the poor, as debtor nations cut social programs. The imposed reforms sparked resentment against the IMF and the West.

## Obstacles to Development

While some developing nations have made progress toward modernization, others have not. Why have they failed to achieve their economic goals? The answers vary from country to country, but many shared problems in five general areas: (1) geography, (2) population and poverty, (3) economic dependence, (4) economic policies, (5) political instability.

**Geography.** In parts of Africa, Asia, and Latin America, geography has posed an obstacle to progress. For example, some newly created African countries are tiny and have few natural resources. Difficult climates, uncertain rainfall, lack of good farmland, and disease have added to the problems of some nations.

**Population and poverty.** The population boom that began in the 1700s has continued. Better medical care and increased food supplies have reduced death rates and led to explosive population growth. In the developing world, though, rapid growth is linked to poverty. Each year, the populations of countries like Nigeria, Egypt, and India increase by millions. All those people need food, housing, education, jobs, and medical care. Meeting the needs of so many people puts a staggering burden on developing nations.

Another result of the population boom is that the world's population has become younger. About half the people alive today are under the age of 25. In developing nations, the percentage can be even higher. Each year, tens of thousands of people in these countries begin looking for work. Often, there are not enough jobs. At the same time, these young people begin raising new families.

Across the developing world, people are caught in a cycle of poverty. Many suffer hunger. An estimated 35 million people die each year from illnesses related to hunger. Children are the most vulnerable. According to the UN, 35,000 children die each day from malnutrition, disease, and other effects of poverty.

Many developing nations have tried to slow population growth. But few countries, except China, want to force people to limit family size. In many cultures, having children is a status symbol. In farming societies, children are a source of labor. They are seen as an insurance policy to support their parents in old age. Religious traditions often encourage large families. Also, despite education efforts, many people still lack information about or access to family planning.

**Economic dependence.** The economic patterns established during the Age of Imperialism did not change after 1945. Most new nations remained dependent on their former colonial rulers. As you read, they sold agricultural products and raw materials to the industrial world. In turn, they relied on the West for manufactured goods, technology, and investment. Also, many new nations had only a single export crop or commodity, such as sugar, cocoa, or copper. Their economies prospered or fell depending on world demand for the product.

As you have read, developing nations borrowed heavily from foreign banks. These funds were intended for development. Once in debt, though, nations had to spend much of their resources to pay interest.

**Economic policies.** After independence, many new nations expected that socialism, rather than capitalism, would help them modernize quickly. They modeled their economic policies on those of China or the Soviet Union, which had made rapid gains in a short period. Under socialism, the government controls the economy. Since these nations had little private capital, only the government could raise the money—through loans, taxes, and controlling profits from labor—to finance large-scale development projects.

Emerging nations made some gains in the 1950s and 1960s. But in the long run, socialism frequently hindered economic growth. As you have read, under international pressure, many emerging nations introduced free-market policies in the 1980s.

**Political instability.** Civil wars and other struggles prevented economic development. El Salvador in Central America, Lebanon in the Middle East, Cambodia in Southeast Asia, and Mozambique in Africa are among a number of nations devastated by civil wars. Military dictators or other authoritarian leaders spent huge sums on weapons and warfare instead of on education, housing, or health care.

War created millions of refugees living in camps both inside and outside their home countries. The loss of their labor has further hurt war-torn countries.

## Economic Development and the Environment

For both rich and poor nations, economic development has been achieved at great cost to the natural environment. Modern industry and agriculture have gobbled up natural resources and polluted the world's water, air, and soil.

**Growing threats.** Since earliest times, people everywhere have taken what they wanted from their environment. In the past, damage was limited because the world's population was relatively small and technology was simple. With the Industrial Revolution and the population explosion, the potential for widespread environmental damage grew.

By the 1970s, conservationists raised the alarm about threats to the planet's fragile environment. Strip mining provided vital ores for industry but destroyed much land. Chemical fertilizers and pesticides produced more food crops but harmed the soil and water. Oil spills polluted oceans, lakes, and rivers. Gases from power plants and factories produced acid rain, a

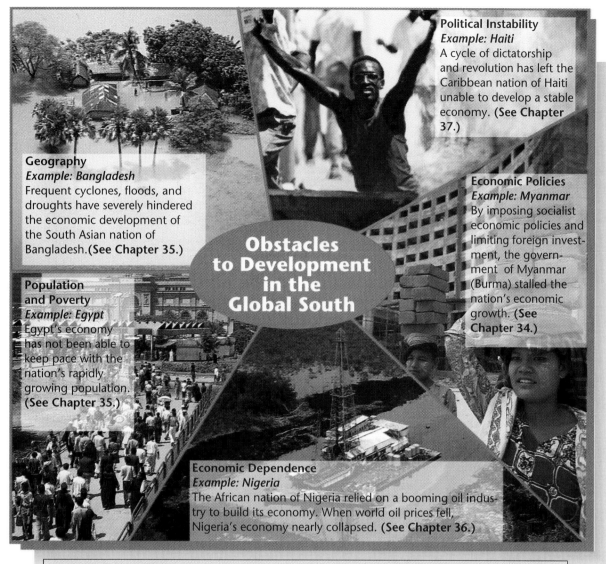

**Geography**
*Example: Bangladesh*
Frequent cyclones, floods, and droughts have severely hindered the economic development of the South Asian nation of Bangladesh. **(See Chapter 35.)**

**Political Instability**
*Example: Haiti*
A cycle of dictatorship and revolution has left the Caribbean nation of Haiti unable to develop a stable economy. **(See Chapter 37.)**

**Obstacles to Development in the Global South**

**Economic Policies**
*Example: Myanmar*
By imposing socialist economic policies and limiting foreign investment, the government of Myanmar (Burma) stalled the nation's economic growth. **(See Chapter 34.)**

**Population and Poverty**
*Example: Egypt*
Egypt's economy has not been able to keep pace with the nation's rapidly growing population. **(See Chapter 35.)**

**Economic Dependence**
*Example: Nigeria*
The African nation of Nigeria relied on a booming oil industry to build its economy. When world oil prices fell, Nigeria's economy nearly collapsed. **(See Chapter 36.)**

**Interpreting a Chart** *This chart gives just one example for each of the five obstacles to development described in this chapter. In Chapters 33–37, you will read about these examples and others in more detail.* ■ *How can political instability contribute to economic instability?*

form of pollution in which toxic chemicals in the air come back to the Earth as rain, snow, or hail. Acid rain damaged forests, lakes, and farmland, especially in industrial Europe and North America. The chart on page 836 outlines other challenges to the world's environment.

Some scientists warned of "global warming" caused by the increased emission of gases into the upper atmosphere. Global warming, they thought, could change the Earth's climate, melting the polar icecaps. This would flood low-lying areas, including most major coastal cities. Not all scientists, however, accepted the global warming theory.

**Industrial accidents.** Major accidents focused attention on threats to the environment. In Bhopal, India, a leak from a pesticide plant in 1984 killed 3,600 people and injured 100,000. In 1986, an accident at the Chernobyl nuclear power plant in the Soviet Union exposed people, crops, and animals to deadly radiation—from Ukraine into other parts of Europe and Turkey. An American oil tanker spill in 1989 destroyed much marine life off the coast of Alaska.

In response to such disasters, technicians have developed measures to increase safety. However, such measures do not always succeed, and companies often resist the expense.

# Global Environmental Challenges

| | Causes | Effects | Outlook for the Future |
|---|---|---|---|
| **Air and Water Pollution** | Auto and factory emissions; dumping of waste; leeching of pesticides into ground water; release of chlorofluorocarbons (CFCs) | Thinning ozone layer; acid rain; poisoned water supplies; human diseases | Although there are few internationally recognized guidelines, nations are seeking ways to reduce pollution while containing costs. Recycling, treatment, and new technologies are promising approaches. |
| **Deforestation** | Overforesting to harvest trees or to build roads, farms, and cities | Change in local weather; less absorption of carbon dioxide; soil erosion; extinction of plants and animals | Balancing economic needs with preservation of forests is a global challenge that requires research and cooperation among local peoples, businesses, governments, and the international community. |
| **Desertification** | Overfarming, overgrazing, and climate shifts that have caused deserts, such as the Sahara, to grow | Reduced arable land; hunger | Famines in Africa have brought the problem to international attention. New farming methods, including improved irrigation, may slow the process of desertification |
| **Endangered Plants and Animals** | Human alterations to landscape through land clearing, river damming, and building; pollution; overfishing; hunting animals for profit; slash-and-burn agriculture | Ecosystem imbalance; loss of resources for food and medicines | International agreements have banned shipment and sale of endangered species. Some people favor preserving habitats as a way of protecting endangered and other species. |
| **Waste Disposal** | Proliferation of waste because of population growth and industrial production; use of nuclear power; overuse of packaging on consumer goods | Pollution of ground water and oceans; health hazards; endangering of plant and animal species; full landfills | Solutions include conservation, recycling, waste reduction, new landfills, and incineration. Cooperation among people can help reduce unnecessary waste. |

*Interpreting a Chart* Identifying environmental problems has been easier than solving them. Often, the long-term effects must be measured against short-term goals, such as preserving jobs or feeding the population. ■ *Describe how rapid population growth has contributed to two of the problems shown on the chart.*

**Protecting the environment.** Rich nations, the greatest consumers of natural resources, produce much of the world's pollution. At the same time, they have also led the campaign to protect the environment. They have passed some laws to control pollution and ensure conservation in their own countries.

In 1992, the UN sponsored the Conference on the Environment, or Earth Summit, in Rio de Janeiro, Brazil. World leaders discussed how to clean up and preserve the planet. They agreed to restrain damage but disagreed over who was responsible and who should pay for it. Many other issues were hotly debated. Should economic development take priority over protecting the environment? Are people, especially in rich nations, willing to do with less in order to preserve the environment? How can emerging nations afford costly safeguards?

As the twentieth century neared its end, many people agreed that permanent damage to the planet was too high a price to pay for economic progress. Agreeing on solutions, however, is a challenge for present and future generations. (☑ See *You Decide*, "What Is the Relationship Between People and the Environment?" pages 980–981.)

## SECTION 2 REVIEW

1. **Identify** (a) OPEC, (b) Chernobyl, (c) Earth Summit.
2. **Define** (a) multinational corporation, (b) privatization, (c) acid rain.
3. How do the global North and global South differ?
4. Why have emerging nations had difficulty reaching their goals?
5. How has economic development increased the potential for widespread damage to the environment? Give two examples.
6. *Critical Thinking* **Applying Information** Describe how each of the following showed interdependence: (a) the oil crisis of the 1970s, (b) the debt crisis of the 1980s.
7. *ACTIVITY* Design a board game on economic development. Spaces on the board might indicate rewards and pitfalls.

# 3 Changing Patterns of Life

## Guide for Reading

- Why has urbanization disrupted older ways of life?
- How has modernization affected the lives of women?
- What are the benefits and limits of modern science and technology?
- How has technology helped shape a new global culture?
- **Vocabulary** *liberation theology*

In recent decades, hundreds of millions of people have migrated from rural villages to urban centers. For many, the anonymity and fast pace of city life required difficult adjustments. The Vietnamese poet Nguyen Sa wrote:

> **❝**I must get far away from this city
> with its soot-streaked curbs
> and people who pass each other
> of a Monday morning
> without a smile or a word.
> 'No time! I have no time!'**❞**

Urbanization has transformed the lives of people in the developing world just as it did in Europe during the Industrial Revolution. First, though, we will look at how the village continues to shape the lives of millions of people.

### The Village: Continuity and Change

The village is close-set houses made of stones, clay bricks, or sticks plastered over with mud, roofed with thatch, palm leaves, tile, or tin. It is hard-packed earthen paths crossed by bare feet, sandals, or perhaps a bicycle or two. It is water from a village well, vegetables from a back garden, chickens or goats in the yard. It is

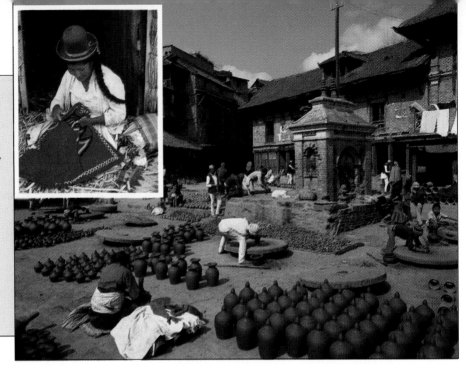

**Village Life** *In villages around the world, economic activities often reflect centuries-old patterns. At right, potters display their wares at an outdoor market in the South Asian kingdom of Nepal. Above, a Peruvian Indian weaves a mat in the doorway of her cottage.* **Continuity and Change** *What forces are changing village life?*

dust, heat, and insects. It is also families, neighbors, and an enduring way of life.

Village people continue to form the largest part of the world's population—about 3.3 billion of the 5.7 billion people on Earth. Most of them live in the global South. Their lives vary widely, depending on climate, geographic isolation, or other factors. Still, similar patterns link village people from Uruguay to Malaysia.

**Enduring ways.** The day may begin before sunrise, with the sound of a rooster crowing. If the village is in a Muslim land, a muezzin may call villagers to predawn prayer. Or the church bells of a Latin American village may announce the start of early mass.

As the morning goes on, children in school uniforms race toward the crossroads to catch the bus, their books swinging behind them in straps or satchels. At the stream, women who do not yet own washing machines slap wet clothes against a rock and lay them out on the grass to dry. Other young women and men labor in fields, workshops, or markets. Many will have sore backs by noon.

Later, people gather at small open-fronted shops around the village square. In tropical regions, lizards may crawl along the walls and ceiling—a welcome addition because each lizard eats several times its weight in flies and mosquitoes. Customers look among the various goods piled here and there. One jokes with the clerk. Another gives news of his daughter attending a university in a far-off city. In times of crisis, villagers gather anxiously around the storekeeper's radio.

**Changing patterns.** Many village ways have endured for centuries. But decades of urbanization, westernization, and new technology have left their mark. Indian writer Prafulla Mohanti noted:

> 66My village is changing. A straight road was built in the mid-1960s to carry iron ore from the mines to the port of Paradip, 40 miles away. . . . Nylon, stainless steel, plastic, fizzy drinks have reached the village. Electricity has come, too . . . there is a cinema and video hall.99

While such changes enrich village life, they also weaken traditional cultures. Supermarkets—efficient but impersonal—threaten village grocers. Worse, more and more young people are leaving the village for the wider vistas of the city.

Still, the village goes on. Life is not easy. Sometimes it is cruelly harsh. Yet for millions of market women and teachers, healers and matchmakers, children and old people, the village remains a vital center of existence. ■

## Old Ways and New

In the western world, industrialization and urbanization began more than 200 years ago during the Industrial Revolution. Since 1945, the rest of the world has experienced similar upheavals.

**Urbanization.** People in the developing world have flocked to the cities to find jobs and escape rural poverty. Cities offer not only economic opportunities but also attractions such as pop music concerts, stores, and sports.

With no money and few jobs, some newcomers cannot afford to ride buses or go to movies. Instead, most settle in shantytowns that ring the cities. These slums are as crowded and dangerous as European cities were in the 1800s. They lack even basic services such as paving, running water, or sewage. Drugs and crime are ever-present threats. Today, millions of people struggle to survive in these conditions.

In cities, the traditional extended family of rural villages is giving way to the nuclear family. As urban children attend school and become literate, they often reject their parents' ways. Without the support of the village and extended family, older beliefs and values are undermined by urban values such as material wealth, education, and job status. People who move from villages to cities frequently suffer a sense of overwhelming stress and isolation, often called culture shock.

**Westernization.** In the cities, people adopted western fashions and ideas. During the Age of Imperialism, you will recall, westerners taught that their civilization was superior. Even after independence, many people in emerging nations felt that the way to modernize was to follow western models.

Some early nationalists, such as Mohandas Gandhi, rejected the rush to abandon traditional ways. Today, leaders in some Muslim lands have called for modernization without westernization. Although they welcome modern technology, they want to preserve older traditions and religious beliefs. They reject western emphasis on material success and the individual, which they feel undermines the community and family.

**Religious influences.** Despite revolutionary changes, many traditions remain strong. The major world religions and their offshoots still shape modern societies. (See the pictures on page 840.) Since the 1980s, religious revivals have swept many regions. Christian, Muslim, Buddhist, and Hindu reformers have offered their own solutions to the problems of today's world. Some of these reformers have been called fundamentalists because they stress what they see as the fundamental, or basic, values of their religions. Many have sought increased political power in an effort to resist changes that they feel threaten their beliefs.

In the West, evangelical Protestant sects have emphasized salvation through faith and preaching, offering spiritual guidelines in a rapidly changing world. In the 1960s, the Second Vatican Council gave Roman Catholics more freedom to discuss issues and promoted cooperation with other Christian faiths. In Latin America, some Roman Catholic clergy adopted a movement called liberation theology. They urged the Church to take a more active role in opposing the social conditions that contributed to poverty. Conservative Catholic forces have often opposed such political activities. (You will read more about the role of the Church in Latin America in Chapter 37.)

In Muslim countries, too, religious reformers called on governments to work for social improvements. Some Muslim leaders rejected westernization and secular goals. Instead, they insisted that government and society should be based on strict obedience to the Sharia, or Islamic religious law. (See Chapter 35.)

## New Rights and Roles for Women

After 1945, women's movements brought changes to both the western and developing worlds. The UN Charter included a commitment to work for "equal rights for men and women." By 1950, women had won the right to

---

**GLOBAL CONNECTIONS**

Urbanization and other changes are threatening many of the world's languages. About 6,000 different languages are spoken in the world today. Many are spoken only in isolated rural areas or remote islands. As families migrate to cities or other countries, their children often grow up speaking a dominant tongue, such as English, Hindi, or Spanish. In the next century, 90 to 95 percent of all current languages may become extinct. Scholars are now working to preserve many of these disappearing languages.

**Enduring Traditions** *In spite of wars, persecutions, and the pressures of modern life, religion remains a powerful force in the modern world. At right, Muslims in Mali engage in their daily prayers. At left, a Roman Catholic bishop conducts a church service in China.* **Religions and Value Systems** *What other religions have millions of followers in the world today?*

vote in most European nations, as well as in Japan, China, Brazil, and other nations. In most African nations, women and men won the vote at the same time, at independence.

A small but growing number of women won elected office. Women headed democratic governments in Britain, Israel, India, Pakistan, the Philippines, and other countries. Yet in 1985, a report to a UN Conference on Women noted that while women represent half of the world's people, "they perform nearly two thirds of all working hours, receive only one tenth of the world's income, and own less than one percent of world property."

**The West.** In the industrial world, more and more women worked outside the home and gradually won equal access to education. By the 1970s, a strong feminist movement sought equal access to jobs and promotions, equal pay for equal work, and an end to sexual harassment on the job. Women moved into high-profile jobs as business owners and executives, astronauts, scientists, or technicians.

Yet new roles for women raised difficult social issues. Working women had to balance jobs outside the home with child rearing and household work. A growing need emerged for affordable day care. Some critics charged that the growth in the female work force was partly responsible for rising divorce rates and a decline in family life. Others responded that many families required two incomes.

**Developing nations.** In emerging nations, women worked actively in the nationalist struggles. Their constitutions spelled out equality between women and men, at least on paper.

While women still had less education than men, the gap was narrowing. Women from the middle and elite classes entered the work force in growing numbers. Their skills and labor contributed to their nations' wealth.

At the same time, women generally shouldered a heavy burden of work inside and around the home. In many places, religious and cultural traditions kept women confined to the home or segregated men and women in the workplace.

In rural areas, especially in Africa, women have traditionally done much of the agricultural work along with household tasks. In recent years, men have gone to the cities to find work, leaving women with added responsibilities. According to one report on Kenya, one third of all rural households are headed by women:

66Everywhere one sees women walking to market with basketloads of vegetables on their heads, infants strapped to their backs, and older children following behind. Even while they walk to market, these women often are weaving baskets or fashioning other handiwork . . . to exchange for cash needed for the family's support or the children's education.99

In other regions, such as Southeast Asia, it is often the women who leave home to work. Their wages go to keep the family on the farm or pay for the education of their brothers.

## Science and Technology

Since 1945, technology has transformed human life and thought. Instant communication via satellites has shrunk the globe. New forms of energy, especially nuclear power, have been added to the steam power, electricity, and gasoline energy of the first industrial age.

**The computer revolution.** The computer is among the most revolutionary developments of the past 50 years. The first electronic computers, built in the 1940s, were huge, slow machines. Later, the computer was miniaturized thanks to inventions like the silicon chip.

Computers led to an information revolution. By the 1990s, a growing computer network linked individuals, governments, and businesses around the world. Computerized robots operated in factories, while computers appeared in more and more homes and schools. Multinational electronics and software companies often depended on labor in developing nations. Still, access to computers added to the gap between the global North and South.

**The space age.** In October 1957, the space age began when the Soviet Union launched *Sputnik,* a tiny satellite, into orbit. *Sputnik* set off a frantic "space race" between the superpowers. In 1969, the United States landed the first man on the moon. Both superpowers explored the military uses of space and sent spy satellites to orbit the Earth. In the post–Cold War world, however, the United States and Russia turned to cooperation and launched joint space ventures.

Other European nations, as well as Japan and China, launched their own satellites. By then, satellites had many peaceful uses. They mapped weather and tracked droughts, livestock diseases, and plagues. In the weightlessness of space, scientists experimented with promising new drugs and vaccines.

**Medical breakthroughs.** In the postwar era, medicine achieved amazing successes. Scientists developed new antibiotics to treat illnesses. Vaccines wiped out some diseases like

**The View From Outer Space** *High above the Earth's atmosphere, American astronauts repair the Hubble Space Telescope in December 1993. Once fixed, the orbiting observatory sent astonishingly clear pictures of faraway galaxies back to scientists on Earth.* **Economics and Technology** *Do you think countries should spend large sums of money learning about outer space? Why or why not?*

smallpox and prevented the spread of others. In the 1980s and 1990s, however, new challenges arose with the spread of deadly new diseases such as ebola and AIDS.

In the 1970s, surgeons learned to transplant organs to save lives. Lasers made surgery safer. Scientists also made headway in treating some cancers. Yet advances in medicine were costly and usually limited to people and nations that could afford them.

A controversial area of research is genetic engineering. It involves altering the chemical codes carried by all living things. In medicine, such research has produced important drug therapies to treat diseases. Still, genetic engineering has raised ethical issues about how far science should go to create and change life.

**The Green Revolution.** Scientists applied new technology to increasing food production for the world's growing population. During the 1960s, they touched off the Green Revolution, developing new kinds of rice and other grains that yielded more food per acre than older strains. In India, Indonesia, and elsewhere, the Green Revolution doubled food output.

The Green Revolution had limits, however. It succeeded only in areas with regular moisture. Also, it required chemical fertilizers and pesticides as well as irrigation systems, which only wealthy farmers with large acreage could afford. Thus, many poor peasants did not benefit from the new technology. Many were forced off their small farms, unable to compete with larger, more efficient agricultural enterprises.

**Enduring issues.** Technology has improved life for people everywhere. Many people, especially in the industrial world, pin their hopes on technology to solve a variety of economic, medical, and environmental problems. Yet it has not solved such basic problems as hunger or poverty. Also, while technology has created many new kinds of jobs, it has threatened others. For example, a single computer can process thousands of telephone calls that were once handled by human operators.

## A New International Culture

"Radio has changed everything," noted Egyptian leader Gamal Abdel Nasser in the 1950s. "Today, people in the most remote villages hear of what is happening and form their opinions." Modern communications technology has indeed created "a new world." Radio, television, satellites, fax machines, and computer networks have put people everywhere in touch and helped create a global culture.

**A westernized popular culture.** The driving force behind this new global culture has been the United States. Since World War II, American fads, fashions, music, and entertainment have captured the world's imagination. American movies and television programs play to audiences in Moscow, Beijing, Buenos Aires, and Cairo. Blue jeans, soft drinks, and fast foods

# PARALLELS THROUGH TIME

## Television

The first public television broadcasts were transmitted in 1936. Since then, television has become the most influential form of communication in the world.

**Linking Past and Present**  Today, more people get their news from television than from newspapers. What do you think are the advantages and disadvantages of television over earlier sources of information?

**PAST**  *In 1949, there were a million television sets in the United States. By 1953, there were over 20 million. That same year, the very first issue of TV Guide (left) had a cover story on television's most popular program,* I Love Lucy.

**PRESENT**  *Today, television reaches almost every corner of the world. Below, an Egyptian family watches a religious program. At right, French television listings include such American programs as* The Simpsons *and* Dr. Quinn, Medicine Woman.

first popularized in the United States are marketed around the world. English has become the leading language of international business.

In some countries, critics have compared this westernization of culture to a foreign invasion. Yet the new global culture sometimes balanced western and nonwestern traditions. From Latin America, popular music such as calypso and reggae gained international popularity. Movie makers like Japan's Akira Kurosawa and India's Satyajit Ray adapted western techniques to express their own distinct traditions.

**The arts.** Global exchanges have influenced literature and the visual arts for hundreds of years. By the 1700s, Europeans were copying Turkish carpets and Chinese pottery. A century later, European painters adapted Japanese printmaking traditions. About the same time, however, Japanese artists were studying the styles of European painters. More recently, writers from Africa to the Middle East to India have adapted western literary forms, such as the novel.

In the twentieth century, the western world gained a new appreciation for the arts of other civilizations. Western artists studied African and Southeast Asian sculptures, dances, and music. Collectors valued Persian or Chinese paintings as well as ancient Mayan or Incan works.

**Preserving ancient cultures.** Global interest in the arts has made nations realize the value of ancient cultural treasures. The UN and other groups are helping countries preserve and restore temples, palaces, manuscripts, and other artifacts. Museums, too, preserve the heritage of past cultures. Traveling exhibits of Egyptian jewelry, Russian icons, Native American carvings, Indian sculpture, or African masks help modern audiences understand cultures from other times and places.

## Looking Ahead

Many current trends and issues emerged long before 1945 and will continue beyond 2000. At the same time, new issues and conflicts will almost certainly take shape in the new millennium, or thousand-year period, that begins after the year 2000.

The next five chapters trace how the trends discussed in this chapter have affected different regions. As you read, notice how two contradic-

ART HISTORY

**M.K. III** *The modern fascination with technology led to a new art form called kinetic, or moving, sculpture. Using parts found in junkyards, Swiss artist Jean Tinguely created elaborate, machinelike constructions like this one. Powered by electric motors, Tinguely's sculptures moved, made noise, or even produced abstract paintings. Others were designed to self-destruct!* **Art and Literature** *How do sculptures like this poke fun at modern machines?*

tory trends are shaping the world. Nationalism is on the rise. Yet global interdependence has become an inescapable fact of life. In many nations and regions, people must reconcile local and global interests.

## SECTION 3 REVIEW

1. **Define** liberation theology.
2. How has urbanization affected people in developing nations?
3. Describe two ways in which women's lives have changed in recent decades.
4. Describe how three developments in science or technology have affected the modern world.
5. How have American influences helped shape a new global culture?
6. *Critical Thinking* **Predicting Consequences** What do you think might be some major global issues of the next century?
7. *ACTIVITY* Imagine that you are a scholar, a business leader, or a teenager in a Third World nation. Draw a cartoon or poster expressing your feelings about westernization.

# Skills for Success

## Interpreting Statistical Tables

Statistics are numerical data. They always answer the questions *how much* or *how many*. Rainfall and temperature figures, bushels of grain produced per year, school enrollments, travel times between cities, population figures—all are examples of statistics.

Statistics can be arranged in a table for quick, easy comparison, analysis, and interpretation. However, you must be very careful when drawing conclusions from statistics. Precisely because the data appear so clear and concise, they can prove misleading in many ways.

The table below contains health statistics for 10 countries. Study the table, then answer the following questions.

**1** **Study the statistical data in the table.** (a) What information does the chart provide for each country? (b) In which country do women have the lowest life expectancy? The highest? (c) Which nation has the most physicians relative to the population? (d) Which country has the highest infant mortality rate?

**2** **Compare the data and look for relationships.** (a) What is the apparent relationship between the number of physicians per person and life expectancy? (b) What is the apparent relationship between hospital beds and life expectancy? (c) What statistics might have a relationship to infant mortality? Why? (d) Look at the map on page 831. Which countries on this chart are part of the global North? Which countries are part of the global South?

**3.** **Interpret the information.** (a) Why does life expectancy not seem to be related to size of the population? (b) Make two generalizations about the global North and the global South based on this table. (c) What other kinds of statistics might help you test this generalization?

*Beyond the Classroom* Consumer magazines often use statistical tables to compare the quality of products. Locate a statistical table in a recent issue of a consumer magazine. Use the table to determine which of the described products you would buy. Then, read the article to find out how your choice compares with the magazine's.

## Health Statistics of Selected Countries, 1994

| Country | Population (thousands) | Life Expectancy at Birth (male/female) | Hospital Beds (per 1,000 people) | Physicians (per 1,000 people) | Infant Mortality (deaths per 1,000) |
|---|---|---|---|---|---|
| Argentina | 33,913 | 68/75 | 4.9 | 3.1 | 29 |
| Australia | 18,077 | 74/81 | 5.0 | 2.3 | 7 |
| Guatemala | 10,721 | 62/67 | * | 0.4 | 54 |
| Japan | 125,107 | 76/82 | 13.5 | 1.7 | 4 |
| Jordan | 3,961 | 70/74 | 1.8 | 1.2 | 32 |
| Myanmar | 44,277 | 58/62 | 0.6 | 0.3 | 64 |
| Netherlands | 15,368 | 75/81 | 5.9 | 2.5 | 6 |
| Poland | 38,655 | 69/77 | 8.5 | 2.2 | 13 |
| United States | 260,714 | 72/79 | 4.7 | 2.5 | 10 |
| Zaire | 42,684 | 46/49 | 2.1 | 0.1 | 111 |

Source: *World Almanac and Book of Facts*                    * Data unavailable

CHAPTER **32** REVIEW

## Building Vocabulary

Choose *four* vocabulary words from this chapter. Then, write a sentence for each word, in which you define the word and describe its relation to the postwar world.

## Reviewing Chapter Themes

1. **Political and Social Systems** Describe how each of the following affected world politics: (a) the great liberation, (b) the Cold War.
2. **Global Interaction** Give three examples of global interdependence in the modern world.
3. **Economics and Technology** (a) How does the global North differ from the global South? (b) What conditions have slowed economic growth in developing nations?
4. **Geography and History** (a) Why has the environment become an area of growing concern in recent years? (b) Describe the causes and effects of one global environmental problem.
5. **Continuity and Change** (a) How has urbanization affected developing nations? (b) Why do some Third World leaders reject westernization?

## Thinking Critically

1. **Analyzing Information** (a) Why might lack of experience with representative government be a problem for developing nations? (b) Do you think democracy will help them solve their problems?
2. **Linking Past and Present** Review pages 473 and 485–486. How does the idea of universal human rights echo the French Declaration of the Rights of Man and the Citizen and the American Bill of Rights?
3. **Recognizing Causes and Effects** List two causes and two effects of the Third World debt crisis. (★ See *Skills for Success,* page 18.)
4. **Distinguishing Facts From Opinions** American President Harry Truman wrote, "The scientific and industrial revolution which began two centuries ago has . . . caught up the peoples of the globe in a common destiny. Two world-shattering wars have proved that no corner of the Earth can be isolated from the affairs of mankind." (a) Which parts of Truman's statement are facts? (b) Which parts are opinions? (c) Do you think Truman's facts support his opinions? Explain. (★ See *Skills for Success,* page 476.)
5. **Applying Information** "Educate a boy," says an African proverb, "and you educate a person. Educate a girl, and you educate a nation." (a) What does the proverb mean? (b) What does it assume about the role of women in society? (c) What goal could this proverb be used to support?
6. **Defending a Position** Do you think a government is justified in spending money to preserve its cultural heritage even when many of its people face poverty, hunger, or disease? Why or why not?

## For Your Portfolio

You are a staff writer on a magazine for teens. Your editor has asked you to do an article on cultural exchanges in contemporary times. Your assignment is to write a two-page feature showing how fashions, foods, music, art, and other aspects of lifestyle have helped create a global culture.

1. Review the information about cultural exchange in this chapter.
2. Check the *Readers' Guide to Periodical Literature* in the library to find other current articles on this subject.
3. As you do your research, look for photographs and other visual materials that will help illustrate your feature. For example, you might find a chart showing sales for reggae music or a photograph showing the popularity of blue jeans in another country.
4. Use your research notes to outline your article. Keep in mind the audience—young people your age—for the magazine.
5. Draft your article. Ask a classmate to act as your editor and make comments.
6. Prepare your revised article for publication. Be sure to include the visual materials that you found.

# CHAPTER 33

# Europe and North America

## (1945–Present)

## CHAPTER OUTLINE

1 The Western World: An Overview
2 The Western European Democracies
3 North American Prosperity
4 The Soviet Union: Rise and Fall
of a Superpower
5 A New Era in Eastern Europe

An East German farm woman told a visitor of her daring adventure in November 1989:

66One day last week, I took my bike and—just went over. I had to stop and laugh! I felt so strange. For 40 years we couldn't do something so simple. I just had to stop and laugh.99

All she had done was to ride a short distance across the border from East Germany into West Germany. But that simple action would have been impossible just a few weeks earlier. For decades, grim-faced guards and police dogs had patrolled the wasteland of barbed wire, mine fields, and concrete that divided east from west.

In the divided city of Berlin, a giant concrete wall kept East Berliners "at home." Time and again, East German guards obeyed orders to "shoot to kill" anyone trying to cross into West Berlin. Then, in November 1989, the unthinkable suddenly happened. As a wave of change engulfed the communist world, a million East Germans protested their communist government. "We are the people!" they chanted. "Democracy, now or never!"

Under growing pressure, the East German government opened the border. Families from both sides clambered up "the Wall" before hammers smashed its weather-pitted concrete into history. (See the picture on page 849.)

For almost a half century after World War II, the Cold War loomed over Europe. Under its shadow, Western Europe and North America enjoyed their most rapid and sustained economic growth since the Industrial Revolution. On both sides of the Atlantic, governments pushed through broad new social programs.

Communist Eastern Europe also rebuilt under the iron hand of Stalin. In the Soviet Union, economic growth slowed and then stagnated in the 1980s. Efforts at major reform unleashed forces that brought the collapse of communism and an end to the Soviet Union. In the post-Cold War world, Europe faced new challenges.

**FOCUS ON** these questions as you read:

■ **Economics and Technology**
How are global economic changes affecting the industrial West?

■ **Continuity and Change**
Why is Western Europe struggling with the issue of unity?

■ **Impact of the Individual**
How did individual leaders in Europe and North America reshape their nations?

■ **Political and Social Systems**
Why did communism collapse in the Soviet Union and Eastern Europe?

■ **Diversity**
Why have ethnic tensions in Europe increased since the end of the Cold War?

## TIME AND PLACE

***Western Prosperity*** *The western world we know today took shape after World War II. In Europe and North America, as well as in Japan, rapid economic growth transformed cities into shimmering temples of glass and steel. Television, satellites, and computers sped up the pace of life. As the world's richest and most powerful nation, the United States strongly influenced the cultures of other nations. American artist Richard Estes captures the look and feel of a modern city in his painting* Central Savings. ***Economics and Technology*** *How does the painting suggest the complexity of modern life?*

## HUMANITIES LINK

***Art History*** Roy Lichtenstein, *Preparedness* (page 859).
***Literature*** In this chapter, you will encounter passages from the following works of literature: Martin Luther King, Jr., "I Have a Dream" (page 861); Yevgeny Yevtushenko, "The Heirs of Stalin" (page 863).

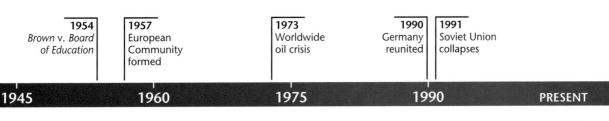

| 1954 | 1957 | 1973 | 1990 | 1991 |
| Brown v. Board of Education | European Community formed | Worldwide oil crisis | Germany reunited | Soviet Union collapses |

| 1945 | 1960 | 1975 | 1990 | PRESENT |

# 1 The Western World: An Overview

## Guide for Reading

- How did the Cold War pose a threat to Europe?

- How have economic cycles affected Europe?

- How did European nations pursue cooperation and peace?

- **Vocabulary** *détente, welfare state, service industry*

Western Europe rebounded out of the rubble of World War II. During the postwar years, standards of living rose dramatically. People earned higher wages, bought homes with central heating and running water, and enjoyed luxuries unheard of in earlier times. Amid these comforts, many other changes were shaping the western world.

## The Cold War in Europe

For more than 40 years, the Cold War divided Europe into two hostile military alliances. The communist nations of Eastern Europe, dominated by the Soviet Union, formed the Warsaw Pact. The western democracies, led by the United States, formed NATO. (See the map on page 811.) In general, the superpowers avoided direct confrontation in Europe. Yet several incidents brought the continent to the brink of war.

**The Berlin Wall.** Berlin remained a focus of Cold War tensions. The city was divided between democratic West Berlin and communist East Berlin. In the 1950s, West Berlin became a showcase for West Germany, whose economy boomed. Thousands of low-paid East Germans, many of them professionals who were discontented with communism, slipped across the border into prosperous West Berlin.

To stop its citizens from fleeing, the East German government built a wall in 1961 that separated the two sectors of the city. The Berlin

Wall grew into a massive concrete barrier, topped with barbed wire and patrolled by guards. It became an ugly symbol of the Cold War and a propaganda defeat for the Soviets. It showed that workers, far from enjoying a communist paradise, had to be forcibly restrained from fleeing. As you will see, revolts in Eastern Europe further shone a negative light on Soviet rule.

**The nuclear peril.** Over a 40-year period, the Cold War sometimes heated up and then cooled off. Each crisis triggered a new round in the arms race. Both sides produced huge arsenals of nuclear weapons. Europe, especially Germany, sat in the middle of this deadly weapons storehouse. If a "shooting" war erupted, it could be destroyed.

Critics denounced the buildup. A nuclear war, they said, would destroy both sides. Yet the superpowers argued that they dared not stop because each side wanted to have the power to deter the other from launching its nuclear weapons. The result was a "balance of terror."

**Disarmament and détente.** Both sides tried to avoid a nuclear showdown by holding disarmament talks. But mutual distrust often blocked progress. In 1963, the superpowers signed the Nuclear Test Ban Treaty, which prohibited the testing of nuclear weapons in the atmosphere. Underground testing was still permitted, however.

By the 1970s, American and Soviet leaders promoted an era of détente (day TAHNT), or relaxation of tensions. Détente brought new agreements to reduce nuclear stockpiles. Détente faced a severe setback, however, when the Soviet Union invaded Afghanistan in 1979.

The arms race had a huge cost. Both superpowers invested fantastic sums of money in

**GLOBAL CONNECTIONS**

In 1959, the United States and the Soviet Union joined 10 other nations—including Argentina, Australia, Japan, France, and South Africa—in signing the Antarctic Treaty. It forbade all parties from building military bases, testing nuclear weapons, or disposing of radioactive wastes on or around Antarctica. It also encouraged cooperation among scientists from all nations who conduct research on the continent. Other nations later agreed to the treaty.

building weapons systems. The Soviet Union spent a large portion of its budget on the military, which meant cutbacks in other areas of the economy. The United States, too, paid a large price to support its military preparedness. In 1953, President Dwight Eisenhower had warned:

66Every gun that is made, every warship launched, every rocket fired, signifies, in the final sense, a theft from those who hunger and are not fed, those who are cold and are not clothed. . . . The cost of one modern heavy bomber is this: a modern brick school in more than 30 cities.99

**A new era.** By the 1990s, as you will read, a new Soviet leader, Mikhail Gorbachev (mee kī EEL gor bah CHAWF), loosened the Soviet grip on Eastern Europe. One after another, communist governments collapsed, setting the stage for the ultimate collapse of the Soviet Union itself.

As the Cold War ended, nations in Western and Eastern Europe sought normal relations. Germany was reunited. The Warsaw Pact dissolved. NATO, originally formed to defend the West against communism, had to redefine its role in a post-Cold War world.

Even as Europeans celebrated the end of the Cold War, new issues arose. Many Eastern Europeans fled economic hardships to find work in the West. The newcomers were not always welcomed. Ethnic clashes, especially in the Balkans, created new tensions that threatened the peace of Europe.

## Recovery and Growth in Western Europe

With Marshall Plan aid, Western European countries recovered fairly quickly from World War II. They rebuilt industries, farms, and transportation networks destroyed by the war. In the 1950s, western economies boomed.

On the political front, right-wing parties, which had supported fascism, were discredited. In France, Italy, and Germany, communists and socialists had often led the resistance against the Nazis. Many postwar governments thus adopted policies favored by the left.

**The welfare state.** A major goal of leftist parties was to extend the welfare state. Under this system, a government keeps most features of a capitalist economy but takes greater responsibility for the social and economic needs of its people. The welfare state had its roots in the late 1800s, when governments passed reforms to ease the hardships of the industrial age. Germany, Britain, and other nations banned child labor, regulated mine safety, and set up public schools, unemployment insurance, and old-age pensions. (See Chapter 22.)

After 1945, governments expanded these programs. Both the middle class and the poor benefited from national health care, unemployment insurance, old-age pensions, and new policies that let any qualified student go to college. Other programs gave aid to the poor and created an economic cushion to help people through hard times. Still, the welfare state was costly, involving many new taxes and greater government regulation.

Socialists supported the welfare state and a larger role for government in the economy. In Britain, France, and elsewhere, governments nationalized basic industries such as railroads, airlines, banks, coal, steel, and nuclear power. Conservatives condemned the drift away from free enterprise toward socialism.

**The oil shock.** As you read in Chapter 32, the West was tied into a complex global economy. In 1973, the West suffered an economic jolt when OPEC cut oil production and raised prices. (See page 832.) Since most Western European countries used imported oil to fuel industries, the higher prices hurt. The oil crisis slowed economic growth. In 1979, OPEC again raised prices, triggering a severe recession. Factories and businesses cut back, and unemployment rose.

**Economic shifts.** At the same time, the West faced growing competition from other parts of the world. For 200 years, western factories had exported basic goods to the world. By the 1980s, however, the pattern changed. Japan, already an industrial power, enjoyed dra-

# PARALLELS THROUGH TIME

## When Leaders Meet

No Roman emperor ever met an emperor of China face to face. Queen Elizabeth I of England never sat down to dinner with the Ottoman sultan Suleiman. But today, leaders of great powers often get together to discuss war, peace, and the challenges of an interdependent world.

**Linking Past and Present**  Why is direct contact between world leaders easier today than in the past?

**PAST** *After World War I, the leaders of the three most powerful nations—David Lloyd George of Britain, Georges Clemenceau of France, and Woodrow Wilson of the United States—met at the Paris peace conference (right). At the height of the Cold War, leaders of the two superpowers held infrequent summit meetings to ease tensions. Below right, President John Kennedy shakes hands with Soviet leader Nikita Khrushchev.*

**PRESENT** *The Group of Seven (G-7), leaders of the seven most prosperous capitalist nations, meet annually to discuss issues of economic cooperation and competition. Above, the leaders of Germany, France, Britain, the United States, Canada, Japan, and Italy pose at their 1991 meeting in London.*

matic growth after World War II. Other countries, such as China and India, also expanded their industries. In addition, western-based multinational corporations set up factories in the developing world, where labor was cheap. From there, they exported goods to the West.

Older industries in the West could not compete with those cheaper production costs. Many factories had to close, throwing workers out of their jobs. Western nations remained rich and powerful, but their economies changed. Most new jobs at home were created not in manufacturing but in service industries. A service industry is one that provides a service rather than a product. Service industries include health care, finance, sales, education, and recreation.

The economic slowdown of the 1970s and 1980s forced governments to cut costs. Some moved away from the welfare state, reducing benefits. Conservative governments privatized state-owned industries. In the new economic climate, the gap between rich and poor grew, but most people still enjoyed a relatively high standard of living.

## Toward European Unity

Europe's recovery from World War II was helped by economic cooperation. In 1952, six nations—France, West Germany, Belgium, Italy, the Netherlands, and Luxembourg—set up the European Coal and Steel Community. This independent agency set prices and otherwise regulated the coal and steel industries of member states. This cooperation spurred economic growth across Western Europe.

**The Common Market.** In 1957, the same six nations signed a treaty to form the European Community (EC), or Common Market, to expand free trade. Over the next decades, the Common Market gradually ended tariffs on goods and allowed labor and capital to move freely across national borders. It set up the European Parliament, a multinational body elected by citizens of the Common Market countries. Its powers were limited, however, since member states remained independent.

**European Union.** Despite disputes between members, the Common Market prospered. In 1973, after much debate, Britain was admitted, along with Denmark and Ireland. In

## European Union

Members by
1957   1973   1981   1986   1995

### GEOGRAPHY AND HISTORY

The European Union, formerly known as the Common Market, created a vast free-trade zone across most of Western Europe.

1. **Location** On the map, locate (a) United Kingdom, (b) France, (c) Germany, (d) Denmark, (e) Ireland, (f) Belgium.
2. **Region** (a) How many nations belonged to the European Union by 1973? (b) Which nations shown on the map joined most recently?
3. **Critical Thinking** **Synthesizing Information** Compare this map to the map on page 990. (a) Which European nations were not members of the European Union by 1995? (b) Based on your reading, why were most of these nations not included?

the 1980s and 1990s, it expanded still further and took the name the European Union (EU). With the end of communism, some Eastern European nations were eager to join the EU.

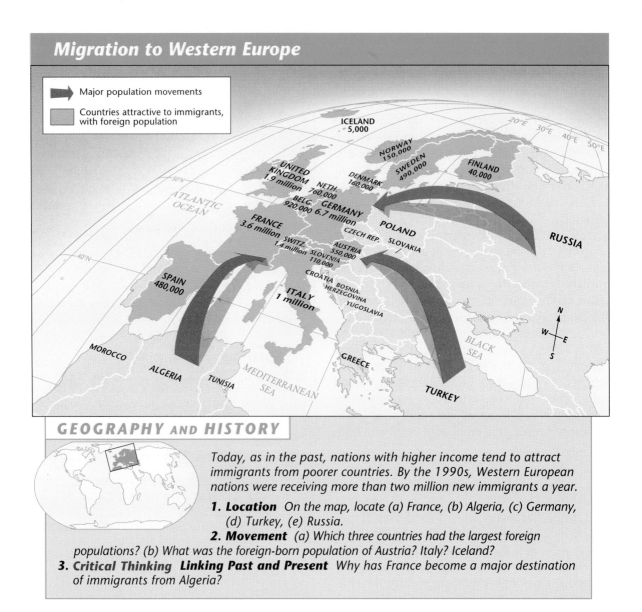

## Migration to Western Europe

**Legend:**
- Major population movements
- Countries attractive to immigrants, with foreign population

ICELAND 5,000
NORWAY 150,000
SWEDEN 490,000
FINLAND 40,000
UNITED KINGDOM 1.9 million
DENMARK 160,000
NETH. 760,000
BELG. 920,000
GERMANY 6.7 million
POLAND
CZECH REP.
SLOVAKIA
RUSSIA
FRANCE 3.6 million
SWITZ. 1.4 million
AUSTRIA 550,000
SLOVENIA 110,000
CROATIA BOSNIA-HERZEGOVINA
YUGOSLAVIA
SPAIN 480,000
ITALY 1 million
ATLANTIC OCEAN
MOROCCO
ALGERIA
TUNISIA
MEDITERRANEAN SEA
GREECE
TURKEY
BLACK SEA

### GEOGRAPHY AND HISTORY

*Today, as in the past, nations with higher income tend to attract immigrants from poorer countries. By the 1990s, Western European nations were receiving more than two million new immigrants a year.*

**1. Location** On the map, locate (a) France, (b) Algeria, (c) Germany, (d) Turkey, (e) Russia.

**2. Movement** (a) Which three countries had the largest foreign populations? (b) What was the foreign-born population of Austria? Italy? Iceland?

**3. Critical Thinking** **Linking Past and Present** Why has France become a major destination of immigrants from Algeria?

---

The EU became a powerful economic force. With just over 6 percent of the world's population, it controlled 37 percent of the world's trade. The EU also promoted regional peace by replacing destructive competition with an amazing degree of cooperation.

**Nationalism versus unity.** By the late 1990s, the EU was pushing for complete economic unity, a single currency, and greater political unity. EU members welcomed the benefits of cooperation. Still, nationalist feelings remained strong. Many British leaders, such as Margaret Thatcher, opposed increased links with Europe. In Denmark, too, voters opposed changes that they feared would destroy their unique identity. Thus, a United States of Europe seemed unlikely to emerge any time soon.

## Social Trends

The pace of social change speeded up after 1945. Class lines blurred as prosperity spread. For most of western history, a tiny wealthy class had dominated the majority of the people. By the 1950s, more and more people in the West belonged to the middle class. As wages rose, working-class people bought homes and cars, and their children could qualify to study at state-funded universities. Although grim pockets of poverty remained, most people had opportunities unknown in earlier times.

**Ethnic diversity.** Since the 1950s, many immigrants from former colonies in Asia, Africa, and the Caribbean settled in Europe. In Germany and elsewhere in Europe, "guest workers"

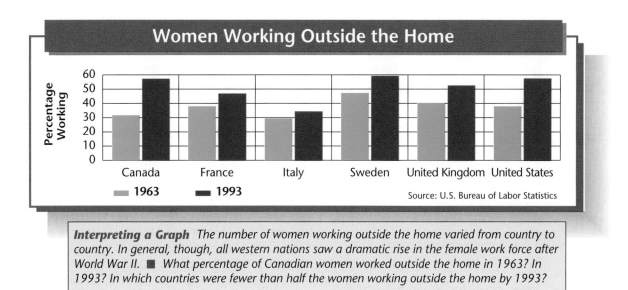

## Women Working Outside the Home

**Percentage Working**

| | Canada | France | Italy | Sweden | United Kingdom | United States |

■ **1963** ■ **1993**

Source: U.S. Bureau of Labor Statistics

**Interpreting a Graph** *The number of women working outside the home varied from country to country. In general, though, all western nations saw a dramatic rise in the female work force after World War II.* ■ *What percentage of Canadian women worked outside the home in 1963? In 1993? In which countries were fewer than half the women working outside the home by 1993?*

from Turkey and the Middle East provided low-wage labor for booming economies. Most lived in segregated areas and faced discrimination.

During later economic recessions, Europeans resented newcomers who competed with them for scarce jobs. In some countries, ultranationalists and racist thugs attacked and sometimes killed foreign workers and immigrants.

**Women.** In 1949, French writer Simone de Beauvoir (boh VWAHR) analyzed the status of women in western society:

66 The two sexes have never shared the world in equality. And even today woman is heavily handicapped, though her situation is beginning to change. Almost nowhere is her legal status the same as man's, and frequently it is much to her disadvantage. 99

Since then, women in Europe and North America have made progress toward legal and economic equality. (See page 840.) A growing number of women worked outside the home. Despite efforts to ensure equality, however, women's pay lagged behind that of men. Women in many careers ran into a "glass ceiling," an invisible barrier that kept them from promotion to top jobs.

A woman's income helped improve her family's standard of living. But while ideals about families survived, family life itself changed. Western families had fewer children than in the past. Children remained in school longer to get skills needed in advanced industrial societies.

Family stability, however, seemed to decline. The divorce rate rose. In cases where a divorced father separated himself from his financial responsibilities, women and children suffered. Dependent only on a mother's income, a growing number of woman-headed families found themselves living in poverty.

## SECTION 1 REVIEW

1. **Identify** (a) Berlin Wall, (b) Nuclear Test Ban Treaty, (c) Common Market, (d) European Union.
2. **Define** (a) détente, (b) welfare state, (c) service industry.
3. (a) Describe two effects of the Cold War on Europe. (b) What were two results of the end of the Cold War?
4. Describe how each of the following affected western economies: (a) oil crisis of 1973, (b) shift of manufacturing jobs to other parts of the world.
5. How did Western European nations achieve greater unity after World War II?
6. *Critical Thinking* **Predicting Consequences** (a) Why did European nations move toward the welfare state? (b) What benefits and drawbacks might this policy have for individuals and nations?
7. *ACTIVITY* Draw a political cartoon about the Berlin Wall, the nuclear arms race, or another Cold War issue from the viewpoint of a small nation in Western Europe.

# 2 The Western European Democracies

## Guide for Reading

- How did Britain's welfare state change in the 1980s?
- What problems did France overcome in the postwar period?
- How did Germany achieve unity?

In July 1994, an army of bicycles snaked through the English countryside, cheered on by a million spectators. The event was the famous Tour de France bicycle race. The cyclists had crossed from France through the new Channel tunnel, nicknamed Chunnel. For the first time since the ice age, a land route linked Britain and continental Europe.

To an English spectator, the Chunnel was an important symbol. "It's all about the future," he said, "about being part of Europe." The Chunnel reflected increased ties between Britain and France as well as improved relations among European nations generally.

After 1945, the Western European democracies operated within a growing framework of regional and global cooperation, including the Common Market, NATO, and the UN. Each nation, however, faced its own problems and made its own contributions to postwar freedom and prosperity.

## Britain: Government and the Economy

World War II left Britain physically battered and economically drained. In 1945, voters put the Labour party in power. The war had helped change old attitudes toward the working class. A Labour official noted that if a working-class boy "can save us in a Spitfire, the same brain can be turned to produce a new world."

That "new world" gave government an ever-larger role in the economy. It nationalized major industries and expanded social welfare bene-

fits such as unemployment insurance and old-age pensions. The government built housing for the poor and opened new state-funded universities. A national health service extended free or low-cost medical care to all citizens. To pay for all these benefits, taxes rose tremendously.

**Welfare rollback.** Later governments generally accepted the welfare state. By 1979, however, Britain, like the rest of Europe, was reeling under economic hard times. The Conservative party won power from the Labour party. Led by Margaret Thatcher, Conservatives denounced the welfare state as costly and inefficient. During 11 years as Britain's prime minister, Thatcher worked to replace government social and economic programs with what she called an "enterprise culture" that promoted individual initiative.

Thatcher privatized government-run industries. She curbed the power of labor unions, reduced the size of the government bureaucracy, and cut back welfare services. These changes did help to slow government spending but did not revive the British economy as much as Thatcher had hoped. And many people who faced unemployment and declining services reacted with demonstrations, strikes, and general unrest.

▲ *Margaret Thatcher*

**A new world role.** After the war, Britain adjusted to a new world role. The British empire shrank as colonies in Asia and Africa won independence. (See page 826.) Still, many former colonies preserved their ties to Britain by joining the Commonwealth of Nations. Immigrants from former British colonies—such as India, Pakistan, and the West Indies—surged into Britain. Increased diversity sometimes led to social tensions.

Weakened by the war and its loss of empire, Britain reluctantly gave up global leadership to its close ally, the United States. Yet it remained a major player in the UN and was active in NATO efforts to resist Soviet power. Britain also sought closer ties within Western Europe. In

1973, it joined the Common Market. By the 1990s, however, surging British nationalism led some people to reject greater European unity.

**Northern Ireland.** When Ireland won independence in 1922, Britain retained control of six northern counties. (See page 767.) Northern Ireland remained a source of bitter conflict. In the face of widespread discrimination, many Catholics demanded civil rights and pressed for the reunification of Ireland. Protestants wanted to remain part of Britain.

Violence escalated in the early 1970s. Extremists on both sides turned to terrorism, killing many people. Betty Williams, co-founder of a joint Catholic-Protestant peace league, described the atmosphere of violence:

> 66 Last week I had a bomb scare. They [radical IRA members] rang me up at one o'clock in the morning and said they were going to come and bomb the house. And me with my cheeky attitude, I said, 'You'd better hurry up, because I want to get to sleep.' Then I sat up all night, because I have two kids and I was really frightened that they would hurt the children. 99

British soldiers were stationed throughout Northern Ireland to keep order. But their presence inflamed tensions, especially as they jailed IRA members and violated their civil rights.

Outbreaks of violence continued for more than 20 years. Then, in 1994, both sides agreed to a cease-fire. Although the outcome of peace talks with Britain remained uncertain, all parties expressed hopes for a lasting peace.

## France: Revival and Prosperity

Like Britain, France was greatly weakened by World War II. The Fourth French Republic, set up in 1946, did little to renew confidence. Ineffective cabinets drew criticism from both communists and conservatives. Bloody colonial wars in Vietnam and Algeria further drained and demoralized France.

**De Gaulle.** In Algeria, longtime French settlers and the French military opposed Algerian nationalists who wanted independence. France itself was so divided over the issue that civil war threatened. Amid the deepening crisis,

**Peace at Last?** Conflict between Catholics and Protestants in Northern Ireland exploded in the 1960s and 1970s. The Irish Republican Army, or IRA, directed attacks against the British army and Protestant groups. Protestant militias attacked the IRA and Catholic civilians. Thousands died in the violence. A breakthrough finally came in 1994, when the IRA announced a cease-fire. Here, a poster in Northern Ireland calls for peace talks and the withdrawal of British troops. **Continuity and Change** Why do you think the conflict in Northern Ireland has lasted so long?

voters turned to General Charles de Gaulle, who had led the Free French during the war.

In 1958, de Gaulle set up the Fifth Republic. Its constitution gave him, as president, great power. Although a staunch nationalist, de Gaulle realized that France must give up Algeria. In 1962, he made peace with the Algerians. Other French colonies in Africa soon won freedom without bloodshed. (See Chapter 36.)

De Gaulle worked hard to restore French prestige and power. He forged new ties with West Germany, ending the long hostility between the two nations. He developed a French nuclear force and challenged American dominance in Europe. For example, he opposed the Cold War stance of the United States and opened talks with communist nations such as China and Cuba.

In 1968, youth revolts shook France. The next year, de Gaulle resigned. Although he was widely disliked by the left, he had successfully asserted French leadership in Europe.

**Student Riots in Paris** *In May 1968, radical students' demands for university reforms sparked a series of riots that paralyzed France. This photograph shows the aftermath of a battle with police, in which students used overturned cars to barricade the street. During the same period, student protests erupted in the United States over the Vietnam War.* **Continuity and Change** *Review pages 531–532. How were the tactics used by the Parisian students in 1968 similar to those used in earlier revolts?*

**Economic revival.** Like Britain, France nationalized some industries and expanded social welfare benefits after the war. With government help, industry and business modernized, leading to new prosperity by the 1970s.

French Socialists, led by François Mitterand, came to power in the early 1980s, just as a global economic recession hit. Mitterand's attempts to nationalize more industries and increase welfare benefits deepened the crisis. A practical man, he then took a more moderate course, encouraging the growth of private business. He was followed in office by conservative Jacques Chirac, who pledged to continue government policies that supported private business.

## Germany: Reunited at Last

The early years after World War II were a desperate time for Germany. People were starving amid a landscape of destruction. German cities lay in ruins. "Nothing is left in Berlin," wrote an American reporter:

66 There are no homes, no shops, no transportation, no government buildings. Only a few walls. . . . Berlin can now be regarded only as a geographical location heaped with mountainous mounds of debris. 99

By 1949, feuds among the Allies divided Germany. (See page 812.) West Germany was a member of the western alliance. East Germany lay in the Soviet orbit. Over the next decades, differences between the two Germanies widened, and the Soviet Union opposed a unified Germany that might pose a new threat to its security.

**West Germany's "economic miracle."** As the Cold War began, the United States rushed aid to its former enemy. It wanted to strengthen West Germany against the communist tide sweeping Eastern Europe. From 1949 to 1963, West Germany was guided by a strong-minded chancellor, Konrad Adenauer (AD ehn ow er). During this time, West Germans rebuilt their cities, factories, and trade. Despite high taxes to pay for the recovery, West Germany created a booming industrial economy.

This "economic miracle" raised European fears of a German revival. But West German leaders worked closely with France and the United States. West Germany also played a key role in NATO and the European Community.

While West Germany remained a capitalist country, later chancellors belonged to the Socialist party. They expanded the welfare state. German workers won unemployment benefits, pensions, and long summer vacations.

**East Germany.** The postwar decades brought no economic miracle to East Germany. Under communist rule, its economy rebuilt but stagnated. The Soviet Union exploited East German workers and industry for its own benefit. Still, unemployment was low, and East German workers did have some basic benefits, such as health care, housing, and free education.

Lured by glittering views of the West, however, many East Germans fled. As you have read, this mass exodus led to the building of the

Berlin Wall in 1961. Overnight, the migration ended. Occasionally, an East German made a dramatic escape. Many died in the attempt.

**Ostpolitik.** In 1969, West German chancellor Willy Brandt tried to ease tensions with communist neighbors to the east. He called his policy *Ostpolitik,* or "eastern policy." While he kept close ties with the West, Brandt signed treaties with the USSR and Poland. He opened economic doors to Eastern Europe and signed a treaty of mutual recognition with East Germany. But Brandt's long-term goal—the reunification of Germany—seemed impossible in the Cold War world.

**Reunification.** By 1989, the decline of communism in the Soviet Union at last made reunification possible. Without Soviet power to back them up, East German communist leaders were forced out of office. The Wall was dismantled, as you read, and Germans set about reuniting their divided land.

West German chancellor Helmut Kohl was the architect of unity. He assured both the Soviet Union and the West that a united Germany would pose no threat to peace. In 1990, German voters approved reunification, and Kohl became chancellor of a united Germany.

**New challenges.** While Germans welcomed unity, the change brought a number of serious problems. Prosperous West Germans had to pay higher taxes to finance the rebuilding of the east. At the same time, East Germans faced a difficult transition to a market economy. As old government-run factories closed, unemployment rose.

The economic shock fed social problems. A few right-wing extremists revived Nazi ideology. Seeing the answer to hard times in racism and hatred, these neo-Nazis viciously attacked foreign workers. Most Germans condemned such actions and worked instead to fulfill the hopes of unity.

## Other Democratic Nations of the West

Other parts of Western Europe slowly recovered from the war. The Scandinavian countries of Norway, Sweden, and Denmark created extensive socialist welfare programs. By the 1990s, rising costs revived debate about how much people were willing to pay for the welfare state. Yet many people saw these social programs as essential to a democratic society.

**Italy.** Postwar Italy was economically divided. In the urban north, industries rebuilt and prospered. In the rural south, the largely peasant population remained much poorer.

**West Germany's Economic Boom**
*The distinctive Volkswagen "beetle" became a symbol of German industry and trade. The first Volkswagen, or people's car, had been designed during the Third Reich as a reliable, low-cost vehicle for the masses. Volkswagen exports soared in the 1950s and 1960s, and the "beetle" became the first foreign car to make a dent in the American automobile market. Here, German workers celebrate the production of the one-millionth Volkswagen.* **Economics and Technology** *What allowed the West German economy to recover quickly after the war?*

Politically, Italy's multiparty system led to instability, as one coalition government succeeded another. The Italian Communist party was strong, although it never won enough votes to become a majority. Corruption and financial scandals shook the major political parties. The Mafia, a violent criminal syndicate, defied government efforts to end its power, especially in the south. Despite these problems, Italy made impressive economic gains and joined the powerful Group of Seven.

**Democratic gains.** Change came more slowly to three other countries of southern Europe: Spain, Portugal, and Greece. In 1945, all were economically undeveloped with large peasant populations. In Spain and Portugal, dictators clung to power for decades. Finally, in the 1970s, both Spain's Francisco Franco and Portugal's Antonio Salazar died. Their authoritarian governments soon collapsed. Both countries adopted democratic governments and eventually won admission to the Common Market. Their economies have grown rapidly.

After World War II, communist rebels unleashed a civil war in Greece. With American aid, the government won. Later military rulers imposed a right-wing government. In 1975, however, Greece returned to civilian rule

## SECTION 2 REVIEW

1. **Identify** (a) Konrad Adenauer, (b) Ostpolitik, (c) Helmut Kohl, (d) neo-Nazis.
2. What impact did Margaret Thatcher's policies have on Britain's welfare state?
3. Describe two steps Charles de Gaulle took to reassert French power in Europe.
4. (a) How did the experiences of West Germany and East Germany differ after World War II? (b) Why was Germany finally able to reunify?
5. *Critical Thinking* **Defending a Position** Some people, especially in France, worried that a reunited Germany would pose a danger to Europe. Using historical evidence, explain why you agree or disagree.
6. *ACTIVITY* Design a banner or write a song about *either* the cease-fire in Northern Ireland or the reunification of Germany, from the viewpoint of someone living there.

# 3 North American Prosperity

## Guide for Reading

■ What world role did the United States take on after World War II?

■ How did economic prosperity and social reforms change American life?

■ What issues have shaped Canada?

■ **Vocabulary** *deficit*

66Let every nation know that we shall pay any price, bear any burden, meet any hardship, support any friend, oppose any foe to assure the survival and the success of liberty.99

John F. Kennedy made this vow when he became President in 1961. In the postwar era, the United States sought to contain communism, extend civil rights, and ensure economic prosperity. To the north, Canada also built democracy and prosperity.

## The United States and the Cold War

In 1945, the United States was the world's greatest military power and the only country with the atomic bomb. Yet it felt threatened by communist expansion, especially after the Soviet Union developed its own atomic bomb. For this and other reasons, the United States gave up its tradition of avoiding foreign alliances. During the Cold War, it used its vast economic and military resources to protect its interests and the security of the free, or non-communist, world.

**Global commitments.** The United States built bases overseas and organized military alliances from Europe to Southeast Asia. Its fleets patrolled the world's oceans and its air power provided a "nuclear umbrella" over its allies. American troops fought in major wars to stop the spread of communism in Korea and Vietnam. They joined UN peacekeeping missions in the Middle East and elsewhere.

**Preparedness** *This painting reflects the position of the United States as the world's dominant military and industrial power. The artist, Roy Lichtenstein, was a leading figure in the 1960s movement known as "pop" art. Pop artists used techniques and images drawn from the mass media and popular culture. Lichtenstein used bold colors, dots, and strong lines to imitate the style of a color comic strip.* **Art and Literature** *Identify three images that Lichtenstein uses to symbolize American might.*

Along with military efforts to contain communism, the United States funneled economic aid to help Europe rebuild and, later, to assist emerging nations. At times, American aid went to nations, such as Zaire and Iran, that were ruled by anti-communist dictators. Yet Presidents such as Jimmy Carter also pressed other countries to end human rights abuses.

**The Cold War at home.** Early in the Cold War, extreme anti-communists in the United States warned that Soviet agents were operating everywhere. Between 1950 and 1954, Senator Joseph McCarthy charged many Americans with harboring communist sympathies. Government probes, however, produced little evidence of subversion. Eventually, the Senate condemned McCarthy's reckless behavior, but not before his unjust charges had ruined the careers of thousands of Americans.

McCarthy's campaign took place while the United States was embroiled in a war to stop communist expansion in Korea. (See pages 888–889.) As the Korean War wound down,

President Eisenhower began to aid another Asian country that seemed threatened by a communist uprising, South Vietnam.

**Turmoil over Vietnam.** American involvement in Vietnam increased under Eisenhower's successors. Between 1964 and 1968, President Lyndon Johnson sent massive aid and a growing number of troops to Southeast Asia. Eventually, American forces there numbered half a million.

By 1967, Americans at home were bitterly divided over the Vietnam War. Many opposed supporting an unpopular regime in South Vietnam. Antiwar protesters disrupted college campuses and filled city streets. In 1968, Richard Nixon, a vigorous anti-communist, was elected President and promised to end American involvement in Vietnam. At first, Nixon widened the war. Actions such as the bombing of Cambodia sparked further protests at home. By 1974, though, Nixon finally negotiated an American withdrawal. The divisions within the nation, though, would take decades to heal.

**The post-Cold War world.** When the Cold War ended in the early 1990s, Americans hoped for a more peaceful world. But as the sole superpower, the United States played a leading role in trying to resolve world conflicts. In 1991, a multinational force led by the United States ousted Iraqi invaders from Kuwait. (See page 919.) American troops restored democracy in Haiti and joined less-successful UN missions in Somalia and elsewhere.

## Economy and the Role of Government

Unlike Europe, the United States emerged from World War II with its cities and industries undamaged. In 1945, it produced 50 percent of the world's manufactured goods. Factories soon shifted from tanks and bombers to peacetime production. With the Cold War looming, however, government military spending increased, creating many jobs in defense industries.

By the early 1950s, the American economy was booming. At home, a growing population demanded homes, cars, refrigerators, and thousands of other products. Overseas, American businesses were investing in Europe's recovery and expanding into markets around the globe.

**A wider role for government.** In the United States, as in Western Europe, government's role in the economy grew. Under President Harry Truman, Congress created generous benefits that helped veterans attend college or buy homes. Other Truman programs expanded FDR's New Deal, providing greater security for the elderly and poor.

Truman's successor, Dwight Eisenhower, tried to reduce the government's role in the economy. At the same time, he approved government funding to build a vast interstate highway system. This program spurred the growth of the auto, trucking, and related industries. Highways and home building changed the face of the nation. Many middle-class Americans moved out of cities to the booming suburbs, while inner-city neighborhoods deteriorated.

**The Great Society.** Reformers urged bold new programs to help the poor and disadvantaged. During the 1960s, the government expanded social programs. President Kennedy wanted to provide health care to the elderly. After his assassination in 1963, Lyndon Johnson pressed ahead with a broad new program, which he called the Great Society. It funded Medicare for the elderly, job training and low-cost housing for the poor, and support for education. Many Americans came to rely on these programs in the next decades.

**The conservative response.** In the 1980s, conservatives challenged costly social programs and the growth of government. Like Margaret Thatcher in Britain, President Ronald Reagan called for cutbacks in government spending on social programs. Congress did end some welfare programs, reduce government regulation of the economy, and cut taxes. At the same time, military spending increased.

Government spending and tax cuts greatly increased the national deficit, the gap between what a government spends and what it takes in through taxes and other sources. As the deficit continued to grow in the 1990s, conservatives crusaded for deeper cuts in social and economic programs. Debate raged about how far to cut spending on programs ranging from education and welfare to environmental protection.

## The Civil Rights Movement

The 1950s seemed a peaceful time at home. Yet major changes were underway that would reshape American society. Among the most far-reaching was the civil rights movement.

**Equality under the law.** Although African Americans had won freedom nearly a century before, many states, especially in the South, denied them equality. Segregation was legal in education and housing. African Americans also faced discrimination in jobs and voting. In the 1950s and 1960s, the civil rights movement renewed earlier efforts to end racial injustice.

In 1954, the Supreme Court issued a landmark ruling in *Brown* v. *Board of Education of Topeka*. It declared that segregated schools were unconstitutional. Some southern states tried to resist court-ordered desegregation, but President Eisenhower and his successors used federal power to uphold the law.

**Martin Luther King, Jr.** By 1956, a gifted preacher, Dr. Martin Luther King, Jr., emerged as a leader of the civil rights movement. Inspired by Gandhi's campaign of civil disobedience in

**I Have a Dream** *Martin Luther King, Jr., was arrested dozens of times for breaking segregation laws. He explained that a person who willingly goes to jail "in order to arouse the conscience of the community over its injustice is in reality expressing the highest respect for law." This 1988 quilt by noted artist Faith Ringgold celebrates King and several women of the civil rights movement.*
**Religions and Value Systems** *Do you think the fact that King was a minister made him a more effective spokesman for civil rights?*

India, King organized boycotts and led peaceful marches throughout the 1960s to end segregation in the United States.

Many black and white Americans joined the civil rights movement. Their courage in the face of sometimes brutal attacks stirred the nation's conscience. In 1963, at a huge civil rights rally in the nation's capital, King declared:

❝I have a dream that one day this nation will rise up and live out the true meaning of its creed: 'We hold these truths to be self-evident, that all men are created equal.'❞

**Progress and problems.** In time, Congress responded. It outlawed segregation in public accommodations, protected the rights of black voters, and required equal access to housing and jobs. Despite these victories, racial prejudice survived, and African Americans faced many economic obstacles. They earned less than whites. Poverty and unemployment plagued African American communities in urban areas. Still, the civil rights movement provided wider opportunities. Many African Americans won elected offices or gained top jobs in business and the military.

**Other groups.** The civil rights movement inspired other groups, such as Native Americans and Hispanics, to campaign for equality. Women, too, renewed their efforts to gain equal rights. The new civil rights laws banned discrimination based on gender as well as race in hiring and promotion. More women ran successfully for political office, and many had begun to make progress toward high positions in business.

## The United States and the Global Economy

In the postwar decades, the United States profited greatly from the growing global economy. But interdependence also brought problems. In the 1970s, OPEC price hikes fed inflation and showed how much Americans relied on imported oil. Inflation also contributed to the Third World debt crisis, which involved American banks. (See Chapter 32.)

American industries faced stiff competition from Asian and other nations. Like Western Europe, the United States lost manufacturing jobs to the developing world. Some American corporations even moved operations to Mexico or Asia to take advantage of lower wages.

Still, the United States remained a rich nation and a magnet for immigrants. Unlike the immigrants of the late 1800s and early 1900s, these newcomers came largely from Latin America and Asia. By the 1980s, however, some Americans were calling for stricter laws to halt illegal immigration. Others even wanted to slow the flow of legal immigrants.

## Postwar Canada

Like the United States, Canada was a nation shaped by immigrants. After gaining independence, it charted its own course but still maintained links with Britain through the Commonwealth of Nations.

Canada ranked among the major democratic, industrial powers. It sided with the Allies in both world wars and was a staunch member of

**Independence for Quebec?** "No room for English speakers in Quebec," declares the graffiti at left. French-speaking Canadians, a minority within Canada, are concentrated in the province of Quebec. To protect their distinct culture, some French Canadians have called for Quebec to secede from Canada. **Diversity** In what ways could the cultural diversity of Canada be seen as an asset instead of a problem?

NATO. Through quiet diplomacy, Canada often worked behind the scenes to ease Cold War tensions. Its troops served in UN peacekeeping missions around the world.

**Economic growth.** Canada, too, enjoyed a postwar economic boom, due in part to rich oil and gas deposits found in the western provinces. In 1959, Canada and the United States completed the St. Lawrence Seaway. It opened the Great Lakes to ocean-going ships and linked the interior of both countries to the Atlantic Ocean.

With a population only a tenth that of the United States, Canada encouraged immigration. Since the 1950s, Canada's population has grown increasingly diverse, with newcomers from Europe, Asia, Africa, Latin America, and the Caribbean.

**Quebec separatism.** Defining a national identity has remained a challenge for Canada. Quebec's French-speaking population saw themselves as a "distinct society." To protect their culture, Quebec demanded more autonomy within Canada.

Government leaders tried hard to meet those demands. But other provinces resisted any solutions that gave Quebec special treatment. Meantime, some people in Quebec wanted to separate from Canada and become an independent nation. In the 1990s, Quebec's future remained a subject of heated debate.

**United States influence.** Another challenge for Canada has been the immense impact of the United States. Although the two nations enjoyed close ties, many Canadians resented their neighbor's cultural domination. Economic competition led to disputes over trade and tariffs. A key step toward solving those issues was a treaty that created a vast free-trade zone between the two nations. NAFTA later extended this zone to Mexico. (See page 963.)

Other issues between Canada and the United States concerned the environment. Chemical pollution from American smokestacks, for example, contributed to acid rain that fell on northeastern Canada. The two nations agreed to work together for a common solution. (See page 834.)

## SECTION 3 REVIEW

1. **Identify** (a) Joseph McCarthy, (b) Great Society, (c) Ronald Reagan, (d) *Brown* v. *Board of Education of Topeka*, (e) Martin Luther King, Jr., (f) St. Lawrence Seaway.
2. **Define** deficit.
3. How did the Cold War affect the role of the United States in the postwar era?
4. What were the goals of the civil rights movement?
5. Give one example of cooperation and one example of conflict between Canada and the United States.
6. *Critical Thinking* **Comparing** How is the situation of French-speaking Canadians similar to or different from that of minority groups within the United States?
7. *ACTIVITY* Interview someone you know who was born before World War II about American life during the postwar years. Topics might include the Cold War era, the civil rights movement, the changing role of women, the Vietnam War and antiwar protests, and economic changes. Prepare eight to ten questions.

# 4 The Soviet Union: Rise and Fall of a Superpower

## Guide for Reading

- What policies did Soviet leaders pursue?
- What were the strengths and weaknesses of the Soviet economy?
- What were the causes and effects of the collapse of the Soviet Union?
- **Vocabulary** *dissident, glasnost, perestroika*

"We shall bury you," Soviet leader Nikita Khrushchev (KROOSH chawf) told the West during the Cold War. His statement was not, he later explained, a military threat. Rather, he believed that capitalism was doomed and Soviet communism was the wave of the future.

Khrushchev's prediction never came true. Instead, in the 1980s, the Soviet economy began to crumble. Efforts at reform led the Soviet empire to disintegrate with stunning speed.

### Stalin's Successors

The Soviet Union emerged from World War II a superpower. Stalin forged a Soviet sphere of influence from the Baltic to the Balkans.

Victory, however, brought few rewards to the Soviet people. Stalin returned to his ruthless prewar policies. He filled slave labor camps with "enemies of the state." He seemed ready to launch a new wave of purges when he died in 1953.

**Khrushchev.** Nikita Khrushchev emerged as the new Soviet leader. In 1956, he shocked top Communist party members when he publicly denounced Stalin's abuse of power. Khrushchev then pursued a policy of de-Stalinization. He did not change Soviet goals but did free many political prisoners and eased censorship. He sought a thaw in the Cold War, calling for "peaceful coexistence" with the West.

The thaw had limits, though. When Hungarians revolted against communist rule in 1956, Khrushchev sent tanks to smash them. When critics at home grew too bold, he clamped down. Soviet poet Yevgeny Yevtushenko (yehv GAY nee yehv tuh SHEHN koh) warned that a return to Stalinism was always a danger:

"But how do we remove Stalin
   from Stalin's heirs?
Some of his heirs . . .
   from platforms rail against Stalin,
but,
   at night,
      yearn for the old days."

**The Brezhnev era.** In 1964, economic and foreign policy setbacks forced Khrushchev to resign. In time, Leonid Brezhnev (BREHSH nehf) took over the Soviet Union, holding power until his death in 1982. Brezhnev rigorously suppressed dissidents, people who spoke out against the government. Critics faced arrest and imprisonment. Some were locked away in insane asylums, a policy once used by czarist Russia.

**Andrei Sakharov** *In the 1950s, Andrei Sakharov was known as a brilliant physicist, the "father of the Soviet hydrogen bomb." By the 1980s, though, he was even better known as a leading Soviet dissident. He campaigned to limit nuclear testing and spoke out against human rights abuses. His efforts won him a Nobel Peace Prize but also angered the repressive Brezhnev government. In 1980, Sakharov was exiled to a remote city. Six years later, as the Soviet Union entered an era of growing freedom, Sakharov was finally released from exile.* **Impact of the Individual** *Why did it take courage for Sakharov and other dissidents to defy the Soviet government?*

## The Soviet Economy

After the war, Stalin rebuilt shattered Soviet industries, using factories and other equipment stripped from Germany. As in the 1930s, he and his successors focused on industries such as steel, coal, and heavy machinery. They also poured resources into science, technology, and weapons.

**Successes.** In 1957, the Soviets launched *Sputnik I*, the first artificial satellite to orbit the Earth. Khrushchev trumpeted *Sputnik* as a victory in the propaganda war against the West. The Soviets claimed other advantages as well. Citizens enjoyed benefits such as low rents, cheap bread, free health care, and day care for their children. Although wages were low, unemployment was almost nonexistent.

**Problems.** Neither Khrushchev nor Brezhnev, however, was able to solve basic Soviet economic problems. The state-run economy could produce impressive results when it poured resources into major projects such as weapons manufacture or the space race. But collectivized agriculture remained so unproductive that the Soviet Union frequently had to import grain to feed its people. Nor could Russia's command economy match the free-market economies of the West in producing consumer goods. Soviet shoes, suits, and television sets were far inferior to those made in the West, and luxuries like frozen food, clothes washers, or automobiles remained rare. People spent many hours of their lives waiting in line to buy food and other goods. The average person might spend years on a waiting list to buy a car.

Low output was due to inefficiencies in central economic planning. A huge bureaucracy, rather than supply and demand, decided what to produce, how much, and for whom. Government planners in Moscow often had little knowledge of the local conditions. Sometimes, factories were forced to shut down because needed supplies never arrived. At the local level, workers set out to meet production quotas, regardless of quality. Since workers had lifetime job security, they had little incentive to produce better-quality goods.

Still, for decades, the system supported the Soviet Union as a superpower. In the late 1980s, however, with military costs skyrocketing, the economy faced major obstacles.

## Foreign Policy Issues

Stalin and his successors forcefully asserted Soviet control over Eastern Europe. In 1955, Khrushchev set up the Warsaw Pact, in theory to defend the communist bloc against NATO. In practice, as you will read, it would be used to suppress dissent within Eastern Europe.

**The developing world.** As nations emerged from colonial rule, the Soviet Union, like the United States, supplied them with military and economic aid. Local conflicts sometimes flared into major Cold War confrontations. In two bitter wars, Soviet-backed governments in North Korea and North Vietnam battled American-backed governments in South Korea and South Vietnam. (See Chapter 34.)

**Rivalry with the United States.** As you saw, Soviet-American relations swung back and forth between confrontation and détente. In 1961, the building of the Berlin Wall increased Cold War tensions. A year later, Khrushchev tried to build nuclear missile bases in Cuba, triggering the dangerous Cuban missile crisis. (See page 957.) The nuclear war that everyone feared almost took place.

Brezhnev invested in a huge military buildup. In the Brezhnev Doctrine, he asserted that the Soviet Union had a right to intervene militarily in any Warsaw Pact nation. At the same time, he also pursued détente and disarmament with the United States.

Détente came to an abrupt end in 1979, after the Soviets invaded Afghanistan to ensure Soviet influence in that neighboring nation. Like the Vietnam War for the United States, the Afghan War drained the Soviet economy and provoked a crisis in morale at home.

▲ *Moscow citizens lining up to buy food*

## Collapse of the Soviet Empire

As the fighting in Afghanistan dragged on, the Soviet economy stagnated. In 1985, an energetic new leader, Mikhail Gorbachev, took up the reins of power. Gorbachev was eager to reform inefficiencies in government and the economy. The changes he unloosed, however, spiraled out of his control, swamping him and the Soviet Union.

**The Gorbachev revolution.** In foreign policy, Gorbachev sought an end to costly Cold War tensions. He renounced the Brezhnev Doctrine, signed arms control treaties with the United States, and eventually pulled Soviet troops out of Afghanistan.

At home, Gorbachev launched a two-pronged effort at reform. First, he called for glasnost, or openness. He ended censorship and encouraged people to discuss publicly the country's problems. Second, he urged the restructuring of government and the economy, called perestroika (pehr uh STROI kuh). Streamlining government and reducing the size of the bureaucracy, he hoped, would boost efficiency and output. He backed some free-market ideas, including limited private enterprise, but wanted to keep the essence of communism.

Corrupt or incompetent officials were dismissed. To produce more and higher-quality consumer goods, factory managers, instead of central planners, were made responsible for decisions. To increase food supplies, farmers were allowed more land on which to grow food to sell on the free market.

**Unexpected results.** Such rapid change brought economic turmoil. Shortages grew worse and prices soared. Factories that could not survive without government help closed, throwing thousands out of work. Old-line Communists and bureaucrats whose careers were at stake denounced the reforms. At the same time, other critics, like the popular Russian leader Boris Yeltsin, demanded even more radical changes.

Gorbachev faced a host of other problems. Glasnost encouraged unrest in the multinational Soviet empire. The Baltic republics of Estonia, Latvia, and Lithuania had been seized by Stalin in 1940. In 1991, they regained full independence. In Eastern Europe, countries from

**Freedom for the Baltic States** As the Soviet Union weakened, the small republics of Latvia, Estonia, and Lithuania declared independence. In a tense standoff, Soviet troops threatened to crush the independence movements. These demonstrators at the United Nations demanded that Gorbachev recognize the independence of the Baltic states. In the end, the Soviet army withdrew. **Geography and History** Look at the map on page 990. Why are Latvia, Estonia, and Lithuania called the Baltic states?

Poland and East Germany to Romania and Bulgaria broke out of the Soviet orbit.

In mid-1991, hardliners tried to overthrow Gorbachev and restore the old order. Their coup failed, but it further weakened Gorbachev. By year's end, as other Soviet republics declared independence, Gorbachev resigned as president. After 74 years, the Soviet Union ceased to exist.

## The Russian Republic

Russia, the largest republic in size and population, had dominated the Soviet Union. After the breakup, Russia and its president, Boris Yeltsin, faced a difficult future.

**Political problems.** Russians approved a new constitution, but they had no democratic traditions. In the 1990s, economic hardships and political turmoil increased. Many Russians feared the growing chaos and longed for a return to order.

Yeltsin clashed repeatedly with parliament. Many members were former Communists who

## The Former Soviet Union

| Country | Major Ethnic Groups | Major Religions |
|---|---|---|
| Armenia | Armenian 93% | Armenian Orthodox Church 94% |
| Azerbaijan | Azeri 83%, Russian 6%, Armenian 6% | Mostly Muslim |
| Belarus | Belarusian 80%, Russian 13% | Mostly Belarusian Orthodox |
| Estonia | Estonian 62%, Russian 30% | Mostly Lutheran |
| Georgia | Georgian 70%, Armenian 8%, Russian 6% | Georgian Orthodox 65%, Muslim 11%, Russian Orthodox 10% |
| Kazakhstan | Kazakh 42%, Russian 37%, Ukrainian 5%, German 4% | Muslim 47%, Russian Orthodox 44% |
| Kyrgyzstan | Kirghiz 52%, Russian 22%, Uzbek 13% | Muslim 70% |
| Latvia | Latvian 52%, Russian 34% | Lutheran, Roman Catholic, Russian Orthodox |
| Lithuania | Lithuanian 80%, Russian 9%, Polish 8% | Mostly Roman Catholic |
| Moldova | Moldovan/Romanian 65%, Ukrainian 14%, Russian 13% | Eastern Orthodox 99% |
| Russia | Russian 82%, Tatar 4% | Russian Orthodox 25%, nonreligious 60% |
| Tajikistan | Tajik 65%, Uzbek 25%, Russian 4% | Mostly Sunni Muslim |
| Turkmenistan | Turkmen 73%, Russian 10%, Uzbek 9% | Muslim 87% |
| Ukraine | Ukrainian 73%, Russian 22% | Orthodox 76%, Ukrainian Catholic 13.5%, Muslim 8.2% |
| Uzbekistan | Uzbek 71%, Russian 8% | Mostly Sunni Muslim |

Source: *The World Almanac and Book of Facts, 1996*

**Interpreting a Chart** *The powerful Soviet government had held together a diverse population of European and Asian peoples. When the Soviet Union collapsed in 1991, it left behind 15 independent states.* ■ *Why do you think Russians are a major ethnic group in almost every nation shown here? Which former Soviet republic seems to have the most diverse population?*

wanted to turn the clock back. Others were extreme nationalists who rejected western ideas and called for a revival of the Russian empire. Whether democracy would survive the turmoil remains to be seen.

Further troubles arose when minorities within Russia sought greater autonomy or independence. In 1994, Yeltsin brutally crushed a revolt in Chechnya (CHAYCH nee ah), a region in the Caucasus Mountains. The conflict revealed divisions within the army and government.

**Economic problems.** To solve Russia's economic problems and gain western aid, Yeltsin had to privatize more state-run industries and collective farms. The changeover to a market economy was painful. Unemployment soared. Without government controls, prices skyrocketed. Older people on fixed pensions were especially hard hit. Unlike East Germany, which got massive aid from West Germany, Russia got relatively little aid from the West.

Some Russians succeeded in the new economy. Their success, however, fanned resentment among poorer Russians. Criminals also flourished, and ruthless gangs preyed on the new business class. In an atmosphere of uncertainty, ultranationalists and old Communists won support at the polls.

**A world power.** Russia reduced its nuclear stockpile after the breakup of the Soviet Union. Still, with its large military and nuclear arsenal, Russia exercised influence as a world power. Its old rival, the United States, hoped Russia might work to resolve global problems. Yet Eastern European nations were alarmed when Russian nationalists and former Communists called for Russia to reassert its power. At the same time, Russia objected to efforts by Eastern European nations to join NATO, fearing a threat to its own security.

### The Other Republics

Like Russia, the other former Soviet republics wanted to build stable governments and improve their standard of living. They, too, faced unrest and divisions between the pro-communist and pro-democracy groups. Ethnic violence erupted in republics that included a mix of national groups. Other conflicts arose over disputed borders. Armenia, for example, tried to seize a small area in neighboring Azerbaijan, where many Armenians lived. The republic of Georgia was torn by a bloody civil war.

These new nations endured hard times as they switched to market economies. In the Central Asian republics, many skilled Russian workers left, causing a shortage of trained managers and technicians. With help from the UN, the World Bank, and the International Monetary Fund, the new nations worked to increase trade and build economic ties with the rest of the world. The republics of Ukraine, Kazakhstan, and Belarus gave up the nuclear weapons left on their soil in return for trading privileges or investments from the West.

### SECTION 4 REVIEW

1. **Identify** (a) Nikita Khrushchev, (b) Leonid Brezhnev, (c) Boris Yeltsin, (d) Chechnya.
2. **Define** (a) dissident, (b) glasnost, (c) perestroika.
3. Give three examples of how Stalin's successors both eased and inflamed Cold War tensions.
4. What problems did the Soviet economy face?
5. (a) What were Mikhail Gorbachev's goals? (b) How did his reforms contribute to the collapse of Soviet communism?
6. *Critical Thinking* **Predicting Consequences** (a) How have former Communist hardliners challenged democracy in the former Soviet republics? (b) What do you think might happen if they came to power again?
7. *ACTIVITY* Using obituaries in a local newspaper as models, write an obituary for the Soviet Union.

## 5 A New Era in Eastern Europe

### Guide for Reading

■ How were Eastern European nations tied to the Soviet Union during the Cold War?

■ How did Eastern European nations achieve democracy?

■ Why did civil war break out in Yugoslavia?

For centuries, the peoples of Eastern Europe lived in the shadow of larger powers. Before 1914, most of the region was divided up among the old German, Russian, Austrian, and Ottoman empires. Many small nations gained independence after World War I, only to be overrun by the Nazis. After the war, the region fell under Soviet domination.

Finally, in 1989, Eastern European nations again won independence. Vaclav Havel, a playwright and the first president of the Czech Republic, spoke about the challenges of freedom:

66Independence is not just a state of being. It is a task. And fresh independence, such as ours, is a particularly complex task. We must . . . ensure that it will not merely be a new burden but that, on the contrary, it will bring benefits to all its citizens, who should experience independence as something worth fighting for, something worth defending, and something worth holding dear.99

### In the Soviet Orbit

In 1945, Soviet armies occupied much of Eastern Europe. Backed by Soviet power, local Communist parties from Hungary to Bulgaria destroyed rival parties, silenced critics, censored the press, and campaigned against religion. As in the Soviet Union, Communist leaders in Eastern Europe ended private ownership of businesses and turned to central economic planning.

Despite Soviet domination, each country kept its own culture and identity. Poland, Hungary, Romania, and other nations also differed in economic wealth.

Stalin forced his satellites to contribute to the rebuilding of Soviet industry. They had to sell natural resources to the Soviet Union on favorable terms and provide troops and money to finance the Warsaw Pact.

**Unrest and repression.** As the Cold War deepened, the Soviet Union tightened its grip on its satellites. More than 30 divisions of Soviet troops were stationed throughout Eastern Europe. Yet in East Germany, Poland, Hungary, and elsewhere, unrest simmered. Despite some economic progress, many people despised the communist monopoly on power. Nationalists resented Moscow's domination.

By 1956, Imre Nagy (NOJ), a communist reformer and strong nationalist, gained power in Hungary. He ended one-party rule, ejected Soviet troops, and withdrew from the Warsaw Pact. Khrushchev responded to this challenge with tanks and troops. Hungarian "freedom fighters" resisted the Soviet advance and called on the West for help. None came. Thousands died in the fighting, and Nagy himself was executed. Many others fled to the West. The failure of western powers to intervene showed that they had accepted the Soviet sphere of influence in Eastern Europe.

A dozen years later, Alexander Dubçek introduced liberal reforms in Czechoslovakia. In easing controls, he called for "socialism with a human face." Once again, the Soviets responded with force. Warsaw Pact troops ousted Dubçek and restored a communist dictatorship. As you have read, under the Brezhnev Doctrine, the Soviet Union claimed the right to intervene in the affairs of any communist nation.

**Tito's independence.** Soviet power did not extend to Yugoslavia. During World War II, a fierce guerrilla leader, Josip Tito, had battled German occupying forces. Later, Tito set up a communist government in Yugoslavia, but he pursued a path independent of Moscow. He refused to join the Warsaw Pact and claimed to be neutral in the Cold War.

## Poland's Struggle Toward Democracy

Poland was the Soviet Union's most troublesome satellite. Like Hungarians and Czechs, Poles wanted greater freedom within the Soviet bloc. Stalin had clamped down hard on Poland. Communist persecution of the Roman Catholic Church, however, backfired. The Church became a rallying point for Poles opposed to the regime.

In 1956, economic woes touched off riots and strikes. To end the turmoil, the Polish government made some reforms. Dissatisfaction with communism, however, would continue to surface.

**Solidarity.** In 1980, economic hardships ignited strikes of shipyard workers in the port of Gdansk. Led by Lech Walesa (vah LEHN sah),

**Hungarian Uprising** In 1956, hundreds of thousands of Hungarians took to the streets to protest Soviet domination. An entire people, one Hungarian said, "rose up without weapons in defense of truth and freedom." Here, Hungarians stand beside a gigantic statue of Stalin, toppled during the revolt. **Art and Literature** What does the size of the statue suggest about the symbolic importance of Stalin?

**A Pope From Poland** In 1978, Polish cardinal Karol Wojtyla became Pope John Paul II—the first non-Italian pope in 456 years. From the Vatican, the pope gave cautious but firm encouragement to anti-communist forces in Eastern Europe. On visits to Poland in 1979 and 1983, he criticized the country's communist rulers. The pope's support inspired Lech Walesa and other members of Solidarity. Here, Walesa holds a photograph of the pope. **Impact of the Individual** Why do you think John Paul II was important to Polish nationalists?

they organized an independent trade union called Solidarity. It soon claimed 10 million members, who pressed for political change.

Under pressure from the Soviets, the Polish government cracked down on Solidarity. It outlawed the union and arrested its leaders, including Walesa. Still, unrest simmered. Walesa became a national hero. Pressure from the world community further strained the communist government.

**Peaceful transition.** In the late 1980s, Gorbachev declared he would not interfere in Eastern Europe. By then, Poland was introducing radical economic reforms similar to Gorbachev's changes in the Soviet Union. It also legalized Solidarity and, in 1989, sponsored the first free elections in 50 years. Solidarity candidates outpolled those of the Communist party. A year later, Lech Walesa was elected president of Poland. The new government began a difficult, but peaceful, transition from socialism to a market economy. It was the beginning of the end for Soviet domination of Eastern Europe.

## Revolution and Freedom

By late 1989, a "democracy movement" was sweeping Eastern Europe. Everywhere, people took to the streets, demanding reform. One by one, communist governments fell. A dissident writer and human rights activist, Vaclav Havel, was elected president of Czechoslovakia. In East Germany, as you have read, the Berlin Wall was toppled and the country reunited.

Most changes came peacefully. Only Romania's brutal longtime dictator, Nicolae Ceausescu (chah SHEHS koo), refused to step down. He was overthrown and executed.

For the first time since 1945, Eastern European countries were free to settle their own affairs. They withdrew from the Warsaw Pact and requested that Soviet troops leave. By then, Soviet power itself was crumbling.

**New struggles.** Like Russia and the former Soviet republics, Eastern European nations set out to build stable governments and free-market economies. Although the experiences of each nation differed, all faced similar challenges.

To attract western investment, governments had to push radical economic reforms. They privatized industries and stopped keeping prices for basic goods and services artificially low. As in Russia, the changes brought high unemployment, soaring prices, and crime waves. Consumer goods were more plentiful, but many people could not afford them.

By the mid-1990s, governments ended many benefits from the old days, such as generous maternity leave and free tuition at universities. Some people became disillusioned with reform. "I don't know why," observed a young Hungarian woman, "but even though we knew that we were a backward country—way behind Western Europe—it somehow felt better then." In some countries, former Communists won seats in the parliaments.

**Return to Europe.** In the 1990s, Eastern European nations looked to the West for aid. Some also hoped to join the European Union and NATO. Western powers applauded the move to market economies, but they were reluctant to assume the responsibility of protecting Eastern European nations if they joined NATO. Russia, too, objected to NATO's expansion into a region within its sphere of influence. Increasing

**Troubled Waters** *After the fall of communism, many East Europeans hoped to enjoy higher wages and new consumer goods right away. In practice, though, the transition to a market economy proved slow and painful. This cartoon shows the dangerous economic waters that Eastern Europe must navigate.* **Economics and Technology** *What does the boat represent? What dangers does it face? What does the cartoon suggest about its destination?*

ethnic violence in some lands created further difficulties between Eastern Europe and the West.

**Ethnic tensions.** Centuries of migration and conquest left most Eastern European countries with ethnically diverse populations. Most countries had a majority population, but with one or more ethnic minorities asserting their own identity. Nationalism has helped unite countries like Poland and Hungary, but it has also been a divisive force. Hungarians in Romania demanded autonomy. Faced with ethnic tensions, Czechoslovakia peacefully split into two countries, the Czech Republic and Slovakia. In 1991, ethnic conflict tore Yugoslavia apart in a long and tragic civil war.

## War Comes to Sarajevo

**UP CLOSE** "I'm trying to concentrate so I can do my homework," 11-year-old Zlata Filipovic wrote in her diary on April 5, 1992. "But I simply can't. Something is going on in town. You can hear gunfire from the hills." Zlata was right. In just a few days, war would come to the beautiful, peaceful city where Zlata lived—Sarajevo.

**Breakup of Yugoslavia.** While Zlata was growing up, Sarajevo was part of Yugoslavia. Its three main ethnic groups were Croats, who were Roman Catholics; Serbs, who were Orthodox Christians; and Muslims. The groups had distinct customs and religions, but they had lived side by side peacefully for years. They all spoke the same language, Serbo-Croatian.

After Tito's death and the fall of communism, however, a wave of nationalism tore Yugoslavia apart. Ambitious extremists, such as Serb leader Slobodan Milosevic, stirred ethnic unrest for their own ends. Croats created the separate countries of Croatia and Slovenia. Sarajevo became the capital of a new nation called Bosnia-Herzegovina. Serbia and Montenegro kept the name Yugoslavia.

**Bosnia.** Although Bosnia, where Zlata lived, became independent, it was still divided. Muslims made up the majority, but there were also many Serbs and Croats. Bosnian Serbs got money and arms from nearby Serbia. As Serbs conquered more and more of Bosnia, neighbors and friends turned against one another.

Serbs practiced "ethnic cleansing," forcibly removing other ethnic groups from the areas they controlled. Hundreds of thousands of Bosnians became refugees, living on food sent by the United Nations and by charities. Others were brutalized or killed. To many, ethnic cleansing recalled the horrors of Nazi Germany and the Holocaust.

**A record of terror.** Zlata watched in horror as shelling and snipers killed thousands of people. On May 7, she wrote:

❝Today a shell fell on the park in front of my house, the park where I used to play and sit with my girlfriends. A lot of people were hurt. . . . AND NINA IS DEAD. A piece of shrapnel lodged in her brain and she died. She was such a sweet, nice little girl.❞

**ISSUES For TODAY** Ethnic conflict has taken many forms—from violence against guest workers in Western Europe to the Quebec separatist movement to "ethnic cleansing" in Bosnia. How can nations encourage harmony among diverse peoples within their borders?

**A Nation Torn Apart**
*In the former Yugoslavia, Serbs, Croats, and Muslims battled to control the new states that were emerging. Above, Muslim refugees are forced to flee their homes after a brutal Serb attack. At right, a woman carries on with her daily routine in the bombed-out streets of Sarajevo.* **Global Interaction** *How do you think Muslim nations elsewhere in the world viewed the conflict in the former Yugoslavia?*

Conditions in Sarajevo became almost unbearable. Serbian troops shelled schools, hospitals, and libraries. They cut off electricity and water supplies for months at a time. "I've forgotten what it's like to have water pouring out of a tap, what it's like to shower," Zlata wrote.

Zlata tried to understand what was causing the war. "I keep asking why? What for? Who's to blame?" She was especially upset about the violence among ethnic groups:

&#x275D;Among my girlfriends, among our friends, in our family, there are Serbs and Croats and Muslims. It's a mixed group and I never knew who was a Serb, a Croat or a Muslim. Now politics has started meddling around. . . . Of course, I'm 'young,' and politics are conducted by 'grown ups.' But I think we 'young' would do it better. We certainly wouldn't have chosen war.&#x275E;

After enduring many months of war, Zlata and her parents finally left Sarajevo for Paris in December 1993. Not everyone could flee the battle. The struggle went on. ▮

## Looking Ahead

By the mid-1990s, much of Eastern Europe was in a state of uncertainty. A long-cherished goal—freedom from Soviet domination—had been achieved. As nations made progress toward a free-market economy, many people looked forward to the future with hope. Yet, at the same time, the region was faced with a pattern of mounting disorder. Communist domination had stifled both nationalism and free enterprise, but it had also imposed order. The civil war in Yugoslavia was an especially horrifying offshoot of the collapse of communism.

Bosnia became a test case for the role of western powers in the post-Cold War world. For three years, UN forces tried unsuccessfully to keep peace. As Serbs advanced, the United States and its NATO allies debated whether or not to intervene militarily or arm the Muslims and Croats. In 1995, an international court indicted two Bosnian Serb leaders for war crimes. Later that year, NATO forces bombarded Serb strongholds. American negotiators assisted all sides in hammering out a cease-fire agreement. However, it was far from certain whether peace would take root in the troubled region.

## SECTION 5 REVIEW

1. **Identify** (a) Imre Nagy, (b) Alexander Dubçek, (c) Josip Tito, (d) Lech Walesa.
2. How did the Soviet Union come to dominate Eastern Europe?
3. (a) What events led to democracy in Poland? (b) Why are some people in Eastern Europe dissatisfied with democracy and free-market economics?
4. Why did civil war break out in Yugoslavia?
5. *Critical Thinking* **Recognizing Causes and Effects** To what extent did Eastern Europe owe its independence to Mikhail Gorbachev?
6. *ACTIVITY* With a classmate, prepare a dialogue between two people in an Eastern European nation. Discuss the changes in your country and the outlook for the future.

# Skills for Success

**Critical Thinking**   **Writing and Researching**   **Maps, Charts, and Graphs**   **Speaking and Listening**

## Planning a Multimedia Presentation

Multimedia presentations communicate through a variety of forms, both audio and visual. Television news programs, for example, convey information through both still and moving images, as well as narration. A documentary may add music, too. A lecturer may enhance his presentation with music, slides, or film.

The preproduction, or planning, stage of a presentation is the most important part. During preproduction, you draft an outline and script, decide what media to use and where, arrange interviews or photography sessions, select images, and choose music. Thorough preproduction makes the production stage—the actual filming and recording—go more smoothly.

Imagine that you have been assigned to produce a multimedia presentation on some aspect of cultural diversity in the United States. Use the preproduction topic analysis sheet below and the following steps to prepare your presentation.

**1** **Plan your content.** Keep in mind what you learned about planning a presentation on page 304. (a) What possible topics might you focus on in your presentation? (b) How could you learn more about the topic? (c) Jot down three specific segments you might include and the order in which you wish to present them. (d) What mood do you want each segment and your overall presentation to convey?

**2** **Plan a script.** First, you must decide what kind of narration you want to have. You may use a running commentary by a single narrator, a dialogue by a pair of narrators, comments by interviewees in each segment, or a combination. Then, create an outline. (a) What are the advantages and disadvantages of using a single narrator? (b) What are the advantages and disadvantages of using several voices?

**3** **Make a list of interviews, images, and music.** (a) What still or moving images would fit the content and mood of each segment?

(b) What kinds of people could you interview?
(c) What pieces or types of music will best enhance the mood of your presentation?

***Beyond the Classroom***  Today, many schools, families, and community organizations videotape important events. Think of an event or occasion you would like to videotape and complete an event analysis sheet for it.

---

**Preproduction Topic Analysis Sheet**

**Assignment:** An aspect of United States cultural diversity

**Possible topics:**
1. _____
2. _____
3. _____
My choice: _____
**Sources for topic information:**
_____
_____

Intended audience: _____
Information to be presented:
_____
_____

**Segment description and sequence:**
1. _____
2. _____
3. _____
Mood: _____
Type of narration: _____

**Graphics/Illustrations, Interviews, Music**
Segment #1 _____  _____
               _____  _____
Segment #2 _____  _____
               _____  _____
Segment #3 _____  _____
               _____  _____

## Building Vocabulary

Select *five* vocabulary words from the chapter. Write each word on a separate slip of paper. Then, write the definition for each word on other slips of paper. Scramble the slips and exchange them with another student. Match the words with their definitions, and then check each other's results.

## Reviewing Chapter Themes

1. **Economics and Technology** Describe one way each of the following developments affected the western economies after World War II: (a) the postwar economic recovery, (b) the rise of the welfare state, (c) increased global interdependence.
2. **Continuity and Change** (a) Describe three steps Western European nations took toward unity after World War II. (b) What benefits have come from European unity? (c) Why have many Europeans objected to increased unity?
3. **Impact of the Individual** (a) How did the policies of Mikhail Gorbachev affect the Soviet Union and the world? (b) Describe the impact of *three* of the following individuals on their nations: Margaret Thatcher; Charles de Gaulle; Willy Brandt; Nikita Khrushchev; Martin Luther King, Jr.; Josip Tito; Lech Walesa.
4. **Political and Social Systems** (a) Describe one economic and one political weakness that contributed to the collapse of the Soviet Union. (b) What problems did the former Soviet republics face?
5. **Diversity** (a) Why is Eastern Europe an ethnically diverse region? (b) What were the causes and effects of the breakup of Yugoslavia?

## Thinking Critically

1. **Defending a Position** If you lived in a Western European country, would you support moves toward a "United States of Europe"? Why or why not?
2. **Analyzing Information** In Germany and other nations, extremist groups attacked foreign refugees and guest workers. Why do you think attacks on immigrants and minorities often increase during economic hard times?

3. **Linking Past and Present** List three ways the civil rights movement of the 1950s and 1960s helped shape American life today.
4. **Analyzing Primary Sources** A Soviet official described how a factory owner ordered supplies: "I need wire. Some nine months before I need the wire I submit a request at the respective office for material-technical supplies. That office sends my request to Moscow to the main Metal Administration. There someone looks at a list of the appropriate industrial enterprises and picks out the plant that can produce such wire." (a) What aspect of the Soviet economy is described here? (b) What could be some disadvantages of this system? (c) Do you think this official favored Gorbachev's policies? Why or why not? ( ★ See *Skills for Success*, page 154.)
5. **Making Decisions** Do you think the western democracies should invest large sums of money in Russia and other former Soviet republics? Why or why not? ( ★ See *Skills for Success*, page 814.)
6. **Applying Information** Reread the words by Vaclav Havel on page 867. (a) Restate his main point in your own words. (b) How do Havel's words apply to the nations of Eastern Europe that have broken free from Soviet influence?

### For Your Portfolio

For this assignment, you will work with a group of classmates to prepare a data file on one of the decades from 1950 to the present.

1. Meet with your team to choose the decade you will research.
2. Review the material in this chapter for information about your decade. Then, use library resources to learn more about significant political, social, religious, and technological events in this time period. You will also want to find out about important leaders and other people.
3. Decide how to organize your decade file. For example, you might group information by topic or by country or region. You might also present it in the order in which events happened.
4. Work with your group to prepare the file on the decade you have chosen.
5. Present your decade file to the class. Be prepared to answer questions.

# CHAPTER
## 34

# East Asia and Southeast Asia
## (1945–Present)

## CHAPTER OUTLINE

1 **Japan Becomes an Economic Superpower**
2 **From Revolution to Reform in China**
3 **The Asian Tigers**
4 **Southeast Asia and the Pacific Rim**

By the end of May 1989, tens of thousands of student demonstrators had packed into Tiananmen Square. The youthful protesters had a list of grievances—inflation, crime, official corruption, the Communist party's monopoly on power. They raised banners calling for democracy:

66China is our motherland.
  We are the people.
  The government should be our
    government.99

Across the world, people watched this historic moment. How would China's totalitarian government respond? Would it agree to political reforms?

The answer came on June 4, with a brutal crackdown. Tanks rolled through Tiananmen Square, followed by armed troops. Soldiers killed hundreds of demonstrators and wounded many more. The Tiananmen Square massacre showed that China's leaders would not allow their authority to be challenged. But it also became a symbol for Chinese who hoped one day to achieve democracy.

Over the past 50 years, China and other nations in East Asia and Southeast Asia have transformed themselves. They cast off foreign control and set out to modernize. In some nations, like China, a totalitarian government remade the economy and society. Other nations made economic progress under authoritarian rule. With its democratic government, Japan was an exception. After a spectacular recovery from the war, Japan claimed a place among the world's top industrial nations.

For decades, Asia was a battleground in the Cold War. As the superpowers jockeyed for position, they fought shooting wars through third parties—Korea and Vietnam. By the 1990s, the Cold War was over. For the first time in years, the major powers in Asia and the United States were at peace. Growing trade and other ties linked the nations of the Pacific Rim from Asia to the Americas.

**FOCUS ON** these questions as you read:

■ **Continuity and Change**
  How did the Cold War affect the nations of East Asia and Southeast Asia?

■ **Economics and Technology**
  How did technology and trade contribute to the success of Japan and the Asian "tigers"?

■ **Political and Social Systems**
  How is the new China created by the communist revolution changing again today?

■ **Impact of the Individual**
  How did leaders like Mao Zedong and Ho Chi Minh remake their nations?

■ **Global Interaction**
  Why did the Pacific Rim become a dynamic center of growth?

## TIME AND PLACE

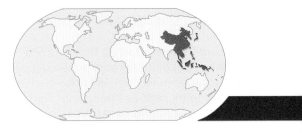

*A New Path for China* In 1949, the Communists won control of China. They proclaimed three main goals for their revolution. They promised a better life for the poor. They called for development of a modern economy. And they pledged to restore China's position as a major world power. Here, a propaganda poster urges the Chinese to "win a good harvest, increase grain production." **Art and Literature** What image of China's farmworkers does this poster present?

## HUMANITIES LINK
*Art History* Indonesian batik (page 894).
*Literature* In this chapter, you will encounter a passage from the following work of literature: Yuan Kejia, "Labor is joy" (page 882).

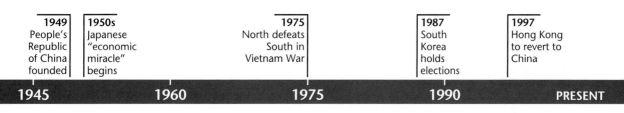

| 1949 | 1950s | 1975 | 1987 | 1997 |
|---|---|---|---|---|
| People's Republic of China founded | Japanese "economic miracle" begins | North defeats South in Vietnam War | South Korea holds elections | Hong Kong to revert to China |

| 1945 | 1960 | 1975 | 1990 | PRESENT |

# Japan Becomes an Economic Superpower

## Guide for Reading

■ What were the goals of American occupation forces in Japan?

■ How did Japan become an economic superpower?

■ What challenges does Japan face today?

■ **Vocabulary** *gross domestic product*

"The wise bamboo sways with the wind," says a Japanese proverb. In 1945, for the first time in its history, Japan had to accept foreign occupation. As in the past, the Japanese learned from outsiders. They selectively borrowed western ideas and technology and put them to their own use. By the 1960s, Japan had emerged as an economic superpower equal to the United States and the Soviet Union.

## On the Road to Recovery

In 1945, Japan lay reeling. It had suffered perhaps the most devastating property damage of any nation involved in World War II. Hiroshima and Nagasaki were leveled. Other Japanese cities were burned-out ruins. Tens of thousands of Japanese were homeless and hungry.

**Occupation goals.** Under General Douglas MacArthur, the American military government set two main goals for the occupation of Japan: to destroy militarism and to ensure democratic government. Japan's armed forces were disbanded. As in Germany, trials were held to punish those responsible for wartime atrocities. Along with Japan's defeat, the trials further discredited the military.

In 1946, a new constitution provided that "the Japanese people forever renounce war as a sovereign right of the nation." Japan, it said, would never maintain military forces except for its own defense.

The constitution stripped the emperor of power. Instead, power was vested in the people, who elected representatives to the Diet, or parliament. The constitution also protected basic rights such as freedom of thought, press, and assembly.

**Social and economic reforms.** To help build Japanese democracy, American occupying forces backed social change. They reformed Japan's education system to open it to all people. They emphasized legal equality for women. Women gained the right to vote and hold office. Marriages had to be based on mutual consent, with equal rights for wife and husband.

**Postwar Japan** *When American troops arrived in Japan at the end of World War II, their first job was to provide emergency food and shelter for their former enemies. Here, village leaders distribute food from the United States in rural Japan.* **Political and Social Systems** *Why do you think the American occupiers used local leaders to give out food?*

The Americans introduced economic reforms designed to promote democracy. The constitution protected the right of workers to organize unions. A sweeping land-reform program divided up large estates among tenant farmers. The former owners received payment, while peasants owned land for the first time. This change erased lingering traces of feudalism in Japan.

Although the Americans tried to disband the zaibatsu, or giant business combines, the Japanese resisted. They felt that large firms were needed to compete internationally.

**The Cold War.** By 1950, Japan was on the road to recovery. At the same time, the Cold War was making the United States eager to end the occupation and turn its World War II enemy into an ally. As the Cold War erupted into an armed conflict in nearby Korea (see Section 3), the United States and Japan signed a peace treaty. In 1952, the occupation ended.

Japan and the United States preserved close ties during the Cold War. The American military operated out of bases that they set up in Japan, while Japan enjoyed the protection of the American "nuclear umbrella." The two nations were also trading partners and, in time, competitors for global markets.

## Japanese Successes

Between 1950 and 1975, Japan produced its own economic miracle, even more spectacular than Germany's. It chalked up huge jumps in gross domestic product (GDP). GDP refers to the total value of all goods and services produced by a nation.

**Manufacturing.** The Japanese success story was built on producing goods for export. At first, Japan manufactured textiles. When other Asian nations entered that field, it shifted to making steel for shipbuilding and machinery.

By the 1970s, Japanese cars, cameras, and television sets found eager buyers on the world market. Its companies also moved into high technology. Soon, Japanese electronic goods—from computers to robots—were competing with western, especially American, products.

**Trade and investment.** As a small island nation with few resources, Japan depended on trade. It had to import oil and other raw materials like iron ore, but it exported the more profitable finished goods, such as steel. It marketed its products so successfully that it built a favorable balance of trade, exporting more goods than it imported. So many Americans bought Japanese-made cars, for example, that American automakers felt a threat to their decades-old dominance.

As Japan's economy expanded, it invested in ventures around the world. The Japanese financed and operated mines and plantations. They built airports and chemical plants. When a tire factory was to be built in East Africa or a dam in Central America, the engineers were as likely to be Japanese as American. Japan's presence everywhere showed that it had not only caught up with the West but was rapidly moving ahead of it.

**Reasons for success.** With few natural resources, how did Japan enjoy such enormous success? After the war, Japan—like Germany—had to rebuild from scratch. Also like Germany, it had the advantage of having successfully industrialized in the past. Now, it quickly built efficient, modern factories that outproduced older industries in the West. It adapted the latest technology from the West to create its own high-quality products.

Japan also benefited from a well-educated and skilled work force. Thanks to the postwar educational reforms, almost all Japanese went to high school and almost 40 percent continued through higher education.

Japanese workers saved much of their pay, which gave banks the capital to invest in industrial growth. Management and labor also tended to work together. Until recently, many large companies guaranteed Japanese workers lifetime employment. In return, workers gave the company total loyalty.

Ironically, Japan also benefited from the restrictions on military development that were forced on it after World War II. Unlike most industrial nations, it spent very little on defense. The government could therefore invest generously in the economy. It helped business and industry develop new products, open new overseas markets, and meet foreign competition. Its high tariffs and many regulations kept foreign imports to a minimum, which in turn gave Japanese products a boost at home.

tween the two nations stumbled along for years, with only limited success.

## A New World Role

Economic success allowed Japan to benefit from the modern global economy. Yet Japan felt the negative effects of interdependence as well, especially because of its need for imported raw materials.

**Dependence on oil.** Nothing brought home Japan's dependence on world markets more than OPEC's price hikes in the 1970s. (See page 832.) Japan's booming industries had fed on cheap imported oil. Higher energy costs sent shock waves through its economy.

In response, Japan sought better relations with oil-producing nations of the Middle East. It also tried to reduce energy use by building more efficient power plants and expanding and improving public transportation. Still, its modern economy required oil.

**Japan and its neighbors.** As Japan sought economic openings in Asia, it had to deal with nations that still held bitter memories of World War II. China, Korea, and parts of Southeast Asia had suffered terribly under Japanese occupation. Japan was slow to apologize for its wartime actions, but it did work hard to regain the trust of neighboring peoples. By the 1980s, Japan was a major investor in China and the emerging nations of Southeast Asia. In the 1990s, Japanese leaders finally offered public regrets for the death and destruction of the war years.

**International politics.** Although Japan was an economic superpower, it took a back seat in international politics. During the Cold War, it supported the western alliance led by the United States. More recently, it has edged toward a larger world role. For decades, it has given huge amounts of foreign aid to emerging

**The trade issue.** Japan's protectionist policies angered its trading partners, who were concerned about their trade deficit with Japan. This trade deficit existed because Japan exported more goods to these nations than it imported from them.

The United States, for example, claimed that Japanese trade barriers deprived American corporations of a fair chance to sell their goods in Japanese markets. To reduce its trade deficit with Japan, the United States threatened to raise tariffs on Japanese imports, making them more expensive for American consumers. That threat was designed to force Japan to open its door to more American imports. Trade talks be-

nations. Today, it ranks as the world's largest donor nation. In 1990, it provided money, but no soldiers, for the Gulf War. (See page 919.) Two years later, its soldiers joined a UN peace-keeping force for the first time.

The United States has urged Japan to rearm and assume more of the costs for its own defense. Asian neighbors oppose Japan's rearmament, and the Japanese themselves are divided on the issue. Some think Japan's status as a world power requires rearmament. Most prefer to avoid the hazards and expense of becoming a military power.

## Changing Patterns

In the past 50 years, Japan has enjoyed many economic successes. In the 1990s, however, Japan faced its worst economic depression since the 1930s. Companies had to make cutbacks, and many workers lost the security of guaranteed lifetime employment.

**Political stresses.** Japan's democracy has survived many crises. The Liberal Democratic party (LDP) has dominated the government since the 1950s. But Japanese political parties differ from those in the United States. The LDP is, in fact, a coalition of conservative factions that compete behind the scenes for top government positions. In the 1990s, charges of corruption greatly weakened the LDP. Some younger, reform-minded politicians broke with the LDP, threatening its monopoly on power.

**Crowded cities.** Today, 80 percent of the Japanese population live in cities, which are hugely overcrowded. Housing is expensive, and space is scarce. Most people live in tiny, cramped apartments. Many space-hungry Japanese move to the suburbs but then face long commutes to work.

In 1995, a severe earthquake badly damaged the city of Kobe (KOH BEE). It also shook Japanese faith in modern "quake-proof" technology. Japan lies in a region often rocked by

# PARALLELS THROUGH TIME

## The Classroom
Public education has changed greatly over the centuries. Until the late 1800s, even in industrialized countries few people got more than an elementary school education. In this century, schools have gone from providing the three R's—reading, 'riting, and 'rithmetic—to offering students a wide variety of specialized and technical courses.

**Linking Past and Present** What subjects that you study in school were taught 50 years ago? What subjects were introduced in recent years?

**PAST** These Japanese students in the late 1940s are learning English. The traditional classroom setting did not differ very much from schools in Africa, Europe, or the Americas.

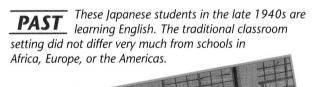

**PRESENT** Modern classrooms like this one in Japan give students a chance to work with the latest technology. Here, students in a language lab use computers to practice English.

earthquakes, and Japanese highways and other structures were supposed to be designed to withstand such quakes. The disaster in Kobe raised questions about just how much technology can protect against natural forces.

**Women.** Japanese women have legal equality and often control the family finances. But traditional attitudes toward women keep them in subordinate positions in the workplace. About half the adult women work outside the home, but most are in low-paying jobs or in family-run businesses. Fewer women than men get a university education, and only a handful have moved into higher-level jobs in business or government.

**Weakening work ethic.** For decades, the Japanese sacrificed family life to work long hours. They also saved large portions of their earnings. Younger Japanese, however, want more time to enjoy the benefits of economic success. Some older Japanese worry that the old work ethic is weakening.

## SECTION 1 REVIEW

1. **Identify** (a) Douglas MacArthur, (b) Diet, (c) Liberal Democratic party.
2. **Define** gross domestic product.
3. (a) What were the main goals of the occupation forces after World War II? (b) Describe three ways that they tried to achieve these goals.
4. (a) How did the Japanese economy grow in the postwar years? (b) What were three reasons for Japan's economic success?
5. What role has Japan played in world affairs in recent years?
6. *Critical Thinking* **Recognizing Points of View** Japan's trading partners complained that unfair Japanese policies caused their large trade deficits with Japan. To the Japanese, however, the trade deficits of these foreign nations were Japan's trade *surplus*. Explain the two points of view. How might these differing perspectives affect efforts to resolve the trade issue?
7. *ACTIVITY* Imagine that you are a Japanese teenager. Write a letter to the prime minister supporting or opposing the rearming of Japan.

## 2 From Revolution to Reform in China

### Guide for Reading

- Why did Mao's forces triumph in China?
- How did the Communists revolutionize China?
- What policies did Mao's successors pursue?
- **Vocabulary** *commune*

On October 1, 1949, to cheering crowds in Beijing, Mao Zedong announced the birth of the People's Republic of China. "The Chinese people have stood up, and the future of our nation is infinitely bright," declared the Communist leader. The government, he pledged, would call on "the great collective strength of the masses . . . to build a new China, independent, democratic, peaceful, unified, prosperous and strong."

In 1911, the collapse of the Qing dynasty marked the end of Confucian China. Mao's triumph in 1949 signaled the start of an even more intense upheaval. China's revolution ranks with Russia's as one of the major revolutionary struggles of our century.

### Triumph of Communism

After World War II, Mao Zedong's Communist forces and Jiang Jieshi's Nationalists resumed the bitter struggle for power that had begun in the 1920s. (See Chapter 29.) Civil war raged until Mao's forces swept to victory and set up the People's Republic of China (PRC) in 1949. The defeated Jiang Jieshi and his supporters fled to the island of Taiwan. After decades of struggle, China was finally united, with the Communists in control.

**Reasons for success.** Why did the Communists triumph? There were a number of reasons for their success.

Mao won the support of China's huge peasant population. Peasants had long suffered from brutal landlords and crushing taxes. The Communists pledged to distribute land to poor peasants and end oppression by landlords.

Women also threw their support behind Mao. The Nationalists had done little to improve their harsh lives. Women were still seen as inferior to men and were often cruelly mistreated. The Communists rejected the inequalities of the old Confucian society. "Women hold up half the sky," Mao said.

Finally, Mao's army was superior to Jiang's. With the guerrilla tactics they had perfected against the Japanese in World War II, they outfought Jiang's armies.

While Mao's support grew, Nationalist popularity dwindled. Chinese of all classes grew disgusted as they watched corrupt officials enrich themselves instead of working to solve China's problems. Peasant-soldiers drafted into the army had little desire to defend a government that oppressed them. Many educated Chinese saw Jiang's government as morally and politically bankrupt. They were drawn to the Communist program for a new China and an end to domination by foreigners who had humiliated their country for so long.

## Remaking Chinese Life

Once in power, the Communists set out to turn China from a backward peasant society into a modern industrial nation. First, however, they had to overcome hunger, poverty, disease, and illiteracy.

**Rebuilding the economy.** To build socialism and repair the economy, China nationalized all businesses. The government also drew up five-year plans designed to increase coal and steel output and develop heavy industry. With Soviet help, the Chinese built hydroelectric plants, railroads, and canals.

To boost agriculture, Mao distributed land to peasants. He encouraged peasants to "speak bitterness" against landlords. Tens of thousands of landlords were attacked and killed. The government urged peasants to pool their land and labor on more efficient cooperative farms.

**Remolding society.** Like Lenin in the Soviet Union, Mao Zedong built a one-party totalitarian state, with the Communist party supreme. Communist ideology replaced Confucian beliefs and traditional religions. The gov-

**Transforming China**  *China set out in a new direction in 1949. Led by Mao Zedong, the Chinese Communists launched revolutionary new programs to change China from a peasant society to a modern, industrial nation. This poster shows peasants hailing the takeover by Mao's Communists.* **Impact of the Individual**  *Do you think that a strong leader is needed to bring about major change? Explain.*

ernment attacked crime and corruption. It did away with the old landlord and business classes. In their place, peasants and workers were honored as the builders of the new China.

To increase literacy, reformers simplified Chinese characters, making it easier to learn to read and write. Schools were opened for young and old. The emphasis was on political education. Students learned to praise the "Great Helmsman," Mao Zedong, who could do no wrong.

The Communists sent health-care workers to remote rural areas. Although many of these "barefoot doctors" had limited training, they did help to reduce disease and teach better hygiene.

**Conflict in Tibet**
High in the mountains of southwestern China lies Tibet. For centuries, Tibetans lived independently, with their own language, culture, and religion, a form of Buddhism led by a spiritual leader called the Dalai Lama (inset picture). In 1950, China seized Tibet—which they call Xizang—setting up collective farms and factories and suppressing Buddhism. Tibetans rebelled against the Chinese in 1959, and in the crackdown that followed, the Dalai Lama fled. From exile, he has worked tirelessly to restore his nation's freedom. At left, Tibetans gather in Lhasa during the 1959 rebellion. **Geography and History** How would its mountain location encourage Tibet's spirit of independence?

**Equality for women.** Under China's new constitution, women won equality under the law. They were expected to work alongside men in fields and factories. State-run nurseries were set up to care for the children. These changes weakened the old ideal of the extended family dominated by the oldest male. In China's cities, as elsewhere in the developing world, the nuclear family became increasingly common.

Although Chinese women made real progress, they did not enjoy full equality. Only a few won promotion to top jobs in government and industry. Women were often paid less than men for the same work. Also, after working at paid jobs, they still were responsible for cleaning, cooking, and child care.

**The Great Leap Forward.** In 1958, Mao launched the Great Leap Forward. He urged people to make a superhuman effort to increase farm and industrial output. In an attempt to make agriculture more efficient, he created communes. A typical commune included several villages, thousands of acres of land, and up to 25,000 people. It had its own schools, factories, housing, and dining halls.

Each commune had production quotas. Communes also mobilized labor brigades to build dams and irrigation systems. Rural communes set up "backyard" industries to produce steel and other products. Poet Yuan Kejia (yoo AHN kuh JYAH) praised the virtues of hard work and self-sacrifice for the new China:

> **"**Labor is joy, how joyful is it?
> Bathed in sweat and two hands
> full of mud,
> Like sweet rain, my sweat waters
> the land
> And the land issues scent,
> better than milk.**"**

The Great Leap Forward was a dismal failure. Backyard industries turned out low-quality, useless goods. The commune system slowed food output. Bad weather added to the problems and led to a terrible famine. Between 1959 and 1961, up to 30 million Chinese are thought to have starved to death. In response, China turned to more moderate policies.

**The Cultural Revolution.** China slowly recovered from the Great Leap Forward. Mao, however, feared that bureaucrats and technicians were slowly replacing revolutionaries in running the country. In 1966, he launched the Great Proletarian Cultural Revolution. Its goal was to purge China of "bourgeois," or nonrevolutionary, tendencies. He urged young Chinese to experience revolution firsthand, as his generation had.

In response, teenagers formed bands of Red Guards. Waving copies of the "Little Red Book" of Mao's sayings, Red Guards attacked those they claimed were counterrevolutionaries. They targeted people in authority, from party leaders and factory managers to teachers, writers, and artists. The accused were publicly humiliated or beaten—sometimes even killed.

The Cultural Revolution convulsed China. Schools and universities closed. Millions of people were driven from their jobs. Government offices ceased to function, the economy slowed, and civil war threatened.

At last, Mao had the army restore order. Many Red Guards were sent to work on communes. They became a lost generation, undereducated and cut off from normal family life and careers. In the end, many became disillusioned with communism.

## China and the Cold War

The Communist victory in China dominated the Cold War in 1949. The United States had supported Jiang Jieshi. After he fled to Taiwan, the Americans continued to support the Nationalist government. They refused to recognize the People's Republic of China, or, as they called it, "Red China."

**Relations with the United States.** The rift between China and the United States deepened when they supported opposing sides in the Korean War. (See Section 3.) For years, the United States tried to isolate China, which it saw as an aggressive communist power expanding across Asia.

In 1971, however, China won admission to the United Nations. A year later, United States President Richard Nixon visited Mao in Beijing,

opening the door to improved relations. Both leaders used this occasion to strengthen their position with the Soviet Union. Formal diplomatic recognition of China by the United States finally came in 1979.

**Split with the Soviet Union.** Despite a treaty of friendship between China and the Soviet Union, the two communist giants were uneasy allies. In the 1950s, Stalin sent economic aid and technical experts to help China modernize. But he and Mao disagreed on many issues, especially ideology.

Mao had adapted Marxism to Chinese conditions. Marx, for example, had predicted that the industrial working class—the proletariat—would lead the revolution. Since China had little industry, Mao relied on peasants rather than factory workers to make the revolution. Stalin rejected Mao's views. Mao, for his part, thought the Soviets were too conservative and accused them of being too willing to "coexist" with the capitalist powers.

China and the Soviet Union were also rivals for influence in the Third World. In addition, border disputes triggered tensions between the two. Their border on the Amur River dated from czarist times, when Russia had seized territory from China. In 1960, border clashes and disputes over ideology led the Soviets to withdraw all aid and advisers from China, thus ending the alliance.

## China After Mao

Mao Zedong died in 1976. Despite disastrous mistakes, he remained the revolutionary hero who had restored order, ended foreign domination, and made China a world power once again.

After Mao, more moderate leaders controlled China. By 1981, Deng Xiaoping (duhng show PIHNG) had set China on a new path. Deng was a practical reformer, more interested in raising output than in political purity. "I don't care if a cat is red [socialist] or white [capitalist]," he declared, "as long as it catches mice."

**Economic reforms.** Deng backed a program called the Four Modernizations. It emphasized agriculture, industry, science, and defense.

◀ Nixon and Mao

**A Call for Democracy** In May 1989, Chinese students and workers rallied for democracy in Beijing's Tiananmen Square. The demonstrators, shown here, carried banners and paraded a statue of the Goddess of Liberty. Hundreds died and many more were injured when the Chinese government sent in troops to put down the protest. **Global Interaction** How did the statue reflect global interaction?

China. The government set up special enterprise zones where foreigners could own and operate industries.

Deng's reforms brought a surge of growth and a better standard of living for some Chinese. They were soon buying motor scooters, televisions, and tape decks. On the down side, crime and corruption grew. Inequalities grew again as a new wealthy class emerged. A gap also grew between poor rural farmers and city dwellers on the coast who were exposed to western influences.

**Tiananmen Square massacre.** By the late 1980s, some Chinese were demanding greater political freedom. In Beijing and other cities, students, workers, and others supported a democracy movement like those sweeping Eastern Europe and the Soviet Union. Unlike Gorbachev in the Soviet Union, however, Deng allowed only economic, not political, reform.

In May 1989, as you have read, demonstrators occupied Tiananmen Square. They built a huge plaster statue called the Goddess of Liberty and waved banners proclaiming, "Give us freedom or give us death." When they refused to disperse, the government sent in troops and tanks. Thousands of demonstrators were killed or wounded. Many others were arrested and tortured, some put to death.

The crackdown showed that China's Communist leaders were determined to maintain control. To them, order was more important than political freedom. During the 1990s, efforts to push China to end human rights violations had limited effects.

### Looking Ahead

By the mid-1990s, China was a major industrial power. Its economy ranked among the fastest growing in the world, and it was building major trade ties with countries worldwide. Yet it faced many unresolved issues. With its leadership in transition, no one knew what direction it would take.

**Population policies.** Population growth posed a challenge for the future. Since 1949, China's population has more than doubled, to 1.2 billion. Such rapid growth strained the economy. In the 1980s, the government instituted a one-child-per-family policy. Parents

As part of the Four Modernizations, Deng introduced economic reforms, including some private ownership of property and free-market policies. In agriculture, the responsibility system replaced the communes. Under it, peasant families were allotted plots of farmland. The government took a share of their crops, but the family could sell the rest on the free market. Entrepreneurs were allowed to set up their own businesses. Managers of state-run factories were given more freedom but were expected to make their plants more efficient.

Deng welcomed foreign capital and technology. Investors from Japan, Hong Kong, Taiwan, and the West organized joint ventures with

who had only one child were given rewards, such as better housing or improved medical benefits. Those who had more children faced fines and other penalties.

The campaign to slow the birthrate worked better in cities, where the government had more control, than in rural areas. Farm families, who wanted children to work the land, often paid fines rather than obey the policy. The one-child policy had a tragic effect in a country that still valued boys over girls. Female infanticide, or the killing of girl babies, increased despite efforts to prevent it.

**Economic and political challenges.** China continued to grapple with economic problems. Many state-run industries were still inefficient but could not be shut down without risking high unemployment and economic chaos. Overcrowded cities were bursting at the seams as millions of peasants arrived each year seeking new opportunities.

China's leaders faced the weakening of communist ideology. Many Chinese—from party officials on down—took more interest in profit than in socialism. China watchers wondered how long China's leaders could continue to promote economic reform without making political change.

## SECTION 2 REVIEW

1. **Identify** (a) People's Republic of China, (b) Great Leap Forward, (c) Cultural Revolution, (d) "Little Red Book," (e) Four Modernizations, (f) Tiananmen Square massacre.
2. **Define** commune.
3. Why were the Communists able to win power in China in 1949?
4. Describe three ways that communism transformed Chinese life.
5. What economic reforms did Deng Xiaoping introduce?
6. *Critical Thinking* **Predicting Consequences** Do you think China can continue to push economic reforms without making political reforms? Why or why not?
7. *ACTIVITY* Imagine that you are an artist working for the Chinese government. Create a poster supporting one of the programs introduced by the People's Republic.

# 3 The Asian Tigers

## Guide for Reading

■ How are Hong Kong and Taiwan linked to China?

■ Why are the Asian tigers an economic success story?

■ How do North Korea and South Korea differ?

At a university in Taiwan, Professor Xu Wenxing worked on what he called a "futuristic dream." After 10 years, he proudly unveiled a computerized fingerprint-recognition device. Xu's invention has many possible uses—it may one day replace passports—and his university set up a company to market the device. To Xu, however, the most satisfying aspect of his success was that "the technology involved was developed in Taiwan."

Taiwan is one of four small Asian lands that have vaulted into the class of "newly industrialized countries." Besides Taiwan, Hong Kong, Singapore, and South Korea are also known for their aggressive growth. The four are often called the "Asian tigers." Although they differ in important ways, all have followed similar roads to modernization since 1945.

### *Greater China: Taiwan and Hong Kong*

The four Asian tigers were all influenced by Confucian traditions and Chinese power. Taiwan and Hong Kong were once ruled by the mainland. Today, the People's Republic still considers them part of China. Neither, however, experienced the Communist revolution and neither is currently part of the People's Republic. Still, historical and other links make them part of "greater China."

**Taiwan.** Taiwan fell to Japan in 1895, during the Age of Imperialism. The Japanese introduced some industry, providing a foundation for later growth. Then, in 1945, Taiwan reverted to China. When Jiang Jieshi fled the mainland, he set up his government there. Despite

Jiang's autocratic rule, Taiwan's economy grew at a phenomenal rate.

First, Taiwan set up light industry such as textiles. Later, it developed heavy industry as well. With new strains of rice brought by the Green Revolution (see page 841), its agriculture also prospered. As trade boomed, industrial cities emerged and the island's standard of living rose to one of Asia's highest. Encouraged by economic success, the government allowed people more freedom.

Hostility between Taiwan and the mainland lessened after the Cold War. Businesses from Taiwan took advantage of Deng Xiaoping's economic reforms to invest in the mainland. Many projects in China's coastal enterprise zones were financed by Taiwan. In addition, extensive trade—some of it illegal—took place between the two countries.

Most residents of Taiwan welcomed closer links with the mainland. Yet some warned against ties that might give Beijing too much power over their economy. Beijing's long-term goal was still to reunite Taiwan with China.

**Hong Kong.** Britain gained the tiny island of Hong Kong after the Opium War, in 1842. (See page 650.) Under British rule, Hong Kong and nearby territories grew into a center for trade. In 1949, refugees from Mao's Communist revolution jammed into Hong Kong. They provided the labor and capital that helped the territory boom.

Today, Hong Kong's economy is based on trade and light industry such as electronics and textiles. With many foreign banks and a busy stock market, it grew into a leading financial center. That wealth helped it modernize.

Hong Kong's amazing growth was due in part to its location on China's doorstep. Hong Kong Chinese built commercial ties to the mainland at a time when the People's Republic was largely isolated by the world community. Today, Hong Kong remains the chief link between the PRC and the rest of the world.

Hong Kong's status is changing, however. On July 1, 1997, Britain must return it to China. The People's Republic has agreed not to alter Hong Kong's social or economic system for 50 years and to allow it self-government. Whether the PRC will honor that pledge remains to be seen. China stands to profit from Hong Kong's bustling free-market economy. But an uncertain future has made many residents nervous.

## Hong Kong's Uncertain Future

The day after Britain announced that Hong Kong would revert to China, panic spread. "Don't try to book a flight out of the city," went one rumor. "They're all taken until after 1997."

**Business as usual.** Gradually, however, the mood subsided. Although Hong Kong's

---

*Interpreting a Graph* Under the British, Hong Kong became a major center of trade, manufacturing, shipping, and finance. As the graph shows, in the 1980s and 1990s its economy was booming. ■ What was Hong Kong's GDP in 1988? In 1992? Approximately what percentage increase was that? What event did Hong Kong residents fear might hurt their economy? Explain.

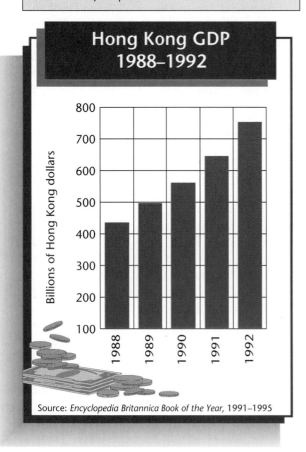

### Hong Kong GDP 1988–1992

*Billions of Hong Kong dollars*

Source: *Encyclopedia Britannica Book of the Year*, 1991–1995

**Gateway to China** *Despite the political differences between Hong Kong and China, their economies are closely linked. Hong Kong has invested some $52 billion in China, while over 2,000 mainland companies have offices in Hong Kong. These mutual economic interests, many hope, will keep the Chinese government from cracking down on Hong Kong after the city reverts to China in 1997.*
**Geography and History** *How has Hong Kong's location helped it to grow into an economic giant?*

newspapers continued to carry a steady stream of stories about the changeover, the issue seemed to have little impact on the daily life of the colony. Despite the uncertain future, the number of residents seeking to emigrate leveled off. Property values continued to rise. Patrons continued to flock to racetracks. Capacity crowds jammed movie houses, restaurants, and other entertainments.

In one of the stranger twists, Hong Kong's business community seemed to look forward to the arrival of China's Communist government. Their optimism was fueled in part by the huge profits that they have made on recent investments in China. They also carefully noted China's new pro-capitalist environment—from the leadership in Beijing to entrepreneurs doing on-the-spot bicycle repairs in the streets of Guangzhou. Said Woo Chia-wei, president of Hong Kong's new University of Science and Technology:

66They see a great opportunity. They see that all Asia is improving, and China is coming along.99

**Concern about democracy.** Still, there is concern about politics and human rights in Hong Kong under China. How much democracy will be allowed to survive when Beijing takes control of the colony?

In the Joint Declaration of 1984 that provided for Hong Kong's return, China agreed to a "one country, two systems" approach. That meant that Hong Kong would keep a high degree of autonomy and continue with the same political, economic, legal, and social systems for the next 50 years. Before the final changeover took place, Hong Kong's last British governor tried to expand the degree of democracy that China would give to Hong Kong.

Many Hong Kong residents said they had little faith in either the Chinese or the British. The Chinese government's repressive policies were the reason that many of them originally fled to Hong Kong from the mainland. Although the British had run Hong Kong efficiently, they kept many of the best jobs for themselves. They also routinely squashed attempts by the majority Chinese to gain a say in government.

Meanwhile, Hong Kong residents clung to the hope that the common goal they share with China—economic prosperity—would overcome all other differences. Jimmy Wong, who fled to Hong Kong from China 40 years ago, expressed the attitude of most Hong Kongers toward 1997:

66We don't believe we have any control over events. So we just wait and see what happens.99 ◼

## Singapore

The smallest Asian tiger is the city-state of Singapore. It sits on a tiny island at the tip of the Malay Peninsula in Southeast Asia. That location gives it command of a busy shipping route.

In the 1800s, the British built a naval base at Singapore, which grew into a center of commerce. Under British rule, many Chinese, brought in to process tin and rubber from Malaya, settled on the island. The Chinese became the dominant ethnic group, and their Confucian traditions shape modern Singapore.

**Order and prosperity.** After independence, Lee Kwan Yew ran a highly authoritarian government based on Confucian traditions. To achieve order, he put many restrictions on citizens—gum chewing, for example, is prohibited. He also introduced strict censorship.

At the same time, Lee launched ambitious programs for economic growth and social welfare. By keeping labor costs low, he attracted foreign capital that helped Singapore's economy boom and boosted its standard of living. By the 1980s, this hub of manufacturing, finance, and trade had the world's busiest harbor.

**Outlook for the future.** Singapore is often seen as a model of successful development. Yet because it is heavily dependent on trade, its economy is influenced by events around the world. Critics also note its limits on individual rights. The government counters with the Confucian argument that order is more important than individual freedom.

Still, Singapore faces demands for more freedom from its well-educated younger generation. It also has to deal with ethnic tensions between the Chinese majority and Malay and Indian minorities.

## The Two Koreas

The fourth Asian tiger is South Korea. It emerged amid Cold War tensions and a devastating "hot" war that involved not only Korea but also China and the United States.

**A Cold War division.** In 1910, Japan annexed Korea and imposed a brutal regime on the peninsula. After the Allied victory in World War II, the Soviet Union and the United States agreed to a temporary division of Korea, along the 38th parallel of latitude. American forces occupied the south. The Soviets held the north.

During the Cold War, Korea's division—like Germany's—seemed to become permanent. North Korea, ruled by Kim Il Sung, became a communist ally of the Soviet Union. In South Korea, the United States backed an authoritarian but noncommunist leader, Syngman Rhee.

**The Korean War.** In 1950, North Korean forces invaded the south, seeking to unify the country. They almost overran the peninsula. Backed by the UN, the United States organized an international force to help South Korea.

UN forces, mostly Americans and South Koreans, were commanded by United States general Douglas MacArthur. After landing troops behind enemy lines, he drove the invaders back across the 38th parallel. He continued to push northward toward the Yalu River on the border of China.

MacArthur's success moved China into action. Mao Zedong feared an American invasion. He sent Chinese troops to help the North Koreans. Together, they pushed the UN forces back to the 38th parallel.

**The long truce.** Fighting continued until an armistice was signed in 1953. That cease-fire has held for more than 40 years. More than a million North Korean and South Korean troops dug in along the truce line. American forces, too, remained in South Korea to guarantee the peace.

## Differences North and South

After the war, the two Koreas slowly rebuilt economies destroyed by the fighting and by years of Japanese occupation. Both remained centers of Cold War rivalry. The United States funneled aid to South Korea, while the Soviets helped the north.

**An economic powerhouse.** Economically, South Korea leaped ahead of the north after the mid-1960s. At first, it exported textiles and

**ISSUES** *For* **TODAY**

Singapore's rulers claimed that they needed to restrict individual freedom in order to achieve economic prosperity for their people. Can developing nations promote economic growth without sacrificing political freedom?

## Korean War, 1950–1953

CHINA

USSR

Chongjin

Yalu R.

Chosan

40°N

Pyongyang

NORTH KOREA

SEA OF JAPAN

Kosong

Yangyang

38th Parallel

Panmunjom · Seoul

Inchon

Samchok

Pyongtaek

YELLOW SEA

SOUTH KOREA

Taegu

Masan

35°N

Pusan

0    50    100 Miles
0    50    100 Kilometers

·········· Line of farthest North Korean advance September 1950

Line of farthest UN advance November 1950

- - - - Line of farthest Chinese and North Korean advance, January 1951

——— Armistice line, 1953

## GEOGRAPHY AND HISTORY

After North Korean troops stormed across the 38th parallel into South Korea, the UN sent an army to aid South Korea. Fighting continued for three years, until a cease-fire was signed in 1953.

1. **Location** On the map, locate (a) North Korea, (b) South Korea, (c) 38th parallel, (d) Yalu River, (e) China.
2. **Movement** Which nation gained territory as a result of the armistice?
3. **Critical Thinking** *Making Inferences* Based on the map, why do you think the UN advance across the 38th parallel worried the Chinese?

inexpensive goods. Then, it shifted to higher-priced exports such as automobiles. Its strong growth was due in part to international loans and investment and in part to low wages paid to workers. By the 1990s, South Korea was an economic powerhouse. As prosperity increased, workers demanded better pay, and South Korea's standard of living rose remarkably.

For decades, a dicatatorial government backed by the military ruled South Korea. By 1987, however, growing prosperity and fierce student protests forced the government to ease controls and hold direct elections. The country also faced new social pressures as urbanization undermined traditional ways.

**The totalitarian north.** Under Kim Il Sung, North Korea recovered from the war. State-owned industries and collective farms increased output. By the late 1960s, however, growth slowed. Kim's emphasis on self-reliance kept North Korea isolated from much of the world. Yet when its old partners, the Soviet Union and China, tried out economic reforms in the 1980s, North Korea clung to hardline communism.

In North Korea, a barrage of propaganda glorified Kim as the "Great Leader." After Kim's death in 1994, his son Kim Jong Il, the "Dear Leader," took charge. Whether Kim Jong Il would opt for change or keep North Korea as isolated as ever remained to be seen. By the 1990s, though, North Korea's longtime ally China was reaching out to the capitalist world. Much to the disgust of North Koreans, China forged economic ties with South Korea.

**The nuclear issue.** Like several other emerging nations, North Korea set up a program to build nuclear power plants and nuclear weapons. Under intense pressure from the United States, the North Koreans agreed to dismantle the program. In exchange, the United States was to supply North Korea with oil and begin the process of diplomatic recognition of North Korea. The agreement remained shaky due in part to deep mistrust on both sides.

**Looking ahead.** Despite differences between the two Koreas, most Koreans want to see their country reunited. After all, they share the same language, culture, and heritage. Reunification on the German model seemed unlikely as long as North Korea insisted on its policy of

**The Great Leader** *During his nearly 50 years in power, Kim Il Sung fostered a powerful cult of personality. Here, a giant portrait of the "Great Leader" looms over a student gathering in Pyongyang.* **Impact of the Individual** *How do you think North Korea's isolation helped to strengthen Kim Il Sung's power?*

isolation. South Korea's growing prosperity also created an economic gulf between the countries. Resolving the issue was of global interest because of Korea's strategic location between three Asian giants—China, Russia, and Japan.

## SECTION 3 REVIEW

1. **Identify** (a) Asian tigers, (b) Lee Kwan Yew, (c) Syngman Rhee, (d) Kim Jong Il.
2. (a) How is Taiwan linked to China today? (b) Why is Hong Kong's future uncertain?
3. (a) Describe Singapore's development as an Asian tiger. (b) What challenges does Singapore face today?
4. (a) How was the division of Korea related to the Cold War? (b) What was one immediate and one long-term result of the Korean War?
5. *Critical Thinking* **Analyzing Information** Why might Korea be harder to reunify than Germany?
6. *ACTIVITY* Singapore leader Lee Kwan Yew argues that economic development is more important than political freedom for developing countries. Write a letter to Lee expressing your opinion on this issue.

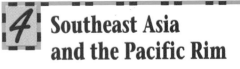

# 4 Southeast Asia and the Pacific Rim

## Guide for Reading

■ What problems did developing nations of Southeast Asia face after World War II?

■ Why was Vietnam plunged into decades of war?

■ Why is the Pacific Rim an economic powerhouse today?

Today, more than 50 years after the end of World War II, Southeast Asia has emerged as a key player in the global economy. In the immediate postwar years, however, the region was shaped by the nationalist drive for independence. Some nations won freedom easily, without much violence. Others, like Vietnam, fought long wars of liberation.

### Sources of Conflict

After World War II, local nationalists rejected European efforts to reclaim their colonial empires in Southeast Asia. Ho Chi Minh, a Vietnamese nationalist, echoed the view of people throughout the region when he declared:

66The whole Vietnamese people, animated by a common purpose, are determined to fight to the bitter end against any attempt by the French colonialists to reconquer their country.99

Cold War tensions complicated the drive for freedom. The United States supported independence for colonial people in principle. But the West was anxious to stop the spread of communism. As a result, the United States helped noncommunists gain power in Southeast Asia even though they had little popular support.

Other problems occurred because emerging Southeast Asian nations lacked experience in self-government. Many faced years of instability as they set out to modernize. Efforts to modernize were further hampered by complex ethnic and regional conflicts.

## Decades of War in Vietnam

In mainland Southeast Asia, an agonizing liberation struggle tore apart the region once known as French Indochina. It affected the emerging nations of Vietnam, Cambodia, and Laos. The 30-year conflict had two major phases: the battle against the French and the Cold War conflict.

**Battle against the French.** The first phase of the struggle lasted from 1946 to 1954. During World War II, Ho Chi Minh, the Vietnamese communist, had organized guerrillas to resist the Japanese. At war's end, Ho controlled much of northern Vietnam.

In 1946, the French set out to regain Indochina. Like Mao in China, however, Ho "swam in the peasant sea." With peasant support, Ho's guerrilla fighters slowly wore down the French and finally forced them to leave.

**Vietnam divided.** By this time, the struggle in Vietnam had become part of the Cold War. At a 1954 conference in Geneva, Switzerland, western and communist powers agreed to a temporary division of Vietnam. Ho and the communists ruled North Vietnam. A noncommunist government, supported by the United States and headed by Ngo Dinh Diem, ruled South Vietnam. Cambodia and Laos became independent nations.

The agreement called for elections to be held in 1956 to reunite Vietnam. The elections never took place, however, largely because the Americans and Diem feared that the communists might win. American officials believed in the "domino theory." It held that a communist victory in South Vietnam would cause noncommunist governments across Southeast Asia to fall to communism, like a row of dominos. To prevent such a disaster, as the French withdrew from Vietnam, the United States stepped in to shore up the Diem government.

**American involvement.** The second phase of the Vietnam War raged from 1959 to 1975. Ho Chi Minh wanted to unite Vietnam under northern rule. He supported the Viet Cong, communist rebels trying to overthrow Diem in South Vietnam.

At first, the United States sent only military advisers and supplies to Diem. Under Presidents Kennedy and Johnson, however, the American

## Vietnam War, 1968–1975

→ Tet Offensive, 1968
■ American bases
////  National Liberation Front base areas
--→ North Vietnam's final offensive, 1975

GEOGRAPHY *AND* HISTORY

In Vietnam, what started as a struggle against colonialism ended up as a major contest of the Cold War. The United States threw its support behind South Vietnam against the communist north. But despite this intervention, the war ended with a North Vietnamese victory.

1. **Location** On the map, locate (a) North Vietnam, (b) South Vietnam, (c) Cambodia, (d) Laos, (e) Saigon, (f) Ho Chi Minh Trail.
2. **Movement** How did North Vietnam's use of the Ho Chi Minh Trail as a supply route help to spread the war beyond Vietnam?
3. **Critical Thinking** **Applying Information** Use the map to describe the "domino theory."

**Generations of Soldiers** *The people of Vietnam were at war for more than 30 years. Generations of young people grew up expecting to fight. These young boys served in the South Vietnamese army.* **Global Interaction** *How did Vietnam's struggle for independence become part of the Cold War?*

the civil war in China that had brought Mao to power in 1949. Diem and his successors in South Vietnam were unpopular leaders of a corrupt government. Ho Chi Minh was widely admired as a hero who had fought the Japanese and the French. Many Vietnamese saw the United States as another foreign power seeking to dominate their land. Also, despite American air power and advanced technology, guerrillas fought well in the jungle terrain.

**Vietnam today.** The communist victors imposed harsh rule on the south. Tens of thousands of Vietnamese fled in small boats. Many of these "boat people" drowned. Survivors landed in refugee camps. Eventually, some were accepted into the United States or other countries.

Vietnam itself had to rebuild a land mangled by decades of war. Recovery was slow due partly to government inefficiency and partly to an American-led boycott of Vietnam. For years, Vietnam was mired in poverty and unable to attract foreign capital.

In the 1990s, a new generation of Vietnamese leaders opened the door to investors by introducing free-market reforms. After the Cold War ended, the United States and Vietnam edged toward better relations. Today, Vietnam seems poised for economic revival.

### Tragedy in Cambodia

During the Vietnam War, fighting spilled over into neighboring Cambodia. The North Vietnamese sent supplies through Cambodia to guerrilla forces in South Vietnam. In 1969, the United States bombed that route and then invaded Cambodia. After the Americans left, Cambodian communist guerrillas, the Khmer Rouge, overthrew the government.

involvement increased, and a local struggle became a major Cold War conflict.

In 1964, the United States began bombing targets in North Vietnam. When air raids failed to force Ho to abandon the war, the United States committed more troops. By 1969, more than 500,000 Americans were serving in Vietnam. Meantime, the Soviet Union and China sent aid but no troops to help North Vietnam.

Even with massive American help, South Vietnam could not defeat the communist guerrillas and their North Vietnamese allies. At the same time, the bombing of North Vietnam and growing American casualties on the ground inflamed antiwar opinion in the United States. Under increasing pressure, President Nixon finally arranged a cease-fire and began withdrawal of American forces in 1973. Two years later, the North Vietnamese captured Saigon, capital of the south, and reunited the country.

**Why the communists won.** Ever since, Americans have debated why the communists won. In some ways, the Vietnam War mirrored

**GLOBAL** **CONNECTIONS**

Ho Chi Minh lived in France for six years, between 1917 and 1923. In 1919, he addressed a petition to the representatives of the Great Powers at the Versailles peace conference that ended World War I. He demanded that the French colonial power grant its subjects in Indochina equal rights with the French rulers. This act brought no response from the peacemakers, but it made him a hero to the Vietnamese.

Led by Pol Pot, the Khmer Rouge unleashed a reign of terror. To destroy all western influences, they drove people from the cities and forced them to work in the fields. They slaughtered or caused the death of more than a million Cambodians, perhaps a third of the population.

In 1979, Vietnam invaded and occupied Cambodia. Pol Pot and his forces retreated to remote areas. In 1993, UN peacekeepers supervised elections. Despite guerrillas who still terrorized parts of the country, a new government began to rebuild Cambodia.

## Independence for the Philippines

In 1946, the island nation of the Philippines gained freedom peacefully after almost five decades of American rule. The United States, however, exerted a strong influence on the country through military and economic aid.

**Rebellions.** Although the Filipino constitution set up a democratic government, a wealthy elite controlled politics and the economy. The peasant majority, meanwhile, was desperately poor. Many peasants threw their support behind the Huks, local communists who promised land reform. With American help, the government crushed the Huks, but new rebellions kept erupting.

In 1965, Ferdinand Marcos was elected president. Marcos had promised reform but instead made himself dictator. He cracked down on free speech and forced opponents into exile. He even had Benigno Aquino (beh NEE nyoh ah KEE noh), a popular rival politician, murdered.

**"People power."** Under heavy pressure, Marcos finally held elections in 1986. At the polls, Corazon Aquino, widow of the slain Benigno, defeated Marcos. When Marcos tried to overturn the results, the people of Manila forced him to leave in what was called the "people power" revolution.

Under Aquino and her successors, the fragile Filipino democracy survived. In

◄ *Corazon Aquino*

the early 1990s, it also saw some economic growth. But the government failed to make the major changes needed to improve life for the poverty-stricken majority. With the election of a new president, Fidel Ramos, who had served in both the Marcos and Aquino governments, there was renewed optimism for the future.

## Developing Nations of Southeast Asia

Other Southeast Asian nations emerged from colonial rule after brief struggles. All pursued the same goal, modernization, but their paths differed. Here, we will look at the experiences of two developing nations: Myanmar (formerly Burma) and Indonesia.

**Myanmar.** Ethnic tensions also plagued Burma after independence. Burmans, who make up the majority of the population, dominated the country. For years, repressive military rulers battled rebel ethnic minorities who wanted autonomy. In 1989, the military renamed the country Myanmar, meaning "the People's Country." By taking that name, the government recognized that other groups besides Burmans lived there.

The military government isolated the country from the world, thus limiting trade and foreign investment. It tried to develop the economy by imposing state socialism modeled on China's system. Its policies brought little improvement in the standard of living.

Under mounting pressure from students and other young people, the government held elections in 1990. The opposition party won. It was led by Aung San Suu Kyi (AWNG SAHN SOO SHEE), whose father had helped Burma win independence. The military rejected the election results and jailed, killed, or exiled many opponents. Suu Kyi was held under house arrest. In 1991, while still a prisoner, she was awarded the Nobel Peace Prize for her "nonviolent struggle for democracy and human rights." Suu Kyi was finally released in 1995 and vowed to continue to fight for democracy in Myanmar.

**Indonesia.** Geography is an obstacle to unity in Indonesia, as in many Third World nations. Indonesia includes more than 13,000 islands splashed across 3,200 miles of ocean—a distance equal to the width of the United States.

**Indonesian Batik** *Indonesians have long been known for their beautiful batik fabrics. Following a centuries-old method, the artist paints a design on cloth with melted wax, then dyes the cloth. The coated areas do not absorb the color, and when the wax is removed the design is revealed. Remains of cloth found on Indonesia's main island of Java indicate that the same or similar designs have been in use for about 1,000 years. A contemporary Indonesian artist created the imaginative batik design shown here.* **Art and Literature** *What mood does the artist convey with this design? Explain.*

recently, the government has silenced protests in East Timor, an island with a large Roman Catholic population that wanted autonomy.

Under military rule, Indonesia made progress toward economic development. It benefited from rich deposits of oil and tin and exported rubber, spices, and coffee. The constant rise and fall of oil prices, however, meant that income was uncertain. Still, Indonesia increased its literacy rate. By the 1990s, economic reforms brought more foreign investment and better times.

**Regional cooperation.** Demands for political freedom and social justice remained an issue in Southeast Asia. Some government leaders, however, asserted that order and economic development must take priority over democracy.

To achieve prosperity and improve regional self-reliance, six Southeast Asian countries formed the Association of Southeast Asian Nations (ASEAN) in 1967. Since then, Singapore, Malaysia, Thailand, the Philippines, Indonesia, and Brunei have worked to promote economic and cultural cooperation. Besides lowering trade barriers, they have increased contacts with other Southeast Asian nations, including Vietnam.

## The Pacific Rim

In the modern global economy, Southeast Asia and East Asia are part of a vast region known as the Pacific Rim. It includes countries in Asia and the Americas that border the Pacific Ocean. (See the map on page 895.)

The Pacific first became an artery for world trade in the 1500s. By the mid-1900s, links across the Pacific had grown dramatically. The end of the Cold War fed a new surge of trade and other contacts.

By the 1990s, the volume of trade across the Pacific was greater than that across the Atlantic. Some analysts predicted that the 2000s will be the "Pacific century" because of this region's potential for further growth.

**Population and markets.** Countries on the Asian Pacific Rim formed a huge market that lured investors, especially multinational corporations. With more than 1.2 billion people, China has a fifth of the world's population. Indonesia, with 190 million people, and Japan, with 125 million, are also among the world's

Its large population is ethnically diverse. The Javanese dominate, but about 300 other groups, with their own languages or dialects, also live in Indonesia. Despite this diversity, about 90 percent of Indonesians are Muslims.

Since independence, an authoritarian government has suppressed rebellions. In 1965, it crushed what looked like a communist uprising and massacred hundreds of thousands of suspected communists. Mobs killed many Chinese whose ancestors had settled in Indonesia. More

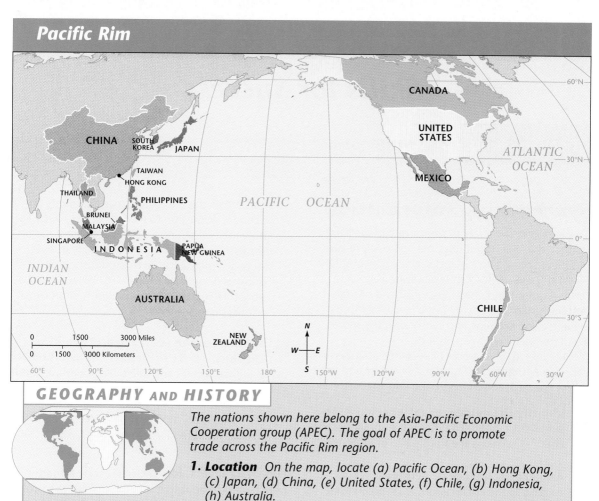

## Pacific Rim

The nations shown here belong to the Asia-Pacific Economic Cooperation group (APEC). The goal of APEC is to promote trade across the Pacific Rim region.

**1. Location** On the map, locate (a) Pacific Ocean, (b) Hong Kong, (c) Japan, (d) China, (e) United States, (f) Chile, (g) Indonesia, (h) Australia.

**2. Movement** What might be some of the effects of trade among the nations of the Pacific Rim?

**3. Critical Thinking Synthesizing Information** The nations of the Pacific Rim are spread out across the globe. What unites them as a region?

---

most populous nations. Vietnam is just emerging as a new market in the region.

Since the 1960s, Japan has dominated the Asian Pacific Rim economically. By the 1990s, however, China was challenging Japan's economic empire. American companies, too, sought a place on the Asian Pacific Rim.

**Cultural exchanges.** Countries on the Pacific Rim are enormously diverse. Indian, Hindu, Buddhist, and Confucian traditions, you will recall, helped shape Southeast Asian cultures. Later, Islam took root in some areas, while the Age of Imperialism brought western and Christian influences.

Today, cultural exchanges occur rapidly as radio and television programs are beamed by satellite throughout Asia. Businesses and tourists aid the exchange of technology and ideas. The development of the Pacific Rim promises to bring the Americas and Asia into closer contact.

## SECTION 4 REVIEW

1. **Identify** (a) Ho Chi Minh, (b) domino theory, (c) Khmer Rouge, (d) Corazon Aquino, (e) Aung San Suu Kyi, (f) ASEAN.
2. How did the Cold War affect Southeast Asia?
3. (a) Describe the two phases of the Vietnam War. (b) Why did North Vietnam triumph?
4. Why is the Pacific Rim seen as an important link in the global economy?
5. *Critical Thinking* **Drawing Conclusions** Why might a country like Indonesia have a hard time creating a national identity?
6. *ACTIVITY* Imagine that you are Aung San Suu Kyi of Myanmar. Prepare a speech accepting the Nobel Peace Prize. Be sure to include remarks about the present state of your nation and your hopes for its future.

# Skills for Success

## Synthesizing Information

To use historical evidence, you must be able to synthesize—that is, put together and analyze various pieces of evidence in order to form a complete picture. The evidence can take a wide variety of forms—graphs and charts, pictures, and primary and secondary sources are just a few. The more evidence you examine and synthesize, the more accurate will be your conclusions.

Below are three pieces of evidence about education in South Korea. Study the evidence and then follow the steps to synthesize the information.

**1** **Identify the evidence.** (a) What is the subject of the graph? (b) What is the subject of the chart? (c) What is the third piece of evidence?

**2** **Analyze each piece of evidence.** (a) According to the circle graph, what percentage of South Korea's total budget is spent for education? (b) How high does spending for education rank in the budget? (c) What item or items have a larger budget than education? (d) According to the table, how many students applied for admission to a university in 1990? For how many openings? (e) What percentage of students who applied to a university in 1990 were accepted? (f) Are these statistics for 1990 unusual or typical? Explain. (g) What does the slogan tell you about competition for university admission in South Korea?

**3** **Synthesize the evidence and draw conclusions.** (a) Based on the three pieces of evidence, what conclusion can you draw about the importance of education in South Korea? (b) How does each piece of evidence support the conclusion? (c) What other pieces of evidence would reinforce your conclusion?

***Beyond the Classroom*** Look through newspapers, magazines, and other sources to collect at least three pieces of evidence about education in the United States today. Then, use the information to draw conclusions about American education.

*Slogan among South Korean high school students:*

"You'll pass with three hours of sleep but you'll fail with four."

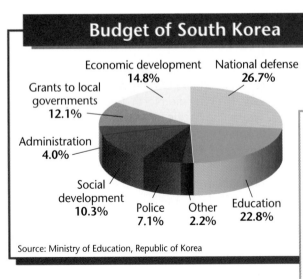

### Budget of South Korea

- National defense 26.7%
- Economic development 14.8%
- Grants to local governments 12.1%
- Administration 4.0%
- Social development 10.3%
- Police 7.1%
- Other 2.2%
- Education 22.8%

Source: Ministry of Education, Republic of Korea

### Applications to Universities in South Korea

| Year | Number of Applicants | Openings | Percentage Accepted |
|------|------------|----------|---------------------|
| 1987 | 732,931 | 271,745 | 37.1 |
| 1988 | 765,604 | 296,820 | 38.8 |
| 1989 | 803,140 | 310,220 | 38.6 |
| 1990 | 889,148 | 334,855 | 38.8 |

Source: *Education Indicators in Korea*

## Building Vocabulary

Review the following vocabulary from this chapter: *zaibatsu, gross domestic product, protectionism, trade deficit, ideology, commune, guerrilla, entrepreneur.* Write sentences using each of these terms, leaving blanks where the terms would go. Exchange your sentences with another student and fill in the blanks on each other's lists.

## Reviewing Chapter Themes

1. **Continuity and Change** (a) Select two nations discussed in the chapter. Describe the effects of the Cold War on their development after World War II. (b) How did the end of the Cold War open new doors across Asia?
2. **Economics and Technology** Describe the role of trade in the development and modernization of one of the following nations: (a) Japan, (b) Taiwan, (c) Singapore.
3. **Political and Social Systems** (a) What economic, social, and political changes did Mao introduce in China? (b) What changes were introduced by Mao's successors?
4. **Impact of the Individual** (a) Why was Mao considered a hero even though some of his programs resulted in the deaths of millions of Chinese? (b) Describe the role of Ho Chi Minh in Vietnam's struggle for independence.
5. **Global Interaction** (a) What nations make up the Pacific Rim community? (b) What role does the Pacific Rim play in today's global economy?

## Thinking Critically

1. **Recognizing Causes and Effects** (a) List the reasons for Japan's economic success after World War II. (b) How might its emergence as an economic superpower threaten some of the values that brought success? (★ See *Skills for Success,* page 18.)
2. **Comparing** Compare Deng's reforms in China to those of Gorbachev in the Soviet Union. (a) How were the reforms similar? (b) How were they different?
3. **Identifying Main Ideas** (a) Describe the development of two of the four Asian tigers after World War II. (b) What factors contributed to

their success? (c) What problems do they face today?
4. **Linking Past and Present** (a) How did Korea become a pawn in the Cold War? (b) How are the effects of the Cold War still felt in Korea today?
5. **Predicting Consequences** Explain how you think the takeover of Hong Kong by the People's Republic of China in 1997 will affect (a) Hong Kong and (b) China. Give reasons for your answers. (★ See *Skills for Success,* page 974.)
6. **Comparing** (a) What problems did developing nations like Indonesia and Myanmar have in common? (b) How were they different?
7. **Synthesizing Information** "Five hundred years ago," notes a contemporary economist, "the world's economic center moved from the Mediterranean to the Atlantic. Today, it has shifted again to the Pacific." Support this statement with evidence from this and earlier chapters. (★ See *Skills for Success,* page 896.)

### For Your Portfolio

Imagine that you work for an Asian trade organization. You have been asked to prepare an agenda for an upcoming meeting on international trade.

1. Review the information on economics and trade in this chapter. Make notes about each issue.
2. Use library resources to update your information. Check the *Reader's Guide to Periodical Literature* for recent magazine articles. Consult the index for business newspapers, such as *The Wall Street Journal,* for other articles.
3. Identify the main issues that nations such as China, Japan, Taiwan, South Korea, Singapore, Hong Kong, Vietnam, and Indonesia might wish to discuss with western nations such as the United States. Keep in mind that the issues will vary depending on the government and economy of the nation.
4. Draw up your agenda, making sure that all important issues are included.
5. Share your agenda with the class. Be prepared to explain why you think each item on the agenda is important.

# South Asia and the Middle East

## (1945–Present)

## CHAPTER OUTLINE

August 15, 1947, was a joyful day in India. Everywhere, parades and mass meetings filled the streets with huge crowds. Speeches hailed Mohandas Gandhi as "father of the nation." Bands played, flags waved, and fireworks exploded. At the stroke of midnight, after decades of struggle, power had passed from British colonial governors to India's own chosen leaders. This was India's Independence Day.

Jawaharlal Nehru, India's first prime minister, greeted the day with hope for the future:

66The Appointed Day has come, the day appointed by destiny, and India stands forth again after a long slumber and struggle, awake, vital, free, and independent. A new star rises, the star of freedom in the East. . . . May the star never set and that hope never be betrayed.99

Sadly, independence would bring tragedy along with joy. Soon, bloody riots exploded between Hindus and Muslims, while Gandhi himself would fall victim to assassination. Less than a year after the celebrations, Nehru wrote:

66Freedom came to us, our long-sought freedom, and it came with a minimum of violence. But immediately after, we had to wade through oceans of blood and tears.99

India and its neighbors on the subcontinent emerged from colonial rule to face many challenges—from religious strife and border conflicts to poverty and limited rights for women.

Developing nations in the Middle East also cast off western rule and set out to modernize. Some had the advantage of great oil wealth. Most did not. In the Middle East, as elsewhere, modernization was linked to a population explosion, urbanization, and disturbing social and economic problems. Nations responded differently to those challenges. In Muslim societies, many people looked for answers in a renewed commitment to Islamic traditions.

**FOCUS ON** these questions as you read:

- **Diversity**
  What impact did diversity have on challenges to nations in South Asia and the Middle East?

- **Economics and Technology**
  How did emerging nations use technology to develop economically?

- **Geography and History**
  Why was geography a significant force in shaping the modern Middle East?

- **Continuity and Change**
  How did modernization pose a challenge to older cultural values and traditions?

- **Religions and Value Systems**
  Why did the Islamic revival have a strong appeal to many Muslims?

## TIME AND PLACE

*Profession of Faith*  This ceramic by Iraqi artist Wasma'a K. Chorbachi repeats the central belief of Islam: "There is no God but God, and Muhammad is his prophet." Like many artists in former European colonies, Chorbachi at first followed western styles. But then, she wrote, "I suddenly felt that these paintings were not me, the Arab and the Muslim. . . . I had not been trained in an artistic language that would enable me to express the inner identity I so strongly felt." *Religions and Value Systems*  Islam has continued to be a major force in both South Asia and the Middle East. What other religions have shaped these regions?

## HUMANITIES LINK

*Art History*  Igael Tumarkin, *War Memories* (page 916).
*Literature*  In this chapter, you will encounter passages from the following works of literature: R. K. Narayan, *The Tale of Nagaraj* (page 902); The First Book of Maccabees (page 916); Liyana Badr, "A Land of Rock and Thyme" (page 918).

| 1947 Independent India and Pakistan created; UN partitions Palestine | 1971 Bangladesh breaks away from Pakistan | 1979 Egypt makes peace with Israel; Iranian revolution begins | 1991 Second Persian Gulf War | 1994 Palestinians gain limited self-rule |

| 1945 | 1960 | 1975 | 1990 | PRESENT |

# 1 Nations of South Asia

## Guide for Reading

- Why was India partitioned in 1947?
- What goals did independent nations of South Asia pursue?
- What obstacles to progress did South Asian nations face?
- What role have India and Pakistan played in world affairs?

In 1950, a new constitution set lofty goals for India:

66 . . . to secure to all its citizens: JUS-TICE, social, economic, and political; LIBERTY of thought expression, belief, faith and worship: EQUALITY of status and opportunity; and to promote among them all FRATERNITY assuring the dignity of the individual and the unity of the Nation. 99

Achieving those goals would prove difficult. In 1950, most Indians were poor and uneducated. They were divided by caste, region, language, and ethnic background. Yet India did make progress toward the promises made at independence. Two other new nations on the subcontinent, Pakistan and Bangladesh, grappled with similar challenges.

## Independence and Partition

As you read in Chapter 29, Indian nationalists had demanded independence since the late 1800s. After World War II, Britain finally agreed to these demands. As independence neared, a long-simmering issue surfaced. What would happen to the Muslim minority in a Hindu-dominated India?

**Two states.** Muhammad Ali Jinnah, leader of the Muslim League, insisted that Muslims have their own state, Pakistan. Riots between Hindus and Muslims helped convince Britain to partition, or divide, the subcontinent. In 1947, British officials hastily drew borders to create Hindu India and Muslim Pakistan. Pakistan was made up of two widely separated areas that had large Muslim populations. (See the map on page 901.)

**A tragedy unfolds.** Drawing fair borders was impossible because Hindus and Muslims lived side by side. In 1947, therefore, millions of Hindus and Muslims crossed the borders of India and Pakistan in both directions. During the mass migration, centuries of mistrust—which the British had exploited to keep the population divided—plunged northern India into savage violence. Hindu and Sikh mobs massacred Muslims fleeing into Pakistan. Muslims slaughtered Hindu and Sikh neighbors. An estimated 10 million refugees fled their homes. As many as a million or more, mostly Muslims, may have died.

Horrified at the partition and the violence, Gandhi turned once more to satyagraha. (See page 748.) On January 30, 1948, he was shot and killed by a Hindu extremist. Jawaharlal Nehru told a stricken nation, "The light has gone out of our lives and there is darkness everywhere." Gandhi's death discredited the extremists and helped end the worst violence. Still, Hindu-Muslim tensions persisted.

**An Extraordinary Family** *This family photograph shows three prime ministers of India. Jawaharlal Nehru, center, led India for 17 years after independence. His daughter Indira Gandhi and his grandson Rajiv Gandhi would in turn succeed Nehru as prime minister. Both would die at the hands of assassins.* **Impact of the Individual** *Why do you think the sons and daughters of political leaders often become politicians themselves?*

The partition of India created two populous new states in South Asia. It also uprooted millions of people and led to widespread violence.

1. **Location** On the map, locate (a) India, (b) West Pakistan, (c) East Pakistan, (d) Kashmir, (e) Ceylon, (f) Afghanistan.
2. **Movement** Using this map, describe the movement of Hindus and Muslims across the India-West Pakistan border during the 1947 partition.
3. **Critical Thinking** *Linking Past and Present* Compare this map to the map on page 988. What has happened to Pakistan since 1947?

## Partition of India, 1947

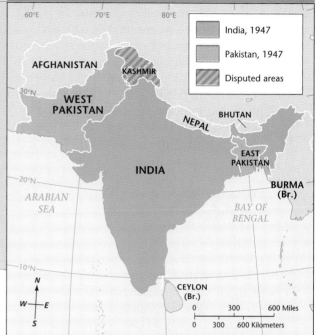

## The World's Largest Democracy

India built on the legacy of British rule, including its system of law and government. Today, with a population of more than 900 million, it is the world's largest democracy.

**Unity and diversity.** Indians had united behind the Congress party in its drive to independence. Still, the new nation was deeply divided. It included hundreds of princely states that had survived British rule. Indians spoke a wide variety of languages and dialects. While most Indians were Hindu, millions of others were Muslim, Christian, Sikh, or Buddhist.

India's constitution set up a federal system, like that of the United States, with powers divided between a strong central government and smaller local governments. In time, the government reorganized the princely states into a smaller number of states. It recognized 15 official languages and 35 major regional languages.

**The Nehru "dynasty."** For 40 years after independence, India was led by members of the Nehru family. As prime minister from 1947 until his death in 1964, Jawaharlal Nehru worked to build a modern, secular state dedicated to promoting social justice.

After he died, his daughter Indira Gandhi, and later his grandson Rajiv Gandhi, served as prime minister. Both were popular, energetic leaders, but their high-handed policies sometimes eroded goodwill. In the end, both fell victim to violence, as you will read. Today, many Indians hope that Rajiv's young son will someday enter politics.

## Economic Growth

Like other developing nations, India wanted to apply modern technology to expand agriculture and industry. The government adopted the socialist model, drawing up five-year plans to set economic goals and manage resources.

**Industrial growth.** British-built railroads gave India a basic transportation network. After independence, Nehru had dams built to produce hydroelectric power and poured resources into heavy industries such as steel. Within a few decades, India edged toward becoming an industrial power. Development, however, remained uneven. India lacked oil and natural gas—two resources essential to economic growth. As a result, it had to rely on costly imported oil.

**Green Revolution.** Seeking to make India self-sufficient in food production, Nehru took advantage of the Green Revolution. (See page 841.) New seeds, chemical fertilizers, and irrigation methods boosted crop output. Still, only farmers with enough land and money could grow the new crops. Most farmers, as in the past, depended on the monsoons and produced enough to survive but little surplus.

**Education.** To turn out the educated work force needed in an industrial economy, the government built schools and universities. India's literacy rate climbed, but unevenly. Boys were more likely to attend school than girls. Also, children from poor families often got little schooling because they were needed to work.

**The population issue.** Rapid population growth hampered efforts to improve conditions for most people. India's population has almost tripled since independence. While food output rose, so did demand. More than a third of Indians live below the poverty level, eating only one meal a day.

As the population boomed and the Green Revolution eliminated many agricultural jobs, millions of people streamed into cities to find work. But cities like Calcutta and Bombay did not have enough jobs and could not provide even basic services such as water or sewage. Families put up shanties in slums that sprawled around the cities.

The government encouraged family planning but did not impose harsh population control measures as China did. (See page 884.) To many Indians, especially in rural areas, children were seen as an economic resource to work the land and care for parents in old age.

**Economic reforms.** An economic slowdown and pressure from international lenders forced India to undertake major reforms. Moving away from the socialist model of development, it looked to the successes of the Asian tigers. (See Chapter 34.) It privatized some industries and made foreign investment easier. By the 1990s, India moved toward taking a significant role in textiles, software production, and other industries.

## Social Change

In India, as elsewhere, urbanization eroded ancient ways. Still, most Indians continued to live in villages, where traditional attitudes and values remained strong.

**The caste system.** In the 1930s, Gandhi had begun a campaign to end the inhuman treatment of the untouchables, or harijans. (See page 87.) At independence, India's constitution banned discrimination against untouchables. The government set aside jobs and places in universities for these long-mistreated groups.

Despite such programs, deep prejudice persisted. Higher-caste Hindus still received better schooling and jobs. In the 1990s, a reform-minded government tried to open more jobs to untouchables. Violent protests by higher-caste Hindus who feared losing their jobs forced the government to back off from its plan.

**Women.** At independence, women gained the right to vote along with other legal rights. A few educated women, like Indira Gandhi, won elected office or entered the professions. In the cities, upper- and middle-class families sought to educate their daughters as a sign of modernization and accomplishment. In R. K. Narayan's novel *The Tale of Nagaraj*, a father brags about his daughter's achievements:

> 66 She is singing a famous song from the latest Hindi film. She has learnt it by herself. . . . Gramophone companies want her to record but I say, 'Not yet.' She must complete her M.A. [graduate degree] first. 99

*Slow Change* As this cartoon shows, the grip of India's caste system has kept untouchables from getting ahead. The government has introduced programs to make up for centuries of discrimination. But when the government announced plans to set aside places in universities for untouchables, some upper-caste students burned their diplomas in protest. *Political and Social Systems* Why do you think upper-caste Indians resented efforts to help untouchables?

# PARALLELS THROUGH TIME

## Love and Marriage

Marriage, like other institutions, has undergone change over the years. Until recently, arranged marriages were common in most of the world. By choosing partners for their children, parents could form alliances with other families, control property, and guide their children's future.

**Linking Past and Present** Why do you think arranged marriages are less common than in the past?

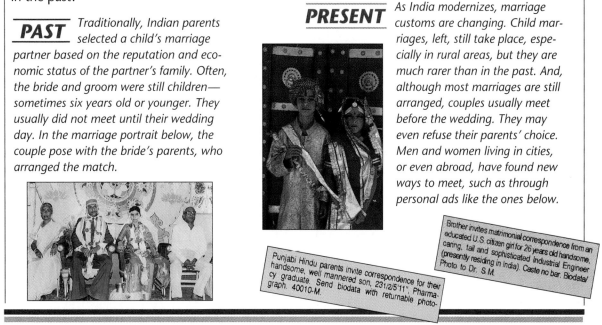

**PAST** Traditionally, Indian parents selected a child's marriage partner based on the reputation and economic status of the partner's family. Often, the bride and groom were still children—sometimes six years old or younger. They usually did not meet until their wedding day. In the marriage portrait below, the couple pose with the bride's parents, who arranged the match.

**PRESENT** As India modernizes, marriage customs are changing. Child marriages, left, still take place, especially in rural areas, but they are much rarer than in the past. And, although most marriages are still arranged, couples usually meet before the wedding. They may even refuse their parents' choice. Men and women living in cities, or even abroad, have found new ways to meet, such as through personal ads like the ones below.

Brother invites matrimonial correspondence from an educated U.S. citizen girl for 26 years old handsome, caring, tall and sophisticated Industrial Engineer (presently residing in India). Caste no bar. Biodata/Photo to Dr. S.M.

Punjabi Hindu parents invite correspondence for their handsome, well mannered son, 231/2/5'11". Pharmacy graduate. Send biodata with returnable photograph. 40010-M.

---

Yet, because of class and caste differences, many girls from poor families receive little or no education. Women on the lower rungs of society cluster in menial, low-paying jobs. In rural areas, women make up a majority of the work force, but few receive wages for their labor.

Indian women have formed organizations and movements to meet their needs. For example, the Self-Employed Women's Association (SEWA) created production and marketing cooperatives, opened banks, and provided classes and legal advice for poor women. Women's groups have also fought violence against women, protested dowry laws, and worked for environmental protection.

## Enduring Issues

As India approached its fiftieth year of independence, it had a record of political and economic achievement in many areas. Yet difficult religious and regional divisions persisted.

**Hindu fundamentalism.** In India, as elsewhere, religious fundamentalism increased in response to the problems of modernization. In the early 1990s, the Bharata Janata party (BJP) won growing support. Unlike the Congress party, which wanted to separate religion and government, the BJP called for a government guided by Hindu principles.

In 1992, the BJP supported calls for the destruction of a mosque in Ayodhya (uh YOHD yuh). Hindu fundamentalists claimed it stood on a sacred Hindu site seized by Muslim invaders centuries ago. The BJP wanted to build a Hindu temple there instead. The conflict touched off rioting at Ayodhya and the mosque was destroyed.

**Sikh separatism.** In the prosperous Punjab region of northern India, some Sikhs demanded a state of their own. In 1983, Sikh separatists occupied the Golden Temple in Amritsar to push their demands. When talks failed, Indira Gandhi sent troops to clear the temple.

◀ *Sikh demonstrators at the Golden Temple*

Thousands of Sikhs died in the fighting. A few months later, Gandhi was killed by two of her own Sikh bodyguards. The assassination ignited battles between Hindus and Sikhs.

## Pakistan's Road to Modernization

At independence, Pakistan faced severe problems. Early on, military leaders seized power and ruled as dictators. The country lacked many natural resources for industry. Ethnic rivalries also fueled conflicts.

**A divided nation.** West and East Pakistan were separated by a wide swath of Indian territory. Although the people of both regions were Muslim, their languages and cultures differed. Bengalis in the east outnumbered Punjabis in the west, but Punjabis dominated the government and economy.

As tensions flared, Bengalis broke away. In 1971, they declared independence for Bangladesh, or "Bengal Nation." Pakistan's military ruler ordered the army to crush the rebels. To escape the bloodbath, millions of Bengalis fled into India. India responded by attacking and defeating the Pakistani army in Bangladesh.

**Political fortunes.** Defeat discredited the ruling general of Pakistan. A civilian politician, Zulfikar Ali Bhutto, became president. He promised to "pick up the pieces" and make a "prosperous and progressive Pakistan." But Bhutto himself was later overthrown, tried, and executed by the military.

By 1988, Pakistan again had a civilian government, with Bhutto's daughter Benazir as prime minister. The first woman to head a modern Muslim state, Benazir Bhutto pledged to continue the reforms begun by her father. But two years later, she was dismissed from office on charges of corruption.

**Economic choices.** Pakistan moved to improve agriculture. It distributed unused lands to landless farmers, experimented with new high-yield crops, and financed irrigation projects. Building dams and clearing land helped boost food output, but at a high cost to the environment. Deforestation caused terrible floods when monsoon rains were very heavy.

To modernize, Pakistan nationalized major industries. More recently, however, the government has encouraged private or mixed government and private ownership of businesses.

## Trials of Bangladesh

Since 1971, Bangladesh has struggled to rise out of poverty, but geography often stands in the way. The large population is crowded on a low-lying coastal plain. Cyclones are a frequent peril. The region is also subject to devastating floods when monsoon rains are too heavy or to droughts if the rains are too light.

Explosive population growth has strained resources still further. More than 50 million people live below the poverty level, many of them women and children. Large amounts of foreign aid have brought little improvement, in part because various military governments misused the assistance.

In the early 1990s, a civilian government encouraged foreign investment. Foreign businesses took advantage of cheap labor costs to make clothes in Bangladesh for export to Japan and the West. Human rights groups, however, showed how textile workers, often young children, were treated like slaves. Development in Bangladesh seemed to mirror the miseries of the early Industrial Revolution in the West.

## South Asia and the World

Fear and mistrust have often guided relations between India and Pakistan. At independence, border conflicts ignited a war over Kashmir, a princely state in the Himalayas. Its Hindu prince signed Kashmir over to India, but its majority Muslim population wanted to be a part of Pakistan. Since then, the two nations have fought several wars over Kashmir.

**The nuclear issue.** The stakes for conflict rose after India tested a nuclear device in 1974. While India was proud of its status as a nuclear power, Pakistan felt threatened. It tried to acquire its own nuclear technology.

ernment. (See page 864.) Millions of Afghan Muslim refugees crossed into Pakistan. The United States funneled weapons and aid to Afghan guerrillas based in Pakistan. Guerrilla attacks and dissent at home eventually forced the Soviets to withdraw. Conflict dragged on, however, among rival rebel factions.

**Sri Lanka.** In the 1970s, ethnic tensions sparked guerrilla war in Sri Lanka (formerly Ceylon), an island nation off the south coast of India. Most Sri Lankans were Buddhists who spoke Singhalese. A Tamil-speaking Hindu minority charged the government with discrimination. When efforts to win equality failed, Tamil rebels waged war to set up a separate nation.

India at first favored Tamil separatists and then opposed them. In the 1980s, Rajiv Gandhi sent troops in an unsuccessful attempt to smash the rebels. His action outraged Tamil extremists, who assassinated him in 1991. Fighting eventually eased, but tensions remained high.

Today, India and Pakistan deny having nuclear weapons. But both nations refused to sign the Non-Proliferation Treaty. (See page 828.) Some people in the world community thought wealthy nations should cut off aid to India and Pakistan if they did not sign the NPT.

**The Cold War.** During the Cold War, India and Pakistan took different paths. Nehru welcomed economic aid from both superpowers but otherwise embraced neutrality. Pakistan, feeling threatened both by India and by the Soviet Union to the north, accepted United States military aid. Partly to counter this alliance, Indira Gandhi signed a treaty of friendship with the Soviet Union in the 1970s.

**Afghanistan.** In 1979, the Soviet Union invaded Afghanistan and set up a puppet gov-

## SECTION 1 REVIEW

1. **Identify** (a) "Nehru dynasty," (b) BJP, (c) Golden Temple, (d) Bhutto family, (e) Kashmir.
2. (a) Why was India divided into two nations? (b) Describe two effects of the partition.
3. (a) What economic goals did India pursue? (b) Why has progress been limited?
4. How has geography affected Bangladesh?
5. Why have India and Pakistan fought several wars?
6. *Critical Thinking* **Applying Information** "The past clings to us still," said Nehru. (a) What do you think he meant? (b) Give two examples that support his view.
7. *ACTIVITY* Design a banner that untouchables might use in their campaign to win full equality.

**GLOBAL CONNECTIONS**

Under Nehru, nonaligned India took a major role in world affairs. India was an active member of the UN and the British Commonwealth. In 1953, India negotiated prisoner-of-war exchanges during the Korean War. Indian troops joined a UN peacekeeping force trying to end a civil war in Zaire. India also led other nonaligned nations—such as Egypt, Ghana, Indonesia, and Yugoslavia—in calling for disarmament talks between Soviet and American leaders.

# 2  Forces Shaping the Modern Middle East

## Guide for Reading

- How have diversity and nationalism shaped the Middle East?

- What resources have had a powerful impact on the region?

- What social and religious forces influence the Middle East today?

In the Arab world, as in South Asia, nations sought to free themselves from the legacy of imperialism. "We are eradicating the traces of the past," declared Egyptian president Gamal Abdel Nasser in the 1950s. "We are building our country on strong and sound bases."

Leaders of Nasser's generation embarked on ambitious reforms. Their policies, however, often failed to bring promised improvements. By the 1970s, Islamic reformers began to offer another route to modernization.

## A Region of Diversity

What do we mean when we speak of the Middle East? Western colonial powers first used the term to refer to the region between Europe and what they called the "Far East"—China, Japan, and Southeast Asia. To avoid this western bias, some people now call the region Southwest Asia. Yet the UN and many experts continue to use the term Middle East.

**Location.** Experts also differ on what areas are part of the Middle East. In this chapter, we refer to the region from Egypt in the west to Iran in the east and from Turkey in the north to the Arabian Peninsula in the south. (See the map on page 988.) Some historians also include Muslim North Africa and Afghanistan.

Throughout history, location has made the Middle East a bridge between Asia, Africa, and Europe. As a world crossroads and a hub of civilization, it became a region of great diversity.

**Diversity.** Judaism, Christianity, and Islam all emerged in the Middle East. Today, most people there are Muslim, but the region is home to Jews and Christians. Different sects within these religions add to the diversity.

Middle Eastern peoples speak more than 30 different languages, including Arabic, Turkish, Persian, Hebrew, Kurdish, and Armenian. Every country has its minority groups—some as many as a dozen. The Kurds, for example, are an ethnic group divided by modern borders among Turkey, Iraq, and Iran. Their efforts to win autonomy have led to repression.

Like Christians in Europe, Muslims share the same faith but belong to different national groups. Arabs, Turks, and Iranians have their own cultures and histories. Often, such differences have created divisions.

## Nationalism and Independence

In the Middle East, as elsewhere, nationalism and imperialism continued to have a strong impact. In the 1920s and 1930s, Arab nationalists opposed European mandates. (See page 746.) Iraq won freedom from Britain in 1932. After World War II, British and French mandate territories won complete independence as the nations of Lebanon, Syria, and Jordan.

The Pan-Arab dream of a united Arab state foundered as nations pursued individual goals. Yet their shared heritage linked Arabs across borders. Pan-Arabism survived in the Arab League, which promoted Arab solidarity in times of crisis and worked for common economic goals.

**Colonial legacy.** Even after independence, Arab nations remained economically dependent on the West. Westerners owned banks and industries. They provided the capital and technology needed for development, as well as the principal market for exports. Ending western economic domination would become a goal of governments in the Middle East.

Imperialism left another legacy. Britain and France had drawn borders to serve their own interests. At independence, Arab nations inherited these borders, leading to disputes. For example, British mapmaking created Iraq, a nation that had never existed before. Within its borders were various groups who had no reason to call themselves Iraqis and were sometimes hostile to one another. Colonial borders also limited Iraq's access to the Persian Gulf. Religious and

ethnic tensions, plus a desire for outlets on the gulf, have fueled conflicts in Iraq to the present.

**The birth of Israel.** The legacy of Britain's Balfour Declaration fueled a conflict over Palestine. (See page 746.) Both Jews and Palestinian Arabs claimed a historical right to the land. Jewish migration to Palestine, which began in the late 1800s, accelerated after World War II. In the United States, the horrors of the Holocaust created strong support for a Jewish homeland. But increased migration and conflicting British policies led to violent clashes.

As the turmoil increased, Britain turned over its mandate to the UN. In 1947, the UN drew up a plan to partition Palestine into an Arab and a Jewish state. Jews accepted the plan, but Arabs rejected it. To them, it was a plan to relocate European Jews on Arab territory.

When Britain withdrew in 1948, Jews proclaimed the independent state of Israel. The United States and Soviet Union both recognized the new nation. Arab states, however, assembled military forces and attacked Israel. Israeli forces fought well against the badly equipped and badly led Arabs, whose governments were not all independent. In the end, Israel almost doubled its territory. Other wars would follow, as you will see.

The nation of Israel developed rapidly after 1948. The government built towns for settlers and provided many services. American aid and high taxes gave Israel the capital to invest in industry and agriculture. Despite scarce natural resources, a skilled work force made rapid progress. Israelis built factories and developed methods to farm their arid land. Kibbutzim, or collective farms, produced crops for export.

**The refugee issue.** The 1948 war uprooted 700,000 Arabs from Palestine. The UN set up temporary shelters for Palestinian refugees. As the Arab-Israeli conflict dragged on, the shelters became permanent homes. In these poverty-stricken camps, new generations of Palestinians grew up bitterly determined to win a homeland of their own.

## Impact of Oil

Parts of the Middle East sit atop the world's largest reserves of oil. Concern over this essential resource has led the United States and other powers to increase their political and military presence in the Middle East. At the same time, the 1973 OPEC oil embargo showed that oil could be a powerful diplomatic weapon. (See page 832.)

Oil is unevenly distributed. Only a few countries, mostly on the Persian Gulf, have large oil reserves. Oil-rich nations include Saudi Arabia and Kuwait, which have small populations. Turkey and Egypt, with much larger populations, have little oil.

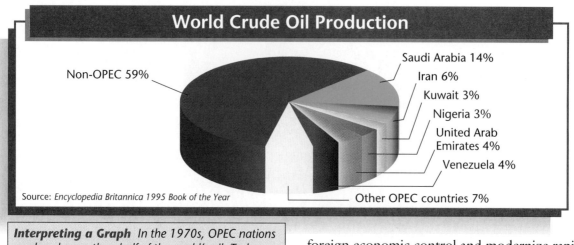

# World Crude Oil Production

Non-OPEC 59%

Saudi Arabia 14%

Iran 6%

Kuwait 3%

Nigeria 3%

United Arab Emirates 4%

Venezuela 4%

Other OPEC countries 7%

Source: *Encyclopedia Britannica 1995 Book of the Year*

*Interpreting a Graph* In the 1970s, OPEC nations produced more than half of the world's oil. Today, that figure is much lower, but many nations still depend on imported OPEC oil to fuel their industries and transportation. ■ *Which OPEC nation produces the largest share of the world's oil? Which OPEC nations shown on this graph are located outside the Middle East?*

Differences between "haves" and "have-nots" contributed to resentments within the region. Oil-rich nations were able to build roads, hospitals, and schools. Poorer countries lacked the capital needed for development.

## Political and Economic Patterns

Middle Eastern nations have worked to modernize their governments and economies. In Egypt and Iraq, revolutionary military leaders toppled monarchs who were closely tied to western powers. In other countries, such as Jordan and Saudi Arabia, hereditary monarchs remained in power but took steps to adapt to the modern world.

**Governments.** Most Middle Eastern nations developed authoritarian governments. Jordan and Saudi Arabia were ruled by hereditary monarchs. In Iraq and Syria, a single party won power. Dictators like Iraq's Saddam Hussein brutally suppressed opponents but enjoyed some popular backing because their social and economic policies improved life for many.

Only Israel and Turkey formed multiparty, democratic systems. In both countries, however, minority groups—Kurds in Turkey and Arabs in Israel—faced restrictions.

**Economic policies.** In the 1950s, some Arab nations turned to socialism as a way to end foreign economic control and modernize rapidly. They nationalized banks, oil companies, and factories. Despite those moves, they still depended on the industrial world for much of their technology.

Governments raised capital with foreign loans. They then used these funds to finance large projects in industry and agriculture, especially irrigation projects. In some countries, they redistributed land to peasants. But small farmers did not produce efficiently, and food output could not keep pace with rapid population growth.

By the 1990s, under pressure from the International Monetary Fund and western banks, many governments eased restrictions on foreign ownership and privatized some state-run enterprises. (See page 833.) The Middle East, like other developing regions, faced grave economic challenges. While nations had built some industry and bustling modern cities, large segments of the people lived in poverty.

## Keep the Water Flowing

A fleet of well over 1,500 trucks and earthmovers crawled across southeastern Anatolia in Turkey. Where Hittites, Persians, and Romans once built forts and palaces, an army of modern workers erected the 600-foot-high (180 m) Atatürk Dam. It was one of 22 dams that Turkey built in the late 1980s to harness the waters of the Tigris and Euphrates rivers.

The goal of this massive project was to turn the region into a breadbasket. Kamren Inan, a Turkish official, noted:

66These rivers have been here for millions of years. We want to put the water to use, to benefit the children of this country. . . . Turkey is increasing by 1.3 million people every year. The requirements are enormous, but if intelligently used, our resources are more than enough to cover these demands.99

**A vital resource.** Water is vital to people the world over. But nowhere is it more valued than in areas like the Middle East, where rainfall is limited and water is often scarce. Since ancient times, farmers have adapted to arid conditions. They planted crops in river valleys and coastal plains, irrigating their fields with water from streams, rivers, and underground springs.

In modern times, growing populations and rising standards of living have increased demands for water. Farmers in the Middle East can produce good crops—if they can get water. Farming accounts for 80 percent of water use in the region.

For Turkey and other nations, the key to irrigation was building dams. Developing nations take pride in such projects that not only water crops but also supply hydroelectric power.

**Whose water is it?** At the same time, dam building has sparked explosive debates over water rights. Many rivers in the Middle East run through several countries. The Nile flows through Ethiopia and Sudan before reaching Egypt. Israel, Jordan, and Syria all have claims on the waters of the Jordan River. The Euphrates rises in Turkey but flows through Syria and Iraq before emptying into the Persian Gulf.

Turkey opened its dams in 1990. For several weeks, they siphoned off 75 percent of the Euphrates water that usually flowed through Syria and Iraq. These nations protested furiously. Turkey's president promised, "We will never use the control of water to coerce or threaten our neighbors."

Today, nations that share river systems seek ways to use water cooperatively. "In the coming decades," predicted Inan, "the most important resource in the Middle East will be water, much more valuable than oil." ▨

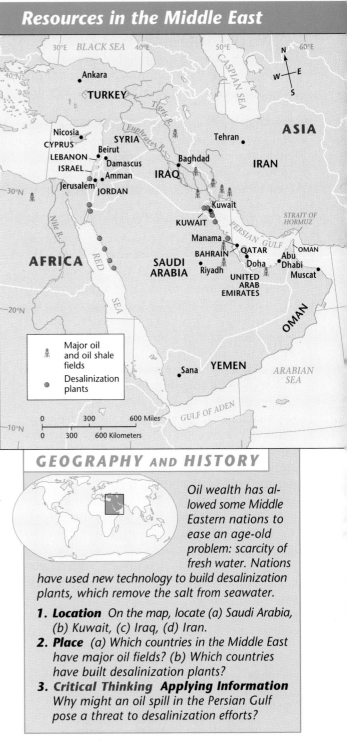

## Resources in the Middle East

Major oil and oil shale fields

Desalinization plants

## GEOGRAPHY AND HISTORY

Oil wealth has allowed some Middle Eastern nations to ease an age-old problem: scarcity of fresh water. Nations have used new technology to build desalinization plants, which remove the salt from seawater.

1. **Location** On the map, locate (a) Saudi Arabia, (b) Kuwait, (c) Iraq, (d) Iran.
2. **Place** (a) Which countries in the Middle East have major oil fields? (b) Which countries have built desalinization plants?
3. **Critical Thinking** **Applying Information** Why might an oil spill in the Persian Gulf pose a threat to desalinization efforts?

## Islamic Revival

Islam has been a shaping force in the Middle East for more than 1,300 years. As in the past, the Quran and Sharia provide guidance to all aspects of life—from government to family relationships. (See Chapter 11.)

**Western influences.** During the Age of Imperialism, westerners urged Muslim lands to modernize. To the West, modernization meant adopting western forms of secular government and law.

After nearly a century of western influence, some Middle Eastern leaders adopted western models of development, promising economic progress and social justice. In the 1950s and 1960s, western cultural influences grew. In the growing cities, people wore western-style clothing, watched American television programs, and bought foreign products. Yet despite government promises, life improved very little. With the failure of their leaders to solve mounting problems, many people became disillusioned.

**Call for reform.** By the 1970s, in the face of failed development and repressive regimes, many Muslim leaders and writers called for a return to the Sharia. They blamed social and economic ills on blind imitation of western models and applied Islamic principles to the search for solutions.

Islamic reformers (often called fundamentalists by westerners) did not reject modernization, but they did reject westernization. They argued that a renewed commitment to Islam was the only way out of their current problems. Offering Islam as an inspiration, the movement appealed to poor and educated Muslims alike.

**Impact.** By the 1990s, the Islamic revival had spread across the Muslim world—from Morocco to Indonesia. Its impact varied from country to country. In Iran, revolutionaries overthrew an unpopular shah. In Algeria, voters supported members of a party that pledged to restore the Sharia. In Egypt and elsewhere, some extremists justified terrorist acts as a weapon against authoritarian governments. Other Muslim groups worked within the system for political reforms and social programs.

Across the Muslim world, the Islamic revival sparked heated debates between reformers and secularists. Issues included science, alcohol use, advertising, teenage crime, and the role of women.

## Women in the Middle East

Conditions for women vary greatly from country to country in the modern Middle East. Since the 1950s, women in most countries have won voting rights and equality before the law. They attend schools and universities in growing numbers. Middle- and upper-class women have entered professions such as law, engineering, and medicine.

The changes have taken place at different rates in different places. In Turkey, Syria, and Egypt, many urban women gave up long-held practices such as wearing *hejab*, or cover.* On the other hand, conservative countries like Saudi Arabia opposed the spread of many western secular influences among women.

**Return to hejab.** In recent decades, many educated Muslim women led a return to wearing hejab. For some women, the movement symbolized resistance to unpopular governments or a refusal to imitate western culture. An Egyptian student said:

> ❝I think of Muslim dress as a kind of uniform. It means I am serious about myself. . . . I can sit in class with men and there is no question of attraction and so on—we are all involved in the same business of learning.❞

Most important, women who elected to return to hejab saw it as an expression of sincere loyalty to Muslim values and practices.

**Issues.** Some women in Muslim countries were dismayed by social and political forces that put severe limits on their lives. Under Sharia

▼ *Muslim children studying the Quran*

---

*The Arabic word *hejab* means following Islamic guidelines for women's dress in public. The practice includes a variety of head coverings as well as a long, loose-fitting garment. In English, the word is often translated as "veiling," though only a small fraction of Muslim women cover their faces.

**Wearing Hejab** *With the growing popularity of hejab, fashionable new forms of Muslim dress have appeared next to traditional styles. Here, a group of Iranian women enjoy an afternoon of boating.* **Continuity and Change** *How does the renewed popularity of traditional dress show continuity in the Muslim world?*

law, women traditionally held powerful positions in the family and played important economic roles. In some countries, however, laws and traditions limited women's right to vote, to work, and to drive. Many Muslim and non-Muslim women spoke out on the need for women to realize their full potential and contribute to national life.

## SECTION 2 REVIEW

1. **Identify** (a) Kurds, (b) Arab League, (c) kibbutzim, (d) hejab.
2. Give one example of how diversity has caused tensions in a Middle Eastern nation.
3. (a) What forces have linked Arab nations? (b) What forces have blocked Arab unity?
4. How was the Islamic revival linked to social and political development?
5. *Critical Thinking* **Defending a Position** (a) How has oil shaped the economies of some Middle Eastern nations? (b) Do you agree that water is "much more valuable than oil" as a resource? Why or why not?
6. *ACTIVITY* Write a four-line verse about hejab from the viewpoint of a Muslim woman.

### Guide for Reading

■ What issues posed challenges to Turkey?

■ How have Egyptian leaders tried to modernize their country?

■ What were the causes and effects of the revolution in Iran?

Ruhollah Khomeini (roo HOH luh koh MAY nee), an Iranian religious leader, angrily denounced the evils of the government. While the shah lived off the riches of the land, claimed Khomeini, most people lived in misery:

> 66When you enter Tehran, you see all the cars and that deceptive exterior, but you haven't gone to the other side of Tehran. . . . Take a look south of the city. Look at those pits, those holes in the ground where people live, dwellings you reach by going down a hundred steps into the ground, homes people have built out of rush matting or clay so their poor children can have somewhere to live.99

Khomeini's fiery speeches against the shah and his American backers helped spur an Iranian revolution in 1979.

In this section, we will see how three nations pursued modernization. Turkey, Egypt, and Iran are the most populous nations in the Middle East. While they have faced similar issues, each followed its own course.

### Turkey Moves Toward Democracy

Turkey had been an independent republic since the 1920s, while its Arab neighbors were still under European control. Kemal Atatürk pushed to build a modern secular state like those in the West. (See Chapter 29.)

After World War II, the Soviets tried to expand southward into Turkey to gain control of the Bosporus. With American military and economic aid, Turkey held off the Soviet threat. In the 1950s, it joined NATO and remained an important western ally in the Mediterranean.

**Government and economy.** Turkey struggled to build a stable government. At first, the military seized power in times of unrest. Later, a multiparty democracy emerged. In the 1990s, Muslim reformers challenged the record of the secular, westernized government.

Turkey transformed its economy, building dams and expanding industry. It exported crops and manufactured goods to Europe and even sought to join the European Union. (See page 851.) While the EU agreed to form closer ties, it denied full membership to Turkey.

*Without a Country* Although Kurds were promised a homeland during World War I, postwar treaties failed to create a Kurdish nation. Since the 1920s, Kurds in Turkey and Iraq have fought for their own nation. That struggle has brought violent reprisals. In the 1980s, Iraq dropped poison gas on Kurdish villages, killing thousands of civilians. The Turkish government has also waged war against Kurdish rebels in eastern Turkey. As a result, thousands of Turkish Kurds like these have become refugees, taking with them only what they can carry.
*Political and Social Systems* Why do you think Turkey and Iraq oppose a separate Kurdish nation?

As elsewhere, modernization and urbanization brought social upheaval. Istanbul could not provide jobs for millions of newcomers. The jobless and the poor lived in shantytowns, where desperate conditions fed unrest.

**Conflicts.** For decades, Turkey tried to force Kurds within its borders to abandon their identity. They were forbidden to speak, broadcast, or publish books in their language. Kurdish revolts were fiercely suppressed. Gradually, the Turkish government agreed to abolish laws against Kurdish culture. Still, that move was unlikely to satisfy Kurdish nationalists who sought autonomy.

Turkey also waged a long struggle over Cyprus, an island in the eastern Mediterranean. The conflict had complex roots dating to Ottoman times. In the 1970s, clashes between the Greek majority and Turkish minority led Turkey to invade. The island was then partitioned. Today, UN peacekeepers monitor the dividing line between Turkish and Greek communities.

## Egypt: A Leader in the Arab World

Egypt has roots both in Africa, where it is located, and in the Arab world, the source of its majority religion. Today, as in the past, geography influences Egypt's destiny. Its location between the Red Sea and the Mediterranean, where Asia and Africa meet, has always been strategically important. Today, it is the most populous Arab state, shares a long border with Israel, and controls the Suez Canal. As in the past, it is a rich agricultural region. But, since most of Egypt is desert, 99 percent of its people live on 4 percent of the land in the fertile Nile Valley.

**Nasser.** In the 1950s, Gamal Abdel Nasser emerged as a towering figure in the Middle East. Like Atatürk, Nasser was a military officer who came to power after the overthrow of a ruler who had allowed foreigners to dominate his country.

Nasser was determined to modernize Egypt and, at the same time, end foreign domination. In 1956, he nationalized the Suez Canal, ending British control. Nasser proclaimed:

66This money is ours. This Canal is the property of Egypt. . . . The Canal was dug by Egypt's sons and 120,000 of them died while working. The Suez Canal Company in Paris is an impostor company.**"**

Britain and France threatened to invade, but Nasser's defiance of the West boosted his prestige in the Arab world. He later formed a union of Egypt and Syria, a step toward the Pan-Arab goal of a United Arab Republic. But the union did not last.

An outspoken enemy of Israel, Nasser led two wars against the Zionist state. Although defeated each time, he remained a symbol of Arab independence and pride.

**Economic development.** Like leaders of other developing nations, Nasser turned to socialism. He nationalized banks and businesses and undertook sweeping land reforms. Large estates were broken up, and land was given to peasant farmers.

In the 1960s, with Soviet help, Nasser built the huge Aswan High Dam on the upper Nile. About 17 times larger than Egypt's Great Pyramid, the dam created a huge reservoir, Lake Nasser, plus more than 2 million acres of new farmland. It also controlled the Nile floodwaters and made year-round irrigation possible.

Like many such projects, however, the blessings of the Aswan High Dam came at a high price. It increased the salt content of the Nile, caused erosion of the delta, and destroyed fish hatcheries in the eastern Mediterranean. Even Egypt's ancient past was threatened. As Lake Nasser rose, many ancient temples had to be relocated to higher ground.

**New directions.** Nasser's economic policies had only limited success. After Nasser's death in 1970, the new president, Anwar Sadat, turned to a policy of *infitah*, or "opening." His goal was to encourage foreign investment and private business.

In foreign affairs, Sadat moved away from the Soviet camp and closer to the United States. In 1979, he became the first Arab leader to make peace with Israel. Although that move angered other Arab states, Sadat promised Egyptians that peace would have economic benefits. It did bring American aid but did not improve life for most Egyptians.

**Unresolved issues.** In 1981, Sadat was assassinated. His successor, Hosni Mubarak, reaf-

**Gamal Abdel Nasser** *In the 1950s and 1960s, Egyptian president Nasser, below, was the foremost spokesman of the Arab world. He used his prominence to promote unity among Arabs living in different nations. Perhaps Nasser's boldest move was to nationalize the Suez Canal, right, giving Egypt control of one of the world's most strategic waterways. Today, more than 50 ships a day pass through the canal.*
**Impact of the Individual**
*How did Nasser pursue both Pan-Arab and nationalist goals?*

firmed the peace with Israel but mended fences with his Arab neighbors. At home, Mubarak faced serious problems. Although farm output and industry expanded, the economy could not keep pace with the population boom. Most rural families who streamed into cities like Cairo ended up in crowded slums, barely managing to survive. Many families set up homes in the City of the Dead, a Cairo cemetery.

Muslim reformers denounced the government's failure to solve social and economic ills. Their emphasis on Islamic solutions seemed to offer a vision for change that Mubarak's government lacked. Islamic organizations developed schools, medical services, and relief for the poor, providing social services for which tight government budgets could no longer pay. A fringe of extremists turned to terrorism against a government they called corrupt and antireligious. Harsh government crackdowns, though, tended to increase support for the dissenters.

## Iran: Goals of the Revolution

Iran is the most ethnically diverse country in the Middle East. About half the people are Iranians, while the rest come from many groups. Unlike their neighbors, most Iranians are Shiite, not Sunni, Muslims and speak Persian, not Arabic or Turkish.

**Nationalism and oil.** The discovery of vast oil fields made Iran a focus for British, Soviet, and American interests. In 1945, the young shah, Muhammad Reza Pahlavi, had western backing but faced opposition from many groups at home. Iranian nationalists wanted to end British control of Iran's oil wealth and limit the shah's dictatorial powers.

Led by Muhammad Mosaddiq (MOH sah dehk), nationalists in the Iranian parliament voted to nationalize the oil industry. That action touched off a long, complex crisis involving the shah, Mosaddiq, Britain, and the United States.

In 1953, the United States helped the shah oust Mosaddiq, an action that angered many Iranians. The United States wanted the anticommunist shah as a solid ally against Soviet influence in the region. For the next 25 years, American weapons and experts helped the shah remain in power.

**Reform from above.** To strengthen Iran and quiet widespread discontent, the shah continued the modernization program begun by his father. He used oil wealth to build roads and industries, redistributed some land to peasants, and granted rights to women. In an attempt to separate religion and government, he reduced the power of the *ulama,* or Islamic scholars, teachers, and legal experts. The shah's "reform from above" was supported by the army, the westernized elite, and others who prospered under the shah. Opposition came from landowners, merchants, students, and religious leaders.

As unrest grew, the shah became more repressive. Savak, his dreaded secret police, arrested, tortured, or executed opponents, especially members of left-wing political groups. Others were forced into exile. The army crushed Kurds and other ethnic minorities who demanded autonomy.

**Revolution.** In the 1970s, the shah's enemies rallied around Shiite leaders, especially the exiled Ayatollah* Ruhollah Khomeini. He accused the shah of violating Islamic law and undermining morality. The ulama also opposed the distribution of land from religious foundations to peasants.

▲ *Ayatollah Ruhollah Khomeini*

Millions of Iranians protested against the shah. As chaos threatened in 1979, he fled Iran and his government toppled. Khomeini returned to guide leaders of a new Islamic republic that would restore the Sharia to a central place in Iranian life. Revolutionaries attacked corruption and banned western books, music, and movies. The Khomeini government abolished all previous legislation favoring women's rights. Still, many women backed the revolution, seeking ways to contribute to national life while following religious law.

At first, the new government allowed some open discussion. Before long, however, like the shah they replaced, the revolutionaries suppressed opponents.

**Foreign policy.** The new leaders bitterly denounced the West. After the shah was allowed into the United States for medical treatment, revolutionaries seized the American embassy in Tehran, holding 53 hostages for over a year. They also tried to export their revolution, urging Muslims in countries like Egypt and Turkey to overthrow secular governments. Although the revolution seemed to strengthen the Islamic revival, it was not reproduced in other Muslim lands.

---

*Ayatollah* is a title given to the most learned Shiite legal experts.

# CAUSE AND EFFECT

## Long-Term Causes

Oil fields discovered in Iran in early 1900s
Oil rights sold to foreigners; Britain and Russia set up spheres of influence in Iran
Iranian nationalists resent western interference
Modernization efforts fail to benefit common people
Muslim religious leaders condemn modernization efforts
Iran becomes focus of Cold War rivalries
Islamic revival begins in 1970s

## Immediate Causes

Shah introduces "reform from above"
As opposition to shah grows, he becomes more repressive
Exiled Ruhollah Khomeini speaks out forcefully against the shah and his American backers
Iranians protest shah's policies

## REVOLUTION IN IRAN

## Immediate Effects

Shah flees Iran
Khomeini returns to Iran to guide leaders of new government
Revolutionaries take 53 Americans hostage
Government imposes strict code of behavior, bans western books and music, and overturns women's rights legislation

## Long-Term Effects

Iran tries to encourage revolution in other Muslim countries
Iran is isolated by international community
Living conditions do not improve a great deal; poverty and unemployment continue
War with Iraq drains resources

## Connections Today

Moderates gain control in Iran
Iran works to improve relations with the West and with other Muslim nations
Debate continues in Iran about how to modernize while remaining loyal to Islamic principles

*Interpreting a Chart* In 1979, a revolution in Iran brought down the shah and set the nation on a new course. The Iranian revolution had worldwide consequences. ■ Why was the discovery of oil fields a long-term cause of the revolution? Why do you think the revolution isolated Iran from the West and from other Muslim nations?

In 1980, as you will read, neighboring Iraq took advantage of the turmoil to invade Iran. In Iran, the war helped rally support for the new government even though the ordeal took a huge economic and human toll.

**Effects.** Since Khomeini's death in 1989, more moderate voices have steered Iran. President Hashemi Rafsanjani (hah SHAY mee rahf sahn JAH nee) worked to rebuild the economy and restore more normal relations with western powers.

The revolution changed Iran's foreign policy and some forms of public behavior. It did not, however, improve life greatly for most people. Corruption resurfaced. Poverty, unemployment, and other problems remained. Still, some reforms did improve conditions in rural areas.

By the mid-1990s, moderates and radicals debated the future of the revolution. They continued seeking ways to achieve modernization while upholding Islamic principles.

## SECTION 3 REVIEW

1. **Identify** (a) Aswan High Dam, (b) Anwar Sadat, (c) Hosni Mubarak, (d) Muhammad Mosaddiq, (e) Ruhollah Khomeini.
2. Describe one step each of these nations took toward modernization: (a) Turkey, (b) Egypt, (c) Iran.
3. How did Nasser challenge the West?
4. (a) Why did discontent spread under the shah? (b) Describe two effects of the Iranian revolution.
5. *Critical Thinking* **Recognizing Points of View** (a) Who might consider the Iranian revolution a success? Why? (b) Who might criticize it? Why?
6. *ACTIVITY* Create a chart comparing the three nations discussed in this section in terms of population, government, economy, and critical issues.

## 4 The Middle East and the World

### Guide for Reading

- Why was the Arab-Israeli conflict difficult to resolve?
- What forces plunged Lebanon into civil war?
- Why did the Persian Gulf become a battleground?
- **Vocabulary** *intifada*

❝The land whereto we have returned to inherit it, it is the inheritance of our fathers and within it no stranger has part or parcel. . . . We have taken unto us our fathers' inheritance and have dwelt in it.❞

With this biblical quotation, David Ben-Gurion, Israel's first prime minister, greeted the birth of modern Israel in 1948. To Arabs then living on the land called Palestine, though, the creation of Israel was an illegal outrage. An official Arab proclamation stated:

❝Palestine is the homeland of the Arab Palestinian people. It is an indivisible part of the Arab homeland, and the Palestinian people are an integral part of the Arab nation.❞

These conflicting claims touched off repeated violence. The Arab-Israeli struggle was one of many issues that focused world attention on the Middle East.

### The Cold War and the Middle East

As in other regions, Cold War rivalries touched the Middle East. The region commanded vital oil resources, as well as strategic waterways such as the Bosporus, the Suez Canal, and the Persian Gulf.

In their global rivalry, each superpower lined up allies in the Middle East. The United States sent aid to stop a communist threat to

**War Memories** *Israeli abstract artist Igael Tumarkin saw the effects of war first in Germany, where he was born, and then through four wars in Israel. In works like* War Memories, *Tumarkin uses splashes of paint and fragments of everyday objects to suggest the psychological damage inflicted by war.* **Art and Literature** *Why have many modern painters experimented with abstract styles instead of reproducing reality?*

Turkey in 1947 and backed the anti-communist shah of Iran. The Soviets found an ally in Egypt during the Nasser years. Iraq, Syria, and Libya joined the Soviet camp, too. They mistrusted their former colonial rulers in the West and condemned western support for Israel.

Each superpower sold arms to its allies in the region. In the Arab-Israeli conflict, the United States helped Israel, while the Soviet Union aided the Arabs. After each Arab-Israeli war, the superpowers rearmed their allies with expensive new weapons.

### The Arab-Israeli Conflict

After the 1948 war, Israel and its Arab neighbors faced off again in 1956, 1967, and 1973. (See the map on page 918.) Between wars, Israel was a center of guerrilla warfare and terrorist activity.

**The occupied territories.** In 1967, Israeli forces won the Golan Heights from Syria, East Jerusalem and the West Bank from Jordan, and the Gaza Strip and Sinai Peninsula from Egypt. In 1973, Arabs attacked Israel but failed to regain the occupied lands.

Israel refused to give up the territories until Arab nations recognized Israel's right to exist. Later, Israel annexed East Jerusalem and the Golan Heights. The government helped Jewish settlers build homes in the occupied territories, displacing more Palestinian Arabs.

**Palestinian resistance.** The number of Palestinians in refugee camps had grown since 1948. Many supported the Palestine Liberation Organization (PLO), headed by Yasir Arafat. The PLO waged guerrilla war against Israelis at home and abroad. PLO bombings, airplane hijackings, and the massacre of Israeli athletes at the 1972 Olympics brought Palestinian demands to the attention of the world.

In 1987, resistance to Israel took another form. Young Palestinians in the occupied territories mounted the *intifada*, or uprising. Teenage boys openly defied Israeli soldiers, throwing rocks and disobeying curfews. When soldiers cracked down on the violence, they were accused of human rights violations. The intifada deepened divisions within Israel. Some Israelis wanted to give up the occupied territories in exchange for peace. Others became even more determined to keep the lands they had won.

**Peace efforts.** During the Cold War, efforts to solve the Arab-Israeli conflict had little success. However, as you have read, Anwar Sadat did take a courageous first step. After the 1979 peace treaty, Israel returned the Sinai Peninsula to Egypt. The collapse of the Soviet Union in 1991 sped up the peace process. Without Soviet aid, some Arab governments accepted the need to negotiate with Israel.

In 1994, Jordan and Israel signed a peace agreement. Talks between Israel and Syria stalled on the issue of the Golan Heights. The status of Jerusalem was another thorny issue. Israel claimed the city as its capital. Arabs insisted that Jerusalem, a holy city to Muslims as well as to Jews and Christians, must be part of any final agreement.

**A historic accord.** In 1993, direct talks were held for the first time between Israel and the PLO. Yasir Arafat and Israeli prime minister Yitzhak Rabin (rah BEEN) signed a historic agreement that gave Palestinians in Gaza and the West Bank city of Jericho limited self-rule in 1994. The following year, a new pact further extended Palestinian self-rule.

The accords raised hopes. But both sides knew that peace would not come quickly. "A bloody conflict, which has been raging for 100 years," warned Rabin, "can only be resolved by means of a process—not a stopwatch."

Some Palestinians were dissatisfied because the agreement promised only limited self-rule, not the independent Palestinian homeland they wanted. The continuing growth of Israeli settlements in the occupied lands also fed Palestinian anger. Radical Palestinian groups, such as Hamas, denounced Arafat as a puppet of Israel and launched new attacks.

*The Intifada* In 1987, Palestinians rebelled against Israeli military rule in a rebellion called the intifada. Young people and even children took to the streets, demanding an end to the 20-year Israeli occupation of the West Bank and the Gaza Strip. "Whatever measures the Israelis take," swore one young Palestinian, "the intifada will not end. The Palestinians have a strong will." **Religions and Value Systems** Why do you think young people led the intifada?

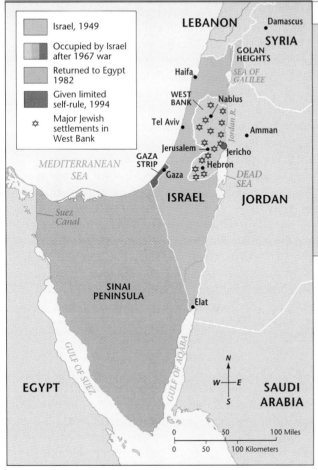

## Arab-Israeli Conflict 1948–1995

Israel, 1949

Occupied by Israel after 1967 war

Returned to Egypt 1982

Given limited self-rule, 1994

☆ Major Jewish settlements in West Bank

LEBANON · Damascus
SYRIA
GOLAN HEIGHTS
Haifa · SEA OF GALILEE
WEST BANK · Nablus
Tel Aviv · Jordan R. · Amman
Jerusalem · Jericho
GAZA STRIP · Hebron
Gaza · DEAD SEA
MEDITERRANEAN SEA
ISRAEL · JORDAN
Suez Canal
SINAI PENINSULA · Elat
GULF OF SUEZ · GULF OF AQABA
EGYPT · SAUDI ARABIA

N W E S

0    50    100 Miles
0  50  100 Kilometers

### GEOGRAPHY AND HISTORY

Israel and its Arab neighbors have fought four wars since 1948. Conflict between Jews and Palestinians in the occupied territories has been an even more explosive issue.

1. **Location** On the map, locate (a) Israel, (b) Egypt, (c) Jordan, (d) Syria, (e) West Bank, (f) Gaza Strip, (g) Sinai Peninsula.
2. **Movement** What territories did Israel gain in the 1967 war?
3. **Critical Thinking  Drawing Conclusions** Why do you think Israel returned the Sinai to Egypt?

Many Israelis, too, bitterly criticized the peace accord. They distrusted Arafat because of past terrorist attacks. Some denounced Rabin as a traitor for agreeing to give up any part of the Jewish "promised land." In November 1995, Rabin was shot and killed by a Jewish law student who opposed his policies. A shocked world waited to see what effect the assassination would have on future peace efforts.

### Civil War in Lebanon

In the 1970s, the Arab-Israeli conflict fueled tensions in nearby Lebanon. After independence, Lebanon had become a thriving center of international commerce. People of diverse ethnic and religious groups lived mostly in harmony. But prosperity masked problems.

**Growing tensions.** The government depended on a delicate balance among Maronites (a Christian sect), Sunni and Shiite Muslims,

Druze (a sect derived from Islam), and others. Maronites held the most power, but local political bosses ran their own districts backed by private armies. Increasing numbers of Palestinian refugees crossed the border, straining resources. As the Muslim population grew to outnumber Maronites, unrest spread. Adding to the tensions, the PLO became an important presence in Palestinian refugee camps. Israel, seeking to end the PLO threat to its security, sought influence in southern Lebanon.

**Tragic violence.** In 1975, Lebanon was plunged into a seemingly endless civil war. Christian and Muslim militias battled for villages and the capital city of Beirut. Israel invaded PLO bases in the south and occupied parts of Lebanon as far as the capital. Syria occupied the east. Lawlessness led to brutal massacres on all sides. At one point, a UN peacekeeping force tried to restore order but withdrew after French and American troops were killed in suicide bombings.

The victims included thousands of Palestinian refugees. Palestinian writer Liyana Badr described life in a besieged refugee camp:

66There was one young man, I remember, who said, 'When I die, put me in this coffin.' They made coffins from cupboard doors and there was a door ready. 'I'll measure it against my body,' the young man said. A moment later a splinter of shrapnel struck him in the back and killed him on the spot. So they did put him in the coffin he'd measured himself for. 99

By 1990, Lebanese leaders finally restored a measure of order. The PLO was forced out of southern Lebanon, private armies began to disarm, and businesses in the devastated city of Beirut rebuilt. Divisions remained, though, and both Syria and Israel still operated in Lebanon.

## Two Wars in the Persian Gulf

Border disputes, oil wealth, foreign intervention, and ambitious rulers fed tensions along the Persian Gulf. In 1980, Iraqi dictator Saddam Hussein took advantage of turmoil in Iran to occupy a disputed border area and then pushed deeper into Iran. Iran launched a counterattack amid calls to spread its revolution to Iraq.

Iraq used its superior weapons, tanks, airplanes, and even poison gas to stop waves of Iranian soldiers. When both sides attacked tankers and oil fields, the United States took steps to protect Persian Gulf shipping lanes. The eight-year Iran-Iraq War drained both sides.

**A second Gulf war.** In 1990, Hussein invaded oil-rich Kuwait, to whom he owed a huge war debt for support against Iran. He claimed Kuwait was a creation of Britain and rightly belonged to Iraq. Control of Kuwait would also expand Iraq's access to the Persian Gulf.

The United States saw the invasion as a threat both to its ally Saudi Arabia and to the oil flow from the Persian Gulf. President George Bush organized a coalition of European and Arab powers to drive Iraqi forces out of Kuwait. In the 1991 Gulf War, American missiles and bombers destroyed targets in Iraq, while ground forces swiftly freed Kuwait.

**Looking ahead.** Defeated and diplomatically isolated, Hussein still held onto power. He managed to suppress revolts by Kurdish and Shiite minorities who had suffered brutally under his rule. Although UN and coalition forces

**Environmental Disaster** *During the Persian Gulf War of 1991, retreating Iraqi soldiers blew up hundreds of oil wells in Kuwait. It took crews of firefighters 10 months to put out the oil fires and cap more than 700 wells.* **Global Interaction** *Why did the burning of the oil fields raise worldwide concern?*

eventually took steps to protect the Kurds, their future remained bleak.

After the war, UN economic sanctions prevented Iraq from selling its oil abroad. The goal was to force Hussein to cease his chemical and nuclear weapons programs. Without oil income and under an import embargo, Iraq suffered great hardships. Yet Hussein increased his support at home by blaming the United States for economic problems. Thus, the Iraqi dictator remained a disruptive force in the region.

## SECTION 4 REVIEW

1. **Identify** (a) PLO, (b) Yasir Arafat, (c) Yitzhak Rabin, (d) Saddam Hussein.
2. **Define** intifada.
3. (a) Why were the occupied territories a source of tension? (b) What steps were taken toward resolving the conflict?
4. Why did civil war break out in Lebanon?
5. What were the effects of the 1991 Gulf War?
6. **Critical Thinking   Solving Problems** If you were organizing a Middle East peace conference, whom would you invite and what issues would you put on the table?
7. **ACTIVITY** Draw a cartoon about the role of oil in fueling tensions on the Persian Gulf.

**ISSUES For TODAY**

The Arab-Israeli conflict, the civil war in Lebanon, and the Iraqi invasion of Kuwait became the focus of worldwide concern. When should the world community intercede in local conflicts to promote peace?

# Skills for Success

## Revising Your Writing

During the revision stage of the writing process, you examine the content, organization, tone, and language of your first draft. You check to make sure that what you have written matches your original thesis. Revision also involves a mechanics check, including grammar, spelling, and punctuation.

Revision often involves rewriting. As you revise, you can make changes as simple as word shuffling, adding, or deleting or as complex as altering sentence or paragraph order. Whatever revisions you make should always be aimed at improving your expression and clarifying your ideas.

Look at the sample composition and the thesis statement to the right. Then, follow these steps.

**1** **Check your introductory paragraph against your original thesis.** (a) What is the original thesis? (b) Is it stated clearly in paragraph A? (c) Is there any detail in the original thesis that the writer omitted in the first paragraph? (d) What changes could you make to the paragraph to present the thesis more clearly?

**2** **Examine each sentence, then each paragraph, to be sure that both content and structure are clear.** Delete unnecessary words or add words for clarity. You may choose to combine simple sentences or rewrite long, unclear sentences. (a) Why has the writer added the words "and resolve" to paragraph A? (b) Why does the writer want to combine paragraphs B and C? (c) What word does the writer think should be explained more fully? (d) How could you condense the three circled sentences in paragraph C? (e) Which information is out of logical order? Explain.

**3** **Correct any mistakes in spelling, punctuation, and grammar.** (a) Why should *madrid* be capitalized as well as set off with commas? (b) Are all punctuation marks at the ends of sentences correct? (c) What word is misspelled in paragraph C?

***Beyond the Classroom*** Choose a news issue that concerns you and write a first draft of a letter to a newspaper editor. Revise your first draft, using the preceding steps to guide you.

---

**ORIGINAL THESIS:**

**Israel and the PLO, bitter long-time enemies, took steps during the first half of the 1990s to resolve their differences.**

**A.** In the Middle East, a willingness by Israel and the Palestinian Liberation Organization (PLO) to discuss ^(and resolve) differences has resulted in ~~real~~ progress toward peace. Following four decades of ~~tragic~~ hostilities, the ^(first half of the) 1990s have been a decade of hope for increasing peace in the Middle East.

**B.** Progress toward peace first began when Israel and PLO leaders, in October 1991 (met) at a conference in madrid Spain to begin peace discussions.

*Combine paragraphs B and C.*

**C.** The Israelis and the Palestinians could finally start talking. "The beginning of the end" was what the Israeli prime minister called it. He was talking about the conflict between his country and the Palestinians. His name is Yitzhak Shamir. In September 1993, Israel and the Palestine Liberation Organization gave each other letters that said they recognized each other. And they signed an agreement on Palestinian autonomy in Israeli-occupied teratories.

*? they began "discussions earlier— aren't discussions "talking"?*

*Condense into one sentence?*

**D.** ~~Although progress was slow, the Israelis were determined to continue the peace process. Going one step further,~~ ^(The next step occurred) in January 1993, ^(when) the Israeli parliament repealed a law prohibiting contacts between Israelis and the PLO. They elected a new, more moderate president in 1992. The new president, Yitzhak Rabin, said he supported a compromise with the Palestinians. If the Palestinians would guarantee peace for Israel, Israel would return lands in the occupied territories to the Palestinians?

## Building Vocabulary

Review the following vocabulary from this chapter: *refugee, secular, caste, nonaligned, guerrilla warfare, ethnic group, autonomy, terrorism, annex, intifada.* Write sentences using each of these terms, leaving blanks where the terms would go. Exchange your sentences with another student and fill in the blanks on each other's lists.

## Reviewing Chapter Themes

1. **Diversity** Describe how *three* of the following illustrate the effects of ethnic or religious conflict: (a) Hindus and Muslims in India, (b) Punjabis and Bengalis in Pakistan, (c) Hindus and Sikhs in India, (d) Kurds in Turkey and Iraq, (e) Jews and Palestinian Arabs in Israel, (f) Muslims and Christians in Lebanon.
2. **Economics and Technology** (a) What steps did India take to modernize its industry and agriculture? (b) How has nuclear technology affected South Asia?
3. **Geography and History** (a) What region do historians mean when they refer to the modern Middle East? (b) Describe two ways that oil resources have affected the region. (c) Why are water rights an explosive issue?
4. **Continuity and Change** Describe how each of these nations modernized after gaining independence: (a) Turkey, (b) Egypt, (c) Iran.
5. **Religions and Value Systems** (a) What were the goals of conservative Muslim reformers like Ruhollah Khomeini in Iran? (b) Why did they win support among many Muslims? (c) Describe two effects of their success.

## Thinking Critically

1. **Linking Past and Present** Give three examples of how the legacy of western imperialism influenced recent developments in South Asia and the Middle East.
2. **Comparing** Review pages 860–861. How is India's attempt to reform the caste system similar to the civil rights movement in the United States? How is it different?
3. **Applying Information** Review the subsection Old Ways and New from Chapter 32, pages

838–839. Give two examples of how the changes described there apply to the Middle East.
4. **Recognizing Points of View** Reread the statement by the Egyptian woman on page 910. According to her, is hejab a restricting or a liberating force? Explain. ( ★ See *Skills for Success,* page 280.)
5. **Analyzing Literature** An Iranian poet wrote: "We were sound asleep/so fast asleep/that the footsteps of thieves/— internal and external thieves—/couldn't wake us up." (a) What situation is the poet describing? (b) Based on these lines, do you think this poet supported the Iranian revolution? Why or why not? ( ★ See *Skills for Success,* page 234.)
6. **Solving Problems** Why do many observers think that solving the Palestinian issue is the key to building peace in the Middle East?

### *For Your Portfolio*

You have been asked to compile a book of collectible quotes from prominent figures of South Asia and the Middle East. You will work with a co-author to complete this project.

1. Reread the chapter to make a preliminary list of the people mentioned. For example, you might include Jawaharlal Nehru, Mohandas Gandhi, Muhammad Ali Jinnah, Indira Gandhi, Rajiv Gandhi, and Benazir Bhutto as representatives of South Asia. Next to each name, make notes about this person's role or contribution.
2. Add to your list by using library resources. You might want to include artists, business leaders, religious leaders, and people from other fields. Keep in mind that not everyone on your list has to be well-known. For example, for Egypt, you might choose to include a farmer in the Nile delta or a slum dweller in Cairo.
3. Do research to find an appropriate quotation from each person on your list. For example, if a person was instrumental in helping a nation gain independence, your quote should reflect that.
4. With your partner decide how to organize your quotations. You might arrange them by country, alphabetically, chronologically, or by topic.
5. Compile your quotations into a book. Share it with the class as a social studies resource.

# CHAPTER
## 36

# Africa
## (1945–Present)

"Kenya regained her *Uhuru* [freedom] from the British on 12 December 1963," writes Ngugi wa Thiong'o in *A Grain of Wheat,* a novel chronicling Kenya's struggle for independence. In one scene, Ngugi describes the moment of independence in Nairobi, Kenya's capital:

66A minute before midnight, lights were put out at the Nairobi stadium. . . . In the dark, the Union Jack was quickly lowered. When next the lights came on the new Kenya flag was flying and fluttering, and waving, in the air. The . . . band played the new National Anthem and the crowd cheered continuously. . . . The cheering sounded like one intense cracking of many trees, falling on the thick mud in the stadium.99

In villages throughout Kenya, men, women, and children celebrated the occasion. Still, people had many questions. In Ngugi's novel, the villagers wonder about the future:

66Men stood or talked in groups about the prospects opened up by Uhuru. . . . Would the government now become less stringent on those who could not pay tax? Would there be more jobs? Would there be more land?99

In the decades after World War II, nationalists across Africa demanded freedom and the power to control their own destinies. Slowly at first and then in rapid succession, African nations emerged from colonial rule. Since 1945, more than 50 new nations have been born.

Leaders of the new nations set out to build strong central governments, achieve economic growth, and raise standards of living to match those in the developed world. Modernization, however, would not be easy. Nations faced a string of problems—from lack of technology, drought, and other natural disasters to economic dependency, political instability, and ethnic rivalries.

Despite repeated setbacks, African nations did not lose hope. They continued to search for workable solutions.

**FOCUS ON** these questions as you read:

■ **Diversity**
How did diversity pose problems for emerging African nations?

■ **Impact of the Individual**
What challenges did liberation leaders face in the struggle for freedom?

■ **Economics and Technology**
Why did developing nations of Africa remain economically dependent on the industrialized world?

■ **Political and Social Systems**
What kinds of governments did the new nations of Africa develop?

■ **Continuity and Change**
Why have many Africans called for their nations to seek African solutions to African problems?

**TIME AND PLACE**

**Independent Africa** *After World War II, dozens of former colonies in Africa emerged as independent nations. The new countries made economic growth a priority. They invested in schools, roads, dams, factories, and other modernization projects. The Kenyatta Center in Nairobi, Kenya, shown here, symbolizes the new Africa at the same time it echoes traditional African designs.* **Global Interaction** *In what ways does the Kenyatta Center reflect a blend of cultural influences?*

## HUMANITIES LINK

*Art History* Voyiya, *Rhythm in 3/4 Time* (page 938).

*Literature* In this chapter, you will encounter passages from the following works of literature: Ngugi wa Thiong'o, *A Grain of Wheat* (page 922); Sembene Ousmane, *God's Bits of Wood* (page 924); John Pepper Clark, "The Casualties" (page 933).

| **Late 1940s** Nationalist movements intensify throughout Africa | **1964** Nyerere becomes president of Tanzania | **1970** Nigerian civil war ends | **1980s** Zimbabwe begins economic and land reforms | **1994** Nelson Mandela is elected president of South Africa |

| 1945 | 1960 | 1975 | 1990 | PRESENT |

# 1 Achieving Independence

## Guide for Reading

- How did African nations win independence?

- How did the colonial legacy hamper development?

- How did nationalist leaders guide the independence movements?

From the town of Thiès, the women march on Dakar, capital of French-ruled Senegal. They want to add their voices to those of their men—railroad workers on strike for equal pay. As they approach the city, they are warned that a column of soldiers has orders not to let them pass. One of their leaders, Penda, speaks up:

66 'The soldiers can't eat us!' she cried. 'They can't even kill us; there are too many of us! Don't be afraid—our friends are waiting for us in Dakar! We'll go on!' 99

Suddenly, shots ring out, and Penda falls. The women, however, continue their march toward the city, where they are welcomed as heroes.

That scene, from *God's Bits of Wood* by Senegalese writer and filmmaker Sembene Ousmane (suhm BEH neh us MAH neh), is based on a real event in 1947. Eventually, the French forced an end to the Senegalese strike. Still, the bravery of the strikers and the women who supported them spurred further campaigns for reform and justice.

By the 1950s, strikes and protests were multiplying. Across the continent, Africans demanded more than reform. They called for freedom from foreign rule.

## The Nationalist Tide

In 1945, four European powers—Britain, France, Belgium, and Portugal—controlled almost all of Africa. (See the map on page 925.) Only Egypt, Ethiopia, Liberia, and white-ruled South Africa were independent nations. The rising tide of nationalism, however, soon swept over European colonial empires, bringing a great liberation in Africa and around the world.

**Impact of World War II.** World War II sharpened the edges of nationalist movements in Africa. Japanese victories in Asia shattered the West's reputation as an unbeatable force. Also, African troops had fought Axis armies in Africa, the Middle East, and other parts of the world. When they returned home to discrimination and second-class citizenship, these ex-soldiers became easy recruits for the growing nationalist movements. Nationalists also found support among workers who had migrated to the cities to work in defense industries during the war.

**The global setting.** After the war, most Europeans were reluctant to fight to hold onto overseas colonies. Faced with growing nationalist demands, Britain and France, the largest imperialist powers, adopted new policies toward their African colonies. They introduced political reforms that would gradually lead to independence. They soon discovered, however, that they could not dictate either the terms or the pace of change.

Pressures for independence built up both within and outside Africa. The two superpowers, you will recall, rejected colonialism. (See page 826.) After India won independence from Britain in 1947, African leaders grew impatient. Everywhere rose the cry "Freedom Now."

**Nationalist leaders.** Most nationalist leaders were western educated. Many were powerful speakers whose words inspired supporters. Kwame Nkrumah in Gold Coast, Jomo Kenyatta in Kenya, and Léopold Senghor in Senegal, to name but a few, were skilled political organizers.

In colonies throughout Africa, leaders organized political parties. In the cities, parties published newspapers, held mass rallies, and mobilized popular support for independence. Demonstrations,

◀ *Léopold Senghor*

# African Independence

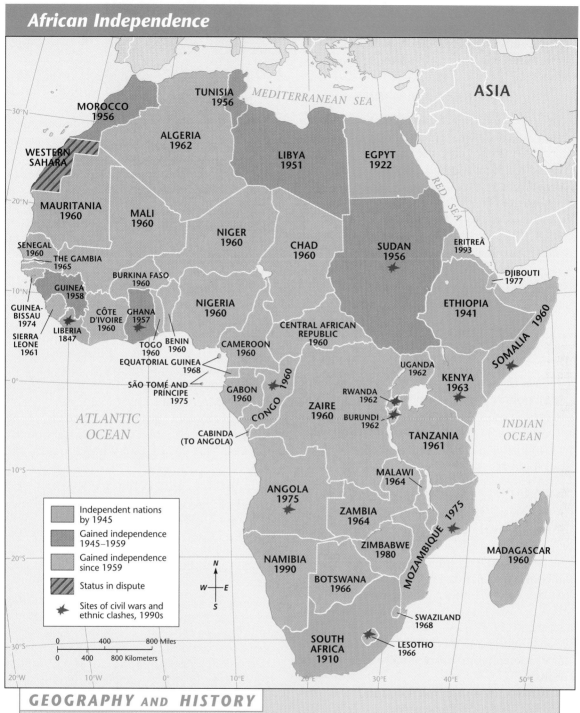

MEDITERRANEAN SEA

ASIA

**TUNISIA** 1956

**MOROCCO** 1956

**ALGERIA** 1962

**WESTERN SAHARA**

**LIBYA** 1951

**EGPYT** 1922

RED SEA

**MAURITANIA** 1960

**MALI** 1960

**NIGER** 1960

**CHAD** 1960

**SUDAN** 1956

**ERITREA** 1993

**SENEGAL** 1960

**THE GAMBIA** 1965

**BURKINA FASO** 1960

**DJIBOUTI** 1977

**GUINEA** 1958

**GUINEA-BISSAU** 1974

**SIERRA LEONE** 1961

**LIBERIA** 1847

**CÔTE D'IVOIRE** 1960

**GHANA** 1957

**NIGERIA** 1960

**CENTRAL AFRICAN REPUBLIC** 1960

**ETHIOPIA** 1941

**TOGO** 1960

**BENIN** 1960

**CAMEROON** 1960

**SOMALIA** 1960

**EQUATORIAL GUINEA** 1968

**SÃO TOMÉ AND PRÍNCIPE** 1975

**GABON** 1960

**CONGO** 1960

**ZAIRE** 1960

**UGANDA** 1962

**RWANDA** 1962

**KENYA** 1963

**ATLANTIC OCEAN**

**BURUNDI** 1962

**CABINDA (TO ANGOLA)**

**TANZANIA** 1961

**INDIAN OCEAN**

**ANGOLA** 1975

**MALAWI** 1964

**ZAMBIA** 1964

**MOZAMBIQUE** 1975

**MADAGASCAR** 1960

**ZIMBABWE** 1980

**NAMIBIA** 1990

**BOTSWANA** 1966

**SWAZILAND** 1968

**SOUTH AFRICA** 1910

**LESOTHO** 1966

Independent nations by 1945

Gained independence 1945–1959

Gained independence since 1959

Status in dispute

Sites of civil wars and ethnic clashes, 1990s

N
W—E
S

0   400   800 Miles
0   400   800 Kilometers

# GEOGRAPHY AND HISTORY

A great liberation took place in Africa following World War II. Slowly at first, and then with increasing speed, the people of Africa regained their independence.

**1. Location**  On the map, locate (a) Egypt, (b) Angola, (c) Tanzania, (d) Zaire, (e) South Africa.

**2. Place**  (a) Which nations were independent before 1945? (b) Which nations regained independence before 1960? (c) When did Zimbabwe gain independence?

**3. Critical Thinking   Drawing Conclusions**  Based on the map, what conclusion can you draw about the fate of European colonial empires in Africa?

strikes, and boycotts helped force European rulers to negotiate timetables for freedom.

## Routes to Freedom

During the great liberation, each African nation had its own leaders and it own story. Here, we will look at three examples: Ghana in West Africa, Kenya in East Africa, and Algeria in North Africa.

**Ghana.** The first African nation south of the Sahara to win freedom was the British colony of Gold Coast. In the late 1940s, young Kwame Nkrumah (kwah MEE ehn KROO muh) was impatient with Britain's policy of gradual movement toward independence. Nkrumah had spent time in the United States, where he was inspired by the Pan-Africanist Marcus Garvey and other civil rights leaders. He also studied the nonviolent methods of Mohandas Gandhi, the Indian leader.

Back in Gold Coast, Nkrumah organized a radical political party. Through strikes and boycotts, he tried to win concessions from Britain. But when mass actions led to riots, Nkrumah was imprisoned. Still, his "Positive Action" movement pressed on.

In 1957, Gold Coast finally won independence. Nkrumah, who had emerged from prison to become prime minister of the new nation, named it Ghana, after the ancient West African empire.* The symbolism was clear. *Gold Coast* reflected European interests in Africa. *Ghana* linked the new nation with the African past that had been denied under colonialism. Before the arrival of the Europeans, Nkrumah said, "our ancestors had attained a great empire. . . . Thus we may take pride in the name of Ghana, not out of romanticism, but as an inspiration for the future."

**Kenya.** In Kenya, freedom came only with armed struggle. White settlers had carved out farms in the fertile highlands, where they displaced African farmers, mostly Kikuyu (kih KOO yoo). Settlers considered Kenya their homeland and had passed laws to ensure their domination. They feared giving up any power to the African majority.

---

\*Ancient Ghana was located to the north and west of modern Ghana.

◀ *Jomo Kenyatta*

Even before World War II, Jomo Kenyatta had become a leading spokesman for the Kikuyu. "The land is ours," he said. "When Europeans came, they kept us back and took our land." Kenyatta supported nonviolent methods to end oppressive laws.

Other, more radical leaders turned to guerrilla warfare. They burned farms and destroyed livestock, hoping to scare whites into leaving. By 1952, they began to attack settlers and Africans who worked with the colonial rulers. The British called the guerrillas Mau Mau and pictured them as savages. To stop the violence, the British arrested Kenyatta and forced thousands of Kikuyu into concentration camps. Kikuyu casualties rose when British bombers pounded Mau Mau fighters armed mostly with swords.

The rebels were crushed, but not the freedom movement. Eventually, the British released Kenyatta, whose years in prison had made him a national hero. In 1963, he became the first prime minister of an independent Kenya.

**Algeria.** From 1954 to 1962, a longer and even costlier war of liberation raged in Algeria. During the 1830s, France had conquered Algeria after a brutal struggle. Over the years, the French had come to see Algeria, located just across the Mediterranean from France, as part of their country. Along with the million Europeans who had settled there, they were determined to keep the Arab-Berber people of Algeria from winning independence.

Muslim Algerian nationalists set up the National Liberation Front (FLN). In 1954, it turned to guerrilla warfare to win freedom. France, which had just lost Vietnam, was unwilling to retreat from Algeria. As the fighting escalated, a half-million French troops went to Algeria. Thousands were killed, but hundreds of thousands of Algerians died during the long war that followed.

Eventually, public opinion in France turned against the war. After Charles de Gaulle, France's World War II leader, became president in 1958, he began talks to end the war. Four years later, Algeria celebrated its freedom.

## High Expectations, Dashed Hopes

More than 50 new nations were born in Africa during the great liberation. Throughout the continent, Africans had great hopes for the future. Karari Njama, a Kenyan, wrote how different people had their own ideas about what freedom meant:

> **66**All the old people think of freedom as the old lives they had prior to the coming of the European . . . while many ignorant young people interpret the freedom as casting down all the present laws with a replacement of liberty to do what he personally wishes. **99**

People looked forward to rapid political and economic development. African leaders knew they had much to do to build modern nations, but they welcomed the chance to deal on an equal footing with the nations of the world. After 70 years of colonial rule, Africans were again in control of their destinies.

During the early decades after independence, the new nations took different paths to modernization. Some made progress despite huge obstacles. Many others were plunged into crisis by civil war, natural disasters, military rule, and corrupt dictators. Projects for economic development failed, and standards of living fell. In many countries, a small elite enjoyed wealth and privileges, while the majority lived in poverty.

## The Colonial Heritage

Scholars trace many of Africa's recent problems to the colonial experience. Western imperialism had a complex and contradictory impact

# PARALLELS THROUGH TIME

## Patterns of Migration

Migration has taken place throughout human history. Beginning in the 1500s, European colonists settled in the Americas, Africa, and Asia. Recently, the flow has reversed, as West Indians, Africans, and Asians moved to Europe. But while European colonists enjoyed many privileges, newcomers to Europe often face discrimination and hardship.

**Linking Past and Present**  Why did Europeans set up colonies in Africa, the Americas, and Asia? Why do you think people from former colonies have moved to Europe?

**PAST**  *France conquered Algeria, in North Africa, in the 1830s. By the 1950s, more than a million French colonists lived in Algeria. The French dominated the economy and granted Algerians few political rights. After a bloody war for independence, most French settlers left Algeria.*

**PRESENT**

*Since World War II, several million Algerians and Moroccans have crossed the Mediterranean to live in France. Although the newcomers speak French, they have held onto their Muslim faith and North African customs. Many have found it difficult to integrate themselves into the mainstream of French life. These children of Algerian-born parents live outside Paris.*

**The Cold War in Africa** Rivalry between the United States and the Soviet Union had devastating effects in Africa. Both sides armed their allies, fueling regional conflicts and civil wars that claimed millions of lives. One of the bloodiest struggles took place in the Horn of Africa, where the United States backed Somalia and the Soviet Union aided Ethiopia. In this cartoon, American and Soviet advisers rushing to help their African allies head for a collision. **Political and Social Systems** Why do you think the United States and the Soviet Union cared about which political system African nations adopted?

ROTHCO

on Africa. Some changes could be considered gains. Others had a destructive effect on African life that is felt down to the present.

**Economic changes.** Colonial rulers introduced new crops, technologies, and cash economies. They built roads, railroads, harbors, and cities. The new forms of transportation were meant to make the colonies profitable by linking plantations and mines to ports. Exporting raw materials and cash crops from Africa helped pay for European rule. For the majority of Africans, who were subsistence farmers, there was little benefit from these facilities.

After liberation, the pattern of economic dependence continued. To pay for expensive development projects, African nations exported minerals and agricultural goods to the industrial world. But most profits flowed out of Africa because the new nations had to buy expensive manufactured goods and technology from the West. Also, many large farms and mines were still owned by westerners.

**Political changes.** During the colonial period, Europeans undermined Africa's traditional political systems. Even when they left African rulers in place, they dictated laws and told Africans how to govern. White officials shared the racial views of their day. They saw Africans as children who needed guidance, overlooking the fact that Africans had ruled themselves for centuries. Europeans denied educated Africans top jobs in colonial governments.

Suddenly, at independence, colonial powers expected African leaders to transform authoritarian colonies into democratic nations. They seemed to forget that western nations themselves had achieved democracy only after centuries of turmoil and with the help of strong industrial economies.

**Education and health care.** In parts of Africa, colonial rulers had paid little attention to schools and health care. Instead, those services were provided by missionary groups. Western doctors, however, did develop vaccines for yellow fever and smallpox and helped to reduce deaths from malaria.

By the 1950s, in response to nationalist demands, colonial rulers built more hospitals and schools. But they emphasized elementary education. There were few secondary schools and only a handful of universities.

**Artificial borders.** The map of Africa after independence was itself a legacy of colonial rule. New nations inherited borders drawn by colonial powers, which caused great problems.

Africa is a continent of enormously diverse societies with more than 1,000 languages and dialects. Colonial borders had forced together people from diverse ethnic groups into countries like Nigeria or Zaire (formerly Belgian

**GLOBAL CONNECTIONS**

Millions of people of African descent are scattered around the world. The slave trade created the African diaspora, carrying Africans across the Atlantic to the Americas. In Brazil, the Caribbean, and North America, especially, many people identify with aspects of African culture. In the United States, African Americans make up about one eighth of the population.

Congo). To herders and traders, such artificial borders were meaningless. Even farming people migrated regardless of lines drawn on a map. Thus, leaders of the new nations often had to create a sense of national unity where there had been none before.

## The Cold War and Africa

Although many African nations supported the nonaligned movement (see page 827), the continent could not avoid the pressures of the Cold War. Leaders who were strongly anticommunist received western aid and support. Those who embraced socialism were looked on with suspicion by the West.

The rival superpowers were drawn into African conflicts. As you will read in Section 4, Soviet- and American-supported forces took part in the liberation struggles in southern Africa. In the Horn of Africa, along the Red Sea, the superpowers became involved in a long, drawn-out war between Ethiopia and Somalia. Elsewhere, the superpowers supplied arms to governments they favored. In the process, they helped increase the power of the military, thus adding to an already unstable situation.

## SECTION 1 REVIEW

1. **Identify** (a) Kwame Nkrumah, (b) Jomo Kenyatta, (c) Mau Mau, (d) National Liberation Front.
2. (a) How did World War II influence nationalist movements in Africa? (b) Why were most African nations able to win freedom peacefully?
3. Describe three ways in which the legacy of colonial rule hampered development after independence.
4. Describe the role of each of the following leaders in winning independence for his country: (a) Kwame Nkrumah, (b) Jomo Kenyatta.
5. *Critical Thinking* **Recognizing Points of View** Many Europeans viewed the Mau Mau as terrorists. Africans viewed them as freedom fighters. How would you explain these different points of view?
6. *ACTIVITY* Select one nation highlighted in this section. Design a logo that might have been used by its independence movement.

## 2 Programs for Development

### Guide for Reading

- What were the main goals of new African nations?
- What obstacles hindered development?
- What political and economic choices did African nations face?
- **Vocabulary** *mixed economy*

"Independence is the beginning of a real struggle," declared one liberation leader in Africa. The new nations faced two critical issues. They needed to create unified states with stable governments, and they needed to build productive economies that would improve the standard of living of their people. Meeting those challenges would be a long, complex process—a process that is still incomplete.

Making accurate generalizations about Africa is difficult. Every nation is different. Some nations have rich resources to help finance progress. Others are poor in resources. Each has its own set of problems and its own history.

In the decades since independence, African governments experimented with various programs. They made some progress but also took some wrong turns. In this section, we will look at the political and economic challenges faced by several new African nations.

### Seeking Unity and Stability

At independence, African nations set up governments modeled on those of departing colonial rulers. But parliamentary systems did not work in Africa as they had in Europe, where they had evolved over centuries.

**Divisions and civil war.** Colonial borders left most African nations a patchwork of people with diverse cultures, languages, and histories. Nationalism had united Africans against colonial rule. But once freedom was won, many Africans felt their first loyalty was to their own people, not to a faceless national government.

Like Eastern European nations, African nations were plagued by ethnic and regional conflict. In Sudan, for example, the majority, Arabic-speaking Muslims, in the north dominated and persecuted the minority, mostly Christian groups, in the south. Southerners tried to break away, which led to civil war.

Westerners often blamed African civil wars on ancient "tribal" rivalries.* But most conflicts were more complex. Some were rooted in colonial history. Britain, for example, found it convenient to rule its African colonies through what it called "tribal" leaders. It assigned Africans in each colony to tribes and then chose one tribe to rule others. The ill-will that was thus fostered lasted long after independence.

Civil wars also resulted when liberation leaders monopolized political and economic power for their own group. In Nigeria and Zaire, civil war erupted when economically successful groups tried to set up their own nations. Civil wars unleashed terrible violence in African societies.

**One-party rule.** Faced with divisions that threatened national unity, many early leaders turned to one-party systems. Multiparty systems, they declared, encouraged disunity. In Tanzania, Julius Nyerere (nyuh RAIR ay) claimed that a one-party system could be democratic and offered voters a choice of candidates within the party.

In fact, most one-party nations became authoritarian states. Some nationalist leaders who had led the struggle for freedom became dictators supported by a privileged elite. Some used their position to enrich themselves, allowed corruption to thrive, and failed to provide justice. Others used force to hold onto power.

▲ *Julius Nyerere*

*The word *tribe* was used by westerners to describe people living in small-scale societies and implied backwardness. The term is misleading, however. Like societies elsewhere, Africans in precolonial times belonged to ethnic or social groups that shared a common culture or loyalty. But these groups changed over time and continue to change today.

**Military rule.** When bad government led to unrest, the military often seized power. More than half of all African nations suffered military coups. Military leaders claimed that they—unlike greedy politicians—were motivated by a sense of duty to their country. Some military rulers, like Idi Amin, who murdered thousands of citizens in Uganda, were brutal tyrants. Others, like Nyerere, sought to end abuses and improve conditions.

Military leaders usually promised to restore civilian rule once they had cleaned up the government. In many cases, however, they gave up power only when they were toppled by other military coups.

**New solutions.** Political and economic woes brought Africa to the brink of crisis in the 1980s. Demands for change came from inside and outside the continent. African thinkers looked for African solutions to their problems. They studied precolonial African societies that had limited a ruler's power and allowed people a share in decision making. (See page 298.) Although they did not propose returning to the past, they did hope to build on traditions that had worked in Africa before.

The call of Africans for "people participation" was matched by demands for democratic reforms from external sources. Western governments and the World Bank often refused badly needed loans without such reforms. Under this pressure, some governments eased autocratic policies, legalized opposition parties, and lifted censorship. In some places, multiparty elections unseated long-ruling leaders.

## Economic Development

African nations, like other developing regions of the world, faced serious obstacles to development. These obstacles fell into five general areas: geography, population and poverty, economic dependence, economic policies, and political instability. (See pages 830–837 for an

**ISSUES** *For* **TODAY**   Some leaders believed African nations should find unique "African" patterns for development. How can developing nations achieve their full potential while preserving their traditions?

overview of the problems facing developing nations in the post-colonial era.)

Developing modern economies meant improving agriculture and developing industry. To achieve those goals, African nations had to build transportation systems, develop resources, increase literacy, and solve problems of rural poverty left by colonial governments. Many had little capital to invest in such projects. As a result, they had to make difficult choices.

**Socialism or capitalism.** At independence, many African nations chose socialism, with an emphasis on government direction of the economy, over the capitalism of colonial rulers. The socialist governments wanted to control scarce resources, using them where they were most needed. They hoped to end foreign economic influence and prevent inequalities between rich and poor. But to regulate the economy, socialism created large, inefficient bureaucracies. Often, the laws imposed by the national government were poorly suited to local farming communities.

Some African nations set up mixed economies, with both private and state-run enterprises. They, too, had problems. These nations relied heavily on foreign aid from the UN, the World Bank, and countries of the global North—as you recall, the industrial nations of Europe, North America, and Japan. Foreign capital was used to build airports, hydroelectric plants, and factories and to improve farming. Some programs succeeded. Many others, like Ghana's Akosombo Dam, were costly failures, due partly to mistakes by government planners or western advisers.

Although African nations did build some industries, they remained dependent on imports. Because most people were subsistence farmers, there was too little demand for goods to make local industries prosper.

Sadly, too, corrupt officials and powerful elites often used aid money to line their own pockets. Bloated bureaucracies and corruption are found in governments everywhere, including the industrial world. In Africa, however, where economies were fragile, waste and greed meant losses to desperately needed development programs.

**Cash crops or food.** In the early years, governments pushed programs to increase earn

**Building Independent Economies** *After independence, African nations struggled to modernize. They invested in transportation links, agricultural projects, new industries, and education. This railroad station was part of a development project in the highlands of Kenya.* **Economics and Technology** *How would a railroad network contribute to economic growth?*

ings by growing more cash crops for export. But land used for cotton, tea, coffee, or sisal did not produce food. As a result, African countries that had once fed their people from their own land had to import food.

**Urban or rural needs.** The food dilemma had another aspect. City dwellers who earned low wages needed cheap food to survive. Farmers, however, would grow food crops only if they received good prices for them. Many governments kept food prices artificially low to satisfy poor city people. As a result, farmers either used their land for export crops or produced only for themselves.

In general, many early government programs neglected rural development in favor of industrial projects. By the 1980s, however, governments realized they must pay more attention to farmers' needs. In Zimbabwe, for example, the government helped small farmers buy tools, fertilizer, and seed. Equally important, it made sure farmers received higher prices for their crops. The policy paid off in higher food output.

**The debt crisis.** Soaring oil prices in the 1970s crushed developing economies. In 1975, a ton of cotton could buy 111 barrels of oil. By 1980, it bought only 60 barrels. As oil prices went up, the world economy slowed down. Prices for African exports fell, plunging the young nations deep into debt. Governments had to pay so much interest on loans that they had little money for development.

The debt crisis led the World Bank and other lenders to require developing nations to make tough economic reforms before granting them new loans. African governments had to privatize businesses and cut spending on development projects. In the long term, the reforms were designed to help economies grow. In the short term, however, they increased unemployment and hurt the poor.

## People and the Environment

The population explosion put a staggering burden on Africa's developing economies. In 1965, Africa's population was about 280 million. By 1990, it had reached 640 million. That number was expected to double before 2020.

**Hardships for farmers.** Rapid population growth worsened rural poverty as more people competed for land. Family land was divided into smaller plots, which made it harder for people to produce enough food.

Today, as in the past, African farmers face harsh conditions, such as irregular rainfall, poor soils, and tropical diseases. Now, as then, when soil is exhausted, farmers migrate to other areas. Because of the growing population, however, many move onto less desirable land in arid steppe regions.

**Drought and famine.** In the early 1970s and again in the 1980s, prolonged drought caused famine in parts of Africa. Livestock died, farmland turned to dust and blew away, and millions of people became refugees. The Sahel was especially hard hit. This semidesert region stretches across Africa just south of the Sahara. There, overgrazing and farming speeded up desertification. (See page 286.)

In countries like Ethiopia and Sudan, civil war intensified the effects of drought and famine. Each side in the conflict tried to keep relief supplies from reaching the other. On several occasions, huge international efforts helped save millions of people facing starvation.

**Deforestation.** Rain forests, too, came under attack. To boost badly needed export earnings, African governments allowed hardwood trees to be cut for shipment to the global North. When forests were cleared, heavy tropical rains washed nutrients from the soil, destroying its fertility. In Kenya, Wangari Maathi challenged government policy by starting the Greenbelt movement. Her aim was to restore the environment while opening up opportunities for women in jobs such as rearing seedlings, planting, marketing, and forestry.

**AIDS.** By the 1990s, many African nations, especially Uganda and Tanzania, were reeling from the staggering effects of the AIDS epidemic. Experts lacked adequate information, but the World Health Organization estimated that up to 20 million Africans would be infected by 2000. Many victims were young people in their twenties and thirties as well as children born to mothers infected with AIDS.

## Outlook and Gains

Despite many setbacks since independence, African nations have made progress in every field. As independent nations, they claimed an equal place on the world scene and won the power to shape their own future. Within each nation, the process of building a national identity went slowly. But education and urbanization did begin to break the localism of the past.

**Education and health care.** As governments sponsored increased schooling, literacy rates rose. Every year, millions of young Africans attended high school. Universities trained a new generation of leaders to provide guidance for a promising future.

Countries that promoted female education, such as Ghana, created the first generation of university-educated women. Those women who achieved university degrees went on to participate at high levels in the modern economy.

Most African nations improved health care and created family planning programs. Governments saw that controlling the rate of population growth was an essential step toward improving standards of living.

**Economic growth.** Despite often depressing economic news, Africa remains a region with enormous potential for growth. By the 1990s,

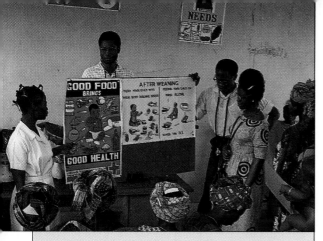

**Improving Health Care** *Providing medical care, especially in rural areas, has been a main goal of African nations. In much of the countryside, doctors are scarce and hospitals nonexistent. As a result, health projects often focus on prevention. Doctors at this rural clinic in Nigeria teach women the importance of good nutrition in raising healthy children.* **Political and Social Systems** *Why is preventive medicine especially important in areas with few doctors or hospitals?*

many nations had learned from failed policies of the past. With free-market reforms, countries like Ghana enjoyed a surge of economic growth. Other nations expanded mining and manufacturing and improved transportation. Some built factories to process agricultural products for export and expanded communication and transportation networks.

## SECTION 2 REVIEW

1. **Define** mixed economy.
2. Describe two goals of the emerging nations of Africa.
3. Why did many African countries have trouble building stable governments?
4. (a) What were two economic obstacles to modernization? (b) Describe two areas in which African nations have made progress since independence.
5. *Critical Thinking* **Applying Information** According to an African saying, "Cotton is the mother of poverty." To what economic problem does this saying apply? Explain.
6. *ACTIVITY* Design a magazine cover highlighting one of the problems facing young African nations. Then, write a short "Message From the Publisher" describing the problem and some possible solutions.

## 3 Four Nations: A Closer Look

### Guide for Reading

■ What problems did Nigeria face at independence?

■ Why has Zaire suffered setbacks in development?

■ What were Nyerere's goals for Tanzania?

■ How did Zimbabwe achieve majority rule?

Nigerian poet John Pepper Clark saw his nation torn by civil war. In "The Casualties," he chronicled both the obvious effects and unseen costs of the war:

**66**The casualties are not only those who
    are dead;
  They are well out of it.
  The casualties are not only those who
    are wounded,
  Though they await burial by
    installment. . . .
  The casualties are not only those led
    away by night;
  The cell is a cruel place . . .
  The casualties are many, and a good
    number well
  Outside the scenes of ravage and
    wreck; . . .

  We fall,
  All casualties of the war,
  Because we cannot hear each
    other speak
  Because eyes have ceased to see the
    face from the crowd.**99**

Nigeria was only one of many African nations that suffered a disastrous civil war after independence. In this section, we will take a closer look at Nigeria, Zaire, Tanzania, and Zimbabwe. Their experiences, resources, populations, and leaders differed. But their efforts to modernize illustrate the patterns that were common during the post-independence years.

## Pressures for Change in Nigeria

When Nigeria won independence in 1960, it hoped to develop rapidly. This large West African nation had rich resources, especially oil. Its population was the largest in Africa south of the Sahara, giving it a potentially strong internal market. Its fertile farming areas produced exports of cocoa and palm oil as well as food crops. The Niger and Benue rivers provided a good transportation network.

**A diverse population.** Following borders drawn in colonial times, Nigeria lumped together 250 ethnic groups. At independence, several large regional groups competed for power. In the north were the Muslim Hausa and Fulani, who had forged a strong empire in the early 1800s. (See page 409.) In the oil-rich southeast, the Christian Ibo were a bustling, energetic people. The Yoruba of the southwest were also mainly Christian.

**Civil war.** After independence, Nigeria drew up a federal constitution to protect the various regional interests. The system did not work well, however.

At first, the Hausa dominated the government. Ethnic rivalries continued, however, and in 1966, after 20,000 Ibo living in the north were massacred, the nation erupted into civil war. In 1967, Ibo leaders in the southeast seceded, declaring the region the independent state of Biafra. For two and a half years, war raged. It ended only after Nigeria imposed a blockade on Biafra, causing countless deaths from starvation. By 1970, when Biafra surrendered, the conflict had taken almost a million lives.

**Economic recovery.** The 1970s oil boom helped Nigeria recover from the war. The government spent lavishly on development projects. It set up industries, including a steel mill, auto assembly plant, and petrochemical works. To pay for prestige projects like a new capital, it borrowed heavily from the West.

Rural people flooded into the cities, hoping to share in the boom. Between 1960 and 1985, Lagos, the capital city, grew from 500,000 to more than six million. But while cities boomed, the government paid little heed to farmers. Nigeria, once a food exporter, bought expensive imported grain. Local food production fell, and rural poverty grew.

**The debt crisis.** Later, when world oil prices fell, the economy came close to collapse. A huge debt burden, combined with waste, mismanagement, and corruption, strangled the young nation. A small elite continued to profit enormously, but the majority of people suffered. A Nigerian editor expressed disgust with the self-serving wealthy class:

> 66It is the elites who have chosen their own narrow interests over everything else. Now the whole place is twisted because you cannot expect justice, and you cannot expect your fair share. They have robbed the country and ruined it.99

**Military rule.** Since independence, Nigeria has often lived under military rule. The military usually took over in the name of reform,

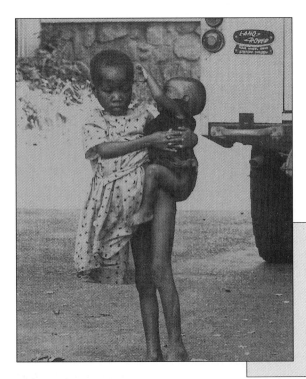

**Tragedy in Biafra** *Ethnic conflicts have taken a heavy toll in some parts of Africa. In 1967, the Ibo people of Nigeria tried to create their own nation, called Biafra. To crush the independence movement, Nigeria blockaded Biafra. In the famine that resulted, nearly a million people died, including hundreds of thousands of children.* **Political and Social Systems** *Why do you think the Nigerian government violently suppressed the independence of Biafra?*

arguing that something needed to be done to end the lavish lifestyle and corrupt practices of civilian politicians. Many citizens welcomed the military as a force for order and honest government even though it imposed censorship and other restrictions.

During Nigeria's debt crisis in the 1980s, General Ibrahim Babangida imposed harsh economic reforms to restore economic stability. He declared war on corruption, inefficiency, and waste. He banned most imports and refocused attention on agriculture, paying farmers higher prices for their crops.

Babangida promised to return the government to civilian rule. Elections were eventually held in 1993, but he and his military successors set aside the results. Many Nigerians feared that the military might remain in power for an indefinite period.

## Zaire: A Dictator's Legacy

After World War II, Belgium was determined to hang on to the Congo, its huge colony in Central Africa. As a result, it did nothing to prepare the colony for freedom. Then, in 1960, fearing a struggle like the French war in Algeria, Belgium suddenly rushed the Congo to independence. The unprepared young nation soon plunged into civil war.

**Freedom—and war.** Physically, the Congo had many advantages. It had rich resources, including vast tropical forests, plantations, and great mineral wealth. And the immense Zaire River and its tributaries flowed from the interior to the coast.

Yet the new nation, made up of some 200 ethnic groups, had no sense of unity. At independence, more than 100 political parties sprang up. They represented diverse regional and ethnic groups. Within months after independence, the nation split apart.

**Mobutu gains power.** Civil war raged for almost three years before United Nations peacekeeping troops ended the worst fighting in 1963. Two years later, an army general, Mobutu Sese Seko, seized power and imposed some kind of order. He renamed the nation Zaire, meaning "big river."

For the next 30 years, Mobutu built an increasingly brutal dictatorship in Zaire. He

▲ *Mobutu Sese Seko*

bilked the treasury of billions, slaughtered rivals, and ran the economy into the ground. The country's roads were left to rot. By 1990, fewer than 10 percent of the nation's roads were passable. Copper and diamond mines closed, and agriculture declined. Zaire's national currency became worthless, and its people resorted to a barter economy. Lawlessness reigned, and most people lived in miserable poverty.

Mobutu survived in power in part because his strong anti-communism won favor in the West during the Cold War. Also, he represented order. A western official noted: "He maintains stability. What would happen without him?" When he was eventually forced to hold elections, Mobutu won an unbelievable 99.9 percent of the vote. In a country where critics seldom lived long, few doubted the reason for his success.

**Looking ahead.** Despite widespread economic misery, Mobutu's grip on power remained strong. But years of bad government worsened ethnic tensions and the economy continued to decline. In the mid-1990s, many experts warned that Zaire was on the verge of disaster.

## Tanzania's Experiment in Socialism

In sharp contrast to Zaire's greedy and corrupt dictator, Tanzania's first president, Julius Nyerere, set out on a high-minded crusade. Nyerere's ambitious goals included improving rural life, building a classless society, and creating a self-reliant economy.

To carry out his program, Nyerere embraced what he called "African socialism." This system was not a western import, he declared, but was based on African village traditions of cooperation and shared responsibility. Nyerere was a strong supporter of women's rights, claiming

that their subservient position was "inconsistent with our socialist conception of the equality of all human beings."

In the 1960s, Nyerere introduced a command economy, nationalizing all banks and foreign-owned businesses. He emphasized the idea that Tanzania was "a rural society where improvement will depend largely upon the efforts of the people in agriculture and village development." He tried to prevent the rise of a wealthy elite through laws that forbade politicians to accumulate riches.

**One-party rule.** At independence, Tanzania was a large country with plenty of land and labor but very little capital or technology. Its main exports were coffee, cotton, tea, and tobacco. Most people were farmers or herders.

Tanzania included about 120 ethnic groups. Most groups were small, however, and the country escaped the worst rivalries that ravaged Nigeria and Zaire.

To promote unity, Nyerere set up a one-party democracy. Several candidates could run for each office. They could debate any topic except those related to ethnic or regional issues.

**Mutual cooperation.** Nyerere promoted the idea of *ujamaa,* a Kiswahili word meaning familyhood or mutual cooperation. Rural farmers were encouraged to live in large villages and to farm the land collectively. The government pledged to build roads and provide technical advice, tools, clean water, health care, and schools. Under this arrangement, Nyerere believed, agricultural output would increase. The govern-

ment would sell the surplus crops to towns or export them to other nations.

Nyerere's bold experiment did not work as planned. Many families refused to leave land they had farmed for generations, and the government had to force them to move to the *ujamaa* villages. Those farmers who did relocate resented experts who tried to teach them to farm. In the end, farm output did not rise.

**Disasters and reforms.** High oil prices, inflation, and a bloated bureaucracy plunged Tanzania into debt. In 1985, Nyerere resigned. His successor, Ali Hassan Mwinyi, introduced reforms. He cut government spending by reducing bureaucracy and privatized some businesses. These moves toward a market economy brought some improvement.

**Successes.** Although it faced serious problems, Tanzania did have some successes. Unlike many African nations, its food output did not decline. With foreign aid, the government provided basic services such as clean water, schools, and health care to its rural villages.

## Zimbabwe and Majority Rule

Southern Rhodesia was a British colony in southern Africa. It had a mild climate and fertile farmland. White settlers had carved out prosperous farms that produced food crops like corn and profitable cash crops such as tea, tobacco, and cotton. Equally valuable were mines that produced gold, copper, nickel, chrome, and coal.

Whites made up only five percent of Rhodesia's population but owned half the land and controlled the government. As the tide of nationalism swept through Africa in the 1960s, white Rhodesians flatly rejected any move to give up power to the black majority. When Britain supported demands for majority rule, conservative whites led by Ian Smith declared independence in 1965.

**Armed struggle.** Smith's white-minority government faced fierce resistance from guerrilla forces led by Robert Mugabe (moo GAH beh) and Joshua Nkomo (uhn KOH moh). The 15-year armed struggle that followed created much suffering in Rhodesia and nearby countries.

By the late 1970s, guerrillas held most of Rhodesia. Many whites had fled, and the UN had imposed economic sanctions that hurt the economy. At last, Smith was forced to accept a negotiated settlement that ensured black majority rule.

**Economic and political challenges.** In 1980, Rhodesia became the independent state of Zimbabwe. The new nation faced severe challenges. Years of war and sanctions had ravaged the economy. Droughts caused further problems. Recovery was also slowed by a bitter power struggle between Mugabe and Nkomo, which pitted the majority Shona people against the minority Ndebele (ehn duh BEH leh).

In the end, Mugabe won, becoming the elected president of Zimbabwe. He pressed for a one-party system, claiming it would promote national unity. Although he did not ban other parties, Mugabe tolerated little opposition.

During the 1980s, Mugabe worked to rebuild agriculture and industry. He encouraged white settlers to stay in Zimbabwe and contribute to its recovery. At the same time, he began to reverse the unequal land arrangement set up in colonial times, transferring some land held by whites to black farmers. To encourage food production, he provided support and higher prices to farmers. The policy helped black farmers increase output, although droughts in the mid-1990s again threatened harvests.

***Rhodesia Becomes Zimbabwe*** *When Rhodesia's white minority refused to share power, black nationalists launched a guerrilla war to oust the government led by Ian Smith. After years of bitter fighting, Smith was forced to seek a compromise. In 1980, Rhodesia became the republic of Zimbabwe, under black majority rule.* **Political and Social Systems** *What problems did Zimbabwe face after independence?*

## SECTION 3 REVIEW

1. **Identify** (a) Biafra, (b) Ibrahim Babangida, (c) Mobutu Sese Seko, (d) Julius Nyerere, (e) *ujamaa*, (f) Ian Smith, (g) Robert Mugabe.
2. (a) List four problems Nigeria has experienced since independence. (b) Why did some Nigerians welcome military rule?
3. (a) Why did civil war erupt in Zaire after independence? (b) How have Mobutu's policies affected Zaire?
4. (a) Describe Nyerere's program of African socialism. (b) Did it succeed? Why or why not?
5. (a) Why did Africans wage guerrilla war in Zimbabwe? (b) How has Mugabe tried to promote economic growth in Zimbabwe?
6. *Critical Thinking* **Defending a Position** (a) What arguments can be made in favor of authoritarian or military rule for a country like Nigeria or Zaire? (b) What arguments can be made against such a system of government?
7. *ACTIVITY* Select one of the nations studied in Section 3. Then, prepare a script for a TV program profiling that nation since independence. You might include interviews with both the nation's leaders and with "people on the street."

# 4 Struggles in Southern Africa

## Guide for Reading

- How did apartheid affect South Africans?
- What steps led to the end of apartheid?
- How did the Cold War affect Angola and Mozambique?

Nelson Mandela stood erect and proud before a crowd of more than 50,000 black and white South Africans. Their cheers hailed the historic moment. It was May 1994, and Mandela had just been inaugurated as South Africa's first president elected by voters of all races.

For 342 years, whites had dominated South Africa, denying blacks the most basic civil rights. Mandela's election set the country on a new track. In his inauguration speech, he spoke of reconciliation, not of revenge for the losses suffered by black South Africans:

> 66The time for the healing of wounds has come. . . . We enter into a covenant that we shall build a society in which all South Africans, both black and white, will be able to walk tall, without any fear in their hearts, assured of their inalienable right to human dignity—a rainbow nation at peace with itself and the world.99

The crowd sang "Nkosi Sikelel' iAfrika" (God Bless Africa)—the anthem that had come to symbolize South Africa's struggle for freedom. In the years ahead, South Africa's successful transition to democratic rule would serve as a beacon to other African nations.

## Crusade for Majority Rule in South Africa

In 1910, South Africa won self-rule from Britain. Freedom, however, was limited to white settlers. Whites also controlled the vast mineral resources and fertile land that made South Africa the richest nation on the African conti-

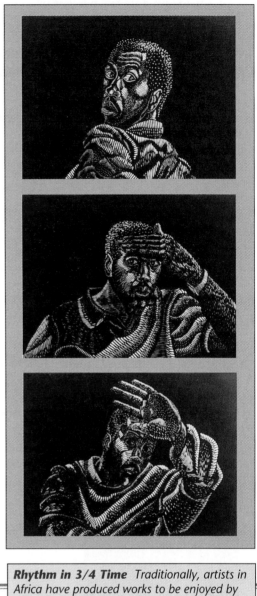

**ART HISTORY**

**Rhythm in 3/4 Time** *Traditionally, artists in Africa have produced works to be enjoyed by the whole community, not sold to private collectors or placed in museums. During the struggle to end apartheid in South Africa, the connection between artists and ordinary people was reinforced. "There can be no line separating the artist from his community," one young South African painter said. In this linocut, Vuyile Cameron Voyiya shows a political prisoner who had been severely beaten by the South African police. In prison, the man lived in fear of more beatings and often raised his arms "like he's evading blows."* **Art and Literature** *How can art like this linocut by Voyiya help to bring about change?*

nent. After independence, the white minority passed racial laws to keep the black majority in a subordinate position.

**Afrikaner nationalism.** After World War II, thousands of blacks moved to towns and cities. There, as elsewhere in Africa, black nationalism stirred demands for rights. In response, Afrikaners, who were descended from Dutch settlers, demanded severe new limits on blacks.

In 1948, the Afrikaner National party won a majority in a "whites-only" parliament. They then extended the system of racial segregation that had grown up over the years, creating what was known as apartheid, or the separation of the races.

Under apartheid, all South Africans were registered by race: Black, White, Colored (people of mixed descent), and Asian. Afrikaners claimed that apartheid would allow each race to develop its own culture. In fact, it was designed to give whites control over South Africa.

**Apartheid in action.** For nonwhites, apartheid meant a life of restrictions. Blacks were treated like foreigners in their own land. They had to get permission to travel and had to carry passbooks or face arrest. The pass laws were an especially heavy burden for women, who had to get permission from their parents, guardian, or husband, as well as from the authorities, in order to move from one district to another.

All blacks were assigned to "homelands," based on their ethnic group. Homelands were located in arid, unproductive parts of the country. More than 80 percent of South Africa, including the richest farmland, mines, and cities, was reserved for the fewer than 20 percent of the population who were white.

Apartheid laws banned mixed marriages and set up segregated restaurants, beaches, schools, and other facilities. Although blacks were needed to work in factories, mines, and other jobs, they were paid less than whites for the same work. Black schools received less funding than white schools. Low wages and inferior schooling condemned blacks to poverty.

**Black resistance.** From the beginning, black South Africans protested apartheid. In 1912, an organization, later called the African National Congress (ANC), was set up to oppose white domination. In the 1950s, as Afrikaner nationalists imposed ever-harsher laws, the ANC organized marches, boycotts, and strikes.

As protests continued, government violence increased. In 1960, police gunned down 69 men, women, and children taking part in a peaceful demonstration in Sharpeville, a black township outside Johannesburg. Another 180 were wounded. In the wake of the incident, the government outlawed the ANC and cracked down on trade unions and other groups opposed to apartheid.

The massacre at Sharpeville stunned the world. At home, it pushed some young ANC activists to shift from nonviolent protest to armed struggle. Some leaders left South Africa to wage the battle for freedom from abroad. Others went underground. Among this last group was a young lawyer, Nelson Mandela.

## Nelson Mandela

Rolihlahla (raw lee LAH luh) Mandela was born in 1918 among the fertile valleys of the Transkei. His father was related to the ruler of the Thembu, a Xhosa-speaking people. As a boy, Mandela enjoyed stories told by the elders about the days before the whites came:

> 66 Then our people lived peacefully, under the democratic rule of their kings and their councillors, and moved freely and confidently up and down the country. . . . Then the country was ours. We . . . operated our own government, we controlled our own armies, and we organized our own trade and commerce. 99

At school, the boy heard tales not of his own people, who were dismissed as savages, but of white warriors. One day, he told his family, "My name is Nelson!" The teacher had given him that name, after Britain's bold admiral Lord Nelson. The boy gave up his Xhosa name Rolihlahla, which means "stirring up trouble." Both names, in fact, would suit Mandela.

**"Stirring up trouble."** Mandela grew up at a time when whites were imposing harsher laws on blacks. Outraged by the plundering of black lands and the restricting of black freedoms, he helped organize the ANC Youth League. With other league leaders, he mobilized young South Africans to take part in acts of civil disobedience against apartheid laws. In time, as government suppression grew, Mandela joined the ANC militants who called for armed struggle against the white regime.

**"An ideal for which I am prepared to die."** By 1964, Mandela had been arrested, tried, and condemned to life in prison for conspiracy against the government. At his trial, he declared:

▲ *Nelson Mandela*

66During my lifetime I have dedicated myself to the struggle of the African people. . . . I have cherished the ideal of a democratic and free society in which all persons live together in harmony and with equal opportunities. It is an ideal which I hope to live for and to achieve. But, if needs be, it is an ideal for which I am prepared to die.99

**A powerful symbol.** Mandela would remain in prison for 27 years. During much of that time, he was permitted only one half-hour visit and one incoming and one outgoing letter every six months. He could not talk to members of the press, and his writings could not be published.

Despite his enforced isolation, Mandela remained a popular leader and a powerful symbol of the struggle against apartheid. Just as he had listened to tales of ancient African warriors as a boy, so young South African children were raised on stories of Nelson Mandela, fighter for freedom. Inspired by his example, these young Africans carried on the struggle in his absence. Both in South Africa and abroad, demands grew for the release of Mandela and an end to apartheid. ▨

## A New South Africa

Over the decades, world attention was increasingly focused on South Africa. During the 1980s, a number of countries, including the United States, imposed economic sanctions on the white-ruled nation. They refused to trade with or invest in businesses there. South African athletes were banned from international sports events such as the Olympic Games. In 1984, the black Anglican bishop Desmond Tutu won the Nobel Peace Prize for his nonviolent opposition to apartheid.

Foreign boycotts hurt South Africa's economy. Even worse, protests and growing violence at home forced the government to impose a state of emergency in 1985. Many South African whites questioned the oppressive measures used by the government and began to call for reform.

**Reform.** By 1989, F. W. de Klerk, newly elected president of South Africa, boldy accepted the need for reform. He abandoned apartheid, repealed the segregation and pass laws, and held talks with the imprisoned Mandela. After lifting the ban on the ANC, he finally freed Mandela in 1990.

For the next four years, Mandela and de Klerk negotiated the terms on which South Africa would move from white rule to majority rule. In 1992, white voters overwhelmingly supported reforms that would allow equal rights for all.

**"Free at last!"** By 1994, Mandela and de Klerk had worked out an arrangement for the nation's first multiracial elections. While the world watched, black South Africans—long barred from voting—lined up with white voters to cast their ballots. They elected Nelson Mandela as the first president of a new democratic South Africa. In a speech to supporters, he echoed a phrase made famous by the African American leader Martin Luther King, Jr.: "We can loudly proclaim from the rooftops: free at last!"

Mandela offered a striking example to other African nations when he welcomed longtime political enemies into his government. If he could work with Afrikaners who had once tyrannized the black majority, perhaps other African leaders could learn to accept opposition and democratic, multiparty systems.

## Looking Ahead

The new government faced the difficult task of meeting its people's high expectations for change. Mandela had promised a better life to the black majority, which had so long been kept in poverty. Once in office, he had a hard time delivering looked-for improvements.

South Africa was a rich country with a strong industrial base. But it could afford only a limited amount of spending for new programs. Mandela soon realized that change would take decades, not just a few years.

The gap in income and education between blacks and whites remained large. Middle-class blacks welcomed the new era of equality, but millions of poor blacks lacked economic power.

Mandela enjoyed great prestige among black and white South Africans. But he would serve only one term as president. People wondered who could succeed a leader who had not only helped end apartheid but had gone on to unite black and white South Africans.

## Freedom for Southern Africa

The colonies of southern Africa were among the last to win independence. From the 1960s to the 1980s, the white-minority government of South Africa interfered to prevent neighboring colonies from gaining their freedom.

**Independence for Namibia.** In 1920, South Africa received German Southwest Africa as a mandate from the League of Nations. After World War II, the UN asked South Africa to prepare the territory for independence. South Africa refused. Instead, it backed the white minority, who imposed an oppressive apartheid regime.

By the 1960s, the Southwest African People's Organization (SWAPO) had turned to armed struggle to win independence. For years, SWAPO guerrillas battled South African troops. The struggle became part of the Cold War, with the Soviet Union and Cuba lending their support to SWAPO.

As the Cold War ground to a halt, an agreement was finally reached to hold free elections. In 1990, Namibia—as the new country was called—celebrated independence.

**Freedom for Portuguese colonies.** As Britain and France bowed to nationalist demands in their African possessions, Portugal clung fiercely to its colonies in southern Africa. During the 1960s, the Portuguese dictator António Salazar had no intention of letting Africans win freedom.

In Angola and Mozambique, nationalists turned to guerrilla warfare. Portugal responded by sending almost its entire army to defend its empire. After 15 years of fighting, however, many Portuguese army officers realized that the struggle could not be won. In Portugal, an army coup toppled the Salazar dictatorship in 1974. A year later, Angola and Mozambique celebrated independence.

*Freedom for Namibia* Like many African peoples, Namibians waged a long armed struggle to win independence. Here, a group of Namibian women celebrate the birth of their nation in 1990. **Global Interaction** How did the Cold War affect Namibia's struggle for independence?

**Wars continue.** Independence did not end the fighting in Angola and Mozambique. Bitter civil wars, fueled by Cold War rivalries among the superpowers, raged for years in both countries.

Both South Africa and the United States had seen the struggles for freedom in southern Africa as a threat because liberation leaders were socialists. To undermine the new governments, South Africa aided rebel groups in both countries that wanted power themselves.

From 1975 to 1992, rebels in Mozambique starved and massacred tens of thousands of civilians. They killed teachers, burned health clinics, and destroyed schools in an effort to topple the government.

In Angola, a complicated power struggle dragged on for years. The Soviet Union helped one side in the struggle by financing more than 50,000 Cuban troops that went to fight in Angola. South Africa supported a rival group and even sent in its own troops. The United States, too, tried to undermine the Soviet-backed government. The war staggered to a halt in 1987. By 1992, both Cuban and South African troops had withdrawn. For both Mozambique and Angola, freedom had been won at an agonizing cost. For these new nations, the 1990s would be a decade for rebuilding after the devastation of war.

## SECTION 4 REVIEW

1. **Identify** (a) Nelson Mandela, (b) ANC, (c) Sharpeville, (d) Desmond Tutu, (e) F. W. de Klerk, (f) SWAPO.
2. Describe three effects of apartheid on South Africa.
3. Why did the South African government end apartheid?
4. (a) Why did Portuguese colonies in Africa have a hard time winning independence? (b) What role did Cold War rivalries play in southern Africa?
5. **Critical Thinking** **Recognizing Causes and Effects** Why do you think economic sanctions helped pressure South Africa to end apartheid?
6. **ACTIVITY** Create a mural portraying the struggle for majority rule in South Africa.

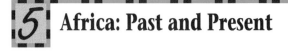

# 5 Africa: Past and Present

## Guide for Reading

- How have African nations helped to shape the UN?
- How are urbanization and modernization affecting social patterns?
- What role do Christianity and Islam play in African societies?

Since the 1950s, Africa has experienced extraordinary changes. It has thrown off the yoke of colonialism and given birth to dozens of new nations. Outside the political sphere, Africans felt the impact of modernization, with its accompanying social upheavals. With independence, noted Kofi Awoonor, a writer from Ghana, "We have had to rediscover ourselves as people."

## African Nations and the World Community

African nations emerged into a world dominated by powerful blocs. As new nations, however, they hoped to carve out their own position in the world. They did so in part through regional and global organizations.

**Organization of African Unity.** At independence, African nations maintained links with the Pan-African movement. While they did not pursue the Pan-Africanist idea of a United States of Africa, African leaders did try to build bridges among their nations.

In 1963, Africans set up the Organization of African Unity (OAU). It encouraged cooperation among members and supported independence for areas still under colonial rule. Members pledged to respect one another's borders and to seek peaceful settlement of disputes.

*Interpreting a Chart* *African writers have won world acclaim. Many write about the conflict between traditional and western ways. Others have challenged the corruption of the new African elite or exposed the evils of apartheid.* ■ *Which authors wrote in African languages? How would this help promote Africans' pride in their heritage?*

# Modern African Writers

| Writer | Career Highlights | Major Works | Major Themes or Subjects | Influence Today |
|---|---|---|---|---|
| **ua Achebe** ia | Writer, radio broadcaster, university professor | **Novels** *Things Fall Apart, A Man of the People* | Encounters between people of different cultures; effects of imperialism | His use of Ibo in his writings encouraged other Africans to write in African languages |
| **ne Gordimer** Africa | Published first story at age 15; Nobel Prize for Literature (1991) | **Novels** *The Lying Days, Burger's Daughter, My Son's Story* **Short Stories** *Friday's Footprint and Other Stories* | Impact of world events on individuals; injustice of apartheid | Helped raise world consciousness to evils of apartheid |
| **iib Mahfouz** t | Government official, journalist; Nobel Prize for Literature (1988) | **Novels** *Midaq Alley, Cairo Trilogy, Miramar* | Sensitivity to human suffering; opposition to repressive governments; struggles for freedom and independence | Popularized novel as literary form in Arab world; used fiction as political commentary |
| **pene nane** gal | Fisherman, plumber, stevedore, union leader, filmmaker | **Novels** *God's Bits of Wood, Tribal Scars* **Films** *Black Girl, The Money Order, Ceddo* | Need for political and social change; conflict between tradition and modernism; tensions among African groups | His use of African languages in films encouraged other African filmmakers to do the same; set the example of using films to fight for reform |
| **: p'Bitek** ida | Teacher, member Ugandan national soccer team, professor, director of Uganda National Theater and Cultural Center | **Poetry** *Song of Lawino* **Nonfiction** *African Religions and Western Scholarship* **Folk Tales** *Hare and Hornbill* | Clash between African and western values; need to preserve traditional culture | Uganda's best-known poet; founded Gulu Arts Festival; helped preserve traditional songs and poetry |
| **e Soyinka** ria | Journal editor, actor, founder of national theater; first African writer to win Nobel Prize for Literature (1986) | **Poetry** *Poems from Prison* **Plays** *The Trials of Brother Jero, Kongi's Harvest, Requiem for a Futurologist* | Need for social change and human rights; conflict between traditional and western values | Leading Nigerian writer; uses his influence to work for justice and political reform |

In the OAU, African nations discussed and tried to settle common problems. The OAU set up the African Development Bank to channel much-needed investment capital from foreign sources into development programs. Its impact was limited, however, because it had no power to enforce decisions and opposed interfering in the internal affairs of member states.

**The UN.** New African nations took pride in joining the United Nations. They contributed to and benefited from the UN and its many agencies. Africans served in UN peacekeeping missions around the world.

Along with other emerging countries, African nations focused world attention on issues important to them, including health care, literacy, and economic development. They also called for an end to racism and imperialism. They pressed nations of the global North to deal with problems such as the unequal distribution of wealth and technology. For example, they sought higher prices for their exports, lower tariffs against their agricultural goods, and more investment capital.

**Disaster relief.** The UN—along with rich industrial nations and private agencies like the International Red Cross, Britain's Oxfam, and the French organization Doctors Without Borders—has responded to famine and other crises in Africa. In the early 1960s, UN peacekeepers helped stop the fighting in Zaire. Later UN efforts helped save millions from starvation in Biafra during Nigeria's civil war.

Some international efforts had limited success. In the early 1990s, Somalia was in chaos as rival factions battled for power. UN forces, backed by a massive American effort, brought food to Somalis caught up in the civil war. However, outsiders were unable to restore peace and were even seen by some as a cause of further violence. In the end, the UN and most foreigners withdrew after they realized that only Somalis could solve their own problems.

## Old and New Patterns

In Africa, as elsewhere, modernization and urbanization disrupted traditional ways of life. Colonial rule had also undermined African traditions by promoting westernization. Today, people across Africa are faced with hard choices.

On the one hand, they want the high standard of living, advanced technology, and other benefits of modern societies. On the other, they value and want to preserve their own traditions.

**Urbanization.** By 1990, a quarter of all Africans lived in towns and cities. That number was expected to double by 2000.

City life weakened traditional cultures. It ruptured the ethnic and kinship ties that held together rural communities. Young urban dwellers who returned to their villages often scorned village customs and traditions. At the same time, many educated Africans looked to their past with pride. Some scholars were urging governments to base policies on African experiences and solutions rather than on western models.

**Women.** Women took part in the great migration to the cities. There, an educated few joined the elite, winning civil service jobs or entering modern professions. Most urban women, however, struggled to feed and keep their families together in poverty-stricken urban slums.

The majority of African women continue to live in rural areas, where they make up the bulk of the population. With the migration of men to cities, these rural women took on sole responsibility for caring and providing for their children. They planted and harvested food crops, collected wood and water, and prepared food. In some areas, they also found work growing cash crops on large farms. In West Africa, their historical role as market traders allowed some women to gain considerable economic power.

After independence, most African nations drafted constitutions that were generous in the area of women's rights. Often, however, these rights have not been enforced, and many aspects of women's lives are still controlled by traditional laws. A small but powerful group of highly educated women have worked to make governments more responsive to women's issues.

In the area of education, tremendous strides were made in providing girls with elementary school education. But few girls continued on to high school. Instead, they were required to stay at home to help their mothers with farm work and household chores. Illiteracy among African women stands at more than 70 percent on the average—and more than 90 percent in rural areas.

**Diverse Traditions** *Diversity marks the religious practices of Africa's people. Sometimes, religious practices intermingle, as in this Catholic church in Ivory Coast, where dancers in traditional dress take part in the service.* **Religions and Value Systems** *How might the incorporation of traditional practices help to strengthen the Catholic Church in a nation such as Ivory Coast?*

**Religion.** Today, as in the past, Africa is home to diverse religious traditions. Colonialism and modernization disrupted many traditional practices, but in rural areas, people remain faithful to their old religious beliefs. They seek the help of ancestors and others in the spirit world who serve as intermediaries for the Creator God.

Centuries ago, Christianity and Islam took root in parts of Africa. Since the population boom of the 1950s, both faiths have grown. The Catholic Church accounts for almost three fourths of African Christians, but many other Africans belong to Orthodox or Protestant sects.

At independence, African clergy replaced white Christian missionaries. Church leaders have risked their lives to stand up to dictators like Mobutu in Zaire and Idi Amin in Uganda. In South Africa, as you have read, Bishop Desmond Tutu preached against apartheid.

**Islamic revival.** Islam has long influenced the northern half of Africa and linked it to the Middle East. From North Africa, Islam also spread along trade routes into both East and West Africa. Nigeria has the largest Muslim population south of the Sahara.

In recent years, Muslim African nations have taken part in the Islamic revival that began in the Middle East. (See Chapter 35.) Its message of reform and call for social justice won a wide welcome. So, too, did its rejection of western influences.

Algeria's Islamic party did well in elections in 1992. The secular party that had ruled Algeria since independence feared an Islamic revolution like Iran's. It encouraged the military to seize power. The government then waged war on Islamic extremists whose attacks on politicians, scholars, and others created turmoil. More than 30,000 people were killed in the fighting, which brought the country to the brink of civil war.

## SECTION 5 REVIEW

1. **Identify** Organization of African Unity.
2. (a) How have African nations influenced the goals of the UN? (b) What role has the UN played in Africa?
3. (a) What effects did urbanization have on African traditions? (b) How have women's lives changed since independence?
4. (a) How have African Christian leaders worked for reform since independence? (b) How did Muslim African nations respond to the Islamic revival of recent years?
5. *Critical Thinking* **Analyzing Information** How does the OAU help to keep alive the idea of Pan-Africanism?
6. *ACTIVITY* Imagine that you are an African farm woman. Write a letter to the leaders of your government explaining why the government should provide you with education and technical training.

# Skills for Success

## Analyzing Cartograms

A cartogram is a special-purpose map used to present statistics geographically. On most maps, the size of a country or state corresponds to its physical dimensions. On a cartogram, however, a statistical feature, such as population or gross domestic product, determines the size of each place. For example, a cartogram of the population of the United States would show Alaska, the state with the largest land area, occupying less than one percent of the area of the map because of its relatively small population.

Study the cartogram at left. Then, follow the steps to read and analyze the cartogram.

**1** **Identify the subject of the cartogram.** As with any map, look first at the title and key. (a) What is the title of the cartogram? (b) In your own words, what information does the cartogram present? (c) According to the key, how is population represented on the cartogram? (d) What is the relationship between the size of a country on the cartogram and its population?

**2** **Compare the cartogram with a conventional map.** A cartogram distorts the size and shape of countries. To recognize the distortion of a cartogram, you will need to compare it to a conventional land area map. Compare the cartogram at right to the map of Africa on page 986. (a) Name one African nation that appears relatively bigger on the cartogram than it does on the land area map. (b) Name one nation that appears relatively smaller on the cartogram than it does on the land area map. (c) Name one nation that appears about the same relative size on the cartogram and the land area map.

**3** **Analyze relationships among the data.** (a) List the nations that you identified in step 2. Write a sentence explaining the relative size of each on the cartogram. (b) What might be one implication of a relatively small land area and a large population? Explain.

*Beyond the Classroom* Cartograms often appear in books of statistics. Locate a cartogram and bring it to class. Explain to the class what the cartogram illustrates and what conclusions can be drawn from it.

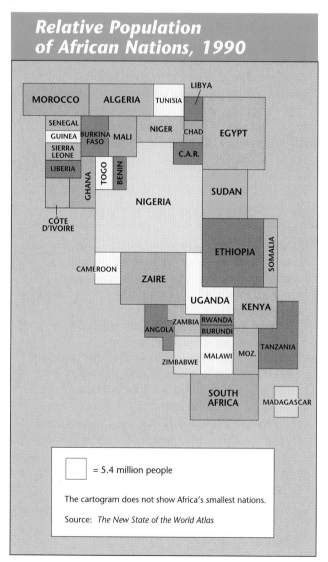

### Relative Population of African Nations, 1990

□ = 5.4 million people

The cartogram does not show Africa's smallest nations.

Source: *The New State of the World Atlas*

## Building Vocabulary

Review the following vocabulary from this chapter: *cash crop, ethnic group, socialism, capitalism, mixed economy, subsistence farmer, desertification, urbanization, apartheid.* Write sentences using each of these terms, leaving blanks where the terms would go. Exchange your sentences with another student and fill in the blanks on each other's lists.

## Reviewing Chapter Themes

1. **Diversity** Explain how multiethnic populations made nation building difficult in each of the following: (a) Nigeria, (b) Zaire
2. **Impact of the Individual** (a) Describe the policies and programs of two of the following African leaders: Mobutuo Sese Seko, Julius Nyerere, Nelson Mandela. (b) What impact did each of these leaders have on his nation?
3. **Economics and Technology** (a) What economic goals did most African nations seek to achieve after independence? (b) Why did many nations find it hard to end their dependence on the industrial world?
4. **Political and Social Systems** (a) Why did many African nations turn to one-party systems? (b) How did military leaders frequently gain control?
5. **Continuity and Change** (a) How has the colonial legacy hindered Africa's development? (b) What do African thinkers mean when they call on Africans to find "African solutions" to African problems?

## Thinking Critically

1. **Synthesizing Information** In Chapter 32, you read that the obstacles hindering modernization of developing nations can be divided into five general areas. (a) Identify the five problem areas. (b) Select *two* problem areas and show how they affect two African nations that you have studied in this chapter. ( ★ See *Skills for Success,* page 896.)
2. **Analyzing Information** How did colonial rule undermine African society?
3. **Analyzing Information** (a) How does rapid population growth make it difficult for develop-

ing African nations to achieve their goals? (b) How were population, famine, and the environment related?
4. **Solving Problems** How do you think leaders can help to develop national feeling among diverse peoples?
5. **Making Inferences** Why were ample resources not a guarantee of a healthy economy and widespread prosperity in some African nations?
6. **Recognizing Causes and Effects** Young African nations faced many difficult problems. (a) Which problems were related to internal forces? (b) Which problems were caused by external forces? Explain. ( ★ See *Skills for Success,* page 18.)
7. **Linking Past and Present** "We have had to rediscover ourselves as people," said Ghanaian writer Kofi Awoonor. What did he mean by this? Give three examples from the chapter to illustrate the statement.

### *For Your Portfolio*

You have been asked to compile an Almanac of African Nations. You will work with an editorial staff of classmates to research and write this resource book.

1. Hold a meeting to select the nations you will include in your almanac.
2. In the library, study almanacs such as *The World Almanac* and *The Information Please Almanac.* Analyze the kinds of information these reference books contain.
3. Decide which facts and statistics you will include in your almanac. For example, for each nation, you might include area, population, capital city, monetary unit, language, and current head of state. You might also include a brief history of each nation, a paragraph about its government, and a summary of current affairs.
4. Use library resources such as encyclopedias and almanacs as well as recent newspaper and magazine articles to compile the information.
5. Decide on a format for your almanac. Then write up each entry.
6. Place your completed almanac in a convenient spot in the classroom where other students can refer to it.

# Latin America

## (1945–Present)

## CHAPTER OUTLINE

Pablo Neruda was outraged. He had worked to help Gabriel González Videla get elected president of Chile in 1946. González Videla had pledged to promote economic and social justice. Once in office, though, he went back on his promises. He cracked down on workers, censored the press, and even persecuted former supporters like Neruda.

Neruda was a highly respected poet and political activist. He wanted to improve the lot of the poor, end injustice, and reduce foreign domination. Faced with González Videla's betrayal, Neruda took an unusual revenge. He included the Chilean president among the villains in his *Canto general.*

In this series of poems, Neruda created an epic for the Americas. He recounts a series of betrayals—from the Spanish conquest to the broken promises of independence that denied equality to the majority. Finally, his accusing finger comes around to González Videla:

> ❝He has *betrayed* everything.
>   He climbed like a rat to my
>     people's shoulders
>   and there, gnawing on my country's
>     sacred
>   flag, he twitches his rodent's tail
>   telling landowners and foreigners,
>     the owners
>   of Chile's subsoil: 'Drink all this
>     nation's blood.'❞

Neruda goes on to deliver a ringing call to the people of Chile:

> ❝Break the bonds, open the walls
>     that enclose you!
>   Crush the ferocious passage
>     of the rat that governs
>   from the Palace.❞

Neruda's poem points up a cycle of dictatorship shared by many Latin American nations.

Like other world regions, Latin America does not lend itself to easy generalizations. Its 33 countries are a complex mosaic of people and cultures. Still, Latin American nations have shared similar problems. They have tried to sustain economic growth and overcome a legacy of repression and poverty.

**FOCUS ON** these questions as you read:

■ **Economics and Technology**
   How did Latin American nations evolve economic policies to meet changing needs?

■ **Political and Social Systems**
   Why did Latin American nations have trouble preserving democratic governments?

■ **Continuity and Change**
   How did colonialism and independence influence present-day Latin America?

■ **Global Interaction**
   How did the Cold War affect Latin America?

■ **Impact of the Individual**
   How did leaders like Juan Perón and Fidel Castro reshape their nations?

## TIME AND PLACE

**Enduring Folkways of Rural Life** Latin American folk traditions have deep roots that can be seen in music, dance, handicrafts, clothing, and religious festivals. This handmade miniature from Mexico shows a bride and groom in a wedding cart being serenaded by a band. Like other centuries-old rural customs, the wedding cart is still used in parts of modern Mexico. But in Latin America, as in other developing regions, older ways of life are increasingly giving way to modern, urban conditions. **Continuity and Change** Why do you think that customs change as people move to urban areas?

## HUMANITIES LINK

*Art History* Marisol, *The Family* (page 954).
*Literature* In this chapter, you will encounter passages from the following works of literature: Pablo Neruda, *Canto general* (page 948); Carolina Maria de Jesus, *Child of the Dark* (page 950); Marta Traba, *Mothers and Shadows* (pages 972–973).

| **1948** | **1962** | **1973** | **1980s** | **1993** |
| Organization of American States formed | Cuban missile crisis | Augusto Pinochet comes to power in Chile | Debates over Brazilian rain forest | NAFTA signed |

| 1945 | 1960 | 1975 | 1990 | PRESENT |

# 1 Forces Shaping Modern Latin America

## Guide for Reading

- What conditions contributed to unrest in Latin America?

- How did the military, the Catholic Church, and Marxist ideology influence political developments in the region?

- How did governments try to promote economic development?

- What forces have contributed to social change in Latin America?

- **Vocabulary** *import substitution, agribusiness*

Like millions of poor people, Carolina Maria de Jesus migrated from the country to the city in the postwar era. For her, life in the slums of São Paulo, Brazil, was filled with hardship. Sometimes she found a job to earn money to feed her family. At other times she combed garbage for paper and other goods to sell. In her published diary, *Child of the Dark*, De Jesus described her daily struggle to move her family out of poverty:

> ❝May 26. At dawn it was raining. I only have four cruzeiros [coins], a little food left over from yesterday, and some bones. I went to look for water to boil the bones. There is still a little macaroni and I made a soup for the children. I saw a neighbor washing beans. How envious I became. It's been two weeks that I haven't washed clothes because I haven't any soap.❞

After years of war and economic dependence, Latin American nations often faced problems that mirrored those of emerging nations in Africa or Asia—rapid population growth, hunger, illiteracy, political instability, and authoritarian governments. In Latin America, as elsewhere, each country pursued its own course toward modernization.

## A Diverse Region

Latin America stretches across a geographically diverse region from Mexico, Central America, and the Caribbean through South America. (See the map on page 992.) It includes 33 independent countries that range from tiny island nations like Grenada and Haiti to giant Brazil, a nation almost as large as the United States.

Conquest, immigration, and intermarriage made Latin America culturally diverse. After 1492, Europeans imposed their civilization on Native Americans and later brought millions of Africans to the region. As these populations mingled, they created vital new cultures. Since the late 1800s, immigrants from Europe and Asia have further contributed to the diversity. Today, people of Indian descent are still the majority population in Mexico, Guatemala, Peru, and Bolivia. Brazil has more people of African descent than any other nation in Latin America. While Spanish is the dominant language of the region, Portuguese, French, English, Creole, and hundreds of Native American languages and African dialects are also spoken.

Most Latin American nations won freedom in the 1800s. However, many Caribbean islands and a few mainland areas—including Jamaica and Belize—did not gain independence until after the "great liberation" of the 1960s. (See page 826.) Despite vast differences, many Latin American nations shared common problems as they pushed to modernize.

## Sources of Unrest

In the decades after World War II, uprisings and revolution shook much of Latin America. They grew in part out of changes brought by modernization and reflected the failure of governments to reform deep-rooted inequalities.

**Gulf between rich and poor.** Since colonial days, a key feature of Latin America has been the uneven distribution of wealth. In most

**ISSUES** *For* **TODAY**

The gulf between rich and poor has fed unrest in many Latin American nations. How can a country reduce poverty without threatening its economic stability?

countries, a tiny elite controlled the land, mines, businesses, and factories. The wealthy few opposed reforms that threatened their economic power. A growing gulf between rich and poor fueled discontent in the postwar era.

**Social classes.** Poverty was linked to the social structure that had survived since colonial times. The upper classes were mostly descended from Europeans. The great majority of the population—the urban and rural poor—were a combination of mestizos, Native Americans, or African Americans.

By the mid-1900s, two social classes were emerging as important forces. As Latin American cities grew, the middle class and urban working class expanded. These classes were less tied to particular ethnic groups than the old aristocracy and peasantry. Both had their own hopes for progress and prosperity.

**Population and poverty.** In Latin America, as elsewhere around the world, the population grew as more people gained access to medical services. The population explosion contributed to poverty. Between 1930 and 1985, for example, the populations of Brazil, the Dominican Republic, and Mexico increased by more than four times. Venezuela's population rose from 3 million to more than 17 million. Growth rates in some countries slowed during the 1980s, but overall populations kept climbing because a large proportion of the people were young and just starting their own families.

Latin America's population, which reached 400 million in 1990, was expected to top 600 million by the year 2000.

In rural areas, where most people were peasant farmers, rapid population growth put stress on the land. A family might own a small plot for growing food. But the majority worked for low wages on the estates of wealthy landlords who held the best land. Although the entire family worked hard, many had to borrow money from their landlords just to get by from harvest to harvest. Burdened by this so-called debt slavery, they were tied to the land unless they ran away to the cities. In Central America and the Andes region, many Indians practiced traditional subsistence farming in isolated villages.

**Urbanization.** Pressure on the land was one cause for the great migration that sent millions of peasants to the cities. Today, 70 percent of Latin Americans live in cities.

Some newcomers found jobs in factories, offices, or stores. Many more survived by working odd jobs such as doing laundry or mending shoes. Others scavenged at the city garbage dump. In the shantytowns that ringed Latin American cities, people lived in tin-roofed shacks without electricity, sewage, or other services. Yet because they were near urban centers, they were more likely to attend school or have access to health care than the rural poor. As a result, the children of the city poor were often in a better position to move ahead than rural children.

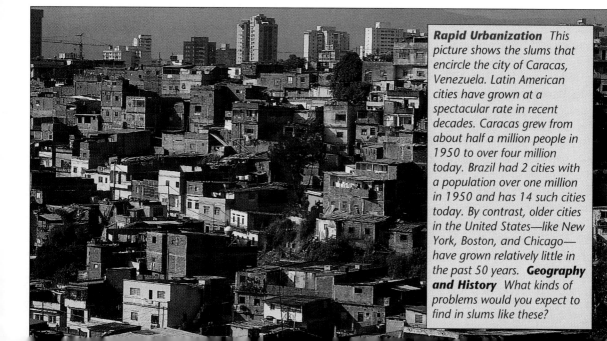

*Rapid Urbanization* This picture shows the slums that encircle the city of Caracas, Venezuela. Latin American cities have grown at a spectacular rate in recent decades. Caracas grew from about half a million people in 1950 to over four million today. Brazil had 2 cities with a population over one million in 1950 and has 14 such cities today. By contrast, older cities in the United States—like New York, Boston, and Chicago—have grown relatively little in the past 50 years. *Geography and History* What kinds of problems would you expect to find in slums like these?

## Reform, Repression, or Revolution?

Most Latin American countries had constitutions modeled on those of the United States or France. On paper, they protected the rights of individuals. Yet building real democracy was difficult in countries plagued by poverty and inequality.

**Competing ideologies.** In the postwar era, various groups pressed for economic and social reforms. They included liberals, socialists, students, labor leaders, peasant organizers, and Catholic priests and nuns. While differing over how to achieve their goals, all wanted to improve conditions for the poor. Most called for schools, housing, health care, and land reform.

Conservative forces, however, resisted reforms that would undermine their power. Among those who supported the status quo were the military, the traditional landed aristocracy, and the growing business middle class. These elite groups were often allied to foreign investors and multinational corporations. Conflict between conservatives and reformers contributed to political instability in many nations.

**Military regimes.** In the mid-1900s, military leaders ruled much of South and Central America. Like the caudillos of the 1800s, military rulers most often served conservative interests. However, some supported modest social and economic reforms, in part because an increasing number of officers came from the lower middle or working classes.

In the 1960s and 1970s, as social unrest increased, military governments seized power in Argentina, Brazil, Chile, Uruguay, and elsewhere. Claiming the need to restore order, they imposed harsh regimes. They outlawed political parties, censored the press, and closed down universities. In Argentina and Chile, the military imprisoned and executed thousands of dissidents. In both these countries, as well as other places such as El Salvador, regimes organized illegal "death squads" to murder opponents.

Military rulers tried to boost growth and solve economic problems by sponsoring capitalism. In Chile, General Augusto Pinochet (pee noh SHAY), who ruled from 1973 to 1990, promoted foreign investment and appointed economists trained in the United States to increase efficiency. The Chilean economy did expand. In general, however, most military regimes were unable to solve basic problems.

**The threat of revolution.** During the 1960s and 1970s, guerrillas and urban terrorists battled military governments in many Latin American countries. Revolutionary groups used bombings, kidnappings, and assassinations as tools against military regimes.

The leaders of many of these revolutionary groups supported Marxist goals. Only a socialist revolution, they said, would be able to end inequalities. Marxism won support among both peasants and urban workers, as well as intellectuals. Still, many revolutionaries were

▶ *Leftist guerrilla in El Salvador*

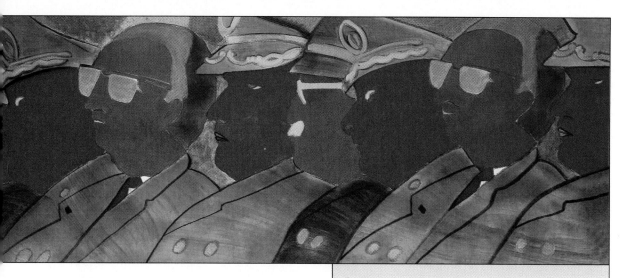

**The Power of the Military** *Military officers ruled many Latin American nations in the 1960s and 1970s. In other countries, elected leaders stayed in power only with the army's support. In this painting, The Parrots, Colombian artist Beatriz González uses the repeating image of a civilian president flanked by generals.* **Art and Literature** *What point do you think the artist is making by repeating the images of the president and his military supporters?*

motivated more by nationalism and local concerns than by the theories of Karl Marx. They condemned economic and cultural domination by the United States.

During the Cold War, the spread of Marxism complicated moderate reform efforts. Conservatives tended to view any effort at reform as a communist threat.

**Revival of democracy.** By the mid-1980s, the debt crisis, inflation, and unpopularity led military leaders to step aside. Argentina, Brazil, Chile, and other countries held multiparty elections to restore civilian governments. Still, elections alone could not solve underlying problems. Since the 1980s, some elected governments have made modest progress, but world economic forces often affected successes. Whether stable democratic governments would survive remained to be seen.

## Economic Development

Except during the Great Depression of the 1930s, most Latin American nations experienced economic growth between 1900 and the 1960s. Their economies were tied into the global economic order, dependent on the industrial world. Many relied on the export of a single crop or commodity, so they were especially hard hit if harvests failed or demand declined. By the 1960s, Latin America faced increased competition from emerging nations elsewhere seeking to export their crops and commodities.

**Economic nationalism.** The trend toward economic nationalism continued after World War II. (See Chapter 29.) To reduce dependence on imported goods, many Latin American governments had begun to set up their own industries in the 1940s. Under this policy, known as import substitution, governments encouraged local manufacturers to produce goods at home to replace imports. In time, many nations produced consumer goods such as textiles or refrigerators. They also set up auto assembly plants, although the parts were mostly imported from overseas.

Efforts to promote industry had mixed success. The middle class prospered, but life did not improve for most people. Many new industries were inefficient and needed government help or foreign capital to survive. Some home products were expensive or poorly made compared to imported products. Also, industry did not expand rapidly enough to produce new jobs for a rapidly growing population. Eventually, governments returned to promoting agricultural exports.

**Expanding agriculture.** In the past 50 years, large amounts of land have been opened up for farming through irrigation and clearing forests. Much of the best farmland belonged to agribusinesses, or large commercial farms that were owned by multinational corporations. They used modern technology, tractors, and irrigation to develop the land and set up food-processing plants. In Brazil and Central America, developers cleared tropical forests and opened new lands for farming and grazing. As you will read, this development had environmental and human costs.

Commercial agriculture also changed the food habits of many people. Advertisers encouraged people to eat hamburgers instead of tortillas and beans. Many traditional foods were no longer grown, as much land was turned over to growing crops for export. As a result, more food had to be imported, at a high cost.

**Crisis and reform.** In the 1980s, Latin American nations were buffeted by economic storms, including higher oil costs, rising interest rates, and a worldwide recession. Nations that had borrowed to develop industry were hurt when interest rates rose. (See Chapter 32.)

To dig out of the debt crisis, nations like Mexico and Brazil had to swallow bitter economic reforms. They cut spending on social programs, raised prices on goods, stopped financing local businesses, and opened their markets to foreign companies. Eventually, most governments got their debt payments under control.

By the 1990s, many nations were enjoying renewed economic growth. Still, for most people, standards of living had fallen. Foreign investments did bring new business, but wages remained low. After all, the chief reason multinational corporations built factories in Latin America was to benefit from cheap labor.

## Changing Social Patterns

In Latin America, as elsewhere, urbanization brought social upheaval. City life weakened the extended family of rural villages, replacing it with the smaller nuclear family. Family members no longer worked the land for food but had to earn cash. To support their families, women

**The Family** The Venezuelan artist Marisol has become world famous for mixed media, that is, using a mix of three-dimensional materials to create a single image. In her 1961 work The Family, *members of a poor family are painted on separate slabs of wood and set against the backdrop of an actual door. Although the work reflects the makeshift shanties common in slums, the expressions on the children's faces suggest a sense of hope for the future.* **Art and Literature** *How does Marisol suggest the strength of the mother?*

took jobs outside the home. Often, families sent their daughters to the city to work as maids, while their sons stayed home to work on the family farm.

In the struggle to survive in the city, some families fell apart. In large cities like Rio de Janeiro, thousands of runaway or abandoned children roamed the streets. Many were caught up in crime and violence.

**Women.** The wars of independence had not improved the status of women during the 1800s. Their role in public life was limited, and they had few legal rights. In this century, women campaigned for equality, including the right to vote. By 1961, they had won the vote throughout the Americas. By the 1990s, women moved into the political arena in small but growing numbers. Both Argentina and Nicaragua had had women as presidents, while Benedita da Silva became the first black woman elected to the Brazilian congress. The fact that "the daughter of a washwoman from a shantytown" could be elected to congress, Da Silva said, was a hopeful sign of change.

Women's status varied according to class and race. All women had responsibilities in the home and for child care. Upper-class women, though, had access to education and professional careers and could hire servants to care for their homes and children. Rural women of Indian or African descent faced prejudice and poverty. They lacked schooling and basic health care, and often labored for low pay.

A peasant woman from El Salvador described her life in the fields. She began harvesting crops when she was 16 years old. Part of each year, she and other women picked coffee. Then, she explained, they would move on to the cotton fields:

66The poisons they use in the fields are very strong and we're always having to take people off to the hospital. They'd give you two and a half sacks as a quota for every day and if you didn't manage it, they didn't pay you anything. Men have always been paid 5 colones more than women or children and we all do exactly the same work.99

When women organized, they became an effective force for change. To protect their families and communities, some peasant women campaigned successfully for schools and health care. In Argentina and elsewhere, women banded together to protest human rights violations by brutal military governments. (See page 969.) Some set up mutual aid networks. During the harsh Pinochet years in Chile, poor women in Santiago organized food kitchens that collected food and served meals to their community. Other groups protested violence against women or challenged the subordinate position of women within the family.

**Religion.** The Catholic Church remained a major influence throughout Latin America. Traditionally, it was a conservative force tied to the ruling class. During the Mexican Revolution, for example, the Church denounced changes that threatened its traditional position and wealth.

Within the Church, however, some people had always spoken up for the poor. During the 1960s and 1970s, a number of priests, nuns, and church workers crusaded for social justice and an end to poverty. Their movement became known as liberation theology. (See page 839.) These activists saw Jesus as a "liberator of the poor." They urged the Church to become a force for reform. Many joined the struggle against oppressive governments. Some became the object of violence themselves. In El Salvador, for example, Archbishop Oscar Romero was assassinated by right-wing death squads.

Some evangelical Protestant groups won a growing following among the poor. Their message, which emphasized the power of faith, had an especially strong appeal among women, who then brought other family members into the faith.

## SECTION 1 REVIEW

1. **Define** (a) import substitution, (b) agribusiness.
2. Describe four conditions that fed unrest in Latin America.
3. (a) What led the military leaders to take control in many Latin American nations? (b) Why did Marxism appeal to some people?
4. (a) Describe two policies Latin American governments adopted to build their economies. (b) Were these policies successful? Why or why not?
5. What were the goals of liberation theology?
6. *Critical Thinking* **Applying Information** Women's movements in Latin America have adopted the slogan "Democracy in the country and in the home." How have women worked for these twin goals?
7. *ACTIVITY* Organize a debate around the following proposition: "In the long run, the rise of agribusiness will probably be a positive development."

# Latin America, the United States, and the World

## Guide for Reading

- What was the impact of the Cuban Revolution?
- What policies did the United States pursue in Latin America?
- What issues have linked Latin America to the world?

"The duty of every revolutionary is to make revolution," declared Cuban dictator Fidel Castro in 1962. After bringing sweeping changes to his island nation, he vowed to export his communist revolution to other nations in Latin America. During the Cold War, Castro's call for revolution had an enormous impact on relations between Latin American nations and their powerful neighbor the United States.

Throughout the century, Latin American nations tried to limit United States influence and exercise greater independence. By the time the Cold War ended, they had carved out new relations in the larger global arena.

## Impact of the Cold War

Between 1933 and 1945, the United States pursued the Good Neighbor Policy, greatly improving relations in the Western Hemisphere. (See page 740.) During the Cold War, however, the United States often saw Latin American reform movements as communist threats. It backed right-wing, anti-communist dictators. At times, it even helped topple leftist leaders.

In Guatemala, for example, a leftist, Jacobo Arbenz, won election in 1950. When his land-reform program threatened United States-owned businesses, the United States helped the army oust Arbenz in 1954. Latin American nations, opposed to foreign intervention, protested this action.

Despite the furor, the United States intervened elsewhere in the hemisphere when it felt its interests were in danger. During the Cold War, Cuba became the chief focus of United States concern.

## Revolution in Cuba

In 1898, Cuba won independence from Spain but was occupied by United States forces until 1902. Over the years, the United States became the chief purchaser of Cuba's major export, sugar, and United States investors bought up Cuban sugar plantations and mills. By the 1930s, the Cuban economy was heavily dependent on the United States. The United States also influenced Cuban politics and for years supported the dictator Fulgencio Batista.

**Castro.** In the 1950s, a young lawyer, Fidel Castro, rallied forces opposed to the corrupt Batista regime. By 1959, Castro had led his tiny guerrilla army to victory. Cubans cheered the bearded young rebel as a hero. For many, the joy soon wore off as Castro introduced radical reforms that turned Cuba into a communist state. He nationalized foreign-owned sugar plantations and businesses. He put most land under government control and distributed the rest to peasant farmers.

While Castro imposed harsh authoritarian rule, he did improve conditions for the poor. During the 1960s, Cuba raised its literacy rate, provided basic health care for all, and backed equality for women. But Castro's revolution angered middle-class Cubans. As in other communist countries, critics were jailed or silenced. Hundreds of thousands of Cubans fled to the United States. Castro's own sister, in exile in Miami, called Cuba "a prison surrounded by water."

**Bay of Pigs disaster.** The Cuban Revolution alarmed the United States, especially as Castro denounced "Yankee imperialism" and turned to the Soviet Union for support. In 1961, the United States backed a plot by anti-Castro exiles to invade Cuba and lead an uprising against Castro.

The poorly planned plot was a disaster. An invasion force landed at the Bay of Pigs in Cuba but was quickly crushed. News of the plot helped Castro rally Cuban popular opinion against foreign interference, and the defeat hurt the reputation of the United States.

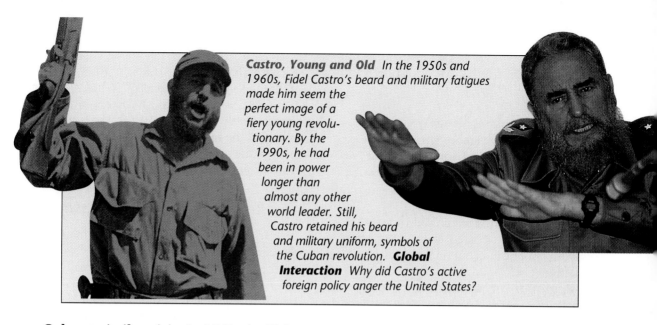

**Castro, Young and Old** In the 1950s and 1960s, Fidel Castro's beard and military fatigues made him seem the perfect image of a fiery young revolutionary. By the 1990s, he had been in power longer than almost any other world leader. Still, Castro retained his beard and military uniform, symbols of the Cuban revolution. **Global Interaction** Why did Castro's active foreign policy anger the United States?

**Cuban missile crisis.** In 1962, the United States imposed a trade embargo on Cuba. The embargo and the Bay of Pigs incident led Castro to seek even closer ties to the Soviet Union. Castro let the Soviets build nuclear missile bases in Cuba, just 90 miles (145 km) off the Florida coast. The threat of Soviet nuclear bases almost in its backyard outraged the United States and touched off a dangerous crisis.

In October 1962, President John Kennedy declared a naval blockade of Cuba. He demanded that the Soviets remove the weapons. For several days, the superpowers stood on the brink of nuclear war. In the end, Soviet leader Nikita Khrushchev backed down. He agreed to remove the missiles from Cuba but won a secret pledge from Kennedy not to invade Cuba. The United States retained its naval base at Guantánamo Bay, Cuba—the only United States military base on communist soil during the Cold War.

**Exporting revolution.** Over the next decades, the Soviets provided massive economic and military aid to Cuba and became its chief trading partner. Castro meanwhile tried to encourage revolution in other Latin American nations. Cuba also sent troops to Africa to help the socialist government of Angola. In response to Castro's policies, the United States continued its efforts to isolate Cuba and undermine Castro. Vowing to prevent "another Cuba," the United States aided anti-communist regimes elsewhere in Latin America.

**After the Cold War.** With the collapse of communism in the Soviet Union and Eastern Europe, Cuba lost its chief allies and trading partners. Even with the Cuban economy in shambles, however, Castro vowed to preserve communism. He encouraged tourism, allowed some features of a market economy, and welcomed foreign investment.

The UN urged the United States to end its embargo. But after years of suspicion and hostility, the United States was unwilling to negotiate with Cuba. Many Latin American leaders who disagreed with Castro's policies nevertheless criticized the United States for its position. They argued that Cuba no longer posed a threat to the hemisphere and that the United States had opened relations with communist governments in China and Vietnam.

## Colossus of the North

A complex network of ties linked Latin America and the United States. Like powerful nations in many times and places, the United States developed a sphere of influence that included a number of smaller neighboring states. The United States was the leading investor and trading partner for most nations in the hemisphere. Profits from United States-owned companies flowed from Latin America to the north. Many cultural influences drifted both north and south.

Still, the United States and its neighbors had very different views of one another. The United States saw itself as the defender of democracy and capitalism and the source of humanitarian aid. Many Latin Americans, however, felt that they lived under the shadow of the "colossus of the north." Mexican poet Octavio Paz wrote:

> 66North Americans are always among us, even when they ignore us or turn their back on us. Their shadow covers the whole hemisphere. It is the shadow of a giant. 99

While Latin Americans admired the wealth and technology of the United States, they often resented its political, economic, military, and cultural influence.

**Regional organizations.** Despite disagreements, Latin American nations and the United States did work together. The Organization of American States (OAS) was formed in 1948 to promote democracy, economic cooperation, and human rights. Members pledged not to interfere "directly or indirectly, for any reason whatever, in the internal or external affairs of any other State." Although the United States often used its power to dominate the OAS, Latin American members did at times pursue an independent line.

The Castro revolution and other Cold War tensions led President Kennedy to launch the ambitious Alliance for Progress in 1961. The United States pledged billions in loans and investments. Latin American governments were to cooperate by introducing genuine reform programs. Jointly, their efforts would promote education and land reform, reduce inequality and poverty, weaken dictatorships, and help countries withstand revolutions.

The alliance accomplished little. Landowners and the business community in many countries opposed basic reforms. Over the decades, the United States did provide economic and other aid to Latin America, but never on the scale originally proposed by Kennedy.

**Intervention.** The United States did invest much aid in training and equipping the military in Latin America. It also returned to a policy of intervention, sending troops to the Dominican Republic in 1965, Grenada in 1983, and Panama in 1989. During the Cold War, it often used secret operations to preserve its power in the hemisphere.

After Salvador Allende (ah YEHN day), a socialist, was elected president of Chile, President Richard Nixon told officials to "make the [Chilean] economy scream." When a military coup overthrew Allende in 1973, the United States quietly lent its support to the coup. Later, it helped the military in Central American countries battle guerrillas. Such undercover operations aroused fierce resentments.

## Regional and Global Issues

By the end of the Cold War, many Latin American nations had reduced their dependence on the United States, although it remained their chief trading partner. They became increasingly tied to the global economy. Oil-rich Venezuela joined Arab nations in OPEC, while Brazil worked with coffee-exporting nations of Africa to support coffee prices.

Many Latin American nations increased trade and cultural links to European countries. Some exported food or minerals to Asian Pacific Rim nations. Japanese investments in Latin America, especially in Brazil, increased.

**Regional ties.** In Latin America, as elsewhere around the world, regional trading blocs gained importance in the 1990s. Such groups created larger markets by lowering trade barriers among neighboring countries.

In 1993, Mexico linked its economy to those of the United States and Canada through NAFTA. (See page 862.) Two years later, a new South American trading bloc, Mercosur, paved the way for increased trade among Argentina, Brazil, Paraguay, and Uruguay. The new groups operated alongside older blocs that linked Andean, Caribbean, or Central American nations. There was even talk of a hemisphere-wide free-trade zone by the year 2005.

**The drug wars.** Regional cooperation played an essential role in efforts to control the illegal drug trade. Indians in Colombia, Peru, and Bolivia had for centuries grown coca for their own uses. As drug use increased in the United States and elsewhere during the 1970s, criminal gangs began producing and smuggling ever-larger quantities of cocaine and other drugs for export.

In the 1980s, the United States declared a "war on drugs" and set out to halt the flow of drugs into the country. It pressed governments in Colombia, Bolivia, and Peru to destroy coca crops and move against drug lords who reaped huge profits from drug trafficking.

Latin American governments recognized the evils of the drug trade. After all, drug lords were bribing government officials and hiring assassins to kill judges, journalists, and others who spoke out against them. But many people in Latin America argued that the root of the problem was not the *supply* of drugs but the growing *demand* for illegal drugs in the United States. Still, countries from Mexico to Colombia accepted aid and cooperated with the United States in the antidrug fight.

**Migration.** Immigration from Latin America to the United States increased rapidly after the 1970s. Poverty, civil war, and repressive governments led many people to flee their homelands. Like earlier immigrants, they sought freedom and economic opportunity.

By the 1990s, the United States had more than 8 million immigrants from Mexico, Central America, the Caribbean, and South America. Many immigrants entered the United States legally and eventually became citizens. A large number, however, were illegal immigrants, which created resentment in the United States. In the 1990s, pressure increased in the United States to halt illegal immigration, deny services to illegal aliens, and return aliens to their country of origin.

## *Development Versus the Environment: No Easy Answers*

Environmental protection also raised troubling issues for Latin America and the world. Developing nations insisted that they needed to exploit their land and other resources if they wanted economic growth. "You cannot talk ecology to people who are struggling to survive," said a Brazilian delegate to the Earth Summit. (See page 837.) Leaders of developing nations pointed out that western powers had long since cleared many of their forests and mined their lands. What right, they asked, did industrial nations have to tell them to stop developing their resources?

The most widely publicized issue was the rapid destruction of the Amazon rain forest, which occupies more than a million square miles in the heart of Brazil. It is rich in mineral re-

**Drug Wars** *Efforts to stop the drug trade have met many obstacles. Often, drug traffickers are able to bribe judges, police, and army officers. At other times, they have murdered officials outright. Still, governments have made a major effort to halt the flow of illegal drugs. Above, a Colombian soldier guards a luxurious house seized from a drug trafficker. Below, Colombian troops burn more than two tons of captured cocaine.* **Global Interaction** *What does the drug trade show about global interaction?*

sources for economic growth. It also could provide land to millions of landless peasants. Since the 1930s, Brazil has tried to open up this vast area to development. By the 1970s and 1980s, vast tracts of tropical forest were being bulldozed and burned for farms, cattle ranches, highways, and even newly planned cities.

Environmentalists argued that deforestation had enormous costs. They called the Amazon rain forest "the lungs of the world" because it plays a key role in absorbing poisonous carbon dioxide from the air and releasing essential oxygen. It has been home to 15 million species of plants and animals, which have been threatened by development. Some forms of plant life might even hold cures for diseases.

**Another Rain Forest** *Some countries have made strong efforts to preserve their rain forests. Costa Rica, in Central America, has had some success by turning its rain forest areas into tourist attractions. With ecological tourism, or "ecotourism," visitors hike through rain forests led by a knowledgeable guide without damaging the fragile environment.* **Geography and History** *Describe one way in which the United States has tried to preserve natural environments.*

Rapid development has also meant disaster for many indigenous peoples. Isolation had protected bands of self-sufficient forest dwellers for centuries. Land-hungry farmers, speculators, or foreign mining companies converged on the forest, threatening these ancient ways of life. Many Indians died of strange diseases introduced by the newcomers or were killed in conflicts provoked by impatient developers.

Debate on the rain forest heated up in the 1980s. In 1988, a murder in a small Brazilian village revealed the explosive nature of the issue.

## A Man of Courage

The night was hot and muggy in Xapuri, a town along the Amazon River in northern Brazil. Francisco "Chico" Mendes, a leader of the local rubber tappers union, had just finished playing dominoes with friends. Dinner was ready. But first, he wanted to cool off at an outdoor water tap.

Mendes never got his dinner. As he stepped out of his small house, he was felled by a shotgun blast.

The murder of Chico Mendes in December 1988 was just another in a series of violent attacks on union activists. In fact, Mendes, like other union leaders, had been living for months under a death threat. But reaction to the murder of this once-obscure rubber tapper was worldwide. Mendes had become a hero to those struggling to save the world's largest remaining tropical rain forest.

**Saving a way of life.** Mendes was an unlikely hero for environmentalists. His chief interest was his small union. Rubber tappers collected raw latex from trees in the rubber plantations of the Amazon rain forest. They worked long hours for low pay. Because Brazil's rubber industry was no longer profitable, ranchers wanted to clear the land for cattle or farming. They tried to buy or push out the rubber tappers. When the tappers would not leave, ranchers hired gunmen to terrorize or kill them.

To save the tappers' way of life, Mendes worked to stop the destruction of the forest. To do so meant standing up to the ranchers. As the conflict raged, environmentalists took up the cause of Mendes and the rubber tappers. They had already sounded the alarm about the burning of the forest by developers. A 1987 satellite photo had shown a smoky haze over the entire Amazon.

Environmentalists praised Mendes as a hero. At the same time, however, he remained clear about his own goals:

Development has threatened indigenous peoples in other parts of the world. The Penan, a nomadic group of hunter-gatherers, live in the rain forest of Borneo, an island in Malaysia. Commercial logging is destroying their ancient way of life. Many Penan have barricaded logging roads and used other forms of nonviolent protest. International environmental groups have asked the Malaysian government to stop logging in areas of the forest where the Penan live.

> **66**I'm not protecting the forest because I'm worried that in 20 years the world will be affected. I'm worried about it because there are thousands of people living here who depend on the forest—and their lives are in danger every day.**99**

**"I want to live."** Along with environmentalists, however, Mendes wanted to create "extractive reserves," protected areas of the forest that tappers and others could use for its resources without destroying it. That goal did not sit well with a local rancher, who issued a death threat against Mendes.

The union leader was brave but not foolhardy. He accepted protection from the police.

> **66**If a messenger came down from heaven and guaranteed that my death would strengthen our struggle, it would even be worth it. But experience teaches us the opposite. . . . I want to live.**99**

Police protection did not save Mendes. Still, his murder helped to focus attention on an issue that has become increasingly important—not only to Brazil but to the world. ■

---

## SECTION 2 REVIEW

**1. Identify** (a) Bay of Pigs, (b) Cuban missile crisis, (c) OAS, (d) Alliance for Progress, (e) Salvador Allende, (f) Chico Mendes.
**2.** What were three results of Castro's revolution in Cuba?
**3.** (a) Describe two ways the United States intervened in Latin American affairs. (b) How did Latin Americans respond?
**4.** Why did Latin American nations join regional trading blocs?
**5.** *Critical Thinking* **Identifying Alternatives** Experts disagree about whether the fight against illegal drugs should focus on supply or demand. List some arguments for and against each approach.
**6.** *ACTIVITY* Draw a political cartoon about the conflict between economic development and environmental protection from the viewpoint of a developing nation.

---

## 3 Mexico, Central America, and the Caribbean

### Guide for Reading

■ What economic successes did Mexico achieve?

■ Why did Central American countries experience civil wars?

■ What problems did democracy face in Haiti?

■ **Vocabulary** *ejidos, maquiladoras*

**66**Today we must fight for a better world, without poverty, without racism, with peace." This message of hope and resolve was delivered at the city hall in Oslo, Norway, by a woman dressed simply in the traditional striped garments of a Guatemalan Indian. Rigoberta Menchu had come to accept the Nobel Peace Prize for her work on behalf of human rights.

Menchu had traveled a difficult road to this moment. From before her birth, the Central American nation of Guatemala had been locked in a struggle between the government and the Indian majority. Tens of thousand of Indians were killed, including Menchu's own parents and brother. Menchu became a leader in the Indians' fight to retain their farmland.

When it was announced that Menchu had won the Nobel Peace Prize in 1992, the Guatemalan government was outraged. To them, Menchu was a revolutionary. To Menchu, however, the award meant that the world recognized her people's cause:

> **66**I consider this prize not as an award to me personally, but rather as one of the greatest conquests in the struggle for peace, for human rights, and for the rights of the indigenous people.**99**

In the postwar era, Guatemala and several other Central American countries were battered by civil wars. To the north, their larger and richer neighbor, Mexico, weathered those decades with relatively little turmoil.

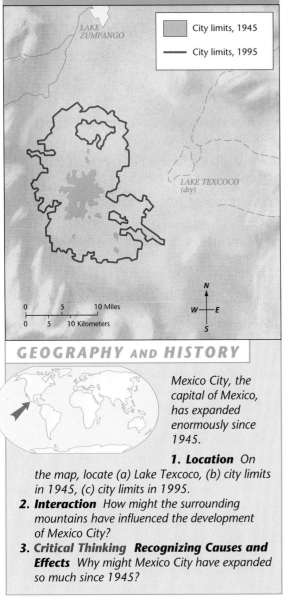

## Growth of Mexico City

LAKE
ZUMPANGO

City limits, 1945

City limits, 1995

LAKE TEXCOCO
(dry)

N

W—E

S

| 0 | 5 | 10 Miles |
| 0 | 5 | 10 Kilometers |

### GEOGRAPHY *AND* HISTORY

Mexico City, the capital of Mexico, has expanded enormously since 1945.

**1. Location** On the map, locate (a) Lake Texcoco, (b) city limits in 1945, (c) city limits in 1995.

**2. Interaction** How might the surrounding mountains have influenced the development of Mexico City?

**3. Critical Thinking** *Recognizing Causes and Effects* Why might Mexico City have expanded so much since 1945?

## Mexico on the Move

As you read in Chapter 29, Mexico had already endured a long, violent revolution. Its government was committed—at least in theory—to improving conditions for the poor.

**The rural poor.** In the 1930s, Mexico's president, Lázaro Cárdenas, had taken steps to fulfill the promises of the Mexican Revolution, especially land reform. He distributed some 44 million acres of land to peasants. Most was given to *ejidos* (eh HEE dohs), or peasant cooperatives. Some families also received small plots to farm themselves.

Much of the land was arid. It needed to be irrigated and fertilized to be productive. As rural populations grew, the land was subdivided and exhausted from overfarming. Presidents after Cárdenas, however, paid less attention to Mexico's rural poor. Instead, they favored agribusinesses that produced cash-earning export crops.

As conditions worsened, many peasants migrated to towns and cities, especially to Mexico City. The population of Mexico's capital mushroomed—from 1.5 million in 1940 to 20 million in 1995—making it the world's largest city. By the year 2000, that number is expected to reach 30 million.

**Politics.** Since the Mexican Revolution, a single party—the Institutional Revolutionary Party (PRI)—has won every election. It claimed to represent all groups—from workers and peasants to business-industrial interests and the military. Although a few small political parties did exist, PRI bosses moved forcefully against any serious opposition.

In part, the PRI held on to power by responding to social ills with programs for education, welfare, and health. As a result, it generally kept discontent from exploding into violence. Yet, in 1968, student protests shook Mexico as they did other western countries. Riot police and the army brutally suppressed the turmoil. The riots and the government's response received worldwide attention because the summer Olympic Games were held in Mexico City that year. Although much criticized, the PRI remained in power.

From time to time, the government also faced guerrilla movements. In 1994, for example, armed Indian rebels in the southern state of Chiapas challenged the government, demanding social and economic reforms. By skillfully using the media, the Chiapas rebels became international heroes. Yet they failed to achieve their goals.

Under pressure from all sides, the PRI did move against corruption and made some election reforms, which helped opposing parties win a larger share of the vote. Some people even predicted that the PRI's monopoly on power might someday end.

**Economic ups and downs.** After World War II, Mexico pushed ahead with efforts to foster import substitution, reduce foreign influence, and expand agriculture. To promote industry, the government worked closely with private businesses. It invested in building roads, dams, and ports and encouraged tourism.

Between 1940 and 1982, both manufacturing and agriculture made huge gains. Mexico became the second largest economy in Latin America after Brazil. That growth turned Mexico from an agricultural economy into a mostly urban, industrial society.

In the late 1970s, new oil discoveries and rising oil prices spurred an economic boom. Mexico borrowed heavily to fund development projects. Then the worldwide recession of the 1980s, falling oil prices, and rising interest rates plunged the country deeply into debt. Like other debtor nations, Mexico was forced to cut spending on social and other programs. (See page 833.) The government also reduced barriers to foreign businesses and privatized some industries.

**Poverty and prosperity.** Mexico remained a disturbing mix of prosperity and poverty. During the 1980s, a system of *maquiladoras* (mah kee luh DOHR uhs), or assembly plants, began to flourish along Mexico's northern border. Maquiladoras, which were owned by multinational corporations, used cheap Mexican labor to assemble imported parts for cars and electronic goods. Finished products were then exported to the United States, Japan, and elsewhere. The maquiladoras system provided jobs for many Mexicans—most of them women. Still, environmental problems in the plants, plus the government's refusal to allow the workers to organize, resulted in a series of worker demonstrations.

Despite economic successes, most Mexicans remained poor. The economy could not produce enough jobs to keep up with rapid population growth. Wealth continued to be unequally distributed. The top 10 percent of the people controlled over 40 percent of the wealth, while the poorest 20 percent earned less than 2 percent of national income.

**Links to the United States.** Mexico has felt the powerful economic and political influence of its northern neighbor. In the 1930s, it set out to reduce economic influence through import substitution. Yet Mexico has continued to rely on investment capital from the United States. In 1995, a $20 billion loan from the United States bailed Mexico out of an economic crisis.

In 1993, Mexico, the United States, and Canada signed NAFTA. Supporters claimed it would boost prosperity by lowering trade barriers, opening up a huge regional market. In its first years, NAFTA did bring some business and investment to Mexico. At the same time, it hurt Mexican manufacturers who could not compete with a flood of goods from the United States.

Issues such as illegal immigration and drug smuggling have created tension between Mexico and the United States. Some employers in the United States, especially commercial farmers, relied on Mexicans to harvest crops

*Earthquake in Mexico City* Many regions of the world—from Japan to Iran—have experienced devastating earthquakes. In September 1985, a powerful quake struck Mexico City. Over a hundred buildings collapsed, and thousands more were damaged. The earthquake killed more than 20,000 people. *Geography and History* Why do you think the effects of an earthquake would be worse in a developing country?

**Factories on the Border** During the 1980s, more than 1,500 maquiladoras sprang up along the United States-Mexican border. Today, these plants employ nearly half a million Mexicans. Many workers in the border factories are women, like those shown here assembling electronic goods. **Economics and Technology** What benefits do the maquiladoras offer Mexico and the United States?

for low wages. But when a growing number of Mexicans crossed the border illegally, many people in the United States came to resent the newcomers. Despite differences, both nations have cooperated on solving issues such as environmental problems.

## War and Peace in Central America

In Central America, unrest threatened the traditional ruling elite of military, business, and landowning interests. Discontent grew in the cities and among rural Indian communities that had long suffered from poverty and oppression. Fearing the spread of communism, the United States intervened repeatedly in the region.

**Nicaragua.** Along with Mexico and Cuba, Nicaragua was the only other Latin American country to have a genuine revolution in this century. From 1936 to 1979, the Somoza family ruled—and looted—Nicaragua. Because of their strong anti-communist stand, they gained United States backing.

In the 1970s, various groups opposed to Anastasio Somoza joined forces. They called themselves Sandinistas after Augusto Sandino, a revolutionary of the 1930s. Like Sandino, they were reform-minded nationalists, including a large number of women and leftist students.

In 1979, the Sandinistas ousted Somoza and set out to reshape Nicaragua. Under Sandinista president Daniel Ortega, they introduced land reform and instituted other socialist policies. Fearing that Nicaragua would become "another Cuba," President Ronald Reagan secretly backed the *contrarevolucionarios,* or contras—guerrillas who opposed the Sandinistas. This pro-contra policy violated OAS policy, sparking bitter debate both within the United States and throughout Latin America.

The long civil war weakened the economy but did not unseat the Sandinistas. Other Central American countries finally helped both sides reach a compromise to stop fighting and hold elections. In 1990, Violeta Chamorro, a moderate, won election as president. The Sandinistas peacefully handed over power, although they kept control of the army. Nicaragua then began the difficult job of rebuilding its economy.

**Guatemala.** The United States helped topple Guatemala's reform government in 1954. The military and landowners then regained power. In the next decades, however, they faced constant challenges from leftist guerrilla movements. During the grueling civil war, the government routinely tortured and murdered critics, including student and labor leaders.

The chief victims were the indigenous Indian majority. An estimated 30,000 died during the 1980s alone. Some were killed fighting for the land they tilled but did not own. Others were shot as military forces exterminated whole villages.

Although a civilian government took power in the mid-1980s, the military remained a powerful force behind the scenes. The 30-year civil war tapered off in the 1990s as the UN worked to negotiate a settlement.

**El Salvador.** In El Salvador, too, reformers and left-wing revolutionaries challenged the wealthy landowners and the military. During a vicious 12-year civil war, right-wing death squads slaughtered student and labor leaders, church workers, and anyone else thought to sympathize with leftists. Although the United States pressed the government to make some re-

forms, it provided weapons and other aid to help the military battle guerrillas.

Eventually, it became clear that neither side could win. In 1991, both agreed to a UN-brokered peace. In the next few years, former enemies met in the congress, not in battle. Joaquín Villalobos, once a guerrilla leader, was grateful to the UN for its help:

66This is a new country. After all we have seen in Bosnia and Rwanda and Somalia, it is good for the world to know there is at least one place where a peace process has been successful.99

Despite the return to peace, many problems remained unsolved, leaving democracy on a shaky footing.

## Struggle in Haiti

The first Latin American country to win independence was the Caribbean nation of Haiti. (See Chapter 21.) But after 1804, this impoverished land endured a stormy history. It was often ruled by dictators who were overthrown by rebellions. A small upper class of mulattoes (people of mixed African and European heritage) controlled the economy and ruled over the majority of the black rural poor.

**A pattern of dictatorship.** From 1957 to 1971, Dr. François Duvalier (doo vahl YAY) ruled Haiti. "Papa Doc," as he was called, created a brutal secret police force that crushed opposition and terrorized the people. After his death in 1971, his son, Jean-Claude Duvalier, took over. "Baby Doc" continued to loot the country until he was driven into exile in 1986. A succession of military leaders then ruled the island nation.

Finally, in 1990, Haiti held its freest elections ever. Jean-Bertrand Aristide (ar ih STEED), a priest and supporter of liberation theology, won 70 percent of the vote. A hero to the poor, Aristide proclaimed, "Our primary objective is to move from misery to dignified poverty." Just months after Aristide took office in 1991, a military coup forced him into exile, and power returned to the wealthy elite. They then launched a reign of terror against Aristide's supporters. Many tried to flee to the United States, where few were accepted.

**An Outspoken Priest** *Oscar Romero was a conservative member of El Salvador's elite until he became archbishop. Then he began to condemn government death squads that were killing students and peasants. Romero's outspokenness cost him his life. On March 24, 1980, as he said mass, shots rang out. Moments later, Romero lay dead, a victim of the death squads he had denounced. These signs and flowers honored Romero on the fourth anniversary of his death.* **Religions and Value Systems** *The sign under Romero's picture says, "If you silence a prophet, he will speak out through his people." What do you think the saying means?*

**Democracy Returns to Haiti** *After the overthrow of Jean-Bertrand Aristide, the United States spearheaded international pressure to restore democracy to Haiti. Aristide's support among poor Haitians was so great that his movement took the name Lavalas, meaning "the flood." Here, Haitians celebrate Aristide's return in 1994.* **Global Interaction** *Why do you think the United States favored the restoration of democracy in Haiti?*

For three years, Aristide sought international help to return democracy to Haiti. When economic pressure failed, the United States used the threat of military action to force the army from power. United States and, later, UN forces helped Aristide's efforts to build a functioning democracy.

**An uncertain future.** On his return to Haiti, an optimistic Aristide declared:

66This is a day on which the sun of democracy rises, never to set. A day of national reconciliation, a day for the eyes of justice to open and never close again. Never, never, never again will blood be shed in this country.99

Despite Aristide's pledge, Haiti's outlook has remained clouded. It is the poorest state in the Western Hemisphere. Past rulers had looted the country, which lacked roads, electricity, and other basic services. Armed gangs, including some former military henchmen, roamed the capital city, Port-au-Prince.

Aristide had little success in reconciling the old ruling elite to his goals for social and economic justice. No one knew who might win elections or whether the fragile democracy would survive after his term expired in 1996.

## SECTION 3 REVIEW

1. **Identify** (a) Lázaro Cárdenas, (b) PRI, (c) Chiapas, (d) Somoza family, (e) Sandinistas, (f) contras, (g) François Duvalier, (h) Jean-Bertrand Aristide.
2. **Define** (a) *ejidos,* (b) *maquiladoras.*
3. (a) How did Mexico develop its economy? (b) What problems did it face?
4. (a) What were the goals of revolutionaries in Nicaragua? (b) How did El Salvador's civil war end?
5. Why did democracy have a hard time taking root in Haiti?
6. *Critical Thinking* **Predicting Consequences** How might the collapse of the Soviet Union and the end of the Cold War affect the prospects for peace in Central America?
7. *ACTIVITY* Write two slogans for a Mexican election—one that might be used by the PRI and one that might be used by a small opposition party.

## 4 | Focus on Argentina and Brazil

### Guide for Reading

- Why was Juan Perón a popular dictator?
- How did economic swings affect Argentina and Brazil?
- What successes and setbacks did democracy experience in Argentina and Brazil?

At carnival every year in Rio de Janeiro, Brazil, groups compete for the best float. In 1991, Joaozinho Trinta helped create a winning entry based on *Alice's Adventures in Wonderland*. Early in her adventures, Alice first shrinks to tiny size, then grows very tall. Later, a caterpillar asks her, "Who are you?" Alice replies:

❝I no longer know who I am. First, I was small like Brazil, underdeveloped, with many problems. Suddenly I grew, became a giant, a great power, but with many problems, a huge foreign debt. I don't know what else I can do.❞

But the caterpillar reassures Alice. "I am a caterpillar, but I turn myself into a butterfly," he says. "This could happen to you." Trinta's float expressed his optimism about his native land. Like Alice, Brazil, too, had experienced disturbing changes. But Trinta was convinced that Brazil would emerge stronger than ever.

Brazil is one of a dozen independent nations of South America, a richly diverse region. Here we will look at the two largest South American republics—Argentina and Brazil. History, geography, and other powerful forces have shaped each country's efforts to develop a stable government and a strong, modern economy.

### Argentina's Drive to Modernize

Argentina fills much of southern South America. In area, it is the largest Spanish-speaking nation in the world.

**Economic Activity in Argentina**

Meatpacking and food processing · Chemicals · Wheat · Textiles · Car assembly · Corn · Metals

### GEOGRAPHY AND HISTORY

Since the 1980s, Argentina has regained its position as the most stable economy in Latin America. Its economic success stems from a wide variety of resources and industries.

1. **Location** On the map, locate (a) Buenos Aires, (b) Falkland Islands, (c) Chile.
2. **Region** Using longitude and latitude, describe the major agricultural region of Argentina.
3. **Critical Thinking** **Making Inferences** Based on this map, name two cities that you might expect to attract a great many workers from rural areas.

By 1900, Argentina was the richest nation in Latin America, with a fairly stable government dominated by the wealthy elite. Its economy was booming, fed by exports of beef and wheat, mostly to Britain. Like the United States at the time, Argentina was a land of promise to millions of immigrants. Many worked in food-processing plants or in other factories being built in Buenos Aires.

Argentina seemed poised to equal the economic giants of Europe and North America. Then the Great Depression shattered its prosperity and led to a military coup. For the next 50 years, Argentina was plagued by economic crises, unrest, and military rule. Since the 1980s, it has worked to rebuild democracy and recover prosperity.

**Perón in power.** In 1946, a former army colonel, Juan Perón, was elected president. He appealed to Argentine nationalism by limiting foreign-owned businesses and pushing ahead with import substitution. By boosting wages, strengthening labor unions, and promoting social reforms, Perón won the loyalty of the working classes. For the first time, the urban poor, whom Perón called the *descamisados,* or "shirtless ones," felt a sense of belonging.

Perón was helped greatly by his glamorous wife Eva Duarte Perón. She had risen from poverty to fame as an actress. She used her position as Perón's chief aide and adviser to help the poor. She once said:

> **❝**I, a humble woman of the people, understood that it was my duty to take my place with the workers, with the descamisados.**❞**

She had clinics and child-care centers built and gave money to the sick and unemployed. To secure more votes for her husband, she helped women gain the right to vote. At the same time, she lined her own pockets and lived an extravagant lifestyle. Still, the descamisados adored their "Evita." "You, too, will have clothes as rich as mine," she promised the poor women of Argentina.

While Juan Perón wooed the urban poor, his authoritarian government stifled opposition. Many educated people fled the repression. Perón increased government power by nationalizing many industries, but his policies led to a huge debt and soaring inflation. After Evita died of cancer in 1952, Perón's power declined. Within three years, he was ousted by a military coup and forced into exile.

**The military takeover.** For two decades, the military was in and out of power, while Perónistas, or supporters of Perón, continued to demand a return to his policies. In 1973, after 21 years in exile, an aging Perón was finally allowed to return. He was again elected president, and his new wife, Isabel, was chosen vice president. When he died the next year, Isabel Perón became president—the first woman head of state in the Western Hemisphere.

Lacking the popularity of Perón's first wife, Isabel Perón also faced a worsening economic and political crisis. Terrorists on the left and right were disrupting the country. In 1976, the military took power and set out to destroy Perón's legacy.

To combat leftist guerrillas, the army waged a "dirty war," terrorizing people they claimed were enemies of the state. They kidnapped, tortured, and murdered thousands of citizens. As many as 20,000 people simply "disappeared" after being taken from their homes. Many more fled the country to escape persecution. (📖 See *World Literature,* "Mothers and Shadows," pages 972–973.)

**War and defeat.** In 1982, the military hoped to mask economic troubles by seizing the British-ruled Falkland Islands. Argentina had long claimed these islands, which it called the Malvinas. The military believed that Britain would not fight to keep the islands. But in a brief but decisive war, the British recaptured the Falklands. Defeat undermined the military's prestige, and it was forced to hold free elections.

◀ *Juan and Eva Perón*

**The "Mothers of the Plaza de Mayo"** Argentina's military kidnapped thousands of opponents, mostly young people. Mothers of the desaparecidos, or the disappeared, marched silently in the Plaza de Mayo in Buenos Aires every Thursday, holding up pictures of their children. Only recently has the military admitted that nearly all the disappeared were murdered—often by being thrown into the ocean from airplanes or helicopters. **Political and Social Systems** Why do you think some of the Mothers of the Plaza de Mayo wore masks?

**Democracy restored.** In 1983, a newly elected government restored democracy to Argentina. Many people wanted the government to investigate and prosecute military leaders for atrocities committed during the "dirty war." Only when people learned the full story of the military's abuses, they insisted, could Argentina heal divisions.

Despite economic setbacks and scandals of corruption, democratic rule survived. Still, like many nations, Argentina was caught up in the debt crisis and took tough measures to reduce inflation and government spending.

In the 1990s, Argentina's economy again grew. The country had strong human resources, including the highest literacy rate in Latin America, and many natural resources. Yet its wealth was still concentrated in the hands of a few. It seemed unlikely to reach its goal of being recognized as a fully developed nation until more people shared in the nation's prosperity.

## Brazil—A Country of the Future

Brazil occupies almost half the continent of South America. Its varied landscapes include the world's largest tropical forest and the mighty Amazon River, fed by thousands of tributaries. Northeastern Brazil, however, is an arid plain.

Brazil's rich resources include minerals, timber, and fertile farmlands that produce cash crops such as coffee, sugar, and cocoa. Size, climate, and differences in resources have contributed to regionalism and uneven settlement patterns. About 90 percent of Brazilians live within 200 miles of the Atlantic coast, many in the fertile, temperate south. To draw settlers inland, the government has encouraged development of the interior.

**Population.** Unlike its South American neighbors, Brazil was settled by Portugal, not Spain. With a population over 155 million, Brazilians outnumber their Spanish-speaking neighbors. Brazil is a melting pot. A Brazilian patriot, Afonso Celso, considered diversity to be a source of national strength:

❝Three elements contributed to the formation of the Brazilian people: the American Indian, the African, and the Portuguese. . . . Any one of these elements . . . possesses qualities of which we should be proud.❞

In this century, many Japanese settled in Brazil, adding to its cultural mix.

Most Brazilians are Roman Catholic, but a growing number embrace evangelical Protestant faiths. Others practice Candomblè, which blends African and Christian beliefs.

Rapid population growth and class divisions have contributed to poverty in Brazil. In the cities, where more than 75 percent of Brazilians live, the contrast between rich and poor is seen everywhere. Teeming, garbage-strewn *favelas*, or slums, ring the cities, which boast luxurious high-rise apartments and wealthy shopping areas. ( ★ See *Skills for Success,* page 974.)

**An unstable giant.** Unlike other South American republics, Brazil won independence peacefully. (See Chapter 21.) Like its neighbors, however, Brazil has had its share of dictators and military rulers. They pursued modernization under the motto "order and progress."

# PARALLELS THROUGH TIME

## Parades

Nearly all societies celebrate holidays or special occasions with public parades. Often, parades express the values and hopes of a society. But mostly, they are a way to have fun.

**Linking Past and Present**   Describe a parade you have participated in or seen. Do you think that the parade reflected the values of your country or community? Explain.

**PRESENT**   *In 1993, Brazil's carnival reflected popular interest in science fiction, as a colorful astronaut floated above the crowd, below. People in the United States enjoy parades, too, such as the Tournament of Roses in Pasadena, California, or Macy's Thanksgiving Day Parade in New York City, above.*

**PAST**   *In Brazil, as well as in many Caribbean nations, millions celebrate carnival just before the start of Lent. Originally a religious holiday, carnival now gives marchers a chance to construct huge, ornate floats and to put on outrageous costumes. Above, a float from a 1940s carnival celebrates Latin American unity.*

Between 1930 and 1945, the dictator Getúlio Vargas allied himself with the working poor. Like Juan Perón in Argentina, he improved wages and benefits, favored labor unions, and gave women the vote. The military eventually toppled Vargas but permitted elected presidents to rule for almost two decades. By 1964, economic problems and fear of communism led the military to take over again.

Backed by the middle and upper classes, the generals ruled with a heavy hand. They tortured and jailed critics, censored the press, and ignored calls for social reform. In the mid-1980s, they gradually eased their grip on power. In 1989, Brazilians were finally able to vote directly for a president for the first time in 29 years.

**Economic development.** "Brazil is a country of the future, and always will be." That familiar saying suggests both Brazil's potential and its many setbacks. In the past century, it has weathered many boom-and-bust cycles. By 1910, the huge demand for Brazilian rubber suddenly fell off, causing economic hardships. Coffee exports then replaced rubber. But again and again, unstable prices or natural disasters wreaked havoc on the economy.

In the 1930s, Brazil diversified its economy. Vargas encouraged industry. He built highways, dams for hydroelectric power, and schools. During and after World War II, industry continued to expand. In the 1950s, president Juscelino Kubitschek (zhooh suh LEE nuh  KOO bih chehk) promised "fifty years of progress in five." He opened up the interior to settlers by carving out a new capital, Brasília, in the wilderness, hundreds of miles from the Atlantic coast.

**"Economic miracle."** Despite their repressive rule, military leaders pushed for economic growth. "Power in the world," said one, "is a great nation that has territory, population, wealth, financial resources, technology, material goods, minerals." Brazil had almost all of these.

Brazil is the fifth largest country in the world in area. Yet its population is very unevenly distributed.

**1. Location** On the map, locate (a) Rio de Janeiro, (b) São Paulo, (c) Brasília, (d) Amazon River.
**2. Interaction** (a) What is the population density of the area around the city of Salvador? (b) What is the density of the area 1,000 miles west of Salvador?
**3. Critical Thinking Drawing Conclusions** Why do you think Brazil's population density is heaviest along the Atlantic coast?

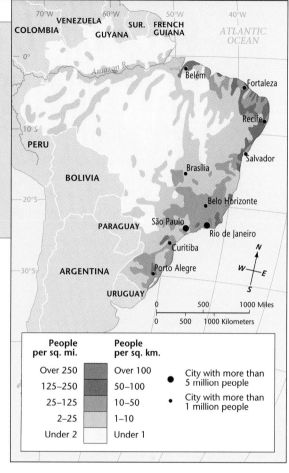

## Brazil: Population Density

| People per sq. mi. | People per sq. km. | |
|---|---|---|
| Over 250 | Over 100 | ● City with more than 5 million people |
| 125–250 | 50–100 | |
| 25–125 | 10–50 | • City with more than 1 million people |
| 2–25 | 1–10 | |
| Under 2 | Under 1 | |

Under the military, experts ran the economy, which for a time chalked up impressive growth. Brazil began producing everything from steel and cars to shoes. People talked of Brazil's "economic miracle," like those in postwar Germany or Japan. The miracle enriched a few. To most Brazilians, however, it brought little or no benefits.

**People on the move.** By the 1980s, Brazil, like other developing nations, faced a host of economic problems—from inflation fed by higher oil prices to a staggering foreign debt. Rapid population growth, too, strained services to the limit. In the 1970s alone, more than 30 million people flooded into cities. (Unlike other Latin American countries that have only one major city, Brazil has more than a dozen.) In the favelas that surrounded São Paulo and Rio de Janeiro, thousands of children survived on the streets without families or education.

By 1990, the government had to curb spending, which further hurt the poor. To spur growth, it again pushed to develop the Amazon region. As you have read, the movement of people into the interior posed problems for the environment.

**Looking ahead.** As world economic conditions improved, so did Brazil's. In the 1990s, it numbered among the top 10 world economies. With ample human and natural resources, this giant of South America was determined to take its place among the world's economic superpowers—and become the country of the future today.

## SECTION 4 REVIEW

1. **Identify** (a) Isabel Perón, (b) "dirty war," (c) Falklands, (d) Getúlio Vargas.
2. (a) Why were Juan and Eva Perón popular figures to many people in Argentina? (b) Describe two policies they pursued.
3. Explain why the military seized power in (a) Argentina, (b) Brazil.
4. (a) Describe the Brazilian economic miracle. (b) Why did it falter?
5. **Critical Thinking Analyzing Information** What benefits and drawbacks might result from building a "cult of personality" around figures like Juan and Eva Perón?
6. **ACTIVITY** Review the section opener story on page 967. Then, design a carnival pageant float that captures some aspect of the current political or economic situation in Brazil.

# World Literature
## Mothers and Shadows
### Marta Traba

**Introduction** *During the early 1980s, a group of determined women assembled each week at the Plaza de Mayo in Buenos Aires, demanding that the government account for their missing sons and daughters. The relentless struggle of the "Mothers of the Plaza de Mayo" inspired Marta Traba's novel* Mothers and Shadows. *In this passage, Irene, an Argentine actress, attends her first demonstration in the Plaza de Mayo.*

S omething felt wrong. She looked and looked again, trying to work out what was out of place in that provincial square whose every detail she knew so well. . . . Everything was as it had always been, drab, bare, and ugly. And then it hit her: apart from the groups of women arriving for the demonstration, there was nobody in the square. No sightseers were standing around, no school children or men going about their daily business were hurrying across it, no old people were sunning themselves on the park benches. There were no street vendors anywhere to be seen. . . .

A woman dashed past with a bundle of duplicated lists and handed her one. It went on for twenty-three pages; she felt an urge to count the names and started to run her forefinger down the columns to work out how many names were on each page. She'd got to the forty-fifth line when someone stopped at her elbow and said: "You needn't bother to count them, sister, there are about a thousand names down here, but the actual number who've disappeared is much higher than that. We've only just started compiling the lists. The job is complicated by the fact that a lot of people are unwilling to give the full names and ages, or the parents' names and phone numbers."

She shrugged her shoulders and walked on. She felt annoyed with the woman for calling her "sister" and poking her nose into what was none of her business, but she took another glance at the list. Only now did she notice the ages: they mostly ranged from fifteen to twenty-five; she went on going through it page by page. A woman of sixty-eight, another of seventy-five. She shuddered. A four-month-old baby, a two-year-old girl, another of five, a brother and sister of three and four. The list in her hand began to quiver. How can a four-month-old baby disappear? The entry read: Anselmo Furco, four months, disappeared on . . . Parents: Juan Gustavo Furco, 23, Alicia, 20, also missing. It was followed by the name, address, and telephone number of the grandparents. A violent lurch in the pit of her stomach made her grope for the nearest wall to lean against.

Someone came up to her and said: "Come on, now, you musn't give up." They steered her back to the square. She felt better in the open air and looked around her. So these were the Madwomen of the Plaza de Mayo. . . .

The number of women was incredible and so was the silence; apart from the rapid footsteps and muffled greetings, there was not a sound. Not a single prison van, not a single policeman, not a single army jeep was in sight. The Casa Rosada looked like a stage set, with thick curtains drawn across its windows. There were no grenadier guards on sentry duty at the gates either. It was the realization that the grenadier guards were not there that gave her a sudden, terrifying insight into the enemy's machinations: *every Thursday, for the two or three hours during which the demonstration took place, the Plaza de Mayo was wiped off the map.* They couldn't fire on the women or lock them all up. It would have undermined the concerted effort they'd made to project a carefree image of "the Argentina I love." Their ploy was simply to ignore them; to ignore the existence of the square and of the madwomen stamping their feet. . . .

**A Tribute to Motherhood** This sculpture of a mother and baby, by the Mexican artist Francisco Zuniga, is titled Maternity. Like Marta Traba in Mothers and Shadows, Zuniga celebrates the strength of mothers and their role in keeping the family together. The fact that mothers, rather than a political organization, led protests about the "disappeared" in Argentina won widespread sympathy for their cause. **Art and Literature** Do you think the sculpture presents a positive image of motherhood? Explain.

[*Irene narrates what happens next.*]

Without a word or command being uttered, the women raised the photographs above their heads. Why, when there was no one there to see them? I expected that, with so much handling and fondling, those childlike faces would soon be disfigured past the point of recognition. Near me, an old woman was holding up a cheap studio portrait with both hands. The girl was smiling stiffly, her head tilted to one side, no doubt obeying the photographer's instructions. She was sitting with her legs crossed, an organdie dress covering her knees. . . . A woman right next to me took out of her handbag a tiny picture in an oval frame. She looked at me and smiled apologetically. The only photos she had of him were taken when he was a child, if only she'd known. . . . I asked her how old he was now. "He'll be twenty next month. We were so proud of him. We were going to hold a party to celebrate." She could barely finish the sentence, but she pulled herself together, sighed and raised the tiny frame as high as she could, along with all the other photographs. I started to feel uncomfortable just standing there with nothing to hold up. I raised the list with both hands and waited expectantly. Was that it? Just this coming together to share one's silent grief with the silent grief of others?

And that was when it started, Dolores. I can't explain to you what it was that happened. How can I find the words? I could say that suddenly someone started to shout and everyone started shouting and in a matter of minutes the whole square was one single shout. But that wouldn't begin to tell you what it was like. . . .

The crowd of women surged forward like a tide. They continued to advance, we knocked into one another, stumbling over each other's feet. The chaos was indescribable as hundreds of sheets of paper were tossed into the air. I did exactly the same as the madwomen, and I couldn't begin to tell you what I felt; it was as if someone was trying to rip my insides out and I was clinging on to them for all I was worth. . . .

I thought I glimpsed a snatch of Elena's jacket in the middle of a circle of women and I elbowed my way toward her. She was part of a chorus chanting in unison, and this time I could clearly hear the words "Where are they? Where are they?"

Source: Marta Traba, *Mothers and Shadows*, translated by Jo Labanyi (Mexico City: Readers International, 1985).

## Thinking About Literature

1. **Vocabulary** Use the dictionary to find the meanings of the following words: *provincial, grenadier, sentry, machinations, concerted.*
2. (a) What surprises Irene when she arrives at the plaza? (b) How does she explain it?
3. Describe how each of the following affects Irene: (a) the list, (b) the photographs, (c) the shouting.
4. *Critical Thinking* **Making Inferences** (a) Why are the Mothers of the Plaza de Mayo called "madwomen"? (b) Why do they represent a threat to the dictatorship?

# Skills for Success

## Predicting Consequences

Historians, business planners, government analysts, and others often try to predict the consequences, or results, of actions or developments. To make informed predictions, experts must analyze what has happened in the past and compare it to the present situation. They also study similar situations in many countries, gathering as much evidence and information as they can find. They then synthesize their information and draw conclusions.

The article below describes the effects of rapid population growth on Rio de Janeiro, one of Brazil's largest cities. Read the article, then follow these steps.

**1** **Identify trends and developments.** (a) According to the article, what long-term population movement has been occurring in Rio de Janeiro? (b) How many new inhabitants have moved to Rio de Janeiro in the last quarter century? (c) While the population was growing, what was happening to the city's industry?

**2** **Analyze the available information.** (a) How has Rio de Janeiro coped with the flood of new arrivals? (b) Identify one major problem that urbanization has caused. (c) How is the population trend related to the industrial trend?

**3** **Predict possible future developments.** (a) What might be the effects if the trends identified continue unchanged? (b) According to the professor quoted in the article below, what change might help solve the city's problems? (c) What other developments might improve the city's prospects?

### Beyond the Classroom
Identify a trend or development that is currently affecting your school or community. Using the steps above, write three predictions about the possible future consequences of this trend or development.

---

*From an October, 1990 article in the São Paulo, Brazil, news magazine* Veja:

❝ Rio de Janeiro, known for its beaches and climate, has been called 'Brazil's treasury of natural beauty.' . . . For decades, the city, once the national capital, attracted the finest human resources of the country: writers, artists, politicians. People with ideas, culture, and talent converged there, delighted by the courtesy, cordiality, and verve of the *cariocas*, the people of Rio.

But Rio has changed a lot—into one of the tragedies of the twentieth century. In 1980, the belt of slums at the edge of Rio was officially recognized by the United Nations as the world's most violent place. More than 2,500 people are murdered there every year. In 1981, 36 percent of *cariocas* declared in a survey that they had been mugged at least once. . . . It is estimated that 1 million *cariocas* earn their daily bread by activities tied, in one way or another, to the growth of crime in the city. . . .

Since the beginning of the century, Rio has played a decreasing role in the nation's development . . . Rio's factories are increasingly out of date. . . . Important financial corporations have moved out. 'The problem of investment in Rio is very simple,' says Congressman Francisco Dornelles. 'No company wants to invest in a city where you never know whether the lights will come on in the morning, or whether your workers can get decent transportation to bring them to work.'

Over the past 25 years, the city's population has increased from 4 million to 6 million. Of these 2 million new inhabitants, 400,000 live in real houses or apartments, made of concrete or bricks, with lights that turn on and water that runs. The others—1.6 million people—have moved into the most famous housing in the country: *favelas*, or slums.

'When the police do their duty,' says one professor, 'investments will return.' ❞

---

# CHAPTER 37 REVIEW

## Building Vocabulary

Review the following vocabulary from this chapter: *caudillo, guerrilla warfare, terrorism, import substitution, agribusiness, multinational corporation, liberation theology, blockade, indigenous, ejidos, maquiladoras, regionalism.* Write sentences using each of these terms, leaving blanks where the terms would go. Exchange your sentences with another student and fill in the blanks on each other's lists.

## Reviewing Chapter Themes

1. **Political and Social Systems** (a) Why did military rulers seize power in many Latin American nations after World War II? (b) Choose *one* of the following nations and describe the challenges it has faced trying to establish a stable democracy: Mexico, El Salvador, Haiti, Argentina, Brazil.
2. **Economics and Technology** How did Latin American countries try to limit economic dependence and develop their economies? Give three examples.
3. **Continuity and Change** (a) How did the legacy of the colonial social class system continue to influence Latin American societies? (b) How did the role of the Catholic Church change?
4. **Global Interaction** (a) How did the Cold War affect relations between the United States and Latin America? (b) What role did regional organizations play in Latin America?
5. **Impact of the Individual** Explain how the policies of each of the following leaders affected their country: (a) Fidel Castro, (b) Lázaro Cárdenas, (c) Juan Perón, (d) Getúlio Vargas.

## Thinking Critically

1. **Drawing Conclusions** How can a wide gap between rich and poor make it difficult for democracy to flourish?
2. **Applying Information** Review the subsection Obstacles to Development on pages 833–834 and the chart on page 835. Which of the obstacles listed on this chart can you apply to Latin American nations? Give one example for each of these obstacles.
3. **Identifying Alternatives** Environmentalists—many of them from industrialized nations—have called on Brazil to stop the destruction of the Amazon rain forest. (a) What possible courses of action can Brazil take? (b) What are the possible consequences of each course? ( ★ See *Skills for Success,* page 654.)
4. **Linking Past and Present** Review pages 738–739. How were the causes of the Mexican Revolution of 1910 similar to the later revolutions in Cuba and Nicaragua?
5. **Synthesizing Information** Review the discussion of women in Latin America on pages 954–955, the picture on page 969, and the literature selection on pages 972–973. In what ways were the Mothers of the Plaza de Mayo typical of women's groups in other Latin American countries? ( ★ See *Skills for Success,* page 896.)

## For Your Portfolio

As you just read, Latin American nations have faced a variety of political, economic, and social challenges in this century. For this assignment, you will work with a small group to describe an action plan for one of these countries.

1. Decide which country you will address. Identify the particular problems this nation has faced and may face in the future.
2. Brainstorm with your group to come up with solutions for these problems. List as many ideas for each issue as you can. Try to look at each issue from the point of view of that nation. For example, why do some Brazilians look at environmental problems differently from the way some North Americans do? Discuss with your group how the various issues and solutions are related.
3. Use library resources to learn more about the needs and problems of the nation you have picked. What solutions are suggested in these books and articles?
4. Decide on a plan for your nation. Work with your group to state the problems as you see them and the solutions that you think would work best. Include facts, statistics, charts, and graphs to support your plan.
5. Share your plan with the class. Be prepared to defend your recommendations.

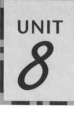

# Unit-in-Brief

## The World Today

**Chapter 32** The World Since 1945:
An Overview
(1945–Present)

Since the end of World War II, the world has changed rapidly. While we cannot yet determine the long-term impact of events of the recent past, we can identify political, social, and economic trends that have shaped the postwar years.

- The collapse of western colonial empires led to the emergence of nearly 100 new countries, mostly in Africa and Asia.
- Nuclear weapons, terrorism, and human rights are enduring issues in an increasingly interdependent world.
- Complex economic ties link the rich nations of the global North and the poor nations of the global South.
- Urbanization, modernization, women's movements, and technology have brought dramatic social changes.
- Technology has revolutionized agriculture and medicine and helped create a global, westernized popular culture.

**Chapter 33** Europe and
North America
(1945–Present)

Within a framework of growing regional cooperation, Western Europe enjoyed tremendous economic growth after World War II. At the same time, the Cold War pitted the West, led by the United States, against the Soviet Union and its allies.

- In the postwar era, Western European nations expanded social programs and introduced the welfare state. By the 1980s, an economic slowdown forced cuts in social programs.
- The United States led world opposition to communism, extended civil rights, and pursued economic prosperity.
- Efforts to reform inefficiencies in government and the economy led to the collapse of the Soviet Union.
- After shaking off Soviet domination, nations of Eastern Europe faced economic challenges and ethnic conflicts.

**Chapter 34** East Asia and
Southeast Asia
(1945–Present)

China, Japan, and other Asian nations have achieved varying degrees of success in their efforts to modernize. Several of these nations enjoy growing trade and other ties, linking the nations of the Pacific Rim from Asia to the Americas.

- After World War II, Japan introduced democratic reforms and by the 1960s had emerged as an economic superpower.
- Under communist rule, the People's Republic of China achieved modest economic gains while sacrificing individual political freedoms.

- The "Asian tigers"—Taiwan, Hong Kong, Singapore, and South Korea—vaulted into the class of newly industrialized nations.
- Cold War tensions sparked long, devastating conflicts in Korea, Vietnam, and Cambodia.

## Chapter 35 South Asia and the Middle East
(1945–Present)

In South Asia and the Middle East, nations cast off western rule and set out to modernize. They have often confronted similar challenges—from religious strife and border conflicts to urbanization and population growth.

- Upon achieving independence, India built on the legacy of British rule to create the world's largest democracy.
- Ethnic and religious rivalries have fueled ongoing conflict among people of South Asia.
- When secular governments in the Middle East did not yield promised improvements, some reformers rejected western models and called for a reaffirmation of Islamic values.
- The long Arab-Israeli struggle and other conflicts have focused world attention on the Middle East.

## Chapter 36 Africa
(1945–Present)

Leaders of new African nations set out to build strong central governments, achieve economic growth, and raise standards of living. They have faced a variety of obstacles, including economic dependency and political instability.

- After independence, many new nations experienced military or one-party rule but have since introduced multiparty democracy.
- African nations experimented with different economic systems, including socialism and mixed economies.

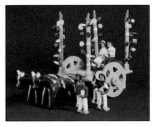

- After decades of conflict, South Africa abandoned its system of apartheid in the 1990s and made a transition to democratic rule.
- In Africa, as elsewhere, modernization and urbanization have disrupted traditional cultures and ways of life.

## Chapter 37 Latin America
(1945–Present)

Despite setbacks, Latin American nations have tried to sustain economic growth and overcome a legacy of poverty and social inequality. Marxism, military rule, and the Roman Catholic Church have been continuing influences in the region.

- In the postwar period, poverty and uneven distribution of wealth fed social unrest in many nations.

- Latin America was a focus of Cold War politics, especially after a communist revolution in Cuba in 1959.
- Through trade, investment, and military intervention, the United States was a dominant force in Latin America.
- Although Mexico enjoyed economic gains in agriculture and manufacturing, most people remained in poverty.
- Argentina and Brazil experienced economic growth and long periods of military rule.

# A Global View

## What Trends Are Influencing the Direction of World History Today?

The world in the second half of the twentieth century has faced many problems and seen many changes. The trends and currents of the past half century will also powerfully influence the shape of things to come.

Three major political trends were the Cold War, the collapse of overseas empires, and the creation of global political organizations, such as the UN. Economic trends included the interdependence of developed and developing countries, as well as the pollution of the global environment.

Social changes were also clear. Conflicts flared between ethnic groups and between old and new ways of life. Urbaniza-tion, rights for women, and the impact of science also shaped twentieth-century society.

### The Developed World

After World War II, two highly industrialized super-powers dominated world politics. The West, led by the United States, defended democratic government and free-enter-prise economies. The eastern bloc, dominated by the Soviet Union, dreamed of a world politically controlled by Communist parties and economically run by government planners.

Economically, the period from the 1940s to the 1970s saw a long boom in Western Europe, North America, and Japan. These prosperous years brought more material goods to more people than ever before in history. The eastern bloc, however, fared less well. In 1989, the Soviet alliance collapsed, and in the early 1990s, both communist dicta-torships and state-run economies disappeared from Europe.

### The Developing World

The story of many develop-ing nations begins with the "great liberation" following World War II. Newly liberated nations of Africa and Asia, as well as the already independ-ent nations of Latin America, followed different paths, linked only by a common concern for economic development.

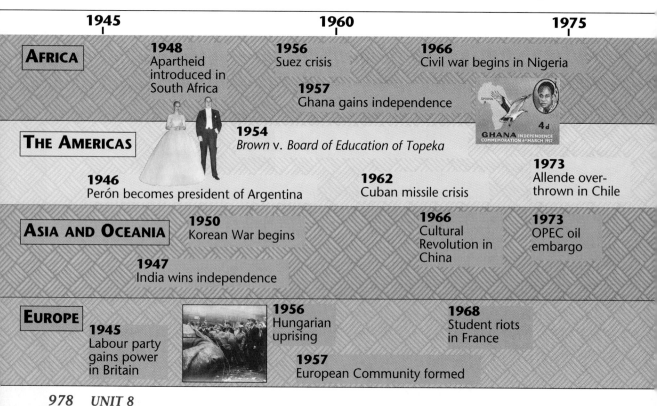

| 1945 | 1960 | 1975 |
|---|---|---|

**AFRICA**
- **1948** Apartheid introduced in South Africa
- **1956** Suez crisis
- **1957** Ghana gains independence
- **1966** Civil war begins in Nigeria

GHANA
GHANA INDEPENDENCE COMMEMORATION 6th MARCH 1957
4d

**THE AMERICAS**
- **1954** Brown v. Board of Education of Topeka
- **1946** Perón becomes president of Argentina
- **1962** Cuban missile crisis
- **1973** Allende over-thrown in Chile

**ASIA AND OCEANIA**
- **1950** Korean War begins
- **1947** India wins independence
- **1966** Cultural Revolution in China
- **1973** OPEC oil embargo

**EUROPE**
- **1945** Labour party gains power in Britain
- **1956** Hungarian uprising
- **1957** European Community formed
- **1968** Student riots in France

Some nations prospered, to varying degrees. A group of Asian "tiger" economies flourished. Oil made the fortunes of a number of Middle Eastern states. Brazil, Argentina, and Mexico were often put in a category of "nearly developed" states.

For other nations—from Bangladesh to Tanzania to Bolivia—the road to development was strewn with obstacles. Foreign economic domination, population pressures, and a worldwide debt crisis were among many factors that hindered growth.

Politically, wars and unrest buffeted the developing world. The United States joined major wars against communist regimes in Korea and Vietnam and supported anti-communist governments in struggles around the world. The Jewish state of Israel was repeatedly locked in combat with its Arab Muslim neighbors. The black majority population of South Africa struggled against the racial system of apartheid.

### Looking Ahead

As the year 2000 drew near, the world seemed to be at a turning point. The peoples of Earth still faced many challenges. Yet some pressing problems had been solved. The collapse of the Soviet Union ended the Cold War. Nelson Mandela's victory in South Africa signaled the end of apartheid. And there were hopes for more advances—from democracy and economic growth in South America and Eastern Europe to peace accords in the Middle East.

Looking ahead to a future that has not yet happened is as hard for a historian as it is for a history student. Studying the past may help you understand how world history works. But it will be up to you to shape the history that is yet to come.

***ACTIVITY*** Choose two events and two pictures from the time line below. For each, write a sentence explaining how it relates to the themes expressed in the Global View essay.

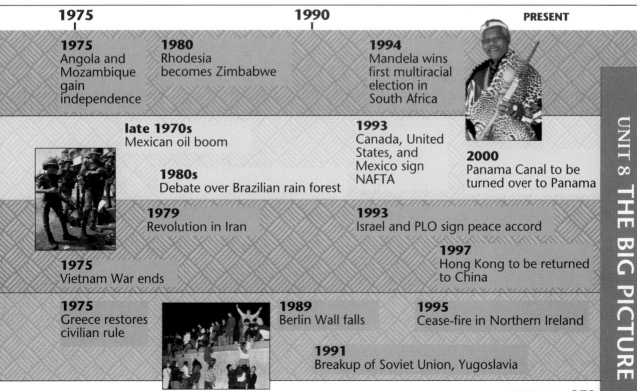

**1975**

**1990**

**PRESENT**

**1975**
Angola and Mozambique gain independence

**1980**
Rhodesia becomes Zimbabwe

**1994**
Mandela wins first multiracial election in South Africa

**late 1970s**
Mexican oil boom

**1993**
Canada, United States, and Mexico sign NAFTA

**2000**
Panama Canal to be turned over to Panama

**1980s**
Debate over Brazilian rain forest

**1979**
Revolution in Iran

**1993**
Israel and PLO sign peace accord

**1997**
Hong Kong to be returned to China

**1975**
Vietnam War ends

**1975**
Greece restores civilian rule

**1989**
Berlin Wall falls

**1995**
Cease-fire in Northern Ireland

**1991**
Breakup of Soviet Union, Yugoslavia

UNIT 8 THE BIG PICTURE

# You Decide

## Exploring Global Issues

### *What Is the Relationship Between People and the Environment?*

In 1972, a team of loggers arrived in a forest in northern India. To their amazement, they were confronted by a group of women who were shielding the trees with their bodies. The women were members of the Chipko, or "Hug-the-Tree," movement. Their admirers saw the Chipko women as heroic defenders of the environment. To critics, however, *tree hugger* became a scornful term for an environmental extremist who stood in the way of economic progress.

Today, environmental issues are getting worldwide attention. Is it more important for a poor nation to protect its environment or to develop its resources? How much right do people have to alter the environment in the first place? To begin your investigation, examine these viewpoints:

**GREECE**

**300s B.C.**

The scientist and philosopher Aristotle used logic to explain relationships in the natural world:

❝Plants exist for the sake of animals, and animals exist for the sake of man—the tame for use and food, the wild, if not all, at least the greater part of them, for food and for the provision of clothing and various instruments. Now, if nature makes nothing in vain, [it follows] that she has made all animals for the sake of man.❞

**JAPAN**

**early 1800s**

The traditions of Zen Buddhism stressed closeness to and respect for nature, as in this print by the artist Hokusai. ▼

**BRAZIL**

**1940s**

President Getúlio Vargas vowed to build Brazil's economy by subduing its mightiest resource—the Amazon River:

❝Nothing will prevent us from accomplishing . . . the highest task of civilized man: the conquest and domination of great valleys of equatorial torrents, transforming their blind force and extraordinary fertility into disciplined energy. The Amazon with the impulse of our will, of our effort, and of our work . . . will become a chapter in the history of civilization.❞

**KENYA**

**1960s**

Perez Olindo, a zoologist, explained why he resigned from the Kenya Game Department:

❝I resigned in protest at having been assigned the duties of 'elephant control' work which, in effect, involved shooting elephants considered to be in conflict with economic activities. . . . I held, and still hold, the view that elephants and other animals have a right to live, and no human has any control over that right.❞

**INDONESIA**

**1980s**

Dr. Sumitro Djojohadikusumo, former minister of trade and industry, gave economic reasons for managing and protecting the environment:

❝We certainly need a healthy natural environment. . . . If we are to make further progress we need the natural resources, we need the timber, we need the water, we need the fish. We can apply science to manage nature so that everyone benefits, even the animals.❞

**UNITED STATES**

**1992**

American cartoonist Tom Toles commented on protecting biodiversity, the wide variety of plant and animal species on the planet.▸

---

## COMPARING VIEWPOINTS

1. How does Aristotle's view of the relationship between people and animals differ from those of Olindo and Toles?
2. Both Vargas and Djojohadikusumo were government officials in developing nations. Compare their views on the environment.
3. What relationship between people and nature is expressed in the Hokusai print? Which other viewpoints seem similar to Hokusai's?

## YOUR INVESTIGATION

**ACTIVITY**

1. Find out more about one of the viewpoints above or another viewpoint related to this topic. You might investigate:

▪ The biblical story of creation in the book of Genesis.

▪ The teachings of the Indian prophet Mahavira, founder of Jainism.
▪ The view of nature in Native American literature.
▪ Poems about nature by British Romantic poets such as William Wordsworth.
▪ The views of an American conservationist such as John Muir, Theodore Roosevelt, or Rachel Carson.
▪ Opposing sides in a recent environmental controversy, such as the damming of the Narmada River in India or the cutting of rain forests in Brazil.

2. Decide which viewpoint you agree with most closely and express it in your own way. You may do so in an essay, a cartoon, a poem, a drawing or painting, a song, a skit, a video, or in some other way.

**UNIT 8 THE BIG PICTURE**

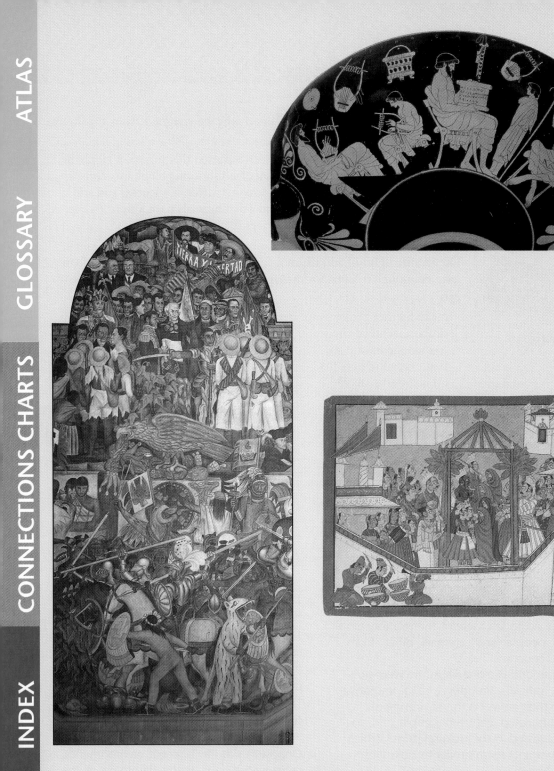

# Reference Section

# The World: Political

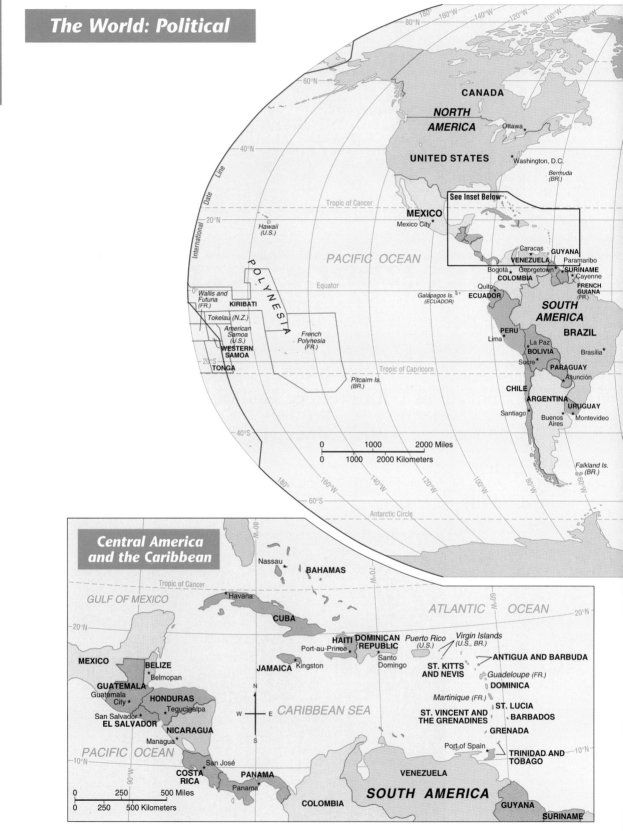

CANADA

**NORTH AMERICA**

Ottawa ★

**UNITED STATES**

Washington, D.C. ★

Bermuda (BR.)

See Inset Below

Tropic of Cancer

**MEXICO**

Mexico City ★

Hawaii (U.S.)

*PACIFIC OCEAN*

Caracas ★ **GUYANA**
**VENEZUELA** ★ Paramaribo
Bogotá ★ Georgetown ★ **SURINAME**
**COLOMBIA** ★ Cayenne
Quito ★ **FRENCH GUIANA (FR.)**
Galápagos Is. (ECUADOR) **ECUADOR**

Equator

Wallis and Futuna (FR.)

0

POLYNESIA

**KIRIBATI**

Tokelau (N.Z.)

American Samoa (U.S.)

French Polynesia (FR.)

**WESTERN SAMOA**

**SOUTH AMERICA**

**BRAZIL**

**PERU**
Lima ★
La Paz ★ **BOLIVIA** Brasília ★
Sucre ★ **PARAGUAY**
Asunción ★

Tropic of Capricorn

**TONGA**

Pitcairn Is. (BR.)

**CHILE**

**ARGENTINA** **URUGUAY**
Santiago ★ Buenos Aires ★ ★ Montevideo

| 0 | 1000 | 2000 Miles |
|---|------|------------|
| 0 | 1000 | 2000 Kilometers |

Falkland Is. (BR.)

International Date Line

Antarctic Circle

---

Nassau ★ **BAHAMAS**

Tropic of Cancer

*GULF OF MEXICO*

Havana ★

**CUBA**

*ATLANTIC OCEAN*

**MEXICO**

**BELIZE**
Belmopan ★

**GUATEMALA**
Guatemala City ★

**HONDURAS**
★ Tegucigalpa

San Salvador ★
**EL SALVADOR**

**NICARAGUA**
Managua ★

*PACIFIC OCEAN*

San José ★

**COSTA RICA**

**PANAMA**
Panama ★

**HAITI** **DOMINICAN REPUBLIC**
Port-au-Prince ★ Santo Domingo ★

**JAMAICA** Kingston ★

Puerto Rico (U.S.)

Virgin Islands (U.S., BR.)

**ANTIGUA AND BARBUDA**

**ST. KITTS AND NEVIS**

Guadeloupe (FR.)

**DOMINICA**

Martinique (FR.)

**ST. LUCIA**

*CARIBBEAN SEA*

**ST. VINCENT AND THE GRENADINES**

**BARBADOS**

**GRENADA**

Port of Spain ★

**TRINIDAD AND TOBAGO**

**VENEZUELA**

**SOUTH AMERICA**

**COLOMBIA**

**GUYANA**

**SURINAME**

| 0 | 250 | 500 Miles |
|---|-----|-----------|
| 0 | 250 | 500 Kilometers |

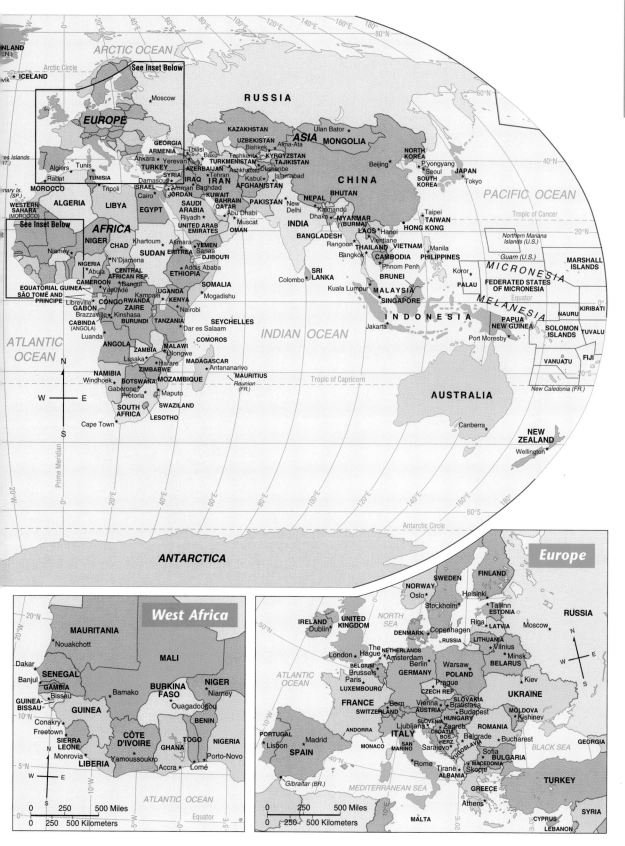

ARCTIC OCEAN

Arctic Circle

★ ICELAND

See Inset Below

EUROPE

★ Moscow

RUSSIA

KAZAKHSTAN

UZBEKISTAN

ASIA

MONGOLIA

GEORGIA

ARMENIA

Tbilisi

Bishkek ★

KYRGYZSTAN

Alma-Ata

NORTH

KOREA

P'yongyang ★

Tashkent ★

Ankara ★ Yerevan ★

TURKMENISTAN

TAJIKISTAN

Beijing ★

Seoul ★

JAPAN

Algiers ★ Tunis ★

TURKEY

AZERBAIJAN

Baku

Ashkhabad Dushanbe ★

SOUTH

KOREA

★ Tokyo

PACIFIC OCEAN

Rabat ★

TUNISIA

Damascus ★

SYRIA

IRAQ

Tehran ★

Kabul ★

Islamabad ★

CHINA

Taipei ★

MOROCCO

Tripoli ★

ISRAEL

Amman ★ Baghdad

IRAN

AFGHANISTAN

NEPAL

BHUTAN

TAIWAN

Tropic of Cancer

WESTERN

SAHARA

(MOROCCO)

ALGERIA

LIBYA

EGYPT

Cairo ★

JORDAN

KUWAIT

BAHRAIN

SAUDI

ARABIA

Riyadh ★

QATAR

Abu Dhabi ★

PAKISTAN

New

Delhi ★

Katmandu

Dhaka ★

INDIA

MYANMAR

(BURMA)

HONG KONG

Northern Mariana

Islands (U.S.)

See Inset Below

AFRICA

NIGER

CHAD

Khartoum ★

UNITED ARAB

EMIRATES

Asmara ★

OMAN

Muscat ★

YEMEN

BANGLADESH

Rangoon ★

LAOS ★ Hanoi

THAILAND

VIETNAM

Manila ★

Guam (U.S.)

MARSHALL

ISLANDS

Niamey ★

NIGERIA

Abuja ★

N'Djamena ★

SUDAN

ERITREA

Sanaa ★

DJIBOUTI

Addis Ababa ★

ETHIOPIA

SRI

LANKA

Colombo ★

Bangkok ★

CAMBODIA

Phnom Penh

PHILIPPINES

Koror ★

PALAU

MICRONESIA

FEDERATED STATES

OF MICRONESIA

EQUATORIAL GUINEA

SÃO TOMÉ AND

PRINCIPE

CAMEROON

Yaoundé ★

CENTRAL

AFRICAN REP.

★ Bangui

UGANDA

Kampala ★

SOMALIA

KENYA

BRUNEI

Kuala Lumpur ★

MALAYSIA

SINGAPORE

Equator

MELANESIA

NAURU

KIRIBATI

Libreville ★

GABON

Brazzaville ★

CONGO

ZAIRE

Kinshasa ★

RWANDA

BURUNDI

Nairobi ★

TANZANIA

SEYCHELLES

INDONESIA

Jakarta ★

PAPUA

NEW GUINEA

Port Moresby ★

SOLOMON

ISLANDS

TUVALU

ATLANTIC

OCEAN

Luanda ★

ANGOLA

ZAMBIA

Kinshasa

Dar es Salaam ★

COMOROS

INDIAN OCEAN

VANUATU

FIJI

N

ZIMBABWE

MALAWI

Lilongwe ★

MADAGASCAR

Antananarivo ★

MAURITIUS

Réunion

(FR.)

Tropic of Capricorn

New Caledonia (FR.)

10°S

W

E

NAMIBIA

Windhoek ★

Lusaka ★

Harare ★

BOTSWANA

MOZAMBIQUE

★ Maputo

AUSTRALIA

S

Gaborone ★

Pretoria ★

Cape Town ★

SOUTH

AFRICA

LESOTHO

SWAZILAND

Canberra ★

NEW

ZEALAND

Wellington ★

ANTARCTICA

Antarctic Circle

## West Africa

20°N

MAURITANIA

★ Nouakchott

MALI

Dakar ★

SENEGAL

Banjul ★

GAMBIA

Bissau ★

GUINEA-

BISSAU

GUINEA

BURKINA

FASO

NIGER

Niamey ★

Bamako ★

Ouagadougou ★

BENIN

10°N

Conakry ★

Freetown ★

SIERRA

LEONE

CÔTE

D'IVOIRE

GHANA

TOGO

NIGERIA

Porto-Novo ★

N

Monrovia ★

Yamoussoukro ★

Accra ★

Lomé ★

W

E

LIBERIA

5°N

S

ATLANTIC OCEAN

Equator

0 250 500 Miles

0 250 500 Kilometers

## Europe

SWEDEN

FINLAND

NORWAY

Oslo ★

Helsinki ★

Stockholm ★

Tallinn ★

ESTONIA

RUSSIA

IRELAND

Dublin ★

UNITED

KINGDOM

NORTH

SEA

DENMARK

Copenhagen ★

Riga ★

LATVIA

Moscow ★

RUSSIA

LITHUANIA

Vilnius ★

The

Hague

NETHERLANDS

Amsterdam ★

Minsk ★

BELARUS

London ★

BELGIUM

Brussels ★

Berlin ★

GERMANY

Warsaw ★

POLAND

Kiev ★

ATLANTIC

OCEAN

Paris ★

LUXEMBOURG

Prague ★

CZECH REP.

UKRAINE

FRANCE

SWITZERLAND

Bern ★

Vienna ★

AUSTRIA

SLOVAKIA

Bratislava ★

Budapest ★

HUNGARY

MOLDOVA

Kishinev ★

ANDORRA

SLOVENIA

Ljubljana ★

Zagreb ★

CROATIA

ITALY

ROMANIA

Bucharest ★

GEORGIA

PORTUGAL

Lisbon ★

Madrid ★

MONACO

SAN

MARINO

BOS.

HERZ.

Sarajevo ★

Belgrade ★

YUGOSLAVIA

BLACK SEA

SPAIN

Rome ★

Sofia ★

BULGARIA

Gibraltar (BR.)

40°N

Tiranë ★

ALBANIA

MACEDONIA

Skopje ★

TURKEY

MEDITERRANEAN SEA

GREECE

Athens ★

MALTA

CYPRUS

SYRIA

LEBANON

0 250 500 Miles

0 250 500 Kilometers

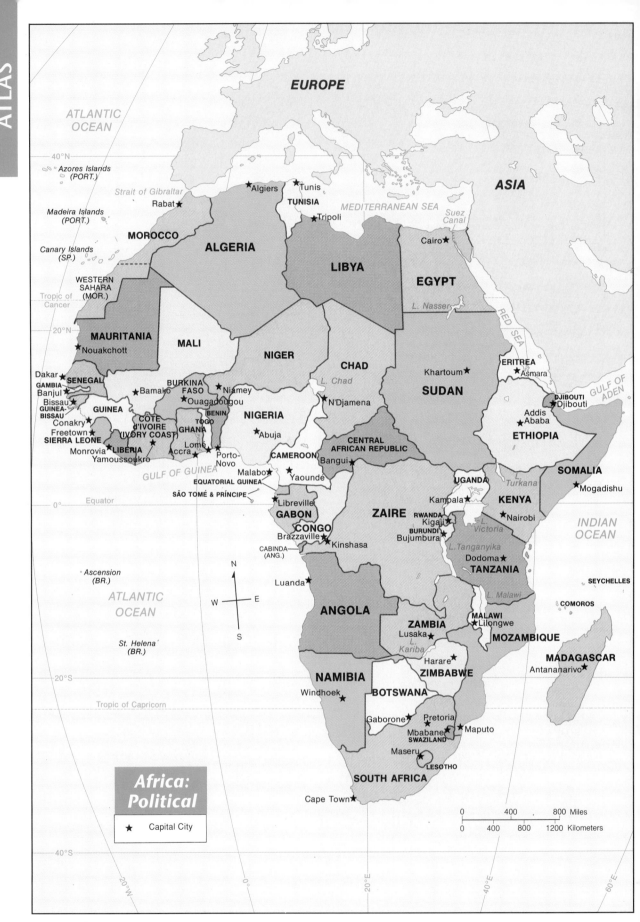

EUROPE

ASIA

ATLANTIC
OCEAN

40°N

Azores Islands
(PORT.)

Madeira Islands
(PORT.)

Strait of Gibraltar

Algiers ★    ★ Tunis
Rabat ★              TUNISIA

MEDITERRANEAN SEA          Suez
                                        Canal

Canary Islands
(SP.)

MOROCCO

ALGERIA

LIBYA

★ Tripoli

Cairo ★

EGYPT

Tropic of
Cancer

WESTERN
SAHARA
(MOR.)

L. Nasser

RED SEA

20°N

MAURITANIA
★ Nouakchott

MALI

NIGER

CHAD

Khartoum ★

SUDAN

ERITREA
★ Asmara

GULF OF
ADEN

Dakar ★
GAMBIA     SENEGAL
Banjul
Bissau ★
GUINEA-
BISSAU     GUINEA
Conakry
Freetown ★
SIERRA LEONE
Monrovia
LIBERIA
Yamoussoukro

★ Bamako

BURKINA
FASO
Ouagadougou

★ Niamey

L. Chad

★ N'Djamena

NIGERIA

CÔTE
d'IVOIRE
(IVORY COAST)   GHANA
TOGO
BENIN
Lomé
Accra
Porto-
Novo

★ Abuja

CENTRAL
AFRICAN REPUBLIC

DJIBOUTI
Djibouti

Addis
Ababa ★

ETHIOPIA

Malabo ★
EQUATORIAL GUINEA
SÃO TOMÉ & PRÍNCIPE

★ Yaoundé
CAMEROON

Bangui ★

UGANDA

SOMALIA
★ Mogadishu

GULF OF GUINEA

0°    Equator

Libreville ★

GABON

CONGO
Brazzaville

ZAIRE

Kinshasa

Kampala ★
RWANDA
Kigali
BURUNDI
Bujumbura

Turkana

L.
Victoria

KENYA
Nairobi ★

L. Tanganyika

INDIAN
OCEAN

Ascension
(BR.)

CABINDA
(ANG.)

N

W    E

S

Luanda ★

ANGOLA

Dodoma ★
TANZANIA

SEYCHELLES

COMOROS

St. Helena
(BR.)

ZAMBIA
Lusaka ★

L.
Kariba

L. Malawi

MALAWI
Lilongwe ★

MOZAMBIQUE

MADAGASCAR
Antananarivo ★

Harare ★
ZIMBABWE

20°S

NAMIBIA
Windhoek ★

BOTSWANA

Tropic of Capricorn

Gaborone ★

Pretoria ★
Mbabane ★   ★ Maputo
SWAZILAND

Maseru ★
LESOTHO

Africa:
Political

★ Capital City

SOUTH AFRICA

Cape Town ★

0    400    800 Miles

0    400    800    1200 Kilometers

40°S

20°W

0°

20°E

40°E

60°E

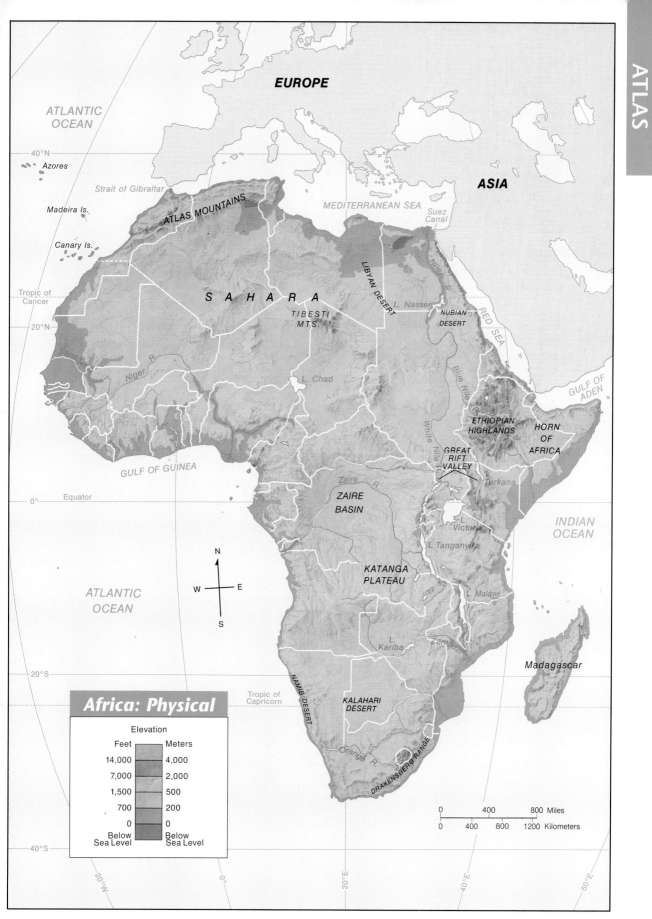

EUROPE

ATLANTIC
OCEAN

40°N

*Azores*

*Strait of Gibraltar*

*Madeira Is.*

ATLAS MOUNTAINS

ASIA

MEDITERRANEAN SEA

*Suez Canal*

*Canary Is.*

Tropic of
Cancer

20°N

S A H A R A

*TIBESTI
MTS.*

LIBYAN DESERT

*Nile R.*

L. Nasser

NUBIAN
DESERT

RED SEA

*Senegal R.*

*Niger R.*

L. Chad

*Blue Nile R.*

GULF OF
ADEN

*ETHIOPIAN
HIGHLANDS*

HORN
OF
AFRICA

GULF OF GUINEA

*White Nile R.*

GREAT
RIFT
VALLEY

L. Turkana

*Zaire R.*

Equator

0°

*ZAIRE
BASIN*

L.
Victoria

INDIAN
OCEAN

L. Tanganyika

N

W — E

S

*KATANGA
PLATEAU*

ATLANTIC
OCEAN

L. Malawi

L.
Kariba

*Zambezi R.*

Madagascar

20°S

Tropic of
Capricorn

NAMIB DESERT

*KALAHARI
DESERT*

Africa: Physical

Elevation

| Feet | | Meters |
|------|---|--------|
| 14,000 | | 4,000 |
| 7,000 | | 2,000 |
| 1,500 | | 500 |
| 700 | | 200 |
| 0 | | 0 |
| Below Sea Level | | Below Sea Level |

*Orange R.*

DRAKENSBERG RANGE

| 0 | 400 | 800 Miles |
|---|-----|-----------|
| 0 | 400 | 800 |
| | 1200 Kilometers | |

40°S

20°W

0°

20°E

40°E

60°E

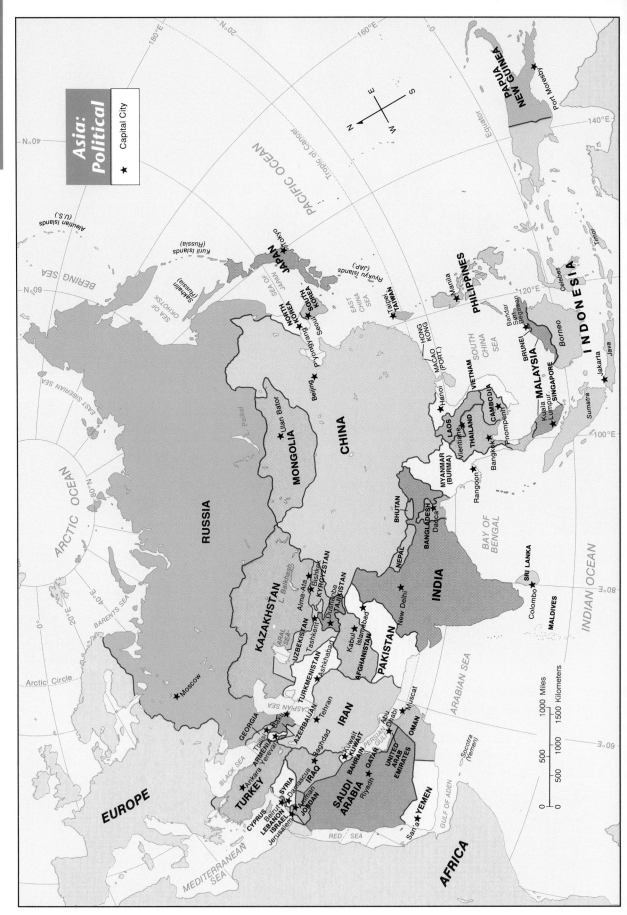

*Asia: Political*

★ Capital City

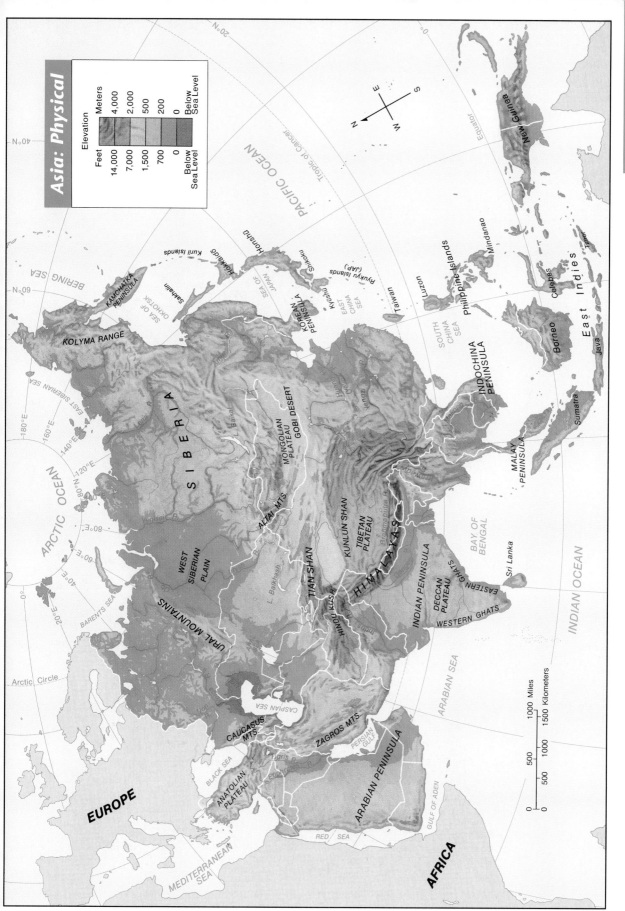

## Asia: Physical

**Elevation**

| Feet | Meters |
|------|--------|
| 14,000 | 4,000 |
| 7,000 | 2,000 |
| 1,500 | 500 |
| 700 | 200 |
| 0 | 0 |
| Below Sea Level | Below Sea Level |

ARCTIC OCEAN

PACIFIC OCEAN

BERING SEA

EAST SIBERIAN SEA

BARENTS SEA

KAMCHATKA PENINSULA

KOLYMA RANGE

S I B E R I A

SEA OF OKHOTSK

Sakhalin

Kuril Islands

Hokkaido

Honshu

SEA OF JAPAN

Shikoku

Kyushu

Ryukyu Islands (JAP.)

KOREAN PENINSULA

EAST CHINA SEA

Taiwan

SOUTH CHINA SEA

Luzon

Mindanao

Philippine Islands

New Guinea

Equator

Celebes

Borneo

Java

Sumatra

East Indies

Timor

MONGOLIAN PLATEAU

GOBI DESERT

ALTAI MTS.

TIAN SHAN

KUNLUN SHAN

TIBETAN PLATEAU

H I M A L A Y A S

HINDU KUSH

WEST SIBERIAN PLAIN

L. Balkhash

L. Baikal

URAL MOUNTAINS

INDOCHINA PENINSULA

MALAY PENINSULA

INDIAN PENINSULA

DECCAN PLATEAU

WESTERN GHATS

EASTERN GHATS

Sri Lanka

BAY OF BENGAL

INDIAN OCEAN

ARABIAN SEA

CASPIAN SEA

CAUCASUS MTS.

ZAGROS MTS.

PERSIAN GULF

ANATOLIAN PLATEAU

ARABIAN PENINSULA

GULF OF ADEN

Tigris R.

Euphrates R.

BLACK SEA

RED SEA

MEDITERRANEAN SEA

EUROPE

AFRICA

Tropic of Cancer

Arctic Circle

20°N

40°N

60°N

80°N

0°

20°E

40°E

60°E

80°E

100°E

120°E

140°E

160°E

180°E

| 0 | 500 | 1000 Miles |
| 0 | 500 | 1000 | 1500 Kilometers |

ICELAND
★ Reykjavik

*Arctic Circle*

*NORWEGIAN SEA*

Faroe Islands
(DEN.)

Shetland Islands
(BR.)

*ATLANTIC
OCEAN*

*NORTH SEA*

SCOTLAND

N.
IRELAND

Dublin ★
IRELAND

UNITED
KINGDOM

WALES  ENGLAND

London ★

*ENGLISH CHANNEL*

Brussels ★
BELGIUM

LUXEMBOURG

Paris ★

FRANCE

*BAY OF
BISCAY*

PORTUGAL

Lisbon ★

SPAIN

Madrid ★

*Corsica
(FR.)*

ANDORRA

MONACO

*Balearic Islands
(SP.)*

*Sardinia
(IT.)*

*Strait of
Gibraltar*

Gibraltar
(BR.)

NORWAY

Oslo ★

SWEDEN

Stockholm ★

DENMARK
Copenhagen ●

*BALTIC SEA*

*GULF OF BOTHNIA*

FINLAND

Helsinki ★

Tallinn ★
ESTONIA

Riga ★
LATVIA

LITHUANIA
Vilnius ★
RUSSIA

●St. Petersburg

RUSSIA

Moscow ★

Minsk ★
BELARUS

Berlin ★

NETHERLANDS
The
Hague ● Amsterdam

GERMANY

Prague ★
CZECH REPUBLIC

POLAND

Warsaw ★

Kiev ★

UKRAINE

SLOVAKIA

Bratislava ★

Vienna ★
AUSTRIA

SWITZERLAND  LIECHTENSTEIN

★ Bern

Ljubljana ●
SLOVENIA

ITALY

SAN
MARINO

VATICAN
CITY  ● Rome

Budapest ●

HUNGARY

Zagreb ●
CROATIA

Belgrade ●

SERBIA

BOSNIA -
HERZEGOVINA
Sarajevo ●  YUGOSLAVIA

MONTENEGRO

ALBANIA

Tirane ●

MOLDOVA
Kishinev ●

ROMANIA

Bucharest ●

*BLACK
SEA*

Sofia ●
BULGARIA

Skopje ●
F.Y.R. OF
MACEDONIA

*ADRIATIC SEA*

GREECE

Athens ★

*MEDITERRANEAN  SEA*

MALTA

Sicily

Istanbul ●

TURKEY

*Bosporus*

*AEGEAN
SEA*

Crete

AFRICA

N
W — E
S

0     200     400 Miles
0   200   400   600 Kilometers

**Europe:
Political**

★ Capital City
● Major City

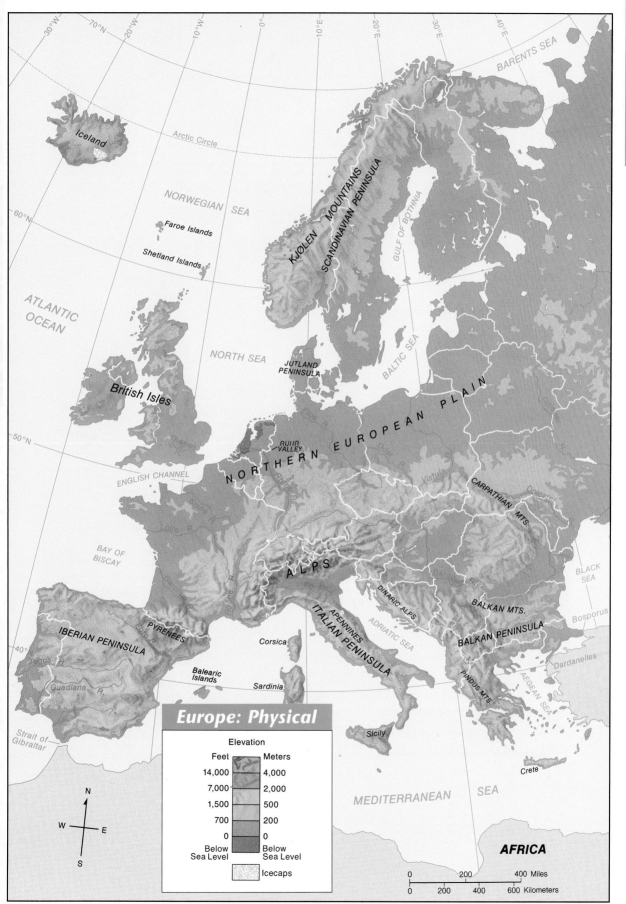

**Europe: Physical**

Elevation

| Feet | Meters |
| --- | --- |
| 14,000 | 4,000 |
| 7,000 | 2,000 |
| 1,500 | 500 |
| 700 | 200 |
| 0 | 0 |
| Below Sea Level | Below Sea Level |

Icecaps

N
W   E
S

| 0 | 200 | 400 Miles |
| 0 | 200 | 400 | 600 Kilometers |

BARENTS SEA

Iceland

NORWEGIAN SEA

Arctic Circle

Faroe Islands

Shetland Islands

ATLANTIC OCEAN

NORTH SEA

British Isles

ENGLISH CHANNEL

BAY OF BISCAY

KJØLEN MOUNTAINS

SCANDINAVIAN PENINSULA

GULF OF BOTHNIA

BALTIC SEA

JUTLAND PENINSULA

NORTHERN EUROPEAN PLAIN

RUHR VALLEY

CARPATHIAN MTS.

Vistula

ALPS

IBERIAN PENINSULA

PYRENEES

Tagus R.

Guadiana R.

Strait of Gibraltar

Corsica

Balearic Islands

Sardinia

APENNINES

ITALIAN PENINSULA

DINARIC ALPS

ADRIATIC SEA

BALKAN MTS.

BALKAN PENINSULA

PINDUS MTS.

BLACK SEA

Bosporus

Dardanelles

AEGEAN SEA

Sicily

Crete

MEDITERRANEAN    SEA

AFRICA

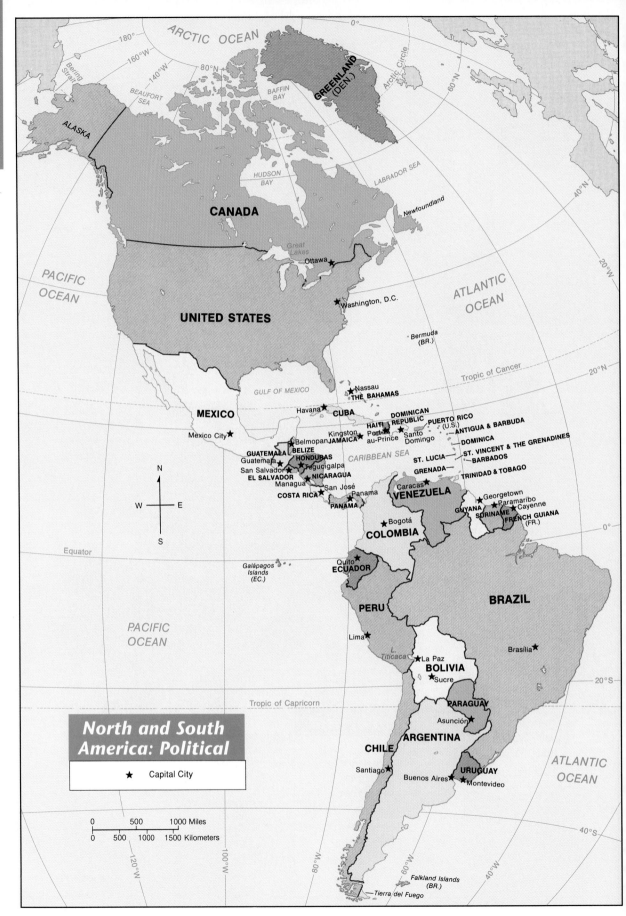

ARCTIC OCEAN

180°
160°W
140°W
80°N

BEAUFORT SEA

BAFFIN BAY

GREENLAND (DEN.)

Arctic Circle

60°W

ALASKA

HUDSON BAY

LABRADOR SEA

CANADA

PACIFIC OCEAN

Great Lakes

Newfoundland

40°N

Ottawa ★

20°W

ATLANTIC OCEAN

UNITED STATES

★ Washington, D.C.

Bermuda (BR.)

20°W

Tropic of Cancer

20°N

GULF OF MEXICO

Nassau •
THE BAHAMAS

MEXICO

Havana • CUBA

DOMINICAN REPUBLIC

PUERTO RICO (U.S.)

★ Mexico City

Kingston •

HAITI • Port- au-Prince

Santo Domingo

ANTIGUA & BARBUDA

BELMOPAN JAMAICA

DOMINICA

GUATEMALA BELIZE

CARIBBEAN SEA

ST. VINCENT & THE GRENADINES

ST. LUCIA

Guatemala
HONDURAS

BARBADOS

San Salvador
Tegucigalpa

GRENADA

N

EL SALVADOR NICARAGUA

TRINIDAD & TOBAGO

Managua

W        E

San José
COSTA RICA

Panama

Caracas •
VENEZUELA

Georgetown •

S

PANAMA

GUYANA

Paramaribo •

SURINAME

Cayenne •
FRENCH GUIANA (FR.)

• Bogotá

COLOMBIA

0°

Equator

Galápagos Islands (EC.)

Quito •
ECUADOR

PERU

BRAZIL

PACIFIC OCEAN

Lima ★

L. Titicaca

La Paz
BOLIVIA

Brasília ★

20°S

Sucre

Tropic of Capricorn

**North and South America: Political**

PARAGUAY

Asunción ★

★ Capital City

ARGENTINA

CHILE

ATLANTIC OCEAN

Santiago ★

URUGUAY

Buenos Aires ★ Montevideo

| 0 | 500 | 1000 Miles |

| 0 | 500 | 1000 | 1500 Kilometers |

40°S

120°W

100°W

80°W

60°W

40°W

Falkland Islands (BR.)

Tierra del Fuego

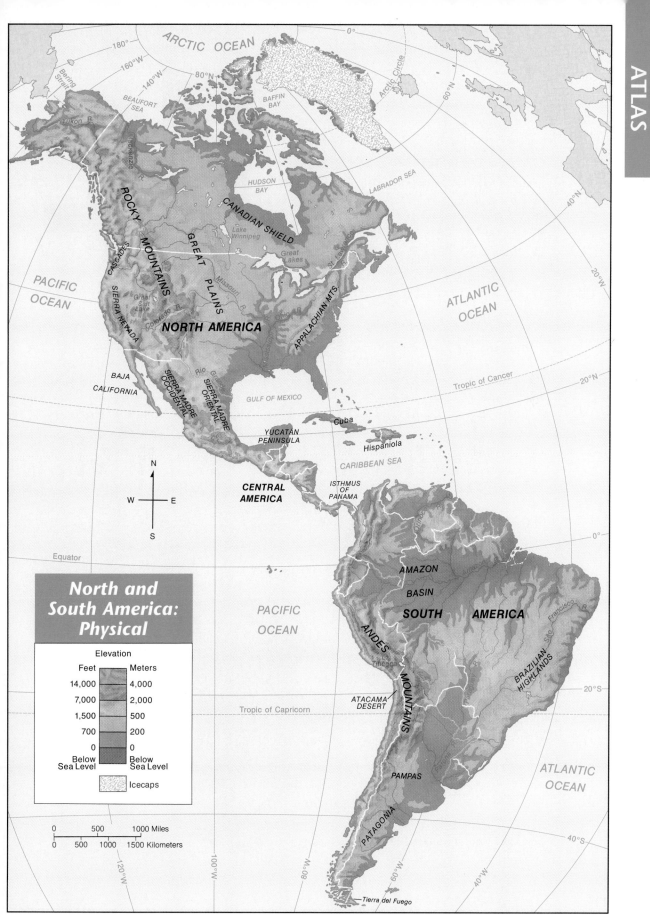

## North and South America: Physical

**Elevation**

| Feet | Meters |
|------|--------|
| 14,000 | 4,000 |
| 7,000 | 2,000 |
| 1,500 | 500 |
| 700 | 200 |
| 0 | 0 |
| Below Sea Level | Below Sea Level |

Icecaps

0 500 1000 Miles
0 500 1000 1500 Kilometers

ARCTIC OCEAN

180°
160°W
140°W
80°N
60°N
0°
Arctic Circle

BERING STRAIT
BEAUFORT SEA
Yukon R.
Mackenzie R.

BAFFIN BAY
HUDSON BAY
LABRADOR SEA

ROCKY MOUNTAINS
CASCADES
SIERRA NEVADA
GREAT PLAINS
CANADIAN SHIELD
Lake Winnipeg
Great Lakes
Missouri R.
St. Lawrence
APPALACHIAN MTS.

PACIFIC OCEAN

Great Salt Lake
Colorado R.

NORTH AMERICA

ATLANTIC OCEAN

40°N
20°W

BAJA CALIFORNIA
SIERRA MADRE OCCIDENTAL
SIERRA MADRE ORIENTAL
Rio Grande

20°N
Tropic of Cancer

YUCATAN PENINSULA
GULF OF MEXICO
Cuba
Hispaniola
CARIBBEAN SEA

N
W E
S

CENTRAL AMERICA
ISTHMUS OF PANAMA

Orinoco R.

0°
Equator

AMAZON BASIN
Amazon R.

SOUTH AMERICA

ANDES MOUNTAINS
Titicaca

PACIFIC OCEAN

São Francisco R.
BRAZILIAN HIGHLANDS

20°S

ATACAMA DESERT
Tropic of Capricorn

PAMPAS

ATLANTIC OCEAN

PATAGONIA

40°S

Tierra del Fuego

120°W
100°W
80°W
60°W
40°W

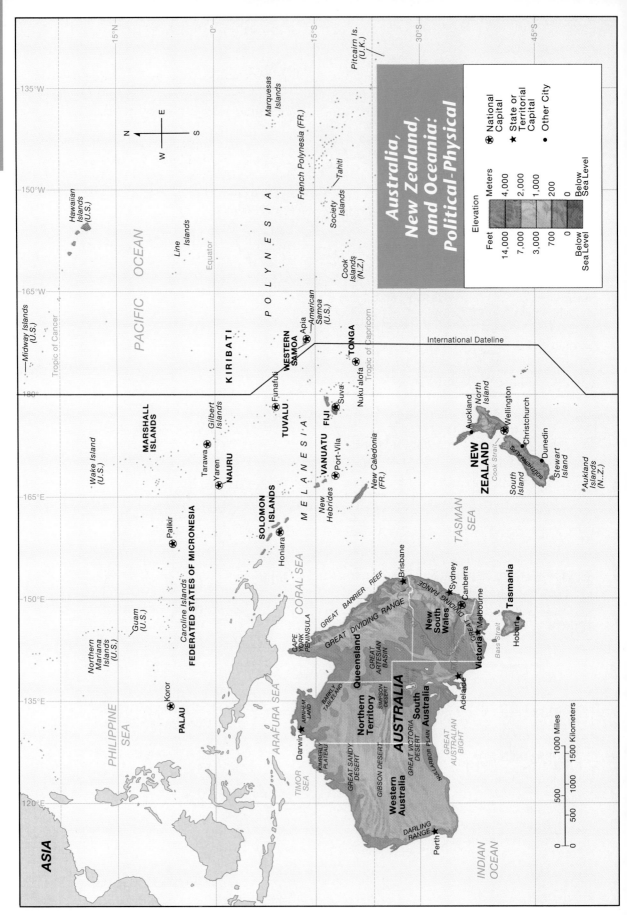

**Australia,
New Zealand,
and Oceania:
Political-Physical**

Elevation

| National Capital | ★ State or Territorial Capital | • Other City |

| Feet | Meters |
| 14,000 | 4,000 |
| 7,000 | 2,000 |
| 3,000 | 1,000 |
| 700 | 200 |
| 0 | 0 |
| Below Sea Level | Below Sea Level |

N
E
W
S

135°W
150°W
165°W
180°
165°E
150°E
135°E
120°E

15°N
0°
15°S
30°S
45°S

Pitcairn Is. (U.K.)

Marquesas Islands

French Polynesia (FR.)

Tahiti

Society Islands

Cook Islands (N.Z.)

Hawaiian Islands (U.S.)

Line Islands

Equator

P O L Y N E S I A

PACIFIC OCEAN

Tropic of Cancer

Midway Islands (U.S.)

American Samoa (U.S.)

Apia
WESTERN SAMOA

TONGA
Nuku'alofa

International Dateline

Tropic of Capricorn

KIRIBATI

Funafuti
TUVALU

Suva
FIJI

Nadi

VANUATU
Port-Vila

New Hebrides

New Caledonia (FR.)

Tarawa
Gilbert Islands

Yaren
NAURU

M E L A N E S I A

MARSHALL ISLANDS

Wake Island (U.S.)

Palikir
Caroline Islands
FEDERATED STATES OF MICRONESIA

SOLOMON ISLANDS

Honiara

Guam (U.S.)

Northern Mariana Islands (U.S.)

Koror
PALAU

PHILIPPINE SEA

ASIA

Auckland
North Island
Wellington
Christchurch
Dunedin
Cook Strait
SOUTHERN ALPS
South Island
Stewart Island
Aukland Islands (N.Z.)

NEW ZEALAND

TASMAN SEA

Brisbane

Sydney
Canberra
New South Wales
Melbourne
Victoria
GREAT DIVIDING RANGE
Tasmania
Hobart
Bass Strait

GREAT BARRIER REEF

Queensland
GREAT ARTESIAN BASIN

GREAT DIVIDING RANGE

CAPE YORK PENINSULA

CORAL SEA

ARAFURA SEA

TIMOR SEA

ARNHEM LAND
Darwin
BARKLY TABLELAND
Northern Territory
SIMPSON DESERT
South Australia
Adelaide

AUSTRALIA

KIMBERLEY PLATEAU
GREAT SANDY DESERT
GIBSON DESERT
Western Australia
GREAT VICTORIA DESERT
NULLARBOR PLAIN
GREAT AUSTRALIAN BIGHT

DARLING RANGE
Perth

INDIAN OCEAN

1000 Miles
500
0

1500 Kilometers
1000
500
0

# UNDERSTANDING MAP PROJECTIONS

Geographers and historians use globes and maps to represent the Earth. A globe is like a small model of the Earth. It shows major geographic features, representing the landmasses and bodies of water accurately. However, a globe is not always convenient to use. A map, on the other hand, which can be printed on a piece of paper or in a book, is a more convenient way to show the Earth. Unfortunately, no map can be an exact picture of the Earth because all maps are flat and the Earth's surface is curved.

Mapmakers have developed many ways of showing the curved Earth on a flat surface. Each of these ways is called a map projection. The three maps on this page show different types of map projections—each with its advantages and disadvantages.

The Robinson projection shows correct shapes and sizes of landmasses for most parts of the world. They are commonly used today by geographers. You will find numerous Robinson projections in this book. They appear at the beginning of each unit, beside the time line at the beginning of each chapter, and as a locator map beneath most other maps in the book.

The Mercator projection, one of the earliest projections developed, accurately shows the directions north, south, east, and west. As you can see, the parallels and meridians are straight lines intersecting each other at right angles. This makes it easy to plot distances on the map. As a result, Mercator projections are useful for showing sailors' routes and ocean currents. Sizes become distorted, however, as you move farther away from the equator.

The Interrupted projection shows the sizes and shapes of landmasses accurately. However, the interruptions in the oceans make it difficult to measure distances and judge directions across water.

## GEOGRAPHY AND HISTORY

Map projections enable mapmakers to show the curved Earth on a flat page. Each of the projections shown here has its advantages and disadvantages.

1. **Location** On the maps, locate (a) North America, (b) Africa, (c) Australia.
2. **Region** (a) On an Interrupted projection, which continent is divided into sections? Why is it divided? (b) List three pages in this textbook on which you can find a Robinson projection.
3. **Critical Thinking Comparing** Locate Antarctica on the Robinson and Mercator projections. On which map is its size shown more accurately? Explain why this is so.

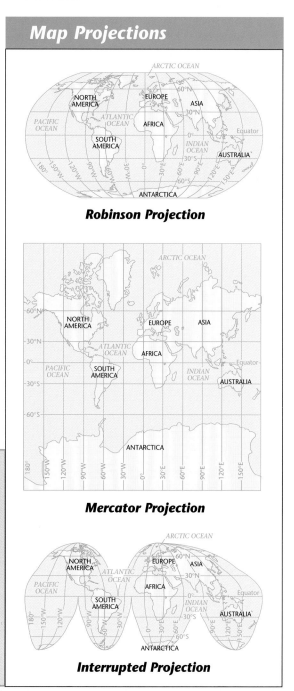

**Map Projections**

**Robinson Projection**

**Mercator Projection**

**Interrupted Projection**

# GLOSSARY

This Glossary defines many important terms and phrases. Some terms are phonetically respelled to aid in pronunciation. See the Pronunciation Key below for an explanation of the respellings. The page number following each definition is the page on which the term or phrase is first discussed in the text. All terms that appear in blue type in the text are included in this Glossary.

**PRONUNCIATION KEY** When difficult terms or names first appear in the text, they are respelled to aid in pronunciation. A syllable in small capital letters receives the most stress. The key below lists the letters used for respelling. It includes examples of words using each sound and shows how they are respelled.

| SYMBOL | EXAMPLE | RESPELLING |
|---|---|---|
| a | hat | (hat) |
| ay | pay, late | (pay), (layt) |
| ah | star, hot | (stahr), (haht) |
| ai | air, dare | (air), (dair) |
| aw | law, all | (law), (awl) |
| eh | met | (meht) |
| ee | bee, eat | (bee), (eet) |
| er | learn, sir, fur | (lern), (ser), (fer) |
| ih | fit | (fiht) |
| i | mile | (mīle) |
| ir | ear | (ir) |
| oh | no | (noh) |
| oi | soil, boy | (soil), (boi) |
| oo | root, rule | (root), rool) |
| or | born, door | (born), (dor) |
| ow | plow, out | (plow), (owt) |
| u | put, book | (put), (buk) |
| uh | fun | (fuhn) |
| yoo | few, use | (fyoo), (yooz) |
| ch | chill, reach | (chihl), (reech) |
| g | go, dig | (goh), (dihg) |
| j | jet, gently, bridge | (jeht), (JEHNT lee), (brihj) |
| k | kite, cup | (kīt), (kuhp) |
| ks | mix | (mihks) |
| kw | quick | (kwihk) |
| ng | bring | (brihng) |
| s | say, cent | (say), (sehnt) |
| sh | she, crash | (shee), (krash) |
| th | three | (three) |
| y | yet, onion | (yeht), (UHN yuhn) |
| z | zip, always | (zihp), (AWL wayz) |
| zh | treasure | (TREH zher) |

# A

**abdicate** to give up a high office (p. 501)

**absolute monarch** ruler with complete authority over the government and lives of the people he or she governs (p. 422)

**acid rain** form of pollution in which toxic chemicals in the air come back to the Earth as rain, snow, or hail (p. 834)

**acropolis** (uh KRAHP uh lihs) hilltop fortress of an ancient Greek city-state (p. 108)

**agribusiness** large commercial farm owned by a multinational corporation (p. 953)

**ahimsa** (uh HIM sah) Hindu belief in nonviolence (p. 79)

**alchemy** (AL kuh mee) medieval science whose aim was to transform ordinary metals into gold (p. 92)

**anarchist** person who wants to abolish all government (p. 595)

**annex** to add a territory onto an existing state or country (p. 497)

**annul** to cancel or invalidate (p. 358)

**anti-Semitism** prejudice against Jews (p. 200)

**apartheid** policy of strict racial separation in South Africa; abolished in 1989 (p. 742)

**appeasement** policy of giving in to an aggressor's demands in order to keep the peace (p. 788)

**apprentice** young person learning a trade from a master (p. 204)

**aqueduct** in ancient Rome, bridgelike stone structure that carried water from the hills into the cities (p. 142) ▲

**archaeology** (ahr kee AHL uh jee) study of the lives of early people through examination of their physical remains (p. 4)

**archipelago** (ahr kuh PEHL uh goh) chain of islands (p. 323)

**aristocracy** in Greek city-states, government headed by a privileged minority or upper class (p. 109)

**armistice** agreement to end fighting in a war (p. 709)

**artifact** object made by human beings (p. 4)

**artisan** skilled craftworker (p. 14)

**assembly line** production method that breaks down a complex job into a series of smaller tasks (p. 557)

**astrolabe** instrument used to determine latitude by measuring the position of the stars (p. 372) ▲

**atman** (AHT muhn) in Hindu belief, a person's essential self (p. 78)

**atrocity** brutal act (p. 706)

**autocrat** ruler who has complete authority (p. 239)

**autonomy** self-rule (p. 529)

# B

**balance of power** distribution of military and economic power that prevents any one nation from becoming too strong (p. 429)

**balance of trade** difference between how much a country imports and how much it exports (p. 649)

**baroque** ornate style of art and architecture popular in the 1600s and 1700s (p. 464)

**barter economy** system in which one set of goods or services is exchanged for another (p. 40)

**bias** prejudice for or against someone or something (p. 390)

**bishop** in the early Christian Church, a high-ranking Church official with authority over a local area, or diocese (p. 147)

**blitzkrieg** lightning war (p. 793)

**blockade** the shutting off of a port to keep people or supplies from moving in or out (p. 498)

**bourgeoisie** (boor zhwah ZEE) the middle class (p. 481)

**boyar** landowning noble in Russia under the czars (p. 247)

**brahman** according to Aryan belief, the single spiritual power that resides in all things (p. 55)

**bureaucracy** system of managing government through departments run by appointed officials (p. 14)

**bushido** (BOO shee doh) code of conduct for samurai during the feudal period in Japan (p. 327)

# C

**caliph** successor to Muhammad as political and religious leader of the Muslims (p. 257)

**calligraphy** beautiful handwriting (p. 61)

**canon law** body of laws of a church (p. 196)

**capital** money for investment (p. 202)

**capitalism** economic system in which the means of production are privately owned and operated for profit (p. 412)

**caravel** improved type of sailing ship in the 1400s (p. 372)

**cartel** association of large corporations formed to fix prices, set production quotas, or divide up markets (p. 561)

**cartographer** mapmaker (p. 372)

**cash crop** crop raised to be sold for money on the world market (p. 647)

**caste** in traditional Indian society, unchangeable social group into which a person is born (p. 55)

**cataract** waterfall (p. 22)

**caudillo** military dictator in Latin America (p. 673)

**charter** in the Middle Ages, a written document that set out the rights and privileges of a town (p. 202)

**chivalry** code of conduct for knights during the Middle Ages (p. 193)

**circumnavigate** to travel all the way around the Earth (p. 377)

**city-state** political unit made up of a city and the surrounding lands (p. 16)

**civil disobedience** refusal to obey unjust laws (p. 748)

**civil law** body of law dealing with private rights of individuals (p. 38)

**clan** group of families with a common ancestor (p. 60)

**coalition** temporary alliance of various political parties (p. 618)

**collaborator** person who cooperates with an enemy (p. 800)

**collective** large farm owned and operated by workers as a group (p. 726)

**colony** territory settled and ruled by people from another land (p. 42)

**comedy** in ancient Greece, play that mocked people or social customs (p. 120)

**command economy** system in which government officials make all basic economic decisions (p. 725)

**common law** system of law based on court decisions that became accepted legal principles (p. 211)

**commune** community in which property is held in common, living quarters are shared, and physical needs are provided in exchange for work at assigned jobs (p. 882)

**communism** form of socialism advocated by Karl Marx; according to Marx, class struggle was inevitable and would lead to the creation of a classless society in which all wealth and property would be owned by the community as a whole (p. 522)

**concentration camp** detention center for civilians considered enemies of a state (p. 782)

**conquistador** (kahn KEES tuh dor) name for the Spanish explorers who claimed lands in the Americas for Spain in the 1500s and 1600s (p. 394)

**constitutional government** a government whose power is defined and limited by law (p. 467)

**consul** in ancient Rome, official from the patrician class who supervised the government and commanded the armies (p. 131)

**containment** Cold War policy of limiting communism to areas already under Soviet control (p. 812)

**corporation** business owned by many investors who buy shares of stock and risk only the amount of their investment (p. 561)

**covenant** binding agreement (p. 44)

**creole** person in Spain's colonies in the Americas who was an American-born descendant of Spanish settlers (p. 399)

**crusade** holy war (p. 218)

**cultural diffusion** the spread of ideas, customs, and technologies from one people to another (p. 17)

**cuneiform** (kyoo NEE uh form) wedge-shaped writing of the ancient Sumerians and other ancient peoples (p. 35) ▲

**czar** title of the ruler of the Russian empire (p. 247)

# D

**daimyo** (DĪ myoh) warrior lords directly below the shogun in feudal Japan (p. 327)

**deficit** gap between what a government spends and what it takes in through taxes and other sources (p. 860)

**deficit spending** situation in which a government spends more money than it takes in (p. 481)

**delta** triangular area of marshland formed by deposits of silt at the mouth of some rivers (p. 22)

**democracy** government in which the people hold ruling power (p. 110)

**demotic** system of ancient Egyptian writing, simpler than hieroglyphics, that was developed for everyday use (p. 29)

**desertification** process by which fertile or semi-desert land becomes desert (p. 286)

**détente** easing of tensions between the United States and the Soviet Union in the 1970s (p. 848)

**dharma** (DAHR muh) in Hindu belief, an individual's religious and moral duties (p. 79)

**diaspora** (dī AS puh ruh) the scattering of the Jewish people from their homeland in Palestine (p. 45); the scattering of African peoples as a result of the slave trade (p. 928)

**dictator** ruler who has complete control over a government; in ancient Rome, a leader appointed to rule for six months in times of emergency (p. 131)

**direct democracy** system of government in which citizens participate directly rather than through elected representatives (p. 114)

**dissident** someone who speaks out against the government (p. 863)

**divine right** belief that a ruler's authority comes directly from God (p. 423)

**dynastic cycle** rise and fall of Chinese dynasties according to the Mandate of Heaven (p. 62)

**dynasty** ruling family (p. 23)

# E

**economic dependence** economic relationship, controlled by a developing nation, in which a less-developed nation exports raw materials to the developed nation and imports manufactured goods, capital, and technological know-how (p. 673)

**ejido** (eh HEE doh) Mexican peasant cooperative (p. 962)

**émigré** (EHM ih gray) person who flees his or her country for political reasons (p. 488)

**empire** group of states or territories controlled by one ruler (p. 16)

**enclosure** in England in the 1700s, the process of taking over and fencing off public lands (p. 509)

**encomienda** right the Spanish government granted to its American colonists to demand labor or tribute from Native Americans (p. 398)

**enlightened despot** absolute ruler who uses his or her power to bring about political and social change (p. 463)

**entrepreneur** person who assumes financial risks in the hope of making a profit (p. 412)

**ethics** moral standards of behavior (p. 45)

**GLOSSARY**

**ethnic group** large group of people who share the same language and cultural heritage (p. 249)

**excommunication** exclusion from the Roman Catholic Church as a penalty for refusing to obey Church laws (p. 196)

**extraterritoriality** right of foreigners to be protected by the laws of their own nation (p. 650)

# F

**factory** place in which workers and machines are brought together to produce large quantities of goods (p. 514)

**feudalism** (FYOOD uhl ihz uhm) loosely organized system of government in which local lords governed their own lands but owed military service and other support to a greater lord (p. 62)

**fief** (FEEF) in the Middle Ages, an estate granted by a lord to a vassal in exchange for service and loyalty (p. 192)

**filial piety** respect for parents (p. 90)

**flapper** in the United States and Europe in the 1920s, a rebellious young woman (p. 773)

**free market** market in which goods are bought and sold without restrictions (p. 460)

# G

**general strike** strike by workers in many different industries at the same time (p. 766)

**genocide** deliberate attempt to destroy an entire religious or ethnic group (p. 642)

**geography** study of people, their environments, and their resources (p. 6)

**ghetto** separate section of a city where members of a minority group are forced to live (p. 362)

**glacier** thick sheet of ice that covered parts of the Earth during the ice age (p. 9)

**glasnost** policy of openness instituted by Soviet leader Mikhail Gorbachev in the 1980s (p. 865)

**gravity** force that tends to pull one mass or object to another (p. 365)

**griot** (GREE oh) professional storyteller in early West Africa (p. 301)

**gross domestic product** total value of all goods and services produced by a nation (p. 877)

**guerrilla warfare** fighting carried on through hit-and-run raids (p. 499)

**guild** in the Middle Ages, association of merchants or artisans who cooperated to protect their economic interests (p. 203)

# H

**habeas corpus** principle that a person cannot be held in prison without first being charged with a specific crime (p. 435)

**haiku** form of Japanese poetry that expresses a feeling, thought, or idea in three lines, or 17 syllables (p. 330)

**hajj** pilgrimage to Mecca that all Muslims are expected to make at least once in their lifetime (p. 258)

**hangul** alphabet that uses symbols to represent the sounds of spoken Korean (p. 322)

**heliocentric** based on the belief that the sun is the center of the universe (p. 364)

**heresy** religious belief that is contrary to the official teachings of a church (p. 148)

**hierarchy** (HĪ uhr ahr kee) system of ranks (p. 34)

**hieroglyphics** (hī er oh GLIHF ihks) form of picture writing developed by the ancient Egyptians (p. 29)

**hijra** Muhammad's flight from Mecca to Medina in 622 (p. 257)

**historian** person who studies how people lived in the past (p. 5)

**home rule** local self-government (p. 615)

**homogeneous society** society that has a common culture and language (p. 662)

**humanism** intellectual movement at the heart of the Italian Renaissance that focused on worldly subjects rather than on religious issues (p. 346)

# I

**icon** holy image of Christ, the Virgin Mary, or a saint venerated in the Eastern Orthodox Church (p. 242) ▲

**ideograph** symbol that represents a thought or an idea (p. 61)

**ideology** system of thought and belief (p. 528)

**imperialism** domination by one country of the political, economic, or cultural life of another country or region (p. 632)

**import substitution** government policy of encouraging local manufacturers to produce goods that would replace imports (p. 953)

**impressionism** school of painting of the late 1800s and early 1900s that tried to capture fleeting visual impressions (p. 577)

**indemnity** payment for losses in war (p. 650)

**indigenous** original or native to a country or region (p. 667)

**indulgence** in the Roman Catholic Church, pardon for sins committed during a person's lifetime (p. 354)

**inflation** economic cycle that involves a rise in prices linked to a sharp increase in the amount of money available (p. 412)

**intendant** official appointed by French king Louis XIV to govern the provinces (p. 428)

**interchangeable parts** identical components that can be used in place of one another in manufacturing (p. 557)

**interdependence** mutual dependence of countries on goods, resources, and knowledge from other parts of the world (p. 828)

**interdict** in the Roman Catholic Church, excommunication of an entire region, town, or kingdom (p. 196)

**intifada** mass uprising mounted in 1987 by Palestinians in territory held by Israel (p. 917)

**isolationism** policy of limited involvement in world affairs (p. 627)

# J

**joint family** family organization in which several generations share a common dwelling (p. 88)

**joint stock company** private trading company in which shares are sold to investors to finance business ventures (p. 412)

**jury** group of people sworn to make a decision in a legal case (p. 211)

# K

**kabuki** (kuh BOO kee) form of Japanese drama developed in the 1600s (p. 330)

**kami** spirit who was believed to be the original ancestor of an early Japanese clan (p. 324)

**kamikaze** Japanese pilot who undertook a suicide mission (p. 806)

**kana** in the Japanese writing system, phonetic symbols representing syllables (p. 325)

**karma** in Hindu belief, all the actions that affect a person's fate in the next life (p. 79)

**kiva** large underground chamber used by the Anasazi for religious ceremonies (p. 170)

**knight** noble in Europe who served as a mounted warrior for a lord in the Middle Ages (p. 192)

**kulak** wealthy peasant in the Soviet Union in the 1930s (p. 727)

# L

**laissez faire** policy allowing business to operate with little or no government interference (p. 460)

**latitude** distance north or south of the Equator (p. 6)

**legion** basic unit of the ancient Roman army, made up of about 5,000 soldiers (p. 132)

**legislature** lawmaking body (p. 111)

GLOSSARY

**legitimacy** the principle by which monarchies that had been unseated by the French Revolution or Napoleon were restored (p. 503)

**liberation theology** in Latin America, movement urging the Roman Catholic Church to take a more active role in changing the social conditions that contribute to poverty and oppression (p. 839)

**limited monarchy** government in which a constitution or legislative body limits the monarch's powers (p. 435)

**lineage** group claiming a common ancestor (p. 299)

**loess** fine windblown yellow soil (p. 59)

**longitude** distance east or west of the Prime Meridian (p. 6)

# M

**mandate** after World War I, a territory that was administered by a western power (p. 712)

**manor** during the Middle Ages in Europe, a lord's estate, which included one or more villages and the surrounding lands (p. 194)

**maquiladora** (mah kee luh DOR uh) foreign-owned industrial plant in Mexico in which local workers assemble imported parts into finished goods (p. 963)

**martyr** person who suffers or dies for his or her beliefs (p. 146)

**matrilineal** term for a family organization in which kinship ties are traced through the mother (p. 299)

**mercantilism** policy by which a nation sought to export more than it imported in order to build its supply of gold and silver (p. 413)

**mercenary** soldier serving in a foreign army for pay (p. 151)

**messiah** savior sent by God (p. 144)

**mestizo** person in Spain's colonies in the Americas who was of Native American and European descent (p. 399)

**militarism** glorification of the military (p. 695)

**millet** in the Ottoman empire, a religious community of non-Muslims (p. 276)

**minaret** slender tower of a mosque, from which Muslims are called to prayer (p. 264)

**mixed economy** economic system with both private and state-run enterprises (p. 931)

**mobilize** to prepare military forces for war (p. 699)

**monarchy** government in which a king or queen exercises central power (p. 108)

**monopoly** complete control of a product or business by one person or group (p. 95)

**monotheistic** believing in one God (p. 44)

**monsoon** seasonal wind; in India, the winter monsoon brings hot, dry weather and the summer monsoon brings rain (p. 50)

**mosque** Muslim house of worship (p. 258)

**mulatto** person in Spain's colonies in the Americas who was of African and European descent (p. 399)

**multinational corporation** enterprise with branches in many countries (p. 832)

**mummification** (muhm mih fih KAY shuhn) practice of preserving the bodies of the dead (p. 27)

**mystic** person who devotes his or her life to seeking spiritual truths (p. 55)

# N

**nationalism** feeling of pride in and devotion to one's country (p. 493)

**nationalization** takeover of property or resources by the government (p. 739)

**natural laws** rules that govern human nature (p. 456)

**natural rights** rights that belong to all humans from birth (p. 457)

**neutrality** policy of supporting neither side in a war (p. 699)

**nirvana** in Buddhism, union with the universe and release from the cycle of rebirth (p. 80)

**nomad** person who moves from place to place in search of food (p. 9)

**nonaligned** not allied with either side in a conflict, such as the Cold War (p. 827)

**nuclear family** family unit consisting of parents and children (p. 299)

# O

**oligarchy** government in which ruling power belongs to a few people (p. 109)

**oracle bone** bone used by priests in Shang China to predict the future (p. 61) ▲

**oral history** collection of people's remembrances about a time or an event (p. 444)

# P

**pacifism** opposition to all war (p. 789)

**pagoda** multistoried Buddhist temple (p. 314)

**papyrus** (puh PĪ ruhs) plant that grows along the banks of the Nile; used by the ancient Egyptians to make a paperlike material (p. 29)

**patriarch** in the Byzantine empire, highest church official in a major city (p. 242)

**patriarchal** describing a family headed by the father or oldest male (p. 88)

**patrician** member of the landholding upper class in ancient Rome (p. 131)

**patrilineal** term for a family organization in which kinship ties are traced through the father (p. 299)

**patron** person who provides financial support for the arts (p. 346)

**penal colony** place where people convicted of crimes are sent (p. 670)

**peninsular** member of the highest class in Spain's colonies in the Americas (p. 399)

**peon** worker forced to labor for a landlord in order to pay off a debt (p. 398)

**peonage** system by which workers owe labor to pay their debts (p. 675)

**perestroika** restructuring of the Soviet government and economy in the 1980s (p. 865)

**perspective** artistic technique used to give drawings and paintings a three-dimensional effect (p. 347)

**phalanx** in ancient Greece, a massive formation of heavily armed foot soldiers (p. 109)

**pharaoh** (FAIR oh) title of the rulers of ancient Egypt (p. 23)

**philosophe** member of a group of Enlightenment thinkers who tried to apply the methods of science to the improvement of society (p. 457)

**physiocrat** an Enlightenment thinker who searched for natural laws to explain economics (p. 460)

**pictogram** drawing used to represent a word (p. 16)

**plantation** large estate run by an owner or overseer and worked by laborers who live there (p. 398)

**plebeian** (plee BEE uhn) member of the lower class in ancient Rome, including farmers, merchants, artisans, and traders (p. 131)

**plebiscite** ballot in which voters have a direct say on an issue (p. 495)

**pogrom** violent attack on a Jewish community (p. 601)

**polis** city-state in ancient Greece (p. 108)

**polytheistic** believing in many gods (p. 14)

**pope** head of the Roman Catholic Church (p. 147)

**potlatch** ceremonial dinners given by wealthy Native Americans of the Northwest Coast (p. 173)

**predestination** idea that God long ago determined who will gain salvation (p. 357)

**prehistory** period of time before writing systems were invented (p. 4)

**primary source** firsthand information about people or events of the past, such as that found in a diary or legal document (p. 100)

**prime minister** head of the cabinet in a parliamentary government; usually the leader of the largest party in the legislature (p. 469)

**privatization** the selling off of state-owned industries to private investors (p. 833)

**proletariat** the working class (p. 523)

**propaganda** the spreading of ideas to promote a certain cause or to damage an opposing cause (p. 706)

**prophet** spiritual leader believed to be interpreting God's will (p. 45)

**protectorate** country with its own government but under the control of an outside power (p. 634)

GLOSSARY

# Q

**quipu**  knotted strings used by Incan officials for record keeping (p. 166)

# R

**racism**  belief that one racial group is superior to another (p. 571)

**raj**  British rule of India (p. 386)

**rajah**  elected chief of an Aryan tribe in ancient India (p. 55)

**realism**  artistic movement whose aim was to represent the world as it is (p. 575)

**recant**  to give up one's views or beliefs (p. 355)

**refugee**  person who flees his or her homeland to seek safety elsewhere (p. 601)

**regionalism**  loyalty to a local area (p. 673)

**reincarnation**  in Hinduism, belief in the rebirth of the soul in another bodily form (p. 79)

**reparations**  payment for war damages (p. 710)

**republic**  system of government in which officials are chosen by the people (p. 130)

**rhetoric**  art of skillful speaking (p. 116)

**romanticism**  nineteenth-century artistic movement that appealed to emotion rather than reason (p. 572)

# S

**sacrament**  sacred ritual of the Roman Catholic Church (p. 196)

**salon**  informal social gathering at which writers, artists, and philosophers exchanged ideas; originated in France in the 1600s (p. 462)

**samurai**  member of the warrior class in Japanese feudal society (p. 327)

**sanction**  penalty (p. 788)

**sans-culotte**  (sanz kyoo LAHT) working-class men and women who called for radical action in France during the French Revolution (p. 489)

**satrap**  governor of a province in the Persian empire (p. 40)

**savanna**  grassy plain with irregular patterns of rainfall (p. 284)

**schism**  permanent division in a church (p. 242)

**scholasticism**  in medieval Europe, school of thought that used logic and reason to support Christian belief (p. 225)

**scribe**  in ancient civilizations, specially trained person who knew how to read and write and kept records (p. 16)

**secondary source**  information about the past that is not based on direct experience (p. 100)

**sect**  small religious group (p. 145)

**secular**  having to do with worldly, rather than religious, matters (p. 195)

**segregation**  separation of the races (p. 625)

**sepoy**  Indian soldier who served in an army set up by the French or English East India company (p. 386)

**serf**  in medieval Europe, peasant bound to the lord's land (p. 194)

**service industry**  industry that provides a service rather than a product (p. 851)

**shogun**  in Japanese feudal society, supreme military commander who held more power than the emperor (p. 327)

**silt**  rich soil carried by flooding rivers (p. 22)

**slash-and-burn agriculture**  farming method in which forest and brush are cut down and burned to create planting fields (p. 298)

**social contract**  agreement by which people give up their freedom to a powerful government in order to avoid chaos (p. 456)

**social gospel**  movement of the 1800s that urged Christians to do social service (p. 572)

**socialism**  system in which the people as a whole rather than private individuals own all property and operate all businesses (p. 522)

**socialist realism**  artistic style whose goal was to promote socialism by showing Soviet life in a positive light (p. 732)

**soviet**  council of workers and soldiers set up by Russian revolutionaries in 1917 (p. 720)

**sphere of influence**  area in which an outside power claims exclusive investment or trading privileges (p. 634)

**steppe**  sparse, dry grassland (p. 17)

**strait**  narrow water passage connecting two bodies of water (p. 105)

**stream of consciousness**  literary technique that probes a character's random thoughts and feelings (p. 771)

**stupa**  large domelike Buddhist shrine (p. 85)

**subcontinent**  large landmass that juts out from a continent (p. 50)

suffrage the right to vote (p. 490)
sultan Muslim ruler (p. 265)

# T

tariff tax on imported goods (p. 414)
technology tools and skills people use to meet their basic needs (p. 4)
terrorism the deliberate use of random violence, especially against civilians, to achieve political goals (p. 829)
theocracy government run by church leaders (p. 357)
theology the study of religion (p. 224)
tithe payment to a church equal to one tenth of a person's income (p. 197)
total war the channeling of a nation's entire resources into a war effort (p. 705)
totalitarian state government in which a one-party dictatorship regulates every aspect of citizens' lives (p. 729)
trade deficit situation in which a country imports more than it exports (p. 649)
tragedy in ancient Greece, a play that focused on human suffering and usually ended in disaster (p. 120)
tribune official in ancient Rome who was elected by the plebeians to protect their interests (p. 132)
tributary state independent state that has to acknowledge the supremacy of another state and pay tribute to its ruler (p. 308)
tribute payment that conquered peoples were forced to make to their conquerors (p. 162)
troubadour wandering poet in Europe in the Middle Ages (p. 193)
turnpike privately built road that charges a fee to travelers who use it (p. 514)
tyrant in ancient Greece, ruler who gained power by force (p. 110)

# U

ultimatum final set of demands (p. 699)
universal manhood suffrage right of all adult men to vote (p. 529)
urbanization movement of people from rural areas to cities (p. 516)

usury (YOO zhuh ree) practice of lending money at interest (p. 203)
utilitarianism idea that the goal of society should be to bring about the greatest happiness for the greatest number of people (p. 521)

# V

vassal in medieval Europe, a lord who was granted land in exchange for service and loyalty to a greater lord (p. 192)
vernacular everyday language of ordinary people (p. 226)
veto power to block a government action (p. 132)
viceroy representative who ruled one of Spain's provinces in the Americas in the king's name (p. 397)
vizier chief minister who supervised the business of government in ancient Egypt (p. 23)

# W

welfare state system in which the government takes responsibility for its citizens' social and economic needs (p. 849)
women's suffrage right of women to vote (p. 569)

# Z

zaibatsu (ZĪ BAHT SOO) since the late 1800s, powerful banking and industrial families in Japan in the late 1800s (p. 662)
zemstvo local elected assembly set up in Russia under Alexander II (p. 600)

ziggurat (ZIHG oo rat) pyramid-temple dedicated to the chief god or goddess of an ancient Sumerian city-state (p. 33) ▲

GLOSSARY

# CONNECTIONS WITH PRENTICE HALL LITERATURE

| Topic | Author | Work/Genre | See Prentice Hall Literature World Masterpieces |
|---|---|---|---|
| **Unit 1 Early Civilizations** | | | |
| The Egyptian Empire, pages 24–25 | unknown | I Think I'll Go Home and Lie Very Still (poetry) | page 33 |
| Sumerian Civilization, pages 32–34 | unknown | Enkindu's Dream of the Underworld (epic poetry) | page 19 |
| A Covenant With God, pages 44–45 | unknown | The Story of the Flood (biblical) | page 47 |
| The Vedic Age, pages 53–55 | unknown | The Mystery of the Brahman (hymn) | page 162 |
| **Unit 2 Empires of the Ancient World** | | | |
| Hinduism: Unity and Diversity, pages 78–79 | unknown | Numskull and the Rabbit (fable) | page 184 |
| The Wisdom of Confucius, pages 90–91 | unknown | I Beg of You, Chung Tze (poetry) | page 220 |
| The Age of Homer, pages 105–107 | Homer | The Quarrel of Achilleus and Agamemnon (epic poetry) | page 335 |
| **Unit 3 Regional Civilizations** | | | |
| The Age of Charlemagne, pages 188–189 | unknown | Song of Roland (epic poetry) | page 569 |
| Lords, Vassals, and Knights, page 192 | Chrétien de Troyes | The Grail (epic poetry) | page 602 |
| Strong Monarchs in England, pages 210-211 | Marie deFrance | The Lay of the Werewolf | page 612 |
| The Brilliant Tang, pages 308–309 | Li Bo (Li Po) | The River-Merchant's Wife: A Letter (poetry) | page 234 |
| The Heian Period, pages 325–326 | Sei Shonagon | The Pillow Book (sketches) | page 296 |
| **Unit 4 Early Modern Times** | | | |
| Humanism, page 346 | Francesco Petrarch | Laura (poetry) | page 676 |
| Literature of the Northern Renaissance, pages 351–352 | Christopher Marlowe | The Tragical History of the Life and Death of Dr. Faustus (play) | page 700 |
| The Golden Century, pages 424–425 | Miguel de Cervantes Saavedra | The Adventures of Don Quixote (fiction) | page 695 |

CONNECTIONS CHARTS

# CONNECTIONS WITH PRENTICE HALL SCIENCE

| Topic | See Prentice Hall Biology or Prentice Hall Chemistry: Connections to Our Changing World |
|---|---|

## Unit 1 Early Civilizations

| | |
|---|---|
| Hunters and Food Gatherers, pages 8–9 (earliest humans) | *Biology,* Developing a Theory of Evolution, pages 291–295 |
| The First Farmers, pages 10–11 (planting seeds) | *Biology,* Seed Development, pages 540–542 |
| Geography: The Nile Valley, page 22 (deserts) | *Biology,* Deserts, page 1015 |
| Warfare and the Spread of Ideas, pages 38–40 (ironworking) | *Chemistry,* Oxidation and Reduction, pages 657–659 |

## Unit 2 Empires of the Ancient World

| | |
|---|---|
| Golden Age of the Guptas, pages 85–87 (vaccinations) | *Biology,* Immunity, pages 973–975 |
| Sparta: A Nation of Soldiers, pages 109–110 (survival of the fittest) | *Biology,* Evolution by Natural Selection, pages 296–298 |
| The Persian Wars, pages 113–114 (fire) | *Chemistry,* Chemistry in Action, pages 3–4 |
| Hellenistic Civilization, pages 124–125 (illnesses and cures) | *Biology,* What Is a Disease? pages 953–954 |
| Greco-Roman Civilization, pages 141–142 (fresh water) | *Chemistry,* Raindrops Keep Falling on My Head, page 568 |

## Unit 3 Regional Civilizations

| | |
|---|---|
| A Land of Great Potential, page 186 (minerals) | *Biology,* Minerals, pages 847–858 |
| An Agricultural Revolution, page 201 (population growth) | *Biology,* Human Population Growth, pages 1038–1039 |
| The Black Death, pages 228–230 (plague) | *Biology,* How Is Infectious Disease Spread? page 954 |
| Masters of Medicine, pages 270–272 (eyesight) | *Biology,* Vision, pages 827–828 |
| Geography: The Continent of Africa, pages 284–286 (gold, diamonds) | *Chemistry,* The Coinage Metals, pages 806–809; Allotropes of Carbon, pages 806–809 |

## Unit 4 Early Modern Times

| | |
|---|---|
| More Scientific Advances, pages 366–367 (scientific method) | *Chemistry,* Scientific Method, pages 7–13 |
| Bacon and Descartes, page 367 (blood circulation) | *Biology,* Blood, pages 905–907 |
| A Global Exchange, pages 410–411 (new foods) | *Biology,* Food and Nutrition, pages (855–866) |

CONNECTIONS CHARTS

## Unit 5 Enlightenment and Revolution

| | |
|---|---|
| A World of Progress and Reason, page 456 (Joseph Priestley, Antoine Lavoisier) | *Chemistry*, Conservation of Matter, pages 72–73; The Pop of Soda, page 604 |
| A Turning Point in History, page 508 (anesthesia) | *Chemistry*, Knockout, page 857 |
| A New Agricultural Revolution, pages 508–509 (soils) | *Biology*, Types of Soil, pages 487–488 |
| The Age of Iron and Coal, page 513 (coal) | *Chemistry*, The Energy Crisis, pages 59–60 |

## Unit 6 Industrialism and a New Global Age

| | |
|---|---|
| Technology and Industry, pages 558–559 (electricity) | *Chemistry*, Static Electricity, pages 95–96 |
| The Shrinking World, pages 559–561 (internal combustion engines) | *Chemistry*, Exothermic Reactions, pages 382–383 |
| Medicine and Population, pages 563–564 (germ theory) | *Biology*, The Germ Theory of Infectious Disease, pages 954–955 |
| The Challenge of Science, page 570 (atomic theory) | *Chemistry*, Atomic Theory, pages 102–111 |
| The Darwin Furor, pages 570–571 (Darwin) | *Biology*, Ideas That Shaped Darwin's Theory of Evolution, pages 293–295 |
| "Ireland of the Irish," pages 614–615 (potato blight) | *Biology*, Diseases Caused by Fungi, pages 421–423 |
| The Trade Issue, pages 649–650 (opium) | *Biology*, How Drugs Affect the Body, pages 987–991 |

## Unit 7 World Wars and Revolutions

| | |
|---|---|
| Death of the Mad Monk, pages 719–720 (hemophilia) | *Biology*, Sex-Linked Genetic Disorders, pages 237–238 |
| New Views of the Universe, pages 770–771 (radioactivity) | *Chemistry*, Radioactivity, pages 99–100 |
| Early Challenges to World Peace, pages 788–789 | *Chemistry*, Petroleum—More Than Just Fuel, page 823 |
| Defeat of Japan, pages 806–808 (atomic bomb) | *Chemistry*, Applications of Nuclear Chemistry, pages 102–111 |

## Unit 8 The World Today

| | |
|---|---|
| The Global North and South: Two Worlds of Development, pages 830–832 (birthrate, deathrate) | *Biology*, Population Growth, pages 1050–1051 |
| Economic Development and the Environment, pages 834–837 (global warming) | *Biology*, Air Pollution, pages 1055–1059 |
| Old Ways and New, pages 838–839 (overcrowded living conditions) | *Biology*, Density-Dependent Limiting Factors, pages 1036–1040 |
| Science and Technology, pages 841–842, (AIDS) | *Biology*, AIDS, pages 979–981 |
| Development Versus the Environment: No Easy Answers, page 959–960 (deforestation) | *Biology*, Forests, pages 1063–1065 |

CONNECTIONS CHARTS

# INDEX

INDEX

INDEX

INDEX

INDEX

INDEX

INDEX

INDEX

INDEX

INDEX

INDEX

**INDEX**

INDEX

**INDEX**

INDEX

*(continued from page ii)*

from "The Second Coming" is reprinted with the permission of **Simon & Schuster, Inc. and A. P. Watt Ltd.** from *The Poems of W. B. Yeats: A New Edition*, edited by Richard J. Finneran. Copyright © 1924 by Macmillan Publishing Company, renewed 1952 by Bertha Georgia Yeats. Excerpts from *Mothers and Shadows* (Readers International, 1985), translated by Jo Labanyi from *Conversación al sur* (Mexico City: Siglo XXI, 1981). Reprinted by permission of **Siglo XXI Editores.** Excerpts from "Gonzalez Videla," from *Canto General* by Pablo Neruda, translated/ edited by Jack Schmitt. Copyright © 1991 Fundacion Pablo Neruda, Regents of the University of California. Used by permission of the publisher, the **University of California Press.** Excerpt from "Black Woman," by Léopold Senghor. Copyright © 1964, 1973, 1979, 1984, and 1990 by Éditions du Seuil, by permission of **George Borchardt, Inc.** Reprinted from *The Collected Poetry* by Léopold Sédar Senghor, translated with an Introduction by Melvin Dixon **(The University Press of Virginia,** Charlottesville, Virginia, 1991). Excerpts from *The Metamorphoses* by Publius Ovidius Naso, translated by Horace Gregory. Translation copyright © 1958 by The Viking Press, Inc., renewed 1986 by Patrick Bolton Gregory. Used by permission of **Viking Penguin, a division of Penguin Books USA Inc.**

Note: Every effort has been made to locate the copyright owner of material reprinted in this book. Omissions brought to our attention will be corrected in subsequent printings.

**ART CREDITS**

**Visual Research:** Photosearch
**Contributing Artists:** Alfred G. Assin, Tammara L. Newnam, Carol Richmond
**Freelance desktop page layout:** David Rosenthal, Rose Sievers

**PHOTOGRAPHIC CREDITS**

**Front Cover:** left © G. Dagli Orti; right © Peter Beck/The Stock Market **Back Cover:** background © G. Dagli Orti; left inset © G. Dagli Orti; right inset © Peter Beck/ The Stock Market **Interior:** title page background and left inset © G. Dagli Orti; right inset © Peter Beck/The Stock Market iii background and left inset © G. Dagli Orti; right inset © Peter Beck/The Stock Market **v** top Dez & Jen Bartlett/Bruce Coleman, Inc.; middle © Archiv/Photo Researchers, Inc.; bottom Dragon Head, late Zhou dynasty. Courtesy of the Freer Gallery of Art, Smithsonian Institution, Washington, D.C. (32.14) **vi** top Archaeological Museum, Sarnath/Robert Harding Picture Library; middle, top © Boltin Picture Library; middle,bottom Scala/Art Resource, NY; bottom © Boltin Picture Library

**vii** left Scala/Art Resource, NY; top, right © Boltin Picture Library; bottom, right © Jose Fuste Raga/The Stock Market **viii** left (detail) Asian Art Museum of San Francisco. Avery Brundage Collection (B60 D23); top, right Scala/Art Resource, NY; bottom, right © 1993 Jason Lauré **ix** top Private Collection Great Britain; middle, top Bibliothèque Nationale de Cartes et Plans/The Bridgeman Art Library, London; middle,bottom The Huntington Library; bottom Archivo Fotographico Oronoz, Madrid **x** top Courtesy of the Peabody Essex Museum, Salem, Mass.; middle, top Musée Carnavalet, Paris/ Giraudon/The Bridgeman Art Library, London; middle,bottom Archiv für Kunst und Geschichte, Berlin; bottom © Jean-Loup Charmet **xi** left The Royal Collection © Her Majesty Queen Elizabeth II; top, right Library of Congress; bottom, right Archiv Für Kunst und Geschichte, Berlin **xii** top Staatliche Museen zu Berlin - Preussischer Kulturbesitz Museum für Volkerkunde; middle, top © Branger-Viollet; middle,bottom The Bettmann Archive; bottom Forbes Magazine Collection/The Bridgeman Art Library, London **xiii** top Nehru Memorial Museum and Library, New Delhi; middle © The London Transport Museum; bottom By permission of the Trustees of the Overlord Embroidery. The Overlord Embroidery is on display at the D-Day Museum, Portsmouth, England. **xiv** top NASA; middle Reuters/ Bettmann; bottom Minick/Jiao **xv** top © Michael Coyne/Black Star; middle © Emory Kristof/National Geographic Image Collection; bottom © Mireille Vautier/Woodfin Camp & Associates **xvi** top (detail) Topkapi Sarayi Museum, Istanbul/Ergun Cagatay/ Tetragon; bottom © Everett C. Johnson/Leo de Wys, Inc. **xvii** © Boltin Picture Library **xxv** top, left Board of Trustees of the National Museums and Galleries on Merseyside (Lady Lever Art Gallery, Port Sunlight); top, right Archiv für Kunst und Geschichte, Berlin; bottom, left JB/Keystone/Hulton Deutsch Collection Ltd.; bottom, right © Tomas Muscionico/Contact Press Images **xxvi** top © Michael Fogden/Animals Animals; bottom © Tom Owen Edmunds/The Image Bank **xxvii** top © Michael Holford; middle © Buu-Hires/Gamma Liaison International; bottom © Palomo/ Cartoonists & Writers Syndicate **xxviii** top, left © André Held; top, middle © Liu Heung Shing/Contact Press Images; top, right (detail) From the collection of Hebrew Union College Skirball Museum, Eric Hockley Photographer; bottom, left Lauros-Giraudon/Art Resource, NY; bottom, middle (detail) Copyright British Museum (PS 192184); bottom, right © Esaias Baitel/Gamma Liaison International **xxix** top © Michael Holford; top, right © Jonathan Wallen/ Harry N. Abrams, Inc.; middle, left The Science Museum/Science & Society Pic-

ture Library; middle, right Whipple Museum of the History of Science; bottom, left Imperial War Museum/E.T. Archive; bottom, right © Somerville/ Cartoonists & Writers Syndicate **xxx** top, left © Michael Holford; top, middle University of British Columbia/The Bridgeman Art Library, London; top, right Library of Congress; bottom, left © Justin Kerr/Brooklyn Museum; bottom,middle Copyright British Museum; bottom, middle Werner Forman Archive, Smithsonian Institution, Washington/Art Resource, NY **xxxi** top, left (detail) The Louvre/The Bridgeman Art Library, London; top, middle Photo Bibliothèque Nationale, Paris; top, right © Hulton Deutsch Collection Ltd; middle, left Bibliothèque Nationale/The Bridgeman Art Library, London; middle, right New York Daily News; bottom, left © John Moss/Black Star; bottom,middle Diplomatic Reception Rooms, United States Department of State; bottom, right (detail) Collection: Congreso Nacional, Salón Eliptico. Photographer: Carlos German Rojas. Courtesy of the Foundation Gallery of National Art, Republic of Venezuela **xxxii** top © Punch/Rothco; bottom, left Nationalmuseet, Copenhagen/The Bridgeman Art Library, London; bottom, right Atkinson Art Gallery/The Bridgeman Art Library, London **xxxiii** top, left Victoria & Albert Museum/Art Resource, NY; top, right Scala/Art Resource, NY; bottom © Elke Walford/Hamburger Kunsthalle, Hamburg **xxxiv** top The Field Museum, Chicago, IL. Photo, Diane Alexander White; bottom © Superstock **1** top, left The Metropolitan Museum of Art, Gift of Norbert Schimmel Trust, 1989. (1989.281.12); top, right Bequest of Alfred F. Pillsbury/The Minneapolis Institute of Arts (50.46.14); bottom © Boltin Picture Library; **3** Dez & Jen Bartlett/Bruce Coleman, Inc. **5** © 1993 Comstock **6** © Punch/Rothco **7** top © Geoffrey Clifford/Woodfin Camp & Associates, Inc.; bottom Novosti Press/The Image Bank **9** © 1985 David L. Brill/Dr. Owen Lovejoy and students, Kent State University **10** © Frank Fournier/Woodfin Camp & Associates, Inc. **11** C. M. Dixon **13** © David A. Harvey/ Woodfin Camp & Associates, Inc. **15** top,left *Ornament*, China, 5th century b.c., late Eastern Zhou dynasty. Courtesy of the Freer Gallery of Art, Smithsonian Institution, Washington, D.C. (30.27); top,right *Choker # 59*, 1980, Mary Lee Hu. Collection of Virginia K. Lewis, Richmond, VA. Courtesy, American Craft Museum. Photo: George Erml; bottom,left The Corning Museum of Glass; bottom,right *Bridal Beads*, 1992, William Harper, Collection: Susan and Steven Turner, Tallahassee, FL. **16** The Kon-Tiki Museum, Oslo **21** © Brian Drake/Photo Researchers, Inc. **24** Art Resource, NY **27** *Mummified Cat*, The Louvre © Photo Réunion des Musées Nationaux **28** top The Metropolitan

Museum of Art, Rogers Fund, 1912 and 1919 (12.182.72); bottom © William Albert Allard/Magnum Photos, Inc. **30** © Archiv/Photo Researchers, Inc. **33** top © George Gerster/Comstock, Inc.; bottom-inset Copyright British Museum (E. 554) **35** © Michael Holford **36** © Michael Holford **37** (detail) The Louvre/The Bridgeman Art Library, London **40** Scala/Art Resource, NY **41** top and top-2 © Michael Holford; top-3 Erich Lessing/Art Resource, NY; bottom-3 The Metropolitan Museum of Art, Purchase, H. Dunscombe Colt Gift, 1961 (61.62); bottom-2 British Museum/The Bridgeman Art Library, London; bottom © Boltin Picture Library; **43** By permission of The British Library **44** (detail) From the collection of Hebrew Union College Skirball Museum, Eric Hockley Photographer. **49** *Dragon Head*, late Zhou dynasty. Courtesy of the Freer Gallery of Art, Smithsonian Institution, Washington, D.C. (32.14) **52** top,left © Jehangir Gazdar/Woodfin Camp & Associates, Inc.; top,right © Jehangir Gazdar/Woodfin Camp & Associates, Inc.; bottom,left Simon and Schuster; bottom,right The Seal of Cotton is a registered servicemark/ trademark of Cotton Incorporated **57** National Museum of India, New Delhi/The Bridgeman Art Library, London **60** © Michael Holford **61** Photo: Wan-go Weng Inc. Archive **65** left Copyright British Museum (PS 164193); right Copyright British Museum (PS 164193) **68** left Dez & Jen Bartlett/Bruce Coleman, Inc.; right © Brian Drake/Photo Researchers, Inc. **69** *Dragon Head*, late Zhou dynasty. Courtesy of the Freer Gallery of Art, Smithsonian Institution, Washington, D.C. (32.14) **70** top Art Resource, NY; bottom, left © Jehangir Gazdar/Woodfin Camp & Associates, Inc.; bottom, right Photo: Wan-go Weng Inc. Archive **71** Top © Boltin Picture Library; bottom, left © Michael Holford; bottom, right Scala/Art Resource, NY **72** Archiv für Kunst und Geschichte, Berlin **73** © Mirror Syndication International/ Hulton Deutsch Collection Ltd. **74** top The Metropolitan Museum of Art, Rogers Fund, 1908. (08.202.47); middle The Metropolitan Museum of Art, Gift of Nathan Cummings, 1964. (64.228.45); bottom © Rapa-Explorer **75** left Copyright British Museum; right Robert Harding Picture Library **77** (detail) Copyright British Museum (PS 192184) **78** Lauros-Giraudon/Art Resource, NY **80** Leo de Wys Inc./W. Hille **83** left Archaeological Museum, Sarnath/Robert Harding Picture Library; right © Viren Desai/Dinodia Picture Agency **86** © Marc Bernheim/ Woodfin Camp & Associates, Inc. **88** SEF/Art Resource, NY **89** Los Angeles County Museum of Art, From the Nasli and Alice Heeramaneck Collection, Museum Associates Purchase **91** Giraudon/ The Bridgeman Art Library, London **92** Copyright British Museum (PS 190954)